Anderson's Business Law and the Legal Environment

Comprehensive Volume

Twenty-First Edition

David P. Twomey | Marianne M. Jennings

CENGAGE
Learning™

Australia • Brazil • Japan • Korea • Mexico • Singapore • Spain • United Kingdom • United States

CENGAGE
Learning™

Anderson's Business Law and the Legal Environment: Comprehensive Volume, Twenty-First Edition

Anderson's Business Law and the Legal Environment, Comprehensive Volume, 21st Edition
David P. Twomey | Marianne M. Jennings

Executive Editors:
Maureen Staudt
Michael Stranz

Senior Project Development Manager:
Linda deStefano

Marketing Specialist:
Courtney Sheldon

Senior Production/Manufacturing Manager:
Donna M. Brown

PreMedia Manager:
Joel Brennecke

Sr. Rights Acquisition Account Manager:
Todd Osborne

Cover Image:
Getty Images*

*Unless otherwise noted, all cover images used by Custom Solutions, a part of Cengage Learning, have been supplied courtesy of Getty Images with the exception of the Earthview cover image, which has been supplied by the National Aeronautics and Space Administration (NASA).

For product information and technology assistance, contact us at
Cengage Learning Customer & Sales Support, 1-800-354-9706
For permission to use material from this text or product,
submit all requests online at **cengage.com/permissions**
Further permissions questions can be emailed to
permissionrequest@cengage.com

This book contains select works from existing Cengage Learning resources and was produced by Cengage Learning Custom Solutions for collegiate use. As such, those adopting and/or contributing to this work are responsible for editorial content accuracy, continuity and completeness.

Compilation © 2010 Cengage Learning
ISBN-13: 978-1-111-29679-7

ISBN-10: 1-111-29679-0

Cengage Learning
5191 Natorp Boulevard
Mason, Ohio 45040
USA
Cengage Learning is a leading provider of customized learning solutions with office locations around the globe, including Singapore, the United Kingdom, Australia, Mexico, Brazil, and Japan. Locate your local office at:
international.cengage.com/region.

Cengage Learning products are represented in Canada by Nelson Education, Ltd.
For your lifelong learning solutions, visit **www.cengage.com/custom.**
Visit our corporate website at **www.cengage.com.**

Printed in the United States of America

Brief Contents

PART 2: Contracts
12. Nature and Classes of Contracts: Contracting on the Internet
13. Formation of Contracts: Offer and Acceptance
14. Capacity and Genuine Assent
15. Consideration
16. Legality and Public Policy
17. Writing, Electronic Forms, and Interpretation of Contracts
18. Third Persons and Contracts
19. Discharge of Contracts
20. Breach of Contract and Remedies
23. Nature and Form of Sales
25. Product Liability: Warranties and Torts
27. Remedies for Breach of Sales Contracts
37. Agency
9. Torts
21. Personal Property and Bailments
49. Real Property

Appendix
Glossary and Index

Chapter 12

NATURE AND CLASSES OF CONTRACTS: CONTRACTING ON THE INTERNET

A. Nature of Contracts

1. DEFINITION OF A CONTRACT
2. ELEMENTS OF A CONTRACT
3. SUBJECT MATTER OF CONTRACTS
4. PARTIES TO A CONTRACT
5. HOW A CONTRACT ARISES
6. INTENT TO MAKE A BINDING AGREEMENT
7. FREEDOM OF CONTRACT

B. Classes of Contracts

8. FORMAL AND INFORMAL CONTRACTS
9. EXPRESS AND IMPLIED CONTRACTS
10. VALID AND VOIDABLE CONTRACTS AND VOID AGREEMENTS
11. EXECUTED AND EXECUTORY CONTRACTS
12. BILATERAL AND UNILATERAL CONTRACTS
13. QUASI CONTRACTS

C. Contracting on the Internet

Practically every business transaction affecting people involves a contract.

A. NATURE OF CONTRACTS

This introductory chapter will familiarize you with the terminology needed to work with contract law. In addition, the chapter introduces quasi contracts, which are not true contracts but obligations imposed by law.

1. Definition of a Contract

contract–a binding agreement based on the genuine assent of the parties, made for a lawful object, between competent parties, in the form required by law, and generally supported by consideration.

A **contract** is a legally binding agreement.[1] By one definition, "a contract is a promise or a set of promises for the breach of which the law gives a remedy, or the performance of which the law in some way recognizes as a duty."[2] Contracts arise out of agreements, so a contract may be defined as an agreement creating an obligation.

The substance of the definition of a contract is that by mutual agreement or assent, the parties create enforceable duties or obligations. That is, each party is legally bound to do or to refrain from doing certain acts.

2. Elements of a Contract

The elements of a contract are (1) an agreement (2) between competent parties (3) based on the genuine assent of the parties that is (4) supported by consideration, (5) made for a lawful objective, and (6) in the form required by law, if any. These elements will be considered in the chapters that follow.

3. Subject Matter of Contracts

The subject matter of a contract may relate to the performance of personal services, such as contracts of employment to work developing computer software or to play professional football. A contract may provide for the transfer of ownership of property, such as a house (real property) or an automobile (personal property), from one person to another.

promisor–person who makes a promise.

promisee–person to whom a promise is made.

obligor–promisor.

obligee–promisee who can claim the benefit of the obligation.

privity–succession or chain of relationship to the same thing or right, such as privity of contract, privity of estate, privity of possession.

4. Parties to a Contract

The person who makes a promise is the **promisor**, and the person to whom the promise is made is the **promisee**. If the promise is binding, it imposes on the promisor a duty or obligation, and the promisor may be called the **obligor**.
The promisee who can claim the benefit of the obligation is called the **obligee**. The parties to a contract are said to stand in **privity** with each other, and the relationship

[1] The Uniform Commercial Code defines *contract* as "the total legal obligation which results from the parties' agreement as affected by [the UCC] and any other applicable rules of law." UCC § 1–201(11).
[2] Restatement (Second) of Contracts § 1.

privity of contract–
relationship between a
promisor and the promisee.

between them is termed **privity of contract.** For Example, when the state of North Carolina and the architectural firm of O'Brien/Atkins Associates executed a contract for the construction of a new building at the University of North Carolina, Chapel Hill, these parties were in privity of contract. However, a building contractor, RPR & Associates, who worked on the project did not have standing to sue on the contract between the architect and the state because the contractor was not in privity of contract.[3]

In written contracts, parties may be referred to by name. More often, however, they are given special names that better identify each party. For example, consider a contract by which one person agrees that another may occupy a house upon the payment of money. The parties to this contract are called *landlord* and *tenant*, or *lessor* and *lessee*, and the contract between them is known as a *lease*. Parties to other types of contracts also have distinctive names, such as *vendor* and *vendee* for the parties to a sales contract, *shipper* and *carrier* for the parties to a transportation contract, and *insurer* and *insured* for the parties to an insurance policy.

A party to a contract may be an individual, a partnership, a limited liability company, a corporation, or a government.[4] One or more persons may be on each side of a contract. Some contracts are three-sided, as in a credit card transaction, which involves the company issuing the card, the holder of the card, and the business furnishing goods and services on the basis of the credit card.

If a contract is written, the persons who are the parties and who are bound by it can ordinarily be determined by reading what the document says and seeing how it is signed. A contract binds only the parties to the contract. It cannot impose a duty on a person who is not a party to it. Ordinarily, only a party to a contract has any rights against another party to the contract.[5] In some cases, third persons have rights on a contract as third-party beneficiaries or assignees. A person cannot be bound, however, by the terms of a contract to which that person is not a party.[6]

CPA ## 5. How a Contract Arises

offeror–person who makes
an offer.

offeree–person to whom
an offer is made.

A contract is based on an agreement. An agreement arises when one person, the **offeror**, makes an offer and the person to whom the offer is made, the **offeree**, accepts. There must be both an offer and an acceptance. If either is lacking, there is no contract.

6. Intent to Make a Binding Agreement

Because a contract is based on the consent of the parties and is a legally binding agreement, it follows that the parties must have an intent to enter into an agreement

---

[3] *RPR & Associates v O'Brien/Atkins Associates, P.A.*, 24 F Supp 2d 515 (MDNC 1998). See also *Roof Techs Int. Inc. v State*, 57P3d 538 (Kan App 2002), where a layer of litigation was avoided regarding lawsuits involving the renovation of the Farrell Library at Kansas State University. The state was the only party in privity of contract with the architectural firm and would thus have to bring claims against the architectural firm on behalf of all of the contractors. Two subcontractors, the general contractor, and the owner of the library, the state of Kansas, used a settlement and liquidation agreement assigning all of the state's claims against the architect to the general contractor.
[4] See *Purina Mills, LLC v Less*, 295 F Supp 2d 1017 (ND Iowa 2003) in which the pig-seller plaintiff, which converted from a corporation to a limited liability company (LLC) while the contract was in effect, was a proper party in interest and could maintain a contract action against defendant buyers.
[5] *Hooper v Yakima County*, 904 P2d 1193 (Wash App 1995).
[6] *Walsh v Telesector Resources Group, Inc.*, 662 NE2d 1043 (Mass App 1996).

that is binding. Sometimes the parties are in agreement, but their agreement does not produce a contract. Sometimes there is merely a preliminary agreement, but the parties never actually make a contract, or there is merely an agreement as to future plans or intentions without any contractual obligation to carry out those plans or intentions.

7. Freedom of Contract

In the absence of some ground for declaring a contract void or voidable, parties may make such contracts as they choose. The law does not require parties to be fair, or kind, or reasonable, or to share gains or losses equitably.

B. Classes of Contracts

formal contracts–written contracts or agreements whose formality signifies the parties' intention to abide by the terms.

Contracts may be classified according to their form, the way in which they were created, their binding character, and the extent to which they have been performed.

`CPA`   **8. Formal and Informal Contracts**

Contracts can be classified as formal or informal.

contract under seal– contract executed by affixing a seal or making an impression on the paper or on some adhering substance such as wax attached to the document.

(A) Formal Contracts. **Formal contracts** are enforced because the formality with which they are executed is considered sufficient to signify that the parties intend to be bound by their terms. Formal contracts include (1) **contracts under seal** where a person's signature or a corporation's name is followed by a scroll, the word *seal*, or the letters *L.S.*;[7] (2) contracts of record, which are obligations that have been entered before a court of record, sometimes called a **recognizance**; and (3)negotiable instruments.

`CPA`   (B) Informal Contracts. All contracts other than formal contracts are called **informal** (or simple) **contracts** without regard to whether they are oral or written. These contracts are enforceable, not because of the form of the transaction but because they represent agreement of the parties.

recognizance–obligation entered into before a court to do some act, such as to appear at a later date for a hearing. Also called a *contract of record.*

informal contract–simple oral or written contract.

9. Express and Implied Contracts

Simple contracts may be classified as express *contracts* or *implied contracts* according to the way they are created.

express contract– agreement of the parties manifested by their words, whether spoken or written.

(A) Express Contracts. An **express contract** is one in which the terms of the agreement of the parties are manifested by their words, whether spoken or written.

implied contract–contract expressed by conduct or implied or deduced from the facts.

(B) Implied Contracts. An **implied contract** (or, as sometimes stated, a *contract implied in fact*) is one in which the agreement is shown not by words, written or spoken, but by the acts and conduct of the parties.[8] Such a contract arises when (1) a person renders services under circumstances indicating that payment for them

---

[7] Some authorities explain *L.S.* as an abbreviation for *locus sigilium* (place for the seal).
[8] *Lindquist Ford, Inc. v Middleton Motors, Inc.*, 557 F3d 469, 481 (7th Cir 2009).

FIGURE 12-1 | *Contractual Liability*

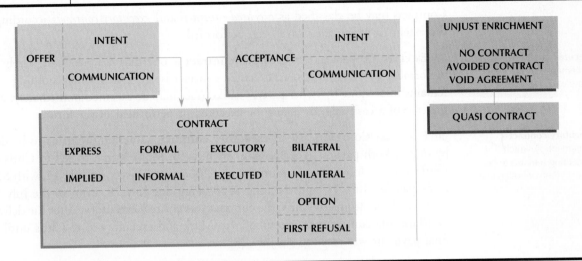

is expected and (2) the other person, knowing such circumstances, accepts the benefit of those services. **For Example,** when a building owner requests a professional roofer to make emergency repairs to the roof of a building, an obligation arises to pay the reasonable value of such services, although no agreement has been made about compensation.

An implied contract cannot arise when there is an existing express contract on the same subject.[9] However, the existence of a written contract does not bar recovery on an implied contract for extra work that was not covered by the contract.

CPA   **10. Valid and Voidable Contracts and Void Agreements**

Contracts may be classified in terms of enforceability or validity.

valid contract–agreement that is binding and enforceable.

(A) VALID CONTRACTS. A **valid contract** is an agreement that is binding and enforceable.

voidable contract–agreement that is otherwise binding and enforceable but may be rejected at the option of one of the parties as the result of specific circumstances.

(B) VOIDABLE CONTRACTS. A **voidable contract** is an agreement that is otherwise binding and enforceable, but because of the circumstances surrounding its execution or the lack of capacity of one of the parties, it may be rejected at the option of one of the parties. **For Example,** a person who has been forced to sign an agreement that that person would not have voluntarily signed may, in some instances, avoid the contract.

void agreement–agreement that cannot be enforced.

(C) VOID AGREEMENTS. A **void agreement** is without legal effect. An agreement that contemplates the performance of an act prohibited by law is usually incapable of enforcement; hence it is void. Likewise, it cannot be made binding by later approval or ratification.

[9] *Pepsi-Cola Bottling Co. of Pittsburgh, Inc., v PepsiCo, Inc.,* 431 F3d 1241 (10th Cir 2000).

11. Executed and Executory Contracts

Contracts may be classified as *executed contracts* and *executory contracts* according to the extent to which they have been performed.

executed contract– agreement that has been completely performed.

(A) EXECUTED CONTRACTS. An **executed contract** is one that has been completely performed. In other words, an executed contract is one under which nothing remains to be done by either party.[10] A contract may be executed immediately, as in the case of a cash sale, or it may be executed or performed in the future.

executory contract– agreement by which something remains to be done by one or both parties.

(B) EXECUTORY CONTRACTS. In an **executory contract**, something remains to be done by one or both parties.[11] **For Example,** on July 10, Mark agreed to sell to Chris his Pearl drum set for $600, the terms being $200 upon delivery on July 14, with $200 to be paid on July 21, and the final $200 being due July 28. Prior to the July 14 delivery of the drums to Chris, the contract was entirely executory. After the delivery by Mark, the contract was executed as to Mark and executory as to Chris until the final payment was received on July 28.

12. Bilateral and Unilateral Contracts

In making an offer, the offeror is in effect extending a promise to do something, such as pay a sum of money, if the offeree will do what the offeror requests. Contracts are classified as *bilateral* or *unilateral*. Some bilateral contracts look ahead to the making of a later contract. Depending on their terms, these are called *option contracts* or *first-refusal contracts*.

CPA

bilateral contract– agreement under which one promise is given in exchange for another.

(A) BILATERAL CONTRACT. If the offeror extends a promise and asks for a promise in return and if the offeree accepts the offer by making the promise, the contract is called a **bilateral contract**. One promise is given in exchange for another, and each party is bound by the obligation. **For Example,** when the house painter offers to paint the owner's house for $3,700 and the owner promises to pay $3,700 for the job, there is an exchange of promises, and the agreement gives rise to a bilateral contract.

unilateral contract– contract under which only one party makes a promise.

(B) UNILATERAL CONTRACT. In contrast with a bilateral contract, the offeror may promise to do something or to pay a certain amount of money only when the offeree does an act.[12] Examples of where **unilateral contracts** commonly appear are when a reward is offered, a contest is announced, or changes are made and disseminated in an employee manual. The offeree does not accept the offer by express agreement, but rather by performance.

option contract–contract to hold an offer to make a contract open for a fixed period of time.

(C) OPTION AND FIRST-REFUSAL CONTRACTS. The parties may make a contract that gives a right to one of them to enter into a second contract at a later date. If one party has an absolute right to enter into the later contract, the initial contract is called an **option contract**. Thus, a bilateral contract may be made today giving one of the parties the right to buy the other party's house for a specified amount. This is an option contract because the party with the privilege has the freedom of choice, or

---

[10] *Marsh v Rheinecker,* 641 NE2d 1256 (Ill App 1994).
[11] *DiGeneraro v Rubbermaid, Inc.,* 214 F Supp 2d 1354 (SO Fla 2002).
[12] See *Young v Virginia Birth-Related Neurological Injury Compensation Program,* 620 SE2d 131 (Va App 2005).

CASE SUMMARY

Unilateral Contract: Pretty Good Bonus!

FACTS: Aon Risk Services, Inc. (ARS Arkansas), and Combined Insurance Companies are subsidiaries of Aon Corporation. The parent corporation issued a "Interdependency Memo" dated February 2000, which encouraged ARS brokerage offices to place insurance business with Aon-affiliated companies. It also set up a bonus pool for revenues generated under the plan, with Combined agreeing to pay "30% of annualized premium on all life products over 15-year term plus 15% 1st year for all other products." John Meadors saw the memo in February 2000, and believed it would entitle him to this compensation over and above his employment contract. Meadors put Combined in touch with Dillard's Department Stores and on March 24, 2000, Dillard's and Combined executed a five-year agreement whereby Dillard's employees could purchase life, disability, and other insurance policies through workplace enrollment. When Meadors did not receive bonus-pool money generated by the transaction, he sued his employer for breach of a unilateral contract. The employer's defense was that the memo was not sufficiently definite to constitute an offer.

DECISION: Judgment for Meadors for $2,406,522.60. A unilateral contract is composed of an offer that invites acceptance in the form of actual performance. For example, in the case of a reward, the offeree accepts by performing the particular task, such as the capture of the fugitive for which the reward is offered. In this case the offer contained in the Interdependency Memo set out specific percentages of provisions that would go into the bonus pool, and required that the pool be distributed annually. It was sufficiently definite to constitute an offer. Meadors was responsible for the production of the Dillard's account, and was entitled to the bonus promised in the memo. [**Aon Risk Services, Inc. v Meadors, 267 SW3d 603 (Ark App 2007)**]

option, to buy or not buy. If the option is exercised, the other party to the contract must follow the terms of the option and enter into the second contract. If the option is never exercised, no second contract ever arises, and the offer protected by the option contract merely expires.

In contrast with an option contract, a contract may merely give a **right of first refusal**. This imposes only the duty to make the first offer to the party having the right of first refusal.

right of first refusal–right of a party to meet the terms of a proposed contract before it is executed, such as a real estate purchase agreement.

13. Quasi Contracts

In some cases, a court will impose an obligation even though there is no contract.[13] Such an obligation is called a **quasi contract**, which is an obligation imposed by law.

quasi contract–court-imposed obligation to prevent unjust enrichment in the absence of a contract.

(A) PREVENTION OF UNJUST ENRICHMENT. A quasi contract is not a true contract reflecting all of the elements of a contract set forth previously in this chapter. The court is not seeking to enforce the intentions of the parties contained in an agreement. Rather, when a person or enterprise receives a benefit from another, even

---

[13] *Thayer v Dial Industrial Sales, Inc.*, 85 F Supp 2d 263 (SDNY 2000).

FIGURE 12-2 | *Contract*

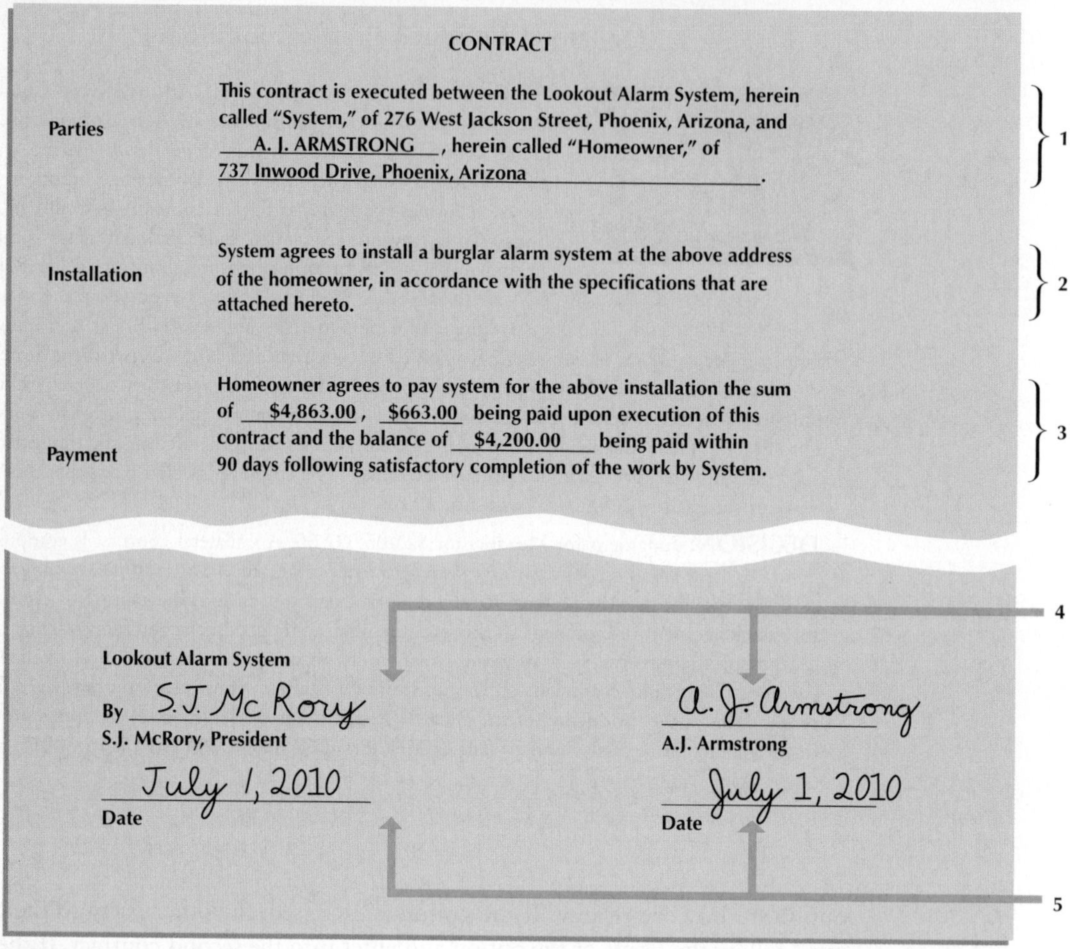

CONTRACT

Parties

This contract is executed between the Lookout Alarm System, herein called "System," of 276 West Jackson Street, Phoenix, Arizona, and ___A. J. ARMSTRONG___, herein called "Homeowner," of 737 Inwood Drive, Phoenix, Arizona_____.

} 1

Installation

System agrees to install a burglar alarm system at the above address of the homeowner, in accordance with the specifications that are attached hereto.

} 2

Payment

Homeowner agrees to pay system for the above installation the sum of ___$4,863.00___, ___$663.00___ being paid upon execution of this contract and the balance of ___$4,200.00___ being paid within 90 days following satisfactory completion of the work by System.

} 3

4

Lookout Alarm System

By *S.J. McRory*
S.J. McRory, President

July 1, 2010
Date

a. J. armstrong
A.J. Armstrong

July 1, 2010
Date

5

Note that this contract includes the following important information: (1) the name and address of each party, (2) the promise or consideration of the seller, (3) the promise or consideration of the buyer, (4) the signature of the two parties, and (5) the date.

in the absence of a promise to pay for the benefit, a court may impose an obligation to pay for the reasonable value of that benefit, to avoid *unjust enrichment*.

A successful claim for unjust enrichment usually requires (1) a benefit conferred on the defendant, (2) the defendant's knowledge of the benefit, and (3) a finding that it would be unjust for the defendant to retain the benefit without payment. The burden of proof is on the plaintiff to prove all of the elements of the claim.

For Example, Hiram College sued Nicholas Courtad for $6,000 plus interest for tuition and other expenses. Because no evidence of a written contract was produced, the court considered it an unjust enrichment claim by the college. Courtad had attended classes for a few weeks and had not paid his tuition due to a problem with his financial aid package. Because he did not receive any credit hours toward a degree, which is the ultimate benefit of attending college, the court found that he did not receive a benefit and that a finding of unjust enrichment was not appropriate.[14]

Sometimes a contract may be unenforceable because of a failure to set forth the contract in writing in compliance with the statute of frauds. In other circumstances, no enforceable contract exists because of a lack of definite and certain terms. Yet in both situations, one party may have performed services for the benefit of the other party and the court will require payment of the reasonable value of services to avoid the unjust enrichment of the party receiving the services without paying for them. These damages are sometimes referred to as *restitution damages*. Some courts refer to this situation as an action or recovery in **quantum meruit** (as much as he or she deserved).

For Example, Arya Group, Inc. (Arya), sued the entertainer Cher for unjust enrichment. In June 1996, Cher negotiated an oral agreement with Arya to design and construct a house on her Malibu property for $4,217,529. The parties' oral agreement was set forth in a written contract with an August 1997 date and was delivered to Cher in October 1997. She never signed it. However, between June 1996 and November 1997, Arya performed and received payment for a number of services discharged under the unsigned contract. In August 1997, Cher requested Arya to meet with a home designer named Bussell who had previously worked with Cher on a Florida project, and Arya showed Bussell the plans and designs for the Malibu property and introduced her to his subcontractors. In November 1997, Cher terminated her agreement with Arya without paying the balance then due, as asserted by Arya, of $415,169.41. Arya claims that Cher and Bussell misappropriated the plans and designs Arya had prepared. Cher and the other defendants demurred to Arya's unjust enrichment complaint, pointing out that construction contracts must be evidenced in a writing signed by both parties under state law in order to be enforceable in a court of law. The appeals court determined that Arya's noncompliance with the state law requiring a signed written contract did not absolutely foreclose Arya from seeking damages for unjust enrichment if he could

quantum meruit—as much as deserved; an action brought for the value of the services rendered the defendant when there was no express contract as to the purchase price.

C A S E   S U M M A R Y

No Free Rides

FACTS: PIC Realty leased farmland to Southfield Farms. After Southfield harvested its crop, it cultivated the land in preparation for the planting in the following year. However, its lease expired, so it did not plant that crop. It then sued PIC for reimbursement for the reasonable value of the services and materials used in preparing the land because this was a benefit to PIC. There was evidence that it was customary for landlords to compensate tenants for such work.

DECISION: Southfield was entitled to recover the reasonable value of the benefit conferred upon PIC. This was necessary in order to prevent the unjust enrichment of PIC. [**PIC Realty Corp. v Southfield Farms, Inc., 832 SW2d 610 (Tex App 1992)**]

[14] *Hiram College v Courtad,* 834 NE2d 432 (Ohio App 2005).

prove the assertions in the complaint that Cher was a sophisticated homeowner with previous involvement in residential construction who had legal representation in negotiating the agreement with Arya, and that Cher would be unjustly enriched if she were not required to compensate Arya for the reasonable value of the work already performed.[15]

A situation may arise over the mistaken conference of a benefit. **For Example,** Nantucket Island has a few approved colors for houses in its historic district. Using the approved gray color, Martin Kane and his crew began painting Sheldon Adams's house in the historic district as the result of a mistaken address. Adams observed the initiation of the work from his office across the street but did nothing to stop the painters. At the end of the day when the work was done, Adams refused to pay for the work, saying, "I signed no contract and never approved this work." The law deems it inequitable that Adams should have received the benefit of this work, having observed the benefit being conferred and knowing that the painters expected payment. Adams would be unjustly enriched if he were allowed to retain the benefit without payment for the reasonable value of the work. If Adams did not have knowledge that the work was being done and thus that payment was expected, quasi-contractual liability would not be imposed.

The mistake that benefits the defendant may be the mistake of a third party.

C A S E   S U M M A R Y

Who Pays the Piper?

FACTS: When improvements or buildings are added to real estate, the real estate tax assessment is usually increased to reflect the increased value of the property. Frank Partipilo and Elmer Hallman owned neighboring tracts of land. In 1977 Hallman made improvements to his land, constructing a new building and driveway on the tract. The tax assessor made a mistake about the location of the boundary line between Partipilo's and Hallman's land and thought the improvements were made on Partipilo's property. Instead of increasing the taxes on Hallman's land, the assessor wrongly increased the taxes on Partipilo's land. Partipilo paid the increased taxes for three years. When he learned why his taxes had been increased, he sued Hallman for the amount of the increase that Partipilo had been paying. Hallman raised the defense that he had not done anything wrong and that the mistake had been the fault of the tax assessor.

DECISION: Judgment for Partipilo. Because the improvements were made to Hallman's land, Hallman should be the one to pay the tax increase. When Partipilo paid it, Hallman received a benefit to which he was not entitled. This was an unjust enrichment. Therefore, Partipilo could recover the amount of the increased taxes without regard to the fact that Hallman was free of any fault and that the only fault in the case was the fault of the tax assessor. [**Partipilo v Hallman, 510 NE2d 8 (Ill App 1987)**]

---

[15] *Arya Group, Inc. v Cher*, 91 Cal Rptr 2d 815 (Cal App 2d 2000). See also *Fischer v Flax*, 816 A2d 1 (2003).

thinking things through
Twelve Years of Litigation

Brown University accepted the bid of Marshall Contractors, Inc. (Marshall), to build the Pizzitola Sports Facility on its Providence, Rhode Island, campus. The parties intended to execute a formal written contract. Brown decided to pay $7,157,051 for the project, but Marshall sought additional payment for items it deemed extras and not contemplated in its bid. Because the parties were unable to agree on the scope of the project as compared to the price Brown was willing to pay, they never executed the formal written contract. Nevertheless, in the context of this disagreement over terms and price, construction began in May 1987. When the parties could not resolve their disagreements as the project neared completion in January 1989, Marshall sued Brown University, seeking to recover the costs for what it deemed "changes." Brown asserted that an implied-in-fact contract existed for all work at the $7,157,051 figure because the contractor went ahead with the project knowing the money Brown would pay. The litigation ended up in the Supreme Court of Rhode Island, and in 1997, the court concluded that no express or implied-in-fact contract had ever been reached by the parties concerning the scope of the project and what costs were to be included in the price stipulated by Brown. The case was remanded to the trial court for a new trial. After a trial on the theories of *quantum meruit* and unjust enrichment, a jury awarded Marshall $1.2 million dollars, which was some $3.1 million less than Marshall sought. Brown University

appealed, and on November 21, 2001, the Supreme Court of Rhode Island affirmed the jury verdict for the contractor, determining that the proper measure of damages on unjust enrichment and *quantum meruit* theories was "the reasonable value of the work done."*

In May 1987 when the parties could not reach agreement enabling the execution of a formal written contract, thinking things through at that point in time should have exposed the potential for significant economic uncertainties to both parties in actually starting the building process under such circumstances. In the spring of 1987 when all parties were unable to reach agreement, mediation or expedited arbitration by construction experts may well have resolved the controversy and yielded an amicable written contract with little or no delay to the project. Instead, the unsettled cost issues during the building process could have had an adverse impact on the "job chemistry" between the contractor and the owner, which may have adversely affected the progress and quality of the job. The 12 years of litigation that, with its economic and human resource costs, yielded just $1.2 million for the contractor was a no-win result for both sides. A primary rule for all managers in projects of this scope is to make sure the written contracts are executed before performance begins! Relying on "implied-in-fact" or quasi-contract legal theories is simply a poor management practice.

* ADP Marshall, Inc. v Brown University, 784 A2d 309 (RI 2001).

(B) **EXTENT OF RECOVERY.** When recovery is allowed in quasi contract, the plaintiff recovers the reasonable value of the benefit conferred on the defendant,[16] or the fair and reasonable[17] value of the work performed, depending on the jurisdiction and the circumstances of the case itself. The customary method of calculating damages in construction contract cases is actual job costs plus an allowance for overhead and profits minus amount paid.[18]

---

[16] *Ramsey v Ellis*, 484 NW2d 331 (Wis 1992).
[17] *ADP Marshall, Inc. v Brown University*, 784 A2d 309 (RI 2001).
[18] *Mirano Contracting, Inc. v Perel*, 871 NYS2d 310 (AD 2008).

C. Contracting on the Internet

Doing business online for consumers is very similar to doing business through a catalog purchase or by phone. Before placing an order, a buyer is commonly concerned about the reputation of the seller. The basic purchasing principle of *caveat emptor* still applies: buyer beware! The Internet provides valuable tools to allow a buyer to research the reputation of the seller and its products. Online evaluations of companies and their products can be found at Web sites, such as Consumer Reports (**www.consumerreports.org**), Consumers Digest (**www.consumersdigest.com**), or the Better Business Bureau (**www.bbb.org**). E-consumers may have access to categorized histories of comments by other e-consumers, such as Planet Feedback ratings at **www.planetfeedback.com**.

The intellectual property principles set forth in Chapter 10—as well as the contractual principles, the law of sales, and privacy laws you are about to study—all apply to e-commerce transactions. When you are purchasing an item online, you must carefully read all of the terms and conditions set forth on the seller's Web site when assessing whether to make a contemplated purchase. The proposed terms may require that any disputes be litigated in a distant state or be resolved through arbitration with restricted remedies, or there may be an unsatisfactory return policy, warranty limitations, or limitation of liability. Generally, the Web site terms become the contract of the parties and are legally enforceable.

The laws you have studied that prevent deceptive advertising by brick-and-mortar businesses also apply to Internet sites.[19] If an in-state site is engaging in false advertising, you may be able to exercise consumer protection rights through your state's attorney general's office, or you may find some therapeutic relief by reporting the misconduct to the Internet Scambusters site (**www.scambusters.com**).

From a seller's perspective, it is exceedingly helpful to have as much information as possible on your potential customers' buying habits. Federal law prohibits the collection of personal information from children without parental consent, and some states restrict the unauthorized collection of personal information. European Union countries have strict laws protecting the privacy of consumers. Sellers intending to collect personal information should obtain the consent of their customers, make certain that children are excluded, and make sure that the information is stored in a secure environment.

Advanced encryption technology has made the use of credit card payments through the Internet very safe. No computer system connected to the Internet is totally secure however. In the worst-case scenario, credit card issuers will not charge a user for more than the first $50 of unauthorized activity.

Internet contracts involve the same types of issues that are addressed in contracts offline but with certain technology-related nuances. The parties to the e-contracts must still negotiate their obligations in clear and unambiguous language, including such terms as quantity, quality, and price as well as warranties, indemnification responsibilities, limitations on liability, and termination procedures. The federal Electronic Signatures in Global and National Commerce Act (E-Sign) and the

---

[19] See *MADCAP I, LLC v McNamee*, 702 NW2d 16 (Wis App 2005) in which the court found genuine issues of material fact as to whether a business Web site falsely represented the size and nature of its business to induce the public to purchase products and services described on its Web site in violation of the state's fraudulent representations statute.

Uniform Electronic Transactions Act (UETA) mandate parity between paper and electronic contracts. The basic legal rules that govern contracts offline are the very same rules that govern online contracts, and basic civil procedure rules apply. **For Example,** California buyer Paul Boschetto bought a 1964 Ford Galaxy that had been advertised on eBay to be "in awesome condition" from a Milton, Wisconsin resident, J. Hansing, for $34,106. On delivery Boschetto discovered that the car had rust, extensive dents, and would not start. His lawsuit against Hansing in U.S. District Court in California was dismissed for lack of personal jurisdiction.[20] (The formation of a contract with a nonresident defendant was not, standing alone, sufficient to create personal jurisdiction in California.)

Boxes identifying special Internet e-commerce topics are strategically placed throughout these chapters.

lawflix

Paper Moon (1973) (PG)

In this movie for which Tatum O'Neal was given an Oscar, the ongoing issue between Annie and her alleged father is her recoupment of the money she says he promised. Discuss the contract issues (voidable [minor], formation, unilateral vs. bilateral, express, informal, etc.).

Check out LawFlix at **www.cengage.com/blaw/dvl** to access movie clips that illustrate business law concepts.

MAKE THE CONNECTION

SUMMARY

A contract is a binding agreement between two or more parties. A contract arises when an offer is accepted with contractual intent (the intent to make a binding agreement).

Contracts may be classified in a number of ways according to form, the way in which they were created, validity, and obligations. With respect to form, a contract may be either informal or formal, such as those under seal or those appearing on the records of courts. Contracts may be classified by the way they were created as those that are expressed by words— written or oral—and those that are implied or deduced from conduct. The question of validity requires distinguishing between contracts that are valid, those that are voidable, and those that are not contracts at all but are merely void agreements. Contracts can be distinguished on the basis of the obligations created as executed contracts, in which everything has been

[20] *Boschetto v. Hansing,* 539 F3d 1011 (9th Cir 2008).

performed, and executory contracts, in which something remains to be done. The bilateral contract is formed by exchanging a promise for a promise, so each party ha the obligation of thereafter rendering the promised performance. In the unilateral contract, which is the doing of an act in exchange for a promise, no further performance is required of the offeree who performed the act.

In certain situations, the law regards it as unjust for a person to receive a benefi and not pay for it. In such a case, the law of quasi contracts allows the performing person to recover the reasonable value of the benefit conferred on the benefited person even though no contract between them requires any payment. Unjust enrichment, which a quasi contract is designed to prevent, sometimes arises when there was never any contract between the persons involved or when there was a contract, but for some reason it was avoided or held to be merely a void agreement

LEARNING OUTCOMES

After studying this chapter, you should be able to clearly explain:

A. NATURE OF CONTRACTS

LO.1 Explain the meaning and importance of privity of a contract
See the example of the subcontractor, RPR & Associates, who worked on a project but could not sue the owner for payment, p. 269.

LO.2 Describe the way in which a contract arises
See the discussion on offer and acceptance on p. 269.

B. CLASSES OF CONTRACTS

LO.3 Distinguish between bilateral and unilateral contracts
See the example of the Nantucket painters on p. 276.
See the *AON Risk Services* case where an insurance agent won his case based on a unilateral contract theory, p. 273.

LO.4 Explain the reasoning behind quasi-contract recovery
See the example whereby Cher had to pay a home designer for certain work even though there was no contract, p. 275.

C. CONTRACTING ON THE INTERNET

LO.5 Explain how Internet contracts involve the same types of issues as offline contracts.
See the eBay example on p. 279.

KEY TERMS

bilateral contract	obligee	quantum meruit
contract	obligor	quasi contract
contracts under seal	offeree	recognizance
executed contract	offeror	right of first refusal
executory contract	option contract	unilateral contract
express contract	privity	valid contract
formal contracts	privity of contract	void agreement
implied contract	promisee	voidable contract
informal contract	promisor	

QUESTIONS AND CASE PROBLEMS

1. What is a contract?

2. Fourteen applicants for a city of Providence, Rhode Island, police academy training class each received from the city a letter stating that it was a "conditional offer of employment" subject to successful completion of medical and psychological exams. The 14 applicants passed the medical and psychological exams. However, these applicants were replaced by others after the city changed the selection criteria. Can you identify an offer and acceptance in this case? Can you make out a bilateral or unilateral contract? [*Ardito et al. v City of Providence,* 213 F Supp 2d 358 (D RI)]

3. Compare an implied contract with a quasi contract.

4. The Jordan Keys law firm represented the Greater Southeast Community Hospital of Washington, D.C., in a medical malpractice suit against the hospital. The hospital was self-insured for the first $1,000,000 of liability and the St. Paul Insurance Co. provided excess coverage up to $4,000,000. The law firm was owed $67,000 for its work on the malpractice suit when the hospital went into bankruptcy. The bankruptcy court ordered the law firm to release its files on the case to St. Paul to defend under the excess coverage insurance, and the Jordan Keys firm sued St. Paul for its legal fees of $67,000 expended prior to the bankruptcy under an "implied-in-fact contract" because the insurance company would have the benefit of all of its work. Decide. [*Jordan Keys v St. Paul Fire,* 870 A2d 58 (DC)]

5. Beck was the general manager of Chilkoot Lumber Co. Haines sold fuel to the company. To persuade Haines to sell on credit, Beck signed a paper by which he promised to pay any debt the lumber company owed Haines. He signed this paper with his name followed by "general manager." Haines later sued Beck on this promise, and Beck raised the defense that the addition of "general manager" showed that Beck, who was signing on behalf of Chilkoot, was not personally liable and did not intend to be bound by the paper. Was Beck liable on the paper? [*Beck v Haines Terminal and Highway Co.,* 843 P2d 1229 (Alaska)]

6. *A* made a contract to construct a house for *B.* Subsequently, *B* sued *A* for breach of contract. *A* raised the defense that the contract was not binding because it was not sealed. Is this a valid defense? [*Cooper v G. E. Construction Co.,* 158 SE2d 305 (Ga App)]

7. Edward Johnson III, the CEO and principal owner of the world's largest mutual fund company, Fidelity Investments, Inc., was a longtime tennis buddy of Richard Larson. In 1995, Johnson asked Larson, who had construction experience, to supervise the construction of a house on Long Pond, Mount Desert Island, Maine. Although they had no written contract, Larson agreed to take on the project for $6,700 per month plus lodging. At the end of the project in 1997, Johnson made a $175,000 cash payment to Larson, and he made arrangements for Larson to live rent-free on another Johnson property in the area called Pray's Meadow in exchange for looking after Johnson's extensive property interests inMaine. In the late summer of 1999, Johnson initiated a new project

on the Long Pond property. Johnson had discussions with Larson about doing this project, but Larson asked to be paid his former rate, and Johnson balked because he had already hired a project manager. According to Johnson, at a later date he again asked Larson to take on the "shop project" as a favor and in consideration of continued rent-free use of the Pray's Meadow home. Johnson stated that Larson agreed to do the job "pro bono" in exchange for the use of the house, and Johnson acknowledged that he told Larson he would "take care" of Larson at the end of the project, which could mean as much or as little as Johnson determined. Larson stated that Johnson told him that he would "take care of" Larson if he would do the project and told him to "trust the Great Oracle" (meaning Johnson, the highly successful businessperson). Larson sought payment in March 2000 and asked Johnson for "something on account" in April. Johnson offered Larson a loan. In August during a tennis match, Larson again asked Johnson to pay him. Johnson became incensed, and through an employee, he ended Larson's participation in the project and asked him to vacate Pray's Meadow. Larson complied and filed suit for payment for work performed at the rate of $6,700 per month. Did Larson have an express contract with Johnson? What legal theory or theories could Larson utilize in his lawsuit? How would you decide this case if you believed Larson's version of the facts? How would you decide the case if you believed Johnson's version of the facts? [*Larson v Johnson*, 196 F Supp 2d 38 (D.Me 2002)]

8. While Clara Novak was sick, her daughter Janie helped her in many ways. Clara died, and Janie then claimed that she was entitled to be paid for the services she had rendered her mother. This claim was opposed by three brothers and sisters who also rendered services to the mother. They claimed that Janie was barred because of the presumption that services rendered between family members are gratuitous. Janie claimed that this presumption was not applicable because she had not lived with her mother but had her own house. Was Janie correct? [*In re Estate of Novak*, 398 NW2d 653 (Minn App)]

9. Dozier and his wife, daughter, and grandson lived in the house Dozier owned. At the request of the daughter and grandson, Paschall made some improvements to the house. Dozier did not authorize these, but he knew that the improvements were being made and did not object to them. Paschall sued Dozier for the reasonable value of the improvements, but Dozier argued that he had not made any contract for such improvements. Was he obligated to pay for such improvements?

10. When Harriet went away for the summer, Landry, a house painter, painted her house. He had a contract to paint a neighbor's house but painted Harriet's house by mistake. When Harriet returned from vacation, Landry billed her for $3,100, which was a fair price for the work. She refused to pay. Landry claimed that she had a quasi-contractual liability for that amount. Was he correct?

11. Margrethe and Charles Pyeatte, a married couple, agreed that she would work so that he could go to law school and that when he finished, she would go back to school for her master's degree. After Charles was admitted to the bar and before Margrethe went back to school, the two were divorced. She sued Charles, claiming that she was entitled to quasi-contractual recovery of the money that

she had paid for Charles's support and law school tuition. He denied liability. Was she entitled to recover for the money she spent for Charles's maintenance and law school tuition? [*Pyeatte v Pyeatte*, 661 P2d 196 (Ariz App)]

12. Carriage Way was a real estate development of approximately 80 houses and 132 apartments. The property owners were members of the Carriage Way Property Owners Association. Each year, the association would take care of certain open neighboring areas, including a nearby lake, that were used by the property owners. The board of directors of the association would make an assessment or charge against the property owners to cover the cost of this work. The property owners paid these assessments for a number of years and then refused to pay any more. In spite of this refusal, the association continued to take care of the areas in question. The association then sued the property owners and claimed that they were liable for the benefit that had been conferred on them. Were the owners liable? [*Board of Directors of Carriage Way Property Owners Ass'n v Western National Bank*, 487 NE2d 974 (Ill App)]

13. Lombard insured his car, and when it was damaged, the insurer sent the car to General Auto Service for repairs. The insurance company went bankrupt and did not pay the repair bill. General Auto Service then sued Lombard for the bill because he had benefited from the repair work. Was he liable?

14. When a college student complained about a particular course, the vice president of the college asked the teacher to prepare a detailed report about the course. The teacher did and then demanded additional compensation for the time spent in preparing the report. He claimed that the college was liable to provide compensation on an implied contract. Was he correct? [*Zadrozny v City Colleges of Chicago*, 581 NE2d 44 (Ill App)]

15. Smith made a contract to sell automatic rifles to a foreign country. Because the sale of such weapons to that country was illegal under an act of Congress, the U.S. government prosecuted Smith for making the contract. He raised the defense that because the contract was illegal, it was void and there is no binding obligation when a contract is void; therefore, no contract for which he could be prosecuted existed. Was he correct?

CPA QUESTIONS

1. Kay, an art collector, promised Hammer, an art student, that if Hammer could obtain certain rare artifacts within two weeks, Kay would pay for Hammer's postgraduate education. At considerable effort and expense, Hammer obtained the specified artifacts within the two-week period. When Hammer requested payment, Kay refused. Kay claimed that there was no consideration for the promise. Hammer would prevail against Kay based on:

   a. Unilateral contract

   b. Unjust enrichment

   c. Public policy

   d. Quasi contract

Chapter 13

FORMATION OF CONTRACTS: OFFER AND ACCEPTANCE

A. Requirements of an Offer

1. CONTRACTUAL INTENTION
2. DEFINITENESS
3. COMMUNICATION OF OFFER TO OFFEREE

B. Termination of Offer

4. REVOCATION OF OFFER BY OFFEROR
5. COUNTEROFFER BY OFFEREE
6. REJECTION OF OFFER BY OFFEREE
7. LAPSE OF TIME
8. DEATH OR DISABILITY OF EITHER PARTY
9. SUBSEQUENT ILLEGALITY

C. Acceptance of Offer

10. WHAT CONSTITUTES AN ACCEPTANCE?
11. PRIVILEGE OF OFFEREE
12. EFFECT OF ACCEPTANCE
13. NATURE OF ACCEPTANCE
14. WHO MAY ACCEPT?
15. MANNER AND TIME OF ACCEPTANCE
16. COMMUNICATION OF ACCEPTANCE
17. AUCTION SALES

A *contract* consists of enforceable obligations that have been voluntarily assumed. Thus, one of the essential elements of a contract is an agreement. This chapter explains how the basic agreement arises, when there is a contract, and how there can be merely unsuccessful negotiations without a resulting contract.

A. REQUIREMENTS OF AN OFFER

offer—expression of an offeror's willingness to enter into a contractual agreement.

An **offer** expresses the willingness of the offeror to enter into a contractual agreement regarding a particular subject. It is a promise that is conditional upon an act, a forbearance (a refraining from doing something one has a legal right to do), or a return promise.

CPA   ## 1. Contractual Intention

To make an offer, the offeror must appear to intend to create a binding obligation. Whether this intent exists is determined by objective standards.[1] This intent may be shown by conduct.

For Example, when one party signs a written contract and sends it to the other party, such action is an offer to enter into a contract on the terms of the writing.

There is no contract when a social invitation is made or when an offer is made in obvious jest or excitement. A reasonable person would not regard such an offer as indicating a willingness to enter into a binding agreement.

(A) INVITATION TO NEGOTIATE. The first statement made by one of two persons is not necessarily an offer. In many instances, there may be a preliminary discussion or an invitation by one party to the other to negotiate or to make an offer. Thus, an inquiry by a school as to whether a teacher wished to continue the following year was merely a survey or invitation to negotiate and was not an offer that could be accepted. Therefore, the teacher's affirmative response did not create a contract.

Ordinarily, a seller sending out circulars or catalogs listing prices is not regarded as making an offer to sell at those prices. The seller is merely indicating a willingness to consider an offer made by a buyer on those terms. The reason for this rule is, in part, the practical consideration that because a seller does not have an unlimited supply of any commodity, the seller cannot possibly intend to make a contract with everyone who sees the circular. The same principle is applied to merchandise that is displayed with price tags in stores or store windows and to most advertisements. An advertisement in a newspaper is ordinarily considered an invitation to negotiate and is not an offer that can be accepted by a reader of the paper.[2] However, some court decisions have construed advertisements as offers that called for an act on the part of the customer thereby forming a unilateral contract, such as the advertisement of a reward for the return of lost property.

Quotations of prices, even when sent on request, are likewise not offers unless the parties have had previous dealings or unless a trade custom exists that would give the recipient of the quotation reason to believe that an offer was being made. Whether a

---

[1] *Glass Service Co. v State Farm Mutual Automobile Ins. Co.,* 530 NW2d 867 (Minn App 1995).
[2] *Pico v Cutter Dodge, Inc.,* 98 Hawaii 309 (2002).

price quotation is to be treated as an offer or merely an invitation to negotiate is a question of the intent of the party giving the quotation.[3]

(B) Agreement to Make a Contract at a Future Date. No contract arises when the parties merely agree that at a future date they will consider making a contract or will make a contract on terms to be agreed on at that time. In such a case, neither party is under any obligation until the future contract is made. Unless an agreement is reached on all material terms and conditions and nothing is left to future negotiations, a contract to enter a contract in the future is of no effect. **For Example,** Hewitt Associates provided employee benefits administrative services to Rollins, Inc. under a contract negotiated in 2001 to run through 2006. Prior to its expiration, the parties negotiated—seeking to agree to a multiyear extension of the 2001 agreement. They agreed to all of the material terms of the contract, except that Rollins balked at a $1.8 million penalty clause. Rollins's employees told Hewitt that the extension "was going to be signed." However, Rollins did not sign and the 2001 agreement expired. Hewitt's contention that the agreement was enforceable at the moment Rollins told Hewitt it was going to sign the new agreement was rejected by the court, stating that an agreement to reach an agreement is a contradiction in terms and imposes no obligation on the parties.[4]

2. Definiteness

An offer, and the resulting contract, must be definite and certain.[5] If an offer is indefinite or vague or if an essential provision is lacking,[6] no contract arises from an attempt to accept it. The reason is that courts cannot tell what the parties are to do. Thus, an offer to conduct a business for as long as it is profitable is too vague to be a valid offer. The acceptance of such an offer does not result in a contract that can be enforced. Statements by a bank that it was "with" the debtors and would "support" them in their proposed business venture were too vague to be regarded as a promise by the bank to make necessary loans to the debtors.

CASE SUMMARY

What is the Meaning of an Agreement for a "Damn Good Job"?

 **FACTS:** Larry Browneller made an oral contract with Hubert Plankenhorn to restore a 1963 Chevrolet Impala convertible. The car was not in good condition. Hubert advised the owner that his work would not yield a car of "show" quality because of the condition of the body, and he accordingly believed that the owner merely wanted a presentable car. Larry, on the other hand, having told Hubert that he wanted a "damn good job," thought this statement would yield a car that would be competitive at the small amateur car shows he attended. When the finished car had what Larry asserted were "waves" in the paint as a result of an uneven surface on the body, Larry brought suit against Hubert for breach of the oral contract.

---

[3] Statutes prohibiting false or misleading advertising may require adherence to advertised prices.
[4] *Hewitt Associates, LLC v Rollins, Inc.,* 669 SE2d 551 (Ga App 2008).
[5] *Graziano v Grant,* 744 A2d 156 (NJ Super AD 1999).
[6] *Peace v Doming Holdings Inc.,* 554 SE2d 314 (Ga App 2001).

C A S E   S U M M A R Y

Continued

DECISION: There was clearly a misunderstanding between the parties over the quality of work that could and would be obtained. *Quality* was a material term of the oral contract between the parties, on which there was no shared understanding. Accordingly, a court will not find an individual in breach of a term of the contract where the term did not exist. **[In re Hubert Plankenhorn 228 BR 638 (ND Ohio 1998)]**

The fact that minor, ministerial, and nonessential terms are left for future determination does not make an agreement too vague to be a contract.[7]

C A S E   S U M M A R Y

Offer to Purchase Is Controlling Legal Document

FACTS: John McCarthy executed an offer to purchase (OTP) real estate on a preprinted form generated by the Greater Boston Real Estate Board. The OTP contained a description of the property, the price to be paid, deposit requirements, limited title requirements, and the time and place for closing. The OTP required the parties to execute the applicable Standard Form Purchase and Sale Agreement recommended by the Greater Boston Real Estate Board that, when executed, was to be the agreement between the parties. An unnumbered paragraph immediately above the signature line stated: "NOTICE: This is a legal document that creates binding obligations. If not understood, consult an attorney." The seller, Ann Tobin, signed the OTP. While lawyers for the parties exchanged drafts of a purchase and sale agreement (PSA), a much higher offer for the property was made to Tobin by the Diminicos. Because she had not yet signed the purchase and sale agreement, Tobin accepted the Diminicos's offer and executed a purchase and sales agreement with them. Before that deal closed, McCarthy filed an action for specific performance of the OTP. McCarthy contended he and Tobin intended to be bound by the OTP and that the execution of a PSA was merely a formality. Tobin contended the OTP language contemplated the execution of a final written document, thus clearly indicating that the parties had not agreed to all material aspects of the transaction, and thus the parties did not intend to be bound until the PSA was signed. From a judgment for Tobin and the Diminicos, McCarthy appealed.

DECISION: Judgment for McCarthy. Although the provisions of the purchase and sale agreement can be the subject of negotiation, norms exist for their customary resolution. The inference that the OTP was legally binding is bolstered by the notice printed on the form. McCarthy and Tobin were alerted to the fact that the OTP "creates binding obligations." The OTP employed familiar contractual language. It stated that McCarthy "hereby offers to buy" the property, and Tobin's signature indicates that "this Offer is hereby accepted." The OTP also details the amount to be paid and when, describes the property bought, and specifies for how long the offer was open. This was a firm offer, the acceptance of which bound Tobin to sell and McCarthy to buy the subject property. **[McCarthy v Tobin, 706 NE2d 629 (Mass 1999)]**

---

[7] *Hsu v Vet-A-Mix, Inc.*, 479 NW2d 336 (Iowa App 1991). But see *Ocean Atlantic Development Corp v Aurora Christian Schools, Inc.*, 322 F3d 983 (7th Cir 2003), where letter offers to purchase (OTP) real estate were signed by both parties, but the offers conditioned the purchase and sale of each property upon the subsequent execution of a purchase and sale agreement. The court held that the parties thus left themselves room to walk away from the deal under Illinois law, and the OTPs were not enforced.

thinking things through

The Rules of Negotiations

Business agreements are often reached after much discussion, study, and posturing by both sides. Many statements may be made by both sides about the price or value placed on the subject of the transaction. Withholding information or presenting selective, self-serving information may be perceived by a party to the negotiations as protective self-interest. Does the law of contracts apply a duty of good faith and fair dealing in the negotiation of contracts? Does the Uniform Commercial Code provide for a general duty of good faith in the negotiation of contracts? Are lawyers under an ethical obligation to inform opposing counsel of relevant facts? The answer to all of these questions is no.

The Restatement (Second) of Contracts applies the duty of good faith and fair dealing to the performance and enforcement of contracts, not their negotiation*; so also does the UCC.** The American Bar Association's Model Rules of Professional Conduct, Rule 4.1 Comment 1 requires a lawyer to be "truthful" when dealing with others on a client's behalf, but it also states that generally a lawyer has "no affirmative duty to inform an opposing party of relevant facts."*** Comment 2 to Rule 4.1 contains an example of a "nonmaterial" statement of a lawyer as "estimates of price or value placed on the subject of a transaction."

The legal rules of negotiations state that—in the absence of fraud, special relationships, or statutory or contractual duties—negotiators are not obligated to divulge pertinent information to the other party to the negotiations. The parties to negotiations themselves must demand and analyze pertinent information and ultimately assess the fairness of the proposed transaction. Should a party conclude that the elements of a final proposal or offer are excessive or dishonest, that party's legal option is to walk away from the deal. Generally, the party has no basis to bring a lawsuit for lack of good faith and fair dealing in negotiations.

However, THINKING THINGS THROUGH, the ethical standards for negotiations set forth in Chapter 3 indicate that establishing a reputation for trustworthiness, candor, and reliability often leads to commercial success for a company's continuing negotiations with its customers, suppliers, distributors, lenders, unions, and employees.****

**** For a contrary example, consider the following story. The Atlanta Braves baseball team's general manager Frank Wren negotiated with free agent baseball player Rafael Furcal's agent Paul Kinzer. When all terms had been negotiated, Kinzer asked for a written terms-of-agreement sheet signed by the Braves, which to Wren meant an agreement had been reached. Kinzer took the sheet to the L.A. Dodgers, who then reached an agreement to sign the shortstop. Braves President John Schuerholz said, "The Atlanta Braves will no longer do business with that company—ever. I told Arn Tellem that we can't trust them to be honest and forthright." "Braves GM Blasts Furcal's Agents," Associated Press, *The Boston Globe*, December 20, 2008, C-7.

* Restatement (Second) of Contracts § 105, comment (c).
** Uniform Commercial Code § 1-203.
*** American Bar Association Model Rule of Professional Conduct 4.1 (a) Comment 1.

The law does not favor the destruction of contracts because that would go against the social force of carrying out the intent of the parties.[8] Consequently, when it is claimed that a contract is too indefinite to be enforced, a court will do its best to find the intent of the parties and thereby reach the conclusion that the contract is not too indefinite. **For Example,** boxing promoter Don King had both a Promotional Agreement and a Bout Agreement with boxer Miguel Angel Gonzalez. The Bout Agreement for a boxing match held on March 7, 1998, with Julio Cesar Chavez gave King the option to promote the next four of Gonzalez's matches. The contract made clear that if Gonzalez won the Chavez match, he would receive at

[8] *Mears v Nationwide Mut, Inc. Co.*, 91 F3d 1118 (8th Cir 1996).

FIGURE 13-1 | *Offer and Acceptance*

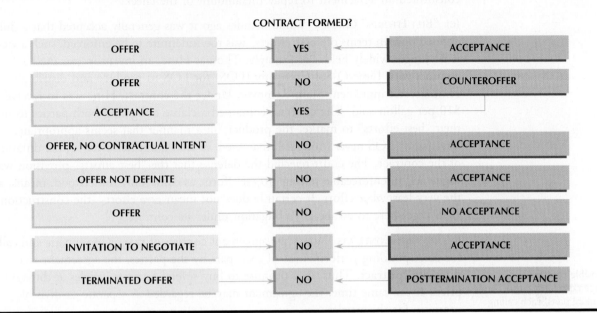

CONTRACT FORMED?

least $75,000 for the next fight unless the parties agreed otherwise, and if he lost, he would receive at least $25,000 for the subsequent fight unless otherwise agreed. The agreement did not explicitly state the purse for the subsequent match in the event of a draw. The Chavez match ended in a draw, and Gonzalez contended that this omission rendered the contract so indefinite that it was unenforceable. The court disagreed, stating that striking down a contract as indefinite and in essence meaningless is at best a last resort. The court held that although the contract was poorly drafted, the Promotional Agreement contained explicit price terms for which a minimum purse for fights following a draw may be inferred.[9] A court may not rewrite the agreement of the parties in order to make it definite.

(A) DEFINITE BY INCORPORATION. An offer and the resulting contract that by themselves may appear "too indefinite" may be made definite by reference to another writing. **For Example,** a lease agreement that was too vague by itself was made definite because the parties agreed that the lease should follow the standard form with which both were familiar. An agreement may also be made definite by reference to the prior dealings of the parties and to trade practices.

(B) IMPLIED TERMS. Although an offer must be definite and certain, not all of its terms need to be expressed. Some omitted terms may be implied by law. **For Example,** an offer "to pay $400" for a certain Movado timepiece does not state the terms of payment. A court, however, would not condemn this provision as too vague but would hold that it required that cash be paid and that the payment be made on delivery of the watch. Likewise, terms may be implied from conduct. As an illustration, when borrowed money was given to the borrower by a check on which

---

[9] *Gonzalez v Don King Productions, Inc.,* 17 F Supp 2d 313 (SDNY 1998); see also *Echols v Pelullo,* 377 F3d 272 (3rd Cir 2004).

the word *loan* was written, the act of the borrower in endorsing the check constituted an agreement to repay the amount of the check.

(c) "Best Efforts" Clauses. While decades ago it was generally accepted that a duty defined only in terms of "best efforts" was too indefinite to be enforced, such a view is no longer widely held. **For Example,** Thomas Hinc, an inventor, executed a contract with Lime-O-Sol Company (LOS) for LOS to produce and distribute Hinc's secret ingredient Stain Remover. Under the contract, Hinc was to receive $10 per gallon sold. The contract contained a clause obligating both parties to use their "best efforts" to market the product "in a manner that seems appropriate." Ultimately, LOS never produced, marketed, or sold Stain Remover for the duration of the contract. The court rejected the defense that the "best efforts" provision was vague and unenforceable stating "[b]est efforts, as commonly understood, means, at the very least *some* effort. It certainly does not mean *zero* effort—the construction LOS urges here to escape any obligation under its contract." [10]

(d) Divisible Contracts. When the agreement consists of two or more parts and calls for corresponding performances of each part by the parties, the agreement is a **divisible contract**. Thus, in a promise to buy several separate articles at different prices at the same time, the agreement may be regarded as separate or divisible promises for the articles.

(e) Exceptions to Definiteness. The law has come to recognize certain situations in which the practical necessity of doing business makes it desirable to have a contract, yet the situation is such that it is either impossible or undesirable to adopt definite terms in advance. In these cases, the indefinite term is often tied to the concept of good-faith performance or to some independent factor that will be definitely ascertainable at some time in the future. The indefinite term might be tied to market price, cost to complete, production, or sales requirements. Thus, the law recognizes binding contracts in the case of a **requirements contract**—that is, a contract to buy all requirements of the buyer from the seller.[11] **For Example,** an agreement between Honeywell International Inc. and Air Products and Chemicals Inc. whereby Air Products would purchase its total requirements of wet process chemicals from Honeywell was held to be an enforceable requirements contract.[12] The law also recognizes as binding an **output contract**—that is, the contract of a producer to sell

divisible contract– agreement consisting of two or more parts, each calling for corresponding performances of each part by the parties.

requirements contract– contract to buy all requirements of the buyer from the seller.

output contract–contract of a producer to sell its entire production or output to a given buyer.

CASE SUMMARY

GM—In The Driver's Seat On Quantity and Timing!

FACTS: Automodular entered into a series of purchase orders that obligated Delphi to purchase and Automodular to provide all of Delphi's requirements deliverable to the original equipment manufacturer (OEM), General Motors. Automodular receives directions from the OEM's final assembly plants, regardless of whether Automodular is under contract to the OEM or Delphi.

---

[10] *Hinc v Lime-O-Sol Company,* 382 F3d 716 (7th Cir 2004).
[11] *Simcala v American Coal Trade, Inc.,* 821 So2d 197 (Ala 2001).
[12] *Honeywell International Inc. v Air Products and Chemicals, Inc.,* 872 A2d 944 (Sup Ct Del 2005).

CASE SUMMARY

Continued

The purchase orders ("Contracts") incorporated Delphi's terms that the Buyer, GM, could require Automodular to implement changes to the specifications or design of the goods or to the scope of any services covered by the Contracts. GM informed Automodular that it needed fewer components and directed Automodular to, among other requirements, reduce shifts, change the assembly line speed, and change the length of workers' shifts. As a result, Automodular requested a price increase per unit assembled from Delphi because Automodular believed that such an increase was warranted pursuant to the Contract's change-in-scope provision. Delphi, however, refused to negotiate any price increase and the matter was litigated.

DECISION: Judgment for Delphi. In a requirements contract, the parties do not fix a quantity term, but instead, the quantity will be the buyer's needs of a specific commodity over the contract's life. Section 2.5 of the Contract states in relevant part that "[d]eliveries will be made in the quantities, on the dates, and at the times specified by Buyer in this Contract or any subsequent releases or instructions Buyer issues under this Contract," and that "[i]f the requirements of Buyer's customers or market, economic or other conditions require changes in delivery schedules, Buyer may change the rate of scheduled shipments or direct temporary suspension of scheduled shipments without entitling [Automodular] to a price adjustment or other compensation." This provision demonstrates the intent of the parties to allow the buyer to effectively control the timing and quantity of deliveries without entitling Automodular to an adjustment in price. [**In re Delphi Corp., 2009 WL 803598, (SDNY 2009).**]

the entire production or output to a given buyer. These are binding contracts even though they do not state the exact quantity of goods that are to be bought or sold.

CPA ## 3. Communication of Offer to Offeree

An offer must be communicated to the offeree. Otherwise, the offeree cannot accept even though knowledge of the offer has been indirectly acquired. Internal management communications of an enterprise that are not intended for outsiders or employees do not constitute offers and cannot be accepted by them. Sometimes, particularly in the case of unilateral contracts, the offeree performs the act called for by the offeror without knowing of the offer's existence. Such performance does not constitute an acceptance. Thus, without knowing that a reward is offered for information leading to the arrest of a particular criminal, a person may provide information that leads to the arrest of the criminal. In most states, if that person subsequently learns of the reward, the reward cannot be recovered.[13]

Not only must the offer be communicated but also it must be communicated by the offeror or at the offeror's direction.

CPA # B. Termination of Offer

An offeree cannot accept a terminated offer. Offers may be terminated by revocation, counteroffer, rejection, lapse of time, death or disability of a party, or subsequent illegality.

---

[13] With respect to the offeror, it should not make any difference, as a practical matter, whether the services were rendered with or without knowledge of the existence of the offer. Only a small number of states have adopted this view, however.

CPA 4. Revocation of Offer by Offeror

Ordinarily, an offeror can revoke the offer before it is accepted. If this is done, the offeree cannot create a contract by accepting the revoked offer. Thus, the bidder at an auction sale may withdraw (revoke) a bid (offer) before it is accepted, and the auctioneer cannot accept that bid later.

An ordinary offer may be revoked at any time before it is accepted even though the offeror has expressly promised that the offer will be good for a stated period and that period has not yet expired. It may also be revoked even though the offeror has expressly promised to the offeree that the offer would not be revoked before a specified later date.

The fact that the offeror expressly promised to keep the offer open has no effect when no consideration was given for that promise.

(A) WHAT CONSTITUTES A REVOCATION? No particular form or words are required to constitute a revocation. Any words indicating the offeror's termination of the offer are sufficient. A notice sent to the offeree that the property that is the subject of the offer has been sold to a third person is a revocation of the offer. A customer's order for goods, which is an offer to purchase at certain prices, is revoked by a notice to the seller of the cancellation of the order, provided that such notice is communicated before the order is accepted.

(B) COMMUNICATION OF REVOCATION. A revocation of an offer is ordinarily effective only when it is made known to the offeree.[14] Until it is communicated to the offeree, directly or indirectly, the offeree has reason to believe that there is still an offer that may be accepted, and the offeree may rely on this belief. A letter revoking an offer made to a particular offeree is not effective until the offeree receives it. It is not a revocation when the offeror writes it or even when it is mailed or dispatched. A written revocation is effective, however, when it is delivered to the offeree's agent or to the offeree's residence or place of business under such circumstances that the offeree may be reasonably expected to be aware of its receipt.

It is ordinarily held that there is a sufficient communication of the revocation when the offeree learns indirectly of the offeror's revocation. This is particularly true in a land sale when the seller-offeror, after making an offer to sell the land to the offeree, sells the land to a third person and the offeree indirectly learns of such sale. The offeree necessarily realizes that the seller cannot perform the original offer and therefore must be considered to have revoked it.

If the offeree accepts an offer before it is effectively revoked, a valid contract is created.

(C) OPTION CONTRACTS. An *option contract* is a binding promise to keep an offer open for a stated period of time or until a specified date. An option contract requires that the promisor receive consideration—that is, something, such as a sum of money—as the price for the promise to keep the offer open. In other words, the option is a contract to refrain from revoking an offer.

(D) FIRM OFFERS. As another exception to the rule that an offer can be revoked at any time before acceptance, statutes in some states provide that an offeror cannot revoke

---

[14] *MD Drilling and Blasting, Inc. v MLS Construction, LLC,* 889 A2d 850 (Conn App 2006).

firm offer–offer stated to be held open for a specified time, which must be so held in some states even in the absence of an option contract, or under the UCC, with respect to merchants.

an offer prior to its expiration when the offeror makes a firm offer. A **firm offer** is an offer that states that it is to be irrevocable, or irrevocable for a stated period of time. Under the Uniform Commercial Code, this doctrine of firm offer applies to a merchant's signed, written offer to buy or sell goods but with a maximum of three months on its period of irrevocability.[15]

5. Counteroffer by Offeree

counteroffer–proposal by an offeree to the offeror that changes the terms of, and thus rejects, the original offer.

The offeree rejects the offer when she ignores the original offer and replies with a different offer.[16] If the offeree purports to accept an offer but in so doing makes any change to the terms of the offer, such action is a **counteroffer** that rejects the original offer. An "acceptance" that changes the terms of the offer or adds new terms is a rejection of the original offer and constitutes a counteroffer.[17]

Ordinarily, if *A* makes an offer, such as to sell a used automobile to *B* for $3,000, and *B* in reply makes an offer to buy at $2,500, the original offer is terminated. *B* is in effect indicating refusal of the original offer and in its place is making a different offer. Such an offer by the offeree is known as a *counteroffer*. No contract arises unless the original offeror accepts the counteroffer.

Counteroffers are not limited to offers that directly contradict the original offers. Any departure from or addition to the original offer is a counteroffer even though the original offer was silent on the point added by the counteroffer.

6. Rejection of Offer by Offeree

If the offeree rejects the offer and communicates this rejection to the offeror, the offer is terminated. Communication of a rejection terminates an offer even though the period for which the offeror agreed to keep the offer open has not yet expired. It may be that the offeror is willing to renew the offer, but unless this is done, there is no longer any offer for the offeree to accept.

7. Lapse of Time

When the offer states that it is open until a particular date, the offer terminates on that date if it has not yet been accepted. This is particularly so when the offeror declares that the offer shall be void after the expiration of the specified time. Such limitations are strictly construed.

If the offer contains a time limitation for acceptance, an attempted acceptance after the expiration of that time has no effect and does not give rise to a contract.[18] When a specified time limitation is imposed on an option, the option cannot be exercised after the expiration of that time, regardless of whether the option was exercised within what would have been held a reasonable time if no time period had been specified.

[15] UCC § 2-205.
[16] *Bourque v FDIC*, 42 F3d 704 (1st Cir 1994).
[17] *McLaughlin v Heikkila*, 697 NW2d 731 (Minn App 2005).
[18] *Century 21 Pinetree Properties, Inc. v Cason*, 469 SE2d 458 (Ga App 1996).

If the offer does not specify a time, it will terminate after the lapse of a reasonable time. What constitutes a reasonable time depends on the circumstances of each case—that is, on the nature of the subject matter, the nature of the market in which it is sold, the time of year, and other factors of supply and demand. If a commodity is perishable or fluctuates greatly in value, the reasonable time will be much shorter than if the subject matter is of a stable value. An offer to sell a harvested crop of tomatoes would expire within a very short time. When a seller purports to accept an offer after it has lapsed by the expiration of time, the seller's acceptance is merely a counteroffer and does not create a contract unless the buyer accepts that counteroffer.

8. Death or Disability of Either Party

If either the offeror or offeree dies or becomes mentally incompetent before the offer is accepted, the offer is automatically terminated. **For Example,** Chet Wilson offers to sell his ranch to Interport, Inc., for $2.5 million. Five days later, Chet is killed in an aviation accident. Interport, Inc., subsequently writes to Chet Wilson Jr., an adult, that his father's offer is accepted. No contract is formed because the offer made by Chet died with him.

CPA   ## 9. Subsequent Illegality

If the performance of the contract becomes illegal after the offer is made, the offer is terminated. **For Example,** if an offer is made to sell six semiautomatic handguns to a commercial firing range for $550 per weapon but a new law prohibiting such sales is enacted before the offer is accepted, the offer is terminated.

CPA   # C. Acceptance of Offer

acceptance–unqualified assent to the act or proposal of another; as the acceptance of a draft (bill of exchange), of an offer to make a contract, of goods delivered by the seller, or of a gift or deed.

An **acceptance** is the assent of the offeree to the terms of the offer. Objective standards determine whether there has been an agreement of the parties.

10. What Constitutes an Acceptance?

No particular form of words or mode of expression is required, but there must be a clear expression that the offeree agrees to be bound by the terms of the offer. If the offeree reserves the right to reject the offer, such action is not an acceptance.[19]

11. Privilege of Offeree

Ordinarily, the offeree may refuse to accept an offer. If there is no acceptance, by definition there is no contract. The fact that there had been a series of contracts between the parties and that one party's offer had always been accepted before by the other does not create any legal obligation to continue to accept subsequent offers.

---

[19] *Pantano v McGowan*, 530 NW2d 912 (Neb 1995).

CPA   ## 12. Effect of Acceptance

The acceptance of an offer creates a binding agreement or contract,[20] assuming that all of the other elements of a contract are present. Neither party can subsequently withdraw from or cancel the contract without the consent of the other party. **For Example,** James Gang refused to honor an oral stock purchase agreement he made with Moshen Sadeghi under terms he assented to and that were announced on the record to a court as a mutual settlement of a dispute. Gang was not allowed subsequently to withdraw from the agreement, because it was an enforceable contract.[21]

CPA   ## 13. Nature of Acceptance

An *acceptance* is the offeree's manifestation of intent to enter into a binding agreement on the terms stated in the offer. Whether there is an acceptance depends on whether the offeree has manifested an intent to accept. It is the objective or outward appearance that is controlling rather than the subjective or unexpressed intent of the offeree.[22]

In the absence of a contrary requirement in the offer, an acceptance may be indicated by an informal "okay," by a mere affirmative nod of the head, or in the case of an offer of a unilateral contract, by performance of the act called for.

The acceptance must be absolute and unconditional. It must accept just what is offered.[23] If the offeree changes any terms of the offer or adds any new term, there is no acceptance because the offeree does not agree to what was offered.

When the offeree does not accept the offer exactly as made, the addition of any qualification converts the "acceptance" into a counteroffer, and no contract arises unless the original offeror accepts such a counteroffer.

CPA   ## 14. Who May Accept?

Only the person to whom an offer is directed may accept it. If anyone else attempts to accept it, no agreement or contract with that person arises.

If the offer is directed to a particular class rather than a specified individual, anyone within that class may accept it. If the offer is made to the public at large, any member of the public at large having knowledge of the existence of the offer may accept it.

When a person to whom an offer was not made attempts to accept it, the attempted acceptance has the effect of an offer. If the original offeror is willing to accept this offer, a binding contract arises. If the original offeror does not accept the new offer, there is no contract.

---

[20] *Ochoa v Ford,* 641 NE2d 1042 (Ind App 1994).
[21] *Sadeghi v Gang,* 270 SW2d 773 (Tex App 2008).
[22] *Cowan v Mervin Mewes, Inc.,* 546 NW2d 104 (SD 1996).
[23] *Jones v Frickey,* 618 SE2d 29 (Ga App 2005).

C A S E   S U M M A R Y

There's No Turning Back

FACTS: As a lease was about to expire, the landlord, CRA Development, wrote the tenant, Keryakos Textiles, setting forth the square footage and the rate terms on which the lease would be renewed. Keryakos sent a reply stating that it was willing to pay the proposed rate but wanted different cancellation and option terms in the renewal contract. CRA rejected Keryakos's terms, and on learning this, Keryakos notified CRA that it accepted the terms of its original letter. CRA sought to evict Keryakos from the property, claiming that no lease contract existed between it and Keryakos.

DECISION: The lease contract is governed by ordinary contract law. When the tenant offered other terms in place of those made by the landlord's offer, the tenant made a counteroffer. This had the effect of rejecting or terminating the landlord's offer. The tenant could not then accept the rejected offer after the tenant's counteroffer was rejected. Therefore, there was no contract. [*Keryakos Textiles, Inc. v CRA Development, Inc.* 563 NYS2d 308 (App Div 1990)]

CPA   ## 15. Manner and Time of Acceptance

The offeror may specify the manner and time for accepting the offer. When the offeror specifies that there must be a written acceptance, no contract arises when the offeree makes an oral acceptance. If the offeror calls for acceptance by a specified time and date, a late acceptance has no legal effect, and a contract is not formed. Where no time is specified in the offer, the offeree has a reasonable period of time to accept the offer. After the time specified in the offer or a reasonable period of time expires (when no time is specified in the offer), the offeree's power to make a contract by accepting the offer "lapses."

When the offeror calls for the performance of an act or of certain conduct, the performance thereof is an acceptance of the offer and creates a unilateral contract.

When the offeror has specified a particular manner and time of acceptance, generally, the offeree cannot accept in any other way. The basic rule applied by the courts is that the offeror is the master of the offer![24]

CPA   (A) SILENCE AS ACCEPTANCE. In most cases, the offeree's silence and failure to act cannot be regarded as an acceptance. Ordinarily, the offeror is not permitted to frame an offer in such a way as to make the silence and inaction of the offeree operate as an acceptance. Nor can a party to an existing contract effect a modification of that agreement without the other party's actual acceptance or approval. **For Example,** H. H. Taylor made a contract with Andy Stricker, a civil engineer, to design a small hotel. The parties agreed on an hourly rate with "total price not to exceed $7,200," and required that additional charges be presented to Taylor prior to proceeding with any changes. Andy was required to dedicate more hours to the project than anticipated but could not present the additional charges to

[24] See *1-800 Contacts, Inc v Weigner,* 127 P3d 1241 (Utah App 2005).

e-commerce&cyberlaw

Contract Formation On The Internet

It is not possible for an online service provider or seller to individually bargain with each person who visits its Web site. The Web site owner, therefore, as offeror, places its proposed terms on its Web site and requires visitors to assent to these terms in order to access the site, download software, or purchase a product or service.

In a written contract, the parties sign a paper document indicating their intention to be bound by the terms of the contract. Online, however, an agreement may be accomplished by the visitor-offeree simply typing the words "I Accept" in an onscreen box and then clicking a "send" or similar button that indicates acceptance. Or the individual clicks an "I Agree" or "I Accept" icon or check box. Access to the site is commonly denied those who do not agree to the terms. Such agreements have come to be known as *clickwrap* agreements and in the case of software license agreements, *SLAs*. The agreements contain fee schedules and other financial terms and may contain terms such as a notice of the proprietary nature of the material contained on the site and of any limitations on the use of the site and the downloading of software. Moreover, the clickwrap agreements may contain limitations on liability, including losses associated with the use of downloaded software or products or services purchased from the site.

To determine whether a clickwrap agreement is enforceable, courts apply traditional principles of contract law and focus on whether the plaintiffs had reasonable notice of and manifested assent to the clickwrap agreement. Failure to read an enforceable clickwrap agreement, as with any binding contract, will not excuse compliance with its terms.

In *Specht v Netscape Communications Corp.,** the Internet users were urged to click on a button to download free software, but the offer did not make clear to the user that clicking the download button would signify assent to restrictive contractual terms and conditions. The court, in its 2002 decision, declined to enforce this clickwrap agreement. Internet sellers and service providers generally learned from the *Specht* decision, and most clickwrap agreements now provide sufficient notice and means for clear assent. For example, in *Feldman v Google, Inc.,*** decided in 2007, the user was unsuccessful in challenging the terms of Google's "AdWords" Program clickwrap agreement. In order to activate an AdWords account, the user had to visit a Web page that displayed the agreement in a scrollable text box. The text of the agreement was immediately visible to the user, as was a prominent admonition in boldface to read the terms and conditions carefully, and with instructions to indicate assent if the user agreed to the terms.

Unlike the impermissible agreement in *Specht*, the user here had to take affirmative action and click the "Yes, I agree to the above terms and conditions" button in order to proceed to the next step. Clicking "Continue" without clicking the "Yes" button would have returned the user to the same Web page. If the user did not agree to all of the terms, he could not have activated his account, placed ads, or incurred charges.

---

* 306 F3d 17 (2d Cir 2002).
** *Feldman v Google. Inc.,* 513 F Supp 2d 229 (ED Pa 2007). See also *A. V. v Iparadigms, LLC,* 554 F Supp 2d 473 (ED Va 2008).

Taylor because Taylor would not return his phone calls. He billed Taylor $9,035 for his services. Taylor's failure to act in not returning phone calls is not a substitute for the assent needed to modify a contract. Stricker is thus only entitled to $7,200. [25]

(B) **UNORDERED GOODS AND TICKETS.** Sometimes a seller writes to a person with whom the seller has not had any prior dealings, stating that unless notified to the contrary, the seller will send specified merchandise and the recipient is obligated to pay for it at stated prices. There is no acceptance if the recipient of the letter ignores the offer

---

[25] *Stricker v Taylor,* 975 P2d 930 (Or App 1999).

and does nothing. The silence of the person receiving the letter is not an acceptance, and the sender, as a reasonable person, should recognize that none was intended.

This rule applies to all kinds of goods, books, magazines, and tickets sent through the mail when they have not been ordered. The fact that the items are not returned does not mean that they have been accepted; that is, the offeree is required neither to pay for nor to return the items. If desired, the recipient of the unordered goods may write "Return to Sender" on the unopened package and put the package back into the mail without any additional postage. The Postal Reorganization Act provides that the person who receives unordered mailed merchandise from a commercial sender has the right "to retain, use, discard, or dispose of it in any manner the recipient sees fit without any obligation whatsoever to the sender."[26] It provides further that any unordered merchandise that is mailed must have attached to it a clear and conspicuous statement of the recipient's right to treat the goods in this manner.

CPA ___ ## 16. Communication of Acceptance

Acceptance by the offeree is the last step in the formation of a bilateral contract. Intuitively, the offeror's receipt of the acceptance should be the point in time when the contract is formed and its terms apply. When the parties are involved in face-to-face negotiations, a contract is formed upon the offeror's receipt of the acceptance. When the offeror hears the offeree's words of acceptance, the parties may shake hands, signifying their understanding that the contract has been formed.

CPA ___ (A) MAILBOX RULE. When the parties are negotiating at a distance from each other, special rules have developed as to when the acceptance takes effect based on the commercial expediency of creating a contract at the earliest period of time and the protection of the offeree. Under the so-called *mailbox rule,* a properly addressed, postage-paid mailed acceptance takes effect when the acceptance is placed into the control of the U.S. Postal Service[27] or, by judicial extension, is placed in the control of a private third-party carrier such as Federal Express or United Parcel Service.[28] That is, the acceptance is effective upon dispatch even before it is received by the offeror.

CASE SUMMARY

When the Mailbox Bangs Shut

FACTS: The Thoelkes owned land. The Morrisons mailed an offer to the Thoelkes to buy their land. The Thoelkes agreed to this offer and mailed back a contract signed by them. While this letter was in transit, the Thoelkes notified the Morrisons that their acceptance was revoked. Were the Thoelkes bound by a contract?

---

[26] Federal Postal Reorganization Act § 3009.

[27] See *Adams v Lindsell,* 106 Eng Rep 250 (KB 1818). Common law jurisdictions have unanimously adopted the mailbox rule, as has the Restatement (Second) of Contracts § 63, and the UCC [see UCC § 1-201(26),(38)].

[28] But see *Baca v. Trejo,* 902 NE2d 1108 (Ill App 2009) whereby an Illinois Court determined that a statute deeming a document to be filed with a state court on the date shown by the U.S. Postal Service cancellation mark—the mailbox rule—does not apply to documents consigned to a private carrier, UPS. The court reasoned that courts should not have the task of deciding which carriers are acceptable.

CASE SUMMARY

Continued

DECISION: The acceptance was effective when mailed, and the subsequent revocation of the acceptance had no effect. [**Morrison v Thoelke, 155 So 2d 889 (Fla App 1963)**]

The offeror may avoid the application of this rule by stating in the offer that acceptance shall take effect upon receipt by the offeror.

CPA   (B) DETERMINING THE APPLICABLE MEANS OF COMMUNICATION. The modern rule on the selection of the appropriate medium of communication of acceptance is that unless otherwise unambiguously indicated in the offer, it shall be construed as inviting acceptance in any manner and by any medium reasonable under the circumstances.[29] A medium of communication is normally reasonable if it is one used by the offeror or if it is customary in similar transactions at the time and place the offer is received. Thus, if the offeror uses the mail to extend an offer, the offeree may accept by using the mail. Indeed, acceptance by mail is ordinarily reasonable when the parties are negotiating at a distance even if the offer is not made by mail.

CASE SUMMARY

Just Be Reasonable

FACTS: Maria Cantu was a special education teacher under a one-year contract with the San Benito School District for the 1990–1991 school year. On Saturday, August 18, just weeks before fall-term classes were to begin, she hand delivered a letter of resignation to her supervisor. Late Monday afternoon the superintendent put in the mail a properly stamped and addressed letter to Cantu accepting her offer of resignation. The next morning at 8:00, before the superintendent's letter reached her, Cantu hand delivered a letter withdrawing her resignation. The superintendent refused to recognize the attempted rescission of the resignation.

DECISION: Cantu was wrong. The resignation became binding when the acceptance of the resignation was mailed. The fact that the offer to resign had been delivered by hand did not require that the offer be accepted by a hand delivery of the acceptance. The use of mail was reasonable under the circumstances, and therefore the mailing of the acceptance made it effective. [**Cantu v Central Education Agency, 884 SW2d 563 (Tex App 1994)**]

CPA   (C) TELEPHONE AND ELECTRONIC COMMUNICATION OF ACCEPTANCE. Although telephonic communication is very similar to face-to-face communication, most U.S. courts, nevertheless, have applied the mailbox rule, holding that telephoned acceptances are effective where and when dispatched.

[29] Restatement (Second) of Contracts § 30; UCC § 2-206(1) (a).

The courts have yet to address the applicability of the mailbox rule to e-mail. However, when the offeree's server is under the control of an independent entity, such as an online service provider, and the offeree cannot withdraw the message, it is anticipated that the courts will apply the mailbox rule, and acceptance will take effect on proper dispatch. In the case of companies that operate their own servers, the acceptance will take effect when the message is passed onto the Internet.

Facsimile transmissions are substantially instantaneous and could be treated as face-to-face communications. However, it is anticipated that U.S. courts, when called upon to deal with this issue, will apply the mailbox acceptance-upon-dispatch rule as they do with telephoned acceptances.

(D) EFFECTS OF THE MAILBOX RULE. If an offer requires that acceptance be communicated by a specific date and the acceptance is properly dispatched by the offeree on the final date, the acceptance is timely and the contract is formed, even though the offeror actually receives the acceptance well after the specified date has passed. **For Example,** by letter dated February 18, 1999, Morton's of Chicago mailed a certified letter to the Crab House accepting the Crab House's offer to terminate its restaurant lease. The Crab House, Inc., sought to revoke its offer to terminate the lease in a certified letter dated February 18, 1999 and by facsimile transmission to Morton's dated February 19, 1999. On February 22, 1999, the Crab House received Morton's acceptance letter; and on the same date Morton's received Crab House's letter revoking the offer to terminate the lease. Acceptance of an offer is effective upon dispatch to the Postal Service, and the contract springs into existence at the time of the mailing. Offers, revocations, and rejections are generally effective only upon the offeree's receipt. Morton's dispatch of its acceptance letter on February 18 formed an agreement to terminate the lease, and the fax dispatched on February 19 was too late to revoke the offer to terminate the lease.[30]

17. Auction Sales

At an auction sale, the statements made by the auctioneer to draw forth bids are merely invitations to negotiate. Each bid is an offer, which is not accepted until the auctioneer indicates that a particular offer or bid is accepted. Usually, this is done by the fall of the auctioneer's hammer, indicating that the highest bid made has been accepted.[31] Because a bid is merely an offer, the bidder may withdraw the bid at any time before it is accepted by the auctioneer.

Ordinarily, the auctioneer who is not satisfied with the amounts of the bids that are being made may withdraw any article or all of the property from the sale. Once a bid is accepted, however, the auctioneer cannot cancel the sale. In addition, if it had been announced that the sale was to be made "without reserve," the property must be sold to the person making the highest bid regardless of how low that bid may be.

In an auction "with reserve," the auctioneer takes bids as agent for the seller with the understanding that no contract is formed until the seller accepts the transaction.[32]

---

[30] *Morton's of Chicago v Crab House Inc.*, 746 NYS2d 317 (2002). *Kass v Grais*, 2007 NY Misc LEXIS 9017.
[31] *Dry Creek Cattle Co. v Harriet Bros. Limited Partnership*, 908 P2d 399 (Wyo 1995).
[32] *Marten v Staab*, 543 NW2d 436 (Neb 1996). Statutes regulate auctions and auctioneers in all states. For example, state of Maine law prohibits an auctioneer from conducting an auction without first having a written contract with the consignor of any property to be sold, including (1) whether the auction is with reserve or without reserve, (2) the commission rate, and (3) a description of all items to be sold. See *Street v Board of Licensing of Auctioneers*, 889 A2d 319 ([Me] 2006).

lawflix

Funny Farm (1988) (PG)

Near the end of this Chevy Chase movie, two couples face a formation issue as one couple attempts to purchase a home. An offer, presented around a friendly kitchen table setting, is declined by the sellers. Do the buyers' threats to sue the sellers have any legal basis? While the buyers had made a special trip to see the land and felt that since they were offering more than the asking price that they had a contract, the sellers were free to reject the offer. Listing a house for a price is not an offer; it is an invitation for an offer.

Check out LawFlix at **www.cengage.com/blaw/dvl** to access movie clips that illustrate business law concepts.

MAKE THE CONNECTION

SUMMARY

Because a contract arises when an offer is accepted, it is necessary to find that there was an offer and that it was accepted. If either element is missing, there is no contract.

An offer does not exist unless the offeror has contractual intent. This intent is lacking if the statement of the person is merely an invitation to negotiate, a statement of intention, or an agreement to agree at a later date. Newspaper ads, price quotations, and catalog prices are ordinarily merely invitations to negotiate and cannot be accepted.

An offer must be definite. If an offer is indefinite, its acceptance will not create a contract because it will be held that the resulting agreement is too vague to enforce. In some cases, an offer that is by itself too indefinite is made definite because some writing or standard is incorporated by reference and made part of the offer. In some cases the offer is made definite by implying terms that were not stated. In other cases, the indefinite part of the offer is ignored when that part can be divided or separated from the balance of the offer.

Assuming that there is in fact an offer that is made with contractual intent and that it is sufficiently definite, it still does not have the legal effect of an offer unless it is communicated to the offeree by or at the direction of the offeror.

In some cases, there was an offer but it was terminated before it was accepted. By definition, an attempted acceptance made after the offer has been terminated has no effect. The offeror may revoke the ordinary offer at any time. All that is required is the showing of the intent to revoke and the communication of that intent to the offeree. The offeror's power to revoke is barred by the existence of an option contract under common law or a firm offer under the Uniform Commercial Code. An offer is also terminated by the express rejection of the offer or by the making of a counteroffer, by the lapse of the time stated in the offer or of a reasonable time when none is stated, by the death or disability of either party, or by a change of law that makes illegal a contract based on the particular offer.

When the offer is accepted, a contract arises. Only the offeree can accept an offer, and the acceptance must be of the offer exactly as made without any qualification or change. Ordinarily, the offeree may accept or reject as the offeree chooses.

The acceptance is any manifestation of intent to agree to the terms of the offer. Ordinarily, silence or failure to act does not constitute acceptance. The recipient of unordered goods and tickets may dispose of the goods or use the goods without such action constituting an acceptance. An acceptance does not exist until the words or conduct demonstrating assent to the offer is communicated to the offeror. Acceptance by mail takes effect at the time and place when and where the letter is mailed or the fax is transmitted.

In an auction sale, the auctioneer asking for bids makes an invitation to negotiate. A person making a bid is making an offer, and the acceptance of the highest bid by the auctioneer is an acceptance of that offer and gives rise to a contract. When the auction sale is without reserve, the auctioneer must accept the highest bid. If the auction is not expressly without reserve, the auctioneer may refuse to accept any of the bids.

LEARNING OUTCOMES

After studying this chapter, you should be able to clearly explain:

A. REQUIREMENTS OF AN OFFER

LO.1 Decide whether an offer contains definite and certain terms
See the *Plankenhorn* case for the meaning of a "damn good job" on p. 286.
See the legal impact of a party's statement that the contract "was going to be signed" in the *Hewitt* example on p. 286.

B. TERMINATION OF AN OFFER

LO.2 Explain the exceptions the law makes to the requirement of definiteness
See the *Delphi* case on requirements contracts, p. 290.

LO.3 Explain all the ways an offer can be terminated
See the discussion of revocation, counteroffer, rejection, lapse of time, death or disability of a party, or subsequent illegality, starting on p. 291.

C. ACCEPTANCE OF AN OFFER

LO.4 Explain what constitutes the acceptance of an offer
See the *Sadeghi* example where acceptance of an offer created a binding contract, p. 295.
See the *Keryakos Textiles* case on the impact of a counteroffer, p. 296.

LO.5 Explain the implications of failing to read a clickwrap agreement
See the *Feldman* case as an example of an enforceable clickwrap agreement containing notice and manifested assent, p. 297.

KEY TERMS

acceptance	firm offer	requirements contract
counteroffer	offer	
divisible contract	output contract	

QUESTIONS AND CASE PROBLEMS

1. Bernie and Phil's Great American Surplus store placed an ad in the *Sunday Times* stating, "Next Saturday at 8:00 A.M. sharp, 3 brand new mink coats worth $5,000 each will be sold for $500 each! First come, First served." Marsha Lufklin was first in line when the store opened and went directly to the coat department, but the coats identified in the ad were not available for sale. She identified herself to the manager and pointed out that she was first in line in conformity with the store's advertised offer and that she was ready to pay the $500 price set forth in the store's offer. The manager responded that a newspaper ad is just an invitation to negotiate and that the store decided to withdraw "the mink coat promotion." Review the text on unilateral contracts in Section 12(b) of Chapter 12. Decide.

2. Brown made an offer to purchase Overman's house on a standard printed form. Underneath Brown's signature was the statement: "ACCEPTANCE ON REVERSE SIDE." Overman did not sign the offer on the back but sent Brown a letter accepting the offer. Later, Brown refused to perform the contract, and Overman sued him for breach of contract. Brown claimed there was no contract because the offer had not been accepted in the manner specified by the offer. Decide. [*Overman v Brown*, 372 NW2d 102 (Neb)]

3. Katherine mailed Paul an offer with definite and certain terms and that was legal in all respects stating that it was good for 10 days. Two days later she sent Paul a letter by certified mail (time stamped by the Postal Service at 1:14 P.M.) stating that the original offer was revoked. That evening Paul e-mailed acceptance of the offer to Katherine. She immediately phoned him to tell him that she had revoked the offer that afternoon, and he would surely receive it in tomorrow's mail. Was the offer revoked by Katherine?

4. Nelson wanted to sell his home. Baker sent him a written offer to purchase the home. Nelson made some changes to Baker's offer and wrote him that he, Nelson, was accepting the offer as amended. Baker notified Nelson that he was dropping out of the transaction. Nelson sued Baker for breach of contract. Decide. What social forces and ethical values are involved? [*Nelson v Baker*, 776 SW2d 52 (Mo App)]

5. Lessack Auctioneers advertised an auction sale that was open to the public and was to be conducted with reserve. Gordon attended the auction and bid $100 for a work of art that was worth much more. No higher bid, however, was

made. Lessack refused to sell the item for $100 and withdrew the item from the sale. Gordon claimed that because he was the highest bidder, Lessack was required to sell the item to him. Was he correct?

6. Willis Music Co. advertised a television set at $22.50 in the Sunday newspaper. Ehrlich ordered a set, but the company refused to deliver it on the grounds that the price in the newspaper ad was a mistake. Ehrlich sued the company. Was it liable? Why or why not? [*Ehrlich v Willis Music Co.,* 113 NE2d 252 (Ohio App)]

7. When a movement was organized to build Charles City College, Hauser and others signed pledges to contribute to the college. At the time of signing, Hauser inquired what would happen if he should die or be unable to pay. The representative of the college stated that the pledge would then not be binding and that it was merely a statement of intent. The college failed financially, and Pappas was appointed receiver to collect and liquidate the assets of the college corporation. He sued Hauser for the amount due on his pledge. Hauser raised the defense that the pledge was not a binding contract. Decide. What ethical values are involved? [*Pappas v Hauser,* 197 NW2d 607 (Iowa)]

8. *A* signed a contract agreeing to sell land he owned but reserved the right to take the hay from the land until the following October. He gave the contract form to *B*, a broker. *C*, a prospective buyer, agreed to buy the land and signed the contract but crossed out the provision regarding the hay crop. Was there a binding contract between *A* and *C*?

9. A. H. Zehmer discussed selling a farm to Lucy. After a 40-minute discussion of the first draft of a contract, Zehmer and his wife, Ida, signed a second draft stating: "We hereby agree to sell to W. O. Lucy the Ferguson farm complete for $50,000 title satisfactory to buyer." Lucy agreed to purchase the farm on these terms. Thereafter, the Zehmers refused to transfer title to Lucy and claimed they had made the contract for sale as a joke. Lucy brought an action to compel performance of the contract. The Zehmers claimed there was no contract. Were they correct? [*Lucy v Zehmer,* 84 SE2d 516 (Va App)]

10. Wheeler operated an automobile service station, which he leased from W. C. Cornitius, Inc. The lease ran for three years. Although the lease did not contain any provision for renewal, it was in fact renewed six times for successive three-year terms. The landlord refused to renew the lease for a seventh time. Wheeler brought suit to compel the landlord to accept his offer to renew the lease. Decide. [*William C. Cornitius, Inc. v Wheeler,* 556 P2d 666 (Or)]

11. Buster Cogdill, a real estate developer, made an offer to the Bank of Benton to have the bank provide construction financing for the development of an outlet mall, with funds to be provided at prime rate plus two percentage points. The bank's president Julio Plunkett thanked Buster for the proposal and said, "I will start the paperwork." Did Cogdill have a contract with the Bank of Benton? [*Bank of Benton v Cogdill,* 454 NE2d 1120 (Ill App)]

12. Ackerley Media Group, Inc., claimed to have a three-season advertising Team Sponsorship Agreement (TSA) with Sharp Electronics Corporation to promote Sharp products at all Seattle Supersonics NBA basketball home games. Sharp contended that a valid agreement did not exist for the third season (2000–2001) because a material price term was missing, thus resulting in an unenforceable "agreement to agree." The terms of the TSA for the 2000–2001 third season called for a base payment of $144,200 and an annual increase "not to exceed 6% [and] to be mutually agreed upon by the parties." No "mutually agreed" increase was negotiated by the parties. Ackerley seeks payment for the base price of $144,200 only. Sharp contends that since no price was agreed upon for the season, the entire TSA is unenforceable, and it is not obligated to pay for the 2000–2001 season. Is Sharp correct? [*Ackerley Media Group, Inc. v Sharp Electronics Corp.,* 170 F Supp 2d 445 (SDNY)]

13. L. B. Foster invited Tie and Track Systems Inc. to submit price quotes on items to be used in a railroad expansion project. Tie and Track responded by e-mail on August 11, 2006, with prices for 9 items of steel ties. The e-mail concluded, "The above prices are delivered/Terms of Payment—to be agreed/Delivery—to be agreed/We hope you are successful with your bid. If you require any additional information please call." Just 3 of the 9 items listed in Tie and Track's price quote were "accepted" by the project. L. B. Foster demanded that Tie and Track provide the items at the price listed in the quote. Tie and Track refused. L. B. Foster sued for breach of contract. Did the August 11 e-mail constitute an offer, acceptance of which could bind the supplier to a contract? If so, was there a valid acceptance? [*L. B. Foster v Tie and Track Systems, Inc.,* 2009 WL 900993 (ND Ill 2009)

14. On August 15, 2003, Wilbert Heikkila signed an agreement with Kangas Realty to sell eight parcels of Heikkila's property. On September 8, 2003, David McLaughlin met with a Kangas agent who drafted McLaughlin's offer to purchase three of the parcels. McLaughlin signed the offer and gave the agent checks for each parcel. On September 9 and 10, 2003, the agent for Heikkila prepared three printed purchase agreements, one for each parcel. On September 14, 2003, David's wife, Joanne McLaughlin, met with the agent and signed the agreements. On September 16, 2003, Heikkila met with his real estate agent. Writing on the printed agreements, Heikkila changed the price of one parcel from $145,000 to $150,000, the price of another parcel from $32,000 to $45,000, and the price of the third parcel from $175,000 to $179,000. Neither of the McLaughlins signed an acceptance of Heikkila's changes to the printed agreements before Heikkila withdrew his offer to sell. The McLaughlins learned that Heikkila had withdrawn his offer on January 1, 2004, when the real estate agent returned the checks to them. Totally shocked at Heikkila's conduct, the McLaughlins brought action to compel specific performance of the purchase agreement signed by Joanne McLaughlin on their behalf. Decide. [*McLaughlin v Heikkila,* 697 NW2d 231 (Minn App)]

CPA QUESTIONS

1. Able Sofa, Inc., sent Noll a letter offering to sell Noll a custom-made sofa for $5,000. Noll immediately sent a telegram to Able purporting to accept the offer. However, the telegraph company erroneously delivered the telegram to Abel Soda, Inc. Three days later, Able mailed a letter of revocation to Noll, which was received by Noll. Able refused to sell Noll the sofa. Noll sued Able for breach of contract. Able:

   a. Would have been liable under the deposited acceptance rule only if Noll had accepted by mail

   b. Will avoid liability since it revoked its offer prior to receiving Noll's acceptance

   c. Will be liable for breach of contract

   d. Will avoid liability due to the telegraph company's error (Law, #2, 9911)

2. On September 27, Summers sent Fox a letter offering to sell Fox a vacation home for $150,000. On October 2, Fox replied by mail agreeing to buy the home for $145,000. Summers did not reply to Fox. Do Fox and Summers have a binding contract?

   a. No, because Fox failed to sign and return Summers's letter

   b. No, because Fox's letter was a counteroffer

   c. Yes, because Summers's offer was validly accepted

   d. Yes, because Summers's silence is an implied acceptance of Fox's letter (Law, #2, 0462)

3. On June 15, Peters orally offered to sell a used lawn mower to Mason for $125. Peters specified that Mason had until June 20 to accept the offer. On June 16, Peters received an offer to purchase the lawn mower for $150 from Bronson, Mason's neighbor. Peters accepted Bronson's offer. On June 17, Mason saw Bronson using the lawn mower and was told the mower had been sold to Bronson. Mason immediately wrote to Peters to accept the June 15 offer. Which of the following statements is correct?

   a. Mason's acceptance would be effective when received by Peters.

   b. Mason's acceptance would be effective when mailed.

   c. Peters's offer had been revoked and Mason's acceptance was ineffective.

   d. Peters was obligated to keep the June 15 offer open until June 20. (Law, #13, 3095)

Chapter 14

CAPACITY AND GENUINE ASSENT

A. Contractual Capacity

   1. CONTRACTUAL CAPACITY DEFINED

   2. MINORS

   3. MENTALLY INCOMPETENT PERSONS

   4. INTOXICATED PERSONS

B. Mistake

   5. UNILATERAL MISTAKE

   6. MUTUAL MISTAKE

   7. MISTAKE IN THE TRANSCRIPTION OR PRINTING OF THE CONTRACT: REFORMATION

C. Deception

   8. INTENTIONAL MISREPRESENTATION

   9. FRAUD

   10. NEGLIGENT MISREPRESENTATION

   11. NONDISCLOSURE

D. Pressure

   12. UNDUE INFLUENCE

   13. DURESS

A *contract* is a binding agreement. This agreement must be made between parties who have the capacity to do so. They must also truly agree so that all parties have really consented to the contract. This chapter explores the elements of contractual capacity of the parties and the genuineness of their assent.

A. CONTRACTUAL CAPACITY

Some persons lack contractual capacity, a lack that embraces both those who have a status incapacity, such as minors, and those who have a factual incapacity, such as persons who are insane.

1. Contractual Capacity Defined

contractual capacity –
ability to understand that a contract is being made and to understand its general meaning.

Contractual capacity is the ability to understand that a contract is being made and to understand its general meaning. However, the fact that a person does not understand the full legal meaning of a contract does not mean that contractual capacity is lacking. Everyone is presumed to have capacity unless it is proven that capacity is lacking or there is status incapacity.[1] **For Example,** Jacqueline, aged 22, entered into a contract with Sunrise Storage Co. but later claimed it was not binding because she did not understand several clauses in the printed contract. The contract was binding. No evidence supported her claim that she lacked capacity to contract or to understand its subject. Contractual capacity can exist even though a party does not understand every provision of the contract.

(A) STATUS INCAPACITY. Over the centuries, the law has declared that some classes of persons lack contractual capacity. The purpose is to protect these classes by giving them the power to get out of unwise contracts. Of these classes, the most important today is the class identified as minors.

Until recent times, some other classes were held to lack contractual capacity in order to discriminate against them. Examples are married women and aliens.

C A S E   S U M M A R Y

We Really Mean Equal Rights

FACTS: An Alabama statute provided that a married woman could not sell her land without the consent of her husband. Montgomery made a contract to sell land she owned to Peddy. Montgomery's husband did not consent to the sale. Montgomery did not perform the contract and Peddy sued her. The defense was raised that the contract was void and could not be enforced because of the statute. Peddy claimed that the statute was unconstitutional.

DECISION: The statute was unconstitutional. Constitutions, both federal and state, guarantee all persons the equal protection of the law. Married women are denied this equal protection when they are treated differently than married men and unmarried women. The fact that such unequal treatment had once been regarded as proper does not justify its modern continuation. **[Peddy v Montgomery 345 So 2d 631 (Ala 1977)]**

---

[1] *In re Adoption of Smith,* 578 So 2d 988 (La App 1991).

Still other classes, such as persons convicted of and sentenced for a felony, were held to lack contractual capacity in order to punish them. Today, these discriminatory and punitive incapacities have largely disappeared. Married women have the same contractual capacity as unmarried persons.[2]

By virtue of international treaties, the discrimination against aliens has been removed.

(B) FACTUAL INCAPACITY. A *factual incapacity* contrasts with incapacity imposed because of the class or group to which a person belongs. A factual incapacity may exist when, because of a mental condition caused by medication, drugs, alcohol, illness, or age, a person does not understand that a contract is being made or understand its general nature. However, mere mental weakness does not incapacitate a person from contracting. It is sufficient if the individual has enough mental capacity to understand, to a reasonable extent, the nature and effect of what he is doing.[3]

2. Minors

Minors may make contracts.[4] To protect them, however, the law has always treated minors as a class lacking contractual capacity.

(A) WHO IS A MINOR? At common law, any person, male or female, under 21 years of age was a minor. At common law, minority ended the day before the twenty-first birthday. The "day before the birthday" rule is still followed, but the age of majority has been reduced from 21 years to 18 years.

CPA (B) MINOR'S POWER TO AVOID CONTRACTS. With exceptions that will be noted later, a contract made by a minor is voidable at the election of the minor. The minor may affirm or ratify the contract on attaining majority by performing the contract, by expressly approving the contract, or by allowing a reasonable time to lapse without avoiding the contract.

CPA *(1) What Constitutes Avoidance?*
A minor may avoid or *disaffirm* a contract by any expression of an intention to repudiate the contract. Any act inconsistent with the continuing validity of the contract is also an avoidance.

CPA *(2) Time for Avoidance.*
A minor can disaffirm a contract only during minority and for a reasonable time after attaining majority. After the lapse of a reasonable time, the contract is deemed ratified and cannot be avoided by the minor.

CPA *(3) Minor's Misrepresentation of Age.*
Generally, the fact that the minor has misrepresented his or her age does not affect the minor's power to disaffirm the contract. Some states hold that such fraud of a

---

[2] A few states have a limitation that a married woman cannot make a binding contract to pay the debt of her husband if he fails to.
[3] *Fisher v Schefers*, 656 NW2d 591 (Minn App 2003).
[4] *Buffington v State Automobile Mut. Ins. Co.*, 384 SE2d 873 (Ga App 1989).

minor bars contract avoidance. Some states permit the minor to disaffirm the contract in such a case but require the minor to pay for any damage to the property received under the contract.

In any case, the other party to the contract may disaffirm it because of the minor's fraud.

CPA (c) RESTITUTION BY MINOR AFTER AVOIDANCE. When a minor disaffirms a contract, the question arises as to what the minor must return to the other contracting party.

(1) Original Consideration Intact.
When a minor still has what was received from the other party, the minor, on avoiding the contract, must return it to the other party or offer to do so. That is, the minor must put things back to the original position or, as it is called, restore the **status quo ante**.

status quo ante–original positions of the parties.

(2) Original Consideration Damaged or Destroyed.
What happens if the minor cannot return what has been received because it has been spent, used, damaged, or destroyed? The minor's right to disaffirm the contract is not affected. The minor can still disaffirm the contract and is required to return only what remains. The fact that nothing remains or that what remains is damaged does not bar the right to disaffirm the contract. In states that follow the common law rule, minors can thus refuse to pay for what has been received under a contract or can get back what had been paid or given even though they do not have anything to return or return property in a damaged condition. There is, however, a trend to limit this rule.

(d) RECOVERY OF PROPERTY BY MINOR ON AVOIDANCE. When a minor disaffirms a contract, the other contracting party must return the money received. Any property received from the minor must also be returned. If the property has been sold to a third person who did not know of the original seller's minority, the minor cannot get the property back. In such cases, however, the minor is entitled to recover the property's monetary value or the money received by the other contracting party.

CPA (e) CONTRACTS FOR NECESSARIES. A minor can disaffirm a contract for necessaries but must pay the reasonable value for furnished necessaries.

(1) What Constitutes Necessaries?
Originally, **necessaries** were limited to those things absolutely necessary for the sustenance and shelter of the minor. Thus limited, the term would extend only to food, clothing, and lodging. In the course of time, the rule was relaxed to extend generally to things relating to the health, education, and comfort of the minor. Thus, the rental of a house used by a married minor is a necessary.

necessaries–things indispensable or absolutely necessary for the sustenance of human life.

(2) Liability of Parent or Guardian.
When a third person supplies the parents or guardian of a minor with goods or services that the minor needs, the minor is not liable for these necessaries because the third person's contract is with the parent or guardian, not with the minor.

When necessary medical care is provided a minor, a parent is liable at common law for the medical expenses provided the minor child. However, at common law, the child can be held contractually liable for her necessary medical expenses when the parent is unable or unwilling to pay.

CASE SUMMARY

The Concussion and Legal Repercussions

FACTS: Sixteen-year-old Michelle Schmidt was injured in an automobile accident and taken to Prince George's Hospital. Although the identities of Michelle and her parents were originally unknown, the hospital provided her emergency medical care for a brain concussion and an open scalp wound. She incurred hospital expenses of $1,756.24. Ms. Schmidt was insured through her father's insurance company. It issued a check to be used to cover medical expenses. However, the funds were used to purchase a car for Ms. Schmidt. Since she was a minor when the services were rendered, she believed that she had no legal obligation to pay. After Ms. Schmidt attained her eighteenth birthday and failed to pay the hospital, it brought suit against her.

DECISION: Judgment for the hospital. The prevailing modern rule is that minors' contracts are voidable except for necessaries. The doctrine of necessaries states that a minor may be held liable for necessaries, including medical necessaries when parents are unwilling to pay. The court concluded that Ms. Schmidt's father demonstrated a clear unwillingness to pay by using the insurance money to purchase a car rather than pay the hospital. The policy behind the necessaries exception is for the benefit of minors because the procurement of such is essential to their existence, and if they were not permitted to bind themselves, they might not be able to obtain the necessaries. [**Schmidt v Prince George's Hospital 784 A2d 1112 (Md 2001)**]

CPA (F) RATIFICATION OF FORMER MINOR'S VOIDABLE CONTRACT. A former minor cannot disaffirm a contract that has been ratified after reaching majority.[5]

CPA *(1) What Constitutes Ratification?*
Ratification consists of any words or conduct of the former minor manifesting an intent to be bound by the terms of a contract made while a minor.

CPA *(2) Form of Ratification.*
Generally, no special form is required for ratification of a minor's voidable contract, although in some states a written ratification or declaration of intention is required.

CPA *(3) Time for Ratification.*
A person can disaffirm a contract any time during minority and for a reasonable time after that but, of necessity, can ratify a contract only after attaining majority. The minor must have attained majority, or the ratification would itself be regarded as voidable.

---

[5] *Fletcher v Marshall*, 632 NE2d 1105 (Ill App 1994).

(G) Contracts That Minors Cannot Avoid. Statutes in many states deprive a minor of the right to avoid an educational loan;[6] a contract for medical care; a contract made while running a business; a contract approved by a court; a contract made in performance of a legal duty; and a contract relating to bank accounts, insurance policies, or corporate stock.

(H) Liability of Third Person for a Minor's Contract. The question arises as to whether parents are bound by the contract of their minor child. The question of whether a person cosigning a minor's contract is bound if the contract is avoided also arises.

(1) Liability of Parent.

Ordinarily, a parent is not liable on a contract made by a minor child. The parent may be liable, however, if the child is acting as the agent of the parent in making the contract. Also, the parent is liable to a seller for the reasonable value of necessaries supplied by the seller to the child if the parent had deserted the child.

(2) Liability of Cosigner.

When the minor makes a contract, another person, such as a parent or a friend, may sign along with the minor to make the contract more acceptable to the third person.

With respect to the other contracting party, the cosigner is bound independently of the minor. Consequently, if the minor disaffirms the contract, the cosigner remains bound by it. When the debt to the creditor is actually paid, the obligation of the cosigner is discharged.

If the minor disaffirms a sales contract but does not return the goods, the cosigner remains liable for the purchase price.

3. Mentally Incompetent Persons

A person with a mental disorder may be so disabled as to lack capacity to make a contract. If the person is so mentally incompetent as to be unable to understand that a contract is being made or the general nature of the contract, the person lacks contractual capacity.

(A) Effect of Incompetency. An incompetent person may ordinarily avoid a contract in the same manner as a minor. Upon the removal of the disability (that is, upon becoming competent), the formerly incompetent person can either ratify or disaffirm the contract.

A mentally incompetent person or his estate is liable for the reasonable value of all necessaries furnished that individual.

A current trend in the law is to treat an incompetent person's contract as binding when its terms and the surrounding circumstances are reasonable and the person is unable to restore the other contracting party to the status quo ante.

---

[6] A Model Student Capacity to Borrow Act makes educational loans binding on minors in Arizona, Mississippi, New Mexico, North Dakota, Oklahoma, and Washington. This act was reclassified from a uniform act to a model act by the Commissioners on Uniform State Law, indicating that uniformity was viewed as unimportant and that the matter was primarily local in character.

C A S E   S U M M A R Y

Friends Should Tell Friends About Medical Leaves

FACTS: Wilcox Manufacturing Group, Inc., did business under the name of Superior Automation Co., and Howard Wilcox served as Superior's president. As part of a loan "lease agreement" of $50,000 executed on December 5, 2000, Superior was to repay Marketing Services of Indiana (MSI) $67,213.80 over the course of 60 months. Wilcox gave a personal guarantee for full and prompt payment. Wilcox had been a patient of psychiatrist Dr. Shaun Wood since May 21, 1999, and was diagnosed as suffering from bipolar disorder during the period from June 2000 to January 2001. On June 9, 2000, Wilcox told Dr. Wood he was having problems functioning at work, and Dr. Wood determined that Wilcox was experiencing lithium toxicity, which lasted for 10 months, during which time he suffered from impaired cognitive functions that limited his capacity to understand the nature and quality of his actions and judgments. Superior made monthly payments though to October 28, 2003, and the balance owed at that time was $33,031.37. MSI sued Wilcox personally and the corporation for breach of contract. The defendants raise the defense of lack of capacity and contend that they are not liable on the loan signed by the corporate president when he was incapacitated.

DECISION: Judgment for MSI. The acts or deeds of a person of unsound mind whose condition has not been judicially ascertained and who is not under guardianship are voidable and not absolutely void. The acts are subject to ratification or disaffirmance on removal of the disability. The latest Wilcox could have been experiencing the effects of lithium toxicity was October 2001. Wilcox thus regained his capacity by that date. No attempt was made to disaffirm the contract. Rather, monthly payments continued to be made for a year and one-half before the payments ceased. The contract was thus ratified by the conduct of the president of Superior after he recovered his ability to understand the nature of the contract. [**Wilcox Manufacturing, Inc. v Marketing Services of Indiana, Inc. 832 NE2d 559 (Ind App 2005)**]

(B) APPOINTMENT OF GUARDIAN. If a court appoints a guardian for the incompetent person, a contract made by that person before the appointment may be ratified or, in some cases, disaffirmed by the guardian. If the incompetent person makes a contract after a guardian has been appointed, the contract is void and not merely voidable.

4. Intoxicated Persons

The capacity of a party to contract and the validity of the contract are not affected by the party's being impaired by alcohol at the time of making the contract so long as the party knew that a contract was being made.

If the degree of intoxication is such that a person does not know that a contract is being made, the contract is voidable by that person. The situation is the same as though the person were insane at the time and did not know what he or she was doing. On becoming sober, the individual may avoid or rescind the contract. However, an unreasonable delay in taking steps to set aside a known contract entered into while intoxicated may bar the intoxicated person from asserting this right.[7]

---

[7] *Diedrich v Diedrich*, 424 NW2d 580 (Minn App 1988).

For Example, Edward made a contract while intoxicated. When he sobered up, he immediately disaffirmed the contract for lack of capacity as the result of his intoxication. The other contracting party claimed that voluntary intoxication cannot void a contract, but Edward could disaffirm the contract because he lacked the legal capacity to enter a contract.

The courts treat impairment caused by the use of drugs the same as impairment caused by the excessive use of alcohol.

ethics & the law

Globe Life Insurance Company undertook a new sales program that targets neighborhoods in Los Angeles where drive-by shootings were a nightly occurrence. In two such shootings, children were killed as they sat in their living rooms.

Globe salespeople were instructed to "hit" the houses surrounding those where children were victims. They were also told to contact the parents of those children to sell policies for their other children.

Tom Raskin, an experienced Globe salesman, read of a drive-by shooting at Nancy Leonard's home, in which Leonard's five-year-old son was killed. The *Los Angeles Times* reported that Leonard was a single parent with four other children.

Raskin traveled to Leonard's home and described the benefits of a Globe policy for her other children. He offered her the $10,000 term life policy for each of the children for a total cost of $21 per month. Leonard was in the process of making funeral arrangements for her son, and Raskin noted, "See how much it costs for a funeral."

Leonard had been given several tranquilizers the night before by a physician at the hospital's emergency room. The physician had also given her 15 more tranquilizers to help her through the following week. She had taken one additional tranquilizer an hour before Raskin arrived, using a Coors Lite beer to take the pill.

Leonard signed the contract for the policy. After her son's funeral, she received the first month's bill for it and exclaimed, "I didn't buy any life insurance! Where did this come from?"

After you discuss Leonard's legal standing, discuss the ethical issues involved in Globe's sales program. Discuss the legal issues involved in Raskin's decision to target Leonard the day after her son's death.

CPA B. MISTAKE

The validity of a contract may be affected by the fact that one or both of the parties made a mistake. In some cases, the mistake may be caused by the misconduct of one of the parties.

5. Unilateral Mistake

A *unilateral mistake*—that is, a mistake by only one of the parties—as to a fact does not affect the contract when the mistake is unknown to the other contracting party.[8] When a contract is made on the basis of a quoted price, the validity of the contract is not affected by the fact that the party furnishing the quotation made a mathematical mistake in computing the price if there was no reason for the other

[8] *Truck South Inc. v Patel*, 528 SE2d 424 (SC 2000).

party to recognize that there had been a mistake.[9] The party making the mistake may avoid the contract if the other contracting party knew or should have known of the mistake.

C A S E   S U M M A R Y

Bumper Sticker: "Mistakes Happen!" (or words to that effect)

FACTS: Lipton-U City, LLC (Lipton), and Shurgard Storage Centers discussed the sale of a self-storage facility for approximately $7 million. Lipton became concerned about an existing environmental condition and as a result, the parties agreed to a lease with an option to buy rather than an outright sale. The contract specified a 10-year lease with an annual rent starting at $636,000 based on a property valuation of $7 million. Section 2.4 of the contract contained the purchase option. Shurgard representatives circulated an e-mail with a copy to Lipton representatives that a purchase option price would be based on six months of *annualized* net operating income. When the lease was submitted to Lipton, inexplicably any language regarding multiplying by 2 or annualizing the net income was omitted. Donn Lipton announced to his attorneys that the lease reflected his successful negotiation of a purchase option based on six months of *unannualized* net operating income. Eight months after signing the lease, Lipton sought to exercise the purchase option under Section 2.4 and stated a price of $2,918,103. Shurgard rejected the offer and filed suit for rescission, citing the misunderstanding about the price terms.

DECISION: Judgment for Shurgard. Under state law, if a material mistake made by one party is known to the other party or is of such a character or circumstances that the other party should know of it, the mistaken party has a right to rescission. Lipton knew or should have known of the mistake of the lessor (Shurgard) in believing that the purchase price would be based on a full year of net operating income rather than six months of net operating income. Lipton was notified by e-mail that the six-month figure was to be annualized and knew that the property was valued at approximately $7 million. [**Shurgard Storage Centers v Lipton-U City, LLC 394 F3d 1041 (8th Cir 2005)**]

6. Mutual Mistake

When both parties enter into a contract under a mutually mistaken understanding concerning a basic assumption of fact or law on which the contract is made, the contract is voidable by the adversely affected party if the mistake has a material effect on the agreed exchange.[10]

A contract based on *a mutual mistake in judgment* is not voidable by the adversely affected party. **For Example,** if both parties believe that a colt is not fast enough to develop into a competitive race horse and effect a sale accordingly, when the animal later develops into the winner of the Preakness as a three-year-old, the seller cannot rescind the contract based on mutual mistake because the mutual mistake was a mistake in judgment. In contrast, when two parties to a contract believe a cow to be barren at the time they contract for its sale, but before delivery of

---

[9] *Procan Construction Co. v Oceanside Development Corp.*, 539 NYS2d 437 (App Div 2d 1989).
[10] See *Browning v Howerton*, 966 P2d 367 (Wash App 1998).

FIGURE 14-1 | *Avoidance of Contract*

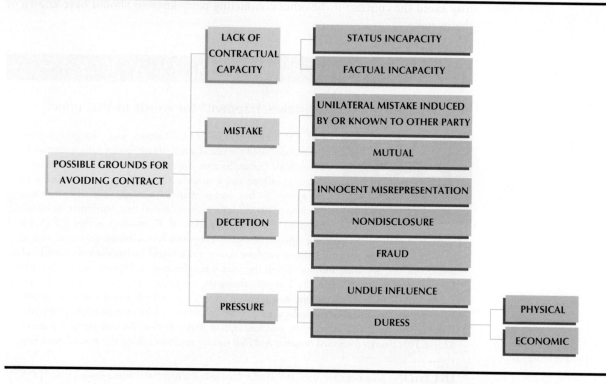

the animal to the buyer, it is discovered that the assumption was mistaken, such is a mutual mistake of fact making the contract void.[11]

7. Mistake in the Transcription or Printing of the Contract: Reformation

In some instances, the parties make an oral agreement, and in the process of committing it to writing or printing it from a manuscript, a phrase, term, or segment is inadvertently left out of the final, signed document. The aggrieved party may petition the court to **reform** the contract to reflect the actual agreement of the parties. However, the burden of proof is heightened to clear and convincing evidence that such a mistake was made. **For Example,** the Printers International Union reached agreement for a new three-year contract with a large regional printing company. As was their practice, the union negotiators then met with Sullivan Brothers Printers, Inc., a small specialty shop employing 10 union printers, and Sullivan Brothers and the union agreed to follow the contractual pattern set by the union and the large printer. That is, Sullivan Brothers agreed to give its workers all of the benefits negotiated for the employees of the large printing company. When the contract was typed, a new benefit of 75 percent employer-paid coverage for a dental plan was inadvertently omitted from the final contract that the parties signed. The mistake was not discovered until later, and Sullivan Brothers, Inc., is now reluctant to

reformation–remedy by which a written instrument is corrected when it fails to express the actual intent of both parties because of fraud, accident, or mistake.

[11] See *Sherwood v Walker*, 66 Mich 568 (1887).

assume the additional expense. Based on the clear and convincing evidence of a practice of following the contractual pattern set by the large printer and Sullivan's assent to again follow the pattern, a court or arbitrator will reform the contract.

C. DECEPTION

One of the parties may have been misled by a fraudulent statement. In such situations, there is no true or genuine assent to the contract, and it is voidable at the innocent party's option.

8. Intentional Misrepresentation

Fraud is a generic term embracing all multifarious means that human ingenuity can devise and that are resorted to by one individual to get advantage over another. It is classified in the law as a *tort*. However, where a party is induced into making a contract by a material misrepresentation of fact, this form of fraudulent activity adversely affects the genuineness of the assent of the innocent party, and this type of fraud is the focus of our discussion in the chapters on contracts.

9. Fraud

fraud—making of a false statement of a past or existing fact, with knowledge of its falsity or with reckless indifference as to its truth, with the intent to cause another to rely thereon, and such person does rely thereon and is harmed thereby.

Fraud is the making of a material misrepresentation (or false statement) of fact with (1) knowledge of its falsity or reckless indifference to its truth, (2) the intent that the listener rely on it, (3) the result that the listener does so rely, and (4) the consequence that the listener is harmed.[12]

To prove fraud, there must be a material misrepresentation of fact. Such a misrepresentation is one that is likely to induce a reasonable person to assent to a contract. **For Example,** Traci Hanson-Suminski purchased a used Honda Civic from Arlington Acura for $10,899. On a test drive with salesperson Mike Dobin, Traci noticed a vibration in the steering wheel and asked if the car had been in an accident. Dobin said, "No, it's fine." The dealer put new tires on the car and Traci bought it. Traci testified that she would not have purchased the car if she had known it had been in an accident. Eight months later when she sought to trade the car for another car, she was shown a Carfax Vehicle History Report which indicated the car had been in an accident. The dealer testified that all its sales associates are trained to respond to questions about vehicle history with "I don't know." It asserted that Dobin's statement was mere puffery. The court found that Dobin's statement was a material misrepresentation of the car's history, inducing the plaintiff to purchase the car. It rejected outright the dealer's assertion of puffery, which it defined as meaningless superlatives that no reasonable person would take seriously.[13]

(A) STATEMENT OF OPINION OR VALUE. Ordinarily, matters of opinion of value or opinions about future events are not regarded as fraudulent. Thus, statements that a building was "very good," it "required only normal maintenance," and the "deal was excellent" were merely matters of opinion. Therefore, a court considered the

---

[12] *Maack v Resource Design & Construction, Inc.,* 875 P2d 570 (Utah 1994); *Bortz v Noon,* 729 A2d 555 (Pa 1999).
[13] *Hanson-Suminski v. Rohrman Midwest Motors Inc.,* 858 NE2d 194 (Ill App 2008).

CASE SUMMARY

Watch Out! Some People Have a Lot of Nerve

FACTS: German citizens Klaus and Gerda Tschira brought suit against Corim, Inc., a U.S. real estate investment firm and its president, Ben Willingham Jr., for fraudulent misrepresentation during a real estate transaction between the Tschiras and Corim. Klaus attended a meeting in Walldorf, Germany, in which Willingham, who speaks fluent German, made a presentation. Willingham explained that Corim proposed to obtain buildings for investors to purchase at a "fair market price"; Corim then intended to enter into management contracts with the new owners. By the terms of the management contracts, Corim and Willingham would lease the buildings from the investors and, in return, would then pay the investors a contractually established rent. The Tschiras subsequently purchased a Nashville, Tennessee, commercial property on December 14, 1990, for $1,985,000. The Tschiras did not visit the property, secure independent counsel, or obtain an appraisal. They later discovered that two closings occurred on December 14, 1990. In the first, One Church Street, Inc., a shell corporation owned by Corim and Willingham, purchased the property from its owner, First Atlanta Services Corporation. The selling price in this deal was $774,000. In the second transaction, One Church Street, Inc., sold the building to the Tschiras for $1,985,000. The title insurance policy Willingham forwarded to the Tschiras indicated that the Ticor Title Insurance Company had provided protection up to $1,985,000. In actuality, Lisa Wilson, the branch manager of Ticor, testified that the policy the company extended for the property was for only $774,000. Willingham and Corim contended that any representations were not material because they "guaranteed" a return on the investment. From a judgment for the Tschiras in the amount of $1,420,000 in compensatory damages and $1,750,000 in punitive damages, Corim and Willingham appealed.

DECISION: Judgment for the Tschiras. Willingham and Corim argue that there was no fraudulent misrepresentation because the representations made were not material because they provided a "guaranteed" return on the Tschiras' investment through the rental income. However, the jury could have reasonably found otherwise. The Tschiras believed they were paying "fair market price" for the purchase of the property in addition to receiving a guaranteed return on their investment. The Tschiras believed, and the jury could have reasonably concluded, that the Tschiras actually paid $1,211,000 over the fair market price of the property and therefore lost that amount on their investment at the time of purchase. The Tschiras reasonably relied on the representations and suffered the damages as a result of that reliance. [**Tschiras v Willingham 133 F3d 1077 (6th Cir 1998)**]

sophistication and expertise of the parties and the commercial setting of the transaction and enforced the contract "as is." The theory is that the person hearing the statement recognizes or should recognize that it is merely the speaker's personal opinion, not a statement of fact. A statement that is mere sales talk cannot be the basis of fraud liability. **For Example,** CEO Bernard Ellis sent a memo to shareholders of his Internet-related services business some four days before the expiration of a lockup period during which these shareholders had agreed not to sell their stock. In the memo, he urged shareholders not to sell their stock on the release date because in the event of a massive sell-off "our stock could plummet." He also stated, "I think our share price will start to stabilize and then rise as our company's strong performance continues." Based on Ellis's "strong performance" statement, a major corporate shareholder did not sell. The price of the stock fell from $40 a share to 29 cents a share over the subsequent nine-month period. The shareholder sued Ellis for fraud, seeking $27 million in damages. The court held that the first half of the sentence in question was framed as a mere opinion as to future events and thus was nonactionable; and as to the characterization of the company's performance as "strong," such a self-congratulatory comment constituted mere puffery on which no reasonable investor would rely.[14]

A statement of opinion may be fraudulent when the speaker knows of past or present facts that make the opinion false. **For Example,** Biff Williams, the sales manager of Abrasives International (AI), sold an exclusive dealership selling AI products to Fred Farkas for $100,000 down and a 3 percent royalty on all gross proceeds. Williams told Farkas, "You have the potential to earn $300,000 to $400,000 a year in this territory." He later added, "We have four dealerships making that kind of money today." Farkas was thus persuaded by the business potential of the territory and executed the purchase contract. He later found out AI had a total of just four distributorships at that time, and the actual earnings of the highest producer was $43,000. Assertions of opinions about the future profit potential alone may not amount to fraud, but the assertion of present fact—that four dealerships were presently earning $300,000 to $400,000 a year—was a material misstatement of fact that made the forecast sales potential for Farkas's territory a material misstatement of fact as well. Because there were reliance and damages, Farkas can rescind the contract based on fraud and recover all damages resulting from it.[15]

(B) Reliance on Statement. A fraudulent statement made by one party has no importance unless the other party relies on the statement's truth. **For Example,** after making thorough tests of Nagel Company's pump, Allstate Services Company ordered 100 pumps. It later sued Nagel on the ground that advertising statements made about the pumps were false. Allstate Services cannot impose fraud liability on Nagel for the advertisements, even if they were false, because it had not relied on them in making the purchase but had acted on the basis of its own tests.

If the alleged victim of the fraud knew that the statements were false because the truth was commonly known, the victim cannot rely on the false statements. When the statements of a seller are so "indefinite and extravagant" that reasonable persons would not rely on them, the statements cannot be the basis of a claim of fraud.[16]

(C) Proof of Harm. For an individual to recover damages for fraud, proof of harm to that individual is required. The injured party may recover the actual losses suffered as a result of the fraud as well as punitive damages when the fraud is gross or oppressive. The injured party has the right to have the court order the rescission or cancellation of the contract that has been induced by fraud.[17]

---

[14] *Next Century Communications v Ellis*, 318 F3d 1023 (11th Cir 2003).

[15] The Federal Trade Commission and state agencies have franchise disclosure rules that will penalize the franchisor in this case. See Chapter 41.

[16] *Eckert v Flair Agency, Inc.*, 909 P2d 1201 (Okla App 1995) (seller's statement that house would never be flooded again).

[17] *Paden v Murray*, 523 SE2d 75 (Ga App 2000).

10. Negligent Misrepresentation

While fraud requires the critical element of a known or recklessly made falsity, a claim of negligent misrepresentation contains similar elements except it is predicated on a negligently made false statement. That is, the speaker failed to exercise due care regarding material information communicated to the listener but did not intend to deceive. When the negligent misrepresentation of a material fact that the listener relies on results in harm to the listener, the contract is voidable at the option of the injured party. If fraud is proven, as opposed to misrepresentation, recovery of punitive damages in addition to actual damages can occur. Because it may be difficult to prove the intentional falsity required for fraud, it is common for a lawsuit to allege both a claim of fraud and a claim of negligent misrepresentation. **For Example,** Marshall Armstrong worked for Fred Collins, owner of Collins Entertainment, Inc., a conglomerate that owns and operates video games. Collins Entertainment's core product video poker was hurt by a court ruling that prohibited cash payouts, which adversely affected its business and resulted in a debt of $13 to $20 million to SouthTrust bank. Chief operating officer Armstrong, on his own time, came up with the idea of modifying bingo machines as a new venture. To exploit this idea, Collins agreed to form a corporation called Skillpins Inc., that was unencumbered by the SouthTrust debt and to give Armstrong a 10 percent ownership interest. After a period, with some 300 Skillpins machines producing income, Armstrong discovered the revenues from the new venture on the debt-laden Collins Entertainment profit and loss statement, not that of Skillpins, Inc. Armstrong's suit for both fraud and intentional misrepresentation was successful. In addition to actual damages, he received $1.8 million in punitive damages for fraud.[18]

11. Nondisclosure

Under certain circumstances, nondisclosure serves to make a contract voidable, especially when the nondisclosure consists of active concealment.

(A) GENERAL RULE OF NONLIABILITY.   Ordinarily, a party to a contract has no duty to volunteer information to the other party. **For Example,** if Fox does not ask Tehan any questions, Tehan is not under any duty to make a full statement of material facts. Consequently, the nondisclosure of information that is not asked for does not impose fraud liability or impair the validity of a contract.

C A S E   S U M M A R Y

Welcome to the Seesaw: Buyer versus Seller

FACTS: Dalarna Management Corporation owned a building constructed on a pier on a lake. There were repeated difficulties with rainwater leaking into the building, and water damage was visible in the interior of the building. Dalarna made a contract to sell the building to Curran. Curran made several inspections of the building and had the building inspected twice by a

---

[18] 621 SE2d 368 (SC App 2005).

C A S E   S U M M A R Y

Continued

licensed engineer. The engineer reported there were signs of water leaks. Curran assigned his contract to Puget Sound Service Corporation, which then purchased the building from Dalarna. Puget Sound spent approximately $118,000 attempting to stop the leaks. Puget Sound then sued Dalarna for damages, claiming that Dalarna's failure to disclose the extent of the water leakage problem constituted fraud.

DECISION: Judgment for Dalarna. Curran was aware there was a water leakage problem, and therefore the burden was on the buyer to ask questions to determine the extent of the problem. There was no duty on the seller to volunteer the extent of the water damage merely because it had been a continuing problem that was more than just a simple leak. The court reached this conclusion because the law "balances the harshness of the former rule of caveat emptor [let the buyer beware] with the equally undesirable alternative of courts standing in loco parentis [in the place of a parent] to parties transacting business." [**Puget Sound Service Corp. v Dalarna Management Corp. 752 P2d 1353 (Wash App 1988)**]

(B) EXCEPTIONS. The following exceptions to the general rule of nonliability for nondisclosure exist.

(1) Unknown Defect or Condition.

A duty may exist in some states for a seller who knows of a serious defect or condition to disclose that information to the other party where the defect or condition is unknown to the other person and is of such a nature that it is unlikely that the other person would discover it. However, a defendant who had no knowledge of the defect cannot be held liable for failure to disclose it.[19]

(2) Confidential Relationship.

confidential relationship– relationship in which, because of the legal status of the parties or their respective physical or mental conditions or knowledge, one party places full confidence and trust in the other.

If parties stand in a **confidential relationship**, failure to disclose information may be regarded as fraudulent. For example, in an attorney-client relationship,[20] the attorney has a duty to reveal anything that is material to the client's interest when dealing with the client. The attorney's silence has the same legal consequence as a knowingly made false statement that there was no material fact to be told the client.

(3) Active Concealment.

Nondisclosure may be more than the passive failure to volunteer information. It may consist of a positive act of hiding information from the other party by physical concealment, or it may consist of knowingly or recklessly furnishing the wrong information. Such conduct constitutes fraud. **For Example,** when Nigel wanted to sell his house, he covered the wooden cellar beams with plywood to hide extensive termite damage. He sold the house to Kuehne, who sued Nigel for damages on later discovering the termite damage. Nigel claimed he had no duty to volunteer information about the termites, but by covering the damage with plywood, he committed active fraud as if he had made a false statement that there were no termites.

[19] *Nesbitt v Dunn*, 672 So 2d 226 (La App 1996).
[20] *In re Boss Trust*, 487 NW2d 256 (Minn App 1992).

D. Pressure

What appears to be an agreement may not in fact be voluntary because one of the parties entered into it as the result of undue influence or physical or economic duress.

CPA

12. Undue Influence

An aged parent may entrust all business affairs to a trusted child; a disabled person may rely on a nurse; a client may follow implicitly whatever an attorney recommends. The relationship may be such that for practical purposes, one person is helpless in the hands of the other. When such a confidential relationship exists, it is apparent that the parent, the disabled person, or the client is not exercising free will in making a contract suggested by the child, nurse, or attorney but is merely following the will of the other person. Because of the great possibility of unfair advantage, the law presumes that the dominating person exerts **undue influence** on the other person whenever the dominating person obtains any benefit from a contract made with the dominated person. The contract is then voidable. It may be set aside by the dominated person unless the dominating person can prove that, at the time the contract was made, no unfair advantage had been taken.

> **undue influence**–influence that is asserted upon another person by one who dominates that person.

The class of confidential relationships is not well defined. It ordinarily includes the relationships of parent and child, guardian and ward, physician and patient, and attorney and client, and any other relationship of trust and confidence in which one party exercises a control or influence over another.

Whether undue influence exists is a difficult question for courts (ordinarily juries) to determine. The law does not regard every influence as undue.

An essential element of undue influence is that the person making the contract does not exercise free will. In the absence of a recognized type of confidential relationship, such as that between parent and child, courts are likely to take the attitude that the person who claims to have been dominated was merely persuaded and there was therefore no undue influence.

C A S E   S U M M A R Y

Cards and Small Talk Sometimes Make the Sale

FACTS: John Lentner owned the farm adjacent to the Schefers. He moved off the farm to a nursing home in 1999. In the fall of 2000, Kristine Schefers visited Lentner at the nursing home some 15 times, engaging in small talk and watching him play cards. In the spring of 2001, Lentner agreed to sell his farm to Kristine and her husband Thomas for $50,000 plus $10,000 for machinery and tools. Kristine drove Lentner to the bank to get the deed from his safe deposit box. She also took him to the abstractor who drafted the transfer documents. Soon after the sale, Earl Fisher was appointed special conservator of Lentner. Fisher sought to set aside the transaction, asserting that Kristine's repeated visits to the nursing home and her failure to involve Lentner's other family members in the transaction unduly influenced Lentner.

CASE SUMMARY

Continued

DECISION: Judgment for Thomas and Kristine Schefers. Undue influence is shown when the person making the contract ceased to act of his own free volition and became a mere puppet of the wielder of that influence. Mere speculation alone that Lentner was a "puppet" acting according to the wishes of Schefers is insufficient to set aside the sale. Undue influence was not established. [**Fisher v Schefers 656 NW2d 592 (Minn App 2003)**]

CPA   ## 13. Duress

A party may enter into a contract to avoid a threatened danger. The danger threatened may be a physical harm to person or property, called **physical duress**, or it may be a threat of financial loss, called **economic duress**.

physical duress–threat of physical harm to person or property.

economic duress–threat of financial loss.

duress–conduct that deprives the victim of free will and that generally gives the victim the right to set aside any transaction entered into under such circumstances.

(A) PHYSICAL DURESS. A person makes a contract under **duress** when there is such violence or threat of violence that the person is deprived of free will and makes the contract to avoid harm. The threatened harm may be directed either at a near relative of the contracting party or against the contracting party. If a contract is made under duress, the resulting agreement is voidable at the victim's election.

Agreements made to bring an end to mass disorder or violence are ordinarily not binding contracts because they were obtained by duress.

One may not void a contract on grounds of duress merely because it was entered into with great reluctance and proves to be very disadvantageous to that individual.[21]

(B) ECONOMIC DURESS. Economic duress is a condition in which one is induced by a wrongful act or threat of another to make a contract under circumstances that deprive one of the exercise of his own free will.[22] **For Example,** Richard Case, an importer of parts used to manufacture high-quality mountain bicycles, had a contractual duty to supply Katahdin Manufacturing Company's needs for specifically manufactured stainless steel brakes for the 2010 season. Katahdin's president, Bill Read, was in constant contact with Case about the delay in delivery of the parts and the adverse consequences it was having on Katahdin's relationship with its retailers. Near the absolute deadline for meeting orders for the 2010 season, Case called Read and said, "I've got the parts in, but I'm not sure I'll be able to send them to you because I'm working on next year's contracts, and you haven't signed yours yet." Case's 2011 contract increased the cost of parts by 38 percent. Read signed the contract to obtain the delivery but later found a new supplier and gave notice to Case of this action. The defense of economic duress would apply in a breach of contract suit brought by Case on the 2011 contract because Case implicitly threatened to commit the wrongful act of not delivering parts due under the prior contract, and Katahdin Company had no means available to obtain parts elsewhere to prevent the economic loss that would occur if it did not receive those parts.

[21] *Miller v Calhoun Johnson Co.*, 497 SE2d 397 (Ga App 1998).
[22] *Hurd v Wildman, Harrold, Allen, and Dixon*, 707 NE2d 609 (Ill App 1999).

lawflix

Jerry Maguire (1996) (R)

Consider the marriage proposal, its validity, and Dorothy's later statement, "I did this. I made this happen. And the thing is, I can do something about it." What was Maguire's state of mind at the time of the proposal? Consider its possible hypothetical nature and the issues of whether it was a joke and the possible presence of undue influence (the young boy).

Matilda (1996)(PG)

A brilliant little girl with a strong moral compass who tries to instruct her family on many things erudite and her father specifically on what constitutes misrepresentation in selling used cars.

You can view a clip of this movie and others that illustrate business law concepts at the LawFlix site, located at **www.cengage.com/blaw/dvl**.

MAKE THE CONNECTION

SUMMARY

An agreement that otherwise appears to be a contract may not be binding because one of the parties lacks contractual capacity. In such a case, the contract is ordinarily voidable at the election of the party who lacks contractual capacity. In some cases, the contract is void. Ordinarily, contractual incapacity is the inability, for mental or physical reasons, to understand that a contract is being made and to understand its general terms and nature. This is typically the case when it is claimed that incapacity exists because of insanity, intoxication, or drug use. The incapacity of minors arises because society discriminates in favor of that class to protect them from unwise contracts.

The age of majority is 18. Minors can disaffirm most contracts. If a minor received anything from the other party, the minor, on avoiding the contract, must return what had been received from the other party if the minor still has it.

When a minor disaffirms a contract for a necessary, the minor must pay the reasonable value of any benefit received.

Minors only are liable for their contracts. Parents of a minor are not liable on the minor's contracts merely because they are the parents. Frequently, an adult enters into the contract as a coparty of the minor and is then liable without regard to whether the minor has avoided the contract.

The contract of an insane person is voidable to much the same extent as the contract of a minor. An important distinction is that if a guardian has been appointed for the insane person, a contract made by the insane person is void, not merely voidable.

An intoxicated person lacks contractual capacity if the intoxication is such that the person does not understand that a contract is being made.

The consent of a party to an agreement is not genuine or voluntary in certain cases of mistake, deception, or pressure. When this occurs, what appears to be a contract can be avoided by the victim of such circumstances or conduct.

As to mistake, it is necessary to distinguish between unilateral mistakes that are unknown to the other contracting party and those that are known. Mistakes that are unknown to the other party usually do not affect the binding character of the agreement. A unilateral mistake of which the other contracting party has knowledge or has reason to know makes the contract avoidable by the victim of the mistake.

The deception situation may be one of negligent misrepresentation or fraud. The law ordinarily does not attach any significance to nondisclosure. Contrary to this rule, there is a duty to volunteer information when a confidential relationship exists between the possessor of the knowledge and the other contracting party.

When concealment goes beyond mere silence and consists of actively taking steps to hide the truth, the conduct may be classified as fraud. A statement of opinion or value cannot ordinarily be the basis for fraud liability.

The voluntary character of a contract may be lacking because the agreement had been obtained by pressure. This may range from undue influence through the array of threats of extreme economic loss (called *economic duress*) to the threat of physical force that would cause serious personal injury or damage to property (called *physical duress*). When the voluntary character of an agreement has been destroyed by deception, or pressure, the victim may avoid or rescind the contract or may obtain money damages from the wrongdoer.

LEARNING OUTCOMES

After studying this chapter, you should be able to clearly explain:

A. CONTRACTUAL CAPACITY

LO.1 Define contractual capacity

> See the example where Jacqueline, age 22, did not understand parts of a storage contract, p. 308.

LO.2 Explain the extent and effect of avoidance of a contract by a minor.

> See the *Prince George's Hospital* case where a minor had to pay for medical necessaries, p. 311.

B. MISTAKE

LO.3 Distinguish unilateral mistakes and mutual mistakes

> See the *Shurgard Storage* case where the "other party" should have known of the unilateral mistake, p. 315.

See the example of the mutual mistake of fact regarding the fertility of a cow on p. 315.

C. DECEPTION

LO.4 Explain the difference between intentional misrepresentation, negligent misrepresentation and puffery.

See the example of the purchase of the used Honda where the misrepresentation was found to be fraud not puffery on p. 317.

D. PRESSURE

LO.5 Explain the difference between undue influence and duress

See the *Fisher v. Schefers* undue influence litigation, p. 322.

See the Katahdin bicycle example on economic duress, p. 323.

KEY TERMS

confidential relationship	fraud	status quo ante
contractual capacity	necessaries	undue influence
duress	physical duress	
economic duress	reform	

QUESTIONS AND CASE PROBLEMS

1. Lester purchased a used automobile from MacKintosh Motors. He asked the seller if the car had ever been in a wreck. The MacKintosh salesperson had never seen the car before that morning and knew nothing of its history but quickly answered Lester's question by stating: "No. It has never been in a wreck." In fact, the auto had been seriously damaged in a wreck and, although repaired, was worth much less than the value it would have had if there had been no wreck. When Lester learned the truth, he sued MacKintosh Motors and the salesperson for damages for fraud. They raised the defense that the salesperson did not know the statement was false and had not intended to deceive Lester. Did the conduct of the salesperson constitute fraud?

2. Helen, age 17, wanted to buy a Harley-Davidson "Sportster" motorcycle. She did not have the funds to pay cash but persuaded the dealer to sell the cycle to her on credit. The dealer did so partly because Helen said that she was 22 and showed the dealer an identification card that falsely stated her age as 22. Helen drove the motorcycle away. A few days later, she damaged it and then returned it to the dealer and stated that she disaffirmed the contract because she was a minor. The dealer said that she could not because (1) she had misrepresented her age and (2) the motorcycle was damaged. Can she avoid the contract?

3. Paden signed an agreement dated May 28 to purchase the Murrays' home. The Murrays accepted Paden's offer the following day, and the sale closed on June 27. Paden and his family moved into the home on July 14, 1997. Paden had the home inspected prior to closing. The report listed four minor repairs

needed by the home, the cost of which was less than $500. Although these repairs had not been completed at the time of closing, Paden decided to go through with the purchase. After moving into the home, Paden discovered a number of allegedly new defects, including a wooden foundation, electrical problems, and bat infestation. The sales agreement allowed extensive rights to inspect the property. The agreement provided:

> *Buyer... shall have the right to enter the property at Buyer's expense and at reasonable times... to thoroughly inspect, examine, test, and survey the Property.... Buyer shall have the right to request that Seller repair defects in the Property by providing Seller within 12 days from Binding Agreement Date with a copy of inspection report(s) and a written amendment to this agreement setting forth the defects in the report which Buyer requests to be repaired and/or replaced.... If Buyer does not timely present the written amendment and inspection report, Buyer shall be deemed to have accepted the Property "as is."*

Paden sued the Murrays for fraudulent concealment and breach of the sales agreement. If Mr. Murray told Paden on May 26 that the house had a concrete foundation, would this be fraud? Decide. [*Paden v Murray*, 523 SE2d 75 (Ga App)]

4. High-Tech Collieries borrowed money from Holland. High-Tech later refused to be bound by the loan contract, claiming the contract was not binding because it had been obtained by duress. The evidence showed that the offer to make the loan was made on a take-it-or-leave-it basis. Was the defense of duress valid? [*Holland v High-Tech Collieries, Inc.*, 911 F Supp 1021 (DC WA)]

5. Thomas Bell, a minor, went to work in the Pittsburgh beauty parlor of Sam Pankas and agreed that when he left the employment, he would not work in or run a beauty parlor business within a 10-mile radius of downtown Pittsburgh for a period of two years. Contrary to this provision, Bell and another employee of Pankas's opened a beauty shop three blocks from Pankas's shop and advertised themselves as Pankas's former employees. Pankas sued Bell to stop the breach of the noncompetition, or restrictive, covenant. Bell claimed that he was not bound because he was a minor when he had agreed to the covenant. Was he bound by the covenant? [*Pankas v Bell*, 198 A2d 312 (Pa)]

6. Aldrich and Co. sold goods to Donovan on credit. The amount owed grew steadily, and finally Aldrich refused to sell any more to Donovan unless Donovan signed a promissory note for the amount due. Donovan did not want to but signed the note because he had no money and needed more goods. When Aldrich brought an action to enforce the note, Donovan claimed that the note was not binding because it had been obtained by economic duress. Was he correct? [*Aldrich & Co. v Donovan*, 778 P2d 397 (Mont)]

7. James Fitl purchased a 1952 Mickey Mantle Topps baseball card from baseball card dealer Mark Strek for $17,750 and placed it in a safe deposit box. Two years later, he had the card appraised, and he was told that the card had been refinished and trimmed, which rendered it valueless. Fitl sued Strek and testified

that he had relied on Strek's position as a sports card dealer and on his representations that the baseball card was authentic. Strek contends that Fitl waited too long to give him notice of the defects that would have enabled Strek to contact the person who sold him the card and obtain relief. Strek asserts that he therefore is not liable. Advise Fitl concerning possible legal theories that apply to his case. How would you decide the case? [See *Fitl v Strek*, 690 NW2d 605 (Neb)]

8. An agent of Thor Food Service Corp. was seeking to sell Makofske a combination refrigerator-freezer and food purchase plan. Makofske was married and had three children. After being informed of the eating habits of Makofske and his family, the agent stated that the cost of the freezer and food would be about $95 to $100 a month. Makofske carefully examined the agent's itemized estimate and made some changes to it. Makofske then signed the contract and purchased the refrigerator-freezer. The cost proved to be more than the estimated $95 to $100 a month, and Makofske claimed that the contract had been obtained by fraud. Decide. [*Thor Food Service Corp. v Makofske*, 218 NYS2d 93]

9. Blubaugh was a district manager of Schlumberger Well Services. Turner was an executive employee of Schlumberger. Blubaugh was told that he would be fired unless he chose to resign. He was also told that if he would resign and release the company and its employees from all claims for wrongful discharge, he would receive about $5,000 in addition to his regular severance pay of approximately $25,000 and would be given job-relocation counseling. He resigned, signed the release, and received about $40,000 and job counseling. Some time thereafter, he brought an action claiming that he had been wrongfully discharged. He claimed that the release did not protect the defendants because the release had been obtained by economic duress. Were the defendants protected by the release? [*Blubaugh v Turner*, 842 P2d 1072 (Wyo)]

10. Sippy was thinking of buying Christich's house. He noticed watermarks on the ceiling, but the agent showing the house stated that the roof had been repaired and was in good condition. Sippy was not told that the roof still leaked and that the repairs had not been able to stop the leaking. Sippy bought the house. Some time later, heavy rains caused water to leak into the house, and Sippy claimed that Christich was liable for damages. What theory would he rely on? Decide. [*Sippy v Christich*, 609 P2d 204 (Kan App)]

11. Pileggi owed Young money. Young threatened to bring suit against Pileggi for the amount due. Pileggi feared the embarrassment of being sued and the possibility that he might be thrown into bankruptcy. To avoid being sued, Pileggi executed a promissory note to pay Young the amount due. He later asserted that the note was not binding because he had executed it under duress. Is this defense valid? [*Young v Pileggi*, 455 A2d 1228 (Pa Super)]

12. Office Supply Outlet, Inc., a single-store office equipment and supply retailer, ordered 100 model RVX-414 computers from Compuserve, Inc. A new staff member made a clerical error on the order form and ordered a quantity that was

far in excess of what Office Supply could sell in a year. Office Supply realized the mistake when the delivery trucks arrived at its warehouse. Its manager called Compuserve and explained that it had intended to order just 10 computers. Compuserve declined to accept the return of the extra machines. Is the contract enforceable? What additional facts would allow the store to avoid the contract for the additional machines?

13. C&J Publishing Co. told a computer salesman that it wanted a computer system that would operate its printing presses. C&J specified that it wanted only new equipment and no used equipment would be acceptable. The seller delivered a system to C&J that was a combination of new and secondhand parts because it did not have sufficient new parts to fill the order. When C&J later learned what had happened, it sued the seller for fraud. The seller contended that no statement or warranty had been made that all parts of the system were new and that it would not therefore be liable for fraud. Decide.

14. The city of Salinas entered into a contract with Souza & McCue Construction Co. to construct a sewer. City officials knew unusual subsoil conditions (including extensive quicksand) existed that would make performance of the contract unusually difficult. This information was not disclosed when city officials advertised for bids. The advertisement for bids directed bidders to examine carefully the site of the work and declared that the submission of a bid would constitute evidence that the bidder had made an examination. Souza & McCue was awarded the contract, but because of the subsoil conditions, it could not complete on time and was sued by Salinas for breach of contract. Souza & McCue counterclaimed on the basis that the city had not revealed its information on the subsoil conditions and was thus liable for the loss. Was the city liable? [*City of Salinas v Souza & McCue Construction Co.*, 424 P2d 921 (Cal App 3d)]

15. Vern Westby inherited a "ticket" from Anna Sjoblom, a survivor of the sinking of the *Titanic*, which had been pinned to the inside of her coat. He also inherited an album of postcards, some of which related to the *Titanic*. The ticket was a one-of-a-kind item in good condition. Westby needed cash and went to the biggest antique dealer in Tacoma, operated by Alan Gorsuch and his family, doing business as Sanford and Sons, and asked about the value of these items. Westby testified that after Alan Gorsuch examined the ticket, he said, "It's not worth nothing." Westby then inquired about the value of the postcard album, and Gorsuch advised him to come back later. On Westby's return, Gorsuch told Westby, "It ain't worth nothing." Gorsuch added that he "couldn't fetch $500 for the ticket." Since he needed money, Westby asked if Gorsuch would give him $1,000 for both the ticket and the album, and Gorsuch did so.

   Six months later, Gorsuch sold the ticket at a nationally advertised auction for $110,000 and sold most of the postcards for $1,200. Westby sued Gorsuch for fraud. Testimony showed that Gorsuch was a major buyer in antiques and collectibles in the Puget Sound area and that he would have had an understanding of the value of the ticket. Gorsuch contends that all elements of fraud are not present since there was no evidence that Gorsuch intended that

Westby rely on the alleged representations, nor did Westby rely on such. Rather, Gorsuch asserts, it was an arm's-length transaction and Westby had access to the same information as Gorsuch. Decide. [*Westby v Gorsuch*, 112 Wash App 558 (2002)]

CPA QUESTIONS

1. A building subcontractor submitted a bid for construction of a portion of a high-rise office building. The bid contained material computational errors. The general contractor accepted the bid with knowledge of the errors. Which of the following statements best represents the subcontractor's liability?

   a. Not liable, because the contractor knew of the errors

   b. Not liable, because the errors were a result of gross negligence

   c. Liable, because the errors were unilateral

   d. Liable, because the errors were material (5/95, Law, #17, 5351)

2. Egan, a minor, contracted with Baker to purchase Baker's used computer for $400. The computer was purchased for Egan's personal use. The agreement provided that Egan would pay $200 down on delivery and $200 thirty days later. Egan took delivery and paid the $200 down payment. Twenty days later, the computer was damaged seriously as a result of Egan's negligence. Five days after the damage occurred and one day after Egan reached the age of majority, Egan attempted to disaffirm the contract with Baker. Egan will:

   a. Be able to disaffirm despite the fact that Egan was *not* a minor at the time of disaffirmance

   b. Be able to disaffirm only if Egan does so in writing

   c. Not be able to disaffirm because Egan had failed to pay the balance of the purchase price

   d. Not be able to disaffirm because the computer was damaged as a result of Egan's negligence (11/93, Law, #21, 4318)

Chapter 15

CONSIDERATION

A. General Principles

1. CONSIDERATION DEFINED AND EXPLAINED
2. GIFTS
3. ADEQUACY OF CONSIDERATION
4. FORBEARANCE AS CONSIDERATION
5. ILLUSORY PROMISES

B. Special Situations

6. PREEXISTING LEGAL OBLIGATION
7. PAST CONSIDERATION
8. MORAL OBLIGATION

C. Exceptions to the Laws of Consideration

9. EXCEPTIONS TO CONSIDERATION

Will the law enforce every promise? Generally, a promise will not be enforced unless something is given or received for the promise.

A. General Principles

As a general rule, one of the elements needed to make an agreement binding is consideration.

1. Consideration Defined and Explained

consideration–promise or performance that the promisor demands as the price of the promise.

Consideration is what each party to a contract gives up to the other in making their agreement.

(A) **Bargained-for Exchange.** *Consideration* is the bargained-for exchange between the parties to a contract. In order for consideration to exist, something of value must be given or promised in return for the performance or promise of performance of the other.[1] The value given or promised can be money, services, property, or the forbearance of a legal right.

For Example, Beth offers to pay Kerry $100 for her used skis, and Kerry accepts. Beth has promised something of value, $100, as consideration for Kerry's promise to sell the skis, and Kerry has promised Beth something of value, the skis, as consideration for the $100. If Kerry offered to *give* Beth the used skis and Beth accepted, these parties would have an agreement but not an enforceable contract because Beth did not provide any consideration in exchange for Kerry's promise of the skis. There was no *bargained-for exchange* because Kerry was not promised anything of value from Beth.

(B) **Benefit-Detriment Approach.** Some jurisdictions analyze consideration from the point of view of a *benefit-detriment approach,* defining *consideration* as a benefit received by the promisor or a detriment incurred by the promisee.

As an example of a unilateral contract analyzed from a benefit-detriment approach to consideration, Mr. Scully, a longtime summer resident of Falmouth, states to George Corfu, a college senior, "I will pay you $3,000 if you paint my summer home." George in fact paints the house. The work of painting the house by George, the promisee, was a legal detriment to him. Also, the painting of the house was a legal benefit to Scully, the promisor. There was consideration in this case, and the agreement is enforceable.

2. Gifts

Promises to make a gift are unenforceable promises under the law of contracts because of lack of consideration, as illustrated previously in the scenario of Kerry promising to give her used skis to Beth without charge. There was no bargained-for

[1] *Brooksbank v Anderson,* 586 NW2d 789 (Minn App 1998).

exchange because Kerry was not promised anything of value from Beth. A completed gift, however, cannot be rescinded for lack of consideration.[2]

Charitable subscriptions by which individuals make pledges to finance the construction of a college building, a church, or another structure for charitable purposes are binding to the extent that the donor (promisor) should have reasonably realized that the charity was relying on the promise in undertaking the building program. Some states require proof that the charity has relied on the subscription.[3]

C A S E   S U M M A R Y

You Can't Back Out Now

FACTS: Salsbury was attempting to establish a new college, Charles City College. Salsbury obtained a pledge from Northwestern Bell Telephone Company to contribute to the college. When the company did not pay, Salsbury sued the company. The company raised the defense that there was no consideration for its promise and that nothing had been done by the college in reliance on the promise.

DECISION: Judgment for Salsbury. As a matter of public policy, a promise of a charitable contribution is binding even though there is no consideration for the promise and without regard for whether the charity had done any acts in reliance on the promise. The company was therefore liable on its promise to contribute. [**Salsbury v Northwestern Bell Telephone Co., 221 NW2d 609 (Iowa 1974)**]

3. Adequacy of Consideration

Ordinarily, courts do not consider the adequacy of the consideration given for a promise. The fact that the consideration supplied by one party is slight when compared with the burden undertaken by the other party is immaterial. It is a matter for the parties to decide when they make their contract whether each is getting a fair return. In the absence of fraud or other misconduct, courts usually will not interfere to make sure that each side is getting a fair return.

C A S E   S U M M A R Y

Who's to Say?

FACTS: On the death of their aunt, a brother and sister became the owners of shares of stock of several corporations. They made an agreement to divide these shares equally between them, although the sister's shares had a value approximately seven times those of the brother. The brother died before the shares were divided. The sister then claimed that the agreement to divide was not binding because the consideration for her promise was not adequate.

---

[2] *Homes v O'Bryant,* 741 So2d 366 (Miss App 1999).
[3] *King v Trustees of Boston University,* 647 NE2d 1176 (Ma 1995).

C A S E S U M M A R Y

Continued

DECISION: The value of stock cannot be determined precisely. It may change with time. In addition, the value that one person may see can be different than that seen by another. The court therefore will not make a comparison of the value that each party was to receive under the agreement. It was sufficient that a promise was exchanged for a promise. The adequacy of the consideration would not be examined. This sister was therefore bound by her promise to divide the shares. [**Emberson v Hartley 762 P2d 364 (Wash App 1988)**]

Because the adequacy of consideration is ignored, it is immaterial that consideration is so slight that the transaction is in part a "gift." However, the Internal Revenue Service may view a given transaction as part consideration, part gift, and assess a gift tax as appropriate.

The fact that the consideration turns out to be disappointing does not affect the binding character of the contract. Thus, the fact that a business purchased by a group of investors proves unprofitable does not constitute a failure of consideration that releases the buyers from their obligation to the seller.

C A S E S U M M A R Y

Expectations versus Consideration

FACTS: Aqua Drilling Company made a contract to drill a well for the Atlas Construction Company. It was expected that this would supply water for a home being constructed by Atlas. Aqua did not make any guarantee or warranty that water would be produced. Aqua drilled the well exactly as required by the contract, but no water was produced. Atlas refused to pay. It asserted that the contract was not binding on the theory that there had been a failure of consideration because the well did not produce water.

DECISION: The contract was binding. Atlas obtained the exact performance required by the contract. While Atlas had expected that water would be obtained, Aqua did not make any guarantee or warranty that this would be so. Hence, there was no failure of consideration. [**Atlas Construction Co., Inc. v Aqua Drilling Co., 559 P2d 39 (Wyo 1977)**]

4. Forbearance as Consideration

In most cases, consideration consists of the performance of an act such as providing a service, or the making of a promise to provide a service or goods, or paying money.[4] Consideration may also consist of **forbearance**, which is refraining from doing an act that an individual has a legal right to do, or it may consist of a promise of forbearance. In other words, the promisor may desire to buy the inaction or a promise of inaction of the other party.

forbearance–refraining from doing an act.

[4] *Prenger v Baumhoer*, 914 SW2d 413 (Mo App 1996).

The giving up of any legal right can be consideration for the promise of the other party to a contract. Thus, the relinquishment of a right to sue for damages will support a promise for the payment of money given in return for the promise to relinquish the right, if such is the agreement of the parties.

The promise of a creditor to forbear collecting a debt is consideration for the promise of the debtor to modify the terms of the transaction.

5. Illusory Promises

In a bilateral contract, each party makes a promise to the other. For a bilateral contract to be enforceable, there must be *mutuality of obligation*. That is, both parties must have created obligations to the other in their respective promises. If one party's promise contains either no obligation or only an apparent obligation to the other, this promise is an **illusory promise**. The party making such a promise is not bound because he or she has made no real promise. The effect is that the other party, who has made a real promise, is also not bound because he or she has received no consideration. It is said that the contract fails for lack of mutuality.

illusory promise–promise that in fact does not impose any obligation on the promisor.

For Example, Mountain Coal Company promises to sell Midwest Power Company all the coal it may order for $48 per ton for the year 2010, and Midwest Power agrees to pay $48 for any coal it orders from Mountain Coal. Mountain Coal in its promise to Midwest Power has obligated itself to supply all coal ordered at a stated price. However, Midwest Power's promise did not obligate it to buy any coal whatsoever from Mountain Coal (note that it was not a requirements contract). Because Midwest has no obligation to Mountain Coal under its promise, there is no mutuality of obligation, and Midwest cannot enforce Mountain Coal's promise when the market price of coal goes to $55 a ton in the winter of 2010 as the result of severe weather conditions.

Consider as well the example of the Jacksonville Fire soccer team's contract with Brazilian soccer star Edmundo. Edmundo signed a contract to play for the Jacksonville franchise of the new International Soccer League for five-years at $25 million. The extensive document signed by Edmundo set forth the details of the team's financial commitment and the details of Edmundo's obligations to the team and its fans. On page 4 of the document, the team inserted a clause reserving the right "to terminate the contract and team obligations at any time in its sole discretion." During the season, Edmundo received a $40 million five-year offer to play for Manchester United of the English Premier League, which he accepted. Because Jacksonville had a free way out of its obligation by the unrestricted cancellation provision in the contract, it thus made its promises to Edmundo illusory. Edmundo was not bound by the Jacksonville contract as a result of a lack of mutuality and was free to sign with Manchester United.

cancellation provision– crossing out of a part of an instrument or a destruction of all legal effect of the instrument, whether by act of party, upon breach by the other party, or pursuant to agreement or decree of court.

(A) CANCELLATION PROVISIONS. Although a promise must impose a binding obligation, it may authorize a party to cancel the agreement under certain circumstances on giving notice by a certain date. Such a provision does not make this party's promise illusory, for the party does not have a free way out and is limited to living up to the terms of the **cancellation provision**. **For Example,** actress Zsa Zsa Gabor made a contract with Hollywood Fantasy Corporation to appear at a fantasy vacation in San

Antonio, Texas, on May 2–4, for a $10,000 appearance fee plus itemized (extravagant) expenses. The last paragraph of the agreement stated: "It is agreed that if a significant acting opportunity in a film comes up, Ms. Gabor will have the right to cancel her appearance in San Antonio by advising Hollywood Fantasy in writing by April 15, 1991." Ms. Gabor sent a telegram on April 15, 1991, canceling her appearance. During the May 2 through 4 period, Ms. Gabor's only acting activity was a 14-second cameo role during the opening credits of *Naked Gun 2½*. In a lawsuit for breach of contract that followed, the jury saw this portion of the movie and concluded that Ms. Gabor had not canceled her obligation on the basis of a "significant acting opportunity," and she was held liable for breach of contract.[5]

(B) CONDITIONAL PROMISES. A *conditional promise* is a promise that depends on the occurrence of a specified condition in order for the promise to be binding. **For Example,** Mary Sparks, in contemplation of her signing a lease to take over a restaurant at Marina Bay, wanted to make certain that she had a highly qualified chef to run the restaurant's food service. She made a contract with John "Grumpy" White to serve as executive chef for a one-year period at a salary of $150,000. The contract set forth White's responsibilities and was conditioned on the successful negotiation of the restaurant lease with Marina Bay Management. Both parties signed it. Although the happening of the condition was within Mary's control because she could avoid the contract with Grumpy White by not acquiring the restaurant lease, she limited her future options by the contract with White. Her promise to White was not illusory because after signing the contract with him, if she acquired the restaurant lease, she was bound to hire White as her executive chef. Before signing the contract with White, she was free to sign any chef for the position. The contract was enforceable.

CPA B. SPECIAL SITUATIONS

The following sections analyze certain common situations in which a lawsuit turns on whether the promisor received consideration for the promise sued on.

6. Preexisting Legal Obligation

Ordinarily, doing or promising to do what one is already under a legal obligation to do is not consideration.[6] Similarly, a promise to refrain from doing what one has no legal right to do is not consideration. This preexisting duty or legal obligation can be based on statute, on general principles of law, on responsibilities of an office held, or on a preexisting contract.

For Example, Officer Mary Rodgers is an undercover police officer in the city of Pasadena, California, assigned to weekend workdays. Officer Rodgers promised Elwood Farnsworth that she would diligently patrol the area of the Farnsworth estate on weekends to keep down the noise and drinking of rowdy young persons who gathered in this area, and Mr. Farnsworth promised to provide a $500 per month gratuity for this extra service. Farnsworth's promise is unenforceable because

---

[5] *Hollywood Fantasy Corp. v Gabor*, 151 F2d 203 (5th Cir 1998).
[6] *Gardiner, Kamya & Associates v Jackson*, 369 F3d 1318 (Fed Cir 2004).

Officer Rodgers has a preexisting official duty as a police officer to protect citizens and enforce the antinoise and public drinking ordinances.

CPA (A) COMPLETION OF CONTRACT. Suppose that a contractor refuses to complete a building unless the owner promises a payment or bonus in addition to the sum specified in the original contract, and the owner promises to make that payment. The question then arises as to whether the owner's promise is binding. Most courts hold that the second promise of the owner is without consideration.

CASE SUMMARY

You're Already Under Contract

 **FACTS:** Crookham & Vessels had a contract to build an extension of a railroad for the Little Rock Port Authority. It made a contract with Larry Moyer Trucking to dig drainage ditches. The ditch walls collapsed because water would not drain off. This required that the ditches be dug over again. Larry Moyer refused to do this unless extra money was paid. Crookham & Vessels agreed to pay the additional compensation, but after the work was done, it refused to pay. Larry Moyer sued for the extra compensation promised.

DECISION: Judgment against Moyer. Moyer was bound by its contract to dig the drainage ditches. Its promise to perform that obligation was not consideration for the promise of Crookham & Vessels to pay additional compensation. Performance of an obligation is not consideration for a promise by a party entitled to that performance. The fact that performance of the contract proved more difficult or costly than originally contemplated does not justify making an exception to this rule. [**Crookham & Vessels, Inc. v Larry Moyer Trucking, Inc. 699 SW2d 414 (Ark App 1985)**]

If the promise of the contractor is to do something that is not part of the first contract, then the promise of the other party is binding. **For Example,** if a bonus of $5,000 is promised in return for the promise of a contractor to complete the building at a date earlier than that specified in the original agreement, the promise to pay the bonus is binding.

CPA *(1) Good-Faith Adjustment*
A current trend is to enforce a second promise to pay a contractor a higher amount for the performance of the original contract when there are extraordinary circumstances caused by unforeseeable difficulties and when the additional amount promised the contractor is reasonable under the circumstances.

(2) Contract for Sale of Goods
When the contract is for the sale of goods, any modification made in good faith by the parties to the contract is binding without regard to the existence of consideration for the modification.

CPA (B) COMPROMISE AND RELEASE OF CLAIMS. The rule that doing or promising to do what one is already legally bound to do is not consideration applies to a part payment made in satisfaction of an admitted or *liquidated debt.* Thus, a promise to pay part of an amount that is admittedly owed is not consideration for a promise to discharge the balance. It will not prevent the creditor from demanding the remainder later. **For Example,** John owes Mark $100,000, which was due on March 1, 2010. On March 15, John offers to pay back $80,000 if Mark will agree to accept this amount as the discharge of the full amount owed. Mark agrees to this proposal, and it is set forth in writing signed by the parties. However, Mark later sues for the $20,000 balance. Mark will be successful in the lawsuit because John's payment of the $80,000 is not consideration for Mark's promise to discharge the full amount owed because John was doing only what he had a preexisting legal duty to do.

If the debtor pays the part payment before the debt is due, there is consideration because, on the day when the payment was made, the creditor was not entitled to demand any payment. Likewise, if the creditor accepts some article (even of slight value) in addition to the part payment, consideration exists.

A debtor and creditor may have a bona fide dispute over the amount owed or whether any amount is owed. Such is called an *unliquidated debt.* In this case, payment by the debtor of less than the amount claimed by the creditor is consideration for the latter's agreement to release or settle the claim. It is generally regarded as sufficient if the claimant believes in the merit of the claim.[7]

(c) **Part-Payment Checks.** When there is a good-faith dispute about the amount of a debt and the debtor tenders a check that states on its face "paid in full" and references the transaction in dispute, but the amount of the check is less than the full amount the creditor asserts is owed, the cashing of the check by the creditor discharges the entire debt.

composition of creditors– agreement among creditors that each shall accept a part payment as full payment in consideration of the other creditors doing the same.

(d) **Composition of Creditors.** In a **composition of creditors**, the various creditors of one debtor mutually agree to accept a fractional part of their claims in full satisfaction of the claims. Such agreements are binding and are supported by consideration. When creditors agree to extend the due date of their debts, the promise of each creditor to forbear is likewise consideration for the promise of other creditors to forbear.

7. Past Consideration

A promise based on a party's past performance lacks consideration.[8] It is said that **past consideration** is no consideration. **For Example,** Fred O'Neal came up with the idea for the formation of the new community bank of Villa Rica and was active in its formation. Just prior to the execution of the documents creating the bank, the organizers discussed that once the bank was formed, it would hire O'Neal, giving him a three-year contract at $65,000 the first year, $67,000 the second year, and $70,000 the third. In a lawsuit against the bank for breach of contract, O'Neal testified that the consideration he gave in exchange for the three-year contract was his past effort to organize the bank. The court stated that past consideration generally will not support a subsequent promise and that the purported consideration was not rendered to the bank, which had not yet been established

past consideration– something that has been performed in the past and which, therefore, cannot be consideration for a promise made in the present.

---

[7] *F. H. Prince & Co. v Towers Financial Corp.,* 656 NE2d 142 (Ill App 1995).
[8] *Smith v Locklear,* 906 So2d 1273 (Fla App 2005).

when his promotion and organization work took place.[9] The presence of a bargained-for exchange is not present when a promise is made in exchange for a past benefit.[10]

8. Moral Obligation

In most states, promises made to another based on "moral obligation" lack consideration and are not enforceable.[11] They are considered gratuitous promises and unenforceable. **For Example,** while on a fishing trip, Tom Snyder, a person of moderate means, met an elderly couple living in near-destitute conditions in a rural area of Texas. He returned to the area often, and he regularly purchased groceries for the couple and paid for their medical needs. Some two years later, the couple's son, David, discovered what Tom had been doing and promised to reimburse Snyder for what he had furnished his parents. This promise, based on a moral obligation, is unenforceable. A "past consideration" analysis also renders David's promise as unenforceable.

---

ethics & the law

Alan Fulkins, who owns a construction company that specializes in single-family residences, is constructing a small subdivision with 23 homes. Tretorn Plumbing, owned by Jason Tretorn, was awarded the contract for the plumbing work on the homes at a price of $4,300 per home.

Plumbing contractors complete their residential projects in three phases. Phase one consists of digging the lines for the plumbing and installing the pipes that are placed in the foundation of the house. Phase two consists of installing the pipes within the walls of the home, and phase three is installing of the surface plumbing, such as sinks and tubs. However, industry practice dictates that the plumbing contractor receive one-half of the contract amount after completion of phase one.

Tretorn completed the digs of phase one for Fulkins and received payment of $2,150. Tretorn then went to Fulkins and demanded an additional $600 per house to complete the work. Fulkins said, "But you already have a contract for $4,300!" Tretorn responded, "I know, but the costs are killing me. I need the additional $600."

Fulkins explained the hardship of the demand, "Look, I've already paid you half. If I hire someone else, I'll have to pay them two-thirds for the work not done. It'll cost me $5,000 per house."

Tretorn responded, "Exactly. I'm a bargain because the additional $600 I want only puts you at $4,900. If you don't pay it, I'll just lien the houses and then you'll be stuck without a way to close the sales. I've got the contract all drawn up. Just sign it and everything goes smoothly."

Should Fulkins sign the agreement? Does Tretorn have the right to the additional $600? Was it ethical for Tretorn to demand the $600? Is there any legal advice you can offer Fulkins?

---

[9] *O'Neal v Home Town Bank of Villa Rica,* 514 SE2d 669 (Ga App 1999).

[10] But see *United Resource Recovery Corp v Ranko Venture Management Inc.,* 854 F Supp 2d 645 (SDNY 2008) where a past work agreement was unenforceable because it was based on past consideration—however, the individual could recover under a signed consulting agreement for which no compensation had been paid. See also *Travis v Paepke,* 3 So3d 131 (Miss App 2009).

[11] *Production Credit Ass'n of Manaan v Rub,* 475 NW2d 532 (ND 1991). As to the Louisiana rule of moral consideration, see *Thomas v Bryant,* 596 So2d 1065 (La App 1992).

FIGURE 15-1 | *Consideration and Promises*

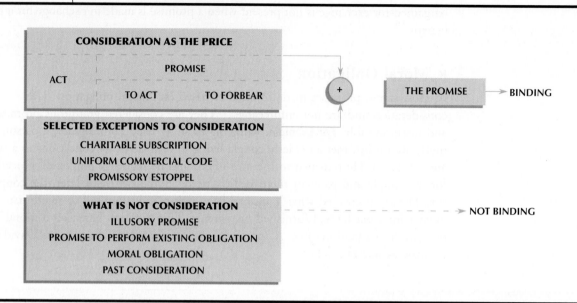

C. EXCEPTIONS TO THE LAWS OF CONSIDERATION

The ever-changing character of law clearly appears in the area of consideration as part of the developing law of contracts.

9. Exceptions to Consideration

By statute or decision, traditional consideration is not required in these situations:

(A) CHARITABLE SUBSCRIPTIONS. Where individuals made pledges to finance the construction of buildings for charitable purposes, consideration is lacking according to technical standards applied in ordinary contract cases. For public policy reasons, the reliance of the charity on the pledge in undertaking the project is deemed a substitute for consideration.

(B) UNIFORM COMMERCIAL CODE. In some situations, the Uniform Commercial Code abolishes the requirement of consideration. **For Example,** under the Code, consideration is not required for (1) a merchant's written, firm offer for goods stated to be irrevocable, (2) a written discharge of a claim for an alleged breach of a commercial contract, or (3) an agreement to modify a contract for the sale of goods.[12]

promissory estoppel–
doctrine that a promise will be enforced although it is not supported by consideration when the promisor should have reasonably expected that the promise would induce action or forbearance of a definite and substantial character on the part of the promised and injustice can be avoided only by enforcement of the promise.

(C) PROMISSORY ESTOPPEL. Under the doctrine of **promissory estoppel**, a promisor may be prevented from asserting that his or her promise is unenforceable because the promisee gave no consideration for the promise. This doctrine, sometimes called the *doctrine of detrimental reliance,* is applicable when (1) the promisor makes a promise that lacks consideration, (2) the promisor intends or should reasonably expect that the promisee will rely on the promise, (3) the promisee in fact relies on

[12] UCC § 2-209(1).

the promise in some definite and substantial manner, and (4) enforcement of the promise is the only way to avoid injustice.[13]

Damages recoverable in a case of promissory estoppel are not the profits that the promisee expected, but only the amount necessary to restore the promisee to the position he or she would have been in had the promisee not relied on the promise.[14]

Legal difficulties often arise because parties take certain things for granted. Frequently, they will be sure that they have agreed to everything and that they have a valid contract. Sometimes, however, they do not. The courts are then faced with the problem of leaving them with their broken dreams or coming to their rescue when promissory estoppel can be established.

CASE SUMMARY

Brits Rescued by Promissory Estoppel

FACTS: Portman Lamborghini, Ltd. (Portman), was owned by Chaplake Holdings, Ltd., a United Kingdom company, which was owned by David Jolliffe and David Lakeman as equal shareholders. Between 1984 and 1987, Portman sold approximately 30 new Lamborghinis each year through its exclusive concession contract with the car maker. It was then the largest Lamborghini dealer in the world since Lamborghini's production was just 250 cars per year. These cars sold at a retail price between $200,000 and $300,000. In 1987, Chrysler Corporation bought Lamborghini, and its chairman, Lee Iacocca, presented a plan to escalate production to 5,000 units within five years. The plan included the introduction of a new model, the P140, with a retail price of $70,000. Between 1987 and 1991, *all* of the Chrysler/Lamborghini top executives with whom Jolliffe and Lakeman and their top advisors came in contact provided the same message to them: Chrysler was committed to the Expansion Plan, and in order for Portman to retain its exclusive U.K. market, it must expand its operational capacity from 35 cars in 1987 to 400 cars by 1992. Accordingly, Portman acquired additional financing, staff, and facilities and built a new distribution center. An economic downturn in the United States and major development and production problems at Lamborghini led Chrysler to reduce its expansion investment by two-thirds. Factory production delays eroded Portman's profitability and success, and it entered into receivership in April 1992. Suit was brought on behalf of the Portman and Chaplake entities on a promissory estoppel theory against Chrysler, a Delaware corporation.

DECISION: Judgment for Portman and Chaplake on the promissory estoppel theory. (1) A promise was made by Chrysler that the Lamborghini line would expand tenfold and that Portman would retain its exclusivity deal *only* if it expanded its operational capacity. (2) The promisor, Chrysler, should have reasonably expected that Portman would rely on this promise. (3) Lakeman and Jolliffe were given the same message and promise by *all* of the top executives involved, and it was therefore not unreasonable for them to rely upon the promises made by these executives and to undertake the detriment of major expansion activity that would have been unnecessary but for the Expansion Plan and the role they were promised. (4) The prevention of injustice is the "fundamental idea" underlying the doctrine of promissory estoppel, and injustice can be avoided in this case only by the enforcement of Chrysler's promise. Portman is entitled to £ 569,321 for its costs to implement its Expansion Plan, and Chaplake is entitled to £ 462,686 for its investment in Portman's expansion. [**Chrysler Corp. v Chaplake Holdings, Ltd. 822 A2d 1024 (Del 2003)**]

---

[13] *Neuhoff v Marvin Lumber and Cedar Co.,* 370 F3d 197 (1st Cir 2004).
[14] *Medistar Corp. v Schmidt,* 267 SW3d 150 (Tex App 2008).

lawflix

Baby Boom (1987) (PG)

Review the scene near the end of the movie when Diane Keaton is presented with an offer for the purchase of her company, Country Baby. List the elements of consideration that Food Giant is paying for the company. Explain what Ms. Keaton's consideration is in exchange.

Check out LawFlix at **www.cengage.com/blaw/dvl** to access movie clips that illustrate business law concepts.

MAKE THE CONNECTION

SUMMARY

A promise is not binding if there is no consideration for the promise. Consideration is what the promisor requires as the price for his promise. That price may be doing an act, refraining from the doing of an act, or merely promising to do or to refrain. In a bilateral contract, it is necessary to find that the promise of each party is supported by consideration. If either promise is not so supported, it is not binding, and the agreement of the parties in not a contract. Consequently, the agreement cannot be enforced. When a promise is the consideration, it must be a binding promise. The binding character of a promise is not affected by the circumstance that there is a condition precedent to the performance promised. A promise to do what one is already obligated to do is not consideration, although some exceptions are made. Such exceptions include the rendering of a partial performance or a modified performance accepted as a good-faith adjustment to a changed situation, a compromise and release of claims, a part-payment check, and a compromise of creditors. Because consideration is the price that is given to obtain the promise, past benefits conferred on the promisor cannot be consideration.

A promise to refrain from doing an act can be consideration. A promise to refrain from suing or asserting a particular claim can be consideration. When consideration is forbearance to assert a claim, it is immaterial whether the claim is valid as long as the claim has been asserted in the good-faith belief that it was valid.

When the promisor obtains the consideration specified for the promise, the law is not ordinarily concerned with the value or adequacy of that consideration.

Under the doctrine of promissory estoppel a court may enforce a promise lacking consideration where it is the only way to avoid injustice.

LEARNING OUTCOMES

After studying this chapter, you should be able to clearly explain:

A. GENERAL PRINCIPLES—CONSIDERATION

LO.1 Explain what constitutes consideration

> See the "bargained for exchange" example involving Beth and Kerry, p. 332.
> See the "benefit-detriment" approach to consideration example, p. 332.
> See the discussion on forbearance as consideration on p. 334.

B. SPECIAL SITUATIONS

LO.2 Distinguish between a "preexisting legal obligation" and "past consideration"

> See the preexisting duty example involving Officer Rogers on p. 336.
> See the example involving Fred O'Neal where he found out the past consideration is no consideration rule, p. 338.

LO.3 Explain why promises based on moral obligations lack consideration.

> See the example of the gratuitous deeds of Tom Synder on p. 336.

C. EXCEPTIONS TO THE LAWS OF CONSIDERATION

LO.4 List the exceptions to the requirement of consideration

> See the discussion on charitable subscriptions, the UCC, and promissory estoppel starting on p. 340.

LO.5 Explain the "fundamental idea" underlying promissory estoppel

> See the *Chaplake Holdings* case where the court enforced Chrysler's promise in order to correct an injustice, p. 341.

KEY TERMS

cancellation provision
composition of creditors
consideration

forbearance
illusory promise

past consideration
promissory estoppel

QUESTIONS AND CASE PROBLEMS

1. Sarah's house caught on fire. Through the prompt assistance of her neighbor Odessa, the fire was quickly extinguished. In gratitude, Sarah promised to pay Odessa $1,000. Can Odessa enforce this promise?

2. William E. Story agreed to pay his nephew, William E. Story II, a large sum of money (roughly equivalent to $50,000 in 2007 dollars) "if he would refrain from drinking liquor, using tobacco, swearing, and playing cards or billiards for money until he should come to be 21 years of age." William II had been using tobacco and occasionally drank liquor but refrained from using these stimulants over several years until he was 21 and also lived up to the other requirements of his uncle's offer. Just after William II's 21st birthday, Story acknowledged that

William II had fulfilled his part of the bargain and advised that the money would be invested for him with interest. Story died, and his executor, Sidway, refused to pay William II because he believed the contract between Story and William II was without consideration. Sidway asserted that Story received no benefit from William II's performance and William II suffered no detriment (in fact, by his refraining from the use of liquor and tobacco, William II was not harmed but benefited, Sidway asserted). Is there any theory of consideration that William II can rely on? How would you decide this case? [*Hamer v Sidway,* 124 NY 538]

3. Dale Dyer, who was employed by National By-Products, Inc., was seriously injured at work as the result of a job-related accident. He agreed to give up his right to sue the employer for damages in consideration of the employer's giving him a lifetime job. The employer later claimed that this agreement was not binding because Dyer's promise not to sue could not be consideration for the promise to employ on the ground that Dyer in fact had no right to sue. Dyer's only remedy was to make a claim under workers' compensation. Was the agreement binding? [*Dyer v National By-Products, Inc.,* 380 NW2d 732 (Iowa)]

4. Charles Sanarwari retained Stan Gissel to prepare his income tax return for the year 2006. The parties agreed on a fee of $400. Charles had done a rough estimate based on last year's return and believed he would owe the IRS approximately $2,000. When Stan's work was completed, it turned out that Charles would receive a $2,321 tax refund. Stan explained how certain legitimate advantages were used to reduce Charles's tax obligation. Charles paid for Stan's services and was so pleased with the work that he promised to pay Stan an additional $400 for the excellent job on the tax return when he received his tax refund. Thereafter, Stan and Charles had a falling out over a golf tournament where Charles was late for his tee time and Stan started without him, causing Charles to lose an opportunity to win the club championship. Stan was not paid the $400 promised for doing an excellent job on the tax return, and he sued Charles as a matter of principle. Decide.

5. Medistar is a real estate development company specializing in the development of medical facilities. Dr. Schmidt, the team physician for the San Antonio Spurs basketball team, sought to develop "The Texas Center for Athletes" medical center next to the Spurs facility and urged Medistar to obtain the real estate and develop the project on his group's behalf. Medistar spent more than $1 million and thousands of man-hours on the project from 2000 to July 12, 2004 when Dr. Schmidt's new group of investors purchased the property next to the Spur's facility for the project; subsequently, Medistar was informed that it would have no role in the project. Medistar asserts that it relied on Dr. Schmidt's assurances that it would be the developer of the project—and after four years and the $1 million in time and expenses it spent, it is unconscionable to be excluded from the project. Dr. Schmidt and associates contend that Medistar has presented no contractual agreement tying it to any legal obligation to Medistar. Is there a viable legal theory available to Medistar? If so what is the remedy? [*Medistar v Schmidt,* 267 SW3d 150 (Tex App)]

6. Fedun rented a building to Gomer, who did business under the name of Mike's Cafe. Later, Gomer was about to sell the business to Brown and requested Fedun to release him from his liability under the lease. Fedun agreed to do so. Brown sold the business shortly thereafter. The balance of the rent due by Gomer under the original lease agreement was not paid, and Fedun sued Gomer on the rent claim. Could he collect after having released Gomer? [*Fedun v Mike's Cafe,* 204 A2d 776 (Pa Super)]

7. Alexander Proudfoot Co. was in the business of devising efficiency systems for industry. It told Sanitary Linen Service Co. that it could provide an improved system for Sanitary Linen that would save Sanitary Linen money. It made a contract with Sanitary Linen to provide a money-saving system. The system was put into operation, and Proudfoot was paid the amount due under the contract. The system failed to work and did not save money. Sanitary Linen sued to get the money back. Was it entitled to do so? [*Sanitary Linen Service Co. v Alexander Proudfoot Co.,* 435 F2d 292 (5th Cir)]

8. Sears, Roebuck and Co. promised to give Forrer permanent employment. Forrer sold his farm at a loss to take the job. Shortly after beginning work, he was discharged by Sears, which claimed that the contract could be terminated at will. Forrer claimed that promissory estoppel prevented Sears from terminating the contract. Was he correct? [*Forrer v Sears, Roebuck & Co.,* 153 NW2d 587 (Wis)]

9. Kemp leased a gas filling station from Baehr. Kemp, who was heavily indebted to Penn-O-Tex Oil Corp., transferred to it his right to receive payments on all claims. When Baehr complained that the rent was not paid, he was assured by the corporation that the rent would be paid to him. Baehr did not sue Kemp for the overdue rent but later sued the corporation. The defense was raised that there was no consideration for the promise of the corporation. Decide. [*Baehr v Penn-O-Tex Corp.,* 104 NW2d 661 (Minn)]

10. Bogart owed several debts to Security Bank & Trust Co. and applied to the bank for a loan to pay the debts. The bank's employee stated that he would take the application for the loan to the loan committee and "within two or three days, we ought to have something here, ready for you to go with." The loan was not made. The bank sued Bogart for his debts. He filed a counterclaim on the theory that the bank had broken its contract to make a loan to him and that promissory estoppel prevented the bank from going back on what the employee had said. Was this counterclaim valid?

11. Kelsoe worked for International Wood Products, Inc., for a number of years. One day Hernandez, a director and major stockholder of the company, promised Kelsoe that the corporation would give her 5 percent of the company's stock. This promise was never kept, and Kelsoe sued International for breach of contract. Had the company broken its contract? [*Kelsoe v International Wood Products, Inc.,* 588 So2d 877 (Ala)]

12. Kathy left her classic 1978 Volkswagen convertible at Freddie's Service Station, requesting a "tune-up." When she returned that evening, Freddie's bill was

$374. Kathy stated that Firestone and Sears advertise tune-ups for $70, and she asked Freddie, "How can you justify this bill?" Freddie responded, "Carburator work." Kathy refused to pay the bill and left. That evening, when the station closed, she took her other set of keys and removed her car, after placing a check in the station's mail slot. The check was made out to Freddie's Service Station for $200 and stated on its face: "This check is in full payment of my account with you regarding the tune-up today on my 1978 Volkswagen convertible." Freddie cashed the check in order to meet his business expenses and then sued Kathy for the difference owed. What result?

13. On the death of their mother, the children of Jane Smith gave their interests in their mother's estate to their father in consideration of his payment of $1 to each of them and his promise to leave them the property on his death. The father died without leaving them the property. The children sued their father's second wife to obtain the property in accordance with the agreement. The second wife claimed that the agreement was not a binding contract because the amount of $1 and future gifts given for the children's interests were so trivial and uncertain. Decide.

14. Radio Station KSCS broadcast a popular music program. It announced that it would pay $25,000 to any listener who detected that it did not play three consecutive songs. Steve Jennings listened to and heard a program in which two songs were followed by a commercial program. He claimed the $25,000. The station refused to pay on the ground that there was no consideration for its promise to pay that amount. Was the station liable? [*Jennings v Radio Station KSCS,* 708 SW2d 60 (Tex App)]

15. Hoffman wanted to acquire a franchise for a Red Owl grocery store. (Red Owl was a corporation that maintained a system of chain stores.) An agent of Red Owl informed Hoffman and his wife that if they would sell their bakery in Wautoma, acquire a certain tract of land in Chilton (another Wisconsin city), and put up $6,000, they would be given a franchise. In reliance on the agent's promise, Hoffman sold his business and acquired the land in Chilton, but he was never granted a franchise. He and his wife sued Red Owl. Red Owl raised the defense that there had been only an assurance that Hoffman would receive a franchise, but because there was no promise supported by consideration, there was no binding contract to give him a franchise. Decide. [*Hoffman v Red Owl Stores, Inc.,* 133 NW2d 267 (Wis)]

Chapter 16

LEGALITY AND PUBLIC POLICY

A. General Principles

1. EFFECT OF ILLEGALITY
2. EXCEPTIONS TO EFFECT OF ILLEGALITY
3. PARTIAL ILLEGALITY
4. CRIMES AND CIVIL WRONGS
5. GOOD FAITH AND FAIRNESS
6. UNCONSCIONABLE CLAUSES

B. Agreements Affecting Public Welfare

7. AGREEMENTS CONTRARY TO PUBLIC POLICY
8. GAMBLING, WAGERS, AND LOTTERIES

C. Regulation of Business

9. EFFECT OF VIOLATION
10. STATUTORY REGULATION OF CONTRACTS
11. LICENSED CALLINGS OR DEALINGS
12. CONTRACTS IN RESTRAINT OF TRADE
13. AGREEMENTS NOT TO COMPETE
14. USURIOUS AGREEMENTS

A court will not enforce a contract if it is illegal, contrary to public policy, or unconscionable.

A. GENERAL PRINCIPLES

An agreement is illegal either when its formation or performance is a crime or a tort or when it is contrary to public policy or unconscionable.

1. Effect of Illegality

Ordinarily, an illegal agreement is void. When an agreement is illegal, the parties are usually not entitled to the aid of the courts. Examples of illegal contracts where the courts have left the parties where they found them include a liquor store owner not being allowed to bring suit for money owed for goods (liquor) sold and delivered on credit in violation of statute and an unlicensed home improvement contractor not being allowed to enforce his contract for progress payments due him. If the illegal agreement has not been performed, neither party can sue the other to obtain performance or damages. If the agreement has been performed, neither party can sue the other to obtain damages or to set the agreement aside.[1]

CASE SUMMARY

The Illegal Paralegal

FACTS: Brian Neiman was involved in the illegal practice of law for over seven years. Having been found guilty of illegally practicing law, he sought to collect disability benefits under his disability insurance policy with Provident Life due to an alleged bipolar disorder, the onset of which occurred during the pendency of criminal and bar proceedings against him. Neiman contends that his bipolar disorder prevents him from working as a paralegal. Provident contends that Neiman should not be indemnified for the loss of income generated from his illegal practice of law.

DECISION: Because all of Neiman's income was derived from the unlawful practice of law in the seven years preceding his claim, as a matter of public policy, a court will not enforce a disability benefits policy that compensates him for his loss of income he was not entitled to earn. Neiman's own wrongdoing caused the contract to be void. Accordingly, Neiman was *in pari delicito* [equally guilty], if not more at fault than the insurance company, in causing the contract to be void and will recover neither benefits nor the premiums he paid. The court must leave the parties where it found them. [**Neiman v Provident Life & Accident Insurance Co., 217 F Supp 2d 1281 SD Fla 2002**]

---

[1] *Sabia v Mattituck Inlet Marina, Inc.*, 805 NYS2d 346 (AD 2005).

Even if a contract appears to be legal on its face, it may be unenforceable if it was entered into for an illegal purpose. **For Example,** if zoning regulations in the special-purpose district of Washington, D.C., require that only a professional can lease space in a given building, and the rental agent suggests that two nonprofessionals take out the lease in their attorney's name, but all parties realize that the premises will be used only by the nonprofessionals, then the lease in question is illegal and unenforceable.[2]

2. Exceptions to Effect of Illegality

To avoid hardship, exceptions are made to the rules stated in Section 1.

(A) PROTECTION OF ONE PARTY. When the law that the agreement violates is intended to protect one of the parties, that party may seek relief. **For Example,** when, in order to protect the public, the law forbids the issuance of securities by certain classes of corporations, a person who has purchased them may recover the money paid.

(B) UNEQUAL GUILT. When the parties are not *in pari delicto*—equally guilty—the least guilty party is granted relief when public interest is advanced by doing so. **For Example,** when a statute is adopted to protect one of the parties to a transaction, such as a usury law adopted to protect borrowers, the person to be protected will not be deemed to be *in pari delicto* with the wrongdoer when entering into a transaction that the statute prohibits.

in pari delicto–equally guilty; used in reference to a transaction as to which relief will not be granted to either party because both are equally guilty of wrongdoing.

3. Partial Illegality

An agreement may involve the performance of several promises, some of which are illegal and some legal. The legal parts of the agreement may be enforced provided that they can be separated from the parts that are illegal.

When the illegal provision of a contract may be ignored without defeating the contract's basic purpose, a court will merely ignore the illegal provision and enforce the balance of the contract. Consequently, when a provision for the payment of an attorney's fee in a car rental agreement was illegal because a local statute prohibited it, the court would merely ignore the fee provision and enforce the balance of the contract.[3]

If a contract is susceptible to two interpretations, one legal and the other illegal, the court will assume that the legal meaning was intended unless the contrary is clearly indicated.

4. Crimes and Civil Wrongs

An agreement is illegal, and therefore void, when it calls for the commission of any act that constitutes a crime. To illustrate, one cannot enforce an agreement by which the other party is to commit an assault, steal property, burn a house, or kill a person.

---

[2] *McMahon v A, H, & B*, 728 A2d 656 (DC 1999).
[3] *Harbour v Arelco, Inc.*, 678 NE2d 381 (Ind 1997).

A contract to obtain equipment for committing a crime is illegal and cannot be enforced. Thus, a contract to manufacture and sell illegal slot machines is void.

An agreement that calls for the commission of a civil wrong is also illegal and void. Examples are agreements to slander a third person; defraud another; infringe another's patent, trademark, or copyright; or fix prices.

5. Good Faith and Fairness

Every contract has an implied obligation that neither party shall do anything that will have the effect of destroying or injuring the right of the other party to receive the fruits of the contract. This means that in every contract there exists an implied covenant of **good faith** and fair dealing. **For Example,** Katy Lesser entered into a 10-year lease of retail space to operate a natural food store in South Burlington, Vermont. Her business prospered and in April of 1999 she signed a lease for additional space. For five years, the landlord continually rebuffed her efforts to meet and discuss plans to renovate the 1999 space to expand the grocery store, motivated solely by a desire to pressure the tenant to pay a portion of his legal fees in an unrelated zoning case. The court found that the landlord breached the obligation of good faith and fair dealing, causing the 1999 space to be essentially unusable from 1999 to 2004. The court awarded the tenant the rent she paid for this period less a storage fee adjustment. [4]

good faith–absence of knowledge of any defects or problems.

6. Unconscionable Clauses

Ordinarily, a court will not consider whether a contract is fair or unfair, is wise or foolish, or operates unequally between the parties. **For Example,** the Kramper Family Farm sold 17.59 acres of land to Dakota Industrial Development, Inc. (DID), for $35,000 per acre if the buyer constructed a paved road along the property by December 31. The contract also provided that if the road was not completed by the date set forth in the contract, the price per acre would be $45,000. When the road was not completed by the December 31 date, Family Farm sued DID for the additional $10,000 per acre. DID defended that to apply the contract according to its plain language would create an unconscionable result and was an unenforceable penalty provision contrary to public policy. The court refused to allow DID to escape its contractual obligations on the pretext of unconscionability and public policy arguments. The parties are at liberty to contract as they see fit, the court concluded, and generally, a court will not inquire into the adequacy of consideration inasmuch as the value of property is a matter of personal judgment by the parties to the contract. In this case, the price consisted of either $45,000 per acre, or $35,000 per acre with the road by a certain date. [5]

However, in certain unusual situations, the law may hold a contract provision unenforceable because it is too harsh or oppressive to one of the parties. This

---

[4] *Century Partners, LP v Lesser Goldsmith Enterprises,* 958 A2d 627 (Vt 2008).
[5] *Kramper Family Farm v Dakota Industrial Development, Inc.,* 603 NW2d 463 (Neb App 1999).

principle may be applied to invalidate a clause providing for the payment by one party of an excessive penalty on the breaking of a contract or a provision inserted by the dominant party that it shall not be liable for the consequences of intentional torts, fraud, or gross negligence. This principle is extended in connection with the sale of goods to provide that "if the court … finds the contract or any clause of the contract to have been unconscionable at the time it was made, the court may refuse to enforce the contract, or it may enforce the remainder of the contract without the unconscionable clause, or it may so limit the application of any unconscionable clause as to avoid any unconscionable result."[6]

(A) WHAT CONSTITUTES UNCONSCIONABILITY? A provision in a contract that gives what the court believes is too much of an advantage over a buyer may be held void as unconscionable.

(B) DETERMINATION OF UNCONSCIONABILITY. Some jurisdictions analyze unconscionability as having two separate elements: procedural and substantive. Both elements must be present for a court to refuse to enforce a contract provision. Other jurisdictions analyze unconscionability by considering the doctrine of adhesion and whether the clause in question is unduly oppressive.

Procedural unconscionability has to do with matters of freedom of assent resulting from inequality of bargaining power and the absence of real negotiations and meaningful choice or a surprise resulting from hiding a disputed term in an unduly long document or fine print. Companywide standardized form contracts imposed on a take-it-or-leave-it basis by a party with superior bargaining strength are called **contracts of adhesion**, and they may sometimes be deemed procedurally unconscionable.

contract of adhesion— contract offered by a dominant party to a party with inferior bargaining power on a take-it-or-leave-it basis.

Substantive unconscionability focuses on the actual terms of the contract itself. Such unconscionability is indicated when the contract terms are so one-sided as to shock the conscience or are so extreme as to appear unconscionable according to the mores and business practices of the time and place.

The U.S. Supreme Court has made clear that arbitration is an acceptable forum for the resolution of employment disputes between employees and their employers, including employment-related claims based on federal and state statutes.[7] The controlling arbitration agreement language is commonly devised and implemented by the employer. Under the Federal Arbitration Act (FAA), the employer can obtain a court order to stay court proceedings and compel arbitration according to the terms of the controlling arbitration agreement. The Supreme Court also made clear that in agreeing to arbitration of a statutory claim, a party does not forgo substantive rights afforded by the statute. In a growing number of court decisions, in effect employers are finding that courts will not enforce arbitration agreements in which the employer has devised an arbitration agreement that functions as a thumb on the employer's side of the scale.[8]

---

[6] UCC § 2-302(1).
[7] *Gilmer v Interstate/Johnson Lane Corp.*, 500 US 20 (1991); *Circuit City Stores, Inc. v Adams*, 532 US 105 (2001).
[8] See *Vassilkouska v Woodfield Nissan Inc.*, 830 NE2d 619 (Ill App 2005).

CASE SUMMARY

Arbitration Agreement Short-Circuited

FACTS: Saint Clair Adams completed an application to work as a salesperson at Circuit City. As part of the application, Adams signed the "Circuit City Dispute Resolution Agreement" (DRA). The DRA requires employees to submit all claims and disputes to binding arbitration. Incorporated into the DRA is a set of "Dispute Resolution Rules and Procedures" that defines the claims subject to arbitration, discovery rules, allocation of fees, and available remedies. Under these rules, the amount of damages is restricted: Back pay is limited to one year, front pay to two years, and punitive damages to the higher of the amount of front and back pay awarded or $5,000. In addition, the employee is required to split the cost of the arbitration, including the daily fees of the arbitrator, the cost of a reporter to transcribe the proceedings, and the expense of renting the room in which the arbitration is held, unless the employee prevails and the arbitrator decides to order Circuit City to pay the employee's share of the costs. Circuit City is not required under the agreement to arbitrate any claims against the employee. An employee cannot work at Circuit City without signing the DRA.

Adams filed a state court lawsuit against Circuit City and three coworkers alleging sexual harassment and related charges. Circuit City responded by filing a petition in federal district court to compel arbitration pursuant to the FAA. The petition was granted by the trial court, reversed by the Ninth Circuit Court of Appeals, which court was reversed by the U.S. Supreme Court (*Circuit City 1*) and the case remanded to the Ninth Circuit Court of Appeals.

DECISION: Judgment for Adams. The arbitration provision is unenforceable. The DRA is procedurally unconscionable because it is a contract of adhesion drafted by the party with superior bargaining power, which relegates to the other party the option of either adhering to its terms without modification or rejecting the contract entirely.

The DRA is substantively unconscionable because employees must arbitrate "any and all employment-related claims" while Circuit City is not obligated to arbitrate their claims against employees and may bring lawsuits against employees, thus depriving the DRA of any modicum of bilaterality. Moreover, the remedies are limited under the DRA, including a one-year back pay limit and a two-year front pay limit, with a cap on punitive damages of an amount up to the higher of the amount of back pay and front pay awarded or $5,000. By contrast, in a civil lawsuit under state law, a plaintiff is entitled to all forms of relief. Further, the DRA requires that the employee split the cost of the arbitrator's fees with the employer while an individual would not be required to split the cost of a judge. [**Circuit City Stores, Inc. v Adams (Circuit City II), 279 F3d 889 9th Cir 2002**]

B. Agreements Affecting Public Welfare

Agreements that may harm the public welfare are condemned as contrary to public policy and are not binding. Agreements that interfere with public service or the duties of public officials, obstruct legal process, or discriminate against classifications of individuals may be considered detrimental to public welfare and, as such, are not enforceable.

7. Agreements Contrary to Public Policy

A given agreement may not violate any statute but may still be so offensive to society that the courts feel that enforcing the contract would be contrary to public policy.

public policy–certain objectives relating to health, morals, and integrity of government that the law seeks to advance by declaring invalid any contract that conflicts with those objectives even though there is no statute expressly declaring such a contract illegal.

Public policy cannot be defined precisely but is loosely described as protection from that which tends to be injurious to the public or contrary to the public good or which violates any established interest of society. Contracts that may be unenforceable as contrary to public policy frequently relate to the protection of the public welfare, health, or safety; to the protection of the person; and to the protection of recognized social institutions. **For Example,** a woman entered into a services contract with a male in exchange for financial support. The record disclosed, however, that the association between the parties was one founded upon the exchange of money for sex. The court determined that the agreement for financial support in exchange for illicit sexual relations was violative of public policy and thus was unenforceable.[9] Courts are cautious in invalidating a contract on the ground that it is contrary to public policy because courts recognize that, on the one hand, they are applying a very vague standard and, on the other hand, they are restricting the freedom of the contracting parties to contract freely as they choose.[10]

8. Gambling, Wagers, and Lotteries

lottery–any plan by which a consideration is given for a chance to win a prize; it consists of three elements: (1) there must be a payment of money or something of value for an opportunity to win, (2) a prize must be available, and (3) the prize must be offered by lot or chance.

Gambling contracts are illegal. Largely as a result of the adoption of antigambling statutes, wagers or bets are generally illegal. Private **lotteries** involving the three elements of prize, chance, and consideration (or similar affairs of chance) are also generally held illegal. In many states, public lotteries (lotteries run by a state government) have been legalized by statute. Raffles are usually regarded as lotteries.

CASE SUMMARY

Horseplay Prohibited

FACTS: Robert Bovard contracted to sell American Horse Enterprises, Inc., to James Ralph. When Ralph did not make payments when due, Bovard brought suit against him. The trial judge raised the question whether the contract was void for illegality. American Horse Enterprises was predominantly engaged in manufacturing devices for smoking marijuana and tobacco, and to a lesser degree in manufacturing jewelry. When the contract was made, there was no statute prohibiting the manufacture of any of these items, but there was a statute making it illegal to possess, use, or transfer marijuana.

DECISION: Although the question of illegality had not been raised by the parties, the trial judge had the duty to question the validity of the contract when it appeared that the contract might be illegal. Although there was no statute expressly making the contract illegal, the statute prohibiting the possession and sale of marijuana manifested a public policy against anything that would further the use of marijuana. It was therefore against public policy to make the devices used in smoking marijuana or to sell a business that engaged in such manufacture. The sales contract was therefore contrary to public policy and void and could not be enforced. [**Bovard v American Horse Enterprises, Inc. 247 Cal Rptr 340 Cal App 1988**]

---

[9] *Anonymous v Anonymous,* 740 NYS2d 341 (App Div 2002).
[10] *Beacon Hill Civic Ass'n v Ristorante Toscano, Inc.,* 662 NE2d 1015 (Mass 1996).

In some states, bingo games, lotteries, and raffles are legalized by statute when the funds raised are used for a charitable purpose.

Sales promotion schemes calling for the distribution of property according to chance among the purchasers of goods are held illegal as lotteries without regard to whether the scheme is called a *guessing contest,* a *raffle,* or a *gift.*

Giveaway plans and games are lawful so long as it is not necessary to buy anything or give anything of value to participate. If participation is free, the element of consideration is lacking, and there is no lottery.

An activity is not gambling when the result is solely or predominantly a matter of skill. In contrast, it is gambling when the result is solely a matter of luck. Rarely is any activity 100 percent skill or 100 percent luck.

C. Regulation of Business

Local, state, and national laws regulate a wide variety of business activities and practices.

9. Effect of Violation

Whether an agreement made in connection with business conducted in violation of the law is binding or void depends on how strongly opposed the public policy is to the prohibited act. Some courts take the view that the agreement is not void unless the statute expressly specifies this. In some instances, a statute expressly preserves the validity of the contract. **For Example,** if someone fails to register a fictitious name under which a business is conducted, the violator, after registering the name as required by statute, is permitted to sue on a contract made while illegally conducting business.

10. Statutory Regulation of Contracts

To establish uniformity or to protect one of the parties to a contract, statutes frequently provide that contracts of a given class must follow a statutory model or must contain specified provisions. **For Example,** statutes commonly specify that particular clauses must be included in insurance policies to protect the persons insured and their beneficiaries. Other statutes require that contracts executed in connection with credit buying and loans contain particular provisions designed to protect the debtor.

Consumer protection legislation gives the consumer the right to rescind the contract in certain situations. Laws relating to truth in lending, installment sales, and home improvement contracts commonly require that an installment-sale contract specify the cash price, the down payment, the trade-in value (if any), the cash balance, the insurance costs, and the interest and finance charges.

CPA 11. Licensed Callings or Dealings

Statutes frequently require that a person obtain a license, certificate, or diploma before practicing certain professions, such as law and medicine.[11] A license may also

---

[11] *Hakimi v Cantwell,* 855 NYS2d 273 (App Div 2008).

be required before carrying on a particular business or trade, such as that of a real estate broker, stockbroker, hotel keeper, or pawnbroker.

If a license is required to protect the public from unqualified persons, a contract made by an unlicensed person is unenforceable. **For Example,** a corporation that does not hold a required real estate broker's license cannot sue to recover fees for services as a broker. An unlicensed insurance broker who cannot recover a fee because of the absence of a license cannot evade the statutory requirement by having a friend who is a licensed broker bill for the services and collect the payment for him.

CASE SUMMARY

How Much for a Brokerage License? How Much Commission Was Lost?

FACTS: Thompson Halbach & Associates, Inc., an Arizona corporation, entered into an agreement with Meteor Motors, Inc., the owner of Palm Beach Acura, to find a buyer for the dealership, and Meteor agreed to pay a 5 percent commission based on the closing price of the sale. Working out of Scottsdale, Arizona, Thompson solicited potential Florida purchasers for the Florida business by phone, fax, and e-mail. Among those contacted was Craig Zinn Automotive Group, which ultimately purchased Palm Beach Acura from Meteor Motors for $5,000,000. Thompson was not paid its $250,000 commission and brought suit against Meteor for breach of contract. Meteor defended that Thompson was an unlicensed broker and that a state statute declares a contract for a commission with an unlicensed broker to be invalid. Thompson responded that the Florida state statue did not apply because it worked out of Scottsdale.

DECISION: Judgment for Meteor. The Florida statute clearly applies to a foreign broker who provides brokerage activities in Florida. Thompson solicited potential Florida purchasers for the Florida business and that purchaser was a Florida corporation. [**Meteor Motors v Thompson Halbach & Associates, 914 So2d 479 Fla App 2005**]

CPA 12. Contracts in Restraint of Trade

An agreement that unreasonably restrains trade is illegal and void on the ground that it is contrary to public policy. Such agreements take many forms, such as a combination to create a monopoly or to obtain a corner on the market or an association of merchants to increase prices. In addition to the illegality of the agreement based on general principles of law, statutes frequently declare monopolies illegal and subject the parties to various civil and criminal penalties.[12]

CPA 13. Agreements Not to Compete

In the absence of a valid restrictive covenant, the seller of a business may compete with the buyer, or an ex-employee may solicit customers of the former employer.

---

[12] Sherman Antitrust Act, 15 USC §§ 1–7; Clayton Act, 15 USC §§ 12–27; Federal Trade Commission Act, 15 USC §§ 41–58.

A noncompetition covenant may be held invalid because of vagueness concerning the duration and geographic area of the restriction.[13] Moreover, if the agreement not to compete is not properly executed in accordance with state law, it will not be enforced. **For Example,** Holly Martinez worked for Avis Rent-A-Car at the New Bern, North Carolina, airport. When hired, she printed her name on the top of the form containing an agreement not to compete but did not sign it. On December 17, she resigned her position to return to school, saying that she planned to get a part-time job. The next day, she began working for Hertz Rent-A-Car at the counter adjacent to the Avis counter. Avis was unsuccessful in obtaining a restraining order to prevent Holly from working for its competitor because the agreement was not signed as required by state law. [14]

CPA   (A) SALE OF BUSINESS. When a going business is sold, it is commonly stated in the contract that the seller shall not go into the same or a similar business again within a certain geographic area or for a certain period of time, or both. In early times, such agreements were held void because they deprived the public of the service of the person who agreed not to compete, impaired the latter's means of earning a livelihood, reduced competition, and exposed the public to monopoly. To modern courts, the question is whether, under the circumstances, the restriction imposed on one party is reasonably necessary to protect the other party. If the restriction is reasonable, it is valid and enforceable. **For Example,** when Scott Gaddy, the majority stockholder of GWC Insurance Brokers, sold his business to Alliant for $4.1 million he agreed to refrain from competing in the insurance business in California for five years. Under California law, contracts not to compete are void, except for noncompetition covenants in connection with the sale of a business. The reason for the exception is to prevent the seller from depriving the buyer of the full value of the acquisition, including the sold company's goodwill. The court enforced the covenant against Gaddy. [15]

(B) EMPLOYMENT CONTRACT. Restrictions to prevent competition by a former employee are held valid when reasonable and necessary to protect the interest of the former employer. **For Example,** a noncompete clause executed by Dr. Samuel Keeley that prohibited his "establishing a competing cardiovascular surgery practice within a 75-mile radius of Albany, Georgia, for a period of two years following the date of termination" was upheld in court and did not include more territory than necessary to protect the professional corporation's business interests. [16]

Public policy requires that noncompetition covenants be strictly construed in favor of freedom of action of the employee.[17] A restrictive covenant is not binding when it places a restriction on the employee that is broader than reasonably necessary to protect the employer. **For Example,** Illinois manufacturer Arcor's noncompete clause, which had a restricted area of "the United States and Canada" precluding competition by a former employee for a one-year period, was found to

---

[13] *Vukovich v Coleman,* 789 NE2d 520 (Ind App 2003).
[14] *New Hanover Rent-A-Car, Inc. v Martinez,* 525 SE2d 487 (NC App 2000).
[15] 72 Cal Rptr 3d 259 (Cal App 2008).
[16] *Keeley v CSA, P.C.,* 510 SE2d 880 (Ga App 1999).
[17] Noncompetition covenants are not valid in California. However, confidentiality agreements protecting trade secrets are enforceable in that state.

be unenforceable as an industrywide ban that constituted a "blanket prohibition on competition."[18] In determining the validity of a restrictive covenant binding an employee, the court balances the aim of protecting the legitimate interests of the employer with the right of the employee to follow gainful employment and provide services required by the public and other employers.

thinking things through

Noncompete Clauses, Cause for Concern?

Some 10 states do not enforce noncompete clauses in employment contracts, according to the research of Matt Marx who has dedicated his doctoral studies at Harvard to this topic. The states are (from west to east): California, Washington, Nevada, Montana, North Dakota, Minnesota, Oklahoma, West Virginia, and Connecticut. (New York and Oregon have significantly limited their applicability). Marx had naively signed a two-year noncompete agreement out of MIT at SpeechWorks, a voice recognition start-up, and when he wanted to leave and continue in the voice recognition field, his options were to sit out the two-year noncompete period or go to work at a California firm, which he did. He is now researching whether enforcing noncompetes in a

state can spur inventors, engineers, and entrepreneurs to move elsewhere to pursue development of their ideas.*

Does a state's innovation suffer when noncompete clauses handcuff employees to an employer, or force employees to take an unpaid leave for the noncompete period before continuing in their field with a new or start-up employer? THINKING THINGS THROUGH, prospective employees should carefully consider the impact noncompetes would have on their lives, and if they must sign one, carefully negotiate its duration and scope.

* *See* Scott Kirsner, "Why 'Noncompete' Means 'Don't Thrive,'" *Boston Globe*, December 30, 2007, E-1; Scott Kirsner, "Start-ups Stifled by Noncompetes," *Boston Globe*, June 21, 2009, G-1.

(c) **Effect of Invalidity.** When a restriction of competition agreed to by the parties is invalid because its scope as to time or geographic area is too great, how does this affect the contract? Some courts trim the restrictive covenant down to a scope they deem reasonable and require the parties to abide by that revision.[19] This rule is nicknamed the "blue-pencil rule." **For Example,** Julie Murray signed a noncompete agreement, which was validly assigned to the purchaser of the Accounting Center of Lucas County, Inc. When the new owner changed from an hourly wage to commission pay for her tax preparation work, she objected and was terminated. The court found the 24-month noncompete restriction exceeded what was reasonable to protect the employer's legitimate business interests, and modified the time period to one year.[20] In the *Arcor* case, the court refused to "blue pencil" the covenant because to render the clause

---

[18] *Arcor, Inc. v Haas*, 842 NE2d 265 (Ill App 2005).
[19] *Unisource Worldwide, Inc. v Valenti*, 196 F Supp 2d 269 (EDNY 2002).
[20] *Murray v Accounting Center of Lucas County, Inc.*, 898 NE2d 89 (Ohio App 2008).

ethics & the law

William Stern and his wife were unable to have children because the wife suffered from multiple sclerosis and pregnancy posed a substantial health risk. Stern's family had been killed in the Holocaust, and he had a strong desire to continue his bloodline.

The Sterns entered into a surrogacy contract with Mary Beth Whitehead through the Infertility Center of New York (ICNY). William Stern and the Whiteheads (husband and wife) signed a contract for Mary Beth to be artificially inseminated and carry Stern's child to term, for which Stern was to pay Mary Beth $10,000 and ICNY $7,500.

Mary Beth was successfully artificially inseminated in 1985, and Baby M was born on March 27, 1986. To avoid publicity, the parents of Baby M were listed as "Mr. and Mrs. Whitehead," and the baby was called Sara Elizabeth Whitehead. On March 30, 1986, Mary Beth turned Baby M over to the Sterns at their home. They renamed the little girl Melissa.

Mary Beth became emotionally distraught and was unable to eat or sleep. The Sterns were so frightened by her behavior that they allowed her to take Baby M for one week to help her adjust. The Whiteheads took the baby and traveled throughout the East, staying in 20 different hotels and motels. Florida authorities found Baby M with Mary Beth's parents and returned her to the Sterns.

Mary Beth said the contract was one to buy a baby and was against public policy and therefore void. She also argued that the contract violated state laws on adoption and the severance of parental rights. The Sterns brought an action to have the contract declared valid and custody awarded to them.

Should the contract be valid or void? What types of behavior would be encouraged if the contract were declared valid? Is it ethical to "rent a womb"? Is it ethical to sell a child? See **In re Baby M, 537 A2d 15 (NJ 1988).**

reasonable, the court would in effect be writing a new agreement, which is inappropriate.[21]

Other courts refuse to apply the blue-pencil rule and hold that the restrictive covenant is void or that the entire contract is void.[22] There is also authority that a court should refuse to apply the blue-pencil rule when the restrictive covenant is manifestly unfair and would virtually keep the employee from earning a living.

14. Usurious Agreements

usury–lending money at an interest rate that is higher than the maximum rate allowed by law.

Usury is committed when money is loaned at a higher rate of interest than the law allows. Most states prohibit by statute charging more than a stated amount of interest. These statutes provide a maximum annual contract rate of interest that can be exacted under the law of a given state. In many states, the usury law does not apply to loans made to corporations.

When a lender incurs expenses in making a loan, such as the cost of appraising property or making a credit investigation of the borrower, the lender will require the

[21] *Arcor Inc.,* 847 NE2d at 374.

[22] *SWAT 24 v Bond,* 759 So2d 1047 (La App 2000). Under California law, any "contract by which anyone is restrained from engaging in a lawful profession, trade or business is to that extent void." Cal B&P Code § 16600. A noncompete provision is permitted, however, when "necessary to protect the employer's trade secrets." See *Lotona v Aetna U.S. Healthcare Inc.,* 82 F Supp 2d 1089 (CD Cal 1999), where Aetna was liable for wrongful termination when it fired a California employee for refusing to sign a noncompete agreement.

thinking things through

Legality and Public Policy

Karl Llewellyn, the principal drafter of the law that governs nearly all sales of goods in the United States—the Uniform Commercial Code (UCC)—once wrote, "Covert tools are never reliable tools." He was referring to unfairness in a contract or between the contracting parties.

The original intent of declaring certain types of contracts void because of issues of imbalance was based in equity. Courts stepped in to help parties who found themselves bound under agreements that were not fair and open in both their written terms and the communications between the parties. One contracts scholar wrote that the original intent could be described as courts stepping in to help "presumptive sillies like sailors and heirs…" and others who, if not crazy, are "pretty peculiar."

However, as the sophistication of contracts and commercial transactions increased, the importance of accuracy, honesty, and fairness increased. Unconscionability is a contracts defense that permits courts to intervene where contracts, if enforced, would "affront the sense of decency." UNCONSCIONABILITY is a term of ethics or moral philosophy used by courts to prevent exploitation and fraud.

borrower to pay the amount of such expenses. Any fee charged by a lender that goes beyond the reasonable expense of making the loan constitutes "interest" for the purposes of determining whether the transaction is usurious.[23]

Penalites for violating usury laws vary from state to state, with a number of states restricting the lender to the recovery of the loan but no interest whatsoever; other states allow recovery of the loan principal and interest up to the maximum contract rate. Some states also impose a penalty on the lender such as the payment of double the interest paid on a usurious loan.

CASE SUMMARY

Would You Recommend Karen Canzoneri as an Investment Advisor?

FACTS: Karen Canzoneri entered into two agreements with Howard Pinchuck. Under the first agreement, Canzoneri advanced $50,000 to be repaid at 12 percent per month for 12 consecutive months "as an investment profit." The second agreement required "$36,000 to be repaid on or before 6/1/01 with an investment profit of $36,000, total being $72,000." The annualized rate of return for the first transaction was 144 percent and for the second transaction was 608 percent. The civil penalty for violating the state's maximum interest rate of 25 percent per annum is forfeiture of the entire principal amount. Canzoneri contends that the transactions were investments not subject to the usury law.

[23] *Lentimo v Cullen Center Bank and Trust Co.,* 919 SW2d 743 (Tex App 1996).

CASE SUMMARY

Continued

DECISION: Judgment for Pinchuck. The four elements of a usurious transaction are present: (1) the transaction was a loan, (2) the money loaned required that it be returned, (3) an interest rate higher than allowed by law was required, and (4) a corrupt intention to take more than the legal rate for the use of the money loaned exists. Even though the terms called for "profit," not "interest," the courts looked to the substance, not the form of the transaction. [**Pinchuck v Canzoneri, 920 So2nd 713 (Fla App 4 Dist 2006)**]

lawflix

Midnight Run (1988) (R)

Is the contract Robert DeNiro has for bringing in Charles Grodin, an embezzler, legal? Discuss the issues of consideration and ethics as the bail bondsman puts another bounty hunter on the case and DeNiro flees from law enforcement agents in order to collect his fee. And finally, discuss the legality of DeNiro's acceptance of money from Grodin and his release of Grodin at the end of the movie.

You can view a clip of this movie and others that illustrate business law concepts at the LawFlix site, located at **www.cengage.com/blaw/dvl**.

MAKE THE CONNECTION

SUMMARY

When an agreement is illegal, it is ordinarily void and no contract arises from it. Courts will not allow one party to an illegal agreement to bring suit against the other party. There are some exceptions to this, such as when the parties are not equally guilty or when the law's purpose in making the agreement illegal is to protect the person who is bringing suit. When possible, an agreement will be interpreted as being lawful. Even when a particular provision is held unlawful, the balance of the agreement may be saved so that the net result is a contract minus the clause that was held illegal.

The term *illegality* embraces situations in unconscionable contract clauses in which the courts hold that contract provisions are unenforceable because they are too harsh or oppressive to one of the parties to a transaction. If the clause is part of a standard form contract drafted by the party having superior bargaining power and is presented on a take-it-or-leave-it basis (a contract of adhesion) and the substantive terms of the clause itself are unduly oppressive, the clause will be found to be unconscionable and not enforced.

Whether a contract is contrary to public policy may be difficult to determine because public policy is not precisely defined. That which is harmful to the public welfare or general good is contrary to public policy. Contracts condemned as contrary to public policy include those designed to deprive the weaker party of a benefit that the lawmaker desired to provide, agreements injuring public service, and wagers and private lotteries. Statutes commonly make the wager illegal as a form of gambling. The private lottery is any plan under which, for a consideration, a person has a chance to win a prize.

Illegality may consist of the violation of a statute or administrative regulation adopted to regulate business. An agreement not to compete may be illegal as a restraint of trade except when reasonable in its terms and when it is incidental to the sale of a business or to a contract of employment.

The charging by a lender of a higher rate of interest than allowed by law is usury. Courts must examine transactions carefully to see whether a usurious loan is disguised as a legitimate transaction.

LEARNING OUTCOMES

After studying this chapter, you should be able to clearly explain:

A. GENERAL PRINCIPLES

LO.1 Explain the general contract principles on "illegality"
> See the unenforceable illegal lease to nonprofessionals example on p. 348. See the example where a contract to manufacture and sell illegal slot machines is void, p. 350.

LO.2 Explain the implied obligation on all parties of good faith and fair dealing
> See the example of the Vermont landlord who deprived a tenant of her rights under a lease, p. 350.

B. AGREEMENTS AFFECTING PUBLIC WELFARE

LO.3 Understand that it is only in unusual situations that a contract provision will be unenforceable because it is unconscionable
> See the *Kramper Family Farm* example where the court refused to consider whether the contract was fair or unfair, wise or foolish, p. 350.

C. REGULATION OF BUSINESS

LO.4 Explain the rationale for requiring licenses to carry on as a business, trade, or profession
> See the discussion requiring licenses to protect the public from unqualified persons, p. 355.

LO.5 Distinguish between noncompete clauses after the sale of a business and noncompete clauses in employment contracts

See the example where the California court enforced a 5 year noncompete clause against the seller of a business, p. 356.

See the example involving Julie Murray's noncompete clause and why it was modified from 24 months to one year, p. 357.

KEY TERMS

contracts of adhesion   *in pari delicto*   public policy
good faith   lotteries   usury

QUESTIONS AND CASE PROBLEMS

1. When are the parties to an illegal agreement *in pari delicto?*

2. John Iwen sued U.S. West Direct because of a negligently constructed yellow pages advertisement. U.S. West Direct moved to stay litigation and compel arbitration under the yellow pages order form, which required advertisers to resolve all controversies through arbitration, but allowed U.S. West (the publisher) to pursue judicial remedies to collect amounts due it. Under the arbitration provision, Iwen's sole remedy was a pro rata reduction or refund of the cost of the advertisement. The order form language was drafted by U.S. West Direct on a take-it-or-leave-it basis and stated in part:

   Any controversy or claim arising out of or relating to this Agreement, or breach thereof, other than an action by Publisher for the collection of amounts due under this Agreement, shall be settled by final, binding arbitration in accordance with the Commercial Arbitration rules of the American Arbitration Association.

   If forced to arbitration, Iwen would be unable to recover damages for the negligently constructed yellow pages ad, nor could he recover damages for infliction of emotional distress and punitive damages related to his many efforts to adjust the matter with the company, which were ignored or rejected. Must Iwen have his case resolved through arbitration rather than a court of law? [*Iwen v U.S. West Direct*, 977 P2d 989 (Mont)]

3. Sutcliffe Banton, dba Nemard Construction, furnished labor and materials (valued at $162,895) for improving Vicky Deafeamkpor's New York City residential property. She paid only $41,718, leaving $121,987 unpaid. Banton sued her and the jury awarded $90,000 in damages. Deafeamkpor moved for an order setting aside the jury's verdict because Banton was not properly licensed by New York City. Under NYC Code an unlicensed contractor may neither enforce a home improvement contract against an owner or recover in *quantum meruit*. The jury heard all the evidence regarding the materials and labor expended on Deafeamkpor's residence and concluded that the plaintiff

performed satisfactory work valued at $90,000 for which he was not paid. Should the court allow the owner to take advantage of Banton and his employees and suppliers? What public policy would support such an outcome? Decide. [*Nemard Construction Corp. v Deafeamkpor*, 863 NY S2d 846]

4. Eugene McCarthy left his position as director of sales for Nike's Brand Jordan division in June 2003 to become vice president of U.S. footwear sales and merchandising at Reebok, one of Nike's competitors. Nike sought a preliminary injunction to prevent McCarthy from working for Reebok for a year, invoking a noncompete agreement McCarthy had signed in Oregon in 1997 when Nike had promoted him to his earlier position as a regional footwear sales manager. The agreement stated in pertinent part:

> During EMPLOYEE'S employment by NIKE … and for one (1) year thereafter, ("the Restriction Period"), EMPLOYEE will not directly or indirectly … be employed by, consult for, or be connected in any manner with, any business engaged anywhere in the world in the athletic footwear, athletic apparel or sports equipment and accessories business, or any other business which directly competes with NIKE or any of its subsidiaries or affiliated corporations.

McCarty contends that such a contract is a restraint of trade and should not be enforced. Nike contends that the agreement is fair and should be enforced. Decide. [*Nike, Inc. v McCarthy*, 379 F3d 576 (9th Cir)]

5. Ewing was employed by Presto-X-Co., a pest exterminator. His contract of employment specified that he would not solicit or attempt to solicit customers of Presto-X for two years after the termination of his employment. After working several years, his employment was terminated. Ewing then sent a letter to customers of Presto-X stating that he no longer worked for Presto-X and that he was still certified by the state. Ewing set forth his home address and phone number, which the customers did not previously have. The letter ended with the statement, "I thank you for your business throughout the past years." Presto-X brought an action to enjoin Ewing from sending such letters. He raised the defense that he was prohibited only from soliciting and there was nothing in the letters that constituted a seeking of customers. Decide. What ethical values are involved? [*Presto-X-Co. v Ewing*, 442 NW2d 85 (Iowa)]

6. The Minnesota adoption statute requires that any agency placing a child for adoption make a thorough investigation and not give a child to an applicant unless the placement is in the best interests of the child. Tibbetts applied to Crossroads, Inc., a private adoption agency, for a child to adopt. He later sued the agency for breach of contract, claiming that the agency was obligated by contract to supply a child for adoption. The agency claimed that it was required only to use its best efforts to locate a child and was not required to supply a child to Tibbetts unless it found him to be a suitable parent. Decide. [*Tibbetts v Crossroads, Inc.*, 411 NW2d 535 (Minn App)]

7. Siddle purchased a quantity of fireworks from Red Devil Fireworks Co. The sale was illegal, however, because Siddle did not have a license to make the

purchase, which the seller knew because it had been so informed by the attorney general of the state. Siddle did not pay for the fireworks, and Red Devil sued him. He defended on the ground that the contract could not be enforced because it was illegal. Was the defense valid? [*Red Devil Fireworks Co. v Siddle,* 648 P2d 468 (Wash App)]

8. Onderdonk entered a retirement home operated by Presbyterian Homes. The contract between Onderdonk and the home required Onderdonk to make a specified monthly payment that could be increased by the home as the cost of operations increased. The contract and the payment plan were thoroughly explained to Onderdonk. As the cost of operations rose, the home continually raised the monthly payments to cover these costs. Onderdonk objected to the increases on the ground that the increases were far more than had been anticipated and that the contract was therefore unconscionable. Was his objection valid?

9. Smith was employed as a salesman for Borden, Inc., which sold food products in 63 counties in Arkansas, 2 counties in Missouri, 2 counties in Oklahoma, and 1 county in Texas. Smith's employment contract prohibited him from competing with Borden after leaving its employ. Smith left Borden and went to work for a competitor, Lady Baltimore Foods. Working for this second employer, Smith sold in 3 counties of Arkansas. He had sold in 2 of these counties while he worked for Borden. Borden brought an injunction action against Smith and Lady Baltimore to enforce the noncompete covenant in Smith's former contract. Was Borden entitled to the injunction? [*Borden, Inc. v Smith,* 478 SW2d 744 (Ark)]

10. Central Water Works Supply, a corporation, had a contract with its shareholders that they would not compete with it. There were only four shareholders, of whom William Fisher was one, but he was not an employee of the corporation. When he sold his shares in the corporation and began to compete with it, the corporation went to court to obtain an injunction to stop such competition. Fisher claimed that the corporation was not entitled to an injunction because he had not obtained any confidential information or made customer contacts. The corporation claimed that such matters were relevant only when an employee had agreed not to compete but were not applicable when there was a noncompetitive covenant in the sale of a business and that the sale-of-a-business rule should be applied to a shareholder. Who was correct?

11. Vodra was employed as a salesperson and contracting agent for American Security Services. As part of his contract of employment, Vodra signed an agreement that for three years after leaving this employment, he would not solicit any customer of American. Vodra had no experience in the security field when he went to work for American. To the extent that he became known to American's customers, it was because of being American's representative rather than because of his own reputation in the security field. After some years, Vodra left American and organized a competing company that solicited American's customers. American sued him to enforce the restrictive covenant. Vodra

claimed that the restrictive covenant was illegal and not binding. Was he correct? [*American Security Services, Inc. v Vodra*, 385 NW2d 73 (Neb)]

12. Potomac Leasing Co. leased an automatic telephone system to Vitality Centers. Claudene Cato signed the lease as guarantor of payments. When the rental was not paid, Potomac Leasing brought suit against Vitality and Cato. They raised the defense that the rented equipment was to be used for an illegal purpose—namely, the random sales solicitation by means of an automatic telephone in violation of state statute; that this purpose was known to Potomac Leasing; and that Potomac Leasing could therefore not enforce the lease. Was this defense valid? [*Potomac Leasing Co. v Vitality Centers, Inc.*, 718 SW2d 928 (Ark)]

13. The English publisher of a book called *Cambridge* gave a New York publisher permission to sell that book any place in the world except in England. The New York publisher made several bulk sales of the book to buyers who sold the book throughout the world, including England. The English publisher sued the New York publisher and its customers for breach of the restriction prohibiting sales in England. Decide.

14. A state law required builders of homes to be licensed and declared that an unlicensed contractor could not recover compensation under a contract made for the construction of a residence. Although Annex Construction, Inc., did not have a license, it built a home for French. When he failed to pay what was owed, Annex sued him. He raised the defense that the unlicensed contractor could not recover for the contract price. Annex claimed that the lack of a license was not a bar because the president of the corporation was a licensed builder and the only shareholder of the corporation, and the construction had been properly performed. Was Annex entitled to recover?

15. Yarde Metals, Inc., owned six season tickets to New England Patriots football games. Gillette Stadium, where the games are played, had insufficient men's restrooms in use for football games at that time, which was the subject of numerous newspaper columns. On October 13, 2002, a guest of Yarde Metals, Mikel LaCroix, along with others, used available women's restrooms to answer the call of nature. As LaCroix left the restroom, however, he was arrested and charged with disorderly conduct. The Patriots organization terminated all six of Yarde's season ticket privileges, incorrectly giving as a reason that LaCroix was ejected "for throwing bottles in the seating section." Yarde sued, contending that "by terminating the plaintiff's season tickets for 2002 and for the future arbitrarily, without cause and based on false information," the Patriots had violated the implicit covenant of good faith and fair dealing of the season tickets contract. The back of each Patriots ticket states:

> *This ticket and all season tickets are revocable licenses. The Patriots reserve the right to revoke such licenses, in their sole discretion, at any time and for any reason.*

How would you decide this case? [*Yarde Metals, Inc. v New England Patriots Ltd.*, 834 NE2d 1233 (Mass App Ct)]

CPA QUESTIONS

1. West, an Indiana real estate broker, misrepresented to Zimmer that West was licensed in Kansas under the Kansas statute that regulates real estate brokers and requires all brokers to be licensed. Zimmer signed a contract agreeing to pay West a 5 percent commission for selling Zimmer's home in Kansas. West did not sign the contract. West sold Zimmer's home. If West sued Zimmer for nonpayment of commission, Zimmer would be:

   a. Liable to West only for the value of services rendered

   b. Liable to West for the full commission

   c. Not liable to West for any amount because West did not sign the contract

   d. Not liable to West for any amount because West violated the Kansas licensing requirements (5/92, Law, #25)

2. Blue purchased a travel agency business from Drye. The purchase price included payment for Drye's goodwill. The agreement contained a covenant prohibiting Drye from competing with Blue in the travel agency business. Which of the following statements regarding the covenant is *not* correct?

   a. The restraint must be *no* more extensive than is reasonably necessary to protect the goodwill purchased by Blue.

   b. The geographic area to which it applies must be reasonable.

   c. The time period for which it is to be effective must be reasonable.

   d. The value to be assigned to it is the excess of the price paid over the seller's cost of all tangible assets. (11/87, Law, #2)

Chapter 17

WRITING, ELECTRONIC FORMS, AND INTERPRETATION OF CONTRACTS

A. Statute of Frauds

   1. VALIDITY OF ORAL CONTRACTS

   2. CONTRACTS THAT MUST BE EVIDENCED BY A WRITING

   3. NOTE OR MEMORANDUM

   4. EFFECT OF NONCOMPLIANCE

B. Parol Evidence Rule

   5. EXCLUSION OF PAROL EVIDENCE

   6. WHEN THE PAROL EVIDENCE RULE DOES NOT APPLY

C. Rules of Construction and Interpretation

   7. INTENTION OF THE PARTIES

   8. WHOLE CONTRACT

   9. CONTRADICTORY AND AMBIGUOUS TERMS

   10. IMPLIED TERMS

   11. CONDUCT AND CUSTOM

   12. AVOIDANCE OF HARDSHIP

W hen must a contract be written? What is the effect of a written contract? These questions lead to the statute of frauds and the parol evidence rule.

A. STATUTE OF FRAUDS

A *contract* is a legally binding agreement. Must the agreement be evidenced by a writing?

1. Validity of Oral Contracts

In the absence of a statute requiring a writing, a contract may be oral or written. Managers and professionals should be more fully aware that their oral communications, including telephone conversations and dinner or breakfast discussions, may be deemed legally enforceable contracts. **For Example,** suppose that Mark Wahlberg, after reviewing a script tentatively entitled *The Bulger Boys*, meets with Steven Spielberg to discuss Mark's playing mobster James "Whitey" Bulger in the film. Steven states, "You *are* 'Whitey,' Marky! The nuns at Gate of Heaven Grammar School in South Boston—or maybe it was St. Augustine's—they don't send for the Boston Police when they are troubled about drug use in the schools; they send for you to talk to the kids. Nobody messes with you, and the kids know it. This is true stuff, I think, and this fugitive's brother Bill comes out of the Southie projects to be president of U Mass." Mark likes the script. Steven and Mark block out two months of time for shooting the film this fall. They agree on Mark's usual fee and a "piece of the action" based on a set percentage of the net income from the film. Thereafter, Mark's agent does not like the deal. He believes there are better scripts for Mark. Incredibly brutal things are coming out about "Whitey" that could severely tarnish the film. And with Hollywood accounting, a percentage of the "net" take is usually of little value. However, all of the essential terms of a contract have been agreed on, and such an oral agreement would be legally enforceable. As set forth in the following text, no writing is required for a services contract that can be performed within one year after the date of the agreement.

Certain contracts, on the other hand, must be evidenced by a writing to be legally enforceable. These contracts are covered by the **statute of frauds.**[1]

Because many oral contracts are legally enforceable, it is a good business practice in the preliminary stages of discussions to stipulate that no binding agreement is intended to be formed until a written contract is prepared and signed by the parties.

statute of frauds–statute that, in order to prevent fraud through the use of perjured testimony, requires that certain kinds of transactions be evidenced in writing in order to be binding or enforceable.

---

[1] The name is derived from the original English Statute of Frauds and Perjuries, which was adopted in 1677 and became the pattern for similar legislation in America. The 17th section of that statute governed the sale of goods, and its modern counterpart is § 2-201 of the UCC. The 4th section of the English statute provided the pattern for U.S. legislation with respect to contracts other than for the sale of goods described in this section of the chapter. The English statute was repealed in 1954 except as to land sale and guarantee contracts. The U.S. statutes remain in force, but the liberalization by UCC § 2-201 of the pre-Code requirements with respect to contracts for the sale of goods lessens the applicability of the writing requirement. Additional movement away from the writing requirement is seen in the 1994 Revision of Article 8, Securities, which abolishes the statute of frauds provision of the original UCC § 8-319 and goes beyond by declaring that the one-year performance provision of the statute of frauds is not applicable to contracts for securities. UCC § 8-113 [1994 Revision].

2. Contracts that Must be Evidenced by a Writing

The statute of frauds requires that certain kinds of contracts be evidenced by a writing or they cannot be enforced. This means that either the contract itself must be in writing and signed by both parties or there must be a sufficient written memorandum of the oral contract signed by the person being sued for breach of contract. A *part performance* doctrine or exception to the statute of frauds may exist when the plaintiff's part performance is "unequivocally referable" to the oral agreement.[2]

(A) AGREEMENT THAT CANNOT BE PERFORMED WITHIN ONE YEAR AFTER THE CONTRACT IS MADE. A writing is required when the contract, by its terms or subject matter, cannot be performed within one year after the date of the agreement. An oral agreement to supply a line of credit for two years cannot be enforced because of the statute of frauds. Likewise, a joint venture agreement to construct a condominium complex was subject to the one-year provision of the statute of frauds when the contract could not reasonably have been performed within one year. The plans of the parties projected a development over the course of three years.

The year runs from the time the oral contract is made rather than from the date when performance is to begin. In computing the year, the day on which the contract was made is excluded.

No *part performance* exception exists to validate an oral agreement not performable within one year. **For Example,** Babyback's Foods negotiated a multiyear oral agreement to comarket its barbecue meat products with the Coca-Cola Co. nationwide and arranged to have several coolers installed at area grocery stores in Louisville under the agreement. Babyback's faxed to Coca-Cola a contract that summarized the oral agreement but Coca-Cola never signed it. Because Coca-Cola did not sign and no part performance exception exists for an oral agreement not performable within one year, Babyback's lawsuit was unsuccessful.[3]

When no time for performance is specified by the oral contract and complete performance could "conceivably occur" within one year, the statute of frauds is not applicable to the oral contract.[4]

When a contract may be terminated at will by either party, the statute of frauds is not applicable because the contract may be terminated within a year. **For Example,** David Ehrlich was hired as manager of Gravediggaz pursuant to an oral management agreement that was terminable at will by either Ehrlich or the group. He was entitled to receive 15 percent of the gross earnings of the group and each of its members, including rap artist Robert Diggs, professionally known as RZA, for all engagements entered into while he was manager under this oral agreement. Such an at-will contract is not barred by the statute of frauds.[5]

---

[2] *Carey & Associates v Ernst,* 802 NYS2d 160 (AD 2005).
[3] *Coca-Cola Co. v Babyback's International Inc.,* 841 NE2d 557 (Ind 2006).
[4] *El Paso Healthcare System v Piping Rock Corp.,* 939 SW2d 695 (Tex App 1997).
[5] See *Ehrlich v Diggs,* 169 F Supp 3d 124 (EDNY 2001). See also *Sterling v Sterling,* 800 NYS2d 463 (AD 2005), in which the statute of frauds was no bar to an oral partnership agreement, deemed to be at will, that continued for an indefinite period of time.

FIGURE 17-1 | *Hurdles in the Path of a Contract*

WRITING REQUIRED	
STATUTE OF FRAUDS	**EXCEPTIONS**
MORE THAN ONE YEAR TO PERFORM SALE OF LAND ANSWER FOR ANOTHER'S DEBT OR DEFAULT PERSONAL REPRESENTATIVE TO PAY DEBT OF DECEDENT FROM PERSONAL FUNDS PROMISE IN CONSIDERATION OF MARRIAGE SALE OF GOODS FOR $500 OR MORE MISCELLANEOUS	PART PERFORMANCE PROMISOR BENEFIT DETRIMENTAL RELIANCE
PAROL EVIDENCE RULE	**EXCEPTIONS**
EVERY COMPLETE, FINAL WRITTEN CONTRACT	INCOMPLETE CONTRACT AMBIGUOUS TERMS FRAUD, ACCIDENT, OR MISTAKE TO PROVE EXISTENCE OR NONBINDING CHARACTER OF CONTRACT MODIFICATION OF CONTRACT ILLEGALITY

(1) Oral Extension of a Contract.

A contract in writing, but not required to be so by the statute of frauds because it is terminable at will, may be varied by a new oral contract, even if the original written contract provided that it should not be varied except by writing. However, the burden of proof on the party asserting the oral modification is a heavy one. The modification must be shown by "clear, unequivocal and convincing evidence, direct or implied." **For Example,** John Boyle is the sole shareholder of numerous entertainment-related companies called the Cellar Door Companies, valued at some $106,000,000. Through these companies, he controls much of the large concert business at outdoor amphitheaters in Virginia and North Carolina. Bill Reid worked for Boyle beginning in 1983 as president of one of Boyle's companies. Boyle conducted financial affairs with an "air of informality." Reid proposed to Boyle the need for an amphitheater in Virginia Beach, and Boyle promised him a "33 percent interest" "if he pulled it off." As a result of Reid's efforts, the 20,000-seat Virginia Beach Amphitheater opened in 1996. The Supreme Court of Virginia determined that clear and convincing evidence did support the oral modification of Reid's written contract, including the following excerpt from the Court's opinion:

> *Thomas J. Lyons, Jr., Boyle's friend for over 35 years, testified on behalf of Reid. Lyons and his wife attended a concert in July 1996 at the newly constructed Virginia Beach Amphitheater as guests of Boyle and his wife. Lyons complimented Boyle for the excellent work and effort that Reid had undertaken in making the amphitheater a reality. According to Lyons, Boyle stated: "Well that's why he's my partner… that's why he owns 35 percent in this—in the Amphitheater or this project." After Lyons finished his testimony, the chancellor remarked on the record that Boyle stood up from his seat and "hugged" Lyons, even though Lyons had just provided testimony detrimental to Boyle.*

Reid was thus entitled to a judgment equivalent to the value of his interest in the project, $3,566,343.[6]

(B) **Agreement to Sell or a Sale of an Interest in Land.** All contracts to sell land, buildings, or interests in land, such as mortgages, must be evidenced by a writing.[7] Leases are also interests in land and must be in writing, except in some states where leases for one year or less do not have to be in writing.[8] **For Example,** if Mrs. O'Toole orally agrees to sell her house to the Gillespies for $250,000 and, thereafter, her children convince her that she could obtain $280,000 for the property if she is patient, Mrs. O'Toole can raise the defense of the statute of frauds should she be sued for breach of the oral agreement. Under the *part performance doctrine,* an exception exists by which an oral contract for the sale of land will be enforced by a court of equity in a suit for specific performance if the buyer has taken possession of the land under an oral contract and has made substantial improvements, the value of which cannot easily be ascertained, or has taken possession and paid part of the purchase price.

(C) **Promise to Answer for the Debt or Default of Another.** If an individual *I* promises a creditor *C* to pay the debt of *D* if *D* does not do so, *I* is promising to answer for the debt of another. Such a promise is sometimes called a **suretyship** contract, and it must be in writing to be enforceable. *I*, the promisor, is obligated to pay only if *D* does not pay. *I*'s promise is a *collateral* or *secondary* promise, and such promises must be in writing under the statute of frauds.[9]

suretyship–undertaking to pay the debt or be liable for the default of another.

(1) Main Purpose of Exception.
When the main purpose of the promisor's promise to pay the debt of another is to benefit the promisor, the statute of frauds is not applicable, and the oral promise to pay the debt is binding.

---

[6] *Reid v Boyle,* 527 SE2d 137 (Va 2000).
[7] *Magnum Real Estate Services, Inc. v Associates, LLC,* 874 NYS2d 435 (App Div 2009).
[8] See, however, *BBQ Blues Texas, Ltd. v Affiliated Business,* 183 SW3d 543 (Tex App 2006), in which Eddie Calagero of Affiliated Business and the owners of BBQ Blues Texas, Ltd. entered an oral commission agreement to pay a 10 percent commission if he found a buyer for the restaurant, and he did so. The oral agreement was held to be outside the statute of frauds because this activity of finding a willing buyer did not involve the transfer of real estate. The second contract between the buyer and seller of the restaurant, which involved the transfer of a lease agreement, was a separate and distinct agreement over which Calagero had no control.
[9] See *Martin Printing, Inc. v Sone,* 873 A2d 232 (Conn App 2005), in which James Kuhe in writing personally guaranteed Martin Printing, Inc, to pay for printing expenses of *Pub Links Golfer Magazine,* if his corporation, Abbey Inc., failed to do so. When Abbey, Inc., failed to pay, the court enforced Kuhe's promise to pay.

For Example, an individual *I* hires a contractor *C* to repair *I*'s building, and the supplier *S* is unwilling to extend credit to *C*. In an oral promise by *I* to pay *S* what is owed for the supplies in question if *C* does not pay, *I* is promising to pay for the debt of another, *C*. However, the *main purpose* of *I*'s promise was not to aid *C* but to get his own house repaired. This promise is not within the statute of frauds.[10]

C A S E   S U M M A R Y

"I Personally Guarantee" Doesn't Mean I'm Personally Liable, Does It?

FACTS: Joel Burgower owned Material Partnerships Inc. (MPI), which supplied Sacos Tubulares del Centro, S.A. de C.V. (Sacos), a Mexican bag manufacturer, essential materials to make its products. When MPI was not paid for shipments, it insisted that Jorge Lopez, Sacos's general manager, personally guarantee all past and future obligations to MPI. In a letter to Burgower dated September 25, 1998, Lopez wrote:

I… want to certify you [sic] that I, personally, guaranty all outstanding [sic] and liabilities of Sacos Tubulares with Material Partnerships as well as future shipments.

Lopez drafted the letter himself and signed it over the designation "Jorge Lopez Venture, General Manager."

After receiving the September 25th letter, MPI resumed shipping product to Sacos, sending additional shipments valued at approximately $200,000. MPI subsequently received one payment of approximately $60,000 from Sacos. When Sacos did not pay for the additional shipments, MPI stopped shipping to it. The Sacos plant closed, and MPI brought suit in a Texas court against Lopez, claiming he was individually liable for the corporate debt of more than $900,000 under the terms of the personal guarantee. Lopez contended that he signed the letter in his capacity as general manager of Sacos as a corporate guarantee and that it was not an enforceable personal guarantee. MPI contended that the letter was a clear personal guarantee.

DECISION: The essential terms of a guarantee agreement required by the statute of frauds were present in this case. Lopez stated in his September 25th letter that "I, personally, guaranty," manifesting an intent to guarantee, and described the obligation being guaranteed as "all outstandings and liabilities of Sacos," as well as "future shipments." Lopez's signature over his corporate office does not render the document ambiguous because the clear intent was expressed in the word "personally." [**MPI v Jorge Lopez Ventura, 102 SW2d 252 (Tex App 2003)**]

personal representative–administrator or executor who represents decedents under UPC.

executor, executrix–person (man, woman) named in a will to administer the estate of the decedent.

administrator, administratrix–person (man, woman) appointed to wind up and settle the estate of a person who has died without a will.

decedent–person whose estate is being administered.

(D) **PROMISE BY THE EXECUTOR OR ADMINISTRATOR OF A DECEDENT'S ESTATE TO PAY A CLAIM AGAINST THE ESTATE FROM PERSONAL FUNDS.** The **personal representative** (**executor** or **administrator**) has the duty of handling the affairs of a deceased person, paying the debts from the proceeds of the estate and distributing any balance remaining. The executor or administrator is not personally liable for the claims against the estate of the **decedent**. If the personal representative promises to pay the decedent's debts

---

[10] See *Christian v Smith*, 759 NW2d 447 (Neb 2008).

with his or her own money, the promise cannot be enforced unless it is evidenced by a writing.

If the personal representative makes a contract on behalf of the estate in the course of administering the estate, a writing is not required. The representative is then contracting on behalf of the estate. Thus, if the personal representative employs an attorney to settle the estate or makes a burial contract with an undertaker, no writing is required.

(e) Promises Made in Consideration of Marriage. Promises to pay a sum of money or give property to another in consideration of marriage must be in writing under the statute of frauds.

For Example, if Mr. John Bradley orally promises to provide Karl Radford $20,000 on Karl's marriage to Mr. Bradley's daughter Michelle—and Karl and Michelle marry—the agreement is not enforceable under the statute of frauds because it was not in writing.

Prenuptial or *antenuptial* agreements are entered into by the parties before their marriage. After full disclosure of each party's assets and liabilities, and in some states, income,[11] the parties set forth the rights of each partner regarding the property and, among other things, set forth rights and obligations should the marriage end in a separation or divorce. Such a contract must be in writing.

For Example, when Susan DeMatteo married her husband M. J. DeMatteo in 1990, she had a 1977 Nova and $5,000 in the bank. M. Joseph DeMatteo was worth as much as $112 million at that time, and he insisted that she sign a prenuptial agreement before their marriage. After full disclosure of each party's assets, the prenuptial agreement was signed and videotaped some five days before their marriage ceremony. The agreement gave Susan $35,000 a year plus cost-of-living increases, as well as a car and a house, should the marriage dissolve. After the couple divorced, Susan argued before the state's highest court that the agreement was not "fair or reasonable" because it gave her less than 1 percent of her former husband's wealth. The court upheld the agreement, however, pointing out that Susan was fully informed about her fiancé's net worth and was represented by counsel.[12] When there is full disclosure and representation, prenuptial agreements, like other contracts, cannot be set aside unless they are unconscionable, which in a domestic relations setting means leaving a former spouse unable to support herself or himself.

(f) Sale of Goods. As will be developed in Chapter 23, Nature and Form of Sales, contracts for the sale of goods priced at $500 or more must ordinarily be in writing under UCC § 2-201.[13]

(g) Promissory Estoppel. The statute of frauds may be circumvented when the party seeking to get around the statute of frauds is able to prove an enhanced promissory estoppel. While one element a of routine promissory estoppel case requires that the promisee rely on the promise in some definite and substantial manner, an enhanced level of reasonable reliance is necessary in order to have enhanced promissory

---

[11] See FLA, STAT § 732·702 (2).
[12] *DeMatteo v DeMatteo,* 762 NE2d 797 (Mass 2002). See also *Waton v Waton,* 887 So2d 419 (Fla App 2004).
[13] As will be presented in Chapter 23, under Revised Article 2, § 2-201, the $500 amount is increased to $5,000. This revision has not yet been adopted by any states.

estoppel, along with proof of an unconscionable injury or unjust enrichment. **For Example,** an Indiana bakery, Classic Cheesecake Inc., was able to interest several hotels and casinos in Las Vegas in buying its products. On July 27, 2004, its principals sought a loan from a local branch office of J. P. Morgan Chase Bank in order to establish a distribution center in Las Vegas. On September 17, local bank officer Dowling told Classic that the loan was a "go." When credit quality issues surfaced, Dowling continued to make assurances that the loan would be approved. On October 12, however, she told Classic that the loan had been turned down. Classic claimed that the bank's breach of its oral promise to make the loan and Classic's detrimental reliance on the promise caused it to lose more than $1 million. The Indiana statute of frauds requires agreements to lend money to be in writing. Classic contended that the oral agreement in this case must be enforced on the basis of promissory estoppel and the company's unconscionable injury. Judge Posner of the Seventh Circuit upheld the dismissal of the claim, writing (in part):

> ...*For the plaintiff to treat the bank loan as a certainty because they were told by the bank officer whom they were dealing with that it would be approved was unreasonable, especially if, as the plaintiffs' damages claim presupposes, the need for the loan was urgent. Rational businessmen know that there is many a slip 'twixt cup and lips,' that a loan is not approved until it is approved, that if a bank's employee tells you your loan application will be approved that is not the same as telling you it has been approved, and that if one does not have a loan commitment in writing yet the need for the loan is urgent one had better be negotiating with other potential lenders at the same time....*[14]

CPA   3. Note or Memorandum

The statute of frauds requires a writing to evidence those contracts that come within its scope. This writing may be a note or memorandum as distinguished from a contract.[15] The statutory requirement is, of course, satisfied if there is a complete written contract signed by both parties.

(A) SIGNING. The note or memorandum must be signed by the party sought to be bound by the contract. **For Example,** in the previous scenario involving Mark Wahlberg and Steven Spielberg, suppose the parties agreed to do the film according to the same terms but agreed to begin shooting the film a year from next April, and Mark wrote the essential terms on a napkin, dated it, and had Steven sign it "to make sure I got it right." Mark then placed the napkin in his wallet for his records. Because the contract could not be performed within one year after the date of the agreement, a writing would be required. If Steven thereafter decided not to pursue the film because of new murder indictments against Whitey Bulger, Mark could enforce the contract against him because the napkin-note had been signed by the party to be bound or "sought to be charged," Steven. However, if Mark later decided not to appear in the film, the agreement to do the film could not be enforced against Mark because no writing existed signed by Mark, the party sought to be charged.

---

[14] *Classic Cheesecake Co. Inc. v J. P. Morgan Chase Bank,* 546 F3d 839 (7th Cir 2008).
[15] *McLinden v Coco,* 765 NE2d 606 (Ind App 2002).

Some states require that the authorization of an agent to execute a contract coming within the statute of frauds must also be in writing. In the case of an auction, it is usual practice for the auctioneer to be the agent of both parties for the purpose of signing the memorandum.

e-commerce&cyberlaw

Electronic Signatures in the Internet Age

A SIGNATURE authenticates a writing by identifying the signers through their distinctive marks. The act of signing a document calls to the attention of the signing parties the legal significance of their act and expresses authorization and assent to the body of the signed writing. An ELECTRONIC SIGNATURE, including technology having digital or wireless capabilities, means any electronic sound, symbol, or process attached to, or logically associated with, a contract or other electronic record and executed with the intent to sign the record. An ELECTRONIC RECORD means any contract or other record created or stored in an electronic medium and retrievable in a perceivable form.

Conducting business electronically over the Internet has many advantages for consumers, businesses, and governments by allowing the instant purchase of goods, information, and services, and the reduction of sales, administrative, and overhead expenses. To facilitate the expansion of electronic commerce and place electronic signatures and electronic contracts on an equal footing with written signatures and paper contracts, Congress enacted a federal electronic signatures law.

Under the Electronic Signatures in Global and National Commerce Act (E-Sign),* electronically signed contracts cannot be denied legal effect because the signatures are in electronic form, nor can they be denied legal effect because they are delivered electronically. Contracts or documents requiring a notarized signature can be satisfied by the electronic signatures of the notaries coupled with the enclosure of all other required information as part of the record.

One of the goals of E-Sign was to spur states to enact the Uniform Electronic Transactions Act (UETA). Under E-Sign, a state may "modify, limit or supersede" the provisions of the federal act by enacting UETA "as approved and recommended for enactment in all the states" by the National Conference of Commissioners on Uniform State Laws or enacting a law that is consistent with E-Sign.** Thus, for those states that enacted the official version of UETA or one consistent with E-Sign, the federal law is superceded by the state law. UETA is similar to E-Sign. It specifies that e-signatures and e-records can be used in contract formation, in audits, and as evidence. Selective differences between E-Sign and UETA are identified below. **For Example,** inventor Stewart Lamle sued toy maker Mattel, Inc., for breach of contract. The U.S. Court of Appeals for the Federal Circuit remanded the case for trial after resolving the motions before it. The facts reveal that after a June 11, 1997, meeting of the parties, Mattel employee Mike Bucher sent an e-mail dated June 26 to Lamle, which set forth the terms agreed to in principle at the meeting with the salutation "Best regards, Mike Bucher" appearing at the end of the e-mail. The court resolved the issue of whether an e-mail is a writing "subscribed by the party to be charged or the party's agent" in Lamle's favor. The court stated that under the UETA, the e-signature satisfies the state's (California's) Statute of Frauds. Because the e-mail was sent in 1997 prior to the effective date on the UETA, January 1, 2000, an evaluation of state common law was necessary. The court stated that it

* Pub L 106-229, 114 Stat 464, 15 USC § 7001.

** § 102(a) and 102(a)(2). Forty-eight states and the District of Columbia have enacted the UETA in some form.

e-commerce&cyberlaw

could see no meaningful difference between a type-written signature on a telegram, which is sufficient to be a signature under state law, and the typed signature on the June 26 e-mail. It concluded that the e-mail satisfies the Statute of Frauds, assuming that there was a binding oral agreement on June 11. ***

(a) General Rule of Parity. E-Sign provides for parity of electronic and paper signatures, contracts, and records. Electronic signatures and contracts satisfy the statute of frauds to the same extent they would if embodied as paper contracts with handwritten signatures. Internet contracts are neither more nor less valid, legal, and binding than are offline paper contracts. The rules are the same! The UETA is comparable to E-Sign in that it treats e-signatures and e-records as if they were handwritten.[†]

(b) Identity Verification. Neither E-Sign nor UETA is a digital signature law in that neither requires security procedures or a certification authority for the verification of electronic signatures. The parties themselves determine how they will verify each other's identity. Some options are a credit card, a password or PIN, public-key cryptographic exchange of digital signatures, or biometric signatures.

(c) Exceptions. The E-Sign Act exempts documents and records on trust and estate law so that it does not cover wills, codicils, and testamentary trusts or commercial law matters such as checks, negotiable instruments, and letters of credit. The act also does not cover court documents and cancellation of health and life insurance. Generally, the UETA also does not apply to these documents and records set forth previously.

(d) Consumer Protection and Notice and Consent Requirements. Consumer protection laws remain intact under E-Sign. Protections exist for consumers to consent to receiving electronic contracts, records, and documents; and businesses must tell consumers of their right to receive hardcopy documents.

Consumers must consent to receiving documents electronically or confirm consent electronically. For example, a consumer and a business may have negotiated terms of a contract by telephone and agreed to execute their agreement by e-mail. The consumer is then sent an e-mail that contains a consent disclosure, which contains a hypertext markup language (HTML) link the consumer can use to test her ability to view the contract in HTML. The consumer then returns the e-mail message to the business, thereby confirming electronically her consent to use this electronic means.

The UETA, like E-Sign, defers to existing substantive law regarding consumer protection.

(e) Time and Place of Sending and Receipt. E-Sign does not contain a provision addressing basic contract requirements such as sending and delivery, leaving such matters to existing contract law. However, the UETA provides that an electronic record is sent when it (1) is properly directed to an information processing system designated or used by the recipient to receive such records and from which the recipient may recover that record; (2) is in a form that the recipient's system is able to process; and (3) enters an information processing system that is in the control of the recipient but outside the control of the sender. An electronic record is received when (1) it enters an information processing system designated or used by the recipient to receive such records and from which the recipient is able to obtain the record and (2) it is in a form that the recipient's system can process.[††]

(f) Errors. Unlike E-Sign, which leaves matters relating to errors to be resolved by existing state contract law, UETA creates a system for dealing with errors. For example, when Marv Hale clicks on "buy" to make an online purchase of 12 bottles of Napa Valley Supreme Chardonnay at $12.90 per bottle, the computer will produce the equivalent of an invoice that includes the product's name, description, quantity, and price to enable Marv to avoid possible error when forming the electronic contract. This procedure gives the buyer an opportunity to identify and immediately correct an error. When such a procedure is not in effect and an error is later discovered, prompt notice to the other party can cure the error under Section 10 of the UETA.[†††]

*** *Lamle v Mattel, Inc.*, 394 F3d 1355 (Fed Cir 2005); see also *Payout v Coral Mortgage Bankers*, 2009 LEXIS 14190 (D Colo 2009).
[†]   UETA § 7(a) and 7(b).

[††]   UETA § 15.
[†††] UETA § 10(2)(A)-(C).

The signature may be an ordinary one or any symbol that is adopted by the party as a signature. It may consist of initials, figures, or a mark. In the absence of a local statute that provides otherwise, a signature may be made by pencil, pen, typewriter, print, or stamp. As will be discussed, electronic signatures have parity with on-paper signatures.

(B) CONTENT. The note or memorandum must contain all of the essential terms of the contract so the court can determine just what was agreed. If any essential term is missing, the writing is not sufficient. A writing evidencing a sale of land that does not describe the land or identify the buyer does not satisfy the statute of frauds. The subject matter must be identified either within the writing itself or in other writings to which it refers. A deposit check given by the buyer to the seller does not take an oral land sales contract out of the statute of frauds. This is so because the check does not set forth the terms of the sale.

The note or memorandum may consist of one writing or of separate papers, such as letters, or a combination of such papers. Separate writings cannot be considered together unless they are linked. Linkage may be express reference in each writing to the other or by the fact that each writing clearly deals with the same subject matter.

4. Effect of Noncompliance

The majority of states hold that a contract that does not comply with the statute of frauds is not enforceable.[16] If an action is brought to enforce the contract, the defendant can raise the defense that the alleged contract is not enforceable because it is not evidenced by a writing, as required by the statute of frauds.

(A) RECOVERY OF VALUE CONFERRED. In most instances, a person who is prevented from enforcing a contract because of the statute of frauds is nevertheless entitled to recover from the other party the value of any services or property furnished or money given under the oral contract. Recovery is not based on the terms of the contract but on a quasi-contractual obligation. The other party is to restore to the plaintiff what was received in order to prevent unjust enrichment at the plaintiff's expense. **For Example,** when an oral contract for services cannot be enforced because of the statute of frauds, the person performing the work may recover the reasonable value of the services rendered.

C A S E   S U M M A R Y

Limited Effect of Oral Contract under Statute of Frauds

FACTS: Richard Golden orally agreed to sell his land to Earl Golden, who paid a deposit of $3,000. The transaction was never completed, and Earl sued for the return of his deposit. Richard claimed that the statute of frauds prevented Earl from proving that there ever was an oral contract under which a deposit of money had been paid.

---

[16] The UCC creates several statutes of frauds of limited applicability, in which it uses the phrase "not enforceable": § 1-206 (sale of intangible personal property); § 2-201 (sale of goods); and § 8-319 (sale of securities).

CASE SUMMARY

Continued

DECISION: Judgment for Earl. The statute of frauds bars enforcement of an oral contract for the sale of land. It does not prevent proof of the contract for the purpose of showing that the seller has received a benefit that would unjustly enrich him if he retained it. Earl could therefore prove the existence of the unperformed oral contract to show that Richard had received a deposit that should be returned. [**Golden v Golden, 541 P2d 1397 (Or 1975)**]

(B) **WHO MAY RAISE THE DEFENSE OF NONCOMPLIANCE?** Only a party to the oral contract may raise a defense that it is not binding because there is no writing that satisfies the statute of frauds. Third persons, such as an insurance company or the Internal Revenue Service, cannot claim that a contract is void because the statute of frauds was not satisfied.

B. PAROL EVIDENCE RULE

When the contract is evidenced by a writing, may the contract terms be changed by the testimony of witnesses?

5. Exclusion of Parol Evidence

The general rule is that parol or extrinsic evidence will not be allowed into evidence to add to, modify, or contradict the terms of a written contract that is fully integrated or complete on its face.[17] Evidence of an alleged earlier oral or written agreement within the scope of the fully integrated written contract or evidence of an alleged contemporaneous oral agreement within the scope of the fully integrated written contract is inadmissible as *parol evidence*.

CASE SUMMARY

Closing the Door on Different Terms

FACTS: Airline Construction, Inc., made a contract with William Barr to build a hotel within 240 calendar days. Barr completed the work 57 days late. Airline Construction sued for damages for delay, and the contractor raised the defense that he had been induced to enter into the contract because it had been agreed that he would have additional time in which to complete the work. Airline Construction objected to the admission of evidence of this agreement.

[17] *Speed v Muhana*, 619 SE2d 324 (Ga App 2005).

C A S E   S U M M A R Y

Continued

DECISION: Parol evidence could not be admitted to show that there was a prior oral agreement that was inconsistent with the terms of the written contract. It was immaterial that the contractor had been "induced" to make the contract because of the alleged agreement. The fact remained that the written contract signed by him specified the time for performance and the parol evidence rule barred proof of any prior inconsistent oral agreement. [**Airline Construction, Inc. v Barr, 807 SW2d 247 (Tenn App 1990)**]

Parol evidence is admissible, however, to show fraud, duress, or mistake and under certain other circumstances to be discussed in the following paragraphs.

parol evidence rule–rule that prohibits the introduction into evidence of oral or written statements made prior to or contemporaneously with the execution of a complete written contract, deed, or instrument, in the absence of clear proof of fraud, accident, or mistake causing the omission of the statement in question.

The **parol evidence rule** is based on the theory that either there never was an oral agreement or, if there was, the parties abandoned it when they reached the stage in negotiations of executing their written contract. The social objective of the parol evidence rule is to give stability to contracts and to prevent the assertion of terms that did not exist or did not survive the bargaining of the parties so as to reach inclusion in the final written contract.

For Example, *L* (landlord), the owner of a new development containing a five-store mall, discusses leasing one of the stores to *T* (tenant), who is viewing the property with his sister *S*, a highly credible poverty worker on leave from her duties in Central America. *L*, in the presence of *S*, agrees to give *T* the exclusive right to sell coffee and soft drinks in the five-store mall. Soon *L* and *T* execute a detailed written lease for the store, which makes no provision for *T*'s exclusive right to sell soft drinks and coffee in the mall. Subsequently, when two of the mall's new tenants begin to sell soft drinks and coffee, *T* brings suit against *L* for the breach of the oral promise granting him exclusive rights to sell soft drinks and coffee. *T* calls *S* as his first witness to prove the existence of the oral promise. *L*, through his attorney, will object to the admission of any evidence of a prior oral agreement that would add to or amend the fully integrated written lease, which set forth all restrictions on the landlord and tenant as to uses of the premises. After study of the matter, the court, based on the parol evidence rule, will not hear testimony from either *S* or *T* about the oral promise *L* made to *T*. In order to preserve his exclusive right to sell the drinks in question, *T* should have made certain that this promise was made part of the lease. His lawsuit will not be successful.

6. When the Parol Evidence Rule Does Not Apply

The parol evidence rule will not apply in certain cases. The most common of these are discussed in the following paragraphs.

ambiguous–having more than one reasonable interpretation.

(A) **AMBIGUITY.** If a written contract is **ambiguous** or may have two or more different meanings, parol evidence may generally be admitted to clarify the meaning.[18]

---

[18] *Berg v Hudesman*, 801 P2d 222 (Wash 1990). This is also the view followed by UCC § 2-202(a), which permits terms in a contract for the sale of goods to be "explained or supplemented by a course of dealing or usage of trade... or by course of performance." Such evidence is admissible not because there is an ambiguity but "in order that the true understanding of the parties as to the agreement may be reached." Official Code Comment to § 2-202.

Parol evidence may also be admitted to show that a word used in a contract has a special trade meaning or a meaning in the particular locality that differs from the common meaning of that word.

(B) FRAUD, DURESS, OR MISTAKE. A contract apparently complete on its face may have omitted a provision that should have been included. Parol evidence may be admitted to show that a provision was omitted as the result of fraud, duress, or mistake and to further show what that provision stated. Parol evidence is admissible to show that a provision of the written contract was a mutual mistake even though the written provision is unambiguous.[19] When one party claims to have been fraudulently induced by the other to enter into a contract, the parol evidence rule does not bar proof that there was a fraud. **For Example,** the parol evidence rule does not bar proof that the seller of land intentionally misrepresented that the land was zoned to permit use as an industrial park. Such evidence does not contradict the terms of the contract but shows that the agreement is unenforceable.[20]

(C) MODIFICATION OF CONTRACT. The parol evidence rule prohibits only the contradiction of a complete written contract. It does not prohibit proof that the contract was thereafter modified or terminated.

CASE SUMMARY

All Sail and No Anchor

FACTS: On April 2, 1990, Christian Bourg hired Bristol Boat Co., Inc., and Bristol Marine Co. (defendants) to construct and deliver a yacht on July 1, 1990. However, the defendants did not live up to their promises and the contract was breached. On October 22, 1990, the defendants executed a written settlement agreement whereby Bourg agreed to pay an additional sum of $135,000 for the delivery of the yacht and to provide the defendants a loan of $80,000 to complete the construction of the vessel. Referencing the settlement agreement, the defendants at the same time executed a promissory note obliging them to repay the $80,000 loan plus interest in annual installments due on November 1 of each year, with the final payment due on November 1, 1994. The court stated in presenting the facts: "However, like the yacht itself, the settlement agreement soon proved to be just another hole in the water into which the plaintiff threw his money." Bourg sued the defendants after they failed to make certain payments on the note, and the court granted a motion for summary judgment in favor of Bourg for $59,081. The defendants appealed.

DECISION: Judgment for Bourg. Because the defendants' affidavit recites that an alleged oral side agreement was entered into at the same time as the settlement agreement and promissory note—the oral side agreement allegedly stated "that the note would be paid for by services rendered by the defendants"—the oral side agreement would have constituted a contemporaneous modification that would merge into the integrated promissory note and settlement agreement and thus be barred from admission into evidence under the parol evidence rule. Although parties to an integrated written contract can modify their understanding by a subsequent oral pact, to be legally effective, there must be evidence of mutual assent to the essential terms of the modification and adequate consideration. Here the defendants adduced no

[19] *Thompson v First Citizens Bank & Trust Co,* 151 NC App 704 (2002).
[20] *Edwards v Centrex Real Estate Corp.,* 61 Cal Rptr 518 (Cal App 1997).

CASE SUMMARY

Continued

competent evidence of either mutual assent to particular terms or a specific consideration that would be sufficiently definite to constitute an enforceable subsequent oral modification to the parties' earlier written agreements. Thus, legally this alleged oral agreement was all sail and no anchor. [**Bourg v Bristol Boat Co., 705 A2d 969 (RI 1998)**]

C. RULES OF CONSTRUCTION AND INTERPRETATION

In interpreting contracts, courts are aided by certain rules.

7. Intention of the Parties

When persons enter into an agreement, it is to be presumed that they intend for their agreement to have some effect. A court will strive to determine the intent of the parties and to give effect to it. A contract, therefore, is to be enforced according to its terms.[21] A court cannot remake or rewrite the contract of the parties under the pretense of interpreting.[22]

No particular form of words is required, and any words manifesting the intent of the parties are sufficient. In the absence of proof that a word has a peculiar meaning or that it was employed by the parties with a particular meaning, a common word is given its ordinary meaning.

(A) MEANING OF WORDS. Ordinary words are to be interpreted according to their ordinary meaning.[23] **For Example,** when a contract requires the gasoline dealer to pay the supplier for "gallons" supplied, the term *gallons* is unambiguous and does not require that an adjustment of the gallonage be made for the temperature.[24] When a contract calls for a businessperson to pay a builder for the builder's "costs," the term *costs* is unambiguous, meaning actual costs, not a lesser amount based on the builder's bid.[25]

If there is a common meaning to a term, that meaning will be followed even though the dictionary may contain additional meanings. If technical or trade terms are used in a contract, they are to be interpreted according to the area of technical knowledge or trade from which the terms are taken.

(B) INCORPORATION BY REFERENCE. The contract may not cover all of the agreed terms. The missing terms may be found in another document. Frequently, the parties executing the contract for storage will simply state that a storage contract is entered into and that the contract applies to the goods listed in the schedule attached to and

[21] See *Greenwald v Kersh*, 621 SE2d 463 (Ga App 2005).
[22] *Abbot v Schnader, Harrison, Segal & Lewis, LLP*, 805 A2d 547 (Pa Super 2002).
[23] *Thorton v D.F.W. Christian Television, Inc.*, 925 SW2d 17 (Tex App 1995).
[24] *Hopkins v BP Oil, Inc.*, 81 F3d 1070 (11th Cir 1996).
[25] *Batzer Construction, Inc. v Boyer*, 125 P3d 773 (Or App 2006).

made part of the contract. Likewise, a contract for the construction of a building may involve plans and specifications on file in a named city office. The contract will simply state that the building is to be constructed according to those plans and specifications that are "incorporated herein and made part of this contract." When there is such an **incorporation by reference**, the contract consists of both the original document and the detailed statement that is incorporated in it.

incorporation by reference–contract consisting of both the original or skeleton document and the detailed statement that is incorporated in it.

When a contract refers to another document, however, the contract must sufficiently describe the document or so much of it as is to be interpreted as part of the contract.

C A S E   S U M M A R Y

Specificity Required

FACTS: Consolidated Credit Counseling Services, Inc. (Consolidated), sued Affinity Internet, Inc., doing business as SkyNet WEB (Affinity), for breach of its contract to provide computer and Web-hosting services. Affinity moved to compel arbitration, and Consolidated argued that the contract between the parties did not contain an arbitration clause. The contract between the parties stated in part: "This contract is subject to all of SkyNet WEB's terms, conditions, user and acceptable use policies located at **http://www.skynetweb.com/ company/legal/legal.php**." By going to the Web site and clicking to paragraph 17 of the User Agreement, an arbitration provision can be found. The contract itself, however, makes no reference to an agreement to arbitrate, nor was paragraph 17 expressly referred to or described in the contract. Nor was a hard copy of the information on the Web site either signed by or furnished to Consolidated.

DECISION: Judgment for Consolidated. Mere reference to another document is not sufficient to incorporate that document into the contract absent specificity describing the portion of the writing to apply to the contract. [**Affinity Internet v Consolidated Credit, 920 So2d 1286 (Fla App 2006)**]

---

8. Whole Contract

The provisions of a contract must be construed as a whole in such a way that every part is given effect.

Every word of a contract is to be given effect if reasonably possible. The contract is to be construed as a whole, and if the plain language of the contract thus viewed solves the dispute, the court is to make no further analysis.[26]

9. Contradictory and Ambiguous Terms

One term in a contract may conflict with another term, or one term may have two different meanings. It is then necessary for the court to determine whether there is a contract and, if so, what the contract really means.

---

[26] *Covensky v Hannah Marine Corp.*, 903 NE2d 422 (Ill App 2009).

CASE SUMMARY

Who Pays the Piper?

FACTS: Olander Contracting Co., developer Gail Wachter, and the City of Bismarck, North Dakota, entered into a water and sewer construction contract including, among other things, connecting a 10-inch sewer line from Wachter's housing development to the city's existing 36-inch concrete sewer main and installing a manhole at the connection, to be paid for by Wachter. Olander installed the manhole, but it collapsed within a few days. Olander installed a second manhole, with a large base supported by pilings, but it too failed a few days after it was installed. Olander then placed a rock bedding under the city's sewer main, replaced 78 feet of the existing concrete pipe with PVC pipe, and installed a manhole a third time on a larger base. Olander sued Wachter and the City of Bismarck for damages of $456,536.25 for extra work it claims it was required to perform to complete its contract. Both defendants denied they were responsible for the amount sued under the contract. The jury returned a special verdict, finding that Olander performed "extra work/unforeseen work… for which it is entitled to be compensated in excess of the contract price" in the amount of $220,849.67, to be paid by the City of Bismarck. Appeals were taken.

DECISION: Judgment for Olander. The trial judge properly made the initial determination that the contract language was ambiguous. That is, the language used by the parties could support good arguments for the positions of both parties. This resolved a question of law. Once this determination had been made, the judge allowed extrinsic evidence from all parties as to what they meant when they negotiated the contract. This evidence related to the questions of fact, which were left to the jury. Testimony was taken from the parties who negotiated the contract, and testimony was also heard about the role of each of the parties in the actual construction of the manhole, the cause for the collapses, and why the contractor had to replace the city's existing concrete pipe with PVC pipe and the city's role in making this determination. The jury then fulfilled its role answering the question whether or not Olander had performed extra work in the affirmative, concluding that the city was required to pay for it. [**Olander Contracting v Wachter, 643 NW2d 29 (2002)**)]

In some instances, apparent conflict between the terms of a contract is eliminated by the introduction of parol evidence or by the application of an appropriate rule of construction.[27]

(A) NATURE OF WRITING. When a contract is partly a printed form or partly typewritten and partly handwritten and the written part conflicts with the printed or typewritten part, the written part prevails. When there is a conflict between a printed part and a typewritten part, the latter prevails. Consequently, when a clause typewritten on a printed form conflicts with what is stated by the print, the conflicting print is ignored and the typewritten clause controls. This rule is based on

---

[27] See *Wilkie v Eutice 36747, LLC*, 669 SE2d 155 (Ga App 2008) where the courts in this jurisdiction resolve contract interpretation issues by first determining whether the language is ambiguous. (1) If it is not, the trial court judge enforces the contract as written; (2) if the contract is ambiguous, the trial court judge will apply the rules of contract construction to resolve this ambiguity; and (3) if the ambiguity cannot be resolved in Step 2, a jury must decide what the parties intended and what the ambiguous language means.

the belief that the parties had given greater thought to what they typed or wrote for the particular contract as contrasted with printed words already in a form designed to cover many transactions. Thus, a typewritten provision to pay 90 cents per unit overrode a preprinted provision setting the price as 45 cents per unit.

When there is a conflict between an amount or quantity expressed both in words and figures, as on a check, the amount or quantity expressed in words prevails. Words control because there is less danger that a word will be wrong than a number.

(B) AMBIGUITY. A contract is *ambiguous* when the intent of the parties is uncertain and the contract is capable of more than one reasonable interpretation.[28] The background from which the contract and the dispute arose may help in determining the intention of the parties. **For Example,** when suit was brought in Minnesota on a Canadian insurance policy, the question arose whether the dollar limit of the policy referred to Canadian or U.S. dollars. The court concluded that Canadian dollars were intended. Both the insurer and the insured were Canadian corporations; the original policy, endorsements to the policy, and policy renewals were written in Canada; over the years, premiums had been paid in Canadian dollars; and a prior claim on the policy had been settled by the payment of an amount computed on the basis of Canadian dollars.

(C) STRICT CONSTRUCTION AGAINST DRAFTING PARTY. An ambiguous contract is interpreted strictly against the party who drafted it.[29] **For Example,** an insurance policy containing ambiguous language regarding coverage or exclusions is interpreted against the insurer and in favor of the insured when two interpretations are reasonably possible. This rule is a secondary rule that may be invoked only after all of the ordinary interpretive guides have been exhausted. The rule basically assigns the risk of an unresolvable ambiguity to the party creating it.[30]

10. Implied Terms

In some cases, a court will imply a term to cover a situation for which the parties failed to provide or, when needed, to give the contract a construction or meaning that is reasonable.

The court often implies details of the performance of a contract not expressly stated in the contract. In a contract to perform work, there is an implied promise to use such skill as is necessary to properly perform the work. When a contract does not specify the time for performance, a reasonable time is implied.

In every contract, there is an implied obligation that neither party shall do anything that will have the effect of destroying or injuring the right of the other party to receive the fruits of the contract. This means that in every contract there exists an implied covenant of **good faith** and fair dealing. When a contract may reasonably be interpreted in different ways, a court should make the interpretation

good faith–absence of knowledge of any defects or problems.

[28] *Kaufman & Stewart v Weinbrenner Shoe Co.,* 589 NW2d 499 (Minn App 1999).
[29] *Idaho Migrant Council, Inc. v Warila,* 89 P2d 39 (Wyo 1995).
[30] *Premier Title Co. v Donahue,* 765 NE2d 513 (Ill App 2002).

that is in harmony with good faith and fair dealing. **For Example,** when a contract is made subject to the condition that one of the parties obtain financing, that party must make reasonable, good-faith efforts to obtain financing. The party is not permitted to do nothing and then claim that the contract is not binding because the condition has not been satisfied. Likewise, when a contract requires a party to obtain government approval, the party must use all reasonable means to obtain it.[31]

The Uniform Commercial Code imposes an obligation of good faith in the performance or enforcement of every contract.[32]

11. Conduct and Custom

The conduct of the parties and the customs and usages of a particular trade may give meaning to the words of the parties and thus aid in the interpretation of their contract.

(A) CONDUCT OF THE PARTIES. The conduct of the parties in carrying out the terms of a contract is the best guide to determine the parties' intent. When performance has been repeatedly tendered and accepted without protest, neither party will be permitted to claim that the contract was too indefinite to be binding. **For Example,** a travel agent made a contract with a hotel to arrange for trips to the hotel. After some 80 trips had already been arranged and paid for by the hotel at the contract price without any dispute about whether the contract obligation was satisfied, any claim by the travel agent that it could charge additional fees must be rejected.

usage of trade–language and customs of an industry.

(B) CUSTOM AND USAGE OF TRADE. The customs and **usages of trade** or commercial activity to which the contract relates may be used to interpret the terms of a contract.[33] **For Example,** when a contract for the construction of a building calls for a "turn-key construction," industry usage is admissible to show what this means: a construction in which all the owner needs to do is to turn the key in the lock to open the building for use and in which all construction risks are assumed by the contractor.[34]

Custom and usage, however, cannot override express provisions of a contract that are inconsistent with custom and usage.

12. Avoidance of Hardship

As a general rule, a party is bound by a contract even though it proves to be a bad bargain. If possible, a court will interpret a contract to avoid hardship. Courts will, if possible, interpret a vague contact in a way to avoid any forfeiture of a party's interest.

When hardship arises because the contract makes no provision for the situation that has occurred, the court will sometimes imply a term to avoid the hardship.

---

[31] *Kroboth v Brent,* 625 NYS2d 748 (App Div 1995).
[32] UCC §§ 1-201(19), 1-203.
[33] *Affiliated FM Ins. Co. v Constitution Reinsurance Corp.,* 626 NE2d 878 (Mass 1994).
[34] *Blue v R.L. Glossen Contracting, Inc.,* 327 SE2d 582 (Ga App 1985).

CASE SUMMARY

Court Glides with Clyde

FACTS: Standard Oil Company made a nonexclusive jobbing or wholesale dealership contract with Perkins, which limited him to selling Standard's products and required Perkins to maintain certain minimum prices. Standard Oil had the right to approve or disapprove Perkins's customers. To be able to perform under his contract, Perkins had to make a substantial monetary investment, and his only income was from the commissions on the sales of Standard's products. Standard Oil made some sales directly to Perkins's customers. When Perkins protested, Standard Oil pointed out that the contract did not contain any provision making his rights exclusive. Perkins sued Standard Oil to compel it to stop dealing with his customers.

DECISION: Judgment for Perkins. In view of the expenditure required of Perkins to operate his business and to perform his part of the contract and because of his dependence on his customers, the interpretation should be made that Standard Oil would not solicit customers of Perkins. This is true even though the contract did not give Perkins an exclusive dealership within the given geographic area. [**Perkins v Standard Oil Co., 383 P2d 107 (Or 1963)**]

lawflix

The Santa Clause (1996) (PG)

When Scott Calvin (Tim Allen) tries on a Santa suit, he discovers that he has assumed all of Santa's responsibility. Calvin tries to challenge his acceptance of the terms of the agreement. Analyze the problems with offer, acceptance, and terms in very fine print (a magnifying glass is required). Do the terms of the suit contract apply when Calvin did not know them at the time he put on the suit?

For movie clips that illustrate business law concepts, see LawFlix at **www.cengage.com/blaw/dvl**.

MAKE THE CONNECTION

SUMMARY

An oral agreement may be a contract unless it is the intention of the parties that they should not be bound by the agreement without a writing executed by them. Certain contracts must be evidenced by a writing, however, or else they cannot be enforced. The statutes that declare this exception are called *statutes of frauds*. Statutes of frauds commonly require that a contract be evidenced by writing in the case of (1) an agreement that cannot be performed within one year after the contract is made, (2) an agreement to sell any interest in land, (3) a promise to answer for the debt or default of another, (4) a promise by the executor or administrator of a decedent's estate to pay a claim against the estate from personal funds, (5) a promise made in consideration of marriage, and (6) a contract for the sale of goods for a purchase price of $500 or more.

To evidence a contract to satisfy a statute of frauds, there must be a writing of all essential terms. The writing must be signed by the defendant against whom suit is brought for enforcement of the contract.

If the applicable statute of frauds is not satisfied, the oral contract cannot be enforced. To avoid unjust enrichment, a plaintiff barred from enforcing an oral contract may in most cases recover from the other contracting party the reasonable value of the benefits conferred by the plaintiff on the defendant.

When there is a written contract, the question arises whether that writing is the exclusive statement of the parties' agreement. If the writing is the complete and final statement of the contract, parol evidence as to matters agreed to before or at the time the writing was signed is not admissible to contradict the writing. This is called the *parol evidence rule*. In any case, the parol evidence rule does not bar parol evidence when (1) the writing is ambiguous, (2) the writing is not a true statement of the agreement of the parties because of fraud, duress, or mistake, or (3) the existence, modification, or illegality of a contract is in controversy.

Because a contract is based on the agreement of the parties, courts must determine the intent of the parties manifested in the contract. The intent that is to be enforced is the intent as it reasonably appears to a third person. This objective intent is followed.

In interpreting a contract, ordinary words are to be given their ordinary meanings. If trade or technical terms have been used, they are interpreted according to their technical meanings. The court must consider the whole contract and not read a particular part out of context. When different writings are executed as part of the same transaction, or one writing refers to or incorporates another, all of the writings are to be read together as the contract of the parties.

When provisions of a contract are contradictory, the court will try to reconcile or eliminate the conflict. If this cannot be done, the conclusion may be that there is no contract because the conflict makes the agreement indefinite as to a material matter. In some cases, conflict is solved by considering the form of conflicting terms. Handwriting prevails over typing and a printed form, and typing prevails over a printed form. Ambiguity will be eliminated in some cases by the admission of parol evidence or by interpreting the provision strictly against the party preparing the contract, particularly when that party has significantly greater bargaining power.

LEARNING OUTCOMES

After studying this chapter, you should be able to clearly explain:

A. STATUTE OF FRAUDS

LO.1 Explain when a contract must be evidenced by a writing
> See the discussion and examples beginning on p. 368.

LO.2 Explain the effect of noncompliance with the statute of frauds
> See the example in which an oral contract cannot be enforced because it is not in writing, but the plaintiff may recover the reasonable value of the services rendered, p. 377.

B. PAROL EVIDENCE RULE

LO.3 Explain the parol evidence rule and the exceptions to this rule
See the example in which the tenant is not allowed to call a witness to testify about a prior oral agreement that would add to and alter the written lease, p. 379.
See the exceptions based on ambiguity, fraud, duress, and mistake discussed on p. 379.

C. RULES OF CONSTRUCTION AND INTERPRETATION

LO.4 Understand the basic rule of contract construction that a contract is enforced according to its terms
See the example of the interpretation of the word "costs" on p. 381.

LO.5 State the rules for interpreting ambiguous terms in a contract
See the discussion on the nature of the writing beginning on p. 383.

KEY TERMS

administrator
ambiguous
decedent
executor
good faith

incorporation by
 reference
parol evidence rule
personal representative
statute of frauds

suretyship
usages of trade

QUESTIONS AND CASE PROBLEMS

1. Kelly made a written contract to sell certain land to Brown and gave Brown a deed to the land. Thereafter, Kelly sued Brown to get back a 20-foot strip of the land. Kelly claimed that before making the written contract, it was agreed that Kelly would sell all of his land to Brown to make it easier for Brown to get a building permit, but after that was done, the 20-foot strip would be reconveyed to Kelly. Was Kelly entitled to the 20-foot strip? What ethical values are involved? [*Brown v Kelly*, 545 So2d 518 (Fla App)]

2. Martin made an oral contract with Cresheim Garage to work as its manager for two years. Cresheim wrote Martin a letter stating that the oral contract had been made and setting forth all of its terms. Cresheim later refused to recognize the contract. Martin sued Cresheim for breach of the contract and offered Cresheim's letter in evidence as proof of the contract. Cresheim claimed that the oral contract was not binding because the contract was not in writing and the letter referring to the contract was not a contract but only a letter. Was the contract binding?

3. Lawrence loaned money to Moore, who died without repaying the loan. Lawrence claimed that when he mentioned the matter to Moore's widow, she promised to pay the debt. She did not pay it, and Lawrence sued her on her promise. Does she have any defense? [*Moore v Lawrence*, 480 SW2d 941 (Ark)]

4. Jackson signed an agreement to sell 79 acres of land to Devenyns. Jackson owned 80 acres and was apparently intending to keep for himself the acre on which his home was located. The written agreement also stated that "Devenyns shall have the option to buy on property _____," but nothing was stated in the blank space. Devenyns sued to enforce the agreement. Was it binding? [*In re Jackson's Estate*, 892 P2d 786 (Wyo)]

5. Boeing Airplane Co. contracted with Pittsburgh–Des Moines Steel Co. for the latter to construct a supersonic wind tunnel. R.H. Freitag Manufacturing Co. sold materials to York-Gillespie Co., which subcontracted to do part of the work. To persuade Freitag to keep supplying materials on credit, Boeing and the principal contractor both assured Freitag that he would be paid. When Freitag was not paid by the subcontractor, he sued Boeing and the contractor. They defended on the ground that the assurances given Freitag were not written. Decide. What ethical values are involved? [*R.H. Freitag Mfg. Co. v Boeing Airplane Co.*, 347 P2d 1074 (Wash)]

6. Louise Pulsifer owned a farm that she wanted to sell and ran an ad in the local newspaper. After Russell Gillespie agreed to purchase the farm, Pulsifer wrote him a letter stating that she would not sell it. He sued her to enforce the contract, and she raised the defense of the statute of frauds. The letter she had signed did not contain any of the terms of the sale. Gillespie, however, claimed that the newspaper ad could be combined with her letter to satisfy the statute of frauds. Was he correct? [*Gillespie v Pulsifer*, 655 SW2d 123 (Mo)]

7. In February or March, Corning Glass Works orally agreed to retain Hanan as management consultant from May 1 of that year to April 30 of the next year for a present value fee of $200,000. Was this agreement binding? Is this decision ethical? [*Hanan v Corning Glass Works*, 314 NYS2d 804 (App Div)]

8. Catherine (wife) and Peter (husband) Mallen had lived together unmarried for some four years when Catherine got pregnant and a marriage was arranged. Peter asked Catherine to sign a prenuptial agreement. Although his financial statement attached to the agreement did not state his income at $560,000 per year, it showed he was wealthy, and she had lived with him for four years and knew from their standard of living that he had significant income. Catherine contends that failure to disclose Peter's income was a nondisclosure of a material fact when the agreement was drawn up and that accordingly the agreement is not valid. Peter contends that he fully disclosed his net worth and that Catherine was well aware of his significant income. Further, he contends that disparities in the parties' financial status and business experience did not make the agreement unconscionable. Decide. [*Mallen v Mallen*, 622 SE2d 812 (Ga Sup Ct)]

9. Panasonic Industrial Co. (PIC) created a contract making Manchester Equipment Co., Inc. (MECI), a nonexclusive wholesale distributor of its products. The contract stated that PIC reserved the unrestricted right to solicit and make direct sales of the products to anyone, anywhere. The contract also stated that it contained the entire agreement of the parties and that any prior agreement or statement was superseded by the contract. PIC subsequently began to make direct sales to two of MECI's established customers. MECI

claimed that this was a breach of the distribution contract and sued PIC for damages. Decide. What ethical values are involved? [*Manchester Equipment Co. Inc. v Panasonic Industrial Co.*, 529 NYS2d 532 (App Div)]

10. A contract made for the sale of a farm stated that the buyer's deposit would be returned "if for any reason the farm cannot be sold." The seller later stated that she had changed her mind and would not sell, and she offered to return the deposit. The buyer refused to take the deposit back and brought suit to enforce the contract. The seller contended that the "any reason" provision extended to anything, including the seller's changing her mind. Was the buyer entitled to recover? [*Phillips v Rogers*, 200 SE2d 676 (W Va)]

11. Integrated, Inc., entered into a contract with the state of California to construct a building. It then subcontracted the electrical work to Alec Fergusson Electrical Contractors. The subcontract was a printed form with blanks filled in by typewriting. The printed payment clause required Integrated to pay Fergusson on the 15th day of the month following the submission of invoices by Fergusson. The typewritten part of the contract required Integrated to pay Fergusson "immediately following payment" (by the state) to the general contractor. When was payment required? [*Integrated, Inc. v Alec Fergusson Electrical Contractors*, 58 Cal Rptr 503 (Cal App)]

12. Norwest Bank had been lending money to Tresch to run a dairy farm. The balance due the bank after several years was $147,000. The loan agreement stated that Tresch would not buy any new equipment in excess of $500 without the express consent of the bank. Some time later, Tresch applied to the bank for a loan of $3,100 to purchase some equipment. The bank refused to make the loan because it did not believe the new equipment would correct the condition for which it would be bought and would not result in significant additional income. Tresch then sued the bank, claiming that its refusal to make the loan was a breach of the implied covenant of good faith and fair dealing. Decide. [*Tresch v Norwest Bank of Lewistown*, 778 P2d 874 (Mont)]

13. Physicians Mutual Insurance Co. issued a policy covering Brown's life. The policy declared that it did not cover any deaths resulting from "mental disorder, alcoholism, or drug addiction." Brown was killed when she fell while intoxicated. The insurance company refused to pay because of the quoted provision. Her executor, Savage, sued the insurance company. Did the insurance company have a defense? [*Physicians Mutual Ins. Co. v Savage*, 296 NE2d 165 (Ind App)]

14. The Dickinson Elks Club conducted an annual Labor Day golf tournament. Charbonneau Buick-Pontiac offered to give a new car as a prize to anyone making "a hole in one on hole no. 8." The golf course of the club was only nine holes. To play 18 holes, the players would go around the course twice, although they would play from different tees or locations for the second nine holes. On the second time around, what was originally the eighth hole became the seventeenth hole. Grove was a contestant in the tournament. He scored 3 on the no. 8 hole, but on approaching it for the second time as the seventeenth hole, he made a hole in one. He claimed the prize car from Charbonneau. The latter claimed that Grove had not won the prize because he did not make the

hole in one on the eighth hole. Decide. [*Grove v Charbonneau Buick-Pontiac, Inc.*, 240 NW2d 8533 (ND)]

15. Tambe Electric Inc. entered into a written agreement with Home Depot to provide copper wire to Tambe at a price set forth in the writing, and allowing the contractor the option of paying for the wire over a period of time. Home Depot did not fulfill this written agreement and Tambe sued for $68,598, the additional cost it had to subsequently pay to obtain copper wire for its work. Home Depot defended that it had made an oral condition precedent requiring payment in full by Tambe at the time it accepted the price quoted in the written agreement. Decide. [*Tambe Electric v Home Depot*, 856 NYS2d 373]

CPA QUESTIONS

1. Which of the following statements is true with regard to the statute of frauds?

   a. All contracts involving consideration of more than $500 must be in writing.

   b. The written contract must be signed by all parties.

   c. The statute of frauds applies to contracts that can be fully performed within one year from the date they are made.

   d. The contract terms may be stated in more than one document.

2. With regard to an agreement for the sale of real estate, the statute of frauds:

   a. Requires that the entire agreement be in a single writing

   b. Requires that the purchase price be fair and adequate in relation to the value of the real estate

   c. Does *not* require that the agreement be signed by all parties

   d. Does *not* apply if the value of the real estate is less than $500

3. In negotiations with Andrews for the lease of Kemp's warehouse, Kemp orally agreed to pay one-half of the cost of the utilities. The written lease, later prepared by Kemp's attorney, provided that Andrews pay all of the utilities. Andrews failed to carefully read the lease and signed it. When Kemp demanded that Andrews pay all of the utilities, Andrews refused, claiming that the lease did not accurately reflect the oral agreement. Andrews also learned that Kemp intentionally misrepresented the condition of the structure of the warehouse during the negotiations between the parties. Andrews sued to rescind the lease and intends to introduce evidence of the parties' oral agreement about sharing the utilities and the fraudulent statements made by Kemp. Will the parol evidence rule prevent the admission of evidence concerning each of the following?

	Oral agreement regarding who pays the utilities	*Fraudulent statements by Kemp*
a.	Yes	Yes
b.	No	Yes
c.	Yes	No
d.	No	No

Chapter 18

THIRD PERSONS AND CONTRACTS

A. Third-Party Beneficiary Contracts

   1. DEFINITION

   2. MODIFICATION OR TERMINATION OF INTENDED THIRD-PARTY BENEFICIARY CONTRACT

   3. LIMITATIONS ON INTENDED THIRD-PARTY BENEFICIARY

   4. INCIDENTAL BENEFICIARIES

B. Assignments

   5. DEFINITIONS

   6. FORM OF ASSIGNMENT

   7. NOTICE OF ASSIGNMENT

   8. ASSIGNMENT OF RIGHT TO MONEY

   9. NONASSIGNABLE RIGHTS

   10. RIGHTS OF ASSIGNEE

   11. CONTINUING LIABILITY OF ASSIGNOR

   12. LIABILITY OF ASSIGNEE

   13. WARRANTIES OF ASSIGNOR

   14. DELEGATION OF DUTIES

A. THIRD-PARTY BENEFICIARY CONTRACTS

Generally, only the parties to a contract may sue on it. However, in some cases a third person who is not a party to the contract may sue on the contract.

CPA   ## 1. Definition

intended beneficiary – third person of a contract whom the contract is intended to benefit.

third-party beneficiary – third person whom the parties to a contract intend to benefit by the making of the contract and to confer upon such person the right to sue for breach of contract.

When a contract is intended to benefit a third person, such a person is an **intended beneficiary** and may bring suit on and enforce the contract. In some states, the right of the intended **third-party beneficiary** to sue on the contract is declared by statute. **For Example,** Ibberson Co., the general contractor hired by AgGrow Oils, LLC to design and build an oilseed processing plant, contracted with subcontractor Anderson International Corp. to supply critical seed processing equipment for the project. Anderson's formal proposal to Ibberson identified the AgGrow Oils Project, and the proposal included drawings of the planned AgGrow plant. Under state law, this contract made between the contractor and subcontractor for the express benefit of the third-party AgGrow Oils could be enforced by the intended third-party beneficiary AgGrow Oils. The project was a failure. AgGrow was successful in the lawsuit against Anderson under the Anderson-Ibberson contract, having the standing to sue as an intended third-party beneficiary of that contract.[1]

(A) CREDITOR BENEFICIARY. The intended beneficiary is sometimes classified as a *creditor beneficiary* when the promisee's primary intent is to discharge a duty owed to the third party.[2] **For Example,** when Max Giordano sold his business, Sameway Laundry, to Harry Phinn, he had three years of payments totaling $14,500 owing to Davco, Inc., on a commercial Davco shirt drying and pressing machine purchased in 2006. Max (the promisee) made a contract with Harry to sell the business for a stipulated sum. A provision in this contract selling the business called for Harry (the promisor) to make the Davco machine payments when due over the next three years. Should Harry fail to make payments, Davco, Inc., as an intended creditor beneficiary under the contract between Max and Harry, would have standing to sue Harry for breach of the payment provision in the contract.

CPA   (B) DONEE BENEFICIARY. The second type of intended beneficiary is a *donee beneficiary* to whom the promisee's primary intent in contracting is to give a benefit. A life insurance contract is such an intended third-party beneficiary contract. The promisee-insured pays premiums to the insurer under the contract of insurance so that, upon the death of the insured, the promisor-insurer would pay the sum designated in the contract to the beneficiary. The beneficiary's rights vest upon the insured's death, and the beneficiary can sue the insurance company upon the insured's death even though the insurance company never made any agreement directly with the beneficiary.

---

[1] *AgGrow Oils, LLC v National Union Fire Ins.,* 420 F3d 751 (8th Cir 2005).
[2] The Restatement (Second) of Contracts § 302 substitutes "intended beneficiary" for the terms "creditor" and "donee" beneficiary. However, some courts continue to use the classifications of creditor and donee third-party beneficiaries. Regardless of the terminology, the law continues to be the same. See *Continental Casualty v Zurich American Insurance,* 2009 WL 455285 (DC Or 2009).

(C) NECESSITY OF INTENT. A third person does not have the status of an intended third-party beneficiary unless it is clear at the time the contract was formed that the parties intended to impose a direct obligation with respect to the third person.[3] In determining whether there is intent to benefit a third party, the surrounding circumstances as well as the contract may be examined.[4] There is a strong presumption that the parties to a contract intend to benefit only themselves.[5]

C A S E   S U M M A R Y

The Pest Control Case

FACTS: Admiral Pest Control had a standing contract with Lodging Enterprises to spray its motel every month to exterminate pests. Copeland, a guest in the motel, was bitten by a spider. She sued Admiral on the ground that she was a third-party beneficiary of the extermination contract.

DECISION: Judgment against Copeland. There was no intent manifested in the contract that guests of the motel were beneficiaries of the contract. The contract was made by the motel to protect itself. The guests were incidental beneficiaries of that contract and therefore could not sue for its breach. [**Copeland v Admiral Pest Control Co., 933 P2d 937 (Okla App 1996)**]

(D) DESCRIPTION. It is not necessary that the intended third-party beneficiary be identified by name. The beneficiary may be identified by class, with the result that any member of that class is a third-party beneficiary. **For Example,** a contract between the promoter of an automobile stock car race and the owner of the racetrack contains a promise by the owner to pay specified sums of money to each driver racing a car in certain races. A person driving in one of the designated races is a third-party beneficiary and can sue the owner on the contract for the promised compensation.

2. Modification or Termination of Intended Third-Party Beneficiary Contract

Can the parties to the contract modify or terminate it so as to destroy the right of the intended third-party beneficiary? If the contract contains an express provision allowing a change of beneficiary or cancellation of the contract without the consent

---

[3] *American United Logistics, Inc. v Catellus,* 319 F3d 921 (7th Cir 2003).
[4] See *Becker v Crispell-Synder, Inc.,* 763 NW2d 192 (Wisc App 2009) for an example of complex circumstances surrounding a third-party beneficiary contract. The town of Somers, Wisconsin, entered into a contract with engineering firm Crispell-Synder (C-S) because it needed an engineering firm to oversee a new subdivision to be developed by the Beckers. Under this contract C-S would submit bills to the town for overseeing the development, and the town would pay C-S through a line of credit from the Beckers. The court held that the Beckers were third-party beneficiaries entitled to sue C-S for overcharging change orders.
[5] *Barney v Unity Paving, Inc.,* 639 NE2d 592 (Ill App 1994).

of the intended third-party beneficiary, the parties to the contract may destroy the rights of the intended beneficiary by acting in accordance with that contract provision.[6]

For Example, Roy obtained a life insurance policy from Phoenix Insurance Company that provided the beneficiary could be changed by the insured. Roy named his son, Harry, as the beneficiary. Later, Roy had a falling out with Harry and removed him as beneficiary. Roy could do this because the right to change the beneficiary was expressly reserved by the contract that created the status of the intended third-party beneficiary.

In addition, the rights of an intended third-party beneficiary are destroyed if the contract is discharged or ended by operation of law, for example, through bankruptcy proceedings.

3. Limitations on Intended Third-Party Beneficiary

Although the intended third-party beneficiary rule gives the third person the right to enforce the contract, it obviously gives no more rights than the contract provides. That is, the intended third-party beneficiary must take the contract as it is. If there is a time limitation or any other restriction in the contract, the intended beneficiary cannot ignore it but is bound by it.

If the contract is not binding for any reason, that defense may be raised against the intended third-party beneficiary suing on the contract.[7]

CPA   4. Incidental Beneficiaries

Not everyone who benefits from the performance of a contract between other persons is entitled to sue as a third-party beneficiary. If the benefit was intended, the third person is an intended beneficiary with the rights described in the preceding sections. If the benefit was not intended, the third person is an *incidental beneficiary*.

For Example, Ensil International (EI), a New York firm, entered a repair agreement in 1998 with a Canadian company (EC) to perform repair work relating to medical imaging devices. EI solicited repair business in the U.S. and shipped the items for repair to the Canadian firm. In 2001 BC Technical (BCT) shipped items for repair to EI who shipped them to EC for the actual repairs. The repair work was not successful and BCT sued both EI and EC under the 1998 repair agreement for damages. BC Technical was not an intended third-party beneficiary of the 1998 agreement that was undertaken several years before BCT and EI contracted for the repairs in 2001. BCT had no standing to sue the Canadian firm under the 1998 contract. BCT was an incidental beneficiary of the 1998 agreement.[8]

Whether or not a third party is an *intended* or *incidental* beneficiary, therefore, comes down to determining whether or not a reasonable person would believe that

---

[6] A common form of reservation is the life insurance policy provision by which the insured reserves the right to change the beneficiary. Section 142 of the Restatement (Second) of Contracts provides that the promisor and the promisee may modify their contract and affect the right of the third-party beneficiary thereby unless the agreement expressly prohibits this or the third-party beneficiary has changed position in reliance on the promise or has manifested assent to it.

[7] *XL Disposal Corp. v John Sexton Contractors Co.,* 659 NE2d 1312 (Ill App 1995).

[8] *BC Technical Inc. v Ensil International,* 2007 WL 2908282 (D Utah 2007).

the promisee intended to confer on the beneficiary an enforceable benefit under the contract in question. The intent must be clear and definite or expressed in the contract itself or in the circumstances surrounding the contract's execution.

CASE SUMMARY

Third Party Must Be Identified in the Four Corners of the Contract

FACTS: Novus International, Inc., manufactures a poultry-feed supplement named Alimet at its plant in Chocolate Bayou, Texas. A key component of Alimet is the chemical MMP. Novus contracted with Union Carbide to secure MMP from Carbide's plant in Taft, Louisiana. Sometime later, Carbide entered into a major rail-transportation contract with the Union Pacific Railroad (UP). The rail contract consisted of nearly 100 pages. Exhibit 2 of the contract delineated inbound and outbound shipments to and from all of Carbide's Texas and Louisiana facilities. Among the hundreds of shipments listed in Exhibit 2 were three outbound MMP shipments from Taft, Louisiana, to Chocolate Bayou, Texas. These shipments were described as "Taft outbound liquid chemicals." Due to difficulties that arose from its merger with the Southern Pacific Railroad, UP experienced severe disruptions in its rail service over parts of two years and was unable to transport sufficient MMP to Chocolate Bayou. As a result, Novus had to utilize more expensive methods of transportation to obtain Alimet. It sued UP to recover the increased costs of premium freight resulting from UP's breach of its rail contract with Carbide. UP asserts that Novus did not have standing to sue; and Novus contends that it had standing to sue as an intended third-party beneficiary.

DECISION: Judgment for UP. Third-party beneficiary claims succeed or fail according to the provisions of the contact upon which suit is brought. The intention to confer a direct benefit on a third party must be clearly and fully spelled out in the four corners of the contract. Otherwise, enforcement of the contract by a third party must be denied. After reviewing the rail contract, no intent to confer a direct benefit on Novus is evident. Novus is never named in the contract, and all obligations flow between UP and Carbide. Nor is it stated anywhere in the contract that the parties are contracting for the benefit of Carbide's customers. Novus, thus, is an incidental beneficiary without standing to sue. [**Union Pacific Railroad v Novus International, Inc., 113 SW3d 418 (Tex App 2003)**]

B. ASSIGNMENTS

The parties to a contract have both rights and duties. Can rights be transferred or sold to another person or entity? Can duties be transferred to another person?

5. Definitions

Contracts create **rights** and **duties** between the parties to the contract. An **assignment** is a transfer of contractual rights to a third party. The party owing a duty or debt under the contract is the **obligor** or **debtor**, and the party to whom the obligation is owed is the **obligee**. The party making the assignment is the **assignor**. The third party to whom the assignment is made is the **assignee**. For Example, Randy Marshall and Marilee Menendez own Huntington Beach Board (HBB) Company,

---

right–legal capacity to require another person to perform or refrain from an action.

duty–obligation of law imposed on a person to perform or refrain from performing a certain act.

assignment–transfer of a right; generally used in connection with personal property rights, as rights under a contract, commercial paper, an insurance policy, a mortgage, or a lease. (Parties—assignor, assignee.)

obligor–promisor.

debtor–buyer on credit (i. e., a borrower).

obligee–promisee who can claim the benefit of the obligation.

assignor–party who assigns contract rights to a third party.

assignee–third party to whom contract benefits are transferred.

FIGURE 18-1 | *Surfboard Transaction Diagram*

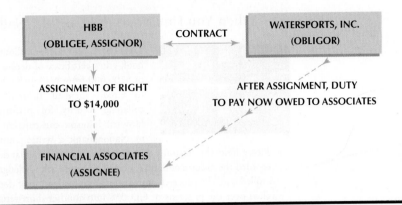

LLC, a five-employee start-up company making top-of-the line surfboards. Marilee was able to sell 100 Duke Kahanamoku–inspired "longboards" to Watersports, Inc., a large retail sporting goods chain, for $140 per board. However, the best payment terms she could obtain were payment in full in 90 days. A contract containing these terms was executed, and the goods were delivered. To meet internal cash flow needs, HBB assigned its right to receive the $14,000 payment from the buyer to West Coast Financial Associates (Associates) and received $12,800 cash from Associates on execution of the assignment documents. Notice was given at that time to Watersports, Inc., of the assignment. The right to receive the payment due in 90 days under the sales contract has thus been transferred by the seller HBB (assignor) to the third party, Associates (the assignee), to whom the buyer, Watersports, Inc. (obligor), now owes the duty of payment. Under the law of assignments, Associates, the assignee, now has direct rights against the obligor, Watersports, Inc. (See Figure 18.1.)

6. Form of Assignment

Generally, an assignment may be in any form. Statutes, however, may require that certain kinds of assignments be in writing or be executed in a particular form. Any words, whether written or spoken, that show an intention to transfer or assign will be given the effect of an assignment.[9]

7. Notice of Assignment

An assignment, if otherwise valid, takes effect the moment it is made. The assignee should give immediate notice of the assignment to the obligor, setting forth the obligor's duty to the assignee, in order to prevent improper payment.[10]

---

[9] *Jom Investments, LLC v Callahan Industries, Inc.*, 667 SE2d 429 (Ga App 2008).
[10] In some cases, an assignee will give notice of the assignment to the obligor in order to obtain priority over other persons who claim the same right or in order to limit the defenses that the obligor may raise against the assignee. UCC § 9-318.

CASE SUMMARY

When You Find Yourself in a Hole, NationsBank, Stop Digging

FACTS: L & S General Contractors, LLC (L & S), purchased a book-entry certificate of deposit (CD 005) in the principal amount of $100,000 from NationsBank, N.A. L & S later assigned CD 005 to Credit General Insurance Company (Credit General) as collateral security for performance and payment bonds on a Howard Johnson construction project. Credit General forwarded to NationsBank a written notice of the assignment that stated, "Please hold this account as assigned to use until demanded or released by us." NationsBank recorded the assignment and executed a written acknowledgment. When CD 005 matured, L & S rolled over the proceeds into a short-term certificate of deposit (CD 058) and, upon maturity, rolled over the proceeds of CD 058 into another short-term certificate of deposit (CD 072).

The bank book entries of CD 058 and CD 072 recorded L & S as the only principal/payee and did not reflect Credit General's assignment interest. NationsBank admitted its failure to show Credit General as assignee on the rollover book entries for CD 058 and CD 072 was a mistake.

Upon maturity, L & S withdrew the proceeds of CD 072 without the knowledge or consent of Credit General. Later Credit General made written demand on NationsBank for the proceeds of CD 005, and NationsBank informed Credit General that CD 005 had been redeemed and refused payment. Credit General sued NationsBank for wrongful payment of proceeds. NationsBank argues that the assignment was limited in time to the completion of the Howard Johnson project.

DECISION: Judgment for the assignee, Credit General. Upon notice and acknowledgment of the assignment, NationsBank incurred a legal duty to pay the account proceeds only to the assignee, Credit General, in whom the account was vested by the terms of the assignment. The assignment was absolute and unambiguous on its face and clearly was not limited as NationsBank proposes. The assignment language controls. [**Credit General Insurance Co. v NationsBank, 299 F3d 943 (8th Cir 2002)**]

If the obligor is notified in any manner that there has been an assignment and that any money due must be paid to the assignee, the obligor's obligation can be discharged only by making payment to the assignee.

If the obligor is not notified that there has been an assignment and that the money due must be paid to the assignee, any payment made by the obligor to the assignor reduces or cancels that portion of the debt. The only remedy for the assignee is to sue the assignor to recover the payments that were made by the obligor.

The Uniform Consumer Credit Code (UCCC) protects consumer-debtors making payments to an assignor without knowledge of the assignment[11] and imposes a penalty for using a contract term that would destroy this protection of consumers.[12]

---

[11] UCCC § 2.412.
[12] UCCC § 5.202.

8. Assignment of Right to Money

Assignments of contracts are generally made to raise money. **For Example,** an automobile dealer assigns a customer's credit contract to a finance company and receives cash for it. Sometimes assignments are made when an enterprise closes and transfers its business to a new owner.

A person entitled to receive money, such as payment for goods sold to a buyer or for work done under a contract, may generally assign that right to another person.[13] A **claim** or **cause of action** against another person may be assigned. Isaac Hayes, an Academy Award®–winning composer, producer, and the original voice of Chef in the television series South Park, assigned his copyright interests in several musical works in exchange for royalties from Stax Records.[14] A contractor entitled to receive payment from a building's owner can assign that right to a bank as security for a loan or can assign it to anyone else.

For Example, Celeste owed Roscoe Painters $5,000 for painting her house. Roscoe assigned this claim to the Main Street Bank. Celeste later refused to pay the bank because she had never consented to the assignment. The fact that Celeste had not consented is irrelevant. Roscoe was the owner of the claim and could transfer it to the bank. Celeste, therefore, is obligated to pay the assignee, Main Street Bank.

(A) FUTURE RIGHTS. By the modern rule, future and expected rights to money may be assigned. Thus, prior to the start of a building, a building contractor may assign its rights to money not yet due under an existing contract's payment on completion-phase schedule.

(B) PURPOSE OF ASSIGNMENT. The assignment of the right to money may be a complete transfer of the right that gives the assignee the right to collect and keep the money. In contrast, the assignment may be held for security. In this case, the assignee may hold the money only as a security for some specified obligation.

(C) PROHIBITION OF ASSIGNMENT OF RIGHTS. A clear and specific contractual prohibition against the assignment of rights is enforceable at common law. However, the UCC favors the assignment of contracts, and express contractual prohibitions on assignments are ineffective against (1) the assignment of rights to payment for goods or services, including accounts receivable,[15] and (2) the assignment of the rights to damages for breach of sales contracts.[16]

9. Nonassignable Rights

If the transfer of a right would materially affect or alter a duty or the rights of the obligor, an assignment is not permitted.[17]

(A) ASSIGNMENT INCREASING BURDEN OF PERFORMANCE. When the assignment of a right would increase the burden of the obligor in performing, an assignment is ordinarily not permitted. To illustrate, if the assignor has the right to buy a certain quantity of

---

claim–right to payment.

cause of action–right to damages or other judicial relief when a legally protected right of the plaintiff is violated by an unlawful act of the defendant.

---

[13] *Pravin Banker Associates v Banco Popular del Peru*, 109 F3d 850 (2d Cir 1997).
[14] *Hayes v Carlin America, Inc.*, 168 F Supp 2d 154 (SDNY 2001).
[15] UCC § 9-318(4). This section of the UCC is applicable to most commercial assignments.
[16] UCC § 2-210(2).
[17] *Aslakson v Home Savings Ass'n*, 416 NW2d 786 (Minn App 1987) (increase of credit risk).

FIGURE 18-2 | *Limitations on Transfer of Rights and Duties*

ASSIGNMENT OF RIGHT TO MONEY	ASSIGNMENT OF RIGHT TO PERFORMANCE	DELEGATION OF DUTIES
GENERALLY NO LIMITATION	INCREASE OF BURDEN PERSONAL SERVICES CREDIT TRANSACTION	PERSONAL OR NONSTANDARDIZED PERFORMANCE

a stated article and to take such property from the seller's warehouse, this right can be assigned. However, if the sales contract stipulates that the seller should deliver to the buyer's premises and the assignee's premises are a substantial distance from the assignor's place of business, the assignment would not be given effect. In this case, the seller would be required to give a different performance by providing greater transportation if the assignment were permitted.

(B) PERSONAL SERVICES. Contracts for personal services are generally not assignable. **For Example,** were golf instructor David Ledbetter to sign a one-year contract to provide instruction for professional golfer Davis Love III, David Ledbetter could not assign his first assistant to provide the instruction, nor could Davis Love assign a protégé to receive instruction from Ledbetter. Professional athletes and their agents commonly deal with assignment or trading rights of the athletes in their contracts with professional sports franchises.

There is a split among jurisdictions regarding whether employee noncompetition covenants are assignable to the new owner of a business absent employee consent. That is, some courts permit a successor employer to enforce an employee's noncompetition agreement as an assignee of the original employer. However, a majority of states that have considered this issue have concluded that restrictive covenants are personal in nature and not assignable. **For Example,** in September 2000, Philip Burkhardt signed a noncompetition agreement with his employer, NES Trench Shoring. On June 30, 2002, United Rentals Purchased NES with all contracts being assigned to United Rentals. Burkhardt stayed on with the new owner for five weeks and thereafter went to work for Traffic Control Services, a direct competitor of United. United was unsuccessful in its action to enforce the noncompetition covenant Burkhardt had signed with NES. Burkhardt's covenant with NES did not contain a clause allowing the covenant to be assigned to a new owner, and the court refused to enforce it, absent an express clause permitting assignment.[18]

(c) CREDIT TRANSACTION. When a transaction is based on extending credit, the person to whom credit is extended cannot assign any rights under the contract to another. **For Example,** Jack Aldrich contracted to sell his summer camp on Lake

---

[18] *Traffic Control Sources, Inc. v United Rentals Northwest, Inc.*, 87 P3d 1054 (Nov 2004).

Sunapee to Pat Norton for $200,000, with $100,000 in cash due at the closing and the balance due on an installment basis secured by a mortgage on the property to be executed by Norton. Several days later, Norton found a more desirable property, and her sister Meg was very pleased to take over the Sunapee contract. Pat assigned her rights to Meg. Jack Aldrich, having received a better offer after contracting with Pat, refused to consent to the assignment. In this situation, the assignment to Meg is prohibited because the assignee, Meg, is a different credit risk even though the property to serve as security remained unchanged.

CPA   10. Rights of Assignee

Unless restricted by the terms of the assignment or applicable law, the assignee acquires all the rights of the assignor.[19]

An assignee stands exactly in the position of the assignor. The assignee's rights are no more or less than those of the assignor. If the assigned right to payment is subject to a condition precedent, that same condition exists for the assignee. **For Example,** when a contractor is not entitled to receive the balance of money due under the contract until all bills of suppliers of materials have been paid, the assignee to whom the contractor assigns the balance due under the contract is subject to the same condition. As set forth previously, in some states the assignee of a business purchasing all of the assets and rights of the business has the right to enforce a confidentiality and noncompetition agreement against a former employee of the assignor, just as though it were the assignor.[20]

11. Continuing Liability of Assignor

The making of an assignment does not relieve the assignor of any obligation of the contract. In the absence of a contrary agreement, an assignor continues to be bound by the obligations of the original contract. **For Example,** boatbuilder Derecktor NY's assignment of obligations to a Connecticut boatbuilder did not release it from all liabilities under its boatbuilding contract with New York Water Taxi (NYWT); and NYWT was allowed to proceed against Derecktor NY for breach of contract–design and breach of contract–workmanship.[21]

When a lease is assigned, the assignee becomes the principal obligor for rent payments, and the leasee becomes a surety toward the lessor for the assignee's performance. **For Example,** Tri-State Chiropractic (TSC) held a five-year lease on premises at 6010 East Main Street in Columbus, Ohio. Without the leasor's consent, TSC assigned that lease to Dr. T. Wilson and Buckeye Chiropractic, LLC, prior to the expiration of the lease. TSC continues to be liable for rent as surety during the term of the lease, even if the leasor (owner) had consented to the assignment or accepted payment from the assignee.[22] In order to avoid liability as a surety, TSC would have to obtain a discharge of the lease by **novation**, in which all three parties agree that the original contract (the lease) would be discharged and a

novation–substitution for an old contract with a new one that either replaces an existing obligation with a new obligation or replaces an original party with a new party.

[19] *Puget Sound National Bank v Washington Department of Revenue,* 868 P2d 127 (Wash 1994).
[20] *Artromick International, Inc. v Koch,* 759 NE2d 385 (Ohio App 2001).
[21] *New York Trans Harbor, LLC v Derecktor Shipyards,* 841 NYS2d 821 (2007).
[22] *Schottenstein Trustees v Carano,* 2000 WL 1455425 (Ohio App 2000).

new lease between Dr. Wilson and the owner would take effect. A novation allows for the discharge of a contractual obligation by the substitution of a new contract involving a new party.[23]

12. Liability of Assignee

It is necessary to distinguish between the question of whether the obligor can assert a particular defense against the assignee and the question of whether any person can sue the assignee. Ordinarily, the assignee is not subject to suit by virtue of the fact that the assignment has been made.

(A) Consumer Protection Liability of Assignee. The assignee of the right to money may have no direct relationship to the original debtor except with respect to receiving payments. Consumer protection laws in most states, however, may subject the assignee to some liability for the assignor's misconduct.

CASE SUMMARY

The Pool and the Agreement Will Not Hold Any Water

FACTS: Homeowner Michael Jackson entered into a contract with James DeWitt for the construction of an in-ground lap pool. The contract provided for a 12 ft. 60 ft. pool at an estimated cost of $21,000. At the time the contract was signed, Jackson paid DeWitt $11,400 in cash and financed $7,500 through a Retail Installment Security Agreement (RISA). Associates Financial Services Company (Associates) provided DeWitt with all of the forms necessary to document the financing of the home improvements. Consumer requests for financing were subject to Associates's approval, which was given for Jackson's lap pool. When the RISA was completed, DeWitt assigned it to Associates. Jackson made two monthly payments of $202.90 and a final payment of $7,094.20 while the lap pool was still under construction. When the pool was filled, it failed to hold water and Jackson had the pool and deck removed. Jackson sued DeWitt for breach of contract. He asserted that all valid claims and defenses he had against DeWitt were also valid against the assignee, Associates. Jackson sought the return of the $7,500 he had financed from Associates. The trial court held that because Jackson had paid the entire balance of the loan before Associates knew of Jackson's claim, he could not obtain relief from Associates under the consumer protection law, section ATCP 110.06 of the Wisconsin Administrative Code. Jackson appealed this decision.

DECISION: Judgment for Jackson. As one commentator has noted, "ch. ATCP 110 deals with virtually a laundry list of unfair or deceptive home improvement practices that have resulted from substantial financial losses to home owners over the years. Jeffries, 57 MARQ. L. REV at 578." Associates is an assignee of a "home improvement contract" that is governed by section ATCP 110.06. The regulation provides that "[e]very assignee of a home improvement contract takes subject to all claims and defenses of the buyer or successors in interest." Therefore, as the assignee of the RISA, Associates is subject to any claims without regard to the negotiability of the contract. [**Jackson v DeWitt, 592 NW2d 262 (Wis App 1999)**]

---

[23] See *Quicksilver Resources, Inc. v Eagle Drilling, LLC*, 2009 LEXIS 39176 (SD Tex 2009).

FIGURE 18-3 | *Can a Third Person Sue on a Contract?*

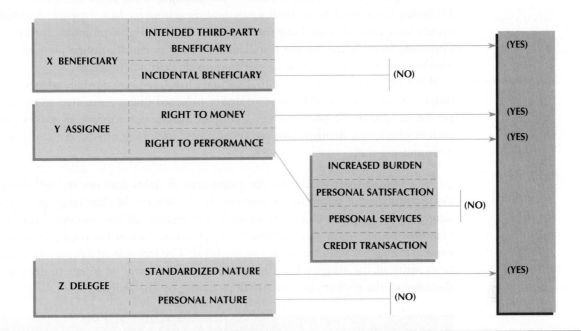

(B) **DEFENSES AND SETOFFS.** The assignee's rights are no greater than those of the assignor.[24] If the obligor could successfully defend against a suit brought by the assignor, the obligor will also prevail against the assignee.

The fact that the assignee has given value for the assignment does not give the assignee any immunity from defenses that the other party, the obligor, could have asserted against the assignor. The rights acquired by the assignee remain subject to any limitations imposed by the contract.

13. Warranties of Assignor

implied warranty–warranty that was not made but is implied by law.

When the assignment is made for a consideration, the assignor is regarded as providing an **implied warranty** that the right assigned is valid. The assignor also warrants that the assignor is the owner of the claim or right assigned and that the assignor will not interfere with the assignee's enforcement of the obligation.

14. Delegation of Duties

delegation of duties– transfer of duties by a contracting party to another person who is to perform them.

delegation–transfer to another of the right and power to do an act.

A **delegation of duties** is a transfer of duties by a contracting party to another person who is to perform them. Under certain circumstances, a contracting party may obtain someone else to do the work. When the performance is standardized and nonpersonal, so that it is not material who performs, the law will permit the **delegation** of the performance of the contract. In such cases, however, the contracting party remains liable in the case of default of the person doing the work just as though no delegation had been made.[25]

---

[24] *Shoreline Communications, Inc. v Norwich Taxi, LCC,* 70 Conn App 60 (2002).
[25] *Orange Bowl Corp. v Warren,* 386 SE2d 293 (SC App 1989).

A contract may prohibit a party owing a duty of performance under a contract from delegating that duty to another.[26] **For Example,** Tom Joyce of Patriot Plumbing Co. contracts to install a new heating system for Mrs. Lawton. A notation on the sales contract that Tom Joyce will do the installation prohibits Patriot Plumbing from delegating the installation to another equally skilled plumber or to another company if a backlog of work occurs at Patriot Plumbing.

If the performance of a party to a contract involves personal skill, talents, judgment, or trust, the delegation of duties is barred unless consented to by the person entitled to the performance. Examples include performance by professionals such as physicians, dentists, lawyers, consultants, celebrities, artists, and craftpersons with unusual skills.

(A) **INTENTION TO DELEGATE DUTIES.** An assignment of rights does not in itself delegate the performance of duties to the assignee. In the absence of clear language in the assignment stating that duties are or are not delegated, all circumstances must be examined to determine whether there is a delegation. When the total picture is viewed, it may become clear what was intended. The fact that an assignment is made for security of the assignee is a strong indication there was no intent to delegate to the assignee the performance of any duty resting on the assignor.[27]

CASE SUMMARY

Duties were Delegated Too, Dude

FACTS: Smith, who owned the Avalon Apartments, a condominium, sold individual apartments under contracts that required each purchaser to pay $15 a month extra for hot and cold water, heat, refrigeration, taxes, and fire insurance. Smith assigned his interest in the apartment house under various contracts to Roberts. When Roberts failed to pay the taxes on the building, the purchasers of the individual apartments sued to compel Roberts to do so.

DECISION: Judgment against Roberts. In the absence of a contrary indication, it is presumed that an assignment of a contract delegates the performance of the duties as well as transfers the rights. Here, there was no indication that a package transfer was not intended, and the assignee was therefore obligated to perform in accordance with the contract terms. [**Radley v Smith and Roberts, 313 P2d 465 (Utah 1957)**]

(B) **DELEGATION OF DUTIES UNDER THE UCC.** With respect to contracts for the sale of goods, "an assignment of 'the contract' or of 'all my rights under the contract' or an assignment in similar general terms is an assignment of rights and, unless the language or the circumstances (as in an assignment for security) indicate the contrary, it is a delegation of performance of the duties of the assignor, and its acceptance by the assignee constitutes a promise ... to perform those duties. This promise is enforceable by either the assignor or the other party to the original contract."[28]

---

[26] See *Physical Distribution Services, Inc. v R. R. Donnelley*, 561 F3d 792 (8th Cir 2009).
[27] *City National Bank of Fort Smith v First National Bank and Trust Co. of Rogers*, 732 SW2d 489 (Ark App 1987).
[28] UCC § 2-210(4).

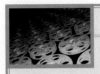

lawflix

It Could Happen to You (1996) (PG)

Discuss the legal, ethical and contract issues involved in the first portion of the film in which a police officer (Nicholas Cage) promises to split a lottery ticket with a coffee shop waitress (Bridget Fonda) as her tip because he does not have enough money. The lottery ticket (purchased by Cage and his wife, Rosie Perez) is a winner, and Cage wrestles with his obligation to tell Fonda. You could discuss whether there was an assignment or whether Fonda was added as a third-party beneficiary after the fact.

Check out LawFlix at **www.cengage.com/blaw/dvl** to access movie clips that illustrate business law concepts.

MAKE THE CONNECTION

SUMMARY

Ordinarily, only the parties to contracts have rights and duties with respect to such contracts. Exceptions are made in the case of third-party beneficiary contracts and assignments.

When a contract shows a clear intent to benefit a third person or class of persons, those persons are called *intended third-party beneficiaries*, and they may sue for breach of the contract. A third-party beneficiary is subject to any limitation or restriction found in the contract. A third-party beneficiary loses all rights when the original contract is terminated by operation of law or if the contract reserves the right to change the beneficiary and such a change is made.

In contrast, an incidental beneficiary benefits from the performance of a contract, but the conferring of this benefit was not intended by the contracting parties. An incidental beneficiary cannot sue on the contract.

An assignment is a transfer of a right; the assignor transfers a right to the assignee. In the absence of a local statute, there are no formal requirements for an assignment. Any words manifesting the intent to transfer are sufficient to constitute an assignment. No consideration is required. Any right to money may be assigned, whether the assignor is entitled to the money at the time of the assignment or will be entitled or expects to be entitled at some time in the future.

A right to a performance may be assigned except when (1) it would increase the burden of performance, (2) the contract involves the performance of personal services, or (3) the transaction is based on extending credit.

When a valid assignment is made, the assignee has the same rights—and only the same rights—as the assignor. The assignee is also subject to the same defenses and setoffs as the assignor had been.

The performance of duties under a contract may be delegated to another person except when a personal element of skill or judgment of the original contracting party is involved. The intent to delegate duties may be expressly stated. The intent may also be found in an "assignment" of "the contract" unless the circumstances make it clear that only the right to money was intended to be transferred. The fact that there has been a delegation of duties does not release the assignor from responsibility for performance. The assignor is liable for breach of the contract if the assignee does not properly perform the delegated duties. In the absence of an effective delegation or the formation of a third-party beneficiary contract, an assignee of rights is not liable to the obligee of the contract for its performance by the assignor.

Notice is not required to effect an assignment. When notice of the assignment is given to the obligor together with a demand that future payments be made to the assignee, the obligor cannot discharge liability by payment to the assignor.

When an assignment is made for a consideration, the assignor makes implied warranties that the right assigned is valid and that the assignor owns that right and will not interfere with its enforcement by the assignee.

LEARNING OUTCOMES

After studying this chapter, you should be able to clearly explain:

A. THIRD-PARTY BENEFICIARY CONTRACTS

LO.1 Explain the two types of intended third-party beneficiaries

See the Sameway Laundry example that illustrates how the "intended creditor beneficiary" can sue the buyer, p. 393.

See the text discussion explaining that a life insurance contract is an "intended" donee third-party beneficiary contract, p. 393.

LO.2 Explain why an incidental beneficiary does not have the right to sue as a third-party beneficiary

See the *Ensil* case in which the owner had no standing to sue as an incidental beneficiary, p. 395.

B. ASSIGNMENTS

LO.3 Define an assignment

See the text discussion explaining that an assignment is the transfer of contractual rights to a third party, p. 396.

See the Hunington *Beach Board* example that discusses the assignee's direct rights against the obligor, p. 396.

LO.4 Explain the general rule that a person entitled to receive money under a contract may generally assign that right to another person

See the example of an automobile dealer assigning a customer's credit contract to a finance company in order to raise cash to buy more inventory, p. 399.

LO.5 List the nonassignable rights to performance
See the text discussion regarding increase of burden, personal services, and credit transactions beginning on p. 399.

KEY TERMS

assignee	delegation of duties	obligee
assignment	delegation	obligor
assignor	duties	rights
cause of action	implied warranty	third-party beneficiary
claim	intended beneficiary	
debtor	novation	

QUESTIONS AND CASE PROBLEMS

1. Give an example of a third-party beneficiary contract.

2. A court order required John Baldassari to make specified payments for the support of his wife and child. His wife needed more money and applied for Pennsylvania welfare payments. In accordance with the law, she assigned to Pennsylvania her right to the support payments from her husband. Pennsylvania then increased her payments. Pennsylvania obtained a court order directing John, in accordance with the terms of the assignment from his wife, to make the support-order payments directly to the Pennsylvania Department of Public Welfare. John refused to pay on the ground that he had not been notified of the assignment or the hearing directing him to make payment to the assignee. Was he correct? [*Pennsylvania v Baldassari*, 421 A2d 306 (Pa Super)]

3. Lee contracts to paint Sally's two-story house for $2,500. Sally realizes that she will not have sufficient money, so she transfers her rights under this agreement to her neighbor Karen, who has a three-story house. Karen notifies Lee that Sally's contract has been assigned to her and demands that Lee paint Karen's house for $2,500. Is Lee required to do so?

4. Assume that Lee agrees to the assignment of the house-painting contract to Karen as stated in question 3. Thereafter, Lee fails to perform the contract to paint Karen's house. Karen sues Sally for damages. Is Sally liable?

5. Jessie borrows $1,000 from Thomas and agrees to repay the money in 30 days. Thomas assigns the right to the $1,000 to Douglas Finance Co. Douglas sues Jessie. Jessie argues that she had agreed to pay the money only to Thomas and that when she and Thomas had entered into the transaction, there was no intention to benefit Douglas Finance Co. Are these objections valid?

6. Washington purchased an automobile from Smithville Motors. The contract called for payment of the purchase price in installments and contained the defense preservation notice required by the Federal Trade Commission regulation. Smithville assigned the contract to Rustic Finance Co. The car was always in need of repairs, and by the time it was half paid for, it would no longer run. Washington canceled the contract. Meanwhile, Smithville had gone out of

business. Washington sued Rustic for the amount she had paid Smithville. Rustic refused to pay on the grounds that it had not been at fault. Decide.

7. Helen obtained an insurance policy insuring her life and naming her niece Julie as beneficiary. Helen died, and about a year later the policy was found in her house. When Julie claimed the insurance money, the insurer refused to pay on the ground that the policy required that notice of death be given to it promptly following the death. Julie claimed that she was not bound by the time limitation because she had never agreed to it, as she was not a party to the insurance contract. Is Julie entitled to recover?

8. Lone Star Life Insurance Co. agreed to make a long-term loan to Five Forty Three Land, Inc., whenever that corporation requested one. Five Forty Three wanted this loan to pay off its short-term debts. The loan was never made, as it was never requested by Five Forty Three, which owed the Exchange Bank & Trust Co. on a short-term debt. Exchange Bank then sued Lone Star for breach of its promise on the theory that the Exchange Bank was a third-party beneficiary of the contract to make the loan. Was the Exchange Bank correct? [*Exchange Bank & Trust Co. v Lone Star Life Ins. Co.*, 546 SW2d 948 (Tex App)]

9. The New Rochelle Humane Society made a contract with the city of New Rochelle to capture and impound all dogs running at large. Spiegler, a minor, was bitten by some dogs while in her schoolyard. She sued the school district of New Rochelle and the Humane Society. With respect to the Humane Society, she claimed that she was a third-party beneficiary of the contract that the Humane Society had made with the city. She claimed that she could therefore sue the Humane Society for its failure to capture the dogs that had bitten her. Was she entitled to recover? [*Spiegler v School District of the City of New Rochelle*, 242 NYS2d 430]

10. Zoya operated a store in premises rented from Peerless. The lease required Zoya to maintain liability insurance to protect Zoya and Peerless. Caswell entered the store, fell through a trap door, and was injured. She then sued Zoya and Peerless on the theory that she was a third-party beneficiary of the lease requirement to maintain liability insurance. Was she correct? [*Caswell v Zoya Int'l*, 654 NE2d 552 (Ill App)]

11. Henry was owed $10,000 by Jones Corp. In consideration of the many odd jobs performed for him over the years by his nephew, Henry assigned the $10,000 claim to his nephew Charles. Henry died, and his widow claimed that the assignment was ineffective so that the claim was part of Henry's estate. She based her assertion on the ground that the past performance rendered by the nephew was not consideration. Was the assignment effective?

12. Industrial Construction Co. wanted to raise money to construct a canning factory in Wisconsin. Various persons promised to subscribe the needed amount, which they agreed to pay when the construction was completed. The construction company assigned its rights and delegated its duties under the agreement to Johnson, who then built the cannery. Vickers, one of the subscribers, refused to pay the amount that he had subscribed on the ground that the contract could not be assigned. Was he correct?

13. The Ohio Department of Public Welfare made a contract with an accountant to audit the accounts of health care providers who were receiving funds under the Medicaid program. Windsor House, which operated six nursing homes, claimed that it was a third-party beneficiary of that contract and could sue for its breach. Was it correct? [*Thornton v Windsor House, Inc.,* 566 NE2d 1220 (Ohio)]

CPA QUESTIONS

1. On August 1, Neptune Fisheries contracted in writing with West Markets to deliver to West 3,000 pounds of lobster at $4.00 a pound. Delivery of the lobsters was due October 1, with payment due November 1. On August 4, Neptune entered into a contract with Deep Sea Lobster Farms that provided as follows: "Neptune Fisheries assigns all the rights under the contract with West Markets dated August 1 to Deep Sea Lobster Farms." The best interpretation of the August 4 contract would be that it was:

   a. Only an assignment of rights by Neptune

   b. Only a delegation of duties by Neptune

   c. An assignment of rights and a delegation of duties by Neptune

   d. An unenforceable third-party beneficiary contract

2. Graham contracted with the city of Harris to train and employ high school dropouts residing in Harris. Graham breached the contract. Long, a resident of Harris and a high school dropout, sued Graham for damages. Under the circumstances, Long will:

   a. Win, because Long is a third-party beneficiary entitled to enforce the contract

   b. Win, because the intent of the contract was to confer a benefit on all high school dropouts residing in Harris

   c. Lose, because Long is merely an incidental beneficiary of the contract

   d. Lose, because Harris did not assign its contract rights to Long

3. Union Bank lent $200,000 to Wagner. Union required Wagner to obtain a life insurance policy naming Union as beneficiary. While the loan was outstanding, Wagner stopped paying the premiums on the policy. Union paid the premiums, adding the amounts paid to Wagner's loan. Wagner died, and the insurance company refused to pay the policy proceeds to Union. Union may:

   a. Recover the policy proceeds because it is a creditor beneficiary

   b. Not recover the policy proceeds because it is a donee beneficiary

   c. Not recover the policy proceeds because it is not in privity of contract with the insurance company

   d. Not recover the policy proceeds because it is only an incidental beneficiary

Chapter 19

DISCHARGE OF CONTRACTS

A. Conditions Relating to Performance

   1. CLASSIFICATIONS OF CONDITIONS

B. Discharge by Performance

   2. NORMAL DISCHARGE OF CONTRACTS

   3. NATURE OF PERFORMANCE

   4. TIME OF PERFORMANCE

   5. ADEQUACY OF PERFORMANCE

C. Discharge by Action of Parties

   6. DISCHARGE BY UNILATERAL ACTION

   7. DISCHARGE BY AGREEMENT

D. Discharge by External Causes

   8. DISCHARGE BY IMPOSSIBILITY

   9. DEVELOPING DOCTRINES

   10. TEMPORARY IMPOSSIBILITY

   11. DISCHARGE BY OPERATION OF LAW

In the preceding chapters, you studied how a contract is formed, what a contract means, and who has rights under a contract. In this chapter, attention is turned to how a contract is ended or discharged. In other words, what puts an end to the rights and duties created by a contract?

A. Conditions Relating to Performance

As developed in the body of this chapter, the ordinary method of discharging obligations under a contract is by performance. Certain promises may be less than absolute and instead come into effect only upon the occurrence of a specified event, or an existing obligation may be extinguished when an event happens. These are conditional promises.

1. Classifications of Conditions

condition—stipulation or prerequisite in a contract, will, or other instrument.

When the occurrence or nonoccurrence of an event, as expressed in a contract, affects the duty of a party to the contract to perform, the event is called a **condition**. Terms such as *if, provided that, when, after, as soon as, subject to,* and *on the condition that* indicate the creation of a condition.[1] Conditions are classified as *conditions precedent, conditions subsequent,* and *concurrent conditions.*

condition precedent—event that if unsatisfied would mean that no rights would arise under a contract.

(A) Condition Precedent. A **condition precedent** is a condition that must occur before a party to a contract has an obligation to perform under the contract. **For Example,** a condition precedent to a contractor's (MasTec's) obligation to pay a subcontractor (MidAmerica) under a "pay-if-paid" by the owner (PathNet) clause in their subcontract agreement is the receipt of payment by MasTec from PathNet. The condition precedent—payment by the owner—did not occur due to bankruptcy, and therefore MasTec did not have an obligation to pay MidAmerica.[2]

CASE SUMMARY

A Blitz on Offense?

FACTS: Richard Blitz owns a piece of commercial property at 4 Old Middle Street. On February 2, 1998, Arthur Subklew entered into a lease with Blitz to rent the rear portion of the property. Subklew intended to operate an auto sales and repair business. Paragraph C of the lease was a zoning contingency clause that stated, "Landlord [plaintiff] will use Landlord's best efforts to obtain a written verification that Tenant can operate [an] Auto Sales and Repair Business at the demised premises. If Landlord is unable to obtain such

---

[1] *Harmon Cable Communications v Scope Cable Television, Inc.,* 468 NW2d 350 (Neb 1990).
[2] *MidAmerica Construction Management, Inc. v MasTec North America, Inc.,* 436 F3d 1257 (10th Cir 2006).

C A S E   S U M M A R Y

Continued

commitment from the municipality, then this agreement shall be deemed null and void and Landlord shall immediately return deposit monies to Tenant." The zoning paraboard approved the location only as a general repair business. When Subklew refused to occupy the premises, Blitz sued him for breach of contract.

DECISION: Judgment for Subklew. A condition precedent is a fact or event that the parties intend must exist before there is right to a performance. If the condition is not fulfilled, the right to enforce the contract does not come into existence. Blitz's obligation to obtain written approval of a used car business was a condition precedent to the leasing agreement. Since it was not obtained, Blitz cannot enforce the leasing agreement. [**Blitz v Subklew, 74 Conn App 183 (2002)**]

(B) **CONDITION SUBSEQUENT.** The parties to a contract may agree that a party is obligated to perform a certain act or pay a certain sum of money, but the contract contains a provision that relieves the obligation on the occurrence of a certain event. That is, on the happening of a **condition subsequent**, such an event extinguishes the duty to thereafter perform. **For Example,** Chad Newly served as the weekend anchor on *Channel 5 News* for several years. The station manager, Tom O'Brien, on reviewing tapes in connection with Newly's contract renewal, believed that Newly's speech on occasion was slightly slurred, and he suspected that it was from alcohol use. In the parties' contract discussions, O'Brien expressed his concerns about an alcohol problem and offered help. Newly denied there was a problem. O'Brien agreed to a new two-year contract with Newly at $167,000 for the first year and $175,000 for the second year with other benefits subject to "the condition" that the station reserved the right to make four unannounced drug-alcohol tests during the contract term; and should Newly test positive for drugs or alcohol under measurements set forth in the contract, then all of Channel 5's obligations to Newly under the contract would cease. When Newly subsequently failed a urinalysis test three months into the new contract, the happening of this event extinguished the station's obligation to employ and pay him under the contract.

condition subsequent–
event whose occurrence or lack there of terminates a contract.

sports&entertainment law

Endorsement Contracts

Sports marketing involves the use of famous athletes to promote the sale of products and services in our economy. Should an athlete's image be tarnished by allegations of immoral or illegal conduct, a company could be subject to financial losses and

corporate embarrassment. Endorsement contracts may extend for multiyear periods, and should a "morals" issue arise, a company would be well served to have had a broad morals clause in its contract that would allow the company at its sole

continued

sports&entertainment law

discretion to summarily terminate the endorsement contract. Representatives of athletes, on the other hand, seek narrow contractual language that allows for termination of endorsement contracts only upon the indictment for a crime, and they seek the right to have an arbitrator, as opposed to the employer, make the determination as to whether the morals clause was violated. NBA player Latrell Spreewell's endorsement contract with Converse Athletic Shoe Co. was terminated by the company following his altercation with his coach P.J. Carlisimo; John Daly's endorsement contract with Callaway Golf

was terminated by the company when he violated his good conduct clause that restricted gambling and drinking activities; and when a photograph of Olympic gold medal swimmer Michael Phelps showed him with a marijuana pipe at a party at the University of South Carolina, Kellogg Co. dropped Phelps's endorsement deal.

Can the courts be utilized to resolve controversies over whether a "morals clause" has been violated? If so, is the occurrence of a morals clause violation a condition precedent or a condition subsequent?

(c) Concurrent Condition. In most bilateral contracts, the performances of the parties are *concurrent conditions*. That is, their mutual duties of performance under the contract are to take place simultaneously. **For Example,** concerning a contract for the sale and delivery of certain goods, the buyer must tender to the seller a certified check at the time of delivery as set forth in the contract, and the seller must tender the goods to the buyer at the same time.

B. Discharge by Performance

When it is claimed that a contract is discharged by performance, questions arise as to the nature, time, and sufficiency of the performance.

2. Normal Discharge of Contracts

A contract is usually discharged by the performance of the terms of the agreement. In most cases, the parties perform their promises and the contract ceases to exist or is thereby discharged. A contract is also discharged by the expiration of the time period specified in the contract.[3]

3. Nature of Performance

Performance may be the doing of an act or the making of payment.

tender–goods have arrived, are available for pickup, and buyer is notified.

(a) Tender. An offer to perform is known as a **tender**. If performance of the contract requires the doing of an act, the refusal of a tender discharges the party offering to perform and is a basis for that party to bring a lawsuit.

[3] *Washington National Ins. Co. v Sherwood Associates,* 795 P2d 665 (Utah App 1990).

A valid tender of payment consists of an unconditional offer of the exact amount due on the date when due. A tender of payment is not just an expression of willingness to pay; it must be an actual offer to perform by making payment of the amount owed.

(B) PAYMENT. When the contract requires payment, performance consists of the payment of money.

(1) Application of Payments

If a debtor owes more than one debt to the creditor and pays money, a question may arise as to which debt has been paid. If the debtor specifies the debt to which the payment is to be applied and the creditor accepts the money, the creditor is bound to apply the money as specified.[4] Thus, if the debtor specifies that a payment is to be made for a current purchase, the creditor may not apply the payment to an older balance.

(2) Payment by Check

Payment by commercial paper, such as a check, is ordinarily a conditional payment. A check merely suspends the debt until the check is presented for payment. If payment is then made, the debt is discharged; if not paid, the suspension terminates, and suit may be brought on either the debt or the check. Frequently, payment must be made by a specified date. It is generally held that the payment is made on time if it is mailed on or before the final date for payment.

C A S E   S U M M A R Y

The Mailed-Check Payment

FACTS: Thomas Cooper was purchasing land from Peter and Ella Birznieks. Cooper was already in possession of the land but was required to pay the amount owed by January 30; otherwise, he would have to vacate the property. The attorney handling the transaction for the Birznieks told Cooper that he could mail the payment to him. On January 30, Cooper mailed to the attorney a personal check drawn on an out-of-state bank for the amount due. The check arrived at the Birznieks' attorney's office on February 1. The Birznieks refused to accept the check on the grounds that it was not a timely payment and moved to evict Cooper from the property.

DECISION: Because of the general custom to regard a check mailed to a creditor as paying the bill that is owed, payment was made by Cooper on January 30 when he mailed the check. Payment was therefore made within the required time even though received after the expiration of the required time. [**Birznieks v Cooper, 275 NW2d 221 (Mich 1979)**]

4. Time of Performance

When the date or period of time for performance is specified in the contract, performance should be made on that date or within that time period.

---

[4] *Oakes Logging, Inc. v Green Crow, Inc.*, 832 P2d 894 (Wash App 1992).

(A) NO TIME SPECIFIED. When the time for performance is not specified in the contract, an obligation to perform within a reasonable time is implied.[5] The fact that no time is specified neither impairs the contract on the ground that it is indefinite nor allows an endless time in which to perform. What constitutes a reasonable time is determined by the nature of the subject matter of the contract and the facts and circumstances surrounding the making of the contract.

(B) WHEN TIME IS ESSENTIAL. If performance of the contract on or within the exact time specified is vital, it is said that "time is of the essence." Time is of the essence when the contract relates to property that is perishable or that is fluctuating rapidly in value. When a contract fixes by unambiguous language a time for performance and where there is no evidence showing that the parties did not intend that time should be of the essence, failure to perform within the specified time is a breach of contract entitling the innocent party to damages. **For Example,** Dixon and Gandhi agreed that Gandhi would close on the purchase of a motel as follows: "Closing Date. The closing shall be held ... on the date which is within twenty (20) days after the closing of Nomura Financing." Gandhi did not close within the time period specified, and Dixon was allowed to retain $100,000 in prepaid closing costs and fees as liquidated damages for Gandhi's breach of contract.[6]

(C) WHEN TIME IS NOT ESSENTIAL. Unless a contract so provides, time is ordinarily not of the essence, and performance within a reasonable time is sufficient. In the case of the sale of property, time is not regarded as of the essence when there has not been any appreciable change in the market value or condition of the property and when the person who delayed does not appear to have done so for the purpose of speculating on a change in market price.

(D) WAIVER OF ESSENCE OF TIME LIMITATION. A provision that time is of the essence may be waived. It is waived when the specified time has expired but the party who could complain requests the delaying party to take steps necessary to perform the contract.

5. Adequacy of Performance

When a party renders exactly the performance called for by the contract, no question arises as to whether the contract has been performed. In other cases, there may not have been a perfect performance, or a question arises as to whether the performance satisfies the standard set by the contract.

CPA

substantial performance— equitable rule that if a good-faith attempt to perform does not precisely meet the terms of the agreement, the agreement will still be considered complete if the essential purpose of the contract is accomplished.

(A) SUBSTANTIAL PERFORMANCE. Perfect performance of a contract is not always possible when dealing with construction projects. A party who in good faith has provided **substantial performance** of the contract may sue to recover the payment specified in the contract. However, because the performance was not perfect, the performing party is subject to a counterclaim for the damages caused the other party. When a building contractor has substantially performed the contract to construct a building, the contractor is responsible for the cost of repairing or correcting the defects as an offset from the contract price.[7]

[5] *First National Bank v Clark,* 447 SE2d 558 (W Va 1994).
[6] *Woodhull Corp. v Saibaba Corp.,* 507 SE2d 493 (Ga App 1998).
[7] Substantial performance is not a defense to a breach of contract claim, however. See *Bentley Systems Inc. v Intergraph Corp.,* 922 So2d 61 (Ala 2005).

FIGURE 19-1 | *Causes of Contract Discharge*

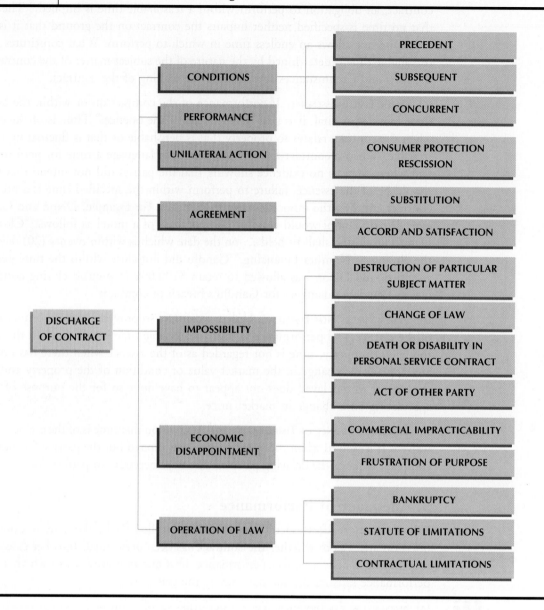

The measure of damages under these circumstances is known as "cost of completion" damages.[8] If, however, the cost of completion would be unreasonably disproportionate to the importance of the defect, the measure of damages is the diminution in value of the building due to the defective performance.

Whether there is substantial performance is a question of degree to be determined by all of the facts, including the particular type of structure involved, its intended purpose, and the nature and relative expense of repairs.

[8] *Hammer Construction Corp. v Phillips*, 994 So2d 1135 (Fla App 2008).

For Example, a certain building contractor (BC) and a certain owner (O) made a contract to construct a home overlooking Vineyard Sound on Martha's Vineyard according to plans and specifications that clearly called for the use of General Plumbing Blue Star piping. The contract price was $1,100,000. Upon inspecting the work before making the final $400,000 payment and accepting the building, O discovered that BC had used Republic piping throughout the house. O explained to BC that his family had made its money by investing in General Plumbing, and he, therefore, would not make the final payment until the breach of contract was remedied. BC explained that Republic pipes were of the same industrial grade and quality as the Blue Star pipes. Moreover, BC estimated that it would cost nearly $300,000 to replace all of the pipes because of the destruction of walls and fixtures necessary to accomplish such a task. BC may sue O for $400,000 for breach of contract, claiming he had substantially performed the contract, and O may counterclaim for $300,000, seeking an offset for the cost of remedying the breach. The court will find in favor of the contractor and will not allow the $300,000 offset but will allow a "nominal" offset of perhaps $100 to $1,000 for the amount by which the Republic pipes diminished the value of the building. [9]

In most jurisdictions, the willfulness of the departure from the specifications of the contract does not by itself preclude some recovery for the contractor on the "cost of completion" basis but rather is a factor in consideration of whether there was substantial performance by the contractor. [10]

CASE SUMMARY

When Perfection is Not Required

FACTS: Beeson Company made a contract to construct a shopping center for Sartori. Before the work was fully completed, Sartori stopped making the payments to Beeson that the contract required. The contract provided for liquidated damages of $1,000 per day if Beeson failed to substantially complete the project within 300 days of the beginning of construction. The contract also provided for a bonus of $1,000 for each day Beeson completed the project ahead of schedule. Beeson then stopped working and sued Sartori for the balance due under the contract, just as though it had been fully performed. Sartori defended on the ground that Beeson had not substantially completed the work. Beeson proved that Sartori had been able to rent most of the stores in the center.

DECISION: The fact that the shopping center could be used for its intended purpose, that of renting stores to others, showed that there had been a substantial performance of the contract. The contractor therefore could recover the contract price less any amount required to complete the construction. **[J.M. Beeson Co. v Sartori, 553 So2d 180 (Fla App 1989)]**

---

[9] See *Jacob & Youngs, Inc. v Kent*, 230 NY 239 (1921).
[10] But see *USX Corp. v M. DeMatteo Construction Co.*, 315 F3d 43 (1st Cir 2002), for application of a common law rule that prohibits a construction contractor guilty of a willful breach of contract from maintaining any suit on the contract against the other party.

(B) FAULT OF COMPLAINING PARTY. A party cannot complain that a performance was defective when the performance follows the terms of the contract required by the complaining party. Thus, a homeowner who supplied the specifications for poured cement walls could not hold a contractor liable for damages when the walls that were poured in exact compliance with those specifications proved defective.

(C) PERFORMANCE TO THE SATISFACTION OF THE CONTRACTING PARTY OR A THIRD PARTY. Sometimes an agreement requires performance to the satisfaction, taste, or judgment of the other party to the contract. When the contract specifically stipulates that the performance must satisfy the contracting party, the courts will ordinarily enforce the plain meaning of the language of the parties and the work must satisfy the contracting party—subject, of course, to the requirement that dissatisfaction be made in good faith. **For Example,** the Perrones' written contract to purchase the Hills' residence contained a clause making performance subject to inspection to the Perrones' satisfaction. During the house inspection, the inspector found a piece of wood in a crawl space that appeared to have been damaged by termites and had possibly been treated some 18 years before with chlordane. At the end of the inspection Mr. Perrone indicated that he would perform on the contract. Thereafter, he went on the Internet and found that chlordane is a highly toxic pesticide now banned from use as a termite treatment. As a result, the Perrones rescinded the contract under the buyer satisfaction clause. The Hills sued, believing that speculation about a pesticide treatment 18 years ago was absurd. They contended that the Perrones had breached the contract without a valid reason. The court decided for the Perrones, since they exercised the "satisfaction clause" in good faith.[11] Good-faith personal satisfaction is generally required when the subject matter of the contract is personal, such as interior design work, tailoring, or the painting of a portrait.

With respect to things mechanical or routine performances, courts require that the performance be such as would satisfy a reasonable person under the circumstances.

When work is to be done subject to the approval of an architect, engineer, or another expert, most courts apply the reasonable person test of satisfaction.

C. DISCHARGE BY ACTION OF PARTIES

Contracts may be discharged by the joint action of both contracting parties or, in some cases, by the action of one party alone.

6. Discharge by Unilateral Action

Ordinarily, a contract cannot be discharged by the action of either party alone. In some cases, however, the contract gives one of either party the right to cancel the

---

[11] *Hill v Perrones,* 42 P3d 210 (Kan App 2002).

contract by unilateral action, such as by notice to the other party. Insurance policies covering loss commonly provide that the insurer may cancel the policy upon giving a specified number of days' notice.

(A) Consumer Protection Rescission. A basic principle of contract law is that once made, a contract between competent persons is a binding obligation. Consumer protection legislation introduces into the law a contrary concept—that of giving the consumer a chance to think things over and to rescind the contract. Thus, the federal Consumer Credit Protection Act (CCPA) gives the debtor the right to rescind a credit transaction within three business days when the transaction would impose a lien on the debtor's home. **For Example,** a homeowner who mortgages his or her home to obtain a loan may cancel the transaction for any reason by notifying the lender before midnight of the third full business day after the loan is made.[12]

A Federal Trade Commission regulation gives the buyer three business days in which to cancel a home-solicited sale of goods or services costing more than $25.[13]

7. Discharge by Agreement

A contract may be discharged by the operation of one of its provisions or by a subsequent agreement. Thus, there may be a discharge by (1) the terms of the original contract, such as a provision that the contract should end on a specified date; (2) a mutual cancellation, in which the parties agree to end their contract; (3) a mutual **rescission**, in which the parties agree to annul the contract and return both parties to their original positions before the contract had been made; (4) the **substitution** of a new contract between the same parties; (5) a novation or substitution of a new contract involving a new party;[14] (6) an **accord and satisfaction**; (7) a release; or (8) a **waiver**.

(A) Substitution. The parties may decide that their contract is not the one they want. They may then replace it with another contract. If they do, the original contract is discharged by substitution.[15]

(B) Accord and Satisfaction. When the parties have differing views as to the performance required by the terms of a contract, they may agree to a different performance. Such an agreement is called an *accord*. When the accord is performed or executed, there is an accord and satisfaction, which discharges the original obligation. To constitute an accord and satisfaction, there must be a bona fide dispute, a proposal to settle the dispute, and performance of the agreement.

rescission–action of one party to a contract to set the contract aside when the other party is guilty of a breach of the contract.

substitution–substitution of a new contract between the same parties.

accord and satisfaction–agreement to substitute for an existing debt some alternative form of discharging that debt, coupled with the actual discharge of the debt by the substituted performance.

waiver–release or relinquishment of a known right or objection.

---

[12] If the owner is not informed of this right to cancel, the three-day period does not begin until that information is given. Consumer Credit Protection Act § 125, 15 USC § 1635(a), (e), (f).

[13] CFR § 429.1. This displaces state laws making similar provisions for rescission, such as UCCC § 2.502.

[14] *Eagle Industries, Inc. v Thompson*, 900 P2d 475 (Or 1995). In a few jurisdictions, the term *novation* is used to embrace the substitution of any new contract, whether between the original parties or not.

[15] *Shawnee Hospital Authority v Dow Construction, Inc.*, 812 P2d 1351 (Okla 1990).

CASE SUMMARY

A Full Court Press to No Avail

FACTS: In September 2002, La Crosse Litho Supply, LLC (La Crosse) entered into a distribution agreement with MKL Pre-Press Electronics (MKL) for the distribution of a printing system. La Crosse purchased a 7000 System unit from MKL for its end user Printing Plus. MKL technicians were to provide service and training for the unit. The 7000 System at Printing Plus failed on three occasions, and ultimately repairs were unsuccessful. On September 30, 2003, La Crosse cancelled the distribution agreement. On October 2, 2003, La Crosse sent a letter to MKL's sales vice president Bill Landwer setting forth an itemized accounting of what it owed MKL Pre-Press with deductions for the purchase price of the failed 7000 System and other offsets. MKL sent a subsequent bill for repairs and services, to which La Crosse objected and stated that it would not pay. MKL's attorney sent a demand letter for $26,453.31. La Crosse's president, Randall Peters, responded by letter dated December 30, 2003, explaining that with an offset for training and warranty work it had performed, "we are sending you the final payment in the amount of $1,696.47." He added, "[w]ith this correspondence, we consider all open issues between La Crosse Litho Supply and MKL Pre-Press closed." Enclosed with the letter was a check for $1,696.47 payable to MKL Pre-Press. In the remittance portion of the check, under the heading "Ref," was typed "FINAL PAYM." The check was endorsed and deposited on either January 26 or 27, 2004. MKL sued La Crosse for $24,756.84. La Crosse defended that the tender and subsequent deposit of the check for $1,696.47 constituted an accord and satisfaction. Jill Fleming, MKL's office manager, stated that it was her duty to process checks and that she did not read Peters' letter. From a judgment for La Crosse, MKL appealed.

DECISION: Judgment for La Crosse. There was an honest dispute as to the amount owed, as evident from the exchange of letters. La Crosse tendered an amount with the explicit understanding that it was the "final payment" of all demands, and the creditor MKL's acceptance and negotiation of a check for that amount constitutes an accord and satisfaction. Ms. Fleming had the authority to endorse checks and deposit them, and her doing so can and should be imputed to her employer, thereby constituting an accord and satisfaction. [**MKL Pre-Press Electronics v La Crosse Litho Supply, LLC, 840 NE2d 687 (Ill App 2005)**]

D. DISCHARGE BY EXTERNAL CAUSES

Circumstances beyond the control of the contracting parties may discharge the contract.

8. Discharge by Impossibility

To establish impossibility a party must show (1) the unexpected occurrence of an intervening act; (2) that the risk of the unexpected occurrence was not allocated by agreement or custom; and (3) that the occurrence made performance impossible. The doctrine of impossibility relieves nonperformance only in extreme circumstances.[16] The party asserting the defense of impossibility bears the burden of proving "a real impossibility and not a mere inconvenience or unexpected difficulty."[17] Moreover, courts will generally only excuse nonperformance where

---

[16] *Island Development Corp. v District of Columbia*, 933 A2d 340, 350 (DC 2007).
[17] *Bergmann v Parker*, 216 A2d 581 (DC 1966).

performance is objectively impossible—that is, incapable performance by anyone. Financial inability to perform a contract that a party voluntarily entered into will rarely, if ever, excuse nonperformance. **For Example,** Ms. Robinson was employed by East Capital Community Development Group under a written employment contract for one year, but was terminated early for lack of funding. The contract did not reference that her continued employment was contingent on continued grant funding. The contract was objectively capable of performance. The defense of impossibility was rejected by the court.[18]

(A) Destruction of Particular Subject Matter. When parties contract expressly for, or with reference to, a particular subject matter, the contract is discharged if the subject matter is destroyed through no fault of either party. When a contract calls for the sale of a wheat crop growing on a specific parcel of land, the contract is discharged if that crop is destroyed by blight.

On the other hand, if there is merely a contract to sell a given quantity of a specified grade of wheat, the seller is not discharged when the seller's crop is destroyed by blight. The seller had made an unqualified undertaking to deliver wheat of a specified grade. No restrictions or qualifications were imposed as to the source. If the seller does not deliver the goods called for by the contract, the contract is broken, and the seller is liable for damages.

(B) Change of Law. A contract is discharged when its performance is made illegal by a subsequent change in the law. Thus, a contract to construct a nonfireproof building at a particular place is discharged by the adoption of a zoning law prohibiting such a building within that area. Mere inconvenience or temporary delay caused by the new law, however, does not excuse performance.

(C) Death or Disability. When the contract obligates a party to render or receive personal services requiring peculiar skill, the death, incapacity, or illness of the party that was either to render or receive the personal services excuses both sides from a duty to perform. It is sometimes said that "the death of either party is the death of the contract."

The rule does not apply, however, when the acts called for by the contract are of such a character that (1) the acts may be as well performed by others, such as the promisor's personal representatives, or (2) the contract's terms contemplate continuance of the obligations after the death of one of the parties. **For Example,** Lynn Jones was under contract to investor Ed Jenkins to operate certain Subway sandwich shops and to acquire new franchises with funding provided by Jenkins. After Jenkins's death, Jones claimed he was no longer bound under the contract and was free to pursue franchise opportunities on his own. The contract between Jones and Jenkins expressed that it was binding on the parties' "heirs and assigns" and that the contract embodied property rights that passed to Jenkins's widow. The agreement's provisions thus established that the agreement survived the death of Jenkins, and Jones was therefore obligated to remit profits from the franchise he acquired for himself after Jenkins's death.[19]

(D) Act of Other Party. Every contract contains "an implied covenant of good faith and fair dealing." As a result of this covenant, a promisee is under an obligation to

[18] *East Capital View Community Development Corp. v Robinson,* 941 A2d 1036 (DC 2008).
[19] *Jenkins Subway, Inc. v Jones,* 990 SW2d 713 (Tenn App 1998).

do nothing that would interfere with the promisor's performance. When the promisee prevents performance or otherwise makes performance impossible, the promisor is discharged from the contract. Thus, a subcontractor is discharged from any obligation when it is unable to do the work because the principal contractor refuses to deliver the material, equipment, or money required by the subcontract. When the default of the other party consists of failing to supply goods or services, the duty may rest on the party claiming a discharge of the contract to show that substitute goods or services could not be obtained elsewhere.

9. Developing Doctrines

Commercial impracticability and frustration of purpose may excuse performance.

(A) **COMMERCIAL IMPRACTICABILITY.** The doctrine of *commercial impracticability* was developed to deal with the harsh rule that a party must perform its contracts unless it is absolutely impossible. However, not every type of impracticability is an excuse for nonperformance. **For Example,** I. Patel was bound by his franchise agreement with Days Inn, Inc., to maintain his 60- room inn on old Route 66 in Lincoln, Illinois, to at least minimum quality assurance standards. His inn failed five consecutive quality inspections over two years, with the inspector noting damaged guest rooms, burns in the bedding, and severely stained carpets. Patel's defense when his franchise was cancelled after the fifth failed inspection was that bridge repairs on the road leading from I-55 to his inn had adversely affected his business and made it commercially impractical to live up to the franchise agreement. The court rejected his defense, determining that while the bridge work might have affected patronage, it had no effect on his duty to comply with the quality assurance standards of his franchise a greement.[20] Commercial impracticability is available only when the performance is made impractical by the subsequent occurrence of an event whose nonoccurrence was a basic assumption on which the contract was made.[21]

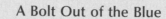

C A S E   S U M M A R Y

A Bolt Out of the Blue

FACTS: CIT, a major equipment leasing company, entered into a sale/leaseback contract with Condere Tire Corporation for 11 tire presses at Condere's tire plant in Natchez, Mississippi. Condere ceased making payments on these presses owned by CIT, and Condere filed for Chapter 11 bankruptcy. CIT thereafter contracted to sell the presses to Specialty Tires, Inc., for $250,000. When the contract was made, CIT, Condere, and Specialty Tires believed that CIT was the owner of the presses and was entitled to immediate possession. When CIT attempted to gain access to the presses to have them shipped, Condere changed its position and refused to allow the equipment to be removed from the plant. When the presses were not delivered, Specialty sued CIT for damages for nondelivery of the presses to date, and CIT asserted the defense of impracticability.

---

[20] *Days Inn of America, Inc. v Patel,* 88 F Supp 2d 928 (CD Ill 2000).
[21] See Restatement (Second) of Contracts § 261; UCC § 2-615.

C A S E   S U M M A R Y

Continued

DECISION: Summary judgment for CIT. The delivery of the presses to Specialty Tires Company was made impracticable by the actions of Condere in refusing to give up the presses. Condere's change of its position and refusal to give up the presses was "a bolt out of the blue" for both CIT and Specialty. It was not a risk that CIT should have expected to either bear or contract against. CIT is excused by the doctrine of impracticability from damages for nondelivery of the presses to date. The impracticability relieves the obligation for only so long as the impracticability lasts. CIT asserts it will perform when it receives possession of the presses. [**Specialty Tires, Inc. v CIT, 82 F Supp 2d 434 (WD Pa 2000)**]

If a subsequent event occurs involving a severe shortage of raw materials or supplies that results in a marked increase in the cost of the materials or supplies and this event was foreseeable, the defense of commercial impracticability is not available.

(B) Frustration of Purpose Doctrine. Because of a change in circumstances, the purpose of the contract may have no value to the party entitled to receive performance. In such a case, performance may be excused if both parties were aware of the purpose and the event that frustrated the purpose was unforeseeable.[22]

For Example, National Southern Bank rents a home near Willowbend Country Club on the southeastern shore of North Carolina for $75,000 a week to entertain business guests at the Ryder Cup matches scheduled for the week in question. Storm damage from Hurricane David the week before the event caused the closing of the course and the transfer of the tournament to another venue in a different state. The bank's duty to pay for the house may be excused by the doctrine of *frustration of purpose,* because the transfer of the tournament fully destroyed the value of the home rental, both parties were aware of the purpose of the rental, and the cancellation of the golf tournament was unforeseeable.

C A S E   S U M M A R Y

Relief for Broken Dreams

FACTS: John J. Paonessa Company made a contract with the state of Massachusetts to reconstruct a portion of highway. Paonessa then made a contract with Chase Precast Corporation to obtain concrete median barriers for use in the highway. Thereafter, the state highway department decided that such barriers would not be used. Paonessa therefore had no reason to go through with the contract to purchase the barriers from Chase because it could not

---

[22] The defense of frustration of purpose, or commercial frustration, is very difficult to invoke because the courts are extremely reluctant to allow parties to avoid obligations to which they have agreed. See *Wal-Mart Stores, Inc. v AIG Life Insurance Co.,* 872 A2d 611 (Del Ch 2005), denying application of the commercial frustration doctrine when the supervening event, the invalidation of hundreds of millions in tax deductions by the IRS, was reasonably foreseeable and could have been provided for in the contract.

CASE SUMMARY

Continued

use them and could not get paid for them by the state. Chase sued Paonessa for the profit Chase would have made on the contract for the barriers.

DECISION: Judgment for Paonessa. The change to the highway construction plan made by the State Department of Highways made the barriers worthless. There was accordingly a frustration of the purpose for which the contract had been made to purchase the barriers. Therefore, the contract for the median barriers was discharged by such frustration of purpose and did not bind Paonessa. [**Chase Precast Corp. v John J. Paonessa Co., Inc. 566 NE2d 603 (Mass 1991)**]

(c) **COMPARISON TO COMMON LAW RULE.** The traditional common law rule refuses to recognize commercial impracticability or frustration of purpose. By the common law rule, the losses and disappointments against which commercial impracticability and frustration of purpose give protection are merely the risks that one takes in entering into a contract. Moreover, the situations could have been guarded against by including an appropriate condition subsequent in the contract. A condition subsequent declares that the contract will be void if a specified event occurs.[23] The contract also could have provided for a readjustment of compensation if there was a basic change of circumstances. The common law approach also rejects these developing concepts because they weaken the stability of a contract.

An indication of a wider recognition of the concept that "extreme" changes of circumstances can discharge a contract is found in the Uniform Commercial Code. The UCC provides for the discharge of a contract for the sale of goods when a condition that the parties assumed existed, or would continue, ceases to exist.[24]

(d) **FORCE MAJEURE.** To avoid litigation over impossibility and impractability issues, modern contracting parties often contract around the doctrine of impossibility, specifying the failures that will excuse performance in their contracts. The clauses in which they do this are called *force majeure*—uncontrollable event—clauses. And they are enforced by courts as written.

CASE SUMMARY

WEPCO Was Not Railroaded, It Was *Force Majeured!*

FACTS: WEPCO, an electric utility, sued the Union Pacific Railroad Co. alleging that the railroad breached the *force majeure* provision of the parties' long-term coal-hauling contract, which ran from 1999 to 2005. The provision at issue provides that if the railroad is prevented by "an event of Force Majeure" from reloading its empty cars (after it has delivered coal to WEPCO) with iron ore destined for Geneva, Utah, it can charge the higher

---

[23] *Wermer v ABI,* 10 SW3d 575 (Mo App 2000).
[24] UCC § 2-615.

C A S E   S U M M A R Y

Continued

rate that the contract makes applicable to shipments that do not involve backhauling. The rate for coal shipped from one of the Colorado coal mines to WEPCO was specified as $13.20 per ton if there was a backhaul shipment but $15.63 if there was not. The iron ore that the railroad's freight trains would have picked up in Minnesota was intended for a steel mill in Utah. The steel company was bankrupt when the parties signed the contract. In November 2001 the steel mill shut down, and closed for good in February 2004. Two months later the railroad wrote WEPCO to declare "an event of Force Majeure" and that henceforth it would be charging WEPCO the higher rate applicable to shipments without a backhaul. WEPCO sued the railroad for breach of the force majeure provision in the contract.

DECISION: Judgment for the railroad. The provision dealt with the foreseeable situation of the steel mill shutdown and the possibility of hauling back to the mine empty coal cars, thereby generating no revenue. The contract clause is enforced as written. [**Wisconsin Electric Power Co. v Union Pacific Railroad Co., 557 F3d 504 (7th Cir 2009)**]

10. Temporary Impossibility

Ordinarily, a temporary impossibility suspends the duty to perform. If the obligation to perform is suspended, it is revived on the termination of the impossibility. If, however, performance at that later date would impose a substantially greater burden on the party obligated to perform, some courts discharge the obligor from the contract.

After the September 11, 2001, terrorist attack on the World Trade Center, New York City courts followed wartime precedents that had developed the law of temporary impossibility. Such impossibility, when of brief duration, excuses performance until it subsequently becomes possible to perform rather than excusing performance altogether. Thus, an individual who was unable to communicate her cancellation of travel 60 days prior to her scheduled travel as required by her contract, which needed to occur on or before September 14, 2001, could expect relief from a cancellation penalty provision in the contract based on credible testimony of attempted phone calls to the travel agent on and after September 12, 2001, even though the calls did not get through due to communication problems in New York City.[25]

(A) **WEATHER.** Acts of God, such as tornadoes, lightning, and floods, usually do not terminate a contract even though they make performance difficult. Thus, weather conditions constitute a risk that is assumed by a contracting party in the absence of a contrary agreement. Consequently, extra expense sustained by a contractor because of weather conditions is a risk that the contractor assumes in the absence of an express provision for additional compensation in such a case. **For Example,** Danielo Contractors made a contract to construct a shopping mall for the Rubicon Center, with construction to begin November 1. Because of abnormal cold and blizzard

[25] See *Bugh v Protravel International, Inc.,* 746 NYS2d 290 (Civ Ct NYC 2002).

conditions, Danielo was not able to begin work until April 1 and was five months late in completing the construction of the project. Rubicon sued Danielo for breach of contract by failing to perform on schedule. Danielo is liable. Because the contract included no provision covering delay caused by weather, Danielo bore the risk of the delay and resulting loss.

Modern contracts commonly contain a "weather clause" and reflect the parties' agreement on this matter. When the parties take the time to discuss weather issues, purchasing insurance coverage is a common resolution.

11. Discharge by Operation of Law

operation of law – attaching of certain consequences to certain facts because of legal principles that operate automatically as contrasted with consequences that arise because of the voluntary action of a party designed to create those consequences.

A contract is discharged by **operation of law** by (1) an alteration or a material change made by a party, (2) the destruction of the written contract with intent to discharge it, (3) bankruptcy, (4) the operation of a statute of limitations, or (5) a contractual limitation.

(A) BANKRUPTCY. As set forth in the chapter on bankruptcy, even though all creditors have not been paid in full, a discharge in **bankruptcy** eliminates ordinary contract claims against the debtor.

CPA

bankruptcy – procedure by which one unable to pay debts may surrender all assets in excess of any exemption claim to the court for administration and distribution to creditors, and the debtor is given a discharge that releases him from the unpaid balance due on most debts.

(B) STATUTE OF LIMITATIONS. A **statute of limitations** provides that after a certain number of years have passed, a contract claim is barred. The time limitation provided by state statutes of limitations varies widely. The time period for bringing actions for breach of an oral contract is two to three years. The period may differ with the type of contract—ranging from a relatively short time for open accounts (ordinary customers' charge accounts) to four years for sales of goods.[26] A somewhat longer period exists for bringing actions for breach of written contracts (usually four to ten years). **For Example,** Prate Installations, Inc., sued homeowners Richard and Rebecca Thomas for failure to pay for a new roof installed by Prate. Prate had sent numerous invoices to the Thomases over a four-year period seeking payment to no avail. The Thomases moved to dismiss the case under a four-year limitation period. However, the court concluded that the state's ten-year limitations period on written contracts applied.[27] The maximum period for judgments of record is usually 10 to 20 years.

statute of limitations – statute that restricts the period of time within which an action may be brought.

(C) CONTRACTUAL LIMITATIONS. Some contracts, particularly insurance contracts, contain a time limitation within which suit must be brought. This is in effect a private statute of limitations created by the agreement of the parties.

A contract may also require that notice of any claim be given within a specified time. A party who fails to give notice within the time specified by the contract is barred from suing on the contract.

A contract provision requiring that suit be brought within one year does not violate public policy, although the statute of limitations would allow two years in the absence of such a contract limitation.[28]

---

[26] UCC § 2-725(1).
[27] *Prate Installations, Inc. v Thomas*, 842 NE2d 1205 (Ill App 2006).
[28] *Keiting v Skauge*, 543 NW2d 565 (Wis App 1995).

lawflix

Uncle Buck (1989) (PG-13)

John Candy plays ne'er-do-well Uncle Buck who promises to go to work at his girlfriend's tire store and marry her. When his brother calls in the middle of the night seeking help with his children, Buck tells his girlfriend (Chenise) that he can no longer honor his promise because he must go to the suburbs to care for his brother's children while his brother and sister-in-law travel to Indiana to be with his sister-in-law's very ill father.

Discuss Buck's excuse. Is it impossibility? Does the change in circumstances excuse Buck?

Check out LawFlix at **www.cengage.com/blaw/dvl** to access movie clips that illustrate business law concepts.

MAKE THE CONNECTION

SUMMARY

A party's duty to perform under a contract can be affected by a condition precedent, which must occur before a party has an obligation to perform; a condition subsequent, that is, a condition or event that relieves the duty to thereafter perform; and concurrent conditions, which require mutual and often simultaneous performance.

Most contracts are discharged by performance. An offer to perform is called a *tender of performance*. If a tender of performance is wrongfully refused, the duty of the tenderer to perform is terminated. When the performance called for by the contract is the payment of money, it must be legal tender that is offered. In actual practice, it is common to pay and to accept payment by checks or other commercial paper.

When the debtor owes the creditor on several accounts and makes a payment, the debtor may specify which account is to be credited with the payment. If the debtor fails to specify, the creditor may choose which account to credit.

When a contract does not state when it is to be performed, it must be performed within a reasonable time. If time for performance is stated in the contract, the contract must be performed at the time specified if such time is essential (is of the essence). Ordinarily, a contract must be performed exactly in the manner specified by the contract. A less-than-perfect performance is allowed if it is a substantial performance and if damages are allowed the other party.

A contract cannot be discharged by unilateral action unless authorized by the contract itself or by statute, as in the case of consumer protection rescission.

Because a contract arises from an agreement, it may also be terminated by an agreement. A contract may also be discharged by the substitution of a new contract for the original contract; by a novation, or making a new contract with a new party; by accord and satisfaction; by release; or by waiver.

A contract is discharged when it is impossible to perform. Impossibility may result from the destruction of the subject matter of the contract, the adoption of a new law that prohibits performance, the death or disability of a party whose personal action was required for performance of the contract, or the act of the other party to the contract. Some courts will also hold that a contract is discharged when its performance is commercially impracticable or there is frustration of purpose. Temporary impossibility, such as a labor strike or bad weather, has no effect on a contract. It is common, though, to include protective clauses that excuse delay caused by temporary impossibility.

A contract may be discharged by operation of law. This occurs when (1) the liability arising from the contract is discharged by bankruptcy, (2) suit on the contract is barred by the applicable statute of limitations, or (3) a time limitation stated in the contract is exceeded.

LEARNING OUTCOMES

After studying this chapter, you should be able to clearly explain:

A. CONDITIONS RELATING TO PERFORMANCE

LO.1 List the three types of conditions that affect a party's duty to perform
See the "pay-if-paid" condition-precedent example on p. 411.
See the TV anchor's "failed urinalysis test" condition-subsequent example on p. 412.

B. DISCHARGE BY PERFORMANCE

LO.2 Explain the on-time performance rule
See the "mailed payment" example on p. 414.
See the "time is of the essence" example on p. 415.

C. DISCHARGE BY ACTION OF PARTIES

LO.3 Explain four ways a contract can be discharged by agreement of the parties
See the text discussion on recession, cancellation, substitution, and novation on p. 419.

D. DISCHARGE BY EXTERNAL CAUSES

LO.4 State the effect on a contract of the death or disability of one of the contracting parties
See the Subway Sandwich Shops example on p. 421.

LO.5 Explain when impossibility or impracticability may discharge a contract
See the *Specialty Tire* impracticability case on p. 422.
See the Ryder Cup frustration-of-purpose example on p. 423.

KEY TERMS

accord and satisfaction   operation of law   tender
bankruptcy   rescission   waiver
condition precedent   statute of limitations
condition subsequent   substantial performance
condition   substitution

QUESTIONS AND CASE PROBLEMS

1. McMullen Contractors made a contract with Richardson to build an apartment house for a specific price. A number of serious apartment house fires broke out in the city, and the city council adopted an ordinance increasing the fire precautions that had to be taken in the construction of a new building. Compliance with these new requirements would make the construction of the apartment house for Richardson more expensive than McMullen had originally contemplated. Is McMullen discharged from the contract to build the apartment house?

2. Lymon Mitchell operated a Badcock Home Furnishings dealership, under which as dealer he was paid a commission on sales and Badcock retained title to merchandise on display. Mitchell sold his dealership to another and to facilitate the sale, Badcock prepared a summary of commissions owed with certain itemized offsets it claimed that Mitchell owed Badcock. Mitchell disagreed with the calculations, but he accepted them and signed the transfer documents closing the sale on the basis of the terms set forth in the summary and was paid accordingly. After pondering the offsets taken by Badcock and verifying the correctness of his position, he brought suit for the additional funds owed. What defense would you expect Badcock to raise? How would you decide the case? Explain fully. [*Mitchell v Badcock Corp.,* 496 SE2d 502 (Ga App)]

3. American Bank loaned Koplik $50,000 to buy equipment for a restaurant about to be opened by Casual Citchen Corp. The loan was not repaid, and Fast Foods, Inc., bought out the interest of Casual Citchen. As part of the transaction, Fast Foods agreed to pay the debt owed to American Bank, and the parties agreed to a new schedule of payments to be made by Fast Foods. Fast Foods did not make the payments, and American Bank sued Koplik. He contended that his obligation to repay $50,000 had been discharged by the execution of the agreement providing for the payment of the debt by Fast Foods. Was this defense valid? [*American Bank & Trust Co. v Koplik,* 451 NYS2d 426 (App Div)]

4. Metalcrafters made a contract to design a new earth-moving vehicle for Lamar Highway Construction Co. Metalcrafters was depending on the genius of Samet, the head of its research department, to design a new product. Shortly after the contract was made between Metalcrafters and Lamar, Samet was killed in an automobile accident. Metalcrafters was not able to design the product without Samet. Lamar sued Metalcrafters for damages for breach of the contract. Metalcrafters claimed that the contract was discharged by Samet's death. Is it correct?

5. The Tinchers signed a contract to sell land to Creasy. The contract specified that the sales transaction was to be completed in 90 days. At the end of the 90 days, Creasy requested an extension of time. The Tinchers refused to grant an extension and stated that the contract was terminated. Creasy claimed that the 90-day clause was not binding because the contract did not state that time was of the essence. Was the contract terminated? [*Creasy v Tincher,* 173 SE2d 332 (W Va)]

6. Christopher Bloom received a medical school scholarship created by the U.S. Department of Health and Human Services to increase the number of doctors serving rural areas. In return for this assistance, Bloom agreed to practice four years in a region identified as being underserved by medical professionals. After some problem with his postgraduation assignment, Bloom requested a repayment schedule from the agency. Although no terms were offered, Bloom tendered to the agency two checks totaling $15,500 and marked "Final Payment." Neither check was cashed, and the government sued Bloom for $480,000, the value of the assistance provided. Bloom claimed that by tendering the checks to the agency, his liability had been discharged by an accord and satisfaction. Decide. [*United States v Bloom,* 112 F3d 200 (7th Cir)]

7. Dickson contracted to build a house for Moran. When it was approximately 25 percent to 40 percent completed, Moran would not let Dickson work any more because he was not following the building plans and specifications and there were many defects. Moran hired another contractor to correct the defects and finish the building. Dickson sued Moran for breach of contract, claiming that he had substantially performed the contract up to the point where he had been discharged. Was Dickson correct? [*Dickson v Moran,* 344 So2d 102 (La App)]

8. A lessor leased a trailer park to a tenant. At the time, sewage was disposed of by a septic tank system that was not connected with the public sewage system. The tenant knew this, and the lease declared that the tenant had examined the premises and that the landlord made no representation or guarantee as to the condition of the premises. Some time thereafter, the septic tank system stopped working properly, and the county health department notified the tenant that he was required to connect the septic tank system with the public sewage system or else the department would close the trailer park. The tenant did not want to pay the additional cost involved in connecting with the public system. The tenant claimed that he was released from the lease and was entitled to a refund of the deposit that he had made. Was he correct? [*Glen R. Sewell Street Metal v Loverde,* 451 P2d 721 (Cal App)]

9. Oneal was a teacher employed by the Colton Consolidated School District. Because of a diabetic condition, his eyesight deteriorated so much that he offered to resign if he would be given pay for a specified number of "sick leave" days. The school district refused to do this and discharged Oneal for nonperformance of his contract. He appealed to remove the discharge from his record. Decide. What ethical values are involved? [*Oneal v Colton Consolidated School District,* 557 P2d 11 (Wash App)]

10. Northwest Construction, Inc., made a contract with the state of Washington for highway construction. Part of the work was turned over under a subcontract to

Yakima Asphalt Paving Co. The contract required that any claim be asserted within 180 days. Yakima brought an action for damages after the expiration of 180 days. The defense was that the claim was too late. Yakima replied that the action was brought within the time allowed by the statute of limitations and that the contractual limitation of 180 days was therefore not binding. Was Yakima correct?

11. The Metropolitan Park District of Tacoma gave Griffith a concession to run the district's parks. The agreement gave the right to occupy the parks and use any improvements found therein. The district later wished to set this agreement aside because it was not making sufficient money from the transaction. While it was seeking to set the agreement aside, a boathouse and a gift shop in one of the parks were destroyed by fire. The district then claimed that the concession contract with Griffith was discharged by impossibility of performance. Was it correct? [*Metropolitan Park District of Tacoma v Griffith,* 723 P2d 1093 (Wash)]

12. Suburban Power Piping Corp., under contract to construct a building for LTV Steel Corp., made a subcontract with Power & Pollution Services, Inc., to do some of the work. The subcontract provided that the subcontractor would be paid when the owner (LTV) paid the contractor. LTV went into bankruptcy before making the full payment to the contractor, who then refused to pay the subcontractor on the ground that the "pay-when-paid" provision of the subcontract made payment by the owner a condition precedent to the obligation of the contractor to pay the subcontractor. Was the contractor correct? [*Power & Pollution Services, Inc. v Suburban Power Piping Corp.,* 598 NE2d 69 (Ohio App)]

13. Ellen borrowed money from Farmers' Bank. As evidence of the loan, she signed a promissory note by which she promised to pay to the bank in installments the amount of the loan together with interest and administrative costs. She was unable to make the payments on the scheduled dates. She and the bank then executed a new agreement that gave her a longer period of time for making the payments. However, after two months, she was unable to pay on this new schedule. The bank then brought suit against her under the terms of the original agreement. She raised the defense that the original agreement had been discharged by the execution of the second agreement and could not be sued on. Decide.

14. Acme Hydraulic Press Co. manufactured large presses and sold them throughout the United States. The agreement-of-sale contract that Acme executed with its customers specified that they could make no claim for breach of contract unless notice of the breach was given within 10 days after the delivery of a press in question to the buyer and that no lawsuit could thereafter be brought if notice had not been given. Was this time limitation valid?

15. New Beginnings provides rehabilitation services for alcohol and drug abuse to both adults and adolescents. New Beginnings entered into negotiation with Adbar for the lease of a building in the city of St. Louis, and subsequently entered into a three-year lease. The total rent due for the three-year term was $273,000. After the lease was executed, the city denied an occupancy permit because Alderman Bosley and residents testified at a hearing in vigorous opposition to the presence

of New Beginnings in the neighborhood. A court ordered the permit issued. Alderman Bosley thereafter contacted the chair of the state's appointment committee and asked her to pull the agency's funding. He received no commitment from her on this matter. After a meeting with the state director of Alcohol and Drug Abuse where it was asserted that the director said the funding would be pulled if New Beginnings moved into the Adbar location, New Beginnings's board decided not to occupy the building. Adbar brought suit for breach of the lease, and New Beginnings asserted it was excused from performance because of commercial impracticability and frustration of purpose. Do you believe the doctrine of commercial impracticability should be limited in its application so as to preserve the certainty of contracts? What rule of law applies to this case? Decide. [*Adbar v New Beginnings*, 103 SW2d 799 (Mo App)]

CPA QUESTIONS

1. Parc hired Glaze to remodel and furnish an office suite. Glaze submitted plans that Parc approved. After completing all the necessary construction and painting, Glaze purchased minor accessories that Parc rejected because they did not conform to the plans. Parc refused to allow Glaze to complete the project and refused to pay Glaze any part of the contract price. Glaze sued for the value of the work performed. Which of the following statements is correct?

   a. Glaze will lose because Glaze breached the contract by not completing performance.

   b. Glaze will win because Glaze substantially performed and Parc prevented complete performance.

   c. Glaze will lose because Glaze materially breached the contract by buying the accessories.

   d. Glaze will win because Parc committed anticipatory breach.

2. Ordinarily, in an action for breach of a construction contract, the statute of limitations time period would be computed from the date the contract is:

   a. Negotiated

   b. Breached

   c. Begun

   d. Signed

3. Which of the following will release all original parties to a contract but will maintain a contractual relationship?

	Novation	Substituted contract
a.	Yes	Yes
b.	Yes	No
c.	No	Yes
d.	No	No

Chapter 20

BREACH OF CONTRACT AND REMEDIES

A. What Constitutes a Breach of Contract?

  1. DEFINITION OF BREACH

  2. ANTICIPATORY BREACH

B. Waiver of Breach

  3. CURE OF BREACH BY WAIVER

  4. EXISTENCE AND SCOPE OF WAIVER

  5. RESERVATION OF RIGHTS

C. Remedies for Breach of Contract

  6. REMEDIES UPON ANTICIPATORY REPUDIATION

  7. REMEDIES IN GENERAL AND THE MEASURE OF DAMAGES

  8. MONETARY DAMAGES

  9. RESCISSION

  10. ACTION FOR SPECIFIC PERFORMANCE

  11. ACTION FOR AN INJUNCTION

  12. REFORMATION OF CONTRACT BY A COURT

D. Contract Provisions Affecting Remedies and Damages

  13. LIMITATION OF REMEDIES

  14. LIQUIDATED DAMAGES

  15. ATTORNEYS' FEES

  16. LIMITATION OF LIABILITY CLAUSES

W

hat can be done when a contract is broken?

A. WHAT CONSTITUTES A BREACH OF CONTRACT?

The question of remedies does not become important until it is first determined that a contract has been violated or breached.

1. Definition of Breach

breach–failure to act or perform in the manner called for in a contract.

A **breach** is the failure to act or perform in the manner called for by the contract. When the contract calls for performance, such as painting an owner's home, the failure to paint or to paint properly is a *breach of contract*. If the contract calls for a creditor's forbearance, the creditor's action in bringing a lawsuit is a breach of the contract.

2. Anticipatory Breach

When the contract calls for performance, a party may make it clear before the time for performance arrives that the contract will not be performed. This is referred to as an **anticipatory breach**.

anticipatory breach– promisor's repudiation of the contract prior to the time that performance is required when such repudiation is accepted by the promisee as a breach of the contract.

anticipatory repudiation– repudiation made in advance of the time for performance of the contract obligations.

(A) ANTICIPATORY REPUDIATION. When a party expressly declares that performance will not be made when required, this declaration is called an **anticipatory repudiation** of the contract. To constitute such a repudiation, there must be a clear, absolute, unequivocal refusal to perform the contract according to its terms. **For Example,** Procter & Gamble (P&G) sought payment on four letters of credit issued by a Serbian bank, Investbanka. P&G presented two letters by June 8, prior to their expiration dates, with the necessary documentation for payment to Beogradska Bank New York, Investbanka's New York agent. A June 11 letter from Beogradska Bank broadly and unequivocally stated that the bank would not pay the letters of credit. Two additional letters of credit totaling $20,000 issued by Investbanka that expired by June 30 were not thereafter submitted to the New York agent bank by P&G. However, a court found that the bank had anticipatorily breached its obligations under those letters of credit by its broad renouncements in the June 11 letter, and judgments were rendered in favor of P&G.[1]

C A S E   S U M M A R Y

Splitting Tips—Contract Price Less Cost of Completion

FACTS: Hartland Developers, Inc., agreed to build an airplane hangar for Robert Tips of San Antonio for $300,000, payable in three installments of $100,000, with the final payment due upon the completion of the building and the issuance of a certificate of completion by the engineer representing Tips. The evidence shows

---

[1] *Procter & Gamble v Investbanka*, 2000 WL 520630 (SDNY 2000).

CASE   SUMMARY

Continued

that Tips's representative, Mr. Lavelle, instructed Hartland to cease work on the building because Tips could no longer afford to make payments. Hartland ceased work as instructed before the final completion of the building, having been paid $200,000 at the time. He sued Tips for breach of contract. On May 6, 1996, the trial court allowed Hartland the amount owing on the contract, $100,000, less the cost of completing the building according to the contract, $65,000, plus attorney fees and prejudgment interest. Tips appealed, pointing out, among other assertions, that he was required to spend $23,000 to provide electrical outlets for the hangar, which were contemplated in the contract.

DECISION: Judgment for Tips, subject to offsets. The trial judge based his damages assessment on anticipatory repudiation of contract. The evidence that Tips's representative, Lavelle, instructed Hartland to cease work on the project because Tips no longer could afford to make payments was sufficient to support this finding. However, Tips is entitled to an offset for electrical connections of $23,000 under a breach of contract theory. [**Tips v Hartland Developers, Inc., 961 SW2d 618 (Tex App 1998)**]

A refusal to perform a contract that is made before performance is required unless the other party to the contract does an act or makes a concession that is not required by the contract, is an anticipatory repudiation of the contract.[2]

sports&entertainment law

Get It While You Can?

In 2000, the cast of *Friends*, one of the hottest shows on television, demanded a pay increase. The demand was made with a valid contract in place and near the time NBC was to announce its fall lineup. The six stars demanded $1,000,000 each per episode. NBC settled for $750,000 per star, up from the stars' $150,000 per episode figure renegotiated in 1998.

When stars seek to renegotiate contracts before their expiration, the network can replace them if they fail to live up to their contracts, and it can enforce the standard contractual clause, which prohibits them from doing other television work until the expiration of their contracts. Recasting six stars for a highly successful show would not be feasible. To offset the stars' bargaining power, NBC prepared a television promotion that would relabel the last show for that season as the "series finale" and announce "See how it all ends on *Friends*." The cast were informed of NBC's threat to end the series in this manner. Renegotiations quickly ensued and led to the $750,000 agreement. Two years later the six stars obtained their goal of $1 million per episode paychecks. Was it ethical for the stars to threaten to strike just before the fall lineup announcements? When Jay Leno was asked about the tactics of the *Friends* stars, he responded, "You have to get what you can while you can in this business." Is Mr. Leno right? Is such an attitude ethical? When the new agreement was reached, was there a mutual rescission of the existing contract and the substitution of a new contract, or did the new contract fail for lack of consideration?

[2] *Chamberlain v Puckett Construction*, 921 P2d 1237 (Mont 1996).

A party making an anticipatory repudiation may retract or take back the repudiation if the other party has not changed position in reliance on the repudiation. However, if the other party has changed position, the party making the anticipatory repudiation cannot retract it. **For Example,** if a buyer makes another purchase when the seller declares that the seller will not perform the contract, the buyer has acted in reliance on the seller's repudiation. The seller will therefore not be allowed to retract the repudiation.

(B) ANTICIPATORY REPUDIATION BY CONDUCT. The anticipatory repudiation may be expressed by conduct that makes it impossible for the repudiating party to perform subsequently. To illustrate, there is a repudiation by conduct if a farmer makes a contract to sell an identified quantity of potatoes nearly equivalent to his entire crop and then sells and delivers them to another buyer before the date specified for the delivery to the first buyer.

B. WAIVER OF BREACH

The breach of a contract may have no importance because the other party to the contract waives the breach.

3. Cure of Breach by Waiver

waiver–release or relinquishment of a known right or objection.

The fact that one party has broken a contract does not necessarily mean that there will be a lawsuit or a forfeiture of the contract. For practical business reasons, one party may be willing to ignore or waive the breach. When it is established that there has been a **waiver** of a breach, the party waiving the breach cannot take any action on the theory that the contract was broken. The waiver, in effect, erases the past breach. The contract continues as though the breach had not existed.

The waiver may be express or it may be implied from the continued recognition of the existence of the contract by the aggrieved party.[3] When the conduct of a party shows an intent to give up a right, it waives that right.[4]

4. Existence and Scope of Waiver

It is a question of fact whether there has been a waiver.

C A S E   S U M M A R Y

Have You Driven a Ford Lately, Jennifer?

FACTS: In 1995, Northland Ford Dealers, an association of dealerships, offered to sponsor a "hole in one" contest at Moccasin Creek Country Club. A banner announced that a hole in one would win a car but gave no other details, and the local dealer parked a Ford Explorer near the banner. Northland paid a $4,602

[3] *Huger v Morrison*, 2000 La App LEXIS 241.
[4] *Stronghaven Inc. v Ingram*, 555 SE2d 49 (Ga App 2001).

C A S E   S U M M A R Y

Continued

premium to Continental Hole-In-One, Inc., to ensure the award of the contest prize. The insurance application stated in capital letters that "ALL AMATEUR MEN AND WOMEN WILL UTILIZE THE SAME TEE." And Continental established the men/women yardage for the hole to be 170 yards, but did not make this known to the participants. Jennifer Harms registered for the tournament and paid her entrance fee. At the contest hole, she teed off from the amateur women's red marker, which was a much shorter distance to the pin than the 170 yards from the men's marker— and she made a hole in one. When she inquired about the prize, she was told that because of insurance requirements, all amateurs had to tee off from the amateur men's tee box, and because she had not done so, she was disqualified. Harms, a collegiate golfer at Concordia College, returned there to complete her last year of athletic eligibility and on graduation sued Northland for breach of contract. Northland contends that under NCAA rules, accepting a prize or agreeing to accept a prize would have disqualified Harms from NCAA competition. It also asserts that her continuation of her NCAA competition evinced intent to waive acceptance of the car.

DECISION: Judgment for Harms. Northland must abide by the rules it announced, not by the ones it left unannounced that disqualified all amateur women from the contest. This was a vintage unilateral contract with performance by the offeree as acceptance. Harms earned the prize when she sank her winning shot. Waiver is a volitional relinquishment, by act or word, of a known existing right conferred in law or contract. Harms could not disclaim the prize; it was not hers to refuse. She was told her shot from the wrong tee disqualified her. One can hardly relinquish what was never conferred. Northland's waiver defense is devoid of merit. [**Harms v Northland Ford Dealers, 602 NW2d 58 (SD 1999)**]

(A) EXISTENCE OF WAIVER. A party may express or declare that the breach of a contract is waived. A waiver of a breach is more often the result of an express forgiving of a breach. Thus, a party allowing the other party to continue performance without objecting that the performance is not satisfactory waives the right to raise that objection when sued for payment by the performing party.

For Example, a contract promising to sell back a parcel of commercial property to Jackson required Jackson to make a $500 payment to Massey's attorney on the first of the month for five months, December through April. It was clearly understood that the payments would be "on time without fail." Jackson made the December payment on time. New Year's Day, a holiday, fell on a Friday, and Jackson made the second payment on January 4. He made $500 payments on February 1, March 1, and March 31, respectively, and the payments were accepted and a receipt issued on each occasion. However, Massey refused to convey title back to Jackson because "the January 4 payment was untimely and the parties' agreement had been breached." The court held that the doctrine of waiver applied due to Massey's acceptance of the late payment and the three subsequent payments without objection, and the court declared that Jackson was entitled to possession of the land.[5]

---

[5] *Massey v Jackson*, 726 So2d 656 (Ala Civ App 1998).

(B) Scope of Waiver. The waiver of a breach of contract extends only to the matter waived. It does not show any intent to ignore other provisions of the contract.

(c) Antimodification Clause. Modern contracts commonly specify that the terms of a contract shall not be deemed modified by waiver as to any breaches. This means that the original contract remains as agreed to. Either party may therefore return to, and insist on, compliance with the original contract.

In the example involving Jackson and Massey's contract, the trial court reviewed the contract to see whether the court was restricted by the contract from applying the waiver. It concluded: "In this case, the parties' contract did not contain any terms that could prevent the application of the doctrine of waiver to the acceptance of late payments."[6]

5. Reservation of Rights

It may be that a party is willing to accept a defective performance but does not wish to surrender any claim for damages for the breach. **For Example,** Midwest Utilities, Inc., accepted 20 carloads of Powder River Basin coal (sometimes called *Western coal*) from its supplier, Maney Enterprises, because its power plants were in short supply of coal. Midwest's requirements contract with Maney called for Appalachian coal, a low-sulfur, highly efficient fuel, which is sold at a premium price per ton. Midwest, in accepting the tendered performance with a **reservation of rights**, gave notice to Maney that it reserved all rights to pursue damages for the tender of a nonconforming shipment.

reservation of rights– assertion by a party to a contract that even though a tendered performance (e.g., a defective product) is accepted, the right to damages for nonconformity to the contract is reserved.

remedy– action or procedure that is followed in order to enforce a right or to obtain damages for injury to a right.

C. Remedies for Breach of Contract

One or more **remedies** may be available to the innocent party in the case of a breach of contract. There is also the possibility that arbitration or a streamlined out-of-court alternative dispute resolution procedure is available or required for determining the rights of the parties.

6. Remedies Upon Anticipatory Repudiation

When an anticipatory repudiation of a contract occurs, the aggrieved person has several options. He may (1) do nothing beyond stating that performance at the proper time will be required, (2) regard the contract as having been definitively broken and bring a lawsuit against the repudiating party without waiting to see whether there will be proper performance when the performance date arrives, or (3) regard the repudiation as an offer to cancel the contract. This offer can be accepted or rejected. If accepted, there is a discharge of the original contract by the subsequent cancellation agreement of the parties.

7. Remedies in General and the Measure of Damages

Courts provide a *quasi-contractual* or *restitution* remedy in which a contract is unenforceable because it lacked definite and certain terms or was not in compliance with the statute of frauds, yet one of the parties performed services for the other.

[6] Id., at 659.

FIGURE 20-1 | *What Follows the Breach*

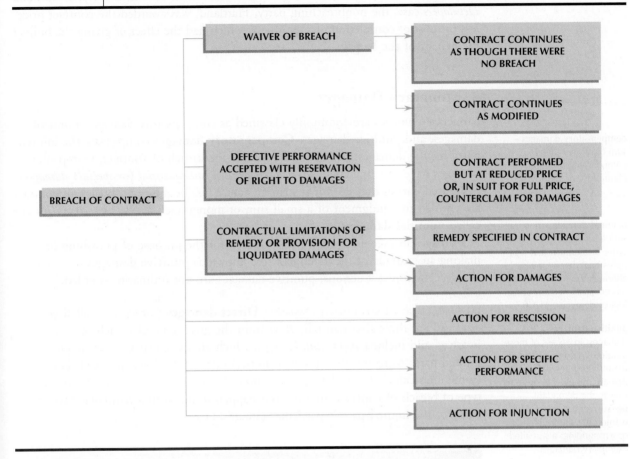

The measure of damages in these and other quasi-contract cases is the reasonable value of the services performed, not an amount derived from the defective contract.

In cases when a person retains money or when a contemplated contract is not properly formed and no work is performed, the party retaining the benefit is obligated to make restitution to the person conferring the benefit. **For Example,** Kramer Associates, Inc. (KAI), a Washington D.C., consulting firm, accepted $75,000 from a Ghana-based corporation, Ikam, Ltd., to secure financing for a Ghana development project. No contract was ever executed, and KAI did virtually nothing to secure financing for the project. Restitution of the $75,000 was required.[7]

When there is a breach of contract, the regular remedy is an award of *monetary damages.* In unusual circumstances, when monetary damages are inadequate, the injured party may obtain **specific performance**, whereby the court will order that the contract terms be carried out.

The measure of monetary damages when there has been a breach of contract is the sum of money that will place the injured party in the same position that would have been attained if the contract had been performed.[8] That is, the injured party

specific performance– action brought to compel the adverse party to perform a contract on the theory that merely suing for damages for its breach will not be an adequate remedy.

---

[7] *Kramer Associates, Inc. v IKAM, Ltd.,* 888 A2d 247 (DC 2005).
[8] *Leingang v City of Mandan Weed Board,* 468 NW2d 397 (ND 1991).

will be given the *benefit of the bargain* by the court. As seen in the *Tips v Hartland Developers* case, the nonbreaching party, Hartland, was awarded the contract price less the cost of completion of the project, which had the effect of giving the builder the benefit of the bargain.

8. Monetary Damages

compensatory damages– sum of money that will compensate an injured plaintiff for actual loss.

Monetary damages are commonly classified as compensatory damages, nominal damages, and punitive damages. **Compensatory damages** compensate the injured party for the damages incurred as a result of the breach of contract. Compensatory damages have two branches, *direct damages* and *consequential* (or *special*) *damages*.

Injured parties that do not sustain an actual loss because of a breach of contract are entitled to a judgment of a small sum of money such as $1; these damages are called **nominal damages**.

nominal damages–nominal sum awarded the plaintiff in order to establish that legal rights have been violated although the plaintiff in fact has not sustained any actual loss or damages.

Damages in excess of actual loss, imposed for the purpose of punishing or making an example of the defendant, are known as **punitive damages** or *exemplary damages*. In contract actions, punitive damages are not ordinarily awarded.[9]

(A) DIRECT AND CONSEQUENTIAL DAMAGES. **Direct damages** (sometimes called *general damages*) are those that naturally flow from the given type of breach of contract involved and include *incidental damages*, which are extra expenditures made by the injured party to rectify the breach or mitigate damages. **Consequential damages** (sometimes called *special damages*) are those that do not necessarily flow from the type of breach of contract involved but happen to do so in a particular case as a result of the injured party's particular circumstances.

punitive damages– damages, in excess of those required to compensate the plaintiff for the wrong done, that are imposed in order to punish the defendant because of the particularly wanton or willful character of wrongdoing; also called *exemplary damages*.

direct damages–losses that are caused by breach of a contract.

consequential damages– damages the buyer experiences as a result of the seller's breach with respect to a third party, also called *special damages*.

C A S E   S U M M A R Y

Who Pays the Expenses?

FACTS: Jerry Birkel was a grain farmer. Hassebrook Farm Service, Inc., made a contract with Jerry to sell to him and install a grain storage and drying bin. Jerry traded in his old dryer to the seller. The new equipment did not work properly, and Jerry had to pay other persons for drying and storing his grain. Jerry sued Hassebrook for damages and claimed the right to be repaid what he had paid to others for drying and storage.

DECISION: Jerry was entitled to recover what he had paid others for drying and storage. Because Jerry had traded in his old dryer to the seller, it was obvious to the seller that if the new equipment did not work properly, Jerry would be forced to pay for alternative drying and storage to prevent the total loss of his crops. The cost of such an alternative was therefore within the seller's contemplation when the contract was made, and so the buyer could recover this cost as an element of damages for the seller's breach of contract. [**Birkel v Hassebrook Farm Service, Inc., 363 NW2d 148 (Neb 1985)**]

---

[9] A party who is not awarded actual damages but wins nominal damages can be considered a "prevailing party" for the purposes of a contractual attorney fee-shifting provision. *Brock v King*, 629 SE2d 829 (Ga App 2006).

Consequential damages may be recovered only if it was reasonably foreseeable to the defendant that the kind of loss in question could be sustained by the nonbreaching party if the contract were broken.

For Example, in early August, Spencer Adams ordered a four-wheel-drive GMC truck with a rear-end hydraulic lift for use on his Aroostook County, Maine, potato farm. The contract price was $58,500. He told Brad Jones, the owner of the dealership, that he had to have the truck by Labor Day so he could use it to bring in his crop from the fields before the first frost, and Brad nodded that he understood. The truck did not arrive by Labor Day as promised in the written contract. After a two-week period of gradually escalating recriminations with the dealership, Adams obtained the same model GMC truck at a dealership 40 minutes away in Houlton but at the cost of $60,500. He was also able to rent a similar truck from the Houlton dealer for $250 for the day while the new truck was being prepared. Farmhands had used other means of harvesting, but because of the lack of the truck, their work was set back by five days. As a result of the delays, 30 percent of the crop was still in the fields when the first frost came, causing damages expertly estimated at $320,000. The *direct damages* for the breach of contract in this case would be the difference between the contract price for the truck of $58,500 and the market price of $60,500, or $2,000. These direct damages naturally flow from the breach of contract for the purchase of a truck. Also, the *incidental damages* of $250 for the truck rental are recoverable direct damages. The $320,000 loss of the potato crop was a consequence of not having the truck, and this sum is arguably recoverable by Spencer Adams as *consequential or special damages.* Adams notified Brad Jones of the reason he needed to have the truck by Labor Day, and it should have been reasonably foreseeable to Jones that loss of a portion of the crop could occur if the truck contract was breached. However, because of Spencer Adams's obligation to mitigate damages (as discussed below), it is unlikely that Adams will recover the full consequential damages. Truck rental availability or the lack of availability within the rural area, alternative tractor usage, and the actual harvesting methods used by Adams all relate to the mitigation issue to be resolved by the jury.

(B) MITIGATION OF DAMAGES. The injured party is under the duty to mitigate damages if reasonably possible.[10] In other words, damages must not be permitted to increase if an increase can be prevented by reasonable efforts. This means that the injured party must generally stop any performance under the contract to avoid running up a larger bill. The duty to mitigate damages may require an injured party to buy or rent elsewhere the goods that the wrongdoer was obligated to deliver under the contract. In the case of breach of an employment contract by the employer, the employee is required to seek other similar employment. The wages earned from other employment must be deducted from the damages claimed. The discharged employee, however, is not required to take employment of less-than-comparable work.

---

[10] *West Pinal Family Health Center, Inc. v McBride*, 785 P2d 66 (Ariz 1989).

(1) Effect of Failure to Mitigate Damages.

The effect of the requirement of mitigating damages is to limit recovery by the nonbreaching party to the damages that would have been sustained had this party mitigated the damages where it was possible to do so. **For Example,** self-described "sports nut" Gary Baker signed up for a three-year club-seat "package" that entitled him and a companion to tickets for 41 Boston Bruins hockey games and 41 Boston Celtics basketball games at the New Boston Garden Corporation's Fleet Center for approximately $18,000 per year. After one year, Baker stopped paying for the tickets, thinking that he would simply lose his $5,000 security deposit. Baker, a CPA, tried to work out a compromise settlement to no avail. New Boston sued Baker for breach of contract, seeking the balance due on the tickets of $34,866. At trial, Baker argued to the jury that although he had breached his contract, New Boston had an obligation to mitigate damages, for example, by treating his empty seats and those of others in the same situation as "rush seats" shortly before game time and selling them at a discount. New Boston argued that just as a used luxury car cannot be returned for a refund, a season ticket cannot be canceled without consequences. The jury accepted Baker's position on mitigation and reduced the amount owed New Boston by $21,176 to $13,690.[11]

9. Rescission

When one party commits a material breach of the contract, the other party may rescind the contract; if the party in default objects, the aggrieved party may bring an action for rescission. A breach is *material* when it is so substantial that it defeats the object of the parties in making the contract.[12]

An injured party who rescinds a contract after having performed services may recover the reasonable value of the performance rendered under restitutionary or quasi-contractual damages. Money paid by the injured party may also be recovered. The purpose is to restore the injured party to the position occupied before the contract was made. However, the party seeking restitutionary damages must also return what this party has received from the party in default.

For Example, Pedro Morena purchased real estate from Jason Alexander after Alexander had assured him that the property did not have a flooding problem. In fact, the property regularly flooded after ordinary rainstorms. Morena was entitled to the return of the purchase price and payment for the reasonable value of the improvements he made to the property. Alexander was entitled to a setoff for the reasonable rental value of the property during the time Morena was in possession of this property.

10. Action for Specific Performance

Under special circumstances, an injured party may obtain the equitable remedy of specific performance, which compels the other party to carry out the terms of a contract. Specific performance is ordinarily granted only if the subject matter of the

---

[11] Sacha Pfeiffer, "Disenchanted Fan Scores Win in Ticket Fight," *Boston Globe*, August 28, 1999, B-4.
[12] *Greentree Properties, Inc. v Kissee*, 92 SW3d 289 (Mo App 2003).

contract is "unique," thereby making an award of money damages an inadequate remedy. Contracts for the purchase of land will be specifically enforced.[13]

Specific performance of a contract to sell personal property can be obtained only if the article is of unusual age, beauty, unique history, or other distinction. **For Example,** Maurice owned a rare Revolutionary War musket that he agreed to sell to Herb. Maurice then changed his mind because of the uniqueness of the musket. Herb can sue and win, requesting the remedy of specific performance of the contract because of the unique nature of the goods.

When the damages sustained by the plaintiff can be measured in monetary terms, specific performance will be refused. Consequently, a contract to sell a television station will not be specifically enforced when the buyer had made a contract to resell the station to a third person; the damages caused by the breach of the first contract would be the loss sustained by being unable to make the resale, and such damages would be adequate compensation to the original buyer.[14]

Ordinarily, contracts for the performance of personal services are not specifically ordered. This is because of the difficulty of supervision by the court and the restriction of the U.S. Constitution's Thirteenth Amendment prohibiting involuntary servitude except as criminal punishment.

11. Action for an Injunction

injunction–order of a court of equity to refrain from doing (negative injunction) or to do (affirmative or mandatory injunction) a specified act. Statute use in labor disputes has been greatly restricted.

When a breach of contract consists of doing an act prohibited by the contract, a possible remedy is an **injunction** against doing the act. **For Example,** when the obligation in an employee's contract is to refrain from competing after resigning from the company and the obligation is broken by competing, a court may order or enjoin the former employee to stop competing. Similarly, when a vocalist breaks a contract to record exclusively for a particular label, she may be enjoined from recording for any other company. This may have the indirect effect of compelling the vocalist to record for the plaintiff.

12. Reformation of Contract by a Court

At times, a written contract does not correctly state the agreement already made by the parties. When this occurs, either party may seek to have the court reform or correct the writing to state the agreement actually made.

A party seeking reformation of a contract must clearly prove both the grounds for reformation and what the agreement actually was. This burden is particularly great when the contract to be reformed is written. This is so because the general rule is that parties are presumed to have read their written contracts and to have intended to be bound by them when they signed the contracts.

When a unilateral mistake is made and it is of such consequence that enforcing the contract according to its terms would be unreasonable, a court may reform the contract to correct the mistake.

---

[13] *English v Muller*, 514 SE2d 195 (Ga 1999).
[14] *Miller v LeSea Broadcasting, Inc.*, 87 F3d 224 (7th Cir 1996).

CASE SUMMARY

Will a Court Correct a Huge Mistake?

FACTS: New York Packaging Corp. (NYPC) manufactured plastic sheets used by Owens Corning (OC) at its asphalt plants throughout the country as dividers to separate asphalt containers and prevent them from sticking to one another. Janet Berry, a customer service representative at Owens Corning, called and received a price from NYPC of "$172.50 per box," with a box containing 200 plastic sheets. Ms. Berry put the information into OC's computer systems, which in turn generated a purchase order. She mistakenly believed that the unit of measurement designated as "EA" on the purchase order was per box when it in fact was per sheet. As a result, the purchase orders likewise reflected a price of $172.50 per sheet rather than per box. The computer automatically calculated the total price of the purchase order and faxed it to NYPC as $1,078,195, without Ms. Berry seeing the huge total price. NYPC filled the order, which included overrun sheets, and billed OC $1,414,605.60. NYPC sought payment at the contract price of $172.50 per sheet. It points out that the purchase order contained a "no oral modification" clause and, by its terms, the order was binding when NYPC accepted. The buyer contends that NYPC is attempting to take advantage of this huge and obvious mistake and that the contract should be reformed.

DECISION: Ms. Berry made a unilateral mistake that was, or should have been, known by NYPC. OC used the sheets after its offer to return them to NYPC was refused. Therefore, the contract could not be rescinded. The drafting error in this case was so huge that to enforce the written contract would be unconscionable. Accordingly, the unit of measurement is amended to read "per box" rather than "EA"; the "Order Qty" is amended to read "41 boxes of 200 sheets per box"; and the overall price is modified to read $7,072.50, not $1,078,195. [**In re Owens Corning et al., Debtors in Possession, 91 BR 329 (2003)**]

D. CONTRACT PROVISIONS AFFECTING REMEDIES AND DAMAGES

The contract of the parties may contain provisions that affect the remedies available or the recovery of damages.

13. Limitation of Remedies

The contract of the parties may limit the remedies of the aggrieved parties. **For Example,** the contract may give one party the right to repair or replace a defective item sold or to refund the contract price. The contract may require both parties to submit any dispute to arbitration or another streamlined out-of-court dispute resolution procedure.

14. Liquidated Damages

liquidated damages–provision stipulating the amount of damages to be paid in the event of default or breach of contract.

The parties may stipulate in their contract that a certain amount should be paid in case of a breach. This amount is known as liquidated damages and may be variously measured by the parties. When delay is possible, **liquidated damages** may be a fixed sum, such as $1,000 for each day of delay. When there is a total default, damages may be a percentage of the contract price or the amount of the down payment.

valid–legal.

liquidated damages clause–specification of exact compensation in case of a breach of contract.

(A) **VALIDITY.** To be **valid**, a **liquidated damages clause** must satisfy two requirements: (1) The situation must be one in which it is difficult or impossible to determine the actual damages and (2) the amount specified must not be excessive when compared with the probable damages that would be sustained.[15] The validity of a liquidated damages clause is determined on the basis of the facts existing when the clause was agreed to.

C A S E   S U M M A R Y

Can We Freeze the Damages?

FACTS: Manny Fakhimi agreed to buy an apartment complex for $697,000 at an auction from David Mason. Fakhimi was obligated to put up 10 percent of the agreed-to price at the auction as a deposit. The agreement signed by Fakhimi allowed Mason to keep this deposit should Fakhimi fail to come up with the remaining 90 percent of the auction price as liquidated damages for the default. Shortly after the auction, Fakhimi heard a rumor that the military base located near the apartment complex might be closing. Fakhimi immediately stopped payment on the check and defaulted on the agreement. Mason sued Fakhimi for the liquidated damages specified in the sales contract.

DECISION: Because of the difficulty of forecasting the loss that might be caused by the breach of a real estate purchase contract, it is held that a liquidated damage clause of 10 percent of the sale price is valid and is not a penalty. The fact that the damages sustained thereafter were less than 10 percent does not convert the 10 percent into an unreasonable forecast. The 10 percent clause remained valid as it would have remained had the damages on resale been more than 10 percent. [**Mason v Fakhimi, 865 P2d 333 (Neb 1993)**]

(B) **EFFECT.** When a liquidated damages clause is held valid, the injured party cannot collect more than the amount specified by the clause. The defaulting party is bound to pay such damages once the fact is established that there has been a default. The injured party is not required to make any proof as to damages sustained, and the defendant is not permitted to show that the damages were not as great as the liquidated sum.

(C) **INVALID CLAUSES.** If the liquidated damages clause calls for the payment of a sum that is clearly unreasonably large and unrelated to the possible actual damages that might be sustained, the clause will be held to be void as a penalty. **For Example,** a settlement agreement between 27 plaintiffs seeking recovery for injuries resulting from faulty breast implants and the implants' manufacturer, Dow Corning Corp., called for seven $200,000 payments to each plaintiff. The agreement also called for a $100 per day payment to each plaintiff for any time when the payments were late as "liquidated damages." The court held that the $100 per day figure was not a reasonable estimate of anticipated damages. Rather, it was an unenforceable "penalty" provision.[16]

---

[15] *Southeast Alaska Construction Co. v Alaska*, 791 P2d 339 (Alaska 1990).
[16] *Bear Stearns v Dow Corning Corp.*, 419 F3d 543 (6th Cir 2005). See *RKR Motors Inc. v Associated Uniform Rentals*, 995 So2d 588 (Fla App 2008).

When a liquidated damages clause is held invalid, the effect is merely to erase the clause from the contract, and the injured party may proceed to recover damages for breach of the contract. Instead of recovering the liquidated damages amount, the injured party will recover whatever actual damages he can prove. **For Example,** JRC

CASE SUMMARY

Could We Make It Any Clearer?

FACTS: Woodside Homes made a contract to build a house for Russ. He and his wife later visited the construction site, where his wife slipped and fell into a hole in the driveway in front of the house. The fall caused a blood clot to form, which caused the wife's death. Russ sued Woodside for damages for his wife's death, claiming that she had been harmed because of Woodside's negligence. There was no evidence of negligence. Woodside raised the defense that the construction contract stated that "the construction site is a dangerous place to visit" and that Woodside would not be liable for any accident, injury, or death resulting from a visit to the jobsite.

DECISION: Judgment for Woodside. The contractor gave adequate warning of the danger, and the wife assumed the risk in visiting the site. The exculpation clause therefore shielded the contractor from liability. [**Russ v Woodside Homes, Inc., 905 P2d 901 (Utah App 1995)**]

Trading Corp (JRC) bought computer software and hardware from Progressive Data Systems (PDS) for $167,935, which it paid in full, to track the movement of its trucks with inventory and to process transactions. The purchase agreement also called for a $7,500 per year licensing fee for an 18-year period, and it stated that in the event of default, PDS could "accelerate and declare all obligations of Customer as a liquidated sum." A dispute arose between the parties, and when the case was litigated, the only actual contract charges owed PDS were license fees of $7,500 for two years. The application of the liquidated damages clause would yield an additional $120,000 cash for PDS for the future fees for 16 years without any reduction for expenses or the present cash value for the not-yet-earned fees. Actual damages were clearly ascertainable and not difficult to determine, and the amount sought was excessive. The court deemed the liquidated damages clause an unenforceable penalty and PDS was relegated to recovering its actual contractual damages.[17]

15. Attorneys' Fees

Attorneys' fees are a very significant factor in contract litigation. In Medistar Corporation's suit against Dr. David Schmidt, the jury awarded it $418,069 in damages under its promissory estoppel claim and in addition thereto the trial court judge allowed Medistar to recover $408,412 for its attorneys' fees. A state statute

---

[17] *Jefferson Randolf Corporation v PDS*, 553 SE2d 304 (Ga App 2001).

allows recovery of attorneys' fees for the prevailing party in a breach of partnership claim. On appeal the recovery of $408,412 in attorneys' fees was reversed since the jury awarded zero damages on Medistars' fees was reveresed since ther jury awarded zero damages on Medistars' breach of partnership claim. The net result after payment of attorneys' fees—and not counting attorneys' fees for the appeal—was $9657 for Medistar, after four years of "successful" litigation.[18]

The so-called "American rule" states that each party is responsible for its own attorneys' fees in the absence of an express contractual or statutory provision to the contrary.[19] Even in the event of a valid contractual provision for attorneys' fees, a trial court has the discretion to exercise its equitable control to allow only such sum as is reasonable, or the court may properly disallow attorneys' fees altogether on the basis that such recovery would be inequitable. **For Example,** although Evergreen Tree Care Services was awarded some monetary damages in its breach of contract suit against JHL, Inc., it was unsuccessful in its claim for attorneys' fees under a provision for attorneys' fees in the contract because the trial court exercised its equitable discretion, finding that both parties to the litigation came to court with "unclean hands," and that Evergreen failed to sufficiently itemize and exclude fees to discovery abuses.[20]

16. Limitation of Liability Clauses

A contract may contain a provision stating that one of the parties shall not be liable for damages in case of breach. Such a provision is called an **exculpatory clause**, or when a monetary limit to damages for breach of contract is set forth in the contract, it may be referred to as a **limitation-of-liability clause**.

exculpatory clause–provision in a contract stating that one of the parties shall not be liable for damages in case of breach; also called a *limitation-of-liability clause.*

limitation-of-liability clause–provision in a contract stating that one of the parties shall not be liable for damages in case of breach; also called an *exculpatory clause.*

(A) CONTENT AND CONSTRUCTION. If an exculpatory clause or a limitation-of-liability clause limits liability for damages caused only by negligent conduct, liability is neither excluded nor limited if the conduct alleged is found to be grossly negligent, willful, or wanton. **For Example,** Security Guards Inc. (SGI) provided services to Dana Corporation, a truck frame manufacturer under a contract that contained a limitation-of-liability clause capping losses at $50,000 per occurrence for damages "caused solely by the negligence" of SGI or its employees. When a critical alarm was activated by a fire in the paint shop at 5:39 P.M., the SGI guard on duty did not follow appropriate procedures, which delayed notification to the fire department for 15 minutes. Royal Indemnity Co., Dana's insurer, paid Dana $16,535,882 for the fire loss and sued SGI for $7 million, contending that the SGI guard's actions were grossly negligent and caused the plant to suffer increased damages. The court held that if SGI were to be found grossly negligent, the liability would not be limited to $50,000, and a jury could find damages far exceeding that amount.[21]

(B) VALIDITY. As a general rule, experienced businesspersons are free to allocate liability in their contracts as they see fit. They have freedom to contract—even to make bad bargains or relinquish fundamental rights. However, courts in most states

[18] *Medistar Corp. v Schmidt,* 267 SW3d 150 (Tex App 2008).
[19] *Centimark v Village Manor Associates, Ltd.,* 967 A2d 550 (Conn App 2009).
[20] *Stafford v JHL, Inc.,* 194 P3d 315 (Wyo 2008). See also *FNBC v Jennessey Group, LLC,* 759 NW2d 808 (Iowa App 2008).
[21] *Royal Indemnity Co. v Security Guards, Inc.,* 255 F Supp 2d 497 (ED Pa 2003).

will not enforce a contract provision that *completely exonerates* a party from gross negligence or intentional acts.

(c) **RELEASES.** Release forms signed by participants in athletic and sporting events declaring that the sponsor, proprietor, or operator of the event shall not be liable for injuries sustained by participants because of its negligence are generally binding.[22] **For Example,** when Merav Sharon sued the city of Newton for negligence as a result of an injury received while participating in a high school cheerleading practice, the city successfully raised a signed exculpatory release as a defense.[23] So also the exculpatory contract Nathan Henderson signed releasing a white-water rafting expedition operator from liability for its negligence barred Henderson's negligence claim against the operator for an injury suffered disembarking from the operator's bus.[24]

lawflix

The Goodbye Girl (1977) (PG)

Richard Dreyfuss plays Elliott Garfield, a struggling Shakespearean actor who lands in New York with a sublease on an apartment still occupied by divorcee Marsha Mason and her daughter. The two work out living arrangements, split rent and food, and deal with the issue of whether Mason has any rights. Review all aspects of contracts as the characters discuss subleases, rent payment, living arrangements, and food costs.

Check out LawFlix at **www.cengage.com/blaw/dvl** to access movie clips that illustrate business law concepts.

MAKE THE CONNECTION

SUMMARY

When a party fails to perform a contract or performs improperly, the other contracting party may sue for damages caused by the breach. What may be recovered by the aggrieved person is stated in terms of being direct or consequential damages. Direct damages are those that ordinarily will result from the breach. Direct damages may be recovered on proof of causation and amount. Consequential

---

[22] But see *Woodman v Kera, LLC*, 760 NW2d 641 (Mich App 2008) where the Court of Appeals of Michigan held that a preinjury waiver signed by a parent on behalf of a five-year-old child was invalid.
[23] *Sharon v City of Newton*, 437 Mass 99 (2002).
[24] *Henderson v Quest Expeditions, Inc.*, 174 SW3d 730 (Tenn App 2005).

damages can be recovered only if, in addition to proving causation and amount, it is shown that they were reasonably within the contemplation of the contracting parties as a probable result of a breach of the contract. The right to recover consequential damages is lost if the aggrieved party could reasonably have taken steps to avoid such damages. In other words, the aggrieved person has a duty to mitigate or reduce damages by reasonable means.

In any case, the damages recoverable for breach of contract may be limited to a specific amount by a liquidated damages clause.

In a limited number of situations, an aggrieved party may bring an action for specific performance to compel the other contracting party to perform the acts called for by the contract. Specific performance by the seller is always obtainable for the breach of a contract to sell land or real estate on the theory that such property has a unique value. With respect to other contracts, specific performance will not be ordered unless it is shown that there was some unique element present so that the aggrieved person would suffer a damage that could not be compensated for by the payment of money damages.

The aggrieved person also has the option of rescinding the contract if (1) the breach has been made concerning a material term and (2) the aggrieved party returns everything to the way it was before the contract was made.

Although there has been a breach of the contract, the effect of this breach is nullified if the aggrieved person by word or conduct waives the right to object to the breach. Conversely, an aggrieved party may accept a defective performance without thereby waiving a claim for breach if the party makes a reservation of rights. A reservation of rights can be made by stating that the defective performance is accepted "without prejudice," "under protest," or "with reservation of rights."

LEARNING OUTCOMES

After studying this chapter, you should be able to clearly explain:

A. WHAT CONSTITUTES A BREACH OF CONTRACT

LO.1 Explain what constitutes a breach of contract and an anticipatory breach of contract

> See the illustration of a painting contractor's failure to properly paint a house, p. 434.
> See the *Tips* case in which damages are assessed for anticipatory repudiation of a contract, p. 434.

B. WAIVER OF BREACH

LO.2 Describe the effect of a waiver of a breach

> See the application of the waiver doctrine as applied in the Massey example on p. 438.

C. REMEDIES FOR BREACH OF CONTRACT

LO.3 Explain the range of remedies available for breach of contract

> See Figure 20.1, "What Follows the Breach," on p. 439.
> See the *Spenser Adams* example involving a range of monetary damages on p. 441.
> See the *Pedro Morena* example involving rescission of a contract on p. 442.

See the rare Revolutionary War musket example of specific performance, p. 443.

D. CONTRACT PROVISIONS AFFECTING REMEDIES AND DAMAGES

LO.4 Explain when liquidated damages clauses are valid and invalid

See the Dow Corning faulty breast implants settlement agreement example in which liquidated damages of a $100 per day late payment were found to be unenforceable penalty provision, p. 445.

LO.5 State when liability-limiting clauses and releases are valid

See the example in which the city of Newton successfully raised a signed exculpatory release as a defense in a high school cheerleading injury case, p. 448.

KEY TERMS

anticipatory breach	injunction	remedies
anticipatory repudiation	limitation-of-liability	reservation of rights
breach	clause	specific performance
compensatory damages	liquidated damages	valid
consequential damages	liquidated damages clause	waiver
direct damages	nominal damages	
exculpatory clause	punitive damages	

QUESTIONS AND CASE PROBLEMS

1. The Forsyth School District contracted with Textor Construction, Inc., to build certain additions and alter school facilities, including the grading of a future softball field. Under the contract, the work was to be completed by August 1. Various delays occurred at the outset of the project attributable to the school district, and the architect's representative on the job, Mr. Hamilton, told Textor's vice president, William Textor, not to be concerned about a clause in the contract of $250 per day liquidated damages for failure to complete the job by August 1. Textor sued the school district for breach of contract regarding payment for the grading of the softball field, and the District counterclaimed for liquidated damages for 84 days at $250 per day for failure to complete the project by the August 1 date. What legal basis exists for Textor to defend against the counter-claim for failure to complete the job on time? Was it ethical for the school district to bring this counterclaim based on the facts before you? [*Textor Construction, Inc. v Forsyth R-III School District*, 60 SW3d 692 (Mo App)]

2. Anthony makes a contract to sell a rare painting to Laura for $100,000. The written contract specifies that if Anthony should fail to perform the contract, he will pay Laura $5,000 as liquidated damages. Anthony fails to deliver the painting and is sued by Laura for $5,000. Can she recover this amount?

3. Rogers made a contract with Salisbury Brick Corp. that allowed it to remove earth and sand from land he owned. The contract ran for four years with provision to renew it for additional four-year terms up to a total of 96 years. The contract provided for compensation to Rogers based on the amount of earth and sand removed. By an unintentional mistake, Salisbury underpaid Rogers the amount of $863 for the months of November and December 1986. Salisbury offered this amount to Rogers, but he refused to accept it and claimed that he had been underpaid in other months. Rogers claimed that he was entitled to rescind the contract. Was he correct? [*Rogers v Salisbury Brick Corp.*, 882 SE2d 915 (SC)]

4. A contractor departed from the specifications at a number of points in a contract to build a house. The cost to put the house in the condition called for by the contract was approximately $14,000. The contractor was sued for $50,000 for breach of contract and emotional disturbance caused by the breach. Decide.

5. Protein Blenders, Inc., made a contract with Gingerich to buy from him the shares of stock of a small corporation. When the buyer refused to take and pay for the stock, Gingerich sued for specific performance of the contract on the ground that the value of the stock was unknown and could not be readily ascertained because it was not sold on the general market. Was he entitled to specific performance? [*Gingerich v Protein Blenders, Inc.*, 95 NW2d 522 (Iowa)]

6. The buyer of real estate made a down payment. The contract stated that the buyer would be liable for damages in an amount equal to the down payment if the buyer broke the contract. The buyer refused to go through with the contract and demanded his down payment back. The seller refused to return it and claimed that he was entitled to additional damages from the buyer because the damages that he had suffered were more than the amount of the down payment. Decide. [*Waters v Key Colony East, Inc.*, 345 So2d 367 (Fla App)]

7. Kuznicki made a contract for the installation of a fire detection system by Security Safety Corp. for $498. The contract was made one night and canceled at 9:00 the next morning. Security then claimed one-third of the purchase price from Kuznicki by virtue of a provision in the contract that "in the event of cancellation of this agreement… the owner agrees to pay $33^{1/3}$ percent of the contract price, as liquidated damages." Was Security Safety entitled to recover the amount claimed? [*Security Safety Corp. v Kuznicki*, 213 NE2d 866 (Mass)]

8. FNBC is a business brokerage firm that assits in the purchase and sale of businesses. Jennings and Hennessey were independent contractors working for FNBC. They left FNBC, and FNBC sued them for breach of their contracts with FNBC. The trial court issued a permanent injuction prohibiting the former contractors from using proprietary information and the court awarded attorneys' fees under a clause in the contract that would obligate Jennings and Hennessey to indemnify FNBC against claims "brought by persons not a party to the provision." Jennings and Hennessey appealed the decision on attorneys' fees. Decide. [*FNBC v Jennessey Group, LLC*, 759 NW2d 808 (Iowa Ap)]

9. Melodee Lane Lingerie Co. was a tenant in a building that was protected against fire by a sprinkler and alarm system maintained by the American District Telegraph Co. (ADT). Because of the latter's fault, the controls on the system were defective and allowed the discharge of water into the building, which damaged Melodee's property. When Melodee sued ADT, its defense was that its service contract limited its liability to 10 percent of the annual service charge made to the customer. Was this limitation valid? [*Melodee Lane Lingerie Co. v American District Telegraph Co.*, 218 NE2d 661 (NY)]

10. In May, a homeowner made a contract with a roofer to make repairs to her house by July 1. The roofer never came to repair the roof, and heavy rains in the fall damaged the interior of the house. The homeowner sued the roofer for breach of contract and claimed damages for the harm done to the interior of the house. Is the homeowner entitled to recover such damages?

11. Ken Sulejmanagic, aged 19, signed up for a course in scuba diving taught by Madison at the YMCA. Before the instruction began, Ken was required to sign a form releasing Madison and the YMCA from liability for any harm that might occur. At the end of the course, Madison, Ken, and another student went into deep water. After Ken made the final dive required by the course program, Madison left him alone in the water while he took the other student for a dive. When Madison returned, Ken could not be found, and it was later determined that he had drowned. Ken's parents sued Madison and the YMCA for negligence in the performance of the teaching contract. The defendants raised the defense that the release Ken signed shielded them from liability. The plaintiffs claimed that the release was invalid. Who was correct? [*Madison v Superior Court*, 250 Cal Rptr 299 (Cal App)]

12. Wassenaar worked for Panos under a three-year contract stating that if the contract were terminated wrongfully by Panos before the end of the three years, he would pay as damages the salary for the remaining time that the contract had to run. After three months, Panos terminated the contract, and Wassenaar sued him for pay for the balance of the contract term. Panos claimed that this amount could not be recovered because the contract provision for the payment was a void penalty. Was this provision valid? [*Wassenaar v Panos*, 331 NW2d 357 (Wis)]

13. Soden, a contractor, made a contract to build a house for Clevert. The sales contract stated that "if either party defaults in the performance of this contract," that party would be liable to the other for attorneys' fees incurred in suing the defaulter. Soden was 61 days late in completing the contract, and some of the work was defective. In a suit by the buyer against the contractor, the contractor claimed that he was not liable for the buyer's attorneys' fees because he had made only a defective performance and because "default" in the phrase quoted meant "nonperformance of the contract." Was the contractor liable for the attorneys' fees? [*Clevert v Soden*, 400 SE2d 181 (Va)]

14. Protection Alarm Co. made a contract to provide burglar alarm security for Fretwell's home. The contract stated that the maximum liability of the alarm

company was the actual loss sustained or $50, whichever was the lesser, and that this provision was agreed to "as liquidated damages and not as a penalty." When Fretwell's home was burglarized, he sued for the loss of approximately $12,000, claiming that the alarm company had been negligent. The alarm company asserted that its maximum liability was $50. Fretwell claimed that this was invalid because it bore no relationship to the loss that could have been foreseen when the contract was made or that in fact "had been sustained." Decide.

15. Shepherd-Will made a contract to sell Emma Cousar:

    5 acres of land adjoining property owned by the purchaser and this being formerly land of Shepherd-Will, Inc., located on north side of Highway 223. This 5 acres to be surveyed at earliest time possible at which time plat will be attached and serve as further description on property.

    Shepherd-Will owned only one 100-acre tract of land that adjoined Emma's property. This tract had a common boundary with her property of 1,140 feet. Shepherd-Will failed to perform this contract. Emma sued for specific performance of the contract. Decide. [*Cousar v Shepherd-Will, Inc.*, 387 SE2d 723 (SC App)]

CPA QUESTIONS

1. Master Mfg., Inc., contracted with Accur Computer Repair Corp. to maintain Master's computer system. Master's manufacturing process depends on its computer system operating properly at all times. A liquidated damages clause in the contract provided that Accur pay $1,000 to Master for each day that Accur was late responding to a service request. On January 12, Accur was notified that Master's computer system had failed. Accur did not respond to Master's service request until January 15. If Master sues Accur under the liquidated damages provision of the contract, Master will:

   a. Win, unless the liquidated damage provision is determined to be a penalty

   b. Win, because under all circumstances liquidated damages provisions are enforceable

   c. Lose, because Accur's breach was *not* material

   d. Lose, because liquidated damage provisions violate public policy
   (5/93, Law, #25)

2. Jones, CPA, entered into a signed contract with Foster Corp. to perform accounting and review services. If Jones repudiates the contract prior to the date performance is due to begin, which of the following is *not* correct?

   a. Foster could successfully maintain an action for breach of contract after the date performance was due to begin.

   b. Foster can obtain a judgment ordering Jones to perform.

c. Foster could successfully maintain an action for breach of contract prior to the date performance is due to begin.

d. Foster can obtain a judgment for the monetary damages it incurred as a result of the repudiation. (5/89, Law, #35)

3. Which of the following concepts affect(s) the amount of monetary damages recoverable by the nonbreaching party when a contract is breached?

	Forseeability of damages	Mitigation of damages
a.	Yes	Yes
b.	Yes	No
c.	No	Yes
d.	No	No

for the value of the furs, $61,045. Emery's offer to pay $2,150, the $10-per-pound rate set forth in the airbill, was rejected. Hopper claimed that the amount of $61,045, which was mistakenly placed in the ZIP Code box, was in fact part of the contract set forth in the airbill and that Emery, on reviewing the contract, must have realized a mistake was made. Decide. [*Hopper Furs, Inc., v Emery Air Freight Corp.*, 749 F2d 1261 (8th Cir)]

13. When de Lema, a Brazilian resident, arrived in New York City, his luggage consisted of three suitcases, an attaché case, and a cylindrical bag. The attaché case and the cylindrical bag contained jewels valued at $300,000. De Lema went from JFK Airport to the Waldorf Astoria Hotel, where he gave the three suitcases to hotel staff in the garage, and then he went to the lobby to register. The assistant manager, Baez, summoned room clerk Tamburino to assist him. De Lema stated, "The room clerk asked me if I had a reservation. I said, 'Yes. The name is José Berga de Lema.' And I said, 'I want a safety deposit box.' He said, 'Please fill out your registration.' " While de Lema was filling out the registration form, paying $300 in cash as an advance, and Tamburino was filling out a receipt for that amount, de Lema had placed the attaché case and the cylindrical bag on the floor. A woman jostled de Lema, apparently creating a diversion, and when he next looked down, he discovered that the attaché case was gone. De Lema brought suit against the hotel for the value of the jewels stolen in the hotel's lobby. The hotel maintained a safe for valuables and posted notices in the lobby, garage, and rooms as required by the New York law that modifies a hotelkeeper's common law liability. The notices stated in part that the hotel was not liable for the loss of valuables that a guest had neglected to deliver to the hotel for safekeeping. The hotel's defense was that de Lema had neglected to inform it of the presence of the jewels and to deliver the jewels to the hotel. Is the hotel liable for the value of the stolen jewels? [*De Lema v Waldorf Astoria Hotel, Inc.*, 588 F Supp 19 (SDNY)]

14. Frosty Land Foods shipped a load of beef from its plant in Montgomery, Alabama, to Scott Meat Co. in Los Angeles via Refrigerated Transport Co. (RTC), a common carrier. Early Wednesday morning, December 7, at 12:55 A.M., two of RTC's drivers left the Frosty Land plant with the load of beef. The bill of lading called for delivery at Scott Meat on Friday, December 9, at 6:00 A.M. The RTC drivers arrived in Los Angeles at approximately 3:30 P.M. on Friday, December 9. Scott notified the drivers that it could not process the meat at that time. The drivers checked into a motel for the weekend, and the load was delivered to Scott on Monday, December 12. After inspecting 65 of the 308 carcasses, Scott determined that the meat was in off condition and refused the shipment. On Tuesday, December 13, Frosty Land sold the meat, after extensive trimming, at a loss of $13,529. Frosty Land brought suit against RTC for its loss. Decide. [*Frosty Land Foods v Refrigerated Transport Co.*, 613 F2d 1344 (5th Cir)]

15. Tate hired Action-Mayflower Moving & Storage to ship his belongings. Action prepared a detailed inventory of Tate's belongings, loaded them on its truck, and received the belongings at its warehouse, where they would be stored until

Tate asked that they be moved. Months later, a dispute arose, and Tate asked Action to release his property to a different mover. Tate had prepaid more than enough to cover all charges to this point. Action refused to release the goods and held them in storage. After allowing storage charges to build up for 15 months, Action sold Tate's property under the warehouser's public sale law. Tate sued Action for damages. Decide. [*Tate v Action-Mayflower Moving & Storage, Inc.*, 383 SE2d 229 (NC App)]

CPA QUESTIONS

1. A common carrier bailee generally would avoid liability for loss of goods entrusted to its care if the goods are:

   a. Stolen by an unknown person

   b. Negligently destroyed by an employee

   c. Destroyed by the derailment of the train carrying them due to railroad employee negligence

   d. Improperly packed by the party shipping them

2. Under a nonnegotiable bill of lading, a carrier who accepts goods for shipment must deliver the goods to:

   a. Any holder of the bill of lading

   b. Any party subsequently named by the seller

   c. The seller who was issued the bill of lading

   d. The consignee of the bill of lading

3. Under the UCC, a warehouse receipt:

   a. Is negotiable if, by its terms, the goods are to be delivered to bearer or to the order of a named person

   b. Will not be negotiable if it contains a contractual limitation on the warehouse's liability

   c. May qualify as both a negotiable warehouse receipt and negotiable commercial paper if the instrument is payable either in cash or by the delivery of goods

   d. May be issued only by a bonded and licensed warehouser

4. Under the Documents of Title Article of the UCC, which of the following acts may limit a common carrier's liability for damages to the goods in transit?

   a. Vandalism

   b. Power outage

   c. Willful acts of third person

   d. Providing for a contractual dollar liability limitation

Chapter 23

NATURE AND FORM OF SALES

A. Nature of Sales
1. SUBJECT MATTER OF SALES
2. SALE DISTINGUISHED FROM OTHER TRANSACTIONS
3. FORMATION OF SALES CONTRACTS
4. TERMS IN THE FORMED CONTRACT
5. BULK TRANSFERS

B. Form of Sales Contract
6. AMOUNT
7. NATURE OF THE WRITING REQUIRED
8. EFFECT OF NONCOMPLIANCE

9. EXCEPTIONS TO REQUIREMENT OF A WRITING
10. NONCODE REQUIREMENTS
11. BILL OF SALE

C. Uniform Law for International Sales
12. SCOPE OF THE CISG

D. Leases of Goods
13. TYPES OF LEASES
14. FORM OF LEASE CONTRACT
15. WARRANTIES
16. DEFAULT

Chapters 12 through 20 examined the common law of contracts. That source of contract law applies to contracts whose subject matter is land or services. However, there is another source of contract law, **Article 2** of the Uniform Commercial Code (UCC).

Article 2 was revised substantially by the National Conference of Commissioners on Uniform State Laws (NCCUSL) and the American Law Institute (ALI) in August 2003. Because no state has adopted Revised Article 2, its future remains a question. Revised Article 2 is covered only briefly in this chapter and Chapters 24–27.

UCC Article 2 governs the sale of everything from boats to televisions to compact discs and applies to contracts for the sale of goods. Article 2 exists as a result of the work of businesspeople, commercial transactions lawyers, and legal experts who together have developed a body of contract law suitable for the fast pace of business. Article 2 continues to be refined and modified to ensure seamless laws for transactions in goods across the country.[1]

A. NATURE OF SALES

A *sale of goods* is defined under Article 2 as transfer of title to tangible personal property for a price.[2] This price may be a payment of money, an exchange of other property, or the performance of services.

The parties to a sale are the person who owns the goods, the seller or vendor, and the person to whom the title is transferred, the buyer or vendee.

CPA ## 1. Subject Matter of Sales

goods–anything movable at the time it is identified as the subject of a transaction.

Goods, as defined under the UCC, consist of all forms of tangible personal property, including specially manufactured goods—everything from a fan to a painting to a yacht.[3] Article 2 does not cover (1) investment securities, such as stocks and bonds, the sale of which is regulated by Article 8 of the UCC; (2) insurance policies, commercial paper, such as checks, and promissory notes because they are

---

[1] The UCC Article 2 (prior to the 2003 revisions) has been adopted in 49 states plus the Virgin Islands and the District of Columbia. Louisiana adopted only Article 1; 1990 Revision of Article 3; 1990 Amendments to Article 4; Article 4A (Funds Transfers); 1995 Revision of Articles 5 and 7; 1994 Revision of Article 8; and 2000 Revision of Article 9. The newest revisions of Article 2 were reconciled in July, 2003. The changes in Revised Article 2 are noted throughout this chapter and Chapters 24–27.

[2] UCC § 2-105(1).

[3] *State v Cardwell*, 718 A2d 594 (Conn 1998) (concert tickets are goods); *Leal v Holtvogh*, 702 NE2d 1246 (Ohio App 1998) (transfer of part interest in a horse is a good); *Bergeron v Aero Sales*, 134 P3d 964 (Or App 2006) (jet fuel is a good); *Rite Aid Corp. v Levy-Gray*, 894A 2d 563 (Md 2006) (prescription drug is a good); *Willis Mining v Noggle*, 509 SE2d 731 (Ga App 1998) (granite blocks are goods); *Sterling Power Partners, L.P. v Niagra Mohawk Power Corp.*, 657 NYS2d 407 (1997) (electricity is a good); *Gladhart v Oregon Vineyard Supply Co.*, 994 P2d 134 (Or App 1999) (grape plants bought from nursery are goods); *Dantzler v S.P. Parks, Inc.*, 1988 WL 131428 (ED Pa 1988) (purchase of ticket to amusement ride is not transaction in goods); *Rossetti v Busch Entm't Corp.*, 87 F Supp 2d 415 (ED Pa 2000) (computer software programs are goods); and *Saxton v Pets Warehouse, Inc.*, 691 NYS2d 872 (1999) (dog is a good).

regulated under Articles 3 and 4 of the UCC; and (3) real estate, such as houses, factories, farms, and land itself.[4]

(A) **NATURE OF GOODS.** Article 2 applies not only to contracts for the sale of familiar items of personal property, such as automobiles or chairs, but also to the transfer of commodities, such as oil, gasoline, milk, and grain.[5]

(B) **EXISTING AND FUTURE GOODS.** Goods that are already manufactured or crops already grown and owned by the seller at the time of the transaction are called **existing goods**. All other goods are called **future goods**, which include both goods that physically exist but are not owned by the seller and goods that have not yet been produced, as when a buyer contracts to purchase custom-made office furniture.

existing goods–goods that physically exist and are owned by the seller at the time of a transaction.

future goods–goods that exist physically but are not owned by the seller and goods that have not yet been produced.

2. Sale Distinguished from Other Transactions

Other types of transactions in goods are not covered by Article 2 because they are not transfers of title to the goods.

(A) **BAILMENT.** A **bailment** is not a sale because only possession is transferred to a **bailee**. Title to the property is not transferred. (For more information on bailments, their nature, and the rights of the parties, see Chapter 21.) A lease of goods, such as an automobile, is governed by Article 2A of the UCC, which is covered later in Section D of this chapter.

bailment–relationship that exists when personal property is delivered into the possession of another under an agreement, express or implied, that the identical property will be returned or will be delivered in accordance with the agreement. (Parties —bailor, bailee)

bailee–person who accepts possession of a property.

gift–title to an owner's personal property voluntarily transferred by a party not receiving anything in exchange.

(B) **GIFT.** A **gift** is a gratuitous (free) transfer of the title to property. The Article 2 definition of a sale requires that the transfer of title be made for a price. Gifts are not covered under Article 2.[6]

(C) **CONTRACT FOR SERVICES.** A contract for services, such as a contract for painting a home, is not a sale of goods and is not covered under Article 2 of the UCC. Contracts for services are governed by common law principles.

(D) **CONTRACT FOR GOODS AND SERVICES.** If a contract calls for both rendering services and supplying materials to be used in performing the services, the contract is classified according to its dominant element. **For Example,** a homeowner may purchase a security system. The homeowner is paying for the equipment that is used in the system as well as for the seller's expertise and installation of that system. Is the homeowner's contract governed by Article 2, or is it a contract for services and covered under the common law of contracts?

If the service element dominates, the contract is a service contract and is governed by common law rather than Article 2. If the goods make up the dominant element of the contract, then the parties' rights are determined under Article 2.[7] In the home security system contract example, the question requires comparing the costs of the

---

[4] However, Article 2 does apply to the sale of rare coins. *Bowers and Merena Auctions, LLC, v James Lull*, 386 BR 261, 65 UCC Rep Serv 2d 194 (Haw 2008).
[5] UCC § 2-105(1)–(2). *Venmar Ventilation, Inc. v Von Weise USA, Inc*, 68 UCC Rep Serv 2d 373 (D Minn 2009); *Marcus Dairy, Inc. v Rollin Dairy Corp.*, 2008 WL 4425954 (D Conn), 67 UCC Rep Serv 2d 777
[6] The adoption of a dog from an animal shelter is not the sale of goods. *Slodov v Animal Protective League*, 628 NE2d 117 (OH App 1993).
[7] Trees and shrubs as part of a landscaping contract are sales of goods. *Kaitz v Landscape Creations, Inc.*, 2000 Mass App Div 140, 2000 WL 694274 (Mass App Div), 42 UCC Rep Serv 2d 691.

CASE SUMMARY

The Question of Goods Pops Up on Pop-Up Ads

FACTS: Click2Boost, Inc. (C2B) entered into an Internet marketing agreement with the *New York Times* (NYT) on May 10, 2002 for C2B to solicit subscribers for home delivery of the *New York Times* newspaper through "pop up ads" at Internet Web sites with which C2B maintained "[m]arketing [a]lliances." The agreement required NYT to pay C2B a fee or commission for each home delivery subscription C2B submitted to NYT. NYT paid C2B more than $1.5 million in subscription submission fees from May 2002 to September 2003, but most of the subscriptions were ended, so NYT terminated the C2B agreement on September 16, 2003.

In October 2003, Wall Street Network (WSN) took over C2B and filed suit for breach of contract against NYT. WSN said that NYT had breached the agreement by terminating it before September 30, 2003 because the contract was one for goods and C2B had furnished those goods. WSN wanted damages under the UCC for breach of a contract because the pop-up ads were sold independently as goods. NYT argued that the contract was one for services for furnishing subscribers, something C2B did not do successfully. WSN countered that the customers generated from the pop-up ads were what was being sold, just like selling a list of names, something that would be considered a good. The trial court granted the NYT summary judgment and WSN appealed.

DECISION: The court held that a contract for subscriber names generated from pop-up ads was the result of a service provided by C2B. The bulk of C2B's work was in providing the service of the pop-ups and collecting the information from them. Such a contract for services falls outside the scope of the UCC. [**Wall Street Network, Ltd. v New York Times Company, 164 Cal App 4th 1171, 80 Cal Rptr 3d 6, 66 UCC Rep Serv 2d 261 (2008)**]

system's parts versus the costs of its installation. In some contracts, the equipment costs are minimal, and installation is key for the customer. In more sophisticated security systems, the installation is a small portion of the overall contract price, and the contract would be governed by the UCC.[8]

One of the critical issues under Article 2 that has resulted from technonlogical advances is whether Article 2 covers computer software included with the sale of a computer, thus subjecting software manufacturers to warranty liability and the damage provisions of the UCC.[9] Whether software would be covered under Article 2 was the most spirited debate in the 2003 revision process.[10] Under the final draft, Revised Article 2 does not cover "information," but information is not defined. Several state legislatures have addressed this issue by modifying their versions of the

---

[8] *TK Power, Inc. v Textron, Inc.,* 433 F Supp 2d 1058 (ND Cal 2006); see also *J. O. Hooker's Sons v Roberts Cabinet,* 683 So 2d 396 (Miss 1996), in which a subcontractor's agreement to dispose of cabinets it removed from a public housing redevelopment project was held to be a service contract not governed by the UCC.

[9] *Multi-Tech Systems, Inc. v Floreat, Inc.,* 47 UCC Rep Serv 2d 924 (D Minn 2002).

[10] Section 2-103(1)(k) of Revised Article 2 defines goods as follows: all things movable at the time of identification to a contract for sale. The term includes future goods, specially manufactured goods, the unborn young of animals, growing crops, and other identified things attached to realty as described in § 2-107. The term does not include information, the money in which the price is to be paid, investment securities under Article 8, the subject matter of foreign exchange transactions and choses in action.

UCC with a section that establishes that "goods" does not cover the sale of "information" not associated with "goods."[11]

CPA   ## 3. Formation of Sales Contracts

(A) NECESSARY DETAIL FOR FORMATION. To streamline business transactions, Article 2 of the UCC does not have standards as rigid as the formation standards of common law contracts.

Under the UCC, a contract can be formed even though one or more terms are left open so long as the parties clearly intend to contract.[12] The minimum terms required for formation of an agreement under the UCC are the subject matter and quantity (if there is more than one).[13] **For Example,** an agreement that described "the sale of my white Scion" would be sufficient, but an agreement to purchase "some white Scions" would require a quantity in order to qualify for formation.[14] Other provisions under Article 2 can cover any missing terms so long as the parties are clear on their intent to contract. Article 2 has provisions that cover price, delivery, time for performance, payment, and other details of performance in the event the parties agree to a sale but have not discussed or reduced to writing their desires in these areas.[15]

(B) THE MERCHANT VERSUS NONMERCHANT PARTIES. Because Article 2 applies to all transactions in goods, it is applicable to sales by both **merchants** and nonmerchants,[16] including consumers. In most instances, the UCC treats all buyers and sellers alike. However, some sections in Article 2 are applicable only to merchants, and as a result, there are circumstances in which merchants are subject to different standards and rules. Generally, these areas of different treatment reflect the UCC's recognition that merchants are experienced, have special knowledge of the relevant commercial practices, and often need to have greater flexibility and speed in their transactions. The sections that have different rules for merchants and nonmerchants are noted throughout Chapters 24–27.

merchant—seller who deals in specific goods classified by the UCC.

offer—expression of an offeror's willingness to enter into a contractual agreement.

CPA   **(C) OFFER.** Just as in common law, the **offer** is the first step in formation of a sales contract under Article 2.[17] The common law contract rules on offers are generally applicable in sales contract formation with the exception of the **firm offer**[18]

firm offer—offer stated to be held open for a specified time, under the UCC, with respect to merchants.

[11] Up through 2002, the UCC revisions included provisions on computer information. However, the original amendments to Section 2-102 (4) and (5) never made their way into the final version of UCC 2-102. We are left only with the comment partially quoted here. The comment basically says "it depends" as to whether Article 2 applies, with the dependency on the nature of the contract.
[12] 5 UCC § 2-204(3); *Cargill v Jorgenson Farms*, 719 NW2d 226 (Minn App 2006). This provision on formation assumes that the agreement the parties do have provides "a reasonably certain basis for giving an appropriate remedy." Revised § 2-204 provides for electronic communication.
[13] *See also, H.P.B.C., Inc. v Nor-Tech Powerboats, Inc.*, 946 So2d 1108 (Fla App 2006).
[14] *Griffith v Clear Lakes Trout Co., Inc.* 200 P3d 1162, 67 UCC Rep Serv 2d 883 (Idaho 2009).
[15] For information on terms, see UCC §§ 2-305 (price), 2-307 to 2-308 (delivery), 2-310 (payment), and 2-311 (performance).
[16] *Merchant* is defined in UCC § 2-104(1). An operator of a turkey farm is not a merchant with regard to heaters used on turkey farms, only for the turkeys themselves. *Jennie-O-Foods, Inc. v Safe-Glo Prods. Corp.*, 582 NW2d 576 (Minn App 1998).
[17] A purchase order is generally considered an offer, but it must have enough information to meet the minimum standards for an offer. *Biotech Pharmacal, Inc. v International Business Connections*, LLC184 SW3d 447, 53 UCC Rep Serv 2d 476 (Ark Ct App 2004). *Westlaw E.C. Styberg Engineering Co. v Eaton Corp.*, 492 F3d 912 (CA 7 2007)
[18] Firm offers are found in UCC § 2-205.

provision, which is a special rule on offers applicable only to merchants: A firm offer by a merchant cannot be revoked if the offer (1) expresses an intention that it will be kept open, (2) is in a writing, and (3) is signed by the merchant.[19]

The period of irrevocability in a merchant's firm offer cannot exceed three months. If no specific time is given in the merchant's firm offer for its duration, it remains irrevocable only for a reasonable time. A firm offer need not have consideration to be irrevocable for a period of three months. **For Example,** a rain check given by a store on advertised merchandise is a merchant's firm offer. The rain check guarantees that you will be able to purchase two bottles of Windex at $1.99 each for a period specified in the rain check.

For nonmerchants' offers and offers in which the parties want firm offer periods that exceed three months, there must be consideration. In these situations, the parties must create an option contract just like those used in common law contracts (see Chapters 12 and 13).

(D) ACCEPTANCE—MANNER. Unlike the common law rules on acceptance, which control with great detail the method of **acceptance**, the UCC rules on acceptance are much more flexible. Under Article 2, an acceptance of an offer may be in any manner and by any medium that is reasonable under the circumstances.[20] Acceptance can occur through written communication or through performance as when a seller accepts an offer for prompt shipment of goods by simply shipping the goods.[21] However, just as under common law, Article 2 requires that if the offer

acceptance–unqualified assent to the act or proposal of another; as the acceptance of an offer to make a contract.

---

ethics&the law

Triple Crown America, Inc., said that it had been involved in extensive discussions with Biosynth AG, a German company, to be Biosynth's exclusive distributor for melatonin to the U.S. "natural food" market. The companies, in fact, began performance of a distribution contract with Biosynth sending melatonin to Triple Crown. Triple Crown, however, said that the amount sent was insufficient for national distribution. Biosynth was, in fact, sending melatonin to other distributors and not honoring what Triple Crown maintained was an exclusive sales arrangement. In addition, an article in the *Chemical Marketing Reporter* quoted a "spokeswoman" for

Biosynth as saying that it had an exclusive distributorship arrangement with Triple Crown.

Biosynth said that it never formalized its arrangements with Triple Crown and was free to deal with others. Should Biosynth be held to its publicly reported statements, or should it be able to rely on contract formation issues and the lack of specifics as a defense to the agreement? Do you think the article is an admission of the contract?*

* Triple Crown America, Inc. v Biosynth AG, 38 UCC Rep Serv 2d 746 (1999).

---

[19] A *quotation* is a firm offer. *Rich Products Corp. v Kemutec, Inc.,* 66 F Supp 2d 937 (ED Wis 1999), but *see Boydstun Metal Works, Inc. v Cottrell, Inc.,* 519 F Supp 2d 1119 (D Or 2007).

[20] UCC § 2-206(1). governs acceptance methods. *See Ardus Medical, Inc. v Emanuel County Hospital Authority,* 558 F Supp 2d 1301, 66 UCC Rep Serv 2d 367 (S D Ga 2008)

[21] UCC § 2-206(1)(b). Shipment of coal in response to an offer is acceptance. *Central Illinois Public Service Co. v Atlas Minerals, Inc.,* 146 F3d 448 (7th Cir 1998).

specifies the manner or medium of acceptance, the offer can be accepted only in that manner.

CPA

mailbox rule–timing for acceptance tied to proper acceptance.

(E) ACCEPTANCE—TIMING. The timing rules of the common law for determining when a contract has been formed are used to determine the formation of a contract under Article 2 with one slight modification. The **mailbox rule** applies under the UCC not just for the use of the same method of communication as that used by the offeror, but also applies when the offeree uses any reasonable method of communication. Under the common law, the offeree had to use the same method of communication in order to have the mailbox rule of acceptance apply. However, a UCC offeree can use any reasonable method for communicating acceptance and still enjoy the priority timing of the mailbox rule, something that makes an acceptance effective when it is sent. **For Example,** suppose that Feather-Light Brownies sent a letter offer to Cane Sugar Suppliers offering to buy 500 pounds of confectioner's sugar at $1 per pound. Cane Sugar Suppliers faxes back an acceptance of the letter offer. Cane Sugar Suppliers' acceptance is effective when it sends the fax.

CPA

mirror image rule– common law contract rule on acceptance that requires language to be absolutely the same as the offer, unequivocal and unconditional.

(F) ACCEPTANCE—LANGUAGE. Under the common law, the **mirror image rule** applies to acceptances. To be valid acceptances under common law, the language of the acceptance must be absolute, unconditional, and unequivocal; that is, the acceptance under common law must be the mirror image of the offer in order for a contract to be formed. However, the UCC has liberalized this rigid rule and permits formation even in circumstances when the acceptance includes terms that vary from the offer. The following sections explain the UCC rules on differing terms in acceptances. These rules for additional terms in acceptance were eliminated under Revised Article 2.[22]

(1) Additional Terms in Acceptance—Nonmerchants.

Under Article 2, unless an offer expressly specifies that an offer to buy or sell goods must be accepted exactly as made, the offeree may accept an offer and at the same time propose an additional term or terms. The additional term or terms in the acceptance does not result in a rejection as it would under common law. A contract is formed with the terms of the original offer. The additional terms are proposals for addition to the contract and may or may not be accepted by the other party.[23] **For Example,** Joe tells Susan, "I'll sell you my X-box for $150," and Susan responds, "I'll take it. The Halo game is included." Susan has added an additional term in her acceptance. At this point, Joe and Susan have a contract for the sale of the X-box for $150. Whether the Halo game is included is up to Joe; Joe is free to accept Susan's proposal or reject it, but his decision does not control whether he has a contract. There is a contract because Susan has made a definite statement of acceptance. To avoid being bound by a contract before she is clear on the terms, Susan should make an inquiry before using the language of acceptance, such as "Would you include the Halo game as part of the sale?" Susan's inquiry is not an acceptance and leaves the original offer still outstanding, which she is free to accept or reject.

---

[22] However, Revised Article 2 has not been adopted widely by the states.
[23] Revised Article 2 provides protections for consumers on terms they would not expect, that were not negotiated, or of which they had no knowledge. Rev UCC § 2-206.

battle of the forms–
merchants' exchanges of
invoices and purchase
orders with differing
boilerplate terms.

(2) Additional Terms in Acceptance—Merchants.

Under Article 2, the use of additional terms in acceptances by merchants is treated slightly differently. The different treatment of merchants in acceptances is the result of a commercial practice known as the **battle of the forms**, which results because a buyer sends a seller a purchase order for the purchase of goods. The seller sends back an invoice to the buyer. Although the buyer and seller may agree on the front of their documents that the subject matter of their contracts is 500 treadmills, the backs of their forms have details on the contracts, often called *boilerplate language,* that will never match. Suppose, for example, that the seller's invoice adds a payment term of "10 days same as cash." Is the payment term now a part of the parties' agreement? The parties have a meeting of the minds on the subject matter of the contract but now have a slight difference in performance terms.

Under Article 2, in a transaction between merchants, the additional term or terms sent back in an acceptance become part of the contract if the additional term or terms do not materially alter the offer and the offeror does not object in a timely fashion.[24] **For Example,** returning to the Joe and Susan example, suppose that they are both now secondary market video game merchants negotiating for the sale and purchase of a used X-box. They would have a contract, and the Halo game would be included as part of the sale. Joe could, however, avoid the problem by adding a limitation to his offer, such as "This offer is limited to these terms." With that limitation, Susan would have a contract, but the contract would not include the Halo game. Joe could also object immediately to Susan's proposal for the Halo game and still have a contract without this additional term.[25]

If the proposed additional term in the acceptance is material, a contract is formed, but the material additional term does not become a part of the contract.[26] **For Example,** if Susan added to her acceptance the statement, "Game system carries one-year warranty," she has probably added a material term because the one-year warranty for a used game system would be unusual in the secondary market and costly for Joe.[27] Again, Joe can avoid this problem by limiting his offer so as to strike any additional terms, whether material or immaterial.

The most significant changes under Revised Article 2 deal with § 2-207. Because there were so many confusing circumstances with additional terms, the effect of the new § 2-207 is to leave the issues of what is or is not included in a contract to the courts. However, because so many businesses and individuals are using the Internet to contract, they are working out their terms through ongoing and immediate exchanges and questions. The result has been a significant reduction in the number

---

[24] UCC § 2-207(2).

[25] *Oakley Fertilizer, Inc. v Continental Ins. Co.,* 276 SW3d 342 (Mo App 2009). Revised UCC Article 2 makes changes in the way these additional terms operate. When there is a record of an agreement, with no objection, the terms in the record are the terms of the contract.

[26] Damage limitations clauses are considered material. *Belden Inc. v American Electronic Components, Inc.,* 885 NE 2d 751 (Ind App 2008). Forum selection clauses are also material. *Hugo Boss Fashions, Inc. v Sam's European Tailoring, Inc.,* 293 AD 2d 296, 297, 742 NYS2d 1 (1st Dept 2002).

[27] A statute of limitations of one year added to the acceptance of an offer is considered a material change because it limits so severely the amount of time for bringing suit on the contract. *American Tempering, Inc. v Craft Architectural Metals Corp.,* 483 NYS2d 304 (1985).

FIGURE 23-1 | *Terms in Contracts under UCC Article § 2-207*

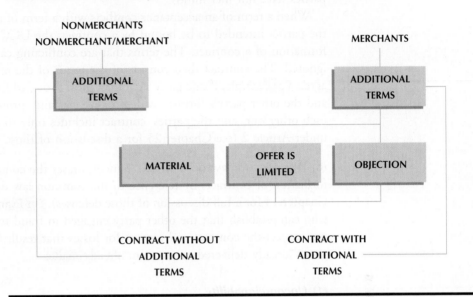

of § 2-207 cases.[28] Revised § 2-207 applies to merchants and nonmerchants alike and regardless of whether the parties use forms.

Figure 23-1 is a graphic picture of the rules on acceptance and contract terms under current Article 2 when additional terms are proposed.

Even without all the UCC provisions on contract terms, an offeror may expressly or by conduct agree to a term added by the offeree to its acceptance of the offer. The offeror may agree orally or in writing to the additional term. There can be acceptance by conduct of the additional term if the parties just perform their obligations under the contract with knowledge that the term has been added by the offeree.[29]

(3) Conflicting Terms in Acceptance.

In some situations, the offeree has not added a different term from the original offer but has instead proposed terms that contradict the terms of the offer. **For Example,** a buyer's purchase order may require the seller to offer full warranty protection, whereas the seller's invoice may include a disclaimer of all warranties. The buyer's purchase order may include a clause that provides "payment in 30 days same as cash," whereas the seller's invoice may include a term that has "10 days same as cash." Once again, it is clear that the parties intended to enter into a contract, and the subject matter is also clear. The task for Article 2 becomes one of establishing the rules that determine the terms of a contract when both sides have used different forms. However, if there are conflicting terms on the basic

---

[28] Francis J. Mootz III, "After the Battle of the Forms: Commercial Contracting in the Electronic Age," 4 *Journal of Law & Policy for the Information Society* 271, Summer, 2008.

[29] Revised UCC §2-207 provides: (3) Conduct by both parties which recognizes the existence of a contract is sufficient to establish a contract for sale although the writings of the parties do not otherwise establish a contract. In such case the terms of the particular contract consist of those terms on which the writings of the parties agree, together with any supplementary terms incorporated under any other provisions of this Act.

requirements (such as price) for formation, the courts may conclude that the parties have not met minds.[30]

When a term of an acceptance conflicts with a term of an offer but it is clear that the parties intended to be bound by a contract, the UCC still recognizes the formation of a contract. The terms that are conflicting cancel each other and are ignored. The contract then consists of the terms of the offer and acceptance that agree. **For Example,** if one party's contract form provided for full warranty protection and the other party's form provided for no warranty protection, the terms cancel each other out, and the parties' contract includes only those warranties provided under Article 2 (see Chapter 25 for a discussion of those warranties).

(G) DEFENSES TO FORMATION. Article 2 incorporates the common law defenses to formation of contracts by reference to the common law defenses in § 1-103 (see Chapter 14 for a full discussion of those defenses). **For Example,** a party to a contract who can establish that the other party engaged in fraud to get the contract formed may cancel the contract and recover for losses that result from any damages for goods already delivered or payment already made.

(1) Unconscionability.

The UCC includes an additional contract defense for parties to a sale contract called *unconscionability*.[31] This section permits a court to refuse to enforce a sales contract that it finds to be **unconscionable**, which is generally defined as grossly unfair.[32] A court may also find a clause or portions of a contract to be unconscionable and refuse to enforce those clauses or sections.[33]

unconscionable –
unreasonable, not guided or restrained by conscience and often referring to a contract grossly unfair to one party because of the superior bargaining powers of the other party.

(2) Illegality.

At common law, a contract is void if its subject matter itself is illegal, such as a contract for hire to murder someone. Under the UCC, a contract for the sale of heroin would be void. Likewise, a contract for the sale of a recalled or banned toy would be void.

(3) The Effect of Illegal Sale.

An illegal sale or contract to sell cannot be enforced. As a general rule, courts will not aid either party in recovering money or property transferred under an illegal agreement.

4. Terms in the Formed Contract

As noted earlier, contracts can be formed under Article 2 with terms of performance still missing or open. A contract is formed with just the quantity agreed on, but

---

[30] *Howard Const. Co. v Jeff-Cole Quarries, Inc.,* App, 669 SW2d 221(1984), where the acceptance changed the price, there was not an acceptance but a counteroffer.

[31] UCC § 2-302. Teri J. Dobbins, "Losing Faith: Extracting the Implied Covenant of Good Faith from (Some) Contracts, 84 Oregon Law Rev 227 (2005). *El Paso Natural Gas Co. v Minco Oil & Gas Co., Inc.,* 8 SW3d 309 (Tex 1999).

[32] Disparity in bargaining power is an issue but is not controlling. In *Intrastate Piping & Controls, Inc. v Robert-James Sales, Inc.,* 39 UCC Rep Serv 2d 347 (Ill Cir Ct 1999), a clause limiting remedies to replacement of defective pipe with no additional damages was upheld because while the seller was a large, national business and the buyer a small, local business, the contract merely incorporated industry practice in terms of remedies.

[33] An example would be voiding exorbitant interest charges but enforcing the underlying sale.

there are issues that must be resolved if the contract is to be completed. Article 2 has provisions for such missing terms.

CPA (A) PRICE. If the price for the goods is not expressly fixed by the contract, the price may be an open term, whereby the parties merely indicate how the price should be determined at a later time. In the absence of any reference to price, the price will be a reasonable price at the time of the delivery of the goods, which is generally the market price.[34]

Parties often use formulas for determining price in sales of goods. The price itself is missing from the contract until the formula is applied at some future time. The so-called **cost plus** formula for determining price has been used a great deal, particularly in commercial contracts. Under this formula, the buyer pays the seller the seller's costs for manufacture or obtaining the goods plus a specified percentage as profit.

cost plus–method of determining the purchase price or contract price equal to the seller's or contractor's costs plus a stated percentage as the profit.

The UCC allows contracts that expressly provide that one of the parties may determine the price. In such a case, that party must act in good faith, another requirement under the UCC that applies to merchants and nonmerchants in the formation and performance of their contracts.[35]

CPA (B) OUTPUT AND REQUIREMENTS CONTRACTS. The **output contract** and the **requirements contract**[36] do not specify the quantity to be sold or purchased. Instead, the contract amount is what the seller produces or the buyer requires. **For Example,** a homeowner may contract to purchase propane fuel for her winter heating needs. The propane company agrees to sell her the amount of propane she needs, which will vary from year to year according to the winter weather, her time at home, and other factors. Although the open quantity in contracts such as these introduces an element of uncertainty, such sales contracts are valid but subject to two limitations: (1) The parties must act in good faith and (2) the quantity offered or demanded must not be unreasonably disproportionate to prior output or requirements or to a stated estimate. With these restrictions, the homeowner will obtain all of the propane she needs for heating but could not use her particularly beneficial price under her open-quantity contract to purchase additional propane to sell to others.

output contract–contract of a producer to sell its entire production or output to a buyer.

requirements contract–contract in which the buyer buys its needs (requirements) from the seller.

(C) INDEFINITE DURATION TERM. When the sales contract is a continuing contract, such as one calling for periodic delivery of coal, but no time is set for the life of the contract, the contract runs for a reasonable time. It may be terminated by notice from either party to the other party.

CPA (D) CHANGES IN TERMS: MODIFICATION OF CONTRACT. An agreement to modify a contract for the sale of goods is binding even though the modification is not supported by consideration.[37] The modification is valid so long as the agreement is voluntary. **For Example,** suppose that Chester's Drug Store has agreed to purchase 300 bottles of vitamins from Pro-Life, Inc., at a price of $3.71 per bottle. Pro-Life has experienced substantial cost increases from its suppliers and asks Chester to pay

---

[34] UCC § 2-305(1) provides, "the price is a reasonable price at the time for delivery."
[35] Good faith requires that the party act honestly and, in the case of a merchant, also requires that the party follow reasonable commercial standards of fair dealing that are recognized in the trade. UCC §§ 1-201(1)(a), 2-103(1)(b);
[36] UCC § 2-306; *XTO Energy Inc. v Smith Production Inc.* 282 SW 3d 672 (Tex App 2009). *ABC Metals & Recycling Co., Inc. v Highland Computer Forms, Inc.,* 2009 WL 1212207, 68 UCC RepServ2d 735 (Iowa App 2009).
[37] UCC § 2-209(1); *Horbach v Kacz Marek,* 934 F Supp 981 (ND Ill 1996), aff'd, 388 F3d 969 (7th Cir 2002).

$3.74 per bottle. Chester is not required to agree to such a price increase because it has a valid contract for the lower price. If Chester agrees to the price increase, however, the agreement for the higher price is valid despite the lack of additional consideration on the part of Pro-Life. Chester may agree to the higher price because Pro-Life's price is still much lower than its competitors and Chester has a longstanding relationship with Pro-Life and values its customer service. However, Pro-Life could not threaten to cut off Chester's supply in order to obtain the price increase because that would be a breach of contract and would also be duress that would invalidate Chester's consent to the higher price. (See Chapter 14 for a discussion of duress.)

(E) CONTRADICTING TERMS: PAROL EVIDENCE RULE. The **parol evidence rule** (see Chapter 17 for a complete discussion) applies to the sale of goods, with the slight modification that a writing is not presumed to represent the entire contract of the parties unless the court specifically decides that it does.[38] If the court so decides, parol evidence is not admissible to add to or contradict the terms of the writing. **For Example,** suppose that Ralph Rhodes and Tana Preuss negotiate the sale of Ralph's 1965 Mustang to Tana. During their discussions, Ralph agrees to pay for an inspection and for new upholstery for the car. However, Tana and Ralph sign a simple sales contract that includes only a description of the Mustang and the price. Tana cannot enforce the two provisions because she failed to have them written into their final agreement. The parol evidence rule requires the parties to be certain that everything they want is in their agreement before they sign. The courts cannot referee disputes over collateral agreements the parties fail to put in writing.

If the court decides that the writing was not intended to represent the entire contract, the writing may be supplemented by additional extrinsic evidence, including the proof of additional terms as long as these terms are not inconsistent with the written terms. Parol evidence may also be admitted to interpret contract terms or show what the parties meant by their words. The parol evidence rule also does not prohibit the proof of fraud, misrepresentation, and any other defenses in formation.

(F) INTERPRETING CONTRACT TERMS: COURSE OF DEALING AND USAGE OF TRADE. The patterns of doing business the parties develop through their prior contractual transactions, or **course of dealing**, become part of their contract.[39] These patterns may be used to find what was intended by the express provisions in their contract and to supply otherwise missing terms. **For Example,** if the parties had 10 previous agreements and payment was always made on the 30th day following delivery, that conduct could be used to interpret the meaning of a clause "payment due in 30 days" when the start of the 30 days is not specifically agreed to in the contract.

In addition, the customs of the industry, or **usage of trade**, are adopted by courts in their interpretation of contract terms. **For Example,** suppose that a contract provides for the sale of mohair. There are two types of mohair: adult and kid. Because adult mohair is cheaper and easier to find, industry custom provides that unless the parties specifically place the term *kid* with the term *mohair* in the contract, the contract is one for the sale of adult mohair. Under Article 2, the court

parol evidence rule– rule that prohibits the introduction in evidence of oral or written statements made prior to or contemporaneously with the execution of a complete written contract, deed, or instrument, in the absence of fraud, accident, or mistake.

course of dealing– pattern of performance between two parties to a contract.

usage of trade– language and customs of an industry.

[38] UCC § 2-202.
[39] UCC § 2-208. Under Revised Article 2, § 2-208 is eliminated for those states that have adopted Revised Article 1 because Revised Article 1 contains the definition for course of performance.

need not find that a contract is ambiguous or incomplete in order to examine the parties' pattern of previous conduct as well as industry custom.[40]

5. Bulk Transfers

Bulk transfer law, Article 6 of the UCC, was created to deal with situations in which sellers of businesses fail to pay the creditors of the business and instead use the proceeds of the sale for their own use.

In 1989, the NCCUSL recommended that UCC Article 6 be repealed because it was obsolete and had little value in the modern business world. At the same time, the commissioners adopted a revised version of Article 6 (Alternative B) for adoption by those states that desired to retain the concept for bulk sales. Rather than relying on the bulk sales law, the trend is for suppliers to use UCC Article 9, Secured Transactions, for protection (See Chapter 34).

B. FORM OF SALES CONTRACT

A contract for the sale of goods may be oral or written. However, under the UCC, certain types of contracts must be evidenced by a record or they cannot be enforced in court.

CPA   ## 6. Amount

Whenever the sales price of goods is $500 or more, the sales contract must be evidenced by a record to be enforceable. Under Revised Article 2, this amount has been increased to $5,000.[41] The section of the UCC that establishes this requirement is known as the **statute of frauds**. (For more details on the statute of frauds and its role in common law contracts, see Chapter 17.)

statute of frauds–statute that, to prevent fraud through the use of perjured testimony, requires that certain kinds of contracts be in writing to be binding or enforceable.

7. Nature of the Writing Required

The requirement for a record for a contract may be satisfied by a complete written contract signed by both parties. Under Article 2, so that the state laws will be consistent with federal laws on electronic signatures (see Chapter 11), the requirement of a writing has been changed to the requirement of a "record." Under Article 2, two merchants can reduce their agreement to a record in much simpler fashion because the detail required under common law is not required to satisfy the UCC standards.

(A) TERMS. To satisfy the UCC statute of frauds, the record must indicate that there has been a completed transaction covering certain goods. Specifically, the record must (1) indicate that a sale or contract to sell has been made and (2) state the quantity of goods involved.[42] Any other missing terms may be supplied by reference to Code sections (discussed earlier) or shown by parol evidence.

(B) SIGNATURE. The record must be signed or authenticated by the person who is being held to the contract or by the authorized agent of that person. Whatever form

---

[40] Revised § 2-202 provides different rules for the use of extrinsic evidence but still includes "course of performance, course of dealing, or usage of trade" as sources for interpretation of contract terms.
[41] Under Revised Article 2, the new amount of $5,000 is found at UCC Rev Art 2, § 2-201.
[42] *Kelly-Stehney & Assoc., Inc. v McDonald's Indus. Products, Inc.,* 893 NW 2d 394 (Mich 2005).

of authentication is being used must be put in place in the record with the intention of authenticating the record. The authentication may consist of initials or may be a printed, stamped, electronic, or typewritten signature placed with the intent to authenticate.[43] **For Example,** when you enter into a contract as part of an online transaction, you are generally asked to check a box that states that you understand you are entering into a contract. Once you check that box, a pop-up appears that explains that you are about to charge your credit card or account and that you have agreed to the purchase. These steps are used to authenticate your electronic version of a signature.

The UCC statute of frauds does provide an important exception to the signature requirement for merchants that enables merchants to expedite their transactions. This exception allows merchants to create a confirmation memorandum of their oral agreement as evidence of an agreement. A merchant's *confirmation memorandum* is a letter, memo, or electronic document signed or authenticated by one of the two merchant parties to an oral agreement.[44] This memorandum can be used by either party to enforce the contract. **For Example,** suppose that Ralph has orally agreed to purchase 1,000 pounds of T-bone steak from Jane for $5.79 per pound. Jane sends Ralph a signed memo that reads, "This is to confirm our telephone conversation earlier today. I will sell you 1,000 pounds of T-bone @ $5.79 per pound." Either Ralph or Jane can use the memo to enforce the contract.

A confirming memo, in various forms of communication, sent by one merchant to another results in a binding and enforceable contract that satisfies the statute of frauds. Such a confirmation binds the nonsigning or nonauthenticating merchant, just as if he had signed the letter or a contract. A merchant can object when he receives the confirmation memo, but he must do so immediately because the confirming memo takes effect in 10 days if there is no objection.[45] This confirmation procedure makes it necessary for merchants to watch their communications and all forms of correspondence and to act within 10 days of receiving a confirmation.

CASE SUMMARY

It's Elementary: A Crayon-Scrawled Contract is Good Enough for the Statute of Frauds

FACTS: Michelle Rosenfeld, an art dealer, went to artist Jean-Michel Basquiat's apartment on October 25, 1982; while she was there, Basquiat agreed to sell her three paintings for $4,000 each, and she picked out three. Basquiat asked for a cash deposit of 10 percent; Rosenfeld left the loft but returned later with $1,000 in cash, which she paid to Basquiat. When she asked for a receipt, he insisted on drawing up a contract and got down on the floor and wrote it out in

---

[43] UCC §§ 1-201(39), 2-201; *CQ, Inc. v TXU Min. Co., LP* 565 F3d 268 (CA5 2009). Revised Article 2 permits electronic forms and signature and "record" includes e-mail, EDI transmissions, faxes, and printouts of screen pages reflecting transactions.
[44] *Siesta Sol, LLC v Brooks Pharmacy, Inc.,* 617 F Supp 2d 38 (D RI 2007).
[45] A confirmation memo is not effective when there is no underlying agreement or the parties did not agree on the terms. *Cargill Inc. v Jorgenson Farms,* 719 NW2d 226 (Minn App 2009)

CASE SUMMARY

Continued

crayon on a large piece of paper, remarking that someday this contract would be worth money. The handwritten document listed the three paintings, bore Rosenfeld's signature and Basquiat's signature, and stated: "$12,000—$1,000 DEPOSIT ¼ Oct 25 82." Rosenfeld later returned to Basquiat's loft to discuss delivery, but Basquiat convinced her to wait for at least two years so that he could show the paintings at exhibitions. After Basquiat's death, the estate argued that there was no contract because the statute of frauds made the agreement unenforceable. The estate contended that a written contract for the sale of goods must include the date of delivery. From a judgment in favor of the estate, Rosenfeld appealed.

DECISION: The contract for the sale of three paintings is governed by the UCC, and its statute of frauds applies to "transactions in goods for $500 which must be in writing or they are unenforceable. All that is required for a writing is that it provide some basis for believing that there is a real transaction." The writing supplied in this case indicated the price, the date, the specific paintings involved, and that Rosenfeld paid a deposit. It also bore the signatures of the buyer and seller and satisfied the requirements of UCC § 2-201. Because the writing, scrawled in crayon by Jean-Michel Basquiat on a large piece of paper, easily satisfied the requirements of § 2-201 of the UCC, the alleged contract is valid. [**Rosenfeld v Basquiat, 78 F3d 84 (2d Cir 1996)**]

(c) **PURPOSE OF EXECUTION.** A writing or record can satisfy a statute of frauds even though it was not made for that purpose. For example, if a buyer writes to the seller to complain that the goods have not been delivered, there is proof of the contract because the buyer's complaint indicates that there was some kind of understanding or an acknowledgment that there was a sale of those goods.

(d) **PARTICULAR WRITINGS.** Formal contracts, bills of sale, letters, and telegrams are common forms of writings that satisfy the record requirement.[46] E-mails, faxes, EDI communications, and verifications through screen printouts will generally satisfy the requirement as to record and authentication so long as they meet minimum formation standards and comply with the requirement of the UCC to specify any quantity. Two or more records grouped together may constitute a record that will be sufficient to satisfy the UCC statute of frauds.[47]

CASE SUMMARY

A Real Basket Case

FACTS: The Greenbrier Basket Company (GBC), a goods distributor, was selling woven baskets to The Pampered Chef (TPC). The ordering process would begin with TPC e-mailing GBC an offer to fill an order. GBC would then go to TPC's Web site and fill out the purchase

---

[46] Contract terms can be pieced together from invoices sent over the period of the agreement and that the buyer paid. *Fleming Companies, Inc. v Krist Oil Co.,* 324 F Supp 2d 933, 54 UCC Rep Serv 2d 120 (WD Wi 2004).
[47] *ReMapp Intern. Corp. v Comfort Keyboard Co., Inc.,* 560 F3d 628, 68 UCC Rep Serv 2d 318 (CA 7 2009). Letters grouped together satisfy UCC § 2-201. *Pepsi-Cola Co. v Steak 'N Shake, Inc.,* 981 F Supp 1149 (SD Ind 1997). Letters and faxes also satisfy the writing requirement. *Den Norske Stats Oljeselskap,* 992 F Supp 913 (SD Tex 1998), aff'd, 161 F3d 8 (5th Cir 1998).

CASE SUMMARY

Continued

order using TPC's purchase order management system and would click on the Accept P.O. button at the end of the terms and conditions field.

TPC sent Mark Beal (a GBC employee) an e-mail with an attachment showing him how to use TPC's purchase order management system, including the following:

> *Clicking on the Accept P.O. button will cause the terms and conditions of the purchase order to pop-up. The user should review these terms and conditions and click the Accept P. O. button at the bottom of the pop-up screen.... If the purchase order is not acceptable in it's [sic] current form, the user may click on the Reject and Request Changes button. This causes a pop-up window to appear where the user may enter a free-form text describing the reason for rejecting the purchase order and request changes that would make the purchase order acceptable.*

Clause 17 of the Terms and Conditions in TPC's purchase management order system provided that all disputes on contracts would be resolved in federal district court in Illinois.

When disputes over orders and payments arose, GBC filed suit against TPC in Kansas for breach of contract. TPC moved to dismiss the suit for improper venue.

DECISION: TPC's e-mails containing purchase order information constituted an offer to buy baskets. The e-mails consisted of information about the quantity of baskets to be bought, price, shipment information, and delivery dates. They also provided that to accept the P.O., GBC should go via Internet to TPC's Web site.

GBC was under a duty to read and understand the terms and conditions prior to clicking the Accept P.O. button because this was the formal acceptance required by TPC's offer to purchase baskets. Failure to read or understand the terms and conditions is not a valid reason to set those provisions aside.

A meeting of the minds requirement is proved when the minds of the parties met on the same matter and agreed upon the terms of the contract. GBC agreed upon these terms and conditions published on TPC's Web site by clicking the Accept P.O. button.

The case was dismissed in Kansas and transferred to Illinois. [**Home Basket Co., LLC v Pampered Chef, Ltd., 55 UCC Rep Serv 2d 792 (D Kan 2005)**]

8. Effect of Noncompliance

A sales agreement that does not satisfy the statute of frauds cannot be enforced. However, the oral contract itself is not unlawful and may be voluntarily performed by the parties.

9. Exceptions to Requirement of a Writing

The absence of a writing does not always mean that a sales contract is unenforceable. Article 2 provides some exceptions for the enforceability of certain oral contracts.

CPA   (A) SPECIALLY MANUFACTURED GOODS. No record is required when the goods are specially made for the buyer and are of such an unusual nature that they are not suitable for sale in the ordinary course of the seller's business. **For Example,** a manufacturer who builds a stair lift for a two-story home cannot resell the $8,000 device to someone else because it is specially built for the stairs in the buyer's home. The manufacturer could enforce the oral contract against the buyer despite the price being in excess of $500 ($5,000 under Revised Article 2).

For this nonresellable goods exception to apply, the seller must have made a substantial beginning in manufacturing the goods or, if a distributor is the seller, in procuring them before the buyer indicates she will not honor the oral contract.[48]

The stair lift manufacturer, for example, must have progressed to a point beyond simply ordering materials for construction of the lift because those materials could be used for any lift.

CPA (B) RECEIPT AND ACCEPTANCE. An oral sales contract may be enforced if it can be shown that the goods were delivered by the seller and were both received and accepted by the buyer even if the amount involved is over $500 ($5,000 Revised) and there is no record. The receipt and acceptance of the goods by the buyer makes the contract enforceable despite the statute of frauds issue. The buyer must actually receive and accept the goods. If only part of the goods have been received and accepted, the contract may be enforced only insofar as it relates to those goods received and accepted.[49] **For Example,** suppose that Wayne ordered 700 baseball jackets at a price of $72 each from Pamela. The order was taken over the telephone, and Wayne emphasized urgency. Pamela shipped the 320 jackets she had on hand and assured Wayne the remainder would be finished during the next two weeks. Wayne received the 320 jackets and sold them to a golf tournament sponsor. Wayne refused to pay Pamela because the contract was oral. Wayne must pay for the 320 jackets, but Pamela will not be able to recover for the remaining 380 jackets she manufactured.

CPA (C) PAYMENT. An oral contract may be enforced if the buyer has made full payment. In the case of partial payment for divisible units of goods, a contract may be enforced only with respect to the goods for which payment has been made and accepted. In the Pamela and Wayne example, if the circumstances were changed so that Pamela agreed to ship only if Wayne sent payment, then Pamela, upon accepting the payment, would be required to perform the contract for the amount of payment received. If partial payment is made for indivisible goods, such as an automobile, a partial payment avoids the statute of frauds and is sufficient proof to permit enforcement of the entire oral contract.

(D) ADMISSION. An oral contract may be enforced against a party if that party admits in pleadings, testimony, or otherwise in court that a contract for sale was made. The contract, however, is not enforceable beyond the quantity of goods admitted.[50]

10. Noncode Requirements

In addition to the UCC requirements for contracts that must be evidenced by a record, other statutes may impose requirements. **For Example,** state consumer

---

[48] *Golden State Porcelain Inc. v Swid Powell Design Inc.,* 37 UCC Rep Serv 2d 928 (NY 1999). Where manufacture has not begun, this exception to the statute of frauds does not apply. *EMSG Sys. Div., Inc. v Miltope Corp.,* 37 UCC Rep Serv 2d 39 (EDNC 1998).
[49] *Allied Grape Growers v Bronco Wine Co.,* 249 Cal Rptr 872 (Ct App 1988).
[50] *Delta Stat, Inc. v Michael's Carpet World,* 276 Va 524, 666 SE2d 331, 66 UCC Rep Serv 2d 897 (Va 2008).

thinking things through

Stop the Presses! Or At Least Stop Printing!

Clinton Press of Tolland provided written materials, including books and pamphlets, for Adelma G. Simmons, a woman who operated a farm known as Caprilands Herb Farm, an attraction for tourists. The books and pamphlets contained informational articles as well as collections of recipes.

Due to limited storage space at Caprilands, Clinton and Simmons agreed that the written materials would remain stored at the print shop until Simmons decided that delivery was necessary. The materials were delivered either routinely or when Simmons requested them. After each delivery, Clinton sent an invoice requesting payment by Simmons, who honored these invoices.

In 1991, the town of Tolland acquired the land on which Simmons resided. She eventually had to close

Caprilands Herb Farm as a result, which she did in 1997. Simmons directed an employee, Jack Lee, to begin to transport the stored printed materials to Caprilands, and he did so.

On December 3, 1997, Simmons died. Clinton submitted a claim against Simmons' estate for $24,599.38 for unpaid deliveries to Caprilands. These deliveries took place from February 12, 1997, to December 11, 1997, with the last two deliveries occurring after Simmons' death. The court denied the claim.*

Why would the court deny the claim? Think through the UCC Article 2 issues you see in the situation. Should the decision be reversed?

* *Kalas v Cook*, 800 A2d 553 (Conn 2002).

protection legislation commonly requires that there be a detailed contract and that a copy of it be given to the consumer.

11. Bill of Sale

bill of sale—writing signed by the seller reciting that the personal property therein described has been sold to the buyer.

Regardless of the requirement of the statute of frauds, the parties may wish to execute a writing as evidence or proof of the sale. Through custom, this writing has become known as a **bill of sale**, but it is neither a bill nor a contract. It is merely a receipt or writing signed by the seller reciting the transfer to the buyer of the title to the described property. A bill of sale can be used as proof of an otherwise oral agreement.

C. Uniform Law for International Sales

Contracts for the International Sale of Goods (CISG)—uniform international contract code contracts for international sale of goods.

The United Nations Convention on **Contracts for the International Sale of Goods (CISG)** applies to contracts between parties in the United States and parties in the other nations that have ratified the convention.[51] The provisions of this convention or international agreement have been strongly influenced by Article 2 of the UCC. The international rules of the convention automatically apply to contracts for the sale of goods if the buyer and seller have places of business in different countries that have ratified the convention. The parties may, however, choose to exclude the convention provisions in their sales contract.

[51] 52 Fed Reg 6262 (1987). While the list of adopting countries is always increasing, those countries involved in NAFTA, GATT, and the European Union (EU) (see Chapter 7) have adopted the CISG. For complete text, commentary, and case law on CISG, go to **www.cisg.law.pace.edu**.

12. Scope of the CISG

The CISG does not govern all contracts between parties in the countries that have ratified it. The CISG does not apply to goods bought for personal, family, or household use.[52] The CISG also does not apply to contracts in which the predominant part of the obligations of the party who furnishes the goods consists of the supply of labor or other services. The CISG has five chapters and 101 articles, and the articles have no titles to them. There is a limited body of case law interpreting the CISG because so many of the decisions under the CISG come through arbitration and other forms of dispute resolution, typical of international commercial arrangements.

D. Leases of Goods

Leases of goods represent a significant part of both contract law and the economy. There are more than $240 billion worth of lease transactions in the United States each year, an amount equal to roughly one-third of all capital investment each year in the United States.[53] One-fourth of all vehicles in the United States are leased. Article 2A of the UCC codifies the law of leases for tangible movable goods. Article 2A applies to any transaction, regardless of form, that creates a lease of personal property or fixtures. Many of the provisions of Article 2 were carried over but changed to reflect differences in style, leasing terminology, or leasing practices.[54] As a practical matter, leases will be of durable goods, such as equipment and vehicles of any kind, computers, boats, airplanes, and household goods and appliances. A **lease** is "a transfer of the right to possession and use of goods for a term in return for consideration."[55]

lease – agreement between the owner of property and a tenant by which the former agrees to give possession of the property to the latter for payment of rent. (Parties— landlord or lessor, tenant or lessee)

13. Types of Leases

Article 2A regulates consumer leases, commercial leases, finance leases, nonfinance leases, and subleases. These categories may overlap in some cases, such as when there is a commercial finance lease.

(A) Consumer Lease. A **consumer lease** is made by a merchant lessor regularly engaged in the business of leasing or selling the kinds of goods involved. A consumer lease is made to a natural person (not a corporation) who takes possession of the goods primarily for personal, family, or household use. Each state places a cap on the amount considered a consumer lease. Section 2A-103(f) simply provides that the state should place its own amount in this section with the admonition to place the cap at a level that ensures that vehicle leases will be covered under the law. During the period from 2002–2007, there were a number of suits brought by individuals injured in auto accidents against the leasing companies of the drivers who were driving their leased autos at the time they caused an accident. Many states were holding the leasing companies liable for those accidents because

consumer lease – lease of goods by a natural person for personal, family, or household use.

---

[52] The UNIDROIT Principles are often used as guidelines for resolving issues in international consumer contracts. M. J. Bonell, "The CISG, European Contract Law and the Development of a World Contract Law," 56 *American Journal of Comparative Law*, 1–28 (2008).

[53] U.S. Department of Commerce, Bureau of Economic Analysis, International Trade Administration and Equipment Leasing Association of America, Trends and Forecasts for Equipment Leasing in the United States (2002).

[54] Forty-nine states (Louisiana has not adopted Article 2A), the District of Columbia, and the Virgin Islands have adopted all or some portions of Article 2A. Not all states have adopted the 1997 version of Article 2A, and some have adopted only selected portions of the 1997 version.

[55] UCC § 2A-103(1)(j). The definition of what constitutes a lease is the subject of continuing examination by the UCC Article 2A drafters and the American Law Institute.

they were title holders of the cars. As a result, leasing companies stopped doing business in certain states because of the liability exposure.

As a result, the federal government passed legislation that preempted all state laws and limited the liability of vehicle leasing companies to a basic level of liability that was limited to mandatory insurance coverage standards.[56]

nonconsumer lease – lease that does not satisfy the definition of a consumer lease; also known as a *commercial lease.*

commercial lease – any nonconsumer lease.

finance lease – three-party lease agreement in which there is a lessor, a lessee, and a financier.

(B) COMMERCIAL LEASE. When a lease does not satisfy the definition of a consumer lease, it may be called a **nonconsumer** or a **commercial lease**. For Example, a contractor's one-year rental of a truck to haul materials is a commercial lease.

(C) FINANCE LEASE. A **finance lease** is a three-party transaction involving a lessor, a lessee, and a supplier. Instead of going directly to a supplier for goods, the customer goes to a financier and tells the financier where to obtain the goods and what to obtain. The financier then acquires the goods and either leases or subleases the goods to its customer. The financier-lessor is in effect a paper channel, or conduit, between the supplier and the customer-lessee. The customer-lessee must approve the terms of the transaction between the supplier and the financier-lessor.[57]

14. Form of Lease Contract

The lease must be evidenced by a record if the total of the payments under the lease will be $1,000 or more. The record must be authenticated by the party against whom enforcement is sought. The record must describe the leased goods, state the term of the lease, and indicate that a lease contract has been formed.[58]

15. Warranties

Under Article 2A, the lessor, except in the case of finance leases, makes all usual warranties that are made by a seller in a sale of goods. In a finance lease, however, the real parties in interest are the supplier, who supplies the lessor with the goods, and the lessee, who leases the goods. The lessee looks to the supplier of the goods for warranties. Any warranties, express or implied, made by the supplier to the lessor are passed on to the lessee, who has a direct cause of action on them against the supplier regardless of the lack of privity.[59] For Example, if a consumer leased an auto and the auto had a defective steering mechanism that resulted in injury to the consumer, the consumer would have a cause of action against the auto manufacturer.

16. Default

The lease agreement and provisions of Article 2A determine whether the lessor or lessee is in default. If either the lessor or the lessee is in default under the lease contract, the party seeking enforcement may obtain a judgment or otherwise enforce the lease contract by any available judicial or nonjudicial procedure. Neither the

---

[56] See, e.g., *Oliveira v Lombardi* 794 A2d 453 (RI 2002). The federal law did not affect all of the suits that were pending at the time of the passage of the federal law. Those suits were permitted to proceed as long as they had been filed by the end of 2005. Those suits should all be concluding 2010. Future recovery will be limited to mandatory policy requirements.

[57] UCC § 2A-103(1)(g). One of the evolving issues in lease financing is the relationship of the parties, the use of liens, and the role of Article 9 security interests (see Chapter 34). The NCCUSL has created Uniform Certificate of Title Act (UCOTA) that makes the interrelationships of lien laws, Article 2, and Article 9 clear. UCOTA was available for adoption by the states in 2006. As of 2009, no states had adopted it, and Oklahoma was the only state to introduce the UCOTA as proposed law.

[58] UCC § 2-201(b).

[59] UCC § 2A-209.

e-commerce&cyberlaw

LOL at Wax Seals: The Electronic Contract

The federal Electronic Signatures in Global and National Commerce Act (E-Sign) took effect October 1, 2000. The *National Law Journal* stated: "Not since notarized written signatures replaced wax and signet rings has history seen such a fundamental change in contract law."*

The states can now use the Uniform Electronic Transactions Act (UETA) for meeting the new federal mandates on E-sign. The UETA was passed as a uniform law in July 1999, and 47 states plus the District of Columbia and the Virgin Islands have adopted it in some form.**

Issues that remain unresolved in this new era of electronic contracting are security and verification. Businesses must be able to verify that the electronic signatures are authentic and that orders from their stated origins are authentic. Furthermore, companies must be able to provide some form of record for auditors to verify transactions.

Consumer signatures have progressed, with more merchants allowing consumers to sign on a telepad at the point of service. However, the issue of identity remains a problem when there are not ongoing relationships as there are in business-to-business transactions.

* Mark Ballard, "E-Sign a Nudge, Not a Revolution," *National Law Journal*, September 25, 2000, B1, B4.
** UETA states are Alabama, Alaska, Arizona, Arkansas, California, Colorado, Connecticut, Delaware, District of Columbia, Florida, Hawaii, Idaho, Indiana, Iowa, Kansas, Kentucky, Louisiana, Maine, Maryland, Massachusetts, Michigan, Minnesota, Mississippi, Montana, Nebraska, Nevada, New Hampshire, New Jersey, New Mexico, North Carolina, North Dakota, Ohio, Oklahoma, Oregon, Pennsylvania, Rhode Island, South Carolina, South Dakota, Tennessee, Texas, Utah, Virginia, West Virginia, Wisconsin, and Wyoming. State legislatures have rejected the Uniform Computer Information Transactions Act (UCITA).

lessor nor the lessee is entitled to notice of default or notice of enforcement from the other party. Both the lessor and the lessee have rights and remedies similar to those given to a seller in a sales contract.[60] If the lessee defaults, the lessor is entitled to recover any rent due, future rent, and incidental damages.[61] (See Chapter 27 for more information on remedies.)

lawflix

Beethoven (1992)(G)

Charles Grodin plays a fussy father who has founded and runs an air freshener company. Part of the plot centers on an investment in the company by some venture capitalists who are interested in using Grodin's company as a supplier. There are contract negotiations as well as issues of warranty and liability.

Check out LawFlix at **www.cengage.com/blaw/dvl** to access movie clips that illustrate business law concepts.

[60] UCC §§ 2A-501, 2A-503; *Torres v Banc One Leasing Corp*, 226 F Supp 2d 1345 (ND Ga 2002).
[61] UCC § 2A-529.

MAKE THE CONNECTION

SUMMARY

Contracts for services and real estate are governed by the common law. Contracts for the sale of goods are governed by Article 2 of the UCC. *Goods* are defined as anything movable at the time they are identified as the subject of the transaction. Goods physically existing and owned by the seller at the time of the transaction are *existing goods*.

A *sale of goods* is the transfer of title to tangible personal property for a price. A *bailment* is a transfer of possession but not title and is therefore not a sale. A *gift* is not a sale because no price is paid for the gift. A contract for services is an ordinary contract and is not governed by the UCC. If a contract calls for both the rendering of services and the supplying of goods, the contract is classified according to its dominant element.

The common law contract rules for intent to contract apply to the formation of contracts under the UCC. However, several formation rules under the UCC differ from common law contract rules. A merchant's firm offer is irrevocable without the payment of consideration. The UCC rules on additional terms in an acceptance permit the formation of a contract despite the changes. These proposals for new terms are not considered counteroffers under the UCC. The terms that are included are determined by detailed rules. If the transaction is between nonmerchants, a contract is formed without the additional terms, which the original offeror is free to accept or reject. If the transaction is between merchants, the additional terms become part of the contract if those terms do not materially alter the offer and no objection is made to them. There is no distinction between merchant and nonmerchant for additional terms under Revised Article 2 and the terms issues is left to the courts.

The same defenses available to formation under common law are incorporated in Article 2. In addition, the UCC recognizes unconscionability as a defense to formation.

The UCC does not require the parties to agree on every aspect of contract performance for the contract to be valid. Provisions in Article 2 will govern the parties' relationship in the event their agreement does not cover all terms. The price term may be expressly fixed by the parties. The parties may make no provision as to price, or they may indicate how the price should be determined later. In output or requirements contracts, the quantity that is to be sold or purchased is not specified, but such contracts are nevertheless valid. A sales contract can be modified even though the modification is not supported by consideration. The parol evidence rule applies to a sale of goods in much the same manner as to ordinary contracts. However, the UCC permits the introduction of evidence of course of dealing and usage of trade for clarification of contract terms and performance.

The UCC's statute of frauds provides that a sales contract for $500 ($5,000 under Revised Article 2) or more must be evidenced by a record. The UCC's merchant's confirmation memorandum allows two merchants to be bound to an otherwise oral agreement by a memo or letter signed by only one party that stands without objection for 10 days. Several exceptions to the UCC statute of frauds exist: when the goods are specially made or procured for the buyer and are nonresellable in the seller's ordinary market; when the buyer has received and accepted the goods; when the buyer has made either full or partial payment; and when the party against whom enforcement is sought admits in court pleadings or testimony that a contract for sale was made.

Uniform rules for international sales are applicable to contracts for sales between parties in countries that have ratified the CISG. Under the CISG, a contract for the sale of goods need not be in any particular form and can be proven by any means.

Article 2A of the UCC regulates consumer leases, commercial leases, finance leases, nonfinance leases, and subleases of tangible movable goods. A lease subject to Article 2A must be in writing if the lease payments will total $1,000 or more.

LEARNING OUTCOMES

After studying this chapter, you should be able to clearly explain:

A. NATURE AND LEGALITY

LO.1 Define a sale of goods and explain when UCC Article 2 applies to contracts
See *Wall Street Network, Ltd. v New York Times Company,* on p. 506.

LO.2 Distinguish between an actual sale of goods and other types of transactions in goods
See the discussion of bailments on p. 505.

LO.3 Describe how contracts are formed under Article 2, and list the differences in formation standards between the UCC and common law
See the **For Example,** discussion of Joe and Susan's X-box transaction on p. 509.
See the *Greenbriar* basket case on p. 517.

B. FORM OF SALES CONTRACT

LO.4 Explain when a contract for the sale of goods must be in writing
See the *Basquiat* case on p. 516.

LO.5 List and explain the exceptions to the requirement that certain contracts be in writing
See the **For Example,** discussion of Wayne and the baseball jackets on p. 519.

C. UNIFORM LAW FOR INTERNATIONAL SALES

LO.6 Discuss the purpose of the United Nations Convention on Contracts for the International Sale of Goods
See the discussion of the CISG on p. 520.

KEY TERMS

acceptance	cost plus	mirror image rule
Article 2	course of dealing	nonconsumer lease
bailee	existing goods	offer
bailment	finance lease	output contract
battle of the forms	firm offer	parol evidence rule
bill of sale	future goods	requirements contract
commercial lease	gift	statute of frauds
consumer lease	goods	unconscionable
Contracts for the	lease	usage of trade
International Sale of	mailbox rule	
Goods (CISG)	merchants	

QUESTIONS AND CASE PROBLEMS

1. Triple H Construction Co. contracted with Hunter's Run Stables, Inc., to erect a horse barn and riding arena on Hunter's Run's property in Big Flats, New York. Hunter's Run got a guarantee in its contract with Triple H that "such design with the span so shown will support its weight and will withstand natural forces including but not limited to snow load and wind." Hunter's Run also got the following guarantee from Rigidply, the manufacturer of the rafters: "Rigidply … hereby guarantees that the design to be used for the construction of a horse barn by Triple H … will support the weight of such barn and to snow load and wind as per drawings." The barn was completed in 1983 and collapsed under the weight of snow in 1994. Hunter's Run has sued Triple H for UCC Article 2 remedies. Does Article 2 apply? [*Hunter's Run Stables, Inc. v Triple H, Inc.*, 938 F Supp 166 (WDNY)]

2. R-P Packaging manufactured cellophane wrapping material that was used by Kern's Bakery in packaging its product. Kern's decided to change its system for packaging cookies from a tied bread bag to a tray covered with printed cellophane wrapping. R-P took measurements to determine the appropriate size for the cellophane wrapping and designed the artwork to be printed on the wrapping. After agreeing that the artwork was satisfactory, Kern placed a verbal order for the cellophane at a total cost of $13,000. When the printed wrapping material was received, Kern complained that it was too short for the trays and the artwork was not centered. The material, however, conformed exactly to the order placed by Kern. Kern returned the material to R-P by overnight express. R-P sued Kern. Kern claimed that because there was no written contract, the suit was barred by the statute of frauds. What result? [*Flowers Baking Co. v R-P Packaging, Inc.*, 329 SE2d 462 (Va)]

3. Smythe wrote to Lasco Dealers inquiring about the price of a certain freezer. Lasco wrote her a letter, signed by its credit manager, stating that Smythe could purchase the freezer in question during the next 30 days for $400. Smythe wrote back the next day ordering a freezer at that price. Lasco received Smythe's letter the following day, but Lasco wrote a response letter stating that it had changed the price to $450. Smythe claims that Lasco could not change its price. Is she correct?

4. Mrs. Downing was fitted for dentures by a dentist, Dr. Cook. After she received her dentures, Mrs. Downing began experiencing mouth pain that she attributed to Dr. Cook's manufacture of dentures that did not fit her properly. Mrs. Downing filed suit against Dr. Cook for breach of warranty under Article 2 of the UCC. Dr. Cook defended on the grounds that his denture work was a service and therefore not covered under Article 2 warranties. The trial court found for Mrs. Downing, and Dr. Cook appealed. Is Dr. Cook correct? Are the dentures a contract for services or goods? [*Cook v Downing*, 891 P2d 611 (Okla App)] Would silicone breast implants be covered by the UCC Article 2 warranties? Does implantation of silicone gel implants constitute a sale of goods by the surgeon? [*In re Breast Implant Product Liability Litigation*, 503 SE2d 445 (SC)]

5. Meyers was under contract with Henderson to install overhead doors in a factory that Henderson was building. Meyers obtained the disassembled doors from the manufacturer. His contract with Henderson required Meyers to furnish all labor, materials, tools, and equipment to satisfactorily complete the installation of all overhead doors. Henderson felt the doors were not installed properly and paid less than one-half of the contract price after subtracting his costs for correcting the installation. Because of a business sale and other complications, Meyers did not sue Henderson for the difference in payment until five years later. Henderson raised the defense that because the contract was for the sale of goods, it was barred by the Code's four-year statute of limitations. Meyers claimed that it was a contract for services and that suit could be brought within six years. Who is correct? Why? [*Meyers v Henderson Construction Co.*, 370 A2d 547 (NJ Super)]

6. Valley Trout Farms ordered fish food from Rangen. Both parties were merchants. The invoice that was sent with the order stated that a specified charge—a percentage common in the industry—would be added to any unpaid bills. Valley Trout Farms did not pay for the food and did not make any objection to the late charge stated in the invoice. When sued by Rangen, Valley Trout Farms claimed that it had never agreed to the late charge and therefore was not required to pay it. Is Valley Trout Farms correct? [*Rangen, Inc. v Valley Trout Farms, Inc.*, 658 P2d 955 (Idaho)]

7. LTV Aerospace Corp. manufactured all-terrain vehicles for use in Southeast Asia. LTV made an oral contract with Bateman under which Bateman would supply the packing cases needed for the vehicles' overseas shipment. Bateman made substantial beginnings in the production of packing cases following LTV's specifications. LTV thereafter stopped production of its vehicles and refused to take delivery of any cases. When Bateman sued for breach of contract, LTV argued that the contract could not be enforced because there was no writing that satisfied the statute of frauds. Was this a valid defense? [*LTV Aerospace Corp. v Bateman*, 492 SW2d 703 (Tex App)]

8. Syrovy and Alpine Resources, Inc., entered into a "Timber Purchase Agreement." Syrovy agreed to sell and Alpine agreed to buy all of the timber produced during a two-year period. The timber to be sold, purchased, and delivered was to be produced by Alpine from timber on Syrovy's land. Alpine

continued harvesting for one year and then stopped after making an initial payment. Syrovy sued Alpine. Alpine alleged there was no contract because the writing to satisfy the statute of frauds must contain a quantity term. Decide. [*Syrovy v Alpine Resources, Inc.*, 841 P2d 1279 (Wash App)]

9. Ray Thomaier placed an order with Hoffman Chevrolet, Inc., for a specifically optioned 1978 Limited Edition Corvette Coupe. The order form described the automobile and the options Mr. Thomaier wanted, included the purchase price, and provided for delivery to the purchaser "A.S.A.P." Thomaier signed the order form in the place designated for his signature and gave the dealer a $1,000 check as a deposit. This check was deposited into the account of Hoffman Chevrolet and cleared. On the same day that Thomaier gave Hoffman the check, Hoffman placed a written order with defendant General Motors Corporation, Chevrolet Motor Division, for the 1978 Limited Edition Corvette Coupe. The order was placed on a form supplied by General Motors, was signed by the dealer and listed Thomaier as the "customer." About a month later, Hoffman sent Thomaier a letter that explained that "market conditions" had made his "offer" unacceptable and that his deposit of $1,000 was being refunded. The vehicle was ultimately manufactured by Chevrolet and delivered to Hoffman. Hoffman sold this specific vehicle to a third party.

  Thomaier filed suit, but Hoffman responded that because it had never signed the order, it was not binding. Hoffman argues there was no acceptance and therefore no binding contract. Is Hoffman correct? [*Thomaier v Hoffman Chevrolet, Inc.*, 410 NYS2d 645 (Supreme Court NY)]

10. Fastener Corp. sent a letter to Renzo Box Co. that was signed by Ronald Lee, Fastener's sales manager, and read as follows: "We hereby offer you 200 type #14 Fastener bolts at $5 per bolt. This offer will be irrevocable for ten days." On the fifth day, Fastener informed Renzo it was revoking the offer, alleging that there was no consideration for the offer. Could Fastener revoke? Explain.

11. Richard, a retailer of video equipment, telephoned Craft Appliances and ordered a $1,000 videotape recorder for his business. Craft accepted Richard's order and sent him a copy of the purchase memorandum that stated the price, quantity, and model ordered and that was stamped "order accepted by Craft." Richard, however, did not sign or return the purchase memorandum and refused to accept delivery of the recorder when Craft delivered it to him three weeks later. Craft sued Richard, who raised the statute of frauds as a defense. Will Richard prevail? Why or why not?

12. REMC furnished electricity to Helvey's home. The voltage furnished was in excess of 135 volts and caused extensive damage to his 110-volt household appliances. Helvey sued REMC for breach of warranty. Helvey argued that providing electrical energy is not a transaction in goods but a furnishing of services, so that he had six years to sue REMC rather than the UCC's four-year statute of limitations, which had expired. Was it a sale of goods or a sale of services? Identify the ethical principles involved in this case. [*Helvey v Wabash County REMC*, 278 NE2d 608 (Ind App)]

13. U.S. Surgical manufactures medical surgical instruments and markets the instruments to hospitals. The packaging for U.S. Surgical's disposable medical instruments is labeled "for single use only." As an example, one label contains the following language: "Unless opened or damaged, contents of package are sterile. DO NOT RESTERILIZE. For multiple use during a SINGLE surgical procedure. DISCARD AFTER USE."

    Orris provides a service to the hospitals that purchase U.S. Surgical's disposable instruments. After the hospitals use or open the instruments, Orris cleans, resterilizes, and/or resharpens the instruments for future use and returns them to the hospitals from which they came. U.S. Surgical filed suit asserting that reprocessing, repackaging, and reuse of its disposable instruments constituted a violation of its patent and trademark rights. Orris says that U.S. Surgical did not prohibit hospitals from re-using the instruments and it was not doing anything that violated the contracts U.S. Surgical had with the hospitals. U.S. Surgical says the language on the packaging was an additional terms that the hospitals accepted by opening the packages and using the instruments. Who is correct? [*U.S. Surgical Corp. v Orris, Inc.*, 5 F Supp 2d 1201 (D Kan); Affirmed 185 F3d 885 (10th Cir) and 230 F3d 1382 (Fed Cir)]

14. Flora Hall went to Rent-A-Center in Milwaukee and signed an agreement to make monthly payments of $77.96 for 19 months in exchange for Rent-A-Center's allowing her to have a Rent-A-Center washer and dryer in her home. In addition, the agreement required Hall to pay tax and a liability waiver fee on the washer and dryer. The total amount she would pay under the agreement was $1,643.15. The agreement provided that Hall would return the washer and dryer at the end of the 19 months, or she could, at that time, pay $161.91 and own the washer and dryer as her own. Is this a sales contract? Is this a consumer lease? At the time Hall leased her washer and dryer, she could have purchased a set for about $600. What do you think about the cost of her agreement with Rent-A-Center? Is it unconscionable? Refer to Chapter 33, and determine whether any other consumer laws apply. Must this contract be in writing? [*Rent-A-Center, Inc. v Hall*, 510 NW2d 789 (Wis)]

CPA QUESTIONS

1. Webstar Corp. orally agreed to sell Northco, Inc., a computer for $20,000. Northco sent a signed purchase order to Webstar confirming the agreement. Webstar received the purchase order and did not respond. Webstar refused to deliver the computer to Northco, claiming that the purchase order did not satisfy the UCC statute of frauds because it was not signed by Webstar. Northco sells computers to the general public, and Webstar is a computer wholesaler. Under the UCC Sales Article, Webstar's position is:

    a. Incorrect, because it failed to object to Northco's purchase order

    b. Incorrect, because only the buyer in a sale-of-goods transaction must sign the contract

c. Correct, because it was the party against whom enforcement of the contract is being sought

d. Correct, because the purchase price of the computer exceeded $500

2. On May 2, Lace Corp., an appliance wholesaler, offered to sell appliances worth $3,000 to Parco, Inc., a household appliances retailer. The offer was signed by Lace's president and provided that it would not be withdrawn before June 1. It also included the shipping terms: "F.O.B.—Parco's warehouse." On May 29, Parco mailed an acceptance of Lace's offer. Lace received the acceptance June 2. Which of the following is correct if Lace sent Parco a telegram revoking its offer and Parco received the telegram on May 25?

a. A contract was formed on May 2.

b. Lace's revocation effectively terminated its offer on May 25.

c. Lace's revocation was ineffective because the offer could not be revoked before June 1.

d. No contract was formed because Lace received Parco's acceptance after June 1.

3. Bond and Spear orally agreed that Bond would buy a car from Spear for $475. Bond paid Spear a $100 deposit. The next day, Spear received an offer of $575, the car's fair market value. Spear immediately notified Bond that Spear would not sell the car to Bond and returned Bond's $100. If Bond sues Spear and Spear defends on the basis of the statute of frauds, Bond will probably:

a. Lose, because the agreement was for less than the fair market value of the car

b. Win, because the agreement was for less than $500

c. Lose, because the agreement was not in writing and signed by Spear

d. Win, because Bond paid a deposit

4. Cookie Co. offered to sell Distrib Markets 20,000 pounds of cookies at $1.00 per pound, subject to certain specified terms for delivery. Distrib replied in writing as follows: "We accept your offer for 20,000 pounds of cookies at $1.00 per pound, weighing scale to have valid city certificate." Under the UCC:

a. A contract was formed between the parties.

b. A contract will be formed only if Cookie agrees to the weighing scale requirement.

c. No contract was formed because Distrib included the weighing scale requirement in its reply.

d. No contract was formed because Distrib's reply was a counteroffer.

Chapter 25

PRODUCT LIABILITY: WARRANTIES AND TORTS

A. General Principles

  1. THEORIES OF LIABILITY

  2. NATURE OF HARM

  3. WHO IS LIABLE IN PRODUCT LIABILITY

B. Express Warranties

  4. DEFINITION OF EXPRESS WARRANTY

  5. FORM OF EXPRESS WARRANTY

  6. SELLER'S OPINION OR STATEMENT OF VALUE

  7. WARRANTY OF CONFORMITY TO DESCRIPTION, SAMPLE, OR MODEL

  8. FEDERAL REGULATION OF EXPRESS WARRANTIES

  9. EFFECT OF BREACH OF EXPRESS WARRANTY

C. Implied Warranties

  10. DEFINITION OF IMPLIED WARRANTY

  11. IMPLIED WARRANTIES OF SELLERS

  12. ADDITIONAL IMPLIED WARRANTIES OF MERCHANT SELLERS

  13. IMPLIED WARRANTIES IN PARTICULAR SALES

  14. NECESSITY OF DEFECT

  15. WARRANTIES IN THE INTERNATIONAL SALE OF GOODS

D. Disclaimer of Warranties

  16. VALIDITY OF DISCLAIMER

  17. PARTICULAR LANGUAGE FOR DISCLAIMERS

  18. EXCLUSION OF WARRANTIES BY EXAMINATION OF GOODS

  19. POSTSALE DISCLAIMER

E. Other Theories of Product Liability

  20. NEGLIGENCE

  21. FRAUD

  22. STRICT TORT LIABILITY

  23. CUMULATIVE THEORIES OF LIABILITY

What happens when goods do not work? Who can recover for injury caused by defective goods? What can you do when the goods are not as promised or pictured?

A. General Principles

When defective goods result in damages or injury to the buyer or other parties, the UCC and tort law provide remedies.

1. Theories of Liability

Two centuries ago, a buyer was limited to recovery from a seller for breach of an express guarantee or for negligence or fraud. After the onset of mass production and distribution, however, these remedies had little value. A guarantee was good, but in the ordinary sales transaction no one stopped to get a guarantee. Few customers remembered to ask the manager of the supermarket to give a guarantee that the loaf of bread purchased was fit to eat. Further, negligence and fraud have become difficult to prove in a mass production world. How can one prove there was a problem in the production process for a can of soup prepared months earlier?

To give buyers protection from economic loss and personal injuries, the concept of warranty liability developed. **Warranties** are either express or implied and can be found in the UCC. As with other UCC areas, there have been changes in warranty liability under the Revised UCC, and those areas of change are discussed in the sections that follow. Many courts have decided that still broader protection beyond the UCC contract remedies is required and have created the additional concept of **strict tort liability** for defective goods.

There are five theories in law for what is often called *product liability*, or the protection of buyers that also allows them recovery for injury and economic loss: express warranty, implied warranty, negligence, fraud, and strict tort liability. Any statutory remedies under consumer law or employment law are additional means of recovery. The plaintiff does not have a choice of all theories in every case; the facts of the case dictate the choices the plaintiff has available for possible theories of recovery.

2. Nature of Harm

A defective product can cause harm to person, property, or economic interests. **For Example,** the buyer of a truck may be injured when, through a defect, the truck goes out of control and plunges down the side of a hill. Passengers in the truck, bystanders, or the driver of a car hit by the truck may also be injured. The defective truck may cause injury to a total stranger who seeks to rescue one of the victims. Property damage could occur if the buyer's truck careens off the road into a fence or even a house and causes damages. Another driver's car may be damaged. Commercial and economic interests of the buyer are affected by the fact that the truck is defective. Even if there is no physical harm, the defective truck is not as valuable as it would have been. The buyer who has paid for the truck on the basis of its value as it should have been has sustained an economic loss. If the buyer is

---

warranty–promise either express or implied about the nature, quality, or performance of the goods.

strict tort liability–product liability theory that imposes liability upon the manufacturer, seller, or distributor of goods for harm caused by defective goods.

required to rent a truck from someone else or loses an opportunity to haul freight for compensation, the fact that the truck was defective also causes economic or commercial loss.

CPA   3. Who is Liable in Product Liability

privity of contract–
relationship between a promisor and the promisee.

Until the early part of the twentieth century, only the parties to a sales contract could recover from each other on product liability issues. A seller was liable to the buyer, but the seller was not liable to others because they were not in **privity of contract** with the seller or in a direct contract relationship with the seller. This requirement of privity of contract has now been widely rejected.[1]

(A) WHO CAN RECOVER UNDER UCC WARRANTIES. Today, not only the buyer but also customers and employees of the buyer and even third persons or bystanders may recover because of harm caused by a defective product. Most states have abolished the requirement of **privity** when the person injured by a product is a member of the buyer's family or household or is a guest of the buyer and has sustained personal injury because of the product.[2] A few states require privity of contract, particularly when the plaintiff does not sustain personal injury or property damage and seeks to recover only economic loss.[3]

privity–succession or chain of relationship to the same thing or right, such as privity of contract, privity of estate, privity of possession.

UCC section 2-318 provides alternatives for who can recover for breach of warranty. Alternative A extends warranty protection to "any individual who is in the family or household of the immediate buyer or the remote purchaser or who is a guest in the home of either…." Alternative B covers "any individual who may reasonably be expected to use, consume, or be affected by the goods." Alternative C covers the same groups as Alternative B but adds that the protections provided cannot be disclaimed.

(B) WHO IS LIABLE UNDER UCC WARRANTIES. Someone who is injured by a defective product can recover from the seller, the manufacturer of the product, and generally even the manufacturer of the component part of the product that caused the harm.[4] **For Example,** when a person is struck by an automobile because the driver has lost control because of the car's defective brakes, the person who was struck and injured may seek recovery from the seller and the manufacturer of the car. The maker of the brake assembly or system that the car manufacturer installed in the car may also be liable.

---

[1] UCC § 2-318, Alternative A. The Code gives the states the option of adopting the provision summarized in this chapter or of making a wide abolition of the requirement of privity by adopting Alternative B or C of § 2-318. As of March 2004, these states/areas had adopted the versions of § 2-318 (not Revised Article 2) as follows: Alternative A adopted in Alaska, Arizona, Arkansas, Connecticut, District of Columbia, Florida, Georgia, Idaho, Illinois, Indiana, Kentucky, Maryland, Michigan, Mississippi, Missouri, Montana, Nebraska, Nevada (has adopted Revised Article 2), New Jersey, New Mexico, North Carolina, Ohio, Oklahoma, Oregon, Pennsylvania, Tennessee, Virgin Islands, Washington, West Virginia, and Wisconsin. Alternative B adopted in Alabama, Colorado, Delaware, Kansas (has adopted Revised Article 2), New York, South Carolina, South Dakota, Vermont, and Wyoming. Alternative C adopted in Hawaii, Iowa, Minnesota, North Dakota, and Utah.

[2] Lack of privity is not a defense in a suit for breach of warranty. *Hyundai Motor America, Inc. v Goodin*, 822 NE2d 947 (Ind 2005) Revised Article 2 expands warranty protection (§§ 2-408 and 2-409).

[3] *Praxair, Inc. v General Insulation Co.* 611 F Supp 2d 318 (WDNY 2009).

[4] However, see *Barnett v Leiserv*, 968 F Supp 690 (ND Ga 1997), where the child of the person who bought coffee for a friend could not sue to recover for burns from coffee spilled on her by the friend. The court also noted that a child who spills coffee on himself could not recover either. Where the coffee maker at the retail store where the coffee was purchased is not defective, the case is one in negligence and requires proof of breach of duty but does not require privity. *McMahon v Bunn-O-Matic Corp.* 150 F3d 651 (CA 7 1998).

B. Express Warranties

A warranty may be express or implied. Both express and implied warranties operate as though the defendant had made an express promise or statement of fact. Both express and implied warranties are governed primarily by the UCC.

CPA   ## 4. Definition of Express Warranty

express warranty – statement by the defendant relating to the goods, which statement is part of the basis of the bargain.

An **express warranty** is a statement by the defendant relating to the goods; the statement is part of the basis of the bargain.[5]

"Basis of the bargain" means that the buyer has purchased the goods because of what the seller has stated about those goods. A statement by the seller regarding the quality, capacity, or other characteristic of the goods is an express warranty. **For Example,** express warranties in sellers' statements are "This cloth is all wool," "This paint is for household woodwork," and "This engine can produce 50 horsepower." A representation that an airplane is a 2007 model is an express warranty. "This computer monitor has a glare-proof screen" is another example of an express warranty.

The manufacturer of the goods cannot isolate itself from claims that are communicated through retailers. **For Example,** WorldWide Wholesalers could purchase Pop-Tarts from Kellogg's. Kellogg's makes warranties to WorldWide Wholesalers directly through their contract relationship, one of privity. WorldWide Wholesalers then sells those Pop-Tarts to grocery stores, convenience stores, and perhaps even to commercial food distributors who then sell them to cafeterias in schools and nursing homes. WorldWide's buyers are remote purchasers. The warranty is not lost through the distribution chain.

5. Form of Express Warranty

No particular group of words is necessary to constitute an express warranty. A seller need not state that a warranty is being made or that one is intended. It is sufficient that the seller asserts a fact that becomes a basis of the bargain or transaction between the parties. UCC § 2-313(2) provides, "It is not necessary to the creation of an express warranty that the seller use formal words such as 'warrant' or 'guarantee' or that the seller have a specific intention to make a warranty."[6] If a warranty is a critical part of the bargain for the buyer, it cannot be disclaimed (see p. 2).

An express warranty can be written or printed as well as oral. The words on the label of a can and in a newspaper ad for "boned chicken" constitute an express warranty that the can contains chicken that is free of bones.

Descriptions of goods, such as the illustrations in a seller's catalog, are express warranties. The express warranty given is that the goods will conform to the catalog illustrations.

---

[5] UCC § 2-313; *Miles v Raymond Corp.* 612 F Supp 2d 913, 68 UCC Rep Serv 2d 405 (ND Oh 2005). *Samsung Electronics America, Inc. v Blu-Ray Class Action Litigation*, 2008 WL 5451024, 67 UCC RepServ2d 794 DNJ 2008). In the UCC Revised Article 2, the "basis of the bargain" requirement is changed to "become part of the agreement." UCC § 2-313(1)(a). Also, § 2-404 is the new express warranty section.
[6] UCC § 2-313(2).

6. Seller's Opinion or Statement of Value

A statement about the value of goods or the seller's opinion or commendation of the goods does not create a warranty.[7] Section 2-313(1)(b) provides, "an affirmation merely of the value of the goods or a statement purporting to be merely the seller's opinion or commendation of goods does not create a warranty."[8] A buyer cannot hold a seller liable for sales talk. **For Example,** sales talk or puffery by a seller that his cloth is "the best piece of cloth on the market" or that her glassware is "as good as anyone else's" is merely an opinion that the buyer cannot ordinarily treat as a warranty. Statements made by a cosmetics seller that its products are "the future of beauty" and are "just the product for [the plaintiff]" are sales talk arising in the ordinary course of merchandising. They do not constitute warranties.

The UCC does permit an exception to the sales talk liability exemption when the circumstances are such that a reasonable person would rely on such a statement. If the buyer has reason to believe that the seller has expert knowledge of the conditions of the market, and the buyer requests the seller's opinion as an expert, the buyer is entitled to accept as a fact the seller's statement of whether a particular good is the best obtainable. The opinion statement could be reasonably regarded as forming part of the basis of the bargain. A statement by a florist that bulbs are of first-grade quality may be a warranty.[9]

7. Warranty of Conformity to Description, Sample, or Model

When the contract is based in part on the understanding that the seller will supply goods according to a particular description or that the goods will be the same as the sample or a model, the seller is bound by an express warranty that the goods conform to the description, sample, or model.[10] Section 2-313 of the UCC provides, "Any sample or model which is made part of the basis of the bargain creates an express warranty that the whole of the goods shall conform to the sample or model."[11] **For Example,** a blender sitting out in a store is a warranty that the blenders in the boxes below are the same. A model of a mobile home is an express warranty that the mobile home being sold contains the same features.

8. Federal Regulation of Express Warranties

A seller who makes a written express warranty for a consumer product costing more than $10 must conform to certain standards imposed by federal statute[12] and by regulations of the Federal Trade Commission (FTC).[13] The seller is not required to make any express warranty. However, if the seller does make an express warranty in a consumer sale, it must be stated in ordinary, understandable language and must be

---

[7] Id.; *Giles v Wyeth, Inc.* 500 F Supp 2d 1063 (SD Ill 2007) *In re Ford Motor Co. E-350 Van Products Liability Litigation,* 2008 WL 4126264 (DNJ), 66 UCC Rep Serv 2d 726 (DNJ 2008).

[8] UCC § 2-313(1)(b).

[9] Likewise, a statement by an art gallery owner that a "painting is by Francis Bacon" is an express warranty. *Rogath v Siebenmann,* 129 F3d 902 (7th Cir 1997).

[10] *Harlan v Roadtrek Motorhomes, Inc.,* 2009 WL 928309, 68 UCC RepServ2d 750 (SD Cal 2009).

[11] UCC § 2-313(1)(c).

[12] The Magnuson-Moss Act, or Federal Consumer Product Warranty Law, can be found at 15 USC § 2301 *et seq.*

[13] 16 CFR § 700.1 *et seq.*

made available for inspection before purchasing so that the consumer may comparison shop.[14]

(A) Full Warranties. If the seller or the label states that a full warranty is made, the seller is obligated to fix or replace a defective product within a reasonable time without cost to the buyer. If the product cannot be fixed or if a reasonable number of repair attempts are unsuccessful, the buyer has the choice of a cash refund or a free replacement. No unreasonable burden may be placed on a buyer seeking to obtain warranty service. **For Example,** a manufacturer offering a full warranty cannot require that the buyer pay the cost of sending the product to or from a warranty service point. A warrantor making a full warranty cannot require the buyer to return the product to a warranty service point if the product weighs over 35 pounds, to return a part for service unless it can be easily removed, or to fill out and return a warranty registration card shortly after purchase to make the warranty effective. If the manufacturer imposes any of these requirements, the warranty is not a "full warranty" under federal law and must be labeled a *limited warranty*. A **full warranty** runs with the product and lasts for its full term regardless of who owns the product.

(B) Limited Warranties. A **limited warranty** is any warranty that does not meet the requirements for a full warranty. **For Example,** a warranty is limited if the buyer must pay any cost for repair or replacement of a defective product, if only the first buyer is covered by the warranty, or if the warranty covers only part of the product. A limited warranty must be conspicuously described as such by the seller.[15]

(C) International Product Safety Laws in the U.S. In 2008, in response to the lead paint discovered in toys imported from China, Congress passed the **Consumer Product Safety Improvement Act (CPSIA)**, which promulgated new standards for product safety.[16] Under CPSIA, the products most affected are those for children under the age of 12. The act provides no discretion for lead levels; it prohibits lead in products for children under 12. Because of the outsourcing issues that resulted in the toys with lead paint making their way into the United States, the CPSIA requires accredited third-party laboratory testing, product tracking, labels, registration, and new warnings in ads and on Web sites about the manufacturing sources of toys. CPSIA increases to $100 million the penalties the Consumer Product Safety Commission can assess.

9. Effect of Breach of Express Warranty

If an express warranty is false, there is a breach of warranty. The warrantor is then liable. It is no defense that the seller or manufacturer who made the express warranty honestly believed that the warranty was true, had exercised due care in manufacturing or handling the product, or had no reason to believe that the warranty was false.

full warranty–obligation of a seller to fix or replace a defective product within a reasonable time without cost to the buyer.

limited warranty–any warranty that does not provide the complete protection of a full warranty.

Consumer Product Safety Improvement Act–federal law that sets standards for the types of paints used in toys; a response to the lead paint found in toys made in China; requires tracking for international production; increases penalties

---

[14] Federal warranty language rules apply only in consumer sales, or sales for personal or home use, not in business purchases.
[15] The federal regulations here do not preempt Article 2 warranty coverage. *Wyeth v Levine,* 129 S Ct 1187 (2009)
[16] 15 USC §1278a

CASE SUMMARY

Fake Tiffany Lamps for $56,200 and a Disclaimer

FACTS: Richard W. La Trace attended an auction at B & B Antiques, Auction & Realty, a business owned and operated by Ray Webster, Deborah Webster, Bo Webster, and Laura Webster (collectively "the Websters"). La Trace purchased five lamps that were identified at the auction as "Tiffany" lamps and one lampshade that was also identified at the auction as a "Tiffany" product. La Trace spent a total of $56,200 on the lamps.

La Trace contacted Fontaine's Auction Gallery in Pittsfield, Massachusetts, to inquire about selling the lamps in an auction. Fontaine's sent Dean Lowry, an expert in Tiffany products, to examine La Trace's lamps and Lowry determined that the lamps were not authentic Tiffany products but were, in fact, reproductions. La Trace filed suit against the Websters and B & B for fraudulent suppression, fraudulent misrepresentation, breach of warranty, breach of contract, negligence, and wantonness.[17] The Websters claimed they thought the lamps were authentic and pointed out that their sales brochure and "Conditions of Auction" document contained the following disclaimer:

1. All property is sold AS IS WHERE IS, and we make NO guarantees, warranties or representations, expressed or implied, with respect to the property or the correctness of the catalog or other description of authenticity of authorship, physical condition, size, quality, rarity, importance, provenance, exhibitions, literature or historical relevance of the property or otherwise. No statement anywhere, whether oral or written, shall be deemed such a guarantee, warranty or representation.

On a motion for summary judgment, the court found for the Websters, indicating that La Trace trusted blindly and should not have done so. La Trace appealed.

DECISION: The Websters' description of the lamps as "Tiffany" products became part of the basis of the bargain because the representations took place during the auction and were not accompanied by any qualifying statements indicating that the authenticity of the lamps was in doubt. Because it is assumed under the UCC that the object of every UCC-regulated sale is describable, the core description is nondisclaimable by a seller, being the basic foundation upon which every sales contract is made. The lamps here were sold with the core description of being Tiffany products. Although disclaimers in a sales brochure and a "Conditions of Auction" document may have been effective to prevent the formation of any express warranties that might otherwise have arisen in those documents, nothing in the language indicated that the disclaimer in the documents was effective to prevent a seller from making express warranties in the future. Judgment for La Trace. [**La Trace v Webster, So2d, 2008 WL 4684147, 67 UCC Rep Serv 2d 78 (Ala Civ App 2008)**]

C. IMPLIED WARRANTIES

Whenever a sale of goods is made, certain warranties are implied unless they are expressly excluded. Implied warranties differ depending on whether the seller is a merchant.

---

[17] B & B was dismissed from the case because it had not yet been properly formed as an LLC. See Chapter 41 for more information on forming a business entity properly.

10. Definition of Implied Warranty

implied warranty–warranty that was not made but is implied by law.

An **implied warranty** is one that was not expressly made by the seller but that is implied in certain circumstances by law. An implied warranty arises automatically from the fact that a sale has been made regardless of the seller's conduct.

Express warranties arise because they form part of the basis on which the sale has been made. Implied warranties can exist independent of express warranties. When both express and implied warranties exist, they are interpreted as consistent, if possible. If the warranties cannot be applied together, then the express warranty prevails over any implied warranty except that an implied warranty of fitness for a particular purpose prevails over an express warranty.

11. Implied Warranties of Sellers

Sellers give different types of implied warranties.

CPA

(A) **WARRANTY OF TITLE.** Every seller, by the mere act of selling, makes an implied warranty that the seller's title to the goods is good and that the seller has the right to transfer title to the goods.[18]

warranty of title–implied warranty that title to the goods is good and transfer is proper.

The **warranty of title** may be disclaimed either by using the words, "There is no warranty of title," or by certain circumstances.[19] If a buyer has reason to know that the seller does not claim to hold the title or that the seller is limited in what can be promised, the warranty of title is disclaimed. **For Example,** no warranty of title arises when the seller makes the sale in a representative capacity, such as a sheriff, an auctioneer, or an administrator of a decedent's estate. Similarly, no warranty arises when the seller makes the sale as a creditor disposing of a debtor's collateral (security). The damages for warranty of title are often the purchase price because the buyer may have to surrender the goods to their rightful owner.[20]

warranty against encumbrances–warranty that there are no liens or other encumbrances to goods except those noted by seller.

(B) **WARRANTY AGAINST ENCUMBRANCES.** Every seller makes an implied **warranty against encumbrances**, that is, that the goods will be delivered free from any security interest or any other lien or encumbrance of which the buyer at the time of the sales transaction had no knowledge. If the seller sells an automobile to the buyer and then delivers a car with an outstanding lien on it that was unknown to the buyer at the time of the sale, there is a breach of the warranty against encumbrances.

CPA

(C) **WARRANTY OF FITNESS FOR A PARTICULAR PURPOSE**[21]. A buyer may intend to use the goods for a particular or unusual purpose, as contrasted with the ordinary use for which they are customarily sold. If the seller states that the goods will be fit for the buyer's purpose with the buyer relying on the seller's skill or judgment to select or furnish suitable goods, and the seller, at the time of contracting, knows or has reason to know of both the buyer's particular purpose and the buyer's reliance on the seller's judgment, then the seller has created an implied warranty of fitness for a

---

[18] UCC § 2-312. The key change in the language in Revised Article 2 is that the seller warrants that the buyer will not be subjected to unreasonable litigation.

[19] *Quality Components Corp. v Kel-Keef Enterprises, Inc.*, 738 NE2d 524 (Ill App 2000).

[20] *Mayberry v Volkswagen of America, Inc.*, 692 NW2d 226 (Wis 2005).

[21] UCC § 2-315. The warranty does not apply when the injury is not caused by any function represented for the product. For example, a buyer could not recover when she hit her head on a wall-mounted fire extinguisher, for the representations were that it would work for home fires, not about mounting it in the home. *Hayes v Larsen Mfg. Co., Inc.*, 871 F Supp 56 (D Me 1996).

C A S E   S U M M A R Y

When the AV Guys Get It Wrong

FACTS: From February through July 2004, Oheka Management, Inc. purchased an audiovisual system from Home Theatre Interiors for $86,000, which included installation of said audiovisual equipment. The system was required to be operational for an event scheduled for July 18, 2004 at Oheka.

Home Theater Interiors did not properly install or maintain the system. Ohkea was left with no alternative but to hire other technicians to complete the set-up and to repair any improper servicing and installations.

Home Theater Interiors argues that it was Oheka's architect, Richard Diller, who caused the problems with the system and its installation. Additionally, Home Theater maintains that because there was no signed contract for the system, Home Theater could not breach it or any warranties. However, the unsigned contract discussed the variety of audiovisual equipment that Oheka purchased from Home Theatre, as well as the installation that Home Theatre would perform. The unsigned contract contained a warranty for on-site parts and labor for this job which was to run for one year's time from date of purchase. Oheka moved for summary judgment for breach of warranty and breach of contract.

DECISION: The court held that the contract was covered under UCC despite its service component. The court also held that an unsigned contract was not controlling. The parties behaved as if there were a contract and the fact that there was no signature does not mean there was no contract or warranties. Exceptions to the documentation requirement for contracts include both parties behaving as if a contract exists. The court also held that Home Theater Interiors gave an implied warranty of merchantability—that a home theater should do the things it was designed to do, including being a working system in the room. [**Oheka Management, Inc. v Home Theater Interiors, LLC, 2007 WL 3325861 (NY Supp)**]

particular purpose.[22] **For Example,** when the seller represents to a buyer that the two hamsters being sold are of the same gender and can safely occupy the same cage with no offspring, an implied warranty of fitness has been given. When the buyer makes the purchase without relying on the seller's skill and judgment, no warranty of fitness for a particular purpose arises.[23]

12. Additional Implied Warranties of Merchant Sellers

A seller who deals in goods of the kind in question is classified as a merchant by the UCC and is held to a higher degree of responsibility for the product than one who is merely making a casual sale.

(A) WARRANTY AGAINST INFRINGEMENT. Unless otherwise agreed, every merchant seller warrants that the goods will be delivered free of the rightful claim of any third person by way of patent, copyright, or trademark infringement.

For Example, if a buyer purchases videos from a seller who is later discovered to be a bootlegger of the films on the videos, the buyer has a cause of action against the

---

[22] UCC § 2-315. This warranty applies to every seller, but ordinarily it is merchant sellers who have such skill and judgment that the UCC provision will apply.
[23] *Walter v George Koch Sons, Inc.*, 610 F Supp 551, 68 UCC Rep Serv 2d 494 (SD Miss 2009). Manufacturing to buyer's specifications precludes recovery for breach of the warranty of fitness for a particular purpose. *Simmons v Washing Equipment Technologies* 857 NYS 2d 412(2008).

e-commerce&cyberlaw

The warranty against infringement has become a critical one because of issues relating to software as well as the downloading of copyrighted music from the Internet. Those who are selling software warrant that they have the rights to do so and would be liable for infringement themselves, as well as the costs their buyers incur in defending themselves against charges of infringement.

Even those who provide the servers for the downloading of music or films can be held liable for infringement if they are aware of the downloading of copyrighted music or copyrighted films and take no steps to stop or prevent it. In fact, those who operate servers must be able to show that they took appropriate precautions to prevent such downloading and warn users against doing it.

seller for any damages he experiences for perhaps renting out the bootlegged videos. Under Revised Article 2, the seller can disclaim the warranty against infringement.

(B) WARRANTY OF MERCHANTABILITY OR FITNESS FOR NORMAL USE. A merchant seller makes an **implied warranty of the merchantability** of the goods sold.[24] This warranty is a group of promises, the most important of which is that the goods are fit for the ordinary purposes for which they are sold. This warranty, unless disclaimed, is given in every sale of goods by a merchant. Section 2-314 provides, "Unless excluded or modified, a warranty that the goods shall be merchantable is implied in a contract for their sale if the seller is a merchant with respect to goods of that kind."[25]

> **implied warranty of merchantability**–group of promises made by the seller, the most important of which is that the goods are fit for the ordinary purposes for which they are sold.

13. Implied Warranties in Particular Sales

Particular types of sales may involve special considerations in terms of the seller's liability and the buyer's rights.

(A) SALE ON BUYER'S SPECIFICATIONS. When the buyer furnishes the seller with exact specifications for the preparation or manufacture of goods, the same warranties arise as in the case of any other sale of such goods by the particular seller. No warranty of fitness for a particular purpose can arise, however. It is clear that the buyer is purchasing on the basis of the buyer's own decision and is not relying on the seller's skill and judgment. Similarly, the manufacturer is not liable for loss caused by a design defect.[26]

(B) SALE OF SECONDHAND OR USED GOODS. Under the UCC, there is a warranty of merchantability in the sale of both new and used goods unless it is specifically disclaimed. However, with respect to used goods, what is considered "fit for normal use" under the

---

[24] UCC § 2-314; Lawson v Hale, 902 NE2d 267 (Ind App 2009) *Trujillo v Apple Comuter, Inc.*, 581 F Supp 2d 935 (ND Ill 2008); limited battery life is not a breach of the implied warranty of merchantability.

[25] UCC § 2-314. Revised Article 2 makes only one change as follows: "(c) are fit for the ordinary purposes for which [deleted word *such* here] goods [added following phrase] *of that description* are used… ." The comment explains the change: "The phrase 'goods of that description' rather than 'for which such goods are used' is used in subsection (2) (c). This emphasizes the importance of the agreed description in determining fitness for ordinary purposes."

[26] *Hallday v Sturm, Ruger, & Co., Inc.*, 792 A2d 1145 (CA MD 2002).

warranty of merchantability will be a lower standard. Some courts still follow their pre-Code law under which no warranties of fitness arise in the sale of used goods.

CPA (c) SALE OF FOOD OR DRINK. The implied warranty of merchantability also applies to the purchase of food in grocery stores and restaurants. The food sold must be of average quality and fit for its ordinary purpose, which is consumption by humans.[27] The types of restaurant and grocery store cases brought under the warranty of merchantability include those in which the buyer or customer finds foreign substances such as grasshoppers in a can of baked beans.[28]

The application of this warranty to food cases becomes more complex when it is not a nail in a can of crabmeat, but crab shell in a can of crabmeat, or a cherry pit in the cherries of a McDonald's cherry pie. Some courts refuse to impose warranty liability if the thing in the food that caused the harm was naturally present, such as crab shell in crabmeat, prune stones in stewed prunes, or bones in canned fish. Other courts reject this foreign substance/natural substance liability test. They hold that there is liability if the seller does not deliver to the buyer goods of the character that the buyer reasonably expected. Under this view, there is a breach of the implied warranty of fitness for normal use if the buyer reasonably expected the food to be free of harm-causing natural things, such as shells and bones that could cause harm.[29]

CASE SUMMARY

Digging for Teeth among the Clams

FACTS: On April 11, 1996, Sandra Mitchell (appellant) was having dinner at T.G.I. Friday's restaurant (hereinafter "Friday's" or appellee). Ms. Mitchell was eating a fried clam strip when she bit into a hard substance that she believed to be a piece of a clam shell. She experienced immediate pain and later sought dental treatment. Some time later, the crown of a tooth came loose. It was determined that the crown could not be reattached, and the remaining root of the tooth was extracted.

Ms. Mitchell filed a product liability action against Friday's, which served the meal, and Pro Source Distributing, the supplier of the fried clams. Both Friday's and Pro Source filed motions for summary judgment, which the trial court granted without explanation. Ms. Mitchell appealed.

DECISION: Two tests can be used for determining whether there should be recovery. One is the "foreign-natural test"; in this case, a clam shell is a natural part of eating clams. The other test is the "reasonable expectation test," and the court ruled that someone eating clams, even fried clams, should reasonably expect that shells might be part of the experience.

The possible presence of a piece of oyster shell in or attached to an oyster is so well known to anyone who eats oysters that all should reasonably anticipate and guard against eating such a piece of shell. The court held that, as a matter of law, one who eats clams can reasonably anticipate and guard against eating a piece of shell. [**Mitchell v T.G.I. Friday's, 748 NE2d 89 (Ohio App 2000)**]

---

[27] Summers v Max & Erma's Restaurant, Inc., 2008 WL 3822437, 66 UCC RepServ2d 664 (Oh App 2008).
[28] *Metty v Shurfine Central Corporation,* 736 SW2d 527 (Mo 1987).
[29] A new type of test for the food cases is called the "duty risk analysis" rule, in which the court examines the injury in light of the risk that comes from the failure to process the items out of the food and weighs that risk with the cost of the processing. *Porteous v St. Ann's Cafe´ & Deli,* 713 So 2d 454 (La 1998). Note that the case is from Louisiana, the nation's non-UCC state.

14. Necessity of Defect

To impose liability for breach of the implied warranty of merchantability, the buyer must show that the product is defective and that defect caused harm. A product may be defective because there is (1) a manufacturing defect, (2) a design defect, (3) inadequate instruction on how to use the product, or (4) inadequate warning against dangers involved in using the product.

For Example, if the manufacturer's blueprint shows that there should be two bolts at a particular place and the factory puts in only one bolt, there is a manufacturing defect. If the two bolts are put in but the product breaks because four bolts are required to provide sufficient strength, there is no manufacturing defect, but there is a design defect. A product that is properly designed and properly manufactured may be dangerous because the user is not given sufficient instructions on how to use the product. Also, a product is defective if there is a danger that is not obvious and there is no warning at all or a warning that does not describe the full danger.[30]

15. Warranties in the International Sale of Goods

The warranties of both merchantability and fitness for a particular purpose exist under the Convention on Contracts for the International Sale of Goods (CISG). In most cases, the provisions are identical to those of the UCC. Sellers, however, can expressly disclaim the convention's warranties without mentioning merchantability or making the disclaimer conspicuous.

thinking things through

What's Foreign to You ...

Based on the discussion and the *T. G. I. Friday's* case, decide which of the following would be considered a breach of the implied warranty of merchantability:

Customer ordered "pecan chicken" from T.G.I. Friday's, described on the menu as chicken with "a breaded mixture of pecans and bread crumbs." He broke a tooth when he bit into a pecan shell that was in the breading. [**Carlton v T.G.I. Friday's, 2006 WL 5129475 (Ohio Com Pl)**]

Customer suffered an injury to the throat as a result of a bone in a chicken sandwich getting stuck in his

throat. [**Ruvolo v Homovich, 778 NE2d 661 (Ohio App 2002)**]

Customer bit into a Baby Ruth candy bar, manufactured by Standard Brands, that contained a "snake bone (vertebrae)" and the customer experienced severe psychological difficulty. [**Gates v Standard Brands Inc., 719 P2d 130 (Wash App 1986)**]

Customer experienced tooth and jaw damage after she bit into a pistachio nut while eating an ice cream cone with pistachio nut ice cream. [**Lewis v Handel's Homemade Ice Cream and Yogurt, 2003 WL 21509258 (Ohio App)**]

[30] *Red Hill Hosiery Mill, Inc. v Magnetek, Inc.* 582 SE2d 632 (NC Ct App 2003). Following government standards does not mean a product is without defect.

D. Disclaimer of Warranties

The seller and the buyer may ordinarily agree that there will be no warranties. In some states, disclaimers of warranties are prohibited for reasons of public policy or consumer protection.

16. Validity of Disclaimer

Warranties may be disclaimed by agreement of the parties, subject to the limitation that such a provision must not be unconscionable, must be conspicuous, and in certain cases must use certain language.[31]

(A) CONSPICUOUSNESS. A disclaimer provision is made conspicuous when it appears in a record under a conspicuous heading that indicates there is an exclusion or modification of warranties. A heading cannot be relied on to make such a provision conspicuous when the heading is misleading and wrongfully gives the impression there is a warranty. **For Example,** the heading "Vehicle Warranty" is misleading if the provision that follows contains a limitation of warranties. A disclaimer that is hidden in a mass of materials or records handed to the buyer is not conspicuous and is not effective to exclude warranties. Similarly, an inconspicuous disclaimer of warranties under a posted notice of "Notice to Retail Buyers" has no effect.

When a disclaimer of warranties fails because it is not conspicuous, the implied warranties apply to the buyer.[32]

(B) UNCONSCIONABILITY AND PUBLIC POLICY. An exclusion of warranties made in the manner specified by the UCC is not unconscionable. In some states, warranty disclaimers are invalid because they are contrary to public policy or because they are prohibited by consumer protection laws.

17. Particular Language for Disclaimers

To waive the warranty of merchantability, the record must contain the following language: "The seller undertakes no responsibility for the quality of the goods except as otherwise provided in this contract."[33] The required language for waiving the warranty of fitness for a particular purpose is as follows: "The seller assumes no responsibility that the goods will be fit for any particular purpose for which you may be buying these goods, except as otherwise provided in the contract."[34]

In consumer contracts, the use of terms such as "as is" can also disclaim the warranties, as it does for merchant transactions, but the disclaimers must be in the record and must be conspicuously set forth in that record.

Figure 25.1 provides a summary of the warranties under Article 2 and the methods for making disclaimers.

---

[31] UCC § 2-316; In *re Rafter Seven Ranches LP*, 546 F3d 1194 (C.A. 10 2008). The revised UCC section is now § 2-406.
[32] A warranty disclaimer written in all caps just below the signature line is conspicuous. *Semitekol v Monaco Coach Corp.*, 582 F Supp 2d 1009 (ND Ill 2008).
[33] Revised UCC § 2-316(2).
[34] *Id.*

18. Exclusion of Warranties by Examination of Goods

For an inspection of goods by the buyer to constitute a waiver, the seller must demand that the buyer inspect the goods as part of the contracting process. The seller may not use inspection as a defense to warranty issues if that demand was not made at the time the parties contracted.[35]

19. Postsale Disclaimer

Frequently, a statement purporting to exclude or modify warranties appears for the first time in a written contract sent to confirm or memorialize an oral contract made earlier. The exclusion or modification may likewise appear in an invoice, a bill, or an instruction manual delivered to the buyer at or after the time the goods are received. Such postsale disclaimers have no effect on warranties that arose at the time of the sale.

E. OTHER THEORIES OF PRODUCT LIABILITY

In addition to recovery for breach of an express guarantee, an express warranty, or an implied warranty, a plaintiff in a given product liability case may be able to recover for negligence, fraud, or strict tort liability.

20. Negligence

negligence–failure to exercise due care under the circumstances that results in harm proximately caused to one owed a duty to exercise due care.

A person injured because of the defective condition of a product may be entitled to recover from the seller or manufacturer for the damages for **negligence**. The injured person must be able to show that the seller was negligent in the preparation or manufacture of the article or failed to provide proper instructions and warnings of dangers. An action for negligence rests on common law tort principles. Negligence does not require privity of contract.

21. Fraud

The UCC expressly preserves the pre-Code law governing fraud. A person defrauded by a distributor's or manufacturer's false statements about a product generally will be able to recover damages for the harm sustained because of such misrepresentations. False statements are fraudulent if the party who made them did so with knowledge that they were false or with reckless indifference to their truthfulness.

CPA   ## 22. Strict Tort Liability

Strict tort liability exists without regard to whether the person injured is a purchaser, a consumer, or a third person, such as a bystander.[36] It is no defense that privity of contract does not exist between the injured party and the defendant. Likewise, it is no defense that the defect was found in a component part purchased from another

---

[35] Revised UCC § 2-316(3)(b).
[36] The concept of strict tort liability was judicially declared in *Greenman v Yuba Power Products*, 377 P2d 897 (Cal 1963). This concept has been incorporated in the Restatement (Second) and (Third) of Torts as § 402A.

FIGURE 25-1 | *UCC Warranties*

NAME OF WARRANTY	CREATION	RESTRICTION	DISCLAIMER
EXPRESS	AFFIRMATION OF FACT, PROMISE OF PERFORMANCE (INCLUDES SAMPLES, MODELS, DESCRIPTIONS)	MUST BE PART OF THE BASIS OF THE BARGAIN	CANNOT MAKE A DISCLAIMER INCONSISTENT WITH AN EXPRESS WARRANTY
IMPLIED WARRANTY OF MERCHANTABILITY	GIVEN IN EVERY SALE OF GOODS BY A MERCHANT ("FIT FOR ORDINARY PURPOSES")	ONLY GIVEN BY MERCHANTS	MUST USE STATUTORY LANGUAGE DISCLAIMER OF "AS IS" OR "WITH ALL FAULTS"; MUST BE CONSPICUOUS IN THE RECORD
IMPLIED WARRANTY OF FITNESS FOR A PARTICULAR PURPOSE	SELLER KNOWS OF BUYER'S RELIANCE FOR A PARTICULAR USE (BUYER IS IGNORANT)	SELLER MUST HAVE KNOWLEDGE; BUYER MUST RELY ON SELLER	(1) MUST HAVE A RECORD (2) MUST BE CONSPICUOUS (3) ALSO DISCLAIMED WITH "AS IS" OR "WITH ALL FAULTS"
TITLE	GIVEN IN EVERY SALE	DOES NOT APPLY IN CIRCUMSTANCES WHERE APPARENT WARRANTY IS NOT GIVEN	MUST SAY "THERE IS NO WARRANTY OF TITLE"
MAGNUSON-MOSS (FEDERAL CONSUMER PRODUCT WARRANTY LAW)	ONLY CONSUMER PRODUCTS OF $10 OR MORE	MUST LABEL "FULL" OR "LIMITED"	

manufacturer.[37] **For Example,** defective tires sold on a new car were probably purchased from a tire supplier by the auto manufacturer. However, the manufacturer is not excused from liability.

Strict tort liability requires that the defect in the product exist at the time it left the control of the manufacturer or distributor. The defective condition is defined in the same way as under negligence: defective by manufacturing error or oversight, defective by design, or defective by the failure to warn.[38] There is liability if the product is defective and unreasonably dangerous and has caused harm. It is immaterial whether the seller was negligent or whether the user was contributorily negligent. Knowledge of

---

[37] *Ford v Beam Radiator, Inc.,* 708 So2d 1158 (La App 1998).
[38] *Lewis v Ariens,* 751 NE2d 862 (Mass 2001).

the defect is not a requirement for liability. Assumption of risk by the injured party, on the other hand, is a defense available to the seller.[39]

23. Cumulative Theories of Liability

The theories of product liability are not mutually exclusive. A given set of facts may give rise to two or more theories of liability. **For Example,** suppose that a manufacturer advertises, "Coaches! Protect your players' eyes! Shatterproof sunglasses for baseball." If the glasses shattered and injured a player, an express warranty, implied warranty, implied warranty for a particular purpose, and strict tort liability could apply for recovery.

C A S E S U M M A R Y

Shocking Warranty Issues

FACTS: Will-Burt builds steel masts used by the military, border control, firefighters, and the television broadcast industry. Will-Burt built one such mast in 1982 for use in the television broadcast industry on an electronic news-gathering van (ENG van). Will-Burt sold the mast in 1982 to Quality Coach of Elkhart, Indiana. In 1989, Alan W. Haines, Custom Construction refurbished the mast and sold it to Mississippi Telecasting Company d/b/a WABG-TV. Barksdale Austin, a 24-year-old college graduate, was employed as a production manager by WABG-TV in Greenville, Mississippi. One of his duties at WABG was to set up the TV station's ENG van for remote broadcasts. This duty entailed operating the telescoping mast on the van. Austin received safety training for keeping a clearance of at least 20 feet from any power line if the mast was to be raised.

On June 17, 1997, Austin was assigned to a live shot at Greenville City Hall. The van was parked underneath visible transformers and power lines by someone other than Austin. The Will-Burt mast, which was attached to the van, contacted an 8,000-volt power line while being raised. The voltage went down the mast and into the van, energizing the van and its extending cables. Austin walked to the van, touched it, and was electrically shocked to death.

The mast still had the following warnings on its base: "DANGER! PLEASE READ INSTRUCTIONS BEFORE RAISING!" and "DANGER. WATCH FOR WIRES. YOU CAN BE KILLED IF THIS PRODUCT COMES NEAR ELECTRICAL POWER LINES." The labels were located on the base of the mast inside the van in bright yellow with red and black lettering. The instructions in the product manual also warned operators never to raise the mast under or near power lines and to check for obstructions within the proximity to the maximum height of the mast.

Austin's family filed suit for breach of warranty and negligence.

DECISION: The court held that no express warranty was breached because no one at WABG had relied on any statements from Will-Burt in purchasing the mast. The court held that while the mast was warranted for a particular purpose of use by an ENG van, that use carried sufficient limitations and warnings that put buyers and users on notice of its limitations for that use. The court did not find negligence because there was no evidence that

[39] *Clark v Mazda Motor Corp.*, 68 P3d 207 (OK 2003).

C A S E   S U M M A R Y

Continued

Will-Burt was aware of any incidents with its masts. Further, the product liability claim was eliminated because of the warning, the fact that the mast had been sold so many times and had been in use for nearly 20 years, and indications that its conducting qualities may have been affected by the failure to keep it clean and maintained. The court granted summary judgment for Will-Burt on all product liability theories under both the UCC and tort law. [**Austin v Will-Burt Company, 232 F Supp 2d 682 (D Miss 2002); affirmed, 361 F3d 862 (5th Cir 2004)**]

ethics&the law

In 2007, the Mattel Corporation had to recall toys it had outsourced for manufacture in China. The recall was necessary because the Chinese factories were using lead paint on the toys, a practice that remains legal in China but is prohibited in the United States. Mattel CEO Robert Eckert of Mattel apologized for Mattel's failure to monitor its suppliers and indicated that Mattel had to "earn back" the trust of consumers.*

Mr. Eckert also used the Senate hearings to announce a new three-step process Mattel was implementing: (1) testing of vendor paint, (2) testing of toys before they reach store shelves, and (3) increased random inspections of vendors and subcontractors for safety and quality compliance.

Class-action lawyers filed suits against Mattel. Discuss what UCC provisions would be the basis of such suits. Did Mr. Eckert do the right thing or do his statements and changes mean Mattel will be held liable? What effect will the information that the use of lead paint reduced production costs by 30 percent have in the litigation?

The U.S. Consumer Product Safety Commission said that of the 39 recalls of toys for the presence of lead-based paint, 38 had been made in China. China produces 70 percent to 80 percent of the world's toys. What lessons should companies learn from international outsourcing?

* Christopher Conkey, "Safety Agency is Grilled," *Wall Street Journal*, Sept. 13, 2007, A12.

lawflix

The Incredible Shrinking Woman (1981) (PG)

Lily Tomlin's exposure to various combinations of products causes her to shrink. Which companies would be liable and how could one go about proving joint and several liability? Discuss privity of contract and whether the interaction with other products would be covered.

Check out LawFlix at **www.cengage.com/blaw/dvl** to access movie clips that illustrate business law concepts.

MAKE THE CONNECTION

SUMMARY

Five theories protect parties from loss caused by nonconforming goods: (1) express warranty, (2) implied warranty, (3) negligence, (4) fraud, and (5) strict tort liability.

Theories of product liability are not mutually exclusive. A given set of facts may give rise to liability under two or more theories.

The requirement of privity of contract (that is, the parties to the sales contract for warranty liability) has been widely rejected. The law is moving toward the conclusion that persons harmed because of an improper product may recover from anyone who is in any way responsible. The requirement of privity has been abolished by most states, and remote buyers as well as their families, members of their households, and guests are covered under the UCC warranties.

Warranties may be express or implied. The types of implied warranties are the warranty of title, the implied warranty of merchantability, and the implied warranty of fitness for a particular purpose. The warranty of title provides that the transfer is lawful, the title is good, and there are no infringement issues. Under Revised Article 2, the warranty of title also protects the buyer against unreasonable litigation. The warranty of merchantability is given by merchants and warrants that the goods are of average quality and will do what those types of goods commonly can do. The implied warranty of fitness for a particular purpose is given in those circumstances in which the buyer relies on the seller's expertise and the seller is aware of that reliance and offers a recommendation on the types of goods.

Express warranties arise from statements of fact and promises of performance made by the seller to the buyer that become a part of the basis for the buyer contracting. Express warranties arise from samples, models, and descriptions.

Warranties may be disclaimed by agreement of the parties provided the disclaimer is not unconscionable. Merchants can have oral disclaimers, but for consumers, warranty disclaimers must be in a record and must be conspicuous. Also for consumers, certain language must be used to disclaim each type of warranty. However, for both merchants and nonmerchants, the use of terms such as "as is" or "with all faults" can disclaim both the warranty of merchantability and the implied warranty of fitness for a particular purpose (although for consumers, there must still be a record and the language must be conspicuous).

The warranties of merchantability and fitness exist under the CISG. However, disclaimers under the CISG need not mention merchantability, nor must such disclaimers be conspicuous.

The strict tort liability plaintiff must show that there was a defect in the product at the time it left the control of the defendant. No negligence need be established on the part of the defendant, nor is the plaintiff's contributory negligence a defense. If negligence is established, however, knowledge by the seller can result in punitive damages. The defendant may show that the injured party assumed the risk.

LEARNING OUTCOMES

After studying this chapter, you should be able to clearly explain:

A. GENERAL PRINCIPLES

LO.1 List the theories of product liability

> See the five theories discussed in the "Theories of Liability" section on p. 556.

LO.2 Identify who may sue and who may be sued when a defective product causes harm

> See the discussion of privity on p. 557.

B. EXPRESS WARRANTIES

LO.3 Define and give examples of an express warranty

> See *La Trace v Webster* on p. 561.

C. IMPLIED WARRANTIES

LO.4 List and explain the types of implied warranties

> See *Oheka Management, Inc. v Home Theater Interiors* on p. 563.
> See *Mitchell v T.G.I. Friday's* on p. 565.

LO.5 Explain warranty protections under federal law

> See the discussion of the Consumer Product Safety Improvement Act (CPSIA) on p. 560.

LO.6 State what constitutes a breach of warranty

> See *Austin v Will-Burt Company* on p. 570.

D. DISCLAIMER OF WARRANTIES

LO.7 Describe the extent and manner in which implied warranties may be disclaimed under the UCC and the CISG

E. OTHER THEORIES OF PRODUCT LIABILITY

> See the **For Example** discussion of the use of the term "Vehicle Warranty" in the "Conspicuousness" section on p. 567.
> See the "Ethics & the Law" discussion of lead paint and toys on p. 571.

KEY TERMS

Consumer Product Safety Improvement Act (CPSIA)	implied warranty	warranty against encumbrances
express warranty	limited warranty	warranty of title
full warranty	negligence	
implied warranty of merchantability	privity of contract	
	privity	
	strict tort liability	
	warranties	

QUESTIONS AND CASE PROBLEMS

1. Maria Gonzalez lived in a rental unit with her sons in Queens, New York. The hot water supplied to their apartment was heated by a Morflo water heater, which had a temperature control device on its exterior manufactured by

Robertshaw and sold to Morflo. Maria Garcia, the owner of the Gonzalezes' apartment, had purchased and installed the water heater. The Morflo heater was located in the basement of the apartment house, which was locked and inaccessible to tenants.

Extensive warnings were on the water heater itself and in the manual given to Garcia at the time of her purchase. The warning on the Robertshaw temperature device read: "CAUTION: Hotter water increases the risk of scald injury." The heater itself contained a picture of hot water coming from a faucet with the word "DANGER" printed above it. In addition, the water heater had a statement on it: "Water temperature over 120 degrees Fahrenheit can cause severe burns instantly or death from scalds. Children, disabled, and elderly are at highest risk of being scalded. Feel water before bathing or showering. Temperature limiting valves are available, see manual."

In the Morflo manual, the following warning appeared:

DANGER! The thermostat is adjusted to its lowest temperature position when shipped from the factory. Adjusting the thermostat past the 120 degree Fahrenheit bar on the temperature dial will increase the risk of scald injury. The normal position is approximately 120 degrees Fahrenheit.

DANGER: WARNING: Hot water can produce first degree burns in 3 seconds at 140 degrees Fahrenheit (60 degrees Celsius), in 20 seconds at 130 degrees Fahrenheit (54 degrees Celsius), in 8 minutes at 120 degrees Fahrenheit (49 degrees Celsius).

On October 1, 1992, 15-month-old Angel Gonzalez was being bathed by his 15-year-old brother, Daniel. When the telephone rang, Daniel left Angel alone in the bathtub. No one else was at home with the boys, and Daniel left the water running. Angel was scalded by the water that came from the tap. Angel and his mother brought suit against Morflo and Robertshaw, alleging defects in the design of the water heater and the failure to warn. Should they recover? [*Gonzalez v Morflo Industries, Inc.*, 931 F Supp 159 (EDNY)]

2. Paul Parrino purchased from Dave's Professional Wheelchair Service a wheelchair manufactured by 21st Century Scientific, Inc. The sales brochure from 21st Century Scientific stated that the wheelchair would "serve [the buyer] well for many years to come." Parrino had problems with the wheelchair within a few years and filed suit against Dave's and 21st Century for breach of express warranty. Both defended on the grounds that the statement on years of service was puffery, not an express warranty. Are they right? [*Parrino v Sperling*, 648 NYS2d 702]

3. Jane Jackson purchased a sealed can of Katydids, chocolate-covered pecan caramel candies manufactured by NestlT. Shortly after, Jackson bit into one of the candies and allegedly broke a tooth on a pecan shell embedded in the candy. She filed a complaint, asserting breach of implied warranty. How would you argue on behalf of the company? How would you argue on behalf of Jackson? In your answer, discuss both the reasonable expectation test and the foreign substance/natural substance test. [*Jackson v NestlT-Beich, Inc.*, 589 NE2d 547 (Ill App)]

4. Webster ordered a bowl of fish chowder at the Blue Ship Tea Room. She was injured by a fish bone in the chowder, and she sued the tea room for breach of the implied warranty of merchantability. The evidence at trial showed that when chowder is made, the entire boned fish is cooked. Should she recover? [*Webster v Blue Ship Tea Room,* 198 NE2d 309]

5. Andy's Sales (owned by Andy Adams) sold a well-built trampoline to Carl and Shirley Wickers. The Wickerses later sold the trampoline to Herbert Bryant. While using the trampoline, Herbert's 14-year-old nephew, Rex, sustained injuries that left him a quadriplegic. Rex's guardian filed suit for breach of express warranty and merchantability. The sales brochure for the round trampoline described it as "safe" because it had a "uniform bounce" and "natural tendency to work the jumper toward the center." The Wickerses had purchased an oval-shaped trampoline. Discuss Rex's ability to recover. Is privity an issue? [*Bryant v Adams,* 448 SE2d 832 (NC App)]

6. Advent purchased ink from Borden. On the labels of the ink drums delivered to Advent, Borden had imprinted in one-sixteenth-inch type in all caps:

   SELLER MAKES NO WARRANTY, EXPRESS OR IMPLIED, CONCERNING THE PRODUCT OR THE MERCHANTABILITY OR FITNESS THEREOF FOR ANY PURPOSE CONCERNING THE ACCURACY OF ANY INFORMATION PROVIDED BY BORDEN.

   This language was printed beneath the following:

   BORDEN PRINTING INKS—"ZERO DEFECTS: THAT'S OUR GOAL"

   All of the printing was in boldface type. The disclaimer was also printed on the sales invoice and on the reverse side of the Borden form, but there was nothing on the front to call attention to the critical nature of the terms on the back because there were simply capital letters reading "SEE REVERSE SIDE." All of the terms on the back were in boldface and although the disclaimer was the first of 19 paragraphs, nothing distinguished it from the other 18 paragraphs of detailed contract terms.

   Advent said that Borden failed to age the black ink that it purchased with the result that the ink separated in Advent's printing machines. Advent refused to pay for the ink and wrote to Borden explaining that it would not tender payment because the ink was defective and demanding that Borden reimburse it for its lost profits from the downtime of printing machines. The trial court held that Borden had disclaimed any and all warranties on the ink and Advent appealed. What would you decide about the disclaimer and why? [*Borden, Inc. v Advent Ink Co.,* 701 A2d 255 (Pa Sup)]

7. Avery purchased a refrigerator from a retail store. The written contract stated that the refrigerator was sold "as is" and that the warranty of merchantability and all warranties of fitness were excluded. This was stated in large capital letters printed just above the line on which Avery signed her name. The refrigerator worked properly for a few weeks and then stopped. The store refused to do anything about it because of the exclusion of the warranties made

by the contract. Avery claimed that this exclusion was not binding because it was unconscionable. Was Avery correct? [*Avery v Aladdin Products Div., Nat'l Service Industries, Inc.*, 196 SE2d 357 (Ga App)]

8. On December 15, 1997, Hilda Forbes and her three grandchildren were traveling to Columbia, Mississippi, in her 1992 Oldsmobile Delta 88. Mrs. Forbes was driving behind a 1981 Chevrolet Chevette, which suddenly stopped and attempted to turn into a private driveway. Mrs. Forbes struck the Chevette from the rear. Both automobiles were damaged. The air bag in Mrs. Forbes's automobile did not inflate.

As a result of the impact, Mrs. Forbes was propelled forward into the windshield. She suffered a subdural hematoma. Dr. Howard Katz, a specialist in physical medicine, rehabilitation, and spinal cord injuries, testified by deposition that Mrs. Forbes suffered significant cognitive dysfunction and never completely recovered from the injury to her brain.

The air bag system and Mrs. Forbes's automobile were manufactured by GM. The owner's manual contains the following statement, "The 'air bag' part of the SIR [Supplemental Inflatable Restraint] system is in the middle of the steering wheel. The SIR system is only for crashes where the front area of your vehicle hits something. If the collision is hard enough, the 'air bag' inflates in a fraction of a second." Mr. Forbes asked the salesman about the air bag and was assured that the car had an effective one.

On December 7, 2000, Hilda and Hoyt Forbes filed suit against Angela Coleman and later added GM as a defendant. GM moved for a directed verdict, which the judge also granted. The Forbeses appealed on the grounds that GM had breached an express warranty. Was there an express warranty made? Discuss the relevant issues in reaching your conclusion. [*Forbes v General Motors Corp.*, 935 So2d 869, (Miss)]

9. In April 1990, Herbert S. Garten went to Valley Motors to purchase a new 1990 Mercedes-Benz Model 300E. Robert Bell, a Mercedes salesman, told Garten that except for some cosmetic changes, the 1990 300E was "identical" to the 1986 300E.

On April 9, 1990, Garten brought in his 1986 car and asked Bell to describe the exact differences between the 1986 model and the new 1990 model of the 300E. Bell explained the changes as only cosmetic; he gave Garten a $17,500 trade-in allowance for his 1986 300E and sold him a 1990 300E for $42,500.

The following morning, Garten had trouble shifting from second to third gear in his new car and called to complain to Bell. Bell convinced him to wait until the 1,000-mile check to see if the problem would work itself out.

On May 3, 1990, Garten brought the 1990 300E to Valley Motors for the 1,000-mile checkup and presented a memorandum describing the problems he was having with the car, focusing on the automobile's delayed upshift from second to third gear. (The delayed upshift was the result of an emissions control system designed to bring the catalytic converter quickly to operating temperature from a cold start.) Garten returned the 1990 300E to Valley Motors on May 9, 1990, and on the same day, Garten delivered two letters to Valley Motors stating that the 1990 300E was defective and he was revoking his acceptance and rescinding the sale. Garten left the keys to the 1990 300E, requested the return of his 1986 300E, and asked Valley Motors how it could retransfer titles to the two cars. Finally, Garten informed Valley Motors that he would be renting a car until this matter was resolved.

The 1990 300E sat parked at Valley Motors for approximately seven months until December 1990, when Garten retrieved the car. He subsequently traded in the 1990 300E for a new 1991 300E he purchased from another Mercedes-Benz dealer. The total purchase price of the 1991 300E was $43,123.50; he also traded in the 1990 300E for $31,500. Garten says the salesman's statement was an express warranty he relied on in buying the car. Can he recover? [*Mercedes-Benz of North America, Inc. v Garten*, 618 A2d 233 (Md App)]

10. Zogarts manufactured and sold a practice device for beginning golfers. According to statements on the package, the device was completely safe, and a player could never be struck by the device's golf ball. Hauter was hit by the ball while using the device. He sued Zogarts, which denied liability on the ground that the statements were merely matters of opinion, so liability could not be based on them. Was this a valid defense? [*Hauter v Zogarts*, 534 P2d 377 (Cal)]

11. A buyer purchased an engine to operate an irrigation pump. The buyer selected the engine from a large number that were standing on the floor of the seller's stockroom. A label on the engine stated that it would produce 100 horsepower. The buyer needed an engine that would generate at least 80 horsepower. In actual use in the buyer's irrigation system, the engine generated only 60 horsepower. The buyer sued the seller for damages. The seller raised the defense that no warranty of fitness for the buyer's particular purpose of operating an irrigation pump had arisen because the seller did not know of the use to which the buyer intended to put the engine. Also, the buyer had not relied on the seller's skill and judgment in selecting the particular engine. Did the seller have any liability based on warranties? [*Potter v Tyndall*, 207 SE2d 762 (NC)]

12. After watching a male horse owned by Terry and Manita Darby perform at a horse show, Ashley Sheffield contacted the Darbys about buying him. The Darbys assured her that the horse had no problems and would make a good show horse for use in competition. In the presence of and in consultation with her father (who raised horses for a business), Sheffield rode the horse and decided to purchase him for $8,500. Within three weeks, Sheffield and her trainer discerned that the horse was lame. Sheffield sued the Darbys for fraud and for breach of express and implied warranties, and the court entered summary judgment in favor of the Darbys on all claims. Sheffield appealed. Was the court correct in granting summary judgment? Was there a breach of an express warranty? [*Sheffield v Darby*, 535 SE2d 776 (Ga App)]

13. On July 27, 2000, Sheldorado Aluminum Products, Inc., installed an aluminum awning on the back of Marie Villette's home for use as a carport. On January 11, 2001, the awning collapsed on top of Ms. Villette's new Mercedes automobile. Ms. Villette brought suit against Sheldorado seeking recovery of the $3,000 she had paid to them for the awning.

There was no formal written contract between the parties; the only writing was a one-page order/bill designated a "contract," dated July 11, 2000, and signed by Ms. Villette and apparently by Jack Finklestein, Sheldorado's salesman. No advertising or promotional material was presented by either party. Ms. Villette testified to no express warranty or representation on the transaction, and none appears in the writing. Sheldorado acknowledges that no instructions or warnings were given to Ms. Villette as to care, maintenance, or use of the awning.

When the awning collapsed, Sheldorado took the position that the cause was an accumulation of snow and high winds and that it bore no responsibility for the loss. Its only response to the incident was to refer Ms. Villette to the insurer on their homeowner's policy. Does Ms. Villette have any rights that would allow her to collect damages? Apply the UCC to answer this question. *Villette v. Sheldorado Aluminum Products, Inc.*, 2001 WL 881055 (NY Supp), 45 UCC Rep Serv. 2d 470 (NY Civ Ct).

14. Drehman Paving & Flooring Co. installed a brick floor at Cumberland Farms that its salesman promised would be "just like" another floor Cumberland had installed several years earlier. The bricks in the new floor came loose because Drehman had failed to install expansion joints. Expansion joints were not included in the second floor contract but were part of the first. Can Cumberland recover? Under what theory? [*Cumberland Farms, Inc. v Drehman Paving & Flooring Co.*, 520 NE2d 1321 (Mass Ct App)]

15. Brian Felley went to the home of Tom and Cheryl Singleton on June 8 to look at a used car that the Singletons had advertised for sale in the local paper. The car was a 1991 Ford with 126,000 miles on it. Following a test drive and the Singletons' representation that the car was "in good mechanical condition," Felley purchased the car for $5,800. By June 18, 1997, Felley had the car in the shop and had paid $942.76 to have its clutch fixed. By July 9, 1997, Felley also had paid $971.18 for a new brake job. By September 16, 1997, Felley had paid another $429.09 for further brake work.

Felley brought suit for breach of express warranty. An auto expert testified that the clutch and brakes were defective when Felley bought the car. Was an express warranty breached? Why or why not? [*Felley v Singleton*, 705 NE2d 930 (Ill App)]

CPA QUESTIONS

1. Under the UCC Sales Article, the warranty of title may be excluded by:

   a. Merchants or nonmerchants, provided the exclusion is in writing

   b. Nonmerchant sellers only

   c. The seller's statement that it is selling only such right or title that it has

   d. Use of an "as is" disclaimer

2. Which of the following factors result(s) in an express warranty with respect to a sale of goods?

   I. The seller's description of the goods is part of the basis of the bargain.

   II. The seller selects goods knowing the buyer's intended use.

   a. I only

   b. II only

   c. Both I and II

   d. Neither I nor II

3. Morgan is suing the manufacturer, wholesaler, and retailer for bodily injuries caused by a power saw Morgan purchased. Which of the following statements is correct under the theory of strict liability?

   a. The manufacturer will avoid liability if it can show it followed the custom of the industry.

   b. Morgan may recover even if he cannot show any negligence was involved.

   c. Contributory negligence on Morgan's part will always be a bar to recovery.

   d. Privity will be a bar to recovery insofar as the wholesaler is concerned if the wholesaler did not have a reasonable opportunity to inspect.

4. On May 2, Handy Hardware sent Ram Industries a signed purchase order that stated, in part: "Ship for May 8 delivery 300 Model A-X socket sets at current dealer price. Terms 2/10/net 30." Ram received Handy's purchase order on May 4. On May 5, Ram discovered that it had only 200 Model A-X socket sets and 100 Model W-Z socket sets in stock. Ram shipped the Model A-X and Model W-Z sets to Handy without explanation concerning the shipment. The sockets were received by Handy on May 8. Assuming a contract exists between Handy and Ram, which of the following implied warranties would result?

   I. Implied warranty of merchantability

   II. Implied warranty of fitness for a particular purpose

   III. Implied warranty of title

   a. I only

   b. III only

   c. I and III only

   d. I, II, and III

Chapter 27

REMEDIES FOR BREACH OF SALES CONTRACTS

A. Statute of Limitations

    1. TIME LIMITS FOR SUITS UNDER THE UCC

    2. TIME LIMITS FOR OTHER SUITS

B. Remedies of the Seller

    3. SELLER'S LIEN

    4. SELLER'S REMEDY OF STOPPING SHIPMENT

    5. RESALE BY SELLER

    6. CANCELLATION BY SELLER

    7. SELLER'S ACTION FOR DAMAGES UNDER THE MARKET PRICE FORMULA

    8. SELLER'S ACTION FOR LOST PROFITS

    9. OTHER TYPES OF DAMAGES

    10. SELLER'S ACTION FOR THE PURCHASE PRICE

    11. SELLER'S NONSALE REMEDIES

C. Remedies of the Buyer

    12. REJECTION OF IMPROPER TENDER

    13. REVOCATION OF ACCEPTANCE

    14. BUYER'S ACTION FOR DAMAGES FOR NONDELIVERY—MARKET PRICE RECOVERY

    15. BUYER'S ACTION FOR DAMAGES FOR NONDELIVERY—COVER PRICE RECOVERY

    16. OTHER TYPES OF DAMAGES

    17. ACTION FOR BREACH OF WARRANTY

    18. CANCELLATION BY BUYER

    19. BUYER'S RESALE OF GOODS

    20. ACTION FOR SPECIFIC PERFORMANCE

    21. NONSALE REMEDIES OF THE BUYER

D. Contract Provisions on Remedies

    22. LIMITATION OF DAMAGES

    23. DOWN PAYMENTS AND DEPOSITS

    24. LIMITATION OF REMEDIES

    25. WAIVER OF DEFENSES

    26. PRESERVATION OF DEFENSES

E. Remedies in the International Sale of Goods

    27. REMEDIES OF THE SELLER

    28. REMEDIES OF THE BUYER

I f one of the parties to a sale fails to perform the contract, the nonbreaching party has remedies under Article 2 of the Uniform Commercial Code (UCC). In addition, the parties may have included provisions on remedies in their contract.

A. Statute of Limitations

statute of limitations– statute that restricts the period of time within which an action may be brought.

Judicial remedies have time limitations. After the expiration of a particular period of time, the party seeking a remedy can no longer resort to the courts. The UCC **statute of limitations** applies to actions brought for remedies on the breach of a sales contract.[1] When a suit is brought on the basis of a tort theory, such as negligence, fraud, or strict tort liability, other general statutes of limitations apply.

CPA ## 1. Time Limits for Suits Under the UCC

breach–failure to act or perform in the manner called for in a contract.

An action for breach of a sales contract must be commenced within four years after the time of the **breach**.[2] The statute of limitations can be reduced as between merchants to as little as one year but cannot be reduced in consumer contracts.

When a cause of action arises depends on the nature of the breach. The UCC has three measurements for determining when a breach occurs. The basic rule is that the time begins to run when the breach occurs, but that rule has exceptions that include special timing rules for repudiation, infringement, breach of warranty, and future performance.

A buyer seeking damages because of a breach of the sales contract must give the seller notice of the breach within a reasonable time after the buyer discovers or should have discovered it.[3]

2. Time Limits for Other Suits

When a party seeks recovery on a non-Code theory, such as on the basis of strict tort liability, fraud, or negligence, the UCC statute of limitations does not apply. The action is subject to each state's tort statute of limitations. Tort statutes of limitations are found in individual state statutes, and the time limitations vary by state. However, the tort statutes of limitations tend to be shorter than the UCC statute of limitations.

B. Remedies of the Seller

When the buyer breaches a sales contract, the seller has different remedies available that are designed to afford the seller compensation for the losses caused by the buyer's breach.[4] Revised Article 2 allows the remedies provided to be used together, and although the various remedies may be called out in separate sections, there is no

---

[1] UCC § 2-703.
[2] The cause of action arises as soon as the breach occurs even if the party is unaware of the breach at that time.
[3] UCC § 2-607(3)(a).
[4] Under Revised Article 2 (§ 2-803), the overall policy change on remedies relates to the parties' expectations. The revision allows courts to deny a remedy if one party thereby benefits to more than a full performance position.

requirement that a party elect only one of the remedies. In many cases of breach, only a combination of the various remedies can make the nonbreaching party whole again.

3. Seller's Lien

In the absence of an agreement for the extension of credit to the buyer for the purchase of goods, and until the buyer pays for the goods or performs whatever actions the contract requires, the seller has the right to retain possession of the goods.[5]

CPA 4. Seller's Remedy of Stopping Shipment

When the buyer has breached the contract prior to the time the goods have arrived at their destination, the seller can stop the goods from coming into the buyer's possession. This remedy is important to sellers because it eliminates the need for sellers to try to recover goods from buyers who have indicated they cannot or will not pay.

A seller has the right to stop shipment if the buyer has received goods on credit and the seller learns that the buyer is insolvent, the buyer has not provided assurances as requested, or the seller has grounds to believe performance by the buyer will not occur.[6] Also, the right to retrieve the goods in the case of a credit buyer's insolvency continues for "a reasonable time after the buyer's receipt of the goods."

CPA 5. Resale by Seller

When the buyer has breached the contract, the seller may resell any of the goods the seller still holds. After the resale, the seller is not liable to the original buyer on the contract and does not have to surrender any profit obtained on the resale. On the other hand, if the proceeds are less than the contract price, the seller may recover the loss from the original buyer.[7] Under Revised UCC, the failure of the seller to resell the goods does not mean the seller cannot recover under the other remedies available under Article 2.

The seller must give reasonable notice to the breaching buyer of the intention to resell the goods. Such notice need not be given if the goods are perishable or could decline rapidly in value. The seller must conduct any method of resale under standards of commercial reasonableness.[8]

6. Cancellation by Seller

When the buyer materially breaches the contract, the seller may cancel the contract. Such a cancellation ends the contract and discharges all unperformed obligations on both sides. Following cancellation, the seller has any remedy with respect to the breach by the buyer that is still available.

---

[5] UCC § 2-703.
[6] UCC § 2-705.
[7] UCC § 2-706(1), (6); *Cook Composites, Inc. v Westlake Styrene Corp.*, 155 W3d 124 (CA Tex 2000).
[8] *Plano Lincoln Mercury, Inc. v Roberts*, 167 SW3d 616 (CA Tex 2005).

7. Seller's Action for Damages Under the Market Price Formula

When the buyer fails to pay for accepted goods, the seller may resell the goods, as discussed earlier, or bring a contract action to recover damages. One formula for a seller's damages is the difference between the market price at the time and place of the tender of the goods and the contract price.[9] Under Revised Article 2, in the case of an anticipatory repudiation, the measurement of damages is the difference between the contract price and the market price "at the expiration of a commercially reasonable time after the seller learned of the repudiation" but not later than the time of tender. Whether the seller chooses to resell or recover the difference between the contract price and the market price is the seller's decision. The flexibility in the remedies under the UCC is provided because certain goods have very high market fluctuations. **For Example,** suppose that Sears has agreed to purchase 10 refrigerators from Whirlpool at a price of $1,000 each, but then Sears notifies Whirlpool that it will not be buying the refrigerators after all. Whirlpool determines the market price at the time of tender to be $850 per refrigerator. The best Whirlpool can find from an alternate buyer after a search is $800. Whirlpool can select the resale remedy ($1,000 − $800, or $200 in damages) to adequately compensate for the change in the market price between the time of tender and the time damages are sought.

CPA   ## 8. Seller's Action for Lost Profits

If the market and resale price measures of damages do not place the seller in the same position in which the seller would have been had the buyer performed, the seller is permitted to recover lost profits.[10] The recovery of lost profits reimburses the seller for costs incurred in gearing up for contract performance.[11] **For Example,** suppose that a buyer has ordered 200 wooden rocking horses from a seller-manufacturer. Before production on the horses begins, the buyer breaches. The seller has nothing to resell, and the goods have not been identified to even permit a market value assessment. Nonetheless, the seller has geared up for production, counted on the contract, and perhaps bypassed other contracts in order to perform. An appropriate remedy for the seller of the rocking horses would be the profits it would have made had the buyer performed.

Some courts also follow the lost volume doctrine that allows sellers to recover for the profits they would have made if the buyer had completed the transaction.[12] **For Example,** suppose that Maytag has a contract to sell 10 washing machines for $600 each to Lakewood Apartment Managers. Lakewood breaches the agreement and refuses to take or pay for the washing machines. Maytag is able to resell them to Suds 'n Duds Laundromat for $600 each. The price is the same, but, the theory of lost volume profits is that Maytag could have sold 20 washers, not just 10, if Lakewood had not breached. Maytag's profit on each machine is $200. Lost volume profits in this situation would be 10 times the $200, or $2,000.

---

[9] UCC § 2-708.
[10] Note that this is a change under Revised Article 2. Prior to this change, the remedy of lost profits was available only under the market price remedy. Now it is available under market price and resale remedies.
[11] UCC § 2-709.
[12] *Sunrich v Pacific Foods of Oregon*, 2004 WL 1124495 (D Or 2004)

CPA   ## 9. Other Types of Damages

incidental damages– incurred by the nonbreaching party as part of the process of trying to cover (buy substitute goods) or sell (selling subject matter of contract to another); includes storage fees, commissions, and the like.

So far, the discussion of remedies has focused on the damages that result because the seller did not sell the goods. However, the seller may incur additional expenses because of the breach. Some of those expenses can be recovered as damages. UCC § 2-710 provides that the seller can also recover, as **incidental damages**, any commercially reasonable charges, expenses, or commissions incurred[13] in recovering damages.[14] **For Example,** the seller may recover expenses for the transportation, care, and storage of the goods after the buyer's breach, as well as any costs incurred in the return or resale of the goods. Such damages are in addition to any others that may be recovered by the seller.

CPA   ## 10. Seller's Action for the Purchase Price

If goods are specially manufactured and the buyer refuses to take them, it is possible for the seller to recover as damages the full purchase price and keep the goods.[15] **For Example,** a printing company that has printed catalogs for a retail mail-order merchant will not be able to sell the catalogs to anyone else. The remedy for the seller is recovery of the purchase price.[16]

11. Seller's Nonsale Remedies

secured transaction– credit sale of goods or a secured loan that provides special protection for the creditor.

In addition to the seller's traditional sales remedies, many sellers enter into other transactions that provide protection from buyer breaches. One such protection is afforded when the seller obtains a security interest from the buyer under UCC Article 9. A **secured transaction** is a pledge of property by the buyer-debtor that enables the seller to take possession of the goods if the buyer fails to pay the amount

---

thinking things through

Bingo: A Breach is a Breach

In 1996, Collins Entertainment Corporation contracted to lease video poker machines to two bingo hall operations known as Ponderosa Bingo and Shipwatch Bingo. The six-year lease required that any purchaser of the premises assume the lease. In 1997, American Bingo and Gaming Corporation purchased the assets of the bingo parlors. American failed to assume the lease and removed Collins' machines from the premises. Collins

had $1.5 million in profits remaining on the lease at the time its machines were removed. However, Collins was able to place the video poker machines in other casinos. Collins filed suit against American Bingo. American Bingo says that Collins has no damages because the machines were already earning money for it. Is American Bingo correct? [**Collins Entertainment Corp. v Coats and Coats Rental Amusement, 629 SE2d 635 (SC 2006)**]

---

[13] UCC § 2-710.
[14] UCC § 2-710; *Purina Mills, L.L.C. v Less*, 295 F Supp 2d 1017 (ND Iowa 2003).
[15] *In re Moltech Power Systems, Inc.*, 326 BR 178 (ND Fla 2005).
[16] UCC § 2-709(1)(a) and (b).

FIGURE 27-1 | *Seller's Remedies under Article 2*

REMEDY	STOP DELIVERY	RESALE PRICE	MARKET PRICE	ACTION FOR PRICE	LOST PROFIT
SECTION NUMBER	2–703	2–706 2–710	2–708 2–710	2–709 2–708	2–708(2)
WHEN AVAILABLE	Insolvency Advance breach by buyer	Buyer fails to take goods	Buyer fails to take goods	Specially manufactured goods	Anticipatory repudiation Breach
NATURE OF REMEDY	Stop delivery of any size shipment or recover goods if buyer insolvent (Revised UCC)	Contract price – Resale price + Incidental damages – Expenses saved + Consequential damages	Contract price – Market price + Incidental damages – Expenses saved + Consequential damages	Contract price + Incidental damages – Expenses saved + Consequential damages	Profits + Incidental damages – Salvage value + Consequential damages

owed. (See Chapter 34.) Figure 27-1 is a summary of the remedies available to the seller under Article 2.

C. REMEDIES OF THE BUYER

When the seller breaches a sales contract, the buyer has a number of remedies under Article 2 of the UCC. Additional remedies based on contract or tort theories of product liability may also be available. (See Chapter 25.)

12. Rejection of Improper Tender

As discussed in Chapter 26, if the goods tendered by the seller do not conform to the contract in some way, the buyer may reject them. However, the rejection is the beginning of the buyer's remedies. Following rejection, the buyer can proceed to recover under the various formulas provided for buyers under the UCC.

13. Revocation of Acceptance

The buyer may revoke acceptance of the goods when they do not conform to the contract, the defect substantially impairs the value of the contract to the buyer, and the buyer either could not discover the problem or kept the goods because of a seller's promise of repair (see Chapter 26). Again, following revocation of acceptance, the buyer has various remedies available under the UCC.

CPA ## 14. Buyer's Action for Damages for Nondelivery—Market Price Recovery

If the seller fails to deliver the goods as required by the contract or repudiates the contract, the buyer is entitled to collect from the seller damages for breach of contract. Under Revised Article 2, the buyer is entitled to recover the difference between the market price at the time of tender and the contract price; this is a change from the previous Article 2 that measured damages at the time the buyer learned of the breach.[17]

CPA ## 15. Buyer's Action for Damages for Nondelivery—Cover Price Recovery

A buyer may also choose, as a remedy for the seller's nondelivery of goods that conform to the contract, to purchase substitute goods or cover.[18] If the buyer acts in good faith, the measure of damages for the seller's nondelivery or repudiation is then the difference between the cost of cover and the contract price.[19]

The buyer need only make a reasonable cover purchase as a substitute for the contract goods. The goods purchased need not be identical to the contract goods. **For Example,** if the buyer could secure only 350 five-speed blenders when the contract called for 350 three-speed blenders, the buyer's cover would be reasonable despite the additional expense of the five-speed blenders.

CPA ## 16. Other Types of Damages

The buyer is also entitled to collect incidental damages in situations in which he must find substitute goods. Those incidental damages could include additional shipping expenses or perhaps commissions paid to find the goods and purchase them. Buyers often also experience **consequential damages**, which are those damages the buyer experiences with respect to a third party as a result of the seller's breach. Revised UCC provides consequential damages for sellers and buyers. The seller's section provides, "Consequential damages resulting from the buyer's breach include any loss resulting from general or particular requirements and needs of which the buyer at the time of contracting had reason to know and which could not reasonably be prevented by resale or otherwise."[20] **For Example,** a seller's failure to deliver the goods may cause the buyer's production line to come to a halt. The buyer might then breach on its sales and delivery contracts with its buyers. In the case of a government contract, the buyer may have to pay a penalty for being late. These types of damages are consequential ones and can be recovered if the seller knew about the consequences or they were foreseeable. Under Revised Article 2, consequential damages cannot be recovered from a consumer.

consequential damages—damages the buyer experiences as a result of the seller's breach with respect to a third party.

17. Action for Breach of Warranty

A remedy available to a buyer when goods are delivered but fail to conform to warranties is an action for breach of warranty.

---

[17] UCC § 2-713.
[18] UCC § 2-712; *Conagra, Inc. v Nierenberg*, 7 P3d 369 (Mont 2000). Buyers are also entitled to recover any deposits paid [*Selectouch Corp. v Perfect Starch, Inc.*, 111 SW3d 830, 51 UCC Rep Serv 2d 1070 (Tex App 2004)].
[19] UCC § 2-712(1) and (2). See *Conductores Monterrey, S.A. de C.V. v Remee Products Corp.*, 45 UCC Rep Serv 2d 111 (SDNY 2000).
[20] UCC § 2-710.

CASE SUMMARY

Showdown over the Silverado Pickup

FACTS: Sonya Kaminski purchased from Billy Cain's Cornelia dealership a truck that was represented to her to be a 1989 Chevrolet Silverado pickup. However, subsequent incidents involving repair of the truck and its parts, as well as a title history, revealed that the truck was a GMC rather than a Chevrolet. Sales agents at the Cornelia dealership misrepresented the truck's character and sold the truck to Kaminski as a Chevrolet.

Kaminski filed suit for intentional fraud and deceit under the Georgia Fair Business Practices Act (FBPA) and for breach of express warranty. The jury awarded Kaminski $2,823.70 for breach of express warranty and $50,000 punitive (exemplary) damages. The judge added damages under the FBPA of $10,913.29 in actual damages and $9,295 in attorney fees and court costs. The dealership appealed.

DECISION: The judgment of the lower court is affirmed. A buyer can collect both incidental and consequential damages. Incidental expenses here included renting a vehicle to get to work. The buyer here was entitled to all forms of damages for the breach, including compensatory, consequential, and incidental damages. The punitive damages were for fraud because the evidence showed that the dealership knew that the truck's make and model were not correct. [**Billy Cain Ford Lincoln Mercury, Inc. v Kaminski, 496 SE2d 521 (Ga App 1998)**]

(A) **NOTICE OF BREACH.** If the buyer has accepted goods that do not conform to the contract or there has been a breach of any warranties given, the buyer must notify the seller of the breach within a reasonable time after the breach is discovered or should have been discovered.[21]

(B) **MEASURE OF DAMAGES.** If the buyer has given the necessary notice of breach, the buyer may recover damages measured by the loss resulting in the normal course of events from the breach. If suit is brought for breach of warranty, the measure of damages is the difference between the value of the goods as they were at the time of tender and the value that they would have had if they had been as warranted. Under Revised Article 2, the buyer is also entitled to any of the other damage remedies necessary to make the buyer whole.

(C) **NOTICE OF THIRD-PARTY ACTION AGAINST BUYER.** When a buyer elects the remedy of resale and sells the contract goods to a third party, that third party has the right of suit against the buyer for breach of warranty. In such a case, it is the buyer's option whether to give the seller notice of the action and request that the seller defend that action.

18. Cancellation by Buyer

The buyer may cancel or rescind the contract if the seller fails to deliver the goods, if the seller has repudiated the contract, or if the goods have been rightfully rejected or

---

[21] *Dunleavey v Paris Ceramics, USA, Inc.,* 819 A2d 945 (Super Ct 2002); *Muehlbauer v General Motors Corp.,* 431 F Supp 2d 847 (ND Ill 2006).

C A S E   S U M M A R Y

The Alpha Chi Omega Battle of the Sweaters

FACTS: Emily Lieberman and Amy Altomondo were members of the Alpha Chi Omega (AXO) sorority at Bowling Green State University. They negotiated with Johnathan James Furlong for the purchase of custom-designed sweaters for themselves and their sorority sisters for a total price of $3,612. Lieberman and Altomondo paid Furlong a $2,000 deposit.

When Lieberman and Altomondo saw the sweaters, they realized that Furlong had made color and design alterations in the lettering imprinted on the sweaters as part of their custom design. Altomondo, as president of AXO, called Furlong and told him that the sweaters were unacceptable and offered to return them. Furlong refused, stating that any changes were immaterial. Altomondo refused to pay the balance due and demanded the return of the $2,000 deposit. Furlong filed suit for breach of contract.

DECISION: The sorority rejected the sweaters within a reasonable time after delivery and notified the seller. The seller breached the contract. The sorority is entitled to cancel the contract, recover the amounts it paid, and hold the sweaters until recovery. The sweaters were altered without authorization and there is a breach of contract. Finally, and alternatively, Furlong should have entered into a contract that gave him discretion to make design changes without AXO's consent. These sweaters, as Furlong himself admits (and describes), were to be "custom-designed" for AXO. Thus, they were to be printed according to AXO's specifications, not according to Furlong's discretion.

The sorority is entitled to a full refund of its deposit and any additional damages it experienced in defending this suit and seeking to collect the amounts it is due. [**Furlong v Alpha Chi Omega Sorority, 657 NE2d 866 (Ohio Mun Ct 1993)**]

their acceptance revoked.[22] A buyer who cancels the contract is entitled to recover as much of the purchase price as has been paid, including the value of any property given as a trade-in as part of the purchase price. The fact that the buyer cancels the contract does not destroy the buyer's cause of action against the seller for breach of that contract. The buyer may recover from the seller not only any payment made on the purchase price but also damages for the breach of the contract. The damages represent the difference between the contract price and the cost of cover.[23]

The right of the buyer to cancel or rescind the sales contract may be lost by a delay in exercising the right. A buyer who, with full knowledge of the defects in the goods, makes partial payments or performs acts of ownership of the goods inconsistent with the decision to cancel may lose certain remedy provisions or be limited in recovery under Article 2.

19. Buyer's Resale of Goods

When the buyer has possession of the goods after rightfully rejecting them or after rightfully revoking acceptance, the buyer is treated as a seller in possession of goods after default by a buyer. When the seller has breached, the buyer has a security

---

[22] UCC § 2-720.
[23] UCC § 2-712(1), (2); *GFSI, Inc. v J-Loong Trading, Ltd.,* 505 F Supp 2d 935 (D Kan 2007).

interest in the goods to protect the claim against the seller for breach and may proceed to resell the goods. From the proceeds of the sale, the aggrieved buyer is entitled to deduct any payments made to the seller and any expenses reasonably incurred in the inspection, receipt, transportation, care and custody, and resale of the goods.[24]

CPA   20. Action for Specific Performance

Under Article 2, specific performance is a remedy available only to buyers in those circumstances in which the goods are specially manufactured, unique, or rare, such as antiques or goods with sentimental value for the buyer. **For Example,** a buyer with a contract to buy a chair from Elvis Presley's home would be entitled to a specific performance remedy of delivery of the chair. Distributors have been granted specific performance against suppliers to deliver goods covered by supply contracts because of the unique dependence of the supply chain and the assumed continuous feeding of that chain.

Specific performance will not be granted, however, merely because the price of the goods purchased from the seller has gone up. In such a case, the buyer can still purchase the goods in the open market. The fact that it will cost more to cover can be compensated for by allowing the buyer to recover the cost increase from the seller.

FIGURE 27-2 | *Buyer's Remedies under Article 2*

REMEDY	SPECIFIC PERFORMANCE (REPLEVIN IDENTIFICATION)	COVER	MARKET PRICE
SECTION NUMBER	2–711	2–712 2–715	2–708 2–710
WHEN AVAILABLE	Rare or unique goods	Seller fails to deliver or goods are defective (rejection) or revocation of acceptance	Seller fails to deliver or goods are defective (rejection or revocation of acceptance)
NATURE OF REMEDY	Buyer gets goods + incidental damages + consequential damages	Cover price – Contract price + Incidental damages + Consequential damages – Expenses saved	Market price – Contract price + Incidental damages + Consequential damages – Expenses saved

[24] UCC § 2-715(1); *Gordon v Gordon*, 929 So2d 981 (Miss App 2006).

21. Nonsale Remedies of the Buyer

In addition to the remedies given the buyer under UCC Article 2, the buyer may have remedies based on contract or tort theories of liability.

The pre-Code law on torts still applies in UCC Article 2 transactions. The seller may therefore be held liable to the buyer for any negligence, fraud, or strict tort liability that occurred in the transaction. (See Chapter 25.)

A defrauded buyer may both avoid the contract and recover damages. The buyer also has the choice of retaining the contract and recovering damages for the losses caused by the fraud.[25]

Figure 27-2 provides a summary of the remedies available to buyers under Article 2.

D. CONTRACT PROVISIONS ON REMEDIES

The parties to a sales contract may modify the remedies provided under Article 2 or limit those remedies.

22. Limitation of Damages

CPA

liquidated damages–
provision stipulating the amount of damages to be paid in the event of default or breach of contract.

(A) LIQUIDATED DAMAGES. The parties may specify the exact amount of damages that may be recovered in case of breach. A **liquidated damages** clause in a contract can be valid if it meets the standards of Article 2. Under Revised Article 2, the enforceability of a liquidated damages clause in a consumer contract is determined by comparing the amount of the liquidated damages specified with the anticipated or actual harm, the difficulties of proof of loss, and the availability of an otherwise adequate remedy. For nonconsumer contracts, the enforceability of a liquidated damages clause depends on whether the amount is reasonable in light of the anticipated or actual harm.

C A S E   S U M M A R Y

The Cost of Breaching a Jet-Set Contract

FACTS: On August 21, 1992, Miguel A. Diaz Rodriguez (Diaz) entered into a contract with Learjet to buy a model 60 jet aircraft for $3,000,000 with a $250,000 deposit made on execution of the contract; $750,000 payment on September 18, 1992; $1,000,000 180 days before delivery of the aircraft; and the balance due on delivery of the aircraft. Diaz paid the $250,000 deposit but made no other payments.

In September 1992, Diaz said he no longer wanted the aircraft and asked for the deposit to be returned. Learjet informed Diaz that the $250,000 deposit was being retained as liquidated damages because their contract provided as follows:

Learjet may terminate this Agreement as a result of the Buyer's failure to make any progress payment when due. If this Agreement is terminated by Learjet for any reason stipulated in

---

[25] *Cooper v Bluff City Mobile Home Sales, Inc.*, 78 SW2d 157(SD 2002).

C A S E   S U M M A R Y

Continued

the previous sentence, Learjet shall retain all payments theretofore made by the Buyer as liquidated damages and not as a penalty and the parties shall thenceforth be released from all further obligations hereunder. Such damages include, but are not limited to, loss of profit on this sale, direct and indirect costs incurred as a result of disruption in production, training expense advance and selling expenses in effecting resale of the Airplane.

After Diaz breached the contract, Circus Circus Enterprises purchased the Learjet Diaz had ordered with some changes that cost $1,326. Learjet realized a $1,887,464 profit on the sale of the aircraft to Circus Circus, which was a larger profit than Learjet had originally budgeted for the sale to Diaz.

Diaz filed suit seeking to recover the $250,000 deposit. The district court granted summary judgment to Learjet, and Diaz appealed. The case was remanded for a determination of the reasonableness of the liquidated damages. The district court upheld the $250,000 as reasonable damages, and Diaz appealed.

DECISION: The lower court's judgment was affirmed. Diaz challenged the reasonableness of the liquidated damages clause. The $250,000 deposit as a liquidated damages clause in a contract in this price range was not unreasonable. Also, the seller was the one that lost its profits on a second sale that it would have made had Diaz not breached. The "lost volume" provision of the UCC permits nonbreaching sellers to recover the lost profits on a contract in which the other remedy sections do not compensate for the breach by the buyer. The evidence indicates that the lost profit from the Diaz contract would have been approximately $1.8 million. [**Rodriguez v Learjet, Inc., 946 P2d 1010 (Kan App 1997)**]

(B) EXCLUSION OF DAMAGES. The sales contract may provide that in case of breach, no damages may be recovered or no consequential damages may be recovered. When goods are sold for consumer use and personal injuries are sustained, such total exclusions are unconscionable and unenforceable. Such a contract limitation is not enforceable in other types of contracts (nonconsumer) unless the party seeking to enforce it is able to prove that the limitation of liability was commercially reasonable and fair rather than oppressive and surprising. As discussed in Chapter 25, limitations on damages for personal injuries resulting from breaches of warranty are not enforceable.

CPA   ## 23. Down Payments and Deposits

A buyer can make a deposit with the seller or an initial or down payment at the time of making the contract. If the contract contains a valid provision for liquidation of damages and the buyer defaults, the seller must return any part of the down payment or deposit in excess of the amount specified by the liquidated damages clause. In the absence of such a liquidated damages clause and in the absence of proof of greater damages, the seller's damages are computed as 20 percent of the purchase price or $500, whichever is smaller.

24. Limitation of Remedies

The parties may limit the remedies that are provided by the Code in the case of breach of contract. A seller may specify that the only remedy of the buyer for breach of warranty will be the repair or replacement of the goods or that the buyer will be limited to returning the goods and obtaining a refund of the purchase price, subject to the restrictions discussed in Chapter 25.

25. Waiver of Defenses

A buyer can be barred from claiming a breach of the contract by the seller if the sales contract expressly states that the buyer will not assert any defenses against the seller.

---

thinking things through

The Gun-Totin' Harley Buyer and His Damages

Wiley Sharbino purchased a 2003 Harley Davidson motorcycle from Cooke Family Enterprises, LLC., d/b/a Renegade Harley-Davidson. He gave a gun as a down payment and financed the remaining amount of the purchase price. Within two days of purchase, the motorcycle  sustained a broken drive belt. When Sharbino took the motorcycle back, Renegade told him that "the drive sprockets on the transmission and the rear wheel of the motorcycle were mismatched, causing the drive belt to break." The problem could not be fixed without changing the appearance of the motorcycle. Sharbino said he would not have purchased the motorcycle if he had known of the problem.

Renegade took back the motorcycle and told Sharbino to pick up his gun at the office where the dealership had kept it in a safe. Sharbino still filed suit seeking as damages the sales price plus interest, reasonable expenses related to the sale and preservation of the motorcycle, and attorney fees. Renegade said that the rescission of the agreement and return of Sharbino's "down payment" made him whole and that he had no other damages. Who is correct? Is rescission and the restoring of the party to his original position enough to compensate for a breach? [**Sharbino v Cooke Family Enterprises, Inc., 6 So 3d 1026 (La App 3d Cir 2009)**]

---

ethics & the law

Do you believe Sharbino is trying to take advantage of the dealership? Should the dealership have conducted a more careful inspection of the motorcycle for the problem before selling it? What  relationships would UCC warranty provisions have in this situation?

26. Preservation of Defenses

Consumer protection law prohibits the waiver of defenses in consumer contracts.

(A) **PRESERVATION NOTICE.** Consumer defenses are preserved by a Federal Trade Commission (FTC) regulation. This regulation requires that the papers signed by a consumer contain a provision that expressly states that the consumer reserves any defense arising from the transaction.[26] A defense of the consumer arising from the original transaction may be asserted against any third person who acquires rights by assignment in the contract (see Chapter 33).

(B) **PROHIBITION OF WAIVER.** When the FTC preservation notice is included in the contract that is obtained by, or transferred to, a third party, a waiver of defenses cannot be made. If the preservation notice is not included, the seller has committed an unfair trade practice.

E. REMEDIES IN THE INTERNATIONAL SALE OF GOODS

The United Nations Convention on Contracts for the International Sale of Goods (CISG) provides remedies for breach of a sales contract between parties from nations that have approved the CISG.

27. Remedies of the Seller

Under the CISG, if the buyer fails to perform any obligations under the contract, the seller may require the buyer to pay the price, take delivery, and perform other obligations under the contract. The seller may also declare the contract void if the

---

e-commerce&cyberlaw

Consequential Damages and Software

Computer systems and software often do not function as intended or have some glitches when installed at a company. For example, suppose that a software company sold to a utility a software package that was represented as one that would simplify the utility's billing processes. The program is installed and tested, and some changes are made as a result of trial runs. When the program is fully implemented and all customers and bills are run through

the new system, there is a complete breakdown. The bills cannot be produced or sent to customers, and the utility company is without cash flow. Without bills going out, no payments are coming in, and the utility must borrow from a high-interest line of credit at an interest cost of $400,000 per month. What damages could the utility collect? Could the software manufacturer limit its liability?

---

[26] 316 CFR § 433.1: It is an unfair or deceptive trade practice to take or receive a consumer credit contract that fails to contain such a preservation notice.

failure of the buyer to perform obligations under the contract amounts to a fundamental breach of contract.

28. Remedies of the Buyer

Under the CISG, a buyer may reject goods only if the tender is a fundamental breach of the contract. This standard of materiality of rejection is in contrast to the UCC requirement of perfect tender. Under the CISG, a buyer may also reduce the price when nonconforming goods are delivered even though no notice of nonconformity is given. However, the buyer must have a reasonable cause for failure to give notice about the nonconformity.

MAKE THE CONNECTION

SUMMARY

The law provides a number of remedies for the breach of a sales contract. Remedies based on UCC theories generally are subject to a four-year statute of limitations, with Revised UCC adding an extension of one additional year (making it five years) in cases in which the breach is discovered in year four. If the remedy sought is based on a non-UCC theory, a tort or contract statute of limitations established by state statute will apply.

Remedies of the seller may include (1) a lien on the goods until the seller is paid, (2) the right to resell the goods, (3) the right to cancel the sales contract, (4) the right to recover the goods from the carrier and the buyer, and (5) the right to bring an action for damages or, in some cases, for the purchase price. The seller may also have remedies because of secured transactions.

Remedies of the buyer may include (1) the rejection of nonconforming goods, (2) the revocation of acceptance, (3) an action for damages for nondelivery of conforming goods, (4) an action for breach of warranty, (5) the cancellation of the sales contract, (6) the right to resell the goods, (7) the right to bring an action for conversion, recovery of goods, or specific performance, and (8) the right to sue for damages and cancel if the seller has made a material breach of the contract.

The parties may modify their remedies by a contractual provision for liquidated damages, for limitations on statutory remedies, or for waiver of defenses. When consumers are involved, this freedom of contract is to some extent limited for their protection.

Under the CISG, the seller may require the buyer to pay the price, take delivery, and perform obligations under the contract, or the seller may avoid the contract if there is a fundamental breach.

A buyer may reject goods under the CISG only if there is a fundamental breach of contract. The buyer may also reduce the price of nonconforming goods.

LEARNING OUTCOMES

After studying this chapter, you should be able to clearly explain:

A. STATUTE OF LIMITATIONS

B. REMEDIES OF THE SELLER

LO.1 List the remedies of the seller when the buyer breaches a sales contract
> See the **For Example,** discussion of the Whirlpool refrigerators on p. 601.

C. REMEDIES OF THE BUYER

LO.2 List the remedies of the buyer when the seller breaches a sales contract
> See the Thinking Things Through discussion of the Harley purchase on p. 610.
> See *Furlong v Alpha Chi Omega Sorority* on p. 606.
> See *Billy Cain Ford Lincoln Mercury, Inc. v Kaminski* on p. 605.

D. CONTRACT PROVISIONS ON REMEDIES

LO.3 Determine the validity of clauses limiting damages
> See *Rodriguez v Learjet, Inc.* on p. 608.
> See the E-Commerce & Cyberlaw discussion of software damages on p. 611.

E. REMEDIES IN THE INTERNATIONAL SALE OF GOODS

KEY TERMS

breach

consequential damages

incidental damages

liquidated damages

secured transaction

statute of limitations

QUESTIONS AND CASE PROBLEMS

1. Firwood Manufacturing Co. had a contract to sell General Tire 55 model 1225 postcure inflators (PCIs). PCIs are $30,000 machines used by General Tire in its manufacturing process. The contract was entered into in 1989, and by April 1990 General Tire had purchased 22 PCIs from Firwood. However, General Tire then closed its Barrie, Michigan, plant. Firwood reminded General Tire that it still had the obligation to purchase the 33 remaining PCIs. General Tire communicated to Firwood that it would not be purchasing the remaining ones. Firwood then was able, over a period of three years, to sell the remaining PCIs. Some of the PCIs were sold as units, and others were broken down and sold to buyers who needed parts. Firwood's sales of the remaining 33 units brought in $187,513 less than the General Tire contract provided, and Firwood filed suit to collect the resale price difference plus interest. Can Firwood recover? Why or why not? [*Firwood Manufacturing Co., Inc. v General Tire, Inc.*, 96 F3d 163 (6th Cir)]

2. Soon after Gast purchased a used auto from a Chevrolet dealer, he experienced a series of mechanical problems with the car. Gast refused to make further payments on the bank note that had financed the purchase. The bank took possession of the automobile and sold it. Gast then brought an action against the dealer, alleging that he had revoked his acceptance. Was Gast correct? Explain your answer. [*Gast v Rodgers-Dingus Chevrolet*, 585 So 2d 725 (Miss)]

3. Formetal Engineering submitted to Presto a sample and specifications for precut polyurethane pads to be used in making air-conditioning units. Formetal paid for the goods as soon as they were delivered but subsequently discovered that the pads did not conform to the sample and specifications in that there were incomplete cuts, color variances, and faulty adherence to the pad's paper backing. Formetal then informed Presto of the defects and notified Presto that it would reject the pads and return them to Presto, but they were not returned for 125 days. Presto argued that it was denied the right to cure because the goods were not returned until some 125 days after Formetal promised to do so. Was there a breach of the contract? Did the buyer (Formetal) do anything wrong in seeking its remedies? [*Presto Mfg. Co. v Formetal Engineering Co.*, 360 NE2d 510 (Ill App)]

4. Lam entered into contracts with Dallas Semiconductor to build six machines, referred to in its contracts as Tools A-F.

   The contracts were entered into in 2000 and in 2001, but Maxim Integrated acquired Dallas Semiconductor in 2001. The employees at Dallas who were in charge of the contracts continued to assure Lam that everything was on track. Lam representatives also had meetings with Maxim representatives. However, those discussions broke down and after Lam issued a demand letter for which there was no response, he filed suit for breach of contract. Lam was able to sell the machines to other customers for an equal or greater price. Lam asked for total damages in the amount of $13,860,847, representing lost profits on all six tools, plus lost profits on the extended warranties and training packages for the tools. Is Lam entitled to such recovery? [*Lam Research Corp. v Dallas Semiconductor Corp.*, 2006 WL 1000573, 59 UCC Rep Serv 2d 716 (Cal App 2006) (Cal App)]

5. McNeely entered into a contract with Wagner to pay $250,000 as a lump sum for all timber present in a given area that Wagner would remove for McNeely. The contract estimated that the volume in the area would be 780,000 board feet. Wagner also had provisions in the contract that made no warranties as to the amount of lumber and that he would keep whatever timber was not harvested if McNeely ended the contract before the harvesting was complete. The $250,000 was to be paid in three advances. McNeely paid two of the three advances but withheld the third payment and ended the contract because he said there was not enough timber. Wagner filed suit for the remaining one-third of the payment. McNeely said Wagner could not have the remaining one-third of the payment as well as the transfer; he had to choose between the two remedies. Is he correct? [*Wagner v McNeely*, 38 UCC2d 1176 (Or)]

6. Brown Machine Company, a division of Kvaerner U.S., Inc., entered into a contract to supply a machine and tools to Hakim Plast, a food

container–producing company based in Cairo, Egypt, to enable Hakim to meet its growing demand for plastic containers. The plastic containers were for customers to use in the ice cream distribution industry. It was understood that the equipment would be ready for delivery before the busy summer ice cream season. Brown Machine was not able to meet the twice extended deadline. It attempted to obtain another extension, but Hakim Plast refused without additional consideration. Brown refused to provide the requested consideration. Hakim Plast declared the contract breached on September 25, 1994. Brown then sold the equipment and brought suit for breach of contract, requesting damages for the loss of the sale. Hakim Plast countersued for Brown's breach seeking out-of-pocket expenses and consequential damages for loss of business. Discuss who breached the contract and determine what possible damages might be recovered. [*Kvaerner U.S., Inc. v Hakim Plast Co.*, 74 F Supp 2d 709 (ED Mich)]

7. When she was 17 years old, Cathy Bishop's parents signed a purchase contract for a new Hyundai automobile on which she made all payments. She was the primary driver of the vehicle, and while it was still under warranty, a manufacturing defect resulted in a fire that damaged it beyond reasonable repair. Although Hyundai was promptly notified and soon acknowledged responsibility for the fire, offers of replacement vehicles were rejected because they were not equivalent to the one destroyed, and monetary offers were rejected as being below its actual value. After Hyundai stated its final offer would expire on June 3, 1992 (some six months after negotiations began), Bishop sued for reimbursement of the vehicle's purchase price, as well as incidental and general damages, asking they be trebled by way of penalty for Hyundai's willful violation of the California "lemon law."

   At trial, Bishop testified at length to her emotional distress resulting from the unavailability of her car upon which she had relied to attend college classes and from her inability to procure new transportation, due in part because of her obligation to make the car payments to the lender. The jury awarded Bishop the value of her car, or $8,312.18, plus damages for "loss of use" in the amount of $17,223, incidental damages of $1,444, and emotional distress damages of $5,000. The jury found Hyundai's lemon law violation to be willful, making its total award $95,937.54. Bishop was awarded more than $50,000 in costs and attorney fees. Discuss all of the damage awards other than the lemon law awards and determine whether they are proper damages under the UCC. [*Bishop v Hyundai Motor America*, 44 Cal App 4th 750, 52 Cal Rptr 2d 134]

8. Mrs. Kirby purchased a wheelchair from NMC/ Continue Care. The wheelchair was customized for her and her home. When the wheelchair arrived, it was too wide to fit through the doorways in her home. What options does Mrs. Kirby have? [*Kirby v NMC Continue Care*, 993 P2d 951 (Wyo)]

9. Wolosin purchased a vegetable and dairy refrigerator case from Evans Manufacturing Corp. When Evans sued Wolosin for the purchase price, Wolosin claimed damages for breach of warranty. The sales contract provided that Evans would replace defective parts free of charge for one year; it also stated, "This warranty is in lieu of any and all other warranties stated or

inferred, and of all other obligations on the part of the manufacturer, which neither assumes nor authorizes anyone to assume for it any other obligations or liability in connection with the sale of its products." Evans claimed that it was liable only for replacement of parts. Wolosin claimed that the quoted clause was not sufficiently specific to satisfy the limitation-of-remedies requirement of UCC § 2-719. Provide some insight on this issue for the parties by discussing damage limitation clauses under the UCC. [*Evans Mfg. Corp. v Wolosin,* 47 Luzerne County Leg Reg 238 (Pa)]

10. McInnis purchased a tractor and scraper as new equipment of the current model year from Western Tractor & Equipment Co. The written contract stated that the seller disclaimed all warranties and that no warranties existed except those stated in the contract. Actually, the equipment was not the current model but that of the prior year. The equipment was not new but had been used for 68 hours as a demonstrator model, after which the hour meter had been reset to zero. The buyer sued the seller for damages. The seller's defense was based on the ground that all liability for warranties had been disclaimed. Was this defense valid? [*McInnis v Western Tractor & Equipment Co.,* 388 P2d 562 (Wash)]

11. Elmore purchased a car from Doenges Brothers Ford. The car had been placed with the dealership by a dealership employee as part of a consignment arrangement. Elmore was unable to obtain title to the car because the Environmental Protection Agency had issues with the car's compliance with emissions equipment requirements. Elmore was unable to drive the car. He brought suit because he was forced to sell the car for $10,300 less than he paid because of the title defect, and the fact that only a salvage dealer would purchase it. Because he lost his transportation, he was out of work for eight months and experienced a $20,000 decline in income. What damages could Elmore recover under the UCC? [*Elmore v Doenges Bros. Ford, Inc.,* 21 P3d 65 (Okla App)]

12. Stock Solution is a "stock photo agency" that leases photographic transparencies produced by professional photographers for use in media advertising. Between October 1, 1994, and May 31, 1995, Stock Solution delivered Axiom 107 color transparencies to be used in Axiom's advertising. The contracts provided that in the event the transparencies were not returned by the specified "return date," Axiom would pay the following fees: (1) an initial "service charge" of $30, (2) "holding fee[s]" in the amount of "$5.00 per week per transparency", (3) "service fees" at a rate of "one and one-half percent per month" on unpaid balances of invoices beginning 30 days after invoice date, and (4) reimbursement for loss or damage of each "original transparency" in the amount of $1,500.

Axiom failed to return 37 of the 107 transparencies in breach of the contracts. Of the 37 missing transparencies, 36 were original color transparencies and 1 was a duplicate color transparency. Stock Solution filed suit seeking damages (1) for the 36 missing original color transparencies, the agreed liquidated value of $54,000 plus sales tax of $3,294; (2) for the 1 missing duplicate color transparency, $1 plus sales tax of $0.06; (3) holding fees on the 37 missing transparencies in the amount of $23,914.83; (4) service fees and charges as provided for in the contracts; and (5) attorney fees.

Discuss whether the liquidated damage clause was enforceable under the law. [*Bair v Axiom Design, LLC*, 20 P3d 388 (Utah)]

13. Ramtreat Metal Technology provided for a "double your money back" remedy in its contracts for the sale of its metal drilling assemblies. A buyer filed suit seeking consequential damages and cost of replacement. Ramtreat said that its clause was a limitation of remedies. Could Ramtreat limit its remedies to "double your money back"? [*Adcock v Ramtreat Metal Technology, Inc.*, 44 UCC Rep Serv 2d 1026 (Wash App)]

14. Joseph Perna purchased a 1981 Oldsmobile at a traffic auction conducted by Locascio. The car had been seized pursuant to action taken by the New York City Parking Violation Bureau against Jose Cruz. Perna purchased the car for $1,800 plus tax and towing fees "subject to the terms and conditions of any and all chattel mortgages, rental agreements, liens, conditional bills of sale, and encumbrances that may be on the motor vehicle of the above judgment debtor." The Olds had 58,103 miles on it at the time of Perna's purchase. On May 7, 1993, Perna sold the car to Elio Marino, a coworker, for $1,200. The vehicle had about 65,000 miles on it at the time of this sale.

During his period of ownership, Marino replaced the radiator ($270), repaired the power steering and valve cover gasket ($117), and replaced a door lock ($97.45). He registered and insured the vehicle. In February 1994, Marino's son was stopped by the police and arrested for driving a stolen vehicle. The son was kept in jail until his arraignment, but the charges were eventually dropped. The Oldsmobile was never returned to Marino, who filed suit for breach of contract because he had been given a car with a defective title. He asked for damages that included the costs of getting his son out of jail and having the theft charges dropped. Is he entitled to those damages? [*Marino v Perna*, 629 NYS2d 669 (NY Cir)]

15. Stephan's Machine & Tool, Inc., purchased a boring mill from D&H Machinery Consultants. The mill was a specialized type of equipment and was essential to the operation of Stephan's plant. The purchase price was $96,000, and Stephan's had to borrow this amount from a bank to finance the sale. The loan exhausted Stephan's borrowing capacity. The mill was unfit, and D&H agreed to replace it with another one. D&H did not keep its promise, and Stephan's sued it for specific performance of the contract as modified by the replacement agreement. Is specific performance an appropriate remedy? Discuss. [*Stephan's Machine & Tool, Inc. v D&H Machinery Consultants, Inc.*, 417 NE2d 579 (Ohio App)]

CPA QUESTIONS

1. On April 5, 1987, Anker, Inc., furnished Bold Corp. with Anker's financial statements dated March 31, 1987. The financial statements contained misrepresentations that indicated that Anker was solvent when in fact it was

insolvent. Based on Anker's financial statements, Bold agreed to sell Anker 90 computers, "F.O.B.— Bold's loading dock." On April 14, Anker received 60 of the computers. The remaining 30 computers were in the possession of the common carrier and in transit to Anker. If, on April 28, Bold discovered that Anker was insolvent, then with respect to the computers delivered to Anker on April 14, Bold may:

a. Reclaim the computers upon making a demand

b. Reclaim the computers irrespective of the rights of any third party

c. Not reclaim the computers since 10 days have elapsed from their delivery

d. Not reclaim the computers since it is entitled to recover the price of the computers

2. February 15, Mazur Corp. contracted to sell 1,000 bushels of wheat to Good Bread, Inc., at $6.00 per bushel with delivery to be made on June 23. On June 1, Good advised Mazur that it would not accept or pay for the wheat. On June 2, Mazur sold the wheat to another customer at the market price of $5.00 per bushel. Mazur had advised Good that it intended to resell the wheat. Which of the following statements is correct?

a. Mazur can successfully sue Good for the difference between the resale price and the contract price.

b. Mazur can resell the wheat only after June 23.

c. Good can retract its anticipatory breach at any time before June 23.

d. Good can successfully sue Mazur for specific performance.

3. Lazur Corp. entered into a contract with Baker Suppliers, Inc., to purchase a used word processor from Baker. Lazur is engaged in the business of selling new and used word processors to the general public. The contract required Baker to ship the goods to Lazur by common carrier pursuant to the following provision in the contract: "FOB Baker Suppliers, Inc., loading dock." Baker also represented in the contract that the word processor had been used for only 10 hours by its previous owner. The contract included the provision that the word processor was being sold "as is," and this provision was in a larger and different type style than the remainder of the contract. Assume that Lazur refused to accept the word processor even though it was in all respects conforming to the contract and that the contract is otherwise silent. Under the UCC Sales Article:

a. Baker can successfully sue for specific performance and make Lazur accept and pay for the word processor.

b. Baker may resell the word processor to another buyer.

c. Baker must sue for the difference between the market value of the word processor and the contract price plus its incidental damages.

d. Baker cannot successfully sue for consequential damages unless it attempts to resell the word processor.

Chapter 37

AGENCY

A. Nature of the Agency Relationship

1. DEFINITIONS AND DISTINCTIONS
2. CLASSIFICATION OF AGENTS
3. AGENCY COUPLED WITH AN INTEREST

B. Creating the Agency

4. AUTHORIZATION BY APPOINTMENT
5. AUTHORIZATION BY CONDUCT
6. AGENCY BY RATIFICATION
7. PROVING THE AGENCY RELATIONSHIP

C. Agent's Authority

8. SCOPE OF AGENT'S AUTHORITY
9. EFFECT OF PROPER EXERCISE OF AUTHORITY
10. DUTY TO ASCERTAIN EXTENT OF AGENT'S AUTHORITY
11. LIMITATIONS ON AGENT'S AUTHORITY

D. Duties and Liabilities of Principal and Agent

12. DUTIES AND LIABILITIES OF AGENT DURING AGENCY

13. DUTIES AND LIABILITIES OF AGENT AFTER TERMINATION OF AGENCY
14. DUTIES AND LIABILITIES OF PRINCIPAL TO AGENT

E. Termination of Agency

15. TERMINATION BY ACT OF PARTIES
16. TERMINATION BY OPERATION OF LAW
17. DISABILITY OF THE PRINCIPAL UNDER THE UDPAA
18. TERMINATION OF AGENCY COUPLED WITH AN INTEREST
19. PROTECTION OF AGENT FROM TERMINATION OF AUTHORITY
20. EFFECT OF TERMINATION OF AUTHORITY

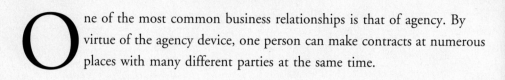

One of the most common business relationships is that of agency. By virtue of the agency device, one person can make contracts at numerous places with many different parties at the same time.

A. Nature of the Agency Relationship

Agency is ordinarily based on the consent of the parties, and for that reason is called a *consensual relationship*. However, the law sometimes imposes an agency relationship. If consideration is present, the agency relationship is contractual.

1. Definitions and Distinctions

agency–relationship that exists between a person identified as a principal and another by virtue of which the latter may make contracts with third persons on behalf of the principal. (Parties—principal, agent, third person)

agent–person or firm who is authorized by the principal or by operation of law to make contracts with third persons on behalf of the principal.

principal–person or firm who employs an agent; person who, with respect to a surety, is primarily liable to the third person or creditor; property held in trust.

Agency is a relationship based on an express or implied agreement by which one person, the **agent**, is authorized to act under the control of and for another, the **principal**, in negotiating and making contracts with third persons.[1] The acts of the agent obligate the principal to third persons and give the principal rights against third persons. (See Figure 37.1.)

The term *agency* is frequently used with other meanings. It is sometimes used to denote the fact that one has the right to sell certain products, such as when a dealer is said to possess an automobile agency. In other instances, the term is used to mean an exclusive right to sell certain articles within a given territory. In these cases, however, the dealer is not an agent in the sense of representing the manufacturer.

It is important to be able to distinguish agencies from other relationships because certain rights and duties in agencies are not present in other relationships.

(A) Employees and Independent Contractors. Control and authority are characteristics that distinguish ordinary employees and independent contractors from agents.

(1) Employees

An agent is distinguished from an ordinary employee who is not hired to represent the employer in making contracts with third persons. It is possible, however, for the same person to be both an agent and an employee. **For Example,** the driver for a spring water delivery service is an agent in making contracts between the company and its customers but is an employee with respect to the work of delivering products.

(2) Independent Contractors

independent contractor– contractor who undertakes to perform a specified task according to the terms of a contract but over whom the other contracting party has no control except as provided for by the contract.

An **independent contractor** is bound by a contract to produce a certain result—for example, to build a house. The actual performance of the work is controlled by the

---

[1] Restatement (Second) of Agency § 1; *Union Miniere, S.A. v Parday Corp.*, 521 NE2d 700 (Ind App 1988).

FIGURE 37-1 | *Agency Relationships*

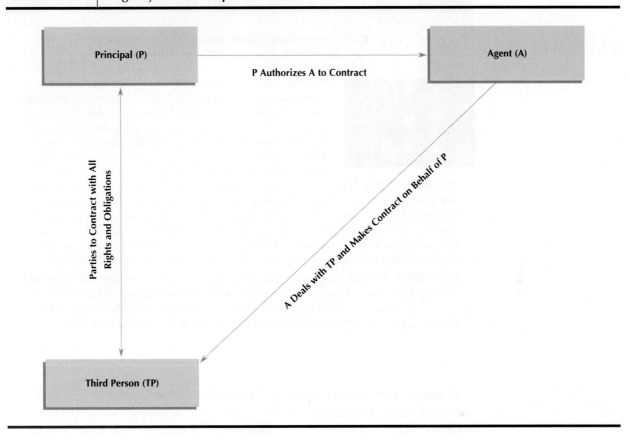

contractor, not the owner. An agent or employee differs from an independent contractor in that the principal or employer has the right to control the agent or employee, but not the contractor, in the performance of the work. **For Example,** Ned and Tracy Seizer contract with Fox Building Company to build a new home on Hilton Head Island, South Carolina, according to referenced plans and specifications. Individuals hired by Fox to work on the home are subject to the authority and control of Fox, the independent contractor, not the Seizers. However, Ned and Tracy could decide to build the home themselves, hiring two individuals from nearby Beaufort, Ted Chase and Marty Bromley, to do the work the Seizers will direct each day. Because Ted and Marty would be employees of the Seizers, the Seizers would be held responsible for any wrongs committed by these employees within the scope of their employment. As a general rule, on the other hand, the Seizers are not responsible for the torts of Fox, the independent contractor, and the contractor's employees. A "right to control" test determines whether an individual is an agent, an employee, or an independent contractor.[2]

---

[2] *NE Ohio College of Massotherapy v Burek,* 759 NE2d 869 (Ohio App 2001).

CASE SUMMARY

Why Some Businesses Use Independent Agents Rather than Employees!

FACTS: Patricia Yelverton died from injuries sustained when an automobile owned and driven by Joseph Lamm crossed the center line of a roadway and struck the automobile driven by Yelverton. Yelverton's executor brought suit against Lamm and Lamm's alleged employer, Premier Industrial Products Inc. The relationship between Lamm and Premier was governed by a written contract entitled "Independent Agent Agreement," in which Lamm, as "Independent Agent," was given the right to sell Premier's products in a designated territory. The agreement provided that all orders were subject to acceptance by Premier and were not binding on Premier until so accepted. Lamm was paid by commission only. He was allowed to work on a self-determined schedule, retain assistants at his own expense, and sell the products of other companies not in competition with Premier. The executor claimed Lamm was an agent or employee of Premier. Premier stated Lamm was an independent contractor.

DECISION: Judgment for Premier. Lamm had no authority to make contracts for Premier but simply took orders. Therefore, he was not an agent. Lamm was not an employee of Premier. Premier had no right to control the way he performed his work and did not in fact do so. Lamm was an independent contractor. [**Yelverton v Lamm, 380 SE2d 621 (NC App 1989)**]

A person who appears to be an independent contractor may in fact be so controlled by the other party that the contractor is regarded as an agent of, or employee of, the controlling person. **For Example,** Pierce, who was under contract to Brookville Carriers, Inc., was involved in a tractor-trailer/car collision with Rich and others. Pierce owned the tractor involved in the accident on a lease from Brookville but could use it only to haul freight for Brookville; he had no authority to carry freight on his own, and all of his operating authority belonged to Brookville. The "owner/operator" was deemed an employee rather than independent contractor for purposes of assessing the liability of the employer.[3] The separate identity of an independent contractor may be concealed so that the public believes that it is dealing with the principal. When this situation occurs, the principal is liable as though the contractor were an agent or employee.

2. Classification of Agents

special agent–agent authorized to transact a specific transaction or to do a specific act.

A **special agent** is authorized by the principal to handle a definite business transaction or to do a specific act. One who is authorized by another to purchase a particular house is a special agent.

general agent–agent authorized by the principal to transact all affairs in connection with a particular type of business or trade or to transact all business at a certain place.

A **general agent** is authorized by the principal to transact all affairs in connection with a particular type of business or trade or to transact all business at a certain place. To illustrate, a person who is appointed as manager by the owner of a store is a general agent.

[3] *Rich v Brookville Carriers, Inc.*, 256 F Supp 2d 26 (D Me 2003).

universal agent–agent authorized by the principal to do all acts that can lawfully be delegated to a representative.

A **universal agent** is authorized by the principal to do all acts that can be delegated lawfully to a representative. This form of agency arises when a person absent because of being in the military service gives another person a blanket power of attorney to do anything that must be done during such absence.

CPA

3. Agency Coupled with an Interest

interest in the authority–form of agency in which an agent has been given or paid for the right to exercise authority.

An agent has an **interest in the authority** when consideration has been given or paid for the right to exercise the authority. To illustrate, when a lender, in return for making a loan of money, is given, as security, authority to collect rents due the borrower and to apply those rents to the payment of the debt, the lender becomes the borrower's agent with an interest in the authority given to collect the rents.

interest in the subject matter–form of agency in which an agent is given an interest in the property with which that agent is dealing.

An agent has an **interest in the subject matter** when, for a consideration, she is given an interest in the property with which she is dealing. Hence, when the agent is authorized to sell property of the principal and is given a lien on such property as security for a debt owed to her by the principal, she has an interest in the subject matter.

B. Creating the Agency

An agency may arise by appointment, conduct, ratification, or operation of law.

4. Authorization by Appointment

express authorization–authorization of an agent to perform a certain act.

The usual method of creating an agency is by **express authorization;** that is, a person is appointed to act for, or on behalf of, another.

In most instances, the authorization of the agent may be oral. However, some appointments must be made in a particular way. A majority of the states, by statute, require the appointment of an agent to be in writing when the agency is created to acquire or dispose of any interest in land. A written authorization of agency is called a **power of attorney.** An agent acting under a power of attorney is referred to as an **attorney in fact.**[4]

power of attorney–written authorization to an agent by the principal.

attorney in fact–agent authorized to act for another under a power of attorney.

5. Authorization by Conduct

Conduct consistent with the existence of an agency relationship may be sufficient to show authorization. The principal may have such dealing with third persons as to cause them to believe that the "agent" has authority. Thus, if the owner of a store places another person in charge, third persons may assume that the person in charge is the agent for the owner in that respect. The "agent" then appears to be authorized and is said to have *apparent authority*, and the principal is estopped from contradicting the appearance that has been created.[5]

[4] *Lamb v Scott,* 643 So2d 972 (Ala 1994).
[5] *Intersparex Leddin KG v AL-Haddad,* 852 SW2d 245 (Tenn App 1992).

CASE SUMMARY

The "Bulletproof Against Rust" Case. Oops: Now What?

FACTS: While constructing a hotel in Lincoln City, Oregon, the owner, Todd Taylor, became concerned about possible rusting in the exterior stucco system manufactured by ChemRex that was being installed at the hotel. The general contractor Ramsay-Gerding arranged a meeting with the owner, the installer, and ChemRex's territory manager for Oregon, Mike McDonald, to discuss Mr. Taylor's concerns. McDonald told those present that the SonoWall system was "bulletproof against rust," and stated that "you're getting a five-year warranty." He followed up with a letter confirming the five-year warranty on parts and labor. A year later rust discoloration appeared, and no one from ChemRex ever fixed the problem. Taylor sued ChemRex for breach of warranty. ChemRex defended that McDonald did not have actual or apparent authority to declare such a warranty.

DECISION: Judgment for Taylor. The evidence indicated that ChemRex clothed Mike McDonald with the title of "territory manager" and gave him the actual authority to visit job sites and resolve problems. Although it denies he had actual authority, ChemRex took sufficient steps to create apparent authority to provide the five-year warranty on the stucco system. [**Taylor v Ramsay-Gerding Construction Co., 196 P3d 532 (Or 2008)**]

The term *apparent authority* is used when there is only the appearance of authority but no actual authority, and that appearance of authority was created by the principal. The test for the existence of apparent authority is an objective test determined by the principal's outward manifestations through words or conduct that lead a third person reasonably to believe that the "agent" has authority. A principal's express restriction on authority not made known to a third person is no defense.

Apparent authority extends to all acts that a person of ordinary prudence, familiar with business usages and the particular business, would be justified in believing that the agent has authority to perform. It is essential to the concept of apparent authority that the third person reasonably believe that the agent has authority. The mere placing of property in the possession of another does not give that person either actual or apparent authority to sell the property.

CPA   6. Agency by Ratification

An agent may attempt, on behalf of the principal, to do an act that was not authorized, or a person who is not the agent of another may attempt to act as such an agent. Generally, in such cases, the principal for whom the agent claimed to act has the choice of ignoring the transaction or of ratifying it. Ordinarily, any unauthorized act may be ratified.

(A) INTENTION TO RATIFY. Initially, ratification is a question of intention. Just as in the case of authorization, when there is a question of whether the principal authorized the agent, there is a question of whether the principal intended to approve or ratify the action of the unauthorized agent.

The intention to ratify may be expressed in words, or it may be found in conduct indicating an intention to ratify.[6] **For Example,** James Reiner signed a five-year lease of commercial space on 320 West Main Street in Avon, Connecticut, because his father Calvin was away on vacation, and the owner, Robert Udolf, told James that if he did not come in and sign the lease, his father would lose the opportunity to rent the space in question. James was aware that his father had an interest in the space, and while telling Robert several times that he had no authority, James did sign his name to the lease. In fact, his father took occupancy of the space and paid rent for three years and then abandoned the space. James is not liable on the remainder of the lease because the owner knew at the time of signing that James did not have authority to act. Although he did not sign the lease, Calvin ratified the lease signed by James by his conduct of moving into the space and doing business there for three years with full knowledge of all material facts relating to the transaction. The owner, therefore, had to bring suit against Calvin, not James.[7]

CPA (B) CONDITIONS FOR RATIFICATION. In addition to the intent to ratify, expressed in some instances with a certain formality, the following conditions must be satisfied for the intention to take effect as a ratification:

1. The agent must have purported to act on behalf of or as agent for the identified principal.

2. The principal must have been capable of authorizing the act both at the time of the act and at the time it was ratified.

3. The principal must have full knowledge of all material facts.

It is not always necessary, however, to show that the principal had actual knowledge. Knowledge will be imputed if a principal knows of other facts that would lead a prudent person to make inquiries or if that knowledge can be inferred from the knowledge of other facts or from a course of business. **For Example,** Stacey, without authorization but knowing that William needed money, contracted to sell one of William's paintings to Courtney for $298. Stacey told William about the contract that evening; William said nothing and helped her wrap the painting in a protective plastic wrap for delivery. A favorable newspaper article about William's art appeared the following morning and dramatically increased the value of all of his paintings. William cannot recover the painting from Courtney on the theory that he never authorized the sale because he ratified the unauthorized contract made by Stacey by his conduct in helping her wrap the painting with full knowledge of the terms of the sale. The effect is a legally binding contract between William and Courtney.

(C) EFFECT OF RATIFICATION. When an unauthorized act is ratified, the effect is the same as though the act had been originally authorized. Ordinarily, this means that the principal and the third party are bound by the contract made by the agent.[8]

---

[6] *Streetscenes, LLC v ITC Entertainment Group, Inc.,*126 Cal Rptr 2d 754 (Cal App 2002).
[7] *Udolf v Reiner,* 2000 WL 726953 (Conn Super 2000).
[8] *Bill McCurley Chevrolet v Rutz,* 808 P2d 1167 (Wash App 1991).

When the principal ratifies the act of the unauthorized person, such ratification releases that person from the liability that would otherwise be imposed for having acted without authority.

CPA **7. Proving the Agency Relationship**

The burden of proving the existence of an agency relationship rests on the person who seeks to benefit by such proof. The third person who desires to bind the principal because of the act of an alleged agent has the burden of proving that the latter person was in fact the authorized agent of the principal and possessed the authority to do the act in question.[9]

C. AGENT'S AUTHORITY

When there is an agent, it is necessary to determine the scope of the agent's authority.

8. Scope of Agent's Authority

The scope of an agent's authority may be determined from the express words of the principal to the agent or it may be implied from the principal's words or conduct or from the customs of the trade or business.

(A) EXPRESS AUTHORITY. If the principal tells the agent to perform a certain act, the agent has express authority to do so. Express authority can be given orally or in writing.

incidental authority– authority of an agent that is reasonably necessary to execute express authority.

(B) INCIDENTAL AUTHORITY. An agent has implied **incidental authority** to perform any act reasonably necessary to execute the express authority given to the agent. **For Example,** if the principal authorizes the agent to purchase goods without furnishing funds to the agent to pay for them, the agent has the implied incidental authority to purchase the goods on credit.[10]

customary authority– authority of an agent to do any act that, according to the custom of the community, usually accompanies the transaction for which the agent is authorized to act.

(C) CUSTOMARY AUTHORITY. An agent has implied **customary authority** to do any act that, according to the custom of the community, usually accompanies the transaction for which the agent is authorized to act. An agent who has express authority to receive payments from third persons, for example, has the implied customary authority to issue receipts.

apparent authority– appearance of authority created by the principal's words or conduct.

(D) APPARENT AUTHORITY. A person has **apparent authority** as an agent when the principal's words or conduct leads a third person to reasonably believe that the person has that authority and the third person relies on that appearance.[11]

---

[9] *Cummings, Inc. v Nelson,* 115 P3d 536 (Alaska 2005).
[10] *Badger v Paulson Investment Co.,* 803 P2d 1178 (Ore 1991).
[11] *Alexander v Chandler,* 179 SW2d 385 (Mo App 2005).

C A S E   S U M M A R Y

CSX Gets Railroaded by Albert Arillotta

FACTS: Recovery Express and Interstate Demolition (IDEC) are two separate corporations located at the same business address in Boston. On August 22, 2003, Albert Arillotta, a "partner" at IDEC, sent an e-mail to Len Whitehead, Jr. of CSX Transportation expressing an interest in buying "rail cars as scrap." Arillotta represented himself to be "from interstate demolition and recovery express" in the e-mail. The e-mail address from which he sent his inquiry was **albert@recoveryexpress.com**. Arillotta went to the CSX rail yard, disassembled the cars, and transported them away. Thereafter CSX sent invoices for the scrap rail cars totaling $115,757.36 addressed to IDEC at its Boston office shared with Recovery Express. Whitehead believed Arillotta was authorized to act for Recovery Express, based on the e-mail's domain name, recoveryexpress.com. Recovery claims that Arillotta never worked for it. Recovery's President Thomas Trafton allowed the "fledgling" company to use telephone, fax, and e-mail services at its offices but never shared anything—assets, funds, books of business, or financials with IDEC—CSX sued Recovery for the invoice amount on the doctrine of "apparent authority." IDEC is now defunct. Recovery claims that Arillotta never worked for it and that it is not liable.

DECISION: Judgment for Recovery. Issuance of an e-mail address with Recovery's domain name to an individual who shared office space with Recovery did not give the individual, Albert Arillotta, apparent authority to enter contracts on Recovery's behalf. No reasonable person could conclude that Arillotta had apparent authority on the basis of an e-mail domain name by itself. Given the anonymity of the Internet, the court warned businesses to take additional action to verify a purported agent's authority to make a deal. [**CSX Transportation, Inc. v Recovery Express, Inc., 415 F Supp 2d 6 (D Mass 2006)**].

9. Effect of Proper Exercise of Authority

When an agent with authority properly makes a contract with a third person that purports to bind the principal, there is by definition a binding contract between the principal and the third person. The agent is not a party to this contract. Consequently, when the owner of goods is the principal, the owner's agent is not liable for breach of warranty with respect to the goods "sold" by the agent. The owner-principal, not the agent, was the "seller" in the sales transaction.

CPA ## 10. Duty to Ascertain Extent of Agent's Authority

A third person who deals with a person claiming to be an agent cannot rely on the statements made by the agent concerning the extent of authority.[12] If the agent is not authorized to perform the act or is not even the agent of the principal, the transaction between the alleged agent and the third person will have no legal effect between the principal and the third person.

Third persons who deal with an agent whose authority is limited to a special purpose are bound at their peril to find out the extent of the agent's authority.

---

[12] *Breed v Hughes Aircraft Col.,* 35 Fed App 864 (Fed Cir 2002).

An attorney is such an agent. Unless the client holds the attorney out as having greater authority than usual, the attorney has no authority to settle a claim without approval from the client.

(A) **Agent's Acts Adverse to Principal.** The third person who deals with an agent is required to take notice of any acts that are clearly adverse to the interest of the principal. Thus, if the agent is obviously using funds of the principal for the agent's personal benefit, persons dealing with the agent should recognize that the agent may be acting without authority and that they are dealing with the agent at their peril.

The only certain way that third persons can protect themselves is to inquire of the principal whether the agent is in fact the agent of the principal and has the necessary authority. **For Example,** Ron Fahd negotiated the sale of a fire truck to the Edinburg Volunteer Fire Company, on behalf of the manufacturer, Danko Company, at a price of $158,000. On Danko forms and letterhead Fahd drafted a "Proposal for Fire Apparatus" and it was signed by the president of the Fire Company and Fahd, as a dealer for Danko. Fahd gave a special $2,000 discount for prepayment of the cost of the chassis. Fahd directed that the prepayment check of $55,000 be made payable to "Ron Fahd Sales" in order to obtain the discount. The Fire Company's treasurer inquired of Fahd why the prepayment check was being made out to Fahd rather than Danko, and he accepted Fahd's answer without contacting Danko to confirm this unusual arrangement. Fahd absconded with the proceeds of the check. The Fire Company sued Danko claiming Fahd had apparent authority to receive the prepayment. While there was some indicia of agency, the court found that the Fire Company had failed to make reasonable inquiry with Danko to verify Fahd's authority to receive the prepayment in Fahd's name, and it rejected the claim that Fahd had apparent authority to accept the prepayment check made out to Fahd as opposed to Danko.[13]

11. Limitations on Agent's Authority

A person who has knowledge of a limitation on the agent's authority cannot ignore that limitation. When the third person knows that the authority of the agent depends on whether financing has been obtained, the principal is not bound by the act of the agent if the financing in fact was not obtained. If the authority of the agent is based on a writing and the third person knows that there is such a writing, the third person is charged with knowledge of limitations contained in it.

(A) **"Obvious" Limitations.** In some situations, it may be obvious to third persons that they are dealing with an agent whose authority is limited. When third persons know that they are dealing with a representative of a government agency, they should recognize that such a person will ordinarily have limited authority. Third persons should recognize that a contract made with such an officer or representative may not be binding unless ratified by the principal.

The federal government places the risk on any individual making arrangements with the government to accurately ascertain that the government agent is within the bounds of his or her authority.

---

[13] *Edinburg Volunteer Fire Company v Danko,* 867 NYS2d 547 (App Div 2008).

C A S E   S U M M A R Y

Humlen was Had?

FACTS: The FBI approached Humlen for assistance in securing the conviction of a drug trafficker. Humlen executed an agreement with the FBI to formalize his status as an informant. The agreement he signed contained compensation figures significantly less than those he had been promised by the FBI agents with whom he was dealing. Humlen claims that five agents repeatedly assured him that he would receive the extra compensation they had discussed with him, despite the wording of the contract. It was explained that the agreement had to be "couched" in that way because it was a discoverable document in any future criminal prosecution and thus could be used to destroy his credibility. Based on the information provided by Humlen, an arrest was made, and Humlen sought the remainder of his promised monetary reward from the FBI. The FBI refused to pay him any more than the contract stipulated. When no additional payment was forthcoming, Humlen sued the U.S. government.

DECISION: Judgment for the United States. The government, unlike private parties, cannot be bound by the apparent authority of its agents. When an agent exceeds his or her authority, the government can disavow the agent's words and is not bound by an implied contract. As a general rule, FBI agents lack the requisite actual authority—either express or implied—to contractually bind the United States to remit rewards to confidential informants. Moreover, Humlen's claims directly collide with the plain language of the agreement. [**Humlen v United States, 49 Fed Cl 497 (2001)**]

(B) **SECRET LIMITATIONS.** If the principal has clothed an agent with authority to perform certain acts but the principal gives secret instructions that limit the agent's authority, the third person is allowed to take the authority of the agent at its face value. The third person is not bound by the secret limitations of which the third person has no knowledge.

D. DUTIES AND LIABILITIES OF PRINCIPAL AND AGENT

The creation of the principal-agent relationship gives rise to duties and liabilities.

12. Duties and Liabilities of Agent during Agency

While the agency relationship exists, the agent owes certain duties to the principal.

(A) **LOYALTY.** An agent must be loyal or faithful to the principal.[14] The agent must not obtain any secret benefit from the agency. If the principal is seeking to buy or rent property, the agent cannot secretly obtain the property and then sell or lease it to the principal at a profit.

---

[14] *Patterson Custom Homes v Bach*, 536 F Supp 2d 1026 (ED ILL 2008).

An agent who owns property cannot sell it to the principal without disclosing that ownership to the principal. If disclosure is not made, the principal may avoid the contract even if the agent's conduct did not cause the principal any financial loss. Alternatively, the principal can approve the transaction and sue the agent for any secret profit obtained by the agent.

A contract is voidable by the principal if the agent who was employed to sell the property purchases the property, either directly or indirectly, without full disclosure to the principal.

An agent cannot act as agent for both parties to a transaction unless both know of the dual capacity and agree to it. If the agent does act in this capacity without the consent of both parties, any principal who did not know of the agent's double status can avoid the transaction.

An agent must not accept secret gifts or commissions from third persons in connection with the agency. If the agent does so, the principal may sue the agent for those gifts or commissions. Such practices are condemned because the judgment of the agent may be influenced by the receipt of gifts or commissions.

It is a violation of an agent's duty of loyalty to make and retain secret profits.

CASE SUMMARY

Was Grappolini a "Bad Boy"?

FACTS: Arthur Frigo, an adjunct professor at the Kellogg Graduate School of Management, formed Lucini Italia Co. (Lucini) to import and sell premium extra virgin olive oil and other products from Italy. Lucini's officers hired Guiseppe Grappolini as their olive oil supplier. They also hired him as their consultant. Grappolini signed an exclusivity agreement and a confidentiality agreement acknowledging the confidential nature of Lucini's product development, plans, and strategies. Grappolini was "branded" as a "master cultivator" in Lucini's literature and commercials.

In 1998, Lucini and Grappolini, as his consultant, discussed adding a line of extra virgin olive oils blended with "essential oils," for example, natural extracts such as lemon and garlic. It spent more than $800,000 developing the market information, testing flavors, designing labels and packaging, creating recipes, and generating trade secrets for the new products. Vegetal-Progress s.r.l. (Vegetal) was identified as the only company in Italy that was capable of producing the superior products Lucini sought, and Grappolini was assigned responsibility to obtain an exclusive supply contract with Vegetal.

In direct contravention of his representations to Lucini, Grappolini secretly negotiated an exclusive supply contract for the Grappolini Co., not for Lucini. Moreover, Grappolini Co. began to sell flavored olive oils in the United States, which coincided with Lucini's market research and recipe development that had been disclosed to Grappolini. When Lucini officers contacted Vegetal, they acknowledged that Grappolini was a "bad boy" in procuring the contract for his own company rather than for Lucini, but they would not renege on the contract. Lucini sued Grappolini.

DECISION: Judgment for Lucini. Grappolini was Lucini's agent and owed Lucini a duty to advance Lucini's interests, not his own. When he obtained an exclusive supply agreement with Vegetal for the Grappolini Co. instead of Lucini, he was disloyal and breached his fiduciary duties. As a result, Lucini suffered lost profits and damages of $4.17 million. In addition to these damages, Grappolini was ordered to pay $1,000,000 in punitive damages to deter similar acts in the future. Additionally, a permanent injunction was issued prohibiting Grappolini from using Lucini's trade secrets. [**Lucini Italia Co. v Grappolini, 2003 WL 1989605 (ND Ill 2003)**]

An agent is, of course, prohibited from aiding the competitors of a principal or disclosing to them information relating to the business of the principal. It is also a breach of duty for the agent to knowingly deceive a principal.[15]

(B) OBEDIENCE AND PERFORMANCE. An agent is under a duty to obey all lawful instructions.[16] The agent is required to perform the services specified for the period and in the way specified. An agent who does not do so is liable to the principal for any harm caused. For example, if an agent is instructed to take cash payments only but accepts a check in payment, the agent is liable for the loss caused the principal if a check is dishonored by nonpayment.

(C) REASONABLE CARE. It is the duty of an agent to act with the care that a reasonable person would exercise under the circumstances. **For Example,** Ethel Wilson applied for fire insurance for her house with St. Paul Reinsurance Co., Ltd., through her agent Club Services Corp. She thought she was fully covered. Unbeknown to her, however, St. Paul had refused coverage and returned her premium to Club Services, who did not refund it to Ms. Wilson or inform her that coverage had been denied. Fire destroyed her garage and St. Paul denied coverage. Litigation resulted, and St. Paul ended up expending $305,406 to settle the Wilson matter. Thereafter, St. Paul successfully sued Club Services Corp. under basic agency law principles that an agent (Club Services) is liable to its principal for all damages resulting from the agent's failure to discharge its duties.[17] In addition, if the agent possesses a special skill, as in the case of a broker or an attorney, the agent must exercise that skill.

(D) ACCOUNTING. An agent must account to the principal for all property or money belonging to the principal that comes into the agent's possession. The agent must, within a reasonable time, give notice of collections made and render an accurate account of all receipts and expenditures. The agency agreement may state at what intervals or on what dates such accountings are to be made. An agent must keep the principal's property and money separate and distinct from that of the agent.

(E) INFORMATION. It is the duty of an agent to keep the principal informed of all facts relating to the agency that are relevant to protecting the principal's interests.[18]

---

[15] *Koontz v Rosener,* 787 P2d 192 (Colo App 1990).
[16] *Stanford v Neiderer,* 341 SE2d 892 (Ga App 1986).
[17] *St. Paul Reinsurance Co., Ltd. v Club Services Corp.,* 30 Fed Appx 834, 2002 WL 203343 (10th Cir 2002).
[18] Restatement (Second) of Agency § 381; *Lumberman's Mutual Ins. Co. v Franey Muha Alliant Ins.,* 388 F Supp 2d 292 (SDNY 2005).

13. Duties and Liabilities of Agent after Termination of Agency

When the agency relationship ends, the duties of the agent continue only to the extent necessary to perform prior obligations. For example, the agent must return to the former principal any property that had been entrusted to the agent for the purpose of the agency. With the exception of such "winding-up" duties, the agency relationship is terminated, and the former agent can deal with the principal as freely as with a stranger.[19]

14. Duties and Liabilities of Principal to Agent

The principal must perform the contract, compensate the agent for services, make reimbursement for proper expenditures and, under certain circumstances, must indemnify the agent for loss.

(A) EMPLOYMENT ACCORDING TO TERMS OF CONTRACT. When the contract is for a specified time, the principal is obligated to permit the agent to act as agent for the term of the contract. Exceptions are made for just cause or contract provisions that permit the principal to terminate the agency sooner. If the principal gives the agent an exclusive right to act in that capacity, the principal cannot give anyone else the authority to act as agent, nor may the principal do the act to which the exclusive agent's authority relates. **For Example,** if Jill Baker gives Brett Stamos the exclusive right for six months to sell her house, she cannot give another real estate agent the right to sell it during the six-month period or undertake to sell the house herself. If the principal or another agent sells the house, the exclusive agent is entitled to full compensation just as though the act had been performed by the exclusive agent.

(B) COMPENSATION. The principal must pay the agent the agreed compensation.[20] If the parties have not fixed the amount of the compensation by their agreement but intended that the agent should be paid, the agent may recover the customary compensation for such services. If there is no established compensation, the agent may recover the reasonable value of the services rendered.

(1) Repeating Transactions

In certain industries, third persons make repeated transactions with the principal. In these cases, the agent who made the original contract with the third person commonly receives a certain compensation or percentage of commissions on all subsequent renewal or additional contracts. In the insurance business, for example, the insurance agent obtaining the policyholder for the insurer receives a substantial portion of the first year's premiums and then receives a smaller percentage of the premiums paid by the policyholder in subsequent years.

(2) Postagency Transactions

An agent is not ordinarily entitled to compensation in connection with transactions, such as sales or renewals of insurance policies, occurring after the termination of the agency even if the postagency transactions are the result of the agent's former

[19] *Corron & Black of Illinois, Inc. v Magner,* 494 NE2d 785 (Ill App 1986).
[20] *American Chocolates, Inc. v Mascot Pecan Co., Inc.,* 592 So2d 93 (Miss 1992).

activities. However, if the parties' employment contract calls for such compensation, it must be paid. **For Example,** real estate agent Laura McLane's contract called for her to receive $1.50 for every square foot the Atlanta Committee for the Olympic Games, Inc. (ACOG), leased at an Atlanta building; and even though she had been terminated at the time ACOG executed a lease amendment for 164,412 additional square feet, she was contractually entitled to a $246,618 commission.[21]

E. TERMINATION OF AGENCY

An agency may be terminated by the act of one or both of the parties to the agency agreement or by operation of law. When the authority of an agent is terminated, the agent loses all right to act for the principal.

15. Termination by Act of Parties

The duration of the agency relationship is commonly stated in the contract creating the relationship. In most cases, either party has the power to terminate the agency relationship at any time. However, the terminating party may be liable for damages to the other if the termination is in violation of the agency contract.

When a principal terminates an agent's authority, it is not effective until the agent receives the notice. Because a known agent will have the appearance of still being an agent, notice must be given to third persons of the termination, and the agent may have the power to bind the principal and third persons until this notice is given.

16. Termination by Operation of Law

The agency relationship is a personal one, and anything that renders one of the parties incapable of performing will result in the termination of the relationship by operation of law. The death of either the principal or the agent ordinarily terminates the authority of an agent automatically even if the death is unknown to the other.[22]

An agency is also terminated by operation of law on the (1) insanity of the principal or agent, (2) bankruptcy of the principal or agent, (3) impossibility of performance, such as the destruction of the subject matter, or (4) when the country of the principal is at war with that of the agent.

C A S E   S U M M A R Y

Missing Out by Minutes

FACTS: William Moore, a fire chief for the city of San Francisco, suffered severe head injuries in a fall while fighting a fire. Moore sued the building owner, Lera, for negligence. The attorneys for the parties held a conference and reached a settlement at 5:15 P.M. Unknown to them, Moore had died at 4:50 P.M. on that day. Was the settlement agreement binding?

---

[21] *McLane v Atlanta Market Center Management Co.*, 486 SE2d 30 (Ga App 1997).
[22] *New York Life Ins. Co. v Estate of Haelen*, 521 NYS2d 970 (Sup Ct AD 1987).

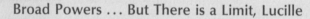

C A S E   S U M M A R Y

Continued

DECISION: No. The death of either the principal or the agent terminates the agency. Thus, the death of a client terminates the authority of his agent to act on his behalf. Because Moore died at 4:50 P.M., his attorney no longer had authority to act on his behalf, and the settlement was not enforceable. [**Moore v Lera Development Inc., 274 Cal Rptr 658 (Cal App 1990)**]

17. Disability of the Principal Under the UDPAA

The Uniform Durable Power of Attorney Act (UDPAA) permits the creation of an agency by specifying that "this power of attorney shall not be affected by subsequent disability or incapacity of the principal." Alternatively, the UDPAA permits the agency to come into existence upon the disability or incapacity of the principal. For this to be effective, the principal must designate the attorney in fact in writing. The writing must contain words showing the intent of the principal that the authority conferred shall continue notwithstanding the disability or incapacity of the principal. The UDPAA, which has been adopted by most states,[23] changes the common law and the general rule that insanity of the principal terminates the agent's authority to act for the principal. Society today recognizes that it may be in the best interest of a principal and good for the business environment for a principal to designate another as an attorney in fact to act for the principal when the principal becomes incapacitated.[24] It may be prudent to grant durable powers of attorney to different persons for property matters and for health care decisions.

Durable powers of attorney grant only those powers that are specified in the instrument. A durable power of attorney may be terminated by revocation by a competent principal and by the death of the principal.

C A S E   S U M M A R Y

Broad Powers ... But There is a Limit, Lucille

FACTS: On May 31, 2000, Thomas Graham made his niece Lucille Morrison his attorney in fact by executing a durable power of attorney. It was notarized and filed at the Registry of Deeds. The power of attorney granted Lucille broad powers and discretion in Graham's affairs. However, it did not contain express authority to make gifts. On October 26, 2000, Lucille conveyed 11.92 acres of property valued at between $400,000 and $700,000 to herself

---

[23] The Uniform Durable Power of Attorney Act has been adopted in some fashion in all states except Connecticut, Florida, Georgia, Illinois, Indiana, Kansas, Louisiana, and Missouri.

[24] The Uniform Probate Code and the Uniform Durable Power of Attorney Act provide for the coexistence of durable powers and guardians or conservators. These acts allow the attorney in fact to continue to manage the principal's financial affairs while the court-appointed fiduciary takes the place of the principal in overseeing the actions of the attorney in fact. See *Rice v Flood*, 768 SW2d 57 (Ky 1989).

C A S E   S U M M A R Y

Continued

based on consideration of services rendered to the principal, Thomas Graham. On June 5, 2001, Lucille, as attorney in fact for Graham, conveyed Graham's house in Charlotte to her son Ladd Morrison. On June 20, 2001, she conveyed Graham's Oakview Terrace property to her brother John Hallman for $3,000 to pay for an attorney to defend Graham in a competency proceeding. Thomas Graham died on August 7, 2001, and his estate sued to set aside the deeds, alleging Lucille's breach of fiduciary duties. After a judgment for the defendants, the estate appealed.

DECISION: Judgment for the estate regarding the 11.92 acre parcel of land Lucille conveyed to herself. When an attorney in fact conveys property to herself based on consideration of services rendered to the principal, the consideration must reflect a fair and reasonable price when compared with the market value of the property. There was no testimony regarding the value of Lucille's services compared with the value of the real property. The deed must be set aside. The conveyance of Graham's home to Ladd Morrison was a gift that was not authorized by her power of attorney and must be set aside. Lucille had authority to sell the principal's property to John Hallman to obtain funds to pay an attorney to represent the principal. The estate's claim of conversion regarding this sale was denied. [**Estate of Graham v Morrison, 607 SE2d 295 (NC App 2005)**]

18. Termination of Agency Coupled with an Interest

An agency coupled with an interest is an exception to the general rule as to the termination of an agency. Such an agency cannot be revoked by the principal before the expiration of the interest. It is not terminated by the death or insanity of either the principal or the agent.

19. Protection of Agent from Termination of Authority

The modern world of business has developed several methods of protecting an agent from the termination of authority for any reason.[25]

These methods include the use of an exclusive agency contract, a secured transaction, an escrow deposit, a standby letter of agreement, or a guarantee agreement.

20. Effect of Termination of Authority

If the principal revokes the agency, the authority to act for the principal is not terminated until the agent receives notice of revocation. As between the principal and the agent, the right of the agent to bind the principal to third persons generally ends immediately upon the termination of the agent's authority. This termination is effective without giving notice to third persons.

When the agency is terminated by the act of the principal, notice must be given to third persons. If this notice is not given, the agent may have the power to make contracts that will bind the principal and third persons. This rule is predicated on

[25] These methods generally replace the concept of an agency coupled with an interest because of the greater protection given to the agent. Typically, the rights of the agent under these modern devices cannot be defeated by the principal, by operation of law, or by claims of other creditors.

the theory that a known agent will have the appearance of still being the agent unless notice to the contrary is given to third persons. **For Example,** Seltzer owns property in Boca Raton that he uses for the month of February and leases the remainder of the year. O'Neil has been Seltzer's rental agent for the past seven years, renting to individuals like Ed Tucker under a power of attorney that gives him authority to lease the property for set seasonal and off-season rates. O'Neil's right to bind Seltzer on a rental agreement ended when Seltzer faxed O'Neil a revocation of the power of attorney on March 1. A rental contract with Ed Tucker signed by O'Neil on behalf of Seltzer on March 2 will bind Seltzer, however, because O'Neil still appeared to be Seltzer's agent and Tucker had no notice to the contrary.

When the law requires giving notice in order to end the power of the agent to bind the principal, individual notice must be given or mailed to all persons who had prior dealings with the agent. In addition, notice to the general public can be given by publishing in a newspaper of general circulation in the affected geographic area a statement that the agency has been terminated.

If a notice is actually received, the power of the agent is terminated without regard to whether the method of giving notice was proper. Conversely, if proper notice is given, it is immaterial that it does not actually come to the attention of the party notified. Thus, a member of the general public cannot claim that the principal is bound on the ground that the third person did not see the newspaper notice stating that the agent's authority had been terminated.

MAKE THE CONNECTION

SUMMARY

An agency relationship is created by an express or implied agreement by which one person, the agent, is authorized to make contracts with third persons on behalf of, and subject to, the control of another person, the principal. An agent differs from an independent contractor in that the principal, who controls the acts of an agent, does not have control over the details of performance of work by the independent contractor. Likewise, an independent contractor does not have authority to act on behalf of the other contracting party.

A special agent is authorized by the principal to handle a specific business transaction. A general agent is authorized by the principal to transact all business affairs of the principal at a certain place. A universal agent is authorized to perform all acts that can be lawfully delegated to a representative.

The usual method of creating an agency is by express authorization. However, an agency relationship may be found to exist when the principal causes or permits a third person to reasonably believe that an agency relationship exists. In such a case, the "agent" appears to be authorized and is said to have apparent authority.

An unauthorized transaction by an agent for a principal may be ratified by the principal.

An agent acting with authority has the power to bind the principal. The scope of an agent's authority may be determined from the express words of the principal to the agent; this is called express authority. An agent has incidental authority to perform any act reasonably necessary to execute the authority given the agent. An agent's authority may be implied so as to enable the agent to perform any act in accordance with the general customs or usages in a business or an industry. This authority is often referred to as customary authority.

The effect of a proper exercise of authority by an agent is to bind the principal and third person to a contract. The agent, not being a party to the contract, is not liable in any respect under the contract. A third person dealing with a person claiming to be an agent has a duty to ascertain the extent of the agent's authority and a duty to take notice of any acts that are clearly adverse to the principal's interests. The third person cannot claim that apparent authority existed when that person has notice that the agent's conduct is adverse to the interests of the principal. A third person who has knowledge of limitations on an agent's authority is bound by those limitations. A third person is not bound by secret limitations.

While the agency relationship exists, the agent owes the principal the duties of (1) being loyal, (2) obeying all lawful instructions, (3) exercising reasonable care, (4) accounting for all property or money belonging to the principal, and (5) informing the principal of all facts relating to the agency that are relevant to the principal's interests. An agency relationship can be terminated by act of either the principal or the agent. However, the terminating party may be liable for damages to the other if the termination is in violation of the agency contract.

Because a known agent will have the appearance of still being an agent, notice must be given to third persons of the termination, and the agent may have the power to bind the principal and third persons until this notice is given.

An agency is terminated by operation of law upon (1) the death of the principal or agent, (2) insanity of the principal or agent, (3) bankruptcy of the principal or agent, (4) impossibility of performance, caused, for example, by the destruction of the subject matter, or (5) war.

In states that have adopted the Uniform Durable Power of Attorney Act (UDPAA), an agency may be created that is not affected by subsequent disability or incapacity of the principal. In UDPAA states, the agency may also come into existence upon the "disability or incapacity of the principal." The designation of an attorney in fact under the UDPAA must be in writing.

LEARNING OUTCOMES

After studying this chapter, you should be able to clearly explain:

A. NATURE OF THE AGENCY RELATIONSHIP

LO.1 Explain the difference between an agent and an independent contractor
See the Ned and Tracy Seizer example and the "right to control" test, beginning on p. 851.

B. CREATING THE AGENCY

LO.2 Explain three methods of creating an agency relationship

See the discussion on the usual method of creating an agency (which is by express authorization), p. 853.

See the *Taylor* case where actual authority to perform some tasks created apparent authority to perform other related tasks, p. 854.

See the agency by ratification example of James and Calvin Reiner on p. 855.

C. AGENT'S AUTHORITY

LO.3 Recognize that third persons who deal with an agent are required to take notice of acts contrary to the interests of the principal

See the example of the Fire Company that failed to verify with the principal an agent's authority to receive a prepayment check of $55,000 made out in the agent's name, p. 858.

D. DUTIES AND LIABILITIES OF PRINCIPAL AND AGENT

LO.4 List and explain the duties an agent owes the principal

See the discussion concerning an agent's duty of loyalty, obedience, reasonable care, accounting, and information beginning on p. 859.

E. TERMINATION OF AGENCY

LO.5 Explain how the Uniform Durable Power of Attorney Act changes the common law rule on incapacity of the principal

See the *Estate of Graham* case on the limits of a durable power of attorney, p. 864.

KEY TERMS

agency	general agent	power of attorney
agent	incidental authority	principal
apparent authority	independent contractor	special agent
attorney in fact	interest in the authority	universal agent
customary authority	interest in the subject	
express authorization	matter	

QUESTIONS AND CASE PROBLEMS

1. How does an agent differ from an independent contractor?

2. Compare authorization of an agent by (a) appointment and (b) ratification.

3. Ernest A. Kotsch executed a durable power of attorney when he was 85 years old, giving his son, Ernie, the power to manage and sell his real estate and personal property "and to do all acts necessary for maintaining and caring for [the father] during his lifetime." Thereafter, Kotsch began "keeping company" with a widow, Margaret Gradl. Ernie believed that the widow was attempting to alienate his father from him, and he observed that she was exerting a great deal of influence over his father. Acting under the durable power of attorney and without informing his father, Ernie created the "Kotsch Family Irrevocable Trust," to which he transferred $700,000, the bulk of his father's liquid assets, with the father as

grantor and initial beneficiary and Ernie's three children as additional beneficiaries. Ernie named himself trustee. His father sued to avoid the trust. Ernie defended his action on the ground that he had authority to create the trust under the durable power of attorney. Decide. [*Kotsch v Kotsch,* 608 So2d 879 (Fla App)]

4. Ken Jones, the number-one-ranked prizefighter in his weight class, signed a two-year contract with Howard Stayword. The contract obligated Stayword to represent and promote Jones in all business and professional matters, including the arrangement of fights. For these services, Jones was to pay Stayword 10 percent of gross earnings. After a year, when Stayword proved unsuccessful in arranging a title match with the champion, Jones fired Stayword. During the following year, Jones earned $4 million. Stayword sued Jones for $400,000. Jones defended himself on the basis that a principal has the absolute power at any time to terminate an agency relationship by discharging the agent, so he was not liable to Stayword. Was Jones correct?

5. Paul Strich did business as an optician in Duluth, Minnesota. Paul used only the products of the Plymouth Optical Co., a national manufacturer of optical products and supplies with numerous retail outlets and some franchise arrangements in areas other than Duluth. To increase business, Paul renovated his office and changed the sign on it to read "Plymouth Optical Co." Paul did business this way for more than three years—advertised under that name, paid bills with checks bearing the name of Plymouth Optical Co., and listed himself in the telephone and city directories by that name. Plymouth immediately became aware of what Paul was doing. However, because Paul used only Plymouth products and Plymouth did not have a franchise in Duluth, it saw no advantage at that time in prohibiting Paul from using the name and losing him as a customer. Paul contracted with the *Duluth Tribune* for advertising, making the contract in the name of Plymouth Optical Co. When the advertising bill was not paid, the *Duluth Tribune* sued Plymouth Optical Co. for payment. Plymouth's defense was that it never authorized Paul to do business under the name, nor authorized him to make a contract with the newspaper. Decide.

6. Record owned a farm that was managed by his agent, Berry, who lived on the farm. Berry hired Wagner to bale the hay and told him to bill Record for this work. Wagner did so and was paid by Record. By the summer of the following year, the agency had been terminated by Record, but Berry remained in possession as tenant of the farm and nothing appeared changed. Late in the summer, Berry asked Wagner to bale the hay as he had done the previous year and bill Record for the work. He did so, but Record refused to pay on the ground that Berry was not then his agent. Wagner sued him. Decide. [*Record v Wagner,* 100 NH 419]

7. Gilbert Church owned Church Farms, Inc., in Manteno, Illinois. Church advertised its well-bred stallion Imperial Guard for breeding rights at $50,000, directing all inquiries to "Herb Bagley, Manager." Herb Bagley lived at Church Farms and was the only person available to visitors. Vern Lundberg answered the ad, and after discussions in which Bagley stated that Imperial Guard would remain in Illinois for at least a two-year period, Lundberg and Bagley executed a two-year breeding rights contract. The contract was signed by Lundberg and by Bagley as "Church Farms, Inc., H. Bagley, Mgr." When Gil Church moved

Imperial Guard to Oklahoma prior to the second year of the contract, Lundberg brought suit for breach of contract. Church testified that Bagley had no authority to sign contracts for Church Farms. Decide. [*Lundberg v Church Farms, Inc.,* 502 NE2d 806 (Ill)]

8. The Holzmans signed an exclusive listing agreement with the Blum real estate brokerage firm. The contract provided that the Holzmans had an obligation to pay a commission "if they enter into a written agreement to sell the property to any person during the term of this exclusive listing agreement." The Holzmans entered into a written agreement to sell their house for $715,000 to the Noravians. On the advice of their attorney, the Holzmans included a default provision in this contract stating that in the event of default by the Holzmans, the Noravians' only remedy would be a refund of their deposit. Subsequently, the Sterns offered $850,000 for the property and the Holzmans canceled their contract with the Noravians and returned their deposit. After the exclusive listing period expired, the Holzmans executed a contract to sell their property to the Sterns at the offered price of $850,000—with the contract calling for the Holzmans to pay half the real estate fee to Blum and half to a cooperating broker. Blum was paid this fee of $21,500. Blum brought suit against the Holzmans seeking the full commission for the Noravian contract under the exclusive listing agreement. Did Blum have a legal obligation or ethical duty to advise the Holzmans when considering the Sterns' offer that he believed they were obligated to him for the full commission under the Novarian contract? Decide. [*Holzman v Blum,* 726 A2d 818 (Md App)]

9. Tillie Flinn properly executed a durable power of attorney designating her nephew James C. Flanders and/or Martha E. Flanders, his wife, as her attorney in fact. Seven months later, Martha Flanders went to the Capitol Federal Savings and Loan Association office. She had the durable power of attorney instrument, five certificates of deposit, and a hand-printed letter identifying Martha as an attorney in fact and stating that Tillie wished to cash her five CDs that Martha had with her. At approximately 10:31 A.M., five checks were given to Martha in the aggregate amount of $135,791.34, representing the funds in the five CDs less penalties for early withdrawal. Some of the checks were drawn to the order of Martha individually and some to the order of James and Martha, as individuals. Tillie was found dead of heart disease later that day. The time of death stated on her death certificate was 11:30 A.M. The Flanderses spent the money on themselves. Bank IV, as administrator of Tillie's estate, sued Capitol Federal to recover the amount of the funds paid to the Flanderses. It contended that Capitol Federal breached its duty to investigate before issuing the checks. Capitol Federal contended that it did all that it had a duty to do. Decide. [*Bank IV v Capitol Federal Savings and Loan Ass'n,* 828 P2d 355 (Kan)]

10. Lew owns a store on Canal Street in New Orleans. He paid a person named Mike and other individuals commissions for customers brought into the store. Lew testified that he had known Mike for less than a week. Boulos and Durso, partners in a wholesale jewelry business, were visiting New Orleans on a business trip when Mike brought them into the store to buy a stereo. While Durso finalized the stereo transaction with the store's manager, Boulos and

Mike negotiated to buy 2 cameras, 3 videos, and 20 gold Dupont lighters. Unknown to the store's manager, Mike was given $8,250 in cash and was to deliver the merchandise later that evening to the Marriott Hotel, where Boulos and Durso were staying. Mike gave a receipt for the cash, but it showed no sales tax or indication that the goods were to be delivered. Boulos testified that he believed Mike was the store owner. Mike never delivered the merchandise and disappeared. Boulos and Durso contended that Lew is liable for the acts of his agent, Mike. Lew denied that Mike was his agent, and the testimony showed that Mike had no actual authority to make a sale, to use a cash register, or even to go behind a sales counter. What ethical principle applies to the conduct of Boulos and Durso? Decide. [*Boulos v Morrison*, 503 So2d 1(La)]

11. Martha Christiansen owns women's apparel stores bearing her name in New Seabury, Massachusetts; Lake Placid, New York; Palm Beach, Florida; and Palm Springs, California. At a meeting with her four store managers, she discussed styles she thought appropriate for the forthcoming season, advised them as always to use their best judgment in the goods they purchased for each of their respective stores, and cautioned "but no blue jeans." Later, Jane Farley, the manager of the Lake Placid store, purchased a line of high-quality blue denim outfits (designer jeans with jacket and vest options) from Women's Wear, Inc., for the summer season. The outfits did not sell. Martha refused to pay for them, contending that she had told all of her managers "no blue jeans" and that if it came to a lawsuit, she would fly in three managers to testify that Jane Farley had absolutely no authority to purchase denim outfits and was, in fact, expressly forbidden to do so. Women's Wear sued Martha, and the three managers testified for her. Is the fact that Martha had explicitly forbidden Farley to purchase the outfits in question sufficient to protect her from liability for the purchases made by Farley?

12. Fred Schilling, the president and administrator of Florence General Hospital, made a contract, dated August 16, 1989, on behalf of the hospital with CMK Associates to transfer the capacity to utilize 25 beds from the hospital to the Faith Nursing Home. Schilling, on behalf of the hospital, had previously made a contract with CMK Associates on May 4, 1987. Schilling had been specifically authorized by the hospital board to make the 1987 contract. The hospital refused to honor the 1989 contract because the board had not authorized it. CMK contended that Schilling had apparent authority to bind the hospital because he was president and administrator of the hospital and he had been the person who negotiated and signed a contract with CMK in 1987. Thus, according to CMK, the hospital had held out Schilling as having apparent authority to make the contract. The hospital disagreed. Decide. [*Pee Dee Nursing Home v Florence General Hospital*, 419 SE2d 843 (SC Ct App)]

13. Barbara Fox was the agent of Burt Hollander, a well-known athlete. She discovered that Tom Lanceford owned a 1957 Chevrolet convertible, which had been stored in a garage for the past 15 years. After demonstrating to Lanceford that she was the authorized agent of Hollander, she made a contract with Lanceford on behalf of Hollander to purchase the Chevrolet. Lanceford later discovered that the car was much more valuable than he originally

believed, and he refused to deliver the car to Fox. Fox sued Lanceford for breach of contract. Can she recover?

14. Francis Gagnon, an elderly gentleman, signed a power of attorney authorizing his daughter, Joan, "to sell any of my real estate and to execute any document needed to carry out the sale…and to add property to a trust of which I am grantor or beneficiary." This power was given in case Gagnon was not available to take care of matters personally because he was traveling. When Joan learned that Gagnon intended to sell his Shelburne property to Cosby for $750,000, she created an irrevocable trust naming Gagnon as beneficiary and herself as trustee. Acting then on the basis of the authority set forth in the power of attorney, she conveyed the Shelburne property to herself as trustee of the irrevocable trust, thus blocking the sale to Cosby. When Gagnon learned of this, he demanded that Joan return the Shelburne property to him, but she refused, saying she had acted within the authority set forth in the power of attorney. Did Joan violate any duty owed to Gagnon? Must she reconvey the property to Gagnon? [*Gagnon v Coombs,* 654 NE2d 54 (Mass App)]

15. Daniels and Julian were employed by the Marriott Hotel in New Orleans and were close personal friends. One day after work, Daniels and Julian went to Werlein's music store to open a credit account. Julian, with Daniels's authorization and in her presence, applied for credit using Daniels's name and credit history. Later, Julian went to Werlein's without Daniels and charged the purchase of a television set to Daniels's account, executing a retail installment contract by signing Daniels's name. Daniels saw the new television in Julian's home and was informed that it was charged to the Werlein's account. Daniels told Julian to continue making payments. When Werlein's credit manager first contacted Daniels to inform her that her account was delinquent, she claimed that a money order for the television was in the mail. On the second call, she asked for a "payment balance." Some four months after the purchase, she informed Werlein's that she had not authorized the purchase of the television nor ratified the purchase. Werlein's sued Daniels for the unpaid balance. Decide. [*Philip Werlein, Ltd. v Daniels,* 536 So 2d 722 (La App)]

CPA QUESTIONS

1. Generally, an agency relationship is terminated by operation of law in all of the following situations except the:

   a. Principal's death

   b. Principal's incapacity

   c. Agent's renunciation of the agency

   d. Agent's failure to acquire a necessary business license

2. Able, on behalf of Pix Corp., entered into a contract with Sky Corp., by which Sky agreed to sell computer equipment to Pix. Able disclosed to Sky that she was acting on behalf of Pix. However, Able had exceeded her actual authority

by entering into the contract with Sky. If Pix wishes to ratify the contract with Sky, which of the following statements is correct?

a. Pix must notify Sky that Pix intends to ratify the contract.

b. Able must have acted reasonably and in Pix's best interest.

c. Able must be a general agent of Pix.

d. Pix must have knowledge of all material facts relating to the contract at the time it is ratified.

3. Which of the following actions requires an agent for a corporation to have a written agency agreement?

a. Purchasing office supplies for the principal's business

b. Purchasing an interest in undeveloped land for the principal

c. Hiring an independent general contractor to renovate the principal's office building

d. Retaining an attorney to collect a business debt owed the principal

4. Simmons, an agent for Jensen, has the express authority to sell Jensen's goods. Simmons also has the express authority to grant discounts of up to 5 percent of list price. Simmons sold Hemple a 10 percent discount. Hemple had not previously dealt with either Simmons or Jensen. Which of the following courses of action may Jensen properly take?

a. Seek to void the sale to Hemple

b. Seek recovery of $50 from Hemple only

c. Seek recovery of $50 from Simmons only

d. Seek recovery of $50 from either Hemple or Simmons

5. Ogden Corp. hired Thorp as a sales representative for nine months at a salary of $3,000 per month plus 4 percent of sales. Which of the following statements is correct?

a. Thorp is obligated to act solely in Ogden's interest in matters concerning Ogden's business.

b. The agreement between Ogden and Thorp formed an agency coupled with an interest.

c. Ogden does not have the power to dismiss Thorp during the nine-month period without cause.

d. The agreement between Ogden and Thorp is not enforceable unless it is in writing and signed by Thorp.

6. Frost's accountant and business manager has the authority to:

a. Mortgage Frost's business property

b. Obtain bank loans for Frost

c. Insure Frost's property against fire loss

d. Sell Frost's business

Chapter 9

TORTS

A. General Principles

1. WHAT IS A TORT?
2. TORT AND CRIME DISTINGUISHED
3. TYPES OF TORTS

B. Intentional Torts

4. ASSAULT
5. BATTERY
6. FALSE IMPRISONMENT
7. INTENTIONAL INFLICTION OF EMOTIONAL DISTRESS
8. INVASION OF PRIVACY

9. DEFAMATION
10. PRODUCT DISPARAGEMENT
11. WRONGFUL INTERFERENCE WITH CONTRACTS
12. TRESPASS

C. Negligence

13. ELEMENTS OF NEGLIGENCE
14. DEFENSES TO NEGLIGENCE

D. Strict Liability

15. WHAT IS STRICT LIABILITY?
16. IMPOSING STRICT LIABILITY

T he law of torts permits individuals and companies to recover from other individuals and companies for wrongs committed against them. Tort law provides rights and remedies for conduct that meets the elements required to establish that a wrong has occurred.

A. GENERAL PRINCIPLES

Civil, or noncriminal, wrongs that are not breaches of contract are governed by tort law. This chapter covers the types of civil wrongs that constitute torts and the remedies available for those wrongs.

1. What is a Tort?

tort–civil wrong that interferes with one's property or person.

Tort comes from the Latin term *tortus,* which means "crooked, dubious, twisted." Torts are actions that are not straight but are crooked, or civil, wrongs. A tort is an interference with someone's person or property. **For Example,** entering someone's house without his or her permission is an interference and constitutes the tort of trespass. Causing someone's character to be questioned is a wrong against the person and is the tort of defamation. The law provides protection against these harms in the form of remedies awarded after the wrongs are committed. These remedies are civil remedies for the acts of interference by others.

2. Tort and Crime Distinguished

A *crime* is a wrong that arises from a violation of a public duty, whereas a *tort* is a wrong that arises from a violation of a private duty. A crime is a wrong of such a serious nature that the appropriate level of government steps in to prosecute and punish the wrongdoer to deter others from engaging in the same type of conduct. However, whenever the act that is committed as a crime causes harm to an identifiable person, that person may recover from the wrongdoer for monetary damages to compensate for the harm. For the person who experiences the direct harm, the act is called a *tort;* for the government, the same act is called a *crime.*

When the same act is both a crime and a tort, the government may prosecute the wrongdoer for a violation of criminal law, and the individual who experiences the direct harm may recover damages. **For Example,** O. J. Simpson was charged by the state of California with the murder of his ex-wife, Nicole Brown Simpson, and her friend Ron Goldman. A criminal trial was held in which O. J. Simpson was acquitted. Simpson was subsequently sued civilly by the families of Nicole Simpson and Ron Goldman for the tort of wrongful death. The jury in the civil case found Simpson civilly liable and the court ordered him to pay nearly $20 million in damages plus interest. Only $382,000 of this judgment has actually been paid to the families.

3. Types of Torts

intentional tort–civil wrong that results from intentional conduct.

There are three types of torts: intentional torts, negligence, and strict liability. **Intentional torts** are those that occur when wrongdoers engage in intentional conduct. **For Example,** striking another person in a fight is an intentional act and would be the tort of battery and possibly also the crime of battery. Your arm striking another person's nose in a fast-moving crowd of people at a rock concert is not a tort or crime because your arm was pushed unintentionally by the force of the crowd. If you stretched out your arms in that crowd or began to swing your arms about and struck another person, you would be behaving carelessly in a crowd of people; and, although you may not have committed an intentional tort, it is possible that your careless conduct constitutes the tort of **negligence**. Careless actions, or actions taken without thinking through their consequences, constitute negligence. The harm to the other person's nose may not have been intended, but there is liability for these accidental harms under negligence. **For Example,** if you run a red light, hit another car, and injure its driver, you did not intend the result. However, your careless behavior of disregarding a traffic signal resulted in the injury, and you would have liability for your negligence to that driver.

negligence–failure to exercise due care under the circumstances in consequence of which harm is proximately caused to one to whom the defendant owed a duty to exercise due care.

strict liability–civil wrong for which there is absolute liability because of the inherent danger in the underlying activity, for example, the use of explosives.

Strict liability is another type of tort that imposes liability without regard to whether there was any intent to harm or any negligence occurred. Strict liability is imposed without regard to fault. Strict or absolute liability is imposed because the activity involved is so dangerous that there must be full accountability. Nonetheless, the activity is necessary and cannot be prohibited. The compromise is to allow the activity but ensure that its dangers and resulting damages are fully covered through the imposition of full liability for all injuries that result. **For Example,** contractors often need to use dynamite to take a roadway through a mountainside or demolish a building that has become a hazard. When the dynamite is used, noise, debris, and possibly dangerous pieces of earth and building will descend on others' land and possibly on people. In most states, contractors are held strictly liable for the resulting damage from the use of dynamite. The activity is necessary and not illegal, but those who use dynamite must be prepared to compensate those who are injured as a result.

Other areas in which there is strict liability for activity include the storage of flammable materials and crop dusting. The federal government and the states have pure food laws that impose absolute liability on manufacturers who fail to meet the statutory standards for their products. Another area of strict liability is *product liability,* which is covered in Chapter 25.

B. INTENTIONAL TORTS

4. Assault

An *assault* is intentional conduct that threatens a person with a well-founded fear of imminent harm coupled with the present ability to carry out the threat of harm. **For Example,** the angry assertion "I'm going to kick your butt" along with aggressive movement in the direction of the victim with the intent to carry out the threat is an assault, even though a third person intervenes to stop the intended action. Mere words, however, although insulting, are ordinarily insufficient to constitute an assault.

5. Battery

A *battery* is the intentional, wrongful touching of another person without that person's consent. Thus, a threat to use force is an assault, and the actual use of force is the battery. The single action of striking an individual can be both a crime and a tort. A lawsuit for the tort of battery provides a plaintiff with the opportunity to recover damages resulting from the battery. The plaintiff must prove damages, however.

CASE SUMMARY

An Exchange of Unpleasantries ...

FACTS: Moore and Beye had an altercation after a public meeting regarding airport expansion. Moore owns a ranch near the airport and staunchly opposes expansion. Beye owns a flying service and avidly supports expansion. Moore and Beye exchanged unpleasantries while leaving the meeting. Beye then punched Moore on the left side of the jaw. Moore stumbled but caught himself before falling. He then exclaimed to the crowd, "You saw that. You are my witnesses. I've been assaulted. I want that man arrested." Ravalli County deputies took Beye into custody, and the state charged him with misdemeanor assault. Moore visited the hospital complaining of back and neck pain two days later and contended that he had injured his back while reeling from Beye's punch. He filed a civil complaint against Beye for damages. Moore's evidence mostly concerned his alleged back injury. Beye did not contest that he had punched Moore. His evidence countered that Moore's back problems had existed before the altercation. The judge instructed the jury that Beye had committed a battery as a matter of law and directed that they answer the question, "Was Moore damaged as a result of the battery?" The jury voted 11 to 1 that the battery did not injure Moore, and Moore appealed.

DECISION: Judgment for Beye. Beye presented the testimony of several eyewitnesses and a medical expert that Moore had sustained no damages. Although Moore presented considerable evidence to the contrary, it was not the court's function to agree or disagree with the verdict. Beye presented sufficient evidence to uphold the jury's verdict. [**Moore v Beye, 122 P3d 1212 (Mont 2005)**]

6. False Imprisonment

false imprisonment– intentional detention of a person without that person's consent; called the *shopkeeper's tort* when shoplifters are unlawfully detained.

False imprisonment is the intentional detention of a person without that person's consent.[1] The detention need not be for any specified period of time, for any detention against one's will is false imprisonment. False imprisonment is often called the *shopkeeper's tort* because so much liability has been imposed on store owners for their unreasonable detention of customers suspected of shoplifting. Requiring a customer to sit in the manager's office or not allowing a customer to

[1] *Forgie-Buccioni v Hannaford Bros. Inc.*, 413 F3d 175 (1st Cir 2005).

leave the store can constitute the tort of false imprisonment. Shop owners do, however, need the opportunity to investigate possible thefts in their stores. As a result, all states have some form of privilege or protection for store owners called a *shopkeeper's privilege.*

shopkeeper's privilege– right of a store owner to detain a suspected shoplifter based on reasonable cause and for a reasonable time without resulting liability for false imprisonment.

The **shopkeeper's privilege** permits the store owner to detain a suspected shoplifter based on reasonable suspicion for a reasonable time without resulting liability for false imprisonment to the accused customer.[2] The privilege applies even if the store owner was wrong about the customer being a shoplifter, so long as the store owner acted based on reasonable suspicions and treated the accused shoplifter in a reasonable manner. These privilege statutes do not protect the store owner from liability for unnecessary physical force or for invasion of privacy.

C A S E   S U M M A R Y

Officer Rivera Flagged for Unnecessary Roughness?

FACTS: Dillard Department Stores, Inc. (Dillard), detained hairstylist Lyndon Silva at its Houston, Texas, store. Silva testified that he was stopped by security guard Kevin Rivera, an off-duty Houston police officer who was in uniform with his "gun on his hip," and he was accused of theft of three shirts. Silva testified that Rivera placed him on the floor, handcuffed him, and emptied his shopping bag onto the floor. Silva testified people were around him when he was taken upstairs in handcuffs and when he was later escorted to the police car. He further stated that the officer and a woman made fun of him while he was being detained upstairs. Silva stated that when the city police came to take him into custody, Rivera again placed him on the floor with his knee in his back and exchanged handcuffs with the city police. He further testified that he asked Rivera many times to check his car for the receipt for the three shirts he was returning, but these requests were ignored, and that during the entire time he was detained, no one asked him for any explanation.

Officer Rivera's testimony was in direct conflict with Silva's, stating that Silva offered no excuse for not having a receipt for the shirts, and disputing that there were a lot of people watching, stating that the store was a "ghost town" at that time of day, 1:30 P.M. Silva later produced a receipt for three shirts. A jury returned a verdict for Silva for $13,121 in damages for physical pain, mental anguish, and attorney fees for false imprisonment and $50,000 in punitive damages. Dillard appealed, contending its employee had a shopkeeper's privilege to detain a customer to investigate the ownership of property.

DECISION: Judgment for Silva. The shopkeeper's privilege is applicable so long as (1) the employee has a reasonable belief that the customer is attempting to steal store merchandise (2) the detention is for a reasonable period of time, and (3) the detention is in a reasonable manner. In this case there was a reasonable belief by a store employee that items were being stolen. The detention for approximately an hour while store employees and Silva were questioned and the police department was called was a reasonable period of time. Regarding the third component, however, the jury found that Silva's story was more credible than Rivera's. It concluded that the detention was not in a reasonable manner and, accordingly, the shopkeeper's privilege did not apply. Since Silva's testimony supported the jury's finding, Dillard's appeal was denied. [**Dillard Department Stores, Inc. v Silva, 106 SW3d 789 (Tex App 2003)**]

---

[2] *Limited Stores, Inc. v Wilson-Robinson*, 876 SW2d 248 (Ark 1994); see also *Wal-Mart Stores, Inc. v Binns*, 15 SW3d 320 (Ark 2000).

7. Intentional Infliction of Emotional Distress

intentional infliction of emotional distress–tort that produces mental anguish caused by conduct that exceeds all bounds of decency.

The **intentional infliction of emotional distress** (IIED) is a tort involving conduct that goes beyond all bounds of decency and produces mental anguish in the harmed individual. This tort requires proof of outrageous conduct and resulting emotional distress in the victim. **For Example,** Erica Schoen, a 16-year employee of Freightliner, returned to work on light duty after surgery for a work-related shoulder injury. She was assigned to work out of the nurse's station under two employees who intentionally worked her beyond her restrictions, assigned her to humiliating work, repeatedly called her worthless, and used her as a personal servant—ordering her to get snacks, sodas, and lunches for them and not reimbursing her. After five months of this treatment, Erica brought the matter to the human resources manager, who told her, in part, "Nobody wants you. You're worthless. We build trucks down here…." Erica became hysterical and thereafter required psychiatric care. The jury awarded $250,000 for IIED, and it was upheld on appeal because the repetitive misconduct and its duration, ratified by the human resource manager, was intolerable.[3]

8. Invasion of Privacy

invasion of privacy–tort of intentional intrusion into the private affairs of another.

The right of privacy is the right to be free of unreasonable intrusion into one's private affairs. The tort of **invasion of privacy** actually consists of three different torts: (1) intrusion into the plaintiff's private affairs (for example, planting a microphone in an office or home); (2) public disclosure of private facts (for example, disclosing private financial information, such as a business posting returned checks from customers near its cash register in a public display); and (3) appropriation of another's name, likeness, or image for commercial advantage. This form of invasion of privacy is generally referred to as the *right to publicity*. The elements of this tort are (1) appropriation of the plaintiff's name or likeness for the value associated with it, and not in an incidental manner or for a newsworthy purpose, (2) identification of the plaintiff in the publication, and (3) an advantage or benefit to the defendant. The right to publicity is designed to protect the commercial interest of celebrities in their identities. **For Example,** popular and critically acclaimed rock and roll musician Don Henley, the founder and member of the band The Eagles, successfully sued a department store chain that ran an international newspaper advertisement for its Henley shirt, which stated in large letters as the focus of the ad "This is Don's henley." The ad (1) used the value associated with the famous name Don Henley to get consumers to read it, (2) the plaintiff was identifiable in the ad, and (3) the ad was created with the belief that use of the words "Don's henley" would help sell the product.[4]

[3] *Schoen v Freightliner LLC,* 199 P3d 332 (Or App 2008).
[4] *Henley v Dillard Department Stores,* 46 F Supp 2d 587 (ND Tex 1999).

C A S E   S U M M A R Y

Cashing in on Catherine's Vacation

FACTS: Catherine Bosley worked as a television news anchor for WKBN, Channel 27, in Youngstown, Ohio. While on vacation with her husband in Florida, she participated in a "wet t-shirt" contest that was videotaped without her consent by DreamGirls, Inc., and licensed to Marvad Corp., which runs a Web site for adult entertainment through a subscription service on the Internet. Marvad used depictions of her in advertisements to promote the materials and services it markets. Web site searches related to Catherine Bosley in 2004 were the most popular search on the World Wide Web. Due to the publicity, she resigned from her position at WKBN and was prevented from seeking other employment. Bosley sought an injunction under the right to publicity theory against the defendants from using her image in any manner that promotes the sale of their goods or services. The defendants contended that an injunction would violate their First Amendment rights.

DECISION: Judgment for Bosley. The First Amendment does not immunize defendants from damages for infringement of the right to publicity. No significant editorial comment or artistic expression involving First Amendment protections applies in this case. If any "speech" interest is involved, it is commercial speech. At its core, the defendants are selling Bosley's image for a profit without her consent. It is in violation of her right to publicity, which protects one's right to be free from the appropriation of one's persona. The injunction sought was granted. [**Bosley v Wildwett.com, 310 F Supp 2d 914 (ND Ohio 2004)**]

9. Defamation

defamation—untrue statement by one party about another to a third party.

slander—defamation of character by spoken words or gestures.

libel—written or visual defamation without legal justification.

Defamation is an untrue statement by one party about another to a third party. **Slander** is oral or spoken defamation, and **libel** is written (and in some cases broadcast) defamation. The elements for defamation are (1) a statement about a person's reputation, honesty, or integrity that is untrue; (2) publication (accomplished when a third party hears or reads the defamatory statement); (3) a statement directed at a particular person; and (4) damages that result from the statement.

For Example, a false statement by the owner of a business that the former manager was fired for stealing when he was not would be defamation, and the former manager's damages could be his inability to find another position because of the statement's impact on his reputation.

In cases in which the victim is a public figure, such as a Hollywood celebrity or a professional sports player, another element is required, the element of malice, which means that what was said or written was done with the knowledge that the information was false or with reckless disregard for whether it was true or false.

The defenses to defamation include the truth. If the statement is true, even if it is harmful to the victim, it is not the tort of defamation.[5]

Some statements are privileged, and this privilege provides a full or partial defense to the tort of defamation. **For Example,** members of Congress enjoy an

---

[5] *See Stark v Zeta Phi Beta Sorority Inc.,* 587 F Supp 2d 170 (D DC 2008).

absolute privilege–
complete defense against
the tort of defamation, as in
the speeches of members of
Congress on the floor and
witnesses in a trial.

absolute privilege when they are speaking on the floor of the Senate or the House because public policy requires a free dialogue on the issues pending in a legislative body. The same absolute privilege applies to witnesses in court proceedings to encourage witnesses with information to come forward and testify. Where a witness granted immunity from prosecution testifies before a governmental agency, the witness is entitled to immunity from defamation lawsuits.

C A S E   S U M M A R Y

Roger Clemens Strikes Out in Texas Court

FACTS: Roger Clemens sued his former trainer Brian McNamee for defamation. He alleged that McNamee falsely stated to the "Mitchell Commission," a congressional investigatory body looking into the use of performance-ehancing drugs in major league baseball, that Clemens had used steroids and human growth hormones during his professional baseball career. Clemens's complaint alleged that McNamee's statements to the Commissioner "injured Clemens's reputation and exposed him to public hatred, contempt, ridicule, and financial injuries." McNamee filed a motion to dismiss for lack of personal jurisdiction and privilege.

DECISION: Motion to dismiss granted in part. McNamee was interviewed by federal agents investigating the use of steroids, human growth hormones, and money laundering; he was given immunity from prosecution for his cooperation, but could be subject to prosecution for making false statements. McNamee's interviews with the Mitchell's Commission were scheduled by U.S. Attorneys and he was told by U.S. Attorneys that his immunity and truth obligations continued to apply to Mitchell interviews. Under Texas law, statements made to government agencies as part of legislative, judicial, or quasi-judicial proceedings may be entitled to absolute immunity, because the proper administration of justice requires full disclosure from witnesses without fear of retaliatory lawsuits for defamation.* **[Clemens V McNamee, 608 F Supp 2d 811 (SDTex, 2009)]**

---

* The court dismissed for lack of personal jurisdiction Clemens's allegations regarding statements made by McNamee to *Sports Illustrated* because they were not made in Texas. A charge of defamation regarding alleged statements made by McNamee to pitcher Andy Pettitte in Texas is still pending before the court.

qualified privilege–media
privilege to print inaccurate
information without liability
for defamation, so long as a
retraction is printed and
there was no malice.

The media enjoy a **qualified privilege** for stories that turn out to be false. Their qualified privilege is a defense to defamation so long as the information was released without malice and a retraction or correction is made when the matter is brought to their attention.

A *qualified privilege* to make a defamatory statement in the workplace exists when the statement is made to protect the interests of the private employer on a work-related matter, especially when reporting actual or suspected wrongdoing. **For Example,** Neda Lewis was fired from her job at Carson Oil Company for allegedly stealing toilet paper. The employee in charge of supplies noticed toilet paper was regularly missing from the ladies room, and one evening from a third-floor window overlooking the parking lot, she observed that the plaintiff's bag contained two rolls of toilet paper. She reported the matter to the executive secretary, who reported it to both the president and the CEO of the firm, who decided to fire her. Two other employees were also informed. The employer was able to successfully raise the defense of a qualified privilege to Ms. Lewis' defamation action for "false accusations of theft" since all of the employees involved were participants in the investigation and termination of the employee.[6]

A new statutory privilege has been evolving with respect to letters of recommendation and references given by employers for employees who are applying for jobs at other companies. Most companies, because of concerns about liability for defamation, will only confirm that a former employee did work at their firm and will provide the time period during which the person was employed. However, many employees who had histories that should have been revealed for safety reasons have been hired because no negative information was released. Numerous states now have statutes that provide employers a qualified privilege with respect to references and recommendations. So long as the employer acts in good faith in providing information, there is no liability for defamation to the former employee as a result of the information provided.

CASE SUMMARY

Putting in an Exaggerated Good Word

FACTS: Randi W., a 13-year-old who attended the Livingston Middle School, was molested and sexually touched by Robert Gadams, a vice principal at the school, in his office at the school. Gadams's prior employer was Muroc Unified School District, where disciplinary actions were taken against him for sexual harassment. When allegations of "sexual touching" of female students were made, Gadams was forced to resign from Muroc. Nonetheless, Gary Rice and David Malcolm, officials at Muroc, provided a letter of recommendation for Gadams that described him as "an upbeat, enthusiastic administrator who relates well to the students" and who was responsible "in large part" for making Boron Junior High School (located in Muroc) "a safe, orderly and clean environment for students and staff." Randi W. filed suit against the school districts, alleging that her injuries from Gadams's sexual touching were proximately caused by their failure to provide full and accurate information about Gadams to the placement service. The trial court dismissed the case, and the Court of Appeals reversed. The districts appealed.

DECISION: One of society's highest priorities is to protect children from sexual or physical abuse. On the other hand, a rule imposing liability in a case like this where a letter of recommendation fails to disclose material information could greatly inhibit the preparation and distribution of reference letters, to the general detriment of employers and employees alike. However, the balancing of these two competing policy issues simply requires that employers prepare recommendation letters stating all "material" facts, positive and negative, and simply decline to write a reference letter or, at most, merely confirm the former employee's position, salary, and dates of employment. Misleading letters of recommendation for potentially dangerous employees present foreseeable risks of harms to others, like the young person harmed here.

The judgment of the Court of Appeals is affirmed as to liability for negligent misrepresentation and fraud. [**Randi W. v Muroc Joint Unified School District, 929 P2d 582 Cal 1997**]

---

[6] *Lewis v Carson Oil Co.*, 127 P3d 1207 (Or App 2006).

10. Product Disparagement

slander of title—malicious making of false statements as to a seller's title.

Although the comparison of products and services is healthy for competition, false statements about another's products constitute a form of slander called **slander of title** or libel called **trade libel**; collectively, these are known as **product disparagement**, which occurs when someone makes false statements about another business, its products, or its abilities.[7] The elements of product disparagement are (1) a false statement about a particular business product or about its service in terms of honesty, reputation, ability, or integrity; (2) communication of the statement to a third party; and (3) damages.

trade libel—written defamation about a product or service.

product disparagement—false statements made about a product or business.

11. Wrongful Interference with Contracts

contract interference—tort in which a third party interferes with others' freedom to contract.

The tort of **contract interference** or (tortious interference with contracts) occurs when parties are not allowed the freedom to contract without interference from third parties. While the elements required to establish the tort of contract interference are complex, a basic definition is that the law affords a remedy when a third party intentionally causes another to break a contract already in existence. **For Example,** Nikke Finke, a newspaper reporter who had a contract with the *New York Post* to write stories about the entertainment industry for the *Post's* business section, wrote two articles about a lawsuit involving a literary agent and the Walt Disney Company over merchandising rights to the Winnie-the-Pooh characters. Finke reported that the trial court sanctioned Disney for engaging in "misuse of the discovery process" and acting in "bad faith" and ordered Disney to pay fees and costs of $90,000. Disney's president, Robert Iger, sent a letter to the *Post's* editor-in-chief, Col Allan, calling Finke's reporting an "absolute distortion" of the record and "absolutely false." Approximately two weeks after the Pooh articles were published, the *Post* fired Finke; her editor told her she was being fired for the Pooh articles. She sued Disney on numerous tort theories, including interference with her contract with the *Post*. Disney sought to have the complaint dismissed, which motion was denied by the court. The Court of Appeals concluded that Finke demonstrated a reasonable probability of proving that Iger's allegations that she made false statements in her article were themselves false; and it concluded that a jury could find Disney liable for intentional interference with contractual relations based on circumstantial evidence and negligent interference with contractual relations because it was reasonably foreseeable to Disney that the nature of its accusations against Finke would result in her termination from employment.[8]

12. Trespass

trespass—unauthorized action with respect to person or property.

A **trespass** is an unauthorized action with respect to land or personal property. A *trespass to land* is any unpermitted entry below, on, across, or above the land of another. **For Example,** Joyce Ameral's home abuts the mid-way point of the 240-yard, par-4 ninth hole of the public Middlebrook Country Club. Balls sliced

---

[7] *Sannerud v Brantz*, 879 P2d 341 (Wyo 1994). See *Suzuki Motor Corp. v Consumers Union*, 230 F3d 1110 (9th Cir 2003), *cert denied* 540 US 983 (2003), for an example of the complexity of a product disparagement action.
[8] *Finke v The Walt Disney Co.*, 2 Cal Rptr 3d 436 (Cal App 2003).

and hooked by golfers have damaged her windows and screens, dented her car, and made her deck too dangerous for daytime use. Her landscapers are forced to wear hard hats when cutting her lawn. In her lawsuit against the country club owner, the court ruled that the projection of golf balls onto Ameral's property constituted a continuing trespass and it enjoined the trespass.[9]

A *trespass to personal property* is the invasion of personal property without the permission of the owner. **For Example,** the use of someone's car without that person's permission is a trespass to personal property.

C. NEGLIGENCE

The widest range of tort liability today arises in the field of negligence. Accidents happen! Property is damaged, and/or injuries result. The fact that an individual suffers an injury does not necessarily mean that the individual will be able to recover damages for the injury. **For Example,** Rhonda Nichols was shopping in the outdoor garden center at a Lowe's Home Center when a "wild bird" flew into the back of her head, causing injuries. Her negligence lawsuit against Lowe's was dismissed because the owner did not have a duty to protect her from a wild bird attack because it was not reasonably foreseeable.[10] Jane Costa was passively watching a Boston Red Sox baseball game at Fenway Park when a foul ball struck her in the face, causing severe and permanent injuries. Her negligence lawsuit against the Boston Red Sox was unsuccessful because it was held that the owners had no duty to warn Ms. Costa of the obvious danger of foul balls being hit into the stands.[11] Although cases involving injury to spectators at baseball games in other jurisdictions have turned on other tort doctrines, injured fans, like Ms. Costa, are left to bear the costs of their injuries. Only when an injured person can demonstrate the following four elements of negligence is a right to recover established: (1) a duty, (2) breach of duty, (3) causation, and (4) damages.[12] Several defenses may be raised in a negligence lawsuit.

13. Elements of Negligence

(A) DUTY TO EXERCISE REASONABLE CARE. The first element of negligence is a *duty*. There is a general duty of care imposed to act as a reasonably prudent person would in similar circumstances. **For Example,** Gustavo Guzman worked for a subcontractor as a chicken catcher at various poultry farms where a Tyson Foods employee, Brian Jones, operated a forklift and worked with the catchers setting up cages to collect birds for processing at a Tyson plant. Contrary to Tyson's instructions "never to allow catchers to move behind the forklift or otherwise out of sight," Brian moved his forklift and struck Guzman, who suffered a serious spinal injury. A general contractor, Tyson Foods, owes a duty to exercise reasonable care to a subcontractor's employee, Gustavo Guzman.[13]

---

9 *Ameral v Pray*, 831 NE2d 915 (Mass App 2005).
10 *Nichols v Lowe's Home Center, Inc.*, 407 F Supp 2d 979 (SD Ill 2006).
11 *Costa v Boston Red Sox Baseball Club*, 809 NE2d 1090 (Mass App 2004).
12 *Alfred v Capital Area Soccer League, Inc.*, 669 SE2d 277 (NC App 2008).
13 *Tyson Foods Inc. v Guzman*, 116 SW3d 233 (Tex App 2003).

malpractice—when services are not properly rendered in accordance with commonly accepted standards; negligence by a professional in performing his or her skill.

Professionals have a duty to perform their jobs at the level of a reasonable professional. For a professional such as an accountant, doctor, lawyer, dentist, or architect to avoid liability for **malpractice,** the professional must perform his or her skill in the same manner as, and at the level of, other professionals in the same field.

Those who own real property have a duty of care to keep their property in a condition that does not create hazards for guests. Businesses have a duty to inspect and repair their property so that their customers are not injured by hazards, such as spills on the floor or uneven walking areas. When customer safety is a concern, businesses have a duty to provide adequate security, such as security patrols in mall parking lots.

(B) BREACH OF DUTY. The second element of negligence is the breach of duty imposed by statute or by the application of the reasonable person standard. The defendant's conduct is evaluated against what a reasonable person would have done under the circumstances. That is, when there is sufficient proof to raise a jury question, the jury decides whether the defendant breached the duty to the injured person from a reasonable person's perspective.[14] **For Example,** the jury in Guzman's lawsuit against Tyson Foods (the *Tyson* case), after weighing all of the facts and circumstances, determined that Tyson's employee's operation of the forklift constituted a breach of Tyson's duty of care to Guzman.

(C) CAUSATION. A third element of negligence is *causation,* the element that connects the duty and the breach of duty to the injuries to the plaintiff. **For Example,** in Guzman's lawsuit, the forklift operator's careless conduct was the cause in fact of this worker's injuries. A "but for" test for causation is used. *But for* Tyson employee Brian Jones' negligent conduct in moving the forklift under the circumstances surrounding the accident, Guzman would not have been injured.

Once the cause in fact is established, the plaintiff must establish *proximate cause.* That is, it must establish that the harm suffered by the injured person was a foreseeable consequence of the defendant's negligent actions. Foreseeability requires only the general danger to be foreseeable. In the *Tyson* case, the court determined that while there was some evidence that a jury could possibly infer that Tyson could not foresee an accident similar to the one involving Guzman, the evidence was legally sufficient to support the jury's finding that Tyson's negligence was foreseeable and the cause in fact of Guzman's injuries.

The landmark *Palsgraf v Long Island Rail Road Co.* case established a limitation on liability for unforeseeable or unusual consequences following a negligent act.

(D) DAMAGES. The plaintiff in a personal injury negligence lawsuit must establish the actual losses caused by the defendant's breach of duty of care and is entitled to be made whole for all losses. The successful plaintiff is entitled to compensation for (1) past and future pain and suffering (mental anguish), (2) past and future physical impairment, (3) past and future medical care, and (4) past and future loss of earning capacity. Life and work life expectancy are critical factors to consider in assessing

---

[14] A breach of duty may be established by the very nature of the harm to the plaintiff. The doctrine of *res ipsa loquitur* ("the event speaks for itself") provides a rebuttable presumption that the defendant was negligent when a defendant owes a duty to the plaintiff, the nature of the harm caused the plaintiff is such that it ordinarily does not happen in the absence of negligence, and the instrument causing the injury was in the defendant's exclusive control. An example of the doctrine is a lawsuit against a surgeon after a surgical device is discovered in a former patient months after the surgery by another physician seeking the cause of the patient's continuing pain subsequent to the operation.

C A S E   S U M M A R Y

The Scales Tipped on Causation

FACTS: Helen Palsgraf lived in Brooklyn. On a summer's day, she purchased tickets to travel to Rockaway Beach on the Long Island Rail Road (LIRR) with her two daughters. She was standing on a platform on the LIRR's East New York station when two men ran to catch another train. One of the men made it onto the train, but the other man, who was carrying a package, was unsteady as the train was about to pull out of the station. The LIRR conductor pulled him up, while the LIRR platform guard pushed him in the train, but in the process, he dropped the package. It contained fireworks and exploded! The concussion from the explosion caused the scales located next to Mrs. Palsgraf to fall over, striking and injuring her. Mrs. Palsgraf sued LIRR for the negligence of the two employees who had assisted the passenger with the package to board the train. A jury awarded her $6,000, which was upheld 3-2 by the Appellate Division. Thereafter the state's highest court considered the railroad's appeal.

DECISION: Recovery for negligence is not available unless there has been some violation of a right. Helen Palsgraf was too remote in distance from the accident for any invasion of rights. To reach a different decision would mean that there could be no end to those who might be harmed. By helping someone onto a moving train, the train employees can anticipate that the passenger himself might be injured, that other passengers might be injured, and that those around the immediate scene might be injured. But Mrs. Palsgraf was too remote for her injuries to be reasonably foreseeable as a consequence of the action of helping a passenger onto a moving train. She was 25 to 30 feet away from the scene, and the explosion cannot be called the proximate cause of her concussion and other injuries. [**Palsgraf v Long Island RR. Co., 162 NE 99 (NY 1928)**]

damage involving permanent disabilities with loss of earning capacity. Expert witnesses are utilized at trial to present evidence based on worklife tables and present value tables to deal with these economic issues. The jury considers all of the evidence in the context of the elements necessary to prove negligence and all defenses raised, and it renders a verdict. **For Example,** in the *Tyson* case, the defendant presented evidence and argued that Gustavo Guzman was himself negligent regarding the accident. The jury found that both parties were negligent and attributed 80 percent of the fault to Tyson and 20 percent to Guzman (this is called *comparative negligence* and is discussed in the following section). The jury awarded Guzman $931,870.51 in damages ($425,000.00 for past physical pain and mental anguish, $150,000.00 for future physical pain and mental anguish, $10,000.00 for past physical impairment, $10,000.00 for future physical impairment, $51,870.51 for past medical care, $5,000.00 for future medical care, $70,000.00 for past lost earning capacity, and $210,000.00 for future lost earning capacity). After deducting 20 percent of the total jury award for Guzman's own negligence, the trial court's final judgment awarded Guzman $745,496.41.

In some situations, the independent actions of two defendants occur to cause harm. **For Example,** Penny Shipler was rendered a quadriplegic as a result of a Chevrolet S-10 Blazer rollover accident. She sued the driver Kenneth Long for negligence and General Motors for negligent design of the Blazer's roof. She was awarded $18.5 million in damages. Because two causes provided a single indivisible injury, the two defendants were held jointly and severally liable.[15] Under *joint and several liability,* each defendant may be held liable to pay the entire judgment. However, should one defendant pay the entire judgment, that party may sue the other for "contribution" for its proportionate share.

In some cases in which the breach of duty was shocking, plaintiffs may be awarded *punitive damages.* However, punitive (also called *exemplary*) damages are ordinarily applied when the defendant's tortious conduct is attended by circumstances of fraud, malice, or willful or wanton conduct.[16]

14. Defenses to Negligence

(A) CONTRIBUTORY NEGLIGENCE. A plaintiff who is also negligent gives the defendant the opportunity to raise the defense of **contributory negligence,** which the defendant establishes by utilizing the elements of negligence previously discussed, including the plaintiff's duty to exercise reasonable care for his or her own safety, the breach of that duty, causation, and harm. Under common law, the defense of contributory negligence, if established, is a complete bar to recovery of damages from the defendant.

contributory negligence– negligence of the plaintiff that contributes to injury and at common law bars from recovery from the defendant although the defendant may have been more negligent than the plaintiff.

CASE SUMMARY

Keep Your Eye on the Ball in Sports: Keep Your Eye on the 300-Pound Boxes in Trucking

FACTS: Lawrence Hardesty is an over-the-road tractor-trailer truck driver who picked up a load of stadium seating equipment for the NFL stadium under construction in Baltimore. The equipment was packaged in large corrugated cardboard boxes weighing several hundred pounds. The shipper, American Seating Co., loaded the trailer while Hardesty remained in the cab of his truck doing "paperwork" and napping. Considerable open space existed between the boxes and the rear door of the trailer. The evidence showed that Hardesty failed to properly examine the load bars used to secure the boxes from movement during transit. When Hardesty arrived at the Baltimore destination, he opened the rear trailer door and boxes at the end of the trailer fell out and injured him. Hardesty brought a personal injury negligence action against the shipper. American Seating Co. responded that Hardesty was contributorily negligent, thus barring his negligence claim.

DECISION: Judgment for American Seating Co. because the claim is barred by Hardesty's contributory negligence. His decision to ignore the loading process by remaining in his truck, oblivious to the manner and means of the loading of the trailer, coupled with his own failure to examine the load bars sufficiently to confirm that they would "adequately secure" the cargo, together with his decision, in the face of his prior omissions, to open the doors of the trailer upon his arrival in Baltimore while standing within the zone of danger created by the possibility (of which he negligently failed to inform himself) of injury from cargo falling out of the trailer, cohered to rise to the level of a cognizable breach of duty—contributory negligence. [**Hardesty v American Seating Co., 194 F Supp 2d 447 D Md 2002**]

---

[15] *Shipler v General Motors Corp.,* 710 NW2d 807 (Neb 2006).
[16] See *Eden Electrical, Ltd. v Amana Co.,* 370 F3d 824 (8th Cir 2004); and *University of Colorado v American Cyanamid Co.,* 342 F3d 1298 (Fed Cir 2003).

The contributory negligence defense has given way to the defense of comparative negligence in most states.

(B) COMPARATIVE NEGLIGENCE. Because contributory negligence produced harsh results with no recovery of damages for an injured plaintiff, most states have adopted a fairer approach to handling situations in which both the plaintiff and the defendant are negligent; it is called *comparative negligence*. Comparative negligence is a defense that permits a negligent plaintiff to recover some damages but only in proportion to the defendant's degree of fault.[17] **For Example,** in the *Tyson* case, both the defendant and the plaintiff were found to be negligent. The jury attributed 80 percent of the fault for the plaintiff's injury to Tyson and 20 percent of the fault to the plaintiff, Guzman. While Guzman's total damages were $931,870, they were reduced by 20 percent, and the final judgment awarded Guzman was $745,496.

Some comparative negligence states refuse to allow the plaintiff to recover damages if the plaintiff's fault was more than 50 percent of the cause of the harm.[18]

(C) ASSUMPTION OF THE RISK. The assumption of the risk defense has two categories. *Express assumption of the risk* involves a written exculpatory agreement under which a plaintiff acknowledges the risks involved in certain activities and releases the defendant from prospective liability for personal injuries sustained as a result of the defendant's negligent conduct. Examples include ski lift tickets, white water rafting contracts, permission for high school cheerleading activities, and parking lot claim checks. In most jurisdictions these agreements are enforceable as written. However, in some jurisdictions they may be considered unenforceable because they violate public policy. **For Example,** Gregory Hanks sued the Powder Ridge Ski Resort for negligence regarding serious injuries he sustained while snowtubing at the defendant's facility. He had signed a release which explicitly provided that the snowtuber: *["fully] assume[s] all risks associated with [s]nowtubing*, even if due to the NEGLIGENCE" of the defendants [emphasis in original]. The Supreme Court of Connecticut found that the release was unenforceable because it violated the public policy by shifting the risk of negligence to the weaker bargainer.[19]

Implied primary assumption of the risk arises when a plaintiff has impliedly consented, often in advance of any negligence by the defendant, to relieve a defendant of a duty to the plaintiff regarding specific known and appreciated risks. It is a subjective standard, one specific to the plaintiff and his or her situation. **For Example,** baseball mom Delinda Taylor took her two boys to a Seattle Mariners baseball game and was injured during the pregame warm-up when a ball thrown by José Mesa got past Freddie Garcia, striking Taylor in the face and causing serious injuries. The defendant baseball team successfully raised the affirmative defense of implied primary assumption of the risk by showing that Mrs. Taylor had full subjective understanding of the specific risk of getting hit by a thrown baseball, and she voluntarily chose to encounter that risk.[20]

---

[17] *City of Chicago v M/V Morgan,* 375 F3d 563 (7th Cir 2004).
[18] *Davenport v Cotton Hope Plantation,* 482 SE2d 569 (SC App 1997).
[19] *Hanks v Powder Ridge,* 885 A2d 734 (Conn 2005).
[20] *Taylor v Baseball Club of Seattle,* 130 P3d 835 (Wash App 2006).

A number of states have either abolished the defense of assumption of the risk, reclassifying the defense as comparative negligence so as not to completely bar a plaintiff's recovery of damages, or have eliminated the use of the assumption of the risk terminology and handle cases under the duty, breach of duty, causation, and harm elements of negligence previously discussed.[21]

(D) **IMMUNITY.** Governments are generally immune from tort liability.[22] This rule has been eroded by decisions and in some instances by statutes, such as the Federal Tort Claims Act. Subject to certain exceptions, this act permits the recovery of damages from the United States for property damage, personal injury, or death action claims arising from the negligent act or omission of any employee of the United States

sports&entertainment law

Liability for Injuries Under the Sports Exception Doctrine

Charles "Booby" Clark played football for the Cincinnati Bengals as a running back on offense. Dale Hackbart played defensive free safety for the Denver Broncos. As a consequence of an interception by the Broncos, Hackbart became an offensive player, threw a block, and was watching the play with one knee on the ground when Clark "acting out of anger and frustration, but without a specific intent to injure," stepped forward and struck a blow to the back of Hackbart's head and neck, causing a serious neck fracture. Is relief precluded for injuries occurring during a professional football game? The answer is no. While proof of mere negligence is insufficient to establish liability during such an athletic contest, liability must instead be premised on heightened proof of reckless or intentional conduct on the part of the defendant. In the *Hackbart* case, the court determined that if the evidence established that the injury was the result of acts of Clark that were in reckless disregard of Hackbart's safety, Hackbart is

entitled to damages.* Why didn't Hackbart pursue recovery under negligence law, contending that Clark had a general duty of care to act as a reasonably prudent person would in similar circumstances? Because football and other contact sports contain within the rules of the games inherent *unreasonable* risks of harm, a negligence theory is not applicable. What contact sports do you believe qualify under this "sports exception" doctrine for which proof of negligence is insufficient to establish liability for injuries sustained during the athletic contest?

PGA golfer Walter Mallin sued PGA golfer John Paesani for injuries that Mallin sustained while competing in a PGA golf tournament when Paesani drove a golf ball that struck Mallin in the head on his right temple. Paesani contends that the "sports exception" doctrine applies and the negligence case must be dismissed. How would you decide this case?**

* *Hackbart v Cincinnati Bengals, Inc.*, 601 F2d 516 (10th Cir 1979).
** *Mallin v Paesani*, 892 A2d 1043 (Conn Super, 2005).

---

[21] See, for example, *Costa v The Boston Red Sox Baseball Club*, 809 NE2d 1090 (Mass App 2004), where the court cites state precedent that"... the abolishment of assumption of the risk as an affirmative defense did not alter the plaintiff's burden ... to prove the defendant owed [the plaintiff] a duty of care ... and thus left intact the open and obvious damages rule, which operates to negate the existence of a duty to care."
[22] *Kirby v Macon County*, 892 SW2d 403 (Tenn 1994).

under such circumstances that the United States, if a private person, would be liable to the claimant in accordance with the law of the place where the act or omission occurred. A rapidly growing number of states have abolished governmental immunity, although many still recognize it.

Until the early 1900s, charities were immune from tort liability, and children and parents and spouses could not sue each other. These immunities are fast disappearing. **For Example,** if a father's negligent driving of his car causes injuries to his minor child passenger, the child may recover from the father for his injuries.[23]

D. Strict Liability

The final form of tort liability is known as *strict liability*. When the standards of strict liability apply, very few defenses are available. Strict liability was developed to provide guaranteed protection for those who are injured by conduct the law deems both serious and inexcusable.

---

thinking things through

Torts and Public Policy

Over a decade ago, a jury awarded 81-year-old Stella Liebeck nearly $3 million because she was burned after she spilled a cup of McDonald's coffee on her lap. Based on these limited facts, a national discussion ensued about a need for tort reform, and to this day "Stella Awards" are given on Web sites for apparently frivolous or excessive lawsuits. Consider the following additional facts and the actual damages awarded Stella Liebeck. Decide whether her recovery was just.

- McDonald's coffee was brewed at 195 to 205 degrees.

- McDonald's quality assurance manager "was aware of the risk [of burns] … and had no plans to turn down the heat."

- Mrs. Liebeck spent seven days in the hospital with third degree burns and had skin grafts. Gruesome photos of burns of the inner thighs, groin, and buttocks were entered as evidence.

- The compensatory damages were $200,000, which were reduced to $160,000 because Mrs. Liebeck was determined to be 20 percent at fault.

- The jury awarded $2.7 million in punitive damages. The trial court judge reduced this amount to $480,000.

- The total recovery at the trial court for Mrs. Liebeck was $640,000. Both parties appealed, and a settlement was reached at what is believed to be close to the $640,000 figure.

Tort remedies have evolved because of public policy incentives for the protection of individuals from physical, mental, and economic damage. Tort remedies provide economic motivation for individuals and businesses to avoid conduct that could harm others.

The amount of the compensation and the circumstances in which compensation for torts should be paid are issues that courts, juries, and legislatures review.

---

[23] *Cates v Cates*, 588 NE2d 330 (Ill App 1992); see also *Doe v McKay*, 700 NE2d 1018 (Ill 1998).

thinking things through

Continued

Many legislatures have examined and continue to review the standards for tort liability and damages.

The U.S. Supreme Court devoted several decisions in recent years to dealing with excessive punitive damages in civil litigation, and it has set "guideposts" to be used by courts in assessing punitive damages.* In *State Farm Mutual Automobile Insurance Co. v Campbell*, compensatory damages for the plaintiffs at the trial court

level were $1 million, and punitive damages, based in part on evidence that State Farm's nationwide policy was to underpay claims regardless of merit to enhance profits, were assessed at $145 million. The Supreme Court concluded that the facts of *Campbell* would likely justify a punitive damages award only at or near the amount of compensatory damages. Thus, even those who act very badly as State Farm Insurance did have a constitutionally protected right under the Due Process Clause of the Fourteenth Amendment to have civil law damages assessed in accordance with the Supreme Court's guideposts.

* *BMW of North America v Gore*, 517 US 559 (1996); *Cooper Industries v Leatherman Tool Group, Inc.*, 532 US 424 (2001); *State Farm Insurance v Campbell*, 538 US 408 (2003); and *Exxon Shipping Co. v Baker*, 128 S Ct 2605, 2621 (2008).

15. What is Strict Liability?

Strict liability is an absolute standard of liability imposed by the law in circumstances the courts or legislatures have determined require a high degree of protection. When strict liability is imposed, the result is that the company or person who has caused injury or damages by the conduct will be required to compensate for those damages in an absolute sense. Few, if any, defenses apply in a situation in which the law imposes a strict liability standard. **For Example,** as noted earlier in the chapter, engaging in ultrahazardous activities, such as using dynamite to excavate a site for new construction, results in strict liability for the contractor performing the demolition. Any damages resulting from the explosion are the responsibility of that contractor, so the contractor is strictly liable.

16. Imposing Strict Liability

Strict liability arises in a number of different circumstances, but the most common are in those situations in which a statutory duty is imposed and in product liability. For example at both the state and federal levels, there are requirements for the use, transportation, and sale of radioactive materials, as well as the disposal of biomedical materials and tools. Any violation of these rules and regulations would result in strict liability for the company or person in violation.

Product liability, while more fully covered in Chapter 25, is another example of strict liability. A product that is defective through its design, manufacture, or instructions and that injures someone results in strict liability for the manufacturer.

lawflix

Class Action (1991) (R)

This movie depicts the magnitude of damages and recovery when multiple injuries occur. The film provides insights on tort reform and the ethics of lawyers. You can learn about the magnitude of discovery and evidence.

Check out LawFlix at [**www.cengage.com/blaw/dvl**] to access movie clips that illustrate business law concepts.

Notting Hill (1999) (PG-13)

A story of famous star gets guy, dumps guy, gets guy back, dumps guy again, and then guy dumps famous star, and on and on. But, the guy owns a bookstore that sells travel books and he has a shoplifter. Hugh Grant, as the guy, illustrates perfection in exercising the shopkeeper's privilege.

You can view a clip of this movie and others that illustrate business law concepts at the LawFlix site, located at **www.cengage.com/blaw/dvl.**

MAKE THE CONNECTION

SUMMARY

A *tort* is a civil wrong that affords recovery for damages that result. The three forms of torts are intentional torts, negligence, and strict liability. A tort differs from a crime in the nature of its remedy. Fines and imprisonment result from criminal violations, whereas money damages are paid to those who are damaged by conduct that constitutes a tort. An action may be both a crime and a tort, but the tort remedy is civil in nature.

Selected intentional torts are false imprisonment, defamation, product disparagement, contract interference or tortious interference, and trespass. False imprisonment is the detention of another without his or her permission. False imprisonment is often called the *shopkeeper's tort* because store owners detain suspected shoplifters. Many states provide a privilege to store owners if they detain shoplifting suspects based on reasonable cause and in a reasonable manner. Defamation is slander (oral) or libel (written) and consists of false statements about another that damage the person's reputation or integrity. Truth is an absolute defense to defamation, and there are some privileges that protect against defamation, such as those for witnesses at trial and for members of Congress during debates on the floor. There is a developing privilege for employers when they give references for former employees. Invasion of privacy is intrusion into private affairs; public disclosure of private facts; or appropriation of someone's name, image, or likeness for commercial purposes.

To establish the tort of negligence, one must show that there has been a breach of duty in the form of a violation of a statute or professional competency standards or of behavior that does not rise to the level of that of a reasonable person. That breach of duty must have caused the foreseeable injuries to the plaintiff, and the plaintiff must be able to quantify the damages that resulted. Possible defenses to negligence include contributory negligence, comparative negligence, and assumption of risk.

Strict liability is absolute liability with few defenses.

LEARNING OUTCOMES

After studying this chapter, you should be able to clearly explain:

A. GENERAL PRINCIPLES

LO.1 Explain the difference between torts and crimes
See the discussion on wrongs that are a violation of a private duty as torts, and wrongs that are a violation of a public duty of crimes, p. 188. See the O.J. Simpson example of his acquittal of the crime of murder and his civil liability for the torts of wrongful death on p. 188.

B. INTENTIONAL TORTS

LO.2 Distinguish between an assault and a battery
See the "kick your butt" threat example of an assault on p. 189.

LO.3 Explain the three different torts of invasion of privacy
See the discussion of the intrusion into a person' private affairs, public disclosure of private facts, and right to publicity torts beginning on p. 192.

LO.4 Explain the torts of defamation and defenses
See the discussion of slander, libel, and trade libel beginning on p. 193. See the discussion of the requirement of the enhanced element of malice for cases in which the victim is a public figure, p. 193. See the defense of privilege raised in the *Clemens* case on p. 194.

C. NEGLIGENCE

LO.5 Explain the elements of negligence and defenses
See the discussion of the elements of negligence: duty, breach of duty, and causation and damages beginning on p. 197. See the discussion of the defenses of contributory negligence, comparative negligence, assumption of risk, and immunity beginning on p. 200.

D. STRICT LIABILITY

LO.6 Explain the tort of strict liability and why very few defenses are avaliable
See the dynamite excavation example, holding the contractor liable for any damages with no defenses because of the hazardous activity, p. 204.

KEY TERMS

absolute privilege

contract interference

contributory negligence,

defamation

false imprisonment

intentional infliction of
emotional distress

intentional torts

invasion of privacy

libel

malpractice,

negligence

product disparagement

qualified privilege

shopkeeper's privilege

slander of title

slander

strict liability

tort

trade libel

trespass

QUESTIONS AND CASE PROBLEMS

1. Christensen Shipyards built a 155-foot yacht for Tiger Woods at its Vancouver, Washington, facilities. It used Tiger's name and photographs relating to the building of the yacht in promotional materials for the shipyard without seeking his permission. Was this a right to publicity tort because Tiger could assert that his name and photos were used to attract attention to the shipyard to obtain commercial advantage? Did the shipyard have a First Amendment right to present the truthful facts regarding their building of the yacht and the owner's identity as promotional materials? Does the fact that the yacht was named *Privacy* have an impact on this case? Would it make a difference as to the outcome of this case if the contract for building the yacht had a clause prohibiting the use of Tiger's name or photo without his permission?

2. ESPN held its Action Sports and Music Awards ceremony in April, at which celebrities in the fields of extreme sports and popular music such as rap and heavy metal converged. Well-known musicians Ben Harper and James Hetfield were there, as were popular rappers Busta Rhymes and LL Cool J. Famed motorcycle stuntman Evel Knievel, who is commonly thought of as the "father of extreme sports," and his wife Krystal were photographed. The photograph depicted Evel, who was wearing a motorcycle jacket and rose-tinted sunglasses, with his right arm around Krystal and his left arm around another young woman. ESPN published the photograph on its "extreme sports" Web site with a caption that read "Evel Knievel proves that you're never too old to be a pimp." The Knievels brought suit against ESPN, contending that the photograph and caption were defamatory because they accused Evel of soliciting prostitution and implied that Krystal was a prostitute. ESPN contends that the caption was a figurative and slang usage and was not defamatory as a matter of law. Decide. [*Knievel v ESPN*, 393 F3d 1068 (9th Cir)]

3. While snowboarding down a slope at Mammoth Mountain Ski Area (Mammoth), 17-year-old David Graham was engaged in a snowball fight with his 14-year-old brother. As he was "preparing to throw a snowball" at his

brother, David slammed into Liam Madigan, who was working as a ski school instructor for Mammoth, and injured him. Madigan sued Graham for damages for reckless and dangerous behavior. The defense contended that the claim was barred under the doctrine of assumption of the risk, applicable in the state, arising from the risk inherent in the sport that allows for vigorous participation and frees a participant from a legal duty to act with due care. Decide. [*Mammoth Mountain Ski Area v Graham*, 38 Cal Rptr 3d 422 (Cal App)]

4. Following a visit to her hometown of Coalinga, Cynthia wrote "An Ode to Coalinga" (Ode) and posted it in her online journal on MySpace.com. Her last name did not appear online. Her page included her picture. The Ode opens with "The older I get, the more I realize how much I despise Coalinga" and then proceeds to make a number of extremely negative comments about Coalinga and its inhabitants. Six days later, Cynthia removed the Ode from her journal. At the time, Cynthia was a student at UC Berkeley, and her parents and sister were living in Coalinga. The Coalinga High School principal, Roger Campbell, submitted the Ode to the local newspaper, the *Coalinga Record*, and it was published in the Letters to the Editor section, using Cynthia's full name. The community reacted violently to the Ode, forcing the family to close its business and move. Cynthia and her family sued Campbell and the newpaper on the right-of-privacy theory of public disclosure of private facts. What are the essential element of this theory? Was Cynthia and her family's right of privacy violated? [*Moreno v Hanford Sentinel, Inc.*, 91 Cal Rptr 3d 858 (Cal App)]

5. JoKatherine Page and her 14-year-old son Jason were robbed at their bank's ATM at 9:30 P.M. one evening by a group of four thugs. The thieves took $300, struck Mrs. Page in the face with a gun, and ran. Mrs. Page and her son filed suit against the bank for its failure to provide adequate security. Should the bank be held liable? [*Page v American National Bank & Trust Co.*, 850 SW2d 133 (Tenn)]

6. A Barberton Glass Co. truck was transporting large sheets of glass down the highway. Elliot Schultz was driving his automobile some distance behind the truck. Because of the negligent way that the sheets of glass were fastened in the truck, a large sheet fell off the truck, shattered on hitting the highway, and then bounced up and broke the windshield of Shultz's car. He was not injured but suffered great emotional shock. He sued Barberton to recover damages for this shock. Barberton denied liability on the ground that Schultz had not sustained any physical injury at the time or as the result of the shock. Should he be able to recover? [*Schultz v Barberton Glass Co.*, 447 NE2d 109 (Ohio)]

7. Mallinckrodt produces nuclear and radioactive medical pharmaceuticals and supplies. Maryland Heights Leasing, an adjoining business owner, claimed that low-level radiation emissions from Mallinckrodt damaged its property and caused a loss in earnings. What remedy should Maryland Heights have? What torts are involved here? [*Maryland Heights Leasing, Inc. v Mallinckrodt, Inc.*, 706 SW2d 218 (Mo App)]

8. An owner abandoned his van in an alley in Chicago. In spite of repeated complaints to the police, the van was allowed to remain in the alley. After several months, it was stripped of most of the parts that could be removed. Jamin Ortiz, age 11, was walking down the alley when the van's gas tank exploded. The flames from the explosion set fire to Jamin's clothing, and he was severely burned. Jamin and his family brought suit brought against the city of Chicago to recover damages for his injuries. Could the city be held responsible for injuries caused by property owned by someone else? Why or why not? [*Ortiz v Chicago*, 398 NE2d 1007 (Ill App)]

9. Carrigan, a district manager of Simples Time Recorder Co., was investigating complaints of mismanagement of the company's Jackson office. He called at the home of Hooks, the secretary of that office, who expressed the opinion that part of the trouble was caused by the theft of parts and equipment by McCall, another employee. McCall was later discharged and sued Hooks for slander. Was she liable? [*Hooks v McCall*, 272 So2d 925 (Miss)]

10. Defendant no. 1 parked his truck in the street near the bottom of a ditch on a dark, foggy night. Iron pipes carried in the truck projected nine feet beyond the truck in back. Neither the truck nor the pipes carried any warning light or flag, in violation of both a city ordinance and a state statute. Defendant no. 2 was a taxicab owner whose taxicab was negligently driven at an excessive speed. Defendant no. 2 ran into the pipes, thereby killing the passenger in the taxicab. The plaintiff brought an action for the passenger's death against both defendants. Defendant no. 1 claimed he was not liable because it was Defendant no. 2's negligence that had caused the harm. Was this defense valid? [*Bumbardner v Allison*, 78 SE2d 752 (NC)]

11. Carl Kindrich's father, a member of the Long Beach Yacht Club before he died, expressed a wish to be "buried at sea." The Yacht Club permitted the Kindrich family the use of one of its boats, without charge, for the ceremony, and Mr. Fuller—a good friend of Carl's father—piloted the boat. Portable stairs on the dock assisted the attendees in boarding. Upon returning, Fuller asked for help to tie up the boat. The steps were not there, and Carl broke his leg while disembarking to help tie up the boat. Carl sued the Yacht Club for negligence in failing to have someone on the dock to ensure that the portable steps were available. The Yacht Club contended that it was not liable because Carl made the conscious decision to jump from the moving vessel to the dock, a primary assumption of risk in the sport of boating. The plaintiff contended that he was not involved in the sport of boating, and at most his actions constituted minimal comparative negligence, the type which a jury could weigh in conjunction with the defendant's negligence in assessing damages. Decide. [*Kindrich v Long Beach Yacht Club*, 84 Cal Rptr 3d 824 (Cal App)]

12. Hegyes was driving her car when it was negligently struck by a Unjian Enterprises truck. She was injured, and an implant was placed in her body to counteract the injuries. She sued Unjian, and the case was settled. Two years later Hegyes became pregnant. The growing fetus pressed against the implant,

making it necessary for her doctor to deliver the child 51 days prematurely by Cesarean section. Because of its premature birth, the child had a breathing handicap. Suit was brought against Unjian Enterprises for the harm sustained by the child. Was the defendant liable? [*Hegyes v Unjian Enterprises, Inc.*, 286 Cal Rptr 85 (Cal App)]

13. Kendra Knight took part in a friendly game of touch football. She had played before and was familiar with football. Michael Jewett was on her team. In the course of play, Michael bumped into Kendra and knocked her to the ground. He stepped on her hand, causing injury to a little finger that later required its amputation. She sued Michael for damages. He defended on the ground that she had assumed the risk. Kendra claimed that assumption of risk could not be raised as a defense because the state legislature had adopted the standard of comparative negligence. What happens if contributory negligence applies? What happens if the defense of comparative negligence applies?

14. A passenger on a cruise ship was injured by a rope thrown while the ship was docking. The passenger was sitting on a lounge chair on the third deck when she was struck by the weighted end of a rope thrown by an employee of Port Everglades, where the boat was docking. These ropes, or heaving lines, were being thrown from the dock to the second deck, and the passenger was injured by a line that was thrown too high.

    The trial court granted the cruise line's motion for directed verdict on the ground there was no evidence that the cruise line knew or should have known of the danger. The cruise line contended that it had no notice that this "freak accident" could occur. What is the duty of a cruise ship line to its passengers? Is there liability here? Does it matter that an employee of the port city, not the cruise lines, caused the injury? Should the passenger be able to recover? Why or why not? [*Kalendareva v Discovery Cruise Line Partnership*, 798 So2d 804 (Fla App)]

15. Blaylock was a voluntary psychiatric outpatient treated by Dr. Burglass, who became aware that Blaylock was violence prone. Blaylock told Dr. Burglass that he intended to do serious harm to Wayne Boynton, Jr., and shortly thereafter he killed Wayne. Wayne's parents then sued Dr. Burglass on grounds that he was liable for the death of their son because he failed to give warning or to notify the police of Blaylock's threat and nature. Was a duty breached here? Should Dr. Burglass be held liable? [*Boynton v Burglass*, 590 So2d 446 (Fla App)]

Chapter 21

PERSONAL PROPERTY AND BAILMENTS

A. Personal Property

1. PERSONAL PROPERTY IN CONTEXT
2. TITLE TO PERSONAL PROPERTY
3. GIFTS
4. FINDING OF LOST PROPERTY
5. OCCUPATION OF PERSONAL PROPERTY
6. ESCHEAT
7. MULTIPLE OWNERSHIP OF PERSONAL PROPERTY
8. COMMUNITY PROPERTY

B. Bailments

9. DEFINITION

10. ELEMENTS OF BAILMENT
11. NATURE OF THE PARTIES' INTERESTS
12. CLASSIFICATION OF ORDINARY BAILMENTS
13. RENTING OF SPACE DISTINGUISHED
14. DUTIES AND RIGHTS OF THE BAILEE
15. BREACH OF DUTY OF CARE: BURDEN OF PROOF
16. LIABILITY FOR DEFECTS IN BAILED PROPERTY
17. CONTRACT MODIFICATION OF LIABILITY

What is personal property? Who owns it? How is it acquired? Think of personal property as all things of value other than real estate. Many instances arise in which the owner of personal property entrusts it to another—a person checks a coat at a restaurant or leaves a watch with a jeweler for repairs; or a company rents a car to a tourist for a weekend. The delivery of personal property to another under such circumstances is a bailment.

A. Personal Property

1. Personal Property in Context

In common usage, the term *property* refers to a piece of land or a thing or an object. As a legal concept, however, property also refers to the rights that an individual may possess in the piece of land or that thing or that object.[1] Property includes the rights of any person to possess, use, enjoy, and dispose of a thing or object of value. A right in a thing is property, without regard to whether this right is absolute or conditional, perfect or imperfect, legal or equitable.

real property–land and all rights in land.

Real property means land and things embedded in the land, such as oil tanks. It also includes things attached to the earth, such as buildings or trees, and rights in any of these things. **Personal property** is property that is movable or intangible, or rights in such things. As described in Chapter 10, rights in intellectual property, such as writings, computer programs, inventions, and trademarks, are valuable business properties that are protected by federal statutes.

personal property– property that is movable or intangible, or rights in such things.

Personal property then consists of (1) whole or fractional rights in things that are tangible and movable, such as furniture and books; (2) claims and debts, which are called **choses in action**; and (3) intangible property rights, such as trademarks, copyrights, and patents.

chose in action–intangible personal property in the nature of claims against another, such as a claim for accounts receivable or wages.

2. Title to Personal Property

Title to personal property may be acquired in different ways. For example, property is commonly purchased. The purchase and sale of goods is governed by the law of sales. In this chapter, the following methods of acquiring personal property will be discussed: gift, finding lost property, occupation, and escheat.

No title is acquired by theft. The thief acquires possession only, and if the thief makes a sale or gift of the property to another, the latter acquires only possession of the property. The true owner may reclaim the property from the thief or a thief's transferee. **For Example,** through a response to a classified ad, Ray purchased a Mongoose bicycle for his son from Kevin for $250, a favorable but fair price for this used bicycle. To protect himself, he obtained from Kevin a handwritten bill of sale that was notarized by a notary public. In fact, Kevin had stolen the bicycle. Its true owner, Juan, can reclaim the bike from Ray, even though Ray has a notarized bill of sale. Ray does not have legal title to the bicycle.

CPA ### 3. Gifts

gift–title to an owner's personal property voluntarily transferred by a party not receiving anything in exchange.

Title to personal property may be transferred by the voluntary act of the owner without receiving anything in exchange—that is, by **gift**. The person making the

---

[1] *Presley Memorial Foundation v Crowell*, 733 SW2d 89 (Tenn App 1987).

FIGURE 21-1 | *Inter Vivos Gift*

| LAW | DONOR | 1. INTENT AND
2. DELIVERY | UNLESS THE GIFT IS DISCLAIMED, TITLE PASSES TO DONEE. |
| APPLICATION | SMITH OWNS THE VAN GOGH PAINTING *THE IRISES* | 1. HE STATES, "THIS IS FOR YOU, MICHAEL," AND
2. PERSONALLY PRESENTS THE PAINTING TO HIS SON, MICHAEL | MICHAEL BECOMES THE OWNER. |

donor—person making a gift.

donee—recipient of a gift.

inter vivos gift—any transaction that takes place between living persons and creates rights prior to the death of any of them.

gift, the **donor**, may do so because of things that the recipient of the gift, the **donee**, has done in the past or is expected to do in the future. However, such things are not deemed consideration and thus do not alter the "free" character of the gift. Five types of gifts are discussed below.

(A) INTER VIVOS GIFTS. The ordinary gift that is made between two living persons is an **inter vivos gift**. For practical purposes, such a gift takes effect when the donor (1) expresses an intent to transfer title and (2) makes delivery, subject to the right of the donee to disclaim the gift within a reasonable time after learning that it has been made.[2] Because there is no consideration for a gift, there is no enforceable contract, and an intended donee cannot sue for breach of contract if the donor fails to complete the gift.[3]

(1) Intent

The intent to make a gift requires an intent to transfer title at that time. **For Example,** former ballet star Rudolf Nureyev made a valid gift when he extended deeds of gift granting ownership of his New York City apartment and its $5 million artwork collection to a nonprofit dance foundation even though he retained the right to visit the apartment and pay for its maintenance. He gave up the right to live in the apartment and executed all documents necessary to divest his domain over it.[4] In contrast, an intent to confer a benefit at a future date is not a sufficient intent to create any right in the intended donee.

A delivery of property without the intent to make a gift does not transfer title. **For Example,** Mrs. Simpson's $80,000 check to her daughter and son-in-law, Shari and Karl Goodman, to help them buy a house was not a gift if the transaction was structured as a loan, notwithstanding Shari and Karl's assertion that it was structured as a loan simply to avoid gift taxes. The legal documents setting up the loan transaction indicated that no gift was intended.[5]

CPA **(2) Delivery**

Ordinarily, the delivery required to make a gift will be an actual handing over to the donee of the thing that is given.

---

[2] *Bishop v Bishop,* 961 SW2d 770 (Ark 1998).
[3] *Dellagrotta v Dellagrotta,* 873 A2d 101 (RI 2005).
[4] *Rudolf Nureyev Dance Foundation v Noureeva-Francois,* 7 F Supp 2d 402 (SDNY 1998).
[5] *Simpson v Goodman,* 727 So2d 555 (La App 1998). See also *Wright v Mallet,* 894 A2d 1016 (Conn App 2006) in which the evidence showed that a transfer in an interest in land was not intended to be a gift.

symbolic delivery–delivery of goods by delivery of the means of control, such as a key or a relevant document of title, such as a negotiable bill of lading; also called constructive delivery.

constructive delivery–see "symbolic delivery."

The delivery of a gift may also be made by a **symbolic** or **constructive delivery**, such as by the delivery of means of control of property. Such means of control might be keys to a lock or keys to a garden tractor or papers that are essential to or closely associated with the ownership of the property, such as documents of title or a ship's papers.

CASE SUMMARY

But You Gave It to Me in Front of All Those People?

FACTS: On March 6, 1999, Colt Manufacturing Co., a handgun manufacturer, sponsored a farewell dinner for one of its officers, Marc Fontane. At the dinner, two Colt officials presented Fontane with a single-action, .45-caliber Colt revolver. After the presentation, an agent of Colt's took possession of the revolver for the purpose of improving it by installing ivory grips and adding engraving. Fontane inquired over a period of months as to when he would receive the revolver and was ultimately told "the gun has been sold and there will be no replacement." Fontane sued Colt for the conversion of the gift, with the promised improvements.

DECISION: Judgment for Fontane. When actual delivery has not occurred, the resolution of whether the donor has made a constructive or symbolic delivery depends on the circumstances of each case. The donor must do that which under the circumstances will in reason be equivalent to actual delivery. The public presentation of the revolver to the departing employee at his retirement dinner constituted a constructive form of delivery. Thus, Fontane is entitled to the value of the revolver with improvements. [**Fontane v Colt Manufacturing Co., 814 A2d 433 (Conn App 2003)**]

Failure to meet the "delivery" requirement will result in an ineffective gift. **For Example,** Walter Brownlee signed a bill of sale and attached a list of valuable construction equipment to it and left it with his attorney with instructions that it be passed to his son Randy after Walter's death. By leaving the bill of sale with his attorney, Walter retained control over the property, and therefore it was never effectively delivered to Randy, resulting in an ineffective gift.[6]

CPA   **(3) Donor's Death**

If the donor dies before doing what is needed to make an effective gift, the gift fails.[7] An agent or the executor or administrator of the estate cannot thereafter perform the missing step on behalf of the decedent.

For Example, Mary Manning, who was in poor health, wanted to give her college-age granddaughter, Phyllis, her antique 1966 Ford Mustang convertible. She sent her daughter, Nel, to obtain the car's title from a file in the basement but was too tired to sign it on Nel's return. Mary passed away the next day without signing the document. Nel, the executrix under Mary's will, cannot complete the delivery of the gift by signing the title because it is beyond the authority of an executrix. Even though donative intent existed, no evidence of transfer of ownership and delivery to Phyllis occurred prior to Mary's death. Therefore, no valid gift was made.

---

[6] *In re Estate of Walter Brownlee, Sr.*, 654 NW2d (SD 2002).
[7] *Laverman v Destocki*, 622 NE2d 1122 (Ohio App 1994).

gift causa mortis–gift, made by the donor in the belief that death was immediate and impending, that is revoked or is revocable under certain circumstances.

(B) GIFTS CAUSA MORTIS. A **gift causa mortis** is made when the donor, contemplating imminent and impending death, delivers personal property to the donee with the intent that the donee shall own it if the donor dies. This is a conditional gift, and the donor is entitled to take the property back if (1) the donor does not die, (2) the donor revokes the gift before dying, or (3) the donee dies before the donor.

(C) GIFTS AND TRANSFERS TO MINORS. Uniform acts provide for transferring property to a custodian to hold for the benefit of a minor.[8] When a custodian holds property for the benefit of a minor under one of the uniform acts, the custodian has discretionary power to use the property "for the support, maintenance, education, and benefit" of the minor, but the custodian may not use the custodial property for the custodian's own personal benefit. The gift is final and irrevocable for tax and all other purposes on complying with the procedures of the acts.

Under the uniform acts, custodianships terminate and the property is distributed when the minor reaches age 21.

CASE SUMMARY

Ignorance Is No Defense

FACTS: In 1980, Larry Heath received $10,000 from his father. With interest, these funds grew to $13,381 by 1983, and in March he used this money to establish two custodian bank accounts for his minor children under the Uniform Gifts to Minors Act (UGMA). Larry was listed as custodian on each account. In August 1984, Larry closed both accounts and returned the proceeds to his mother while his father was then in Europe. The children's mother, Pamela, brought suit to recover the funds on behalf of the children, contending that the deposits were irrevocable gifts. Larry contended that the money was his father's and was never intended as a gift. Larry testified that he was a mere factory worker and was ignorant of the legal effect of his signing the signature cards for the custodian accounts.

DECISION: Judgment for Pamela on behalf of the children. To find that an inter vivos gift has been made, there must be donative intent and delivery. The UGMA expressly deals with "delivery" and provides that this element of a gift is satisfied by documentary compliance with the procedures of the statute. The issue of "donative intent" is not conclusively resolved by making a determination that there was documentary compliance with the statute. However, documentary compliance with the procedures set forth by the UGMA is highly probative on the issue of intent. Larry's testimony that he was ignorant of the legal effect of his signing the signature cards was unworthy of belief and insufficient to rebut the strong documentary showing that he had created irrevocable gifts. [**Heath v Heath, 493 NE2d 97 (Ill App 1986)**]*

---

* See *Wasniewski v Quick and Reilly, Inc.*, 940 A2d 811 (Conn App 2008) where a minor's father opened a brokerage account on November 15, 1989, at Quick and Reilly in his minor son James's name funded with $30,000 in bonds. The account was closed on July 5,2001, and all funds were transferred to a joint account in the name of the father and another son. The court determined that a contract had existed between James, the owner of the account, and the brokerage firm, and that the brokerage firm had breached its contract with James when it transferred funds to someone other than James. James was awarded principal and interest of $52,085 from Quick and Reilly.

---

[8] The Uniform Gifts to Minors Act (UGMA) is in effect in South Carolina and Vermont.
The Uniform Transfers to Minors Act, which expands the type of property that can be made the subject of a gift, was originally proposed in 1983. It has been adopted, often with minor variations, in all states and the District of Columbia except South Carolina and Vermont.

(D) **CONDITIONAL GIFTS.** A gift may be made subject to a condition, such as "This car is yours when you graduate" or "This car is yours unless you drop out of school." In the first example, the gift is subject to a condition precedent—graduation. A condition precedent must be satisfied before any gift or transfer takes place. In the second example, the gift is subject to a condition subsequent—dropping out of school.

Absent a finding of an intent to create a trust, a donative transaction will be analyzed as a gift subject to conditions. **For Example,** the gift by the Tennessee United Daughters of the Confederacy (UDC) to a building fund for Peabody College expressly reserved the right to recall the gift if the college failed to comply with the conditions of placing an inscription on the 1935 building naming it Confederate Memorial Hall. Peabody College for Teachers was merged into Vanderbilt University in 1979. In 2002, Vanderbilt decided to rename Confederate Memorial Hall. The Tennessee UDC's suit for the return of its gift was successful; the court decided it was not at liberty to relieve a party from its contractual obligations.[9]

Most courts regard an engagement ring as a conditional gift subject to the condition subsequent of a failure to marry. The inherent symbolism of the gift itself is deemed to foreclose the need to establish an express condition that there be a marriage.

Some jurisdictions require return of engagement rings only if the donor has not unjustifiably broken off the engagement. Most states now reject considerations of "fault" in the breaking of an engagement and always require the return of the ring to the donor when an engagement is broken. This "modern trend" is based on the theory that, in most cases, "fault" is impossible to determine.

CASE SUMMARY

Your Honor, Marriages Are Not Made in Heaven, You Say?

FACTS: Dr. Barry Meyer and Robyn Mitnick became engaged on August 9, 1996, at which time Barry gave Robyn a custom-designed engagement ring that he purchased for $19,500. On November 8, 1996, Barry asked Robyn to sign a prenuptial agreement and Robyn refused. The engagement was broken during that meeting, with both Barry and Robyn contending the other party caused the breakup. Robyn did not return the ring, and Barry sued for its return. Robyn filed a countercomplaint, alleging that the ring was an unconditional gift and that because Barry broke the engagement, she was entitled to keep the ring.

DECISION: Judgment for Barry Meyer. Following the "modern trend," the court decided that an engagement ring given in contemplation of marriage is an impliedly conditional gift that is completed only upon marriage. If the engagement is called off, regardless of fault, the gift is not complete and must be returned to the donor. The court rejected the "older view" of returning the gift to the donor only when the engagement is unjustifiably broken off by the donee, or by mutual agreement. As stated by the court in *Aronow v Silver*, 223 NJ Super 344 (1987):

What fact justifies the breaking of an engagement? The absence of a sense of humor? Differing musical tastes? Differing political views? The painfully-learned fact is that marriages are made on earth, not in heaven. They must be approached with intelligent

[9] *Tennessee UDC v Vanderbilt University,* 174 SW3d 98 (Tenn Ct App 2005).

C A S E   S U M M A R Y

Continued

care and should not happen without a decent assurance of success. When either party lacks that assurance, for whatever reason, the engagement should be broken. No justification is needed. Either party may act. Fault, impossible to fix, does not count. [**Meyer v Mitnick, 625 NW2d 136 (Mich App 2001)**]*

---

* Texas courts apply the fault-based conditional gift rule when a donee breaks the engagement. When the giver of the ring violates his promise to marry, it would seem to Texas courts that a similar result should follow; that is, he should lose, not gain, rights to the ring. [See *Curtis v Anderson*, 2003 WL 1832257 (Tex App)]

(E) **ANATOMICAL GIFTS.** Persons may make gifts of parts of their bodies, as in the case of kidney transplants. Persons may also make postdeath gifts. The Uniform Anatomical Gift Act[10] permits persons 18 years or older to make gifts of their bodies or any parts thereof. The gift takes effect on the death of the donor. The gift may be made to a school, a hospital, an organ bank, or a named patient. Such a gift may also be made, subject to certain restrictions, by the spouse, adult child, parent, adult brother or sister, or guardian of a deceased person. If a hospital misleads family members into consenting to tissue or organ donations that exceed their express wishes, such misconduct is sufficiently outrageous to support a claim for intentional infliction of emotional distress.[11]

CPA ## 4. Finding of Lost Property

Personal property is lost when the owner does not know where it is located but intends to retain title to or ownership of it. The person finding lost property does not acquire title but only possession. Ordinarily, the finder of lost property is required to surrender the property to the true owner when the latter establishes ownership. Meanwhile, the finder is entitled to retain possession as against everyone else.

Without a contract with the owner or a statute so providing, the finder of lost property usually is not entitled to a reward or to compensation for finding or caring for the property.

(A) **FINDING IN PUBLIC PLACE.** If the lost property is found in a public place, such as a hotel, under such circumstances that to a reasonable person it would appear the property had been intentionally placed there by the owner and the owner would be likely to recall where the property had been left and to return for it, the finder is not entitled to possession of the property. The finder must give it to the proprietor or manager of the public place to keep it for the owner. This exception does not apply if it appears that the property was not intentionally placed where it was found. In that case, it is not likely that the owner will recall having left it there.

---

[10] This act has been adopted in every state.
[11] See *Perry v Saint Francis Hospital*, 886 F Supp 1551 (D Kan 1995).

(B) STATUTORY CHANGE. Some states have adopted statutes permitting the finder to sell the property or keep it if the owner does not appear within a stated period of time. In this case, the finder is required to give notice—for example, by newspaper publication—to attempt to reach the owner.

5. Occupation of Personal Property

In some cases, title to personal property may be acquired by occupation—that is, by taking and retaining possession of the property.

(A) WILD ANIMALS. Wild animals, living in a state of nature, are not owned by any individual. In the absence of restrictions imposed by game laws, the person who acquires dominion or control over a wild animal becomes its owner. What constitutes sufficient dominion or control varies with the nature of the animal and the surrounding circumstances. If the animal is killed, tied, imprisoned, or otherwise prevented from going at its will, the hunter exercises sufficient dominion or control over the animal and becomes its owner. If the wild animal, subsequent to its capture, should escape and return to its natural state, it resumes the status of a wild animal.

As a qualification to the ordinary rule, the following exception developed. If an animal is killed or captured on the land of another while the hunter is on the land without permission of the landowner, the animal, when killed or captured, belongs not to the hunter but to the landowner.

(B) ABANDONED PERSONAL PROPERTY. Personal property is deemed abandoned when the owner relinquishes possession with the intention to disclaim title to it. Yesterday's newspaper thrown out in the trash is abandoned personal property. Title to abandoned property may be acquired by the first person who obtains possession and control of it. A person becomes the owner at the moment of taking possession of the abandoned personal property. If, however, the owner of property flees in the face of an approaching peril, property left behind is not abandoned. An abandonment occurs only when the owner voluntarily leaves the property.

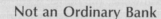

CASE SUMMARY

Not an Ordinary Bank

FACTS: Charles and Rosa Nelson owned a home in Selma, Iowa, for over one-half a century. After their death, the property was abandoned because of the substantial unpaid real estate taxes. The Selma United Methodist Church purchased the property at a tax sale. When the church razed the dwelling, it found $24,547 in cash and coins that had been buried in the ground in glass jars by Charles many years before. The heirs of the Nelson family claimed the money. The church claimed that because the real estate was abandoned by the estate, the church was now the true owner of the money.

DECISION: Judgment for the heirs. Although the real estate was abandoned, the money found by the church had not been abandoned by its owner, Charles Nelson. The fact that it was buried in glass jars indicates that the owner was trying to preserve it. Therefore, the money had not been abandoned and was owned by Nelson's heirs. [**Ritz v Selma United Methodist Church, 467 NW2d 266 (Iowa 1991)**]

(c) **CONVERSION.** The tort of conversion has its origins in the ancient common law writ of trover, created "as a remedy against the finder of lost goods who refused to return them."[12] Because of that origin, the tort of conversion was limited to property that could be lost and found (i.e., tangible personalty as opposed to real property).

CASE SUMMARY

Hey! That's My Stuff on the North Star Web Site!

FACTS: In 2003 Paul and Arthur Williams moved personal property from the Skinner Gallery to Smith Storage, which was operated by the Faeber family. After the death of a Faeber parent in March 2006, Smith Storage customers were notified that the business was being discontinued. Gary and Robert Faeber, sons who were not active in the business, removed property from Smith Storage in March 2006 and consigned it to North Star Auction Galleries, Inc. When Arthur Williams became aware that some of his property was listed on North Star's Web site, the Williamses sued Gary and Robert for conversion. Gary contended that he was not liable for conversion because he in good faith believed that the property consigned and sold on North Star belonged to his mother. He and Robert also asserted that the Williamses did not provide sufficient proof that the stored property belonged to them.

DECISION: Judgment for Paul and Arthur Williams. They presented documentation of their ownership interest. While the defendants assert that the property belonged to their mother, they presented no admissible evidence to support this assertion. Gary Faeber's argument that the consignment was done in "good faith" based on the belief that the property belonged to his mother is of no merit, for good faith is not a defense to conversion. The defendant's assertion that the plaintiffs did not provide sufficient evidence of ownership is irrelevant. A bailee cannot deny a bailor's title as an excuse for refusing to redeliver the property. [**Williams v Smith Avenue Moving Co., 528 F Supp 2d 316 (NDNY 2008)**]

As the nature of personal property evolved to the point that tangible documents represented highly valuable rights, such as promissory notes, stock certificates, insurance policies, and bank books, common law courts expanded the tort of conversion to include such documents within its definitional scope despite their intangible aspects, which, invariably, are primary components of the document's value. The concept of conversion today, which is the wrongful exclusionary retention of an owner's physical property, applies to an electronic record as much as it does to a paper record such as valuable stock certificates and bank books. **For Example,** a computerized client /investor list created by a real estate agent is "property" protected by the law of conversion.[13]

6. Escheat

Who owns unclaimed property? In the case of personal property, the practical answer is that the property will probably "disappear" after a period of time, or if in the possession of a carrier, hotel, or warehouse, it may be sold for unpaid storage charges. A growing problem arises with respect to unclaimed corporate dividends, bank deposits, insurance payments, and refunds. Most states have a statute

---

[12] Restatement, Second of Torts § 242, comment d.
[13] *Shmueli v Corcoran Group*, 802 NYS2d 871 (2005).

escheat–transfer to the state of the title to a decedent's property when the owner of the property dies intestate and is not survived by anyone capable of taking the property as heir.

providing for the transfer of such unclaimed property to the state government. This transfer to the government is often called by its feudal name of **escheat**.

For Example, when James Canel's 280 shares of stock in Patrick Industries were turned over to the state treasurer's office by Harris Bank because his account at the bank had been inactive for more than five years, the property was presumed to be abandoned. Once Canel claimed the property, however, he was entitled to the return of the stock and the past dividends. The state was not entitled to retain the dividends under the court's reading of the state's Unclaimed Property Act.[14] Funds held by stores for layaway items for customers who fail to complete the layaway purchases are subject to escheat to the state. To provide for unclaimed property, many states have adopted the Uniform Unclaimed Property Act (UUPA),[15] formerly called the Uniform Disposition of Unclaimed Property Act.

CASE SUMMARY

The King Is Dead! Who Gets the Unrefunded Ticket Proceeds?

FACTS: Elvis Presley contracted with the Mid-South Coliseum Board (City of Memphis) for the rental of the Coliseum and for personnel to sell tickets for concerts on August 27 and 28, 1977. Subsequently, $325,000 worth of tickets were sold. On August 16, 1977, Elvis Presley died. Refunds were given to those who returned their tickets to the coliseum board. Ten years after his death, however, $152,279 worth of ticket proceeds remained unclaimed in the custody of the board. This fund had earned $223,760 in interest. Priscilla Presley and the coexecutors of the estate of Elvis Presley brought an action claiming the unrefunded ticket proceeds for the canceled concerts. The state of Tennessee claimed that it was entitled to the proceeds under the Uniform Disposition of Unclaimed Property Act (UDUPA).

DECISION: Judgment for the state. Elvis Presley's estate has no legal claim to the ticket proceeds because his death discharged the contract represented by each ticket sold. Ticket holders would have claimed the refunds if it had not been for Presley's legendary status, and they chose to keep the tickets as memorabilia. The drafters of the UDUPA intended that windfalls such as the unrefunded proceeds in this case benefit the public rather than individuals. [**Presley v City of Memphis, 769 SW2d 221 (Tenn App 1988)**]

7. Multiple Ownership of Personal Property

severalty–ownership of property by one person.

cotenancy–when two or more persons hold concurrent rights and interests in the same property.

tenancy in common–relationship that exists when two or more persons own undivided interests in property.

When all rights in a particular object of property are held by one person, that property is held in **severalty**. However, two or more persons may hold concurrent rights and interests in the same property. In that case, the property is said to be held in **cotenancy**. The various forms of cotenancy include (1) tenancy in common, (2) joint tenancy, (3) tenancy by entirety, and (4) community property.

(A) TENANCY IN COMMON. A **tenancy in common** is a form of ownership by two or more persons. The interest of a tenant in common may be transferred or inherited,

[14] *Canel v Topinka*, 818 NE2d 311 (Ill 2004).

[15] The 1981 or 1995 version of the Act has been adopted in Alaska, Arizona, Arkansas, Colorado, Florida, Hawaii, Idaho, Illinois, Indiana, Kansas, Louisiana, Maine, Michigan, Montana, Nevada, New Hampshire, New Jersey, New Mexico, North Carolina, North Dakota, Oklahoma, Oregon, Rhode Island, South Carolina, South Dakota, U.S. Virgin Islands, Utah, Virginia, Washington, West Virginia, Wisconsin, and Wyoming.

in which case the taker becomes a tenant in common with the others. **For Example,** Brandt and Vincent restored an 18-foot 1940 mahogany-hulled Chris Craft runabout and own it as tenants in common. If Brandt sold his interest in the boat to Andrea, then Vincent and Andrea would be co-owners as tenants in common. If Brandt died before Vincent, a one-half interest in the boat would become the property of Brandt's heirs.

CPA

joint tenancy—estate held jointly by two or more with the right of survivorship as between them, unless modified by statute.

(B) Joint Tenancy. A **joint tenancy** is another form of ownership by two or more persons, but a joint tenancy has a *right of survivorship.*[16] On the death of a joint tenant, the remaining tenants take the share of the deceased tenant. The last surviving joint tenant takes the property as a holder in severalty. **For Example,** in Brandt and Vincent's Chris Craft case, if the boat were owned as joint tenants with a right of survivorship, Vincent would own the boat outright upon Brandt's death, and Brandt's heirs would obtain no interest in it.

A joint tenant's interest may be transferred to a third person, but this destroys the joint tenancy. If the interest of one of two joint tenants is transferred to a third person, the remaining joint tenant becomes a tenant in common with the third person. **For Example,** if Brandt sold his interest to Andrea, Vincent and Andrea would be co-owners as tenants in common.

Statutes in many states have modified the common law by adding a formal requirement to the creation of a joint tenancy with survivorship. At common law, such an estate would be created by a transfer of property to "*A* and *B* as joint tenants."[17] Under these statutes, however, it is necessary to add the words "with right of survivorship" or other similar words if a right of survivorship is desired.

C A S E   S U M M A R Y

Honor Thy Mother's Wishes?

FACTS: Rachel Auffert purchased a $10,000 certificate of deposit on January 7, 1981, creating a joint tenancy in this bank deposit payable to herself or either of two children, Leo or Mary Ellen, "either or the survivor." When Rachel died, a note dated January 7, 1981, written in Rachel's handwriting and signed by her, was found with the certificate of deposit. The note stated:

Leo: If I die this goes to Sr. Mary Ellen,
Wanted another name on it.
S/Rachel Auffert
Jan 7 1981

Mary Ellen cashed the certificate of deposit and retained the proceeds. Leo sued to recover one-half the value of the certificate.

[16] *Estate of Munier v Jacquemin*, 899 SW2d 114 (Mo App 1995).
[17] Some states have modified the common law by creating a condition that whenever two or more persons are listed as owners of a bank account or certificate of deposit, a presumption of joint tenancy with right of survivorship arises unless expressly negated by the signature card or another instrument or by extrinsic proof. Thus, when Herbert H. Herring had his bank change the designated owners of a certificate of deposit to read, "Herbert H. Herring or [his grandson] Robert J. Herring," and no words indicating survivorship upon the death of either were on the certificate, nevertheless under a 1992 Florida statute creating a presumption of survivorship, which presumption was not rebutted, grandson Robert was declared the owner of the certificate. *In re Estate of H. H. Herring*, 670 So2d 145 (Fla App 1996).

C A S E   S U M M A R Y

Continued

DECISION: Judgment for Leo. There was statutory compliance when the certificate of deposit was purchased, and thus a statutory joint tenancy was created. The only means available to Rachel to alter the joint tenants' proportionate interests was to change the names on the account during her lifetime. Because Rachel failed to do so, the law presumes that Leo and Mary Ellen equally owned the certificate of deposit. [**Auffert v Auffert, 829 SW2d 95 (Mo App 1992)**]

If no words of survivorship are used, the transfer of property to two or more persons will be construed as creating a tenancy in common. Under such a statute, a certificate of deposit issued only in the name of "*A* or *B*" does not create a joint tenancy because it does not contain words of survivorship.

tenancy by entirety or **tenancy by the entireties**– transfer of property to both husband and wife.

(C) TENANCY BY ENTIRETY. At common law, a **tenancy by entirety** or **tenancy by the entireties** was created when property was transferred to both husband and wife. It differs from joint tenancy in that it exists only when the transfer is to husband and wife. Also, the right of survivorship cannot be extinguished, and one spouse's interest cannot be transferred to a third person. However, in some jurisdictions, a spouse's right to share the possession and the profits may be transferred. This form of property holding is popular in common law jurisdictions because creditors of only one of the spouses cannot reach the property while both are living. Only a creditor of both the husband and the wife under the same obligation can obtain execution against the property.

For Example, a husband and wife, Rui and Carla Canseco, purchased a 2007 Lexus LS 430 for cash. It was titled in the names of "Rui J. *and* Carla T. Canseco." Later that year, State National Bank obtained a money judgment against Rui for $200,000, and the bank claimed entitlement to half the value of the Cansecos' car, which it asserted was Rui's share as a joint tenant. A tenancy by entirety had been created, however, so the bank could not levy against the auto. If the car had been titled "Rui *or* Carla T. Canseco," in most states the use of the word "or" would indicate that the vehicle was held in joint tenancy even if the co-owners are husband and wife. As such, Rui's half interest could be reached by the bank.

The tenancy by entirety is, in effect, a substitute for a will because the surviving spouse acquires the complete property interest on the death of the other. There are usually other reasons, however, why each spouse should make a will.

In many states, the granting of an absolute divorce converts a tenancy by the entireties into a tenancy in common.

8. Community Property

community property– cotenancy held by husband and wife in property acquired during their marriage under the law of some of the states, principally in the southwestern United States.

In some states, property acquired during the period of marriage is the **community property** of the husband and wife. Some statutes provide for the right of survivorship; others provide that half of the property of the deceased husband or wife shall go to the heirs of that spouse or permit such half to be disposed of by will. It is commonly provided that property acquired by either spouse during the

prima facie—evidence that, if believed, is sufficient by itself to lead to a particular conclusion.

marriage is **prima facie** community property, even though title is taken in the spouse's individual name, unless it can be shown that it was obtained with property possessed by the spouse prior to the marriage.

B. Bailments

9. Definition

bailment—relationship that exists when personal property is delivered into the possession of another under an agreement, express or implied, that the identical property will be returned or will be delivered in accordance with the agreement. (Parties—bailor, bailee)

bailor—person who turns over the possession of a property.

bailee—person who accepts possession of a property.

A **bailment** is the relationship that arises when one person delivers possession of personal property to another under an agreement, express or implied, by which the latter is under a duty to return the property or to deliver it or dispose of it as agreed. The person who turns over the possession of the property is the **bailor**. The person who accepts is the **bailee**. **For Example,** Arthur Grace, a world renowned photojournalist, had an agreement with Sygma-Paris and Sygma-New York whereby Grace turned over his photographs to Sygma, and Sygma agreed to act as Grace's agent to license the images and administer the fee-setting process and delivery and return of the images. The *bailor*, Grace, terminated its agreement with the *bailee*, Sygma, in 2001, and the *bailee* was unable to return all of the photographs to Grace as obligated under the agreement. Sygma's system of keeping track of images was "completely inadequate"; hence, it was liable for $472,000 in damages to the *bailor* for the failure to return some 40,000 images.[18]

10. Elements of Bailment

A bailment is created when the following elements are present.

(A) AGREEMENT. The bailment is based on an *agreement*. This agreement may be express or implied. Generally, it contains all of the elements of a contract. The bailment transaction in fact consists of (1) a contract to bail and (2) the actual bailing of the property. Ordinarily, there is no requirement that the contract of

FIGURE 21-2 | **Bailment of Personal Property**

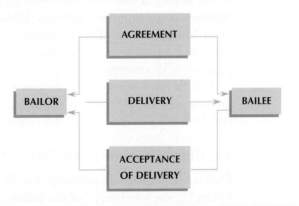

---

[18] *Grace v Corbis Sygma*, 403 F Supp 2d 337 (SDNY 2005).

bailment be in writing. The subject of a bailment may be any personal property of which possession may be given.[19] Real property cannot be bailed.

(B) DELIVERY AND ACCEPTANCE. The bailment arises when, pursuant to the agreement of the parties, the property is delivered to the bailee and accepted by the bailee as subject to the bailment agreement.

In the absence of a prior agreement to the contrary, a valid delivery and acceptance generally require that the bailee be aware that goods have been placed within the bailee's exclusive possession or control. **For Example,** photography equipment belonging to Bill Bergey, the photographer of Roosevelt University's student newspaper, was stolen from the newspaper's campus office. Bergey believes that the university breached its duty as bailee because records showed that no campus police officer checked the building on the night of the theft. Bergey's case against the university on this bailment theory will fail, however, because the university did not know the equipment was left in the office. Without this knowledge, there was neither a bailment agreement nor acceptance of delivery by the university as a bailee.

11. Nature of the Parties' Interests

The bailor and bailee have different legal interests in the bailed property.

(A) BAILOR'S INTEREST. The bailor is usually the owner, but ownership by the bailor is not required. It is sufficient that the bailor have physical possession. **For Example,** Crella Magee delivered a blue fox jacket for summer storage to Walbro, Inc. When it was not returned, she sued Walbro for the replacement cost of the jacket, $3,400. Walbro's defense that Magee was not entitled to recover the replacement cost of the lost jacket because she did not prove ownership was rejected as irrelevant by the court, and the case was decided in favor of Magee.[20]

(B) BAILEE'S INTEREST. The bailee has possession of the property only. **For Example,** the Lackawanna Chapter for the Railway & Locomotive Historical Society, Inc. and its predecessor held title to Engine No. 952, a now-rare camelback locomotive built in 1905 and retired in 1938. It was placed in the care of the St. Louis Transportation Museum in 1953 for "permanent exhibition." The Lackawanna Chapter sought the return of Engine No. 952 after more than 50 years, and the successor St. Louis Museum raised numerous defenses. Possession and control do not entitle the St. Louis Museum to continued possession that overcomes a lender's good title. The museum, as a bailee in a gratuitous bailment, has the duty to return the bailment property to the owner.[21]

Title to the property does not pass to the bailee, and the bailee cannot sell the property to a third person. If the bailee attempts to sell the property, such sale transfers only possession, and the owner may recover the property from the buyer.

12. Classification of Ordinary Bailments

Ordinary bailments are generally classified as being for (1) the sole benefit of the bailor, (2) the sole benefit of the bailee, or (3) the mutual benefit of both.

---

[19] *Stone v CDI Corp.,* 9 SW3d 699 (Mo App 1999).
[20] *Magee v Walbro, Inc.,* 525 NE2d 975 (Ill App 1988).
[21] *Lackawanna Chapter v St. Louis County,* 497 F3d 832 (8th Cir 2007).

bailment for mutual benefit–bailment in which the bailor and bailee derive a benefit from the bailment.

gratuitous bailment–bailment in which the bailee does not receive any compensation or advantage.

constructive bailment–bailment imposed by law as opposed to one created by contract, whereby the bailee must preserve the property and redeliver it to the owner.

Bailments may or may not provide for compensation to the bailee. On the basis of compensation, bailments may be classified as (1) **bailments for mutual benefit** in which one party takes the personal property of another into her care or custody in exchange for payment or other benefit and (2) **gratuitous bailments** in which the transfer of possession and use of the bailed property is without compensation. Bailments for the sole benefit of the bailor or for the sole benefit of the bailee are sometimes described as gratuitous. The fact that no charge is made by the bailor does not necessarily make the transaction a gratuitous bailment. If the bailment is made to further a business interest of the bailor, as when something is loaned free to a customer, the bailment is not gratuitous.

A **constructive bailment** arises when one person has lawfully acquired possession of another's personal property other than by virtue of a bailment contract and holds it under such circumstances that the law imposes on the recipient of the property the obligation to keep it safely and redeliver it to the owner. **For Example,** the City of Chicago is the constructive bailee of an automobile impounded by Chicago police at the time of a driver's arrest for drunk driving. It has a duty to keep the automobile safely and turn it over to the owner upon payment of towing and storage fees. When this duty is delegated to a private contractor to tow and store, a constructive bailment for the mutual benefit of the contractor and the owner exists.

13. Renting of Space Distinguished

When a person rents space in a locker or building under an agreement that gives the renter the exclusive right to use that space, the placing of goods by the renter in that space does not create a bailment, for it does not constitute a delivery of goods into the possession of the owner of the space. **For Example,** Winston Hutton entered into a rental agreement for a storage space at Public Storage Management's self-storage facility in New York City, and his stored property was stolen from the space. Hutton had procured his own lock for the storage space, and the rental agreement provided that management would not have a key. Hutton's lawsuit was unsuccessful because the defendant did not take possession of the property. The legal relationship was not a bailment.[22]

14. Duties and Rights of the Bailee

The bailee has certain duties concerning performance, care, and return of the bailed property. The bailee must perform his part of a contract and is liable for ordinary contract damages for failure to perform the contract.

The bailee is under a duty to care for the bailed property, and the duty of care owed differs according to classification, based in terms of "benefit." A bailment may be for the sole benefit of the bailor. **For Example,** when Fred allows Mary, a college classmate from out of state, to store her books and furniture in his basement over the summer, Fred, the bailee, is liable only for gross negligence relating to damage to these stored belongings. A bailment may be for the sole benefit of the bailee, as when Mary allows Fred to borrow her Les Paul Gibson guitar. Fred, the bailee, is liable even for slight negligence in the case of any damage to the guitar. Most bailments, however,

---

[22] *Hutton v Public Storage Management, Inc.,* 676 NYS2d 887 (NY City Civ Ct 1998).

are mutual benefit bailments. **For Example,** when Harry rents for a fee a trailer from U-Haul, Inc., to transport his son's belongings to college, Harry, the bailee, is responsible for using reasonable or ordinary care under the circumstances while possessing and using the trailer. U-Haul, the bailor, has a duty to warn Harry of any known defects or defects that could be discovered on reasonable inspection.

A bailee has a right to receive payment for charges due for storage or repairs. A **bailee's lien** gives the bailee the right to keep possession of the bailed property until charges are paid. A bailee who is authorized by statute to sell the bailed property to enforce a charge or claim against the bailor must give such notice as is required by the statute. A bailee who sells without giving the required notice is liable for conversion of the property.

bailee's lien–specific, possessory lien of the bailee upon the goods for work done to them. Commonly extended by statute to any bailee's claim for compensation, eliminating the necessity of retention of possession.

15. Breach of Duty of Care: Burden of Proof

Although a bailment is contractual in nature, an action for breach of duty of care by a bailee "sounds in tort." That is, the true nature of the liability is not contractual at all but based on tort principles.

When the bailor sues the bailee for damages to the bailed property, the bailor has the burden of proving that the bailee was at fault and that such fault was the proximate cause of the loss.[23] A prima facie right of the bailor to recover is established, however, by proof that the bailor delivered the property to the bailee in good condition and subsequently could not be returned by the bailee or was returned in a damaged condition. When this is done, the bailee has the burden of proving that the loss or damage was not caused by the bailee's failure to exercise the care required by law, which in the case of a mutual benefit bailment is that of an ordinary or due care, under all of the circumstances.

C A S E   S U M M A R Y

Towed into Court

FACTS: Mark Hadfield, a medical student in Charleston, South Carolina, went to retrieve his 1988 Lincoln Continental from a parking space on private property near the medical school where his wife had parked the car earlier that day without permission. The property owner had called Gilchrist Towing Co., and the auto had been removed. When Hadfield discovered that the car had been towed, he telephoned Gilchrist Towing and was told that he would have to wait until the next morning to retrieve the car after paying towing and storage fees. The next morning, after paying the charges, he went to the storage lot and found that his car had been extensively vandalized along with a number of other vehicles. The owner of the company, S.S. Gilchrist, refused to pay the estimated cost of repairs, $4,021.43. Hadfield brought suit, contending that a constructive bailment for the mutual benefit of Hadfield and Gilchrist had been created, and that Gilchrist breached his duty of care to Hadfield. Gilchrist contended that he towed the vehicle pursuant to Charleston Municipal Ordinances, which are for the sole benefit of the vehicle owners, intended to preserve their property. As such, the relationship created was a gratuitous bailment, which limited his duty of care. Gilchrist contended he was not liable for damages caused by unknown vandals.

---

[23] *Fedrick v Nichols*, 2008 WL 4117208 (Tex App 2008).

C A S E   S U M M A R Y

Continued

DECISION: Judgment for Hadfield. Where a city ordinance is utilized as the legal justification for taking possession of a vehicle on private property, the person or entity lawfully acquiring possession of the property under the ordinance becomes a constructive bailee as a matter of law. A constructive bailment, for the mutual benefit of Hadfield and Gilchrist, was created. The burden of proof in a constructive bailment case rests upon a bailor to prove a prima facie case, and once so proven, the burden shifts to the bailee to show the use of ordinary care in the storage and safekeeping of the property. The fact that a guard was not on duty at the impound lot and the only other security for the vehicles was a chain-link fence, a reasonable basis existed to conclude that Gilchrist failed to exercise ordinary care. [**Hadfield v Gilchrist, 343 SC 88 (SC App 2000)**]

16. Liability for Defects in Bailed Property

In the case of a mutual benefit bailment, the bailor must not only inform the bailee of known defects but also make a reasonable investigation to discover defects. The bailor is liable for harm resulting from any such defects. If the bailment is for the sole benefit of the bailee, the bailor must inform the bailee of known defects.

In bailments for hire where the bailor is in the business of renting vehicles, machines, or equipment for use by bailees, such as Hertz or Avis car rental companies, Article 2A of the Uniform Commercial Code provides an implied warranty of merchantability and fitness for a particular purpose for the protection of bailee customers.[24]

17. Contract Modification of Liability

An ordinary bailee may limit liability (except for willful misconduct) by agreement or contract. If the bailee seeks to limit liability for its own negligence, the wording of the contract must clearly express this intention so that the other party will know what is being contracted away.[25] In some states, statutes prohibit certain kinds of paid bailees, such as automobile parking garages, from limiting their liability for negligence. Statutes in some states declare that a party cannot bar liability for negligent violations of common law standards of care where a public interest is involved. **For Example,** Bruce Gardner left his Porsche 911 automobile to be repaired at Downtown Porsche Auto, signing a repair order standardized adhesion contract that stated Downtown was "not responsible for loss of cars ... in case of ... theft." The car was stolen while in the garage for repairs due to Downtown's negligence. The California appeals court determined that because automobile repair contracts "affect the public interest," Downtown's exculpatory clause was invalid as to public policy.[26]

When a bailee attempts to limit liability by printing a limitation on a claim check, the limitation must be called to the attention of the bailor in some reasonable fashion, such as a sign at point of purchase, before it may become part of the bailment contract. **For Example,** a claim check for a coat that purports to limit liability is ineffective without a reasonably placed sign notifying customers of the limitation.

---

[24] UCC §§ 2A-212, 2A-213.
[25] *Hertz v Klein Mfg., Inc.,* 636 So2d 189 (Fla App 1994).
[26] *Gardner v Downtown Porsche Auto,* 225 Cal Rptr 757 (1986).

lawflix

The Goonies (1985)(PG)

This story is about children finding a lost treasure they wish to claim as theirs and use to stop the condemnation of their parents' properties by developers. The issue of who owns the treasure is a fascinating one for discussion.

For movie clips that illustrate business law concepts, see LawFlix at **www.cengage.com/blaw/dvl**.

MAKE THE CONNECTION

SUMMARY

Personal property consists of whole or fractional ownership rights in things that are tangible and movable, as well as rights in things that are intangible.

Personal property may be acquired by purchase. Personal property may also be acquired by gift when the donor has present intent to make a gift and delivers possession to the donee or makes a constructive delivery. Personal property may be acquired by occupation and under some statutes may be acquired by finding. The state may acquire property by escheat.

All rights in a particular object of property can be held by one individual, in which case it is said to be held *in severalty*. Ownership rights may be held concurrently by two or more individuals, in which case it is said to be held in cotenancy. The major forms of cotenancy are (1) tenancy in common, (2) joint tenancy, (3) tenancy by entirety, and (4) community property.

A bailment is the relationship that exists when tangible personal property is delivered by the bailor into the possession of the bailee under an agreement, express or implied, that the identical property will be returned or delivered in accordance with the agreement. No title is transferred by a bailment. The bailee has the right of possession. When a person comes into the possession of the personal property of another without the owner's consent, the law classifies the relationship as a constructive bailment.

Bailments may be classified in terms of benefit—that is, for the (1) sole benefit of the bailor, (2) sole benefit of the bailee, or (3) benefit of both parties (mutual benefit bailment). Some courts state the standard of care required of a bailee in terms of the class of bailment. Thus, if the bailment is for the sole benefit of the bailor, the bailee is required to exercise only slight care and is liable for gross negligence only. When the bailment is for the sole benefit of the bailee, the bailee is liable for the slightest negligence. When the bailment is for the mutual benefit of the parties, as in a commercial bailment, the bailee is liable for ordinary negligence. An ordinary bailee may limit liability except for willful misconduct or where prohibited by law.

A bailee must perform the bailee's part of the contract. The bailee has a lien on the bailed property until they have paid for storage or repair charges.

In a mutual benefit bailment, the bailor is under a duty to furnish goods reasonably fit for the purposes contemplated by the parties. The bailor may be held liable for damages or injury caused by the defective condition of the bailed property.

LEARNING OUTCOMES

After studying this chapter, you should be able to clearly explain:

A. PERSONAL PROPERTY

LO.1 Explain how title to personal property is acquired

> See the discussion of the acquisition of property by gift, the finding of lost property, occupation, and escheat, p. 458.
>
> See the example of Steam Engine No. 952 where the museum had possession and control of the locomotive for over 50 years but could not overcome the lender's good title, p. 470.

LO.2 List and explain the various types of gifts

> See the discussion of inter vivos gifts, gifts causa mortis, gifts and transfers to minors, conditional gifts, and anatomical gifts, p. 459.

LO.3 Explain the legal theory whereby an owner can recover his or her property from the wrongful exclusionary retention of another

> See the example of the real estate agent who recovered her computerized client investment list from a former employer under the legal theory called "conversion," p. 465.

B. BAILMENTS

LO.4 Identify the elements necessary to create a bailment

> See the Roosevelt University example in which there could be no bailment created because there was no agreement or acceptance of delivery, p. 470.

LO.5 Explain the standard of care a bailee is required to exercise over bailed property

> See the examples of duties owed according to classifications based in terms of benefits, p. 471.

KEY TERMS

bailee	constructive delivery	joint tenancy
bailee's lien	cotenancy	personal property
bailment	donee	prima facie
bailments for mutual benefit	donor	real property
bailor	escheat	severalty
choses in action	gift	symbolic delivery
community property	gift causa mortis	tenancy by entirety
constructive bailment	gratuitous bailments	tenancy by the entireties
	inter vivos gift	tenancy in common

QUESTIONS AND CASE PROBLEMS

1. Can a creditor of both the husband and wife under the same obligation obtain an execution against a Winnebago mobile home owned by the husband and wife in tenancy by entirety?

2. Joe obtained a box of antique Lenox china dishes that had been left at the Mashpee town dump. He supplemented the sizable but incomplete set of dishes with other Lenox pieces found at antique dealers. At dinner parties, he proudly told of the origin of his china. When Marlene discovered that Joe had taken her dishes from the dump, she hired an attorney to obtain their return. What result?

3. Joyce Clifford gave a check for $5,000 to her nephew Carl to help with living expenses for his last year of college. The face of the check stated, "As a loan." Years later, Carl wrote to his aunt asking what he should do about the loan. She responded on her Christmas card simply, "On money—keep it—no return." After Joyce's death, her administrator sued Carl after discovering the "As a loan" canceled check. Decide.

4. Ruth and Stella were sisters. They owned a house as joint tenants with right of survivorship. Ruth sold her half interest to Roy. Thereafter, Stella died, and Roy claimed the entire property by survivorship. Was he entitled to it?

5. Mona found a wallet on the floor of an elevator in the office building where she worked. She posted several notices in the building about finding the wallet, but no one appeared to claim it. She waited for six months and then spent the money in the wallet in the belief that she owned it. Jason, the person who lost the wallet, subsequently brought suit to recover the money. Mona's defense was that the money was hers because Jason did not claim it within a reasonable time after she posted the notices. Is she correct? (Assume that the common law applies.)

6. In 1971, Harry Gordon turned over $40,000 to his son, Murray Gordon. Murray opened two $20,000 custodial bank accounts under the Uniform Gifts to Minors Act for his minor children, Eden and Alexander. Murray was listed as the custodian of both accounts. On January 9, 1976, both accounts were closed, and a single bank check representing the principal of the accounts was drawn to the order of Harry Gordon. In April 1976, Murray and his wife, Joan, entered into a separation agreement and were later divorced. Thereafter, Joan, on behalf of her children, Eden and Alexander, brought suit against Murray to recover the funds withdrawn in January 1976, contending that the deposits in both accounts were irrevocable gifts. Murray contended that the money was his father's and that it was never intended as a gift but was merely a means of avoiding taxes. Decide. [*Gordon v Gordon*, 419 NYS2d 684 (App Div)]

7. New York's banking law provides that a presumption arises that a joint tenancy has been created when a bank account is opened in the names of two persons "payable to either or the survivor." While he was still single, Richard Coddington opened a savings account with his mother, Amelia. The signature card they signed stated that the account was owned by them as joint tenants with the right of survivorship. No statement as to survivorship was made on the passbook. Richard later married Margaret. On Richard's death, Margaret claimed a share of the account on the ground that it was not held in joint

tenancy because the passbook did not contain words of survivorship and because the statutory presumption of a joint tenancy was overcome by the fact that Richard had withdrawn substantial sums from the account during his life. Decide. [*Coddington v Coddington*, 391 NYS2d 760 (Sup Ct App Div)]

8. Martin Acampora purchased a shotgun at a garage sale years ago, never used the weapon, and did not know of any defects in it. His 31-year-old son Marty borrowed the shotgun to go duck hunting. As Marty attempted to engage the safety mechanism, the shotgun fired. The force of the shotgun's firing caused it to fall to the ground and to discharge another shot, which struck Marty in the hand. Classify the bailment in this case. What duty of care was owed by the bailor in this case? Is Martin liable to his son for the injury?

9. Baena Brothers agreed to reupholster and reduce the size of the arms of Welge's sofa and chair. The work was not done according to the contract, and the furniture when finished had no value to Welge and was not accepted by him. Baena sued him for the contract price. Welge counterclaimed for the value of the furniture. Decide. [*Baena Brothers v Welge*, 3 Conn Cir 67, 207 A2d 749]

10. Schroeder parked his car in a parking lot operated by Allright, Inc. On the parking stub given him was printed in large, heavy type that the lot closed at 6:00 P.M. Under this information, printed in smaller, lighter type, was a provision limiting the liability of Allright for theft or loss. A large sign at the lot stated that after 6:00 P.M. patrons could obtain their car keys at another location. Schroeder's car was stolen from the lot sometime after the 6:00 P.M. closing, and he sued Allright for damages. Allright defended on the basis of the limitation-of-liability provision contained in the parking stub and the notice given Schroeder that the lot closed at 6:00 P.M. Decide. [*Allright, Inc. v Schroeder*, 551 SW2d 745 (Tex Civ App)]

11. John Hayes and Lynn Magosian, auditors for a public accounting firm, went to lunch at the Bay View Restaurant in San Francisco. John left his raincoat with a coatroom attendant, but Lynn took her new raincoat with her to the dining room, where she hung it on a coat hook near her booth. When leaving the restaurant, Lynn discovered that someone had taken her raincoat. When John sought to claim his raincoat at the coatroom, it could not be found. The attendant advised that it might have been taken while he was on his break. John and Lynn sued the restaurant, claiming that the restaurant was a bailee of the raincoats and had a duty to return them. Are both John and Lynn correct?

12. Rhodes parked his car in the self-service park-and-lock lot of Pioneer Parking Lot, Inc. The ticket that he received from the ticket meter stated the following: "NOTICE. THIS CONTRACT LIMITS OUR LIABILITY. READ IT. WE RENT SPACE ONLY. NO BAILMENT IS CREATED." Rhodes parked the car himself and kept the keys. There was no attendant at the lot. The car was stolen from the lot. Rhodes sued the parking lot on the theory that it had breached its duty as a bailee. Was there a bailment? [*Rhodes v Pioneer Parking Lot, Inc.*, 501 SW2d 569 (Tenn)]

13. Newman underwent physical therapy at Physical Therapy Associates of Rome, Inc. (PTAR), in Rome, Georgia, for injuries sustained in an auto accident. At a therapy session on February 6, it was necessary for Newman to take off two

necklaces. She placed one of the necklaces on a peg on the wall in the therapy room, and the therapist placed the other necklace on another peg. After the session, Newman forgot to retrieve her jewelry from the wall pegs. When she called the next day for the forgotten jewelry, it could not be found. She sued PTAR for the value of the jewelry on a bailment theory. PTAR raised the defense that there was no bailment because Newman retained the right to remove the jewelry from the wall pegs. Decide. [*Newman v Physical Therapy Associates of Rome, Inc.*, 375 SE2d 253 (Ga App)]

14. Contract Packers rented a truck from Hertz Truck Leasing. The brakes of the truck did not function properly. This resulted in injuring Packers' employee Cintrone while he was riding in the truck as it was driven by his helper. Cintrone sued Hertz for breach of the implied warranty that the truck was fit for normal use on public highways. Hertz contended that implied warranties apply only to sales, not to bailments for hire. Decide. [*Cintrone v Hertz Truck Leasing & Rental Service*, 212 A2d 769 (NJ)]

15. Charter Apparel, Inc., supplied fabric to Marco Apparel, Inc., in December to manufacture finished articles of clothing at its Walnut Grove, Mississippi, facilities. The fabric arrived just before the Christmas holiday shutdown and was stacked on cutting tables in the old building, which was known to have a roof that leaked. The evidence showed that no precautions were taken to cover the fabric and no guard was posted at the plant during the shutdown. Severe weather and freezing rain occurred during the shutdown, and it was discovered that the rain had leaked through the roof and destroyed more than $400,000 worth of the fabric. Marco denied that it was negligent and argued that it exercised ordinary care. It offered no evidence to rebut Charter's prima facie case or to rebut Charter's evidence of negligence. It asserted, however, that as a bailee it was not an insurer of goods against severe weather conditions. Decide. [*California Union Ins. v City of Walnut Grove*, 857 F Supp 515 (SD Miss)]

CPA QUESTIONS

The topic of insurance has been eliminated from the content outline for the CPA exam as of October 2009. However, the exam lags behind the content change, so this topic may continue to appear on the exam for six to 18 months.

1. Which of the following requirements must be met to create a bailment?

   I. Delivery of personal property to the intended bailee

   II. Possession by the intended bailee

   III. An absolute duty on the intended bailee to return or dispose of the property according to the bailor's directions

      a. I and II only

      b. I and III only

      c. II and III only

      d. I, II, and III

Chapter 49

REAL PROPERTY

A. Nature of Real Property
1. LAND
2. EASEMENTS
3. PROFITS
4. LICENSES
5. LIENS
6. FIXTURES

B. Nature and Form of Real Property Ownership
7. FEE SIMPLE ESTATE
8. LIFE ESTATE
9. FUTURE INTERESTS

C. Liability to Third Persons for Condition of Real Property
10. COMMON LAW RULE

D. Co-Ownership of Real Property
11. MULTIPLE OWNERSHIP
12. CONDOMINIUMS

E. Transfer of Real Property by Deed
13. DEFINITIONS
14. CLASSIFICATION OF DEEDS

15. EXECUTION OF DEEDS
16. DELIVERY AND ACCEPTANCE OF DEEDS
17. RECORDING OF DEEDS
18. ADDITIONAL PROTECTION OF BUYERS
19. GRANTORS WARRANTIES
20. GRANTEES COVENANTS

F. Other Methods of Transferring Real Property
21. EMINENT DOMAIN
22. ADVERSE POSSESSION

G. Mortgages
23. CHARACTERISTICS OF A MORTGAGE
24. PROPERTY SUBJECT TO MORTGAGE
25. FORM OF MORTGAGE
26. CREATIVE FORMS OF FINANCING
27. RECORDING OR FILING OF MORTGAGE
28. RESPONSIBILITIES OF THE PARTIES
29. TRANSFER OF INTEREST
30. RIGHTS OF MORTGAGEE AFTER DEFAULT
31. RIGHTS OF MORTGAGOR AFTER DEFAULT

T he law of real property can be highly technical and still relies on vocabulary drawn from the days of feudal lords and castles. This chapter presents a simplified look at the law of real property.

A. NATURE OF REAL PROPERTY

real property–land and all rights in land.

Real property has special characteristics of permanence and uniqueness. These characteristics have strongly influenced the rules that society has developed to resolve disputes concerning real property.

1. Land

land–earth, including all things embedded in or attached thereto, whether naturally or by the act of humans.

Land means more than the surface of the earth. It is composed of the soil and all things of a permanent nature affixed to the ground, such as herbs, grass, trees, and other growing, natural products. The word also includes the waters on the ground and things that are embedded beneath the surface.

Technically, land extends downward to the earth's center and upward indefinitely. The general view is that the owner of the land owns the space above that land subject to the right of flying aircraft that do not interfere with the use of the land and are not dangerous to persons or property on the land.

CPA 2. Easements

easement–permanent right that one has in the land of another, as the right to cross another's land or an easement of way.

An **easement** is the right to use another's property, such as the right to cross another's land. Rights in another person's land also include profits. The easement belongs to the land that is benefited. The benefited land is called the **dominant tenement**, and the land that is subject to the easement is called the **servient tenement**.[1]

dominant tenement– land that is benefited by an easement.

servient tenement– land that is subject to an easement.

easement by implication– easement not specifically created by deed that arises from the circumstances of the parties and the land location and access.

(A) CREATION OF EASEMENT. Because an easement is an interest in land, an oral promise to create an easement is not binding because of the statute of frauds. An oral grant of an easement would be a license (see Section 4). An easement created by agreement is transferred by deed. However, an easement may also be created by implication. An **easement by implication** arises when one conveys part of the land that has been used as a dominant estate in relation to the part retained. **For Example,** if water pipes or drain pipes run from the part of the land conveyed through the part retained, there is an implied right to continue using the pipes. For an easement to be implied, the use, as in this case with the pipes, must be apparent, continuous, and reasonably necessary.

An easement by implication arises when one subdivides land and sells a portion to which no entry can be made except over the land retained or over the land of a stranger. The grantee's right to use the land retained by the grantor for the purpose of going to and from the land conveyed is known as a **way of necessity**.

way of necessity–grantee's right to use land retained by the grantor for going to and from the conveyed land.

[1] *City of Aurora v ACJ Partnership*, 209 P3d 1076 (Colo 2009).

CASE SUMMARY

Brick Walls Do Not Make for Good Neighbors

FACTS: The Friersons have a two-story building in Easley, South Carolina that shares a common wall with an adjacent two-story building owned by David and Patricia Watson. An outdoor stairway located on the Watsons' property provides access to the second floor of both buildings. A dispute arose when David Watson began to construct apartments on the second floor of his building and proposed to close off a connecting indoor hallway between the two properties at the top of the stairs located inside the building. The Friersons maintained that they had an easement to use both the outdoor stairway and the indoor hallway for access.

The Friersons' predecessors-in-interest, E. C., E. O., and D. M. Frierson, purchased the building in 1929 from the "Estate of R. F. Smith, Inc." The 1929 deed, dated January 14 and recorded on January 23, expressly conveyed "an easement in a certain four foot stairway in the back of the building, with right of ingress and egress on said stairway to the second story of said building." On January 21, 1929, two days before the deed was recorded, the parties to the sale executed a "Memorandum of Agreement" that granted an easement for the use of the hallway. The memo was not recorded.

The Friersons brought suit to stop Watson's construction. The Friersons claimed Watson's construction violated their easement by eliminating the hallway, which denied them access to the second floor of their building.

The circuit court determined that the Friersons had established an easement for use of the hallway by grant and by prescription and granted the Friersons' motion. David Watson appealed.

DECISION: The court held that the memo granted an easement that did not need to be recorded to be valid. Also, the ongoing use of the indoor easement by the parties indicated it had always existed. Recording would have helped, but it was not required to grant the easement. Affirmed. **[Frierson v Watson, 636 SE2d 872 (SC App 2006)]**

---

prescription–acquisition of a right to use the land of another, as an easement, by making hostile, visible, and notorious use of the land, continuing for the period specified by the local law.

An easement may be created by **prescription**. Under prescription, a person acquires an easement by adverse use, or use contrary to the landowner's use, for a statutory period. No easement is acquired by prescription if the use of the land is with the permission of the owner.

(B) TERMINATION OF EASEMENT. Once an easement has been granted, it cannot be destroyed by the act of the grantor. A "revocation" attempted without the easement owner's consent has no effect.

An easement may be lost by nonuse when surrounding circumstances show an intent to abandon the easement.[2] **For Example,** when a surface transit system had an easement to maintain trolley tracks but abandoned the easement when the tracks were removed and all surface transportation was discontinued, the easement was lost through abandonment. Likewise, when the owner of the easement planted a flower bed on the land across the end of the path of the easement, the intent to abandon the easement was evident.

[2] *Backman v Lawrence*, 210 P3d 75 (Idaho 2009).

CPA 3. Profits

profit–right to take a part of the soil or produce of another's land, such as timber or water.

Profits are rights to take part of the soil, subsurface materials, or resources or produce from land that belongs to another. **For Example,** profits could include the right to remove coal from the land of another and the right to use the water from another's land.

CPA 4. Licenses

license–personal privilege to do some act or series of acts upon the land of another, as the placing of a sign thereon, not amounting to an easement or a right of possession.

A **license** is a personal, revocable privilege to perform an act or series of acts on the land of another. Unlike an easement, a license is not an interest in land. **For Example,** the person allowed to come into the house to use the telephone has a license. The advertising company that has permission to paint a sign on the side of a building also has a license.

A license may be terminated at the will of the licensor. It continues only as long as the licensor is the owner of the land.

CPA 5. Liens

Real property may be subject to **liens** that arise by the voluntary act of the owner of the land. **For Example,** the lien of a mortgage is created when the owner borrows money and uses the land as security for repayment of the debt.

---

thinking things through

The Dryer Vent that Dumped on the Doc

Danetta Garfink owns a condominium unit at The Cloisters at Charles Condominiums. Garfink purchased her unit (one of the model units) in 1991 during the development and construction phase of the project. The original construction included installed household appliances in each unit, a clothes dryer among them. As originally installed, the clothes dryer was connected and vented into the furnace room, rather than to the outside of the building, contrary to the terms of the construction contract, and in violation of prevailing building codes and regulations.

In 2000, the clothes dryer malfunctioned and Garfink purchased a replacement from Sears, Roebuck & Co. After viewing the existing vent system, however,

Sears refused to install the replacement because a "fire hazzard [sic] was identified."

Garfink took it upon herself to have the venting system rerouted. The new system was routed from the dryer through the wall of the laundry room into the adjoining garage, then through the garage and then the exterior wall. Garfink's immediate neighbor, Dr. Oscar Kantt, found that the new vent was within 17 feet of the front door of his residence, and Dr. Kantt complained about the discharge. Garfink says she has an easement for the dryer vent. Analyze whether she does have an easement. Be sure to think through the types of easements. [***Garfink v Cloisters at Charles, Inc.,*** **897 A2d 206 (Md 2006)**]

lien–claim or right, against property, existing by virtue of the entry of a judgment against its owner or by the entry of a judgment and a levy thereunder on the property, or because of the relationship of the claimant to the particular property, such as an unpaid seller.

tax lien–lien on property by a government agency for nonpayment of taxes.

CPA

judgment lien–lien by a creditor who has won a verdict against the landowner in court.

mechanic's lien–protection afforded by statute to various kinds of laborers and persons supplying materials, by giving them a lien on the building and land that has been improved or added to by them.

fixture–personal property that has become so attached to or adapted to real estate that it has lost its character as personal property and is part of the real estate.

Liens may also arise involuntarily, as in the case of **tax liens**, **judgment liens**, and **mechanic's liens**. In the case of taxes and judgments, the liens provide a means for enforcing the obligations of the owner of the land to pay the taxes or the judgment. Mechanic's liens give persons furnishing labor and materials in the improvement of real estate the right to proceed against the real estate for the collection of the amounts due them.

6. Fixtures

Under the laws relating to fixtures, personal property becomes real property.

(A) DEFINITION. A **fixture** is personal property that is attached to the earth or placed in a building in such a way or under such circumstances that it is considered part of the real property.

A person may buy a refrigerator, an air conditioner, a furnace, or some other item that is used in a building and then have the item installed. The question of whether such an item is a fixture, and therefore part of a building, can arise in a variety of situations: (1) The real estate tax assessor assesses the building and adds in the value of the item on the theory that it is part of the building, (2) the buyer of the item owns and then sells the building, and the new owner of the building claims that the item stays with the building, (3) the buyer places a mortgage on the building, and the mortgagee claims that the item is bound by the mortgage, (4) the buyer is a tenant in the building in which the item is installed, and the landlord claims that the item must stay in the building when the tenant leaves, and (5) the buyer does not pay in full for the item, and the seller of the item has a security interest that the seller wishes to enforce against the buyer or against the landlord of the building in which the buyer installs the item. The seller of the item may also assert a claim against the mortgagee of the building or against the buyer of the building. The determination of the rights of these parties depends on the common law of fixtures, as occasionally modified by statute.

sports&entertainment law

Using a View as Easement or a License in Lieu of a Ticket

There are 13 rooftops on buildings that surround Wrigley Field. When the Chicago Cubs play at Wrigley, the rooftops are packed with folks who, with coolers full of drinks and plenty of food stacked on tables, are watching the games. Kayakers pack McCovey's Cove near San Francisco's SBC Park's right field to watch the Giants. Hot tubs and roofs overlook the Arizona Diamondback's games in Chase Ballpark (once BankOne Ballpark or BOB).

Do the folks using these areas need a license? An easement? If they own the property or are there with the owner's permission, are they permitted to watch the games?*

* Lee Jenkins, "The Best Seats in the House Are Just Outside Wrigley," *New York Times*, June 12, 2005, 8-1 (Sports 1).

CPA   (B) TESTS OF A FIXTURE. In the absence of an agreement between the parties, the courts apply three tests to determine whether personal property has become a fixture.

(1) Annexation.

Generally, personal property becomes a fixture if it is so attached to the realty that it cannot be removed without materially damaging the real property or destroying the personal property itself. If the property is so affixed as to lose its specific identity, such as bricks in a wall, it becomes part of the realty. When cabinets are attached to kitchen walls so as to be immovable, they are fixtures.

(2) Adaptation.

Personal property especially adapted or suited to the use made of the building may constitute a fixture such as the pipes for a church organ.

(3) Intent.

One controlling test is the intention of the person affixing the property.[3] Intent is considered as of the time the property was affixed. In the absence of direct proof of such intent, courts resort to the nature of the property, the method of its attachment, and all the surrounding circumstances to determine intent.

The fact that machinery installed in a plant would be very difficult and expensive to move or is so delicate that the moving would cause damage is significant in reaching the conclusion that the owner installed the equipment as a permanent addition and intented to make the equipment fixtures. **For Example,** when the floors in a large apartment house are made of concrete and covered with a thin sheet of plywood to which wall-to-wall carpeting is stapled, the carpeting constitutes a fixture that cannot be removed from the building. Removal would probably destroy the carpeting because it was cut to size. In addition, the carpeting is necessary to make the building livable as an apartment.

CPA   (C) MOVABLE MACHINERY AND EQUIPMENT. Machinery and equipment that are movable are ordinarily held not to be fixtures even though, in order to move them, it is necessary to unbolt them from the floor or to disconnect electrical wires or water pipes. **For Example,** refrigerators, freezers, and gas and electric ranges are not fixtures. They do not lose their character as personal property when they are readily removable after disconnecting pipes or unplugging wires. A portable window air conditioner that rests on a rack that is affixed to the windowsill by screws and is connected directly to the building only by an electric cord plug is not a fixture.

The mere fact that an item may be unplugged, however, does not establish that it is not a fixture. **For Example,** a computer and its related hardware constitute fixtures when there is such a mass of wires and cables under the floor that the installation gives the impression of permanence.

CPA   (D) TRADE FIXTURES. Equipment that a tenant attaches to a rented building and uses in a trade or business is ordinarily removable by the tenant when the tenant permanently leaves the premises. Such equipment is commonly called a *trade fixture.*[4]

---

[3] *Englewood v Miami Valley Lighting, L.L.C.,* 911 NE2d 913 (Oh App 2009).
[4] *In re City of New York,* 899 NE 2d 933, 870 NYS 2d 827 (2008).

CASE SUMMARY

Falling Through the Cracks for the Home Team

FACTS: On September 29, 2000, Elaine Kohn and her then four-year-old daughter, Lori Kohn, attended the homecoming football game at Darlington High School. At about 2:30 P.M. on a glorious Wisconsin Saturday afternoon, young Lori fell through the space at the foot of her seat in the home bleachers to the ground 15 feet below and was injured. The home bleachers are a huge structure. They are 15 rows tall, over 100 feet long, and contain a 50-inch-wide walkway elevated 30 inches above the ground. They can seat nearly 1,500 individuals. They adjoin a rather large press box and incorporate a wheelchair access ramp. While it is unclear whether they are anchored to the ground, they clearly are not readily moveable. The Kohns brought suit in 2001 against Standard Steel Industries, Inc. (Standard was later purchased by Illinois Tool Works), a company that sold Darlington the bleachers for $16,167 in 1969. However, the suit was dismissed initially because Wisconsin has a 10-year statute of limitations (statute of repose) on recovery for injuries caused by improvements to real property.

The Wisconsin Court of Appeals reversed the lower court's dismissal, concluding that the bleachers were not an improvement to real property because there was no evidence that the bleachers were anchored to the ground. The Court of Appeals held that the Kohns' claims were governed by the three-year statute of limitations on personal injury and product liability actions rather than by the 10-year statute of repose. The Wisconsin Supreme Court then stepped, carefully, as it were, into the fray.

DECISION: The court held that the bleachers were fixtures and as improvements to real property could not be the basis for a lawsuit after 1979 (the 10-year limit). The bleachers had never been moved in the 30 years since their placement. Ramps and others structures were attached to them. The bleachers were an integral part of the facility and games could not take place without them being there. There was no evidence that the bleachers were annexed, but that test is not controlling in determining whether an item is a fixture. [**Kohn v Darlington Community School District, 686 NW2d 794 (Wis 2005)**]

CPA ## B. NATURE AND FORM OF REAL PROPERTY OWNERSHIP

> **fee simple estate**–highest level of land ownership; full interest of unlimited duration.
>
> **life estate**–an estate for the duration of a life.
>
> **leasehold estate**–interest of a tenant in rented land.
>
> **estate in fee**–largest estate possible, in which the owner has absolute and entire interest in the land.

A person's interest in real property may be defined in terms of the period of time for which the person will remain the owner as (1) a **fee simple estate** or (2) a **life estate**. These estates are termed *freehold estates*, which are interests of uncertain duration. At the time of creation of a freehold estate, a termination date is not known. When a person owns property for a specified period of time, this interest is not regarded as a freehold estate; it is a **leasehold estate**, subject to special rules of law.

CPA ### 7. Fee Simple Estate

An **estate in fee**, a fee simple, or a fee simple absolute lasts forever. The owner of such a land interest held in fee simple has the absolute and entire interest in the land. The important characteristics of this estate are that (1) it is alienable, or transferable, during life, (2) it is alienable by will, (3) it passes to heirs of the owner if it is not specifically devised (transferred by will), (4) it is subject to rights of the owner's surviving spouse, and (5) it can be attached or used to satisfy debts of the owner before or after death.

fee simple defeasibles—fee simple interest can be lost if restrictions on its use are violated.

There are other forms of the fee simple estate generally used for control of land use. **Fee simple defeasibles** are interests that give the grantee all the rights of a fee simple holder provided that the grantee complies with certain restrictions. **For Example,** the grant "To Ralph Watkins so long as he uses the property for school purposes" is an example of a fee simple defeasible. Watkins will have all the rights of a fee simple holder provided that he uses the property for school purposes. If Watkins ever stops using the property for school purposes, the property reverts back to the grantor.

CPA   **8. Life Estate**

A *life estate* (or life tenancy), as its name indicates, lasts only during the life of a person (ordinarily its owner). Upon the death of the person by whose life the estate was measured, the owner of the life estate has no interest remaining to pass to heirs or by will. **For Example,** a grant of a life estate would be "To my husband, Nathan Jones, for life, and then to my children." Jones would hold title to the property only for the time he is alive. When Jones dies, he cannot give the property away by will. If Jones conveys the property while he is alive, the grantee for the property holds title to the land only until Jones's death.

CPA   **9. Future Interests**

In several of the examples given to illustrate fee simple and life estates, interests were created in more than one person. **For Example,** in the preceding life estate example, the children of the grantor are given an interest in the land at the same time that Jones is. However, the interests of the children will not take effect until Jones dies. The children have a future interest in the land. Their interest is referred to as a **remainder interest** because they have the remaining interest in the land once the life estate ends.

remainder interest—land interest that follows a life estate.

possibility of reverter—nature of the interest held by the grantor after conveying land outright but subject to a condition or provision that may cause the grantee's interest to become forfeited and the interest to revert to the grantor or heirs.

In the Watkins fee simple defeasible example, the grantor has a future interest if Watkins violates the restriction. The grantor's interest is called a **possibility of reverter**. It is a future interest because it cannot exist unless Watkins violates the use restriction placed on his present interest.

C. LIABILITY TO THIRD PERSONS FOR CONDITION OF REAL PROPERTY

A person entering the land of another may be injured by the condition of the land. Who is liable for such harm?

CPA ## 10. Common Law Rule

Under the common law, liability to a person entering onto land was controlled by the status of the injured person—that is, whether the person injured was a **trespasser**, a **licensee**, or an **invitee**. A different duty was owed by the owner (or occupier, as when a tenant is leasing property) of land to persons in each of these three categories.

trespass–an unauthorized action with respect to person or property.

(A) TRESPASSERS. For a trespasser, the landowner ordinarily owes the duty of refraining from causing intentional harm only once the presence of the trespasser is known. The landowner is not under any duty to warn of dangers or to make the premises safe to protect the trespasser from harm. The most significant exception to this rule arises in the case of small children. Even when children are trespassers, they are generally afforded greater protection through the **attractive nuisance doctrine**. **For Example,** the owner of a tract of land was held liable for the death of a seven-year-old child who drowned in a creek on that land. Snow had covered the ice on the creek, and children running across the land did not know of the creek's location or the danger of the ice. The landowner had a duty to fence the creek, put up warnings, or control the children's access.[5]

licensee–someone on another's premises with the permission of the occupier, whose duty is to warn the licensee of nonobvious dangers.

invitee–person who enters another's land by invitation.

attractive nuisance doctrine–a rule imposing liability upon a landowner for injuries sustained by small children playing on the land when the landowner permits a condition to exist or maintains equipment that a reasonable person should realize would attract small children who could not realize the danger. The rule does not apply if an unreasonable burden would be imposed upon the landowner in taking steps to protect the children.

(B) LICENSEES. *Licensees* are on the premises with the permission of the landowner, who owes the duty of warning of nonobvious dangers that are known to the owner. A host must warn a guest of such dangers. **For Example,** when a sliding glass door is "invisible" if the patio lights are on and the house lights are off, the owner must warn guests of the presence of the glass. The owner is liable if he has not warned guests of the danger and a guest is injured in shattering the glass. An owner, however, owes no duty to a licensee to take any steps to learn of the presence of dangers that are unknown to the owner.

(C) INVITEES. *Invitees* are persons who enter another's land by invitation. The entry is connected with the owner's business or with an activity the occupier conducts on the land. Business customers, for example, are invitees.

Owners have a duty to take reasonable steps to discover any danger and a duty to warn the invitee or to correct the danger. **For Example,** a store must make a reasonable inspection of the premises to determine that there is nothing on the floor that would be dangerous, such as a slippery substance that might cause a patron to fall. The store must correct the condition, appropriately rope off the danger area, or give suitable warning. If the owner of the premises fails to take the degree of care required and an invitee is harmed as a result, then the owner is liable for such harm.

In most states, the courts have expanded the concept of invitees beyond the category of customers, or those whose presence will economically benefit the occupier. Invitees now usually include members of the public who are invited onto the premises and who cannot be reasonably expected to make an inspection of the premises before using them and would not be able to make necessary repairs to dangerous conditions. Some courts have also made inroads into the prior law by treating a recurring licensee, such as a letter carrier, as an invitee. For more information on landowner liability, refer to Chapter 9 on torts.

[5] *Foss v. Kincade*, 766 NW 2d 317 (Minn 2009).

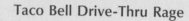

CASE SUMMARY

Taco Bell Drive-Thru Rage

FACTS: At approximately 3:00 A.M., on February 3, 2000, Sonya Winchell was driving two of her friends through a Fort Wayne Taco Bell drive-thru. When Winchell arrived in line, there was one car in front of her at the speaker. Winchell noticed that the occupants of the car, Remco Guy and Ariel Graham, were taking a long time placing their order and then got out of their car. At that point, Winchell yelled out her window, "Can we get moving, we are hungry!" Guy approached Winchell's car, stuck his head in the window, and "started cussing everybody out." Guy removed his head from the window, stuck it back in, and asked, "You got an F-ing problem?" Winchell responded by "drill[ing] him in the nose." Guy then pulled a gun out of his pants and shot Winchell. One of Winchell's passengers and others summoned police officers who were in a nearby parking lot.

Winchell survived the shooting, and Guy was convicted of attempted murder. Winchell filed a civil action against Guy and Graham, and against Taco Bell, alleging negligence. Taco Bell moved for summary judgment and the trial court granted it.

DECISION: Landowners have a duty to take reasonable precautions to protect their invitees from foreseeable criminal attacks. Taco Bell did owe a duty to its customers, including Winchell, to use reasonable care to protect them from injuries caused by other patrons and guests on their premises.

The line of sight between the employees of Taco Bell and the drive-thru was obstructed, that the video monitoring system was in a closet and not readily accessible to Taco Bell employees. No security guard was on duty that night. There had been previous calls to the police from the Taco Bell, including one in which there was also violence.

Taco Bell owed Winchell a duty as a matter of law and there were questions of fact regarding the elements of breach and causation. The trial court improperly granted Taco Bell's motion for summary judgment. Reversed. [**Winchell v Guy, 857 NE2d 1024 (Ind 2006)**]

D. Co-Ownership of Real Property

Real property may be owned by one or several persons, and the method of co-ownership determines the extent of the owners' rights.

11. Multiple Ownership

Several persons may have *concurrent interests* (or interests that exist at the same time) in the same real property. The forms of multiple ownership for real property are the same as those for personal property. Real property can be held by tenants in common, by joint tenants with right of survivorship, by tenants by the entirety, or under community property rights. When co-owners sell property, they hold the proceeds of sale by the same kind of tenancy as that in which they held the original property.

12. Condominiums

condominium–
combination of
co-ownership and
individual ownership.

A **condominium** is a combination of co-ownership and individual ownership.
For Example, persons owning an office building or an apartment house by condominium are co-owners of the land and of the halls, lobby, elevators, stairways, exits, surrounding land, incinerator, laundry rooms, and other areas used in

common. Each apartment or office in the building, however, is individually owned and is transferred in the same way as other forms of real property.

(A) CONTROL AND EXPENSE. In some states, owners of the various units in the condominium have equal voice in its management and share an equal part of its expenses. In others, control and liability for expenses are shared by a unit owner in the same ratio that the value of the unit bears to the value of the entire condominium project. In all states, unit owners have equal rights to use the common areas. An owners' association is created by the condominium owners to operate the common areas of the condominium property and resolve any disputes among owners.

The owner of each condominium unit makes the repairs required by the owner's deed or contract of ownership. The owner is prohibited from making any major change that would impair or damage the safety or value of an adjoining unit.

(B) COLLECTION OF EXPENSES FROM UNIT OWNER. When a unit owner fails to pay the owner's share of taxes, operating expenses, and repairs, the owners' association generally has the right to a lien against that owner's unit for the amount due.

(C) TORT LIABILITY. Most condominium projects fail to make provision for the liability of unit owners for a tort occurring in the common areas. A few states expressly provide that when a third person is injured in a common area, a suit may be brought only against the condominium association. Any judgment recovered is a charge against the association to be paid off as a common expense. When the condominium association is incorporated, the same result should be obtained by applying ordinary principles of corporation law. Under principles of corporation law, liability for torts occurring on the premises of the corporation would not be the liability of individual shareholders.

cooperative – group of two or more persons or enterprises that acts through a common agent with respect to a common objective, such as buying or selling.

(D) COOPERATIVES DISTINGUISHED. Ownership in a condominium is different from ownership in a **cooperative**. An apartment cooperative is typically a corporation that owns an apartment complex. The "ownership" interests of the apartment occupants are as stockholders of the corporation.

---

e-commerce&cyberlaw
Web Listings

The Internet has proven to be a help in selling real property. Real estate agents use the Web to post listings and provide potential buyers with virtual tours of properties that interest them. Visit the

National Association of Realtors Web site at **www.nar.com** and view its materials related to selling real property.

E. Transfer of Real Property by Deed

Although many of the technical limitations of the feudal system and earlier common law on transfer of land have disappeared, much of the law relating to the modern deed originated in those days.

deed–an instrument by which the grantor (owner of land) conveys or transfers the title to a grantee.

CPA   13. Definitions

A **deed** is an instrument or writing by which an owner or **grantor** transfers or conveys an interest in land to a new owner. The new owner is called a **grantee** or **transferee**. Real property may be either sold or given as a gift. A deed, however, is necessary to transfer title to land, even if it is a gift.

In contrast to the situation with a contract, no consideration is required to make a deed effective. Although consideration is not required to make a deed valid or to transfer title by deed, the absence of consideration may show that the owner makes the transfer to defraud creditors. The creditors may then be able to set aside the fraudulent transfer.

grantor–owner who transfers or conveys an interest in land to a new owner.

grantee–new owner of a land conveyance.

transferee–buyer or vendee.

CPA   14. Classification of Deeds

Deeds may be classified according to the interest conveyed as **quitclaim deeds** or **warranty deeds**. A quitclaim deed merely transfers whatever interest, if any, the grantor may have in the property without specifying that interest in any way. A warranty deed transfers a specified interest and warrants or guarantees that such interest is transferred. Figure 49.1 is a sample warranty deed.

quitclaim deed–deed by which the grantor purports to give up only whatever right or title the grantor may have in the property without specifying or warranting transfer of any particular interest.

CPA   15. Execution of Deeds

Ordinarily, the grantor must sign, by signature or mark, a deed. A deed must be executed and delivered by a person having capacity. A deed may be set aside by the grantor for fraud by the grantee if third persons have not acquired rights in the land in good faith.

warranty deed–deed by which the grantor conveys a specific estate or interest to the grantee and makes one or more of the covenants of title.

CPA   16. Delivery and Acceptance of Deeds

A deed has no effect and title does not pass until the deed has been delivered. Delivery is a matter of intent as shown by words and conduct; no particular form of ceremony is required. The essential intent in delivering a deed is not merely that the grantor intends to hand over physical control and possession of the paper on which the deed is written but also that the grantor intends thereby to transfer the ownership of the property described in the deed. That intent can be shown by handing it to the grantee or placing the deed, addressed to the grantee, in the mail or by giving it to a third person with directions to give it to the grantee.

An effective delivery of a deed may be made symbolically, or constructively, such as by delivering to the grantee the key to a locked box and informing the grantee that the deed to the property is in the box. **For Example,** the delivery of a safe deposit box key has been held to constitute delivery of a deed that was in the box.

FIGURE 49-1 | *Form of Warranty Deed*

THIS DEED, made the twentieth day of November, two thousand and . . . between James K. Damron, residing at 132 Spring Street in the Borough of Manhattan, City and State of New York, party of the first part, and Terrence S. Bloemker, residing at 14 Steinway Street in the Borough of Queens, City and State of New York, party of the second part,

WITNESSETH, that the party of the first part, in consideration of the sum of one dollar ($1), lawful money of the United States, and other good and valuable consideration paid by the party of the second part, does hereby grant and release unto the party of the second part, his heirs and assigns forever,

ALL that certain lot, piece, and parcel of land situated in the Borough of Manhattan, City and County of New York, and State of New York, and bounded and described as follows:

Beginning at a point on the northerly side of Spring Street, distant two hundred (200) feet westerly from the corner formed by the intersection of the northerly side of Spring Street with the westerly side of 6th Avenue, running thence northerly parallel with 6th Avenue one hundred (100) feet, thence westerly and parallel with said Spring Street one hundred (100) feet; thence southerly, again parallel with said 6th Avenue one hundred (100) feet to the northerly side of Spring Street, and thence easterly along the said northerly side of Spring Street one hundred (100) feet to the point or place of beginning.

Together with the appurtenances and all the estate and rights of the party of the first part in and to said premises.

TO HAVE AND TO HOLD the premises herein granted unto the party of the second part, his heirs and assigns forever.

AND the party of the first part covenants as follows:

First. That the party of the first part is seised of the said premises in fee simple, and has good right to convey the same;

Second. That the party of the second part shall quietly enjoy the said premises;

Third. That the said premises are free from encumbrances except as expressly stated;

Fourth. That the party of the first part will execute or procure any further necessary assurance of the title to said premises;

IN WITNESS WHEREOF, the party of the first part has hereunto set his hand and seal the day and year first above written.

JAMES K. DAMRON

(L.S.)

In presence of:

DIANA L. REILMAN

State of New York ⎫
                 ⎬ s.s.:*
County of New York ⎭

On the twentieth day of November in the year two thousand and . . . , before me personally came James K. Damron, to me known and known to me to be the individual described in, and who executed, the foregoing instrument, and he acknowledged that he executed the same.

DIANA L. REILMAN
Notary Public, New York County

*Note: Acknowledgment before a notary public is not essential to the effectiveness of a deed, but it is typically required to qualify the deed for recording.

Generally, there must be an **acceptance** by the grantee. In all cases, an acceptance is presumed unless the grantee disclaims the transfer.

17. Recording of Deeds

acceptance – unqualified assent to the act or proposal of another, such as the acceptance of a draft (bill of exchange), of an offer to make a contract, of goods delivered by the seller, or of a gift or deed.

recorder – public official in charge of deeds.

The owner of land may record the deed in the office of a public official, sometimes called a **recorder** or *commissioner of deeds*. The recording is not required to make the deed effective to pass title, but it is done so that the public will know that the grantee is the present owner and thereby prevent the former owner from making any future transfer or transaction relating to the property.

When no document is recorded, states have statutes for determining who obtains title and who will be left to take action against the party that has conveyed the property to more than one person. **For Example,** suppose that Grant conveys a tract of land to Dee. Dee does not record her deed. Grant then conveys the same tract of land to Joe, who also does not record his deed, but Joe is unaware of Dee's acquisition. Then Grant conveys the same property to Larry who knows about Dee and Joe but records his deed. Who will hold title, and who will be left to pursue Grant for remedies? Under **race statutes**, the first party to record the deed holds title, so Larry holds title. Under **notice statutes**, the last good-faith or bona fide purchaser (BFP), someone who does not know about the previous conveyances, takes title. Under notice, Joe holds title because he is the last BFP. Larry knows about the prior transactions and that fact controls title, not the recording of his deed under notice statutes. Under **notice-race** or **race-notice statutes**, the first BFP to record the deed holds title. So, if Dee records first, she holds title. If Joe records first, he will. Larry has recorded but does not meet the second requirement of race-notice, which is that one must be the first BFP to record to take title in a race-notice statute. Suppose that Larry is a BFP, but Joe is not because he is aware of the conveyance to Dee. Under race, Larry holds title. Under notice, Larry holds title. Under race-notice, Larry wins again. If Dee records her deed, all of these issues are moot because recording the deed is complete notice for all subsequent purchasers.

race statute – statute under which the first party to record the deed holds the title.

notice statute – statute under which the last good faith or bona fide purchaser holds the title.

notice-race statute – statute under which the first bona fide purchaser to record the deed holds the title.

race-notice statute – see *notice-race statute*.

The fact that a deed is recorded provides notice to the world about who holds title. The recording of a deed, however, is only such notice if the deed was properly executed. Likewise, the grantee of land cannot claim any protection by virtue of the recording of a deed when (1) a claim is made by one whose title is superior to that of the owner of record, (2) the grantee had notice or knowledge of the adverse claim when title was acquired, (3) a person acting under a hostile claim was then in possession of the land, (4) the grantee received the land as a gift, or (5) the transfer to the grantee was fraudulent.

18. Additional Protection of Buyers

abstract of title – history of the transfers of title to a given piece of land, briefly stating the parties to and the effect of all deeds, wills, and judicial proceedings relating to the land.

In addition to the protection given to buyers and third persons by the recorded title to property, a buyer is generally protected by procuring title insurance or an abstract of title. An **abstract of title** is a summarized report of the title to the property as shown by the records, together with a report of all judgments, mortgages, and similar recorded claims against the property.

CASE SUMMARY

Selling the Same Property Twice and Then Disappearing

FACTS: Wallace Salls was the recorded owner of a 12.56-acre parcel of real property in Hunt County, Texas. In October 1984, Salls sold two adjoining tracts from the parcel. Tract I, consisting of 3.675 acres, was sold to Paula Malecek and her husband for $14,700. Tract II, consisting of 3.676 acres, was sold to David Minton and his wife for $14,704.

In September 1994, Salls sold the property again. This sale involved the entire 12.56-acre parcel, including the two tracts previously conveyed to Minton and Malecek. Shannon Cook, the purchaser of the entire parcel, did not record the deed until 1997. In 1999, Cook sold the 12.56-acre parcel to Fletcher.

An attorney named Robert Crouch handled all legal matters for both Malecek and Salls, including the drafting of the contract for deed for Tract I. Crouch also drafted the deeds when the property was conveyed to Cook and Fletcher. Crouch is now deceased. Salls filed bankruptcy sometime prior to 1989, and no one has been able to locate him for a number of years.

Fletcher filed a lawsuit against Minton seeking to quiet title to Tracts I and II. Minton denied Fletcher's allegations of ownership. Malecek intervened in the lawsuit and asserted that she was the owner of Tract I. The trial court held that Malecek was the owner of Tract I; Minton was the owner of Tract II; and Fletcher was entitled to reimbursement from Malecek for ad valorem taxes paid on Tract I. Fletcher appealed.

DECISION: An unrecorded conveyance is binding on those who have knowledge of the conveyance.. A person who acquires property in good faith, for value, and without notice of any third-party claim or interest is a bona fide purchaser. Status as a bona fide purchaser is an affirmative defense to a title dispute.

Fletcher, through her agent, had constructive, if not actual, notice of Minton's claims to both tracts at the time she purchased the property. Minton's use and occupation of the property was sufficiently open, visible, exclusive, and unequivocal to put Fletcher on notice of a competing claim. Fletcher is not entitled to the protection of a bona fide purchaser as to Tract I. Malecek is the owner of Tract I. Also, the trial court properly found that Minton is the owner of Tract II. Affirmed. [**Fletcher v Minton, 217 SW3d 755 (Tex App 2007)**]

warranty of title–implied warranty that title to the goods is good and transfer is proper.

covenants of title–grantor's covenants of a deed that guarantee such matters as the right to make the conveyance, to ownership of the property, to freedom of the property from encumbrances, or that the grantee will not be disturbed in the quiet enjoyment of the land.

covenant of seisin– guarantee that the grantor of an interest in land owns the estate conveyed to a new owner.

covenant of right to convey–guarantee that the grantor of an interest in land, if not the owner, has the right or authority to make the conveyance to a new owner.

covenant against encumbrances–guarantee that conveyed land is not subject to any right or interest of a third person.

covenant of quiet enjoyment–covenant by the grantor of an interest in land that the grantee's possession of the land shall not be disturbed.

19. Grantor's Warranties

The warranties of the grantor relate to the title transferred by the grantor and to the fitness of the property for use.

CPA (A) WARRANTIES OF TITLE. In the common law deed, the grantor may expressly warrant or make certain *covenants* as to the title conveyed. The statutes authorizing a short form of deed provide that, unless otherwise stated in the deed, the grantor is presumed to have made certain **warranties of title**.

The more important of the **covenants (or warranties) of title** that the grantor may make are (1) **covenant of seisin**, or guarantee that the grantor owns the estate conveyed, (2) **covenant of right to convey**, or guarantee that the grantor, if not the owner as in the case of an agent, has the right or authority to make the conveyance, (3) **covenant against encumbrances**, or guarantee that the land is not subject to any right or interest of a third person, such as a lien or an easement, (4) **covenant of quiet enjoyment**, or

limited covenant–any covenant that does not provide the complete protection of a full covenant.

covenant of further assurances–promise that the grantor of an interest in land will execute any additional documents required to perfect the title of the grantee.

guarantee by the grantor that the grantee's possession of the land will not be disturbed either by the grantor, in the case of a **limited covenant**, or by the grantor or any person claiming title under the grantor, in the case of a general covenant, and (5) **covenant of further assurances**, or guarantee that the grantor will execute any additional documents that may be required to perfect the title of the grantee.

(B) FITNESS FOR USE. Courts in most states hold that when a builder or real estate developer sells a new house to a home buyer, the buyer gets an implied warranty that the house and foundation are fit for occupancy or use. This warranty arises regardless of whether the house was purchased before, during, or after completion of construction.[6] This first buyer is not responsible for the builder warranty when the house is resold. However, there is authority that the second buyer may recover from the original contractor for breach of the implied warranty even though there is no privity of contract.[7]

20. Grantee's Covenants

In a deed, the grantee may agree to do or to refrain from doing certain acts. Such an agreement becomes a binding contract between the grantor and the grantee. The grantor may recover from the grantee for its breach.

run with the land–concept that certain covenants in a deed to land are deemed to run or pass with the land so that whoever owns the land is bound by or entitled to the benefit of the covenants.

The right to enforce the covenant also **runs with the land** owned by the grantor to whom the promise was made. **For Example,** a promise not to use a tract of land for a parking lot between two adjoining landowners would be passed (conveyed) to any buyers who subsequently acquire these tracts. For more information on covenants, see Chapter 50, Environmental Law and Land Use Controls.

F. OTHER METHODS OF TRANSFERRING REAL PROPERTY

Title to real property can also be acquired by eminent domain and by adverse possession.

CPA   ### 21. Eminent Domain

eminent domain–power of government and certain kinds of corporations to take private property against the objection of the owner, provided the taking is for a public purpose and just compensation is made for it.

Under **eminent domain**, property is taken from its private owner for a public purpose. The title is then taken by a government or public authority. There are constitutionally protected rights of property owners under eminent domain. Known as the "takings clause," this portion of the Fifth Amendment to the U.S. Constitution requires compensation when private property is taken for public use. Two important issues arise under the takings clause: (1) whether there is a taking of property and (2) whether the property is taken for a public use. With respect to whether a taking has occurred, it is not necessary that the owner be physically

---

[6] *Richards v Powercraft Homes, Inc., 678 P2d 427 (Ariz 1984), but see Long v Jeb Breithaupt Design Build Inc.,* 4 So 3d 930 (La App 2009).
[7] Many states have passed statutes that govern the extent of the implied warranty of habitability. Although the statutes vary, the types of defects covered include defects in construction, design, and appearance.

CASE SUMMARY

Little Pink Houses, for You, but Not for Me ... Anymore

FACTS: In 1978, the city of New London, Connecticut, undertook a redevelopment plan for purposes of creating a redeveloped area in and around the existing park at Fort Trumball. The plan had the goals of achieving all the related ambience a state park should have, including the absence of pink cottages and other architecturally eclectic homes. Part of the redevelopment plan was the city's deal with Pfizer Corporation for the location of its research facility in the area. The preface to the city's development plan stated that it would "*create jobs, increase tax and other revenues, encourage public access to and use of the city's waterfront, and eventually "build momentum" for the revitalization of the rest of the city, including its downtown area.*"

Susette Kelo, and other property owners whose homes would be razed and whose land would be taken to allow for the park, Pfizer's facility, and other redevelopment (15 total owners including Kelo), asked to be permitted to stay in the area. The city refused their request.

Kelo and the other homeowners filed suit challenging New London's legal authority to take their homes. The trial court issued an injunction preventing New London from taking certain of the properties but allowing others to be taken. Those property owners who were held subject to eminent domain appealed.

The appellate court found for New London on all claims; the landowners appealed.

DECISION: In a 5-4 decision delivered by Justice Stevens, joined by Justices Kennedy, Souter, Ginsberg, and Breyer, the U.S. Supreme Court upheld the decision of the Connecticut Supreme Court. New London's taking of the homes of Kelo and others qualifies as a "public use." Local governments cannot take private land simply to give to a particular private party, but when the takings are part of a carefully considered economic development plan, then the takings are constitutional. Public purpose is a broad category for purposes of determining when takings are constitutional. Economic development is a legitimate and constitutionally protected public purpose. Local governments' determinations that areas are economically distressed is enough to justify a program of economic development and local authorities are entitled to make that determination. The courts will not second-guess local authorities. [**Kelo v City of New London, 545 US 469 (2005)**]

---

deprived of the property but that normal use of the property has been impaired or lost. Whether there is a public use for the taking is a question that continues to be challenged in court because the definition of public purpose is so broad.

For Example, property can be taken to build a freeway as well as for the preservation of a historic site. In the eminent domain cases after 2000, much of the litigation centered on whether revitalization of areas with urban blight were permissible takings. Eminent domain has activated a concerned public as state and local governments take more and more houses and land for purposes of economic development.

22. Adverse Possession

adverse possession–hostile possession of real estate, which when actual, visible, notorious, exclusive, and continued for the required time, will vest the title to the land in the person in such adverse possession.

Title to land may be acquired by possessing it adversely for a statutorily prescribed period of time. A possessor who complies with the requirements for **adverse possession** can gain title. Those who adversely possess property gain title to property even though they had no right to use the property at the beginning of their use or possession.

To acquire title by adverse possession, the possession must be (1) actual, (2) visible and notorious, (3) exclusive, (4) hostile, and (5) continuous for a required period of time.

State statutes control the required time period, but the typical range is 10 to 20 years. Use or possession of land under a mistaken belief that one is the owner still qualifies for the "hostile" possession required under the fourth element listed.[8]

G. Mortgages

mortgage–interest in land given by the owner to a creditor as security for the payment of the creditor for a debt, the nature of the interest depending upon the law of the state where the land is located. (Parties—mortgagor, mortgagee)

An agreement that creates an interest in real property as security for an obligation until that obligation is repaid is a **mortgage**.

The property owner, whose interest in the property is given as security, is the *mortgagor*.

The person who receives the security is the *mortgagee*.

CPA   ## 23. Characteristics of a Mortgage

A mortgage has three characteristics: (1) the termination of the mortgagee's interest on the performance of the obligation secured by the mortgage, (2) the right of the mortgagee to enforce the mortgage by foreclosure on the mortgagor's failure to perform, and (3) the mortgagor's right to redeem or regain the property.

thinking things through
Putting the Brakes on Eminent Domain

Bailey's Brake Service, a bit of an eyesore at a main intersection near a failing downtown area of Mesa, Arizona, was a family-founded, owned, and operated business that had been open in its existing location since 1970. Lenhart's True Value Hardware store was also a longstanding Mesa business with a location south and east of Bailey's and a desire for a better location. The Lenharts purchased the property abutting Bailey's but felt that the street facing Bailey's property was necessary for its location.

The city did a taking by eminent domain and then "reissued" the property to Lenhart's for its store. The Baileys challenged the city's taking in the Superior Court as unconstitutional, but the court held that the taking was constitutional as part of the city's plan for redevelopment and revitalization of the area. The Baileys appealed the trial court decision. Should the Baileys get their property back? Was this a proper eminent domain taking? [**Bailey v Myers, 76 P3d 398 (Az Ct App 2003)**]

[8] The state with the shortest period for adverse possession is Texas, whose adverse possession period can be as short as 3 years. The state with the longest adverse possession period is Wyoming, with 40 years.

ethics&the law

Hell Hath No Fury Like a NOWMP

The NIMBYs (Not In My Backyard) challenge the placement of everything from power plants to refineries to Wal-Marts. There are also the BANANAs (Build Absolutely Nothing Anywhere Near Anything). Finally, the NOWMPs (Not With My Property) are opposed to eminent domain, the taking of their property for a public use.

Think back to your readings on ethics in Chapter 3. What ethical principles could you apply in favor of the

NIMBYs, the BANANAs, and the NOWMPs? What ethical principles could you apply that find that the NIMBYs, the BANANAs and the NOWMPs are acting unethically?

Source: For more information, see Marianne M. Jennings, "NIMBYs, BANANAs, LULUs, NOPEs, and NOWMPs: The Percolating World of Eminent Domain (The Par Boil Stage or Part I)," 33 Real Estate Law Journal *(no. 4), 445–457 (2005).*

24. Property Subject to Mortgage

In general, any form of property that may be sold or conveyed may be mortgaged. It is immaterial whether the right is a present right, a future interest, or merely a right in the land of another. It is not necessary that the mortgagor have complete or absolute ownership in the property. Mortgagors may mortgage any type of land interest they own.

CPA

25. Form of Mortgage

Because a mortgage of real property transfers an interest in the property, it must be in writing under the statute of frauds. As a general rule, no particular form of language is required if the language used expresses the intent of the parties to create a mortgage. Many state statutes provide a standardized form for mortgage language that may be used.

26. Creative Forms of Financing

In many situations in which a buyer seeks to purchase property, the conventional methods for obtaining a mortgage are not available because of affordability or qualifications required for a loan. Many creative forms of financing have been developed to help buyers purchase property. **For Example,** residential land buyers, particularly during the real estate boom in 2005–2006, obtain an **adjustable rate mortgage (ARM)**, in which the lower interest rates applied at the beginning of the mortgage help the buyer qualify for the loan. The ARM changes interest rates along with the market, going up and down, unless the ARM has a fixed minimum rate. Other buyers may have the seller finance their purchase through the use of a land or an installment contract. Some new forms of financing, such as the **reverse mortgage**, permit those who have paid off their mortgages on their property to get the value out of their property by having a mortgage company take a mortgage out on the property and pay them money over time. Many senior citizens are able to

adjustable rate mortgage (ARM)–mortgage with variable financing charges over the life of the loan.

reverse mortgage–mortgage in which the owners get their equity out of their home over a period of time and return the house to the lender upon their deaths.

obtain the additional monthly income they may need by this form of financing, which permits them to draw on their equity in their land. Because of the collapse of the subprime mortgage market in 2007–2008, these creative forms of financing are now under extensive state and federal regulation. In addition, state and federal reforms require additional disclosures about the full cost of financing a real property purchase through a mortgage, especially in the types of mortgages in which payments and interest rates fluctuate.

27. Recording or Filing of Mortgage

An unrecorded mortgage is still a valid and binding between and among the parties. A mortgage cannot be set aside on the ground that it has not been recorded. However, recording the mortgage does protect the mortgagee in terms of priority as against other creditors. The recording statutes discussed earlier also apply to mortgages.

28. Responsibilities of the Parties

The mortgagor and mortgagee have the following duties and liabilities when a mortgage is placed on real property.

CPA (A) TAXES, ASSESSMENTS, AND INSURANCE. The duty to pay taxes and assessments rests with the mortgagor. In the absence of an agreement, neither party is under a duty to insure the mortgaged property. Both parties, however, may insure their respective interests. It is common practice for the mortgagor to obtain a single policy of insurance on the property payable to the mortgagee and the mortgagor generally according to the standard mortgagee clause that pays the outstanding loan balance first.

(B) IMPAIRMENT OF SECURITY. The mortgagor is liable to the mortgagee for any damage to the property caused by the mortgagor that impairs the security of the mortgage by materially reducing the value of the property. Both the mortgagor and the mortgagee have a right of action against a third person who wrongfully injures the property.

29. Transfer of Interest

Questions arise as to transfers by the mortgagor and the mortgagee of their respective interests and of the liability of a transferee of the mortgagor.

CPA (A) TRANSFER BY MORTGAGOR. The mortgagor may ordinarily transfer the property without the consent of the mortgagee. Such a transfer passes only the interest of the mortgagor and does not divest or impair a properly recorded mortgage.

The transfer of the property by the mortgagor does not affect the liability of the mortgagor to the mortgagee. Unless the mortgagee has agreed to substitute the mortgagor's grantee for the mortgagor, the mortgagor remains liable for the mortgage debt as though no transfer had been made.[9]

CPA (B) LIABILITY OF THE PARTIES IN A TRANSFER BY A MORTGAGOR. There are two ways to transfer mortgaged property, and each way has different results in terms of personal liability for the transferee. In the assumption of a mortgage, the transferee agrees to

[9] *Williams v Countrywide Home Loans, Inc.*, 504 F Supp 2d 176 (WD Tex 2007).

assumption–mortgage transfers in which the transferee and mortgagor are liable and the property is subject to foreclosure by the mortgagee if payments are not made.

assume liability. In an **assumption**, the mortgagor remains liable, the transferee is liable, and the property is subject to foreclosure by the mortgagee in the event the payments are not made. **For Example,** if Bob sold his house with a $175,000 mortgage for $200,000 to Jane, Jane could pay Bob $25,000 cash and then agree to assume Bob's mortgage. Jane may get the benefit of a lower interest rate by assuming Bob's mortgage. Both Bob and Jane are personally liable, and the mortgagee may foreclose on the property if the payments are not made.

The second method of transfer is called a "subject to" transfer. In this type of transfer, the property is subject to foreclosure, but the transferee does not agree to assume the mortgage personally. The mortgagor remains liable in this type of transfer, too.

(c) Transfer by Mortgagee. In most states, a mortgage may be transferred or assigned by the mortgagee.

30. Rights of Mortgagee After Default

foreclosure–procedure for enforcing a mortgage resulting in the public sale of the mortgaged property and, less commonly, in merely barring the right of the mortgagor to redeem the property from the mortgage.

Upon the mortgagor's default, the mortgagee in some states is entitled to obtain possession of the property and collect the rents or to have a receiver appointed for that purpose. In all states, the mortgagee may enforce the mortgage by **foreclosure**, a judicial procedure resulting in sale of the mortgaged property.

Generally, upon any default under the terms of the mortgage agreement, the mortgagee has the right to accelerate the debt or declare that the entire mortgage debt is due. The mortgagee generally has this right even though the default related only to paying an installment or to doing some act, such as maintaining insurance on the property or producing receipts for taxes.

A sale resulting from the foreclosure of the mortgage ends the mortgage lien (subject to rights of redemption), and the property passes free of the mortgage to the buyer at the sale. However, the extinction of the mortgage by foreclosure does not destroy the debt that was secured by the mortgage. The mortgagor remains liable for any unpaid balance or deficiency. In many states, the mortgagor is generally given credit for the fair value of the property if it was purchased by the mortgagee.[10]

stay of foreclosure–delay of foreclosure obtained by the mortgagor to prevent undue hardship.

31. Rights of Mortgagor After Default

redemption–buying back of one's property, which has been sold because of a default, upon paying the amount that had been originally due together with interest and costs.

After default, the mortgagor may seek to stop or stay foreclosure or to redeem the mortgaged land.

(a) Stay of Foreclosure. In certain cases authorized by statute, a **stay (or delay) of foreclosure** may be obtained by the mortgagor to prevent undue hardship.

CPA

(b) Redemption. The right of **redemption** is the right of the mortgagor to pay off the mortgage lien and all foreclosure expenses and, by so doing, acquire title to the property. State laws vary, but the right of redemption generally runs from the time of default through to six months after the foreclosure sale.

[10] *Carolina Bank v Chatham Station, Inc.*, 651 SE2d 386 (NC App 2007).

MAKE THE CONNECTION

SUMMARY

Real property includes land, buildings, fixtures, and rights in the land of another. Some land interests include the right to use the land, such as easements. Easements can be granted or arise by implication or prescription.

The interest held by a person in real property may be defined in terms of the period of time for which the person will remain the owner. The interest may be a fee simple estate, which lasts forever, or a life estate, which lasts for the life of a person. These estates are known as *freehold estates*. If the ownership interest exists for a specified number of days, months, or years, the interest is a leasehold estate.

Personal property may be attached to, or associated with, real property in such a way that it becomes real property. In such a case, it is called a *fixture*. To determine whether property has in fact become a fixture, the courts look to the method of attachment, to how the property is adapted to the realty, and to the intent of the person originally owning the personal property.

Under common law, the liability of a land owner for injury to third persons on the premises depends on the status of the third persons as trespassers, licensees, or invitees. Many jurisdictions, however, are ignoring these common law distinctions in favor of an ordinary negligence standard or are giving licensees the same protection as invitees.

Real property may be the subject of multiple ownership. The forms of multiple ownership are the same as those for personal property. In addition, there are special forms of co-ownership for real property, such as condominiums and cooperatives.

A *deed* is an instrument by which a grantor transfers an interest in land to a grantee. A deed can be a quitclaim deed or a warranty deed. To be effective, a deed must be signed or sealed by the grantor and delivered to the grantee. Recording the deed is not required to make the deed effective to pass title, but recording provides notice to the public that the grantee is the present owner. The warranties of the grantor relate to the title transferred by the grantor and to the fitness of the property for use. In the absence of any express warranty in the deed, no warranty of fitness arises under the common law in the sale or the conveyance of real estate. Most states today hold that when a builder or real estate developer sells a new home to a buyer, an implied warranty of habitability arises. Title to real estate may also be acquired by eminent domain and adverse possession.

An agreement that creates an interest in real property as security for an obligation and that ends upon the performance of the obligation is a mortgage. A mortgage must be in writing under the statute of frauds. If the mortgage is unrecorded, it is valid between the parties. The mortgage should be recorded to put good-faith purchasers on notice of the mortgage. A purchaser of the mortgaged property does not become liable for the mortgage debt unless the purchaser assumes the mortgage. The mortgagor still remains liable unless the mortgagee agrees to a substitution of parties. If the mortgagor defaults, the mortgagee may enforce the mortgage by foreclosure. Such foreclosure may be delayed because of undue hardship.

LEARNING OUTCOMES

After studying this chapter, you should be able to clearly explain:

A. NATURE OF REAL PROPERTY

LO.1 List the types of real property interests, the rights of the parties and their liabilities

See *Kelo v City of New London* on p. 1179.
See *Winchell v Guy* on p. 1172.

LO.2 Distinguish between liens, licenses, and easements

See *Frierson v Watson* on p. 1165.
See the Sports & Entertainment Law discussion of Wrigley Field on p. 1167.

B. NATURE AND FORM OF REAL PROPERTY OWNERSHIP

LO.3 Discuss the nature and form of real property ownership

See **For Example**, on Ralph Watkins on p. 1170

C. LIABILITY TO THIRD PERSONS FOR CONDITION OF REAL PROPERTY

LO.4 Explain the liability of landowners for injury to others on their property.

See the slip-and-fall example on p. 1171

D. CO-OWNERSHIP OF REAL PROPERTY

LO.5 Discuss the forms of co-ownership and parties' rights.

See the example on p. 1172 of the rights of condominium owners.

E. TRANSFER OF REAL PROPERTY BY DEED

LO.6 Describe how deeds convey title to land

See *Fletcher v Minton* on p. 1177.

F. OTHER METHODS OF TRANSFERRING REAL PROPERTY

G. MORTGAGES

LO.7 Describe the characteristics and effect of a mortgage

See the **For Example**, discussion of Bob and Jane on p. 1183.

KEY TERMS

abstract of title
acceptance
adjustable rate mortgage (ARM)
adverse possession
assumption
attractive nuisance doctrine
condominium
cooperative
covenant against encumbrances
covenant of further assurances

covenant of quiet enjoyment
covenant of right to convey
covenant of seisin
covenants (or warranties) of title
deed
dominant tenement
easement
easement by implication
eminent domain
estate in fee
fee simple defeasibles

fee simple estate
fixture
foreclosure
grantee
grantor
invitee
judgment liens
land
leasehold estate
license
licensee
liens
life estate
limited covenant

mechanic's liens
mortgage
notice statutes
notice-race
possibility of reverter
prescription
profits
quitclaim deeds
race statutes

race-notice statutes
real property
recorder
redemption
remainder interest
reverse mortgage
runs with the land
servient tenement

stay (or delay) of
    foreclosure
tax liens
transferee
trespasser
warranties of title
warranty deeds
way of necessity

QUESTIONS AND CASE PROBLEMS

1. In 1972, Donald and Joyce Carnahan purchased a 1-acre lot located on a 22-acre lake. The purchase included a portion of the lake bed. The Carnahans used the lake for recreational activity in both winter and summer, and their activities included motorboats, jet skis, and wave runners. In 1991, the Moriah Property Owners Association, Inc., acquired title to the majority of the lots along the lake and imposed restrictive covenants on the use of the lake, including one that prohibited all motors on the lake except for those powered by 12-volt batteries. The Carnahans filed suit to establish a prescriptive easement in their right to use the lake for all their activities. Do you think the Carnahans acquired an easement by prescription? [*Carnahan v Moriah Property Owners Association, Inc.*, 716 NE2d 437 (Ind)]

2. Bunn and his wife claimed that they had an easement to enter and use the swimming pool on neighboring land. A contract between the former owners of the Bunns' property and the adjacent apartment complex contained a provision that the use of the apartment complex's swimming pool would be available to the purchaser and his family. No reference to the pool was made in the contract between the former owners and the Bunns, nor was there any reference to it in the deed conveying the property to the Bunns. Decide. [*Bunn v Offutt*, 222 SE2d 522 (Va)]

3. After executing the various deeds, J. M. Fernandez Jr. placed them in a closet (with other valuable papers) for safekeeping until they could be physically delivered to the various grantees, including Sylvia Sheppard, when she returned to Key West. This closet was in the home that Fernandez shared with Betty DeMerritt. They were not married but lived together the final 15 years of Fernandez's life. Shortly thereafter, Fernandez was debilitated by a stroke and became a total invalid. He never regained his health and died before Sylvia Sheppard could return to Key West to receive physical delivery of the deed personally from him. When Sylvia Sheppard did arrive in Key West, Betty DeMerritt gave her the deed. This took place two or three days after the death of Fernandez. When questioned as to why she turned the deed over to Sylvia, Betty DeMerritt stated, "I knew he wanted me to do it … because he couldn't do it." She was speaking of Fernandez's physical disability. Does Sylvia have title to the property? Was there delivery? [*Kerr v Fernandez*, 792 So2d 685 (Fla)]

4. Kenneth Corson, 10, lived with his mother, Lynda Lontz, in an apartment building owned by Bruno and Carolyn Kosinski. While playing with other children who lived in the same building, Corson was drawn to a stairwell that provided access to the building's laundry room and roof. Corson and the other children climbed to the roof and discovered an area where they could jump from the roof of their building to that of the building next door. The children engaged in roof hopping for several days. On the last day, Corson misjudged his jump and fell the three stories to the ground below. Corson and his mother filed suit against the Kosinskis to collect damages for Corson's injuries. What theory might be used to hold the Kosinskis liable? [*Corson by Lontz v Kosinski*, 801 F Supp 75 (ND Ill)]

5. Determine whether the following would be fixtures or personal property.

   a. Refrigerator in a home

   b. Refrigerators in an apartment complex with furnished units

   c. Refrigerators in a restaurant kitchen

   d. Refrigeration/freezer units in a grocery store

   e. Mini-refrigerator in a student dorm

6. What is the relationship between trespass and adverse possession?

7. Bradham and other members and trustees of the Mount Olivet Church brought an action to cancel a mortgage on the church property. The mortgage had been executed previously by Davis and other former trustees of the church and given to Robinson as mortgagee. The court found that the church was not indebted to the mortgagee for any amount. Should the mortgage be canceled? [*Bradham v Robinson*, 73 SE2d 555 (NC)]

8. Miller executed a deed to real estate, naming Zieg as grantee. He placed the deed in an envelope on which was written "To be filed at my death" and put the envelope and deed in a safe deposit box in the National Bank that had been rented in the names of Miller and Zieg. After Miller's death, Zieg removed the deed from the safe deposit box. Moseley, as executor under Miller's will, brought an action against Zieg to declare the deed void. Decide. [*Moseley v Zieg*, 146 NW2d 72 (Neb)]

9. Henry Lile owned a house. When the land on which it was situated was condemned for a highway, he moved the house to the land of his daughter, Sarah Crick. In the course of construction work, blasting damaged the house. Sarah Crick sued the contractors, Terry & Wright, who claimed that Lile should be joined in the action as a plaintiff and that Sarah could not sue by herself because it was Lile's house. Were the defendants correct? [*Terry & Wright v Crick*, 418 SW2d 217 (Ky)]

10. Bradt believed his backyard ran all the way to a fence. Actually, a strip on Bradt's side of the fence belonged to his neighbor Giovannone, but Bradt never intended to take land away from anyone. Bradt later brought an action against

Giovannone to determine who owned the strip on Bradt's side of the fence. Who is the owner? Why? [*Bradt v Giovannone*, 315 NYS2d 96]

11. Robert E. Long owned land in the City of Hampton that he leased to Adams Outdoor Advertising Limited Partnership. Adams had an advertising billboard placed on the property. On October 6, 1993, Long notified Adams that he was terminating the lease. Adams accepted the termination and told Long that it would have the electrical service disconnected and would schedule demolition of the billboard for the first week in November. Long wanted to use the billboard to advertise his own business and filed suit to enjoin Adams from destroying the billboard. Long maintained the billboard was part of the land and belonged to him. Adams asserted that it owned the billboard as a lessee. The trial court found for Long, and Adams appealed. Decide. [*Adams Outdoor Adv., Ltd., Part. v Long*, 483 SE2d 224 (Va)]

12. Smikahl sold Hansen a tract of land on which were two houses and four trailer lots equipped with concrete patios and necessary connections for utility lines. The tract Hansen purchased was completely surrounded by the land owned by Smikahl and third persons. To get onto the highway, it was necessary to cross the Smikahl tract. Several years after the sale, Smikahl put a barbed wire fence around his land. Hansen sued to prevent obstruction to travel between his land and the highway over the Smikahl land. Smikahl's defense was that no such right of travel had been given to Hansen. Was he correct? [*Hansen v Smikahl*, 113 NW2d 210 (Neb)]

13. Martin Manufacturing decided to raise additional long-term capital by mortgaging an industrial park it owned. First National Loan Co. agreed to lend Martin $1 million and to take a note and first mortgage on the land and building. The mortgage was duly recorded. Martin sold the property to Marshall, who took the property and assumed the mortgage debt. Does Marshall have any personal liability on the mortgage debt? Is Martin still liable on the mortgage debt? Explain.

14. Christine and Steve Mallock buried their son in a burial plot purchased at Southern Memorial Park, Inc. Each year the Mallocks conducted a memorial service for their son at his burial plot. On the seventh anniversary of their son's death, the Mallocks went to their son's grave at 11:00 A.M. for the annual service, which generally took 30 minutes. When they arrived, they discovered that a tent and chairs set up for funeral services on the plot next to their son's grave were actually resting on his gravesite. The Mallocks asked Southern's management if the tent and chairs could be moved until they could conduct their service. The managers refused, and the Mallocks went ahead with their ceremony, cutting it to five minutes, after they moved the chairs and tents by themselves.

Southern's managers called the police and had the Mallocks evicted. Southern claimed the Mallocks had no rights on the property except for the grave and that their deed for the plot did not award an easement for access. Did the Mallocks have the right to access to the gravesite? [*Mallock v Southern Memorial Park, Inc.*, 561 So2d 330 (Fla Ct App)]

15. *O* conveys property to *A* on December 1, 2006. *O* conveys the same property to *B* who does not know about *A* and who records his deed on December 2, 2006. *O* then conveys the same property to *C*. Who has title to the property?

CPA QUESTIONS

The topic of insurance has been eliminated from the content outline for the CPA exam as of october 2009. However, the exam lags behind the content change, so this topic may continue to appear on the exam for six to 18 months.

1. Which of the following statements is correct with respect to a real estate mortgage?

    a. It must be signed only by the mortgagor (borrower).

    b. It must be recorded in order to be effective between the mortgagor and the mortgagee.

    c. It does *not* have to be recorded to be effective against third parties without notice if it is a purchase money mortgage.

    d. It is effective even if *not* delivered to the mortgagee.

2. To be enforceable against the mortgagor, a mortgage must meet all the following requirements *except:*

    a. Be delivered to the mortgagee

    b. Be in writing and signed by the mortgagor

    c. Be recorded by the mortgagee

    d. Include a description of the debt and land involved

3. Ritz owned a building in which there was a duly recorded first mortgage held by Lyn and a recorded second mortgage held by Jay. Ritz sold the building to Nunn. Nunn assumed the Jay mortgage and had no actual knowledge of the Lyn mortgage. Nunn defaulted on the payments to Jay. If both Lyn and Jay foreclosed and the proceeds of the sale were insufficient to pay both Lyn and Jay, then:

    a. Jay would be paid after Lyn was fully paid.

    b. Jay and Lyn would be paid proportionately.

    c. Nunn would be personally liable to Lyn but not to Jay.

    d. Nunn would be personally liable to Lyn and Jay.

4. Which of the following deeds will give a real property purchaser the greatest protection?

    a. Quitclaim

    b. Bargain and sale

    c. Special warranty

    d. General warranty

HOW TO FIND THE LAW

In order to determine what the law on a particular question or issue is, it may be necessary to examine (1) compilations of constitutions, treaties, statutes, executive orders, proclamations, and administrative regulations; (2) reports of state and federal court decisions; (3) digests of opinions; (4) treatises on the law; and (5) loose-leaf services. These sources can be either researched traditionally or using fee-and/or non-fee-based computerized legal research accessed through the World Wide Web.

A. COMPILATIONS

In the consideration of a legal problem in business it is necessary to determine whether the matter is affected or controlled by a constitution, national or state; by a national treaty; by an Act of Congress or a state legislature, or by a city ordinance; by a decree or proclamation of the President of the United States, a governor, or a mayor; or by a regulation of a federal, state, or local administrative agency.

Each body or person that makes laws, regulations, or ordinances usually compiles and publishes at the end of each year or session all of the matter that it has adopted. In addition to the periodical or annual volumes, it is common to compile all the treaties, statutes, regulations, or ordinances in separate volumes. To illustrate, the federal Anti-Injunction Act may be cited as the Act of March 23, 1932, 47 Stat 70, 29 USC Sections 101 et seq. This means that this law was enacted on March 23, 1932, and that it can be found at page 70 in Volume 47 of the reports that contain all of the statutes adopted by the Congress.

The second part of the citation, 29 USC Sections 101 et seq., means that in the collection of all of the federal statutes, which is known as the United States Code, the full text of the statute can be found in the sections of the 29th title beginning with Section 101.

B. COURT DECISIONS

For complicated or important legal cases or when an appeal is to be taken, a court will generally write an opinion, which explains why the court made the decision. Appellate courts as a rule write opinions. The great majority of these decisions, particularly in the case of the appellate courts, are collected and printed. In order to avoid confusion, the opinions of each court are ordinarily printed in a separate set of reports, either by official reporters or private publishers.

In the reference "Pennoyer v Neff, 95 US 714, 24 LEd 565," the first part states the names of the parties. It does not necessarily tell who was the plaintiff and who was the defendant. When an action is begun in a lower court, the first name is that of the plaintiff and the second name that of the defendant. When the case is appealed, generally the name of the person taking the appeal appears on the records of the higher court as the first one and that of the adverse party as the second. Sometimes, therefore, the original order of the names of the parties is reversed.

The balance of the reference consists of two citations. The first citation, 95 US 714, means that the opinion which the court filed in the case of Pennoyer v Neff may be found on page 714 of the 95th volume of a series of books in which are printed officially the opinions of the United States Supreme Court. Sometimes the same opinion is printed in two different sets of volumes. In the example, 24 LEd 565 means that in the 24th volume of another set of books, called Lawyer's Edition, of the United States Supreme Court Reports, the same opinion begins on page 565.

In opinions by a state court there may also be two citations, as in the case of "Morrow v Corbin, 122 Tex 553, 62 SW2d 641." This means that the opinion in the lawsuit between Morrow and Corbin may be found in the 122d volume of the reports of the highest court of Texas, beginning on page 553; and also in Volume 62 of the Southwestern Reporter, Second Series, at page 641.

The West Publishing Company publishes a set of sectional reporters covering the entire United States. They are called "sectional" because each reporter, instead of being limited to a particular court or a particular state, covers the decisions of the courts of a particular section of the country. Thus the decisions of the courts of Arkansas, Kentucky, Missouri, Tennessee, and Texas are printed by the West Publishing company as a group in a sectional reporter called the Southwestern Reporter.[1] Because of the large number of decisions involved, generally only the opinions of the state appellate courts are printed. A number of states[2] have discontinued publication of the opinions of their courts, and those opinions are now found only in the West reporters.

The reason for the "Second Series" in the Southwestern citation is that when there were 300 volumes in the original series, instead of calling the next volume 301, the publisher called it Volume 1, Second Series. Thus 62 SW2d Series really means the 362d volume of the Southwestern Reporter. Six to eight volumes appear in a year for each geographic section.

In addition to these state reporters, the West Publishing Company publishes a Federal Supplement, which primarily reports the opinions of the Federal District Courts; the Federal Reporter, which primarily reports the decisions of the United States Courts of Appeals; and the Supreme Court Reporter, which reports the decisions of the United States Supreme Court. The Supreme Court decisions are also reported in a separate set called the Lawyers' Edition, published by the Lawyers Cooperative Publishing Company.

The reports published by the West Publishing Company and Lawyers Cooperative Publishing Company are unofficial reports, while those bearing the name or abbreviation of the United States or of a state, such as "95 US 714" or "122 Tex 553" are official reports. This means that in the case of the latter, the particular court, such as the United States Supreme Court, has officially authorized that its decisions be printed and that by federal statute such official printing is made. In the case of the unofficial reporters, the publisher prints the decisions of a court on its own initiative. Such opinions are part of the public domain and not subject to any copyright or similar restriction.

C. Digests of Opinions

The reports of court decisions are useful only if one has the citation, that is, the name and volume number of the book and the page number of the opinion one is seeking. For this reason, digests of the decisions have been prepared. These digests organize the entire field of law under major headings, which are then arranged in alphabetical order. Under each heading, such as "Contracts," the subject is divided into the different questions that can arise with respect to that field. A master outline is thus created on the subject. This outline includes short paragraphs describing what each case holds and giving its citation.

D. Treatises and Restatements

Very helpful in finding a case or a statute are the treatises on the law. These may be special books, each written by an author on a particular subject, such as Williston on Contracts, Bogert on Trusts, Fletcher on Corporations, or they may be general encyclopedias, as in the case of American Jurisprudence, American Jurisprudence, Second, and Corpus Juris Secundum.

Another type of treatise is found in the restatements of the law prepared by the American Law Institute. Each restatement consists of one or more volumes devoted to a particular phase of the law, such as the Restatement of the Law of Contracts, Restatement of the Law of Agency, and Restatement of the Law of Property. In each restatement, the American Law Institute, acting through special committees of judges, lawyers, and professors of law, has set forth what the law is; and in many areas where there is no law or the present rule is regarded as unsatisfactory, the restatement specifies what the Institute deems to be the desirable rule.

E. Loose-Leaf Services

A number of private publishers, notably Commerce Clearing House and Prentice-Hall, publish loose-leaf books devoted to particular branches of the law. Periodically, the publisher sends to the purchaser a number of pages that set forth any decision, regulation, or statute made or adopted since the prior set of pages was prepared. Such services are unofficial.

F. Computerized Legal Research

National and local computer services are providing constantly widening assistance for legal research. The database in such a system may be opinions, statutes, or administrative regulations stored word for word; or the later history of a particular case giving its full citation and

---

[1] The sectional reporters are: Atlantic—A. (Connecticut, Delaware, District of Columbia, Maine, Maryland, New Hampshire, New Jersey, Pennsylvania, Rhode Island, Vermont); Northeastern—N.E. (Illinois, Indiana, Massachusetts, New York, Ohio); N.W. (Iowa, Michigan, Minnesota, Nebraska, North Dakota, South Dakota, Wisconsin); Pacific—P. (Alaska, Arizona, California, Colorado, Hawaii, Idaho, Kansas, Montana, Nevada, New Mexico, Oklahoma, Oregon, Utah, Washington, Wyoming); Southeastern—S.E. (Georgia, North Carolina, South Carolina, Virginia, West Virginia); Southwestern— S.W. (Arkansas, Kentucky, Missouri, Tennessee, Texas); and Southern—So. (Alabama, Florida, Louisiana, Mississippi). There is also a special New York State reporter known as the New York Supplement and a special California State reporter known as the California Reporter.

[2] See, for example, Alaska, Florida, Iowa, Kentucky, Louisiana, Maine, Mississippi, Missouri, North Dakota, Oklahoma, Texas, and Wyoming.

showing whether the case has been followed by other courts; or the text of forms and documents. By means of a terminal connected to the system, the user can retrieve the above information at a great saving of time and with the assurance that it is up-to-date.

There are two leading, fee-based systems for computer-aided research. Listed alphabetically, they are LEXIS and WESTLAW.

A specialized service of legal forms for business is provided by Shepard's BUSINESS LAW CASE MANAGEMENT SYSTEM. A monthly fee is required for usage.

Numerous free, private sites offer a lot of legal resources. The federal government offers a variety of case law, regulations, and code enactments, either pending or newly promulgated. To find the most comprehensive source of government-maintained legal information, go to **http://www.house.gov**.

Increasingly, some states offer their regulations and codes online. As an example, go to the State of California's site, **www.leginfo.ca.gov**, as an example of a government-based legal information provider. For a complete listing of state homepages, go to **http://www.house.gov/house/govsites.shtml**.

For sources of all types of law, and legal resources, the internet site, Hieros Gamos, **www.hg.org** claims that "virtually all online and offline (published) legal information is accessible within three levels." It is important to note, however, that non-fee-based services do not guarantee the integrity of the information provided. Therefore, when accessing free information over the Internet, one should be careful to double-check the authority of the provider and the accuracy of the data obtained. This caution extends to sites maintained by federal and state governments as well.

The computer field has expanded to such an extent that there is now a Legal Software Review of over 500 pages prepared by Lawyers Library, 12761 New Hall Ferry, Florissant, MO 63033.

THE CONSTITUTION OF THE UNITED STATES

We the people of the United States of America, in order to form a more perfect union, establish justice, insure domestic tranquility, provide for the common defense, promote the general welfare, and secure the blessings of liberty to ourselves and our posterity, do ordain and establish this Constitution for the United States of America.

Article I

SECTION 1

All legislative powers herein granted shall be vested in a Congress of the United States, which shall consist of a Senate and House of Representatives.

SECTION 2

1. The House of Representatives shall be composed of members chosen every second year by the people of the several States, and the electors in each State shall have the qualifications requisite for electors of the most numerous branch of the State legislature.

2. No person shall be a representative who shall not have attained to the age of twenty-five years, and been seven years a citizen of the United States, and who shall not, when elected, be an inhabitant of that State in which he shall be chosen.

3. Representatives and direct taxes shall be apportioned among the several States which may be included within this Union, according to their respective numbers, which shall be determined by adding to the whole number of free persons, including those bound to service for a term of years, and excluding Indians not taxed, three fifths of all other persons.[1] The actual enumeration shall be made within three years after the first meeting of the Congress of the United States, and within every subsequent term of ten years, in such manner as they shall by law direct. The number of representatives shall not exceed one for every thirty thousand, but each State shall have at least one representative; and until such enumeration shall be made, the State of New Hampshire shall be entitled to choose three, Massachusetts eight, Rhode Island and Providence Plantations one, Connecticut five, New York six, New Jersey four, Pennsylvania eight, Delaware one, Maryland six, Virginia ten, North Carolina five, South Carolina five, and Georgia three.

4. When vacancies happen in the representation from any State, the executive authority thereof shall issue writs of election to fill such vacancies.

5. The House of Representatives shall choose their speaker and other officers; and shall have the sole power of impeachment.

SECTION 3

1. The Senate of the United States shall be composed of two senators from each State, chosen by the legislature thereof, for six years; and each senator shall have one vote.

2. Immediately after they shall be assembled in consequence of the first election, they shall be divided as equally as may be into three classes. The seats of the senators of the first class shall be vacated at the expiration of the second year, of the second class at the expiration of the fourth year, and of the third class at the expiration of the sixth year, so that one third may be chosen every second year; and if vacancies happen by resignation, or otherwise, during the recess of the legislature of any State, the executive thereof may make temporary appointments until the next meeting of the legislature, which shall then fill such vacancies.[2]

3. No person shall be a senator who shall not have attained to the age of thirty years, and been nine years a citizen of the United States, and who shall not, when elected, be an inhabitant of that State for which he shall be chosen.

4. The Vice President of the United States shall be President of the Senate, but shall have no vote, unless they be equally divided.

[1] See the 14th Amendment.

[2] See the 17th Amendment.

5. The Senate shall choose their other officers, and also a president pro tempore, in the absence of the Vice President, or when he shall exercise the office of the President of the United States.

6. The Senate shall have the sole power to try all impeachments. When sitting for that purpose, they shall be on oath or affirmation. When the President of the United States is tried, the chief justice shall preside: and no person shall be convicted without the concurrence of two thirds of the members present.

7. Judgment in cases of impeachment shall not extend further than to removal from office, and disqualification to hold and enjoy any office of honor, trust or profit under the United States: but the party convicted shall nevertheless be liable and subject to indictment, trial, judgment and punishment, according to law.

SECTION 4

1. The times, places, and manner of holding elections for senators and representatives, shall be prescribed in each State by the legislature thereof; but the Congress may at any time by law make or alter such regulations, except as to the places of choosing senators.

2. The Congress shall assemble at least once in every year, and such meeting shall be on the first Monday in December, unless they shall by law appoint a different day.

SECTION 5

1. Each House shall be the judge of the elections, returns and qualifications of its own members, and a majority of each shall constitute a quorum to do business; but a smaller number may adjourn from day to day, and may be authorized to compel the attendance of absent members, in such manner, and under such penalties as each House may provide.

2. Each House may determine the rules of its proceedings, punish its members for disorderly behavior, and, with the concurrence of two thirds, expel a member.

3. Each House shall keep a journal of its proceedings, and from time to time publish the same, excepting such parts as may in their judgment require secrecy; and the yeas and nays of the members of either House on any question shall, at the desire of one fifth of those present, be entered on the journal.

4. Neither House, during the session of Congress, shall, without the consent of the other, adjourn for more than three days, nor to any other place than that in which the two Houses shall be sitting.

SECTION 6

1. The senators and representatives shall receive a compensation for their services, to be ascertained by law, and paid out of the Treasury of the United States. They shall in all cases, except treason, felony, and breach of the peace, be privileged from arrest during their attendance at the session of their respective Houses, and in going to and returning from the same; and for any speech or debate in either House, they shall not be questioned in any other place.

2. No senator or representative shall, during the time for which he was elected, be appointed to any civil office under the authority of the United States, which shall have been created, or the emoluments whereof shall have been increased during such time; and no person holding any office under the United States shall be a member of either House during his continuance in office.

SECTION 7

1. All bills for raising revenue shall originate in the House of Representatives; but the Senate may propose or concur with amendments as on other bills.

2. Every bill which shall have passed the House of Representatives and the Senate, shall, before it becomes a law, be presented to the President of the United States; if he approves he shall sign it, but if not he shall return it, with his objections to that House in which it shall have originated, who shall enter the objections at large on their journal, and proceed to reconsider it. If after such reconsideration two thirds of that House shall agree to pass the bill, it shall be sent, together with the objections, to the other House, by which it shall likewise be reconsidered, and if approved by two thirds of that House, it shall become a law. But in all such cases the votes of both Houses shall be determined by yeas and nays, and the names of the persons voting for and against the bill shall be entered on the journal of each House respectively. If any bill shall not be returned by the President within ten days (Sundays excepted) after it shall have been presented to him, the same shall be a law, in like manner as if he had signed it, unless the Congress by their adjournment prevent its return, in which case it shall not be a law.

3. Every order, resolution, or vote to which the concurrence of the Senate and the House of Representatives may be necessary (except on a question of adjournment) shall be presented to the President of the United States; and before the same shall take effect, shall be approved by him, or being disapproved by him, shall be repassed by two thirds of the Senate and House of Representatives, according to the rules and limitations prescribed in the case of a bill.

SECTION 8

The Congress shall have the power

1. To lay and collect taxes, duties, imposts, and excises, to pay the debts and provide for the common defense and general welfare of the United States; but all duties, imposts, and excises shall be uniform throughout the United States;

2. To borrow money on the credit of the United States;

3. To regulate commerce with foreign nations, and among the several States, and with the Indian tribes;

4. To establish a uniform rule of naturalization, and uniform laws on the subject of bankruptcies throughout the United States;

5. To coin money, regulate the value thereof, and of foreign coin, and fix the standard of weights and measures;

6. To provide for the punishment of counterfeiting the securities and current coin of the United States;

7. To establish post offices and post roads;

8. To promote the progress of science and useful arts, by securing for limited times to authors and inventors the exclusive rights to their respective writings and discoveries;

9. To constitute tribunals inferior to the Supreme Court;

10. To define and punish piracies and felonies committed on the high seas, and offenses against the law of nations;

11. To declare war, grant letters of marque and reprisal, and make rules concerning captures on land and water;

12. To raise and support armies, but no appropriation of money to that use shall be for a longer term than two years;

13. To provide and maintain a navy;

14. To make rules for the government and regulation of the land and naval forces;

15. To provide for calling forth the militia to execute the laws of the Union, suppress insurrections and repel invasions;

16. To provide for organizing, arming, and disciplining the militia, and for governing such part of them as may be employed in the service of the United States, reserving to the States respectively, the appointment of the officers, and the authority of training the militia according to the discipline prescribed by Congress;

17. To exercise exclusive legislation in all cases whatsoever, over such district (not exceeding ten miles square) as may, by cession of particular States, and the acceptance of Congress, become the seat of the government of the United States, and to exercise like authority over all places purchased by the consent of the legislature of the State in which the same shall be, for the erection of forts, magazines, arsenals, dockyards, and other needful buildings; and

18. To make all laws which shall be necessary and proper for carrying into execution the foregoing powers, and all other powers vested by this Constitution in the government of the United States, or in any department or officer thereof.

SECTION 9

1. The migration or importation of such persons as any of the States now existing shall think proper to admit, shall not be prohibited by the Congress prior to the year one thousand eight hundred and eight, but a tax or duty may be imposed on such importation, not exceeding ten dollars for each person.

2. The privilege of the writ of habeas corpus shall not be suspended, unless when in cases of rebellion or invasion the public safety may require it.

3. No bill of attainder or ex post facto law shall be passed.

4. No capitation, or other direct, tax shall be laid, unless in proportion to the census or enumeration hereinbefore directed to be taken.[3]

5. No tax or duty shall be laid on articles exported from any State.

6. No preference shall be given by any regulation of commerce or revenue to the ports of one State over those of another: nor shall vessels bound to, or from, one State be obliged to enter, clear, or pay duties in another.

7. No money shall be drawn from the treasury, but in consequence of appropriations made by law; and a regular statement and account of the receipts and expenditures of all public money shall be published from time to time.

8. No title of nobility shall be granted by the United States: and no person holding any office of profit or trust under them, shall, without the consent of the Congress, accept of any present, emolument, office, or title, of any kind whatever, from any king, prince, or foreign State.

SECTION 10

1. No State shall enter into any treaty, alliance, or confederation; grant letters of marque and reprisal; coin money; emit bills of credit; make anything but gold and silver coin a tender in payment of debts; pass any bill of attainder, ex post facto law, or law impairing the obligation of contracts, or grant any title of nobility.

2. No State shall, without the consent of the Congress, lay any imposts or duties on imports or exports, except what may be absolutely necessary for executing its inspection laws: and the net produce of all duties and imposts laid by any State on imports or exports, shall be for the use of the treasury of the United States; and all such laws shall be subject to the revision and control of the Congress.

3. No State shall, without the consent of the Congress, lay any duty of tonnage, keep troops, or ships of war in time of peace, enter into any agreement or compact with another State, or with a foreign power, or engage in war, unless actually invaded, or in such imminent danger as will not admit of delay.

Article II

SECTION 1

1. The executive power shall be vested in a President of the United States of America. He shall hold his office during the term of four years, and, together with the Vice President, chosen for the same term, be elected as follows:

2. Each State shall appoint, in such manner as the legislature thereof may direct, a number of electors, equal to the whole number of senators and representatives to which the State may be entitled in the Congress: but no senator or representative, or person holding an office of trust or profit under the United States, shall be appointed an elector.

[3] See the 16th Amendment.

The electors shall meet in their respective States, and vote by ballot for two persons, of whom one at least shall not be an inhabitant of the same State with themselves. And they shall make a list of all the persons voted for, and of the number of votes for each; which list they shall sign and certify, and transmit sealed to the seat of the government of the United States, directed to the president of the Senate. The president of the Senate shall, in the presence of the Senate and House of Representatives, open all the certificates, and the votes shall then be counted. The person having the greatest number of votes shall be the President, if such number be a majority of the whole number of electors appointed; and if there be more than one who have such majority, and have an equal number of votes, then the House of Representatives shall immediately choose by ballot one of them for President; and if no person have a majority, then from the five highest on the list the said House shall in like manner choose the President. But in choosing the President, the votes shall be taken by States, the representation from each State having one vote; a quorum for this purpose shall consist of a member or members from two thirds of the States, and a majority of all the States shall be necessary to a choice. In every case, after the choice of the President, the person having the greatest number of votes of the electors shall be the Vice President. But if there should remain two or more who have equal votes, the Senate shall choose from them by ballot the Vice President.[4]

3. The Congress may determine the time of choosing the electors, and the day on which they shall give their votes; which day shall be the same throughout the United States.

4. No person except a natural born citizen, or a citizen of the United States, at the time of the adoption of this Constitution, shall be eligible to the office of President; neither shall any person be eligible to that office who shall not have attained to the age of thirty-five years, and been fourteen years a resident within the United States.

5. In the case of removal of the President from office, or of his death, resignation, or inability to discharge the powers and duties of the said office, the same shall devolve on the Vice President, and the Congress may by law provide for the case of removal, death, resignation, or inability, both of the President and Vice President, declaring what officer shall then act as President, and such officer shall act accordingly, until the disability be removed, or a President shall be elected.

6. The President shall, at stated times, receive for his services a compensation, which shall neither be increased nor diminished during the period for which he shall have been elected, and he shall not receive within that period any other emolument from the United States, or any of them.

7. Before he enter on the execution of his office, he shall take the following oath or affirmation:—"I do solemnly swear (or affirm) that I will faithfully execute the office of President of the United States, and will to the best of my ability, preserve, protect and defend the Constitution of the United States."

SECTION 2

1. The President shall be commander in chief of the army and navy of the United States, and of the militia of the several States, when called into the actual service of the United States; he may require the opinion, in writing, of the principal officer in each of the executive departments, upon any subject relating to the duties of their respective office, and he shall have power to grant reprieves and pardons for offenses against the United States, except in cases of impeachment.

2. He shall have power, by and with the advice and consent of the Senate, to make treaties, provided two thirds of the senators present concur; and he shall nominate, and by and with the advice and consent of the Senate, shall appoint ambassadors, other public ministers and consuls, judges of the Supreme Court, and all other officers of the United States, whose appointments are not herein otherwise provided for, and which shall be established by law: but the Congress may by law vest the appointment of such inferior officers, as they think proper, in the President alone, in the courts of law, or in the heads of departments.

3. The President shall have power to fill up all vacancies that may happen during the recess of the Senate, by granting commissions which shall expire at the end of their next session.

SECTION 3

He shall from time to time give to the Congress information of the state of the Union, and recommend to their consideration such measures as he shall judge necessary and expedient; he may, on extraordinary occasions, convene both Houses, or either of them, and in case of disagreement between them with respect to the time of adjournment, he may adjourn them to such time as he shall think proper; he shall receive ambassadors and other public ministers; he shall take care that the laws be faithfully executed, and shall commission all the officers of the United States.

SECTION 4

The President, Vice President, and all civil officers of the United States, shall be removed from office on impeachment for, and conviction of, treason, bribery, or other high crimes and misdemeanors.

Article III

SECTION 1

The judicial power of the United States shall be vested in one Supreme Court, and in such inferior courts as the Congress may from time to time ordain and establish. The judges, both of the Supreme and inferior courts, shall hold their offices during good behavior, and shall, at stated

---

[4] Superseded by the 12th Amendment.

times, receive for their services, a compensation, which shall not be diminished during their continuance in office.

SECTION 2

1. The judicial power shall extend to all cases, in law and equity, arising under this Constitution, the laws of the United States, and treaties made, or which shall be made, under their authority;—to all cases affecting ambassadors, other public ministers and consuls;—to all cases of admiralty and maritime jurisdiction;—to controversies to which the United States shall be a party;—to controversies between two or more States; between a State and citizens of another State;[5]—between citizens of different States;—between citizens of the same State claiming lands under grants of different States, and between a State, or the citizens thereof, and foreign States, citizens or subjects.

2. In all cases affecting ambassadors, other public ministers and consuls, and those in which a State shall be party, the Supreme Court shall have original jurisdiction. In all the other cases before mentioned, the Supreme Court shall have appellate jurisdiction, both as to law and to fact, with such exceptions, and under such regulations as the Congress shall make.

3. The trial of all crimes, except in cases of impeachment, shall be by jury; and such trial shall be held in the State where the said crimes shall have been committed; but when not committed within any State, the trial shall be at such place or places as the Congress may by law have directed.

SECTION 3

1. Treason against the United States shall consist only in levying war against them, or in adhering to their enemies, giving them aid and comfort. No person shall be convicted of treason unless on the testimony of two witnesses to the same overt act, or on confession in open court.

2. The Congress shall have power to declare the punishment of treason, but no attainder of treason shall work corruption of blood, or forfeiture except during the life of the person attainted.

Article IV

SECTION 1

Full faith and credit shall be given in each State to the public acts, records, and judicial proceedings of every other State. And the Congress may by general laws prescribe the manner in which such acts, records and proceedings shall be proved, and the effect thereof.

SECTION 2

1. The citizens of each State shall be entitled to all privileges and immunities of citizens in the several States.[6]

2. A person charged in any State with treason, felony, or other crime, who shall flee from justice, and be found in another State, shall on demand of the executive authority of the State from which he fled, be delivered up to be removed to the State having jurisdiction of the crime.

3. No person held to service or labor in one State under the laws thereof, escaping into another, shall in consequence of any law or regulation therein, be discharged from such service or labor, but shall be delivered up on claim of the party to whom such service or labor may be due.[7]

SECTION 3

1. New States may be admitted by the Congress into this Union; but no new State shall be formed or erected within the jurisdiction of any other State, nor any State be formed by the junction of two or more States, or parts of States, without the consent of the legislatures of the States concerned as well as of the Congress.

2. The Congress shall have power to dispose of and make all needful rules and regulations respecting the territory or other property belonging to the United States; and nothing in this Constitution shall be so construed as to prejudice any claims of the United States, or of any particular State.

SECTION 4

The United States shall guarantee to every State in this Union a republican form of government, and shall protect each of them against invasion; and on application of the legislature, or of the executive (when the legislature cannot be convened) against domestic violence.

Article V

The Congress, whenever two thirds of both Houses shall deem it necessary, shall propose amendments to this Constitution, or, on the application of the legislature of two thirds of the several States, shall call a convention for proposing amendments, which in either case, shall be valid to all intents and purposes, as part of this Constitution when ratified by the legislatures of three fourths of the several States, or by conventions in three fourths thereof, as the one or the other mode of ratification may be proposed by the Congress; provided that no amendment which may be made prior to the year one thousand eight hundred and eight shall in any manner affect the first and fourth clauses in the ninth section of the first article; and that no State, without its consent, shall be deprived of its equal suffrage in the Senate.

Article VI

1. All debts contracted and engagements entered into, before the adoption of this Constitution, shall be as valid

---

[5] See the 11th Amendment.
[6] See the 14th Amendment, Sec. 1.

[7] See the 13th Amendment.

against the United States under this Constitution, as under the Confederation.[8]

2. This Constitution, and the laws of the United States which shall be made in pursuance thereof; and all treaties made, or which shall be made, under the authority of the United States, shall be the supreme law of the land; and the judges in every State shall be bound thereby, anything in the Constitution or laws of any State to the contrary notwithstanding.

3. The senators and representatives before mentioned, and the members of the several State legislatures, and all executive and judicial officers, both of the United States and of the several States, shall be bound by oath or affirmation to support this Constitution; but no religious test shall ever be required as a qualification to any office or public trust under the United States.

Article VII

The ratification of the conventions of nine States shall be sufficient for the establishment of this Constitution between the States so ratifying the same.

Done in Convention by the unanimous consent of the States present the seventeenth day of September in the year of our Lord one thousand seven hundred and eighty-seven, and of the independence of the United States of America the twelfth. In witness whereof we have hereunto subscribed our names.

A. AMENDMENTS

First Ten Amendments passed by Congress Sept. 25, 1789.
Ratified by three-fourths of the States December 15, 1791.

Amendment I

Congress shall make no law respecting an establishment of religion, or prohibiting the free exercise thereof; or abridging the freedom of speech, or of the press; or the right of the people peaceably to assemble, and to petition the government for a redress of grievances.

Amendment II

A well regulated militia, being necessary to the security of a free State, the right of the people to keep and bear arms, shall not be infringed.

Amendment III

No soldier shall, in time of peace be quartered in any house, without the consent of the owner, nor in time of war, but in a manner to be prescribed by law.

Amendment IV

The right of the people to be secure in their persons, houses, papers, and effects, against unreasonable searches and seizures, shall not be violated, and no warrants shall issue, but upon probable cause, supported by oath or affirmation, and particularly describing the place to be searched, and the person or things to be seized.

Amendment V

No person shall be held to answer for a capital, or otherwise infamous crime, unless on a presentment or indictment of a grand jury, except in cases arising in the land or naval forces, or in the militia, when in actual service in time of war or public danger; nor shall any person be subject for the same offense to be twice put in jeopardy of life or limb; nor shall be compelled in any criminal case to be a witness against himself, nor be deprived of life, liberty, or property, without due process of law; nor shall private property be taken for public use without just compensation.

Amendment VI

In all criminal prosecutions, the accused shall enjoy the right to a speedy and public trial, by an impartial jury of the State and district wherein the crime shall have been committed, which district shall have been previously ascertained by law, and to be informed of the nature and cause of the accusation; to be confronted with the witnesses against him; to have compulsory process for obtaining witnesses in his favor, and to have the assistance of counsel for his defense.

Amendment VII

In suits at common law, where the value in controversy shall exceed twenty dollars, the right of trial by jury shall be preserved, and no fact tried by a jury shall be otherwise reexamined in any court of the United States, then according to the rules of the common law.

Amendment VIII

Excessive bail shall not be required, nor excessive fines imposed, nor cruel and unusual punishments inflicted.

[8] See the 14th Amendment, Sec. 4.

Amendment IX

The enumeration in the Constitution of certain rights shall not be construed to deny or disparage others retained by the people.

Amendment X

The powers not delegated to the United States by the Constitution, nor prohibited by it to the States, are reserved to the States respectively, or to the people.

Amendment XI

Passed by Congress March 5, 1794. Ratified January 8, 1798.

The judicial power of the United States shall not be construed to extend to any suit in law or equity, commenced or prosecuted against one of the United States by citizens of another State, or by citizens or subjects of any foreign State.

Amendment XII

Passed by Congress December 12, 1803. Ratified September 25, 1804.

The electors shall meet in their respective States, and vote by ballot for President and Vice President, one of whom, at least, shall not be an inhabitant of the same State with themselves; they shall name in their ballots the person voted for as President, and in distinct ballots, the person voted for as Vice President, and they shall make distinct lists of all persons voted for as President and of all persons voted for as Vice President, and of the number of votes for each, which lists they shall sign and certify, and transmit sealed to the seat of the government of the United States, directed to the President of the Senate;—The President of the Senate shall, in the presence of the Senate and House of Representatives, open all the certificates and the votes shall then be counted;—The person having the greatest number of votes for President, shall be the President, if such number be a majority of the whole number of electors appointed; and if no person have such majority, then from the persons having the highest numbers not exceeding three on the list of those voted for as President, the House of Representatives shall choose immediately, by ballot, the President. But in choosing the President, the votes shall be taken by States, the representation from each State having one vote; a quorum for this purpose shall consist of a member or members from two thirds of the States, and a majority of all the States shall be necessary to a choice. And if the House of Representatives shall not choose a President whenever the right of choice shall devolve upon them, before the fourth day of March next following, then the Vice President shall act as President, as in the case of the death or other constitutional disability of the President. The person having the greatest number of votes as Vice President shall be the Vice President, if such number be a majority of the whole number of electors appointed, and if no person have a majority, then from the two highest numbers on the list, the Senate shall choose the Vice President; a quorum for the purpose shall consist of two thirds of the whole number of Senators, and a majority of the whole number shall be necessary to a choice. But no person constitutionally ineligible to the office of President shall be eligible to that of Vice President of the United States.

Amendment XIII

Passed by Congress February 1, 1865. Ratified December 18, 1865.

SECTION 1

Neither slavery nor involuntary servitude, except as punishment for crime whereof the party shall have been duly convicted, shall exist within the United States, or any place subject to their jurisdiction.

SECTION 2

Congress shall have power to enforce this article by appropriate legislation.

Amendment XIV

Passed by Congress June 16, 1866. Ratified July 23, 1868.

SECTION 1

All persons born or naturalized in the United States, and subject to the jurisdiction thereof, are citizens of the United States and of the State wherein they reside. No State shall make or enforce any law which shall abridge the privileges or immunities of citizens of the United States; nor shall any State deprive any person of life, liberty, or property, without due process of law; nor deny to any person within its jurisdiction the equal protection of the laws.

SECTION 2

Representatives shall be apportioned among the several States according to their respective numbers, counting the whole number of persons in each State, excluding Indians not taxed. But when the right to vote at any election for the choice of electors for President and Vice President of the United States, representatives in Congress, the executive and judicial officers of a State, or the members of the legislature thereof, is denied to any of the male inhabitants of such State, being twenty-one years of age, and citizens of the United States, or in any way abridged, except for participation in rebellion, or other crime, the basis of representation therein shall be reduced in the proportion which the number of such male citizens shall bear to the whole number of male citizens twenty-one years of age in such State.

SECTION 3

No person shall be a senator or representative in Congress, or elector of President and Vice President, or hold any office, civil or military, under the United States, or under any State, who having previously taken an oath, as a member of Congress, or as an officer of the United States, or as a member of any State legislature, or as an executive or judicial officer of any State, to support the Constitution of the United States, shall have engaged in insurrection or rebellion against the same, or given aid or comfort to the enemies thereof. But Congress may by a vote of two thirds of each House, remove such disability.

SECTION 4

The validity of the public debt of the United States, authorized by law, including debts incurred for payment of pensions and bounties for services in suppressing insurrection or rebellion, shall not be questioned. But neither the United States nor any State shall assume or pay any debt or obligation incurred in aid of insurrection or rebellion against the United States, or any claim for the loss or emancipation of any slave; but all such debts, obligations, and claims shall be held illegal and void.

SECTION 5

The Congress shall have power to enforce, by appropriate legislation, the provisions of this article.

Amendment XV

Passed by Congress February 27, 1869. Ratified March 30, 1870.

SECTION 1

The right of citizens of the United States to vote shall not be denied or abridged by the United States or by any State on account of race, color, or previous condition of servitude.

SECTION 2

The Congress shall have power to enforce this article by appropriate legislation.

Amendment XVI

Passed by Congress July 12, 1909. Ratified February 25, 1913.

The Congress shall have power to lay and collect taxes on incomes, from whatever source derived, without apportionment among the several States, and without regard to any census or enumeration.

Amendment XVII

Passed by Congress May 16, 1912. Ratified May 31, 1913.

The Senate of the United States shall be composed of two senators from each State, elected by the people thereof, for six years; and each senator shall have one vote. The electors in each State shall have the qualifications requisite for electors of the most numerous branch of the State legislature.

When vacancies happen in the representation of any State in the Senate, the executive authority of such State shall issue writs of election to fill such vacancies: Provided, That the legislature of any State may empower the executive thereof to make temporary appointments until the people fill the vacancies by election as the legislature may direct.

This amendment shall not be so construed as to affect the election or term of any senator chosen before it becomes valid as part of the Constitution.

Amendment XVIII

Passed by Congress December 17, 1917. Ratified January 29, 1919.

After one year from the ratification of this article, the manufacture, sale, or transportation of intoxicating liquors within, the importation thereof into, or the exportation thereof from the United States and all territory subject to the jurisdiction thereof for beverage purposes is hereby prohibited.

The Congress and the several States shall have concurrent power to enforce this article by appropriate legislation.

This article shall be inoperative unless it shall have been ratified as an amendment to the Constitution by the legislatures of the several States, as provided in the Constitution, within seven years from the date of the submission hereof to the States by Congress.

Amendment XIX

Passed by Congress June 5, 1919. Ratified August 26, 1920.

The right of citizens of the United States to vote shall not be denied or abridged by the United States or by any State on account of sex.

The Congress shall have power by appropriate legislation to enforce the provisions of this article.

Amendment XX

Passed by Congress March 3, 1932. Ratified January 23, 1933.

SECTION 1

The terms of the President and Vice President shall end at noon on the 20th day of January, and the terms of Senators and Representatives at noon on the 3d day of January, of the years in which such terms would have ended if this article had not been ratified; and the terms of their successors shall then begin.

SECTION 2

The Congress shall assemble at least once in every year, and such meeting shall begin at noon on the 3d day of January, unless they shall by law appoint a different day.

SECTION 3

If, at the time fixed for the beginning of the term of the President, the President-elect shall have died, the Vice President-elect shall become President. If a President shall not have been chosen before the time fixed for the beginning of his term, or if the President-elect shall have failed to qualify, then the Vice President-elect shall act as President until a President shall have qualified; and the Congress may by law provide for the case wherein neither a President-elect nor a Vice President-elect shall have qualified, declaring who shall then act as President, or the manner in which one who is to act shall be selected, and such person shall act accordingly until a President or Vice President shall have qualified.

SECTION 4

The Congress may by law provide for the case of the death of any of the persons from whom the House of Representatives may choose a President whenever the right of choice shall have devolved upon them, and for the case of the death of any of the persons from whom the Senate may choose a Vice President whenever the right of choice shall have devolved upon them.

SECTION 5

Sections 1 and 2 shall take effect on the 15th day of October following the ratification of this article.

SECTION 6

This article shall be inoperative unless it shall have been ratified as an amendment to the Constitution by the legislatures of three-fourths of the several States within seven years from the date of its submission.

Amendment XXI

Passed by Congress February 20, 1933. Ratified December 5, 1933.

SECTION 1

The eighteenth article of amendment to the Constitution of the United States is hereby repealed.

SECTION 2

The transportation or importation into any State, Territory, or possession of the United States for delivery or use therein of intoxicating liquors in violation of the laws thereof, is hereby prohibited.

SECTION 3

This article shall be inoperative unless it shall have been ratified as an amendment to the Constitution by conventions in the several States, as provided in the Constitution, within seven years from the date of the submission thereof to the States by the Congress.

Amendment XXII

Passed by Congress March 24, 1947. Ratified February 26, 1951.

SECTION 1

No person shall be elected to the office of the President more than twice, and no person who has held the office of President, or acted as President, for more than two years of a term to which some other person was elected President shall be elected to the office of the President more than once. But this article shall not apply to any person holding the office of President when this article was proposed by the Congress, and shall not prevent any person who may be holding the office of President, or acting as President, during the term within which this article becomes operative from holding the office of President or acting as President during the remainder of such term.

SECTION 2

This article shall be inoperative unless it shall have been ratified as an amendment to the Constitution by the legislatures of three-fourths of the several States within seven years from the date of its submission to the States by the Congress.

Amendment XXIII

Passed by Congress June 16, 1960. Ratified April 3, 1961.

SECTION 1

The District constituting the seat of Government of the United States shall appoint in such manner as the Congress may direct:

A number of electors of President and Vice President equal to the whole number of Senators and Representatives in Congress to which the District would be entitled if it were a State, but in no event more than the least populous State; they shall be in addition to those appointed by the States, but they shall be considered, for the purposes of the election of President and Vice President, to be electors appointed by a State; and they shall meet in the District and perform such duties as provided by the twelfth article of amendment.

SECTION 2

The Congress shall have power to enforce this article by appropriate legislation.

Amendment XXIV

Passed by Congress August 27, 1962. Ratified February 4, 1964.

SECTION 1

The right of citizens of the United States to vote in any primary or other election for President or Vice President, for electors for President or Vice President, or for Senator or Representative in Congress, shall not be denied or abridged by the United States or any State by reason of failure to pay any poll tax or other tax.

SECTION 2

The Congress shall have power to enforce this article by appropriate legislation.

Amendment XXV

Passed by Congress July 6, 1965. Ratified February 23, 1967.

SECTION 1

In case of the removal of the President from office or of his death or resignation, the Vice President shall become President.

SECTION 2

Whenever there is a vacancy in the office of the Vice President, the President shall nominate a Vice President who shall take office upon confirmation by a majority vote of both Houses of Congress.

SECTION 3

Whenever the President transmits to the President pro tempore of the Senate and the Speaker of the House of Representatives his written declaration that he is unable to discharge the powers and duties of his office, and until he transmits to them a written declaration to the contrary, such powers and duties shall be discharged by the Vice President as Acting President.

SECTION 4

Whenever the Vice President and a majority of either the principal officers of the executive departments or of such other body as Congress may by law provide, transmit to the President pro tempore of the Senate and the Speaker of the House of Representatives their written declaration that the President is unable to discharge the powers and duties of his office, the Vice President shall immediately assume the powers and duties of the office as Acting President.

Thereafter, when the President transmits to the President pro tempore of the Senate and the Speaker of the House of Representatives his written declaration that no inability exists, he shall resume the powers and duties of his office unless the Vice President and a majority of either the principal officers of the executive department or of such other body as Congress may by law provide, transmit within four days to the President pro tempore of the Senate and the Speaker of the House of Representatives their written declaration that the President is unable to discharge the powers and duties of his office. Thereupon Congress shall decide the issue, assembling within forty-eight hours for that purpose if not in session. If the Congress, within twenty-one days after receipt of the latter written declaration, or, if Congress is not in session, within twenty-one days after Congress is required to assemble, determines by two-thirds vote of both Houses that the President is unable to discharge the powers and duties of his office, the Vice President shall continue to discharge the same as Acting President; otherwise, the President shall resume the powers and duties of his office.

Amendment XXVI

Passed by Congress March 23, 1971. Ratified July 5, 1971.

SECTION 1

The right of citizens of the United States, who are eighteen years of age or older, to vote shall not be denied or abridged by the United States or by any State on account of age.

Amendment XXVII

Passed by Congress September 25, 1789. Ratified May 18, 1992.

No law, varying the compensation for the services of the Senators and Representatives, shall take effect, until an election of Representatives shall have intervened.

UNIFORM COMMERCIAL CODE

(Adopted in fifty-two jurisdictions; all fifty States, although Louisiana has adopted only Articles 1, 3, 4, 7, 8, and 9; the District of Columbia; and the Virgin Islands.)
The Code consists of the following articles:

Art.

1. General Provisions

2. Sales

2A. Leases

3. Negotiable Instruments

4. Bank Deposits and Collections

4A. Funds Transfers

5. Letters of Credit

6. Repealer of Article 6—Bulk Transfers and [Revised] Article 6—Bulk Sales

7. Warehouse Receipts, Bills of Lading and Other Documents of Title

8. Investment Securities

9. Secured Transactions

10. Effective Date and Repealer

11. Effective Date and Transition Provisions

ARTICLE 1 GENERAL PROVISIONS

Part 1 Short Title, Construction, Application and Subject Matter of the Act

§1—101. SHORT TITLE

This Act shall be known and may be cited as Uniform Commercial Code.

§1—102. PURPOSES; RULES OF CONSTRUCTION; VARIATION BY AGREEMENT

(1) This Act shall be liberally construed and applied to promote its underlying purposes and policies.

(2) Underlying purposes and policies of this Act are
(a) to simplify, clarify and modernize the law governing commercial transactions;
(b) to permit the continued expansion of commercial practices through custom, usage and agreement of the parties;
(c) to make uniform the law among the various jurisdictions.

(3) The effect of provisions of this Act may be varied by agreement, except as otherwise provided in this Act and except that the obligations of good faith, diligence, reasonableness and care prescribed by this Act may not be disclaimed by agreement but the parties may by agreement determine the standards by which the performance of such obligations is to be measured if such standards are not manifestly unreasonable.

(4) The presence in certain provisions of this Act of the words "unless otherwise agreed" or words of similar import does not imply that the effect of other provisions may not be varied by agreement under subsection (3).

(5) In this Act unless the context otherwise requires
(a) words in the singular number include the plural, and in the plural include the singular;
(b) words of the masculine gender include the feminine and the neuter, and when the sense so indicates words of the neuter gender may refer to any gender.

§1—103. SUPPLEMENTARY GENERAL PRINCIPLES OF LAW APPLICABLE

Unless displaced by the particular provisions of this Act, the principles of law and equity, including the law merchant and the law relative to capacity to contract, principal and agent, estoppel, fraud, misrepresentation, duress, coercion, mistake, bankruptcy, or other validating or invalidating cause shall supplement its provisions.

§1—104. CONSTRUCTION AGAINST IMPLICIT REPEAL

This Act being a general act intended as a unified coverage of its subject matter, no part of it shall be deemed to be impliedly repealed by subsequent legislation if such construction can reasonably be avoided.

§1—105. TERRITORIAL APPLICATION OF THE ACT; PARTIES' POWER TO CHOOSE APPLICABLE LAW

(1) Except as provided hereafter in this section, when a transaction bears a reasonable relation to this state and also to another state or nation the parties may agree that the law either of this state or of such other state or nation shall govern their rights and duties. Failing such agreement this Act applies to transactions bearing an appropriate relation to this state.

    (2) Where one of the following provisions of this Act specifies the applicable law, that provision governs and a contrary agreement is effective only to the extent permitted by the law (including the conflict of laws rules) so specified:

Rights of creditors against sold goods. Section 2—402.

> Applicability of the Article on Leases. Sections 2A—105 and 2A—106.
> Applicability of the Article on Bank Deposits and Collections. Section 4—102.
> Governing law in the Article on Funds Transfers. Section 4A—507.
> Letters of Credit, Section 5—116.
> Bulk sales subject to the Article on Bulk Sales. Section 6—103.
> Applicability of the Article on Investment Securities. Section 8—106.
> Law governing perfection, the effect of perfection or nonperfection, and the priority of security interests and agricultural liens. Sections 9—301 through 9—307.
> As amended in 1972, 1987, 1988, 1989, 1994, 1995, and 1999.

§1—106. REMEDIES TO BE LIBERALLY ADMINISTERED

(1) The remedies provided by this Act shall be liberally administered to the end that the aggrieved party may be put in as good a position as if the other party had fully performed but neither consequential or special nor penal damages may be had except as specifically provided in this Act or by other rule of law.

    (2) Any right or obligation declared by this Act is enforceable by action unless the provision declaring it specifies a different and limited effect.

§1—107. WAIVER OR RENUNCIATION OF CLAIM OR RIGHT AFTER BREACH

Any claim or right arising out of an alleged breach can be discharged in whole or in part without consideration by a written waiver or renunciation signed and delivered by the aggrieved party.

§1—108. SEVERABILITY

If any provision or clause of this Act or application thereof to any person or circumstances is held invalid, such invalidity shall not affect other provisions or applications of the Act which can be given effect without the invalid provision or application, and to this end the provisions of this Act are declared to be severable.

§1—109. SECTION CAPTIONS

Section captions are parts of this Act.

Part 2 General Definitions and Principles of Interpretation

§1—201. GENERAL DEFINITIONS

Subject to additional definitions contained in the subsequent Articles of this Act which are applicable to specific Articles or Parts thereof, and unless the context otherwise requires, in this Act:

(1) "Action" in the sense of a judicial proceeding includes recoupment, counterclaim, set-off, suit in equity and any other proceedings in which rights are determined.

    (2) "Aggrieved party" means a party entitled to resort to a remedy.

    (3) "Agreement" means the bargain of the parties in fact as found in their language or by implication from other circumstances including course of dealing or usage of trade or course of performance as provided in this Act (Sections 1—205 and 2—208). Whether an agreement has legal consequences is determined by the provisions of this Act, if applicable; otherwise by the law of contracts (Section 1—103). (Compare "Contract".)

    (4) "Bank" means any person engaged in the business of banking.

    (5) "Bearer" means the person in possession of an instrument, document of title, or certificated security payable to bearer or indorsed in blank.

    (6) "Bill of lading" means a document evidencing the receipt of goods for shipment issued by a person engaged in the business of transporting or forwarding goods, and includes an airbill. "Airbill" means a document serving for air transportation as a bill of lading does for marine or rail transportation, and includes an air consignment note or air waybill.

    (7) "Branch" includes a separately incorporated foreign branch of a bank.

(8) "Burden of establishing" a fact means the burden of persuading the triers of fact that the existence of the fact is more probable than its non-existence.

(9) "Buyer in ordinary course of business" means a person that buys goods in good faith, without knowledge that the sale violates the rights of another person in the goods, and in the ordinary course from a person, other than a pawnbroker, in the business of selling goods of that kind. A person buys goods in the ordinary course if the sale to the person comports with the usual or customary practices in the kind of business in which the seller is engaged or with the seller's own usual or customary practices. A person that sells oil, gas, or other minerals at the wellhead or minehead is a person in the business of selling goods of that kind. A buyer in ordinary course of business may buy for cash, by exchange of other property, or on secured or unsecured credit, and may acquire goods or documents of title under a pre-existing contract for sale. Only a buyer that takes possession of the goods or has a right to recover the goods from the seller under Article 2 may be a buyer in ordinary course of business. A person that acquires goods in a transfer in bulk or as security for or in total or partial satisfaction of a money debt is not a buyer in ordinary course of business.

(10) "Conspicuous": A term or clause is conspicuous when it is so written that a reasonable person against whom it is to operate ought to have noticed it. A printed heading in capitals (as: NON-NEGOTIABLE BILL OF LADING) is conspicuous. Language in the body of a form is "conspicuous" if it is in larger or other contrasting type or color. But in a telegram any stated term is "conspicuous". Whether a term or clause is "conspicuous" or not is for decision by the court.

(11) "Contract" means the total legal obligation which results from the parties' agreement as affected by this Act and any other applicable rules of law. (Compare "Agreement".)

(12) "Creditor" includes a general creditor, a secured creditor, a lien creditor and any representative of creditors, including an assignee for the benefit of creditors, a trustee in bankruptcy, a receiver in equity and an executor or administrator of an insolvent debtor's or assignor's estate.

(13) "Defendant" includes a person in the position of defendant in a cross-action or counterclaim.

(14) "Delivery" with respect to instruments, documents of title, chattel paper, or certificated securities means voluntary transfer of possession.

(15) "Document of title" includes bill of lading, dock warrant, dock receipt, warehouse receipt or order for the delivery of goods, and also any other document which in the regular course of business or financing is treated as adequately evidencing that the person in possession of it is entitled to receive, hold and dispose of the document and the goods it covers. To be a document of title a document must purport to be issued by or addressed to a bailee and purport to cover goods in the bailee's possession which are either identified or are fungible portions of an identified mass.

(16) "Fault" means wrongful act, omission or breach.

(17) "Fungible" with respect to goods or securities means goods or securities of which any unit is, by nature or usage of trade, the equivalent of any other like unit. Goods which are not fungible shall be deemed fungible for the purposes of this Act to the extent that under a particular agreement or document unlike units are treated as equivalents.

(18) "Genuine" means free of forgery or counterfeiting.

(19) "Good faith" means honesty in fact in the conduct or transaction concerned.

(20) "Holder" with respect to a negotiable instrument, means the person in possession if the instrument is payable to bearer or, in the cases of an instrument payable to an identified person, if the identified person is in possession. "Holder" with respect to a document of title means the person in possession if the goods are deliverable to bearer or to the order of the person in possession.

(21) To "honor" is to pay or to accept and pay, or where a credit so engages to purchase or discount a draft complying with the terms of the credit.

(22) "Insolvency proceedings" includes any assignment for the benefit of creditors or other proceedings intended to liquidate or rehabilitate the estate of the person involved.

(23) A person is "insolvent" who either has ceased to pay his debts in the ordinary course of business or cannot pay his debts as they become due or is insolvent within the meaning of the federal bankruptcy law.

(24) "Money" means a medium of exchange authorized or adopted by a domestic or foreign government and includes a monetary unit of account established by an intergovernmental organization or by agreement between two or more nations.

(25) A person has "notice" of a fact when
    (a) he has actual knowledge of it; or
    (b) he has received a notice or notification of it; or
    (c) from all the facts and circumstances known to him at the time in question he has reason to know that it exists.

A person "knows" or has "knowledge" of a fact when he has actual knowledge of it. "Discover" or "learn" or a word or phrase of similar import refers to knowledge rather than to reason to know. The time and circumstances under which a notice or notification may cease to be effective are not determined by this Act.

(26) A person "notifies" or "gives" a notice or notification to another by taking such steps as may be reasonably required to inform the other in ordinary course whether or not such other actually comes to know of it. A person "receives" a notice or notification when

(a) it comes to his attention; or

(b) it is duly delivered at the place of business through which the contract was made or at any other place held out by him as the place for receipt of such communications.

(27) Notice, knowledge or a notice or notification received by an organization is effective for a particular transaction from the time when it is brought to the attention of the individual conducting that transaction, and in any event from the time when it would have been brought to his attention if the organization had exercised due diligence. An organization exercises due diligence if it maintains reasonable routines for communicating significant information to the person conducting the transaction and there is reasonable compliance with the routines. Due diligence does not require an individual acting for the organization to communicate information unless such communication is part of his regular duties or unless he has reason to know of the transaction and that the transaction would be materially affected by the information.

(28) "Organization" includes a corporation, government or governmental subdivision or agency, business trust, estate, trust, partnership or association, two or more persons having a joint or common interest, or any other legal or commercial entity.

(29) "Party", as distinct from "third party", means a person who has engaged in a transaction or made an agreement within this Act.

(30) "Person" includes an individual or an organization (See Section 1—102).

(31) "Presumption" or "presumed" means that the trier of fact must find the existence of the fact presumed unless and until evidence is introduced which would support a finding of its non-existence.

(32) Purchase" includes taking by sale, discount, negotiation, mortgage, pledge, lien, issue or re-issue, gift or any other voluntary transaction creating an interest in property.

(33) "Purchaser" means a person who takes by purchase.

(34) "Remedy" means any remedial right to which an aggrieved party is entitled with or without resort to a tribunal.

(35) "Representative" includes an agent, an officer of a corporation or association, and a trustee, executor or administrator of an estate, or any other person empowered to act for another.

(36) "Rights" includes remedies.

(37) "Security interest" means an interest in personal property or fixtures which secures payment or performance of an obligation. The term also includes any interest of a consignor and a buyer of accounts, chattel paper, a payment intangible, or a promissory note in a transaction that is subject to Article 9. The special property interest of a buyer of goods on identification of those goods to a contract for sale under Section 2—401 is not a "security interest", but a buyer may also acquire a "security interest" by complying

with Article 9. Except as otherwise provided in Section 2—505, the right of a seller or lessor of goods under Article 2 or 2A to retain or acquire possession of the goods is not a "security interest", but a seller or lessor may also acquire a "security interest" by complying with Article 9. The retention or reservation of title by a seller of goods notwithstanding shipment or delivery to the buyer (Section 2—401) is limited in effect to a reservation of a "security interest".

Whether a transaction creates a lease or security interest is determined by the facts of each case; however, a transaction creates a security interest if the consideration the lessee is to pay the lessor for the right to possession and use of the goods is an obligation for the term of the lease not subject to termination by the lessee, and

(a) the original term of the lease is equal to or greater than the remaining economic life of the goods,

(b) the lessee is bound to renew the lease for the remaining economic life of the goods or is bound to become the owner of the goods,

(c) the lessee has an option to renew the lease for the remaining economic life of the goods for no additional consideration or nominal additional consideration upon compliance with the lease agreement, or

(d) the lessee has an option to become the owner of the goods for no additional consideration or nominal additional consideration upon compliance with the lease agreement.

A transaction does not create a security interest merely because it provides that

(a) the present value of the consideration the lessee is obligated to pay the lessor for the right to possession and use of the goods is substantially equal to or is greater than the fair market value of the goods at the time the lease is entered into,

(b) the lessee assumes risk of loss of the goods, or agrees to pay taxes, insurance, filing, recording, or registration fees, or service or maintenance costs with respect to the goods,

(c) the lessee has an option to renew the lease or to become the owner of the goods,

(d) the lessee has an option to renew the lease for a fixed rent that is equal to or greater than the reasonably predictable fair market rent for the use of the goods for the term of the renewal at the time the option is to be performed, or

(e) the lessee has an option to become the owner of the goods for a fixed price that is equal to or greater than the reasonably predictable fair market value of the goods at the time the option is to be performed.

For purposes of this subsection (37):

(x) Additional consideration is not nominal if (i) when the option to renew the lease is granted to the lessee the rent is stated to be the fair market rent for the use of the goods for the term of the renewal determined at the time the option is to be performed, or (ii) when the option to become the owner of the goods is granted to the lessee the price is stated to be the fair market value of the goods determined at the time the option is to be performed. Additional consideration is nominal if it is less than the lessee's reasonably predictable cost of performing under the lease agreement if the option is not exercised;

(y) "Reasonably predictable" and "remaining economic life of the goods" are to be determined with reference to the facts and circumstances at the time the transaction is entered into; and

(z) "Present value" means the amount as of a date certain of one or more sums payable in the future, discounted to the date certain. The discount is determined by the interest rate specified by the parties if the rate is not manifestly unreasonable at the time the transaction is entered into; otherwise, the discount is determined by a commercially reasonable rate that takes into account the facts and circumstances of each case at the time the transaction was entered into.

(38) "Send" in connection with any writing or notice means to deposit in the mail or deliver for transmission by any other usual means of communication with postage or cost of transmission provided for and properly addressed and in the case of an instrument to an address specified thereon or otherwise agreed, or if there be none to any address reasonable under the circumstances. The receipt of any writing or notice within the time at which it would have arrived if properly sent has the effect of a proper sending.

(39) "Signed" includes any symbol executed or adopted by a party with present intention to authenticate a writing.

(40) "Surety" includes guarantor.

(41) "Telegram" includes a message transmitted by radio, teletype, cable, any mechanical method of transmission, or the like.

(42) "Term" means that portion of an agreement which relates to a particular matter.

(43) "Unauthorized" signature means one made without actual, implied or apparent authority and includes a forgery.

(44) "Value". Except as otherwise provided with respect to negotiable instruments and bank collections (Sections 3—303, 4—210 and 4—211) a person gives "value" for rights if he acquires them

(a) in return for a binding commitment to extend credit or for the extension of immediately available credit whether or not drawn upon and whether or not a chargeback is provided for in the event of difficulties in collection; or

(b) as security for or in total or partial satisfaction of a pre-existing claim; or

(c) by accepting delivery pursuant to a preexisting contract for purchase; or

(d) generally, in return for any consideration sufficient to support a simple contract.

(45) "Warehouse receipt" means a receipt issued by a person engaged in the business of storing goods for hire.

(46) "Written" or "writing" includes printing, typewriting or any other intentional reduction to tangible form.

§1—202. PRIMA FACIE EVIDENCE BY THIRD PARTY DOCUMENTS

A document in due form purporting to be a bill of lading, policy or certificate of insurance, official weigher's or inspector's certificate, consular invoice, or any other document authorized or required by the contract to be issued by a third party shall be prima facie evidence of its own authenticity and genuineness and of the facts stated in the document by the third party.

§1—203. OBLIGATION OF GOOD FAITH

Every contract or duty within this Act imposes an obligation of good faith in its performance or enforcement.

§1—204. TIME; REASONABLE TIME; "SEASONABLY"

(1) Whenever this Act requires any action to be taken within a reasonable time, any time which is not manifestly unreasonable may be fixed by agreement.

(2) What is a reasonable time for taking any action depends on the nature, purpose and circumstances of such action.

(3) An action is taken "seasonably" when it is taken at or within the time agreed or if no time is agreed at or within a reasonable time.

§1—205. COURSE OF DEALING AND USAGE OF TRADE

(1) A course of dealing is a sequence of previous conduct between the parties to a particular transaction which is fairly to be regarded as establishing a common basis of understanding for interpreting their expressions and other conduct.

(2) A usage of trade is any practice or method of dealing having such regularity of observance in a place, vocation or trade as to justify an expectation that it will be

observed with respect to the transaction in question. The existence and scope of such a usage are to be proved as facts. If it is established that such a usage is embodied in a written trade code or similar writing the interpretation of the writing is for the court.

(3) A course of dealing between parties and any usage of trade in the vocation or trade in which they are engaged or of which they are or should be aware give particular meaning to and supplement or qualify terms of an agreement.

(4) The express terms of an agreement and an applicable course of dealing or usage of trade shall be construed wherever reasonable as consistent with each other; but when such construction is unreasonable express terms control both course of dealing and usage of trade and course of dealing controls usage trade.

(5) An applicable usage of trade in the place where any part of performance is to occur shall be used in interpreting the agreement as to that part of the performance.

(6) Evidence of a relevant usage of trade offered by one party is not admissible unless and until he has given the other party such notice as the court finds sufficient to prevent unfair surprise to the latter.

§1—206. STATUTE OF FRAUDS FOR KINDS OF PERSONAL PROPERTY NOT OTHERWISE COVERED

(1) Except in the cases described in subsection (2) of this section a contract for the sale of personal property is not enforceable by way of action or defense beyond five thousand dollars in amount or value of remedy unless there is some writing which indicates that a contract for sale has been made between the parties at a defined or stated price, reasonably identifies the subject matter, and is signed by the party against whom enforcement is sought or by his authorized agent.

(2) Subsection (1) of this section does not apply to contracts for the sale of goods (Section 2—201) nor of securities (Section 8—113) nor to security agreements (Section 9—203).

As amended in 1994.

§1—207. PERFORMANCE OR ACCEPTANCE UNDER RESERVATION OF RIGHTS

(1) A party who with explicit reservation of rights performs or promises performance or assents to performance in a manner demanded or offered by the other party does not thereby prejudice the rights reserved. Such words as "without prejudice", "under protest" or the like are sufficient.

(2) Subsection (1) does not apply to an accord and satisfaction.

As amended in 1990.

§1—208. OPTION TO ACCELERATE AT WILL

A term providing that one party or his successor in interest may accelerate payment or performance or require collateral or additional collateral "at will" or "when he deems himself insecure" or in words of similar import shall be construed to mean that he shall have power to do so only if he in good faith believes that the prospect of payment or performance is impaired. The burden of establishing lack of good faith is on the party against whom the power has been exercised.

§1—209. SUBORDINATED OBLIGATIONS

An obligation may be issued as subordinated to payment of another obligation of the person obligated, or a creditor may subordinate his right to payment of an obligation by agreement with either the person obligated or another creditor of the person obligated. Such a subordination does not create a security interest as against either the common debtor or a subordinated creditor. This section shall be construed as declaring the law as it existed prior to the enactment of this section and not as modifying it.

Added 1966.

Note: *This new section is proposed as an optional provision to make it clear that a subordination agreement does not create a security interest unless so intended.*

ARTICLE 2 SALES

Part 1 Short Title, General Construction and Subject Matter

§2—101. SHORT TITLE

This Article shall be known and may be cited as Uniform Commercial Code—Sales.

§2—102. SCOPE; CERTAIN SECURITY AND OTHER TRANSACTIONS EXCLUDED FROM THIS ARTICLE

Unless the context otherwise requires, this Article applies to transactions in goods; it does not apply to any transaction which although in the form of an unconditional contract to sell or present sale is intended to operate only as a security transaction nor does this Article impair or repeal any statute regulating sales to consumers, farmers or other specified classes of buyers.

§2—103. DEFINITIONS AND INDEX OF DEFINITIONS

(1) In this Article unless the context otherwise requires
    (a) "Buyer" means a person who buys or contracts to buy goods.
    (b) "Good faith" in the case of a merchant means honesty in fact and the observance of reasonable commercial standards of fair dealing in the trade.

(c) "Receipt" of goods means taking physical possession of them.

(d) "Seller" means a person who sells or contracts to sell goods.

(2) Other definitions applying to this Article or to specified Parts thereof, and the sections in which they appear are:

"Acceptance". Section 2—606.
"Banker's credit". Section 2—325.
"Between merchants". Section 2—104.
"Cancellation". Section 2—106(4).
"Commercial unit". Section 2—105.
"Confirmed credit". Section 2—325.
"Conforming to contract". Section 2—106.
"Contract for sale". Section 2—106.
"Cover". Section 2—712.
"Entrusting". Section 2—403.
"Financing agency". Section 2—104.
"Future goods". Section 2—105.
"Goods". Section 2—105.
"Identification". Section 2—501.
"Installment contract". Section 2—612.
"Letter of Credit". Section 2—325.
"Lot". Section 2—105.
"Merchant". Section 2—104.
"Overseas". Section 2—323.
"Person in position of seller". Section 2—707.
"Present sale". Section 2—106.
"Sale". Section 2—106.
"Sale on approval". Section 2—326.
"Sale or return". Section 2—326.
"Termination". Section 2—106.

(3) The following definitions in other Articles apply to this Article:

"Check". Section 3—104.
"Consignee". Section 7—102.
"Consignor". Section 7—102.
"Consumer goods". Section 9—109.
"Dishonor". Section 3—507.
"Draft". Section 3—104.

(4) In addition Article 1 contains general definitions and principles of construction and interpretation applicable throughout this Article.

As amended in 1994 and 1999.

§2—104. DEFINITIONS: "MERCHANT"; "BETWEEN MERCHANTS"; "FINANCING AGENCY"

(1) "Merchant" means a person who deals in goods of the kind or otherwise by his occupation holds himself out as having knowledge or skill peculiar to the practices or goods involved in the transaction or to whom such knowledge or skill may be attributed by his employment of an agent or broker or other intermediary who by his occupation holds himself out as having such knowledge or skill.

(2) "Financing agency" means a bank, finance company or other person who in the ordinary course of business makes advances against goods or documents of title or who by arrangement with either the seller or the buyer intervenes in ordinary course to make or collect payment due or claimed under the contract for sale, as by purchasing or paying the seller's draft or making advances against it or by merely taking it for collection whether or not documents of title accompany the draft. "Financing agency" includes also a bank or other person who similarly intervenes between persons who are in the position of seller and buyer in respect to the goods (Section 2—707).

(3) "Between merchants" means in any transaction with respect to which both parties are chargeable with the knowledge or skill of merchants.

§2—105. DEFINITIONS: TRANSFERABILITY; "GOODS"; "FUTURE" GOODS; "LOT"; "COMMERCIAL UNIT"

(1) "Goods" means all things (including specially manufactured goods) which are movable at the time of identification to the contract for sale other than the money in which the price is to be paid, investment securities (Article 8) and things in action. "Goods" also includes the unborn young of animals and growing crops and other identified things attached to realty as described in the section on goods to be severed from realty (Section 2—107).

(2) Goods must be both existing and identified before any interest in them can pass. Goods which are not both existing and identified are "future" goods. A purported present sale of future goods or of any interest therein operates as a contract to sell.

(3) There may be a sale of a part interest in existing identified goods.

(4) An undivided share in an identified bulk of fungible goods is sufficiently identified to be sold although the quantity of the bulk is not determined. Any agreed proportion of such a bulk or any quantity thereof agreed upon by number, weight or other measure may to the extent of the seller's interest in the bulk be sold to the buyer who then becomes an owner in common.

(5) "Lot" means a parcel or a single article which is the subject matter of a separate sale or delivery, whether or not it is sufficient to perform the contract.

(6) "Commercial unit" means such a unit of goods as by commercial usage is a single whole for purposes of sale and division of which materially impairs its character or value on the market or in use. A commercial unit may be a single article (as a machine) or a set of articles (as a suite of furniture or an assortment of sizes) or a quantity (as a bale, gross, or carload) or any other unit treated in use or in the relevant market as a single whole.

§2—106. DEFINITIONS: "CONTRACT"; "AGREEMENT"; "CONTRACT FOR SALE"; "SALE"; "PRESENT SALE"; "CONFORMING TO CONTRACT; "TERMINATION"; "CANCELLATION"

(1)   In this Article unless the context otherwise requires "contract" and "agreement" are limited to those relating to the present or future sale of goods. "Contract for sale" includes both a present sale of goods and a contract to sell goods at a future time. A "sale" consists in the passing of title from the seller to the buyer for a price (Section 2—401). A "present sale" means a sale which is accomplished by the making of the contract.

(2)   Goods or conduct including any part of a performance are "conforming" or conform to the contract when they are in accordance with the obligations under the contract.

(3)   "Termination" occurs when either party pursuant to a power created by agreement or law puts an end to the contract otherwise than for its breach. On "termination" all obligations which are still executory on both sides are discharged but any right based on prior breach or performance survives.

(4)   "Cancellation" occurs when either party puts an end to the contract for breach by the other and its effect is the same as that of "termination" except that the cancelling party also retains any remedy for breach of the whole contract or any unperformed balance.

§2—107. GOODS TO BE SEVERED FROM REALTY: RECORDING

(1)   A contract for the sale of minerals or the like (including oil and gas) or a structure or its materials to be removed from realty is a contract for the sale of goods within this Article if they are to be severed by the seller but until severance a purported present sale thereof which is not effective as a transfer of an interest in land is effective only as a contract to sell.

(2)   A contract for the sale apart from the land of growing crops or other things attached to realty and capable of severance without material harm thereto but not described in subsection (1) or of timber to be cut is a contract for the sale of goods within this Article whether the subject matter is to be severed by the buyer or by the seller even though it forms part of the realty at the time of contracting, and the parties can by identification effect a present sale before severance.

(3)   The provisions of this section are subject to any third party rights provided by the law relating to realty records, and the contract for sale may be executed and recorded as a document transferring an interest in land and shall then constitute notice to third parties of the buyer's rights under the contract for sale.

As amended in 1972.

Part 2 Form, Formation and Readjustment of Contract

§2—201. FORMAL REQUIREMENTS; STATUTE OF FRAUDS

(1)   Except as otherwise provided in this section a contract for the sale of goods for the price of $500 or more is not enforceable by way of action or defense unless there is some writing sufficient to indicate that a contract for sale has been made between the parties and signed by the party against whom enforcement is sought or by his authorized agent or broker. A writing is not insufficient because it omits or incorrectly states a term agreed upon but the contract is not enforceable under this paragraph beyond the quantity of goods shown in such writing.

(2)   Between merchants if within a reasonable time a writing in confirmation of the contract and sufficient against the sender is received and the party receiving it has reason to know its contents, its satisfies the requirements of subsection (1) against such party unless written notice of objection to its contents is given within ten days after it is received.

(3)   A contract which does not satisfy the requirements of subsection (1) but which is valid in other respects is enforceable

(a)   if the goods are to be specially manufactured for the buyer and are not suitable for sale to others in the ordinary course of the seller's business and the seller, before notice of repudiation is received and under circumstances which reasonably indicate that the goods are for the buyer, has made either a substantial beginning of their manufacture or commitments for their procurement; or

(b)   if the party against whom enforcement is sought admits in his pleading, testimony or otherwise in court that a contract for sale was made, but the contract is not enforceable under this provision beyond the quantity of goods admitted; or

(c)   with respect to goods for which payment has been made and accepted or which have been received and accepted (Sec. 2—606).

§2—202. FINAL WRITTEN EXPRESSION: PAROL OR EXTRINSIC EVIDENCE

Terms with respect to which the confirmatory memoranda of the parties agree or which are otherwise set forth in a writing intended by the parties as a final expression of their agreement with respect to such terms as are included therein may not be contradicted by evidence of any prior agreement or of a contemporaneous oral agreement but may be explained or supplemented

(a) by course of dealing or usage of trade (Section 1—205) or by course of performance (Section 2—208); and

(b) by evidence of consistent additional terms unless the court finds the writing to have been intended also as a complete and exclusive statement of the terms of the agreement.

§2—203. SEALS INOPERATIVE

The affixing of a seal to a writing evidencing a contract for sale or an offer to buy or sell goods does not constitute the writing a sealed instrument and the law with respect to sealed instruments does not apply to such a contract or offer.

§2—204. FORMATION IN GENERAL

(1) A contract for sale of goods may be made in any manner sufficient to show agreement, including conduct by both parties which recognizes the existence of such a contract.

(2) An agreement sufficient to constitute a contract for sale may be found even though the moment of its making is undetermined.

(3) Even though one or more terms are left open a contract for sale does not fail for indefiniteness if the parties have intended to make a contract and there is a reasonably certain basis for giving an appropriate remedy.

§2—205. FIRM OFFERS

An offer by a merchant to buy or sell goods in a signed writing which by its terms gives assurance that it will be held open is not revocable, for lack of consideration, during the time stated or if no time is stated for a reasonable time, but in no event may such period of irrevocability exceed three months; but any such term of assurance on a form supplied by the offeree must be separately signed by the offeror.

§2—206. OFFER AND ACCEPTANCE IN FORMATION OF CONTRACT

(1) Unless other unambiguously indicated by the language or circumstances

(a) an offer to make a contract shall be construed as inviting acceptance in any manner and by any medium reasonable in the circumstances;

(b) an order or other offer to buy goods for prompt or current shipment shall be construed as inviting acceptance either by a prompt promise to ship or by the prompt or current shipment of conforming or nonconforming goods, but such a shipment of non-conforming goods does not constitute an acceptance if the seller seasonably notifies the buyer that the shipment is offered only as an accommodation to the buyer.

(2) Where the beginning of a requested performance is a reasonable mode of acceptance an offeror who is not notified of acceptance within a reasonable time may treat the offer as having lapsed before acceptance.

§2—207. ADDITIONAL TERMS IN ACCEPTANCE OR CONFIRMATION

(1) A definite and seasonable expression of acceptance or a written confirmation which is sent within a reasonable time operates as an acceptance even though it states terms additional to or different from those offered or agreed upon, unless acceptance is expressly made conditional on assent to the additional or different terms.

(2) The additional terms are to be construed as proposals for addition to the contract. Between merchants such terms become part of the contract unless:

(a) the offer expressly limits acceptance to the terms of the offer;

(b) they materially alter it; or

(c) notification of objection to them has already been given or is given within a reasonable time after notice of them is received.

(3) Conduct by both parties which recognizes the existence of a contract is sufficient to establish a contract for sale although the writings of the parties do not otherwise establish a contract. In such case the terms of the particular contract consist of those terms on which the writings of the parties agree, together with any supplementary terms incorporated under any other provisions of this Act.

§2—208. COURSE OF PERFORMANCE OR PRACTICAL CONSTRUCTION

(1) Where the contract for sale involves repeated occasions for performance by either party with knowledge of the nature of the performance and opportunity for objection to it by the other, any course of performance accepted or acquiesced in without objection shall be relevant to determine the meaning of the agreement.

(2) The express terms of the agreement and any such course of performance, as well as any course of dealing and usage of trade, shall be construed whenever reasonable as consistent with each other; but when such construction is unreasonable, express terms shall control course of performance and course of performance shall control both course of dealing and usage of trade (Section 1—205).

(3) Subject to the provisions of the next section on modification and waiver, such course of performance shall be relevant to show a waiver or modification of any term inconsistent with such course of performance.

§2—209. MODIFICATION, RESCISSION AND WAIVER

(1) An agreement modifying a contract within this Article needs no consideration to be binding.

(2) A signed agreement which excludes modification or rescission except by a signed writing cannot be otherwise modified or rescinded, but except as between merchants such a requirement on a form supplied by the merchant must be separately signed by the other party.

(3) The requirements of the statute of frauds section of this Article (Section 2—201) must be satisfied if the contract as modified is within its provisions.

(4) Although an attempt at modification or rescission does not satisfy the requirements of subsection (2) or (3) it can operate as a waiver.

(5) A party who has made a waiver affecting an executory portion of the contract may retract the waiver by reasonable notification received by the other party that strict performance will be required of any term waived, unless the retraction would be unjust in view of a material change of position in reliance on the waiver.

§2—210. DELEGATION OF PERFORMANCE; ASSIGNMENT OF RIGHTS

(1) A party may perform his duty through a delegate unless otherwise agreed or unless the other party has a substantial interest in having his original promisor perform or control the acts required by the contract. No delegation of performance relieves the party delegating of any duty to perform or any liability for breach.

(2) Except as otherwise provided in Section 9—406, unless otherwise agreed, all rights of either seller or buyer can be assigned except where the assignment would materially change the duty of the other party, or increase materially the burden or risk imposed on him by his contract, or impair materially his chance of obtaining return performance. A right to damages for breach of the whole contract or a right arising out of the assignor's due performance of his entire obligation can be assigned despite agreement otherwise.

(3) The creation, attachment, perfection, or enforcement of a security interest in the seller's interest under a contract is not a transfer that materially changes the duty of or increases materially the burden or risk imposed on the buyer or impairs materially the buyer's chance of obtaining return performance within the purview of subsection (2) unless, and then only to the extent that, enforcement actually results in a delegation of material performance of the seller. Even in that event, the creation, attachment, perfection, and enforcement of the security interest remain effective, but (i) the seller is liable to the buyer for damages caused by the delegation to the extent that the damages could not reasonably by prevented by the buyer, and (ii) a court having jurisdiction may grant other appropriate relief, including cancellation of the contract for sale or an injunction against enforcement of the security interest or consummation of the enforcement.

(4) Unless the circumstnaces indicate the contrary a prohibition of assignment of "the contract" is to be construed as barring only the delegation to the assignees of the assignor's performance.

(5) An assignment of "the contract" or of "all my rights under the contract" or an assignment in similar general terms is an assignment of rights and unless the language or the circumstances (as in an assignment for security) indicate the contrary, it is a delegation of performance of the duties of the assignor and its acceptance by the assignee constitutes a promise by him to perform those duties. This promise is enforceable by either the assignor or the other party to the original contract.

(6) The other party may treat any assignment which delegates performance as creating reasonable grounds for insecurity and may without prejudice to his rights against the assignor demand assurances from the assignee (Section 2—609).

As amended in 1999.

Part 3 General Obligation and Construction of Contract

§2—301. GENERAL OBLIGATIONS OF PARTIES

The obligation of the seller is to transfer and deliver and that of the buyer is to accept and pay in accordance with the contract.

§2—302. UNCONSCIONABLE CONTRACT OR CLAUSE

(1) If the court as a matter of law finds the contract or any clause of the contract to have been unconscionable at the time it was made the court may refuse to enforce the contract, or it may enforce the remainder of the contract without the unconscionable clause, or it may so limit the application of any unconscionable clause as to avoid any unconscionable result.

(2) When it is claimed or appears to the court that the contract or any clause thereof may be unconscionable the parties shall be afforded a reasonable opportunity to present evidence as to its commercial setting, purpose and effect to aid the court in making the determination.

§2—303. ALLOCATIONS OR DIVISION OF RISKS

Where this Article allocates a risk or a burden as between the parties "unless otherwise agreed", the agreement may not only shift the allocation but may also divide the risk or burden.

§2—304. PRICE PAYABLE IN MONEY, GOODS, REALTY, OR OTHERWISE

(1) The price can be made payable in money or otherwise. If it is payable in whole or in part in goods each party is a seller of the goods which he is to transfer.

(2) Even though all or part of the price is payable in an interest in realty the transfer of the goods and the seller's obligations with reference to them are subject to this Article, but not the transfer of the interest in realty or the transferor's obligations in connection therewith.

§2—305. OPEN PRICE TERM

(1) The parties if they so intend can conclude a contract for sale even though the price is not settled. In such a case the price is a reasonable price at the time for delivery if

(a) nothing is said as to price; or

(b) the price is left to be agreed by the parties and they fail to agree; or

(c) the price is to be fixed in terms of some agreed market or other standard as set or recorded by a third person or agency and it is not so set or recorded.

(2) A price to be fixed by the seller or by the buyer means a price for him to fix in good faith.

(3) When a price left to be fixed otherwise than by agreement of the parties fails to be fixed through fault of one party the other may at his option treat the contract as cancelled or himself fix a reasonable price.

(4) Where, however, the parties intend not to be bound unless the price be fixed or agreed and it is not fixed or agreed there is no contract. In such a case the buyer must return any goods already received or if unable so to do must pay their reasonable value at the time of delivery and the seller must return any portion of the price paid on account.

§2—306. OUTPUT, REQUIREMENTS AND EXCLUSIVE DEALINGS

(1) A term which measures the quantity by the output of the seller or the requirements of the buyer means such actual output or requirements as may occur in good faith, except that no quantity unreasonably disproportionate to any stated estimate or in the absence of a stated estimate to any normal or otherwise comparable prior output or requirements may be tendered or demanded.

(2) A lawful agreement by either the seller or the buyer for exclusive dealing in the kind of goods concerned imposes unless otherwise agreed an obligation by the seller to use best efforts to supply the goods and by the buyer to use best efforts to promote their sale.

§2—307. DELIVERY IN SINGLE LOT OR SEVERAL LOTS

Unless otherwise agreed all goods called for by a contract for sale must be tendered in a single delivery and payment is due only on such tender but where the circumstances give either party the right to make or demand delivery in lots the price if it can be apportioned may be demanded for each lot.

§2—308. ABSENCE OF SPECIFIED PLACE FOR DELIVERY

Unless otherwise agreed

(a) the place for delivery of goods is the seller's place of business or if he has none his residence; but

(b) in a contract for sale of identified goods which to the knowledge of the parties at the time of contracting are in some other place, that place is the place for their delivery; and

(c) documents of title may be delivered through customary banking channels.

§2—309. ABSENCE OF SPECIFIC TIME PROVISIONS; NOTICE OF TERMINATION

(1) The time for shipment or delivery or any other action under a contract if not provided in this Article or agreed upon shall be a reasonable time.

(2) Where the contract provides for successive performances but is indefinite in duration it is valid for a reasonable time but unless otherwise agreed may be terminated at any time by either party.

(3) Termination of a contract by one party except on the happening of an agreed event requires that reasonable notification be received by the other party and an agreement dispensing with notification is invalid if its operation would be unconscionable.

§2—310. OPEN TIME FOR PAYMENT OR RUNNING OF CREDIT; AUTHORITY TO SHIP UNDER RESERVATION

Unless otherwise agreed

(a) payment is due at the time and place at which the buyer is to receive the goods even though the place of shipment is the place of delivery; and

(b) if the seller is authorized to send the goods he may ship them under reservation, and may tender the documents of title, but the buyer may inspect the goods after their arrival before payment is due unless such inspection is inconsistent with the terms of the contract (Section 2—513); and

(c) if delivery is authorized and made by way of documents of title otherwise than by subsection (b) then payment is due at the time and place at which the buyer is to receive the documents regardless of where the goods are to be received; and

(d) where the seller is required or authorized to ship the goods on credit the credit period runs from the time of shipment but post-dating the invoice or delaying its dispatch will correspondingly delay the starting of the credit period.

§2—311. OPTIONS AND COOPERATION RESPECTING PERFORMANCE

(1) An agreement for sale which is otherwise sufficiently definite (subsection (3) of Section 2—204) to be a contract is not made invalid by the fact that it leaves particulars of performance to be specified by one of the parties. Any such specification must be made in good faith and within limits set by commercial reasonableness.

(2) Unless otherwise agreed specifications relating to assortment of the goods are at the buyer's option and except as otherwise provided in subsections (1)(c) and (3) of Section 2—319 specifications or arrangements relating to shipment are at the seller's option.

(3) Where such specification would materially affect the other party's performance but is not seasonably made or where one party's cooperation is necessary to the agreed performance of the other but is not seasonably forthcoming, the other party in addition to all other remedies

   (a) is excused for any resulting delay in his own performance; and

   (b) may also either proceed to perform in any reasonable manner or after the time for a material part of his own performance treat the failure to specify or to cooperate as a breach by failure to deliver or accept the goods.

§2—312. WARRANTY OF TITLE AND AGAINST INFRINGEMENT; BUYER'S OBLIGATION AGAINST INFRINGEMENT

(1) Subject to subsection (2) there is in a contract for sale a warranty by the seller that

   (a) the title conveyed shall be good, and its transfer rightful; and

   (b) the goods shall be delivered free from any security interest or other lien or encumbrance of which the buyer at the time of contracting has no knowledge.

(2) A warranty under subsection (1) will be excluded or modified only by specific language or by circumstances which give the buyer reason to know that the person selling does not claim title in himself or that he is purporting to sell only such right or title as he or a third person may have.

(3) Unless otherwise agreed a seller who is a merchant regularly dealing in goods of the kind warrants that the goods shall be delivered free of the rightful claim of any third person by way of infringement or the like but a buyer who furnishes specifications to the seller must hold the seller harmless against any such claim which arises out of compliance with the specifications.

§2—313. EXPRESS WARRANTIES BY AFFIRMATION, PROMISE, DESCRIPTION, SAMPLE

(1) Express warranties by the seller are created as follows:

   (a) Any affirmation of fact or promise made by the seller to the buyer which relates to the goods and becomes part of the basis of the bargain creates an express warranty that the goods shall conform to the affirmation or promise.

   (b) Any description of the goods which is made part of the basis of the bargain creates an express warranty that the goods shall conform to the description.

   (c) Any sample or model which is made part of the basis of the bargain creates an express warranty that the whole of the goods shall conform to the sample or model.

(2) It is not necessary to the creation of an express warranty that the seller use formal words such as "warrant" or "guarantee" or that he have a specific intention to make a warranty, but an affirmation merely of the value of the goods or a statement purporting to be merely the seller's opinion or commendation of the goods does not create a warranty.

§2—314. IMPLIED WARRANTY: MERCHANTABILITY; USAGE OF TRADE

(1) Unless excluded or modified (Section 2—316), a warranty that the goods shall be merchantable is implied in a contract for their sale if the seller is a merchant with respect to goods of that kind. Under this section the serving for value of food or drink to be consumed either on the premises or elsewhere is a sale.

(2) Goods to be merchantable must be at least such as

   (a) pass without objection in the trade under the contract description; and

   (b) in the case of fungible goods, are of fair average quality within the description; and

   (c) are fit for the ordinary purposes for which such goods are used; and

   (d) run, within the variations permitted by the agreement, of even kind, quality and quantity within each unit and among all units involved; and

   (e) are adequately contained, packaged, and labeled as the agreement may require; and

   (f) conform to the promises or affirmations of fact made on the container or label if any.

(3) Unless excluded or modified (Section 2—316) other implied warranties may arise from course of dealing or usage of trade.

§2—315. IMPLIED WARRANTY: FITNESS FOR PARTICULAR PURPOSE

Where the seller at the time of contracting has reason to know any particular purpose for which the goods are required and that the buyer is relying on the seller's skill or judgment to select or furnish suitable goods, there is unless excluded or modified under the next section an implied warranty that the goods shall be fit for such purpose.

§2—316. EXCLUSION OR MODIFICATION OF WARRANTIES

(1) Words or conduct relevant to the creation of an express warranty and words or conduct tending to negate or limit warranty shall be construed wherever reasonable as consistent with each other; but subject to the provisions of this Article on parol or extrinsic evidence (Section 2—202) negation or limitation is inoperative to the extent that such construction is unreasonable.

(2) Subject to subsection (3), to exclude or modify the implied warranty of merchantability or any part of it the language must mention merchantability and in case of a writing must be conspicuous, and to exclude or modify any implied warranty of fitness the exclusion must be by a writing and conspicuous. Language to exclude all implied warranties of fitness is sufficient if it states, for example, that "There are no warranties which extend beyond the description on the face hereof."

(3) Notwithstanding subsection (2)

(a) unless the circumstances indicate otherwise, all implied warranties are excluded by expressions like "as is", "with all faults" or other language which in common understanding calls the buyer's attention to the exclusion of warranties and makes plain that there is no implied warranty; and

(b) when the buyer before entering into the contract has examined the goods or the sample or model as fully as he desired or has refused to examine the goods there is no implied warranty with regard to defects which an examination ought in the circumstances to have revealed to him; and

(c) an implied warranty can also be excluded or modified by course of dealing or course of performance or usage of trade.

(4) Remedies for breach of warranty can be limited in accordance with the provisions of this Article on liquidation or limitation of damages and on contractual modification of remedy (Sections 2—718 and 2—719).

§2—317. CUMULATION AND CONFLICT OF WARRANTIES EXPRESS OR IMPLIED

Warranties whether express or implied shall be construed as consistent with each other and as cumulative, but if such construction is unreasonable the intention of the parties shall determine which warranty is dominant. In ascertaining that intention the following rules apply:

(a) Exact or technical specifications displace an inconsistent sample or model or general language of description.

(b) A sample from an existing bulk displaces inconsistent general language of description.

(c) Express warranties displace inconsistent implied warranties other than an implied warranty of fitness for a particular purpose.

§2—318. THIRD PARTY BENEFICIARIES OF WARRANTIES EXPRESS OR IMPLIED

Note: If this Act is introduced in the Congress of the United States this section should be omitted. (States to select one alternative.)

Alternative A

A seller's warranty whether express or implied extends to any natural person who is in the family or household of his buyer or who is a guest in his home if it is reasonable to expect that such person may use, consume or be affected by the goods and who is injured in person by breach of the warranty. A seller may not exclude or limit the operation of this section.

Alternative B

A seller's warranty whether express or implied extends to any natural person who may reasonably be expected to use, consume or be affected by the goods and who is injured in person by breach of the warranty. A seller may not exclude or limit the operation of this section.

Alternative C

A seller's warranty whether express or implied extends to any person who may reasonably be expected to use, consume or be affected by the goods and who is injured by breach of the warranty. A seller may not exclude or limit the operation of this section with respect to injury to the person of an individual to whom the warranty extends.

As amended 1966.

§2—319. F.O.B. AND F.A.S. TERMS

(1) Unless otherwise agreed the term F.O.B. (which means "free on board") at a named place, even though used only in connection with the stated price, is a delivery term under which

(a) when the term is F.O.B. the place of shipment, the seller must at that place ship the goods in the manner provided in this Article (Section 2—504) and bear the expense and risk of putting them into the possession of the carrier; or

(b) when the term is F.O.B. the place of destination, the seller must at his own expense and risk transport the goods to that place and there tender delivery of them in the manner provided in this Article (Section 2—503);

(c) when under either (a) or (b) the term is also F.O.B. vessel, car or other vehicle, the seller must in addition at his own expense and risk load the goods on board. If the term is F.O.B. vessel the buyer must name the vessel and in an appropriate case the seller must comply with the provisions of this Article on the form of bill of lading (Section 2—323).

(2) Unless otherwise agreed the term F.A.S. vessel (which means "free alongside") at a named port, even though used only in connection with the stated price, is a delivery term under which the seller must

(a) at his own expense and risk deliver the goods alongside the vessel in the manner usual in that port or on a dock designated and provided by the buyer; and

(b) obtain and tender a receipt for the goods in exchange for which the carrier is under a duty to issue a bill of lading.

(3) Unless otherwise agreed in any case falling within subsection (1)(a) or (c) or subsection (2) the buyer must seasonably give any needed instructions for making delivery, including when the term is F.A.S. or F.O.B. the loading berth of the vessel and in an appropriate case its name and sailing date. The seller may treat the failure of needed instructions as a failure of cooperation under this Article (Section 2—311). He may also at his option move the goods in any reasonable manner preparatory to delivery or shipment.

(4) Under the term F.O.B. vessel or F.A.S. unless otherwise agreed the buyer must make payment against tender of the required documents and the seller may not tender nor the buyer demand delivery of the goods in substitution for the documents.

§2—320. C.I.F. AND C. & F. TERMS

(1) The term C.I.F. means that the price includes in a lump sum the cost of the goods and the insurance and freight to the named destination. The term C. & F. or C.F. means that the price so includes cost and freight to the named destination.

(2) Unless otherwise agreed and even though used only in connection with the stated price and destination, the term C.I.F. destination or its equivalent requires the seller at his own expense and risk to

(a) put the goods into the possession of a carrier at the port for shipment and obtain a negotiable bill or bills of lading covering the entire transportation to the named destination; and

(b) load the goods and obtain a receipt from the carrier (which may be contained in the bill of

lading) showing that the freight has been paid or provided for; and

(c) obtain a policy or certificate of insurance, including any war risk insurance, of a kind and on terms then current at the port of shipment in the usual amount, in the currency of the contract, shown to cover the same goods covered by the bill of lading and providing for payment of loss to the order of the buyer or for the account of whom it may concern; but the seller may add to the price the amount of the premium for any such war risk insurance; and

(d) prepare an invoice of the goods and procure any other documents required to effect shipment or to comply with the contract; and

(e) forward and tender with commercial promptness all the documents in due form and with any indorsement necessary to perfect the buyer's rights.

(3) Unless otherwise agreed the term C. & F. or its equivalent has the same effect and imposes upon the seller the same obligations and risks as a C.I.F. term except the obligation as to insurance.

(4) Under the term C.I.F. or C. & F. unless otherwise agreed the buyer must make payment against tender of the required documents and the seller may not tender nor the buyer demand delivery of the goods in substitution for the documents.

§2—321. C.I.F. OR C. & F.: "NET LANDED WEIGHTS"; "PAYMENT ON ARRIVAL"; WARRANTY OF CONDITION ON ARRIVAL

Under a contract containing a term C.I.F. or C.& F.

(1) Where the price is based on or is to be adjusted according to "net landed weights", "delivered weights", "out turn" quantity or quality or the like, unless otherwise agreed the seller must reasonably estimate the price. The payment due on tender of the documents called for by the contract is the amount so estimated, but after final adjustment of the price a settlement must be made with commercial promptness.

(2) An agreement described in subsection (1) or any warranty of quality or condition of the goods on arrival places upon the seller the risk of ordinary deterioration, shrinkage and the like in transportation but has no effect on the place or time of identification to the contract for sale or delivery or on the passing of the risk of loss.

(3) Unless otherwise agreed where the contract provides for payment on or after arrival of the goods the seller must before payment allow such preliminary inspection as is feasible; but if the goods are lost delivery of the documents and payment are due when the goods should have arrived.

§2—322. DELIVERY "EX-SHIP"

(1) Unless otherwise agreed a term for delivery of goods "ex-ship" (which means from the carrying vessel) or in equivalent language is not restricted to a particular ship and requires delivery from a ship which has reached a place at the named port of destination where goods of the kind are usually discharged.

> (2) Under such a term unless otherwise agreed
>> (a) the seller must discharge all liens arising out of the carriage and furnish the buyer with a direction which puts the carrier under a duty to deliver the goods; and
>> (b) the risk of loss does not pass to the buyer until the goods leave the ship's tackle or are otherwise properly unloaded.

§2—323. FORM OF BILL OF LADING REQUIRED IN OVERSEAS SHIPMENT; "OVERSEAS"

(1) Where the contract contemplates overseas shipment and contains a term C.I.F. or C. & F. or F.O.B. vessel, the seller unless otherwise agreed must obtain a negotiable bill of lading stating that the goods have been loaded on board or, in the case of a term C.I.F. or C. & F., received for shipment.

> (2) Where in a case within subsection (1) a bill of lading has been issued in a set of parts, unless otherwise agreed if the documents are not to be sent from abroad the buyer may demand tender of the full set; otherwise only one part of the bill of lading need be tendered. Even if the agreement expressly requires a full set
>> (a) due tender of a single part is acceptable within the provisions of this Article on cure of improper delivery (subsection (1) of Section 2—508); and
>> (b) even though the full set is demanded, if the documents are sent from abroad the person tendering an incomplete set may nevertheless require payment upon furnishing an indemnity which the buyer in good faith deems adequate.

(3) A shipment by water or by air or a contract contemplating such shipment is "overseas" insofar as by usage of trade or agreement it is subject to the commercial, financing or shipping practices characteristic of international deep water commerce.

§2—324. "NO ARRIVAL, NO SALE" TERM

Under a term "no arrival, no sale" or terms of like meaning, unless otherwise agreed,

(a) the seller must properly ship conforming goods and if they arrive by any means he must tender them on arrival but he assumes no obligation that the goods will arrive unless he has caused the non-arrival; and

> (b) where without fault of the seller the goods are in part lost or have so deteriorated as no longer to conform to the contract or arrive after the contract time, the buyer may proceed as if there had been casualty to identified goods (Section 2—613).

§2—325. "LETTER OF CREDIT" TERM; "CONFIRMED CREDIT"

(1) Failure of the buyer seasonably to furnish an agreed letter of credit is a breach of the contract for sale.

> (2) The delivery to seller of a proper letter of credit suspends the buyer's obligation to pay. If the letter of credit is dishonored, the seller may on seasonable notification to the buyer require payment directly from him.

> (3) Unless otherwise agreed the term "letter of credit" or "banker's credit" in a contract for sale means an irrevocable credit issued by a financing agency of good repute and, where the shipment is overseas, of good international repute. The term "confirmed credit" means that the credit must also carry the direct obligation of such an agency which does business in the seller's financial market.

§2—326. SALE ON APPROVAL AND SALE OR RETURN; RIGHTS OF CREDITORS

(1) Unless otherwise agreed, if delivered goods may be returned by the buyer even though they conform to the contract, the transaction is
>> (a) a "sale on approval" if the goods are delivered primarily for use, and
>> (b) a "sale or return" if the goods are delivered primarily for resale.

> (2) Goods held on approval are not subject to the claims of the buyer's creditors until acceptance; goods held on sale or return are subject to such claims while in the buyer's possession.

> (3) Any "or return" term of a contract for sale is to be treated as a separate contract for sale within the statute of frauds section of this Article (Section 2—201) and as contradicting the sale aspect of the contract within the provisions of this Article or on parol or extrinsic evidence (Section 2—202).

As amended in 1999.

§2—327. SPECIAL INCIDENTS OF SALE ON APPROVAL AND SALE OR RETURN

(1) Under a sale on approval unless otherwise agreed
>> (a) although the goods are identified to the contract the risk of loss and the title do not pass to the buyer until acceptance; and
>> (b) use of the goods consistent with the purpose of trial is not acceptance but failure seasonably to notify the seller of election to return the goods is acceptance, and if the goods conform to the contract acceptance of any part is acceptance of the whole; and

(c) after due notification of election to return, the return is at the seller's risk and expense but a merchant buyer must follow any reasonable instructions.

(2) Under a sale or return unless otherwise agreed

(a) the option to return extends to the whole or any commercial unit of the goods while in substantially their original condition, but must be exercised seasonably; and

(b) the return is at the buyer's risk and expense.

§2—328. SALE BY AUCTION

(1) In a sale by auction if goods are put up in lots each lot is the subject of a separate sale.

(2) A sale by auction is complete when the auctioneer so announces by the fall of the hammer or in other customary manner. Where a bid is made while the hammer is falling in acceptance of a prior bid the auctioneer may in his discretion reopen the bidding or declare the goods sold under the bid on which the hammer was falling.

(3) Such a sale is with reserve unless the goods are in explicit terms put up without reserve. In an auction with reserve the auctioneer may withdraw the goods at any time until he announces completion of the sale. In an auction without reserve, after the auctioneer calls for bids on an article or lot, that article or lot cannot be withdrawn unless no bid is made within a reasonable time. In either case a bidder may retract his bid until the auctioneer's announcement of completion of the sale, but a bidder's retraction does not revive any previous bid.

(4) If the auctioneer knowingly receives a bid on the seller's behalf or the seller makes or procures such as bid, and notice has not been given that liberty for such bidding is reserved, the buyer may at his option avoid the sale or take the goods at the price of the last good faith bid prior to the completion of the sale. This subsection shall not apply to any bid at a forced sale.

Part 4 Title, Creditors and Good Faith Purchasers

§2—401. PASSING OF TITLE; RESERVATION FOR SECURITY; LIMITED APPLICATION OF THIS SECTION

Each provision of this Article with regard to the rights, obligations and remedies of the seller, the buyer, purchasers or other third parties applies irrespective of title to the goods except where the provision refers to such title. Insofar as situations are not covered by the other provisions of this Article and matters concerning title became material the following rules apply:

(1) Title to goods cannot pass under a contract for sale prior to their identification to the contract (Section 2—501), and

unless otherwise explicitly agreed the buyer acquires by their identification a special property as limited by this Act. Any retention or reservation by the seller of the title (property) in goods shipped or delivered to the buyer is limited in effect to a reservation of a security interest. Subject to these provisions and to the provisions of the Article on Secured Transactions (Article 9), title to goods passes from the seller to the buyer in any manner and on any conditions explicitly agreed on by the parties.

(2) Unless otherwise explicitly agreed title passes to the buyer at the time and place at which the seller completes his performance with reference to the physical delivery of the goods, despite any reservation of a security interest and even though a document of title is to be delivered at a different time or place; and in particular and despite any reservation of a security interest by the bill of lading

(a) if the contract requires or authorizes the seller to send the goods to the buyer but does not require him to deliver them at destination, title passes to the buyer at the time and place of shipment; but

(b) if the contract requires delivery at destination, title passes on tender there.

(3) Unless otherwise explicitly agreed where delivery is to be made without moving the goods,

(a) if the seller is to deliver a document of title, title passes at the time when and the place where he delivers such documents; or

(b) if the goods are at the time of contracting already identified and no documents are to be delivered, title passes at the time and place of contracting.

(4) A rejection or other refusal by the buyer to receive or retain the goods, whether or not justified, or a justified revocation of acceptance revests title to the goods in the seller. Such revesting occurs by operation of law and is not a "sale".

§2—402. RIGHTS OF SELLER'S CREDITORS AGAINST SOLD GOODS

(1) Except as provided in subsections (2) and (3), rights of unsecured creditors of the seller with respect to goods which have been identified to a contract for sale are subject to the buyer's rights to recover the goods under this Article (Sections 2—502 and 2—716).

(2) A creditor of the seller may treat a sale or an identification of goods to a contract for sale as void if as against him a retention of possession by the seller is fraudulent under any rule of law of the state where the goods are situated, except that retention of possession in good faith and current course of trade by a merchant-seller for a commercially reasonable time after a sale or identification is not fraudulent.

(3) Nothing in this Article shall be deemed to impair the rights of creditors of the seller

(a) under the provisions of the Article on Secured Transactions (Article 9); or

(b) where identification to the contract or delivery is made not in current course of trade but in satisfaction of or as security for a pre-existing claim for money, security or the like and is made under circumstances which under any rule of law of the state where the goods are situated would apart from this Article constitute the transaction a fraudulent transfer or voidable preference.

§2—403. POWER TO TRANSFER; GOOD FAITH PURCHASE OF GOODS; "ENTRUSTING"

(1) A purchaser of goods acquires all title which his transferor had or had power to transfer except that a purchaser of a limited interest acquires rights only to the extent of the interest purchased. A person with voidable title has power to transfer a good title to a good faith purchaser for value. When goods have been delivered under a transaction of purchase the purchaser has such power even though

(a) the transferor was deceived as to the identity of the purchaser, or

(b) the delivery was in exchange for a check which is later dishonored, or

(c) it was agreed that the transaction was to be a "cash sale", or

(d) the delivery was procured through fraud punishable as larcenous under the criminal law.

(2) Any entrusting of possession of goods to a merchant who deals in goods of that kind gives him power to transfer all rights of the entruster to a buyer in ordinary course of business.

(3) "Entrusting" includes any delivery and any acquiescence in retention of possession regardless of any condition expressed between the parties to the delivery or acquiescence and regardless of whether the procurement of the entrusting or the possessor's disposition of the goods have been such as to be larcenous under the criminal law.

(4) The rights of other purchasers of goods and of lien creditors are governed by the Articles on Secured Transactions (Article 9), Bulk Transfers (Article 6) and Documents of Title (Article 7).

As amended in 1988.

Part 5 Performance

§2—501. INSURABLE INTEREST IN GOODS; MANNER OF IDENTIFICATION OF GOODS

(1) The buyer obtains a special property and an insurable interest in goods by identification of existing goods as goods to which the contract refers even though the goods so identified are non-conforming and he has an option to return or reject them. Such identification can be made at any time and in any manner explicitly agreed to by the parties. In the absence of explicit agreement identification occurs

(a) when the contract is made if it is for the sale of goods already existing and identified;

(b) if the contract is for the sale of future goods other than those described in paragraph (c), when goods are shipped, marked or otherwise designated by the seller as goods to which the contract refers;

(c) when the crops are planted or otherwise become growing crops or the young are conceived if the contract is for the sale of unborn young to be born within twelve months after contracting or for the sale of crops to be harvested within twelve months or the next normal harvest season after contracting whichever is longer.

(2) The seller retains an insurable interest in goods so long as title to or any security interest in the goods remains in him and where the identification is by the seller alone he may until default or insolvency or notification to the buyer that the identification is final substitute other goods for those identified.

(3) Nothing in this section impairs any insurable interest recognized under any other statute or rule of law.

§2—502. BUYER'S RIGHT TO GOODS ON SELLER'S INSOLVENCY

(1) Subject to subsections (2) and (3) and even though the goods have not been shipped a buyer who has paid a part or all of the price of goods in which he has a special property under the provisions of the immediately preceding section may on making and keeping good a tender of any unpaid portion of their price recover them from the seller if:

(a) in the case of goods bought for personal, family, or household purposes, the seller repudiates or fails to deliver as required by the contract; or

(b) in all cases, the seller becomes insolvent within ten days after receipt of the first installment on their price.

(2) The buyer's right to recover the goods under subsection (1)(a) vests upon acquisition of a special property, even if the seller had not then repudiated or failed to deliver.

(3) If the identification creating his special property has been made by the buyer he acquires the right to recover the goods only if they conform to the contract for sale.

As amended in 1999.

§2—503. MANNER OF SELLER'S TENDER OF DELIVERY

(1) Tender of delivery requires that the seller put and hold conforming goods at the buyer's disposition and give the

buyer any notification reasonably necessary to enable him to take delivery. The manner, time and place for tender are determined by the agreement and this Article, and in particular

(a) tender must be at a reasonable hour, and if it is of goods they must be kept available for the period reasonably necessary to enable the buyer to take possession; but

(b) unless otherwise agreed the buyer must furnish facilities reasonably suited to the receipt of the goods.

(2) Where the case is within the next section respecting shipment tender requires that the seller comply with its provisions.

(3) Where the seller is required to deliver at a particular destination tender requires that he comply with subsection (1)and also in any appropriate case tender documents as described in subsections (4) and (5) of this section.

(4) Where goods are in the possession of a bailee and are to be delivered without being moved

(a) tender requires that the seller either tender a negotiable document of title covering such goods or procure acknowledgment by the bailee of the buyer's right to possession of the goods; but

(b) tender to the buyer of a non-negotiable document of title or of a written direction to the bailee to deliver is sufficient tender unless the buyer seasonably objects, and receipt by the bailee of notification of the buyer's rights fixes those rights as against the bailee and all third persons; but risk of loss of the goods and of any failure by the bailee to honor the non-negotiable document of title or to obey the direction remains on the seller until the buyer has had a reasonable time to present the document or direction, and a refusal by the bailee to honor the document or to obey the direction defeats the tender.

(5) Where the contract requires the seller to deliver documents

(a) he must tender all such documents in correct form, except as provided in this Article with respect to bills of lading in a set (subsection (2) of Section 2—323); and

(b) tender through customary banking channels is sufficient and dishonor of a draft accompanying the documents constitutes non-acceptance or rejection.

§2—504. SHIPMENT BY SELLER

Where the seller is required or authorized to send the goods to the buyer and the contract does not require him to deliver them at a particular destination, then unless otherwise agreed he must

(a) put the goods in the possession of such a carrier and make such a contract for their transportation as may be reasonable having regard to the nature of the goods and other circumstances of the case; and

(b) obtain and promptly deliver or tender in due form any document necessary to enable the buyer to obtain possession of the goods or otherwise required by the agreement or by usage of trade; and

(c) promptly notify the buyer of the shipment.

Failure to notify the buyer under paragraph (c) or to make a proper contract under paragraph (a) is a ground for rejection only if material delay or loss ensues.

§2—505. SELLER'S SHIPMENT UNDER RESERVATION

(1) Where the seller has identified goods to the contract by or before shipment:

(a) his procurement of a negotiable bill of lading to his own order or otherwise reserves in him a security interest in the goods. His procurement of the bill to the order of a financing agency or of the buyer indicates in addition only the seller's expectation of transferring that interest to the person named.

(b) a non-negotiable bill of lading to himself or his nominee reserves possession of the goods as security but except in a case of conditional delivery (subsection (2)of Section 2—507) a non-negotiable bill of lading naming the buyer as consignee reserves no security interest even though the seller retains possession of the bill of lading.

(2) When shipment by the seller with reservation of a security interest is in violation of the contract for sale it constitutes an improper contract for transportation within the preceding section but impairs neither the rights given to the buyer by shipment and identification of the goods to the contract nor the seller's powers as a holder of a negotiable document.

§2—506. RIGHTS OF FINANCING AGENCY

(1) A financing agency by paying or purchasing for value a draft which relates to a shipment of goods acquires to the extent of the payment or purchase and in addition to its own rights under the draft and any document of title securing it any rights of the shipper in the goods including the right to stop delivery and the shipper's right to have the draft honored by the buyer.

(2) The right to reimbursement of a financing agency which has in good faith honored or purchased the draft under commitment to or authority from the buyer is not impaired by subsequent discovery of defects with reference to any relevant document which was apparently regular on its face.

§2—507. EFFECT OF SELLER'S TENDER; DELIVERY ON CONDITION

(1) Tender of delivery is a condition to the buyer's duty to accept the goods and, unless otherwise agreed, to his duty to pay for them. Tender entitles the seller to acceptance of the goods and to payment according to the contract.

(2) Where payment is due and demanded on the delivery to the buyer of goods or documents of title, his right as against the seller to retain or dispose of them is conditional upon his making the payment due.

§2—508. CURE BY SELLER OF IMPROPER TENDER OR DELIVERY; REPLACEMENT

(1) Where any tender or delivery by the seller is rejected because non-conforming and the time for performance has not yet expired, the seller may seasonably notify the buyer of his intention to cure and may then within the contract time make a conforming delivery.

(2) Where the buyer rejects a non-conforming tender which the seller had reasonable grounds to believe would be acceptable with or without money allowance the seller may if he seasonably notifies the buyer have a further reasonable time to substitute a conforming tender.

§2—509. RISK OF LOSS IN THE ABSENCE OF BREACH

(1) Where the contract requires or authorizes the seller to ship the goods by carrier

    (a) if it does not require him to deliver them at a particular destination, the risk of loss passes to the buyer when the goods are duly delivered to the carrier even though the shipment is under reservation (Section 2—505); but

    (b) if it does require him to deliver them at a particular destination and the goods are there duly tendered while in the possession of the carrier, the risk of loss passes to the buyer when the goods are there duly so tendered as to enable the buyer to take delivery.

(2) Where the goods are held by a bailee to be delivered without being moved, the risk of loss passes to the buyer

    (a) on his receipt of a negotiable document of title covering the goods; or

    (b) on acknowledgment by the bailee of the buyer's right to possession of the goods; or

    (c) after his receipt of a non-negotiable document of title or other written direction to deliver, as provided in subsection (4)(b) of Section 2—503.

(3) In any case not within subsection (1) or (2), the risk of loss passes to the buyer on his receipt of the goods if the seller is a merchant; otherwise the risk passes to the buyer on tender of delivery.

(4) The provisions of this section are subject to contrary agreement of the parties and to the provisions of this Article on sale on approval (Section 2—327) and on effect of breach on risk of loss (Section 2—510).

§2—510. EFFECT OF BREACH ON RISK OF LOSS

(1) Where a tender or delivery of goods so fails to conform to the contract as to give a right of rejection the risk of their loss remains on the seller until cure or acceptance.

(2) Where the buyer rightfully revokes acceptance he may to the extent of any deficiency in his effective insurance coverage treat the risk of loss as having rested on the seller from the beginning.

(3) Where the buyer as to conforming goods already identified to the contract for sale repudiates or is otherwise in breach before risk of their loss has passed to him, the seller may to the extent of any deficiency in his effective insurance coverage treat the risk of loss as resting on the buyer for a commercially reasonable time.

§2—511. TENDER OF PAYMENT BY BUYER; PAYMENT BY CHECK

(1) Unless otherwise agreed tender of payment is a condition to the seller's duty to tender and complete any delivery.

(2) Tender of payment is sufficient when made by any means or in any manner current in the ordinary course of business unless the seller demands payment in legal tender and gives any extension of time reasonably necessary to procure it.

(3) Subject to the provisions of this Act on the effect of an instrument on an obligation (Section 3—310), payment by check is conditional and is defeated as between the parties by dishonor of the check on due presentment.

As amended in 1994.

§2—512. PAYMENT BY BUYER BEFORE INSPECTION

(1) Where the contract requires payment before inspection non-conformity of the goods does not excuse the buyer from so making payment unless

    (a) the non-conformity appears without inspection; or

    (b) despite tender of the required documents the circumstances would justify injunction against honor under this Act (Section 5—109(b)).

(2) Payment pursuant to subsection (1) does not constitute an acceptance of goods or impair the buyer's right to inspect or any of his remedies.

As amended in 1995.

§2—513. BUYER'S RIGHT TO INSPECTION OF GOODS

(1) Unless otherwise agreed and subject to subsection (3), where goods are tendered or delivered or identified to the contract for sale, the buyer has a right before payment or acceptance to inspect them at any reasonable place and time and in any reasonable manner. When the seller is required or authorized to send the goods to the buyer, the inspection may be after their arrival.

(2) Expenses of inspection must be borne by the buyer but may be recovered from the seller if the goods do not conform and are rejected.

(3) Unless otherwise agreed and subject to the provisions of this Article on C.I.F. contracts (subsection (3) of Section 2—321), the buyer is not entitled to inspect the goods before payment of the price when the contract provides

  (a) for delivery "C.O.D." or on other like terms; or

  (b) for payment against documents of title, except where such payment is due only after the goods are to become available for inspection.

(4) A place or method of inspection fixed by the parties is presumed to be exclusive but unless otherwise expressly agreed it does not postpone identification or shift the place for delivery or for passing the risk of loss. If compliance becomes impossible, inspection shall be as provided in this section unless the place or method fixed was clearly intended as an indispensable condition failure of which avoids the contract.

§2—514. WHEN DOCUMENTS DELIVERABLE ON ACCEPTANCE; WHEN ON PAYMENT

Unless otherwise agreed documents against which a draft is drawn are to be delivered to the drawee on acceptance of the draft if it is payable more than three days after presentment; otherwise, only on payment.

§2—515. PRESERVING EVIDENCE OF GOODS IN DISPUTE

In furtherance of the adjustment of any claim or dispute

(a) either party on reasonable notification to the other and for the purpose of ascertaining the facts and preserving evidence has the right to inspect, test and sample the goods including such of them as may be in the possession or control of the other; and

  (b) the parties may agree to a third party inspection or survey to determine the conformity or condition of the goods and may agree that the findings shall be binding upon them in any subsequent litigation or adjustment.

Part 6 Breach, Repudiation and Excuse

§2—601. BUYER'S RIGHTS ON IMPROPER DELIVERY

Subject to the provisions of this Article on breach in installment contracts (Section 2—612) and unless otherwise agreed under the sections on contractual limitations of remedy (Sections 2—718 and 2—719), if the goods or the tender of delivery fail in any respect to conform to the contract, the buyer may

(a) reject the whole; or

  (b) accept the whole; or

  (c) accept any commercial unit or units and reject the rest.

§2—602. MANNER AND EFFECT OF RIGHTFUL REJECTION

(1) Rejection of goods must be within a reasonable time after their delivery or tender. It is ineffective unless the buyer seasonably notifies the seller.

(2) Subject to the provisions of the two following sections on rejected goods (Sections 2—603 and 2—604),

  (a) after rejection any exercise of ownership by the buyer with respect to any commercial unit is wrongful as against the seller; and

  (b) if the buyer has before rejection taken physical possession of goods in which he does not have a security interest under the provisions of this Article (subsection (3) of Section 2—711), he is under a duty after rejection to hold them with reasonable care at the seller's disposition for a time sufficient to permit the seller to remove them; but

  (c) the buyer has no further obligations with regard to goods rightfully rejected.

(3) The seller's rights with respect to goods wrongfully rejected are governed by the provisions of this Article on Seller's remedies in general (Section 2—703).

§2—603. MERCHANT BUYER'S DUTIES AS TO RIGHTFULLY REJECTED GOODS

(1) Subject to any security interest in the buyer (subsection (3) of Section 2—711), when the seller has no agent or place of business at the market of rejection a merchant buyer is under a duty after rejection of goods in his possession or control to follow any reasonable instructions received from the seller with respect to the goods and in the absence of such instructions to make reasonable efforts to sell them for the seller's account if they are perishable or threaten to decline in value speedily. Instructions are not reasonable if on demand indemnity for expenses is not forthcoming.

(2) When the buyer sells goods under subsection (1), he is entitled to reimbursement from the seller or out of the

proceeds for reasonable expenses of caring for and selling them, and if the expenses include no selling commission then to such commission as is usual in the trade or if there is none to a reasonable sum not exceeding ten per cent on the gross proceeds.

(3) In complying with this section the buyer is held only to good faith and good faith conduct hereunder is neither acceptance nor conversion nor the basis of an action for damages.

§2—604. BUYER'S OPTIONS AS TO SALVAGE OF RIGHTFULLY REJECTED GOODS

Subject to the provisions of the immediately preceding section on perishables if the seller gives no instructions within a reasonable time after notification of rejection the buyer may store the rejected goods for the seller's account or reship them to him or resell them for the seller's account with reimbursement as provided in the preceding section. Such action is not acceptance or conversion.

§2—605. WAIVER OF BUYER'S OBJECTIONS BY FAILURE TO PARTICULARIZE

(1) The buyer's failure to state in connection with rejection a particular defect which is ascertainable by reasonable inspection precludes him from relying on the unstated defect to justify rejection or to establish breach

(a) where the seller could have cured it if stated seasonably; or

(b) between merchants when the seller has after rejection made a request in writing for a full and final written statement of all defects on which the buyer proposes to rely.

(2) Payment against documents made without reservation of rights precludes recovery of the payment for defects apparent on the face of the documents.

§2—606. WHAT CONSTITUTES ACCEPTANCE OF GOODS

(1) Acceptance of goods occurs when the buyer

(a) after a reasonable opportunity to inspect the goods signifies to the seller that the goods are conforming or that he will take or retain them in spite of their nonconformity; or

(b) fails to make an effective rejection (subsection (1) of Section 2—602), but such acceptance does not occur until the buyer has had a reasonable opportunity to inspect them; or

(c) does any act inconsistent with the seller's ownership; but if such act is wrongful as against the seller it is an acceptance only if ratified by him.

(2) Acceptance of a part of any commercial unit is acceptance of that entire unit.

§2—607. EFFECT OF ACCEPTANCE; NOTICE OF BREACH; BURDEN OF ESTABLISHING BREACH AFTER ACCEPTANCE; NOTICE OF CLAIM OR LITIGATION TO PERSON ANSWERABLE OVER

(1) The buyer must pay at the contract rate for any goods accepted.

(2) Acceptance of goods by the buyer precludes rejection of the goods accepted and if made with knowledge of a non-conformity cannot be revoked because of it unless the acceptance was on the reasonable assumption that the non-conformity would be seasonably cured but acceptance does not of itself impair any other remedy provided by this Article for non-conformity.

(3) Where a tender has been accepted

(a) the buyer must within a reasonable time after he discovers or should have discovered any breach notify the seller of breach or be barred from any remedy; and

(b) if the claim is one for infringement or the like (subsection (3) of Section 2—312) and the buyer is sued as a result of such a breach he must so notify the seller within a reasonable time after he receives notice of the litigation or be barred from any remedy over for liability established by the litigation.

(4) The burden is on the buyer to establish any breach with respect to the goods accepted.

(5) Where the buyer is sued for breach of a warranty or other obligation for which his seller is answerable over

(a) he may give his seller written notice of the litigation. If the notice states that the seller may come in and defend and that if the seller does not do so he will be bound in any action against him by his buyer by any determination of fact common to the two litigations, then unless the seller after seasonable receipt of the notice does come in and defend he is so bound.

(b) if the claim is one for infringement or the like (subsection (3) of Section 2—312) the original seller may demand in writing that his buyer turn over to him control of the litigation including settlement or else be barred from any remedy over and if he also agrees to bear all expense and to satisfy any adverse judgment, then unless the buyer after seasonable receipt of the demand does turn over control the buyer is so barred.

(6) The provisions of subsections (3), (4) and (5) apply to any obligation of a buyer to hold the seller harmless against infringement or the like (subsection (3) of Section 2—312).

§2—608. REVOCATION OF ACCEPTANCE IN WHOLE OR IN PART

(1) The buyer may revoke his acceptance of a lot or commercial unit whose non-conformity substantially impairs its value to him if he has accepted it

    (a) on the reasonable assumption that its non-conformity would be cured and it has not been seasonably cured; or

    (b) without discovery of such non-conformity if his acceptance was reasonably induced either by the difficulty of discovery before acceptance or by the seller's assurances.

(2) Revocation of acceptance must occur within a reasonable time after the buyer discovers or should have discovered the ground for it and before any substantial change in condition of the goods which is not caused by their own defects. It is not effective until the buyer notifies the seller of it.

(3) A buyer who so revokes has the same rights and duties with regard to the goods involved as if he had rejected them.

§2—609. RIGHT TO ADEQUATE ASSURANCE OF PERFORMANCE

(1) A contract for sale imposes an obligation on each party that the other's expectation of receiving due performance will not be impaired. When reasonable grounds for insecurity arise with respect to the performance of either party the other may in writing demand adequate assurance of due performance and until he receives such assurance may if commercially reasonable suspend any performance for which he has not already received the agreed return.

(2) Between merchants the reasonableness of grounds for insecurity and the adequacy of any assurance offered shall be determined according to commercial standards.

(3) Acceptance of any improper delivery or payment does not prejudice the party's right to demand adequate assurance of future performance.

(4) After receipt of a justified demand failure to provide within a reasonable time not exceeding thirty days such assurance of due performance as is adequate under the circumstances of the particular case is a repudiation of the contract.

§2—610. ANTICIPATORY REPUDIATION

When either party repudiates the contract with respect to a performance not yet due the loss of which will substantially impair the value of the contract to the other, the aggrieved party may

(a) for a commercially reasonable time await performance by the repudiating party; or

(b) resort to any remedy for breach (Section 2—703 or Section 2—711), even though he has notified the repudiating party that he would await the latter's performance and has urged retraction; and

(c) in either case suspend his own performance or proceed in accordance with the provisions of this Article on the seller's right to identify goods to the contract notwithstanding breach or to salvage unfinished goods (Section 2—704).

§2—611. RETRACTION OF ANTICIPATORY REPUDIATION

(1) Until the repudiating party's next performance is due he can retract his repudiation unless the aggrieved party has since the repudiation cancelled or materially changed his position or otherwise indicated that he considers the repudiation final.

(2) Retraction may be by any method which clearly indicates to the aggrieved party that the repudiating party intends to perform, but must include any assurance justifiably demanded under the provisions of this Article (Section 2—609).

(3) Retraction reinstates the repudiating party's rights under the contract with due excuse and allowance to the aggrieved party for any delay occasioned by the repudiation.

§2—612. "INSTALLMENT CONTRACT"; BREACH

(1) An "installment contract" is one which requires or authorizes the delivery of goods in separate lots to be separately accepted, even though the contract contains a clause "each delivery is a separate contract" or its equivalent.

(2) The buyer may reject any installment which is non-conforming if the non-conformity substantially impairs the value of that installment and cannot be cured or if the non-conformity is a defect in the required documents; but if the non-conformity does not fall within subsection (3) and the seller gives adequate assurance of its cure the buyer must accept that installment.

(3) Whenever non-conformity or default with respect to one or more installments substantially impairs the value of the whole contract there is a breach of the whole. But the aggrieved party reinstates the contract if he accepts a non-conforming installment without seasonably notifying of cancellation or if he brings an action with respect only to past installments or demands performance as to future installments.

§2—613. CASUALTY TO IDENTIFIED GOODS

Where the contract requires for its performance goods identified when the contract is made, and the goods suffer casualty without fault of either party before the risk of loss passes to the buyer, or in a proper case under a "no arrival, no sale" term (Section 2—324) then

(a) if the loss is total the contract is avoided; and

(b) if the loss is partial or the goods have so deteriorated as no longer to conform to the contract the buyer may nevertheless demand inspection and at his option either treat the contract as voided or accept the goods with due allowance from the contract price for the deterioration or the deficiency in quantity but without further right against the seller.

§2—614. SUBSTITUTED PERFORMANCE

(1) Where without fault of either party the agreed berthing, loading, or unloading facilities fail or an agreed type of carrier becomes unavailable or the agreed manner of delivery otherwise becomes commercially impracticable but a commercially reasonable substitute is available, such substitute performance must be tendered and accepted.

(2) If the agreed means or manner of payment fails because of domestic or foreign governmental regulation, the seller may withhold or stop delivery unless the buyer provides a means or manner of payment which is commercially a substantial equivalent. If delivery has already been taken, payment by the means or in the manner provided by the regulation discharges the buyer's obligation unless the regulation is discriminatory, oppressive or predatory.

§2—615. EXCUSE BY FAILURE OF PRESUPPOSED CONDITIONS

Except so far as a seller may have assumed a greater obligation and subject to the preceding section on substituted performance:

(a) Delay in delivery or non-delivery in whole or in part by a seller who complies with paragraphs (b) and (c) is not a breach of his duty under a contract for sale if performance as agreed has been made impracticable by the occurrence of a contingency the nonoccurrence of which was a basic assumption on which the contract was made or by compliance in good faith with any applicable foreign or domestic governmental regulation or order whether or not it later proves to be invalid.

(b) Where the causes mentioned in paragraph (a) affect only a part of the seller's capacity to perform, he must allocate production and deliveries among his customers but may at his option include regular customers not then under contract as well as his own requirements for further manufacture. He may so allocate in any manner which is fair and reasonable.

(c) The seller must notify the buyer seasonably that there will be delay or non-delivery and, when allocation is required under paragraph (b), of the estimated quota thus made available for the buyer.

§2—616. PROCEDURE ON NOTICE CLAIMING EXCUSE

(1) Where the buyer receives notification of a material or indefinite delay or an allocation justified under the preceding section he may by written notification to the seller as to any delivery concerned, and where the prospective deficiency substantially impairs the value of the whole contract under the provisions of this Article relating to breach of installment contracts (Section 2—612), then also as to the whole,

(a) terminate and thereby discharge any unexecuted portion of the contract; or

(b) modify the contract by agreeing to take his available quota in substitution.

(2) If after receipt of such notification from the seller the buyer fails so to modify the contract within a reasonable time not exceeding thirty days the contract lapses with respect to any deliveries affected.

(3) The provisions of this section may not be negated by agreement except in so far as the seller has assumed a greater obligation under the preceding section.

Part 7 Remedies

§2—701. REMEDIES FOR BREACH OF COLLATERAL CONTRACTS NOT IMPAIRED

Remedies for breach of any obligation or promise collateral or ancillary to a contract for sale are not impaired by the provisions of this Article.

§2—702. SELLER'S REMEDIES ON DISCOVERY OF BUYER'S INSOLVENCY

(1) Where the seller discovers the buyer to be insolvent he may refuse delivery except for cash including payment for all goods theretofore delivered under the contract, and stop delivery under this Article (Section 2—705).

(2) Where the seller discovers that the buyer has received goods on credit while insolvent he may reclaim the goods upon demand made within ten days after the receipt, but if misrepresentation of solvency has been made to the particular seller in writing within three months before delivery the ten day limitation does not apply. Except as provided in this subsection the seller may not base a right to reclaim goods on the buyer's fraudulent or innocent misrepresentation of solvency or of intent to pay.

(3) The seller's right to reclaim under subsection (2) is subject to the rights of a buyer in ordinary course or other good faith purchaser under this Article (Section 2—403). Successful reclamation of goods excludes all other remedies with respect to them.

§2—703. SELLER'S REMEDIES IN GENERAL

Where the buyer wrongfully rejects or revokes acceptance of goods or fails to make a payment due on or before delivery or repudiates with respect to a part or the whole, then with respect to any goods directly affected and, if the breach is of the whole contract (Section 2—612), then also with respect to the whole undelivered balance, the aggrieved seller may

(a) withhold delivery of such goods;

(b) stop delivery by any bailee as hereafter provided (Section 2—705);

(c) proceed under the next section respecting goods still unidentified to the contract;

(d) resell and recover damages as hereafter provided (Section 2—706);

(e) recover damages for non-acceptance (Section 2—708) or in a proper case the price (Section 2—709);

(f) cancel.

§2—704. SELLER'S RIGHT TO IDENTIFY GOODS TO THE CONTRACT NOTWITHSTANDING BREACH OR TO SALVAGE UNFINISHED GOODS

(1) An aggrieved seller under the preceding section may

(a) identify to the contract conforming goods not already identified if at the time he learned of the breach they are in his possession or control;

(b) treat as the subject of resale goods which have demonstrably been intended for the particular contract even though those goods are unfinished.

(2) Where the goods are unfinished an aggrieved seller may in the exercise of reasonable commercial judgment for the purposes of avoiding loss and of effective realization either complete the manufacture and wholly identify the goods to the contract or cease manufacture and resell for scrap or salvage value or proceed in any other reasonable manner.

§2—705. SELLER'S STOPPAGE OF DELIVERY IN TRANSIT OR OTHERWISE

(1) The seller may stop delivery of goods in the possession of a carrier or other bailee when he discovers the buyer to be insolvent (Section 2—702) and may stop delivery of carload, truckload, planeload or larger shipments of express or freight when the buyer repudiates or fails to make a payment due before delivery or if for any other reason the seller has a right to withhold or reclaim the goods.

(2) As against such buyer the seller may stop delivery until

(a) receipt of the goods by the buyer; or

(b) acknowledgment to the buyer by any bailee of the goods except a carrier that the bailee holds the goods for the buyer; or

(c) such acknowledgment to the buyer by a carrier by reshipment or as warehouseman; or

(d) negotiation to the buyer of any negotiable document of title covering the goods.

(3) (a) To stop delivery the seller must so notify as to enable the bailee by reasonable diligence to prevent delivery of the goods.

(b) After such notification the bailee must hold and deliver the goods according to the directions of the seller but the seller is liable to the bailee for any ensuing charges or damages.

(c) If a negotiable document of title has been issued for goods the bailee is not obliged to obey a notification to stop until surrender of the document.

(d) A carrier who has issued a non-negotiable bill of lading is not obliged to obey a notification to stop received from a person other than the consignor.

§2—706. SELLER'S RESALE INCLUDING CONTRACT FOR RESALE

(1) Under the conditions stated in Section 2—703 on seller's remedies, the seller may resell the goods concerned or the undelivered balance thereof. Where the resale is made in good faith and in a commercially reasonable manner the seller may recover the difference between the resale price and the contract price together with any incidental damages allowed under the provisions of this Article (Section 2—710), but less expenses saved in consequence of the buyer's breach.

(2) Except as otherwise provided in subsection (3) or unless otherwise agreed resale may be at public or private sale including sale by way of one or more contracts to sell or of identification to an existing contract of the seller. Sale may be as a unit or in parcels and at any time and place and on any terms but every aspect of the sale including the method, manner, time, place and terms must be commercially reasonable. The resale must be reasonably identified as referring to the broken contract, but it is not necessary that the goods be in existence or that any or all of them have been identified to the contract before the breach.

(3) Where the resale is at private sale the seller must give the buyer reasonable notification of his intention to resell.

(4) Where the resale is at public sale

(a) only identified goods can be sold except where there is a recognized market for a public sale of futures in goods of the kind; and

(b) it must be made at a usual place or market for public sale if one is reasonably available and except in the case of goods which are perishable or threaten to decline in value speedily the seller must give the buyer reasonable notice of the time and place of the resale; and

(c) if the goods are not to be within the view of those attending the sale the notification of sale must state the place where the goods are located and provide for their reasonable inspection by prospective bidders; and

(d) the seller may buy.

(5) A purchaser who buys in good faith at a resale takes the goods free of any rights of the original buyer even though the seller fails to comply with one or more of the requirements of this section.

(6) The seller is not accountable to the buyer for any profit made on any resale. A person in the position of a seller (Section 2—707) or a buyer who has rightfully rejected or justifiably revoked acceptance must account for any excess over the amount of his security interest, as hereinafter defined (subsection (3) of Section 2—711).

§2—707. "PERSON IN THE POSITION OF A SELLER"

(1) A "person in the position of a seller" includes as against a principal an agent who has paid or become responsible for the price of goods on behalf of his principal or anyone who otherwise holds a security interest or other right in goods similar to that of a seller.

(2) A person in the position of a seller may as provided in this Article withhold or stop delivery (Section 2—705) and resell (Section 2—706) and recover incidental damages (Section 2—710).

§2—708. SELLER'S DAMAGES FOR NON-ACCEPTANCE OR REPUDIATION

(1) Subject to subsection (2) and to the provisions of this Article with respect to proof of market price (Section 2—723), the measure of damages for non-acceptance or repudiation by the buyer is the difference between the market price at the time and place for tender and the unpaid contract price together with any incidental damages provided in this Article (Section 2—710), but less expenses saved in consequence of the buyer's breach.

(2) If the measure of damages provided in subsection (1) is inadequate to put the seller in as good a position as performance would have done then the measure of damages is the profit (including reasonable overhead) which the seller would have made from full performance by the buyer, together with any incidental damages provided in this Article (Section 2—710), due allowance for costs reasonably incurred and due credit for payments or proceeds of resale.

§2—709. ACTION FOR THE PRICE

(1) When the buyer fails to pay the price as it becomes due the seller may recover, together with any incidental damages under the next section, the price

(a) of goods accepted or of conforming goods lost or damaged within a commercially reasonable time after risk of their loss has passed to the buyer; and

(b) of goods identified to the contract if the seller is unable after reasonable effort to resell them at a reasonable price or the circumstances reasonably indicate that such effort will be unavailing.

(2) Where the seller sues for the price he must hold for the buyer any goods which have been identified to the contract and are still in his control except that if resale becomes possible he may resell them at any time prior to the collection of the judgment. The net proceeds of any such resale must be credited to the buyer and payment of the judgment entitles him to any goods not resold.

(3) After the buyer has wrongfully rejected or revoked acceptance of the goods or has failed to make a payment due or has repudiated (Section 2—610), a seller who is held not entitled to the price under this section shall nevertheless be awarded damages for non-acceptance under the preceding section.

§2—710. SELLER'S INCIDENTAL DAMAGES

Incidental damages to an aggrieved seller include any commercially reasonable charges, expenses or commissions incurred in stopping delivery, in the transportation, care and custody of goods after the buyer's breach, in connection with return or resale of the goods or otherwise resulting from the breach.

§2—711. BUYER'S REMEDIES IN GENERAL; BUYER'S SECURITY INTEREST IN REJECTED GOODS

(1) Where the seller fails to make delivery or repudiates or the buyer rightfully rejects or justifiably revokes acceptance then with respect to any goods involved, and with respect to the whole if the breach goes to the whole contract (Section 2—612), the buyer may cancel and whether or not he has done so may in addition to recovering so much of the price as has been paid

(a) "cover" and have damages under the next section as to all the goods affected whether or not they have been identified to the contract; or

(b) recover damages for non-delivery as provided in this Article (Section 2—713).

(2) Where the seller fails to deliver or repudiates the buyer may also

(a) if the goods have been identified recover them as provided in this Article (Section 2—502); or

(b) in a proper case obtain specific performance or replevy the goods as provided in this Article (Section 2—716).

(3) On rightful rejection or justifiable revocation of acceptance a buyer has a security interest in goods in his possession or control for any payments made on their price and any expenses reasonably incurred in their inspection, receipt, transportation, care and custody and may hold such goods and resell them in like manner as an aggrieved seller (Section 2—706).

§2—712. "COVER"; BUYER'S PROCUREMENT OF SUBSTITUTE GOODS

(1) After a breach within the preceding section the buyer may "cover" by making in good faith and without unreasonable delay any reasonable purchase of or contract to purchase goods in substitution for those due from the seller.

(2) The buyer may recover from the seller as damages the difference between the cost of cover and the contract price together with any incidental or consequential damages as hereinafter defined (Section 2—715), but less expenses saved in consequence of the seller's breach.

(3) Failure of the buyer to effect cover within this section does not bar him from any other remedy.

§2—713. BUYER'S DAMAGES FOR NON-DELIVERY OR REPUDIATION

(1) Subject to the provisions of this Article with respect to proof of market price (Section 2—723), the measure of damages for non-delivery or repudiation by the seller is the difference between the market price at the time when the buyer learned of the breach and the contract price together with any incidental and consequential damages provided in this Article (Section 2—715), but less expenses saved in consequence of the seller's breach.

(2) Market price is to be determined as of the place for tender or, in cases of rejection after arrival or revocation of acceptance, as of the place of arrival.

§2—714. BUYER'S DAMAGES FOR BREACH IN REGARD TO ACCEPTED GOODS

(1) Where the buyer has accepted goods and given notification (subsection (3) of Section 2—607) he may recover as damages for any non-conformity of tender the loss resulting in the ordinary course of events from the seller's breach as determined in any manner which is reasonable.

(2) The measure of damages for breach of warranty is the difference at the time and place of acceptance between the value of the goods accepted and the value they would have had if they had been as warranted, unless special circumstances show proximate damages of a different amount.

(3) In a proper case any incidental and consequential damages under the next section may also be recovered.

§2—715. BUYER'S INCIDENTAL AND CONSEQUENTIAL DAMAGES

(1) Incidental damages resulting from the seller's breach include expenses reasonably incurred in inspection, receipt, transportation and care and custody of goods rightfully rejected, any commercially reasonable charges, expenses or commissions in connection with effecting cover and any other reasonable expense incident to the delay or other breach.

(2) Consequential damages resulting from the seller's breach include

(a) any loss resulting from general or particular requirements and needs of which the seller at the time of contracting had reason to know and which could not reasonably be prevented by cover or otherwise; and

(b) injury to person or property proximately resulting from any breach of warranty.

§2—716. BUYER'S RIGHT TO SPECIFIC PERFORMANCE OR REPLEVIN

(1) Specific performance may be decreed where the goods are unique or in other proper circumstances.

(2) The decree for specific performance may include such terms and conditions as to payment of the price, damages, or other relief as the court may deem just.

(3) The buyer has a right of replevin for goods identified to the contract if after reasonable effort he is unable to effect cover for such goods or the circumstances reasonably indicate that such effort will be unavailing or if the goods have been shipped under reservation and satisfaction of the security interest in them has been made or tendered. In the case of goods bought for personal, family, or household purposes, the buyer's right of replevin vests upon acquisition of a special property, even if the seller had not then repudiated or failed to deliver.

As amended in 1999.

§2—717. DEDUCTION OF DAMAGES FROM THE PRICE

The buyer on notifying the seller of his intention to do so may deduct all or any part of the damages resulting from any breach of the contract from any part of the price still due under the same contract.

§2—718. LIQUIDATION OR LIMITATION OF DAMAGES; DEPOSITS

(1) Damages for breach by either party may be liquidated in the agreement but only at an amount which is

reasonable in the light of the anticipated or actual harm caused by the breach, the difficulties of proof of loss, and the inconvenience or nonfeasibility of otherwise obtaining an adequate remedy. A term fixing unreasonably large liquidated damages is void as a penalty.

(2) Where the seller justifiably withholds delivery of goods because of the buyer's breach, the buyer is entitled to restitution of any amount by which the sum of his payments exceeds

(a) the amount to which the seller is entitled by virtue of terms liquidating the seller's damages in accordance with subsection (1), or

(b) in the absence of such terms, twenty per cent of the value of the total performance for which the buyer is obligated under the contract or $500, whichever is smaller.

(3) The buyer's right to restitution under subsection (2) is subject to offset to the extent that the seller establishes

(a) a right to recover damages under the provisions of this Article other than subsection (1), and

(b) the amount or value of any benefits received by the buyer directly or indirectly by reason of the contract.

(4) Where a seller has received payment in goods their reasonable value or the proceeds of their resale shall be treated as payments for the purposes of subsection (2); but if the seller has notice of the buyer's breach before reselling goods received in part performance, his resale is subject to the conditions laid down in this Article on resale by an aggrieved seller (Section 2—706).

§2—719. CONTRACTUAL MODIFICATION OR LIMITATION OF REMEDY

(1) Subject to the provisions of subsections (2) and (3) of this section and of the preceding section on liquidation and limitation of damages,

(a) the agreement may provide for remedies in addition to or in substitution for those provided in this Article and may limit or alter the measure of damages recoverable under this Article, as by limiting the buyer's remedies to return of the goods and repayment of the price or to repair and replacement of nonconforming goods or parts; and

(b) resort to a remedy as provided is optional unless the remedy is expressly agreed to be exclusive, in which case it is the sole remedy.

(2) Where circumstances cause an exclusive or limited remedy to fail of its essential purpose, remedy may be had as provided in this Act.

(3) Consequential damages may be limited or excluded unless the limitation or exclusion is unconscionable. Limitation of consequential damages for injury to the

person in the case of consumer goods is prima facie unconscionable but limitation of damages where the loss is commercial is not.

§2—720. EFFECT OF "CANCELLATION" OR "RESCISSION" ON CLAIMS FOR ANTECEDENT BREACH

Unless the contrary intention clearly appears, expressions of "cancellation" or "rescission" of the contract or the like shall not be construed as a renunciation or discharge of any claim in damages for an antecedent breach.

§2—721. REMEDIES FOR FRAUD

Remedies for material misrepresentation or fraud include all remedies available under this Article for non-fraudulent breach. Neither rescission or a claim for rescission of the contract for sale nor rejection or return of the goods shall bar or be deemed inconsistent with a claim for damages or other remedy.

§2—722. WHO CAN SUE THIRD PARTIES FOR INJURY TO GOODS

Where a third party so deals with goods which have been identified to a contract for sale as to cause actionable injury to a party to that contract

(a) a right of action against the third party is in either party to the contract for sale who has title to or a security interest or a special property or an insurable interest in the goods; and if the goods have been destroyed or converted a right of action is also in the party who either bore the risk of loss under the contract for sale or has since the injury assumed that risk as against the other;

(b) if at the time of the injury the party plaintiff did not bear the risk of loss as against the other party to the contract for sale and there is no arrangement between them for disposition of the recovery, his suit or settlement is, subject to his own interest, as a fiduciary for the other party to the contract;

(c) either party may with the consent of the other sue for the benefit of whom it may concern.

§2—723. PROOF OF MARKET PRICE: TIME AND PLACE

(1) If an action based on anticipatory repudiation comes to trial before the time for performance with respect to some or all of the goods, any damages based on market price (Section 2—708 or Section 2—713) shall be determined according to the price of such goods prevailing at the time when the aggrieved party learned of the repudiation.

(2) If evidence of a price prevailing at the times or places described in this Article is not readily available the price prevailing within any reasonable time before or after the time described or at any other place which in commercial judgment or under usage of trade would serve as a reasonable substitute for the one described may be used, making any proper allowance for the cost of transporting the goods to or from such other place.

(3) Evidence of a relevant price prevailing at a time or place other than the one described in this Article offered by one party is not admissible unless and until he has given the other party such notice as the court finds sufficient to prevent unfair surprise.

§2—724. ADMISSIBILITY OF MARKET QUOTATIONS

Whenever the prevailing price or value of any goods regularly bought and sold in any established commodity market is in issue, reports in official publications or trade journals or in newspapers or periodicals of general circulation published as the reports of such market shall be admissible in evidence. The circumstances of the preparation of such a report may be shown to affect its weight but not its admissibility.

§2—725. STATUTE OF LIMITATIONS IN CONTRACTS FOR SALE

(1) An action for breach of any contract for sale must be commenced within four years after the cause of action has accrued. By the original agreement the parties may reduce the period of limitation to not less than one year but may not extend it.

(2) A cause of action accrues when the breach occurs, regardless of the aggrieved party's lack of knowledge of the breach. A breach of warranty occurs when tender of delivery is made, except that where a warranty explicitly extends to future performance of the goods and discovery of the breach must await the time of such performance the cause of action accrues when the breach is or should have been discovered.

(3) Where an action commenced within the time limited by subsection (1) is so terminated as to leave available a remedy by another action for the same breach such other action may be commenced after the expiration of the time limited and within six months after the termination of the first action unless the termination resulted from voluntary discontinuance or from dismissal for failure or neglect to prosecute.

(4) This section does not alter the law on tolling of the statute of limitations nor does it apply to causes of action which have accrued before this Act becomes effective.

ARTICLE 2 AMENDMENTS (EXCERPTS)

Part 1 Short Title, General Construction and Subject Matter
* * * *

§2—103. DEFINITIONS AND INDEX OF DEFINITIONS

(1) In this article unless the context otherwise requires
* * * *

(b) "Conspicuous", with reference to a term, means so written, displayed, or presented that a reasonable person against which it is to operate ought to have noticed it. A term in an electronic record intended to evoke a response by an electronic agent is conspicuous if it is presented in a form that would enable a reasonably configured electronic agent to take it into account or react to it without review of the record by an individual. Whether a term is "conspicuous" or not is a decision for the court. Conspicuous terms include the following:
    (i) for a person:
        (A) a heading in capitals equal to or greater in size than the surrounding text, or in contrasting type, font, or color to the surrounding text of the same or lesser size;
        (B) language in the body of a record or display in larger type than the surrounding text, or in contrasting type, font, or color to the surrounding text of the same size, or set off from surrounding text of the same size by symbols or other marks that call attention to the language; and
    (ii) for a person or an electronic agent, a term that is so placed in a record or display that the person or electronic agent cannot proceed without taking action with respect to the particular term.
(c) "Consumer" means an individual who buys or contracts to buy goods that, at the time of contracting, are intended by the individual to be used primarily for personal, family, or household purposes.
(d) "Consumer contract" means a contract between a merchant seller and a consumer.
* * * *

(j) "Good faith" means honesty in fact and the observance of reasonable commercial standards of fair dealing.

(k) "Goods" means all things that are movable at the time of identification to a contract for sale. The term includes future goods, specially manufactured goods, the unborn young of animals, growing crops, and other identified things attached to realty as described in Section 2—107. The term does not include information, the money in which the price is to be paid, investment securities under Article 8, the subject matter of foreign exchange transactions, and choses in action.

* * * *

(m) "Record" means information that is inscribed on a tangible medium or that is stored in an electronic or other medium and is retrievable in perceivable form.

(n) "Remedial promise" means a promise by the seller to repair or replace the goods or to refund all or part of the price upon the happening of a specified event.

* * * *

(p) "Sign" means, with present intent to authenticate or adopt a record,

   (i) to execute or adopt a tangible symbol; or

   (ii) to attach to or logically associate with the record an electronic sound, symbol, or process.

* * * *

Part 2 Form, Formation, Terms and Readjustment of Contract; Electronic Contracting

§2—201. FORMAL REQUIREMENTS; STATUTE OF FRAUDS

(1) A contract for the sale of goods for the price of $5,000 or more is not enforceable by way of action or defense unless there is some record sufficient to indicate that a contract for sale has been made between the parties and signed by the party against whom which enforcement is sought or by the party's authorized agent or broker. A record is not insufficient because it omits or incorrectly states a term agreed upon but the contract is not enforceable under this subsection beyond the quantity of goods shown in the record.

(2) Between merchants if within a reasonable time a record in confirmation of the contract and sufficient against the sender is received and the party receiving it has reason to know its contents, it satisfies the requirements of subsection (1) against such party the recipient unless notice of objection to its contents is given in a record within 10 days after it is received.

(3) A contract which does not satisfy the requirements of subsection (1) but which is valid in other respects is enforceable

(a) if the goods are to be specially manufactured for the buyer and are not suitable for sale to others in the ordinary course of the seller's business and the seller, before notice of repudiation is received and under circumstances which reasonably indicate that the goods are for the buyer, has made either a substantial beginning of their manufacture or commitments for their procurement; or

(b) if the party against whom which enforcement is sought admits in the party's pleading, or in the party's testimony or otherwise under oath that a contract for sale was made, but the contract is not enforceable under this paragraph beyond the quantity of goods admitted; or

(c) with respect to goods for which payment has been made and accepted or which have been received and accepted (Sec. 2—606).

(4) A contract that is enforceable under this section is not rendered unenforceable merely because it is not capable of being performed within one year or any other applicable period after its making.

* * * *

§2—207. TERMS OF CONTRACT; EFFECT OF CONFIRMATION

If (i) conduct by both parties recognizes the existence of a contract although their records do not otherwise establish a contract, (ii) a contract is formed by an offer and acceptance, or (iii) a contract formed in any manner is confirmed by a record that contains terms additional to or different from those in the contract being confirmed, the terms of the contract, subject to Section 2—202, are:

(a) terms that appear in the records of both parties;

(b) terms, whether in a record or not, to which both parties agree; and

(c) terms supplied or incorporated under any provision of this Act.

* * * *

Part 3 General Obligation and Construction of Contract

* * * *

§2—312. WARRANTY OF TITLE AND AGAINST INFRINGEMENT; BUYER'S OBLIGATION AGAINST INFRINGEMENT

(1) Subject to subsection (2) there is in a contract for sale a warranty by the seller that

(a) the title conveyed shall be good, good and its transfer rightful and shall not, because of any colorable claim to or interest in the goods, unreasonably expose the buyer to litigation; and

(b) the goods shall be delivered free from any security interest or other lien or encumbrance of which the buyer at the time of contracting has no knowledge.

(2) Unless otherwise agreed a seller that is a merchant regularly dealing in goods of the kind warrants that the goods shall be delivered free of the rightful claim of any third person by way of infringement or the like but a buyer that furnishes specifications to the seller must hold the seller harmless against any such claim that arises out of compliance with the specifications.

(3) A warranty under this section may be disclaimed or modified only by specific language or by circumstances that give the buyer reason to know that the seller does not claim title, that the seller is purporting to sell only the right or title as the seller or a third person may have, or that the seller is selling subject to any claims of infringement or the like.

§2—313. EXPRESS WARRANTIES BY AFFIRMATION, PROMISE, DESCRIPTION, SAMPLE; REMEDIAL PROMISE

(1) In this section, "immediate buyer" means a buyer that enters into a contract with the seller.

* * * *

(4) Any remedial promise made by the seller to the immediate buyer creates an obligation that the promise will be performed upon the happening of the specified event.

§2—313A. OBLIGATION TO REMOTE PURCHASER CREATED BY RECORD PACKAGED WITH OR ACCOMPANYING GOODS

(1) This section applies only to new goods and goods sold or leased as new goods in a transaction of purchase in the normal chain of distribution. In this section:

(a) "Immediate buyer" means a buyer that enters into a contract with the seller.

(b) "Remote purchaser" means a person that buys or leases goods from an immediate buyer or other person in the normal chain of distribution.

(2) If a seller in a record packaged with or accompanying the goods makes an affirmation of fact or promise that relates to the goods, provides a description that relates to the goods, or makes a remedial promise, and the seller reasonably expects the record to be, and the record is, furnished to the remote purchaser, the seller has an obligation to the remote purchaser that:

(a) the goods will conform to the affirmation of fact, promise or description unless a reasonable person in the position of the remote purchaser would not believe that the affirmation of fact, promise or description created an obligation; and

(b) the seller will perform the remedial promise.

(3) It is not necessary to the creation of an obligation under this section that the seller use formal words such as "warrant" or "guarantee" or that the seller have a specific intention to undertake an obligation, but an affirmation merely of the value of the goods or a statement purporting to be merely the seller's opinion or commendation of the goods does not create an obligation.

(4) The following rules apply to the remedies for breach of an obligation created under this section:

(a) The seller may modify or limit the remedies available to the remote purchaser if the modification or limitation is furnished to the remote purchaser no later than the time of purchase or if the modification or limitation is contained in the record that contains the affirmation of fact, promise or description.

(b) Subject to a modification or limitation of remedy, a seller in breach is liable for incidental or consequential damages under Section 2—715, but the seller is not liable for lost profits.

(c) The remote purchaser may recover as damages for breach of a seller's obligation arising under subsection (2) the loss resulting in the ordinary course of events as determined in any manner that is reasonable.

(5) An obligation that is not a remedial promise is breached if the goods did not conform to the affirmation of fact, promise or description creating the obligation when the goods left the seller's control.

§2—313B. OBLIGATION TO REMOTE PURCHASER CREATED BY COMMUNICATION TO THE PUBLIC

(1) This section applies only to new goods and goods sold or leased as new goods in a transaction of purchase in the normal chain of distribution. In this section:

(a) "Immediate buyer" means a buyer that enters into a contract with the seller.

(b) "Remote purchaser" means a person that buys or leases goods from an immediate buyer or other person in the normal chain of distribution.

(2) If a seller in advertising or a similar communication to the public makes an affirmation of fact or promise that relates to the goods, provides a description that relates to the goods, or makes a remedial promise, and the remote purchaser enters into a transaction of purchase with knowledge of and with the expectation that the goods will conform to the affirmation of fact, promise, or description, or that the seller will perform the remedial promise, the seller has an obligation to the remote purchaser that:

(a) the goods will conform to the affirmation of fact, promise or description unless a reasonable person in the position of the remote purchaser would not believe that the affirmation of fact, promise or description created an obligation; and

(b) the seller will perform the remedial promise.

(3) It is not necessary to the creation of an obligation under this section that the seller use formal words such as "warrant" or "guarantee" or that the seller have a specific intention to undertake an obligation, but an affirmation merely of the value of the goods or a statement purporting to be merely the seller's opinion or commendation of the goods does not create an obligation.

(4) The following rules apply to the remedies for breach of an obligation created under this section:

(a) The seller may modify or limit the remedies available to the remote purchaser if the modification or limitation is furnished to the remote purchaser no later than the time of purchase. The modification or limitation may be furnished as part of the communication that contains the affirmation of fact, promise or description.

(b) Subject to a modification or limitation of remedy, a seller in breach is liable for incidental or consequential damages under Section 2—715, but the seller is not liable for lost profits.

(c) The remote purchaser may recover as damages for breach of a seller's obligation arising under subsection (2) the loss resulting in the ordinary course of events as determined in any manner that is reasonable.

(5) An obligation that is not a remedial promise is breached if the goods did not conform to the affirmation of fact, promise or description creating the obligation when the goods left the seller's control.

* * * *

§2—316. EXCLUSION OR MODIFICATION OF WARRANTIES.

* * * *

(2) Subject to subsection (3), to exclude or modify the implied warranty of merchantability or any part of it in a consumer contract the language must be in a record, be conspicuous and state "The seller undertakes no responsibility for the quality of the goods except as otherwise provided in this contract," and in any other contract the language must mention merchantability and in case of a record must be conspicuous. Subject to subsection (3), to exclude or modify the implied warranty of fitness the exclusion must be in a record and be conspicuous. Language to exclude all implied warranties of fitness in a consumer contract must state "The seller assumes no responsibility that the goods will be fit for any particular purpose for which you may be buying these goods, except as otherwise provided in the contract," and in any other contract the language is sufficient if it states, for example, that "There are no warranties which extend beyond the

description on the face hereof." Language that satisfies the requirements of this subsection for the exclusion and modification of a warranty in a consumer contract also satisfies the requirements for any other contract.

(3) Notwithstanding subsection (2):

(a) unless the circumstances indicate otherwise, all implied warranties are excluded by expressions like "as is", "with all faults" or other language which in common understanding calls the buyer's attention to the exclusion of warranties, makes plain that there is no implied warranty, and in a consumer contract evidenced by a record is set forth conspicuously in the record; and

(b) when the buyer before entering into the contract has examined the goods or the sample or model as fully as desired or has refused to examine the goods after a demand by the seller there is no implied warranty with regard to defects which an examination ought in the circumstances to have revealed to the buyer; and

(c) an implied warranty can also be excluded or modified by course of dealing or course of performance or usage of trade.

* * * *

§2—318. THIRD PARTY BENEFICIARIES OF WARRANTIES EXPRESS OR IMPLIED

(1) In this section:

(a) "Immediate buyer" means a buyer that enters into a contract with the seller.

(b) "Remote purchaser" means a person that buys or leases goods from an immediate buyer or other person in the normal chain of distribution.

Alternative A to subsection (2)

(2) A seller's warranty whether express or implied to an immediate buyer, a seller's remedial promise to an immediate buyer, or a seller's obligation to a remote purchaser under Section 2—313A or 2—313B extends to any natural person who is in the family or household of the immediate buyer or the remote purchaser or who is a guest in the home of either if it is reasonable to expect that the person may use, consume or be affected by the goods and who is injured in person by breach of the warranty, remedial promise or obligation. A seller may not exclude or limit the operation of this section.

Alternative B to subsection (2)

(2) A seller's warranty whether express or implied to an immediate buyer, a seller's remedial promise to an immediate buyer, or a seller's obligation to a remote purchaser under Section 2—313A or 2—313B extends to any natural

person who may reasonably be expected to use, consume or be affected by the goods and who is injured in person by breach of the warranty, remedial promise or obligation. A seller may not exclude or limit the operation of this section.

Alternative C to subsection (2)

(2) A seller's warranty whether express or implied to an immediate buyer, a seller's remedial promise to an immediate buyer, or a seller's obligation to a remote purchaser under Section 2—313A or 2—313B extends to any person that may reasonably be expected to use, consume or be affected by the goods and that is injured by breach of the warranty, remedial promise or obligation. A seller may not exclude or limit the operation of this section with respect to injury to the person of an individual to whom the warranty, remedial promise or obligation extends.
* * * *

Part 5 Performance
* * * *

§2—502. BUYER'S RIGHT TO GOODS ON SELLER'S INSOLVENCY

(1) Subject to subsections (2) and (3) and even though the goods have not been shipped a buyer who that has paid a part or all of the price of goods in which the buyer has a special property under the provisions of the immediately preceding section may on making and keeping good a tender of any unpaid portion of their price recover them from the seller if:

    (a) in the case of goods bought by a consumer, the seller repudiates or fails to deliver as required by the contract; or

    (b) in all cases, the seller becomes insolvent within ten days after receipt of the first installment on their price.

(2) The buyer's right to recover the goods under subsection (1) vests upon acquisition of a special property, even if the seller had not then repudiated or failed to deliver.

(3) If the identification creating the special property has been made by the buyer, the buyer acquires the right to recover the goods only if they conform to the contract for sale.
* * * *

§2—508. CURE BY SELLER OF IMPROPER TENDER OR DELIVERY; REPLACEMENT

(1) Where the buyer rejects goods or a tender of delivery under Section 2—601 or 2—612 or except in a consumer contract justifiably revokes acceptance under Section 2—608(1)(b) and the agreed time for performance has not expired, a seller that has performed in good faith, upon seasonable notice to the buyer and at the seller's own expense, may cure the breach of contract by making a conforming tender of delivery within the agreed time. The seller shall compensate the buyer for all of the buyer's reasonable expenses caused by the seller's breach of contract and subsequent cure.

(2) Where the buyer rejects goods or a tender of delivery under Section 2—601 or 2—612 or except in a consumer contract justifiably revokes acceptance under Section 2—608(1)(b) and the agreed time for performance has expired, a seller that has performed in good faith, upon seasonable notice to the buyer and at the seller's own expense, may cure the breach of contract, if the cure is appropriate and timely under the circumstances, by making a tender of conforming goods. The seller shall compensate the buyer for all of the buyer's reasonable expenses caused by the seller's breach of contract and subsequent cure.

§2—509. RISK OF LOSS IN THE ABSENCE OF BREACH

(1) Where the contract requires or authorizes the seller to ship the goods by carrier

    (a) if it does not require the seller to deliver them at a particular destination, the risk of loss passes to the buyer when the goods are delivered to the carrier even though the shipment is under reservation (Section 2—505); but

    (b) if it does require the seller to deliver them at a particular destination and the goods are there tendered while in the possession of the carrier, the risk of loss passes to the buyer when the goods are there so tendered as to enable the buyer to take delivery.

(2) Where the goods are held by a bailee to be delivered without being moved, the risk of loss passes to the buyer

    (a) on the buyer's receipt of a negotiable document of title covering the goods; or

    (b) on acknowledgment by the bailee to the buyer of the buyer's right to possession of the goods; or

    (c) after the buyer's receipt of a non-negotiable document of title or other direction to deliver in a record, as provided in subsection (4)(b) of Section 2—503.

(3) In any case not within subsection (1) or (2), the risk of loss passes to the buyer on the buyer's receipt of the goods.
* * * *

§2—513. BUYER'S RIGHT TO INSPECTION OF GOODS
* * * *

(3) Unless otherwise agreed, the buyer is not entitled to inspect the goods before payment of the price when the contract provides

    (a) for delivery on terms that under applicable course of performance, course of dealing, or usage of trade are interpreted to preclude inspection before payment; or

(b) for payment against documents of title, except where such payment is due only after the goods are to become available for inspection.

* * * *

Part 6 Breach, Repudiation and Excuse
* * * *

§2—605. WAIVER OF BUYER'S OBJECTIONS BY FAILURE TO PARTICULARIZE

(1) The buyer's failure to state in connection with rejection a particular defect or in connection with revocation of acceptance a defect that justifies revocation precludes the buyer from relying on the unstated defect to justify rejection or revocation of acceptance if the defect is ascertainable by reasonable inspection

    (a) where the seller had a right to cure the defect and could have cured it if stated seasonally; or

    (b) between merchants when the seller has after rejection made a request in a record for a full and final statement in record form of all defects on which the buyer proposes to rely.

    (2) A buyer's payment against documents tendered to the buyer made without reservation of rights precludes recovery of the payment for defects apparent on the face of the documents.

* * * *

§2—607. EFFECT OF ACCEPTANCE; NOTICE OF BREACH; BURDEN OF ESTABLISHING BREACH AFTER ACCEPTANCE; NOTICE OF CLAIM OR LITIGATION TO PERSON ANSWERABLE OVER

* * * *

(3) Where a tender has been accepted

(a) the buyer must within a reasonable time after the buyer discovers or should have discovered any breach notify the seller; however, failure to give timely notice bars the buyer from a remedy only to the extent that the seller is prejudiced by the failure and

(b) if the claim is one for infringement or the like (subsection (3) of Section 2—312) and the buyer is sued as a result of such a breach the buyer must so notify the seller within a reasonable time after the buyer receives notice of the litigation or be barred from any remedy over for liability established by the litigation.

* * * *

§2—608. REVOCATION OF ACCEPTANCE IN WHOLE OR IN PART

* * * *

(4) If a buyer uses the goods after a rightful rejection or justifiable revocation of acceptance, the following rules apply:

(a) Any use by the buyer that is unreasonable under the circumstances is wrongful as against the seller and is an acceptance only if ratified by the seller.

(b) Any use of the goods that is reasonable under the circumstances is not wrongful as against the seller and is not an acceptance, but in an appropriate case the buyer shall be obligated to the seller for the value of the use to the buyer.

* * * *

§2—612. "INSTALLMENT CONTRACT"; BREACH

* * * *

(2) The buyer may reject any installment which is non-conforming if the non-conformity substantially impairs the value of that installment to the buyer or if the non-conformity is a defect in the required documents; but if the non-conformity does not fall within subsection (3) and the seller gives adequate assurance of its cure the buyer must accept that installment.

    (3) Whenever non-conformity or default with respect to one or more installments substantially impairs the value of the whole contract there is a breach of the whole. But the aggrieved party reinstates the contract if the party accepts a non-conforming installment without seasonably notifying of cancellation or if the party brings an action with respect only to past installments or demands performance as to future installments.

* * * *

Part 7 Remedies

§2—702. SELLER'S REMEDIES ON DISCOVERY OF BUYER'S INSOLVENCY

* * * *

(2) Where the seller discovers that the buyer has received goods on credit while insolvent the seller may reclaim the goods upon demand made within a reasonable time after the buyer's receipt of the goods. Except as provided in this subsection the seller may not base a right to reclaim goods on the buyer's fraudulent or innocent misrepresentation of solvency or of intent to pay.

* * * *

§2—705. SELLER'S STOPPAGE OF DELIVERY IN TRANSIT OR OTHERWISE

(1) The seller may stop delivery of goods in the possession of a carrier or other bailee when the seller discovers the buyer to be insolvent (Section 2—702) or when the buyer repudiates or fails to make a payment due before delivery or if for any other reason the seller has a right to withhold or reclaim the goods.

* * * *

§2—706. SELLER'S RESALE INCLUDING CONTRACT FOR RESALE

(1) In an appropriate case involving breach by the buyer, the seller may resell the goods concerned or the undelivered

balance thereof. Where the resale is made in good faith and in a commercially reasonable manner the seller may recover the difference between the contract price and the resale price together with any incidental or consequential damages allowed under the provisions of this Article (Section 2—710), but less expenses saved in consequence of the buyer's breach.

* * * *

§2—708. SELLER'S DAMAGES FOR NON-ACCEPTANCE OR REPUDIATION

(1) Subject to subsection (2) and to the provisions of this Article with respect to proof of market price (Section 2—723)

(a) the measure of damages for non-acceptance by the buyer is the difference between the contract price and the market price at the time and place for tender together with any incidental or consequential damages provided in this Article (Section 2—710), but less expenses saved in consequence of the buyer's breach; and

(b) the measure of damages for repudiation by the buyer is the difference between the contract price and the market price at the place for tender at the expiration of a commercially reasonable time after the seller learned of the repudiation, but no later than the time stated in paragraph (a), together with any incidental or consequential damages provided in this Article (Section 2—710), but less expenses saved in consequence of the buyer's breach.

(2) If the measure of damages provided in subsection (1) or in Section 2—706 is inadequate to put the seller in as good a position as performance would have done then the measure of damages is the profit (including reasonable overhead) which the seller would have made from full performance by the buyer, together with any incidental or consequential damages provided in this Article (Section 2—710).

§2—709. ACTION FOR THE PRICE

(1) When the buyer fails to pay the price as it becomes due the seller may recover, together with any incidental or consequential damages under the next section, the price

(a) of goods accepted or of conforming goods lost or damaged within a commercially reasonable time after risk of their loss has passed to the buyer; and

(b) of goods identified to the contract if the seller is unable after reasonable effort to resell them at a reasonable price or the circumstances reasonably indicate that such effort will be unavailing.

* * * *

§2—710. SELLER'S INCIDENTAL AND CONSEQUENTIAL DAMAGES

(1) Incidental damages to an aggrieved seller include any commercially reasonable charges, expenses or commissions incurred in stopping delivery, in the transportation, care and custody of goods after the buyer's breach, in connection with return or resale of the goods or otherwise resulting from the breach.

(2) Consequential damages resulting from the buyer's breach include any loss resulting from general or particular requirements and needs of which the buyer at the time of contracting had reason to know and which could not reasonably be prevented by resale or otherwise.

(3) In a consumer contract, a seller may not recover consequential damages from a consumer.

* * * *

§2—713. BUYER'S DAMAGES FOR NON-DELIVERY OR REPUDIATION

(1) Subject to the provisions of this Article with respect to proof of market price (Section 2—723), if the seller wrongfully fails to deliver or repudiates or the buyer rightfully rejects or justifiably revokes acceptance

(a) the measure of damages in the case of wrongful failure to deliver by the seller or rightful rejection or justifiable revocation of acceptance by the buyer is the difference between the market price at the time for tender under the contract and the contract price together with any incidental or consequential damages provided in this Article (Section 2—715), but less expenses saved in consequence of the seller's breach; and

(b) the measure of damages for repudiation by the seller is the difference between the market price at the expiration of a commercially reasonable time after the buyer learned of the repudiation, but no later than the time stated in paragraph (a), and the contract price together with any incidental or consequential damages provided in this Article (Section 2—715), but less expenses saved in consequence of the seller's breach.

* * * *

§2—725. STATUTE OF LIMITATIONS IN CONTRACTS FOR SALE

(1) Except as otherwise provided in this section, an action for breach of any contract for sale must be commenced within the later of four years after the right of action has accrued under subsection (2) or (3) or one year after the breach was or should have been discovered, but no longer than five years after the right of action accrued. By the original agreement the parties may reduce the period of limitation to not less than one year but may not extend it; however, in a consumer contract, the period of limitation may not be reduced.

(2) Except as otherwise provided in subsection (3), the following rules apply:

(a) Except as otherwise provided in this subsection, a right of action for breach of a contract accrues when the breach occurs, even if the aggrieved party did not have knowledge of the breach.

(b) For breach of a contract by repudiation, a right of action accrues at the earlier of when the aggrieved party elects to treat the repudiation as a breach or when a commercially reasonable time for awaiting performance has expired.

(c) For breach of a remedial promise, a right of action accrues when the remedial promise is not performed when due.

(d) In an action by a buyer against a person that is answerable over to the buyer for a claim asserted against the buyer, the buyer's right of action against the person answerable over accrues at the time the claim was originally asserted against the buyer.

(3) If a breach of a warranty arising under Section 2—312, 2—313(2), 2—314, or 2—315, or a breach of an obligation other than a remedial promise arising under Section 2—313A or 2—313B, is claimed the following rules apply:

(a) Except as otherwise provided in paragraph (c), a right of action for breach of a warranty arising under Section 2—313(2), 2—314 or 2—315 accrues when the seller has tendered delivery to the immediate buyer, as defined in Section 2—313, and has completed performance of any agreed installation or assembly of the goods.

(b) Except as otherwise provided in paragraph (c), a right of action for breach of an obligation other than a remedial promise arising under Section 2—313A or 2—313B accrues when the remote purchaser, as defined in sections 2—313A and 2—313B, receives the goods.

(c) Where a warranty arising under Section 2—313(2) or an obligation other than a remedial promise arising under 2—313A or 2—313B explicitly extends to future performance of the goods and discovery of the breach must await the time for performance the right of action accrues when the immediate buyer as defined in Section2—313 or the remote purchaser as defined in Sections 2—313A and 2—313B discovers or should have discovered the breach.

(d) A right of action for breach of warranty arising under Section 2—312 accrues when the aggrieved party discovers or should have discovered the breach. However, an action for breach of the warranty of non-infringement may not be commenced more than six years after tender of delivery of the goods to the aggrieved party.

* * * *

Article 2A Leases

Part 1 General Provisions

§2A—101. SHORT TITLE

This Article shall be known and may be cited as the Uniform Commercial Code—Leases.

§2A—102. SCOPE

This Article applies to any transaction, regardless of form, that creates a lease.

§2A—103. DEFINITIONS AND INDEX OF DEFINITIONS

(1) In this Article unless the context otherwise requires:

(a) "Buyer in ordinary course of business" means a person who in good faith and without knowledge that the sale to him [or her] is in violation of the ownership rights or security interest or leasehold interest of a third party in the goods buys in ordinary course from a person in the business of selling goods of that kind but does not include a pawnbroker. "Buying" may be for cash or by exchange of other property or on secured or unsecured credit and includes receiving goods or documents of title under a pre-existing contract for sale but does not include a transfer in bulk or as security for or in total or partial satisfaction of a money debt.

(b) "Cancellation" occurs when either party puts an end to the lease contract for default by the other party.

(c) "Commercial unit" means such a unit of goods as by commercial usage is a single whole for purposes of lease and division of which materially impairs its character or value on the market or in use. A commercial unit may be a single article, as a machine, or a set of articles, as a suite of furniture or a line of machinery, or a quantity, as a gross or carload, or any other unit treated in use or in the relevant market as a single whole.

(d) "Conforming" goods or performance under a lease contract means goods or performance that are in accordance with the obligations under the lease contract.

(e) "Consumer lease" means a lease that a lessor regularly engaged in the business of leasing or selling makes to a lessee who is an individual and who takes under the lease primarily for a personal, family, or household purpose [, if the total payments to be made under the lease contract, excluding payments for options to renew or buy, do not exceed $____].

(f) "Fault" means wrongful act, omission, breach, or default.

(g) "Finance lease" means a lease with respect to which:

   (i) the lessor does not select, manufacture or supply the goods;

   (ii) the lessor acquires the goods or the right to possession and use of the goods in connection with the lease; and

   (iii) one of the following occurs:

     (A) the lessee receives a copy of the contract by which the lessor acquired the goods or the right to possession and use of the goods before signing the lease contract;

     (B) the lessee's approval of the contract by which the lessor acquired the goods or the right to possession and use of the goods is a condition to effectiveness of the lease contract;

     (C) the lessee, before signing the lease contract, receives an accurate and complete statement designating the promises and warranties, and any disclaimers of warranties, limitations or modifications of remedies, or liquidated damages, including those of a third party, such as the manufacturer of the goods, provided to the lessor by the person supplying the goods in connection with or as part of the contract by which the lessor acquired the goods or the right to possession and use of the goods; or

     (D) if the lease is not a consumer lease, the lessor, before the lessee signs the lease contract, informs the lessee in writing (a) of the identity of the person supplying the goods to the lessor, unless the lessee has selected that person and directed the lessor to acquire the goods or the right to possession and use of the goods from that person, (b) that the lessee is entitled under this Article to any promises and warranties, including those of any third party, provided to the lessor by the person supplying the goods in connection with or as part of the contract by which the lessor acquired the goods or the right to possession and use of the goods, and (c) that the lessee may communicate with the person supplying the goods to the lessor and receive an accurate and complete statement of those promises and warranties, including any disclaimers and limitations of them or of remedies.

(h) "Goods" means all things that are movable at the time of identification to the lease contract, or are fixtures (Section 2A—309), but the term does not include money, documents, instruments, accounts, chattel paper, general intangibles, or minerals or the like, including oil and gas, before extraction. The term also includes the unborn young of animals.

(i) "Installment lease contract" means a lease contract that authorizes or requires the delivery of goods in separate lots to be separately accepted, even though the lease contract contains a clause "each delivery is a separate lease" or its equivalent.

(j) "Lease" means a transfer of the right to possession and use of goods for a term in return for consideration, but a sale, including a sale on approval or a sale or return, or retention or creation of a security interest is not a lease. Unless the context clearly indicates otherwise, the term includes a sublease.

(k) "Lease agreement" means the bargain, with respect to the lease, of the lessor and the lessee in fact as found in their language or by implication from other circumstances including course of dealing or usage of trade or course of performance as provided in this Article. Unless the context clearly indicates otherwise, the term includes a sublease agreement.

(l) "Lease contract" means the total legal obligation that results from the lease agreement as affected by this Article and any other applicable rules of law. Unless the context clearly indicates otherwise, the term includes a sublease contract.

(m) "Leasehold interest" means the interest of the lessor or the lessee under a lease contract.

(n) "Lessee" means a person who acquires the right to possession and use of goods under a lease. Unless the context clearly indicates otherwise, the term includes a sublessee.

(o) "Lessee in ordinary course of business" means a person who in good faith and without knowledge that the lease to him [or her] is in violation of the ownership rights or security interest or leasehold interest of a third party in the goods, leases in ordinary course from a person in the business of selling or leasing goods of that kind but does not include a pawnbroker. "Leasing" may be for cash or by exchange of other property or on secured or unsecured credit and includes receiving goods or documents of title under a pre-existing lease contract but does not include a transfer in bulk or as security for or in total or partial satisfaction of a money debt.

(p) "Lessor" means a person who transfers the right to possession and use of goods under a lease.

Unless the context clearly indicates otherwise, the term includes a sublessor.

(q) "Lessor's residual interest" means the lessor's interest in the goods after expiration, termination, or cancellation of the lease contract.

(r) "Lien" means a charge against or interest in goods to secure payment of a debt or performance of an obligation, but the term does not include a security interest.

(s) "Lot" means a parcel or a single article that is the subject matter of a separate lease or delivery, whether or not it is sufficient to perform the lease contract.

(t) "Merchant lessee" means a lessee that is a merchant with respect to goods of the kind subject to the lease.

(u) "Present value" means the amount as of a date certain of one or more sums payable in the future, discounted to the date certain. The discount is determined by the interest rate specified by the parties if the rate was not manifestly unreasonable at the time the transaction was entered into; otherwise, the discount is determined by a commercially reasonable rate that takes into account the facts and circumstances of each case at the time the transaction was entered into.

(v) "Purchase" includes taking by sale, lease, mortgage, security interest, pledge, gift, or any other voluntary transaction creating an interest in goods.

(w) "Sublease" means a lease of goods the right to possession and use of which was acquired by the lessor as a lessee under an existing lease.

(x) "Supplier" means a person from whom a lessor buys or leases goods to be leased under a finance lease.

(y) "Supply contract" means a contract under which a lessor buys or leases goods to be leased.

(z) "Termination" occurs when either party pursuant to a power created by agreement or law puts an end to the lease contract otherwise than for default.

(2) Other definitions applying to this Article and the sections in which they appear are:

"Accessions". Section 2A—310(1).
"Construction mortgage". Section 2A—309(1)(d).
"Encumbrance". Section 2A—309(1)(e).
"Fixtures". Section 2A—309(1)(a).
"Fixture filing". Section 2A—309(1)(b).
"Purchase money lease". Section 2A—309(1)(c).

(3) The following definitions in other Articles apply to this Article:

"Accounts". Section 9—106.

"Between merchants". Section 2—104(3).
"Buyer". Section 2—103(1)(a).
"Chattel paper". Section 9—105(1)(b).
"Consumer goods". Section 9—109(1).
"Document". Section 9—105(1)(f).
"Entrusting". Section 2—403(3).
"General intangibles". Section 9—106.
"Good faith". Section 2—103(1)(b).
"Instrument". Section 9—105(1)(i).
"Merchant". Section 2—104(1).
"Mortgage". Section 9—105(1)(j).
"Pursuant to commitment". Section 9—105(1)(k).
"Receipt". Section 2—103(1)(c).
"Sale". Section 2—106(1).
"Sale on approval". Section 2—326.
"Sale or return". Section 2—326.
"Seller". Section 2—103(1)(d).

(4) In addition Article 1 contains general definitions and principles of construction and interpretation applicable throughout this Article.

As amended in 1990 and 1999.

§2A—104. LEASES SUBJECT TO OTHER LAW

(1) A lease, although subject to this Article, is also subject to any applicable:

(a) certificate of title statute of this State: (list any certificate of title statutes covering automobiles, trailers, mobile homes, boats, farm tractors, and the like);

(b) certificate of title statute of another jurisdiction (Section 2A—105); or

(c) consumer protection statute of this State, or final consumer protection decision of a court of this State existing on the effective date of this Article.

(2) In case of conflict between this Article, other than Sections 2A—105, 2A—304(3), and 2A—305(3), and a statute or decision referred to in subsection (1), the statute or decision controls.

(3) Failure to comply with an applicable law has only the effect specified therein.

As amended in 1990.

§2A—105. TERRITORIAL APPLICATION OF ARTICLE TO GOODS COVERED BY CERTIFICATE OF TITLE

Subject to the provisions of Sections 2A—304(3) and 2A—305(3), with respect to goods covered by a certificate of title issued under a statute of this State or of another jurisdiction, compliance and the effect of compliance or noncompliance with a certificate of title statute are governed by the law (including the conflict of laws rules) of the jurisdiction issuing the certificate until the earlier of (a) surrender of the certificate, or (b) four months after the goods are removed from that jurisdiction and thereafter until a new certificate of title is issued by another jurisdiction.

§2A—106. LIMITATION ON POWER OF PARTIES TO CONSUMER LEASE TO CHOOSE APPLICABLE LAW AND JUDICIAL FORUM

(1) If the law chosen by the parties to a consumer lease is that of a jurisdiction other than a jurisdiction in which the lessee resides at the time the lease agreement becomes enforceable or within 30 days thereafter or in which the goods are to be used, the choice is not enforceable.

(2) If the judicial forum chosen by the parties to a consumer lease is a forum that would not otherwise have jurisdiction over the lessee, the choice is not enforceable.

§2A—107. WAIVER OR RENUNCIATION OF CLAIM OR RIGHT AFTER DEFAULT

Any claim or right arising out of an alleged default or breach of warranty may be discharged in whole or in part without consideration by a written waiver or renunciation signed and delivered by the aggrieved party.

§2A—108. UNCONSCIONABILITY

(1) If the court as a matter of law finds a lease contract or any clause of a lease contract to have been unconscionable at the time it was made the court may refuse to enforce the lease contract, or it may enforce the remainder of the lease contract without the unconscionable clause, or it may so limit the application of any unconscionable clause as to avoid any unconscionable result.

(2) With respect to a consumer lease, if the court as a matter of law finds that a lease contract or any clause of a lease contract has been induced by unconscionable conduct or that unconscionable conduct has occurred in the collection of a claim arising from a lease contract, the court may grant appropriate relief.

(3) Before making a finding of unconscionability under subsection (1) or (2), the court, on its own motion or that of a party, shall afford the parties a reasonable opportunity to present evidence as to the setting, purpose, and effect of the lease contract or clause thereof, or of the conduct.

(4) In an action in which the lessee claims unconscionability with respect to a consumer lease:

(a) If the court finds unconscionability under subsection (1) or (2), the court shall award reasonable attorney's fees to the lessee.

(b) If the court does not find unconscionability and the lessee claiming unconscionability has brought or maintained an action he [or she] knew to be groundless, the court shall award reasonable

attorney's fees to the party against whom the claim is made.

(c) In determining attorney's fees, the amount of the recovery on behalf of the claimant under subsections (1) and (2) is not controlling.

§2A—109. OPTION TO ACCELERATE AT WILL

(1) A term providing that one party or his [or her] successor in interest may accelerate payment or performance or require collateral or additional collateral "at will" or "when he [or she] deems himself [or herself] insecure" or in words of similar import must be construed to mean that he [or she] has power to do so only if he [or she] in good faith believes that the prospect of payment or performance is impaired.

(2) With respect to a consumer lease, the burden of establishing good faith under subsection (1) is on the party who exercised the power; otherwise the burden of establishing lack of good faith is on the party against whom the power has been exercised.

Part 2 Formation and Construction of Lease Contract

§2A—201. STATUTE OF FRAUDS

(1) A lease contract is not enforceable by way of action or defense unless:

(a) the total payments to be made under the lease contract, excluding payments for options to renew or buy, are less than $1,000; or

(b) there is a writing, signed by the party against whom enforcement is sought or by that party's authorized agent, sufficient to indicate that a lease contract has been made between the parties and to describe the goods leased and the lease term.

(2) Any description of leased goods or of the lease term is sufficient and satisfies subsection (1)(b), whether or not it is specific, if it reasonably identifies what is described.

(3) A writing is not insufficient because it omits or incorrectly states a term agreed upon, but the lease contract is not enforceable under subsection (1)(b) beyond the lease term and the quantity of goods shown in the writing.

(4) A lease contract that does not satisfy the requirements of subsection (1), but which is valid in other respects, is enforceable:

(a) if the goods are to be specially manufactured or obtained for the lessee and are not suitable for lease or sale to others in the ordinary course of the lessor's business, and the lessor, before notice of repudiation is received and under circumstances that reasonably indicate that the goods are for the lessee, has made either a substantial beginning of their manufacture or commitments for their procurement;

(b) if the party against whom enforcement is sought admits in that party's pleading, testimony or otherwise in court that a lease contract was made, but the lease contract is not enforceable under this provision beyond the quantity of goods admitted; or

(c) with respect to goods that have been received and accepted by the lessee.

(5) The lease term under a lease contract referred to in subsection (4) is:

(a) if there is a writing signed by the party against whom enforcement is sought or by that party's authorized agent specifying the lease term, the term so specified;

(b) if the party against whom enforcement is sought admits in that party's pleading, testimony, or otherwise in court a lease term, the term so admitted; or

(c) a reasonable lease term.

§2A—202. FINAL WRITTEN EXPRESSION: PAROL OR EXTRINSIC EVIDENCE

Terms with respect to which the confirmatory memoranda of the parties agree or which are otherwise set forth in a writing intended by the parties as a final expression of their agreement with respect to such terms as are included therein may not be contradicted by evidence of any prior agreement or of a contemporaneous oral agreement but may be explained or supplemented:

(a) by course of dealing or usage of trade or by course of performance; and

(b) by evidence of consistent additional terms unless the court finds the writing to have been intended also as a complete and exclusive statement of the terms of the agreement.

§2A—203. SEALS INOPERATIVE

The affixing of a seal to a writing evidencing a lease contract or an offer to enter into a lease contract does not render the writing a sealed instrument and the law with respect to sealed instruments does not apply to the lease contract or offer.

§2A—204. FORMATION IN GENERAL

(1) A lease contract may be made in any manner sufficient to show agreement, including conduct by both parties which recognizes the existence of a lease contract.

(2) An agreement sufficient to constitute a lease contract may be found although the moment of its making is undetermined.

(3) Although one or more terms are left open, a lease contract does not fail for indefiniteness if the parties have intended to make a lease contract and there is a reasonably certain basis for giving an appropriate remedy.

§2A—205. FIRM OFFERS

An offer by a merchant to lease goods to or from another person in a signed writing that by its terms gives assurance it will be held open is not revocable, for lack of consideration, during the time stated or, if no time is stated, for a reasonable time, but in no event may the period of irrevocability exceed 3 months. Any such term of assurance on a form supplied by the offeree must be separately signed by the offeror.

§2A—206. OFFER AND ACCEPTANCE IN FORMATION OF LEASE CONTRACT

(1) Unless otherwise unambiguously indicated by the language or circumstances, an offer to make a lease contract must be construed as inviting acceptance in any manner and by any medium reasonable in the circumstances.

(2) If the beginning of a requested performance is a reasonable mode of acceptance, an offeror who is not notified of acceptance within a reasonable time may treat the offer as having lapsed before acceptance.

§2A—207. COURSE OF PERFORMANCE OR PRACTICAL CONSTRUCTION

(1) If a lease contract involves repeated occasions for performance by either party with knowledge of the nature of the performance and opportunity for objection to it by the other, any course of performance accepted or acquiesced in without objection is relevant to determine the meaning of the lease agreement.

(2) The express terms of a lease agreement and any course of performance, as well as any course of dealing and usage of trade, must be construed whenever reasonable as consistent with each other; but if that construction is unreasonable, express terms control course of performance, course of performance controls both course of dealing and usage of trade, and course of dealing controls usage of trade.

(3) Subject to the provisions of Section 2A—208 on modification and waiver, course of performance is relevant to show a waiver or modification of any term inconsistent with the course of performance.

§2A—208. MODIFICATION, RESCISSION AND WAIVER

(1) An agreement modifying a lease contract needs no consideration to be binding.

(2) A signed lease agreement that excludes modification or rescission except by a signed writing may not be otherwise modified or rescinded, but, except as between merchants, such a requirement on a form supplied by a merchant must be separately signed by the other party.

(3) Although an attempt at modification or rescission does not satisfy the requirements of subsection (2), it may operate as a waiver.

(4) A party who has made a waiver affecting an executory portion of a lease contract may retract the waiver by reasonable notification received by the other party that strict performance will be required of any term waived, unless the retraction would be unjust in view of a material change of position in reliance on the waiver.

§2A—209. LESSEE UNDER FINANCE LEASE AS BENEFICIARY OF SUPPLY CONTRACT

(1) The benefit of the supplier's promises to the lessor under the supply contract and of all warranties, whether express or implied, including those of any third party provided in connection with or as part of the supply contract, extends to the lessee to the extent of the lessee's leasehold interest under a finance lease related to the supply contract, but is subject to the terms warranty and of the supply contract and all defenses or claims arising therefrom.

(2) The extension of the benefit of supplier's promises and of warranties to the lessee (Section 2A—209(1)) does not: (i) modify the rights and obligations of the parties to the supply contract, whether arising therefrom or otherwise, or (ii) impose any duty or liability under the supply contract on the lessee.

(3) Any modification or rescission of the supply contract by the supplier and the lessor is effective between the supplier and the lessee unless, before the modification or rescission, the supplier has received notice that the lessee has entered into a finance lease related to the supply contract. If the modification or rescission is effective between the supplier and the lessee, the lessor is deemed to have assumed, in addition to the obligations of the lessor to the lessee under the lease contract, promises of the supplier to the lessor and warranties that were so modified or rescinded as they existed and were available to the lessee before modification or rescission.

(4) In addition to the extension of the benefit of the supplier's promises and of warranties to the lessee under subsection (1), the lessee retains all rights that the lessee may have against the supplier which arise from an agreement between the lessee and the supplier or under other law.

As amended in 1990.

§2A—210. EXPRESS WARRANTIES

(1) Express warranties by the lessor are created as follows:
    (a) Any affirmation of fact or promise made by the lessor to the lessee which relates to the goods and becomes part of the basis of the bargain creates an express warranty that the goods will conform to the affirmation or promise.
    (b) Any description of the goods which is made part of the basis of the bargain creates an express warranty that the goods will conform to the description.
    (c) Any sample or model that is made part of the basis of the bargain creates an express warranty that the whole of the goods will conform to the sample or model.

(2) It is not necessary to the creation of an express warranty that the lessor use formal words, such as "warrant" or "guarantee," or that the lessor have a specific intention to make a warranty, but an affirmation merely of the value of the goods or a statement purporting to be merely the lessor's opinion or commendation of the goods does not create a warranty.

§2A—211. WARRANTIES AGAINST INTERFERENCE AND AGAINST INFRINGEMENT; LESSEE'S OBLIGATION AGAINST INFRINGEMENT

(1) There is in a lease contract a warranty that for the lease term no person holds a claim to or interest in the goods that arose from an act or omission of the lessor, other than a claim by way of infringement or the like, which will interfere with the lessee's enjoyment of its leasehold interest.

(2) Except in a finance lease there is in a lease contract by a lessor who is a merchant regularly dealing in goods of the kind a warranty that the goods are delivered free of the rightful claim of any person by way of infringement or the like.

(3) A lessee who furnishes specifications to a lessor or a supplier shall hold the lessor and the supplier harmless against any claim by way of infringement or the like that arises out of compliance with the specifications.

§2A—212. IMPLIED WARRANTY OF MERCHANTABILITY

(1) Except in a finance lease, a warranty that the goods will be merchantable is implied in a lease contract if the lessor is a merchant with respect to goods of that kind.

(2) Goods to be merchantable must be at least such as
    (a) pass without objection in the trade under the description in the lease agreement;
    (b) in the case of fungible goods, are of fair average quality within the description;
    (c) are fit for the ordinary purposes for which goods of that type are used;
    (d) run, within the variation permitted by the lease agreement, of even kind, quality, and quantity within each unit and among all units involved;
    (e) are adequately contained, packaged, and labeled as the lease agreement may require; and

(f) conform to any promises or affirmations of fact made on the container or label.

(3) Other implied warranties may arise from course of dealing or usage of trade.

§2A—213. IMPLIED WARRANTY OF FITNESS FOR PARTICULAR PURPOSE

Except in a finance of lease, if the lessor at the time the lease contract is made has reason to know of any particular purpose for which the goods are required and that the lessee is relying on the lessor's skill or judgment to select or furnish suitable goods, there is in the lease contract an implied warranty that the goods will be fit for that purpose.

§2A—214. EXCLUSION OR MODIFICATION OF WARRANTIES

(1) Words or conduct relevant to the creation of an express warranty and words or conduct tending to negate or limit a warranty must be construed wherever reasonable as consistent with each other; but, subject to the provisions of Section 2A—202 on parol or extrinsic evidence, negation or limitation is inoperative to the extent that the construction is unreasonable.

(2) Subject to subsection (3), to exclude or modify the implied warranty of merchantability or any part of it the language must mention "merchantability", be by a writing, and be conspicuous. Subject to subsection (3), to exclude or modify any implied warranty of fitness the exclusion must be by a writing and be conspicuous. Language to exclude all implied warranties of fitness is sufficient if it is in writing, is conspicuous and states, for example, "There is no warranty that the goods will be fit for a particular purpose".

(3) Notwithstanding subsection (2), but subject to subsection (4),

    (a) unless the circumstances indicate otherwise, all implied warranties are excluded by expressions like "as is" or "with all faults" or by other language that in common understanding calls the lessee's attention to the exclusion of warranties and makes plain that there is no implied warranty, if in writing and conspicuous;

    (b) if the lessee before entering into the lease contract has examined the goods or the sample or model as fully as desired or has refused to examine the goods, there is no implied warranty with regard to defects that an examination ought in the circumstances to have revealed; and

    (c) an implied warranty may also be excluded or modified by course of dealing, course of performance, or usage of trade.

(4) To exclude or modify a warranty against interference or against infringement (Section 2A—211) or any part of it, the language must be specific, be by a writing, and be conspicuous, unless the circumstances, including course of performance, course of dealing, or usage of trade, give the lessee reason to know that the goods are being leased subject to a claim or interest of any person.

§2A—215. CUMULATION AND CONFLICT OF WARRANTIES EXPRESS OR IMPLIED

Warranties, whether express or implied, must be construed as consistent with each other and as cumulative, but if that construction is unreasonable, the intention of the parties determines which warranty is dominant. In ascertaining that intention the following rules apply:

(a) Exact or technical specifications displace an inconsistent sample or model or general language of description.

    (b) A sample from an existing bulk displaces inconsistent general language of description.

    (c) Express warranties displace inconsistent implied warranties other than an implied warranty of fitness for a particular purpose.

§2A—216. THIRD-PARTY BENEFICIARIES OF EXPRESS AND IMPLIED WARRANTIES

Alternative A

A warranty to or for the benefit of a lessee under this Article, whether express or implied, extends to any natural person who is in the family or household of the lessee or who is a guest in the lessee's home if it is reasonable to expect that such person may use, consume, or be affected by the goods and who is injured in person by breach of the warranty. This section does not displace principles of law and equity that extend a warranty to or for the benefit of a lessee to other persons. The operation of this section may not be excluded, modified, or limited, but an exclusion, modification, or limitation of the warranty, including any with respect to rights and remedies, effective against the lessee is also effective against any beneficiary designated under this section.

Alternative B

A warranty to or for the benefit of a lessee under this Article, whether express or implied, extends to any natural person who may reasonably be expected to use, consume, or be affected by the goods and who is injured in person by breach of the warranty. This section does not displace principles of law and equity that extend a warranty to or for the benefit of a lessee to other persons. The operation of this section may not be excluded, modified, or limited, but an exclusion, modification, or limitation of the warranty, including any with respect to rights and remedies, effective against the lessee is also effective against the beneficiary designated under this section.

Alternative C

A warranty to or for the benefit of a lessee under this Article, whether express or implied, extends to any person who may reasonably be expected to use, consume, or be affected by the goods and who is injured by breach of the warranty. The operation of this section may not be excluded, modified, or limited with respect to injury to the person of an individual to whom the warranty extends, but an exclusion, modification, or limitation of the warranty, including any with respect to rights and remedies, effective against the lessee is also effective against the beneficiary designated under this section.

§2A—217. IDENTIFICATION

Identification of goods as goods to which a lease contract refers may be made at any time and in any manner explicitly agreed to by the parties. In the absence of explicit agreement, identification occurs:

(a) when the lease contract is made if the lease contract is for a lease of goods that are existing and identified;

(b) when the goods are shipped, marked, or otherwise designated by the lessor as goods to which the lease contract refers, if the lease contract is for a lease of goods that are not existing and identified; or

(c) when the young are conceived, if the lease contract is for a lease of unborn young of animals.

§2A—218. INSURANCE AND PROCEEDS

(1) A lessee obtains an insurable interest when existing goods are identified to the lease contract even though the goods identified are nonconforming and the lessee has an option to reject them.

(2) If a lessee has an insurable interest only by reason of the lessor's identification of the goods, the lessor, until default or insolvency or notification to the lessee that identification is final, may substitute other goods for those identified.

(3) Notwithstanding a lessee's insurable interest under subsections (1) and (2), the lessor retains an insurable interest until an option to buy has been exercised by the lessee and risk of loss has passed to the lessee.

(4) Nothing in this section impairs any insurable interest recognized under any other statute or rule of law.

(5) The parties by agreement may determine that one or more parties have an obligation to obtain and pay for insurance covering the goods and by agreement may determine the beneficiary of the proceeds of the insurance.

§2A—219. RISK OF LOSS

(1) Except in the case of a finance lease, risk of loss is retained by the lessor and does not pass to the lessee. In the case of a finance lease, risk of loss passes to the lessee.

(2) Subject to the provisions of this Article on the effect of default on risk of loss (Section 2A—220), if risk of loss is to pass to the lessee and the time of passage is not stated, the following rules apply:

(a) If the lease contract requires or authorizes the goods to be shipped by carrier

(i) and it does not require delivery at a particular destination, the risk of loss passes to the lessee when the goods are duly delivered to the carrier; but

(ii) if it does require delivery at a particular destination and the goods are there duly tendered while in the possession of the carrier, the risk of loss passes to the lessee when the goods are there duly so tendered as to enable the lessee to take delivery.

(b) If the goods are held by a bailee to be delivered without being moved, the risk of loss passes to the lessee on acknowledgment by the bailee of the lessee's right to possession of the goods.

(c) In any case not within subsection (a) or (b), the risk of loss passes to the lessee on the lessee's receipt of the goods if the lessor, or, in the case of a finance lease, the supplier, is a merchant; otherwise the risk passes to the lessee on tender of delivery.

§2A—220. EFFECT OF DEFAULT ON RISK OF LOSS

(1) Where risk of loss is to pass to the lessee and the time of passage is not stated:

(a) If a tender or delivery of goods so fails to conform to the lease contract as to give a right of rejection, the risk of their loss remains with the lessor, or, in the case of a finance lease, the supplier, until cure or acceptance.

(b) If the lessee rightfully revokes acceptance, he [or she], to the extent of any deficiency in his [or her] effective insurance coverage, may treat the risk of loss as having remained with the lessor from the beginning.

(2) Whether or not risk of loss is to pass to the lessee, if the lessee as to conforming goods already identified to a lease contract repudiates or is otherwise in default under the lease contract, the lessor, or, in the case of a finance lease, the supplier, to the extent of any deficiency in his [or her] effective insurance coverage may treat the risk of loss as resting on the lessee for a commercially reasonable time.

§2A—221. CASUALTY TO IDENTIFIED GOODS

If a lease contract requires goods identified when the lease contract is made, and the goods suffer casualty without fault of the lessee, the lessor or the supplier before delivery, or the goods suffer casualty before risk of loss passes to the lessee pursuant to the lease agreement or Section 2A—219, then:

(a) if the loss is total, the lease contract is avoided; and

(b) if the loss is partial or the goods have so deteriorated as to no longer conform to the lease contract, the lessee may nevertheless demand inspection and at his [or her] option either treat the lease contract as avoided or, except in a finance lease that is not a consumer lease, accept the goods with due allowance from the rent payable for the balance of the lease term for the deterioration or the deficiency in quantity but without further right against the lessor.

Part 3 Effect of Lease Contract

§2A—301. ENFORCEABILITY OF LEASE CONTRACT

Except as otherwise provided in this Article, a lease contract is effective and enforceable according to its terms between the parties, against purchasers of the goods and against creditors of the parties.

§2A—302. TITLE TO AND POSSESSION OF GOODS

Except as otherwise provided in this Article, each provision of this Article applies whether the lessor or a third party has title to the goods, and whether the lessor, the lessee, or a third party has possession of the goods, notwithstanding any statute or rule of law that possession or the absence of possession is fraudulent.

§2A—303. ALIENABILITY OF PARTY'S INTEREST UNDER LEASE CONTRACT OR OF LESSOR'S RESIDUAL INTEREST IN GOODS; DELEGATION OF PERFORMANCE; TRANSFER OF RIGHTS

(1) As used in this section, "creation of a security interest" includes the sale of a lease contract that is subject to Article9, Secured Transactions, by reason of Section 9—109(a)(3).

(2) Except as provided in subsections (3) and Section 9—407, a provision in a lease agreement which (i) prohibits the voluntary or involuntary transfer, including a transfer by sale, sublease, creation or enforcement of a security interest, or attachment, levy, or other judicial process, of an interest of a party under the lease contract or of the lessor's residual interest in the goods, or (ii) makes such a transfer an event of default, gives rise to the rights and remedies provided in subsection (4), but a transfer that is prohibited or is an event of default under the lease agreement is otherwise effective.

(3) A provision in a lease agreement which (i) prohibits a transfer of a right to damages for default with respect to the whole lease contract or of a right to payment arising out of the transferor's due performance of the transferor's entire obligation, or (ii) makes such a transfer an event of default, is not enforceable, and such a transfer is not a transfer that materially impairs the propsect of obtaining return performance by, materially changes the duty of, or materially increases the burden or risk imposed on, the other party to the lease contract within the purview of subsection (4).

(4) Subject to subsection (3) and Section 9—407:

(a) if a transfer is made which is made an event of default under a lease agreement, the party to the lease contract not making the transfer, unless that party waives the default or otherwise agrees, has the rights and remedies described in Section 2A—501(2);

(b) if paragraph (a) is not applicable and if a transfer is made that (i) is prohibited under a lease agreement or (ii) materially impairs the prospect of obtaining return performance by, materially changes the duty of, or materially increases the burden or risk imposed on, the other party to the lease contract, unless the party not making the transfer agrees at any time to the transfer in the lease contract or otherwise, then, except as limited by contract, (i) the transferor is liable to the party not making the transfer for damages caused by the transfer to the extent that the damages could not reasonably be prevented by the party not making the transfer and (ii) a court having jurisdiction may grant other appropriate relief, including cancellation of the lease contract or an injunction against the transfer.

(5) A transfer of "the lease" or of "all my rights under the lease", or a transfer in similar general terms, is a transfer of rights and, unless the language or the circumstances, as in a transfer for security, indicate the contrary, the transfer is a delegation of duties by the transferor to the transferee. Acceptance by the transferee constitutes a promise by the transferee to perform those duties. The promise is enforceable by either the transferor or the other party to the lease contract.

(6) Unless otherwise agreed by the lessor and the lessee, a delegation of performance does not relieve the transferor as against the other party of any duty to perform or of any liability for default.

(7) In a consumer lease, to prohibit the transfer of an interest of a party under the lease contract or to make a transfer an event of default, the language must be specific, by a writing, and conspicuous.

As amended in 1990 and 1999.

§2A—304. SUBSEQUENT LEASE OF GOODS BY LESSOR

(1) Subject to Section 2A—303, a subsequent lessee from a lessor of goods under an existing lease contract obtains, to the extent of the leasehold interest transferred, the leasehold interest in the goods that the lessor had or had power to transfer, and except as provided in subsection (2)

and Section 2A—527(4), takes subject to the existing lease contract. A lessor with voidable title has power to transfer a good leasehold interest to a good faith subsequent lessee for value, but only to the extent set forth in the preceding sentence. If goods have been delivered under a transaction of purchase the lessor has that power even though:

(a) the lessor's transferor was deceived as to the identity of the lessor;

(b) the delivery was in exchange for a check which is later dishonored;

(c) it was agreed that the transaction was to be a "cash sale"; or

(d) the delivery was procured through fraud punishable as larcenous under the criminal law.

(2) A subsequent lessee in the ordinary course of business from a lessor who is a merchant dealing in goods of that kind to whom the goods were entrusted by the existing lessee of that lessor before the interest of the subsequent lessee became enforceable against that lessor obtains, to the extent of the leasehold interest transferred, all of that lessor's and the existing lessee's rights to the goods, and takes free of the existing lease contract.

(3) A subsequent lessee from the lessor of goods that are subject to an existing lease contract and are covered by a certificate of title issued under a statute of this State or of another jurisdiction takes no greater rights than those provided both by this section and by the certificate of title statute.

As amended in 1990.

§2A—305. SALE OR SUBLEASE OF GOODS BY LESSEE

(1) Subject to the provisions of Section 2A—303, a buyer or sublessee from the lessee of goods under an existing lease contract obtains, to the extent of the interest transferred, the leasehold interest in the goods that the lessee had or had power to transfer, and except as provided in subsection (2)and Section 2A—511(4), takes subject to the existing lease contract. A lessee with a voidable leasehold interest has power to transfer a good leasehold interest to a good faith buyer for value or a good faith sublessee for value, but only to the extent set forth in the preceding sentence. When goods have been delivered under a transaction of lease the lessee has that power even though:

(a) the lessor was deceived as to the identity of the lessee;

(b) the delivery was in exchange for a check which is later dishonored; or

(c) the delivery was procured through fraud punishable as larcenous under the criminal law.

(2) A buyer in the ordinary course of business or a sublessee in the ordinary course of business from a lessee who is a merchant dealing in goods of that kind to whom the goods were entrusted by the lessor obtains, to the extent of the interest transferred, all of the lessor's and lessee's rights to the goods, and takes free of the existing lease contract.

(3) A buyer or sublessee from the lessee of goods that are subject to an existing lease contract and are covered by a certificate of title issued under a statute of this State or of another jurisdiction takes no greater rights than those provided both by this section and by the certificate of title statute.

§2A—306. PRIORITY OF CERTAIN LIENS ARISING BY OPERATION OF LAW

If a person in the ordinary course of his [or her] business furnishes services or materials with respect to goods subject to a lease contract, a lien upon those goods in the possession of that person given by statute or rule of law for those materials or services takes priority over any interest of the lessor or lessee under the lease contract or this Article unless the lien is created by statute and the statute provides otherwise or unless the lien is created by rule of law and the rule of law provides otherwise.

§2A—307. PRIORITY OF LIENS ARISING BY ATTACHMENT OR LEVY ON, SECURITY INTERESTS IN, AND OTHER CLAIMS TO GOODS

(1) Except as otherwise provided in Section 2A—306, a creditor of a lessee takes subject to the lease contract.

(2) Except as otherwise provided in subsection (3) and in Sections 2A—306 and 2A—308, a creditor of a lessor takes subject to the lease contract unless the creditor holds a lien that attached to the goods before the lease contract became enforceable.

(3) Except as otherwise provided in Sections 9—317, 9—321, and 9—323, a lessee takes a leasehold interest subject to a security interest held by a creditor of the lessor.

As amended in 1990 and 1999.

§2A—308. SPECIAL RIGHTS OF CREDITORS

(1) A creditor of a lessor in possession of goods subject to a lease contract may treat the lease contract as void if as against the creditor retention of possession by the lessor is fraudulent under any statute or rule of law, but retention of possession in good faith and current course of trade by the lessor for a commercially reasonable time after the lease contract becomes enforceable is not fraudulent.

(2) Nothing in this Article impairs the rights of creditors of a lessor if the lease contract (a) becomes enforceable, not in current course of trade but in satisfaction of or as security for a pre-existing claim for money, security, or the like, and (b) is made under circumstances which under any statute or rule of law apart from this Article would constitute the transaction a fraudulent transfer or voidable preference.

(3)   A creditor of a seller may treat a sale or an identification of goods to a contract for sale as void if as against the creditor retention of possession by the seller is fraudulent under any statute or rule of law, but retention of possession of the goods pursuant to a lease contract entered into by the seller as lessee and the buyer as lessor in connection with the sale or identification of the goods is not fraudulent if the buyer bought for value and in good faith.

§2A—309. LESSOR'S AND LESSEE'S RIGHTS WHEN GOODS BECOME FIXTURES

(1)   In this section:

(a)   goods are "fixtures" when they become so related to particular real estate that an interest in them arises under real estate law;

(b)   a "fixture filing" is the filing, in the office where a mortgage on the real estate would be filed or recorded, of a financing statement covering goods that are or are to become fixtures and conforming to the requirements of Section 9—502(a) and (b);

(c)   a lease is a "purchase money lease" unless the lessee has possession or use of the goods or the right to possession or use of the goods before the lease agreement is enforceable;

(d)   a mortgage is a "construction mortgage" to the extent it secures an obligation incurred for the construction of an improvement on land including the acquisition cost of the land, if the recorded writing so indicates; and

(e)   "encumbrance" includes real estate mortgages and other liens on real estate and all other rights in real estate that are not ownership interests.

(2)   Under this Article a lease may be of goods that are fixtures or may continue in goods that become fixtures, but no lease exists under this Article of ordinary building materials incorporated into an improvement on land.

(3)   This Article does not prevent creation of a lease of fixtures pursuant to real estate law.

(4)   The perfected interest of a lessor of fixtures has priority over a conflicting interest of an encumbrancer or owner of the real estate if:

(a)   the lease is a purchase money lease, the conflicting interest of the encumbrancer or owner arises before the goods become fixtures, the interest of the lessor is perfected by a fixture filing before the goods become fixtures or within ten days thereafter, and the lessee has an interest of record in the real estate or is in possession of the real estate; or

(b)   the interest of the lessor is perfected by a fixture filing before the interest of the encumbrancer or owner is of record, the lessor's interest has priority over any conflicting interest of a predecessor in title of the encumbrancer or owner, and the lessee has an interest of record in the real estate or is in possession of the real estate.

(5)   The interest of a lessor of fixtures, whether or not perfected, has priority over the conflicting interest of an encumbrancer or owner of the real estate if:

(a)   the fixtures are readily removable factory or office machines, readily removable equipment that is not primarily used or leased for use in the operation of the real estate, or readily removable replacements of domestic appliances that are goods subject to a consumer lease, and before the goods become fixtures the lease contract is enforceable; or

(b)   the conflicting interest is a lien on the real estate obtained by legal or equitable proceedings after the lease contract is enforceable; or

(c)   the encumbrancer or owner has consented in writing to the lease or has disclaimed an interest in the goods as fixtures; or

(d)   the lessee has a right to remove the goods as against the encumbrancer or owner. If the lessee's right to remove terminates, the priority of the interest of the lessor continues for a reasonable time.

(6)   Notwithstanding paragraph (4)(a) but otherwise subject to subsections (4) and (5), the interest of a lessor of fixtures, including the lessor's residual interest, is subordinate to the conflicting interest of an encumbrancer of the real estate under a construction mortgage recorded before the goods become fixtures if the goods become fixtures before the completion of the construction. To the extent given to refinance a construction mortgage, the conflicting interest of an encumbrancer of the real estate under a mortgage has this priority to the same extent as the encumbrancer of the real estate under the construction mortgage.

(7)   In cases not within the preceding subsections, priority between the interest of a lessor of fixtures, including the lessor's residual interest, and the conflicting interest of an encumbrancer or owner of the real estate who is not the lessee is determined by the priority rules governing conflicting interests in real estate.

(8)   If the interest of a lessor of fixtures, including the lessor's residual interest, has priority over all conflicting interests of all owners and encumbrancers of the real estate, the lessor or the lessee may (i) on default, expiration, termination, or cancellation of the lease agreement but subject to the agreement and this Article, or (ii) if necessary to enforce other rights and remedies of the lessor or lessee under this Article, remove the goods from the real estate, free and clear of all conflicting interests of all owners and encumbrancers of the real estate, but the lessor or lessee must reimburse any encumbrancer or owner of the real estate who is not the lessee and who has not otherwise

agreed for the cost of repair of any physical injury, but not for any diminution in value of the real estate caused by the absence of the goods removed or by any necessity of replacing them. A person entitled to reimbursement may refuse permission to remove until the party seeking removal gives adequate security for the performance of this obligation.

(9) Even though the lease agreement does not create a security interest, the interest of a lessor of fixtures, including the lessor's residual interest, is perfected by filing a financing statement as a fixture filing for leased goods that are or are to become fixtures in accordance with the relevant provisions of the Article on Secured Transactions (Article 9).

As amended in 1990 and 1999.

§2A—310. LESSOR'S AND LESSEE'S RIGHTS WHEN GOODS BECOME ACCESSIONS

(1) Goods are "accessions" when they are installed in or affixed to other goods.

(2) The interest of a lessor or a lessee under a lease contract entered into before the goods became accessions is superior to all interests in the whole except as stated in subsection (4).

(3) The interest of a lessor or a lessee under a lease contract entered into at the time or after the goods became accessions is superior to all subsequently acquired interests in the whole except as stated in subsection (4) but is subordinate to interests in the whole existing at the time the lease contract was made unless the holders of such interests in the whole have in writing consented to the lease or disclaimed an interest in the goods as part of the whole.

(4) The interest of a lessor or a lessee under a lease contract described in subsection (2) or (3) is subordinate to the interest of

(a) a buyer in the ordinary course of business or a lessee in the ordinary course of business of any interest in the whole acquired after the goods became accessions; or

(b) a creditor with a security interest in the whole perfected before the lease contract was made to the extent that the creditor makes subsequent advances without knowledge of the lease contract.

(5) When under subsections (2) or (3) and (4) a lessor or a lessee of accessions holds an interest that is superior to all interests in the whole, the lessor or the lessee may (a) on default, expiration, termination, or cancellation of the lease contract by the other party but subject to the provisions of the lease contract and this Article, or (b) if necessary to enforce his [or her] other rights and remedies under this Article, remove the goods from the whole, free and clear of all interests in the whole, but he [or she] must reimburse any holder of an interest in the whole who is not the lessee and who has not otherwise agreed for the cost of repair of any physical injury but not for any diminution in value of the whole caused by the absence of the goods removed or by any necessity for replacing them. A person entitled to reimbursement may refuse permission to remove until the party seeking removal gives adequate security for the performance of this obligation.

§2A—311. PRIORITY SUBJECT TO SUBORDINATION

Nothing in this Article prevents subordination by agreement by any person entitled to priority.

As added in 1990.

Part 4 Performance of Lease Contract: Repudiated, Substituted and Excused

§2A—401. INSECURITY: ADEQUATE ASSURANCE OF PERFORMANCE

(1) A lease contract imposes an obligation on each party that the other's expectation of receiving due performance will not be impaired.

(2) If reasonable grounds for insecurity arise with respect to the performance of either party, the insecure party may demand in writing adequate assurance of due performance. Until the insecure party receives that assurance, if commercially reasonable the insecure party may suspend any performance for which he [or she] has not already received the agreed return.

(3) A repudiation of the lease contract occurs if assurance of due performance adequate under the circumstances of the particular case is not provided to the insecure party within a reasonable time, not to exceed 30 days after receipt of a demand by the other party.

(4) Between merchants, the reasonableness of grounds for insecurity and the adequacy of any assurance offered must be determined according to commercial standards.

(5) Acceptance of any nonconforming delivery or payment does not prejudice the aggrieved party's right to demand adequate assurance of future performance.

§2A—402. ANTICIPATORY REPUDIATION

If either party repudiates a lease contract with respect to a performance not yet due under the lease contract, the loss of which performance will substantially impair the value of the lease contract to the other, the aggrieved party may:

(a) for a commercially reasonable time, await retraction of repudiation and performance by the repudiating party;

(b) make demand pursuant to Section 2A—401 and await assurance of future performance adequate under the circumstances of the particular case; or

(c) resort to any right or remedy upon default under the lease contract or this Article, even though the aggrieved party has notified the repudiating party that the aggrieved party would await the repudiating party's performance and assurance and has urged retraction. In addition, whether or not the aggrieved party is pursuing one of the foregoing remedies, the aggrieved party may suspend performance or, if the aggrieved party is the lessor, proceed in accordance with the provisions of this Article on the lessor's right to identify goods to the lease contract notwithstanding default or to salvage unfinished goods (Section 2A—524).

§2A—403. RETRACTION OF ANTICIPATORY REPUDIATION

(1) Until the repudiating party's next performance is due, the repudiating party can retract the repudiation unless, since the repudiation, the aggrieved party has cancelled the lease contract or materially changed the aggrieved party's position or otherwise indicated that the aggrieved party considers the repudiation final.

(2) Retraction may be by any method that clearly indicates to the aggrieved party that the repudiating party intends to perform under the lease contract and includes any assurance demanded under Section 2A—401.

(3) Retraction reinstates a repudiating party's rights under a lease contract with due excuse and allowance to the aggrieved party for any delay occasioned by the repudiation.

§2A—404. SUBSTITUTED PERFORMANCE

(1) If without fault of the lessee, the lessor and the supplier, the agreed berthing, loading, or unloading facilities fail or the agreed type of carrier becomes unavailable or the agreed manner of delivery otherwise becomes commercially impracticable, but a commercially reasonable substitute is available, the substitute performance must be tendered and accepted.

(2) If the agreed means or manner of payment fails because of domestic or foreign governmental regulation:

(a) the lessor may withhold or stop delivery or cause the supplier to withhold or stop delivery unless the lessee provides a means or manner of payment that is commercially a substantial equivalent; and

(b) if delivery has already been taken, payment by the means or in the manner provided by the regulation discharges the lessee's obligation unless the regulation is discriminatory, oppressive, or predatory.

§2A—405. EXCUSED PERFORMANCE

Subject to Section 2A—404 on substituted performance, the following rules apply:

(a) Delay in delivery or nondelivery in whole or in part by a lessor or a supplier who complies with paragraphs (b) and (c) is not a default under the lease contract if performance as agreed has been made impracticable by the occurrence of a contingency the nonoccurrence of which was a basic assumption on which the lease contract was made or by compliance in good faith with any applicable foreign or domestic governmental regulation or order, whether or not the regulation or order later proves to be invalid.

(b) If the causes mentioned in paragraph (a) affect only part of the lessor's or the supplier's capacity to perform, he [or she] shall allocate production and deliveries among his [or her] customers but at his [or her] option may include regular customers not then under contract for sale or lease as well as his [or her] own requirements for further manufacture. He [or she] may so allocate in any manner that is fair and reasonable.

(c) The lessor seasonably shall notify the lessee and in the case of a finance lease the supplier seasonably shall notify the lessor and the lessee, if known, that there will be delay or nondelivery and, if allocation is required under paragraph (b), of the estimated quota thus made available for the lessee.

§2A—406. PROCEDURE ON EXCUSED PERFORMANCE

(1) If the lessee receives notification of a material or indefinite delay or an allocation justified under Section 2A—405, the lessee may by written notification to the lessor as to any goods involved, and with respect to all of the goods if under an installment lease contract the value of the whole lease contract is substantially impaired (Section 2A—510):

(a) terminate the lease contract (Section 2A—505(2)); or

(b) except in a finance lease that is not a consumer lease, modify the lease contract by accepting the available quota in substitution, with due allowance from the rent payable for the balance of the lease term for the deficiency but without further right against the lessor.

(2) If, after receipt of a notification from the lessor under Section 2A—405, the lessee fails so to modify the lease agreement within a reasonable time not exceeding 30 days, the lease contract lapses with respect to any deliveries affected.

§2A—407. IRREVOCABLE PROMISES: FINANCE LEASES

(1) In the case of a finance lease that is not a consumer lease the lessee's promises under the lease contract become irrevocable and independent upon the lessee's acceptance of the goods.

(2) A promise that has become irrevocable and independent under subsection (1):

    (a) is effective and enforceable between the parties, and by or against third parties including assignees of the parties, and

    (b) is not subject to cancellation, termination, modification, repudiation, excuse, or substitution without the consent of the party to whom the promise runs.

(3) This section does not affect the validity under any other law of a covenant in any lease contract making the lessee's promises irrevocable and independent upon the lessee's acceptance of the goods.

As amended in 1990.

Part 5 Default A. In General

§2A—501. DEFAULT: PROCEDURE

(1) Whether the lessor or the lessee is in default under a lease contract is determined by the lease agreement and this Article.

(2) If the lessor or the lessee is in default under the lease contract, the party seeking enforcement has rights and remedies as provided in this Article and, except as limited by this Article, as provided in the lease agreement.

(3) If the lessor or the lessee is in default under the lease contract, the party seeking enforcement may reduce the party's claim to judgment, or otherwise enforce the lease contract by self-help or any available judicial procedure or nonjudicial procedure, including administrative proceeding, arbitration, or the like, in accordance with this Article.

(4) Except as otherwise provided in Section 1—106 (1) or this Article or the lease agreement, the rights and remedies referred to in subsections (2) and (3) are cumulative.

(5) If the lease agreement covers both real property and goods, the party seeking enforcement may proceed under this Part as to the goods, or under other applicable law as to both the real property and the goods in accordance with that party's rights and remedies in respect of the real property, in which case this Part does not apply.

As amended in 1990.

§2A—502. NOTICE AFTER DEFAULT

Except as otherwise provided in this Article or the lease agreement, the lessor or lessee in default under the lease contract is not entitled to notice of default or notice of enforcement from the other party to the lease agreement.

§2A—503. MODIFICATION OR IMPAIRMENT OF RIGHTS AND REMEDIES

(1) Except as otherwise provided in this Article, the lease agreement may include rights and remedies for default in addition to or in substitution for those provided in this Article and may limit or alter the measure of damages recoverable under this Article.

(2) Resort to a remedy provided under this Article or in the lease agreement is optional unless the remedy is expressly agreed to be exclusive. If circumstances cause an exclusive or limited remedy to fail of its essential purpose, or provision for an exclusive remedy is unconscionable, remedy may be had as provided in this Article.

(3) Consequential damages may be liquidated under Section 2A—504, or may otherwise be limited, altered, or excluded unless the limitation, alteration, or exclusion is unconscionable. Limitation, alteration, or exclusion of consequential damages for injury to the person in the case of consumer goods is prima facie unconscionable but limitation, alteration, or exclusion of damages where the loss is commercial is not prima facie unconscionable.

(4) Rights and remedies on default by the lessor or the lessee with respect to any obligation or promise collateral or ancillary to the lease contract are not impaired by this Article.

As amended in 1990.

§2A—504. LIQUIDATION OF DAMAGES

(1) Damages payable by either party for default, or any other act or omission, including indemnity for loss or diminution of anticipated tax benefits or loss or damage to lessor's residual interest, may be liquidated in the lease agreement but only at an amount or by a formula that is reasonable in light of the then anticipated harm caused by the default or other act or omission.

(2) If the lease agreement provides for liquidation of damages, and such provision does not comply with subsection (1), or such provision is an exclusive or limited remedy that circumstances cause to fail of its essential purpose, remedy may be had as provided in this Article.

(3) If the lessor justifiably withholds or stops delivery of goods because of the lessee's default or insolvency (Section 2A—525 or 2A—526), the lessee is entitled to restitution of any amount by which the sum of his [or her] payments exceeds:

    (a) the amount to which the lessor is entitled by virtue of terms liquidating the lessor's damages in accordance with subsection (1); or

    (b) in the absence of those terms, 20 percent of the then present value of the total rent the lessee was obligated to pay for the balance of the lease term, or, in the case of a consumer lease, the lesser of such amount or $500.

(4) A lessee's right to restitution under subsection (3) is subject to offset to the extent the lessor establishes:

    (a) a right to recover damages under the provisions of this Article other than subsection (1); and

(b) the amount or value of any benefits received by the lessee directly or indirectly by reason of the lease contract.

§2A—505. CANCELLATION AND TERMINATION AND EFFECT OF CANCELLATION, TERMINATION, RESCISSION, OR FRAUD ON RIGHTS AND REMEDIES

(1) On cancellation of the lease contract, all obligations that are still executory on both sides are discharged, but any right based on prior default or performance survives, and the cancelling party also retains any remedy for default of the whole lease contract or any unperformed balance.

(2) On termination of the lease contract, all obligations that are still executory on both sides are discharged but any right based on prior default or performance survives.

(3) Unless the contrary intention clearly appears, expressions of "cancellation," "rescission," or the like of the lease contract may not be construed as a renunciation or discharge of any claim in damages for an antecedent default.

(4) Rights and remedies for material misrepresentation or fraud include all rights and remedies available under this Article for default.

(5) Neither rescission nor a claim for rescission of the lease contract nor rejection or return of the goods may bar or be deemed inconsistent with a claim for damages or other right or remedy.

§2A—506. STATUTE OF LIMITATIONS

(1) An action for default under a lease contract, including breach of warranty or indemnity, must be commenced within 4 years after the cause of action accrued. By the original lease contract the parties may reduce the period of limitation to not less than one year.

(2) A cause of action for default accrues when the act or omission on which the default or breach of warranty is based is or should have been discovered by the aggrieved party, or when the default occurs, whichever is later. A cause of action for indemnity accrues when the act or omission on which the claim for indemnity is based is or should have been discovered by the indemnified party, whichever is later.

(3) If an action commenced within the time limited by subsection (1) is so terminated as to leave available a remedy by another action for the same default or breach of warranty or indemnity, the other action may be commenced after the expiration of the time limited and within 6 months after the termination of the first action unless the termination resulted from voluntary discontinuance or from dismissal for failure or neglect to prosecute.

(4) This section does not alter the law on tolling of the statute of limitations nor does it apply to causes of action that have accrued before this Article becomes effective.

§2A—507. PROOF OF MARKET RENT: TIME AND PLACE

(1) Damages based on market rent (Section 2A—519 or 2A—528) are determined according to the rent for the use of the goods concerned for a lease term identical to the remaining lease term of the original lease agreement and prevailing at the times specified in Sections 2A—519 and 2A—528.

(2) If evidence of rent for the use of the goods concerned for a lease term identical to the remaining lease term of the original lease agreement and prevailing at the times or places described in this Article is not readily available, the rent prevailing within any reasonable time before or after the time described or at any other place or for a different lease term which in commercial judgment or under usage of trade would serve as a reasonable substitute for the one described may be used, making any proper allowance for the difference, including the cost of transporting the goods to or from the other place.

(3) Evidence of a relevant rent prevailing at a time or place or for a lease term other than the one described in this Article offered by one party is not admissible unless and until he [or she] has given the other party notice the court finds sufficient to prevent unfair surprise.

(4) If the prevailing rent or value of any goods regularly leased in any established market is in issue, reports in official publications or trade journals or in newspapers or periodicals of general circulation published as the reports of that market are admissible in evidence. The circumstances of the preparation of the report may be shown to affect its weight but not its admissibility.

As amended in 1990.

B. Default by Lessor

§2A—508. LESSEE'S REMEDIES

(1) If a lessor fails to deliver the goods in conformity to the lease contract (Section 2A—509) or repudiates the lease contract (Section 2A—402), or a lessee rightfully rejects the goods (Section 2A—509) or justifiably revokes acceptance of the goods (Section 2A—517), then with respect to any goods involved, and with respect to all of the goods if under an installment lease contract the value of the whole lease contract is substantially impaired (Section 2A—510), the lessor is in default under the lease contract and the lessee may:

(a) cancel the lease contract (Section 2A—505(1));

(b) recover so much of the rent and security as has been paid and is just under the circumstances;

(c) cover and recover damages as to all goods affected whether or not they have been identified to the lease contract (Sections 2A—518 and 2A—520), or recover damages for nondelivery (Sections 2A—519 and 2A—520);

(d) exercise any other rights or pursue any other remedies provided in the lease contract.

(2) If a lessor fails to deliver the goods in conformity to the lease contract or repudiates the lease contract, the lessee may also:

(a) if the goods have been identified, recover them (Section 2A—522); or

(b) in a proper case, obtain specific performance or replevy the goods (Section 2A—521).

(3) If a lessor is otherwise in default under a lease contract, the lessee may exercise the rights and pursue the remedies provided in the lease contract, which may include a right to cancel the lease, and in Section 2A—519(3).

(4) If a lessor has breached a warranty, whether express or implied, the lessee may recover damages (Section 2A—519(4)).

(5) On rightful rejection or justifiable revocation of acceptance, a lessee has a security interest in goods in the lessee's possession or control for any rent and security that has been paid and any expenses reasonably incurred in their inspection, receipt, transportation, and care and custody and may hold those goods and dispose of them in good faith and in a commercially reasonable manner, subject to Section 2A—527(5).

(6) Subject to the provisions of Section 2A—407, a lessee, on notifying the lessor of the lessee's intention to do so, may deduct all or any part of the damages resulting from any default under the lease contract from any part of the rent still due under the same lease contract.

As amended in 1990.

§2A—509. LESSEE'S RIGHTS ON IMPROPER DELIVERY; RIGHTFUL REJECTION

(1) Subject to the provisions of Section 2A—510 on default in installment lease contracts, if the goods or the tender or delivery fail in any respect to conform to the lease contract, the lessee may reject or accept the goods or accept any commercial unit or units and reject the rest of the goods.

(2) Rejection of goods is ineffective unless it is within a reasonable time after tender or delivery of the goods and the lessee seasonably notifies the lessor.

§2A—510. INSTALLMENT LEASE CONTRACTS: REJECTION AND DEFAULT

(1) Under an installment lease contract a lessee may reject any delivery that is nonconforming if the nonconformity substantially impairs the value of that delivery and cannot be cured or the nonconformity is a defect in the required documents; but if the nonconformity does not fall within subsection (2) and the lessor or the supplier gives adequate assurance of its cure, the lessee must accept that delivery.

(2) Whenever nonconformity or default with respect to one or more deliveries substantially impairs the value of the installment lease contract as a whole there is a default with respect to the whole. But, the aggrieved party reinstates the installment lease contract as a whole if the aggrieved party accepts a nonconforming delivery without seasonably notifying of cancellation or brings an action with respect only to past deliveries or demands performance as to future deliveries.

§2A—511. MERCHANT LESSEE'S DUTIES AS TO RIGHTFULLY REJECTED GOODS

(1) Subject to any security interest of a lessee (Section 2A—508(5)), if a lessor or a supplier has no agent or place of business at the market of rejection, a merchant lessee, after rejection of goods in his [or her] possession or control, shall follow any reasonable instructions received from the lessor or the supplier with respect to the goods. In the absence of those instructions, a merchant lessee shall make reasonable efforts to sell, lease, or otherwise dispose of the goods for the lessor's account if they threaten to decline in value speedily. Instructions are not reasonable if on demand indemnity for expenses is not forthcoming.

(2) If a merchant lessee (subsection (1)) or any other lessee (Section 2A—512) disposes of goods, he [or she] is entitled to reimbursement either from the lessor or the supplier or out of the proceeds for reasonable expenses of caring for and disposing of the goods and, if the expenses include no disposition commission, to such commission as is usual in the trade, or if there is none, to a reasonable sum not exceeding 10 percent of the gross proceeds.

(3) In complying with this section or Section 2A—512, the lessee is held only to good faith. Good faith conduct hereunder is neither acceptance or conversion nor the basis of an action for damages.

(4) A purchaser who purchases in good faith from a lessee pursuant to this section or Section 2A—512 takes the goods free of any rights of the lessor and the supplier even though the lessee fails to comply with one or more of the requirements of this Article.

§2A—512. LESSEE'S DUTIES AS TO RIGHTFULLY REJECTED GOODS

(1) Except as otherwise provided with respect to goods that threaten to decline in value speedily (Section 2A—511) and subject to any security interest of a lessee (Section 2A—508(5)):

(a) the lessee, after rejection of goods in the lessee's possession, shall hold them with reasonable care at the lessor's or the supplier's disposition for a reasonable time after the lessee's seasonable notification of rejection;

(b) if the lessor or the supplier gives no instructions within a reasonable time after notification of rejection, the lessee may store the rejected goods for the lessor's or the supplier's account or ship them to the lessor or the supplier or dispose of them for the lessor's or the supplier's account with reimbursement in the manner provided in Section 2A—511; but

(c) the lessee has no further obligations with regard to goods rightfully rejected.

(2) Action by the lessee pursuant to subsection (1) is not acceptance or conversion.

§2A—513. CURE BY LESSOR OF IMPROPER TENDER OR DELIVERY; REPLACEMENT

(1) If any tender or delivery by the lessor or the supplier is rejected because nonconforming and the time for performance has not yet expired, the lessor or the supplier may seasonably notify the lessee of the lessor's or the supplier's intention to cure and may then make a conforming delivery within the time provided in the lease contract.

(2) If the lessee rejects a nonconforming tender that the lessor or the supplier had reasonable grounds to believe would be acceptable with or without money allowance, the lessor or the supplier may have a further reasonable time to substitute a conforming tender if he [or she] seasonably notifies the lessee.

§2A—514. WAIVER OF LESSEE'S OBJECTIONS

(1) In rejecting goods, a lessee's failure to state a particular defect that is ascertainable by reasonable inspection precludes the lessee from relying on the defect to justify rejection or to establish default:

(a) if, stated seasonably, the lessor or the supplier could have cured it (Section 2A—513); or

(b) between merchants if the lessor or the supplier after rejection has made a request in writing for a full and final written statement of all defects on which the lessee proposes to rely.

(2) A lessee's failure to reserve rights when paying rent or other consideration against documents precludes recovery of the payment for defects apparent on the face of the documents.

§2A—515. ACCEPTANCE OF GOODS

(1) Acceptance of goods occurs after the lessee has had a reasonable opportunity to inspect the goods and

(a) the lessee signifies or acts with respect to the goods in a manner that signifies to the lessor or the supplier that the goods are conforming or that the lessee will take or retain them in spite of their nonconformity; or

(b) the lessee fails to make an effective rejection of the goods (Section 2A—509(2)).

(2) Acceptance of a part of any commercial unit is acceptance of that entire unit.

§2A—516. EFFECT OF ACCEPTANCE OF GOODS; NOTICE OF DEFAULT; BURDEN OF ESTABLISHING DEFAULT AFTER ACCEPTANCE; NOTICE OF CLAIM OR LITIGATION TO PERSON ANSWERABLE OVER

(1) A lessee must pay rent for any goods accepted in accordance with the lease contract, with due allowance for goods rightfully rejected or not delivered.

(2) A lessee's acceptance of goods precludes rejection of the goods accepted. In the case of a finance lease, if made with knowledge of a nonconformity, acceptance cannot be revoked because of it. In any other case, if made with knowledge of a nonconformity, acceptance cannot be revoked because of it unless the acceptance was on the reasonable assumption that the nonconformity would be seasonably cured. Acceptance does not of itself impair any other remedy provided by this Article or the lease agreement for nonconformity.

(3) If a tender has been accepted:

(a) within a reasonable time after the lessee discovers or should have discovered any default, the lessee shall notify the lessor and the supplier, if any, or be barred from any remedy against the party notified;

(b) except in the case of a consumer lease, within a reasonable time after the lessee receives notice of litigation for infringement or the like (Section 2A—211) the lessee shall notify the lessor or be barred from any remedy over for liability established by the litigation; and

(c) the burden is on the lessee to establish any default.

(4) If a lessee is sued for breach of a warranty or other obligation for which a lessor or a supplier is answerable over the following apply:

(a) The lessee may give the lessor or the supplier, or both, written notice of the litigation. If the notice states that the person notified may come in and defend and that if the person notified does not do so that person will be bound in any action against that person by the lessee by any determination of fact common to the two litigations, then unless the person notified after seasonable receipt of the notice does come in and defend that person is so bound.

(b) The lessor or the supplier may demand in writing that the lessee turn over control of the litigation including settlement if the claim is one for infringement or the like (Section 2A—211) or else be barred from any remedy over. If the demand states that the lessor or the supplier agrees to bear all expense and to satisfy any adverse judgment, then unless the lessee after seasonable receipt of the demand does turn over control the lessee is so barred.

(5) Subsections (3) and (4) apply to any obligation of a lessee to hold the lessor or the supplier harmless against infringement or the like (Section 2A—211).

As amended in 1990.

§2A—517. REVOCATION OF ACCEPTANCE OF GOODS

(1) A lessee may revoke acceptance of a lot or commercial unit whose nonconformity substantially impairs its value to the lessee if the lessee has accepted it:

    (a) except in the case of a finance lease, on the reasonable assumption that its nonconformity would be cured and it has not been seasonably cured; or

    (b) without discovery of the nonconformity if the lessee's acceptance was reasonably induced either by the lessor's assurances or, except in the case of a finance lease, by the difficulty of discovery before acceptance.

(2) Except in the case of a finance lease that is not a consumer lease, a lessee may revoke acceptance of a lot or commercial unit if the lessor defaults under the lease contract and the default substantially impairs the value of that lot or commercial unit to the lessee.

(3) If the lease agreement so provides, the lessee may revoke acceptance of a lot or commercial unit because of other defaults by the lessor.

(4) Revocation of acceptance must occur within a reasonable time after the lessee discovers or should have discovered the ground for it and before any substantial change in condition of the goods which is not caused by the nonconformity. Revocation is not effective until the lessee notifies the lessor.

(5) A lessee who so revokes has the same rights and duties with regard to the goods involved as if the lessee had rejected them.

As amended in 1990.

§2A—518. COVER; SUBSTITUTE GOODS

(1) After a default by a lessor under the lease contract of the type described in Section 2A—508(1), or, if agreed, after other default by the lessor, the lessee may cover by making any purchase or lease of or contract to purchase or lease goods in substitution for those due from the lessor.

(2) Except as otherwise provided with respect to damages liquidated in the lease agreement (Section 2A—504) or otherwise determined pursuant to agreement of the parties (Sections 1—102(3) and 2A—503), if a lessee's cover is by lease agreement substantially similar to the original lease agreement and the new lease agreement is made in good faith and in a commercially reasonable manner, the lessee may recover from the lessor as damages (i) the present value, as of the date of the commencement of the term of the new lease agreement, of the rent under the new lease agreement applicable to that period of the new lease term which is comparable to the then remaining term of the original lease agreement minus the present value as of the same date of the total rent for the then remaining lease term of the original lease agreement, and (ii) any incidental or consequential damages, less expenses saved in consequence of the lessor's default.

(3) If a lessee's cover is by lease agreement that for any reason does not qualify for treatment under subsection (2), or is by purchase or otherwise, the lessee may recover from the lessor as if the lessee had elected not to cover and Section 2A—519 governs.

As amended in 1990.

§2A—519. LESSEE'S DAMAGES FOR NON-DELIVERY, REPUDIATION, DEFAULT, AND BREACH OF WARRANTY IN REGARD TO ACCEPTED GOODS

(1) Except as otherwise provided with respect to damages liquidated in the lease agreement (Section 2A—504) or otherwise determined pursuant to agreement of the parties (Sections 1—102(3) and 2A—503), if a lessee elects not to cover or a lessee elects to cover and the cover is by lease agreement that for any reason does not qualify for treatment under Section 2A—518(2), or is by purchase or otherwise, the measure of damages for non-delivery or repudiation by the lessor or for rejection or revocation of acceptance by the lessee is the present value, as of the date of the default, of the then market rent minus the present value as of the same date of the original rent, computed for the remaining lease term of the original lease agreement, together with incidental and consequential damages, less expenses saved in consequence of the lessor's default.

(2) Market rent is to be determined as of the place for tender or, in cases of rejection after arrival or revocation of acceptance, as of the place of arrival.

(3) Except as otherwise agreed, if the lessee has accepted goods and given notification (Section 2A—516 (3)), the measure of damages for non-conforming tender or delivery or other default by a lessor is the loss resulting in the ordinary course of events from the lessor's default as determined in any manner that is reasonable together with incidental and consequential damages, less expenses saved in consequence of the lessor's default.

(4) Except as otherwise agreed, the measure of damages for breach of warranty is the present value at the time and place of acceptance of the difference between the value of the use of the goods accepted and the value if they had been as warranted for the lease term, unless special circumstances show proximate damages of a different amount, together with incidental and consequential damages, less expenses saved in consequence of the lessor's default or breach of warranty.

As amended in 1990.

§2A—520. LESSEE'S INCIDENTAL AND CONSEQUENTIAL DAMAGES

(1) Incidental damages resulting from a lessor's default include expenses reasonably incurred in inspection, receipt, transportation, and care and custody of goods rightfully rejected or goods the acceptance of which is justifiably revoked, any commercially reasonable charges, expenses or commissions in connection with effecting cover, and any other reasonable expense incident to the default.

(2) Consequential damages resulting from a lessor's default include:

(a) any loss resulting from general or particular requirements and needs of which the lessor at the time of contracting had reason to know and which could not reasonably be prevented by cover or otherwise; and

(b) injury to person or property proximately resulting from any breach of warranty.

§2A—521. LESSEE'S RIGHT TO SPECIFIC PERFORMANCE OR REPLEVIN

(1) Specific performance may be decreed if the goods are unique or in other proper circumstances.

(2) A decree for specific performance may include any terms and conditions as to payment of the rent, damages, or other relief that the court deems just.

(3) A lessee has a right of replevin, detinue, sequestration, claim and delivery, or the like for goods identified to the lease contract if after reasonable effort the lessee is unable to effect cover for those goods or the circumstances reasonably indicate that the effort will be unavailing.

§2A—522. LESSEE'S RIGHT TO GOODS ON LESSOR'S INSOLVENCY

(1) Subject to subsection (2) and even though the goods have not been shipped, a lessee who has paid a part or all of the rent and security for goods identified to a lease contract (Section 2A—217) on making and keeping good a tender of any unpaid portion of the rent and security due under the lease contract may recover the goods identified from the lessor if the lessor becomes insolvent within 10 days after receipt of the first installment of rent and security.

(2) A lessee acquires the right to recover goods identified to a lease contract only if they conform to the lease contract.

C. Default by Lessee

§2A—523. LESSOR'S REMEDIES

(1) If a lessee wrongfully rejects or revokes acceptance of goods or fails to make a payment when due or repudiates with respect to a part or the whole, then, with respect to any goods involved, and with respect to all of the goods if under an installment lease contract the value of the whole lease contract is substantially impaired (Section 2A—510), the lessee is in default under the lease contract and the lessor may:

(a) cancel the lease contract (Section 2A—505 (1));

(b) proceed respecting goods not identified to the lease contract (Section 2A—524);

(c) withhold delivery of the goods and take possession of goods previously delivered (Section 2A—525);

(d) stop delivery of the goods by any bailee (Section 2A—526);

(e) dispose of the goods and recover damages (Section 2A—527), or retain the goods and recover damages (Section 2A—528), or in a proper case recover rent (Section 2A—529)

(f) exercise any other rights or pursue any other remedies provided in the lease contract.

(2) If a lessor does not fully exercise a right or obtain a remedy to which the lessor is entitled under subsection (1), the lessor may recover the loss resulting in the ordinary course of events from the lessee's default as determined in any reasonable manner, together with incidental damages, less expenses saved in consequence of the lessee's default.

(3) If a lessee is otherwise in default under a lease contract, the lessor may exercise the rights and pursue the remedies provided in the lease contract, which may include a right to cancel the lease. In addition, unless otherwise provided in the lease contract:

(a) if the default substantially impairs the value of the lease contract to the lessor, the lessor may exercise the rights and pursue the remedies provided in subsections (1) or (2); or

(b) if the default does not substantially impair the value of the lease contract to the lessor, the lessor may recover as provided in subsection (2).

As amended in 1990.

§2A—524. LESSOR'S RIGHT TO IDENTIFY GOODS TO LEASE CONTRACT

(1) After default by the lessee under the lease contract of the type described in Section 2A—523(1) or 2A—523(3) (a) or, if agreed, after other default by the lessee, the lessor may:

(a) identify to the lease contract conforming goods not already identified if at the time the lessor learned of the default they were in the lessor's or the supplier's possession or control; and

(b) dispose of goods (Section 2A—527(1)) that demonstrably have been intended for the particular lease contract even though those goods are unfinished.

(2) If the goods are unfinished, in the exercise of reasonable commercial judgment for the purposes of avoiding loss and of effective realization, an aggrieved lessor or the supplier may either complete manufacture and wholly identify the goods to the lease contract or cease manufacture and lease, sell, or otherwise dispose of the goods for scrap or salvage value or proceed in any other reasonable manner.

As amended in 1990.

§2A—525. LESSOR'S RIGHT TO POSSESSION OF GOODS

(1) If a lessor discovers the lessee to be insolvent, the lessor may refuse to deliver the goods.

(2) After a default by the lessee under the lease contract of the type described in Section 2A—523(1) or 2A—523(3)(a) or, if agreed, after other default by the lessee, the lessor has the right to take possession of the goods. If the lease contract so provides, the lessor may require the lessee to assemble the goods and make them available to the lessor at a place to be designated by the lessor which is reasonably convenient to both parties. Without removal, the lessor may render unusable any goods employed in trade or business, and may dispose of goods on the lessee's premises (Section 2A—527).

(3) The lessor may proceed under subsection (2) without judicial process if that can be done without breach of the peace or the lessor may proceed by action.

As amended in 1990.

§2A—526. LESSOR'S STOPPAGE OF DELIVERY IN TRANSIT OR OTHERWISE

(1) A lessor may stop delivery of goods in the possession of a carrier or other bailee if the lessor discovers the lessee to be insolvent and may stop delivery of carload, truckload, planeload, or larger shipments of express or freight if the lessee repudiates or fails to make a payment due before delivery, whether for rent, security or otherwise under the lease contract, or for any other reason the lessor has a right to withhold or take possession of the goods.

(2) In pursuing its remedies under subsection (1), the lessor may stop delivery until

> (a) receipt of the goods by the lessee;
> (b) acknowledgment to the lessee by any bailee of the goods, except a carrier, that the bailee holds the goods for the lessee; or
> (c) such an acknowledgment to the lessee by a carrier via reshipment or as warehouseman.

> (3) (a) To stop delivery, a lessor shall so notify as to enable the bailee by reasonable diligence to prevent delivery of the goods.

> (b) After notification, the bailee shall hold and deliver the goods according to the directions of the lessor, but the lessor is liable to the bailee for any ensuing charges or damages.
> (c) A carrier who has issued a nonnegotiable bill of lading is not obliged to obey a notification to stop received from a person other than the consignor.

§2A—527. LESSOR'S RIGHTS TO DISPOSE OF GOODS

(1) After a default by a lessee under the lease contract of the type described in Section 2A—523(1) or 2A—523(3)(a) or after the lessor refuses to deliver or takes possession of goods (Section 2A—525 or 2A—526), or, if agreed, after other default by a lessee, the lessor may dispose of the goods concerned or the undelivered balance thereof by lease, sale, or otherwise.

(2) Except as otherwise provided with respect to damages liquidated in the lease agreement (Section 2A—504) or otherwise determined pursuant to agreement of the parties (Sections 1—102(3) and 2A—503), if the disposition is by lease agreement substantially similar to the original lease agreement and the new lease agreement is made in good faith and in a commercially reasonable manner, the lessor may recover from the lessee as damages (i) accrued and unpaid rent as of the date of the commencement of the term of the new lease agreement, (ii) the present value, as of the same date, of the total rent for the then remaining lease term of the original lease agreement minus the present value, as of the same date, of the rent under the new lease agreement applicable to that period of the new lease term which is comparable to the then remaining term of the original lease agreement, and (iii) any incidental damages allowed under Section 2A—530, less expenses saved in consequence of the lessee's default.

(3) If the lessor's disposition is by lease agreement that for any reason does not qualify for treatment under subsection (2), or is by sale or otherwise, the lessor may recover from the lessee as if the lessor had elected not to dispose of the goods and Section 2A—528 governs.

(4) A subsequent buyer or lessee who buys or leases from the lessor in good faith for value as a result of a disposition under this section takes the goods free of the original lease contract and any rights of the original lessee even though the lessor fails to comply with one or more of the requirements of this Article.

(5) The lessor is not accountable to the lessee for any profit made on any disposition. A lessee who has rightfully rejected or justifiably revoked acceptance shall account to the lessor for any excess over the amount of the lessee's security interest (Section 2A—508(5)).

As amended in 1990.

§2A—528. LESSOR'S DAMAGES FOR NON-ACCEPTANCE, FAILURE TO PAY, REPUDIATION, OR OTHER DEFAULT

(1) Except as otherwise provided with respect to damages liquidated in the lease agreement (Section 2A—504) or otherwise determined pursuant to agreement of the parties (Section 1—102(3) and 2A—503), if a lessor elects to retain the goods or a lessor elects to dispose of the goods and the disposition is by lease agreement that for any reason does not qualify for treatment under Section 2A—527(2), or is by sale or otherwise, the lessor may recover from the lessee as damages for a default of the type described in Section 2A—523(1) or 2A—523(3)(a), or if agreed, for other default of the lessee, (i) accrued and unpaid rent as of the date of the default if the lessee has never taken possession of the goods, or, if the lessee has taken possession of the goods, as of the date the lessor repossesses the goods or an earlier date on which the lessee makes a tender of the goods to the lessor, (ii) the present value as of the date determined under clause (i) of the total rent for the then remaining lease term of the original lease agreement minus the present value as of the same date of the market rent as the place where the goods are located computed for the same lease term, and (iii) any incidental damages allowed under Section 2A—530, less expenses saved in consequence of the lessee's default.

(2) If the measure of damages provided in subsection (1) is inadequate to put a lessor in as good a position as performance would have, the measure of damages is the present value of the profit, including reasonable overhead, the lessor would have made from full performance by the lessee, together with any incidental damages allowed under Section 2A—530, due allowance for costs reasonably incurred and due credit for payments or proceeds of disposition.

As amended in 1990.

§2A—529. LESSOR'S ACTION FOR THE RENT

(1) After default by the lessee under the lease contract of the type described in Section 2A—523(1) or 2A—523(3)(a) or, if agreed, after other default by the lessee, if the lessor complies with subsection (2), the lessor may recover from the lessee as damages:

> (a) for goods accepted by the lessee and not repossessed by or tendered to the lessor, and for conforming goods lost or damaged within a commercially reasonable time after risk of loss passes to the lessee (Section 2A—219), (i) accrued and unpaid rent as of the date of entry of judgment in favor of the lessor (ii) the present value as of the same date of the rent for the then remaining lease term of the lease agreement, and (iii) any incidental damages allowed under

Section 2A—530, less expenses saved in consequence of the lessee's default; and

> (b) for goods identified to the lease contract if the lessor is unable after reasonable effort to dispose of them at a reasonable price or the circumstances reasonably indicate that effort will be unavailing, (i) accrued and unpaid rent as of the date of entry of judgment in favor of the lessor, (ii) the present value as of the same date of the rent for the then remaining lease term of the lease agreement, and (iii) any incidental damages allowed under Section 2A—530, less expenses saved in consequence of the lessee's default.

(2) Except as provided in subsection (3), the lessor shall hold for the lessee for the remaining lease term of the lease agreement any goods that have been identified to the lease contract and are in the lessor's control.

(3) The lessor may dispose of the goods at any time before collection of the judgment for damages obtained pursuant to subsection (1). If the disposition is before the end of the remaining lease term of the lease agreement, the lessor's recovery against the lessee for damages is governed by Section 2A—527 or Section 2A—528, and the lessor will cause an appropriate credit to be provided against a judgment for damages to the extent that the amount of the judgment exceeds the recovery available pursuant to Section 2A—527 or 2A—528.

(4) Payment of the judgment for damages obtained pursuant to subsection (1) entitles the lessee to the use and possession of the goods not then disposed of for the remaining lease term of and in accordance with the lease agreement.

(5) After default by the lessee under the lease contract of the type described in Section 2A—523(1) or Section 2A—523(3)(a) or, if agreed, after other default by the lessee, a lessor who is held not entitled to rent under this section must nevertheless be awarded damages for non-acceptance under Sections 2A—527 and 2A—528.

As amended in 1990.

§2A—530. LESSOR'S INCIDENTAL DAMAGES

Incidental damages to an aggrieved lessor include any commercially reasonable charges, expenses, or commissions incurred in stopping delivery, in the transportation, care and custody of goods after the lessee's default, in connection with return or disposition of the goods, or otherwise resulting from the default.

§2A—531. STANDING TO SUE THIRD PARTIES FOR INJURY TO GOODS

(1) If a third party so deals with goods that have been identified to a lease contract as to cause actionable injury to a party to the lease contract (a) the lessor has a right of

action against the third party, and (b) the lessee also has a right of action against the third party if the lessee:

    (i) has a security interest in the goods;

    (ii) has an insurable interest in the goods; or

    (iii) bears the risk of loss under the lease contract or has since the injury assumed that risk as against the lessor and the goods have been converted or destroyed.

(2) If at the time of the injury the party plaintiff did not bear the risk of loss as against the other party to the lease contract and there is no arrangement between them for disposition of the recovery, his [or her] suit or settlement, subject to his [or her] own interest, is as a fiduciary for the other party to the lease contract.

(3) Either party with the consent of the other may sue for the benefit of whom it may concern.

§2A—532. LESSOR'S RIGHTS TO RESIDUAL INTEREST

In addition to any other recovery permitted by this Article or other law, the lessor may recover from the lessee an amount that will fully compensate the lessor for any loss of or damage to the lessor's residual interest in the goods caused by the default of the lessee.

As added in 1990.

REVISED ARTICLE 3
NEGOTIABLE INSTRUMENTS

Part 1 General Provisions and Definitions

§3—101. SHORT TITLE

This Article may be cited as Uniform Commercial Code— Negotiable Instruments.

§3—102. SUBJECT MATTER

(a) This Article applies to negotiable instruments. It does not apply to money, to payment orders governed by Article 4A, or to securities governed by Article 8.

(b) If there is conflict between this Article and Article 4 or 9, Articles 4 and 9 govern.

(c) Regulations of the Board of Governors of the Federal Reserve System and operating circulars of the Federal Reserve Banks supersede any inconsistent provision of this Article to the extent of the inconsistency.

§3—103. DEFINITIONS

(a) In this Article:

    (1) "Acceptor" means a drawee who has accepted a draft.

    (2) "Drawee" means a person ordered in a draft to make payment.

    (3) "Drawer" means a person who signs or is identified in a draft as a person ordering payment.

    (4) "Good faith" means honesty in fact and the observance of reasonable commercial standards of fair dealing.

    (5) "Maker" means a person who signs or is identified in a note as a person undertaking to pay.

    (6) "Order" means a written instruction to pay money signed by the person giving the instruction. The instruction may be addressed to any person, including the person giving the instruction, or to one or more persons jointly or in the alternative but not in succession. An authorization to pay is not an order unless the person authorized to pay is also instructed to pay.

    (7) "Ordinary care" in the case of a person engaged in business means observance of reasonable commercial standards, prevailing in the area in which the person is located, with respect to the business in which the person is engaged. In the case of a bank that takes an instrument for processing for collection or payment by automated means, reasonable commercial standards do not require the bank to examine the instrument if the failure to examine does not violate the bank's prescribed procedures and the bank's procedures do not vary unreasonably from general banking usage not disapproved by this Article or Article 4.

    (8) "Party" means a party to an instrument.

    (9) "Promise" means a written undertaking to pay money signed by the person undertaking to pay. An acknowledgment of an obligation by the obligor is not a promise unless the obligor also undertakes to pay the obligation.

    (10) "Prove" with respect to a fact means to meet the burden of establishing the fact (Section 1—201(8)).

    (11) "Remitter" means a person who purchases an instrument from its issuer if the instrument is payable to an identified person other than the purchaser.

(b) [Other definitions' section references deleted.]

(c) [Other definitions' section references deleted.]

(d) In addition, Article 1 contains general definitions and principles of construction and interpretation applicable throughout this Article.

§3—104. NEGOTIABLE INSTRUMENT

(a) Except as provided in subsections (c) and (d), "negotiable instrument" means an unconditional promise or order to pay a fixed amount of money, with or without interest or other charges described in the promise or order, if it:

> (1) is payable to bearer or to order at the time it is issued or first comes into possession of a holder;
>
> (2) is payable on demand or at a definite time; and
>
> (3) does not state any other undertaking or instruction by the person promising or ordering payment to do any act in addition to the payment of money, but the promise or order may contain (i) an undertaking or power to give, maintain, or protect collateral to secure payment, (ii) an authorization or power to the holder to confess judgment or realize on or dispose of collateral, or (iii) a waiver of the benefit of any law intended for the advantage or protection of an obligor.

(b) "Instrument" means a negotiable instrument.

(c) An order that meets all of the requirements of subsection (a), except paragraph (1), and otherwise falls within the definition of "check" in subsection (f) is a negotiable instrument and a check.

(d) A promise or order other than a check is not an instrument if, at the time it is issued or first comes into possession of a holder, it contains a conspicuous statement, however expressed, to the effect that the promise or order is not negotiable or is not an instrument governed by this Article.

(e) An instrument is a "note" if it is a promise and is a "draft" if it is an order. If an instrument falls within the definition of both "note" and "draft," a person entitled to enforce the instrument may treat it as either.

(f) "Check" means (i) a draft, other than a documentary draft, payable on demand and drawn on a bank or (ii) a cashier's check or teller's check. An instrument may be a check even though it is described on its face by another term, such as "money order."

(g) "Cashier's check" means a draft with respect to which the drawer and drawee are the same bank or branches of the same bank.

(h) "Teller's check" means a draft drawn by a bank (i) on another bank, or (ii) payable at or through a bank.

(i) "Traveler's check" means an instrument that (i) is payable on demand, (ii) is drawn on or payable at or through a bank, (iii) is designated by the term "traveler's check" or by a substantially similar term, and (iv) requires, as a condition to payment, a countersignature by a person whose specimen signature appears on the instrument.

(j) "Certificate of deposit" means an instrument containing an acknowledgment by a bank that a sum of money has been received by the bank and a promise by the bank to repay the sum of money. A certificate of deposit is a note of the bank.

§3—105. ISSUE OF INSTRUMENT

(a) "Issue" means the first delivery of an instrument by the maker or drawer, whether to a holder or nonholder, for the purpose of giving rights on the instrument to any person.

(b) An unissued instrument, or an unissued incomplete instrument that is completed, is binding on the maker or drawer, but nonissuance is a defense. An instrument that is conditionally issued or is issued for a special purpose is binding on the maker or drawer, but failure of the condition or special purpose to be fulfilled is a defense.

(c) "Issuer" applies to issued and unissued instruments and means a maker or drawer of an instrument.

§3—106. UNCONDITIONAL PROMISE OR ORDER

(a) Except as provided in this section, for the purposes of Section 3—104(a), a promise or order is unconditional unless it states (i) an express condition to payment, (ii) that the promise or order is subject to or governed by another writing, or (iii) that rights or obligations with respect to the promise or order are stated in another writing. A reference to another writing does not of itself make the promise or order conditional.

(b) A promise or order is not made conditional (i) by a reference to another writing for a statement of rights with respect to collateral, prepayment, or acceleration, or (ii) because payment is limited to resort to a particular fund or source.

(c) If a promise or order requires, as a condition to payment, a countersignature by a person whose specimen signature appears on the promise or order, the condition does not make the promise or order conditional for the purposes of Section 3—104(a). If the person whose specimen signature appears on an instrument fails to countersign the instrument, the failure to countersign is a defense to the obligation of the issuer, but the failure does not prevent a transferee of the instrument from becoming a holder of the instrument.

(d) If a promise or order at the time it is issued or first comes into possession of a holder contains a statement, required by applicable statutory or administrative law, to the effect that the rights of a holder or transferee are subject to claims or defenses that the issuer could assert against the original payee, the promise or order is not thereby made conditional for the purposes of Section 3—104(a); but if the promise or order is an instrument, there cannot be a holder in due course of the instrument.

§3—107. INSTRUMENT PAYABLE IN FOREIGN MONEY

Unless the instrument otherwise provides, an instrument that states the amount payable in foreign money may be paid in the foreign money or in an equivalent amount in dollars calculated by using the current bank-offered spot rate at the place of payment for the purchase of dollars on the day on which the instrument is paid.

§3—108. PAYABLE ON DEMAND OR AT DEFINITE TIME

(a) A promise or order is "payable on demand" if it (i) states that it is payable on demand or at sight, or otherwise indicates that it is payable at the will of the holder, or (ii) does not state any time of payment.

(b) A promise or order is "payable at a definite time" if it is payable on elapse of a definite period of time after sight or acceptance or at a fixed date or dates or at a time or times readily ascertainable at the time the promise or order is issued, subject to rights of (i) prepayment, (ii) acceleration, (iii) extension at the option of the holder, or (iv) extension to a further definite time at the option of the maker or acceptor or automatically upon or after a specified act or event.

(c) If an instrument, payable at a fixed date, is also payable upon demand made before the fixed date, the instrument is payable on demand until the fixed date and, if demand for payment is not made before that date, becomes payable at a definite time on the fixed date.

§3—109. PAYABLE TO BEARER OR TO ORDER

(a) A promise or order is payable to bearer if it:

(1) states that it is payable to bearer or to the order of bearer or otherwise indicates that the person in possession of the promise or order is entitled to payment;

(2) does not state a payee; or

(3) states that it is payable to or to the order of cash or otherwise indicates that it is not payable to an identified person.

(b) A promise or order that is not payable to bearer is payable to order if it is payable (i) to the order of an identified person or (ii) to an identified person or order. A promise or order that is payable to order is payable to the identified person.

(c) An instrument payable to bearer may become payable to an identified person if it is specially indorsed pursuant to Section 3—205(a). An instrument payable to an identified person may become payable to bearer if it is indorsed in blank pursuant to Section 3—205(b).

§3—110. IDENTIFICATION OF PERSON TO WHOM INSTRUMENT IS PAYABLE

(a) The person to whom an instrument is initially payable is determined by the intent of the person, whether or not authorized, signing as, or in the name or behalf of, the issuer of the instrument. The instrument is payable to the person intended by the signer even if that person is identified in the instrument by a name or other identification that is not that of the intended person. If more than one person signs in the name or behalf of the issuer of an instrument and all the signers do not intend the same person as payee, the instrument is payable to any person intended by one or more of the signers.

(b) If the signature of the issuer of an instrument is made by automated means, such as a check-writing machine, the payee of the instrument is determined by the intent of the person who supplied the name or identification of the payee, whether or not authorized to do so.

(c) A person to whom an instrument is payable may be identified in any way, including by name, identifying number, office, or account number. For the purpose of determining the holder of an instrument, the following rules apply:

(1) If an instrument is payable to an account and the account is identified only by number, the instrument is payable to the person to whom the account is payable. If an instrument is payable to an account identified by number and by the name of a person, the instrument is payable to the named person, whether or not that person is the owner of the account identified by number.

(2) If an instrument is payable to:

(i) a trust, an estate, or a person described as trustee or representative of a trust or estate, the instrument is payable to the trustee, the representative, or a successor of either, whether or not the beneficiary or estate is also named;

(ii) a person described as agent or similar representative of a named or identified person, the instrument is payable to the represented person, the representative, or a successor of the representative;

(iii) a fund or organization that is not a legal entity, the instrument is payable to a representative of the members of the fund or organization; or

(iv) an office or to a person described as holding an office, the instrument is payable to the named person, the incumbent of the office, or a successor to the incumbent.

(d) If an instrument is payable to two or more persons alternatively, it is payable to any of them and may be negotiated, discharged, or enforced by any or all of them in possession of the instrument. If an instrument is payable to two or more persons not alternatively, it is payable to all of them and may be negotiated, discharged, or enforced only by all of them. If an instrument payable to two or more persons is ambiguous as to whether it is payable to the persons alternatively, the instrument is payable to the persons alternatively.

§3—111. PLACE OF PAYMENT

Except as otherwise provided for items in Article 4, an instrument is payable at the place of payment stated in the instrument. If no place of payment is stated, an instrument is payable at the address of the drawee or maker stated in the instrument. If no address is stated, the place of payment is the place of business of the drawee or maker. If a drawee or maker has more than one place of business, the place of payment is any place of business of the drawee or maker chosen by the person entitled to enforce the instrument. If the drawee or maker has no place of business, the place of payment is the residence of the drawee or maker.

§3—112. INTEREST

(a) Unless otherwise provided in the instrument, (i) an instrument is not payable with interest, and (ii) interest on an interest-bearing instrument is payable from the date of the instrument.

(b) Interest may be stated in an instrument as a fixed or variable amount of money or it may be expressed as a fixed or variable rate or rates. The amount or rate of interest may be stated or described in the instrument in any manner and may require reference to information not contained in the instrument. If an instrument provides for interest, but the amount of interest payable cannot be ascertained from the description, interest is payable at the judgment rate in effect at the place of payment of the instrument and at the time interest first accrues.

§3—113. DATE OF INSTRUMENT

(a) An instrument may be antedated or postdated. The date stated determines the time of payment if the instrument is payable at a fixed period after date. Except as provided in Section 4—401(c), an instrument payable on demand is not payable before the date of the instrument.

(b) If an instrument is undated, its date is the date of its issue or, in the case of an unissued instrument, the date it first comes into possession of a holder.

§3—114. CONTRADICTORY TERMS OF INSTRUMENT

If an instrument contains contradictory terms, typewritten terms prevail over printed terms, handwritten terms prevail over both, and words prevail over numbers.

§3—115. INCOMPLETE INSTRUMENT

(a) "Incomplete instrument" means a signed writing, whether or not issued by the signer, the contents of which show at the time of signing that it is incomplete but that the signer intended it to be completed by the addition of words or numbers.

(b) Subject to subsection (c), if an incomplete instrument is an instrument under Section 3—104, it may be enforced according to its terms if it is not completed, or according to its terms as augmented by completion. If an incomplete instrument is not an instrument under Section 3—104, but, after completion, the requirements of Section 3—104 are met, the instrument may be enforced according to its terms as augmented by completion.

(c) If words or numbers are added to an incomplete instrument without authority of the signer, there is an alteration of the incomplete instrument under Section 3—407.

(d) The burden of establishing that words or numbers were added to an incomplete instrument without authority of the signer is on the person asserting the lack of authority.

§3—116. JOINT AND SEVERAL LIABILITY; CONTRIBUTION

(a) Except as otherwise provided in the instrument, two or more persons who have the same liability on an instrument as makers, drawers, acceptors, indorsers who indorse as joint payees, or anomalous indorsers are jointly and severally liable in the capacity in which they sign.

(b) Except as provided in Section 3—419(e) or by agreement of the affected parties, a party having joint and several liability who pays the instrument is entitled to receive from any party having the same joint and several liability contribution in accordance with applicable law.

(c) Discharge of one party having joint and several liability by a person entitled to enforce the instrument does not affect the right under subsection (b) of a party having the same joint and several liability to receive contribution from the party discharged.

§3—117. OTHER AGREEMENTS AFFECTING INSTRUMENT

Subject to applicable law regarding exclusion of proof of contemporaneous or previous agreements, the obligation of a party to an instrument to pay the instrument may be modified, supplemented, or nullified by a separate agreement of the obligor and a person entitled to enforce the instrument, if the instrument is issued or the obligation is incurred in reliance on the agreement or as part of the same transaction giving rise to the agreement. To the extent an obligation is modified, supplemented, or nullified by an agreement under this section, the agreement is a defense to the obligation.

§3—118. STATUTE OF LIMITATIONS

(a) Except as provided in subsection (e), an action to enforce the obligation of a party to pay a note payable at a definite time must be commenced within six years after the due date or dates stated in the note or, if a due date is accelerated, within six years after the accelerated due date.

(b) Except as provided in subsection (d) or (e), if demand for payment is made to the maker of a note payable on demand, an action to enforce the obligation of a party to pay the note must be commenced within six years after the demand. If no demand for payment is made to the maker, an action to enforce the note is barred if neither principal nor interest on the note has been paid for a continuous period of 10 years.

(c) Except as provided in subsection (d), an action to enforce the obligation of a party to an unaccepted draft to pay the draft must be commenced within three years after dishonor of the draft or 10 years after the date of the draft, whichever period expires first.

(d) An action to enforce the obligation of the acceptor of a certified check or the issuer of a teller's check, cashier's check, or traveler's check must be commenced within three years after demand for payment is made to the acceptor or issuer, as the case may be.

(e) An action to enforce the obligation of a party to a certificate of deposit to pay the instrument must be commenced within six years after demand for payment is made to the maker, but if the instrument states a due date and the maker is not required to pay before that date, the six-year period begins when a demand for payment is in effect and the due date has passed.

(f) An action to enforce the obligation of a party to pay an accepted draft, other than a certified check, must be commenced (i) within six years after the due date or dates stated in the draft or acceptance if the obligation of the acceptor is payable at a definite time, or (ii) within six years after the date of the acceptance if the obligation of the acceptor is payable on demand.

(g) Unless governed by other law regarding claims for indemnity or contribution, an action (i) for conversion of an instrument, for money had and received, or like action based on conversion, (ii) for breach of warranty, or (iii) to enforce an obligation, duty, or right arising under this Article and not governed by this section must be commenced within three years after the [cause of action] accrues.

§3—119. NOTICE OF RIGHT TO DEFEND ACTION

In an action for breach of an obligation for which a third person is answerable over pursuant to this Article or Article 4, the defendant may give the third person written notice of the litigation, and the person notified may then give similar notice to any other person who is answerable over. If the notice states (i) that the person notified may come in and defend and (ii) that failure to do so will bind the person notified in an action later brought by the person giving the notice as to any determination of fact common to the two litigations, the person notified is so bound unless after seasonable receipt of the notice the person notified does come in and defend.

Part 2 Negotiation, Transfer, and Indorsement

§3—201. NEGOTIATION

(a) "Negotiation" means a transfer of possession, whether voluntary or involuntary, of an instrument by a person other than the issuer to a person who thereby becomes its holder.

(b) Except for negotiation by a remitter, if an instrument is payable to an identified person, negotiation requires transfer of possession of the instrument and its indorsement by the holder. If an instrument is payable to bearer, it may be negotiated by transfer of possession alone.

§3—202. NEGOTIATION SUBJECT TO RESCISSION

(a) Negotiation is effective even if obtained (i) from an infant, a corporation exceeding its powers, or a person without capacity, (ii) by fraud, duress, or mistake, or (iii) in breach of duty or as part of an illegal transaction.

(b) To the extent permitted by other law, negotiation may be rescinded or may be subject to other remedies, but those remedies may not be asserted against a subsequent holder in due course or a person paying the instrument in good faith and without knowledge of facts that are a basis for rescission or other remedy.

§3—203. TRANSFER OF INSTRUMENT; RIGHTS ACQUIRED BY TRANSFER

(a) An instrument is transferred when it is delivered by a person other than its issuer for the purpose of giving to the person receiving delivery the right to enforce the instrument.

(b) Transfer of an instrument, whether or not the transfer is a negotiation, vests in the transferee any right of the transferor to enforce the instrument, including any right as a holder in due course, but the transferee cannot acquire rights of a holder in due course by a transfer, directly or indirectly, from a holder in due course if the transferee engaged in fraud or illegality affecting the instrument.

(c) Unless otherwise agreed, if an instrument is transferred for value and the transferee does not become a holder because of lack of indorsement by the transferor, the transferee has a specifically enforceable right to the unqualified indorsement of the transferor, but negotiation of the instrument does not occur until the indorsement is made.

(d) If a transferor purports to transfer less than the entire instrument, negotiation of the instrument does not occur. The transferee obtains no rights under this Article and has only the rights of a partial assignee.

§3—204. INDORSEMENT

(a) "Indorsement" means a signature, other than that of a signer as maker, drawer, or acceptor, that alone or accompanied by other words is made on an instrument for the purpose of (i) negotiating the instrument, (ii) restricting payment of the instrument, or (iii) incurring indorser's liability on the instrument, but regardless of the intent of the signer, a signature and its accompanying words is an indorsement unless the accompanying words, terms of the instrument, place of the signature, or other circumstances unambiguously indicate that the signature was made for a purpose other than indorsement. For the purpose of determining whether a signature is made on an instrument, a paper affixed to the instrument is a part of the instrument.

(b) "Indorser" means a person who makes an indorsement.

(c) For the purpose of determining whether the transferee of an instrument is a holder, an indorsement that transfers a security interest in the instrument is effective as an unqualified indorsement of the instrument.

(d) If an instrument is payable to a holder under a name that is not the name of the holder, indorsement may be made by the holder in the name stated in the instrument or in the holder's name or both, but signature in both names may be required by a person paying or taking the instrument for value or collection.

§3—205. SPECIAL INDORSEMENT; BLANK INDORSEMENT; ANOMALOUS INDORSEMENT

(a) If an indorsement is made by the holder of an instrument, whether payable to an identified person or payable to bearer, and the indorsement identifies a person to whom it makes the instrument payable, it is a "special indorsement." When specially indorsed, an instrument becomes payable to the identified person and may be negotiated only by the indorsement of that person. The principles stated in Section 3—110 apply to special indorsements.

(b) If an indorsement is made by the holder of an instrument and it is not a special indorsement, it is a "blank indorsement." When indorsed in blank, an instrument becomes payable to bearer and may be negotiated by transfer of possession alone until specially indorsed.

(c) The holder may convert a blank indorsement that consists only of a signature into a special indorsement by writing, above the signature of the indorser, words identifying the person to whom the instrument is made payable.

(d) "Anomalous indorsement" means an indorsement made by a person who is not the holder of the instrument. An anomalous indorsement does not affect the manner in which the instrument may be negotiated.

§3—206. RESTRICTIVE INDORSEMENT

(a) An indorsement limiting payment to a particular person or otherwise prohibiting further transfer or negotiation of the instrument is not effective to prevent further transfer or negotiation of the instrument.

(b) An indorsement stating a condition to the right of the indorsee to receive payment does not affect the right of the indorsee to enforce the instrument. A person paying the instrument or taking it for value or collection may disregard the condition, and the rights and liabilities of that person are not affected by whether the condition has been fulfilled.

(c) If an instrument bears an indorsement (i) described in Section 4—201(b), or (ii) in blank or to a particular bank using the words "for deposit," "for collection," or other words indicating a purpose of having the instrument collected by a bank for the indorser or for a particular account, the following rules apply:

(1) A person, other than a bank, who purchases the instrument when so indorsed converts the instrument unless the amount paid for the instrument is received by the indorser or applied consistently with the indorsement.

(2) A depositary bank that purchases the instrument or takes it for collection when so indorsed converts the instrument unless the amount paid by the bank with respect to the instrument is received by the indorser or applied consistently with the indorsement.

(3) A payor bank that is also the depositary bank or that takes the instrument for immediate payment over the counter from a person other than a collecting bank converts the instrument unless the proceeds of the instrument are received by the indorser or applied consistently with the indorsement.

(4) Except as otherwise provided in paragraph (3), a payor bank or intermediary bank may disregard the indorsement and is not liable if the proceeds of the instrument are not received by the indorser or applied consistently with the indorsement.

(d) Except for an indorsement covered by subsection (c), if an instrument bears an indorsement using words to the effect that payment is to be made to the indorsee as agent, trustee, or other fiduciary for the benefit of the indorser or another person, the following rules apply:

(1) Unless there is notice of breach of fiduciary duty as provided in Section 3—307, a person who purchases the instrument from the indorsee or takes the instrument from the indorsee for collection or payment may pay the proceeds of payment or the value given for the instrument to the indorsee without regard to whether the indorsee violates a fiduciary duty to the indorser.

(2) A subsequent transferee of the instrument or person who pays the instrument is neither given notice nor otherwise affected by the restriction in the indorsement unless the transferee or payor knows that the fiduciary dealt with the instrument or its proceeds in breach of fiduciary duty.

(e) The presence on an instrument of an indorsement to which this section applies does not prevent a purchaser of the instrument from becoming a holder in due course of the instrument unless the purchaser is a converter under subsection (c) or has notice or knowledge of breach of fiduciary duty as stated in subsection (d).

(f) In an action to enforce the obligation of a party to pay the instrument, the obligor has a defense if payment would violate an indorsement to which this section applies and the payment is not permitted by this section.

§3—207. REACQUISITION

Reacquisition of an instrument occurs if it is transferred to a former holder, by negotiation or otherwise. A former holder who reacquires the instrument may cancel indorsements made after the reacquirer first became a holder of the instrument. If the cancellation causes the instrument to be payable to the reacquirer or to bearer, the reacquirer may negotiate the instrument. An indorser whose indorsement is canceled is discharged, and the discharge is effective against any subsequent holder.

Part 3 Enforcement of Instruments

§3—301. PERSON ENTITLED TO ENFORCE INSTRUMENT

"Person entitled to enforce" an instrument means (i) the holder of the instrument, (ii) a nonholder in possession of the instrument who has the rights of a holder, or (iii) a person not in possession of the instrument who is entitled to enforce the instrument pursuant to Section 3—309 or 3—418(d). A person may be a person entitled to enforce the instrument even though the person is not the owner of the instrument or is in wrongful possession of the instrument.

§3—302. HOLDER IN DUE COURSE

(a) Subject to subsection (c) and Section 3—106(d), "holder in due course" means the holder of an instrument if:

(1) the instrument when issued or negotiated to the holder does not bear such apparent evidence of forgery or alteration or is not otherwise so irregular or incomplete as to call into question its authenticity; and
(2) the holder took the instrument (i) for value, (ii) in good faith, (iii) without notice that the instrument is overdue or has been dishonored or that there is an uncured default with respect to payment of another instrument issued as part of the same series, (iv) without notice that the instrument contains an unauthorized signature or has been altered, (v) without notice of any claim to the instrument described in Section 3—306, and (vi) without notice that any party has a defense or claim in recoupment described in Section 3—305(a).

(b) Notice of discharge of a party, other than discharge in an insolvency proceeding, is not notice of a defense under subsection (a), but discharge is effective against a person who became a holder in due course with notice of the discharge. Public filing or recording of a document does not of itself constitute notice of a defense, claim in recoupment, or claim to the instrument.

(c) Except to the extent a transferor or predecessor in interest has rights as a holder in due course, a person does not acquire rights of a holder in due course of an instrument taken (i) by legal process or by purchase in an execution, bankruptcy, or creditor's sale or similar proceeding, (ii) by purchase as part of a bulk transaction not in ordinary course of business of the transferor, or (iii) as the successor in interest to an estate or other organization.

(d) If, under Section 3—303(a)(1), the promise of performance that is the consideration for an instrument has been partially performed, the holder may assert rights as a holder in due course of the instrument only to the fraction of the amount payable under the instrument equal to the value of the partial performance divided by the value of the promised performance.

(e) If (i) the person entitled to enforce an instrument has only a security interest in the instrument and (ii) the person obliged to pay the instrument has a defense, claim in recoupment, or claim to the instrument that may be asserted against the person who granted the security interest, the person entitled to enforce the instrument may assert rights as a holder in due course only to an amount payable under the instrument which, at the time of enforcement of the instrument, does not exceed the amount of the unpaid obligation secured.

(f) To be effective, notice must be received at a time and in a manner that gives a reasonable opportunity to act on it.

(g) This section is subject to any law limiting status as a holder in due course in particular classes of transactions.

§3—303. VALUE AND CONSIDERATION

(a) An instrument is issued or transferred for value if:
(1) the instrument is issued or transferred for a promise of performance, to the extent the promise has been performed;

(2) the transferee acquires a security interest or other lien in the instrument other than a lien obtained by judicial proceeding;

(3) the instrument is issued or transferred as payment of, or as security for, an antecedent claim against any person, whether or not the claim is due;

(4) the instrument is issued or transferred in exchange for a negotiable instrument; or

(5) the instrument is issued or transferred in exchange for the incurring of an irrevocable obligation to a third party by the person taking the instrument.

(b) "Consideration" means any consideration sufficient to support a simple contract. The drawer or maker of an instrument has a defense if the instrument is issued without consideration. If an instrument is issued for a promise of performance, the issuer has a defense to the extent performance of the promise is due and the promise has not been performed. If an instrument is issued for value as stated in subsection (a), the instrument is also issued for consideration.

§3—304. OVERDUE INSTRUMENT

(a) An instrument payable on demand becomes overdue at the earliest of the following times:

(1) on the day after the day demand for payment is duly made;

(2) if the instrument is a check, 90 days after its date; or

(3) if the instrument is not a check, when the instrument has been outstanding for a period of time after its date which is unreasonably long under the circumstances of the particular case in light of the nature of the instrument and usage of the trade.

(b) With respect to an instrument payable at a definite time the following rules apply:

(1) If the principal is payable in installments and a due date has not been accelerated, the instrument becomes overdue upon default under the instrument for nonpayment of an installment, and the instrument remains overdue until the default is cured.

(2) If the principal is not payable in installments and the due date has not been accelerated, the instrument becomes overdue on the day after the due date.

(3) If a due date with respect to principal has been accelerated, the instrument becomes overdue on the day after the accelerated due date.

(c) Unless the due date of principal has been accelerated, an instrument does not become overdue if there is default in payment of interest but no default in payment of principal.

§3—305. DEFENSES AND CLAIMS IN RECOUPMENT

(a) Except as stated in subsection (b), the right to enforce the obligation of a party to pay an instrument is subject to the following:

(1) a defense of the obligor based on (i) infancy of the obligor to the extent it is a defense to a simple contract, (ii) duress, lack of legal capacity, or illegality of the transaction which, under other law, nullifies the obligation of the obligor, (iii) fraud that induced the obligor to sign the instrument with neither knowledge nor reasonable opportunity to learn of its character or its essential terms, or (iv) discharge of the obligor in insolvency proceedings;

(2) a defense of the obligor stated in another section of this Article or a defense of the obligor that would be available if the person entitled to enforce the instrument were enforcing a right to payment under a simple contract; and

(3) a claim in recoupment of the obligor against the original payee of the instrument if the claim arose from the transaction that gave rise to the instrument; but the claim of the obligor may be asserted against a transferee of the instrument only to reduce the amount owing on the instrument at the time the action is brought.

(b) The right of a holder in due course to enforce the obligation of a party to pay the instrument is subject to defenses of the obligor stated in subsection (a)(1), but is not subject to defenses of the obligor stated in subsection (a)(2) or claims in recoupment stated in subsection (a)(3) against a person other than the holder.

(c) Except as stated in subsection (d), in an action to enforce the obligation of a party to pay the instrument, the obligor may not assert against the person entitled to enforce the instrument a defense, claim in recoupment, or claim to the instrument (Section 3—306) of another person, but the other person's claim to the instrument may be asserted by the obligor if the other person is joined in the action and personally asserts the claim against the person entitled to enforce the instrument. An obligor is not obliged to pay the instrument if the person seeking enforcement of the instrument does not have rights of a holder in due course and the obligor proves that the instrument is a lost or stolen instrument.

(d) In an action to enforce the obligation of an accommodation party to pay an instrument, the accommodation party may assert against the person entitled to enforce the instrument any defense or claim in recoupment under subsection (a) that the accommodated party could assert against the person entitled to enforce the instrument, except the defenses of discharge in insolvency proceedings, infancy, and lack of legal capacity.

§3—306. CLAIMS TO AN INSTRUMENT

A person taking an instrument, other than a person having rights of a holder in due course, is subject to a claim of a property or possessory right in the instrument or its proceeds, including a claim to rescind a negotiation and to recover the instrument or its proceeds. A person having rights of a holder in due course takes free of the claim to the instrument.

§3—307. NOTICE OF BREACH OF FIDUCIARY DUTY

(a) In this section:

(1) "Fiduciary" means an agent, trustee, partner, corporate officer or director, or other representative owing a fiduciary duty with respect to an instrument.

(2) "Represented person" means the principal, beneficiary, partnership, corporation, or other person to whom the duty stated in paragraph (1) is owed.

(b) If (i) an instrument is taken from a fiduciary for payment or collection or for value, (ii) the taker has knowledge of the fiduciary status of the fiduciary, and (iii) the represented person makes a claim to the instrument or its proceeds on the basis that the transaction of the fiduciary is a breach of fiduciary duty, the following rules apply:

(1) Notice of breach of fiduciary duty by the fiduciary is notice of the claim of the represented person.

(2) In the case of an instrument payable to the represented person or the fiduciary as such, the taker has notice of the breach of fiduciary duty if the instrument is (i) taken in payment of or as security for a debt known by the taker to be the personal debt of the fiduciary, (ii) taken in a transaction known by the taker to be for the personal benefit of the fiduciary, or (iii) deposited to an account other than an account of the fiduciary, as such, or an account of the represented person.

(3) If an instrument is issued by the represented person or the fiduciary as such, and made payable to the fiduciary personally, the taker does not have notice of the breach of fiduciary duty unless the taker knows of the breach of fiduciary duty.

(4) If an instrument is issued by the represented person or the fiduciary as such, to the taker as payee, the taker has notice of the breach of fiduciary duty if the instrument is (i) taken in payment of or as security for a debt known by the taker to be the personal debt of the fiduciary, (ii) taken in a transaction known by the taker to be for the personal benefit of the fiduciary, or

(iii) deposited to an account other than an account of the fiduciary, as such, or an account of the represented person.

§3—308. PROOF OF SIGNATURES AND STATUS AS HOLDER IN DUE COURSE

(a) In an action with respect to an instrument, the authenticity of, and authority to make, each signature on the instrument is admitted unless specifically denied in the pleadings. If the validity of a signature is denied in the pleadings, the burden of establishing validity is on the person claiming validity, but the signature is presumed to be authentic and authorized unless the action is to enforce the liability of the purported signer and the signer is dead or incompetent at the time of trial of the issue of validity of the signature. If an action to enforce the instrument is brought against a person as the undisclosed principal of a person who signed the instrument as a party to the instrument, the plaintiff has the burden of establishing that the defendant is liable on the instrument as a represented person under Section 3—402(a).

(b) If the validity of signatures is admitted or proved and there is compliance with subsection (a), a plaintiff producing the instrument is entitled to payment if the plaintiff proves entitlement to enforce the instrument under Section 3—301, unless the defendant proves a defense or claim in recoupment. If a defense or claim in recoupment is proved, the right to payment of the plaintiff is subject to the defense or claim, except to the extent the plaintiff proves that the plaintiff has rights of a holder in due course which are not subject to the defense or claim.

§3—309. ENFORCEMENT OF LOST, DESTROYED, OR STOLEN INSTRUMENT

(a) A person not in possession of an instrument is entitled to enforce the instrument if (i) the person was in possession of the instrument and entitled to enforce it when loss of possession occurred, (ii) the loss of possession was not the result of a transfer by the person or a lawful seizure, and (iii) the person cannot reasonably obtain possession of the instrument because the instrument was destroyed, its whereabouts cannot be determined, or it is in the wrongful possession of an unknown person or a person that cannot be found or is not amenable to service of process.

(b) A person seeking enforcement of an instrument under subsection (a) must prove the terms of the instrument and the person's right to enforce the instrument. If that proof is made, Section 3—308 applies to the case as if the person seeking enforcement had produced the instrument. The court may not enter judgment in favor of the person seeking enforcement unless it finds that the person required to pay the instrument is adequately protected against loss that might occur by reason of a claim by another person to enforce the instrument. Adequate protection may be provided by any reasonable means.

§3—310. EFFECT OF INSTRUMENT ON OBLIGATION FOR WHICH TAKEN

(a) Unless otherwise agreed, if a certified check, cashier's check, or teller's check is taken for an obligation, the obligation is discharged to the same extent discharge would result if an amount of money equal to the amount of the instrument were taken in payment of the obligation. Discharge of the obligation does not affect any liability that the obligor may have as an indorser of the instrument.

(b) Unless otherwise agreed and except as provided in subsection (a), if a note or an uncertified check is taken for an obligation, the obligation is suspended to the same extent the obligation would be discharged if an amount of money equal to the amount of the instrument were taken, and the following rules apply:

(1) In the case of an uncertified check, suspension of the obligation continues until dishonor of the check or until it is paid or certified. Payment or certification of the check results in discharge of the obligation to the extent of the amount of the check.

(2) In the case of a note, suspension of the obligation continues until dishonor of the note or until it is paid. Payment of the note results in discharge of the obligation to the extent of the payment.

(3) Except as provided in paragraph (4), if the check or note is dishonored and the obligee of the obligation for which the instrument was taken is the person entitled to enforce the instrument, the obligee may enforce either the instrument or the obligation. In the case of an instrument of a third person which is negotiated to the obligee by the obligor, discharge of the obligor on the instrument also discharges the obligation.

(4) If the person entitled to enforce the instrument taken for an obligation is a person other than the obligee, the obligee may not enforce the obligation to the extent the obligation is suspended. If the obligee is the person entitled to enforce the instrument but no longer has possession of it because it was lost, stolen, or destroyed, the obligation may not be enforced to the extent of the amount payable on the instrument, and to that extent the obligee's rights against the obligor are limited to enforcement of the instrument.

(c) If an instrument other than one described in subsection (a) or (b) is taken for an obligation, the effect is (i) that stated in subsection (a) if the instrument is one on which a bank is liable as maker or acceptor, or (ii) that stated in subsection (b) in any other case.

§3—311. ACCORD AND SATISFACTION BY USE OF INSTRUMENT

(a) If a person against whom a claim is asserted proves that (i) that person in good faith tendered an instrument to the claimant as full satisfaction of the claim, (ii) the amount of the claim was unliquidated or subject to a bona fide dispute, and (iii) the claimant obtained payment of the instrument, the following subsections apply.

(b) Unless subsection (c) applies, the claim is discharged if the person against whom the claim is asserted proves that the instrument or an accompanying written communication contained a conspicuous statement to the effect that the instrument was tendered as full satisfaction of the claim.

(c) Subject to subsection (d), a claim is not discharged under subsection (b) if either of the following applies:

(1) The claimant, if an organization, proves that (i) within a reasonable time before the tender, the claimant sent a conspicuous statement to the person against whom the claim is asserted that communications concerning disputed debts, including an instrument tendered as full satisfaction of a debt, are to be sent to a designated person, office, or place, and (ii) the instrument or accompanying communication was not received by that designated person, office, or place.

(2) The claimant, whether or not an organization, proves that within 90 days after payment of the instrument, the claimant tendered repayment of the amount of the instrument to the person against whom the claim is asserted. This paragraph does not apply if the claimant is an organization that sent a statement complying with paragraph (1)(i).

(d) A claim is discharged if the person against whom the claim is asserted proves that within a reasonable time before collection of the instrument was initiated, the claimant, or an agent of the claimant having direct responsibility with respect to the disputed obligation, knew that the instrument was tendered in full satisfaction of the claim.

§3—312. LOST, DESTROYED, OR STOLEN CASHIER'S CHECK, TELLER'S CHECK, OR CERTIFIED CHECK.*

(a) In this section:

(1) "Check" means a cashier's check, teller's check, or certified check.

---

*[Section 3—312 was not adopted as part of the 1990 Official Text of Revised Article 3. It was officially approved and recommended for enactment in all states in August 1991 by the National Conference of Commissioners on Uniform State Laws.]

(2) "Claimant" means a person who claims the right to receive the amount of a cashier's check, teller's check, or certified check that was lost, destroyed, or stolen.

(3) "Declaration of loss" means a written statement, made under penalty of perjury, to the effect that (i) the declarer lost possession of a check, (ii) the declarer is the drawer or payee of the check, in the case of a certified check, or the remitter or payee of the check, in the case of a cashier's check or teller's check, (iii) the loss of possession was not the result of a transfer by the declarer or a lawful seizure, and (iv) the declarer cannot reasonably obtain possession of the check because the check was destroyed, its whereabouts cannot be determined, or it is in the wrongful possession of an unknown person or a person that cannot be found or is not amenable to service of process.

(4) "Obligated bank" means the issuer of a cashier's check or teller's check or the acceptor of a certified check.

(b) A claimant may assert a claim to the amount of a check by a communication to the obligated bank describing the check with reasonable certainty and requesting payment of the amount of the check, if (i) the claimant is the drawer or payee of a certified check or the remitter or payee of a cashier's check or teller's check, (ii) the communication contains or is accompanied by a declaration of loss of the claimant with respect to the check, (iii) the communication is received at a time and in a manner affording the bank a reasonable time to act on it before the check is paid, and (iv) the claimant provides reasonable identification if requested by the obligated bank. Delivery of a declaration of loss is a warranty of the truth of the statements made in the declaration. If a claim is asserted in compliance with this subsection, the following rules apply:

(1) The claim becomes enforceable at the later of (i) the time the claim is asserted, or (ii) the 90th day following the date of the check, in the case of a cashier's check or teller's check, or the 90th day following the date of the acceptance, in the case of a certified check.

(2) Until the claim becomes enforceable, it has no legal effect and the obligated bank may pay the check or, in the case of a teller's check, may permit the drawee to pay the check. Payment to a person entitled to enforce the check discharges all liability of the obligated bank with respect to the check.

(3) If the claim becomes enforceable before the check is presented for payment, the obligated bank is not obliged to pay the check.

(4) When the claim becomes enforceable, the obligated bank becomes obliged to pay the amount of the check to the claimant if payment of the check has not been made to a person entitled to enforce the check. Subject to Section 4—302(a)(1), payment to the claimant discharges all liability of the obligated bank with respect to the check.

(c) If the obligated bank pays the amount of a check to a claimant under subsection (b)(4) and the check is presented for payment by a person having rights of a holder in due course, the claimant is obliged to (i) refund the payment to the obligated bank if the check is paid, or (ii) pay the amount of the check to the person having rights of a holder in due course if the check is dishonored.

(d) If a claimant has the right to assert a claim under subsection (b) and is also a person entitled to enforce a cashier's check, teller's check, or certified check which is lost, destroyed, or stolen, the claimant may assert rights with respect to the check either under this section or Section 3—309.

Added in 1991.

Part 4 Liability of Parties

§3—401. SIGNATURE

(a) A person is not liable on an instrument unless (i) the person signed the instrument, or (ii) the person is represented by an agent or representative who signed the instrument and the signature is binding on the represented person under Section 3—402.

(b) A signature may be made (i) manually or by means of a device or machine, and (ii) by the use of any name, including a trade or assumed name, or by a word, mark, or symbol executed or adopted by a person with present intention to authenticate a writing.

§3—402. SIGNATURE BY REPRESENTATIVE

(a) If a person acting, or purporting to act, as a representative signs an instrument by signing either the name of the represented person or the name of the signer, the represented person is bound by the signature to the same extent the represented person would be bound if the signature were on a simple contract. If the represented person is bound, the signature of the representative is the "authorized signature of the represented person" and the represented person is liable on the instrument, whether or not identified in the instrument.

(b) If a representative signs the name of the representative to an instrument and the signature is an authorized signature of the represented person, the following rules apply:

(1) If the form of the signature shows unambiguously that the signature is made on behalf of the represented person who is identified in the instrument, the representative is not liable on the instrument.

(2) Subject to subsection (c), if (i) the form of the signature does not show unambiguously that the signature is made in a representative capacity or (ii) the represented person is not identified in the instrument, the representative is liable on the instrument to a holder in due course that took the instrument without notice that the representative was not intended to be liable on the instrument. With respect to any other person, the representative is liable on the instrument unless the representative proves that the original parties did not intend the representative to be liable on the instrument.

(c) If a representative signs the name of the representative as drawer of a check without indication of the representative status and the check is payable from an account of the represented person who is identified on the check, the signer is not liable on the check if the signature is an authorized signature of the represented person.

§3—403. UNAUTHORIZED SIGNATURE

(a) Unless otherwise provided in this Article or Article 4, an unauthorized signature is ineffective except as the signature of the unauthorized signer in favor of a person who in good faith pays the instrument or takes it for value. An unauthorized signature may be ratified for all purposes of this Article.

(b) If the signature of more than one person is required to constitute the authorized signature of an organization, the signature of the organization is unauthorized if one of the required signatures is lacking.

(c) The civil or criminal liability of a person who makes an unauthorized signature is not affected by any provision of this Article which makes the unauthorized signature effective for the purposes of this Article.

§3—404. IMPOSTORS; FICTITIOUS PAYEES

(a) If an impostor, by use of the mails or otherwise, induces the issuer of an instrument to issue the instrument to the impostor, or to a person acting in concert with the impostor, by impersonating the payee of the instrument or a person authorized to act for the payee, an indorsement of the instrument by any person in the name of the payee is effective as the indorsement of the payee in favor of a person who, in good faith, pays the instrument or takes it for value or for collection.

(b) If (i) a person whose intent determines to whom an instrument is payable (Section 3—110(a) or (b)) does not intend the person identified as payee to have any interest in the instrument, or (ii) the person identified as payee of an instrument is a fictitious person, the following rules apply until the instrument is negotiated by special indorsement:

(1) Any person in possession of the instrument is its holder.

(2) An indorsement by any person in the name of the payee stated in the instrument is effective as the indorsement of the payee in favor of a person who, in good faith, pays the instrument or takes it for value or for collection.

(c) Under subsection (a) or (b), an indorsement is made in the name of a payee if (i) it is made in a name substantially similar to that of the payee or (ii) the instrument, whether or not indorsed, is deposited in a depositary bank to an account in a name substantially similar to that of the payee.

(d) With respect to an instrument to which subsection (a) or (b) applies, if a person paying the instrument or taking it for value or for collection fails to exercise ordinary care in paying or taking the instrument and that failure substantially contributes to loss resulting from payment of the instrument, the person bearing the loss may recover from the person failing to exercise ordinary care to the extent the failure to exercise ordinary care contributed to the loss.

§3—405. EMPLOYER'S RESPONSIBILITY FOR FRAUDULENT INDORSEMENT BY EMPLOYEE

(a) In this section:

(1) "Employee" includes an independent contractor and employee of an independent contractor retained by the employer.

(2) "Fraudulent indorsement" means (i) in the case of an instrument payable to the employer, a forged indorsement purporting to be that of the employer, or (ii) in the case of an instrument with respect to which the employer is the issuer, a forged indorsement purporting to be that of the person identified as payee.

(3) "Responsibility" with respect to instruments means authority (i) to sign or indorse instruments on behalf of the employer, (ii) to process instruments received by the employer for bookkeeping purposes, for deposit to an account, or for other disposition, (iii) to prepare or process instruments for issue in the name of the employer, (iv) to supply information determining the names or addresses of payees of instruments to be issued in the name of the employer, (v) to control the disposition of instruments to be issued in the name of the employer, or (vi) to act otherwise with respect to instruments in a responsible capacity. "Responsibility" does not include authority that merely allows an employee to have access to instruments or blank or incomplete instrument forms that are being stored or transported or are part of incoming or outgoing mail, or similar access.

(b) For the purpose of determining the rights and liabilities of a person who, in good faith, pays an instrument or takes it for value or for collection, if an employer entrusted an employee with responsibility with respect to the instrument and the employee or a person acting in concert with the employee makes a fraudulent indorsement of the instrument, the indorsement is effective as the indorsement of the person to whom the instrument is payable if it is made in the name of that person. If the person paying the instrument or taking it for value or for collection fails to exercise ordinary care in paying or taking the instrument and that failure substantially contributes to loss resulting from the fraud, the person bearing the loss may recover from the person failing to exercise ordinary care to the extent the failure to exercise ordinary care contributed to the loss.

(c) Under subsection (b), an indorsement is made in the name of the person to whom an instrument is payable if (i) it is made in a name substantially similar to the name of that person or (ii) the instrument, whether or not indorsed, is deposited in a depository bank to an account in a name substantially similar to the name of that person.

§3—406. NEGLIGENCE CONTRIBUTING TO FORGED SIGNATURE OR ALTERATION OF INSTRUMENT

(a) A person whose failure to exercise ordinary care substantially contributes to an alteration of an instrument or to the making of a forged signature on an instrument is precluded from asserting the alteration or the forgery against a person who, in good faith, pays the instrument or takes it for value or for collection.

(b) Under subsection (a), if the person asserting the preclusion fails to exercise ordinary care in paying or taking the instrument and that failure substantially contributes to loss, the loss is allocated between the person precluded and the person asserting the preclusion according to the extent to which the failure of each to exercise ordinary care contributed to the loss.

(c) Under subsection (a), the burden of proving failure to exercise ordinary care is on the person asserting the preclusion. Under subsection (b), the burden of proving failure to exercise ordinary care is on the person precluded.

§3—407. ALTERATION

(a) "Alteration" means (i) an unauthorized change in an instrument that purports to modify in any respect the obligation of a party, or (ii) an unauthorized addition of words or numbers or other change to an incomplete instrument relating to the obligation of a party.

(b) Except as provided in subsection (c), an alteration fraudulently made discharges a party whose obligation is affected by the alteration unless that party assents or is precluded from asserting the alteration. No other alteration discharges a party, and the instrument may be enforced according to its original terms.

(c) A payor bank or drawee paying a fraudulently altered instrument or a person taking it for value, in good faith and without notice of the alteration, may enforce rights with respect to the instrument (i) according to its original terms, or (ii) in the case of an incomplete instrument altered by unauthorized completion, according to its terms as completed.

§3—408. DRAWEE NOT LIABLE ON UNACCEPTED DRAFT

A check or other draft does not of itself operate as an assignment of funds in the hands of the drawee available for its payment, and the drawee is not liable on the instrument until the drawee accepts it.

§3—409. ACCEPTANCE OF DRAFT; CERTIFIED CHECK

(a) "Acceptance" means the drawee's signed agreement to pay a draft as presented. It must be written on the draft and may consist of the drawee's signature alone. Acceptance may be made at any time and becomes effective when notification pursuant to instructions is given or the accepted draft is delivered for the purpose of giving rights on the acceptance to any person.

(b) A draft may be accepted although it has not been signed by the drawer, is otherwise incomplete, is overdue, or has been dishonored.

(c) If a draft is payable at a fixed period after sight and the acceptor fails to date the acceptance, the holder may complete the acceptance by supplying a date in good faith.

(d) "Certified check" means a check accepted by the bank on which it is drawn. Acceptance may be made as stated in subsection (a) or by a writing on the check which indicates that the check is certified. The drawee of a check has no obligation to certify the check, and refusal to certify is not dishonor of the check.

§3—410. ACCEPTANCE VARYING DRAFT

(a) If the terms of a drawee's acceptance vary from the terms of the draft as presented, the holder may refuse the acceptance and treat the draft as dishonored. In that case, the drawee may cancel the acceptance.

(b) The terms of a draft are not varied by an acceptance to pay at a particular bank or place in the United States, unless the acceptance states that the draft is to be paid only at that bank or place.

(c) If the holder assents to an acceptance varying the terms of a draft, the obligation of each drawer and indorser that does not expressly assent to the acceptance is discharged.

§3—411. REFUSAL TO PAY CASHIER'S CHECKS, TELLER'S CHECKS, AND CERTIFIED CHECKS

(a) In this section, "obligated bank" means the acceptor of a certified check or the issuer of a cashier's check or teller's check bought from the issuer.

(b) If the obligated bank wrongfully (i) refuses to pay a cashier's check or certified check, (ii) stops payment of a teller's check, or (iii) refuses to pay a dishonored teller's check, the person asserting the right to enforce the check is entitled to compensation for expenses and loss of interest resulting from the nonpayment and may recover consequential damages if the obligated bank refuses to pay after receiving notice of particular circumstances giving rise to the damages.

(c) Expenses or consequential damages under subsection (b) are not recoverable if the refusal of the obligated bank to pay occurs because (i) the bank suspends payments, (ii) the obligated bank asserts a claim or defense of the bank that it has reasonable grounds to believe is available against the person entitled to enforce the instrument, (iii) the obligated bank has a reasonable doubt whether the person demanding payment is the person entitled to enforce the instrument, or (iv) payment is prohibited by law.

§3—412. OBLIGATION OF ISSUER OF NOTE OR CASHIER'S CHECK

The issuer of a note or cashier's check or other draft drawn on the drawer is obliged to pay the instrument (i) according to its terms at the time it was issued or, if not issued, at the time it first came into possession of a holder, or (ii) if the issuer signed an incomplete instrument, according to its terms when completed, to the extent stated in Sections 3—115 and 3—407. The obligation is owed to a person entitled to enforce the instrument or to an indorser who paid the instrument under Section 3—415.

§3—413. OBLIGATION OF ACCEPTOR

(a) The acceptor of a draft is obliged to pay the draft (i) according to its terms at the time it was accepted, even though the acceptance states that the draft is payable "as originally drawn" or equivalent terms, (ii) if the acceptance varies the terms of the draft, according to the terms of the draft as varied, or (iii) if the acceptance is of a draft that is an incomplete instrument, according to its terms when completed, to the extent stated in Sections 3—115 and 3—407. The obligation is owed to a person entitled to enforce the draft or to the drawer or an indorser who paid the draft under Section 3—414 or 3—415.

(b) If the certification of a check or other acceptance of a draft states the amount certified or accepted, the obligation of the acceptor is that amount. If (i) the certification or acceptance does not state an amount, (ii) the amount of the instrument is subsequently raised, and (iii) the instrument is then negotiated to a holder in due course, the obligation of the acceptor is the amount of the instrument at the time it was taken by the holder in due course.

§3—414. OBLIGATION OF DRAWER

(a) This section does not apply to cashier's checks or other drafts drawn on the drawer.

(b) If an unaccepted draft is dishonored, the drawer is obliged to pay the draft (i) according to its terms at the time it was issued or, if not issued, at the time it first came into possession of a holder, or (ii) if the drawer signed an incomplete instrument, according to its terms when completed, to the extent stated in Sections 3—115 and 3—407. The obligation is owed to a person entitled to enforce the draft or to an indorser who paid the draft under Section 3—415.

(c) If a draft is accepted by a bank, the drawer is discharged, regardless of when or by whom acceptance was obtained.

(d) If a draft is accepted and the acceptor is not a bank, the obligation of the drawer to pay the draft if the draft is dishonored by the acceptor is the same as the obligation of an indorser under Section 3—415(a) and (c).

(e) If a draft states that it is drawn "without recourse" or otherwise disclaims liability of the drawer to pay the draft, the drawer is not liable under subsection (b) to pay the draft if the draft is not a check. A disclaimer of the liability stated in subsection (b) is not effective if the draft is a check.

(f) If (i) a check is not presented for payment or given to a depositary bank for collection within 30 days after its date, (ii) the drawee suspends payments after expiration of the 30-day period without paying the check, and (iii) because of the suspension of payments, the drawer is deprived of funds maintained with the drawee to cover payment of the check, the drawer to the extent deprived of funds may discharge its obligation to pay the check by assigning to the person entitled to enforce the check the rights of the drawer against the drawee with respect to the funds.

§3—415. OBLIGATION OF INDORSER

(a) Subject to subsections (b), (c), and (d) and to Section 3—419(d), if an instrument is dishonored, an indorser is obliged to pay the amount due on the instrument (i) according to the terms of the instrument at the time it was indorsed, or (ii) if the indorser indorsed an incomplete instrument, according to its terms when completed, to the extent stated in Sections 3—115 and 3—407. The obligation of the indorser is owed to a person entitled to enforce the instrument or to a subsequent indorser who paid the instrument under this section.

(b) If an indorsement states that it is made "without recourse" or otherwise disclaims liability of the indorser, the indorser is not liable under subsection (a) to pay the instrument.

(c) If notice of dishonor of an instrument is required by Section 3—503 and notice of dishonor complying with that section is not given to an indorser, the liability of the indorser under subsection (a) is discharged.

(d) If a draft is accepted by a bank after an indorsement is made, the liability of the indorser under subsection (a) is discharged.

(e) If an indorser of a check is liable under subsection (a) and the check is not presented for payment, or given to a depositary bank for collection, within 30 days after the day the indorsement was made, the liability of the indorser under subsection (a) is discharged.

As amended in 1993.

§3—416. TRANSFER WARRANTIES

(a) A person who transfers an instrument for consideration warrants to the transferee and, if the transfer is by indorsement, to any subsequent transferee that:

(1) the warrantor is a person entitled to enforce the instrument;

(2) all signatures on the instrument are authentic and authorized;

(3) the instrument has not been altered;

(4) the instrument is not subject to a defense or claim in recoupment of any party which can be asserted against the warrantor; and

(5) the warrantor has no knowledge of any insolvency proceeding commenced with respect to the maker or acceptor or, in the case of an unaccepted draft, the drawer.

(b) A person to whom the warranties under subsection (a) are made and who took the instrument in good faith may recover from the warrantor as damages for breach of warranty an amount equal to the loss suffered as a result of the breach, but not more than the amount of the instrument plus expenses and loss of interest incurred as a result of the breach.

(c) The warranties stated in subsection (a) cannot be disclaimed with respect to checks. Unless notice of a claim for breach of warranty is given to the warrantor within 30 days after the claimant has reason to know of the breach and the identity of the warrantor, the liability of the warrantor under subsection (b) is discharged to the extent of any loss caused by the delay in giving notice of the claim.

(d) A [cause of action] for breach of warranty under this section accrues when the claimant has reason to know of the breach.

§3—417. PRESENTMENT WARRANTIES

(a) If an unaccepted draft is presented to the drawee for payment or acceptance and the drawee pays or accepts the draft, (i) the person obtaining payment or acceptance, at the time of presentment, and (ii) a previous transferor of the draft, at the time of transfer, warrant to the drawee making payment or accepting the draft in good faith that:

(1) the warrantor is, or was, at the time the warrantor transferred the draft, a person entitled to enforce the draft or authorized to obtain payment or acceptance of the draft on behalf of a person entitled to enforce the draft;

(2) the draft has not been altered; and

(3) the warrantor has no knowledge that the signature of the drawer of the draft is unauthorized.

(b) A drawee making payment may recover from any warrantor damages for breach of warranty equal to the amount paid by the drawee less the amount the drawee received or is entitled to receive from the drawer because of the payment. In addition, the drawee is entitled to compensation for expenses and loss of interest resulting from the breach. The right of the drawee to recover damages under this subsection is not affected by any failure of the drawee to exercise ordinary care in making payment. If the drawee accepts the draft, breach of warranty is a defense to the obligation of the acceptor. If the acceptor makes payment with respect to the draft, the acceptor is entitled to recover from any warrantor for breach of warranty the amounts stated in this subsection.

(c) If a drawee asserts a claim for breach of warranty under subsection (a) based on an unauthorized indorsement of the draft or an alteration of the draft, the warrantor may defend by proving that the indorsement is effective under Section 3—404 or 3—405 or the drawer is precluded under Section 3—406 or 4—406 from asserting against the drawee the unauthorized indorsement or alteration.

(d) If (i) a dishonored draft is presented for payment to the drawer or an indorser or (ii) any other instrument is presented for payment to a party obliged to pay the instrument, and (iii) payment is received, the following rules apply:

(1) The person obtaining payment and a prior transferor of the instrument warrant to the person making payment in good faith that the warrantor is, or was, at the time the warrantor transferred the instrument, a person entitled to enforce the instrument or authorized to obtain payment on behalf of a person entitled to enforce the instrument.

(2) The person making payment may recover from any warrantor for breach of warranty an amount equal to the amount paid plus expenses and loss of interest resulting from the breach.

(e) The warranties stated in subsections (a) and (d) cannot be disclaimed with respect to checks. Unless notice of a claim for breach of warranty is given to the warrantor within 30 days after the claimant has reason to know of the breach and the identity of the warrantor, the liability of the warrantor under subsection (b) or (d) is discharged to the extent of any loss caused by the delay in giving notice of the claim.

(f) A [cause of action] for breach of warranty under this section accrues when the claimant has reason to know of the breach.

§3—418. PAYMENT OR ACCEPTANCE BY MISTAKE

(a) Except as provided in subsection (c), if the drawee of a draft pays or accepts the draft and the drawee acted on the mistaken belief that (i) payment of the draft had not been stopped pursuant to Section 4—403 or (ii) the signature of the drawer of the draft was authorized, the drawee may recover the amount of the draft from the person to whom or for whose benefit payment was made or, in the case of acceptance, may revoke the acceptance. Rights of the drawee under this subsection are not affected by failure of the drawee to exercise ordinary care in paying or accepting the draft.

(b) Except as provided in subsection (c), if an instrument has been paid or accepted by mistake and the case is not covered by subsection (a), the person paying or accepting may, to the extent permitted by the law governing mistake and restitution, (i) recover the payment from the person to whom or for whose benefit payment was made or (ii) in the case of acceptance, may revoke the acceptance.

(c) The remedies provided by subsection (a) or (b) may not be asserted against a person who took the instrument in good faith and for value or who in good faith changed position in reliance on the payment or acceptance. This subsection does not limit remedies provided by Section 3—417 or 4—407.

(d) Notwithstanding Section 4—215, if an instrument is paid or accepted by mistake and the payor or acceptor recovers payment or revokes acceptance under subsection (a) or (b), the instrument is deemed not to have been paid or accepted and is treated as dishonored, and the person from whom payment is recovered has rights as a person entitled to enforce the dishonored instrument.

§3—419. INSTRUMENTS SIGNED FOR ACCOMMODATION

(a) If an instrument is issued for value given for the benefit of a party to the instrument ("accommodated party") and another party to the instrument ("accommodation party") signs the instrument for the purpose of incurring liability on the instrument without being a direct beneficiary of the value given for the instrument, the instrument is signed by the accommodation party "for accommodation."

(b) An accommodation party may sign the instrument as maker, drawer, acceptor, or indorser and, subject to subsection (d), is obliged to pay the instrument in the capacity in which the accommodation party signs. The obligation of an accommodation party may be enforced notwithstanding any statute of frauds and whether or not the accommodation party receives consideration for the accommodation.

(c) A person signing an instrument is presumed to be an accommodation party and there is notice that the instrument is signed for accommodation if the signature is an anomalous indorsement or is accompanied by words indicating that the signer is acting as surety or guarantor with respect to the obligation of another party to the instrument. Except as provided in Section 3—605, the obligation of an accommodation party to pay the instrument is not affected by the fact that the person enforcing the obligation had notice when the instrument was taken by that person that the accommodation party signed the instrument for accommodation.

(d) If the signature of a party to an instrument is accompanied by words indicating unambiguously that the party is guaranteeing collection rather than payment of the obligation of another party to the instrument, the signer is obliged to pay the amount due on the instrument to a person entitled to enforce the instrument only if (i) execution of judgment against the other party has been returned unsatisfied, (ii) the other party is insolvent or in an insolvency proceeding, (iii) the other party cannot be served with process, or (iv) it is otherwise apparent that payment cannot be obtained from the other party.

(e) An accommodation party who pays the instrument is entitled to reimbursement from the accommodated party and is entitled to enforce the instrument against the accommodated party. An accommodated party who pays the instrument has no right of recourse against, and is not entitled to contribution from, an accommodation party.

§3—420. CONVERSION OF INSTRUMENT

(a) The law applicable to conversion of personal property applies to instruments. An instrument is also converted if it is taken by transfer, other than a negotiation, from a person not entitled to enforce the instrument or a bank makes or obtains payment with respect to the instrument for a person not entitled to enforce the instrument or receive payment. An action for conversion of an instrument may not be brought by (i) the issuer or acceptor of the instrument or (ii) a payee or indorsee who did not receive delivery of the instrument either directly or through delivery to an agent or a co-payee.

(b) In an action under subsection (a), the measure of liability is presumed to be the amount payable on the instrument, but recovery may not exceed the amount of the plaintiff's interest in the instrument.

(c) A representative, other than a depository bank, who has in good faith dealt with an instrument or its proceeds on behalf of one who was not the person entitled to enforce the instrument is not liable in conversion to that person beyond the amount of any proceeds that it has not paid out.

Part 5 Dishonor

§3—501. PRESENTMENT

(a) "Presentment" means a demand made by or on behalf of a person entitled to enforce an instrument (i) to pay the instrument made to the drawee or a party obliged to pay the instrument or, in the case of a note or accepted draft payable at a bank, to the bank, or (ii) to accept a draft made to the drawee.

(b) The following rules are subject to Article 4, agreement of the parties, and clearing-house rules and the like:

(1) Presentment may be made at the place of payment of the instrument and must be made at the place of payment if the instrument is payable at a bank in the United States; may be made by any commercially reasonable means, including an oral, written, or electronic communication; is effective when the demand for payment or acceptance is received by the person to whom presentment is made; and is effective if made to any one of two or more makers, acceptors, drawees, or other payors.

(2) Upon demand of the person to whom presentment is made, the person making presentment must (i) exhibit the instrument, (ii) give reasonable identification and, if presentment is made on behalf of another person, reasonable evidence of authority to do so, and (…) sign a receipt on the instrument for any payment made or surrender the instrument if full payment is made.

(3) Without dishonoring the instrument, the party to whom presentment is made may (i) return the instrument for lack of a necessary indorsement, or (ii) refuse payment or acceptance for failure of the presentment to comply with the terms of the instrument, an agreement of the parties, or other applicable law or rule.

(4) The party to whom presentment is made may treat presentment as occurring on the next business day after the day of presentment if the party to whom presentment is made has established a cut-off hour not earlier than 2 P.M. for the receipt and processing of instruments presented for payment or acceptance and presentment is made after the cut-off hour.

§3—502. DISHONOR

(a) Dishonor of a note is governed by the following rules:

(1) If the note is payable on demand, the note is dishonored if presentment is duly made to the maker and the note is not paid on the day of presentment.

(2) If the note is not payable on demand and is payable at or through a bank or the terms of the note require presentment, the note is dishonored if presentment is duly made and the note is not paid on the day it becomes payable or the day of presentment, whichever is later.

(3) If the note is not payable on demand and paragraph (2) does not apply, the note is dishonored if it is not paid on the day it becomes payable.

(b) Dishonor of an unaccepted draft other than a documentary draft is governed by the following rules:

(1) If a check is duly presented for payment to the payor bank otherwise than for immediate payment over the counter, the check is dishonored if the payor bank makes timely return of the check or sends timely notice of dishonor or nonpayment under Section 4—301 or 4—302, or becomes accountable for the amount of the check under Section 4—302.

(2) If a draft is payable on demand and paragraph (1) does not apply, the draft is dishonored if presentment for payment is duly made to the drawee and the draft is not paid on the day of presentment.

(3) If a draft is payable on a date stated in the draft, the draft is dishonored if (i) presentment for payment is duly made to the drawee and payment is not made on the day the draft becomes payable or the day of presentment, whichever is later, or (ii) presentment for acceptance is duly made before the day the draft becomes payable and the draft is not accepted on the day of presentment.

(4) If a draft is payable on elapse of a period of time after sight or acceptance, the draft is dishonored if presentment for acceptance is duly made and the draft is not accepted on the day of presentment.

(c) Dishonor of an unaccepted documentary draft occurs according to the rules stated in subsection (b)(2), (3), and (4), except that payment or acceptance may be delayed without dishonor until no later than the close of the third business day of the drawee following the day on which payment or acceptance is required by those paragraphs.

(d) Dishonor of an accepted draft is governed by the following rules:

(1) If the draft is payable on demand, the draft is dishonored if presentment for payment is duly

made to the acceptor and the draft is not paid on the day of presentment.

(2) If the draft is not payable on demand, the draft is dishonored if presentment for payment is duly made to the acceptor and payment is not made on the day it becomes payable or the day of presentment, whichever is later.

(e) In any case in which presentment is otherwise required for dishonor under this section and presentment is excused under Section 3—504, dishonor occurs without presentment if the instrument is not duly accepted or paid.

(f) If a draft is dishonored because timely acceptance of the draft was not made and the person entitled to demand acceptance consents to a late acceptance, from the time of acceptance the draft is treated as never having been dishonored.

§3—503. NOTICE OF DISHONOR

(a) The obligation of an indorser stated in Section 3—415 (a) and the obligation of a drawer stated in Section 3—414 (d) may not be enforced unless (i) the indorser or drawer is given notice of dishonor of the instrument complying with this section or (ii) notice of dishonor is excused under Section 3—504(b).

(b) Notice of dishonor may be given by any person; may be given by any commercially reasonable means, including an oral, written, or electronic communication; and is sufficient if it reasonably identifies the instrument and indicates that the instrument has been dishonored or has not been paid or accepted. Return of an instrument given to a bank for collection is sufficient notice of dishonor.

(c) Subject to Section 3—504(c), with respect to an instrument taken for collection by a collecting bank, notice of dishonor must be given (i) by the bank before midnight of the next banking day following the banking day on which the bank receives notice of dishonor of the instrument, or (ii) by any other person within 30 days following the day on which the person receives notice of dishonor. With respect to any other instrument, notice of dishonor must be given within 30 days following the day on which dishonor occurs.

§3—504. EXCUSED PRESENTMENT AND NOTICE OF DISHONOR

(a) Presentment for payment or acceptance of an instrument is excused if (i) the person entitled to present the instrument cannot with reasonable diligence make presentment, (ii) the maker or acceptor has repudiated an obligation to pay the instrument or is dead or in insolvency proceedings, (iii) by the terms of the instrument presentment is not necessary to enforce the obligation of indorsers or the drawer, (iv) the drawer or indorser whose obligation is being enforced has waived presentment or otherwise has no reason to expect or right to require that the instrument

be paid or accepted, or (v) the drawer instructed the drawee not to pay or accept the draft or the drawee was not obligated to the drawer to pay the draft.

(b) Notice of dishonor is excused if (i) by the terms of the instrument notice of dishonor is not necessary to enforce the obligation of a party to pay the instrument, or (ii) the party whose obligation is being enforced waived notice of dishonor. A waiver of presentment is also a waiver of notice of dishonor.

(c) Delay in giving notice of dishonor is excused if the delay was caused by circumstances beyond the control of the person giving the notice and the person giving the notice exercised reasonable diligence after the cause of the delay ceased to operate.

§3—505. EVIDENCE OF DISHONOR

(a) The following are admissible as evidence and create a presumption of dishonor and of any notice of dishonor stated:

(1) a document regular in form as provided in subsection (b) which purports to be a protest;

(2) a purported stamp or writing of the drawee, payor bank, or presenting bank on or accompanying the instrument stating that acceptance or payment has been refused unless reasons for the refusal are stated and the reasons are not consistent with dishonor;

(3) a book or record of the drawee, payor bank, or collecting bank, kept in the usual course of business which shows dishonor, even if there is no evidence of who made the entry.

(b) A protest is a certificate of dishonor made by a United States consul or vice consul, or a notary public or other person authorized to administer oaths by the law of the place where dishonor occurs. It may be made upon information satisfactory to that person. The protest must identify the instrument and certify either that presentment has been made or, if not made, the reason why it was not made, and that the instrument has been dishonored by nonacceptance or nonpayment. The protest may also certify that notice of dishonor has been given to some or all parties.

Part 6 Discharge and Payment

§3—601. DISCHARGE AND EFFECT OF DISCHARGE

(a) The obligation of a party to pay the instrument is discharged as stated in this Article or by an act or agreement with the party which would discharge an obligation to pay money under a simple contract.

(b) Discharge of the obligation of a party is not effective against a person acquiring rights of a holder in due course of the instrument without notice of the discharge.

§3—602. PAYMENT

(a) Subject to subsection (b), an instrument is paid to the extent payment is made (i) by or on behalf of a party obliged to pay the instrument, and (ii) to a person entitled to enforce the instrument. To the extent of the payment, the obligation of the party obliged to pay the instrument is discharged even though payment is made with knowledge of a claim to the instrument under Section 3—306 by another person.

(b) The obligation of a party to pay the instrument is not discharged under subsection (a) if:

(1) a claim to the instrument under Section 3—306 is enforceable against the party receiving payment and (i) payment is made with knowledge by the payor that payment is prohibited by injunction or similar process of a court of competent jurisdiction, or (ii) in the case of an instrument other than a cashier's check, teller's check, or certified check, the party making payment accepted, from the person having a claim to the instrument, indemnity against loss resulting from refusal to pay the person entitled to enforce the instrument; or

(2) the person making payment knows that the instrument is a stolen instrument and pays a person it knows is in wrongful possession of the instrument.

§3—603. TENDER OF PAYMENT

(a) If tender of payment of an obligation to pay an instrument is made to a person entitled to enforce the instrument, the effect of tender is governed by principles of law applicable to tender of payment under a simple contract.

(b) If tender of payment of an obligation to pay an instrument is made to a person entitled to enforce the instrument and the tender is refused, there is discharge, to the extent of the amount of the tender, of the obligation of an indorser or accommodation party having a right of recourse with respect to the obligation to which the tender relates.

(c) If tender of payment of an amount due on an instrument is made to a person entitled to enforce the instrument, the obligation of the obligor to pay interest after the due date on the amount tendered is discharged. If presentment is required with respect to an instrument and the obligor is able and ready to pay on the due date at every place of payment stated in the instrument, the obligor is deemed to have made tender of payment on the due date to the person entitled to enforce the instrument.

§3—604. DISCHARGE BY CANCELLATION OR RENUNCIATION

(a) A person entitled to enforce an instrument, with or without consideration, may discharge the obligation of a party to pay the instrument (i) by an intentional voluntary act, such as surrender of the instrument to the party, destruction, mutilation, or cancellation of the instrument, cancellation or striking out of the party's signature, or the addition of words to the instrument indicating discharge, or (ii) by agreeing not to sue or otherwise renouncing rights against the party by a signed writing.

(b) Cancellation or striking out of an indorsement pursuant to subsection (a) does not affect the status and rights of a party derived from the indorsement.

§3—605. DISCHARGE OF INDORSERS AND ACCOMMODATION PARTIES

(a) In this section, the term "indorser" includes a drawer having the obligation described in Section 3—414(d).

(b) Discharge, under Section 3—604, of the obligation of a party to pay an instrument does not discharge the obligation of an indorser or accommodation party having a right of recourse against the discharged party.

(c) If a person entitled to enforce an instrument agrees, with or without consideration, to an extension of the due date of the obligation of a party to pay the instrument, the extension discharges an indorser or accommodation party having a right of recourse against the party whose obligation is extended to the extent the indorser or accommodation party proves that the extension caused loss to the indorser or accommodation party with respect to the right of recourse.

(d) If a person entitled to enforce an instrument agrees, with or without consideration, to a material modification of the obligation of a party other than an extension of the due date, the modification discharges the obligation of an indorser or accommodation party having a right of recourse against the person whose obligation is modified to the extent the modification causes loss to the indorser or accommodation party with respect to the right of recourse. The loss suffered by the indorser or accommodation party as a result of the modification is equal to the amount of the right of recourse unless the person enforcing the instrument proves that no loss was caused by the modification or that the loss caused by the modification was an amount less than the amount of the right of recourse.

(e) If the obligation of a party to pay an instrument is secured by an interest in collateral and a person entitled to enforce the instrument impairs the value of the interest in collateral, the obligation of an indorser or accommodation party having a right of recourse against the obligor is discharged to the extent of the impairment. The value of an interest in collateral is impaired to the extent (i) the value of the interest is reduced to an amount less than the amount of the right of recourse of the party asserting discharge, or (ii) the reduction in value of the interest causes an increase in the amount by which the amount of the right of recourse exceeds the value of the interest.

The burden of proving impairment is on the party asserting discharge.

(f) If the obligation of a party is secured by an interest in collateral not provided by an accommodation party and a person entitled to enforce the instrument impairs the value of the interest in collateral, the obligation of any party who is jointly and severally liable with respect to the secured obligation is discharged to the extent the impairment causes the party asserting discharge to pay more than that party would have been obliged to pay, taking into account rights of contribution, if impairment had not occurred. If the party asserting discharge is an accommodation party not entitled to discharge under subsection (e), the party is deemed to have a right to contribution based on joint and several liability rather than a right to reimbursement. The burden of proving impairment is on the party asserting discharge.

(g) Under subsection (e) or (f), impairing value of an interest in collateral includes (i) failure to obtain or maintain perfection or recordation of the interest in collateral, (ii) release of collateral without substitution of collateral of equal value, (iii) failure to perform a duty to preserve the value of collateral owed, under Article 9 or other law, to a debtor or surety or other person secondarily liable, or (iv) failure to comply with applicable law in disposing of collateral.

(h) An accommodation party is not discharged under subsection (c), (d), or (e) unless the person entitled to enforce the instrument knows of the accommodation or has notice under Section 3—419(c) that the instrument was signed for accommodation.

(i) A party is not discharged under this section if (i) the party asserting discharge consents to the event or conduct that is the basis of the discharge, or (ii) the instrument or a separate agreement of the party provides for waiver of discharge under this section either specifically or by general language indicating that parties waive defenses based on suretyship or impairment of collateral.

ADDENDUM TO REVISED ARTICLE 3 NOTES TO LEGISLATIVE COUNSEL

(1) If revised Article 3 is adopted in your state, the reference in Section 2—511 to Section 3—802 should be changed to Section 3—310.

(2) If revised Article 3 is adopted in your state and the Uniform Fiduciaries Act is also in effect in your state, you may want to consider amending Uniform Fiduciaries Act @3:§9 to conform to Section 3—307(b)(2)(iii) and (4)(iii). See Official Comment 3 to Section 3—307.

REVISED ARTICLE 4 BANK DEPOSITS AND COLLECTIONS

Part 1 General Provisions and Definitions

§4—101. SHORT TITLE

This Article may be cited as Uniform Commercial Code—Bank Deposits and Collections.

As amended in 1990.

§4—102. APPLICABILITY

(a) To the extent that items within this Article are also within Articles 3 and 8, they are subject to those Articles. If there is conflict, this Article governs Article 3, but Article 8 governs this Article.

(b) The liability of a bank for action or non-action with respect to an item handled by it for purposes of presentment, payment, or collection is governed by the law of the place where the bank is located. In the case of action or non-action by or at a branch or separate office of a bank, its liability is governed by the law of the place where the branch or separate office is located.

§4—103. VARIATION BY AGREEMENT; MEASURE OF DAMAGES; ACTION CONSTITUTING ORDINARY CARE

(a) The effect of the provisions of this Article may be varied by agreement, but the parties to the agreement cannot disclaim a bank's responsibility for its lack of good faith or failure to exercise ordinary care or limit the measure of damages for the lack or failure. However, the parties may determine by agreement the standards by which the bank's responsibility is to be measured if those standards are not manifestly unreasonable.

(b) Federal Reserve regulations and operating circulars, clearing-house rules, and the like have the effect of agreements under subsection (a), whether or not specifically assented to by all parties interested in items handled.

(c) Action or non-action approved by this Article or pursuant to Federal Reserve regulations or operating circulars is the exercise of ordinary care and, in the absence of special instructions, action or non-action consistent with clearing-house rules and the like or with a general banking usage not disapproved by this Article, is prima facie the exercise of ordinary care.

(d) The specification or approval of certain procedures by this Article is not disapproval of other procedures that may be reasonable under the circumstances.

(e) The measure of damages for failure to exercise ordinary care in handling an item is the amount of the item reduced by an amount that could not have been realized by the exercise of ordinary care. If there is also bad faith it includes any other damages the party suffered as a proximate consequence.

As amended in 1990.

§4—104. DEFINITIONS AND INDEX OF DEFINITIONS

(a) In this Article, unless the context otherwise requires:

(1) "Account" means any deposit or credit account with a bank, including a demand, time, savings, passbook, share draft, or like account, other than an account evidenced by a certificate of deposit;

(2) "Afternoon" means the period of a day between noon and midnight;

(3) "Banking day" means the part of a day on which a bank is open to the public for carrying on substantially all of its banking functions;

(4) "Clearing house" means an association of banks or other payors regularly clearing items;

(5) "Customer" means a person having an account with a bank or for whom a bank has agreed to collect items, including a bank that maintains an account at another bank;

(6) "Documentary draft" means a draft to be presented for acceptance or payment if specified documents, certificated securities (Section 8—102) or instructions for uncertificated securities (Section 8—102), or other certificates, statements, or the like are to be received by the drawee or other payor before acceptance or payment of the draft;

(7) "Draft" means a draft as defined in Section 3—104 or an item, other than an instrument, that is an order;

(8) "Drawee" means a person ordered in a draft to make payment;

(9) "Item" means an instrument or a promise or order to pay money handled by a bank for collection or payment. The term does not include a payment order governed by Article 4A or a credit or debit card slip;

(10) "Midnight deadline" with respect to a bank is midnight on its next banking day following the banking day on which it receives the relevant item or notice or from which the time for taking action commences to run, whichever is later;

(11) "Settle" means to pay in cash, by clearing-house settlement, in a charge or credit or by remittance, or otherwise as agreed. A settlement may be either provisional or final;

(12) "Suspends payments" with respect to a bank means that it has been closed by order of the supervisory authorities, that a public officer has been appointed to take it over, or that it ceases or refuses to make payments in the ordinary course of business.

(b) [Other definitions' section references deleted.]

(c) [Other definitions' section references deleted.]

(d) In addition, Article 1 contains general definitions and principles of construction and interpretation applicable throughout this Article.

§4—105. "BANK"; "DEPOSITARY BANK"; "PAYOR BANK"; "INTERMEDIARY BANK"; "COLLECTING BANK"; "PRESENTING BANK"

In this Article:

(1) "Bank" means a person engaged in the business of banking, including a savings bank, savings and loan association, credit union, or trust company;

(2) "Depositary bank" means the first bank to take an item even though it is also the payor bank, unless the item is presented for immediate payment over the counter;

(3) "Payor bank" means a bank that is the drawee of a draft;

(4) "Intermediary bank" means a bank to which an item is transferred in course of collection except the depositary or payor bank;

(5) "Collecting bank" means a bank handling an item for collection except the payor bank;

(6) "Presenting bank" means a bank presenting an item except a payor bank.

§4—106. PAYABLE THROUGH OR PAYABLE AT BANK: COLLECTING BANK

(a) If an item states that it is "payable through" a bank identified in the item, (i) the item designates the bank as a collecting bank and does not by itself authorize the bank to pay the item, and (ii) the item may be presented for payment only by or through the bank.

Alternative A

(b) If an item states that it is "payable at" a bank identified in the item, the item is equivalent to a draft drawn on the bank.

Alternative B

(b) If an item states that it is "payable at" a bank identified in the item, (i) the item designates the bank as a collecting bank and does not by itself authorize the bank to pay the item, and (ii) the item may be presented for payment only by or through the bank.

(c) If a draft names a nonbank drawee and it is unclear whether a bank named in the draft is a co-drawee or a collecting bank, the bank is a collecting bank.

As added in 1990.

§4—107. SEPARATE OFFICE OF BANK

A branch or separate office of a bank is a separate bank for the purpose of computing the time within which and determining the place at or to which action may be taken or notices or orders shall be given under this Article and under Article 3.

As amended in 1962 and 1990.

§4—108. TIME OF RECEIPT OF ITEMS

(a) For the purpose of allowing time to process items, prove balances, and make the necessary entries on its books to determine its position for the day, a bank may fix an afternoon hour of 2 P.M. or later as a cutoff hour for the handling of money and items and the making of entries on its books.

(b) An item or deposit of money received on any day after a cutoff hour so fixed or after the close of the banking day may be treated as being received at the opening of the next banking day.

As amended in 1990.

§4—109. DELAYS

(a) Unless otherwise instructed, a collecting bank in a good faith effort to secure payment of a specific item drawn on a payor other than a bank, and with or without the approval of any person involved, may waive, modify, or extend time limits imposed or permitted by this [act] for a period not exceeding two additional banking days without discharge of drawers or indorsers or liability to its transferor or a prior party.

(b) Delay by a collecting bank or payor bank beyond time limits prescribed or permitted by this [act] or by instructions is excused if (i) the delay is caused by interruption of communication or computer facilities, suspension of payments by another bank, war, emergency conditions, failure of equipment, or other circumstances beyond the control of the bank, and (ii) the bank exercises such diligence as the circumstances require.

§4—110. ELECTRONIC PRESENTMENT

(a) "Agreement for electronic presentment" means an agreement, clearing-house rule, or Federal Reserve regulation or operating circular, providing that presentment of an item may be made by transmission of an image of an item or information describing the item ("presentment notice") rather than delivery of the item itself. The agreement may provide for procedures governing retention, presentment, payment, dishonor, and other matters concerning items subject to the agreement.

(b) Presentment of an item pursuant to an agreement for presentment is made when the presentment notice is received.

(c) If presentment is made by presentment notice, a reference to "item" or "check" in this Article means the presentment notice unless the context otherwise indicates.

As added in 1990.

§4—111. STATUTE OF LIMITATIONS

An action to enforce an obligation, duty, or right arising under this Article must be commenced within three years after the [cause of action] accrues.

As added in 1990.

Part 2 Collection of Items: Depositary and Collecting Banks

§4—201. STATUS OF COLLECTING BANK AS AGENT AND PROVISIONAL STATUS OF CREDITS; APPLICABILITY OF ARTICLE; ITEM INDORSED "PAY ANY BANK"

(a) Unless a contrary intent clearly appears and before the time that a settlement given by a collecting bank for an item is or becomes final, the bank, with respect to an item, is an agent or sub-agent of the owner of the item and any settlement given for the item is provisional. This provision applies regardless of the form of indorsement or lack of indorsement and even though credit given for the item is subject to immediate withdrawal as of right or is in fact withdrawn; but the continuance of ownership of an item by its owner and any rights of the owner to proceeds of the item are subject to rights of a collecting bank, such as those resulting from outstanding advances on the item and rights of recoupment or setoff. If an item is handled by banks for purposes of presentment, payment, collection, or return, the relevant provisions of this Article apply even though action of the parties clearly establishes that a particular bank has purchased the item and is the owner of it.

(b) After an item has been indorsed with the words "pay any bank" or the like, only a bank may acquire the rights of a holder until the item has been:

(1) returned to the customer initiating collection; or

(2) specially indorsed by a bank to a person who is not a bank.

As amended in 1990.

§4—202. RESPONSIBILITY FOR COLLECTION OR RETURN; WHEN ACTION TIMELY

(a) A collecting bank must exercise ordinary care in:

(1) presenting an item or sending it for presentment;

(2) sending notice of dishonor or nonpayment or returning an item other than a documentary draft to the bank's transferor after learning that the item has not been paid or accepted, as the case may be;

(3) settling for an item when the bank receives final settlement; and

(4) notifying its transferor of any loss or delay in transit within a reasonable time after discovery thereof.

(b) A collecting bank exercises ordinary care under subsection (a) by taking proper action before its midnight deadline following receipt of an item, notice, or settlement. Taking proper action within a reasonably longer time may constitute the exercise of ordinary care, but the bank has the burden of establishing timeliness.

(c) Subject to subsection (a)(1), a bank is not liable for the insolvency, neglect, misconduct, mistake, or default of another bank or person or for loss or destruction of an item in the possession of others or in transit.

As amended in 1990.

§4—203. EFFECT OF INSTRUCTIONS

Subject to Article 3 concerning conversion of instruments (Section 3—420) and restrictive indorsements (Section 3—206), only a collecting bank's transferor can give instructions that affect the bank or constitute notice to it, and a collecting bank is not liable to prior parties for any action taken pursuant to the instructions or in accordance with any agreement with its transferor.

§4—204. METHODS OF SENDING AND PRESENTING; SENDING DIRECTLY TO PAYOR BANK

(a) A collecting bank shall send items by a reasonably prompt method, taking into consideration relevant instructions, the nature of the item, the number of those items on hand, the cost of collection involved, and the method generally used by it or others to present those items.

(b) A collecting bank may send:

(1) an item directly to the payor bank;

(2) an item to a nonbank payor if authorized by its transferor; and

(3) an item other than documentary drafts to a nonbank payor, if authorized by Federal Reserve regulation or operating circular, clearing-house rule, or the like.

(c) Presentment may be made by a presenting bank at a place where the payor bank or other payor has requested that presentment be made.

As amended in 1990.

§4—205. DEPOSITARY BANK HOLDER OF UNINDORSED ITEM

If a customer delivers an item to a depositary bank for collection:

(1) the depositary bank becomes a holder of the item at the time it receives the item for collection if the customer at the time of delivery was a holder of the item, whether or not the customer indorses the item, and, if the bank satisfies the other requirements of Section 3—302, it is a holder in due course; and

(2) the depositary bank warrants to collecting banks, the payor bank or other payor, and the drawer that the amount of the item was paid to the customer or deposited to the customer's account.

As amended in 1990.

§4—206. TRANSFER BETWEEN BANKS

Any agreed method that identifies the transferor bank is sufficient for the item's further transfer to another bank.

As amended in 1990.

§4—207. TRANSFER WARRANTIES

(a) A customer or collecting bank that transfers an item and receives a settlement or other consideration warrants to the transferee and to any subsequent collecting bank that:

(1) the warrantor is a person entitled to enforce the item;

(2) all signatures on the item are authentic andauthorized;

(3) the item has not been altered;

(4) the item is not subject to a defense or claim in recoupment (Section 3—305(a)) of any party that can be asserted against the warrantor; and

(5) the warrantor has no knowledge of any insolvency proceeding commenced with respect to the maker or acceptor or, in the case of an unaccepted draft, the drawer.

(b) If an item is dishonored, a customer or collecting bank transferring the item and receiving settlement or other consideration is obliged to pay the amount due on the item (i) according to the terms of the item at the time it was transferred, or (ii) if the transfer was of an incomplete item, according to its terms when completed as stated in Sections 3—115 and 3—407. The obligation of a transferor is owed to the transferee and to any subsequent collecting bank that takes the item in good faith. A transferor cannot disclaim its obligation under this subsection by an indorsement stating that it is made "without recourse" or otherwise disclaiming liability.

(c) A person to whom the warranties under subsection (a) are made and who took the item in good faith may recover from the warrantor as damages for breach of warranty an amount equal to the loss suffered as a result of the breach, but not more than the amount of the item plus expenses and loss of interest incurred as a result of the breach.

(d) The warranties stated in subsection (a) cannot be disclaimed with respect to checks. Unless notice of a claim for breach of warranty is given to the warrantor within 30 days after the claimant has reason to know of the breach and the identity of the warrantor, the warrantor is discharged to the extent of any loss caused by the delay in giving notice of the claim.

(e) A cause of action for breach of warranty under this section accrues when the claimant has reason to know of the breach.

As amended in 1990.

§4—208. PRESENTMENT WARRANTIES

(a) If an unaccepted draft is presented to the drawee for payment or acceptance and the drawee pays or accepts the draft, (i) the person obtaining payment or acceptance, at the time of presentment, and (ii) a previous transferor of the draft, at the time of transfer, warrant to the drawee that pays or accepts the draft in good faith that:

(1) the warrantor is, or was, at the time the warrantor transferred the draft, a person entitled to enforce the draft or authorized to obtain payment or acceptance of the draft on behalf of a person entitled to enforce the draft;

(2) the draft has not been altered; and

(3) the warrantor has no knowledge that the signature of the purported drawer of the draft is unauthorized.

(b) A drawee making payment may recover from a warrantor damages for breach of warranty equal to the amount paid by the drawee less the amount the drawee received or is entitled to receive from the drawer because of the payment. In addition, the drawee is entitled to compensation for expenses and loss of interest resulting from the breach. The right of the drawee to recover damages under this subsection is not affected by any failure of the drawee to exercise ordinary care in making payment. If the drawee accepts the draft (i) breach of warranty is a defense to the obligation of the acceptor, and (ii) if the acceptor makes payment with respect to the draft, the acceptor is entitled to recover from a warrantor for breach of warranty the amounts stated in this subsection.

(c) If a drawee asserts a claim for breach of warranty under subsection (a) based on an unauthorized indorsement of the draft or an alteration of the draft, the warrantor may defend by proving that the indorsement is effective under Section 3—404 or 3—405 or the drawer is precluded under Section 3—406 or 4—406 from asserting against the drawee the unauthorized indorsement or alteration.

(d) If (i) a dishonored draft is presented for payment to the drawer or an indorser or (ii) any other item is presented for payment to a party obliged to pay the item, and the item is paid, the person obtaining payment and a prior transferor of the item warrant to the person making payment in good faith that the warrantor is, or was, at the time the warrantor transferred the item, a person entitled to enforce the item or authorized to obtain payment on

behalf of a person entitled to enforce the item. The person making payment may recover from any warrantor for breach of warranty an amount equal to the amount paid plus expenses and loss of interest resulting from the breach.

(e) The warranties stated in subsections (a) and (d) cannot be disclaimed with respect to checks. Unless notice of a claim for breach of warranty is given to the warrantor within 30 days after the claimant has reason to know of the breach and the identity of the warrantor, the warrantor is discharged to the extent of any loss caused by the delay in giving notice of the claim.

(f) A cause of action for breach of warranty under this section accrues when the claimant has reason to know of the breach.

As amended in 1990.

§4—209. ENCODING AND RETENTION WARRANTIES

(a) A person who encodes information on or with respect to an item after issue warrants to any subsequent collecting bank and to the payor bank or other payor that the information is correctly encoded. If the customer of a depositary bank encodes, that bank also makes the warranty.

(b) A person who undertakes to retain an item pursuant to an agreement for electronic presentment warrants to any subsequent collecting bank and to the payor bank or other payor that retention and presentment of the item comply with the agreement. If a customer of a depositary bank undertakes to retain an item, that bank also makes this warranty.

(c) A person to whom warranties are made under this section and who took the item in good faith may recover from the warrantor as damages for breach of warranty an amount equal to the loss suffered as a result of the breach, plus expenses and loss of interest incurred as a result of the breach.

As added in 1990.

§4—210. SECURITY INTEREST OF COLLECTING BANK IN ITEMS, ACCOMPANYING DOCUMENTS AND PROCEEDS

(a) A collecting bank has a security interest in an item and any accompanying documents or the proceeds of either:

(1) in case of an item deposited in an account, to the extent to which credit given for the item has been withdrawn or applied;

(2) in case of an item for which it has given credit available for withdrawal as of right, to the extent of the credit given, whether or not the credit is drawn upon or there is a right of charge-back; or

(3) if it makes an advance on or against the item.

(b) If credit given for several items received at one time or pursuant to a single agreement is withdrawn or applied in part, the security interest remains upon all the items, any accompanying documents or the proceeds of either. For the purpose of this section, credits first given are first withdrawn.

(c) Receipt by a collecting bank of a final settlement for an item is a realization on its security interest in the item, accompanying documents, and proceeds. So long as the bank does not receive final settlement for the item or give up possession of the item or accompanying documents for purposes other than collection, the security interest continues to that extent and is subject to Article 9, but:

(1) no security agreement is necessary to make the security interest enforceable (Section 9—203 (1)(a));

(2) no filing is required to perfect the security interest; and

(3) the security interest has priority over conflicting perfected security interests in the item, accompanying documents, or proceeds.

As amended in 1990 and 1999.

§4—211. WHEN BANK GIVES VALUE FOR PURPOSES OF HOLDER IN DUE COURSE

For purposes of determining its status as a holder in due course, a bank has given value to the extent it has a security interest in an item, if the bank otherwise complies with the requirements of Section 3—302 on what constitutes a holder in due course.

As amended in 1990.

§4—212. PRESENTMENT BY NOTICE OF ITEM NOT PAYABLE BY, THROUGH, OR AT BANK; LIABILITY OF DRAWER OR INDORSER

(a) Unless otherwise instructed, a collecting bank may present an item not payable by, through, or at a bank by sending to the party to accept or pay a written notice that the bank holds the item for acceptance or payment. The notice must be sent in time to be received on or before the day when presentment is due and the bank must meet any requirement of the party to accept or pay under Section 3—501 by the close of the bank's next banking day after it knows of the requirement.

(b) If presentment is made by notice and payment, acceptance, or request for compliance with a requirement under Section 3—501 is not received by the close of business on the day after maturity or, in the case of demand items, by the close of business on the third banking day after notice was sent, the presenting bank may treat the item as dishonored and charge any drawer or indorser by sending it notice of the facts.

As amended in 1990.

§4—213. MEDIUM AND TIME OF SETTLEMENT BY BANK

(a) With respect to settlement by a bank, the medium and time of settlement may be prescribed by Federal Reserve regulations or circulars, clearing-house rules, and the like, or agreement. In the absence of such prescription:

(1) the medium of settlement is cash or credit to an account in a Federal Reserve bank of or specified by the person to receive settlement; and

(2) the time of settlement is:

(i) with respect to tender of settlement by cash, a cashier's check, or teller's check, when the cash or check is sent or delivered;

(ii) with respect to tender of settlement by credit in an account in a Federal Reserve Bank, when the credit is made;

(iii) with respect to tender of settlement by a credit or debit to an account in a bank, when the credit or debit is made or, in the case of tender of settlement by authority to charge an account, when the authority is sent or delivered; or

(iv) with respect to tender of settlement by a funds transfer, when payment is made pursuant to Section 4A—406(a) to the person receiving settlement.

(b) If the tender of settlement is not by a medium authorized by subsection (a) or the time of settlement is not fixed by subsection (a), no settlement occurs until the tender of settlement is accepted by the person receiving settlement.

(c) If settlement for an item is made by cashier's check or teller's check and the person receiving settlement, before its midnight deadline:

(1) presents or forwards the check for collection, settlement is final when the check is finally paid; or

(2) fails to present or forward the check for collection, settlement is final at the midnight deadline of the person receiving settlement.

(d) If settlement for an item is made by giving authority to charge the account of the bank giving settlement in the bank receiving settlement, settlement is final when the charge is made by the bank receiving settlement if there are funds available in the account for the amount of the item.

As amended in 1990.

§4—214. RIGHT OF CHARGE-BACK OR REFUND; LIABILITY OF COLLECTING BANK: RETURN OF ITEM

(a) If a collecting bank has made provisional settlement with its customer for an item and fails by reason of dishonor, suspension of payments by a bank, or otherwise to receive settlement for the item which is or becomes final, the bank may revoke the settlement given by it, charge back the amount of any credit given for the item to its customer's account, or obtain refund from its customer, whether or not it is able to return the item, if by its midnight deadline or within a longer reasonable time after it learns the facts it returns the item or sends notification of the facts. If the return or notice is delayed beyond the bank's midnight deadline or a longer reasonable time after it learns the facts, the bank may revoke the settlement, charge back the credit, or obtain refund from its customer, but it is liable for any loss resulting from the delay. These rights to revoke, charge back, and obtain refund terminate if and when a settlement for the item received by the bank is or becomes final.

(b) A collecting bank returns an item when it is sent or delivered to the bank's customer or transferor or pursuant to its instructions.

(c) A depositary bank that is also the payor may charge back the amount of an item to its customer's account or obtain refund in accordance with the section governing return of an item received by a payor bank for credit on its books (Section 4—301).

(d) The right to charge back is not affected by:
   (1) previous use of a credit given for the item; or
   (2) failure by any bank to exercise ordinary care with respect to the item, but a bank so failing remains liable.

(e) A failure to charge back or claim refund does not affect other rights of the bank against the customer or any other party.

(f) If credit is given in dollars as the equivalent of the value of an item payable in foreign money, the dollar amount of any charge-back or refund must be calculated on the basis of the bank-offered spot rate for the foreign money prevailing on the day when the person entitled to the charge-back or refund learns that it will not receive payment in ordinary course.

As amended in 1990.

(3) made a provisional settlement for the item and failed to revoke the settlement in the time and manner permitted by statute, clearing-house rule, or agreement.

(b) If provisional settlement for an item does not become final, the item is not finally paid.

(c) If provisional settlement for an item between the presenting and payor banks is made through a clearing house or by debits or credits in an account between them, then to the extent that provisional debits or credits for the item are entered in accounts between the presenting and payor banks or between the presenting and successive prior collecting banks seriatim, they become final upon final payment of the item by the payor bank.

(d) If a collecting bank receives a settlement for an item which is or becomes final, the bank is accountable to its customer for the amount of the item and any provisional credit given for the item in an account with its customer becomes final.

(e) Subject to (i) applicable law stating a time for availability of funds and (ii) any right of the bank to apply the credit to an obligation of the customer, credit given by a bank for an item in a customer's account becomes available for withdrawal as of right:
   (1) if the bank has received a provisional settlement for the item, when the settlement becomes final and the bank has had a reasonable time to receive return of the item and the item has not been received within that time;
   (2) if the bank is both the depositary bank and the payor bank, and the item is finally paid, at the opening of the bank's second banking day following receipt of the item.

(f) Subject to applicable law stating a time for availability of funds and any right of a bank to apply a deposit to an obligation of the depositor, a deposit of money becomes available for withdrawal as of right at the opening of the bank's next banking day after receipt of the deposit.

As amended in 1990.

§4—215. FINAL PAYMENT OF ITEM BY PAYOR BANK; WHEN PROVISIONAL DEBITS AND CREDITS BECOME FINAL; WHEN CERTAIN CREDITS BECOME AVAILABLE FOR WITHDRAWAL

(a) An item is finally paid by a payor bank when the bank has first done any of the following:
   (1) paid the item in cash;
   (2) settled for the item without having a right to revoke the settlement under statute, clearing-house rule, or agreement; or

§4—216. INSOLVENCY AND PREFERENCE

(a) If an item is in or comes into the possession of a payor or collecting bank that suspends payment and the item has not been finally paid, the item must be returned by the receiver, trustee, or agent in charge of the closed bank to the presenting bank or the closed bank's customer.

(b) If a payor bank finally pays an item and suspends payments without making a settlement for the item with its customer or the presenting bank which settlement is or becomes final, the owner of the item has a preferred claim against the payor bank.

(c) If a payor bank gives or a collecting bank gives or receives a provisional settlement for an item and thereafter suspends payments, the suspension does not prevent or interfere with the settlement's becoming final if the finality occurs automatically upon the lapse of certain time or the happening of certain events.

(d) If a collecting bank receives from subsequent parties settlement for an item, which settlement is or becomes final and the bank suspends payments without making a settlement for the item with its customer which settlement is or becomes final, the owner of the item has a preferred claim against the collecting bank.

As amended in 1990.

Part 3 Collection of Items: Payor Banks

§4—301. DEFERRED POSTING; RECOVERY OF PAYMENT BY RETURN OF ITEMS; TIME OF DISHONOR; RETURN OF ITEMS BY PAYOR BANK

(a) If a payor bank settles for a demand item other than a documentary draft presented otherwise than for immediate payment over the counter before midnight of the banking day of receipt, the payor bank may revoke the settlement and recover the settlement if, before it has made final payment and before its midnight deadline, it

(1) returns the item; or

(2) sends written notice of dishonor or nonpayment if the item is unavailable for return.

(b) If a demand item is received by a payor bank for credit on its books, it may return the item or send notice of dishonor and may revoke any credit given or recover the amount thereof withdrawn by its customer, if it acts within the time limit and in the manner specified in subsection (a).

(c) Unless previous notice of dishonor has been sent, an item is dishonored at the time when for purposes of dishonor it is returned or notice sent in accordance with this section.

(d) An item is returned:

(1) as to an item presented through a clearing house, when it is delivered to the presenting or last collecting bank or to the clearing house or is sent or delivered in accordance with clearing-house rules; or

(2) in all other cases, when it is sent or delivered to the bank's customer or transferor or pursuant to instructions.

As amended in 1990.

§4—302. PAYOR BANK'S RESPONSIBILITY FOR LATE RETURN OF ITEM

(a) If an item is presented to and received by a payor bank, the bank is accountable for the amount of:

(1) a demand item, other than a documentary draft, whether properly payable or not, if the bank, in any case in which it is not also the depositary bank, retains the item beyond midnight of the banking day of receipt without settling for it or, whether or not it is also the depositary bank, does not pay or return the item or send notice of dishonor until after its midnight deadline; or

(2) any other properly payable item unless, within the time allowed for acceptance or payment of that item, the bank either accepts or pays the item or returns it and accompanying documents.

(b) The liability of a payor bank to pay an item pursuant to subsection (a) is subject to defenses based on breach of a presentment warranty (Section 4—208) or proof that the person seeking enforcement of the liability presented or transferred the item for the purpose of defrauding the payor bank.

As amended in 1990.

§4—303. WHEN ITEMS SUBJECT TO NOTICE, STOP-PAYMENT ORDER, LEGAL PROCESS, OR SETOFF; ORDER IN WHICH ITEMS MAY BE CHARGED OR CERTIFIED

(a) Any knowledge, notice, or stop-payment order received by, legal process served upon, or setoff exercised by a payor bank comes too late to terminate, suspend, or modify the bank's right or duty to pay an item or to charge its customer's account for the item if the knowledge, notice, stop-payment order, or legal process is received or served and a reasonable time for the bank to act thereon expires or the setoff is exercised after the earliest of the following:

(1) the bank accepts or certifies the item;

(2) the bank pays the item in cash;

(3) the bank settles for the item without having a right to revoke the settlement under statute, clearing-house rule, or agreement;

(4) the bank becomes accountable for the amount of the item under Section 4—302 dealing with the payor bank's responsibility for late return of items; or

(5) with respect to checks, a cutoff hour no earlier than one hour after the opening of the next banking day after the banking day on which the bank received the check and no later than the close of that next banking day or, if no cutoff hour is fixed, the close of the next banking day after the banking day on which the bank received the check.

(b) Subject to subsection (a), items may be accepted, paid, certified, or charged to the indicated account of its customer in any order.

As amended in 1990.

Part 4 Relationship Between Payor Bank and Its Customer

§4—401. WHEN BANK MAY CHARGE CUSTOMER'S ACCOUNT

(a) A bank may charge against the account of a customer an item that is properly payable from the account even though the charge creates an overdraft. An item is properly payable if it is authorized by the customer and is in accordance with any agreement between the customer and bank.

(b) A customer is not liable for the amount of an overdraft if the customer neither signed the item nor benefited from the proceeds of the item.

(c) A bank may charge against the account of a customer a check that is otherwise properly payable from the account, even though payment was made before the date of the check, unless the customer has given notice to the bank of the postdating describing the check with reasonable certainty. The notice is effective for the period stated in Section 4—403(b) for stop-payment orders, and must be received at such time and in such manner as to afford the bank a reasonable opportunity to act on it before the bank takes any action with respect to the check described in Section 4—303. If a bank charges against the account of a customer a check before the date stated in the notice of postdating, the bank is liable for damages for the loss resulting from its act. The loss may include damages for dishonor of subsequent items under Section 4—402.

(d) A bank that in good faith makes payment to a holder may charge the indicated account of its customer according to:

  (1) the original terms of the altered item; or
  (2) the terms of the completed item, even though the bank knows the item has been completed unless the bank has notice that the completion was improper.

As amended in 1990.

§4—402. BANK'S LIABILITY TO CUSTOMER FOR WRONGFUL DISHONOR; TIME OF DETERMINING INSUFFICIENCY OF ACCOUNT

(a) Except as otherwise provided in this Article, a payor bank wrongfully dishonors an item if it dishonors an item that is properly payable, but a bank may dishonor an item that would create an overdraft unless it has agreed to pay the overdraft.

(b) A payor bank is liable to its customer for damages proximately caused by the wrongful dishonor of an item. Liability is limited to actual damages proved and may include damages for an arrest or prosecution of the customer or other consequential damages. Whether any consequential damages are proximately caused by the wrongful dishonor is a question of fact to be determined in each case.

(c) A payor bank's determination of the customer's account balance on which a decision to dishonor for insufficiency of available funds is based may be made at any time between the time the item is received by the payor bank and the time that the payor bank returns the item or gives notice in lieu of return, and no more than one determination need be made. If, at the election of the payor bank, a subsequent balance determination is made for the purpose of reevaluating the bank's decision to dishonor the item, the account balance at that time is determinative of whether a dishonor for insufficiency of available funds is wrongful.

As amended in 1990.

§4—403. CUSTOMER'S RIGHT TO STOP PAYMENT; BURDEN OF PROOF OF LOSS

(a) A customer or any person authorized to draw on the account if there is more than one person may stop payment of any item drawn on the customer's account or close the account by an order to the bank describing the item or account with reasonable certainty received at a time and in a manner that affords the bank a reasonable opportunity to act on it before any action by the bank with respect to the item described in Section 4—303. If the signature of more than one person is required to draw on an account, any of these persons may stop payment or close the account.

(b) A stop-payment order is effective for six months, but it lapses after 14 calendar days if the original order was oral and was not confirmed in writing within that period. A stop-payment order may be renewed for additional six-month periods by a writing given to the bank within a period during which the stop-payment order is effective.

(c) The burden of establishing the fact and amount of loss resulting from the payment of an item contrary to a stop-payment order or order to close an account is on the customer. The loss from payment of an item contrary to a stop-payment order may include damages for dishonor of subsequent items under Section 4—402.

As amended in 1990.

§4—404. BANK NOT OBLIGED TO PAY CHECK MORE THAN SIX MONTHS OLD

A bank is under no obligation to a customer having a checking account to pay a check, other than a certified check, which is presented more than six months after its date, but it may charge its customer's account for a payment made thereafter in good faith.

§4—405. DEATH OR INCOMPETENCE OF CUSTOMER

(a) A payor or collecting bank's authority to accept, pay, or collect an item or to account for proceeds of its collection, if otherwise effective, is not rendered ineffective by incompetence of a customer of either bank existing at the time the item is issued or its collection is undertaken if the bank does not know of an adjudication of incompetence. Neither death nor incompetence of a customer revokes the authority to accept, pay, collect, or account until the bank knows of the fact of death or of an adjudication of incompetence and has reasonable opportunity to act on it.

(b) Even with knowledge, a bank may for 10 days after the date of death pay or certify checks drawn on or before the date unless ordered to stop payment by a person claiming an interest in the account.

As amended in 1990.

§4—406. CUSTOMER'S DUTY TO DISCOVER AND REPORT UNAUTHORIZED SIGNATURE OR ALTERATION

(a) A bank that sends or makes available to a customer a statement of account showing payment of items for the account shall either return or make available to the customer the items paid or provide information in the statement of account sufficient to allow the customer reasonably to identify the items paid. The statement of account provides sufficient information if the item is described by item number, amount, and date of payment.

(b) If the items are not returned to the customer, the person retaining the items shall either retain the items or, if the items are destroyed, maintain the capacity to furnish legible copies of the items until the expiration of seven years after receipt of the items. A customer may request an item from the bank that paid the item, and that bank must provide in a reasonable time either the item or, if the item has been destroyed or is not otherwise obtainable, a legible copy of the item.

(c) If a bank sends or makes available a statement of account or items pursuant to subsection (a), the customer must exercise reasonable promptness in examining the statement or the items to determine whether any payment was not authorized because of an alteration of an item or because a purported signature by or on behalf of the customer was not authorized. If, based on the statement or items provided, the customer should reasonably have discovered the unauthorized payment, the customer must promptly notify the bank of the relevant facts.

(d) If the bank proves that the customer failed, with respect to an item, to comply with the duties imposed on the customer by subsection (c), the customer is precluded from asserting against the bank:

(1) the customer's unauthorized signature or any alteration on the item, if the bank also proves that it suffered a loss by reason of the failure; and

(2) the customer's unauthorized signature or alteration by the same wrongdoer on any other item paid in good faith by the bank if the payment was made before the bank received notice from the customer of the unauthorized signature or alteration and after the customer had been afforded a reasonable period of time, not exceeding 30 days, in which to examine the item or statement of account and notify the bank.

(e) If subsection (d) applies and the customer proves that the bank failed to exercise ordinary care in paying the item and that the failure substantially contributed to loss, the loss is allocated between the customer precluded and the bank asserting the preclusion according to the extent to which the failure of the customer to comply with subsection (c) and the failure of the bank to exercise ordinary care contributed to the loss. If the customer proves that the bank did not pay the item in good faith, the preclusion under subsection (d) does not apply.

(f) Without regard to care or lack of care of either the customer or the bank, a customer who does not within one year after the statement or items are made available to the customer (subsection (a)) discover and report the customer's unauthorized signature on or any alteration on the item is precluded from asserting against the bank the unauthorized signature or alteration. If there is a preclusion under this subsection, the payor bank may not recover for breach or warranty under Section 4—208 with respect to the unauthorized signature or alteration to which the preclusion applies.

As amended in 1990.

§4—407. PAYOR BANK'S RIGHT TO SUBROGATION ON IMPROPER PAYMENT

If a payor has paid an item over the order of the drawer or maker to stop payment, or after an account has been closed, or otherwise under circumstances giving a basis for objection by the drawer or maker, to prevent unjust enrichment and only to the extent necessary to prevent loss to the bank by reason of its payment of the item, the payor bank is subrogated to the rights

(1) of any holder in due course on the item against the drawer or maker;

(2) of the payee or any other holder of the item against the drawer or maker either on the item or under the transaction out of which the item arose; and

(3) of the drawer or maker against the payee or any other holder of the item with respect to the transaction out of which the item arose.

As amended in 1990.

Part 5 Collection of Documentary Drafts

§4—501. HANDLING OF DOCUMENTARY DRAFTS; DUTY TO SEND FOR PRESENTMENT AND TO NOTIFY CUSTOMER OF DISHONOR

A bank that takes a documentary draft for collection shall present or send the draft and accompanying documents for presentment and, upon learning that the draft has not been paid or accepted in due course, shall seasonably notify its customer of the fact even though it may have discounted or bought the draft or extended credit available for withdrawal as of right.

As amended in 1990.

§4—502. PRESENTMENT OF "ON ARRIVAL" DRAFTS

If a draft or the relevant instructions require presentment "on arrival", "when goods arrive" or the like, the collecting bank need not present until in its judgment a reasonable time for arrival of the goods has expired. Refusal to pay or accept because the goods have not arrived is not dishonor; the bank must notify its transferor of the refusal but need not present the draft again until it is instructed to do so or learns of the arrival of the goods.

§4—503. RESPONSIBILITY OF PRESENTING BANK FOR DOCUMENTS AND GOODS; REPORT OF REASONS FOR DISHONOR; REFEREE IN CASE OF NEED

Unless otherwise instructed and except as provided in Article 5, a bank presenting a documentary draft:

(1) must deliver the documents to the drawee on acceptance of the draft if it is payable more than three days after presentment, otherwise, only on payment; and

(2) upon dishonor, either in the case of presentment for acceptance or presentment for payment, may seek and follow instructions from any referee in case of need designated in the draft or, if the presenting bank does not choose to utilize the referee's services, it must use diligence and good faith to ascertain the reason for dishonor, must notify its transferor of the dishonor and of the results of its effort to ascertain the reasons therefor, and must request instructions.

However, the presenting bank is under no obligation with respect to goods represented by the documents except to follow any reasonable instructions seasonably received; it has a right to reimbursement for any expense incurred in following instructions and to prepayment of or indemnity for those expenses.

As amended in 1990.

§4—504. PRIVILEGE OF PRESENTING BANK TO DEAL WITH GOODS; SECURITY INTEREST FOR EXPENSES

(a) A presenting bank that, following the dishonor of a documentary draft, has seasonably requested instructions but does not receive them within a reasonable time may store, sell, or otherwise deal with the goods in any reasonable manner.

(b) For its reasonable expenses incurred by action under subsection (a) the presenting bank has a lien upon the goods or their proceeds, which may be foreclosed in the same manner as an unpaid seller's lien.

As amended in 1990.

ARTICLE 4A FUNDS TRANSFERS

Part 1 Subject Matter and Definitions

§4A—101. SHORT TITLE

This Article may be cited as Uniform Commercial Code-Funds Transfers.

§4A—102. SUBJECT MATTER

Except as otherwise provided in Section 4A—108, this Article applies to funds transfers defined in Section 4A—104.

§4A—103. PAYMENT ORDER—DEFINITIONS

(a) In this Article:

(1) "Payment order" means an instruction of a sender to a receiving bank, transmitted orally, electronically, or in writing, to pay, or to cause another bank to pay, a fixed or determinable amount of money to a beneficiary if:

(i) the instruction does not state a condition to payment to the beneficiary other than time of payment,

(ii) the receiving bank is to be reimbursed by debiting an account of, or otherwise receiving payment from, the sender, and

(iii) the instruction is transmitted by the sender directly to the receiving bank or to an agent, funds-transfer system, or communication system for transmittal to the receiving bank.

(2) "Beneficiary" means the person to be paid by the beneficiary's bank.

(3) "Beneficiary's bank" means the bank identified in a payment order in which an account of the beneficiary is to be credited pursuant to the order or which otherwise is to make payment to

the beneficiary if the order does not provide for payment to an account.

(4) "Receiving bank" means the bank to which the sender's instruction is addressed.

(5) "Sender" means the person giving the instruction to the receiving bank.

(b) If an instruction complying with subsection (a)(1) is to make more than one payment to a beneficiary, the instruction is a separate payment order with respect to each payment.

(c) A payment order is issued when it is sent to the receiving bank.

§4A—104. FUNDS TRANSFER—DEFINITIONS

In this Article:

(a) "Funds transfer" means the series of transactions, beginning with the originator's payment order, made for the purpose of making payment to the beneficiary of the order. The term includes any payment order issued by the originator's bank or an intermediary bank intended to carry out the originator's payment order. A funds transfer is completed by acceptance by the beneficiary's bank of a payment order for the benefit of the beneficiary of the originator's payment order.

(b) "Intermediary bank" means a receiving bank other than the originator's bank or the beneficiary's bank.

(c) "Originator" means the sender of the first payment order in a funds transfer.

(d) "Originator's bank" means (i) the receiving bank to which the payment order of the originator is issued if the originator is not a bank, or (ii) the originator if the originator is a bank.

§4A—105. OTHER DEFINITIONS

(a) In this Article:

(1) "Authorized account" means a deposit account of a customer in a bank designated by the customer as a source of payment of payment orders issued by the customer to the bank. If a customer does not so designate an account, any account of the customer is an authorized account if payment of a payment order from that account is not inconsistent with a restriction on the use of that account.

(2) "Bank" means a person engaged in the business of banking and includes a savings bank, savings and loan association, credit union, and trust company. A branch or separate office of a bank is a separate bank for purposes of this Article.

(3) "Customer" means a person, including a bank, having an account with a bank or from whom a bank has agreed to receive payment orders.

(4) "Funds-transfer business day" of a receiving bank means the part of a day during which the receiving bank is open for the receipt, processing, and transmittal of payment orders and cancellations and amendments of payment orders.

(5) "Funds-transfer system" means a wire transfer network, automated clearing house, or other communication system of a clearing house or other association of banks through which a payment order by a bank may be transmitted to the bank to which the order is addressed.

(6) "Good faith" means honesty in fact and the observance of reasonable commercial standards of fair dealing.

(7) "Prove" with respect to a fact means to meet the burden of establishing the fact (Section 1—201(8)).

(b) Other definitions applying to this Article and the sections in which they appear are:

"Acceptance"	Section 4A—209
"Beneficiary"	Section 4A—103
"Beneficiary's bank"	Section 4A—103
"Executed"	Section 4A—301
"Execution date"	Section 4A—301
"Funds transfer"	Section 4A—104
"Funds-transfer system rule"	Section 4A—501
"Intermediary bank"	Section 4A—104
"Originator"	Section 4A—104
"Originator's bank"	Section 4A—104
"Payment by beneficiary's bank to beneficiary"	Section 4A—405
"Payment by originator to beneficiary"	Section 4A—406
"Payment by sender to receiving bank"	Section 4A—403
"Payment date"	Section 4A—401
"Payment order"	Section 4A—103
"Receiving bank"	Section 4A—103
"Security procedure"	Section 4A—201
"Sender"	Section 4A—103

(c) The following definitions in Article 4 apply to this Article:

"Clearing house"	Section 4—104
"Item"	Section 4—104
"Suspends payments"	Section 4—104

(d) In addition, Article 1 contains general definitions and principles of construction and interpretation applicable throughout this Article.

§4A—106. TIME PAYMENT ORDER IS RECEIVED

(a) The time of receipt of a payment order or communication cancelling or amending a payment order is determined by the rules applicable to receipt of a notice stated in Section 1—201(27). A receiving bank may fix a cut-off time or times on a funds-transfer business day for the receipt and processing of payment orders and communications cancelling or amending payment orders. Different cut-off times may apply to payment orders, cancellations, or amendments, or to different categories of payment orders, cancellations, or amendments. A cut-off time may apply to senders generally or different cut-off times may apply to different senders or categories of payment orders. If a payment order or communication cancelling or amending a payment order is received after the close of a funds-transfer business day or after the appropriate cut-off time on a funds-transfer business day, the receiving bank may treat the payment order or communication as received at the opening of the next funds-transfer business day.

(b) If this Article refers to an execution date or payment date or states a day on which a receiving bank is required to take action, and the date or day does not fall on a funds-transfer business day, the next day that is a funds-transfer business day is treated as the date or day stated, unless the contrary is stated in this Article.

§4A—107. FEDERAL RESERVE REGULATIONS AND OPERATING CIRCULARS

Regulations of the Board of Governors of the Federal Reserve System and operating circulars of the Federal Reserve Banks supersede any inconsistent provision of this Article to the extent of the inconsistency.

§4A—108. EXCLUSION OF CONSUMER TRANSACTIONS GOVERNED BY FEDERAL LAW

This Article does not apply to a funds transfer any part of which is governed by the Electronic Fund Transfer Act of 1978 (Title XX, Public Law 95—630, 92 Stat. 3728, 15 U.S.C. §1693 et seq.) as amended from time to time.

Part 2 Issue and Acceptance of Payment Order

§4A—201. SECURITY PROCEDURE

"Security procedure" means a procedure established by agreement of a customer and a receiving bank for the purpose of (i) verifying that a payment order or communication amending or cancelling a payment order is that of the customer, or (ii) detecting error in the transmission or the content of the payment order or communication. A security procedure may require the use of algorithms or other codes, identifying words or numbers, encryption, callback procedures, or similar security devices. Comparison of a signature on a payment order or communication with an authorized specimen signature of the customer is not by itself a security procedure.

§4A—202. AUTHORIZED AND VERIFIED PAYMENT ORDERS

(a) A payment order received by the receiving bank is the authorized order of the person identified as sender if that person authorized the order or is otherwise bound by it under the law of agency.

(b) If a bank and its customer have agreed that the authenticity of payment orders issued to the bank in the name of the customer as sender will be verified pursuant to a security procedure, a payment order received by the receiving bank is effective as the order of the customer, whether or not authorized, if (i) the security procedure is a commercially reasonable method of providing security against unauthorized payment orders, and (ii) the bank proves that it accepted the payment order in good faith and in compliance with the security procedure and any written agreement or instruction of the customer restricting acceptance of payment orders issued in the name of the customer. The bank is not required to follow an instruction that violates a written agreement with the customer or notice of which is not received at a time and in a manner affording the bank a reasonable opportunity to act on it before the payment order is accepted.

(c) Commercial reasonableness of a security procedure is a question of law to be determined by considering the wishes of the customer expressed to the bank, the circumstances of the customer known to the bank, including the size, type, and frequency of payment orders normally issued by the customer to the bank, alternative security procedures offered to the customer, and security procedures in general use by customers and receiving banks similarly situated. A security procedure is deemed to be commercially reasonable if (i) the security procedure was chosen by the customer after the bank offered, and the customer refused, a security procedure that was commercially reasonable for that customer, and (ii) the customer expressly agreed in writing to be bound by any payment order, whether or not authorized, issued in its name and accepted by the bank in compliance with the security procedure chosen by the customer.

(d) The term "sender" in this Article includes the customer in whose name a payment order is issued if the order is the authorized order of the customer under subsection (a), or it is effective as the order of the customer under subsection (b).

(e) This section applies to amendments and cancellations of payment orders to the same extent it applies to payment orders.

(f) Except as provided in this section and in Section 4A—203(a)(1), rights and obligations arising under this section or Section 4A—203 may not be varied by agreement.

§4A—203. UNENFORCEABILITY OF CERTAIN VERIFIED PAYMENT ORDERS

(a) If an accepted payment order is not, under Section 4A—202(a), an authorized order of a customer identified as sender, but is effective as an order of the customer pursuant to Section 4A—202(b), the following rules apply:

(1) By express written agreement, the receiving bank may limit the extent to which it is entitled to enforce or retain payment of the payment order.

(2) The receiving bank is not entitled to enforce or retain payment of the payment order if the customer proves that the order was not caused, directly or indirectly, by a person (i) entrusted at any time with duties to act for the customer with respect to payment orders or the security procedure, or (ii) who obtained access to transmitting facilities of the customer or who obtained, from a source controlled by the customer and without authority of the receiving bank, information facilitating breach of the security procedure, regardless of how the information was obtained or whether the customer was at fault. Information includes any access device, computer software, or the like.

(b) This section applies to amendments of payment orders to the same extent it applies to payment orders.

§4A—204. REFUND OF PAYMENT AND DUTY OF CUSTOMER TO REPORT WITH RESPECT TO UNAUTHORIZED PAYMENT ORDER

(a) If a receiving bank accepts a payment order issued in the name of its customer as sender which is (i) not authorized and not effective as the order of the customer under Section 4A—202, or (ii) not enforceable, in whole or in part, against the customer under Section 4A—203, the bank shall refund any payment of the payment order received from the customer to the extent the bank is not entitled to enforce payment and shall pay interest on the refundable amount calculated from the date the bank received payment to the date of the refund. However, the customer is not entitled to interest from the bank on the amount to be refunded if the customer fails to exercise ordinary care to determine that the order was not authorized by the customer and to notify the bank of the relevant facts within a reasonable time not exceeding 90 days after the date the customer received notification from the bank that the order was accepted or that the customer's account was debited with respect to the order. The bank is not entitled to any recovery from the customer on account of a failure by the customer to give notification as stated in this section.

(b) Reasonable time under subsection (a) may be fixed by agreement as stated in Section 1—204(1), but the obligation of a receiving bank to refund payment as stated in subsection (a) may not otherwise be varied by agreement.

§4A—205. ERRONEOUS PAYMENT ORDERS

(a) If an accepted payment order was transmitted pursuant to a security procedure for the detection of error and the payment order (i) erroneously instructed payment to a beneficiary not intended by the sender, (ii) erroneously instructed payment in an amount greater than the amount intended by the sender, or (iii) was an erroneously transmitted duplicate of a payment order previously sent by the sender, the following rules apply:

(1) If the sender proves that the sender or a person acting on behalf of the sender pursuant to Section 4A—206 complied with the security procedure and that the error would have been detected if the receiving bank had also complied, the sender is not obliged to pay the order to the extent stated in paragraphs (2) and (3).

(2) If the funds transfer is completed on the basis of an erroneous payment order described in clause (i) or (iii) of subsection (a), the sender is not obliged to pay the order and the receiving bank is entitled to recover from the beneficiary any amount paid to the beneficiary to the extent allowed by the law governing mistake and restitution.

(3) If the funds transfer is completed on the basis of a payment order described in clause (ii) of subsection (a), the sender is not obliged to pay the order to the extent the amount received by the beneficiary is greater than the amount intended by the sender. In that case, the receiving bank is entitled to recover from the beneficiary the excess amount received to the extent allowed by the law governing mistake and restitution.

(b) If (i) the sender of an erroneous payment order described in subsection (a) is not obliged to pay all or part of the order, and (ii) the sender receives notification from the receiving bank that the order was accepted by the bank or that the sender's account was debited with respect to the order, the sender has a duty to exercise ordinary care, on the basis of information available to the sender, to discover the error with respect to the order and to advise the bank of the relevant facts within a reasonable time, not exceeding 90 days, after the bank's notification was received by the sender. If the bank proves that the sender failed to perform that duty, the sender is liable to the bank for the loss the bank proves it incurred as a result of the failure, but the liability of the sender may not exceed the amount of the sender's order.

(c) This section applies to amendments to payment orders to the same extent it applies to payment orders.

§4A—206. TRANSMISSION OF PAYMENT ORDER THROUGH FUNDS-TRANSFER OR OTHER COMMUNICATION SYSTEM

(a) If a payment order addressed to a receiving bank is transmitted to a funds-transfer system or other third party communication system for transmittal to the bank, the system is deemed to be an agent of the sender for the purpose of transmitting the payment order to the bank. If there is a discrepancy between the terms of the payment order transmitted to the system and the terms of the payment order transmitted by the system to the bank, the terms of the payment order of the sender are those transmitted by the system. This section does not apply to a funds-transfer system of the Federal Reserve Banks.

(b) This section applies to cancellations and amendments to payment orders to the same extent it applies to payment orders.

§4A—207. MISDESCRIPTION OF BENEFICIARY

(a) Subject to subsection (b), if, in a payment order received by the beneficiary's bank, the name, bank account number, or other identification of the beneficiary refers to a nonexistent or unidentifiable person or account, no person has rights as a beneficiary of the order and acceptance of the order cannot occur.

(b) If a payment order received by the beneficiary's bank identifies the beneficiary both by name and by an identifying or bank account number and the name and number identify different persons, the following rules apply:

(1) Except as otherwise provided in subsection (c), if the beneficiary's bank does not know that the name and number refer to different persons, it may rely on the number as the proper identification of the beneficiary of the order. The beneficiary's bank need not determine whether the name and number refer to the same person.

(2) If the beneficiary's bank pays the person identified by name or knows that the name and number identify different persons, no person has rights as beneficiary except the person paid by the beneficiary's bank if that person was entitled to receive payment from the originator of the funds transfer. If no person has rights as beneficiary, acceptance of the order cannot occur.

(c) If (i) a payment order described in subsection (b) is accepted, (ii) the originator's payment order described the beneficiary inconsistently by name and number, and (iii) the beneficiary's bank pays the person identified by number as permitted by subsection (b)(1), the following rules apply:

(1) If the originator is a bank, the originator is obliged to pay its order.

(2) If the originator is not a bank and proves that the person identified by number was not entitled to receive payment from the originator, the originator is not obliged to pay its order unless the originator's bank proves that the originator, before acceptance of the originator's order, had notice that payment of a payment order issued by the originator might be made by the beneficiary's bank on the basis of an identifying or bank account number even if it identifies a person different from the named beneficiary. Proof of notice may be made by any admissible evidence. The originator's bank satisfies the burden of proof if it proves that the originator, before the payment order was accepted, signed a writing stating the information to which the notice relates.

(d) In a case governed by subsection (b)(1), if the beneficiary's bank rightfully pays the person identified by number and that person was not entitled to receive payment from the originator, the amount paid may be recovered from that person to the extent allowed by the law governing mistake and restitution as follows:

(1) If the originator is obliged to pay its payment order as stated in subsection (c), the originator has the right to recover.

(2) If the originator is not a bank and is not obliged to pay its payment order, the originator's bank has the right to recover.

§4A—208. MISDESCRIPTION OF INTERMEDIARY BANK OR BENEFICIARY'S BANK

(a) This subsection applies to a payment order identifying an intermediary bank or the beneficiary's bank only by an identifying number.

(1) The receiving bank may rely on the number as the proper identification of the intermediary or beneficiary's bank and need not determine whether the number identifies a bank.

(2) The sender is obliged to compensate the receiving bank for any loss and expenses incurred by the receiving bank as a result of its reliance on the number in executing or attempting to execute the order.

(b) This subsection applies to a payment order identifying an intermediary bank or the beneficiary's bank both by name and an identifying number if the name and number identify different persons.

(1) If the sender is a bank, the receiving bank may rely on the number as the proper identification of the intermediary or beneficiary's bank if

the receiving bank, when it executes the sender's order, does not know that the name and number identify different persons. The receiving bank need not determine whether the name and number refer to the same person or whether the number refers to a bank. The sender is obliged to compensate the receiving bank for any loss and expenses incurred by the receiving bank as a result of its reliance on the number in executing or attempting to execute the order.

(2) If the sender is not a bank and the receiving bank proves that the sender, before the payment order was accepted, had notice that the receiving bank might rely on the number as the proper identification of the intermediary or beneficiary's bank even if it identifies a person different from the bank identified by name, the rights and obligations of the sender and the receiving bank are governed by subsection (b)(1), as though the sender were a bank. Proof of notice may be made by any admissible evidence. The receiving bank satisfies the burden of proof if it proves that the sender, before the payment order was accepted, signed a writing stating the information to which the notice relates.

(3) Regardless of whether the sender is a bank, the receiving bank may rely on the name as the proper identification of the intermediary or beneficiary's bank if the receiving bank, at the time it executes the sender's order, does not know that the name and number identify different persons. The receiving bank need not determine whether the name and number refer to the same person.

(4) If the receiving bank knows that the name and number identify different persons, reliance on either the name or the number in executing the sender's payment order is a breach of the obligation stated in Section 4A—302(a)(1).

§4A—209. ACCEPTANCE OF PAYMENT ORDER

(a) Subject to subsection (d), a receiving bank other than the beneficiary's bank accepts a payment order when it executes the order.

(b) Subject to subsections (c) and (d), a beneficiary's bank accepts a payment order at the earliest of the following times:

(1) When the bank (i) pays the beneficiary as stated in Section 4A—405(a) or 4A—405(b), or (ii) notifies the beneficiary of receipt of the order or that the account of the beneficiary has been credited with respect to the order unless the notice indicates that the bank is rejecting the order or that funds with respect to the order may not be withdrawn or used until receipt of payment from the sender of the order;

(2) When the bank receives payment of the entire amount of the sender's order pursuant to Section 4A—403(a)(1) or 4A—403(a)(2); or

(3) The opening of the next funds-transfer business day of the bank following the payment date of the order if, at that time, the amount of the sender's order is fully covered by a withdrawable credit balance in an authorized account of the sender or the bank has otherwise received full payment from the sender, unless the order was rejected before that time or is rejected within (i) one hour after that time, or (ii) one hour after the opening of the next business day of the sender following the payment date if that time is later. If notice of rejection is received by the sender after the payment date and the authorized account of the sender does not bear interest, the bank is obliged to pay interest to the sender on the amount of the order for the number of days elapsing after the payment date to the day the sender receives notice or learns that the order was not accepted, counting that day as an elapsed day. If the withdrawable credit balance during that period falls below the amount of the order, the amount of interest payable is reduced accordingly.

(c) Acceptance of a payment order cannot occur before the order is received by the receiving bank. Acceptance does not occur under subsection (b)(2) or (b)(3) if the beneficiary of the payment order does not have an account with the receiving bank, the account has been closed, or the receiving bank is not permitted by law to receive credits for the beneficiary's account.

(d) A payment order issued to the originator's bank cannot be accepted until the payment date if the bank is the beneficiary's bank, or the execution date if the bank is not the beneficiary's bank. If the originator's bank executes the originator's payment order before the execution date or pays the beneficiary of the originator's payment order before the payment date and the payment order is subsequently cancelled pursuant to Section 4A—211(b), the bank may recover from the beneficiary any payment received to the extent allowed by the law governing mistake and restitution.

§4A—210. REJECTION OF PAYMENT ORDER

(a) A payment order is rejected by the receiving bank by a notice of rejection transmitted to the sender orally, electronically, or in writing. A notice of rejection need not use any particular words and is sufficient if it indicates that the receiving bank is rejecting the order or will not execute or pay the order. Rejection is effective when the notice is given if transmission is by a means that is reasonable in the circumstances. If notice of rejection is given by a means that is not reasonable, rejection is effective when the notice is received. If an agreement of the sender and receiving bank establishes the means to be used to reject a payment order, (i) any means complying with the agreement is reasonable and (ii) any means not complying is not reasonable unless no significant delay in receipt of the notice resulted from the use of the noncomplying means.

(b) This subsection applies if a receiving bank other than the beneficiary's bank fails to execute a payment order despite the existence on the execution date of a withdrawable credit balance in an authorized account of the sender sufficient to cover the order. If the sender does not receive notice of rejection of the order on the execution date and the authorized account of the sender does not bear interest, the bank is obliged to pay interest to the sender on the amount of the order for the number of days elapsing after the execution date to the earlier of the day the order is cancelled pursuant to Section 4A—211(d) or the day the sender receives notice or learns that the order was not executed, counting the final day of the period as an elapsed day. If the withdrawable credit balance during that period falls below the amount of the order, the amount of interest is reduced accordingly.

(c) If a receiving bank suspends payments, all unaccepted payment orders issued to it are are deemed rejected at the time the bank suspends payments.

(d) Acceptance of a payment order precludes a later rejection of the order. Rejection of a payment order precludes a later acceptance of the order.

§4A—211. CANCELLATION AND AMENDMENT OF PAYMENT ORDER

(a) A communication of the sender of a payment order cancelling or amending the order may be transmitted to the receiving bank orally, electronically, or in writing. If a security procedure is in effect between the sender and the receiving bank, the communication is not effective to cancel or amend the order unless the communication is verified pursuant to the security procedure or the bank agrees to the cancellation or amendment.

(b) Subject to subsection (a), a communication by the sender cancelling or amending a payment order is effective to cancel or amend the order if notice of the communication is received at a time and in a manner affording the receiving bank a reasonable opportunity to act on the communication before the bank accepts the payment order.

(c) After a payment order has been accepted, cancellation or amendment of the order is not effective unless the receiving bank agrees or a funds-transfer system rule allows cancellation or amendment without agreement of the bank.

(1) With respect to a payment order accepted by a receiving bank other than the beneficiary's bank, cancellation or amendment is not effective unless a conforming cancellation or amendment of the payment order issued by the receiving bank is also made.

(2) With respect to a payment order accepted by the beneficiary's bank, cancellation or amendment is not effective unless the order was issued in execution of an unauthorized payment order, or because of a mistake by a sender in the funds transfer which resulted in the issuance of a payment order (i) that is a duplicate of a payment order previously issued by the sender, (ii) that orders payment to a beneficiary not entitled to receive payment from the originator, or (iii) that orders payment in an amount greater than the amount the beneficiary was entitled to receive from the originator. If the payment order is cancelled or amended, the beneficiary's bank is entitled to recover from the beneficiary any amount paid to the beneficiary to the extent allowed by the law governing mistake and restitution.

(d) An unaccepted payment order is cancelled by operation of law at the close of the fifth funds-transfer business day of the receiving bank after the execution date or payment date of the order.

(e) A cancelled payment order cannot be accepted. If an accepted payment order is cancelled, the acceptance is nullified and no person has any right or obligation based on the acceptance. Amendment of a payment order is deemed to be cancellation of the original order at the time of amendment and issue of a new payment order in the amended form at the same time.

(f) Unless otherwise provided in an agreement of the parties or in a funds-transfer system rule, if the receiving bank, after accepting a payment order, agrees to cancellation or amendment of the order by the sender or is bound by a funds-transfer system rule allowing cancellation or amendment without the bank's agreement, the sender, whether or not cancellation or amendment is effective, is liable to the bank for any loss and expenses, including reasonable attorney's fees, incurred by the bank as a result of the cancellation or amendment or attempted cancellation or amendment.

(g) A payment order is not revoked by the death or legal incapacity of the sender unless the receiving bank knows of the death or of an adjudication of incapacity by a court of competent jurisdiction and has reasonable opportunity to act before acceptance of the order.

(h) A funds-transfer system rule is not effective to the extent it conflicts with subsection (c)(2).

§4A—212. LIABILITY AND DUTY OF RECEIVING BANK REGARDING UNACCEPTED PAYMENT ORDER

If a receiving bank fails to accept a payment order that it is obliged by express agreement to accept, the bank is liable for breach of the agreement to the extent provided in the agreement or in this Article, but does not otherwise have any duty to accept a payment order or, before acceptance, to take any action, or refrain from taking action, with respect to the order except as provided in this Article or by express agreement. Liability based on acceptance arises only when acceptance occurs as stated in Section 4A—209, and liability is limited to that provided in this Article. A receiving bank is not the agent of the sender or beneficiary of the payment order it accepts, or of any other party to the funds transfer, and the bank owes no duty to any party to the funds transfer except as provided in this Article or by express agreement.

Part 3 Execution of Sender's Payment Order by Receiving Bank

§4A—301. EXECUTION AND EXECUTION DATE

(a) A payment order is "executed" by the receiving bank when it issues a payment order intended to carry out the payment order received by the bank. A payment order received by the beneficiary's bank can be accepted but cannot be executed.

(b) "Execution date" of a payment order means the day on which the receiving bank may properly issue a payment order in execution of the sender's order. The execution date may be determined by instruction of the sender but cannot be earlier than the day the order is received and, unless otherwise determined, is the day the order is received. If the sender's instruction states a payment date, the execution date is the payment date or an earlier date on which execution is reasonably necessary to allow payment to the beneficiary on the payment date.

§4A—302. OBLIGATIONS OF RECEIVING BANK IN EXECUTION OF PAYMENT ORDER

(a) Except as provided in subsections (b) through (d), if the receiving bank accepts a payment order pursuant to Section 4A—209(a), the bank has the following obligations in executing the order:

(1) The receiving bank is obliged to issue, on the execution date, a payment order complying with the sender's order and to follow the sender's instructions concerning (i) any intermediary bank or funds-transfer system to be used in carrying out the funds transfer, or (ii) the means by which payment orders are to be transmitted in the funds transfer. If the originator's bank issues a payment order to an intermediary bank, the originator's bank is obliged to instruct the intermediary bank according to the instruction of the originator. An intermediary bank in the funds transfer is

similarly bound by an instruction given to it by the sender of the payment order it accepts.

(2) If the sender's instruction states that the funds transfer is to be carried out telephonically or by wire transfer or otherwise indicates that the funds transfer is to be carried out by the most expeditious means, the receiving bank is obliged to transmit its payment order by the most expeditious available means, and to instruct any intermediary bank accordingly. If a sender's instruction states a payment date, the receiving bank is obliged to transmit its payment order at a time and by means reasonably necessary to allow payment to the beneficiary on the payment date or as soon thereafter as is feasible.

(b) Unless otherwise instructed, a receiving bank executing a payment order may (i) use any funds-transfer system if use of that system is reasonable in the circumstances, and (ii) issue a payment order to the beneficiary's bank or to an intermediary bank through which a payment order conforming to the sender's order can expeditiously be issued to the beneficiary's bank if the receiving bank exercises ordinary care in the selection of the intermediary bank. A receiving bank is not required to follow an instruction of the sender designating a funds-transfer system to be used in carrying out the funds transfer if the receiving bank, in good faith, determines that it is not feasible to follow the instruction or that following the instruction would unduly delay completion of the funds transfer.

(c) Unless subsection (a)(2) applies or the receiving bank is otherwise instructed, the bank may execute a payment order by transmitting its payment order by first class mail or by any means reasonable in the circumstances. If the receiving bank is instructed to execute the sender's order by transmitting its payment order by a particular means, the receiving bank may issue its payment order by the means stated or by any means as expeditious as the means stated.

(d) Unless instructed by the sender, (i) the receiving bank may not obtain payment of its charges for services and expenses in connection with the execution of the sender's order by issuing a payment order in an amount equal to the amount of the sender's order less the amount of the charges, and (ii) may not instruct a subsequent receiving bank to obtain payment of its charges in the same manner.

§4A—303. ERRONEOUS EXECUTION OF PAYMENT ORDER

(a) A receiving bank that (i) executes the payment order of the sender by issuing a payment order in an amount greater than the amount of the sender's order, or (ii) issues a payment order in execution of the sender's order and then issues a duplicate order, is entitled to payment of the amount of the sender's order under Section 4A—402(c) if that subsection is otherwise satisfied. The bank is entitled to recover from the beneficiary of the erroneous order the excess payment received to the extent allowed by the law governing mistake and restitution.

(b) A receiving bank that executes the payment order of the sender by issuing a payment order in an amount less than the amount of the sender's order is entitled to payment of the amount of the sender's order under Section 4A—402(c) if (i) that subsection is otherwise satisfied and (ii) the bank corrects its mistake by issuing an additional payment order for the benefit of the beneficiary of the sender's order. If the error is not corrected, the issuer of the erroneous order is entitled to receive or retain payment from the sender of the order it accepted only to the extent of the amount of the erroneous order. This subsection does not apply if the receiving bank executes the sender's payment order by issuing a payment order in an amount less than the amount of the sender's order for the purpose of obtaining payment of its charges for services and expenses pursuant to instruction of the sender.

(c) If a receiving bank executes the payment order of the sender by issuing a payment order to a beneficiary different from the beneficiary of the sender's order and the funds transfer is completed on the basis of that error, the sender of the payment order that was erroneously executed and all previous senders in the funds transfer are not obliged to pay the payment orders they issued. The issuer of the erroneous order is entitled to recover from the beneficiary of the order the payment received to the extent allowed by the law governing mistake and restitution.

§4A—304. DUTY OF SENDER TO REPORT ERRONEOUSLY EXECUTED PAYMENT ORDER

If the sender of a payment order that is erroneously executed as stated in Section 4A—303 receives notification from the receiving bank that the order was executed or that the sender's account was debited with respect to the order, the sender has a duty to exercise ordinary care to determine, on the basis of information available to the sender, that the order was erroneously executed and to notify the bank of the relevant facts within a reasonable time not exceeding 90 days after the notification from the bank was received by the sender. If the sender fails to perform that duty, the bank is not obliged to pay interest on any amount refundable to the sender under Section 4A—402(d) for the period before the bank learns of the execution error. The bank is not entitled to any recovery from the sender on account of a failure by the sender to perform the duty stated in this section.

§4A—305. LIABILITY FOR LATE OR IMPROPER EXECUTION OR FAILURE TO EXECUTE PAYMENT ORDER

(a) If a funds transfer is completed but execution of a payment order by the receiving bank in breach of Section 4A—302 results in delay in payment to the beneficiary, the bank is obliged to pay interest to either the originator or the beneficiary of the funds transfer for the period of delay caused by the improper execution. Except as provided in subsection (c), additional damages are not recoverable.

(b) If execution of a payment order by a receiving bank in breach of Section 4A—302 results in (i) noncompletion of the funds transfer, (ii) failure to use an intermediary bank designated by the originator, or (iii) issuance of a payment order that does not comply with the terms of the payment order of the originator, the bank is liable to the originator for its expenses in the funds transfer and for incidental expenses and interest losses, to the extent not covered by subsection (a), resulting from the improper execution. Except as provided in subsection (c), additional damages are not recoverable.

(c) In addition to the amounts payable under subsections (a) and (b), damages, including consequential damages, are recoverable to the extent provided in an express written agreement of the receiving bank.

(d) If a receiving bank fails to execute a payment order it was obliged by express agreement to execute, the receiving bank is liable to the sender for its expenses in the transaction and for incidental expenses and interest losses resulting from the failure to execute. Additional damages, including consequential damages, are recoverable to the extent provided in an express written agreement of the receiving bank, but are not otherwise recoverable.

(e) Reasonable attorney's fees are recoverable if demand for compensation under subsection (a) or (b) is made and refused before an action is brought on the claim. If a claim is made for breach of an agreement under subsection (d) and the agreement does not provide for damages, reasonable attorney's fees are recoverable if demand for compensation under subsection (d) is made and refused before an action is brought on the claim.

(f) Except as stated in this section, the liability of a receiving bank under subsections (a) and (b) may not be varied by agreement.

Part 4 Payment

§4A—401. PAYMENT DATE

"Payment date" of a payment order means the day on which the amount of the order is payable to the beneficiary by the beneficiary's bank. The payment date may be determined by instruction of the sender but cannot be earlier than the day the order is received by the beneficiary's bank and, unless otherwise determined, is the day the order is received by the beneficiary's bank.

§4A—402. OBLIGATION OF SENDER TO PAY RECEIVING BANK

(a) This section is subject to Sections 4A—205 and 4A—207.

(b) With respect to a payment order issued to the beneficiary's bank, acceptance of the order by the bank obliges the sender to pay the bank the amount of the order, but payment is not due until the payment date of the order.

(c) This subsection is subject to subsection (e) and to Section 4A—303. With respect to a payment order issued to a receiving bank other than the beneficiary's bank, acceptance of the order by the receiving bank obliges the sender to pay the bank the amount of the sender's order. Payment by the sender is not due until the execution date of the sender's order. The obligation of that sender to pay its payment order is excused if the funds transfer is not completed by acceptance by the beneficiary's bank of a payment order instructing payment to the beneficiary of that sender's payment order.

(d) If the sender of a payment order pays the order and was not obliged to pay all or part of the amount paid, the bank receiving payment is obliged to refund payment to the extent the sender was not obliged to pay. Except as provided in Sections 4A—204 and 4A—304, interest is payable on the refundable amount from the date of payment.

(e) If a funds transfer is not completed as stated in subsection (c) and an intermediary bank is obliged to refund payment as stated in subsection (d) but is unable to do so because not permitted by applicable law or because the bank suspends payments, a sender in the funds transfer that executed a payment order in compliance with an instruction, as stated in Section 4A—302(a)(1), to route the funds transfer through that intermediary bank is entitled to receive or retain payment from the sender of the payment order that it accepted. The first sender in the funds transfer that issued an instruction requiring routing through that intermediary bank is subrogated to the right of the bank that paid the intermediary bank to refund as stated in subsection (d).

(f) The right of the sender of a payment order to be excused from the obligation to pay the order as stated in subsection (c) or to receive refund under subsection (d) may not be varied by agreement.

§4A—403. PAYMENT BY SENDER TO RECEIVING BANK

(a) Payment of the sender's obligation under Section 4A—402 to pay the receiving bank occurs as follows:

(1) If the sender is a bank, payment occurs when the receiving bank receives final settlement of the obligation through a Federal Reserve Bank or through a funds-transfer system.

(2) If the sender is a bank and the sender (i) credited an account of the receiving bank with the sender, or (ii) caused an account of the receiving bank in another bank to be credited, payment occurs when the credit is withdrawn or, if not withdrawn, at midnight of the day on which the credit is withdrawable and the receiving bank learns of that fact.

(3) If the receiving bank debits an account of the sender with the receiving bank, payment occurs when the debit is made to the extent the debit is covered by a withdrawable credit balance in the account.

(b) If the sender and receiving bank are members of a funds-transfer system that nets obligations multilaterally among participants, the receiving bank receives final settlement when settlement is complete in accordance with the rules of the system. The obligation of the sender to pay the amount of a payment order transmitted through the funds-transfer system may be satisfied, to the extent permitted by the rules of the system, by setting off and applying against the sender's obligation the right of the sender to receive payment from the receiving bank of the amount of any other payment order transmitted to the sender by the receiving bank through the funds-transfer system. The aggregate balance of obligations owed by each sender to each receiving bank in the funds-transfer system may be satisfied, to the extent permitted by the rules of the system, by setting off and applying against that balance the aggregate balance of obligations owed to the sender by other members of the system. The aggregate balance is determined after the right of setoff stated in the second sentence of this subsection has been exercised.

(c) If two banks transmit payment orders to each other under an agreement that settlement of the obligations of each bank to the other under Section 4A—402 will be made at the end of the day or other period, the total amount owed with respect to all orders transmitted by one bank shall be set off against the total amount owed with respect to all orders transmitted by the other bank. To the extent of the setoff, each bank has made payment to the other.

(d) In a case not covered by subsection (a), the time when payment of the sender's obligation under Section 4A—402(b) or 4A—402(c) occurs is governed by applicable principles of law that determine when an obligation is satisfied.

§4A—404. OBLIGATION OF BENEFICIARY'S BANK TO PAY AND GIVE NOTICE TO BENEFICIARY

(a) Subject to Sections 4A—211(e), 4A—405(d), and 4A—405(e), if a beneficiary's bank accepts a payment order, the bank is obliged to pay the amount of the order to the beneficiary of the order. Payment is due on the payment date of the order, but if acceptance occurs on the payment date after the close of the funds-transfer business day of the bank, payment is due on the next funds-transfer business day. If the bank refuses to pay after demand by the beneficiary and receipt of notice of particular circumstances that will give rise to consequential damages as a result of nonpayment, the beneficiary may recover damages resulting from the refusal to pay to the extent the bank had notice of the damages, unless the bank proves that it did not pay because of a reasonable doubt concerning the right of the beneficiary to payment.

(b) If a payment order accepted by the beneficiary's bank instructs payment to an account of the beneficiary, the bank is obliged to notify the beneficiary of receipt of the order before midnight of the next funds-transfer business day following the payment date. If the payment order does not instruct payment to an account of the beneficiary, the bank is required to notify the beneficiary only if notice is required by the order. Notice may be given by first class mail or any other means reasonable in the circumstances. If the bank fails to give the required notice, the bank is obliged to pay interest to the beneficiary on the amount of the payment order from the day notice should have been given until the day the beneficiary learned of receipt of the payment order by the bank. No other damages are recoverable. Reasonable attorney's fees are also recoverable if demand for interest is made and refused before an action is brought on the claim.

(c) The right of a beneficiary to receive payment and damages as stated in subsection (a) may not be varied by agreement or a funds-transfer system rule. The right of a beneficiary to be notified as stated in subsection (b) may be varied by agreement of the beneficiary or by a funds-transfer system rule if the beneficiary is notified of the rule before initiation of the funds transfer.

§4A—405. PAYMENT BY BENEFICIARY'S BANK TO BENEFICIARY

(a) If the beneficiary's bank credits an account of the beneficiary of a payment order, payment of the bank's obligation under Section 4A—404(a) occurs when and to the extent (i) the beneficiary is notified of the right to withdraw the credit, (ii) the bank lawfully applies the credit to a debt of the beneficiary, or (iii) funds with respect to the order are otherwise made available to the beneficiary by the bank.

(b) If the beneficiary's bank does not credit an account of the beneficiary of a payment order, the time when payment of the bank's obligation under Section 4A—404(a) occurs is governed by principles of law that determine when an obligation is satisfied.

(c) Except as stated in subsections (d) and (e), if the beneficiary's bank pays the beneficiary of a payment order under a condition to payment or agreement of the beneficiary giving the bank the right to recover payment from the beneficiary if the bank does not receive payment of the order, the condition to payment or agreement is not enforceable.

(d) A funds-transfer system rule may provide that payments made to beneficiaries of funds transfers made through the system are provisional until receipt of payment by the beneficiary's bank of the payment order it accepted. A beneficiary's bank that makes a payment that is provisional under the rule is entitled to refund from the beneficiary if (i) the rule requires that both the beneficiary and the originator be given notice of the provisional nature of the payment before the funds transfer is initiated, (ii) the beneficiary, the beneficiary's bank, and the originator's bank agreed to be bound by the rule, and (iii) the beneficiary's bank did not receive payment of the payment order that it accepted. If the beneficiary is obliged to refund payment to the beneficiary's bank, acceptance of the payment order by the beneficiary's bank is nullified and no payment by the originator of the funds transfer to the beneficiary occurs under Section 4A—406.

(e) This subsection applies to a funds transfer that includes a payment order transmitted over a funds-transfer system that (i) nets obligations multilaterally among participants, and (ii) has in effect a loss-sharing agreement among participants for the purpose of providing funds necessary to complete settlement of the obligations of one or more participants that do not meet their settlement obligations. If the beneficiary's bank in the funds transfer accepts a payment order and the system fails to complete settlement pursuant to its rules with respect to any payment order in the funds transfer, (i) the acceptance by the beneficiary's bank is nullified and no person has any right or obligation based on the acceptance, (ii) the beneficiary's bank is entitled to recover payment from the beneficiary, (iii) no payment by the originator to the beneficiary occurs under Section 4A—406, and (iv) subject to Section 4A—402(e), each sender in the funds transfer is excused from its obligation to pay its payment order under Section 4A—402 (c) because the funds transfer has not been completed.

§4A—406. PAYMENT BY ORIGINATOR TO BENEFICIARY; DISCHARGE OF UNDERLYING OBLIGATION

(a) Subject to Sections 4A—211(e), 4A—405(d), and 4A—405(e), the originator of a funds transfer pays the beneficiary of the originator's payment order (i) at the time a payment order for the benefit of the beneficiary is accepted by the beneficiary's bank in the funds transfer and (ii) in an amount equal to the amount of the order accepted by the beneficiary's bank, but not more than the amount of the originator's order.

(b) If payment under subsection (a) is made to satisfy an obligation, the obligation is discharged to the same extent discharge would result from payment to the beneficiary of the same amount in money, unless (i) the payment under subsection (a) was made by a means prohibited by the contract of the beneficiary with respect to the obligation, (ii) the beneficiary, within a reasonable time after receiving notice of receipt of the order by the beneficiary's bank, notified the originator of the beneficiary's refusal of the payment, (iii) funds with respect to the order were not withdrawn by the beneficiary or applied to a debt of the beneficiary, and (iv) the beneficiary would suffer a loss that could reasonably have been avoided if payment had been made by a means complying with the contract. If payment by the originator does not result in discharge under this section, the originator is subrogated to the rights of the beneficiary to receive payment from the beneficiary's bank under Section 4A—404(a).

(c) For the purpose of determining whether discharge of an obligation occurs under subsection (b), if the beneficiary's bank accepts a payment order in an amount equal to the amount of the originator's payment order less charges of one or more receiving banks in the funds transfer, payment to the beneficiary is deemed to be in the amount of the originator's order unless upon demand by the beneficiary the originator does not pay the beneficiary the amount of the deducted charges.

(d) Rights of the originator or of the beneficiary of a funds transfer under this section may be varied only by agreement of the originator and the beneficiary.

Part 5 Miscellaneous Provisions

§4A—501. VARIATION BY AGREEMENT AND EFFECT OF FUNDS-TRANSFER SYSTEM RULE

(a) Except as otherwise provided in this Article, the rights and obligations of a party to a funds transfer may be varied by agreement of the affected party.

(b) "Funds-transfer system rule" means a rule of an association of banks (i) governing transmission of payment orders by means of a funds-transfer system of the association or rights and obligations with respect to those orders, or (ii) to the extent the rule governs rights and obligations between banks that are parties to a funds transfer in which a Federal Reserve Bank, acting as an intermediary bank, sends a payment order to the beneficiary's bank. Except as otherwise provided in this Article, a funds-transfer system rule governing rights and obligations between participating banks using the system may be effective even if the rule conflicts with this Article and indirectly affects another party to the funds transfer who does not consent to the rule. A funds-transfer system rule may also govern rights and obligations of parties other than participating banks using the system to the extent stated in Sections 4A—404(c), 4A—405(d), and 4A—507(c).

§4A—502. CREDITOR PROCESS SERVED ON RECEIVING BANK; SETOFF BY BENEFICIARY'S BANK

(a) As used in this section, "creditor process" means levy, attachment, garnishment, notice of lien, sequestration, or similar process issued by or on behalf of a creditor or other claimant with respect to an account.

(b) This subsection applies to creditor process with respect to an authorized account of the sender of a payment order if the creditor process is served on the receiving bank. For the purpose of determining rights with respect to the creditor process, if the receiving bank accepts the payment order the balance in the authorized account is deemed to be reduced by the amount of the payment order to the extent the bank did not otherwise receive payment of the order, unless the creditor process is served at a time and in a manner affording the bank a reasonable opportunity to act on it before the bank accepts the payment order.

(c) If a beneficiary's bank has received a payment order for payment to the beneficiary's account in the bank, the following rules apply:

(1) The bank may credit the beneficiary's account. The amount credited may be set off against an obligation owed by the beneficiary to the bank or may be applied to satisfy creditor process served on the bank with respect to the account.

(2) The bank may credit the beneficiary's account and allow withdrawal of the amount credited unless creditor process with respect to the account is served at a time and in a manner affording the bank a reasonable opportunity to act to prevent withdrawal.

(3) If creditor process with respect to the beneficiary's account has been served and the bank has had a reasonable opportunity to act on it, the bank may not reject the payment order except for a reason unrelated to the service of process.

(d) Creditor process with respect to a payment by the originator to the beneficiary pursuant to a funds transfer may be served only on the beneficiary's bank with respect to the debt owed by that bank to the beneficiary. Any other bank served with the creditor process is not obliged to act with respect to the process.

§4A—503. INJUNCTION OR RESTRAINING ORDER WITH RESPECT TO FUNDS TRANSFER

For proper cause and in compliance with applicable law, a court may restrain (i) a person from issuing a payment order to initiate a funds transfer, (ii) an originator's bank from executing the payment order of the originator, or (iii) the beneficiary's bank from releasing funds to the beneficiary or the beneficiary from withdrawing the funds. A court may not otherwise restrain a person from issuing a payment order, paying or receiving payment of a payment order, or otherwise acting with respect to a funds transfer.

§4A—504. ORDER IN WHICH ITEMS AND PAYMENT ORDERS MAY BE CHARGED TO ACCOUNT; ORDER OF WITHDRAWALS FROM ACCOUNT

(a) If a receiving bank has received more than one payment order of the sender or one or more payment orders and other items that are payable from the sender's account, the bank may charge the sender's account with respect to the various orders and items in any sequence.

(b) In determining whether a credit to an account has been withdrawn by the holder of the account or applied to a debt of the holder of the account, credits first made to the account are first withdrawn or applied.

§4A—505. PRECLUSION OF OBJECTION TO DEBIT OF CUSTOMER'S ACCOUNT

If a receiving bank has received payment from its customer with respect to a payment order issued in the name of the customer as sender and accepted by the bank, and the customer received notification reasonably identifying the order, the customer is precluded from asserting that the bank is not entitled to retain the payment unless the customer notifies the bank of the customer's objection to the payment within one year after the notification was received by the customer.

§4A—506. RATE OF INTEREST

(a) If, under this Article, a receiving bank is obliged to pay interest with respect to a payment order issued to the bank, the amount payable may be determined (i) by agreement of the sender and receiving bank, or (ii) by a funds-transfer system rule if the payment order is transmitted through a funds-transfer system.

(b) If the amount of interest is not determined by an agreement or rule as stated in subsection (a), the amount is calculated by multiplying the applicable Federal Funds rate by the amount on which interest is payable, and then multiplying the product by the number of days for which interest is payable. The applicable Federal Funds rate is the average of the Federal Funds rates published by the Federal Reserve Bank of New York for each of the days for which interest is payable divided by 360. The Federal Funds rate for any day on which a published rate is not available is the same as the published rate for the next preceding day for which there is a published rate. If a receiving bank that accepted a payment order is required to refund payment to the sender of the order because the funds transfer was not completed, but the failure to complete was not due to any fault by the bank, the interest payable is reduced by a percentage equal to the reserve requirement on deposits of the receiving bank.

§4A—507. CHOICE OF LAW

(a) The following rules apply unless the affected parties otherwise agree or subsection (c) applies:

(1) The rights and obligations between the sender of a payment order and the receiving bank are governed by the law of the jurisdiction in which the receiving bank is located.

(2) The rights and obligations between the beneficiary's bank and the beneficiary are governed by the law of the jurisdiction in which the beneficiary's bank is located.

(3) The issue of when payment is made pursuant to a funds transfer by the originator to the beneficiary is governed by the law of the jurisdiction in which the beneficiary's bank is located.

(b) If the parties described in each paragraph of subsection (a) have made an agreement selecting the law of a particular jurisdiction to govern rights and obligations between each other, the law of that jurisdiction governs those rights and obligations, whether or not the payment order or the funds transfer bears a reasonable relation to that jurisdiction.

(c) A funds-transfer system rule may select the law of a particular jurisdiction to govern (i) rights and obligations between participating banks with respect to payment orders transmitted or processed through the system, or (ii) the rights and obligations of some or all parties to a funds transfer any part of which is carried out by means of the system. A choice of law made pursuant to clause (i) is binding on participating banks. A choice of law made pursuant to clause (ii) is binding on the originator, other sender, or a receiving bank having notice that the funds-transfer system might be used in the funds transfer and of the choice of law by the system when the originator, other sender, or receiving bank issued or accepted a payment order. The beneficiary of a funds transfer is bound by the choice of law if, when the funds transfer is initiated, the beneficiary has notice that the funds-transfer system might be used in the funds transfer and of the choice of law by the system. The law of a jurisdiction selected pursuant to this subsection may govern, whether or not that law bears a reasonable relation to the matter in issue.

(d) In the event of inconsistency between an agreement under subsection (b) and a choice-of-law rule under subsection (c), the agreement under subsection (b) prevails.

(e) If a funds transfer is made by use of more than one funds-transfer system and there is inconsistency between choice-of-law rules of the systems, the matter in issue is governed by the law of the selected jurisdiction that has the most significant relationship to the matter in issue.

* * * *

REVISED ARTICLE 9 SECURED TRANSACTIONS

Part 1 General Provisions [Subpart 1. Short Title, Definitions, and General Concepts]

§9—101. SHORT TITLE

This article may be cited as Uniform Commercial Code—Secured Transactions.

§9—102. DEFINITIONS AND INDEX OF DEFINITIONS

(a) In this article:

(1) "Accession" means goods that are physically united with other goods in such a manner that the identity of the original goods is not lost.

(2) "Account", except as used in "account for", means a right to payment of a monetary obligation, whether or not earned by performance, (i) for property that has been or is to be sold, leased, licensed, assigned, or otherwise disposed of, (ii) for services rendered or to be rendered, (iii) for a policy of insurance issued or to be issued, (iv) for a secondary obligation incurred or to be incurred, (v) for energy provided or to be provided, (vi) for the use or hire of a vessel under a charter or other contract, (vii) arising out of the use of a credit or charge card or information contained on or for use with the card, or (viii) as winnings in a lottery or other game of chance operated or sponsored by a State, governmental unit of a State, or person licensed or authorized to operate the game by a State or governmental unit of a State. The term includes health-care insurance receivables. The term does not include (i) rights to payment evidenced by chattel paper or an instrument, (ii) commercial tort claims, (iii) deposit accounts, (iv) investment property, (v) letter-of-credit rights or letters of credit, or (vi) rights to payment for money or funds advanced or sold, other than rights arising out of the use of a credit or charge card or information contained on or for use with the card.

(3) "Account debtor" means a person obligated on an account, chattel paper, or general intangible. The term does not include persons obligated to pay a negotiable instrument, even if the instrument constitutes part of chattel paper.

(4) "Accounting", except as used in "accounting for", means a record:

(A) authenticated by a secured party;

(B) indicating the aggregate unpaid secured obligations as of a date not more than 35 days earlier or 35 days later than the date of the record; and

(C) identifying the components of the obligations in reasonable detail.

(5) "Agricultural lien" means an interest, other than a security interest, in farm products:

(A) which secures payment or performance of an obligation for:

(i) goods or services furnished in connection with a debtor's farming operation; or

(ii) rent on real property leased by a debtor in connection with its farming operation;

(B) which is created by statute in favor of a person that:

(i) in the ordinary course of its business furnished goods or services to a debtor in connection with a debtor's farming operation; or

(ii) leased real property to a debtor in connection with the debtor's farming operation; and

(C) whose effectiveness does not depend on the person's possession of the personal property.

(6) "As-extracted collateral" means:

(A) oil, gas, or other minerals that are subject to a security interest that:

(i) is created by a debtor having an interest in the minerals before extraction; and

(ii) attaches to the minerals as extracted; or

(B) accounts arising out of the sale at the wellhead or minehead of oil, gas, or other minerals in which the debtor had an interest before extraction.

(7) "Authenticate" means:

(A) to sign; or

(B) to execute or otherwise adopt a symbol, or encrypt or similarly process a record in whole or in part, with the present intent of the authenticating person to identify the person and adopt or accept a record.

(8) "Bank" means an organization that is engaged in the business of banking. The term includes savings banks, savings and loan associations, credit unions, and trust companies.

(9) "Cash proceeds" means proceeds that are money, checks, deposit accounts, or the like.

(10) "Certificate of title" means a certificate of title with respect to which a statute provides for

the security interest in question to be indicated on the certificate as a condition or result of the security interest's obtaining priority over the rights of a lien creditor with respect to the collateral.

(11) "Chattel paper" means a record or records that evidence both a monetary obligation and a security interest in specific goods, a security interest in specific goods and software used in the goods, a security interest in specific goods and license of software used in the goods, a lease of specific goods, or a lease of specific goods and license of software used in the goods. In this paragraph, "monetary obligation" means a monetary obligation secured by the goods or owed under a lease of the goods and includes a monetary obligation with respect to software used in the goods. The term does not include (i) charters or other contracts involving the use or hire of a vessel or (ii) records that evidence a right to payment arising out of the use of a credit or charge card or information contained on or for use with the card. If a transaction is evidenced by records that include an instrument or series of instruments, the group of records taken together constitutes chattel paper.

(12) "Collateral" means the property subject to a security interest or agricultural lien. The term includes:

(A) proceeds to which a security interest attaches;

(B) accounts, chattel paper, payment intangibles,and promissory notes that have been sold; and

(C) goods that are the subject of a consignment.

(13) "Commercial tort claim" means a claim arising in tort with respect to which:

(A) the claimant is an organization; or

(B) the claimant is an individual and the claim:

(i) arose in the course of the claimant's business or profession; and

(ii) does not include damages arising out of personal injury to or the death of an individual.

(14) "Commodity account" means an account maintained by a commodity intermediary in which a commodity contract is carried for a commodity customer.

(15) "Commodity contract" means a commodity futures contract, an option on a commodity futures contract, a commodity option, or another contract if the contract or option is:

(A) traded on or subject to the rules of a board of trade that has been designated as a contract market for such a contract pursuant to federal commodities laws; or

(B) traded on a foreign commodity board of trade,exchange, or market, and is carried on the books of a commodity intermediary for a commodity customer.

(16) "Commodity customer" means a person for which a commodity intermediary carries a commodity contract on its books.

(17) "Commodity intermediary" means a person that:

(A) is registered as a futures commission merchant under federal commodities law; or

(B) in the ordinary course of its business provides clearance or settlement services for a board of trade that has been designated as a contract market pursuant to federal commodities law.

(18) "Communicate" means:

(A) to send a written or other tangible record;

(B) to transmit a record by any means agreed upon by the persons sending and receiving the record; or

(C) in the case of transmission of a record to or by a filing office, to transmit a record by any means prescribed by filing-office rule.

(19) "Consignee" means a merchant to which goods are delivered in a consignment.

(20) "Consignment" means a transaction, regardless of its form, in which a person delivers goods to a merchant for the purpose of sale and:

(A) the merchant:

(i) deals in goods of that kind under a name other than the name of the person making delivery;

(ii) is not an auctioneer; and

(iii) is not generally known by its creditors to be substantially engaged in selling the goods of others;

(B) with respect to each delivery, the aggregate value of the goods is $1,000 or more at the time of delivery;

(C) the goods are not consumer goods immediately before delivery; and

(D) the transaction does not create a security interest that secures an obligation.

(21) "Consignor" means a person that delivers goods to a consignee in a consignment.

(22) "Consumer debtor" means a debtor in a consumer transaction.

(23) "Consumer goods" means goods that are used or bought for use primarily for personal, family, or household purposes.

(24) "Consumer-goods transaction" means a consumer transaction in which:

(A) an individual incurs an obligation primarily for personal, family, or household purposes; and

(B) a security interest in consumer goods secures the obligation.

(25) "Consumer obligor" means an obligor who is an individual and who incurred the obligation as part of a transaction entered into primarily for personal, family, or household purposes.

(26) "Consumer transaction" means a transaction in which (i) an individual incurs an obligation primarily for personal, family, or household purposes, (ii) a security interest secures the obligation, and (iii) the collateral is held or acquired primarily for personal, family, or household purposes. The term includes consumer-goods transactions.

(27) "Continuation statement" means an amendment of a financing statement which:

(A) identifies, by its file number, the initial financing statement to which it relates; and

(B) indicates that it is a continuation statement for, or that it is filed to continue the effectiveness of, the identified financing statement.

(28) "Debtor" means:

(A) a person having an interest, other than a security interest or other lien, in the collateral, whether or not the person is an obligor;

(B) a seller of accounts, chattel paper, payment intangibles, or promissory notes; or

(C) a consignee.

(29) "Deposit account" means a demand, time, savings, passbook, or similar account maintained with a bank. The term does not include investment property or accounts evidenced by an instrument.

(30) "Document" means a document of title or a receipt of the type described in Section 7—201(2).

(31) "Electronic chattel paper" means chattel paper evidenced by a record or records consisting of information stored in an electronic medium.

(32) "Encumbrance" means a right, other than an ownership interest, in real property. The term includes mortgages and other liens on real property.

(33) "Equipment" means goods other than inventory, farm products, or consumer goods.

(34) "Farm products" means goods, other than standing timber, with respect to which the debtor is engaged in a farming operation and which are:

(A) crops grown, growing, or to be grown, including:

(i) crops produced on trees, vines, and bushes; and

(ii) aquatic goods produced in aquacultural operations;

(B) livestock, born or unborn, including aquatic goods produced in aquacultural operations;

(C) supplies used or produced in a farming operation; or

(D) products of crops or livestock in their unmanufactured states.

(35) "Farming operation" means raising, cultivating, propagating, fattening, grazing, or any other farming, livestock, or aquacultural operation.

(36) "File number" means the number assigned to an initial financing statement pursuant to Section 9—519(a).

(37) "Filing office" means an office designated in Section 9—501 as the place to file a financing statement.

(38) "Filing-office rule" means a rule adopted pursuant to Section 9—526.

(39) "Financing statement" means a record or records composed of an initial financing statement and any filed record relating to the initial financing statement.

(40) "Fixture filing" means the filing of a financing statement covering goods that are or are to become fixtures and satisfying Section 9—502(a) and (b). The term includes the filing of a financing statement covering goods of a transmitting utility which are or are to become fixtures.

(41) "Fixtures" means goods that have become so related to particular real property that an interest in them arises under real property law.

(42) "General intangible" means any personal property, including things in action, other than accounts, chattel paper, commercial tort claims, deposit accounts, documents, goods, instruments, investment property, letter-of-credit rights, letters of credit, money, and oil, gas, or other minerals before extraction. The term includes payment intangibles and software.

(43) "Good faith" means honesty in fact and the observance of reasonable commercial standards of fair dealing.

(44) "Goods" means all things that are movable when a security interest attaches. The term includes (i) fixtures, (ii) standing timber that is to be cut and removed under a conveyance or contract for sale, (iii) the unborn young of animals, (iv) crops grown, growing, or to be grown, even if the crops are produced on trees, vines, or bushes, and (v) manufactured homes.

The term also includes a computer program embedded in goods and any supporting information provided in connection with a transaction relating to the program if (i) the program is associated with the goods in such a manner that it customarily is considered part of the goods, or (ii) by becoming the owner of the goods, a person acquires a right to use the program in connection with the goods. The term does not include a computer program embedded in goods that consist solely of the medium in which the program is embedded. The term also does not include accounts, chattel paper, commercial tort claims, deposit accounts, documents, general intangibles, instruments, investment property, letter-of-credit rights, letters of credit, money, or oil, gas, or other minerals before extraction.

(45) "Governmental unit" means a subdivision, agency, department, county, parish, municipality, or other unit of the government of the United States, a State, or a foreign country. The term includes an organization having a separate corporate existence if the organization is eligible to issue debt on which interest is exempt from income taxation under the laws of the United States.

(46) "Health-care-insurance receivable" means an interest in or claim under a policy of insurance which is a right to payment of a monetary obligation for health-care goods or services provided.

(47) "Instrument" means a negotiable instrument or any other writing that evidences a right to the payment of a monetary obligation, is not itself a security agreement or lease, and is of a type that in ordinary course of business is transferred by delivery with any necessary indorsement or assignment. The term does not include (i) investment property, (ii) letters of credit, or (iii) writings that evidence a right to payment arising out of the use of a credit or charge card or information contained on or for use with the card.

(48) "Inventory" means goods, other than farm products, which:
  (A) are leased by a person as lessor;
  (B) are held by a person for sale or lease or to be furnished under a contract of service;
  (C) are furnished by a person under a contract of service; or
  (D) consist of raw materials, work in process, or materials used or consumed in a business.

(49) "Investment property" means a security, whether certificated or uncertificated, security

entitlement, securities account, commodity contract, or commodity account.

(50) "Jurisdiction of organization", with respect to a registered organization, means the jurisdiction under whose law the organization is organized.

(51) "Letter-of-credit right" means a right to payment or performance under a letter of credit, whether or not the beneficiary has demanded or is at the time entitled to demand payment or performance. The term does not include the right of a beneficiary to demand payment or performance under a letter of credit.

(52) "Lien creditor" means:
  (A) a creditor that has acquired a lien on the property involved by attachment, levy, or the like;
  (B) an assignee for benefit of creditors from the time of assignment;
  (C) a trustee in bankruptcy from the date of the filing of the petition; or
  (D) a receiver in equity from the time of appointment.

(53) "Manufactured home" means a structure, transportable in one or more sections, which, in the traveling mode, is eight body feet or more in width or 40 body feet or more in length, or, when erected on site, is 320 or more square feet, and which is built on a permanent chassis and designed to be used as a dwelling with or without a permanent foundation when connected to the required utilities, and includes the plumbing, heating, air-conditioning, and electrical systems contained therein. The term includes any structure that meets all of the requirements of this paragraph except the size requirements and with respect to which the manufacturer voluntarily files a certification required by the United States Secretary of Housing and Urban Development and complies with the standards established under Title 42 of the United States Code.

(54) "Manufactured-home transaction" means a secured transaction:
  (A) that creates a purchase-money security interest in a manufactured home, other than a manufactured credit home held as inventory; or
  (B) in which a manufactured home, other than a manufactured home held as inventory, is the primary collateral.

(55) "Mortgage" means a consensual interest in real property, including fixtures, which secures payment or performance of an obligation.

(56) "New debtor" means a person that becomes bound as debtor under Section 9—203(d) by a security agreement previously entered into by another person.

(57) "New value" means (i) money, (ii) money's worth in property, services, or new credit, or (iii) release by a transferee of an interest in property previously transferred to the transferee. The term does not include an obligation substituted for another obligation.

(58) "Noncash proceeds" means proceeds other than cash proceeds.

(59) "Obligor" means a person that, with respect to an obligation secured by a security interest in or an agricultural lien on the collateral, (i) owes payment or other performance of the obligation, (ii) has provided property other than the collateral to secure payment or other performance of the obligation, or (iii) is otherwise accountable in whole or in part for payment or other performance of the obligation. The term does not include issuers or nominated persons under a letter of credit.

(60) "Original debtor", except as used in Section 9—310(c), means a person that, as debtor, entered into a security agreement to which a new debtor has become bound under Section 9—203(d).

(61) "Payment intangible" means a general intangible under which the account debtor's principal obligation is a monetary obligation.

(62) "Person related to", with respect to an individual, means:
   (A) the spouse of the individual;
   (B) a brother, brother-in-law, sister, or sister-in-law of the individual;
   (C) an ancestor or lineal descendant of the individual or the individual's spouse; or
   (D) any other relative, by blood or marriage, of the individual or the individual's spouse who shares the same home with the individual.

(63) "Person related to", with respect to an organization, means:
   (A) a person directly or indirectly controlling, controlled by, or under common control with the organization;
   (B) an officer or director of, or a person performing similar functions with respect to, the organization;
   (C) an officer or director of, or a person performing similar functions with respect to, a person described in subparagraph (A);
   (D) the spouse of an individual described in subparagraph (A), (B), or (C); or
   (E) an individual who is related by blood or marriage to an individual described in subparagraph (A), (B), (C), or (D) and shares the same home with the individual.

(64) "Proceeds", except as used in Section 9—609 (b), means the following property:
   (A) whatever is acquired upon the sale, lease, license, exchange, or other disposition of collateral;
   (B) whatever is collected on, or distributed on account of, collateral;
   (C) rights arising out of collateral;
   (D) to the extent of the value of collateral, claims arising out of the loss, nonconformity, or interference with the use of, defects or infringement of rights in, or damage to, the collateral; or
   (E) to the extent of the value of collateral and to the extent payable to the debtor or the secured party, insurance payable by reason of the loss or nonconformity of, defects or infringement of rights in, or damage to, the collateral.

(65) "Promissory note" means an instrument that evidences a promise to pay a monetary obligation, does not evidence an order to pay, and does not contain an acknowledgment by a bank that the bank has received for deposit a sum of money or funds.

(66) "Proposal" means a record authenticated by a secured party which includes the terms on which the secured party is willing to accept collateral in full or partial satisfaction of the obligation it secures pursuant to Sections 9—620, 9—621, and 9—622.

(67) "Public-finance transaction" means a secured transaction in connection with which:
   (A) debt securities are issued;
   (B) all or a portion of the securities issued have an initial stated maturity of at least 20 years; and
   (C) the debtor, obligor, secured party, account debtor or other person obligated on collateral, assignor or assignee of a secured obligation, or assignor or assignee of a security interest is a State or a governmental unit of a State.

(68) "Pursuant to commitment", with respect to an advance made or other value given by a secured party, means pursuant to the secured party's obligation, whether or not a subsequent event of default or other event not within the secured party's control has relieved or may relieve the secured party from its obligation.

(69) "Record", except as used in "for record", "of record", "record or legal title", and "record owner", means information that is inscribed on a tangible medium or which is stored in an electronic or other medium and is retrievable in perceivable form.

(70) "Registered organization" means an organization organized solely under the law of a single State or the United States and as to which the State or the United States must maintain a public record showing the organization to have been organized.

(71) "Secondary obligor" means an obligor to the extent that:

(A) the obligor's obligation is secondary; or

(B) the obligor has a right of recourse with respect to an obligation secured by collateral against the debtor, another obligor, or property of either.

(72) "Secured party" means:

(A) a person in whose favor a security interest is created or provided for under a security agreement, whether or not any obligation to be secured is outstanding;

(B) a person that holds an agricultural lien;

(C) a consignor;

(D) a person to which accounts, chattel paper, payment intangibles, or promissory notes have been sold;

(E) a trustee, indenture trustee, agent, collateral agent, or other representative in whose favor a security interest or agricultural lien is created or provided for; or

(F) a person that holds a security interest arising under Section 2—401, 2—505, 2—711(3), 2A—508(5), 4—210, or 5—118.

(73) "Security agreement" means an agreement that creates or provides for a security interest.

(74) "Send", in connection with a record or notification, means:

(A) to deposit in the mail, deliver for transmission, or transmit by any other usual means of communication, with postage or cost of transmission provided for, addressed to any address reasonable under the circumstances; or

(B) to cause the record or notification to be received within the time that it would have been received if properly sent under subparagraph (A).

(75) "Software" means a computer program and any supporting information provided in connection with a transaction relating to the program. The term does not include a computer program that is included in the definition of goods.

(76) "State" means a State of the United States, the District of Columbia, Puerto Rico, the United States Virgin Islands, or any territory or insular possession subject to the jurisdiction of the United States.

(77) "Supporting obligation" means a letter-of-credit right or secondary obligation that supports the payment or performance of an account, chattel paper, a document, a general intangible, an instrument, or investment property.

(78) "Tangible chattel paper" means chattel paper evidenced by a record or records consisting of information that is inscribed on a tangible medium.

(79) "Termination statement" means an amendment of a financing statement which:

(A) identifies, by its file number, the initial financing statement to which it relates; and

(B) indicates either that it is a termination statement or that the identified financing statement is no longer effective.

(80) "Transmitting utility" means a person primarily engaged in the business of:

(A) operating a railroad, subway, street railway, or trolley bus;

(B) transmitting communications electrically, electromagnetically, or by light;

(C) transmitting goods by pipeline or sewer; or

(D) transmitting or producing and transmitting electricity, steam, gas, or water.

(b) The following definitions in other articles apply to this article:

"Applicant."	Section 5—102
"Beneficiary."	Section 5—102
"Broker."	Section 8—102
"Certificated security."	Section 8—102
"Check."	Section 3—104
"Clearing corporation."	Section 8—102
"Contract for sale."	Section 2—106
"Customer."	Section 4—104
"Entitlement holder."	Section 8—102
"Financial asset."	Section 8—102
"Holder in due course."	Section 3—302
"Issuer" (with respect to a letter of credit or letter-of-credit right).	Section 5—102
"Issuer" (with respect to a security).	Section 8—201
"Lease."	Section 2A—103
"Lease agreement."	Section 2A—103
"Lease contract."	Section 2A—103
"Leasehold interest."	Section 2A—103
"Lessee."	Section 2A—103
"Lessee in ordinary course of business."	Section 2A—103
"Lessor."	Section 2A—103

"Lessor's residual interest."	Section 2A—103
"Letter of credit."	Section 5—102
"Merchant."	Section 2—104
"Negotiable instrument."	Section 3—104
"Nominated person."	Section 5—102
"Note."	Section 3—104
"Proceeds of a letter of credit."	Section 5—114
"Prove."	Section 3—103
"Sale."	Section 2—106
"Securities account."	Section 8—501
"Securities intermediary."	Section 8—102
"Security."	Section 8—102
"Security certificate."	Section 8—102
"Security entitlement."	Section 8—102
"Uncertificated security."	Section 8—102

(c) Article 1 contains general definitions and principles of construction and interpretation applicable throughout this article.

Amended in 1999 and 2000.

§9—103. PURCHASE-MONEY SECURITY INTEREST; APPLICATION OF PAYMENTS; BURDEN OF ESTABLISHING

(a) In this section:

(1) "purchase-money collateral" means goods or software that secures a purchase-money obligation incurred with respect to that collateral; and

(2) "purchase-money obligation" means an obligation of an obligor incurred as all or part of the price of the collateral or for value given to enable the debtor to acquire rights in or the use of the collateral if the value is in fact so used.

(b) A security interest in goods is a purchase-money security interest:

(1) to the extent that the goods are purchase-money collateral with respect to that security interest;

(2) if the security interest is in inventory that is or was purchase-money collateral, also to the extent that the security interest secures a purchase-money obligation incurred with respect to other inventory in which the secured party holds or held a purchase-money security interest; and

(3) also to the extent that the security interest secures a purchase-money obligation incurred with respect to software in which the secured party holds or held a purchase-money security interest.

(c) A security interest in software is a purchase-money security interest to the extent that the security interest also secures a purchase-money obligation incurred with respect to goods in which the secured party holds or held a purchase-money security interest if:

(1) the debtor acquired its interest in the software in an integrated transaction in which it acquired an interest in the goods; and

(2) the debtor acquired its interest in the software for the principal purpose of using the software in the goods.

(d) The security interest of a consignor in goods that are the subject of a consignment is a purchase-money security interest in inventory.

(e) In a transaction other than a consumer-goods transaction, if the extent to which a security interest is a purchase-money security interest depends on the application of a payment to a particular obligation, the payment must be applied:

(1) in accordance with any reasonable method of application to which the parties agree;

(2) in the absence of the parties' agreement to a reasonable method, in accordance with any intention of the obligor manifested at or before the time of payment; or

(3) in the absence of an agreement to a reasonable method and a timely manifestation of the obligor's intention, in the following order:

(A) to obligations that are not secured; and

(B) if more than one obligation is secured, to obligations secured by purchase-money security interests in the order in which those obligations were incurred.

(f) In a transaction other than a consumer-goods transaction, a purchase-money security interest does not lose its status as such, even if:

(1) the purchase-money collateral also secures an obligation that is not a purchase-money obligation;

(2) collateral that is not purchase-money collateral also secures the purchase-money obligation; or

(3) the purchase-money obligation has been renewed, refinanced, consolidated, or restructured.

(g) In a transaction other than a consumer-goods transaction, a secured party claiming a purchase-money security interest has the burden of establishing the extent to which the security interest is a purchase-money security interest.

(h) The limitation of the rules in subsections (e), (f), and (g) to transactions other than consumer-goods transactions is intended to leave to the court the determination of the proper rules in consumer-goods transactions. The court may not infer from that limitation the nature of the proper rule in consumer-goods transactions and may continue to apply established approaches.

§9—104. CONTROL OF DEPOSIT ACCOUNT

(a) A secured party has control of a deposit account if:

(1) the secured party is the bank with which the deposit account is maintained;

(2) the debtor, secured party, and bank have agreed in an authenticated record that the bank will comply with instructions originated by the secured party directing disposition of the funds in the deposit account without further consent by the debtor; or

(3) the secured party becomes the bank's customer with respect to the deposit account.

(b) A secured party that has satisfied subsection (a) has control, even if the debtor retains the right to direct the disposition of funds from the deposit account.

§9—105. CONTROL OF ELECTRONIC CHATTEL PAPER

A secured party has control of electronic chattel paper if the record or records comprising the chattel paper are created, stored, and assigned in such a manner that:

(1) a single authoritative copy of the record or records exists which is unique, identifiable and, except as otherwise provided in paragraphs (4), (5), and (6), unalterable;

(2) the authoritative copy identifies the secured party as the assignee of the record or records;

(3) the authoritative copy is communicated to and maintained by the secured party or its designated custodian;

(4) copies or revisions that add or change an identified assignee of the authoritative copy can be made only with the participation of the secured party;

(5) each copy of the authoritative copy and any copy of a copy is readily identifiable as a copy that is not the authoritative copy; and

(6) any revision of the authoritative copy is readily identifiable as an authorized or unauthorized revision.

§9—106. CONTROL OF INVESTMENT PROPERTY

(a) A person has control of a certificated security, uncertificated security, or security entitlement as provided in Section 8—106.

(b) A secured party has control of a commodity contract if:

(1) the secured party is the commodity intermediary with which the commodity contract is carried; or

(2) the commodity customer, secured party, and commodity intermediary have agreed that the commodity intermediary will apply any value distributed on account of the commodity contract as directed by the secured party without further consent by the commodity customer.

(c) A secured party having control of all security entitlements or commodity contracts carried in a securities account or commodity account has control over the securities account or commodity account.

§9—107. CONTROL OF LETTER-OF-CREDIT RIGHT

A secured party has control of a letter-of-credit right to the extent of any right to payment or performance by the issuer or any nominated person if the issuer or nominated person has consented to an assignment of proceeds of the letter of credit under Section 5—114(c) or otherwise applicable law or practice.

§9—108. SUFFICIENCY OF DESCRIPTION

(a) Except as otherwise provided in subsections (c), (d), and (e), a description of personal or real property is sufficient, whether or not it is specific, if it reasonably identifies what is described.

(b) Except as otherwise provided in subsection (d), a description of collateral reasonably identifies the collateral if it identifies the collateral by:

(1) specific listing;

(2) category;

(3) except as otherwise provided in subsection (e), a type of collateral defined in [the Uniform Commercial Code];

(4) quantity;

(5) computational or allocational formula or procedure; or

(6) except as otherwise provided in subsection (c), any other method, if the identity of the collateral is objectively determinable.

(c) A description of collateral as "all the debtor's assets" or "all the debtor's personal property" or using words of similar import does not reasonably identify the collateral.

(d) Except as otherwise provided in subsection (e), a description of a security entitlement, securities account, or commodity account is sufficient if it describes:

(1) the collateral by those terms or as investment property; or

(2) the underlying financial asset or commodity contract.

(e) A description only by type of collateral defined in [the Uniform Commercial Code] is an insufficient description of:

(1) a commercial tort claim; or

(2) in a consumer transaction, consumer goods, a security entitlement, a securities account, or a commodity account.

[Subpart 2. Applicability of Article]

§9—109. SCOPE

(a) Except as otherwise provided in subsections (c) and (d), this article applies to:

    (1) a transaction, regardless of its form, that creates a security interest in personal property or fixtures by contract;

    (2) an agricultural lien;

    (3) a sale of accounts, chattel paper, payment intangibles, or promissory notes;

    (4) a consignment;

    (5) a security interest arising under Section 2—401, 2—505, 2—711(3), or 2A—508(5), as provided in Section 9—110; and

    (6) a security interest arising under Section 4—210 or 5—118.

(b) The application of this article to a security interest in a secured obligation is not affected by the fact that the obligation is itself secured by a transaction or interest to which this article does not apply.

(c) This article does not apply to the extent that:

    (1) a statute, regulation, or treaty of the United States preempts this article;

    (2) another statute of this State expressly governs the creation, perfection, priority, or enforcement of a security interest created by this State or a governmental unit of this State;

    (3) a statute of another State, a foreign country, or a governmental unit of another State or a foreign country, other than a statute generally applicable to security interests, expressly governs creation, perfection, priority, or enforcement of a security interest created by the State, country, or governmental unit; or

    (4) the rights of a transferee beneficiary or nominated person under a letter of credit are independent and superior under Section 5—114.

(d) This article does not apply to:

    (1) a landlord's lien, other than an agricultural lien;

    (2) a lien, other than an agricultural lien, given by statute or other rule of law for services or materials, but Section 9—333 applies with respect to priority of the lien;

    (3) an assignment of a claim for wages, salary, or other compensation of an employee;

    (4) a sale of accounts, chattel paper, payment intangibles, or promissory notes as part of a sale of the business out of which they arose;

    (5) an assignment of accounts, chattel paper, payment intangibles, or promissory notes which is for the purpose of collection only;

    (6) an assignment of a right to payment under a contract to an assignee that is also obligated to perform under the contract;

    (7) an assignment of a single account, payment intangible, or promissory note to an assignee in full or partial satisfaction of a preexisting indebtedness;

    (8) a transfer of an interest in or an assignment of a claim under a policy of insurance, other than an assignment by or to a health-care provider of a health-care-insurance receivable and any subsequent assignment of the right to payment, but Sections 9—315 and 9—322 apply with respect to proceeds and priorities in proceeds;

    (9) an assignment of a right represented by a judgment, other than a judgment taken on a right to payment that was collateral;

    (10) a right of recoupment or set-off, but:

        (A) Section 9—340 applies with respect to the effectiveness of rights of recoupment or set-off against deposit accounts; and

        (B) Section 9—404 applies with respect to defenses or claims of an account debtor;

    (11) the creation or transfer of an interest in or lien on real property, including a lease or rents thereunder, except to the extent that provision is made for:

        (A) liens on real property in Sections 9—203 and 9—308;

        (B) fixtures in Section 9—334;

        (C) fixture filings in Sections 9—501, 9—502, 9—512, 9—516, and 9—519; and

        (D) security agreements covering personal and real property in Section 9—604;

    (12) an assignment of a claim arising in tort, other than a commercial tort claim, but Sections 9—315 and 9—322 apply with respect to proceeds and priorities in proceeds; or

    (13) an assignment of a deposit account in a consumer transaction, but Sections 9—315 and 9—322 apply with respect to proceeds and priorities in proceeds.

§9—110. SECURITY INTERESTS ARISING UNDER ARTICLE 2 OR 2A

A security interest arising under Section 2—401, 2—505, 2—711(3), or 2A—508(5) is subject to this article. However, until the debtor obtains possession of the goods:

(1) the security interest is enforceable, even if Section 9—203(b)(3) has not been satisfied;

(2) filing is not required to perfect the security interest;

(3) the rights of the secured party after default by the debtor are governed by Article 2 or 2A; and

(4) the security interest has priority over a conflicting security interest created by the debtor.

Part 2 Effectiveness of Security Agreement; Attachment of Security Interest; Rights of Parties to Security Agreement [Subpart 1. Effectiveness and Attachment]

§9—201. GENERAL EFFECTIVENESS OF SECURITY AGREEMENT

(a) Except as otherwise provided in [the Uniform Commercial Code], a security agreement is effective according to its terms between the parties, against purchasers of the collateral, and against creditors.

(b) A transaction subject to this article is subject to any applicable rule of law which establishes a different rule for consumers and [insert reference to (i) any other statute or regulation that regulates the rates, charges, agreements, and practices for loans, credit sales, or other extensions of credit and (ii) any consumer-protection statute or regulation].

(c) In case of conflict between this article and a rule of law, statute, or regulation described in subsection (b), the rule of law, statute, or regulation controls. Failure to comply with a statute or regulation described in subsection (b) has only the effect the statute or regulation specifies.

(d) This article does not:

(1) validate any rate, charge, agreement, or practice that violates a rule of law, statute, or regulation described in subsection (b); or

(2) extend the application of the rule of law, statute, or regulation to a transaction not otherwise subject to it.

§9—202. TITLE TO COLLATERAL IMMATERIAL

Except as otherwise provided with respect to consignments or sales of accounts, chattel paper, payment intangibles, or promissory notes, the provisions of this article with regard to rights and obligations apply whether title to collateral is in the secured party or the debtor.

§9—203. ATTACHMENT AND ENFORCEABILITY OF SECURITY INTEREST; PROCEEDS; SUPPORTING OBLIGATIONS; FORMAL REQUISITES

(a) A security interest attaches to collateral when it becomes enforceable against the debtor with respect to the collateral, unless an agreement expressly postpones the time of attachment.

(b) Except as otherwise provided in subsections (c) through (i), a security interest is enforceable against the debtor and third parties with respect to the collateral only if:

(1) value has been given;

(2) the debtor has rights in the collateral or the power to transfer rights in the collateral to a secured party; and

(3) one of the following conditions is met:

(A) the debtor has authenticated a security agreement that provides a description of the collateral and, if the security interest covers timber to be cut, a description of the land concerned;

(B) the collateral is not a certificated security and is in the possession of the secured party under Section 9—313 pursuant to the debtor's security agreement;

(C) the collateral is a certificated security in registered form and the security certificate has been delivered to the secured party under Section 8—301 pursuant to the debtor's security agreement; or

(D) the collateral is deposit accounts, electronic chattel paper, investment property, or letter-of-credit rights, and the secured party has control under Section 9—104, 9—105, 9—106, or 9—107 pursuant to the debtor's security agreement.

(c) Subsection (b) is subject to Section 4—210 on the security interest of a collecting bank, Section 5—118 on the security interest of a letter-of-credit issuer or nominated person, Section 9—110 on a security interest arising under Article 2 or 2A, and Section 9—206 on security interests in investment property.

(d) A person becomes bound as debtor by a security agreement entered into by another person if, by operation of law other than this article or by contract:

(1) the security agreement becomes effective to create a security interest in the person's property; or

(2) the person becomes generally obligated for the obligations of the other person, including the obligation secured under the security agreement, and acquires or succeeds to all or substantially all of the assets of the other person.

(e) If a new debtor becomes bound as debtor by a security agreement entered into by another person:

(1) the agreement satisfies subsection (b)(3) with respect to existing or after-acquired property of the new debtor to the extent the property is described in the agreement; and

(2) another agreement is not necessary to make a security interest in the property enforceable.

(f) The attachment of a security interest in collateral gives the secured party the rights to proceeds provided by Section 9—315 and is also attachment of a security interest in a supporting obligation for the collateral.

(g) The attachment of a security interest in a right to payment or performance secured by a security interest or other lien on personal or real property is also attachment of a security interest in the security interest, mortgage, or other lien.

(h) The attachment of a security interest in a securities account is also attachment of a security interest in the security entitlements carried in the securities account.

(i) The attachment of a security interest in a commodity account is also attachment of a security interest in the commodity contracts carried in the commodity account.

§9—204. AFTER-ACQUIRED PROPERTY; FUTURE ADVANCES

(a) Except as otherwise provided in subsection (b), a security agreement may create or provide for a security interest in after-acquired collateral.

(b) A security interest does not attach under a term constituting an after-acquired property clause to:
>(1) consumer goods, other than an accession when given as additional security, unless the debtor acquires rights in them within 10 days after the secured party gives value; or
>(2) a commercial tort claim.

(c) A security agreement may provide that collateral secures, or that accounts, chattel paper, payment intangibles, or promissory notes are sold in connection with, future advances or other value, whether or not the advances or value are given pursuant to commitment.

§9—205. USE OR DISPOSITION OF COLLATERAL PERMISSIBLE

(a) A security interest is not invalid or fraudulent against creditors solely because:
>(1) the debtor has the right or ability to:
>>(A) use, commingle, or dispose of all or part of the collateral, including returned or repossessed goods;
>>(B) collect, compromise, enforce, or otherwise deal with collateral;
>>(C) accept the return of collateral or make repossessions; or
>>(D) use, commingle, or dispose of proceeds; or
>(2) the secured party fails to require the debtor to account for proceeds or replace collateral.

(b) This section does not relax the requirements of possession if attachment, perfection, or enforcement of a security interest depends upon possession of the collateral by the secured party.

§9—206. SECURITY INTEREST ARISING IN PURCHASE OR DELIVERY OF FINANCIAL ASSET

(a) A security interest in favor of a securities intermediary attaches to a person's security entitlement if:
>(1) the person buys a financial asset through the securities intermediary in a transaction in which the person is obligated to pay the purchase price to the securities intermediary at the time of the purchase; and
>(2) the securities intermediary credits the financial asset to the buyer's securities account before the buyer pays the securities intermediary.

(b) The security interest described in subsection (a) secures the person's obligation to pay for the financial asset.

(c) A security interest in favor of a person that delivers a certificated security or other financial asset represented by a writing attaches to the security or other financial asset if:
>(1) the security or other financial asset:
>>(A) in the ordinary course of business is transferred by delivery with any necessary indorsement or assignment; and
>>(B) is delivered under an agreement between persons in the business of dealing with such securities or financial assets; and
>(2) the agreement calls for delivery against payment.

(d) The security interest described in subsection (c) secures the obligation to make payment for the delivery.

[Subpart 2. Rights and Duties]

§9—207. RIGHTS AND DUTIES OF SECURED PARTY HAVING POSSESSION OR CONTROL OF COLLATERAL

(a) Except as otherwise provided in subsection (d), a secured party shall use reasonable care in the custody and preservation of collateral in the secured party's possession. In the case of chattel paper or an instrument, reasonable care includes taking necessary steps to preserve rights against prior parties unless otherwise agreed.

(b) Except as otherwise provided in subsection (d), if a secured party has possession of collateral:
>(1) reasonable expenses, including the cost of insurance and payment of taxes or other charges, incurred in the custody, preservation, use, or operation of the collateral are chargeable to the debtor and are secured by the collateral;
>(2) the risk of accidental loss or damage is on the debtor to the extent of a deficiency in any effective insurance coverage;
>(3) the secured party shall keep the collateral identifiable, but fungible collateral may be commingled; and
>(4) the secured party may use or operate the collateral:
>>(A) for the purpose of preserving the collateral or its value;
>>(B) as permitted by an order of a court having competent jurisdiction; or

(C) except in the case of consumer goods, in the manner and to the extent agreed by the debtor.

(c) Except as otherwise provided in subsection (d), a secured party having possession of collateral or control of collateral under Section 9—104, 9—105, 9—106, or 9—107:

(1) may hold as additional security any proceeds, except money or funds, received from the collateral;

(2) shall apply money or funds received from the collateral to reduce the secured obligation, unless remitted to the debtor; and

(3) may create a security interest in the collateral.

(d) If the secured party is a buyer of accounts, chattel paper, payment intangibles, or promissory notes or a consignor:

(1) subsection (a) does not apply unless the secured party is entitled under an agreement:

(A) to charge back uncollected collateral; or

(B) otherwise to full or limited recourse against the debtor or a secondary obligor based on the nonpayment or other default of an account debtor or other obligor on the collateral; and

(2) subsections (b) and (c) do not apply.

§9—208. ADDITIONAL DUTIES OF SECURED PARTY HAVING CONTROL OF COLLATERAL

(a) This section applies to cases in which there is no outstanding secured obligation and the secured party is not committed to make advances, incur obligations, or otherwise give value.

(b) Within 10 days after receiving an authenticated demand by the debtor:

(1) a secured party having control of a deposit account under Section 9—104(a)(2) shall send to the bank with which the deposit account is maintained an authenticated statement that releases the bank from any further obligation to comply with instructions originated by the secured party;

(2) a secured party having control of a deposit account under Section 9—104(a)(3) shall:

(A) pay the debtor the balance on deposit in the deposit account; or

(B) transfer the balance on deposit into a deposit account in the debtor's name;

(3) a secured party, other than a buyer, having control of electronic chattel paper under Section 9—105 shall:

(A) communicate the authoritative copy of the electronic chattel paper to the debtor or its designated custodian;

(B) if the debtor designates a custodian that is the designated custodian with which the authoritative copy of the electronic chattel paper is maintained for the secured party, communicate to the custodian an authenticated record releasing the designated custodian from any further obligation to comply with instructions originated by the secured party and instructing the custodian to comply with instructions originated by the debtor; and

(C) take appropriate action to enable the debtor or its designated custodian to make copies of or revisions to the authoritative copy which add or change an identified assignee of the authoritative copy without the consent of the secured party;

(4) a secured party having control of investment property under Section 8—106(d)(2) or 9—106 (b) shall send to the securities intermediary or commodity intermediary with which the security entitlement or commodity contract is maintained an authenticated record that releases the securities intermediary or commodity intermediary from any further obligation to comply with entitlement orders or directions originated by the secured party; and

(5) a secured party having control of a letter-of-credit right under Section 9—107 shall send to each person having an unfulfilled obligation to pay or deliver proceeds of the letter of credit to the secured party an authenticated release from any further obligation to pay or deliver proceeds of the letter of credit to the secured party.

§9—209. DUTIES OF SECURED PARTY IF ACCOUNT DEBTOR HAS BEEN NOTIFIED OF ASSIGNMENT

(a) Except as otherwise provided in subsection (c), this section applies if:

(1) there is no outstanding secured obligation; and

(2) the secured party is not committed to make advances, incur obligations, or otherwise give value.

(b) Within 10 days after receiving an authenticated demand by the debtor, a secured party shall send to an account debtor that has received notification of an assignment to the secured party as assignee under Section 9—406(a) an authenticated record that releases the account debtor from any further obligation to the secured party.

(c) This section does not apply to an assignment constituting the sale of an account, chattel paper, or payment intangible.

§9—210. REQUEST FOR ACCOUNTING; REQUEST REGARDING LIST OF COLLATERAL OR STATEMENT OF ACCOUNT

(a) In this section:

(1) "Request" means a record of a type described in paragraph (2), (3), or (4).

(2) "Request for an accounting" means a record authenticated by a debtor requesting that the recipient provide an accounting of the unpaid obligations secured by collateral and reasonably identifying the transaction or relationship that is the subject of the request.

(3) "Request regarding a list of collateral" means a record authenticated by a debtor requesting that the recipient approve or correct a list of what the debtor believes to be the collateral securing an obligation and reasonably identifying the transaction or relationship that is the subject of the request.

(4) "Request regarding a statement of account" means a record authenticated by a debtor requesting that the recipient approve or correct a statement indicating what the debtor believes to be the aggregate amount of unpaid obligations secured by collateral as of a specified date and reasonably identifying the transaction or relationship that is the subject of the request.

(b) Subject to subsections (c), (d), (e), and (f), a secured party, other than a buyer of accounts, chattel paper, payment intangibles, or promissory notes or a consignor, shall comply with a request within 14 days after receipt:

(1) in the case of a request for an accounting, by authenticating and sending to the debtor an accounting; and

(2) in the case of a request regarding a list of collateral or a request regarding a statement of account, by authenticating and sending to the debtor an approval or correction.

(c) A secured party that claims a security interest in all of a particular type of collateral owned by the debtor may comply with a request regarding a list of collateral by sending to the debtor an authenticated record including a statement to that effect within 14 days after receipt.

(d) A person that receives a request regarding a list of collateral, claims no interest in the collateral when it receives the request, and claimed an interest in the collateral at an earlier time shall comply with the request within 14 days after receipt by sending to the debtor an authenticated record:

(1) disclaiming any interest in the collateral; and

(2) if known to the recipient, providing the name and mailing address of any assignee of or successor to the recipient's interest in the collateral.

(e) A person that receives a request for an accounting or a request regarding a statement of account, claims no interest in the obligations when it receives the request, and claimed an interest in the obligations at an earlier time shall comply with the request within 14 days after receipt by sending to the debtor an authenticated record:

(1) disclaiming any interest in the obligations; and

(2) if known to the recipient, providing the name and mailing address of any assignee of or successor to the recipient's interest in the obligations.

(f) A debtor is entitled without charge to one response to a request under this section during any six-month period. The secured party may require payment of a charge not exceeding $25 for each additional response.

As amended in 1999.

Part 3 Perfection and Priority [Subpart 1. Law Governing Perfection and Priority]

§9—301. LAW GOVERNING PERFECTION AND PRIORITY OF SECURITY INTERESTS

Except as otherwise provided in Sections 9—303 through 9—306, the following rules determine the law governing perfection, the effect of perfection or nonperfection, and the priority of a security interest in collateral:

(1) Except as otherwise provided in this section, while a debtor is located in a jurisdiction, the local law of that jurisdiction governs perfection, the effect of perfection or nonperfection, and the priority of a security interest in collateral.

(2) While collateral is located in a jurisdiction, the local law of that jurisdiction governs perfection, the effect of perfection or nonperfection, and the priority of a possessory security interest in that collateral.

(3) Except as otherwise provided in paragraph (4), while negotiable documents, goods, instruments, money, or tangible chattel paper is located in a jurisdiction, the local law of that jurisdiction governs:

(A) perfection of a security interest in the goods by filing a fixture filing;

(B) perfection of a security interest in timber to be cut; and

(C) the effect of perfection or nonperfection and the priority of a nonpossessory security interest in the collateral.

(4) The local law of the jurisdiction in which the wellhead or minehead is located governs perfection, the effect of perfection or nonperfection, and the priority of a security interest in as-extracted collateral.

§9—302. LAW GOVERNING PERFECTION AND PRIORITY OF AGRICULTURAL LIENS

While farm products are located in a jurisdiction, the local law of that jurisdiction governs perfection, the effect of perfection or nonperfection, and the priority of an agricultural lien on the farm products.

§9—303. LAW GOVERNING PERFECTION AND PRIORITY OF SECURITY INTERESTS IN GOODS COVERED BY A CERTIFICATE OF TITLE

(a) This section applies to goods covered by a certificate of title, even if there is no other relationship between the jurisdiction under whose certificate of title the goods are covered and the goods or the debtor.

(b) Goods become covered by a certificate of title when a valid application for the certificate of title and the applicable fee are delivered to the appropriate authority. Goods cease to be covered by a certificate of title at the earlier of the time the certificate of title ceases to be effective under the law of the issuing jurisdiction or the time the goods become covered subsequently by a certificate of title issued by another jurisdiction.

(c) The local law of the jurisdiction under whose certificate of title the goods are covered governs perfection, the effect of perfection or nonperfection, and the priority of a security interest in goods covered by a certificate of title from the time the goods become covered by the certificate of title until the goods cease to be covered by the certificate of title.

§9—304. LAW GOVERNING PERFECTION AND PRIORITY OF SECURITY INTERESTS IN DEPOSIT ACCOUNTS

(a) The local law of a bank's jurisdiction governs perfection, the effect of perfection or nonperfection, and the priority of a security interest in a deposit account maintained with that bank.

(b) The following rules determine a bank's jurisdiction for purposes of this part:

    (1) If an agreement between the bank and the debtor governing the deposit account expressly provides that a particular jurisdiction is the bank's jurisdiction for purposes of this part, this article, or [the Uniform Commercial Code], that jurisdiction is the bank's jurisdiction.

    (2) If paragraph (1) does not apply and an agreement between the bank and its customer governing the deposit account expressly provides that the agreement is governed by the law of a particular jurisdiction, that jurisdiction is the bank's jurisdiction.

    (3) If neither paragraph (1) nor paragraph (2) applies and an agreement between the bank and its customer governing the deposit account expressly provides that the deposit account is maintained at an office in a particular jurisdiction, that jurisdiction is the bank's jurisdiction.

    (4) If none of the preceding paragraphs applies, the bank's jurisdiction is the jurisdiction in which the office identified in an account statement as the office serving the customer's account is located.

    (5) If none of the preceding paragraphs applies, the bank's jurisdiction is the jurisdiction in which the chief executive office of the bank is located.

§9—305. LAW GOVERNING PERFECTION AND PRIORITY OF SECURITY INTERESTS IN INVESTMENT PROPERTY

(a) Except as otherwise provided in subsection (c), the following rules apply:

    (1) While a security certificate is located in a jurisdiction, the local law of that jurisdiction governs perfection, the effect of perfection or nonperfection, and the priority of a security interest in the certificated security represented thereby.

    (2) The local law of the issuer's jurisdiction as specified in Section 8—110(d) governs perfection, the effect of perfection or nonperfection, and the priority of a security interest in an uncertificated security.

    (3) The local law of the securities intermediary's jurisdiction as specified in Section 8—110(e) governs perfection, the effect of perfection or nonperfection, and the priority of a security interest in a security entitlement or securities account.

    (4) The local law of the commodity intermediary's jurisdiction governs perfection, the effect of perfection or nonperfection, and the priority of a security interest in a commodity contract or commodity account.

(b) The following rules determine a commodity intermediary's jurisdiction for purposes of this part:

    (1) If an agreement between the commodity intermediary and commodity customer governing the commodity account expressly provides that a particular jurisdiction is the commodity intermediary's jurisdiction for purposes of this part, this article, or [the Uniform Commercial Code], that jurisdiction is the commodity intermediary's jurisdiction.

    (2) If paragraph (1) does not apply and an agreement between the commodity intermediary and commodity customer governing the commodity account expressly provides that the

agreement is governed by the law of a particular jurisdiction, that jurisdiction is the commodity intermediary's jurisdiction.

(3) If neither paragraph (1) nor paragraph (2) applies and an agreement between the commodity intermediary and commodity customer governing the commodity account expressly provides that the commodity account is maintained at an office in a particular jurisdiction, that jurisdiction is the commodity intermediary's jurisdiction.

(4) If none of the preceding paragraphs applies, the commodity intermediary's jurisdiction is the jurisdiction in which the office identified in an account statement as the office serving the commodity customer's account is located.

(5) If none of the preceding paragraphs applies, the commodity intermediary's jurisdiction is the jurisdiction in which the chief executive office of the commodity intermediary is located.

(c) The local law of the jurisdiction in which the debtor is located governs:

(1) perfection of a security interest in investment property by filing;

(2) automatic perfection of a security interest in investment property created by a broker or securities intermediary; and

(3) automatic perfection of a security interest in a commodity contract or commodity account created by a commodity intermediary.

§9—306. LAW GOVERNING PERFECTION AND PRIORITY OF SECURITY INTERESTS IN LETTER-OF-CREDIT RIGHTS

(a) Subject to subsection (c), the local law of the issuer's jurisdiction or a nominated person's jurisdiction governs perfection, the effect of perfection or nonperfection, and the priority of a security interest in a letter-of-credit right if the issuer's jurisdiction or nominated person's jurisdiction is a State.

(b) For purposes of this part, an issuer's jurisdiction or nominated person's jurisdiction is the jurisdiction whose law governs the liability of the issuer or nominated person with respect to the letter-of-credit right as provided in Section 5—116.

(c) This section does not apply to a security interest that is perfected only under Section 9—308(d).

§9—307. LOCATION OF DEBTOR

(a) In this section, "place of business" means a place where a debtor conducts its affairs.

(b) Except as otherwise provided in this section, the following rules determine a debtor's location:

(1) A debtor who is an individual is located at the individual's principal residence.

(2) A debtor that is an organization and has only one place of business is located at its place of business.

(3) A debtor that is an organization and has more than one place of business is located at its chief executive office.

(c) Subsection (b) applies only if a debtor's residence, place of business, or chief executive office, as applicable, is located in a jurisdiction whose law generally requires information concerning the existence of a nonpossessory security interest to be made generally available in a filing, recording, or registration system as a condition or result of the security interest's obtaining priority over the rights of a lien creditor with respect to the collateral. If subsection (b) does not apply, the debtor is located in the District of Columbia.

(d) A person that ceases to exist, have a residence, or have a place of business continues to be located in the jurisdiction specified by subsections (b) and (c).

(e) A registered organization that is organized under the law of a State is located in that State.

(f) Except as otherwise provided in subsection (i), a registered organization that is organized under the law of the United States and a branch or agency of a bank that is not organized under the law of the United States or a State are located:

(1) in the State that the law of the United States designates, if the law designates a State of location;

(2) in the State that the registered organization, branch, or agency designates, if the law of the United States authorizes the registered organization, branch, or agency to designate its State of location; or

(3) in the District of Columbia, if neither paragraph (1) nor paragraph (2) applies.

(g) A registered organization continues to be located in the jurisdiction specified by subsection (e) or (f) notwithstanding:

(1) the suspension, revocation, forfeiture, or lapse of the registered organization's status as such in its jurisdiction of organization; or

(2) the dissolution, winding up, or cancellation of the existence of the registered organization.

(h) The United States is located in the District of Columbia.

(i) A branch or agency of a bank that is not organized under the law of the United States or a State is located in the State in which the branch or agency is licensed, if all branches and agencies of the bank are licensed in only one State.

(j) A foreign air carrier under the Federal Aviation Act of 1958, as amended, is located at the designated office of the agent upon which service of process may be made on behalf of the carrier.

(k) This section applies only for purposes of this part.

[Subpart 2. Perfection]

§9—308. WHEN SECURITY INTEREST OR AGRICULTURAL LIEN IS PERFECTED; CONTINUITY OF PERFECTION

(a) Except as otherwise provided in this section and Section 9—309, a security interest is perfected if it has attached and all of the applicable requirements for perfection in Sections 9—310 through 9—316 have been satisfied. A security interest is perfected when it attaches if the applicable requirements are satisfied before the security interest attaches.

(b) An agricultural lien is perfected if it has become effective and all of the applicable requirements for perfection in Section 9—310 have been satisfied. An agricultural lien is perfected when it becomes effective if the applicable requirements are satisfied before the agricultural lien becomes effective.

(c) A security interest or agricultural lien is perfected continuously if it is originally perfected by one method under this article and is later perfected by another method under this article, without an intermediate period when it was unperfected.

(d) Perfection of a security interest in collateral also perfects a security interest in a supporting obligation for the collateral.

(e) Perfection of a security interest in a right to payment or performance also perfects a security interest in a security interest, mortgage, or other lien on personal or real property securing the right.

(f) Perfection of a security interest in a securities account also perfects a security interest in the security entitlements carried in the securities account.

(g) Perfection of a security interest in a commodity account also perfects a security interest in the commodity contracts carried in the commodity account.

Legislative Note: Any statute conflicting with subsection (e) must be made expressly subject to that subsection.

§9—309. SECURITY INTEREST PERFECTED UPON ATTACHMENT

The following security interests are perfected when they attach:

(1) a purchase-money security interest in consumer goods, except as otherwise provided in Section 9—311(b) with respect to consumer goods that are subject to a statute or treaty described in Section 9—311(a);

(2) an assignment of accounts or payment intangibles which does not by itself or in conjunction with other assignments to the same assignee transfer a significant part of the assignor's outstanding accounts or payment intangibles;

(3) a sale of a payment intangible;

(4) a sale of a promissory note;

(5) a security interest created by the assignment of a health-care-insurance receivable to the provider of the health-care goods or services;

(6) a security interest arising under Section 2—401, 2—505, 2—711(3), or 2A—508(5), until the debtor obtains possession of the collateral;

(7) a security interest of a collecting bank arising under Section 4—210;

(8) a security interest of an issuer or nominated person arising under Section 5—118;

(9) a security interest arising in the delivery of a financial asset under Section 9—206(c);

(10) a security interest in investment property created by a broker or securities intermediary;

(11) a security interest in a commodity contract or a commodity account created by a commodity intermediary;

(12) an assignment for the benefit of all creditors of the transferor and subsequent transfers by the assignee thereunder; and

(13) a security interest created by an assignment of a beneficial interest in a decedent's estate; and

(14) a sale by an individual of an account that is a right to payment of winnings in a lottery or other game of chance.

§9—310. WHEN FILING REQUIRED TO PERFECT SECURITY INTEREST OR AGRICULTURAL LIEN; SECURITY INTERESTS AND AGRICULTURAL LIENS TO WHICH FILING PROVISIONS DO NOT APPLY

(a) Except as otherwise provided in subsection (b) and Section 9—312(b), a financing statement must be filed to perfect all security interests and agricultural liens.

(b) The filing of a financing statement is not necessary to perfect a security interest:

(1) that is perfected under Section 9—308(d), (e), (f), or (g);

(2) that is perfected under Section 9—309 when it attaches;

(3) in property subject to a statute, regulation, or treaty described in Section 9—311(a);

(4) in goods in possession of a bailee which is perfected under Section 9—312(d)(1) or (2);

(5) in certificated securities, documents, goods, or instruments which is perfected without filing or possession under Section 9—312(e), (f), or (g);

(6) in collateral in the secured party's possession under Section 9—313;

(7) in a certificated security which is perfected by delivery of the security certificate to the secured party under Section 9—313;

(8) in deposit accounts, electronic chattel paper, investment property, or letter-of-credit rights

which is perfected by control under Section 9—314;

(9) in proceeds which is perfected under Section 9—315; or

(10) that is perfected under Section 9—316.

(c) If a secured party assigns a perfected security interest or agricultural lien, a filing under this article is not required to continue the perfected status of the security interest against creditors of and transferees from the original debtor.

§9—311. PERFECTION OF SECURITY INTERESTS IN PROPERTY SUBJECT TO CERTAIN STATUTES, REGULATIONS, AND TREATIES

(a) Except as otherwise provided in subsection (d), the filing of a financing statement is not necessary or effective to perfect a security interest in property subject to:

(1) a statute, regulation, or treaty of the United States whose requirements for a security interest's obtaining priority over the rights of a lien creditor with respect to the property preempt Section 9—310(a);

(2) [list any certificate-of-title statute covering automobiles, trailers, mobile homes, boats, farm tractors, or the like, which provides for a security interest to be indicated on the certificate as a condition or result of perfection, and any non-Uniform Commercial Code central filing statute]; or

(3) a certificate-of-title statute of another jurisdiction which provides for a security interest to be indicated on the certificate as a condition or result of the security interest's obtaining priority over the rights of a lien creditor with respect to the property.

(b) Compliance with the requirements of a statute, regulation, or treaty described in subsection (a) for obtaining priority over the rights of a lien creditor is equivalent to the filing of a financing statement under this article. Except as otherwise provided in subsection (d) and Sections 9—313 and 9—316(d) and (e) for goods covered by a certificate of title, a security interest in property subject to a statute, regulation, or treaty described in subsection (a) may be perfected only by compliance with those requirements, and a security interest so perfected remains perfected notwithstanding a change in the use or transfer of possession of the collateral.

(c) Except as otherwise provided in subsection (d) and Section 9—316(d) and (e), duration and renewal of perfection of a security interest perfected by compliance with the requirements prescribed by a statute, regulation, or treaty described in subsection (a) are governed by the statute, regulation, or treaty. In other respects, the security interest is subject to this article.

(d) During any period in which collateral subject to a statute specified in subsection (a)(2) is inventory held for sale or lease by a person or leased by that person as lessor and that person is in the business of selling goods of that kind, this section does not apply to a security interest in that collateral created by that person.

Legislative Note: This Article contemplates that perfection of a security interest in goods covered by a certificate of title occurs upon receipt by appropriate State officials of a properly tendered application for a certificate of title on which the security interest is to be indicated, without a relation back to an earlier time. States whose certificate-of-title statutes provide for perfection at a different time or contain a relation-back provision should amend the statutes accordingly.

§9—312. PERFECTION OF SECURITY INTERESTS IN CHATTEL PAPER, DEPOSIT ACCOUNTS, DOCUMENTS, GOODS COVERED BY DOCUMENTS, INSTRUMENTS, INVESTMENT PROPERTY, LETTER-OF-CREDIT RIGHTS, AND MONEY; PERFECTION BY PERMISSIVE FILING; TEMPORARY PERFECTION WITHOUT FILING OR TRANSFER OF POSSESSION

(a) A security interest in chattel paper, negotiable documents, instruments, or investment property may be perfected by filing.

(b) Except as otherwise provided in Section 9—315 (c) and (d) for proceeds:

(1) a security interest in a deposit account may be perfected only by control under Section 9—314;

(2) and except as otherwise provided in Section 9—308(d), a security interest in a letter-of-credit right may be perfected only by control under Section 9—314; and

(3) a security interest in money may be perfected only by the secured party's taking possession under Section 9—313.

(c) While goods are in the possession of a bailee that has issued a negotiable document covering the goods:

(1) a security interest in the goods may be perfected by perfecting a security interest in the document; and

(2) a security interest perfected in the document has priority over any security interest that becomes perfected in the goods by another method during that time.

(d) While goods are in the possession of a bailee that has issued a nonnegotiable document covering the goods, a security interest in the goods may be perfected by:

    (1) issuance of a document in the name of the secured party;

    (2) the bailee's receipt of notification of the secured party's interest; or

    (3) filing as to the goods.

(e) A security interest in certificated securities, negotiable documents, or instruments is perfected without filing or the taking of possession for a period of 20 days from the time it attaches to the extent that it arises for new value given under an authenticated security agreement.

(f) A perfected security interest in a negotiable document or goods in possession of a bailee, other than one that has issued a negotiable document for the goods, remains perfected for 20 days without filing if the secured party makes available to the debtor the goods or documents representing the goods for the purpose of:

    (1) ultimate sale or exchange; or

    (2) loading, unloading, storing, shipping, trans-shipping, manufacturing, processing, or otherwise dealing with them in a manner preliminary to their sale or exchange.

(g) A perfected security interest in a certificated security or instrument remains perfected for 20 days without filing if the secured party delivers the security certificate or instrument to the debtor for the purpose of:

    (1) ultimate sale or exchange; or

    (2) presentation, collection, enforcement, renewal, or registration of transfer.

(h) After the 20-day period specified in subsection (e), (f), or (g) expires, perfection depends upon compliance with this article.

§9—313. WHEN POSSESSION BY OR DELIVERY TO SECURED PARTY PERFECTS SECURITY INTEREST WITHOUT FILING

(a) Except as otherwise provided in subsection (b), a secured party may perfect a security interest in negotiable documents, goods, instruments, money, or tangible chattel paper by taking possession of the collateral. A secured party may perfect a security interest in certificated securities by taking delivery of the certificated securities under Section 8—301.

(b) With respect to goods covered by a certificate of title issued by this State, a secured party may perfect a security interest in the goods by taking possession of the goods only in the circumstances described in Section 9—316(d).

(c) With respect to collateral other than certificated securities and goods covered by a document, a secured party takes possession of collateral in the possession of a person other than the debtor, the secured party, or a lessee of the collateral from the debtor in the ordinary course of the debtor's business, when:

    (1) the person in possession authenticates a record acknowledging that it holds possession of the collateral for the secured party's benefit; or

    (2) the person takes possession of the collateral after having authenticated a record acknowledging that it will hold possession of collateral for the secured party's benefit.

(d) If perfection of a security interest depends upon possession of the collateral by a secured party, perfection occurs no earlier than the time the secured party takes possession and continues only while the secured party retains possession.

(e) A security interest in a certificated security in registered form is perfected by delivery when delivery of the certificated security occurs under Section 8—301 and remains perfected by delivery until the debtor obtains possession of the security certificate.

(f) A person in possession of collateral is not required to acknowledge that it holds possession for a secured party's benefit.

(g) If a person acknowledges that it holds possession for the secured party's benefit:

    (1) the acknowledgment is effective under subsection (c) or Section 8—301(a), even if the acknowledgment violates the rights of a debtor; and

    (2) unless the person otherwise agrees or law other than this article otherwise provides, the person does not owe any duty to the secured party and is not required to confirm the acknowledgment to another person.

(h) A secured party having possession of collateral does not relinquish possession by delivering the collateral to a person other than the debtor or a lessee of the collateral from the debtor in the ordinary course of the debtor's business if the person was instructed before the delivery or is instructed contemporaneously with the delivery:

    (1) to hold possession of the collateral for the secured party's benefit; or

    (2) to redeliver the collateral to the secured party.

(i) A secured party does not relinquish possession, even if a delivery under subsection (h) violates the rights of a debtor. A person to which collateral is delivered under subsection (h) does not owe any duty to the secured party and is not required to confirm the delivery to another person unless the person otherwise agrees or law other than this article otherwise provides.

§9—314. PERFECTION BY CONTROL

(a) A security interest in investment property, deposit accounts, letter-of-credit rights, or electronic chattel paper may be perfected by control of the collateral under Section 9—104, 9—105, 9—106, or 9—107.

(b) A security interest in deposit accounts, electronic chattel paper, or letter-of-credit rights is perfected by control under Section 9—104, 9—105, or 9—107 when the secured party obtains control and remains perfected by control only while the secured party retains control.

(c) A security interest in investment property is perfected by control under Section 9—106 from the time the secured party obtains control and remains perfected by control until:

    (1) the secured party does not have control; and

    (2) one of the following occurs:

        (A) if the collateral is a certificated security, the debtor has or acquires possession of the security certificate;

        (B) if the collateral is an uncertificated security, the issuer has registered or registers the debtor as the registered owner; or

        (C) if the collateral is a security entitlement, the debtor is or becomes the entitlement holder.

§9—315. SECURED PARTY'S RIGHTS ON DISPOSITION OF COLLATERAL AND IN PROCEEDS

(a) Except as otherwise provided in this article and in Section 2—403(2):

    (1) a security interest or agricultural lien continues in collateral notwithstanding sale, lease, license, exchange, or other disposition thereof unless the secured party authorized the disposition free of the security interest or agricultural lien; and

    (2) a security interest attaches to any identifiable proceeds of collateral.

(b) Proceeds that are commingled with other property are identifiable proceeds:

    (1) if the proceeds are goods, to the extent provided by Section 9—336; and

    (2) if the proceeds are not goods, to the extent that the secured party identifies the proceeds by a method of tracing, including application of equitable principles, that is permitted under law other than this article with respect to commingled property of the type involved.

(c) A security interest in proceeds is a perfected security interest if the security interest in the original collateral was perfected.

(d) A perfected security interest in proceeds becomes unperfected on the 21st day after the security interest attaches to the proceeds unless:

    (1) the following conditions are satisfied:

        (A) a filed financing statement covers the original collateral;

        (B) the proceeds are collateral in which a security interest may be perfected by filing in the office in which the financing statement has been filed; and

        (C) the proceeds are not acquired with cash proceeds;

    (2) the proceeds are identifiable cash proceeds; or

    (3) the security interest in the proceeds is perfected other than under subsection (c) when the security interest attaches to the proceeds or within 20 days thereafter.

(e) If a filed financing statement covers the original collateral, a security interest in proceeds which remains perfected under subsection (d)(1) becomes unperfected at the later of:

    (1) when the effectiveness of the filed financing statement lapses under Section 9—515 or is terminated under Section 9—513; or

    (2) the 21st day after the security interest attaches to the proceeds.

§9—316. CONTINUED PERFECTION OF SECURITY INTEREST FOLLOWING CHANGE IN GOVERNING LAW

(a) A security interest perfected pursuant to the law of the jurisdiction designated in Section 9—301(1) or 9—305(c) remains perfected until the earliest of:

    (1) the time perfection would have ceased under the law of that jurisdiction;

    (2) the expiration of four months after a change of the debtor's location to another jurisdiction; or

    (3) the expiration of one year after a transfer of collateral to a person that thereby becomes a debtor and is located in another jurisdiction.

(b) If a security interest described in subsection (a) becomes perfected under the law of the other jurisdiction before the earliest time or event described in that subsection, it remains perfected thereafter. If the security interest does not become perfected under the law of the other jurisdiction before the earliest time or event, it becomes unperfected and is deemed never to have been perfected as against a purchaser of the collateral for value.

(c) A possessory security interest in collateral, other than goods covered by a certificate of title and as-extracted collateral consisting of goods, remains continuously perfected if:

    (1) the collateral is located in one jurisdiction and subject to a security interest perfected under the law of that jurisdiction;

    (2) thereafter the collateral is brought into another jurisdiction; and

    (3) upon entry into the other jurisdiction, the security interest is perfected under the law of the other jurisdiction.

(d) Except as otherwise provided in subsection (e), a security interest in goods covered by a certificate of title which is perfected by any method under the law of another jurisdiction when the goods become covered by a certificate of title from this State remains perfected until the security interest would have become unperfected under the law of the other jurisdiction had the goods not become so covered.

(e) A security interest described in subsection (d) becomes unperfected as against a purchaser of the goods for value and is deemed never to have been perfected as against a purchaser of the goods for value if the applicable requirements for perfection under Section 9—311(b) or 9—313 are not satisfied before the earlier of:

(1) the time the security interest would have become unperfected under the law of the other jurisdiction had the goods not become covered by a certificate of title from this State; or

(2) the expiration of four months after the goods had become so covered.

(f) A security interest in deposit accounts, letter-of-credit rights, or investment property which is perfected under the law of the bank's jurisdiction, the issuer's jurisdiction, a nominated person's jurisdiction, the securities intermediary's jurisdiction, or the commodity intermediary's jurisdiction, as applicable, remains perfected until the earlier of:

(1) the time the security interest would have become unperfected under the law of that jurisdiction; or

(2) the expiration of four months after a change of the applicable jurisdiction to another jurisdiction.

(g) If a security interest described in subsection (f) becomes perfected under the law of the other jurisdiction before the earlier of the time or the end of the period described in that subsection, it remains perfected thereafter. If the security interest does not become perfected under the law of the other jurisdiction before the earlier of that time or the end of that period, it becomes unperfected and is deemed never to have been perfected as against a purchaser of the collateral for value.

[Subpart 3. Priority]

§9—317. INTERESTS THAT TAKE PRIORITY OVER OR TAKE FREE OF SECURITY INTEREST OR AGRICULTURAL LIEN

(a) A security interest or agricultural lien is subordinate to the rights of:

(1) a person entitled to priority under Section 9—322; and

(2) except as otherwise provided in subsection (e), a person that becomes a lien creditor before the earlier of the time:

(A) the security interest or agricultural lien is perfected; or

(B) one of the conditions specified in Section 9—203(b)(3) is met and a financing statement covering the collateral is filed.

(b) Except as otherwise provided in subsection (e), a buyer, other than a secured party, of tangible chattel paper, documents, goods, instruments, or a security certificate takes free of a security interest or agricultural lien if the buyer gives value and receives delivery of the collateral without knowledge of the security interest or agricultural lien and before it is perfected.

(c) Except as otherwise provided in subsection (e), a lessee of goods takes free of a security interest or agricultural lien if the lessee gives value and receives delivery of the collateral without knowledge of the security interest or agricultural lien and before it is perfected.

(d) A licensee of a general intangible or a buyer, other than a secured party, of accounts, electronic chattel paper, general intangibles, or investment property other than a certificated security takes free of a security interest if the licensee or buyer gives value without knowledge of the security interest and before it is perfected.

(e) Except as otherwise provided in Sections 9—320 and 9—321, if a person files a financing statement with respect to a purchase-money security interest before or within 20 days after the debtor receives delivery of the collateral, the security interest takes priority over the rights of a buyer, lessee, or lien creditor which arise between the time the security interest attaches and the time of filing.

As amended in 2000.

§9—318. NO INTEREST RETAINED IN RIGHT TO PAYMENT THAT IS SOLD; RIGHTS AND TITLE OF SELLER OF ACCOUNT OR CHATTEL PAPER WITH RESPECT TO CREDITORS AND PURCHASERS

(a) A debtor that has sold an account, chattel paper, payment intangible, or promissory note does not retain a legal or equitable interest in the collateral sold.

(b) For purposes of determining the rights of creditors of, and purchasers for value of an account or chattel paper from, a debtor that has sold an account or chattel paper, while the buyer's security interest is unperfected, the debtor is deemed to have rights and title to the account or chattel paper identical to those the debtor sold.

§9—319. RIGHTS AND TITLE OF CONSIGNEE WITH RESPECT TO CREDITORS AND PURCHASERS

(a) Except as otherwise provided in subsection (b), for purposes of determining the rights of creditors of, and purchasers for value of goods from, a consignee, while the goods are in the possession of the consignee, the consignee is deemed to have rights and title to the goods identical to those the consignor had or had power to transfer.

(b) For purposes of determining the rights of a creditor of a consignee, law other than this article determines the rights and title of a consignee while goods are in the consignee's possession if, under this part, a perfected security interest held by the consignor would have priority over the rights of the creditor.

§9—320. BUYER OF GOODS

(a) Except as otherwise provided in subsection (e), a buyer in ordinary course of business, other than a person buying farm products from a person engaged in farming operations, takes free of a security interest created by the buyer's seller, even if the security interest is perfected and the buyer knows of its existence.

(b) Except as otherwise provided in subsection (e), a buyer of goods from a person who used or bought the goods for use primarily for personal, family, or household purposes takes free of a security interest, even if perfected, if the buyer buys:

(1) without knowledge of the security interest;

(2) for value;

(3) primarily for the buyer's personal, family, or household purposes; and

(4) before the filing of a financing statement covering the goods.

(c) To the extent that it affects the priority of a security interest over a buyer of goods under subsection (b), the period of effectiveness of a filing made in the jurisdiction in which the seller is located is governed by Section 9—316(a) and (b).

(d) A buyer in ordinary course of business buying oil, gas, or other minerals at the wellhead or minehead or after extraction takes free of an interest arising out of an encumbrance.

(e) Subsections (a) and (b) do not affect a security interest in goods in the possession of the secured party under Section 9—313.

§9—321. LICENSEE OF GENERAL INTANGIBLE AND LESSEE OF GOODS IN ORDINARY COURSE OF BUSINESS

(a) In this section, "licensee in ordinary course of business" means a person that becomes a licensee of a general intangible in good faith, without knowledge that the license violates the rights of another person in the general intangible, and in the ordinary course from a person in the business of licensing general intangibles of that kind. A person becomes a licensee in the ordinary course if the license to the person comports with the usual or customary practices in the kind of business in which the licensor is engaged or with the licensor's own usual or customary practices.

(b) A licensee in ordinary course of business takes its rights under a nonexclusive license free of a security interest in the general intangible created by the licensor, even if the security interest is perfected and the licensee knows of its existence.

(c) A lessee in ordinary course of business takes its leasehold interest free of a security interest in the goods created by the lessor, even if the security interest is perfected and the lessee knows of its existence.

§9—322. PRIORITIES AMONG CONFLICTING SECURITY INTERESTS IN AND AGRICULTURAL LIENS ON SAME COLLATERAL

(a) Except as otherwise provided in this section, priority among conflicting security interests and agricultural liens in the same collateral is determined according to the following rules:

(1) Conflicting perfected security interests and agricultural liens rank according to priority in time of filing or perfection. Priority dates from the earlier of the time a filing covering the collateral is first made or the security interest or agricultural lien is first perfected, if there is no period thereafter when there is neither filing nor perfection.

(2) A perfected security interest or agricultural lien has priority over a conflicting unperfected security interest or agricultural lien.

(3) The first security interest or agricultural lien to attach or become effective has priority if conflicting security interests and agricultural liens are unperfected.

(b) For the purposes of subsection (a)(1):

(1) the time of filing or perfection as to a security interest in collateral is also the time of filing or perfection as to a security interest in proceeds; and

(2) the time of filing or perfection as to a security interest in collateral supported by a supporting obligation is also the time of filing or perfection as to a security interest in the supporting obligation.

(c) Except as otherwise provided in subsection (f), a security interest in collateral which qualifies for priority over a conflicting security interest under Section 9—327, 9—328, 9—329, 9—330, or 9—331 also has priority over a conflicting security interest in:

(1) any supporting obligation for the collateral; and

(2) proceeds of the collateral if:

(A) the security interest in proceeds is perfected;

(B) the proceeds are cash proceeds or of the same type as the collateral; and

(C) in the case of proceeds that are proceeds of proceeds, all intervening proceeds are cash proceeds, proceeds of the same type as the collateral, or an account relating to the collateral.

(d) Subject to subsection (e) and except as otherwise provided in subsection (f), if a security interest in chattel paper, deposit accounts, negotiable documents, instruments, investment property, or letter-of-credit rights is perfected by a method other than filing, conflicting perfected security interests in proceeds of the collateral rank according to priority in time of filing.

(e) Subsection (d) applies only if the proceeds of the collateral are not cash proceeds, chattel paper, negotiable documents, instruments, investment property, or letter-of-credit rights.

(f) Subsections (a) through (e) are subject to:

(1) subsection (g) and the other provisions of this part;

(2) Section 4—210 with respect to a security interest of a collecting bank;

(3) Section 5—118 with respect to a security interest of an issuer or nominated person; and

(4) Section 9—110 with respect to a security interest arising under Article 2 or 2A.

(g) A perfected agricultural lien on collateral has priority over a conflicting security interest in or agricultural lien on the same collateral if the statute creating the agricultural lien so provides.

§9—323. FUTURE ADVANCES

(a) Except as otherwise provided in subsection (c), for purposes of determining the priority of a perfected security interest under Section 9—322(a)(1), perfection of the security interest dates from the time an advance is made to the extent that the security interest secures an advance that:

(1) is made while the security interest is perfected only:

(A) under Section 9—309 when it attaches; or

(B) temporarily under Section 9—312(e), (f), or (g); and

(2) is not made pursuant to a commitment entered into before or while the security interest is perfected by a method other than under Section 9—309 or 9—312(e), (f), or (g).

(b) Except as otherwise provided in subsection (c), a security interest is subordinate to the rights of a person that becomes a lien creditor to the extent that the security interest secures an advance made more than 45 days after the person becomes a lien creditor unless the advance is made:

(1) without knowledge of the lien; or

(2) pursuant to a commitment entered into without knowledge of the lien.

(c) Subsections (a) and (b) do not apply to a security interest held by a secured party that is a buyer of accounts, chattel paper, payment intangibles, or promissory notes or a consignor.

(d) Except as otherwise provided in subsection (e), a buyer of goods other than a buyer in ordinary course of business takes free of a security interest to the extent that it secures advances made after the earlier of:

(1) the time the secured party acquires knowledge of the buyer's purchase; or

(2) 45 days after the purchase.

(e) Subsection (d) does not apply if the advance is made pursuant to a commitment entered into without knowledge of the buyer's purchase and before the expiration of the 45-day period.

(f) Except as otherwise provided in subsection (g), a lessee of goods, other than a lessee in ordinary course of business, takes the leasehold interest free of a security interest to the extent that it secures advances made after the earlier of:

(1) the time the secured party acquires knowledge of the lease; or

(2) 45 days after the lease contract becomes enforceable.

(g) Subsection (f) does not apply if the advance is made pursuant to a commitment entered into without knowledge of the lease and before the expiration of the 45-day period.

As amended in 1999.

§9—324. PRIORITY OF PURCHASE-MONEY SECURITY INTERESTS

(a) Except as otherwise provided in subsection (g), a perfected purchase-money security interest in goods other than inventory or livestock has priority over a conflicting security interest in the same goods, and, except as otherwise provided in Section 9—327, a perfected security interest in its identifiable proceeds also has priority, if the purchase-money security interest is perfected when the debtor receives possession of the collateral or within 20 days thereafter.

(b) Subject to subsection (c) and except as otherwise provided in subsection (g), a perfected purchase-money security interest in inventory has priority over a conflicting security interest in the same inventory, has priority over a conflicting security interest in chattel paper or an instrument constituting proceeds of the inventory and in proceeds of the chattel paper, if so provided in Section 9—330, and, except as otherwise provided in Section 9—327, also has priority in identifiable cash proceeds of the inventory to the extent the identifiable cash proceeds are received on or before the delivery of the inventory to a buyer, if:

    (1) the purchase-money security interest is perfected when the debtor receives possession of the inventory;

    (2) the purchase-money secured party sends an authenticated notification to the holder of the conflicting security interest;

    (3) the holder of the conflicting security interest receives the notification within five years before the debtor receives possession of the inventory; and

    (4) the notification states that the person sending the notification has or expects to acquire a purchase-money security interest in inventory of the debtor and describes the inventory.

(c) Subsections (b)(2) through (4) apply only if the holder of the conflicting security interest had filed a financing statement covering the same types of inventory:

    (1) if the purchase-money security interest is perfected by filing, before the date of the filing; or

    (2) if the purchase-money security interest is temporarily perfected without filing or possession under Section 9—312(f), before the beginning of the 20-day period thereunder.

(d) Subject to subsection (e) and except as otherwise provided in subsection (g), a perfected purchase-money security interest in livestock that are farm products has priority over a conflicting security interest in the same livestock, and, except as otherwise provided in Section 9—327, a perfected security interest in their identifiable proceeds and identifiable products in their unmanufactured states also has priority, if:

    (1) the purchase-money security interest is perfected when the debtor receives possession of the livestock;

    (2) the purchase-money secured party sends an authenticated notification to the holder of the conflicting security interest;

    (3) the holder of the conflicting security interest receives the notification within six months before the debtor receives possession of the livestock; and

    (4) the notification states that the person sending the notification has or expects to acquire a purchase-money security interest in livestock of the debtor and describes the livestock.

(e) Subsections (d)(2) through (4) apply only if the holder of the conflicting security interest had filed a financing statement covering the same types of livestock:

    (1) if the purchase-money security interest is perfected by filing, before the date of the filing; or

    (2) if the purchase-money security interest is temporarily perfected without filing or possession under Section 9—312(f), before the beginning of the 20-day period thereunder.

(f) Except as otherwise provided in subsection (g), a perfected purchase-money security interest in software has priority over a conflicting security interest in the same collateral, and, except as otherwise provided in Section 9—327, a perfected security interest in its identifiable proceeds also has priority, to the extent that the purchase-money security interest in the goods in which the software was acquired for use has priority in the goods and proceeds of the goods under this section.

(g) If more than one security interest qualifies for priority in the same collateral under subsection (a), (b), (d), or (f):

    (1) a security interest securing an obligation incurred as all or part of the price of the collateral has priority over a security interest securing an obligation incurred for value given to enable the debtor to acquire rights in or the use of collateral; and

    (2) in all other cases, Section 9—322(a) applies to the qualifying security interests.

§9—325. PRIORITY OF SECURITY INTERESTS IN TRANSFERRED COLLATERAL

(a) Except as otherwise provided in subsection (b), a security interest created by a debtor is subordinate to a security interest in the same collateral created by another person if:

    (1) the debtor acquired the collateral subject to the security interest created by the other person;

    (2) the security interest created by the other person was perfected when the debtor acquired the collateral; and

    (3) there is no period thereafter when the security interest is unperfected.

(b) Subsection (a) subordinates a security interest only if the security interest:

    (1) otherwise would have priority solely under Section 9—322(a) or 9—324; or

    (2) arose solely under Section 2—711(3) or 2A—508(5).

§9—326. PRIORITY OF SECURITY INTERESTS CREATED BY NEW DEBTOR

(a) Subject to subsection (b), a security interest created by a new debtor which is perfected by a filed financing statement that is effective solely under Section 9—508 in collateral in which a new debtor has or acquires rights is subordinate to a security interest in the same collateral which is perfected other than by a filed financing statement that is effective solely under Section 9—508.

(b) The other provisions of this part determine the priority among conflicting security interests in the same collateral perfected by filed financing statements that are effective solely under Section 9—508. However, if the security agreements to which a new debtor became bound as debtor were not entered into by the same original debtor, the conflicting security interests rank according to priority in time of the new debtor's having become bound.

§9—327. PRIORITY OF SECURITY INTERESTS IN DEPOSIT ACCOUNT

The following rules govern priority among conflicting security interests in the same deposit account:

(1) A security interest held by a secured party having control of the deposit account under Section 9—104 has priority over a conflicting security interest held by a secured party that does not have control.

(2) Except as otherwise provided in paragraphs (3) and (4), security interests perfected by control under Section 9—314 rank according to priority in time of obtaining control.

(3) Except as otherwise provided in paragraph (4), a security interest held by the bank with which the deposit account is maintained has priority over a conflicting security interest held by another secured party.

(4) A security interest perfected by control under Section 9—104(a)(3) has priority over a security interest held by the bank with which the deposit account is maintained.

§9—328. PRIORITY OF SECURITY INTERESTS IN INVESTMENT PROPERTY

The following rules govern priority among conflicting security interests in the same investment property:

(1) A security interest held by a secured party having control of investment property under Section 9—106 has priority over a security interest held by a secured party that does not have control of the investment property.

(2) Except as otherwise provided in paragraphs (3) and (4), conflicting security interests held by secured parties each of which has control under Section 9—106 rank according to priority in time of:

    (A) if the collateral is a security, obtaining control;

    (B) if the collateral is a security entitlement carried in a securities account and:

      (i) if the secured party obtained control under Section 8—106(d)(1), the secured party's becoming the person for which the securities account is maintained;

      (ii) if the secured party obtained control under Section 8—106(d)(2), the securities intermediary's agreement to comply with the secured party's entitlement orders with respect to security entitlements carried or to be carried in the securities account; or

      (iii) if the secured party obtained control through another person under Section 8—106(d)(3), the time on which priority would be based under this paragraph if the other person were the secured party; or

    (C) if the collateral is a commodity contract carried with a commodity intermediary, the satisfaction of the requirement for control specified in Section 9—106(b)(2) with respect to commodity contracts carried or to be carried with the commodity intermediary.

(3) A security interest held by a securities intermediary in a security entitlement or a securities account maintained with the securities intermediary has priority over a conflicting security interest held by another secured party.

(4) A security interest held by a commodity intermediary in a commodity contract or a commodity account maintained with the commodity intermediary has priority over a conflicting security interest held by another secured party.

(5) A security interest in a certificated security in registered form which is perfected by taking delivery under Section 9—313(a) and not by control under Section 9—314 has priority over a conflicting security interest perfected by a method other than control.

(6) Conflicting security interests created by a broker, securities intermediary, or commodity intermediary which are perfected without control under Section 9—106 rank equally.

(7) In all other cases, priority among conflicting security interests in investment property is governed by Sections 9—322 and 9—323.

§9—329. PRIORITY OF SECURITY INTERESTS IN LETTER-OF-CREDIT RIGHT

The following rules govern priority among conflicting security interests in the same letter-of-credit right:

(1) A security interest held by a secured party having control of the letter-of-credit right under Section 9—107 has priority to the extent of its control over a conflicting security interest held by a secured party that does not have control.

(2) Security interests perfected by control under Section 9—314 rank according to priority in time of obtaining control.

§9—330. PRIORITY OF PURCHASER OF CHATTEL PAPER OR INSTRUMENT

(a) A purchaser of chattel paper has priority over a security interest in the chattel paper which is claimed merely as proceeds of inventory subject to a security interest if:

    (1) in good faith and in the ordinary course of the purchaser's business, the purchaser gives new

value and takes possession of the chattel paper or obtains control of the chattel paper under Section 9—105; and

(2) the chattel paper does not indicate that it has been assigned to an identified assignee other than the purchaser.

(b) A purchaser of chattel paper has priority over a security interest in the chattel paper which is claimed other than merely as proceeds of inventory subject to a security interest if the purchaser gives new value and takes possession of the chattel paper or obtains control of the chattel paper under Section 9—105 in good faith, in the ordinary course of the purchaser's business, and without knowledge that the purchase violates the rights of the secured party.

(c) Except as otherwise provided in Section 9—327, a purchaser having priority in chattel paper under subsection (a) or (b) also has priority in proceeds of the chattel paper to the extent that:

(1) Section 9—322 provides for priority in the proceeds; or

(2) the proceeds consist of the specific goods covered by the chattel paper or cash proceeds of the specific goods, even if the purchaser's security interest in the proceeds is unperfected.

(d) Except as otherwise provided in Section 9—331 (a), a purchaser of an instrument has priority over a security interest in the instrument perfected by a method other than possession if the purchaser gives value and takes possession of the instrument in good faith and without knowledge that the purchase violates the rights of the secured party.

(e) For purposes of subsections (a) and (b), the holder of a purchase-money security interest in inventory gives new value for chattel paper constituting proceeds of the inventory.

(f) For purposes of subsections (b) and (d), if chattel paper or an instrument indicates that it has been assigned to an identified secured party other than the purchaser, a purchaser of the chattel paper or instrument has knowledge that the purchase violates the rights of the secured party.

§9—331. PRIORITY OF RIGHTS OF PURCHASERS OF INSTRUMENTS, DOCUMENTS, AND SECURITIES UNDER OTHER ARTICLES; PRIORITY OF INTERESTS IN FINANCIAL ASSETS AND SECURITY ENTITLEMENTS UNDER ARTICLE 8

(a) This article does not limit the rights of a holder in due course of a negotiable instrument, a holder to which a negotiable document of title has been duly negotiated, or a protected purchaser of a security. These holders or purchasers take priority over an earlier security interest, even if perfected, to the extent provided in Articles 3, 7, and 8.

(b) This article does not limit the rights of or impose liability on a person to the extent that the person is protected against the assertion of a claim under Article 8.

(c) Filing under this article does not constitute notice of a claim or defense to the holders, or purchasers, or persons described in subsections (a) and (b).

§9—332. TRANSFER OF MONEY; TRANSFER OF FUNDS FROM DEPOSIT ACCOUNT

(a) A transferee of money takes the money free of a security interest unless the transferee acts in collusion with the debtor in violating the rights of the secured party.

(b) A transferee of funds from a deposit account takes the funds free of a security interest in the deposit account unless the transferee acts in collusion with the debtor in violating the rights of the secured party.

§9—333. PRIORITY OF CERTAIN LIENS ARISING BY OPERATION OF LAW

(a) In this section, "possessory lien" means an interest, other than a security interest or an agricultural lien:

(1) which secures payment or performance of an obligation for services or materials furnished with respect to goods by a person in the ordinary course of the person's business;

(2) which is created by statute or rule of law in favor of the person; and

(3) whose effectiveness depends on the person's possession of the goods.

(b) A possessory lien on goods has priority over a security interest in the goods unless the lien is created by a statute that expressly provides otherwise.

§9—334. PRIORITY OF SECURITY INTERESTS IN FIXTURES AND CROPS

(a) A security interest under this article may be created in goods that are fixtures or may continue in goods that become fixtures. A security interest does not exist under this article in ordinary building materials incorporated into an improvement on land.

(b) This article does not prevent creation of an encumbrance upon fixtures under real property law.

(c) In cases not governed by subsections (d) through (h), a security interest in fixtures is subordinate to a conflicting interest of an encumbrancer or owner of the related real property other than the debtor.

(d) Except as otherwise provided in subsection (h), a perfected security interest in fixtures has priority over a conflicting interest of an encumbrancer or owner of the real property if the debtor has an interest of record in or is in possession of the real property and:

>   (1) the security interest is a purchase-money security interest;

>   (2) the interest of the encumbrancer or owner arises before the goods become fixtures; and

>   (3) the security interest is perfected by a fixture filing before the goods become fixtures or within 20 days thereafter.

(e) A perfected security interest in fixtures has priority over a conflicting interest of an encumbrancer or owner of the real property if:

>   (1) the debtor has an interest of record in the real property or is in possession of the real property and the security interest:

>>   (A) is perfected by a fixture filing before the interest of the encumbrancer or owner is of record; and

>>   (B) has priority over any conflicting interest of a predecessor in title of the encumbrancer or owner;

>   (2) before the goods become fixtures, the security interest is perfected by any method permitted by this article and the fixtures are readily removable:

>>   (A) factory or office machines;

>>   (B) equipment that is not primarily used or leased for use in the operation of the real property; or

>>   (C) replacements of domestic appliances that are consumer goods;

>   (3) the conflicting interest is a lien on the real property obtained by legal or equitable proceedings after the security interest was perfected by any method permitted by this article; or

>   (4) the security interest is:

>>   (A) created in a manufactured home in a manufactured-home transaction; and

>>   (B) perfected pursuant to a statute described in Section 9—311(a)(2).

(f) A security interest in fixtures, whether or not perfected, has priority over a conflicting interest of an encumbrancer or owner of the real property if:

>   (1) the encumbrancer or owner has, in an authenticated record, consented to the security interest or disclaimed an interest in the goods as fixtures; or

>   (2) the debtor has a right to remove the goods as against the encumbrancer or owner.

(g) The priority of the security interest under paragraph (f)(2) continues for a reasonable time if the debtor's right to remove the goods as against the encumbrancer or owner terminates.

(h) A mortgage is a construction mortgage to the extent that it secures an obligation incurred for the construction of an improvement on land, including the acquisition cost of the land, if a recorded record of the mortgage so indicates. Except as otherwise provided in subsections (e) and (f), a security interest in fixtures is subordinate to a construction mortgage if a record of the mortgage is recorded before the goods become fixtures and the goods become fixtures before the completion of the construction. A mortgage has this priority to the same extent as a construction mortgage to the extent that it is given to refinance a construction mortgage.

(i) A perfected security interest in crops growing on real property has priority over a conflicting interest of an encumbrancer or owner of the real property if the debtor has an interest of record in or is in possession of the real property.

(j) Subsection (i) prevails over any inconsistent provisions of the following statutes:

>   [List here any statutes containing provisions inconsistent with subsection (i).]

>   *Legislative Note: States that amend statutes to remove provisions inconsistent with subsection (i) need not enact subsection (j).*

§9—335. ACCESSIONS

(a) A security interest may be created in an accession and continues in collateral that becomes an accession.

(b) If a security interest is perfected when the collateral becomes an accession, the security interest remains perfected in the collateral.

(c) Except as otherwise provided in subsection (d), the other provisions of this part determine the priority of a security interest in an accession.

(d) A security interest in an accession is subordinate to a security interest in the whole which is perfected by compliance with the requirements of a certificate-of-title statute under Section 9—311(b).

(e) After default, subject to Part 6, a secured party may remove an accession from other goods if the security interest in the accession has priority over the claims of every person having an interest in the whole.

(f) A secured party that removes an accession from other goods under subsection (e) shall promptly reimburse any holder of a security interest or other lien on, or owner of, the whole or of the other goods, other than the debtor, for the cost of repair of any physical injury to the whole or the other goods. The secured party need not reimburse the holder or owner for any diminution in value of the whole or the other goods caused by the absence of the accession removed or by any necessity for replacing it. A person entitled to reimbursement may refuse permission to remove until the secured party gives adequate assurance for the performance of the obligation to reimburse.

§9—336. COMMINGLED GOODS

(a) In this section, "commingled goods" means goods that are physically united with other goods in such a manner that their identity is lost in a product or mass.

(b) A security interest does not exist in commingled goods as such. However, a security interest may attach to a product or mass that results when goods become commingled goods.

(c) If collateral becomes commingled goods, a security interest attaches to the product or mass.

(d) If a security interest in collateral is perfected before the collateral becomes commingled goods, the security interest that attaches to the product or mass under subsection (c) is perfected.

(e) Except as otherwise provided in subsection (f), the other provisions of this part determine the priority of a security interest that attaches to the product or mass under subsection (c).

(f) If more than one security interest attaches to the product or mass under subsection (c), the following rules determine priority:

(1) A security interest that is perfected under subsection (d) has priority over a security interest that is unperfected at the time the collateral becomes commingled goods.

(2) If more than one security interest is perfected under subsection (d), the security interests rank equally in proportion to the value of the collateral at the time it became commingled goods.

§9—337. PRIORITY OF SECURITY INTERESTS IN GOODS COVERED BY CERTIFICATE OF TITLE

If, while a security interest in goods is perfected by any method under the law of another jurisdiction, this State issues a certificate of title that does not show that the goods are subject to the security interest or contain a statement that they may be subject to security interests not shown on the certificate:

(1) a buyer of the goods, other than a person in the business of selling goods of that kind, takes free of the security interest if the buyer gives value and receives delivery of the goods after issuance of the certificate and without knowledge of the security interest; and

(2) the security interest is subordinate to a conflicting security interest in the goods that attaches, and is perfected under Section 9—311(b), after issuance of the certificate and without the conflicting secured party's knowledge of the security interest.

§9—338. PRIORITY OF SECURITY INTEREST OR AGRICULTURAL LIEN PERFECTED BY FILED FINANCING STATEMENT PROVIDING CERTAIN INCORRECT INFORMATION

If a security interest or agricultural lien is perfected by a filed financing statement providing information described in Section 9—516(b)(5) which is incorrect at the time the financing statement is filed:

(1) the security interest or agricultural lien is subordinate to a conflicting perfected security interest in the collateral to the extent that the holder of the conflicting security interest gives value in reasonable reliance upon the incorrect information; and

(2) a purchaser, other than a secured party, of the collateral takes free of the security interest or agricultural lien to the extent that, in reasonable reliance upon the incorrect information, the purchaser gives value and, in the case of chattel paper, documents, goods, instruments, or a security certificate, receives delivery of the collateral.

§9—339. PRIORITY SUBJECT TO SUBORDINATION

This article does not preclude subordination by agreement by a person entitled to priority.

[Subpart 4. Rights of Bank]

§9—340. EFFECTIVENESS OF RIGHT OF RECOUPMENT OR SET-OFF AGAINST DEPOSIT ACCOUNT

(a) Except as otherwise provided in subsection (c), a bank with which a deposit account is maintained may exercise any right of recoupment or set-off against a secured party that holds a security interest in the deposit account.

(b) Except as otherwise provided in subsection (c), the application of this article to a security interest in a deposit account does not affect a right of recoupment or set-off of the secured party as to a deposit account maintained with the secured party.

(c) The exercise by a bank of a set-off against a deposit account is ineffective against a secured party that holds a security interest in the deposit account which is perfected by control under Section 9—104(a)(3), if the set-off is based on a claim against the debtor.

§9—341. BANK'S RIGHTS AND DUTIES WITH RESPECT TO DEPOSIT ACCOUNT

Except as otherwise provided in Section 9—340(c), and unless the bank otherwise agrees in an authenticated record, a bank's rights and duties with respect to a deposit account maintained with the bank are not terminated, suspended, or modified by:

(1) the creation, attachment, or perfection of a security interest in the deposit account;

(2) the bank's knowledge of the security interest; or

(3) the bank's receipt of instructions from the secured party.

§9—342. BANK'S RIGHT TO REFUSE TO ENTER INTO OR DISCLOSE EXISTENCE OF CONTROL AGREEMENT

This article does not require a bank to enter into an agreement of the kind described in Section 9—104(a)(2), even if its customer so requests or directs. A bank that has entered into such an agreement is not required to confirm the existence of the agreement to another person unless requested to do so by its customer.

Part 4 Rights of Third Parties

§9—401. ALIENABILITY OF DEBTOR'S RIGHTS

(a) Except as otherwise provided in subsection (b) and Sections 9—406, 9—407, 9—408, and 9—409, whether a debtor's rights in collateral may be voluntarily or involuntarily transferred is governed by law other than this article.

(b) An agreement between the debtor and secured party which prohibits a transfer of the debtor's rights in collateral or makes the transfer a default does not prevent the transfer from taking effect.

§9—402. SECURED PARTY NOT OBLIGATED ON CONTRACT OF DEBTOR OR IN TORT

The existence of a security interest, agricultural lien, or authority given to a debtor to dispose of or use collateral, without more, does not subject a secured party to liability in contract or tort for the debtor's acts or omissions.

§9—403. AGREEMENT NOT TO ASSERT DEFENSES AGAINST ASSIGNEE

(a) In this section, "value" has the meaning provided in Section 3—303(a).

(b) Except as otherwise provided in this section, an agreement between an account debtor and an assignor not to assert against an assignee any claim or defense that the account debtor may have against the assignor is enforceable by an assignee that takes an assignment:

(1) for value;

(2) in good faith;

(3) without notice of a claim of a property or possessory right to the property assigned; and

(4) without notice of a defense or claim in recoupment of the type that may be asserted against a person entitled to enforce a negotiable instrument under Section 3—305(a).

(c) Subsection (b) does not apply to defenses of a type that may be asserted against a holder in due course of a negotiable instrument under Section 3—305(b).

(d) In a consumer transaction, if a record evidences the account debtor's obligation, law other than this article requires that the record include a statement to the effect that the rights of an assignee are subject to claims or defenses that the account debtor could assert against the original obligee, and the record does not include such a statement:

(1) the record has the same effect as if the record included such a statement; and

(2) the account debtor may assert against an assignee those claims and defenses that would have been available if the record included such a statement.

(e) This section is subject to law other than this article which establishes a different rule for an account debtor who is an individual and who incurred the obligation primarily for personal, family, or household purposes.

(f) Except as otherwise provided in subsection (d), this section does not displace law other than this article which gives effect to an agreement by an account debtor not to assert a claim or defense against an assignee.

§9—404. RIGHTS ACQUIRED BY ASSIGNEE; CLAIMS AND DEFENSES AGAINST ASSIGNEE

(a) Unless an account debtor has made an enforceable agreement not to assert defenses or claims, and subject to subsections (b) through (e), the rights of an assignee are subject to:

(1) all terms of the agreement between the account debtor and assignor and any defense or claim in recoupment arising from the transaction that gave rise to the contract; and

(2) any other defense or claim of the account debtor against the assignor which accrues before the account debtor receives a notification of the assignment authenticated by the assignor or the assignee.

(b) Subject to subsection (c) and except as otherwise provided in subsection (d), the claim of an account debtor against an assignor may be asserted against an assignee under subsection (a) only to reduce the amount the account debtor owes.

(c) This section is subject to law other than this article which establishes a different rule for an account debtor who is an individual and who incurred the obligation primarily for personal, family, or household purposes.

(d) In a consumer transaction, if a record evidences the account debtor's obligation, law other than this article requires that the record include a statement to the effect that the account debtor's recovery against an assignee with respect to claims and defenses against the assignor may not exceed amounts paid by the account debtor under the record, and the record does not include such a statement, the extent to which a claim of an account debtor against the assignor may be asserted against an assignee is determined as if the record included such a statement.

(e) This section does not apply to an assignment of a health-care-insurance receivable.

§9—405. MODIFICATION OF ASSIGNED CONTRACT

(a) A modification of or substitution for an assigned contract is effective against an assignee if made in good faith. The assignee acquires corresponding rights under the modified or substituted contract. The assignment may provide that the modification or substitution is a breach of contract by the assignor. This subsection is subject to subsections (b) through (d).

   (b) Subsection (a) applies to the extent that:
      (1) the right to payment or a part thereof under an assigned contract has not been fully earned by performance; or
      (2) the right to payment or a part thereof has been fully earned by performance and the account debtor has not received notification of the assignment under Section 9—406(a).

   (c) This section is subject to law other than this article which establishes a different rule for an account debtor who is an individual and who incurred the obligation primarily for personal, family, or household purposes.

   (d) This section does not apply to an assignment of a health-care-insurance receivable.

§9—406. DISCHARGE OF ACCOUNT DEBTOR; NOTIFICATION OF ASSIGNMENT; IDENTIFICATION AND PROOF OF ASSIGNMENT; RESTRICTIONS ON ASSIGNMENT OF ACCOUNTS, CHATTEL PAPER, PAYMENT INTANGIBLES, AND PROMISSORY NOTES INEFFECTIVE

(a) Subject to subsections (b) through (i), an account debtor on an account, chattel paper, or a payment intangible may discharge its obligation by paying the assignor until, but not after, the account debtor receives a notification, authenticated by the assignor or the assignee, that the amount due or to become due has been assigned and that payment is to be made to the assignee. After receipt of the notification, the account debtor may discharge its obligation by paying the assignee and may not discharge the obligation by paying the assignor.

   (b) Subject to subsection (h), notification is ineffective under subsection (a):
      (1) if it does not reasonably identify the rights assigned;
      (2) to the extent that an agreement between an account debtor and a seller of a payment intangible limits the account debtor's duty to pay a person other than the seller and the limitation is effective under law other than this article; or
      (3) at the option of an account debtor, if the notification notifies the account debtor to make

less than the full amount of any installment or other periodic payment to the assignee, even if:
      (A) only a portion of the account, chattel paper, or payment intangible has been assigned to that assignee;
      (B) a portion has been assigned to another assignee; or
      (C) the account debtor knows that the assignment to that assignee is limited.

   (c) Subject to subsection (h), if requested by the account debtor, an assignee shall seasonably furnish reasonable proof that the assignment has been made. Unless the assignee complies, the account debtor may discharge its obligation by paying the assignor, even if the account debtor has received a notification under subsection (a).

   (d) Except as otherwise provided in subsection (e) and Sections 2A—303 and 9—407, and subject to subsection (h), a term in an agreement between an account debtor and an assignor or in a promissory note is ineffective to the extent that it:
      (1) prohibits, restricts, or requires the consent of the account debtor or person obligated on the promissory note to the assignment or transfer of, or the creation, attachment, perfection, or enforcement of a security interest in, the account, chattel paper, payment intangible, or promissory note; or
      (2) provides that the assignment or transfer or the creation, attachment, perfection, or enforcement of the security interest may give rise to a default, breach, right of recoupment, claim, defense, termination, right of termination, or remedy under the account, chattel paper, payment intangible, or promissory note.

   (e) Subsection (d) does not apply to the sale of a payment intangible or promissory note.

   (f) Except as otherwise provided in Sections 2A—303 and 9—407 and subject to subsections (h) and (i), a rule of law, statute, or regulation that prohibits, restricts, or requires the consent of a government, governmental body or official, or account debtor to the assignment or transfer of, or creation of a security interest in, an account or chattel paper is ineffective to the extent that the rule of law, statute, or regulation:
      (1) prohibits, restricts, or requires the consent of the government, governmental body or official, or account debtor to the assignment or transfer of, or the creation, attachment, perfection, or enforcement of a security interest in the account or chattel paper; or
      (2) provides that the assignment or transfer or the creation, attachment, perfection, or enforcement of the security interest may give rise to a default, breach, right of recoupment, claim,

defense, termination, right of termination, or remedy under the account or chattel paper.

(g) Subject to subsection (h), an account debtor may not waive or vary its option under subsection (b)(3).

(h) This section is subject to law other than this article which establishes a different rule for an account debtor who is an individual and who incurred the obligation primarily for personal, family, or household purposes.

(i) This section does not apply to an assignment of a health-care-insurance receivable.

(j) This section prevails over any inconsistent provisions of the following statutes, rules, and regulations: [List here any statutes, rules, and regulations containing provisions inconsistent with this section.] *Legislative Note: States that amend statutes, rules, and regulations to remove provisions inconsistent with this section need not enact subsection (j).*

As amended in 1999 and 2000.

§9—407. RESTRICTIONS ON CREATION OR ENFORCEMENT OF SECURITY INTEREST IN LEASEHOLD INTEREST OR IN LESSOR'S RESIDUAL INTEREST

(a) Except as otherwise provided in subsection (b), a term in a lease agreement is ineffective to the extent that it:

(1) prohibits, restricts, or requires the consent of a party to the lease to the assignment or transfer of, or the creation, attachment, perfection, or enforcement of a security interest in an interest of a party under the lease contract or in the lessor's residual interest in the goods; or

(2) provides that the assignment or transfer or the creation, attachment, perfection, or enforcement of the security interest may give rise to a default, breach, right of recoupment, claim, defense, termination, right of termination, or remedy under the lease.

(b) Except as otherwise provided in Section 2A—303 (7), a term described in subsection (a)(2) is effective to the extent that there is:

(1) a transfer by the lessee of the lessee's right of possession or use of the goods in violation of the term; or

(2) a delegation of a material performance of either party to the lease contract in violation of the term.

(c) The creation, attachment, perfection, or enforcement of a security interest in the lessor's interest under the lease contract or the lessor's residual interest in the goods is not a transfer that materially impairs the lessee's prospect of obtaining return performance or materially changes the duty of or materially increases the burden or risk imposed on the lessee within the purview of Section 2A—303(4)

unless, and then only to the extent that, enforcement actually results in a delegation of material performance of the lessor.

As amended in 1999.

§9—408. RESTRICTIONS ON ASSIGNMENT OF PROMISSORY NOTES, HEALTH-CARE-INSURANCE RECEIVABLES, AND CERTAIN GENERAL INTANGIBLES INEFFECTIVE

(a) Except as otherwise provided in subsection (b), a term in a promissory note or in an agreement between an account debtor and a debtor which relates to a health-care-insurance receivable or a general intangible, including a contract, permit, license, or franchise, and which term prohibits, restricts, or requires the consent of the person obligated on the promissory note or the account debtor to, the assignment or transfer of, or creation, attachment, or perfection of a security interest in, the promissory note, health-care-insurance receivable, or general intangible, is ineffective to the extent that the term:

(1) would impair the creation, attachment, or perfection of a security interest; or

(2) provides that the assignment or transfer or the creation, attachment, or perfection of the security interest may give rise to a default, breach, right of recoupment, claim, defense, termination, right of termination, or remedy under the promissory note, health-care-insurance receivable, or general intangible.

(b) Subsection (a) applies to a security interest in a payment intangible or promissory note only if the security interest arises out of a sale of the payment intangible or promissory note.

(c) A rule of law, statute, or regulation that prohibits, restricts, or requires the consent of a government, governmental body or official, person obligated on a promissory note, or account debtor to the assignment or transfer of, or creation of a security interest in, a promissory note, health-care-insurance receivable, or general intangible, including a contract, permit, license, or franchise between an account debtor and a debtor, is ineffective to the extent that the rule of law, statute, or regulation:

(1) would impair the creation, attachment, or perfection of a security interest; or

(2) provides that the assignment or transfer or the creation, attachment, or perfection of the security interest may give rise to a default, breach, right of recoupment, claim, defense, termination, right of termination, or remedy under the promissory note, health-care-insurance receivable, or general intangible.

(d) To the extent that a term in a promissory note or in an agreement between an account debtor and a debtor which relates to a health-care-insurance receivable or general intangible or a rule of law, statute, or regulation described in subsection (c) would be effective under law other than this article but is ineffective under subsection (a) or (c), the creation, attachment, or perfection of a security interest in the promissory note, health-care-insurance receivable, or general intangible:

(1) is not enforceable against the person obligated on the promissory note or the account debtor;

(2) does not impose a duty or obligation on the person obligated on the promissory note or the account debtor;

(3) does not require the person obligated on the promissory note or the account debtor to recognize the security interest, pay or render performance to the secured party, or accept payment or performance from the secured party;

(4) does not entitle the secured party to use or assign the debtor's rights under the promissory note, health-care-insurance receivable, or general intangible, including any related information or materials furnished to the debtor in the transaction giving rise to the promissory note, health-care-insurance receivable, or general intangible;

(5) does not entitle the secured party to use, assign, possess, or have access to any trade secrets or confidential information of the person obligated on the promissory note or the account debtor; and

(6) does not entitle the secured party to enforce the security interest in the promissory note, health-care-insurance receivable, or general intangible.

(e) This section prevails over any inconsistent provisions of the following statutes, rules, and regulations:

[List here any statutes, rules, and regulations containing provisions inconsistent with this section.]

Legislative Note: States that amend statutes, rules, and regulations to remove provisions inconsistent with this section need not enact subsection (e).

As amended in 1999.

§9—409. RESTRICTIONS ON ASSIGNMENT OF LETTER-OF-CREDIT RIGHTS INEFFECTIVE

(a) A term in a letter of credit or a rule of law, statute, regulation, custom, or practice applicable to the letter of credit which prohibits, restricts, or requires the consent of an applicant, issuer, or nominated person to a beneficiary's assignment of or creation of a security interest in a letter-of-credit right is ineffective to the extent that the term or rule of law, statute, regulation, custom, or practice:

(1) would impair the creation, attachment, or perfection of a security interest in the letter-of-credit right; or

(2) provides that the assignment or the creation, attachment, or perfection of the security interest may give rise to a default, breach, right of recoupment, claim, defense, termination, right of termination, or remedy under the letter-of-credit right.

(b) To the extent that a term in a letter of credit is ineffective under subsection (a) but would be effective under law other than this article or a custom or practice applicable to the letter of credit, to the transfer of a right to draw or otherwise demand performance under the letter of credit, or to the assignment of a right to proceeds of the letter of credit, the creation, attachment, or perfection of a security interest in the letter-of-credit right:

(1) is not enforceable against the applicant, issuer, nominated person, or transferee beneficiary;

(2) imposes no duties or obligations on the applicant, issuer, nominated person, or transferee beneficiary; and

(3) does not require the applicant, issuer, nominated person, or transferee beneficiary to recognize the security interest, pay or render performance to the secured party, or accept payment or other performance from the secured party.

As amended in 1999.

Part 5 Filing [Subpart 1. Filing Office; Contents and Effectiveness of Financing Statement]

§9—501. FILING OFFICE

(a) Except as otherwise provided in subsection (b), if the local law of this State governs perfection of a security interest or agricultural lien, the office in which to file a financing statement to perfect the security interest or agricultural lien is:

(1) the office designated for the filing or recording of a record of a mortgage on the related real property, if:

(A) the collateral is as-extracted collateral or timber to be cut; or

(B) the financing statement is filed as a fixture filing and the collateral is goods that are or are to become fixtures; or

(2) the office of [ ] [or any office duly authorized by [ ]], in all other cases, including a case in which the collateral is goods that are or are to become fixtures and the financing statement is not filed as a fixture filing.

(b) The office in which to file a financing statement to perfect a security interest in collateral, including fixtures, of a transmitting utility is the office of [ ]. The financing statement also constitutes a fixture filing as to the collateral indicated in the financing statement which is or is to become fixtures.

Legislative Note: The State should designate the filing office where the brackets appear. The filing office may be that of a governmental official (e.g., the Secretary of State) or a private party that maintains the State's filing system.

§9—502. CONTENTS OF FINANCING STATEMENT; RECORD OF MORTGAGE AS FINANCING STATEMENT; TIME OF FILING FINANCING STATEMENT

(a) Subject to subsection (b), a financing statement is sufficient only if it:

(1) provides the name of the debtor;

(2) provides the name of the secured party or a representative of the secured party; and

(3) indicates the collateral covered by the financing statement.

(b) Except as otherwise provided in Section 9—501 (b), to be sufficient, a financing statement that covers as-extracted collateral or timber to be cut, or which is filed as a fixture filing and covers goods that are or are to become fixtures, must satisfy subsection (a) and also:

(1) indicate that it covers this type of collateral;

(2) indicate that it is to be filed [for record] in the real property records;

(3) provide a description of the real property to which the collateral is related [sufficient to give constructive notice of a mortgage under the law of this State if the description were contained in a record of the mortgage of the real property]; and

(4) if the debtor does not have an interest of record in the real property, provide the name of a record owner.

(c) A record of a mortgage is effective, from the date of recording, as a financing statement filed as a fixture filing or as a financing statement covering as-extracted collateral or timber to be cut only if:

(1) the record indicates the goods or accounts that it covers;

(2) the goods are or are to become fixtures related to the real property described in the record or the collateral is related to the real property described in the record and is as-extracted collateral or timber to be cut;

(3) the record satisfies the requirements for a financing statement in this section other than an indication that it is to be filed in the real property records; and

(4) the record is [duly] recorded.

(d) A financing statement may be filed before a security agreement is made or a security interest otherwise attaches.

Legislative Note: Language in brackets is optional. Where the State has any special recording system for real property other than the usual grantor-grantee index (as, for instance, a tract system or a title registration or Torrens system) local adaptations of subsection (b) and Section 9—519(d) and (e) may be necessary. See, e.g., Mass. Gen. Laws Chapter 106, Section 9—410.

§9—503. NAME OF DEBTOR AND SECURED PARTY

(a) A financing statement sufficiently provides the name of the debtor:

(1) if the debtor is a registered organization, only if the financing statement provides the name of the debtor indicated on the public record of the debtor's jurisdiction of organization which shows the debtor to have been organized;

(2) if the debtor is a decedent's estate, only if the financing statement provides the name of the decedent and indicates that the debtor is an estate;

(3) if the debtor is a trust or a trustee acting with respect to property held in trust, only if the financing statement:

(A) provides the name specified for the trust in its organic documents or, if no name is specified, provides the name of the settlor and additional information sufficient to distinguish the debtor from other trusts having one or more of the same settlors; and

(B) indicates, in the debtor's name or otherwise, that the debtor is a trust or is a trustee acting with respect to property held in trust; and

(4) in other cases:

(A) if the debtor has a name, only if it provides the individual or organizational name of the debtor; and

(B) if the debtor does not have a name, only if it provides the names of the partners, members, associates, or other persons comprising the debtor.

(b) A financing statement that provides the name of the debtor in accordance with subsection (a) is not rendered ineffective by the absence of:

(1) a trade name or other name of the debtor; or

(2) unless required under subsection (a)(4)(B), names of partners, members, associates, or other persons comprising the debtor.

(c) A financing statement that provides only the debtor's trade name does not sufficiently provide the name of the debtor.

(d) Failure to indicate the representative capacity of a secured party or representative of a secured party does not affect the sufficiency of a financing statement.

(e) A financing statement may provide the name of more than one debtor and the name of more than one secured party.

§9—504. INDICATION OF COLLATERAL

A financing statement sufficiently indicates the collateral that it covers if the financing statement provides:

(1) a description of the collateral pursuant to Section 9—108; or

(2) an indication that the financing statement covers all assets or all personal property.

As amended in 1999.

§9—505. FILING AND COMPLIANCE WITH OTHER STATUTES AND TREATIES FOR CONSIGNMENTS, LEASES, OTHER BAILMENTS, AND OTHER TRANSACTIONS

(a) A consignor, lessor, or other bailor of goods, a licensor, or a buyer of a payment intangible or promissory note may file a financing statement, or may comply with a statute or treaty described in Section 9—311(a), using the terms "consignor", "consignee", "lessor", "lessee", "bailor", "bailee", "licensor", "licensee", "owner", "registered owner", "buyer", "seller", or words of similar import, instead of the terms "secured party" and "debtor".

(b) This part applies to the filing of a financing statement under subsection (a) and, as appropriate, to compliance that is equivalent to filing a financing statement under Section 9—311(b), but the filing or compliance is not of itself a factor in determining whether the collateral secures an obligation. If it is determined for another reason that the collateral secures an obligation, a security interest held by the consignor, lessor, bailor, licensor, owner, or buyer which attaches to the collateral is perfected by the filing or compliance.

§9—506. EFFECT OF ERRORS OR OMISSIONS

(a) A financing statement substantially satisfying the requirements of this part is effective, even if it has minor errors or omissions, unless the errors or omissions make the financing statement seriously misleading.

(b) Except as otherwise provided in subsection (c), a financing statement that fails sufficiently to provide the name of the debtor in accordance with Section 9—503(a) is seriously misleading.

(c) If a search of the records of the filing office under the debtor's correct name, using the filing office's standard search logic, if any, would disclose a financing statement that fails sufficiently to provide the name of the debtor in accordance with Section 9—503(a), the name provided does not make the financing statement seriously misleading.

(d) For purposes of Section 9—508(b), the "debtor's correct name" in subsection (c) means the correct name of the new debtor.

§9—507. EFFECT OF CERTAIN EVENTS ON EFFECTIVENESS OF FINANCING STATEMENT

(a) A filed financing statement remains effective with respect to collateral that is sold, exchanged, leased, licensed, or otherwise disposed of and in which a security interest or agricultural lien continues, even if the secured party knows of or consents to the disposition.

(b) Except as otherwise provided in subsection (c) and Section 9—508, a financing statement is not rendered ineffective if, after the financing statement is filed, the information provided in the financing statement becomes seriously misleading under Section 9—506.

(c) If a debtor so changes its name that a filed financing statement becomes seriously misleading under Section 9—506:

(1) the financing statement is effective to perfect a security interest in collateral acquired by the debtor before, or within four months after, the change; and

(2) the financing statement is not effective to perfect a security interest in collateral acquired by the debtor more than four months after the change, unless an amendment to the financing statement which renders the financing statement not seriously misleading is filed within four months after the change.

§9—508. EFFECTIVENESS OF FINANCING STATEMENT IF NEW DEBTOR BECOMES BOUND BY SECURITY AGREEMENT

(a) Except as otherwise provided in this section, a filed financing statement naming an original debtor is effective to perfect a security interest in collateral in which a new debtor has or acquires rights to the extent that the financing statement would have been effective had the original debtor acquired rights in the collateral.

(b) If the difference between the name of the original debtor and that of the new debtor causes a filed financing statement that is effective under subsection (a) to be seriously misleading under Section 9—506:

(1) the financing statement is effective to perfect a security interest in collateral acquired by the new debtor before, and within four months after, the new debtor becomes bound under Section 9B—203(d); and

(2) the financing statement is not effective to perfect a security interest in collateral acquired by the new debtor more than four months after the new debtor becomes bound under Section 9—203(d) unless an initial financing statement providing the name of the new debtor is filed before the expiration of that time.

(c) This section does not apply to collateral as to which a filed financing statement remains effective against the new debtor under Section 9—507(a).

§9—509. PERSONS ENTITLED TO FILE A RECORD

(a) A person may file an initial financing statement, amendment that adds collateral covered by a financing statement, or amendment that adds a debtor to a financing statement only if:

    (1) the debtor authorizes the filing in an authenticated record or pursuant to subsection (b) or (c); or

    (2) the person holds an agricultural lien that has become effective at the time of filing and the financing statement covers only collateral in which the person holds an agricultural lien.

(b) By authenticating or becoming bound as debtor by a security agreement, a debtor or new debtor authorizes the filing of an initial financing statement, and an amendment, covering:

    (1) the collateral described in the security agreement; and

    (2) property that becomes collateral under Section 9—315(a)(2), whether or not the security agreement expressly covers proceeds.

(c) By acquiring collateral in which a security interest or agricultural lien continues under Section 9—315(a)(1), a debtor authorizes the filing of an initial financing statement, and an amendment, covering the collateral and property that becomes collateral under Section 9—315(a)(2).

(d) A person may file an amendment other than an amendment that adds collateral covered by a financing statement or an amendment that adds a debtor to a financing statement only if:

    (1) the secured party of record authorizes the filing; or

    (2) the amendment is a termination statement for a financing statement as to which the secured party of record has failed to file or send a termination statement as required by Section 9—513(a) or (c), the debtor authorizes the filing, and the termination statement indicates that the debtor authorized it to be filed.

(e) If there is more than one secured party of record for a financing statement, each secured party of record may authorize the filing of an amendment under subsection (d).

As amended in 2000.

§9—510. EFFECTIVENESS OF FILED RECORD

(a) A filed record is effective only to the extent that it was filed by a person that may file it under Section 9—509.

(b) A record authorized by one secured party of record does not affect the financing statement with respect to another secured party of record.

(c) A continuation statement that is not filed within the six-month period prescribed by Section 9—515(d) is ineffective.

§9—511. SECURED PARTY OF RECORD

(a) A secured party of record with respect to a financing statement is a person whose name is provided as the name of the secured party or a representative of the secured party in an initial financing statement that has been filed. If an initial financing statement is filed under Section 9—514 (a), the assignee named in the initial financing statement is the secured party of record with respect to the financing statement.

(b) If an amendment of a financing statement which provides the name of a person as a secured party or a representative of a secured party is filed, the person named in the amendment is a secured party of record. If an amendment is filed under Section 9—514(b), the assignee named in the amendment is a secured party of record.

(c) A person remains a secured party of record until the filing of an amendment of the financing statement which deletes the person.

§9—512. AMENDMENT OF FINANCING STATEMENT

[Alternative A]

(a) Subject to Section 9—509, a person may add or delete collateral covered by, continue or terminate the effectiveness of, or, subject to subsection (e), otherwise amend the information provided in, a financing statement by filing an amendment that:

    (1) identifies, by its file number, the initial financing statement to which the amendment relates; and

    (2) if the amendment relates to an initial financing statement filed [or recorded] in a filing office described in Section 9—501(a)(1), provides the information specified in Section 9—502(b).

[Alternative B]

(a) Subject to Section 9—509, a person may add or delete collateral covered by, continue or terminate the effectiveness of, or, subject to subsection (e), otherwise amend the information provided in, a financing statement by filing an amendment that:

    (1) identifies, by its file number, the initial financing statement to which the amendment relates; and

(2) if the amendment relates to an initial financing statement filed [or recorded] in a filing office described in Section 9—501(a)(1), provides the date [and time] that the initial financing statement was filed [or recorded] and the information specified in Section 9—502(b).

[End of Alternatives]

(b) Except as otherwise provided in Section 9—515, the filing of an amendment does not extend the period of effectiveness of the financing statement.

(c) A financing statement that is amended by an amendment that adds collateral is effective as to the added collateral only from the date of the filing of the amendment.

(d) A financing statement that is amended by an amendment that adds a debtor is effective as to the added debtor only from the date of the filing of the amendment.

(e) An amendment is ineffective to the extent it:

(1) purports to delete all debtors and fails to provide the name of a debtor to be covered by the financing statement; or

(2) purports to delete all secured parties of record and fails to provide the name of a new secured party of record.

Legislative Note: States whose real-estate filing offices require additional information in amendments and cannot search their records by both the name of the debtor and the file number should enact Alternative B to Sections 9—512(a), 9—518(b), 9—519(f), and 9—522(a).

§9—513. TERMINATION STATEMENT

(a) A secured party shall cause the secured party of record for a financing statement to file a termination statement for the financing statement if the financing statement covers consumer goods and:

(1) there is no obligation secured by the collateral covered by the financing statement and no commitment to make an advance, incur an obligation, or otherwise give value; or

(2) the debtor did not authorize the filing of the initial financing statement.

(b) To comply with subsection (a), a secured party shall cause the secured party of record to file the termination statement:

(1) within one month after there is no obligation secured by the collateral covered by the financing statement and no commitment to make an advance, incur an obligation, or otherwise give value; or

(2) if earlier, within 20 days after the secured party receives an authenticated demand from a debtor.

(c) In cases not governed by subsection (a), within 20 days after a secured party receives an authenticated demand from a debtor, the secured party shall cause the secured party of record for a financing statement to send to the debtor a termination statement for the financing statement or file the termination statement in the filing office if:

(1) except in the case of a financing statement covering accounts or chattel paper that has been sold or goods that are the subject of a consignment, there is no obligation secured by the collateral covered by the financing statement and no commitment to make an advance, incur an obligation, or otherwise give value;

(2) the financing statement covers accounts or chattel paper that has been sold but as to which the account debtor or other person obligated has discharged its obligation;

(3) the financing statement covers goods that were the subject of a consignment to the debtor but are not in the debtor's possession; or

(4) the debtor did not authorize the filing of the initial financing statement.

(d) Except as otherwise provided in Section 9—510, upon the filing of a termination statement with the filing office, the financing statement to which the termination statement relates ceases to be effective. Except as otherwise provided in Section 9—510, for purposes of Sections 9—519(g), 9—522(a), and 9—523(c), the filing with the filing office of a termination statement relating to a financing statement that indicates that the debtor is a transmitting utility also causes the effectiveness of the financing statement to lapse.

As amended in 2000.

§9—514. ASSIGNMENT OF POWERS OF SECURED PARTY OF RECORD

(a) Except as otherwise provided in subsection (c), an initial financing statement may reflect an assignment of all of the secured party's power to authorize an amendment to the financing statement by providing the name and mailing address of the assignee as the name and address of the secured party.

(b) Except as otherwise provided in subsection (c), a secured party of record may assign of record all or part of its power to authorize an amendment to a financing statement by filing in the filing office an amendment of the financing statement which:

(1) identifies, by its file number, the initial financing statement to which it relates;

(2) provides the name of the assignor; and

(3) provides the name and mailing address of the assignee.

(c) An assignment of record of a security interest in a fixture covered by a record of a mortgage which is effective as a financing statement filed as a fixture filing under

Section 9—502(c) may be made only by an assignment of record of the mortgage in the manner provided by law of this State other than [the Uniform Commercial Code].

§9—515. DURATION AND EFFECTIVENESS OF FINANCING STATEMENT; EFFECT OF LAPSED FINANCING STATEMENT

(a) Except as otherwise provided in subsections (b), (e), (f), and (g), a filed financing statement is effective for a period of five years after the date of filing.

(b) Except as otherwise provided in subsections (e), (f), and (g), an initial financing statement filed in connection with a public-finance transaction or manufactured-home transaction is effective for a period of 30 years after the date of filing if it indicates that it is filed in connection with a public-finance transaction or manufactured-home transaction.

(c) The effectiveness of a filed financing statement lapses on the expiration of the period of its effectiveness unless before the lapse a continuation statement is filed pursuant to subsection (d). Upon lapse, a financing statement ceases to be effective and any security interest or agricultural lien that was perfected by the financing statement becomes unperfected, unless the security interest is perfected otherwise. If the security interest or agricultural lien becomes unperfected upon lapse, it is deemed never to have been perfected as against a purchaser of the collateral for value.

(d) A continuation statement may be filed only within six months before the expiration of the five-year period specified in subsection (a) or the 30-year period specified in subsection (b), whichever is applicable.

(e) Except as otherwise provided in Section 9—510, upon timely filing of a continuation statement, the effectiveness of the initial financing statement continues for a period of five years commencing on the day on which the financing statement would have become ineffective in the absence of the filing. Upon the expiration of the five-year period, the financing statement lapses in the same manner as provided in subsection (c), unless, before the lapse, another continuation statement is filed pursuant to subsection (d). Succeeding continuation statements may be filed in the same manner to continue the effectiveness of the initial financing statement.

(f) If a debtor is a transmitting utility and a filed financing statement so indicates, the financing statement is effective until a termination statement is filed.

(g) A record of a mortgage that is effective as a financing statement filed as a fixture filing under Section 9—502(c) remains effective as a financing statement filed as a fixture filing until the mortgage is released or satisfied of record or its effectiveness otherwise terminates as to the real property.

§9—516. WHAT CONSTITUTES FILING; EFFECTIVENESS OF FILING

(a) Except as otherwise provided in subsection (b), communication of a record to a filing office and tender of the filing fee or acceptance of the record by the filing office constitutes filing.

(b) Filing does not occur with respect to a record that a filing office refuses to accept because:

(1) the record is not communicated by a method or medium of communication authorized by the filing office;

(2) an amount equal to or greater than the applicable filing fee is not tendered;

(3) the filing office is unable to index the record because:

   (A) in the case of an initial financing statement, the record does not provide a name for the debtor;

   (B) in the case of an amendment or correction statement, the record:

      (i) does not identify the initial financing statement as required by Section 9—512 or 9—518, as applicable; or

      (ii) identifies an initial financing statement whose effectiveness has lapsed under Section 9—515;

   (C) in the case of an initial financing statement that provides the name of a debtor identified as an individual or an amendment that provides a name of a debtor identified as an individual which was not previously provided in the financing statement to which the record relates, the record does not identify the debtor's last name; or

   (D) in the case of a record filed [or recorded] in the filing office described in Section 9—501(a)(1), the record does not provide a sufficient description of the real property to which it relates;

(4) in the case of an initial financing statement or an amendment that adds a secured party of record, the record does not provide a name and mailing address for the secured party of record;

(5) in the case of an initial financing statement or an amendment that provides a name of a debtor which was not previously provided in the financing statement to which the amendment relates, the record does not:

   (A) provide a mailing address for the debtor;

   (B) indicate whether the debtor is an individual or an organization; or

   (C) if the financing statement indicates that the debtor is an organization, provide:

      (i) a type of organization for the debtor;

(ii) a jurisdiction of organization for the debtor; or

(iii) an organizational identification number for the debtor or indicate that the debtor has none;

(6) in the case of an assignment reflected in an initial financing statement under Section 9—514(a) or an amendment filed under Section 9—514(b), the record does not provide a name and mailing address for the assignee; or

(7) in the case of a continuation statement, the record is not filed within the six-month period prescribed by Section 9—515(d).

(c) For purposes of subsection (b):

(1) a record does not provide information if the filing office is unable to read or decipher the information; and

(2) a record that does not indicate that it is an amendment or identify an initial financing statement to which it relates, as required by Section 9—512, 9—514, or 9—518, is an initial financing statement.

(d) A record that is communicated to the filing office with tender of the filing fee, but which the filing office refuses to accept for a reason other than one set forth in subsection (b), is effective as a filed record except as against a purchaser of the collateral which gives value in reasonable reliance upon the absence of the record from the files.

§9—517. EFFECT OF INDEXING ERRORS

The failure of the filing office to index a record correctly does not affect the effectiveness of the filed record.

§9—518. CLAIM CONCERNING INACCURATE OR WRONGFULLY FILED RECORD

(a) A person may file in the filing office a correction statement with respect to a record indexed there under the person's name if the person believes that the record is inaccurate or was wrongfully filed.

[Alternative A]

(b) A correction statement must:

(1) identify the record to which it relates by the file number assigned to the initial financing statement to which the record relates;

(2) indicate that it is a correction statement; and

(3) provide the basis for the person's belief that the record is inaccurate and indicate the manner in which the person believes the record should be amended to cure any inaccuracy or provide the basis for the person's belief that the record was wrongfully filed.

[Alternative B]

(b) A correction statement must:

(1) identify the record to which it relates by:

(A) the file number assigned to the initial financing statement to which the record relates; and

(B) if the correction statement relates to a record filed [or recorded] in a filing office described in Section 9—501(a)(1), the date [and time] that the initial financing statement was filed [or recorded] and the information specified in Section 9—502(b);

(2) indicate that it is a correction statement; and

(3) provide the basis for the person's belief that the record is inaccurate and indicate the manner in which the person believes the record should be amended to cure any inaccuracy or provide the basis for the person's belief that the record was wrongfully filed.

[End of Alternatives]

(c) The filing of a correction statement does not affect the effectiveness of an initial financing statement or other filed record.

Legislative Note: States whose real-estate filing offices require additional information in amendments and cannot search their records by both the name of the debtor and the file number should enact Alternative B to Sections 9—512(a), 9—518(b), 9—519(f), and 9—522(a).

[Subpart 2. Duties and Operation of Filing Office]

§9—519. NUMBERING, MAINTAINING, AND INDEXING RECORDS; COMMUNICATING INFORMATION PROVIDED IN RECORDS

(a) For each record filed in a filing office, the filing office shall:

(1) assign a unique number to the filed record;

(2) create a record that bears the number assigned to the filed record and the date and time of filing;

(3) maintain the filed record for public inspection; and

(4) index the filed record in accordance with subsections (c), (d), and (e).

(b) A file number [assigned after January 1, 2002,] must include a digit that:

(1) is mathematically derived from or related to the other digits of the file number; and

(2) aids the filing office in determining whether a number communicated as the file number includes a single-digit or transpositional error.

(c) Except as otherwise provided in subsections (d) and (e), the filing office shall:

(1) index an initial financing statement according to the name of the debtor and index all filed records relating to the initial financing statement in a manner that associates with one another an initial financing statement and all filed records relating to the initial financing statement; and

(2) index a record that provides a name of a debtor which was not previously provided in the financing statement to which the record relates also according to the name that was not previously provided.

(d) If a financing statement is filed as a fixture filing or covers as-extracted collateral or timber to be cut, [it must be filed for record and] the filing office shall index it:

(1) under the names of the debtor and of each owner of record shown on the financing statement as if they were the mortgagors under a mortgage of the real property described; and

(2) to the extent that the law of this State provides for indexing of records of mortgages under the name of the mortgagee, under the name of the secured party as if the secured party were the mortgagee thereunder, or, if indexing is by description, as if the financing statement were a record of a mortgage of the real property described.

(e) If a financing statement is filed as a fixture filing or covers as-extracted collateral or timber to be cut, the filing office shall index an assignment filed under Section 9—514(a) or an amendment filed under Section 9—514(b):

(1) under the name of the assignor as grantor; and

(2) to the extent that the law of this State provides for indexing a record of the assignment of a mortgage under the name of the assignee, under the name of the assignee.

[Alternative A]

(f) The filing office shall maintain a capability:

(1) to retrieve a record by the name of the debtor and by the file number assigned to the initial financing statement to which the record relates; and

(2) to associate and retrieve with one another an initial financing statement and each filed record relating to the initial financing statement.

[Alternative B]

(f) The filing office shall maintain a capability:

(1) to retrieve a record by the name of the debtor and:

(A) if the filing office is described in Section 9—501(a)(1), by the file number assigned to the initial financing statement to which the record relates and the date [and time] that the record was filed [or recorded]; or

(B) if the filing office is described in Section 9—501(a)(2), by the file number assigned to the initial financing statement to which the record relates; and

(2) to associate and retrieve with one another an initial financing statement and each filed record relating to the initial financing statement.

[End of Alternatives]

(g) The filing office may not remove a debtor's name from the index until one year after the effectiveness of a financing statement naming the debtor lapses under Section 9—515 with respect to all secured parties of record.

(h) The filing office shall perform the acts required by subsections (a) through (e) at the time and in the manner prescribed by filing-office rule, but not later than two business days after the filing office receives the record in question.

[(i) Subsection[s] [(b)] [and] [(h)] do[es] not apply to a filing office described in Section 9—501(a)(1).]

Legislative Notes:

1. States whose filing offices currently assign file numbers that include a verification number, commonly known as a "check digit," or can implement this requirement before the effective date of this Article should omit the bracketed language in subsection (b).

2. In States in which writings will not appear in the real property records and indices unless actually recorded the bracketed language in subsection (d) should be used.

3. States whose real-estate filing offices require additional information in amendments and cannot search their records by both the name of the debtor and the file number should enact Alternative B to Sections 9—512(a), 9—518(b), 9—519(f), and 9—522(a).

4. A State that elects not to require real-estate filing offices to comply with either or both of subsections (b) and (h) may adopt an applicable variation of subsection (i) and add "Except as otherwise provided in subsection (i)," to the appropriate subsection or subsections.

§9—520. ACCEPTANCE AND REFUSAL TO ACCEPT RECORD

(a) A filing office shall refuse to accept a record for filing for a reason set forth in Section 9—516(b) and may refuse to accept a record for filing only for a reason set forth in Section 9—516(b).

(b) If a filing office refuses to accept a record for filing, it shall communicate to the person that presented the record the fact of and reason for the refusal and the date and time the record would have been filed had the filing office accepted it. The communication must be made at the time and in the manner prescribed by filing-office rule but [, in the case of a filing office described in Section 9—501(a)(2),] in no event more than two business days after the filing office receives the record.

(c) A filed financing statement satisfying Section 9—502(a) and (b) is effective, even if the filing office is required to refuse to accept it for filing under subsection (a). However, Section 9—338 applies to a filed financing statement providing information described in Section 9—516(b)(5) which is incorrect at the time the financing statement is filed.

(d) If a record communicated to a filing office provides information that relates to more than one debtor, this part applies as to each debtor separately.

Legislative Note: A State that elects not to require real-property filing offices to comply with subsection (b) should include the bracketed language.

§9—521. UNIFORM FORM OF WRITTEN FINANCING STATEMENT AND AMENDMENT

(a) A filing office that accepts written records may not refuse to accept a written initial financing statement in the following form and format except for a reason set forth in Section 9—516(b):

[NATIONAL UCC FINANCING STATEMENT (FORM UCC1)(REV. 7/29/98)]
[NATIONAL UCC FINANCING STATEMENT ADDENDUM (FORM UCC1Ad)(REV. 07/29/98)]

(b) A filing office that accepts written records may not refuse to accept a written record in the following form and format except for a reason set forth in Section 9—516(b):

[NATIONAL UCC FINANCING STATEMENT AMENDMENT (FORM UCC3)(REV. 07/29/98)]
[NATIONAL UCC FINANCING STATEMENT AMENDMENT ADDENDUM (FORM UCC3Ad) (REV. 07/29/98)]

§9—522. MAINTENANCE AND DESTRUCTION OF RECORDS

[Alternative A]

(a) The filing office shall maintain a record of the information provided in a filed financing statement for at least one year after the effectiveness of the financing statement has lapsed under Section 9—515 with respect to all secured parties of record. The record must be retrievable by using the name of the debtor and by using the file

number assigned to the initial financing statement to which the record relates.

[Alternative B]

(a) The filing office shall maintain a record of the information provided in a filed financing statement for at least one year after the effectiveness of the financing statement has lapsed under Section 9—515 with respect to all secured parties of record. The record must be retrievable by using the name of the debtor and:

(1) if the record was filed [or recorded] in the filing office described in Section 9—501(a)(1), by using the file number assigned to the initial financing statement to which the record relates and the date [and time] that the record was filed [or recorded]; or

(2) if the record was filed in the filing office described in Section 9—501(a)(2), by using the file number assigned to the initial financing statement to which the record relates.

[End of Alternatives]

(b) Except to the extent that a statute governing disposition of public records provides otherwise, the filing office immediately may destroy any written record evidencing a financing statement. However, if the filing office destroys a written record, it shall maintain another record of the financing statement which complies with subsection (a).

Legislative Note: States whose real-estate filing offices require additional information in amendments and cannot search their records by both the name of the debtor and the file number should enact Alternative B to Sections 9—512(a), 9—518(b), 9—519(f), and 9—522(a).

§9—523. INFORMATION FROM FILING OFFICE; SALE OR LICENSE OF RECORDS

(a) If a person that files a written record requests an acknowledgment of the filing, the filing office shall send to the person an image of the record showing the number assigned to the record pursuant to Section 9—519(a)(1) and the date and time of the filing of the record. However, if the person furnishes a copy of the record to the filing office, the filing office may instead:

(1) note upon the copy the number assigned to the record pursuant to Section 9—519(a)(1) and the date and time of the filing of the record; and

(2) send the copy to the person.

(b) If a person files a record other than a written record, the filing office shall communicate to the person an acknowledgment that provides:

(1) the information in the record;

(2) the number assigned to the record pursuant to Section 9—519(a)(1); and

(3) the date and time of the filing of the record.

(c) The filing office shall communicate or otherwise make available in a record the following information to any person that requests it:

(1) whether there is on file on a date and time specified by the filing office, but not a date earlier than three business days before the filing office receives the request, any financing statement that:

(A) designates a particular debtor [or, if the request so states, designates a particular debtor at the address specified in the request];

(B) has not lapsed under Section 9—515 with respect to all secured parties of record; and

(C) if the request so states, has lapsed under Section 9—515 and a record of which is maintained by the filing office under Section 9—522(a);

(2) the date and time of filing of each financing statement; and

(3) the information provided in each financing statement.

(d) In complying with its duty under subsection (c), the filing office may communicate information in any medium. However, if requested, the filing office shall communicate information by issuing [its written certificate] [a record that can be admitted into evidence in the courts of this State without extrinsic evidence of its authenticity].

(e) The filing office shall perform the acts required by subsections (a) through (d) at the time and in the manner prescribed by filing-office rule, but not later than two business days after the filing office receives the request.

(f) At least weekly, the [insert appropriate official or governmental agency] [filing office] shall offer to sell or license to the public on a nonexclusive basis, in bulk, copies of all records filed in it under this part, in every medium from time to time available to the filing office.

Legislative Notes:
1. *States whose filing office does not offer the additional service of responding to search requests limited to a particular address should omit the bracketed language in subsection (c) (1)(A).*

2. *A State that elects not to require real-estate filing offices to comply with either or both of subsections (e) and (f) should specify in the appropriate subsection(s) only the filing office described in Section 9—501(a)(2).*

§9—524. DELAY BY FILING OFFICE

Delay by the filing office beyond a time limit prescribed by this part is excused if:

(1) the delay is caused by interruption of communication or computer facilities, war, emergency conditions, failure of equipment, or other circumstances beyond control of the filing office; and

(2) the filing office exercises reasonable diligence under the circumstances.

§9—525. FEES

(a) Except as otherwise provided in subsection (e), the fee for filing and indexing a record under this part, other than an initial financing statement of the kind described in subsection (b), is [the amount specified in subsection (c), if applicable, plus]:

(1) $[X] if the record is communicated in writing and consists of one or two pages;

(2) $[2X] if the record is communicated in writing and consists of more than two pages; and

(3) $[1/2X] if the record is communicated by another medium authorized by filing-office rule.

(b) Except as otherwise provided in subsection (e), the fee for filing and indexing an initial financing statement of the following kind is [the amount specified in subsection (c), if applicable, plus]:

(1) $____ if the financing statement indicates that it is filed in connection with a public-finance transaction;

(2) $____ if the financing statement indicates that it is filed in connection with a manufactured-home transaction.

[Alternative A]

(c) The number of names required to be indexed does not affect the amount of the fee in subsections (a) and (b).

[Alternative B]

(c) Except as otherwise provided in subsection (e), if a record is communicated in writing, the fee for each name more than two required to be indexed is $____.

[End of Alternatives]

(d) The fee for responding to a request for information from the filing office, including for [issuing a certificate showing] [communicating] whether there is on file any financing statement naming a particular debtor, is:

(1) $____ if the request is communicated in writing; and

(2) $____ if the request is communicated by another medium authorized by filing-office rule.

(e) This section does not require a fee with respect to a record of a mortgage which is effective as a financing statement filed as a fixture filing or as a financing statement covering as-extracted collateral or timber to be cut under Section 9—502(c). However, the recording and satisfaction fees that otherwise would be applicable to the record of the mortgage apply.

Legislative Notes:

1. *To preserve uniformity, a State that places the provisions of this section together with statutes setting fees for other services should do so without modification.*

2. *A State should enact subsection (c), Alternative A, and omit the bracketed language in subsections (a) and (b) unless its indexing system entails a substantial additional cost when indexing additional names.*

As amended in 2000.

§9—526. FILING-OFFICE RULES

(a)   The [insert appropriate governmental official or agency] shall adopt and publish rules to implement this article. The filing-office rules must be[:

(1)   ] consistent with this article[; and

(2)   adopted and published in accordance with the [insert any applicable state administrative procedure act]].

(b)   To keep the filing-office rules and practices of the filing office in harmony with the rules and practices of filing offices in other jurisdictions that enact substantially this part, and to keep the technology used by the filing office compatible with the technology used by filing offices in other jurisdictions that enact substantially this part, the [insert appropriate governmental official or agency], so far as is consistent with the purposes, policies, and provisions of this article, in adopting, amending, and repealing filing-office rules, shall:

(1)   consult with filing offices in other jurisdictions that enact substantially this part; and

(2)   consult the most recent version of the Model Rules promulgated by the International Association of Corporate Administrators or any successor organization; and

(3)   take into consideration the rules and practices of, and the technology used by, filing offices in other jurisdictions that enact substantially this part.

§9—527. DUTY TO REPORT

The [insert appropriate governmental official or agency] shall report [annually on or before _____] to the [Governor and Legislature] on the operation of the filing office. The report must contain a statement of the extent to which:

(1)   the filing-office rules are not in harmony with the rules of filing offices in other jurisdictions that enact substantially this part and the reasons for these variations; and

(2)   the filing-office rules are not in harmony with the most recent version of the Model Rules promulgated by the International Association of Corporate Administrators, or any successor organization, and the reasons for these variations.

Part 6 Default [Subpart 1. Default and Enforcement of Security Interest]

§9—601. RIGHTS AFTER DEFAULT; JUDICIAL ENFORCEMENT; CONSIGNOR OR BUYER OF ACCOUNTS, CHATTEL PAPER, PAYMENT INTANGIBLES, OR PROMISSORY NOTES

(a)   After default, a secured party has the rights provided in this part and, except as otherwise provided in Section 9—602, those provided by agreement of the parties. A secured party:

(1)   may reduce a claim to judgment, foreclose, or otherwise enforce the claim, security interest, or agricultural lien by any available judicial procedure; and

(2)   if the collateral is documents, may proceed either as to the documents or as to the goods they cover.

(b)   A secured party in possession of collateral or control of collateral under Section 9—104, 9—105, 9—106, or 9—107 has the rights and duties provided in Section 9—207.

(c)   The rights under subsections (a) and (b) are cumulative and may be exercised simultaneously.

(d)   Except as otherwise provided in subsection (g) and Section 9—605, after default, a debtor and an obligor have the rights provided in this part and by agreement of the parties.

(e)   If a secured party has reduced its claim to judgment, the lien of any levy that may be made upon the collateral by virtue of an execution based upon the judgment relates back to the earliest of:

(1)   the date of perfection of the security interest or agricultural lien in the collateral;

(2)   the date of filing a financing statement covering the collateral; or

(3)   any date specified in a statute under which the agricultural lien was created.

(f)   A sale pursuant to an execution is a foreclosure of the security interest or agricultural lien by judicial procedure within the meaning of this section. A secured party may purchase at the sale and thereafter hold the collateral free of any other requirements of this article.

(g)   Except as otherwise provided in Section 9—607 (c), this part imposes no duties upon a secured party that is a consignor or is a buyer of accounts, chattel paper, payment intangibles, or promissory notes.

§9—602. WAIVER AND VARIANCE OF RIGHTS AND DUTIES

Except as otherwise provided in Section 9—624, to the extent that they give rights to a debtor or obligor and impose duties on a secured party, the debtor or obligor may not waive or vary the rules stated in the following listed sections:

(1) Section 9—207(b)(4)(C), which deals with use and operation of the collateral by the secured party;

(2) Section 9—210, which deals with requests for an accounting and requests concerning a list of collateral and statement of account;

(3) Section 9—607(c), which deals with collection and enforcement of collateral;

(4) Sections 9—608(a) and 9—615(c) to the extent that they deal with application or payment of noncash proceeds of collection, enforcement, or disposition;

(5) Sections 9—608(a) and 9—615(d) to the extent that they require accounting for or payment of surplus proceeds of collateral;

(6) Section 9—609 to the extent that it imposes upon a secured party that takes possession of collateral without judicial process the duty to do so without breach of the peace;

(7) Sections 9—610(b), 9—611, 9—613, and 9—614, which deal with disposition of collateral;

(8) Section 9—615(f), which deals with calculation of a deficiency or surplus when a disposition is made to the secured party, a person related to the secured party, or a secondary obligor;

(9) Section 9—616, which deals with explanation of the calculation of a surplus or deficiency;

(10) Sections 9—620, 9—621, and 9—622, which deal with acceptance of collateral in satisfaction of obligation;

(11) Section 9—623, which deals with redemption of collateral;

(12) Section 9—624, which deals with permissible waivers; and

(13) Sections 9—625 and 9—626, which deal with the secured party's liability for failure to comply with this article.

§9—603. AGREEMENT ON STANDARDS CONCERNING RIGHTS AND DUTIES

(a) The parties may determine by agreement the standards measuring the fulfillment of the rights of a debtor or obligor and the duties of a secured party under a rule stated in Section 9—602 if the standards are not manifestly unreasonable.

(b) Subsection (a) does not apply to the duty under Section 9—609 to refrain from breaching the peace.

§9—604. PROCEDURE IF SECURITY AGREEMENT COVERS REAL PROPERTY OR FIXTURES

(a) If a security agreement covers both personal and real property, a secured party may proceed:

(1) under this part as to the personal property without prejudicing any rights with respect to the real property; or

(2) as to both the personal property and the real property in accordance with the rights with respect to the real property, in which case the other provisions of this part do not apply.

(b) Subject to subsection (c), if a security agreement covers goods that are or become fixtures, a secured party may proceed:

(1) under this part; or

(2) in accordance with the rights with respect to real property, in which case the other provisions of this part do not apply.

(c) Subject to the other provisions of this part, if a secured party holding a security interest in fixtures has priority over all owners and encumbrancers of the real property, the secured party, after default, may remove the collateral from the real property.

(d) A secured party that removes collateral shall promptly reimburse any encumbrancer or owner of the real property, other than the debtor, for the cost of repair of any physical injury caused by the removal. The secured party need not reimburse the encumbrancer or owner for any diminution in value of the real property caused by the absence of the goods removed or by any necessity of replacing them. A person entitled to reimbursement may refuse permission to remove until the secured party gives adequate assurance for the performance of the obligation to reimburse.

§9—605. UNKNOWN DEBTOR OR SECONDARY OBLIGOR

A secured party does not owe a duty based on its status as secured party:

(1) to a person that is a debtor or obligor, unless the secured party knows:

(A) that the person is a debtor or obligor;

(B) the identity of the person; and

(C) how to communicate with the person; or

(2) to a secured party or lienholder that has filed a financing statement against a person, unless the secured party knows:

(A) that the person is a debtor; and

(B) the identity of the person.

§9—606. TIME OF DEFAULT FOR AGRICULTURAL LIEN

For purposes of this part, a default occurs in connection with an agricultural lien at the time the secured party becomes entitled to enforce the lien in accordance with the statute under which it was created.

§9—607. COLLECTION AND ENFORCEMENT BY SECURED PARTY

(a) If so agreed, and in any event after default, a secured party:

(1) may notify an account debtor or other person obligated on collateral to make payment or otherwise render performance to or for the benefit of the secured party;

(2) may take any proceeds to which the secured party is entitled under Section 9—315;

(3) may enforce the obligations of an account debtor or other person obligated on collateral and exercise the rights of the debtor with respect to the obligation of the account debtor or other person obligated on collateral to make payment or otherwise render performance to the debtor, and with respect to any property that secures the obligations of the account debtor or other person obligated on the collateral;

(4) if it holds a security interest in a deposit account perfected by control under Section 9—104(a)(1), may apply the balance of the deposit account to the obligation secured by the deposit account; and

(5) if it holds a security interest in a deposit account perfected by control under Section 9—104(a)(2) or (3), may instruct the bank to pay the balance of the deposit account to or for the benefit of the secured party.

(b) If necessary to enable a secured party to exercise under subsection (a)(3) the right of a debtor to enforce a mortgage nonjudicially, the secured party may record in the office in which a record of the mortgage is recorded:

(1) a copy of the security agreement that creates or provides for a security interest in the obligation secured by the mortgage; and

(2) the secured party's sworn affidavit in recordable form stating that:

(A) a default has occurred; and

(B) the secured party is entitled to enforce the mortgage nonjudicially.

(c) A secured party shall proceed in a commercially reasonable manner if the secured party:

(1) undertakes to collect from or enforce an obligation of an account debtor or other person obligated on collateral; and

(2) is entitled to charge back uncollected collateral or otherwise to full or limited recourse against the debtor or a secondary obligor.

(d) A secured party may deduct from the collections made pursuant to subsection (c) reasonable expenses of collection and enforcement, including reasonable attorney's fees and legal expenses incurred by the secured party.

(e) This section does not determine whether an account debtor, bank, or other person obligated on collateral owes a duty to a secured party.

As amended in 2000.

§9—608. APPLICATION OF PROCEEDS OF COLLECTION OR ENFORCEMENT; LIABILITY FOR DEFICIENCY AND RIGHT TO SURPLUS

(a) If a security interest or agricultural lien secures payment or performance of an obligation, the following rules apply:

(1) A secured party shall apply or pay over for application the cash proceeds of collection or enforcement under Section 9—607 in the following order to:

(A) the reasonable expenses of collection and enforcement and, to the extent provided for by agreement and not prohibited by law, reasonable attorney's fees and legal expenses incurred by the secured party;

(B) the satisfaction of obligations secured by the security interest or agricultural lien under which the collection or enforcement is made; and

(C) the satisfaction of obligations secured by any subordinate security interest in or other lien on the collateral subject to the security interest or agricultural lien under which the collection or enforcement is made if the secured party receives an authenticated demand for proceeds before distribution of the proceeds is completed.

(2) If requested by a secured party, a holder of a subordinate security interest or other lien shall furnish reasonable proof of the interest or lien within a reasonable time. Unless the holder complies, the secured party need not comply with the holder's demand under paragraph (1)(C).

(3) A secured party need not apply or pay over for application noncash proceeds of collection and enforcement under Section 9—607 unless the failure to do so would be commercially unreasonable. A secured party that applies or pays over for application noncash proceeds shall do so in a commercially reasonable manner.

(4) A secured party shall account to and pay a debtor for any surplus, and the obligor is liable for any deficiency.

(b) If the underlying transaction is a sale of accounts, chattel paper, payment intangibles, or promissory notes, the debtor is not entitled to any surplus, and the obligor is not liable for any deficiency.

As amended in 2000.

§9—609. SECURED PARTY'S RIGHT TO TAKE POSSESSION AFTER DEFAULT

(a) After default, a secured party:
>   (1) may take possession of the collateral; and
>   (2) without removal, may render equipment unusable and dispose of collateral on a debtor's premises under Section 9—610.

(b) A secured party may proceed under subsection (a):
>   (1) pursuant to judicial process; or
>   (2) without judicial process, if it proceeds without breach of the peace.

(c) If so agreed, and in any event after default, a secured party may require the debtor to assemble the collateral and make it available to the secured party at a place to be designated by the secured party which is reasonably convenient to both parties.

§9—610. DISPOSITION OF COLLATERAL AFTER DEFAULT

(a) After default, a secured party may sell, lease, license, or otherwise dispose of any or all of the collateral in its present condition or following any commercially reasonable preparation or processing.

(b) Every aspect of a disposition of collateral, including the method, manner, time, place, and other terms, must be commercially reasonable. If commercially reasonable, a secured party may dispose of collateral by public or private proceedings, by one or more contracts, as a unit or in parcels, and at any time and place and on any terms.

(c) A secured party may purchase collateral:
>   (1) at a public disposition; or
>   (2) at a private disposition only if the collateral is of a kind that is customarily sold on a recognized market or the subject of widely distributed standard price quotations.

(d) A contract for sale, lease, license, or other disposition includes the warranties relating to title, possession, quiet enjoyment, and the like which by operation of law accompany a voluntary disposition of property of the kind subject to the contract.

(e) A secured party may disclaim or modify warranties under subsection (d):
>   (1) in a manner that would be effective to disclaim or modify the warranties in a voluntary disposition of property of the kind subject to the contract of disposition; or
>   (2) by communicating to the purchaser a record evidencing the contract for disposition and including an express disclaimer or modification of the warranties.

(f) A record is sufficient to disclaim warranties under subsection (e) if it indicates "There is no warranty relating to title, possession, quiet enjoyment, or the like in this disposition" or uses words of similar import.

§9—611. NOTIFICATION BEFORE DISPOSITION OF COLLATERAL

(a) In this section, "notification date" means the earlier of the date on which:
>   (1) a secured party sends to the debtor and any secondary obligor an authenticated notification of disposition; or
>   (2) the debtor and any secondary obligor waive the right to notification.

(b) Except as otherwise provided in subsection (d), a secured party that disposes of collateral under Section 9—610 shall send to the persons specified in subsection (c) a reasonable authenticated notification of disposition.

(c) To comply with subsection (b), the secured party shall send an authenticated notification of disposition to:
>   (1) the debtor;
>   (2) any secondary obligor; and
>   (3) if the collateral is other than consumer goods:
>>   (A) any other person from which the secured party has received, before the notification date, an authenticated notification of a claim of an interest in the collateral;
>>   (B) any other secured party or lienholder that, 10 days before the notification date, held a security interest in or other lien on the collateral perfected by the filing of a financing statement that:
>>>   (i) identified the collateral;
>>>   (ii) was indexed under the debtor's name as of that date; and
>>>   (iii) was filed in the office in which to file a financing statement against the debtor covering the collateral as of that date; and
>>   (C) any other secured party that, 10 days before the notification date, held a security interest in the collateral perfected by compliance with a statute, regulation, or treaty described in Section 9—311(a).

(d) Subsection (b) does not apply if the collateral is perishable or threatens to decline speedily in value or is of a type customarily sold on a recognized market.

(e) A secured party complies with the requirement for notification prescribed by subsection (c)(3)(B) if:
>   (1) not later than 20 days or earlier than 30 days before the notification date, the secured party requests, in a commercially reasonable manner, information concerning financing statements indexed under the debtor's name in the office indicated in subsection (c)(3)(B); and
>   (2) before the notification date, the secured party:
>>   (A) did not receive a response to the request for information; or
>>   (B) received a response to the request for information and sent an authenticated

notification of disposition to each secured party or other lienholder named in that response whose financing statement covered the collateral.

§9—612. TIMELINESS OF NOTIFICATION BEFORE DISPOSITION OF COLLATERAL

(a) Except as otherwise provided in subsection (b), whether a notification is sent within a reasonable time is a question of fact.

(b) In a transaction other than a consumer transaction, a notification of disposition sent after default and 10 days or more before the earliest time of disposition set forth in the notification is sent within a reasonable time before the disposition.

§9—613. CONTENTS AND FORM OF NOTIFICATION BEFORE DISPOSITION OF COLLATERAL: GENERAL

Except in a consumer-goods transaction, the following rules apply:

(1) The contents of a notification of disposition are sufficient if the notification:

(A) describes the debtor and the secured party;

(B) describes the collateral that is the subject of the intended disposition;

(C) states the method of intended disposition;

(D) states that the debtor is entitled to an accounting of the unpaid indebtedness and states the charge, if any, for an accounting; and

(E) states the time and place of a public disposition or the time after which any other disposition is to be made.

(2) Whether the contents of a notification that lacks any of the information specified in paragraph (1) are nevertheless sufficient is a question of fact.

(3) The contents of a notification providing substantially the information specified in paragraph (1) are sufficient, even if the notification includes:

(A) information not specified by that paragraph; or

(B) minor errors that are not seriously misleading.

(4) A particular phrasing of the notification is not required.

(5) The following form of notification and the form appearing in Section 9—614(3), when completed, each provides sufficient information:

NOTIFICATION OF DISPOSITION OF COLLATERAL

To: *[Name of debtor, obligor, or other person to which the notification is sent]*

From: *[Name, address, and telephone number of secured party]*

Name of Debtor(s): *[Include only if debtor(s) are not an addressee]*

[For a public disposition:]

We will sell [or lease or license, *as applicable*] the *[describe collateral]* [to the highest qualified bidder] in public as follows:

Day and Date: _____
Time: _____
Place: _____

[For a private disposition:]

We will sell [or lease or license, *as applicable*] the *[describe collateral]* privately sometime after *[day and date]*.

You are entitled to an accounting of the unpaid indebtedness secured by the property that we intend to sell [or lease or license, *as applicable*] [for a charge of $_____]. You may request an accounting by calling us at *[telephone number]*.

[End of Form]

As amended in 2000.

§9—614. CONTENTS AND FORM OF NOTIFICATION BEFORE DISPOSITION OF COLLATERAL: CONSUMER-GOODS TRANSACTION

In a consumer-goods transaction, the following rules apply:

(1) A notification of disposition must provide the following information:

(A) the information specified in Section 9—613(1);

(B) a description of any liability for a deficiency of the person to which the notification is sent;

(C) a telephone number from which the amount that must be paid to the secured party to redeem the collateral under Section 9—623 is available; and

(D) a telephone number or mailing address from which additional information concerning the disposition and the obligation secured is available.

(2) A particular phrasing of the notification is not required.

(3) The following form of notification, when completed, provides sufficient information:

[Name and address of secured party]
[Date]

NOTICE OF OUR PLAN TO SELL PROPERTY

[Name and address of any obligor who is also a debtor]

Subject: *[Identification of Transaction]*

We have your *[describe collateral]*, because you broke promises in our agreement.

[For a public disposition:]

We will sell *[describe collateral]* at public sale. A sale could include a lease or license. The sale will be held as follows:

    Date: _____

    Time: _____

    Place: _____

    You may attend the sale and bring bidders if you want.

[For a private disposition:]

We will sell *[describe collateral]* at private sale sometime after *[date]*. A sale could include a lease or license.

The money that we get from the sale (after paying our costs) will reduce the amount you owe. If we get less money than you owe, you *[will or will not, as applicable]* still owe us the difference. If we get more money than you owe, you will get the extra money, unless we must pay it to someone else.

You can get the property back at any time before we sell it by paying us the full amount you owe (not just the past due payments), including our expenses. To learn the exact amount you must pay, call us at *[telephone number]*.

If you want us to explain to you in writing how we have figured the amount that you owe us, you may call us at *[telephone number]* [or write us at *[secured party's address]*] and request a written explanation. [We will charge you $_____ for the explanation if we sent you another written explanation of the amount you owe us within the last six months.]

If you need more information about the sale call us at *[telephone number]* [or write us at *[secured party's address]*].

We are sending this notice to the following other people who have an interest in *[describe collateral]* or who owe money under your agreement:

[Names of all other debtors and obligors, if any]

[End of Form]

(4) A notification in the form of paragraph (3) is sufficient, even if additional information appears at the end of the form.

(5) A notification in the form of paragraph (3) is sufficient, even if it includes errors in information not required by paragraph (1), unless the error is misleading with respect to rights arising under this article.

(6) If a notification under this section is not in the form of paragraph (3), law other than this article determines the effect of including information not required by paragraph (1).

§9—615. APPLICATION OF PROCEEDS OF DISPOSITION; LIABILITY FOR DEFICIENCY AND RIGHT TO SURPLUS

(a) A secured party shall apply or pay over for application the cash proceeds of disposition under Section 9—610 in the following order to:

    (1) the reasonable expenses of retaking, holding, preparing for disposition, processing, and disposing, and, to the extent provided for by agreement and not prohibited by law, reasonable attorney's fees and legal expenses incurred by the secured party;

    (2) the satisfaction of obligations secured by the security interest or agricultural lien under which the disposition is made;

    (3) the satisfaction of obligations secured by any subordinate security interest in or other subordinate lien on the collateral if:

        (A) the secured party receives from the holder of the subordinate security interest or other lien an authenticated demand for proceeds before distribution of the proceeds is completed; and

        (B) in a case in which a consignor has an interest in the collateral, the subordinate security interest or other lien is senior to the interest of the consignor; and

    (4) a secured party that is a consignor of the collateral if the secured party receives from the consignor an authenticated demand for proceeds before distribution of the proceeds is completed.

(b) If requested by a secured party, a holder of a subordinate security interest or other lien shall furnish reasonable proof of the interest or lien within a reasonable time. Unless the holder does so, the secured party need not comply with the holder's demand under subsection (a)(3).

(c) A secured party need not apply or pay over for application noncash proceeds of disposition under Section 9—610 unless the failure to do so would be commercially unreasonable. A secured party that applies or pays over for application noncash proceeds shall do so in a commercially reasonable manner.

(d) If the security interest under which a disposition is made secures payment or performance of an obligation, after making the payments and applications required by subsection (a) and permitted by subsection (c):

    (1) unless subsection (a)(4) requires the secured party to apply or pay over cash proceeds to a consignor, the secured party shall account to and pay a debtor for any surplus; and

    (2) the obligor is liable for any deficiency.

(e) If the underlying transaction is a sale of accounts, chattel paper, payment intangibles, or promissory notes:

    (1) the debtor is not entitled to any surplus; and

(2) the obligor is not liable for any deficiency.

(f) The surplus or deficiency following a disposition is calculated based on the amount of proceeds that would have been realized in a disposition complying with this part to a transferee other than the secured party, a person related to the secured party, or a secondary obligor if:

(1) the transferee in the disposition is the secured party, a person related to the secured party, or a secondary obligor; and

(2) the amount of proceeds of the disposition is significantly below the range of proceeds that a complying disposition to a person other than the secured party, a person related to the secured party, or a secondary obligor would have brought.

(g) A secured party that receives cash proceeds of a disposition in good faith and without knowledge that the receipt violates the rights of the holder of a security interest or other lien that is not subordinate to the security interest or agricultural lien under which the disposition is made:

(1) takes the cash proceeds free of the security interest or other lien;

(2) is not obligated to apply the proceeds of the disposition to the satisfaction of obligations secured by the security interest or other lien; and

(3) is not obligated to account to or pay the holder of the security interest or other lien for any surplus.

As amended in 2000.

§9—616. EXPLANATION OF CALCULATION OF SURPLUS OR DEFICIENCY

(a) In this section:

(1) "Explanation" means a writing that:

(A) states the amount of the surplus or deficiency;

(B) provides an explanation in accordance with subsection (c) of how the secured party calculated the surplus or deficiency;

(C) states, if applicable, that future debits, credits, charges, including additional credit service charges or interest, rebates, and expenses may affect the amount of the surplus or deficiency; and

(D) provides a telephone number or mailing address from which additional information concerning the transaction is available.

(2) "Request" means a record:

(A) authenticated by a debtor or consumer obligor;

(B) requesting that the recipient provide an explanation; and

(C) sent after disposition of the collateral under Section 9—610.

(b) In a consumer-goods transaction in which the debtor is entitled to a surplus or a consumer obligor is liable for a deficiency under Section 9—615, the secured party shall:

(1) send an explanation to the debtor or consumer obligor, as applicable, after the disposition and:

(A) before or when the secured party accounts to the debtor and pays any surplus or first makes written demand on the consumer obligor after the disposition for payment of the deficiency; and

(B) within 14 days after receipt of a request; or

(2) in the case of a consumer obligor who is liable for a deficiency, within 14 days after receipt of a request, send to the consumer obligor a record waiving the secured party's right to a deficiency.

(c) To comply with subsection (a)(1)(B), a writing must provide the following information in the following order:

(1) the aggregate amount of obligations secured by the security interest under which the disposition was made, and, if the amount reflects a rebate of unearned interest or credit service charge, an indication of that fact, calculated as of a specified date:

(A) if the secured party takes or receives possession of the collateral after default, not more than 35 days before the secured party takes or receives possession; or

(B) if the secured party takes or receives possession of the collateral before default or does not take possession of the collateral, not more than 35 days before the disposition;

(2) the amount of proceeds of the disposition;

(3) the aggregate amount of the obligations after deducting the amount of proceeds;

(4) the amount, in the aggregate or by type, and types of expenses, including expenses of retaking, holding, preparing for disposition, processing, and disposing of the collateral, and attorney's fees secured by the collateral which are known to the secured party and relate to the current disposition;

(5) the amount, in the aggregate or by type, and types of credits, including rebates of interest or credit service charges, to which the obligor is known to be entitled and which are not reflected in the amount in paragraph (1); and

(6) the amount of the surplus or deficiency.

(d) A particular phrasing of the explanation is not required. An explanation complying substantially with the requirements of subsection (a) is sufficient, even if it includes minor errors that are not seriously misleading.

(e) A debtor or consumer obligor is entitled without charge to one response to a request under this section during any six-month period in which the secured party did not send to the debtor or consumer obligor an explanation pursuant to subsection (b)(1). The secured party may require payment of a charge not exceeding $25 for each additional response.

§9—617. RIGHTS OF TRANSFEREE OF COLLATERAL

(a) A secured party's disposition of collateral after default:

(1) transfers to a transferee for value all of the debtor's rights in the collateral;

(2) discharges the security interest under which the disposition is made; and

(3) discharges any subordinate security interest or other subordinate lien [other than liens created under [cite acts or statutes providing for liens, if any, that are not to be discharged]].

(b) A transferee that acts in good faith takes free of the rights and interests described in subsection (a), even if the secured party fails to comply with this article or the requirements of any judicial proceeding.

(c) If a transferee does not take free of the rights and interests described in subsection (a), the transferee takes the collateral subject to:

(1) the debtor's rights in the collateral;

(2) the security interest or agricultural lien under which the disposition is made; and

(3) any other security interest or other lien.

§9—618. RIGHTS AND DUTIES OF CERTAIN SECONDARY OBLIGORS

(a) A secondary obligor acquires the rights and becomes obligated to perform the duties of the secured party after the secondary obligor:

(1) receives an assignment of a secured obligation from the secured party;

(2) receives a transfer of collateral from the secured party and agrees to accept the rights and assume the duties of the secured party; or

(3) is subrogated to the rights of a secured party with respect to collateral.

(b) An assignment, transfer, or subrogation described in subsection (a):

(1) is not a disposition of collateral under Section 9—610; and

(2) relieves the secured party of further duties under this article.

§9—619. TRANSFER OF RECORD OR LEGAL TITLE

(a) In this section, "transfer statement" means a record authenticated by a secured party stating:

(1) that the debtor has defaulted in connection with an obligation secured by specified collateral;

(2) that the secured party has exercised its post-default remedies with respect to the collateral;

(3) that, by reason of the exercise, a transferee has acquired the rights of the debtor in the collateral; and

(4) the name and mailing address of the secured party, debtor, and transferee.

(b) A transfer statement entitles the transferee to the transfer of record of all rights of the debtor in the collateral specified in the statement in any official filing, recording, registration, or certificate-of-title system covering the collateral. If a transfer statement is presented with the applicable fee and request form to the official or office responsible for maintaining the system, the official or office shall:

(1) accept the transfer statement;

(2) promptly amend its records to reflect the transfer; and

(3) if applicable, issue a new appropriate certificate of title in the name of the transferee.

(c) A transfer of the record or legal title to collateral to a secured party under subsection (b) or otherwise is not of itself a disposition of collateral under this article and does not of itself relieve the secured party of its duties under this article.

§9—620. ACCEPTANCE OF COLLATERAL IN FULL OR PARTIAL SATISFACTION OF OBLIGATION; COMPULSORY DISPOSITION OF COLLATERAL

(a) Except as otherwise provided in subsection (g), a secured party may accept collateral in full or partial satisfaction of the obligation it secures only if:

(1) the debtor consents to the acceptance under subsection (c);

(2) the secured party does not receive, within the time set forth in subsection (d), a notification of objection to the proposal authenticated by:

(A) a person to which the secured party was required to send a proposal under Section 9—621; or

(B) any other person, other than the debtor, holding an interest in the collateral subordinate to the security interest that is the subject of the proposal;

(3) if the collateral is consumer goods, the collateral is not in the possession of the debtor when the debtor consents to the acceptance; and

(4) subsection (e) does not require the secured party to dispose of the collateral or the debtor waives the requirement pursuant to Section 9—624.

(b) A purported or apparent acceptance of collateral under this section is ineffective unless:

(1) the secured party consents to the acceptance in an authenticated record or sends a proposal to the debtor; and

(2) the conditions of subsection (a) are met.

(c) For purposes of this section:

(1) a debtor consents to an acceptance of collateral in partial satisfaction of the obligation it secures only if the debtor agrees to the terms of the acceptance in a record authenticated after default; and

(2) a debtor consents to an acceptance of collateral in full satisfaction of the obligation it secures only if the debtor agrees to the terms of the acceptance in a record authenticated after default or the secured party:

(A) sends to the debtor after default a proposal that is unconditional or subject only to a condition that collateral not in the possession of the secured party be preserved or maintained;

(B) in the proposal, proposes to accept collateral in full satisfaction of the obligation it secures; and

(C) does not receive a notification of objection authenticated by the debtor within 20 days after the proposal is sent.

(d) To be effective under subsection (a)(2), a notification of objection must be received by the secured party:

(1) in the case of a person to which the proposal was sent pursuant to Section 9—621, within 20 days after notification was sent to that person; and

(2) in other cases:

(A) within 20 days after the last notification was sent pursuant to Section 9—621; or

(B) if a notification was not sent, before the debtor consents to the acceptance under subsection (c).

(e) A secured party that has taken possession of collateral shall dispose of the collateral pursuant to Section 9—610 within the time specified in subsection (f) if:

(1) 60 percent of the cash price has been paid in the case of a purchase-money security interest in consumer goods; or

(2) 60 percent of the principal amount of the obligation secured has been paid in the case of a non-purchase-money security interest in consumer goods.

(f) To comply with subsection (e), the secured party shall dispose of the collateral:

(1) within 90 days after taking possession; or

(2) within any longer period to which the debtor and all secondary obligors have agreed in an agreement to that effect entered into and authenticated after default.

(g) In a consumer transaction, a secured party may not accept collateral in partial satisfaction of the obligation it secures.

§9—621. NOTIFICATION OF PROPOSAL TO ACCEPT COLLATERAL

(a) A secured party that desires to accept collateral in full or partial satisfaction of the obligation it secures shall send its proposal to:

(1) any person from which the secured party has received, before the debtor consented to the acceptance, an authenticated notification of a claim of an interest in the collateral;

(2) any other secured party or lienholder that, 10 days before the debtor consented to the acceptance, held a security interest in or other lien on the collateral perfected by the filing of a financing statement that:

(A) identified the collateral;

(B) was indexed under the debtor's name as of that date; and

(C) was filed in the office or offices in which to file a financing statement against the debtor covering the collateral as of that date; and

(3) any other secured party that, 10 days before the debtor consented to the acceptance, held a security interest in the collateral perfected by compliance with a statute, regulation, or treaty described in Section 9—311(a).

(b) A secured party that desires to accept collateral in partial satisfaction of the obligation it secures shall send its proposal to any secondary obligor in addition to the persons described in subsection (a).

§9—622. EFFECT OF ACCEPTANCE OF COLLATERAL

(a) A secured party's acceptance of collateral in full or partial satisfaction of the obligation it secures:

(1) discharges the obligation to the extent consented to by the debtor;

(2) transfers to the secured party all of a debtor's rights in the collateral;

(3) discharges the security interest or agricultural lien that is the subject of the debtor's consent and any subordinate security interest or other subordinate lien; and

(4) terminates any other subordinate interest.

(b) A subordinate interest is discharged or terminated under subsection (a), even if the secured party fails to comply with this article.

§9—623. RIGHT TO REDEEM COLLATERAL

(a) A debtor, any secondary obligor, or any other secured party or lienholder may redeem collateral.

(b) To redeem collateral, a person shall tender:
(1) fulfillment of all obligations secured by the collateral; and
(2) the reasonable expenses and attorney's fees described in Section 9—615(a)(1).

(c) A redemption may occur at any time before a secured party:
(1) has collected collateral under Section 9—607;
(2) has disposed of collateral or entered into a contract for its disposition under Section 9—610; or
(3) has accepted collateral in full or partial satisfaction of the obligation it secures under Section 9—622.

§9—624. WAIVER

(a) A debtor or secondary obligor may waive the right to notification of disposition of collateral under Section 9—611 only by an agreement to that effect entered into and authenticated after default.

(b) A debtor may waive the right to require disposition of collateral under Section 9—620(e) only by an agreement to that effect entered into and authenticated after default.

(c) Except in a consumer-goods transaction, a debtor or secondary obligor may waive the right to redeem collateral under Section 9—623 only by an agreement to that effect entered into and authenticated after default.

[Subpart 2. Noncompliance with Article]

§9—625. REMEDIES FOR SECURED PARTY'S FAILURE TO COMPLY WITH ARTICLE

(a) If it is established that a secured party is not proceeding in accordance with this article, a court may order or restrain collection, enforcement, or disposition of collateral on appropriate terms and conditions.

(b) Subject to subsections (c), (d), and (f), a person is liable for damages in the amount of any loss caused by a failure to comply with this article. Loss caused by a failure to comply may include loss resulting from the debtor's inability to obtain, or increased costs of, alternative financing.

(c) Except as otherwise provided in Section 9—628:
(1) a person that, at the time of the failure, was a debtor, was an obligor, or held a security interest in or other lien on the collateral may recover damages under subsection (b) for its loss; and
(2) if the collateral is consumer goods, a person that was a debtor or a secondary obligor at the time a secured party failed to comply with this part may recover for that failure in any event an amount not less than the credit service charge plus 10 percent of the principal amount of the obligation or the time-price differential plus 10 percent of the cash price.

(d) A debtor whose deficiency is eliminated under Section 9—626 may recover damages for the loss of any surplus. However, a debtor or secondary obligor whose deficiency is eliminated or reduced under Section 9—626 may not otherwise recover under subsection (b) for noncompliance with the provisions of this part relating to collection, enforcement, disposition, or acceptance.

(e) In addition to any damages recoverable under subsection (b), the debtor, consumer obligor, or person named as a debtor in a filed record, as applicable, may recover $500 in each case from a person that:
(1) fails to comply with Section 9—208;
(2) fails to comply with Section 9—209;
(3) files a record that the person is not entitled to file under Section 9—509(a);
(4) fails to cause the secured party of record to file or send a termination statement as required by Section 9—513(a) or (c);
(5) fails to comply with Section 9—616(b)(1) and whose failure is part of a pattern, or consistent with a practice, of noncompliance; or
(6) fails to comply with Section 9—616(b)(2).

(f) A debtor or consumer obligor may recover damages under subsection (b) and, in addition, $500 in each case from a person that, without reasonable cause, fails to comply with a request under Section 9—210. A recipient of a request under Section 9—210 which never claimed an interest in the collateral or obligations that are the subject of a request under that section has a reasonable excuse for failure to comply with the request within the meaning of this subsection.

(g) If a secured party fails to comply with a request regarding a list of collateral or a statement of account under Section 9—210, the secured party may claim a security interest only as shown in the list or statement included in the request as against a person that is reasonably misled by the failure.

As amended in 2000.

§9—626. ACTION IN WHICH DEFICIENCY OR SURPLUS IS IN ISSUE

(a) In an action arising from a transaction, other than a consumer transaction, in which the amount of a deficiency or surplus is in issue, the following rules apply:
(1) A secured party need not prove compliance with the provisions of this part relating to collection, enforcement, disposition, or acceptance unless the debtor or a secondary obligor places the secured party's compliance in issue.
(2) If the secured party's compliance is placed in issue, the secured party has the burden of

establishing that the collection, enforcement, disposition, or acceptance was conducted in accordance with this part.

(3) Except as otherwise provided in Section 9—628, if a secured party fails to prove that the collection, enforcement, disposition, or acceptance was conducted in accordance with the provisions of this part relating to collection, enforcement, disposition, or acceptance, the liability of a debtor or a secondary obligor for a deficiency is limited to an amount by which the sum of the secured obligation, expenses, and attorney's fees exceeds the greater of:

(A) the proceeds of the collection, enforcement, disposition, or acceptance; or

(B) the amount of proceeds that would have been realized had the noncomplying secured party proceeded in accordance with the provisions of this part relating to collection, enforcement, disposition, or acceptance.

(4) For purposes of paragraph (3)(B), the amount of proceeds that would have been realized is equal to the sum of the secured obligation, expenses, and attorney's fees unless the secured party proves that the amount is less than that sum.

(5) If a deficiency or surplus is calculated under Section 9—615(f), the debtor or obligor has the burden of establishing that the amount of proceeds of the disposition is significantly below the range of prices that a complying disposition to a person other than the secured party, a person related to the secured party, or a secondary obligor would have brought.

(b) The limitation of the rules in subsection (a) to transactions other than consumer transactions is intended to leave to the court the determination of the proper rules in consumer transactions. The court may not infer from that limitation the nature of the proper rule in consumer transactions and may continue to apply established approaches.

§9—627. DETERMINATION OF WHETHER CONDUCT WAS COMMERCIALLY REASONABLE

(a) The fact that a greater amount could have been obtained by a collection, enforcement, disposition, or acceptance at a different time or in a different method from that selected by the secured party is not of itself sufficient to preclude the secured party from establishing that the collection, enforcement, disposition, or acceptance was made in a commercially reasonable manner.

(b) A disposition of collateral is made in a commercially reasonable manner if the disposition is made:

(1) in the usual manner on any recognized market;

(2) at the price current in any recognized market at the time of the disposition; or

(3) otherwise in conformity with reasonable commercial practices among dealers in the type of property that was the subject of the disposition.

(c) A collection, enforcement, disposition, or acceptance is commercially reasonable if it has been approved:

(1) in a judicial proceeding;

(2) by a bona fide creditors' committee;

(3) by a representative of creditors; or

(4) by an assignee for the benefit of creditors.

(d) Approval under subsection (c) need not be obtained, and lack of approval does not mean that the collection, enforcement, disposition, or acceptance is not commercially reasonable.

§9—628. NONLIABILITY AND LIMITATION ON LIABILITY OF SECURED PARTY; LIABILITY OF SECONDARY OBLIGOR

(a) Unless a secured party knows that a person is a debtor or obligor, knows the identity of the person, and knows how to communicate with the person:

(1) the secured party is not liable to the person, or to a secured party or lienholder that has filed a financing statement against the person, for failure to comply with this article; and

(2) the secured party's failure to comply with this article does not affect the liability of the person for a deficiency.

(b) A secured party is not liable because of its status as secured party:

(1) to a person that is a debtor or obligor, unless the secured party knows:

(A) that the person is a debtor or obligor;

(B) the identity of the person; and

(C) how to communicate with the person; or

(2) to a secured party or lienholder that has filed a financing statement against a person, unless the secured party knows:

(A) that the person is a debtor; and

(B) the identity of the person.

(c) A secured party is not liable to any person, and a person's liability for a deficiency is not affected, because of any act or omission arising out of the secured party's reasonable belief that a transaction is not a consumer-goods transaction or a consumer transaction or that goods are not consumer goods, if the secured party's belief is based on its reasonable reliance on:

(1) a debtor's representation concerning the purpose for which collateral was to be used, acquired, or held; or

(2) an obligor's representation concerning the purpose for which a secured obligation was incurred.

(d) A secured party is not liable to any person under Section 9—625(c)(2) for its failure to comply with Section 9—616.

(e) A secured party is not liable under Section 9—625(c)(2) more than once with respect to any one secured obligation.

Part 7 Transition

§9—701. EFFECTIVE DATE

This [Act] takes effect on July 1, 2001.

§9—702. SAVINGS CLAUSE

(a) Except as otherwise provided in this part, this [Act] applies to a transaction or lien within its scope, even if the transaction or lien was entered into or created before this [Act] takes effect.

(b) Except as otherwise provided in subsection (c) and Sections 9—703 through 9—709:

(1) transactions and liens that were not governed by [former Article 9], were validly entered into or created before this [Act] takes effect, and would be subject to this [Act] if they had been entered into or created after this [Act] takes effect, and the rights, duties, and interests flowing from those transactions and liens remain valid after this [Act] takes effect; and

(2) the transactions and liens may be terminated, completed, consummated, and enforced as required or permitted by this [Act] or by the law that otherwise would apply if this [Act] had not taken effect.

(c) This [Act] does not affect an action, case, or proceeding commenced before this [Act] takes effect.

As amended in 2000.

§9—703. SECURITY INTEREST PERFECTED BEFORE EFFECTIVE DATE

(a) A security interest that is enforceable immediately before this [Act] takes effect and would have priority over the rights of a person that becomes a lien creditor at that time is a perfected security interest under this [Act] if, when this [Act] takes effect, the applicable requirements for enforceability and perfection under this [Act] are satisfied without further action.

(b) Except as otherwise provided in Section 9—705, if, immediately before this [Act] takes effect, a security interest is enforceable and would have priority over the rights of a person that becomes a lien creditor at that time, but the applicable requirements for enforceability or perfection under this [Act] are not satisfied when this [Act] takes effect, the security interest:

(1) is a perfected security interest for one year after this [Act] takes effect;

(2) remains enforceable thereafter only if the security interest becomes enforceable under Section 9—203 before the year expires; and

(3) remains perfected thereafter only if the applicable requirements for perfection under this [Act] are satisfied before the year expires.

§9—704. SECURITY INTEREST UNPERFECTED BEFORE EFFECTIVE DATE

A security interest that is enforceable immediately before this [Act] takes effect but which would be subordinate to the rights of a person that becomes a lien creditor at that time:

(1) remains an enforceable security interest for one year after this [Act] takes effect;

(2) remains enforceable thereafter if the security interest becomes enforceable under Section 9—203 when this [Act] takes effect or within one year thereafter; and

(3) becomes perfected:

(A) without further action, when this [Act] takes effect if the applicable requirements for perfection under this [Act] are satisfied before or at that time; or

(B) when the applicable requirements for perfection are satisfied if the requirements are satisfied after that time.

§9—705. EFFECTIVENESS OF ACTION TAKEN BEFORE EFFECTIVE DATE

(a) If action, other than the filing of a financing statement, is taken before this [Act] takes effect and the action would have resulted in priority of a security interest over the rights of a person that becomes a lien creditor had the security interest become enforceable before this [Act] takes effect, the action is effective to perfect a security interest that attaches under this [Act] within one year after this [Act] takes effect. An attached security interest becomes unperfected one year after this [Act] takes effect unless the security interest becomes a perfected security interest under this [Act] before the expiration of that period.

(b) The filing of a financing statement before this [Act] takes effect is effective to perfect a security interest to the extent the filing would satisfy the applicable requirements for perfection under this [Act].

(c) This [Act] does not render ineffective an effective financing statement that, before this [Act] takes effect, is filed and satisfies the applicable requirements for perfection under the law of the jurisdiction governing perfection as provided in [former Section 9—103]. However, except as otherwise provided in subsections (d) and (e) and

Section 9—706, the financing statement ceases to be effective at the earlier of:

(1) the time the financing statement would have ceased to be effective under the law of the jurisdiction in which it is filed; or

(2) June 30, 2006.

(d) The filing of a continuation statement after this [Act] takes effect does not continue the effectiveness of the financing statement filed before this [Act] takes effect. However, upon the timely filing of a continuation statement after this [Act] takes effect and in accordance with the law of the jurisdiction governing perfection as provided in Part 3, the effectiveness of a financing statement filed in the same office in that jurisdiction before this [Act] takes effect continues for the period provided by the law of that jurisdiction.

(e) Subsection (c)(2) applies to a financing statement that, before this [Act] takes effect, is filed against a transmitting utility and satisfies the applicable requirements for perfection under the law of the jurisdiction governing perfection as provided in [former Section 9—103] only to the extent that Part 3 provides that the law of a jurisdiction other than the jurisdiction in which the financing statement is filed governs perfection of a security interest in collateral covered by the financing statement.

(f) A financing statement that includes a financing statement filed before this [Act] takes effect and a continuation statement filed after this [Act] takes effect is effective only to the extent that it satisfies the requirements of Part 5 for an initial financing statement.

§9—706. WHEN INITIAL FINANCING STATEMENT SUFFICES TO CONTINUE EFFECTIVENESS OF FINANCING STATEMENT

(a) The filing of an initial financing statement in the office specified in Section 9—501 continues the effectiveness of a financing statement filed before this [Act] takes effect if:

(1) the filing of an initial financing statement in that office would be effective to perfect a security interest under this [Act];

(2) the pre-effective-date financing statement was filed in an office in another State or another office in this State; and

(3) the initial financing statement satisfies subsection (c).

(b) The filing of an initial financing statement under subsection (a) continues the effectiveness of the pre-effective-date financing statement:

(1) if the initial financing statement is filed before this [Act] takes effect, for the period provided in [former Section 9—403] with respect to a financing statement; and

(2) if the initial financing statement is filed after this [Act] takes effect, for the period provided in Section 9—515 with respect to an initial financing statement.

(c) To be effective for purposes of subsection (a), an initial financing statement must:

(1) satisfy the requirements of Part 5 for an initial financing statement;

(2) identify the pre-effective-date financing statement by indicating the office in which the financing statement was filed and providing the dates of filing and file numbers, if any, of the financing statement and of the most recent continuation statement filed with respect to the financing statement; and

(3) indicate that the pre-effective-date financing statement remains effective.

§9—707. AMENDMENT OF PRE-EFFECTIVE-DATE FINANCING STATEMENT

(a) In this section, "Pre-effective-date financing statement" means a financing statement filed before this [Act] takes effect.

(b) After this [Act] takes effect, a person may add or delete collateral covered by, continue or terminate the effectiveness of, or otherwise amend the information provided in, a pre-effective-date financing statement only in accordance with the law of the jurisdiction governing perfection as provided in Part 3. However, the effectiveness of a pre-effective-date financing statement also may be terminated in accordance with the law of the jurisdiction in which the financing statement is filed.

(c) Except as otherwise provided in subsection (d), if the law of this State governs perfection of a security interest, the information in a pre-effective-date financing statement may be amended after this [Act] takes effect only if:

(1) the pre-effective-date financing statement and an amendment are filed in the office specified in Section 9—501;

(2) an amendment is filed in the office specified in Section 9—501 concurrently with, or after the filing in that office of, an initial financing statement that satisfies Section 9—706(c); or

(3) an initial financing statement that provides the information as amended and satisfies Section 9—706(c) is filed in the office specified in Section 9—501.

(d) If the law of this State governs perfection of a security interest, the effectiveness of a pre-effective-date financing statement may be continued only under Section 9—705(d) and (f) or 9—706.

(e) Whether or not the law of this State governs perfection of a security interest, the effectiveness of a pre-effective-date financing statement filed in this State may be terminated after this [Act] takes effect by filing a termination statement in the office in which the pre-effective-date financing statement is filed, unless an initial financing statement that satisfies Section 9—706(c) has been filed in the office specified by the law of the jurisdiction governing perfection as provided in Part 3 as the office in which to file a financing statement.

As amended in 2000.

§9—708. PERSONS ENTITLED TO FILE INITIAL FINANCING STATEMENT OR CONTINUATION STATEMENT

A person may file an initial financing statement or a continuation statement under this part if:

(1) the secured party of record authorizes the filing; and
　　(2) the filing is necessary under this part:
　　　　(A) to continue the effectiveness of a financing statement filed before this [Act] takes effect; or
　　　　(B) to perfect or continue the perfection of a security interest.
　　As amended in 2000.

§9—709. PRIORITY

(a) This [Act] determines the priority of conflicting claims to collateral. However, if the relative priorities of the claims were established before this [Act] takes effect, [former Article 9] determines priority.

(b) For purposes of Section 9—322(a), the priority of a security interest that becomes enforceable under Section 9—203 of this [Act] dates from the time this [Act] takes effect if the security interest is perfected under this [Act] by the filing of a financing statement before this [Act] takes effect which would not have been effective to perfect the security interest under [former Article 9]. This subsection does not apply to conflicting security interests each of which is perfected by the filing of such a financing statement.

As amended in 2000.

glossary

A

abate—put a stop to a nuisance; reduce or cancel a legacy because the estate of the decedent is insufficient to make payment in full.

absolute guaranty—agreement that creates the same obligation for the guarantor as a suretyship does for the surety; a guaranty of payment creates an absolute guaranty.

absolute privilege—complete defense against the tort of defamation, as in the speeches of members of Congress on the floor and witnesses in a trial.

abstract of title—history of the transfers of title to a given piece of land, briefly stating the parties to and the effect of all deeds, wills, and judicial proceedings relating to the land.

acceptance—unqualified assent to the act or proposal of another; as the acceptance of a draft (bill of exchange), of an offer to make a contract, of goods delivered by the seller, or of a gift or deed.

acceptor—drawee who has accepted the liability of paying the amount of money specified in a draft.

accommodation party—person who signs an instrument to lend credit to another party to the paper.

accord and satisfaction—agreement to substitute for an existing debt some alternative form of discharging that debt, coupled with the actual discharge of the debt by the substituted performance.

acknowledgment—admission or confirmation, generally of an instrument and usually made before a person authorized to administer oaths, such as a notary public; used to establish that the instrument was executed by the person making the instrument, that it was a voluntary act, or that the instrument is recorded.

acquired distinctiveness—through advertising, use and association, over time, an ordinary descriptive word or phase has taken on a new source-identifying meaning and functions as a mark in the eyes of the public

act-of-state doctrine—doctrine whereby every sovereign state is bound to respect the independence of every other sovereign state, and the courts of one country will not sit in judgment of another government's acts done within its own territory.

adeemed—canceled; as in a specifically bequeathed property being sold or given away by the testator prior to death, thus canceling the bequest.

adjustable rate mortgage (ARM)—mortgage with variable financing charges over the life of the loan.

administrative agency—government body charged with administering and implementing legislation.

administrative law—law governing administrative agencies.

Administrative Procedure Act—federal law that establishes the operating rules for administrative agencies.

administrative regulations—rules made by state and federal administrative agencies.

administrator, administratrix—person (man, woman) appointed to wind up and settle the estate of a person who has died without a will.

admissibility—the quality of the evidence in a case that allows it to be presented to the jury.

adverse possession—hostile possession of real estate, which when actual, visible, notorious, exclusive, and continued for the required time, will vest the title to the land in the person in such adverse possession.

advising bank—bank that tells beneficiary that letter of credit has been issued.

affidavit—statement of facts set forth in written form and supported by the oath or affirmation of the person making the statement setting forth that such facts are true on the basis of actual knowledge or on information and belief. The affidavit is executed before a notary public or other person authorized to administer oaths.

affirm—action taken by an appellate court that approves the decision of the court below.

affirmative action plan (AAP)—plan to have a diverse and representative workforce.

after-acquired goods—goods acquired after a security interest has attached.

agency—the relationship that exists between a person identified as a principal and another by virtue of which the latter may make contracts with third persons on behalf of the principal. (Parties—principal, agent, third person)

agent—person or firm who is authorized by the principal or by operation of law to make contracts with third persons on behalf of the principal.

airbill—document of title issued to a shipper whose goods are being sent via air.

alteration—unauthorized change or completion of a negotiable instrument designed to modify the obligation of a party to the instrument.

alternative payees—those persons to whom a negotiable instrument is made payable, any one of whom may indorse and take delivery of it.

ambiguous—having more than one reasonable interpretation.

answer—what a defendant must file to admit or deny facts asserted by the plaintiff.

anticipatory breach—promisor's repudiation of the contract prior to the time that performance is required when such repudiation is accepted by the promisee as a breach of the contract.

anticipatory repudiation—repudiation made in advance of the time for performance of the contract obligations.

antilapse statutes—statutes providing that the children or heirs of a deceased beneficiary may take the legacy in the place of the deceased beneficiary.

apparent authority—appearance of authority created by the principal's words or conduct.

appeal—taking a case to a reviewing court to determine whether the judgment of the lower court or administrative agency was correct. (Parties—appellant, appellee)

appellate jurisdiction—the power of a court to hear and decide a given class of cases on appeal from another court or administrative agency.

appropriation—taking of an image, likeness, or name for commercial advantage.

arbitration—the settlement of disputed questions, whether of law or fact, by one or more arbitrators by whose decision the parties agree to be bound.

Article 2—section of the Uniform Commercial Code that governs contracts for the sale of goods.

articles of copartnership—See *Partnership Agreement.*

articles of incorporation—document filed to create a corporation; the basic structure of a company and the rights of its owners.

articles of partnership—See *Partnership Agreement.*

assignee—third party to whom contract benefits are transferred.

assignment—transfer of a right. Generally used in connection with personal property rights, as rights under a contract, commercial paper, an insurance policy, a mortgage, or a lease. (Parties—assignor, assignee)

assignor—party who assigns contract rights to a third party.

association tribunal—a court created by a trade association or group for the resolution of disputes among its members.

assumption—mortgage transfers in which the transferee and mortgagor are liable and the property is subject to foreclosure by the mortgagee if payments are not made.

attestation clause—clause that indicates a witness has observed either the execution of the will or the testator's acknowledgment of the writing as the testator's will.

attorney in fact—agent authorized to act for another under a power of attorney.

attorney-client privilege—right of individual to have discussions with his/her attorney kept private and confidential

attractive nuisance doctrine—a rule imposing liability upon a landowner for injuries sustained by small children playing on the land when the landowner permits a condition to exist or maintains equipment that a reasonable person should realize would attract small children who could not realize the danger. The rule does not apply if an unreasonable burden would be imposed upon the landowner in taking steps to protect the children.

authorities—corporations formed by government that perform public service.

automatic perfection—perfection given by statute without specific filing or possession requirements on the part of the creditor.

automatic stay—order to prevent creditors from taking action such as filing suits or seeking foreclosure against the debtor.

B

bad check laws—laws making it a criminal offense to issue a bad check with intent to defraud.

bailee—person who accepts possession of a property.

bailee's lien—specific, possessory lien of the bailee upon the goods for work done to them. Commonly extended by statute to any bailee's claim for compensation, eliminating the necessity of retention of possession.

bailment—relationship that exists when personal property is delivered into the possession of another under an agreement, express or implied, that the identical property will be returned or will be delivered in accordance with the agreement. (Parties—bailor, bailee)

bailment for mutual benefit—bailment in which the bailor and bailee derive a benefit from the bailment.

bailor—person who turns over the possession of a property.

balance sheet test—comparison of assets to liabilities made to determine solvency.

bankruptcy—procedure by which one unable to pay debts may surrender all assets in excess of any exemption claim to the court for administration and distribution to creditors, and the debtor is given a discharge that releases him from the unpaid balance due on most debts.

bankruptcy courts—court of special jurisdiction to determine bankruptcy issues.

battle of the forms—merchants' exchanges of invoices and purchase orders with differing boilerplate terms.

bearer—person in physical possession of commercial paper payable to bearer, a document of title directing delivery to bearer, or an investment security in bearer form.

bearer paper—instrument with no payee, payable to cash or payable to bearer.

bedrock view—a strict constructionist interpretation of a constitution.

beneficiary—person to whom the proceeds of a life insurance policy are payable, a person for whose benefit property is held in trust, or a person given property by a will; the ultimate recipient of the benefit of a funds transfer.

beneficiary's bank—the final bank, which carries out the payment order, in the chain of a transfer of funds.

bequest—gift of personal property by will.

bicameral—a two-house form of the legislative branch of government.

bilateral contract—agreement under which one promise is given in exchange for another.

bill of lading—document issued by a carrier acknowledging the receipt of goods and the terms of the contract of transportation.

bill of sale—writing signed by the seller reciting that the personal property therein described has been sold to the buyer.

blackmail—extortion demands made by a nonpublic official.

blank indorsement—an indorsement that does not name the person to whom the paper, document of title, or investment security is negotiated.

blocking laws—laws that prohibit the disclosure, copying, inspection, or removal of documents located in the enacting country in compliance with orders from foreign authorities.

blue sky laws—state statutes designed to protect the public from the sale of worthless stocks and bonds.

bona fide—in good faith; without any fraud or deceit.

bond—obligation or promise in writing and sealed, generally of corporations, personal representatives, and trustees; fidelity bonds.

bond indenture—agreement setting forth the contractual terms of a particular bond issue.

book value—value found by dividing the value of the corporate assets by the number of shares outstanding.

breach—failure to act or perform in the manner called for in a contract.

breach of the peace—violation of the law in the repossession of the collateral.

brownfields—land that is a designated Superfund cleanup site but which lies fallow because no one is willing to risk liability by buying the property, even when the hazardous waste has been removed or property no one is willing to spend the money to remove the hazardous waste.

bubble concept—method for determining total emissions in one area; all sources are considered in an area.

business ethics—balancing the goal of profits with values of individuals and society.

business judgment rule (BJR)—rule that allows management immunity from liability for corporate acts where there is a reasonable indication that the acts were made in good faith with due care.

bylaws—rules and regulations enacted by a corporation to govern the affairs of the corporation and its shareholders, directors, and officers.

C

cancellation provision—crossing out of a part of an instrument or a destruction of all legal effect of the instrument, whether by act of party, upon breach by the other party, or pursuant to agreement or decree of court.

capital stock—declared money value of the outstanding stock of the corporation.

cargo insurance—insurance that protects a cargo owner against financial loss if goods being shipped are lost or damaged at sea.

carrier—individual or organization undertaking the transportation of goods.

case law—law that includes principles that are expressed for the first time in court decisions.

cash surrender value—sum paid the insured upon the surrender of a policy to the insurer.

cash tender offer—general offer to all shareholders of a target corporation to purchase their shares for cash at a specified price.

cashier's check—draft drawn by a bank on itself.

cause of action—right to damages or other judicial relief when a legally protected right of the plaintiff is violated by an unlawful act of the defendant.

cease-and-desist order—order issued by a court or administrative agency to stop a practice that it decides is improper.

certificate of deposit (CD)—promise-to- pay instrument issued by a bank.

certificate of incorporation—written approval from the state or national government for a corporation to be formed.

certificate of stock—document evidencing a shareholder's ownership of stock issued by a corporation.

certified check—check for which the bank has set aside in a special account sufficient funds to pay it; payment is made when check is presented regardless of amount in drawer's account at that time; discharges all parties except certifying bank when holder requests certification.

cestui que trust—beneficiary or person for whose benefit the property is held in trust.

CF—cost and freight.

Chapter 11 bankruptcy—reorganization form of bankruptcy under federal law.

Chapter 7 bankruptcy—liquidation form of bankruptcy under federal law.

Chapter 13 bankruptcy—proceeding of consumer debt readjustment plan bankruptcy.

charging order—order by a court, after a business partner's personal assets are exhausted, requiring that the partner's share of the profits be paid to a creditor until the debt is discharged.

charter—grant of authority from a government to exist as a corporation. Generally replaced today by a certificate of incorporation approving the articles of incorporation.

check—order by a depositor on a bank to pay a sum of money to a payee; a bill of exchange drawn on a bank and payable on demand.

choice-of-law clause—clause in an agreement that specifies which law will govern should a dispute arise.

chose in action—intangible personal property in the nature of claims

against another, such as a claim for accounts receivable or wages.

CIF—cost, insurance, and freight.

civil disobedience—the term used when natural law proponents violate positive law.

claim—right to payment.

Clayton Act—a federal law that prohibits price discrimination.

Clean Air Act—federal legislation that establishes standards for air pollution levels and prevents further deterioration of air quality.

Clean Water Act—federal legislation that regulates water pollution through a control system.

close corporation—corporation whose shares are held by a single shareholder or a small group of shareholders.

close-connection doctrine—circumstantial evidence, such as an ongoing or a close relationship, that can serve as notice of a problem with an instrument.

COD—cash on delivery.

coinsurance clause—clause requiring the insured to maintain insurance on property up to a stated amount and providing that to the extent that this is not done, the insured is to be deemed a coinsurer with the insurer, so that the latter is liable only for its proportionate share of the amount of insurance required to be carried.

collateral—property pledged by a borrower as security for a debt.

comity—principle of international and national law that the laws of all nations and states deserve the respect legitimately demanded by equal participants.

commerce clause—that section of the U.S. Constitution allocating business regulation.

commercial impracticability—situation that occurs when costs of performance rise suddenly and performance of a contract will result in a substantial loss.

commercial lease—any nonconsumer lease.

commercial paper—written, transferable, signed promise or order to pay a specified sum of money; a negotiable instrument.

commercial unit—standard of the trade for shipment or packaging of a good.

commission merchant—bailee to whom goods are consigned for sale.

commission or factorage—consignee's compensation.

common carrier—carrier that holds out its facilities to serve the general public for compensation without discrimination.

common law—the body of unwritten principles originally based upon the usages and customs of the community that were recognized and enforced by the courts.

common stock—stock that has no right or priority over any other stock of the corporation as to dividends or distribution of assets upon dissolution.

community property—cotenancy held by husband and wife in property acquired during their marriage under the law of some of the states, principally in the southwestern United States.

comparative negligence—defense to negligence that allows plaintiff to recover reduced damages based on his level of fault.

compensatory damages—sum of money that will compensate an injured plaintiff for actual loss.

complaint—the initial pleading filed by the plaintiff in many actions, which in many states may be served as original process to acquire jurisdiction over the defendant.

composition of creditors—agreement among creditors that each shall accept a partial payment as full payment in consideration of the other creditors doing the same.

Comprehensive Environmental Response, Compensation, and Liability Act (CERCLA)—federal law that authorizes the president to issue funds for the cleanup of areas that were once disposal sites for hazardous wastes.

computer crimes—wrongs committed using a computer or with knowledge of computers.

concealment—failure to volunteer information not requested.

condition—stipulation or prerequisite in a contract, will, or other instrument.

condition precedent—event that if unsatisfied would mean that no rights would arise under a contract.

condition subsequent—event whose occurrence or lack thereof terminates a contract.

condominium—combination of co-ownership and individual ownership.

confidential relationship—relationship in which, because of the legal status of the parties or their respective physical or mental conditions or knowledge, one party places full confidence and trust in the other.

conflict of interest—conduct that compromises an employee's allegiance to that company.

conglomerate—relationship of a parent corporation to subsidiary corporations engaged in diversified fields of activity unrelated to the field of activity of the parent corporation.

consent decrees—informal settlements of enforcement actions brought by agencies.

consequential damages—damages the buyer experiences as a result of the seller's breach with respect to a third party; also called *special damages*.

consideration—promise or performance that the promisor demands as the price of the promise.

consignee—(1) person to whom goods are shipped, (2) dealer who sells goods for others.

consignment—bailment made for the purpose of sale by the bailee. (Parties—consignor, consignee)

consignor—(1) person who delivers goods to the carrier for shipment, (2) party with title who turns goods over to another for sale.

consolidation (of corporations)—combining of two or more corporations in which the corporate existence of each one ceases and a new corporation is created.

conspiracy—agreement between two or more persons to commit an unlawful act.

constitution—a body of principles that establishes the structure of a government and the relationship of the government to the people who are governed.

constructive bailment—bailment imposed by law as opposed to one created by contract, whereby the bailee must preserve the property and redeliver it to the owner.

constructive delivery—See *Symbolic Delivery*.

constructive eviction—act or omission of the landlord that substantially deprives the tenant of the use and enjoyment of the premises.

consumer—any buyer afforded special protections by statute or regulation.

consumer credit—credit for personal, family, and household use.

consumer goods—goods used or bought primarily for personal, family, or household use.

consumer lease—lease of goods by a natural person for personal, family, or household use.

Consumer Product Safety Improvement Act—federal law that sets standards for the types of paints used in toys; a response to the lead paint found in toys made in China; requires tracking for international production; increases penalties

contract—a binding agreement based on the genuine assent of the parties, made for a lawful object, between competent parties, in the form required by law, and generally supported by consideration.

contract carrier—carrier that transports on the basis of individual contracts that it makes with each shipper.

contract interference—tort in which a third party interferes with others' freedom to contract.

contract of adhesion—contract offered by a dominant party to a party with inferior bargaining power on a take-it-or-leave-it basis.

contract under seal—contract executed by affixing a seal or making an impression on the paper or on some adhering substance such as wax attached to the document.

contracting agent—agent with authority to make contracts; person with whom the buyer deals.

Contracts for the International Sale of Goods (CISG)—uniform international contract code contracts for international sale of goods.

contractual capacity—ability to understand that a contract is being made and to understand its general meaning.

contribution—right of a co-obligor who has paid more than a proportionate share to demand that the other obligor pay the amount of the excess payment made.

contributory negligence—negligence of the plaintiff that contributes to injury and at common law bars recovery from the defendant although the defendant may have been more negligent than the plaintiff.

conversion—act of taking personal property by a person not entitled to it and keeping it from its true owner or prior possessor without consent.

cooperative—group of two or more persons or enterprises that acts through a common agent with respect to a common objective, such as buying or selling.

copyright—exclusive right given by federal statute to the creator of a literary or an artistic work to use, reproduce, and display the work.

corporation—artificial being created by government grant, which for many purposes is treated as a natural person.

corporation by estoppel—corporation that comes about when parties estop themselves from denying that the corporation exists.

corporation de jure—corporation with a legal right to exist by virtue of law.

correspondent bank—will honor the letter of credit from the domestic bank of the buyer.

cost plus—method of determining the purchase price or contract price equal to the seller's or contractor's costs plus a stated percentage as the profit.

co-sureties—sureties for the same debtor and obligor.

cotenancy—when two or more persons hold concurrent rights and interests in the same property.

Council on Environmental Quality (CEQ)—federal agency that establishes national policies on environmental quality and then recommends legislation to implement these policies.

counterclaim—a claim that the defendant in an action may make against the plaintiff.

counteroffer—proposal by an offeree to the offeror that changes the terms of, and thus rejects, the original offer.

course of dealing—pattern of performance between two parties to a contract.

court—a tribunal established by government to hear and decide matters properly brought to it.

covenant against encumbrances—guarantee that conveyed land is not subject to any right or interest of a third person.

covenant of further assurances—promise that the grantor of an interest in land will execute any additional documents required to perfect the title of the grantee.

covenant of quiet enjoyment—covenant by the grantor of an interest in land to not disturb the grantee's possession of the land.

covenant of right to convey—guarantee that the grantor of an interest in land, if not the owner, has the right or authority to make the conveyance to a new owner.

covenant of seisin—guarantee that the grantor of an interest in land owns the estate conveyed to a new owner.

covenants of title—grantor's covenants of a deed that guarantee such matters as the right to make the conveyance, to ownership of the property, to freedom of the property from encumbrances, or that the grantee will not be disturbed in the quiet enjoyment of the land.

credit transfer—transaction in which a person making payment, such as a buyer, requests payment be made to the beneficiary's bank.

creditor—person (seller or lender) who is owed money; also may be a secured party.

crime—violation of the law that is punished as an offense against the state or government.

cross-examination—the examination made of a witness by the attorney for the adverse party.

cumulative voting—system of voting for directors in which each shareholder has as many votes as the number of voting shares owned multiplied by the number of directors to be elected, and such votes can be distributed for the various candidates as desired.

customary authority—authority of an agent to do any act that, according to the custom of the community, usually accompanies the transaction for which the agent is authorized to act.

cybercrime—crimes committed via the Internet.

cyberlaw—laws and precedent applicable to Internet transactions and communications.

cyberspace—World Wide Web and Internet communication.

cybersquatters—term for those who register and set up domain names on the Internet for resale to the famous users of the names in question.

D

de facto—existing in fact as distinguished from as of right, as in the case of an officer or a corporation purporting to act as such without being elected to the office or having been properly incorporated.

debenture—unsecured bond of a corporation, with no specific corporate assets pledged as security for payment.

debit transfer—transaction in which a beneficiary entitled to money requests payment from a bank according to a prior agreement.

debtor—buyer on credit (i.e., a borrower).

decedent—person whose estate is being administered.

deed—instrument by which the grantor (owner of land) conveys or transfers the title to a grantee.

defamation—untrue statement by one party about another to a third party.

defendant—party charged with a violation of civil or criminal law in a proceeding.

definite time—time of payment computable from the face of the instrument.

delegated powers—powers expressly granted the national government by the Constitution.

delegation—transfer to another of the right and power to do an act.

delegation of duties—transfer of duties by a contracting party to another person who is to perform them.

delivery—constructive or actual possession.

demand draft—draft that is payable upon presentment.

demurrer—a pleading to dismiss the adverse party's pleading for not stating a cause of action or a defense.

deposition—the testimony of a witness taken out of court before a person authorized to administer oaths.

depositor—person, or bailor, who gives property for storage.

derivative action—secondary action for damages or breach of contract brought by one or more corporate shareholders against directors, officers, or third persons.

development statement—statement that sets forth significant details of a real estate or property development as required by the federal Land Sales Act.

devise—gift of real estate made by will.

devisee—beneficiary of a devise.

direct damages—losses that are caused by breach of a contract.

direct examination—examination of a witness by his or her attorney.

directed verdict—a direction by the trial judge to the jury to return a verdict in favor of a specified party to the action.

disability—any incapacity resulting from bodily injury or disease to engage in any occupation for remuneration or profit.

discharge in bankruptcy—order of the bankruptcy court relieving the debtor from obligation to pay the unpaid balance of most claims.

disclosed principal—principal whose identity is made known by the agent as well as the fact that the agent is acting on the principal's behalf.

discovery—procedures for ascertaining facts prior to the time of trial in order to eliminate the element of surprise in litigation.

dishonor—status when the primary party refuses to pay the instrument according to its terms.

disinherited—excluded from sharing in the estate of a decedent.

Dispute Settlement Body—means, provided by the World Trade Organization, for member countries to resolve trade disputes rather than engage in unilateral trade sanctions or a trade war.

distinctiveness—capable of serving the source-identifying function of a mark.

distribution per stirpes—distribution of an estate made in as many equal parts as there are family lines represented in the nearest generation; also known as stirpital distribution.

distributor—entity that takes title to goods and bears the financial and commercial risks for the subsequent sale of the goods.

divestiture order—a court order to dispose of interests that could lead to a monopoly.

divisible contract—agreement consisting of two or more parts, each calling for corresponding performances of each part by the parties.

document of title—document treated as evidence that a person is entitled to receive, hold, and dispose of the document and the goods it covers.

domestic corporation—corporation that has been incorporated by the state in question as opposed to incorporation by another state.

dominant tenement—land that is benefited by an easement.

donee—recipient of a gift.

donor—person making a gift.

double indemnity—provision for payment of double the amount specified by the insurance contract if death is caused by an accident and occurs under specified circumstances.

draft or bill of exchange—an unconditional order in writing by one person upon another, signed by the person giving it, and ordering the person to whom it is directed to pay upon demand or at a definite time a sum certain in money to order or to bearer.

drawee—person to whom the draft is addressed and who is ordered to pay the amount of money specified in the draft.

drawer—person who writes out and creates a draft or bill of exchange, including a check.

due diligence—process of checking the environmental history and nature of land prior to purchase.

due process—the constitutional right to be heard, question witnesses, and present evidence.

due process clause—in the Fifth and Fourteenth Amendments, a guarantee of protection from unreasonable procedures and unreasonable laws.

dumping—selling goods in another country at less than their fair value.

duress—conduct that deprives the victim of free will and that generally gives the victim the right to set aside any transaction entered into under such circumstances.

duty—an obligation of law imposed on a person to perform or refrain from performing a certain act.

E

easement—permanent right that one has in the land of another, as the right to cross another's land or an easement of way.

easement by implication—easement not specifically created by deed that arises from the circumstances of the parties and the land location and access.

economic duress—threat of financial loss.

Economic Espionage Act (EEA)—federal law that makes it a felony to copy, download, transmit, or in any way transfer proprietary files, documents, and information from a computer to an unauthorized person.

economic strikers—union strikers trying to enforce bargaining demands when an impasse has been reached in the negotiation process for a collective bargaining agreement.

effects doctrine—doctrine that states that U.S. courts will assume jurisdiction and will apply antitrust laws to conduct outside of the United States when the activity of business firms has direct and substantial effect on U.S. commerce; the rule has been modified to require that the effect on U.S. commerce also be foreseeable.

effluent guidelines—EPA standards for maximum ranges of discharge into water.

electronic funds transfer (EFT)—any transfer of funds (other than a transaction originated by a check, draft, or similar paper instrument) that is initiated through an electronic terminal, telephone, computer, or magnetic tape so as to authorize a financial institution to debit or credit an account.

Electronic Funds Transfer Act (EFTA)—federal law that provides consumers with rights and protections in electronic funds transfers.

eleemosynary corporation—corporation organized for a charitable or benevolent purpose.

embezzlement—statutory offense consisting of the unlawful conversion of property entrusted to the wrongdoer.

eminent domain—power of government and certain kinds of corporations to take private property against the objection of the owner, provided the taking is for a public purpose and just compensation is made for it.

emissions offset policy—controls whether new factories can be built in a nonattainment area.

employment-at-will doctrine—doctrine in which the employer has historically been allowed to terminate the employment contract at any time for any reason or for no reason.

en banc—the term used when the full panel of judges on the appellate court hears a case.

encoding warranty—warranty made by any party who encodes electronic information on an instrument; a warranty of accuracy.

Endangered Species Act (ESA)—federal law that identifies and protects species that are endangered from development or other acts that threaten their existence.

endowment insurance—insurance that pays the face amount of the policy if the insured dies within the policy period.

environmental impact statement (EIS)—formal report prepared under NEPA to document findings on the impact of a federal project on the environment.

equitable title—beneficial interest in a trust.

equity—the body of principles that originally developed because of the inadequacy of the rules then applied by the common law courts of England.

escalation clause—provision for the automatic increase of the rent at periodic intervals.

escheat—transfer to the state of the title to a decedent's property when the owner of the property dies intestate and is not survived by anyone capable of taking the property as heir.

E-sign—signature over the Internet.

estate in fee—largest estate possible, in which the owner has absolute and entire interest in the land.

estoppel—principle by which a person is barred from pursuing a certain course of action or of disputing the truth of certain matters.

ethics—a branch of philosophy dealing with values that relate to the nature of human conduct and values associated with that conduct.

ex post facto *law*—a law making criminal an act that was lawful when done or that increases the penalty when done. Such laws are generally prohibited by constitutional provisions.

exculpatory clause—provision in a contract stating that one of the parties is not liable for damages in case of breach; also called *limitation-of-liability clause*.

executed contract—agreement that has been completely performed.

execution—the carrying out of a judgment of a court, generally directing that property owned by the defendant be sold and the proceeds first be used to pay the execution or judgment creditor.

executive branch—the branch of government (e.g., the president) formed to execute the laws.

executor, executrix—person (man, woman) named in a will to administer the estate of the decedent.

executory contract—agreement by which something remains to be done by one or both parties.

exhaustion of administrative remedies—requirement that an agency make its final decision before the parties can go to court.

existing goods—goods that physically exist and are owned by the seller at the time of a transaction.

exoneration—agreement or provision in an agreement that one party shall not be held liable for loss; the right of the surety to demand that those primarily liable pay the claim for which the surety is secondarily liable.

expert witness—one who has acquired special knowledge in a particular field as through practical experience or study, or both, whose opinion is admissible as an aid to the trier of fact.

export sale—direct sale to customers in a foreign country.

express authorization—authorization of an agent to perform a certain act.

express contract—agreement of the parties manifested by their words, whether spoken or written.

express warranty—statement by the defendant relating to the goods, which statement is part of the basis of the bargain.

extortion—illegal demand by a public officer acting with apparent authority.

F

facilitation payments—(or grease payments) legal payments to speed up or ensure performance of normal government duties.

factor—bailee to whom goods are consigned for sale.

fair use—principle that allows the limited use of copyrighted material for teaching, research, and news reporting.

false imprisonment—intentional detention of a person without that person's consent; called the shopkeeper's tort when shoplifters are unlawfully detained.

FAS—free alongside the named vessel.

federal district court—a general trial court of the federal system.

Federal Register—government publication issued five days a week that lists all administrative regulations, all presidential proclamations and executive orders, and other documents and classes of documents that the president or Congress direct to be published.

Federal Register Act—federal law requiring agencies to make public disclosure of proposed rules, passed rules, and activities.

Federal Sentencing Guidelines—federal standards used by judges in determining mandatory sentence terms for those convicted of federal crimes.

federal system—the system of government in which a central government is given power to administer to national concerns while individual states retain the power to administer to local concerns.

fee simple defeasibles—fee simple interest can be lost if restrictions on its use are violated.

fee simple estate—highest level of land ownership; full interest of unlimited duration.

felony—criminal offense that is punishable by confinement in prison for more than one year or by death, or that is expressly stated by statute to be a felony.

field warehousing—stored goods under the exclusive control of a warehouse but kept on the owner's premises rather than in a warehouse.

Fifth Amendment—constitutional protection against self-incrimination; also guarantees due process.

finance lease—three-party lease agreement in which there is a lessor, a lessee, and a financier.

financing statement—brief statement (record) that gives sufficient information to alert third persons that a particular creditor may have a security interest in the collateral described.

fire insurance policy—a contract that indemnifies the insured for property destruction or damage caused by fire.

firm offer—offer stated to be held open for a specified time, which must be so held in some states even in the absence of an option contract, or under the UCC, with respect to merchants.

first-in-time provision—creditor whose interest attached first has priority in the collateral when two creditors have a secured interest.

first-to-perfect basis—rule of priorities that holds that first in time in perfecting a security interest, mortgage, judgment, lien, or other property attachment right should have priority.

fixture—personal property that has become so attached to or adapted to real estate that it has lost its character as personal property and is part of the real estate.

floating lien—claim in a changing or shifting stock of goods of the buyer.

FOB place of destination—general commercial language for delivery to the buyer.

FOB place of shipment—"ship to" contract.

forbearance—refraining from doing an act.

forcible entry and detainer—action by the landlord to have the tenant removed for nonpayment of rent.

foreclosure—procedure for enforcing a mortgage resulting in the public sale of the mortgaged property and, less commonly, in merely barring the right of the mortgagor to redeem the property from the mortgage.

foreign corporation—corporation incorporated under the laws of another state.

Foreign Corrupt Practices Act (FCPA)—federal law that makes it a felony to influence decision makers in other countries for the purpose of obtaining business, such as contracts for sales and services; also imposes financial reporting requirements on certain U.S. corporations.

forged or unauthorized indorsement—instrument indorsed by an agent for a principal without authorization or authority.

forgery—fraudulently making or altering an instrument that apparently creates or alters a legal liability of another.

formal contracts—written contracts or agreements whose formality signifies the parties' intention to abide by the terms.

Fourth Amendment—privacy protection in the U.S. Constitution; prohibits unauthorized searches and seizures.

franchise—(1) privilege or authorization, generally exclusive, to engage in a particular activity within a particular geographic area, such as a government franchise to operate a taxi company within a specified city, or a private franchise as the grant by a manufacturer of a right to sell products within a particular territory or for a particular number of years; (2) right to vote.

franchise agreement—sets forth rights of franchisee to use trademarks, etc., of franchisor.

franchisee—person to whom franchise is granted.

franchising—granting of permission to use a trademark, trade name, or copyright under specified conditions; a form of licensing.

franchisor—party granting the franchise.

fraud—making of a false statement of a past or existing fact, with knowledge of its falsity or with reckless indifference as to its truth, with the intent to cause another to rely thereon, and such person does rely thereon and is harmed thereby.

fraud in factum—fraud committed through deception on documents or the nature of the transaction as opposed to the subject matter or parties in the transaction (fraud in the inducement).

fraud in the inducement—fraud that occurs when a person is persuaded or induced to execute an instrument because of fraudulent statements.

fraud-on-the-market—a theory that in an open and developed securities market, the price of a stock is determined by the information on the company available to the public, and misleading statements will defraud purchasers of stock even if they do not directly rely on these statements.

Freedom of Information Act—federal law permitting citizens to request documents and records from administrative agencies.

freight forwarder—one who contracts to have goods transported and, in turn, contracts with carriers for such transportation.

freight insurance—insures that shipowner will receive payment for transportation charges.

full warranty—obligation of a seller to fix or replace a defective product within a reasonable time without cost to the buyer.

funds transfer—communication of instructions or requests to pay a specific sum of money to the credit of a specified account or person without an actual physical passing of money.

fungible goods—homogeneous goods of which any unit is the equivalent of any other unit.

future goods—goods that exist physically but are not owned by the seller and goods that have not yet been produced.

G

garnishment—the name given in some states to attachment proceedings.

general agent—agent authorized by the principal to transact all affairs in connection with a particular type of business or trade or to transact all business at a certain place.

general corporation code—state's code listing certain requirements for creation of a corporation.

general jurisdiction—the power to hear and decide most controversies involving legal rights and duties.

general legacies—certain sums of money bequeathed to named persons by the testator; to be paid out of the decedent's assets generally without specifying any particular fund or source from which the payment is to be made.

general partnership—partnership in which the partners conduct as co-owners a business for profit, and each partner has a right to take part in the management of the business and has unlimited liability.

general partners—partners who publicly and actively engage in the transaction of firm business.

gift—title to an owner's personal property voluntarily transferred by a party not receiving anything in exchange.

gift causa mortis—gift, made by the donor in the belief that death was immediate and impending, that is revoked or is revocable under certain circumstances.

good faith—absence of knowledge of any defects in or problems; "pure heart and an empty head."

goods—anything movable at the time it is identified as the subject of a transaction.

grantee—new owner of a land conveyance.

grantor—owner who transfers or conveys an interest in land to a new owner.

gratuitous bailment—bailment in which the bailee does not receive any compensation or advantage.

gray market goods—foreign-made goods with U.S. trademarks brought into the United States by a third party without the consent of the trademark owners to compete with these owners.

grease payments—(or facilitation payments) legal payments to speed up or ensure performance of normal government duties.

guarantor—one who undertakes the obligation of guaranty.

guaranty—agreement or promise to answer for a debt; an undertaking to pay the debt of another if the creditor first sues the debtor.

guaranty of collection—form of guaranty in which creditor cannot proceed against guarantor until after proceeding against debtor.

guaranty of payment—absolute promise to pay when a debtor defaults.

guest—transient who contracts for a room or site at a hotel.

H

hearsay evidence—statements made out of court that are offered in court as proof of the information contained in the statements and that, subject to many exceptions, are not admissible in evidence.

holder—someone in possession of an instrument that runs to that person (i.e., is made payable to that person, is indorsed to that person, or is bearer paper).

holder in due course—a holder who has given value, taken in good faith without notice of dishonor, defenses, or that instrument is overdue, and who is afforded special rights or status.

holder through a holder in due course—holder of an instrument who attains holder-in-due-course status because a holder in due course has held it previous to him or her.

holographic will—unwitnessed will written by hand.

homeowners insurance policy—combination of standard fire insurance and comprehensive personal liability insurance.

hotelkeeper—one regularly engaged in the business of offering living accommodations to all transient persons.

hull insurance—insurance that covers physical damage on a freight-moving vessel.

I

identification—point in the transaction when the buyer acquires an interest in the goods subject to the contract.

identified—term applied to particular goods selected by either the buyer or the seller as the goods called for by the sales contract.

identity theft—use of another's credit tools, social security number, or other IDs to obtain cash, goods, or credit without permission.

illusory promise—promise that in fact does not impose any obligation on the promisor.

impeach—using prior inconsistent evidence to challenge the credibility of a witness.

implied contract—contract expressed by conduct or implied or deduced from the facts.

implied warranty—warranty that was not made but is implied by law.

implied warranty of merchantability—group of promises made by the seller, the most important of which is that the goods are fit for the ordinary purposes for which they are sold.

impostor rule—an exception to the rules on liability for forgery that covers situations such as the embezzling payroll clerk.

in pari delicto—equally guilty; used in reference to a transaction as to which relief will not be granted to either party because both are equally guilty of wrongdoing.

incidental authority—authority of an agent that is reasonably necessary to execute express authority.

incidental damages—incurred by the nonbreaching party as part of the process of trying to cover (buy substitute goods) or sell (selling subject matter of contract to another); includes storage fees, commissions, and the like.

income—money earned by the principal, or property in trust, and distributed by the trustee.

incontestability clause—provision that after the lapse of a specified time the insurer cannot dispute the policy on the ground of misrepresentation or fraud of the insured or similar wrongful conduct.

incorporation by reference—contract consisting of both the original or skeleton document and the detailed statement that is incorporated in it.

incorporator—one or more natural persons or corporations who sign and file appropriate incorporation forms with a designated government official.

indemnity—right of a person secondarily liable to require that a person primarily liable pay for loss sustained when the secondary party discharges the obligation that the primary party should have discharged; the right of an agent to be paid the amount of any loss or damage sustained without fault because of obedience to the principal's instructions; an undertaking by one person for a consideration to pay another person a sum of money to indemnify that person when a specified loss is incurred.

indemnity contract—agreement by one person, for consideration, to pay another person a sum of money in the event that the other person sustains a specified loss.

indenture trustee—usually a commercial banking institution, to represent the interests of the bondholders and ensure that the terms and covenants of the bond issue are met by the corporation.

independent contractor—contractor who undertakes to perform a specified task according to the terms of a contract but over whom the other contracting party has no control except as provided for by the contract.

indorsee—party to whom special indorsement is made.

indorsement—signature of the payee on an instrument.

indorser—secondary party (or obligor) on a note.

informal contract—simple oral or written contract.

informal settlements—negotiated disposition of a matter before an administrative agency, generally without public sanctions.

infringement—violation of trademarks, patents, or copyrights by copying or using material without permission.

injunction—order of a court of equity to refrain from doing (negative injunction) or to do

(affirmative or mandatory injunction) a specified act.

inland marine—insurance that covers domestic shipments of goods over land and inland waterways.

insider—full-time corporate employee or a director or their relatives.

insider information—privileged information on company business only known to employees.

insolvency—excess of debts and liabilities over assets, or inability to pay debts as they mature.

instruction—summary of the law given to jurors by the judge before deliberation begins.

insurable interest—the right to hold a valid insurance policy on a person or property.

insurance—a plan of security against risks by charging the loss against a fund created by the payments made by policyholders.

insurance agent—agent of an insurance company.

insurance broker—independent contractor who is not employed by any one insurance company.

insured—person to whom the promise in an insurance contract is made.

insurer—promisor in an insurance contract.

integrity—the adherence to one's values and principles despite the costs and consequences.

intellectual property rights—trademark, copyright, and patent rights protected by law.

intended beneficiary—third person of a contract whom the contract is intended to benefit.

intentional infliction of emotional distress—tort that produces mental anguish caused by conduct that exceeds all bounds of decency.

intentional tort—civil wrong that results from intentional conduct.

inter vivos gift—any transaction that takes place between living persons and creates rights prior to the death of any of them.

interest in the authority—form of agency in which an agent has been given or paid for the right to exercise authority.

interest in the subject matter—form of agency in which an agent is given an interest in the property with which that agent is dealing.

interlineation—writing between the lines or adding to the provisions of a document, the effect thereof depending upon the nature of the document.

intermediary bank—bank between the originator and the beneficiary bank in the transfer of funds.

interrogatories—written questions used as a discovery tool that must be answered under oath.

intestate—condition of dying without a will as to any property.

intestate succession—distribution, made as directed by statute, of a decedent's property not effectively disposed of by will.

invasion of privacy—tort of intentional intrusion into the private affairs of another.

investigative consumer report—report on a person based on personal investigation and interviews.

invitee—person who enters another's land by invitation.

involuntary bankruptcy—proceeding in which a creditor or creditors file the petition for relief with the bankruptcy court.

issuer—party who issues a document such as a letter of credit or a document of title such as a warehouse receipt or bill of lading.

J

joint tenancy—estate held jointly by two or more with the right of survivorship as between them, unless modified by statute.

joint venture—relationship in which two or more persons or firms combine their labor or property for a single undertaking and share profits and losses equally unless otherwise agreed.

judge—primary officer of the court.

judgment lien—lien by a creditor who has won a verdict against the landowner in court.

judgment n.o.v. (or *non obstante veredicto,* "notwithstanding the verdict") — a judgment entered after verdict upon the motion of the losing party on the ground that the verdict is so wrong that a judgment should be entered the opposite of the verdict.

judicial branch—the branch of government (courts) formed to interpret the laws.

judicial or execution sale—sale made under order of court by an officer appointed to make the sale or by an officer having such authority as incident to the office. The sale may have the effect of divesting liens on the property.

judicial triage—court management tool used by judges to expedite certain cases in which time is of the essence, such as asbestos cases in which the plaintiffs are gravely ill.

jurisdiction—the power of a court to hear and determine a given class of cases; the power to act over a particular defendant.

jurisdictional rule of reason—rule that balances the vital interests, including laws and policies, of the United States with those of a foreign country.

jury—a body of citizens sworn by a court to determine by verdict the issues of fact submitted to them.

L

land—earth, including all things embedded in or attached thereto, whether naturally or by the act of humans.

landlord—one who leases real property to another.

law—the order or pattern of rules that society establishes to govern the conduct of individuals and the relationships among them.

lease—agreement between the owner of property and a tenant by which the former agrees to give possession of the property to the latter in consideration of the payment of rent. (Parties—landlord or lessor, tenant or lessee)

leasehold estate—interest of a tenant in rented land.

legacy—gift of money made by will.

legal title—title held by the trustee in a trust situation.

legatee—beneficiary who receives a gift of personal property by will.

legislative branch—the branch of government (e.g., Congress) formed to make the laws.

lessee—one who has a possessory interest in real or personal property under a lease; a tenant.

lessor—one who conveys real or personal property by a lease; a landlord.

letter of credit—commercial device used to guarantee payment to a seller, primarily in an international business transaction.

letters of administration—written authorization given to an administrator of an estate as evidence of appointment and authority.

letters testamentary—written authorization given to an executor of an estate as evidence of appointment and authority.

liability insurance—covers the shipowner's liability if the ship causes damage to another ship or its cargo.

libel—written or visual defamation without legal justification.

license—personal privilege to do some act or series of acts upon the land of another, as the placing of a sign thereon, not amounting to an easement or a right of possession.

licensee—someone on another's premises with the permission of the occupier, whose duty is to warn the licensee of nonobvious dangers.

licensing—transfer of technology rights to a product so that it may be produced by a different business organization in a foreign country in exchange for royalties and other payments as agreed.

lien—claim or right, against property, existing by virtue of the entry of a judgment against its owner or by the entry of a judgment and a levy thereunder on the property, or because of the relationship of the claimant to the particular property, such as an unpaid seller.

life estate—an estate for the duration of a life.

limitation-of-liability clause—provision in a contract stating that one of the parties shall not be liable for damages in case of breach; also called an exculpatory clause.

limited covenant—any covenant that does not provide the complete protection of a full covenant.

limited defenses—defenses available to secondary parties if the presenting party is a holder in due course.

limited liability partnership (LLP)—partnership in which at least one partner has a liability limited to the loss of the capital contribution made to the partnership.

limited partner—partner who neither takes part in the management of the partnership nor appears to the public to be a general partner.

limited partnership—partnership that can be formed by "one or more general partners and one or more limited partners."

limited (special) jurisdiction—the authority to hear only particular kinds of cases.

limited warranty—any warranty that does not provide the complete protection of a full warranty.

lineals—relationship that exists when one person is a direct descendant of the other; also called lineal descendants.

liquidated damages—damages established in advance of breach as an alternative to establishing compensatory damages at the time of the breach.

liquidated damages clause—specification of exact compensation in case of a breach of contract.

liquidation—process of converting property into money whether of particular items of property or of all the assets of a business or an estate.

living trust—trust created to take effect within the lifetime of the settlor; also called inter vivos trust.

living will—document by which individuals may indicate that if they become unable to express their wishes and are in an irreversible, incurable condition, they do not want life-sustaining medical treatments.

living-document view—the term when a constitution is interpreted according to changes in conditions.

lottery—any plan by which a consideration is given for a chance to win a prize; it consists of three elements: (1) there must be a payment of money or something of value for an opportunity to win, (2) a prize must be available, and (3) the prize must be offered by lot or chance.

M

mailbox rule—timing for acceptance tied to proper acceptance.

maker—party who writes or creates a promissory note.

malpractice—when services are not properly rendered in accordance with commonly accepted standards; negligence by a professional in performing his or her skill.

marine insurance—policies that cover perils relating to the transportation of goods.

market power—the ability to control price and exclude competitors.

market value—price at which a share of stock can be voluntarily bought or sold in the open market.

mask work—specific form of expression embodied in a chip design, including the stencils used in manufacturing semiconductor chip products.

mass picketing—illegal tactic of employees massing together in great numbers to effectively shut down entrances of the employer's facility.

maturity date—date that a corporation is required to repay a loan to a bondholder.

means test—new standard under the Reform Act that requires the court to find that the debtor does not have the means to repay creditors; goes beyond the past requirement of petitions being granted on the simple assertion of the debtor saying, "I have debts."

mechanic's lien—protection afforded by statute to various kinds of laborers and persons supplying materials, by giving them a lien on the building and land that has been improved or added to by them.

mediation—the settlement of a dispute through the use of a messenger who carries to each side of the dispute the issues and offers in the case.

merchant—seller who deals in specific goods classified by the UCC.

merger (of corporations)—combining of corporations by which one absorbs the other and continues to exist, preserving its original charter and identity while the other corporation ceases to exist.

minitrial—a trial held on portions of the case or certain issues in the case.

Miranda *warnings*—warnings required to prevent self-incrimination in a criminal matter.

mirror image rule—common law contract rule on acceptance that requires language to be absolutely the same as the offer, unequivocal and unconditional.

misdemeanor—criminal offense with a sentence of less than one year that is neither treason nor a felony.

misrepresentation—false statement of fact made innocently without any intent to deceive.

mistrial—a court's declaration that terminates a trial and postpones it to a later date; commonly entered when evidence has been of a highly prejudicial character or when a juror has been guilty of misconduct.

money—medium of exchange.

money order—draft issued by a bank or a nonbank.

moral relativism—takes into account motivation and circumstance to determine whether an act was ethical.

mortgage—interest in land given by the owner to a creditor as security for the payment of the creditor for a debt, the nature of the interest depending upon the law of the state where the land is located. (Parties—mortgagor, mortgagee) *most-favored-nation clause*—clause in treaties between countries whereby any privilege subsequently granted to a third country in relation to a given treaty subject is extended to the other party to the treaty.

motion for summary judgment—request that the court decide a case on basis of law only because there are no material issues disputed by the parties.

motion to dismiss—a pleading that may be filed to attack the adverse party's pleading as not stating a cause of action or a defense.

N

National Environmental Policy Act (NEPA)—federal law that mandates study of a project's impact on the environment before it can be undertaken by any federal agency.

natural law—a system of principles to guide human conduct independent of, and sometimes contrary to, enacted law and discovered by man's rational intelligence.

necessaries—things indispensable or absolutely necessary for the sustenance of human life.

negligence—failure to exercise due care under the circumstances in consequence of which harm is proximately caused to one to whom the defendant owed a duty to exercise due care.

negotiability—quality of an instrument that affords special rights and standing.

negotiable bill of lading—document of title that by its terms calls for goods to be delivered "to the bearer" or "to the order of" a named person.

negotiable instruments—drafts, promissory notes, checks, and certificates of deposit that, in proper form, give special rights as "negotiable commercial paper."

negotiable warehouse receipt—receipt that states the covered goods will be delivered "to the bearer" or "to the order of."

negotiation—the transfer of commercial paper by indorsement and delivery by the person to whom it is then payable in the case of order paper and by physical transfer in the case of bearer paper.

Noise Control Act—federal law that controls noise emissions from low-flying aircraft.

nominal damages—nominal sum awarded the plaintiff in order to establish that legal rights have been violated although the plaintiff in fact has not sustained any actual loss or damages.

nonattainment areas—"dirty" areas that do not meet federal standards under the Clean Air Act.

nonconforming use—use of land that conflicts with a zoning ordinance at the time the ordinance goes into effect.

nonconsumer lease—lease that does not satisfy the definition of a consumer lease; also known as a commercial lease.

nonnegotiable bill of lading—See *Straight Bill of Lading.*

nonnegotiable instrument—contract, note, or draft that does not meet negotiability requirements of Article 3.

nonnegotiable warehouse receipt—receipt that states the covered goods received will be delivered to a specific person.

notice of dishonor—notice that an instrument has been dishonored; such notice can be oral, written, or electronic but is subject to time limitations.

notice statute—statute under which the last good faith or bona fide purchaser holds the title.

notice-race statute—statute under which the first bona fide purchaser to record the deed holds the title.

novation—substitution for an old contract with a new one that either replaces an existing obligation with a new obligation or replaces an original party with a new party.

nuisance—conduct that harms or prejudices another in the use of land or that harms or prejudices the public.

O

obligee—promisee who can claim the benefit of the obligation.

obligor—promisor.

ocean marine—policies that cover transportation of goods in vessels in international and coastal trade.

offer—expression of an offeror's willingness to enter into a contractual agreement.

offeree—person to whom an offer is made.

offeror—person who makes an offer.

Oil Pollution Act—federal law that assigns cleanup liability for oil spills in U.S. waters.

ombudsman—a government official or organization employee designated by statute or the organization/company to examine citizen and/or employee complaints.

open meeting law—law that requires advance notice of agency meeting and public access.

opening statements—statements by opposing attorneys that tell the jury what their cases will prove.

operation of law—attaching of certain consequences to certain facts because of legal principles that operate automatically as contrasted with consequences that arise because of the voluntary action of a party designed to create those consequences.

option contract—contract to hold an offer to make a contract open for a fixed period of time.

order of relief—the order from the bankruptcy judge that starts the protection for the debtor; when the order of relief is entered by the court, the debtor's creditors must stop all proceedings and work through the bankruptcy court to recover debts (if possible). Court finding that creditors have met the standards for bankruptcy petitions.

order paper—instrument payable to the order of a party.

original jurisdiction—the authority to hear a controversy when it is first brought to court.

originator—party who originates the funds transfer.

output contract—contract of a producer to sell its entire production or output to a buyer.

outstanding—name for shares of a company that have been issued to stockholders.

overdraft—negative balance in a drawer's account.

P

par value—specified monetary amount assigned by an issuing corporation for each share of its stock.

parol evidence rule—rule that prohibits the introduction into evidence of oral or written statements made prior to or contemporaneously with the execution of a complete written contract, deed, or instrument, in the absence of clear proof of fraud, accident, or mistake causing the omission of the statement in question.

partially disclosed principal—principal whose existence is made known but whose identity is not.

partner—one of two or more persons who jointly own and carry on a business for profit.

partnership—pooling of capital resources and the business or professional talents of two or more individuals (partners) with the goal of making a profit.

partnership agreement—document prepared to evidence the contract of the parties. (Parties—partners or general partners)

party—person involved in a legal transaction; may be a natural person, an artificial person (e.g., a corporation), or an unincorporated enterprise (e.g., a government agency).

past consideration—something that has been performed in the past and which, therefore, cannot be consideration for a promise made in the present.

payable to order—term stating that a negotiable instrument is payable to the order of any person described in it or to a person or order.

payee—party to whom payment is to be made.

payment order—direction given by an originator to his or her bank or by any bank to a subsequent bank to make a specified funds transfer.

per capita—method of distributing estate assets on an equal-per-person basis.

per stirpes—method for distribution of an estate that divides property equally down family lines.

perfected security interest—security interest with priority because of filing, possession, automatic or temporary priority status.

periodic tenancy—tenancy that continues indefinitely for a specified rental period until terminated; often called a month-to- month tenancy.

personal property—property that is movable or intangible, or rights in such things.

personal representative—administrator or executor who represents decedents under UPC.

physical duress—threat of physical harm to person or property.

plaintiff—the party who initiates a lawsuit.

pleadings—the papers filed by the parties in an action in order to set forth the facts and frame the issues to be tried, although, under some systems, the pleadings merely give notice or a general indication of the nature of the issues.

pledge—bailment given as security for the payment of a debt or the performance of an obligation owed to the pledgee. (Parties—pledgor, pledgee)

police power—the power to govern; the power to adopt laws for the protection of the public health, welfare, safety, and morals.

policy—paper evidencing the contract of insurance.

positive law—law enacted and codified by governmental authority.

possession—exclusive dominion and control of property.

possibility of reverter—nature of the interest held by the grantor after conveying land outright but subject to a condition or provision that may cause the grantee's interest to become forfeited and the interest to revert to the grantor or heirs.

postdate—to insert or place on an instrument a later date than the actual date on which it was executed.

power of attorney—written authorization to an agent by the principal.

precedent—a decision of a court that stands as the law for a particular problem in the future.

predatory lending—a practice on the part of the subprime lending market whereby lenders take advantage of less sophisticated consumers or those who are desperate for funds by using the lenders' superior bargaining positions to obtain credit terms that go well beyond compensating them for their risk.

predicate act—qualifying underlying offense for RICO liability.

preemption—the federal government's superior regulatory position over state laws on the same subject area.

preemptive right—shareholder's right upon the increase of a corporation's capital stock to be allowed to subscribe to such a percentage of the new shares as the shareholder's old shares bore to the former total capital stock.

preferences—transfers of property by a debtor to one or more specific creditors to enable these creditors to obtain payment for debts owed.

preferential transfers—certain transfers of money or security interests in the time frame just prior to bankruptcy that can be set aside if voidable.

preferred stock—stock that has a priority or preference as to payment of dividends or upon liquidation, or both.

prescription—acquisition of a right to use the land of another, as an easement, by making hostile, visible, and notorious use of the land, continuing for the period specified by the local law.

presentment—formal request for payment on an instrument.

price discrimination—the charging practice by a seller of different prices to different buyers for commodities of similar grade and quality, resulting in reduced competition or a tendency to create a monopoly.

prima facie—evidence that, if believed, is sufficient by itself to lead to a particular conclusion.

primary party—party to whom the holder or holder in due course must turn first to obtain payment.

primary picketing—legal presentations in front of a business notifying the public of a labor dispute.

primum non nocere—"above all do no harm."

principal—person or firm who employs an agent; person who, with

respect to a surety, is primarily liable to the third person or creditor; property held in trust.

principal debtor—original borrower or debtor.

prior art—a showing that an invention as a whole would have been obvious to a person of ordinary skill in the art when the invention was patented

private carrier—carrier owned by the shipper, such as a company's own fleet of trucks.

private corporation—corporation organized for charitable and benevolent purposes or for purposes of finance, industry, and commerce.

private law—the rules and regulations parties agree to as part of their contractual relationships.

private nuisance—nuisance that affects only one or a few individuals.

privileges and immunities clause—a clause that entitles a person going into another state to make contracts, own property, and engage in business to the same extent as citizens of that state.

privity—succession or chain of relationship to the same thing or right, such as privity of contract, privity of estate, privity of possession.

privity of contract—relationship between a promisor and the promisee.

privity rule—succession or chain of relationship to the same thing or right, such as privity of contract, privity of estate, privity of possession.

pro rata—proportionately, or divided according to a rate or standard.

probate—procedure for formally establishing or proving that a given writing is the last will and testament of the person who purportedly signed it.

procedural law—the law that must be followed in enforcing rights and liabilities.

process—paperwork served personally on a defendant in a civil case.

product disparagement—false statements made about a product or business.

profit—right to take a part of the soil or produce of another's land, such as timber or water.

promisee—person to whom a promise is made.

promisor—person who makes a promise.

promissory estoppel—doctrine that a promise will be enforced although it is not supported by consideration when the promisor should have reasonably expected that the promise would induce action or forbearance of a definite and substantial character on the part of the promised and injustice can be avoided only by enforcement of the promise.

promissory note—unconditional promise in writing made by one person to another, signed by the maker engaging to pay on demand, or at a definite time, a sum certain in money to order or to bearer. (Parties—maker, payee)

promoters—persons who plan the formation of the corporation and sell or promote the idea to others.

proof of claim—written statement, signed by the creditor or an authorized representative, setting forth any claim made against the debtor and the basis for it.

property report—condensed version of a property development statement filed with the secretary of HUD and given to a prospective customer at least 48 hours before signing a contract to buy or lease property.

prosecutor—party who originates a criminal proceeding.

prospectus—information provided to each potential purchaser of securities setting forth the key information contained in the registration statement.

proxy—written authorization by a shareholder to another person to vote the stock owned by the shareholder; the person who is the holder of such a written authorization.

public corporation—corporation that has been established for governmental purposes and for the administration of public affairs.

public nuisance—nuisance that affects the community or public at large.

public policy—certain objectives relating to health, morals, and integrity of government that the law seeks to advance by declaring invalid any contract that conflicts with those objectives even though there is no statute expressly declaring such a contract illegal.

public warehouses—entities that serve the public generally without discrimination.

pump-and-dump—self-touting a stock to drive its price up and then selling it.

punitive damages—damages, in excess of those required to compensate the plaintiff for the wrong done, that are imposed in order to punish the defendant because of the particularly wanton or willful character of wrongdoing; also called exemplary damages.

purchase money security interest (PMSI)—the security interest in the goods a seller sells on credit that become the collateral for the creditor/seller.

Q

qualified indorsement—an indorsement that includes words such as "without recourse" that disclaims certain liability of the indorser to a maker or a drawee.

qualified privilege—media privilege to print inaccurate information without liability for defamation, so long as a

retraction is printed and there was no malice.

quantum meruit—"as much as deserved;" an action brought for the value of the services rendered the defendant when there was no express contract as to the purchase price.

quasi contract—court-imposed obligation to prevent unjust enrichment in the absence of a contract.

quasi-judicial proceedings—forms of hearings in which the rules of evidence and procedure are more relaxed but each side still has a chance to be heard.

quasi-public corporation—private corporation furnishing services on which the public is particularly dependent, for example, a gas and electric company.

quitclaim deed—deed by which the grantor purports to give up only whatever right or title the grantor may have in the property without specifying or warranting transfer of any particular interest.

quorum—minimum number of persons, shares represented, or directors who must be present at a meeting in order to lawfully transact business.

R

race statute—statute under which the first party to record the deed holds the title.

race-notice statute—See *Notice-Race Statute.*

Racketeer Influenced and Corrupt Organizations (RICO) Act—federal law, initially targeting organized crime, that has expanded in scope and provides penalties and civil recovery for multiple criminal offenses, or a pattern of racketeering.

real property—land and all rights in land.

recognizance—obligation entered into before a court to do some act,

such as to appear at a later date for a hearing. Also called a *contract of record.*

recorder—public official in charge of deeds.

recross-examination—an examination by the other side's attorney that follows the redirect examination.

redemption—buying back of one's property, which has been sold because of a default, upon paying the amount that had been originally due together with interest and costs.

redirect examination—questioning after cross-examination, in which the attorney for the witness testifying may ask the same witness other questions to overcome effects of the cross-examination.

reference to a third person—settlement that allows a nonparty to resolve the dispute.

reformation—remedy by which a written instrument is corrected when it fails to express the actual intent of both parties because of fraud, accident, or mistake.

registered bonds—bonds held by owners whose names and addresses are registered on the books of the corporation.

registration requirements—provisions of the Securities Act of 1933 requiring advance disclosure to the public of a new securities issue through filing a statement with the SEC and sending a prospectus to each potential purchaser.

registration statement—document disclosing specific financial information regarding the security, the issuer, and the underwriter.

remainder interest—land interest that follows a life estate.

remand—term used when an appellate court sends a case back to trial court for additional hearings or a new trial.

remedy—action or procedure that is followed in order to enforce a right or to obtain damages for injury to a right.

rent-a-judge plan—dispute resolution through private courts with judges paid to be referees for the cases.

representative capacity—action taken by one on behalf of another, as the act of a personal representative on behalf of a decedent's estate, or action taken both on one's behalf and on behalf of others, as a shareholder bringing a representative action.

repudiation—result of a buyer or seller refusing to perform the contract as stated.

request for production of documents—discovery tool for uncovering paper evidence in a case.

requirements contract—contract in which the buyer buys its needs (requirements) from the seller.

rescission—action of one party to a contract to set the contract aside when the other party is guilty of a breach of the contract.

reservation of rights—assertion by a party to a contract that even though a tendered performance (e.g., a defective product) is accepted, the right to damages for nonconformity to the contract is reserved.

Resource Conservation and Recovery Act (RCRA)—federal law that regulates the disposal of potentially harmful substances and encourages resource conservation and recovery.

Resource Recovery Act—early federal solid waste disposal legislation that provided funding for states and local governments with recycling programs.

respondeat superior—doctrine that the principal or employer is vicariously liable for the unauthorized torts committed by an agent or employee while acting within the scope of the agency

or the course of the employment, respectively.

restrictive covenants—covenants in a deed by which the grantee agrees to refrain from doing specified acts.

restrictive indorsement—an indorsement that restricts further transfer, such as in trust for or to the use of some other person, is conditional, or for collection or deposit.

reverse—the term used when the appellate court sets aside the verdict or judgment of a lower court.

reverse mortgage—mortgage in which the owners get their equity out of their home over a period of time and return the house to the lender upon their deaths.

reversible error—an error or defect in court proceedings of so serious a nature that on appeal the appellate court will set aside the proceedings of the lower court.

reversionary interest—interest that a lessor has in property that is subject to an outstanding lease.

revoke—testator's act of taking back his or her will and its provisions.

right—legal capacity to require another person to perform or refrain from an action.

right of escheat—right of the state to take the property of a decedent that has not been distributed.

right of first refusal—right of a party to meet the terms of a proposed contract before it is executed, such as a real estate purchase agreement.

right of privacy—the right to be free from unreasonable intrusion by others.

right to cure—second chance for a seller to make a proper tender of conforming goods.

right-to-work laws—laws restricting unions and employees from negotiating clauses in their collective

bargaining agreements that make union membership compulsory.

risk—peril or contingency against which the insured is protected by the contract of insurance.

risk of loss—in contract performance, the cost of damage or injury to the goods contracted for.

Robinson-Patman Act—a federal statute designed to eliminate price discrimination in interstate commerce.

run with the land—concept that certain covenants in a deed to land are deemed to run or pass with the land so that whoever owns the land is bound by or entitled to the benefit of the covenants.

S

Safe Drinking Water Act—a federal law that establishes national standards for contaminants in drinking water.

sale on approval—term indicating that no sale takes place until the buyer approves or accepts the goods.

sale or return—sale in which the title to the property passes to the buyer at the time of the transaction but the buyer is given the option of returning the property and restoring the title to the seller.

search engine—Internet service used to locate Web sites.

search warrant—judicial authorization for a search of property where there is the expectation of privacy.

seasonable—timely.

secondary meaning—a legal term signifying the words in question have taken on a new meaning with the public, capable of serving a source-identifying function of a mark.

secondary parties—called secondary obligors under Revised Article 3; parties to an instrument to whom holders turn when the primary party, for whatever reason, fails to pay the instrument.

secondary picketing—picketing an employer with which a union has no dispute to persuade the employer to stop doing business with a party to the dispute; generally illegal under the NLRA.

secrecy laws—confidentiality laws applied to home-country banks.

secured party—person owed the money, whether as a seller or a lender, in a secured transaction in personal property.

secured transaction—credit sale of goods or a secured loan that provides special protection for the creditor.

securities—stocks and bonds issued by a corporation. Under some investor protection laws, the term includes any interest in an enterprise that provides unearned income to its owner.

security agreement—agreement of the creditor and the debtor that the creditor will have a security interest.

security interest—property right that enables the creditor to take possession of the property if the debtor does not pay the amount owed.

self-help repossession—creditor's right to repossess the collateral without judicial proceedings.

self-proved wills—wills that eliminate some formalities of proof by being executed according to statutory requirements.

selling on consignment—entrusting a person with possession of property for the purpose of sale.

semiconductor chip product—product placed on a piece of semiconductor material in accordance with a predetermined pattern that is intended to perform electronic circuitry functions.

service mark—mark that identifies a service.

servient tenement—land that is subject to an easement.

settlor—one who settles property in trust or creates a trust estate.

severalty—ownership of property by one person.

shared powers—powers that are held by both state and national governments.

Sherman Antitrust Act—a federal statute prohibiting combinations and contracts in restraint of interstate trade, now generally inapplicable to labor union activity.

shop right—right of an employer to use in business without charge an invention discovered by an employee during working hours and with the employer's material and equipment.

shopkeeper's privilege—right of a store owner to detain a suspected shoplifter based on reasonable cause and for a reasonable time without resulting liability for false imprisonment.

short-swing profit—profit realized by a corporate insider from selling securities less than six months after purchase.

sinking fund—fixed amount of money set aside each year by the borrowing corporation toward the ultimate payment of bonds.

situational ethics—a flexible standard of ethics that permits an examination of circumstances and motivation before attaching the label of right or wrong to conduct.

Sixth Amendment—the U.S. constitutional amendment that guarantees a speedy trial.

slander—defamation of character by spoken words or gestures.

slander of title—malicious making of false statements as to a seller's title.

small claims courts—courts that resolve disputes between parties when those disputes do not exceed a minimal

level; no lawyers are permitted; the parties represent themselves.

sole or individual proprietorship—form of business ownership in which one individual owns the business.

soliciting agent—salesperson.

sovereign compliance doctrine—doctrine that allows a defendant to raise as an affirmative defense to an antitrust action the fact that the defendant's actions were compelled by a foreign state.

sovereign immunity doctrine—doctrine that states that a foreign sovereign generally cannot be sued unless an exception to the Foreign Sovereign Immunities Act of 1976 applies.

special agent—agent authorized to transact a specific transaction or to do a specific act.

special drawing rights (SDRs)—rights that allow a country to borrow enough money from other International Money Fund (IMF) members to permit that country to maintain the stability of its currency's relationship to other world currencies.

special indorsement—an indorsement that specifies the person to whom the instrument is indorsed.

specific legacies—identified property bequeathed by a testator; also called specific devises.

specific lien—right of a creditor to hold particular property or assert a lien on particular property of the debtor because of the creditor's having done work on or having some other association with the property, as distinguished from having a lien generally against the assets of the debtor merely because the debtor is indebted to the lien holder.

specific performance—action brought to compel the adverse party to perform a contract on the theory that merely suing for damages for its breach will not be an adequate remedy.

spendthrift trust—a trust that, to varying degrees, provides that creditors of the beneficiary shall not be able to reach the principal or income held by the trustee and that the beneficiary shall not be able to assign any interest in the trust.

spot zoning—allowing individual variation in zoning.

stakeholder analysis—the term used when a decision maker views a problem from different perspectives and measures the impact of a decision on various groups.

stakeholders—those who have a stake, or interest, in the activities of a corporation; stakeholders include employees, members of the community in which the corporation operates, vendors, customers, and any others who are affected by the actions and decisions of the corporation.

stale check—a check whose date is longer than six months ago.

standby letter—letter of credit for a contractor ensuring he will complete the project as contracted.

stare decisis—"let the decision stand" ; the principle that the decision of a court should serve as a guide or precedent and control the decision of a similar case in the future.

status quo ante—original positions of the parties.

statute of frauds—statute that, in order to prevent fraud through the use of perjured testimony, requires that certain kinds of transactions be evidenced in writing in order to be binding or enforceable.

statute of limitations—statute that restricts the period of time within which an action may be brought.

statutory law—legislative acts declaring, commanding, or prohibiting something.

stay of foreclosure—delay of foreclosure obtained by the mortgagor to prevent undue hardship.

stirpes—family lines; distribution per stirpes refers to the manner in which descendants take property by right of representation.

stock subscription—contract or agreement to buy a specific number and kind of shares when they are issued by the corporation.

stop payment order—order by a depositor to the bank to refuse to make payment of a check when presented for payment.

straight (or nonnegotiable) bill of lading—document of title that consigns transported goods to a named person.

strict liability—civil wrong for which there is absolute liability because of the inherent danger in the underlying activity, for example, the use of explosives.

strict tort liability—product liability theory that imposes liability upon the manufacturer, seller, or distributor of goods for harm caused by defective goods.

subject matter jurisdiction—judicial authority to hear a particular type of case.

sublease—a transfer of the premises by the lessee to a third person, the sublessee or subtenant, for a period of less than the term of the original lease.

sublessee—person with lease rights for a period of less than the term of the original lease; also known as subtenant.

subprime lending market—a credit market that makes loans to high-risk consumers (those who have bankruptcies, no credit history, or a poor credit history), often loaning money to pay off other debts the consumer has due.

subrogation—right of a party secondarily liable to stand in the place of the creditor after making payment to the creditor and to enforce the creditor's

right against the party primarily liable in order to obtain indemnity from such primary party.

substantial impairment—material defect in a good.

substantial performance—equitable rule that if a good-faith attempt to perform does not precisely meet the terms of the agreement, the agreement will still be considered complete if the essential purpose of the contract is accomplished.

substantive law—the law that defines rights and liabilities.

substitute check—electronic image of a paper check that a bank can create and that has the same legal effect as the original instrument.

substitution—substitution of a new contract between the same parties.

sum certain—amount due under an instrument that can be computed from its face with only reference to interest rates.

summary jury trial—a mock or dry-run trial for parties to get a feel for how their cases will play to a jury.

summation—the attorney address that follows all the evidence presented in court and sums up a case and recommends a particular verdict be returned by the jury.

Superfund Amendment and Reauthorization Act—federal law that authorizes the EPA to collect cleanup costs from those responsible for the ownership, leasing, dumping, or security of hazardous waste sites.

Superfund sites—areas designated by the EPA for cleanup of hazardous waste.

surety—obligor of a suretyship; primarily liable for the debt or obligation of the principal debtor.

suretyship—undertaking to pay the debt or be liable for the default of another.

symbolic delivery—delivery of goods by delivery of the means of control, such as a key or a relevant document of title, such as a negotiable bill of lading; also called constructive delivery.

T

takeover laws—laws that guard against unfairness in corporate takeover situations.

tariff—(1) domestically—government-approved schedule of charges that may be made by a regulated business, such as a common carrier or warehouser; (2) internationally—tax imposed by a country on goods crossing its borders, without regard to whether the purpose is to raise revenue or to discourage the traffic in the taxed goods.

tax lien—lien on property by a government agency for nonpayment of taxes.

teller's check—draft drawn by a bank on another bank in which it has an account.

temporary insider—someone retained by a corporation for professional services on an as-needed basis, such as an attorney, accountant, or investment banker.

temporary perfection—perfection given for a limited period of time to creditors.

tenancy at sufferance—lease arrangement in which the tenant occupies the property at the discretion of the landlord.

tenancy at will—holding of land for an indefinite period that may be terminated at any time by the landlord or by the landlord and tenant acting together.

tenancy by entirety or tenancy by entireties—transfer of property to both husband and wife.

tenancy for years—tenancy for a fixed period of time, even though the time is less than a year.

tenancy in common—relationship that exists when two or more persons own undivided interests in property.

tenancy in partnership—ownership relationship that exists between partners under the Uniform Partnership Act.

tenant—one who holds or possesses real property by any kind of right or title; one who pays rent for the temporary use and occupation of another's real property under a lease.

tender—goods have arrived, are available for pickup, and buyer is notified.

term insurance—policy written for a specified number of years that terminates at the end of that period.

termination statement—document (record), which may be requested by a paid-up debtor, stating that a security interest is no longer claimed under the specified financing statement.

testamentary capacity—sufficient mental capacity to understand that a writing being executed is a will and what that entails.

testamentary intent—designed to take effect at death, as by disposing of property or appointing a personal representative.

testamentary trust—trust that becomes effective only when the settlor's will takes effect after death.

testate—condition of leaving a will upon death.

testate distribution—distribution of an estate in accordance with the will of the decedent.

testator, testatrix—man, woman who makes a will.

third-party beneficiary—third person whom the parties to a contract intend to benefit by the making of the contract and to confer upon such person the right to sue for breach of contract.

time draft—bill of exchange payable at a stated time after sight or at a definite time.

tippee—individual who receives information about a corporation from an insider or temporary insider.

tort—civil wrong that interferes with one's property or person.

Toxic Substances Control Act (TOSCA)—first federal law to control the manufacture, use, and disposal of toxic substances.

trade dress—product's total image including its overall packaging look.

trade libel—written defamation about a product or service.

trade name—name under which a business is carried on and, if fictitious, must be registered.

trade secret—any formula, device, or compilation of information that is used in one's business and is of such a nature that it provides an advantage over competitors who do not have the information.

trademark—mark that identifies a product.

transferee—buyer or vendee.

traveler's check—check that is payable on demand provided it is countersigned by the person whose specimen signature appears on the check.

treasury stock—corporate stock that the corporation has reacquired.

treble damages—three times the damages actually sustained.

trespass—an unauthorized action with respect to person or property.

trial de novo—a trial required to preserve the constitutional right to a jury trial by allowing an appeal to proceed as though there never had been any prior hearing or decision.

tripartite—three-part division (of government).

trust—transfer of property by one person to another with the understanding or declaration that such property be held for the benefit of another; the holding of property by the owner in trust for another, upon a declaration of trust, without a transfer to another person. (Parties—settlor, trustee, beneficiary)

trust agreement—instrument creating a trust; also called deed of trust.

trust corpus—fund or property that is transferred to the trustee or held by the settlor as the body or subject matter of the trust; also called *trust fund, trust estate,* and *trust res.*

trustee—party who has legal title to estate and manages it.

trustee in bankruptcy—impartial person elected to administer the debtor's estate.

trustor—donor or settlor who is the owner of property and creates a trust in the property.

tying—the anticompetitive practice of requiring buyers to purchase one product in order to get another.

U

ultra vires—act or contract that the corporation does not have authority to do or make.

unconscionable—unreasonable, not guided or restrained by conscience and often referring to a contract grossly unfair to one party because of the superior bargaining powers of the other party.

underwriter—insurer.

undisclosed principal—principal on whose behalf an agent acts without disclosing to the third person the fact of agency or the identity of the principal.

undue influence—influence that is asserted upon another person by one who dominates that person.

Uniform Probate Code (UPC)—uniform statute on wills and administration of estates.

Uniform Simultaneous Death Act—law providing that when survivorship

cannot be established, the property of each person shall be disposed of as though he or she had survived the other.

unilateral contract—contract under which only one party makes a promise.

unincorporated association—combination of two or more persons for the furtherance of a common nonprofit purpose.

universal agent—agent authorized by the principal to do all acts that can lawfully be delegated to a representative.

universal defenses—defenses that are regarded as so basic that the social interest in preserving them outweighs the social interest of giving negotiable instruments the freely transferable qualities of money; accordingly, such defenses are given universal effect and may be raised against all holders.

USA Patriot Act—federal law that, among other things, imposes reporting requirements on banks.

usage of trade—language and customs of an industry.

usury—lending money at an interest rate that is higher than the maximum rate allowed by law.

uttering—crime of issuing or delivering a forged instrument to another person.

V

valid—legal.

valid contract—agreement that is binding and enforceable.

value—consideration or antecedent debt or security given in exchange for the transfer of a negotiable instrument or creation of a security interest.

variance—permission of a landowner to use the land in a specified manner that is inconsistent with the zoning ordinance.

vicarious liability—imposing liability for the fault of another.

void agreement—agreement that cannot be enforced.

voidable contract—agreement that is otherwise binding and enforceable but may be rejected at the option of one of the parties as the result of specific circumstances.

voidable title—title of goods that carries with it the contingency of an underlying problem.

voir dire examination—the preliminary examination of a juror or a witness to ascertain fitness to act as such.

voluntary bankruptcy—proceeding in which the debtor files the petition for relief.

voting by proxy—authorizing someone else to vote the shares owned by the shareholder.

voting trust—transfer by two or more persons of their shares of stock of a corporation to a trustee who is to vote the shares and act for such shareholders.

W

waiver—release or relinquishment of a known right or objection.

warehouse—entity engaged in the business of storing the goods of others for compensation.

warehouse receipt—receipt issued by the warehouse for stored goods. Regulated by the UCC, which clothes the receipt with some degree of negotiability.

warrant—authorization via court order to search private property for tools or evidence of a crime.

warranty—promise either express or implied about the nature, quality, or performance of the goods.

warranty against encumbrances—warranty that there are no liens or other encumbrances to goods except those noted by seller.

warranty deed—deed by which the grantor conveys a specific estate or interest to the grantee and makes one or more of the covenants of title.

warranty of habitability—implied warranty that the leased property is fit for dwelling by tenants.

warranty of title—implied warranty that title to the goods is good and transfer is proper.

wasting assets corporation—corporation designed to exhaust or use up the assets of the corporation, such as by extracting oil, coal, iron, and other ores.

way of necessity—grantee's right to use land retained by the grantor for going to and from the conveyed land.

White-Collar Crime Penalty Enhancement Act of 2002—federal reforms passed as a result of the collapses of companies such as Enron; provides for longer sentences and higher fines for both executives and companies.

white-collar crimes—crimes that do not use nor threaten to use force or violence or do not cause injury to persons or property.

whole life insurance—ordinary life insurance providing lifetime insurance protection.

will—instrument executed with the formality required by law by which a person makes a disposition of his or her property to take effect upon death.

writ of certiorari—order by the U.S. Supreme Court granting a right of review by the court of a lower court decision.

wrongfully dishonored—error by a bank in refusing to pay a check.

Z

zoning—restrictions imposed by government on the use of designated land to ensure an orderly physical development of the regulated area.

Opinion cases are in italic type for the case summary; cited cases are in roman type. Cases new to this edition are in red.

14 Penn Plaza, LLC v Pyett, 938

1-800 Contacts, Inc. v Weigner, 296

35 Park Ave. Corp. v Campagna, 1214

99 Commercial Street, Inc. v Goldberg, 1104

A

A. B. & S. Auto Service, Inc. v South Shore Bank of Chicago, 752

A. E. Staley Manufacturing Co. v Chao, 920

Abbot v Schnader, Harrison, Segal & Lewis, LLP, 381

Abbott Thinlite Corp. v Redmont, 1159

ABC Metals & Recycling Co., Inc. v Highland Computer Forms, Inc., 513

Abeles Inc. v Creekstone Farms Premium Beef, LLC, 965

Abrahim & Sons, Inc. v Equilon Enterprises, LLC, 1020

Abrams v General Start Indemnity, 537

Accurate Printers, Inc. v Stark, 1032

Ackerley Media Group, Inc. v Sharp Electronics Corp., 305

Acushnet Company v Mohasco, 1194

Adams v Lindsell, 298

Adams v National Engineering Service Corp., 742

Adams v Uno Restaurants, Inc., 898–899

Adams v Wacaster Oil Co., Inc., 585

Adams Outdoor Adv., Ltd., Part. v Long, 1188

Adarand Constructors, Inc. v Pena (Adarand I), 947

Adbar v New Beginnings, 431–432

Adcock v Ramtreat Metal Technology, Inc., 617

ADP Marshall, Inc. v Brown University, 277

Advanced Alloys, Inc. v Sergeant Steel Corp., 712

Aetna Casualty & Surety Co. v Garza, 828

Aetna Chemical Co. v Spaulding & Kimball Co., 594

Affiliated FM Ins. Co. v Constitution Reinsurance Corp., 385

Affinity Internet v Consolidated Credit, 382

AgGrow Oils, LLC v National Union Fire Ins., 393

Agriliance, LLC v Farmpro Services, Inc., 668

AIG Global Securities Lending Corp. v Banc of America Securities LLC, 675

AIG, Inc. v Greenberg, 1070, 1077, 1113

Airline Construction, Inc. v Barr, 378–379

Akron v Akron Center for Reproductive Health, Inc., 79

Alamance County Board of Education v Bobby Murray Chevrolet, Inc., 593

Alamo Rent-A-Car v Mendenhall, 551

Albemale Paper Co. v Moody, 942

Aldrich & Co. v Donovan, 327

Alexander v Chandler, 856

Alexander v Gardner-Denver Co., 938

Alfred v Capital Area Soccer League, Inc., 197

Alien, Inc. v Futterman, 731

Allegheny Ludlum Corp. v United States, 144

Allied Capital Partners L.P. v Bank One, Texas, N.A., 662

Allied Grape Growers v Bronco Wine Co., 519

Allright, Inc. v Schroeder, 477

Allstate Ins. Co. v Winnebago County Fair Ass'n, Inc., 499–500

Allstate Life Ins. Co. v Miller, 838

Alpert v 28 Williams Street Corp., 1052

Altera Corp. v Clear Logic Inc., 235

Am South Bank v Holland, 1041

Amato v KPMG LLP, 1114

Ameral v Pray, 197

America Online, Inc. v Anonymous Publicly Traded Co., 263–264

American Bank & Trust Co. v Koplik, 429

American Chocolates, Inc. v Mascot Pecan Co., Inc., 862

American Concept Ins. Co. v Lloyds of London, 835

American Cyanamid Co. v New Penn Motor Express, Inc., 498

American Family Mutual Ins. Co. v Shelter Mutual Ins. Co., 836

American Geophysical Union v Texaco Inc., 223

American Home Insurance Co. v First Speciality Insurance Corp., 835

American National Ins. Co. v Gilroy Associates, Ltd., 1016, 1026

American Nat'l Bank v Touche Ross & Co., 1123

American Power & Light Co. v Securities and Exchange Commission, 72

American Security Services, Inc. v Vodra, 364–365

American Standard Inc. v Meehan, 969

American States Insurance Co. v Capital Associates of Jackson County Inc., 832

American Telephone and Telegraph Co. v Hitachi, 152

American Tempering, Inc. v Craft Architectural Metals Corp., 510

American Truck Lines, Inc. v Albino, 1032

American Trucking Associations, Inc. v Michigan Public Service Com'n, 83

American United Logistics, Inc. v Catellus, 394

American Vending Services, Inc. v Morse, 1042

Amex Life Assurance Co. v Superior Court, 838

Amica Life Insurance Co. v Barbor, 837

Amoco Oil Co. v DZ Enterprises, Inc., 493

Amstar Corp. v Domino's Pizza Inc., 215

Amwest Sur. Ins. Co. v Concord Bank, 728

Andersen, LLP v US, 1128

Anderson v Bellino, 1149

Anderson v Little League Baseball, Inc., 1222

Anderson Development Co. v Travelers Indemnity Co., 831

Andres v Roswell-Windsor Village Apartments, 1231

Andrews v Elwell, 988

Animazing Entertainment, Inc. v Louis Lofredo Associates, Inc., 1043

Anonymous v Anonymous, 353

Antaeus Enterprises, Inc. v SD-Barn Real Estate, LLC, 646

Any Kind Checks Cashed, Inc. v Talcott, 670–671, 680

Aon Risk Services, Inc. v Meadors, 273, 280

Apache Bohai Corp. LDC v Texaco China BV, 30

APL Co. Pte. Ltd. v UK Aerosols Ltd., Inc., 543

Apodaca v Discover Financial Services, 756

Apple Computer Inc. v Franklin Computer Corp., 232, 236

Application of Mostek Corp., 36–37

Arban v West Publishing Co., 917

Arciniaga v General Motors Corp., 970

Arcor, Inc. v Haas, 357

Arcor Inc., 358

Ardito et al. v City of Providence, 281

Ardus Medical, Inc. v Emanuel County Hospital Authority, 508

Arias v Mutual Central Alarm Services, Inc., 924

Aries Information Systems, Inc. v Pacific Management Systems Corp., 239–240

Arizona Public Service v Apache County, 802

Arizona v Gant, 177

Armstrong v Guccione, 114

Arnlund v Deloitte & Touche LLP, 1134

Aronow v Silver, 462–463

Arthur Andersen LLP v U.S., 170

Artromick International, Inc. v Koch, 401

Arvest Bank v SpiritBank, N.A., 777

Arya Group, Inc. v Cher, 275–276

Ashcroft v Free Speech Coalition, 257

Asher v Chase Bank USA, N.A., 750

Aslakson v Home Savings Ass'n, 399

Aspen Skiing Co. v Aspen Highlands Skiing Corp., 102–103

Associated Industries of Missouri v Lohman, 78

Associates Home Equity Services, Inc. v Troup, 669

AT&T Corporation v Hulteen, 941

Atlas Construction Co., Inc. v Aqua Drilling Co., 334

Attia v New York Hospital, 220

Auffert v Auffert, 467–468

AUSA Life Insurance Co. v Ernst & Young, 1118, 1131

Austin v New Hampshire, 86

Austin v Will-Burt Company, 570–571, 573

A.V. v iParadigms, LLC, 252, 297

Avery v Aladdin Products Div., Nat'l Service Industries, Inc., 575–576

Avery v Whitworth, 638

Aydin Corp. v First State Ins. Co., 831

B

B. P. Dev. & Management Corp. v Lafer Enterprises, Inc., 593–594

Babbitt v Sweet Home Chapter of Communities for a Great Oregon, 1197

Baca v Trejo, 298

Backman v Lawrence, 1165

Bacon & Associates, Inc. v Rolly Tasker Sails Co. Ltd. (Thailand), 493

Badger v Paulson Investment Co., 856

Baehr v Penn-O-Tex Corp., 345

Baena Brothers v Welge, 477

Bailey v Myers, 1180

Bair v Axiom Design, LLC, 616–617

Baldwin v Castro County Feeders I, Ltd., 765

Ball v Carlson, 991

Banco General Runinahui, S.A. v Citibank International, 733

Banderas v Banco Central del Ecuador, 186

Bank IV v Capitol Federal Savings and Loan Ass'n, 870

Bank of America Nat'l Trust & Savings Ass'n v Allstate Insurance Co., 661

Bank of Benton v Cogdill, 304

Bank of Glen Burnie v Elkridge Bank, 653

Bank of Hoven v Rausch, 674

Bank of Nichols Hills v Bank of Oklahoma, 653, 698

Bank of Niles v American State Bank, 683

Bank of the Sierra v Kallis, 785

Bankers Security Life Ins. Society v Kane, 843

Bankers Trust v 236 Beltway Investment, 630

Banque de Depots v Bozel, 488

Barclays Bank, P.L.C. v Johnson, 639

Barlow Lane Holdings Ltd. v Applied Carbon Technology (America), Inc., 765

Barnett v Leiserv, 557

Barney v Unity Paving, Inc., 394

Barnsley v Empire Mortgage, Ltd. Partnership, 630

Barrett v Brian Bemis Auto World, 586

Bartomeli v Bartomeli, 1010

Barton v Moore, 1072

Basic Inc. v Levinson, 1094–1095

Batzer Construction, Inc. v Boyer, 381

Baurer v Mountain West Farm Bureau Ins., 843–844

Bausch & Lomb Inc. v Commissioner, 133

Bay Harbour Management LLC v Carothers, 1121

Bayne v Smith, 1215

Baysprings Forest Products, Inc. v Wade, 553

BBQ Blues Texas, Ltd. v Affiliated Business, 371

BC Technical Inc. v Ensil International, 395, 406

B.D.G.S., Inc. v Balio, 654, 658

Beacon Hill Civic Ass'n v Ristorante Toscano, Inc., 353

Beall Transport Equipment Co. v Southern Pacific Transportation, 537

Beam v Stewart, 1077–1078

Bear Stearns v Dow Corning Corp., 445

Beard v Summit Institute of Pulmonary Medicine and Rehabilitation, Inc., 903

Bechtel v Competitive Technologies, Inc., 902

Beck v Haines Terminal and Highway Co., 281

Beck v Roper Whitney, Inc., 1047

Becker v Crispell-Synder, Inc., 394

Beckman v Kansas Dep't. of Human Resources, 903

Belden Inc. v American Electronic Components, Inc., 510

Bellum v PCE Constructors Inc., 916

Benbow v The Ferryboat James Johns, 1011

Bender v Green, 1221, 1228

Bennett v Spear, 1197–1198

Bentley Systems Inc. v Intergraph Corp., 415

Berg Chilling Systems Inc. v Hull Corp., 1047

Berg v Hudesman, 379

Bergeron v Aero Sales, 504

Bergmann v Parker, 420

Bering Strait School District v RLT Ins. Co., 827

Bermuda Run Country Club, Inc. v Atwell, 1209–1210

Berry v Lucas, 545

Bettner Trust v Bettner, 1065

Bill McCurley Chevrolet v Rutz, 855

Billy Cain Ford Lincoln Mercury, Inc. v Kaminski, 605, 613

Bily v Arthur Young & Co., 1120

Biotech Pharmacal, Inc. v International Business Connections, LLC, 507

Birkel v Hassebrook Farm Services, Inc., 440

Birt v St. Mary Mercy Hospital, 1081

Birznieks v Cooper, 414

Bishop v Bishop, 459

Bishop v Hyundai Motor America, 615

Bixby's Food Systems, Inc. v McKay, 973–974

Black v Graham, 1051

Blackwell v Kenworth Truck Co., 980

Blitz v Agean, Inc., 746

Blitz v Subklew, 411–412

Bloom v G.P.F., 652

Blubaugh v Turner, 328

Blue v R.L. Glossen Contracting, Inc., 385

Blue Bell, Inc. v Peat, Marwick, Mitchell & Co., 1119

BMW of North America, Inc. v Gore, 9, 204

Board of Directors of Carriage Way Property Owners Ass'n v Western National Bank, 283

Board of Regents of Wisconsin System v Southworth, 84

Bohach v City of Reno, 933

Boles v National Development Co. Inc., 1072, 1077

Borden, Inc. v Advent Ink Co., 575

Borden, Inc. v Smith, 364
Boros v Carter, 878
Boschetto v Hansing, 279
Bosley v Wildwett.com, 193
Boston Athletic Ass'n v
    Sullivan, 238
*Boston Athletic Association v
    International Marathon,
    Inc., 1140*
Boston Beer Co. v Slesar Bros.
    Brewing Co., 214
Botsee Gates v Houston, 987
Boulos v Morrison, 870–871
Bourdeau Bros. v International
    Trade Commission, 137
*Bourg v Bristol Boat Co.,
    380–381*
Bourque v FDIC, 293
*Bovard v American Horse
    Enterprises, Inc., 353*
Bowers and Merena Auctions,
    LLC, v James Lull, 505
Boydstun Metal Works, Inc. v
    Cottrell, Inc., 508
Boykin v Arthur Andersen &
    Co., 1119
Boyne v Town of Glastonbury,
    1201
Boynton v Burglass, 210
BPR Group v Bendetson, 1000
Bracewell v Bracewell,
    1253–1254
Bradham v Robinson, 1187
Bradt v Giovannone,
    1187–1188
Brady v Wal-Mart Stores, Inc.,
    953
Brady-Lunny v Massey, 106
Braswell v United States, 114
Brazil Quality Stones, Inc. v
    Chertoff, 927
Breed v Hughes Aircraft Co., 857
Brenlla v LaSorsa Buick, 916
Brenner v Plitt, 980
Brigham v Dillon Companies,
    Inc., 898
Brittingham v Cerasimo, Inc.,
    750
Brock v King, 440
Brooke v Mt. Hood Meadows,
    Ltd., 1014
Brooksbank v Anderson, 332
Brosseau v Ranzau, 995
Brown v Board of Education, 8
Brown v Johnston, 1222
Brown v Kelly, 388
Brown v KPMG Peat Marwick,
    1117
Brown v Twentieth Century
    Fox Film Corp., 238–239

Browning v Howerton, 315
Brunette v Humane Society of
    Ventura County, 12
Brunfield v Horn, 1074
Bryant v Adams, 575
Bryant v Livigni, 886
Bryant v Wal-Mart Stores, Inc.,
    922
B.T. Lazarus & Co. v
    Christofides, 789
Bucci v Wachovia Bank, N.A.,
    697
Buck v Hankin, 500
Buehner v IBM Corp., 1116
Buente v Allstate Ins. Co., 827
Buffington v State Automobile
    Mut. Ins. Co., 309
Buffo v Baltimore & Ohio
    Railroad Co., 932
Bugh v Protravel International,
    Inc., 425
Bumbardner v Allison, 209
Bumgarner v Wood, 643, 658
Bunn v Offutt, 1186
Burger King Corp. v E-Z
    Corporations, 970, 976
Burger King Corp. v Hinton,
    Inc., 969
Burgess v Lee Acceptance
    Corp., 887
Burke v Oxford House of
    Oregon Chapter V, 1214
Burlington Industries, Inc. v
    Ellerth, 943
*Burlington Northern Railway/
    Shell Oil Co. v U.S.,
    1194–1195*
*Burlington Northern Santa Fe
    Railroad Co. v White, 944,
    955*
*Burns v Neiman Marcus Group,
    Inc., 702, 709*
Bursey v CFX Bank, 698
Bush v Gore, 78
Bush v Sage Health Care, LLC,
    1019
Byker v Mannes, 986, 1007

C

C & E Services, Inc. v Ashland
    Inc., 581
C&N Contractors, Inc. v
    Community Bancshares,
    Inc., 658–659
Cable News Network v CNN
    News.com, 237
Cablevision Systems Corp. v
    F.C.C., 1204
Cadle Co. v DeVincent, 669

California Union Ins. v City of
    Walnut Grove, 478
California v American Stores
    Co., 95
California v Ravenscroft, 172
Callahan & Sons, Inc. v
    Dykeman Electric Co. Inc.,
    1047
Callaway v Whittenton, 783
Campbell Soup Co., Inc. v
    United States, 153
Canel v Topinka, 466
*Cantu v Central Education
    Agency, 299*
Capano v Wilmington Country
    Club, Inc., 1060
Caparos v Morton, 995
Capithorne v Framingham
    Union Hospital, 886
Capshaw v Hickman, 542
Carey & Associates v Ernst, 369
Cargill Inc. v Jorgenson Farms,
    507, 516
Carlson v Lake Chelan
    Community Hospital, 899
*Carlson v Xerox Corp., 1124,
    1131*
Carlton v T.G.I. Friday's, 566
Carman Tool & Abrasives, Inc.
    v Evergreen Lines, 844–845
Carnahan v Moriah Property
    Owners Association, Inc.,
    1186
Carolina Bank v Chatham
    Station, Inc., 1183
Carpenter v United States,
    1099
Carter & Grimsley v Omni
    Trading, Inc., 684
Carter v Wilson Construction
    Co., Inc., 1079
Casey v Brennan, 1142, 1156
Cassiani v Bellino, 638
Castle Cheese Inc. v MS
    Produce Inc., 877
Caswell v Zoya Int'l, 408
Catellus Development Corp. v
    United States, 1209
Cates v Cates, 203
CBS Corporation, Inc. v FCC,
    121, 125
CBS Outdoor Group, Inc. v
    Biefeld, 876
Centimark v Village Manor
    Associates, Ltd., 447
Central Bank of Denver v First
    Interstate Bank of Denver,
    1096
Central District Alarm, Inc. v
    Hal-Tuc, Inc., 592–593

Central Illinois Public Service
    Co. v Atlas Minerals, Inc.,
    508
*Central Missouri Professional
    Services v Shoemaker, 877*
Central New Jersey
    Freightliner, Inc., v
    Freightliner Corp., 970
Century 21 Pinetree Properties,
    Inc. v Cason, 293
Century Partners, LP v Lesser
    Goldsmith Enterprises, 350
Chaiken v Employment
    Security Comm'n,
    1009–1010
Cham, Hill, Inc., v Block &
    Veatch, 992
Chamberlain v Puckett
    Construction, 435
Chaney v Burdett, 1004
Chao v Mallard Bay Drilling
    Co., 919
Chappone v First Florence
    Corp., 495
Charles v Lundgren &
    Associates, P.C., 760–761
Charter Oak Fire Ins. Co. v
    Heedon & Cos., 831
*Chase Precast Corp. v John J.
    Paonessa Co., Inc., 423–424*
Chemical Leaman Tank Lines,
    Inc. v Aetna Casualty Co.,
    831
Chestnut Corp. v Pestine,
    Brinati, Gamer, Ltd., 1117
Chevron v Echazabal, 951
Chevron v El-Khoury, 971
Chevron,U.S.A., Inc. v
    National Resources Defense
    Council, Inc., 108
Chicago District Council of
    Carpenters Welfare Fund v
    Gleason's Fritzshall, 659
Chicago Title Ins. Co. v Allfirst
    Bank, 646, 693
Choo Choo Tire Service, Inc. v
    Union Planters National
    Bank, 668
Christian v Smith, 372
Christner v Anderson, Nietzke
    & Co., 1153
*Chrysler Corp. v Chaplake
    Holdings, Ltd., 341, 343*
*Chrysler Credit v Koontz, 782,
    787*
Cintrone v Hertz Truck
    Leasing & Rental Service,
    478
Circuit City Stores, Inc. v
    Adams, 937

Circuit City Stores, Inc. v Adams (Circuit City II), 352, 938
Citibank v Bank of Salem, 649
Citibank v Shen, 689
Citizens Bank v Parkman Woodman Medical Associates, 998
Citizens Bank, Booneville v National Bank of Commerce, 682
Citizens State Bank v Timm, Schmidt & Co., 1131
City and County of San Francisco v Sainez, 1218
City Check Cashing, Inc. v Manufacturers Hanover Trust Co., 692
City National Bank of Fort Smith v First National Bank and Trust Co. of Rogers, 404
City of Aurora v ACJ Partnership, 1164
City of Chicago v M/V Morgan, 201
City of Salinas v Souza & McCue Construction Co., 329
Clark v Mazda Motor Corp., 570
Classic Cheesecake Co. Inc. v J.P. Morgan Chase Bank, 374
Cleland v Thirion, 985
Clemens v McNamee, 194, 206
Clerical-Technical Union of Michigan State University v Board of Trustees of Michigan State University, 124
Cleveland Board of Education v Loudermill, 115
Clevert v Soden, 452
Clicks Billiards v Sixshooters, Inc., 217
Cliffstar Corp. v Elmar Industries, Inc., 586
Clinton Investors Co. v Watkins, 1039, 1050
Cloud Corp. v Hasbro, Inc., 534
Cloutier v Costco, 940
Cobin v Rice, 995
Coca-Cola Co. v Babyback's International Inc., 369
Coddington v Coddington, 476–477
Coeur Alaska v Southeast Alaska Conservation, 1193

Coggins v New England Patriots Football Club, 1053–1054
Coleman v Casey County Board of Education, 960
Collier v Cobalt, LLC, 1018
Collins Entertainment Corp. v Coats and Coats Rental Amusement, 602
Colorado v Hill, 79
Columbia Pictures, Inc. v Bunnell, 248
Comdata Network, Inc. v First Interstate Bank of Fort Dodge, 730
Command Communications v Fritz Cos., 142
Commissioner of Revenue v J.C. Penney Co., Inc., 83–84
Commodities Reserve Co. v St. Paul Fire & Marine Ins. Co., 832–833
Commonwealth v Proetto, 261
Commonwealth v Thompson, 753, 759
Commonwealth Capital Investment Corp. v McElmurry, 1010–1011
Commonwealth Edison Co. v Montana, 85
Community Bank & Trust, S.S.B. v Fleck, 702
Compagnie Européenne des Pétroles v Sensor Nederland, 154
Conagra, Inc. v Nierenberg, 604
Conductores Monterrey, S.A. de C.V. v Remee Products Corp., 604
Connecticut Community Bank v The Bank of Greenwich, 239
Connes v Molalla Transportation Systems, 885
Continental Casualty v Zurich American Insurance, 393
Continental Photo, Inc., 956–957
Conway v Larsen Jewelry, 552
Cook v Columbia Sussex Corp., 495
Cook Composites, Inc. v Westlake Styrene Corp., 600
Cooper v Bluff City Mobile Home Sales, Inc., 608
Cooper v G. E. Construction Co., 281

Cooper Industries v Leatherman Tool Group, Inc., 204
Cooperative Resources, Inc. v Dynasty Software, Inc., 587
Copeland v Admiral Pest Control Co., 394
Coregis Insurance Co. v Fleet National Bank, 659
Corley v Ott, 1004–1005
Corporate Express Office Products, Inc. v Phillips, 1046
Corron & Black of Illinois, Inc. v Magner, 862
Corson by Lontz v Kosinski, 1187
Costa v The Boston Red Sox Baseball Club, 197, 202
County of Westchester v Town of Greenwich, Connecticut, 1202
Cousar v Shepherd-Will, Inc., 453
Covad Communications Co. v FCC, 108
Covensky v Hannah Marine Corp., 382
Cowan v Mervin Mewes, Inc., 295
Craig v Bossenberry, 1210
Crane Brothers, Inc. v May, 883
Creasy v Tincher, 430
Creative Computing v Getloaded.com LLC, 249
Credit Alliance Corp. v Arthur Andersen & Co., 1118
Credit General Insurance Co. v NationsBank, 398
Crookham & Vessels, Inc. v Larry Moyer Trucking, Inc., 337
Crowder v Kitagawa, 1219
Crowe v Tull, 739
Crown Controls, Inc. v Smiley, 881
CSX Transportation, Inc. v Recovery Express, Inc., 857
Culver v Maryland Ins. Com'r, 88
Cumberland Farms, Inc. v Drehman Paving & Flooring Co., 578
Cummings, Inc. v Nelson, 856
Cunico v Pueblo School District No. 6, 959
Cuomo v Clearinghouse Ass'n, LLC, 69

Curtis v Anderson, 463
Cusimano v Metro Auto, Inc., 1073

D

D. E. Rogers Assoc., Inc. v Gardner-Denver Co., 102
Dagesse v Plant Hotel N.V., 262
DaimlerChrysler Corp. v U.S., 131
Dale v Cologiovani, 139
Dalessio v Kressler, 691
Dal-Tile Corp. v Cash N' Go, 682
Dantzler v S.P. Parks, Inc., 504
Darden v Peters, 222
Darnall v Petersen, 675
Darr v Town of Telluride, Colo., 115
Daubert v Merrell Dow Pharmaceuticals, Inc., 25
Davenport v Cotton Hope Plantation, 201
David Tunick, Inc. v Kornfeld, 596
Davis v Passman, 79
Days Inn of America, Inc. v Patel, 422
DCM Ltd. Partnership v Wang, 643, 649
de Guerrero v John Hancock Mutual Life Ins. Co., 845
De Lema v Waldorf Astoria Hotel, Inc., 501
Deal v Spears, 924
Dean v Eastern Shore Trust Co., 712
Delavau v Eastern American Trading & Warehousing, Inc., 485
Delaware Open MRI Radiology v Kessler, 1044
Della Ratta v Dyas, 1001–1002, 1007
Dellagrotta v Dellagrotta, 459
Deloitte, Haskins, & Sells v Green, 1114
Delta Stat, Inc. v Michael's Carpet World, 519
DeMatteo v DeMatteo, 373
Demoulas v Demoulas Super Markets, Inc., 1148, 1155
Den Norske Stats Oljeselskap, 517
Department of Housing and Urban Development v Rucker, 1220

Design Data Corp. v Maryland Casualty Co., 544

DeWeldon, Ltd. v McKean, 551

Diamond v Chakrabarty, 227

Diamond v Diehr, 239

Dickerson v United States, 180, 182

Dickson v Moran, 430

Diedrich v Diedrich, 313

DiGeneraro v Rubbermaid, Inc., 272

Dillard Department Stores, Inc. v Silva, 191

DIRECTV, Inc. v Robson, 164

Dirks v SEC, 1099, 1106

Dishon v Ponthie, 1073

District of Columbia v Heller, 79

D.L.S. v Maybin, 972–973, 976

Doe v America Online, Inc., 264

Doe v Cahill, 257

Doe v U.S. Dept. of Treasury, 107

Doeblers' Pennsylvania Hybrids, Inc. v Doebler, 216

Dole Food Co. v Patrickson, 139

Donaghue v Natural Microsystems Corp., 1101

Don-Linn Jewelry Co. v The Westin Hotel Co., 495

Dorchester Associates LLC v District of Columbia Bd. of Zoning Adjustment, 117

Dow Chemical Co. v United States, 113, 178, 182

Dry Creek Cattle Co. v Harriet Bros. Limited Partnership, 300

Duarte v Agilent Technologies, Inc., 918

Dubuque Packing Co. and UFCWIU, Local 150A, 910

Dugan v FedEx Corp., 490

Dunaway v Parker, 1156

Dunkin Donuts of America v Minerva, Inc., 978

Dunleavey v Paris Ceramics, USA, Inc., 605

Dyer v National By-Products, Inc., 344

E

Eagle Industries, Inc. v Thompson, 419

Earth Island Institute v Christopher, 143

East Capital View Community Development Corp. v Robinson, 421

East Market v Tycorp Pizza IV, Inc., 1072

Eastern Airlines Inc. v Airline Pilots Association Int'l, 911

eBay, Inc. v MercExchange, LLC, 229–230

Eberhard Manufacturing Co. v Brown, 553

E.C. Styberg Engineering Co. v Eaton Corp., 507

Echols v Pelullo, 289

Eckert v Flair Agency, Inc., 319

Ecology Services Inc. v GranTurk Equipment, Inc., 590, 592

Economy Forms Corp. v Kandy, Inc., 594–595

Eddins v Redstone, 91

Edelman v Lynchburg College, 937

Eden Electrical, Ltd. v Amana Co., 200

Edinburg Volunteer Fire Company v Danko, 585

Edwards v Centrex Real Estate Corp., 380

Eenkhoorn v New York Telephone Co., 930

EEOC v Dial Corp., 956

EEOC v Liggett and Meyers, Inc., 959–960

EEOC v Red Robin Gourmet Burger, Inc., 940

EEOC v Sidley, Austen, Brown and Wood, 112

Eggett v Wasatch Energy Corp., 1057

Egyptian Goddess, Inc. v SWISA, Inc., 226

Ehrlich v Diggs, 369

Ehrlich v Willis Music Co., 304

E.I. Du Pont de Nemours & Co. v United States, 134

El Fenix v Serrano Gutierrez, 842

El Paso Healthcare System v Piping Rock Corp., 369

El Paso Natural Gas Co. v Minco Oil & Gas Co., Inc., 512

Elenkrieg v Siebrecht, 1079

Elf Atochem N. America, Inc. v Jaffari, 1018

Elf Atochem North America, Inc. v Celco, Inc., 787–788

Elkgrove Unified School District v Newdow, 19

Ellis v City of Lakewood, 85

Ellis v Edwards, 1050–1051

Ellis v Grant Thornton LLP, 1120, 1131

Elmore v Doenges Bros. Ford, Inc., 616

Emberson v Hartley, 333–334

Empire of American v Arthur Andersen & Co., 1118

EMSG Sys. Div., Inc. v Miltope Corp., 519

Englewood v Miami Valley Lighting, L.L.C., 1168

English v Muller, 443

Enstar Group, Inc., v Grassgreen, 1157

Entregy Corporation v Riverkeeper, Inc., 1193

Environmental Defense v Duke Energy, 1192

ESS Entertainment 2000, Inc. v Rockstar Videos Inc., 219

Estate of Graham v Morrison, 864–865, 868

Estate of Munier v Jacquemin, 467

Eutsler v First Nat'l Bank, Pawhuska, 661

Evans Mfg. Corp. v Wolosin, 615–616

Evjen v Employment Agency, 915

Ex parte Lewis, 163

Exchange Bank & Trust Co. v Lone Star Life Ins. Co., 408

Exxon Shipping Co. v. Baker, 204, 1198

F

F. H. Prince & Co. v Towers Financial Corp., 338

Faber Industries, Ltd. v Dori Leeds Witek, 730–731

Fabrica de Tejidos Imperial v Brandon Apparel Group, Inc., 585

Fabry Partnership v Christensan, 1015

Fairchild Publications v Rosston, 877

Famous Music Corp. v Bay State Harness Horse Racing and Breeding Association, Inc., 894

Faragher v City of Boca Raton, 942, 943, 957

Fawzy v Fawzy, 29

Fayad v Clarenden National Insurance Co., 826

F.C.C. v Fox Television Stations, Inc., 119

Federal Crop Ins. Corp. v Merrill, 122

Federal Financial Co. v Gerard, 669

Federal Services Finance Corp. v Bishop Nat'l Bank of Hawaii, 1158

Federal Trade Commission v AmeriDebt, Inc., DebtWorks, Inc., Andris Pukke, and Pamela Pukke, 797

Federal Trade Commission v Colgate-Palmolive Co., 760

Fedrick v Nichols, 472

Fedun v Mike's Cafe, 345

Feigenbaum v Guaracini, 720, 730

Feist Publications Inc. v Rural Telephone Services Co., 222

Feldman v Google. Inc., 297, 302

Felley v Singleton, 578

Ferris v Tennessee Log Homes, Inc., 889

Festo Corp. v Shoketsu, 230

Fidenas v Honeywell Bull, S.A., 153

Fifth Third Bank v Jones, 676

Filasky v Preferred Risk Mut. Ins. Co., 843

Financial Associates v Impact Marketing, 682

Finke v The Walt Disney Co., 196

First Coinvestors, Inc. v Coppola, 552

First Interstate Bank of Oregon v Bergendahl, 994

First National Bank v Clark, 415

First National Bank of Boston v Belotti, 80

First National Maintenance v NLRB, 910

First Nat'l Bank of Lacon v Strong, 789

First of America-Bank Northeast Illinois v Bocian, 681

First Options v Kaplan, 30

Firwood Manufacturing Co., Inc. v General Tire, Inc., 613

Fischer v Unipac Service Corp., 754

Fisher v City of Berkeley, California, 1218

Fisher v Schefers, 309, 322–323, 326

Fisher v State Mutual Insurance Co., 1141

Fiss Corp. v National Safety Bank and Trust Co., 713

Fitl v Strek, 328

Fitzgerald v Salsbury Chemical, Inc., 898

Flatiron Linen, Inc. v First American State Bank, 668

Fleet National Bank v Phillips, 722

Fleming Companies, Inc. v Krist Oil Co., 517

Fletcher v Marshall, 311

Fletcher v Minton, 1177, 1185

Flinn v Indiana, 183

Flora v Hughes, 1254

Flowers Baking Co. v R-P Packaging, Inc., 526

Fly v Cannon, 552

FNBC v Jennessey Group, LLC, 447, 451

Fode v Capital RV Center, Inc., 586

Fonar Corp. v Domenick, 233

Fontaine v Gordon Contractors Building Supply, Inc., 731–732

Fontane v Colt Manufacturing Co., 460

Forbes v General Motors Corp., 576

Ford v Beam Radiator, Inc., 569

Ford v Mitcham, 984

Forgie-Buccioni v Hannaford Bros. Inc., 190

Former Employees of Merrill Corp. v U.S., 145

Forrer v Sears, Roebuck & Co., 345

Foss v. Kincade, 1171

Foster v United Ins. Co., 842

Fought v Morris, 1060

Fragante v City and County of Honolulu, 945

Frank v Hershey National Bank, 636

Franklin v Maclean, 1254–1255

Franklin National Bank v Sidney Gotowner, 682

Fraser v Nationwide Mut. Ins. Co., 245, 924

Frasier v Trans-western Land Corp., 1074

Free Speech Coalition v Reno, 257

French v Chosin Few, Inc., 1147

Frierson v Watson, 1165, 1185

Frito-Lay, Inc. v Ramos, 893

Front-Line Inc. v Mayweather Promotions, LLC, 966

Frosty Land Foods v Refrigerated Transport Co., 501

FTC v Tiny Doubles Int'l, Inc., 977

FTC v Wolf, 977

Furlong v Alpha Chi Omega Sorority, 606, 613

Future Tech Int'l, Inc. v Tae II Media, Ltd., 552–553

G

Gabelli & Co. v Liggett Group, Inc., 1069

Gagliardo v Connaught Laboratories, Inc., 953

Gagnon v Coombs, 872

Gale v North Meadow Associates, 1229–1230

Gall v U.S., 160

Gallant v Kanterman, 1062

Galyen Petroleum Co. v Hixson, 714

Garcetti v Ceballos, 898

Gardiner, Kamya & Associates v Jackson, 336

Gardner v Downtown Porsche Auto, 473

Garfink v Cloisters at Charles, Inc., 1166

Garrett v Impac Hotels, LLC, 494

Garrido v Empty Nester Homes, Ltd., 1217

Garrity v John Hancock Mut. Life Ins. Co., 244

Gast v Rodgers-Dingus Chevrolet, 614

Gates v Standard Brands Inc., 566

Gates, Duncan, and VanCamp v Levatino, 995

Geer v Farquhar, 638

Geier v American Honda Motor Co., 84–85

Gelfman v Weeden Investors, L.P., 1017

General Accident Fire & Life Assur. Corp. v Citizens Fidelity Bank & Trust Co., 661

General Elec. Capital Corp. v Union Planters Bank, NA, 778

General Motors Acceptance Corp. v Bank of Richmondville, 692

General Motors Acceptance Corp. v Lincoln Nat'l Bank, 777, 787

General Motors Corp. v Cadillac Marine and Boat Co., 215

Georgia v Randolph, 179

Getty Petroleum Corp. v American Exp. Travel Related Services Co., Inc., 660

GFSI, Inc. v J-Loong Trading, Ltd., 582, 606

Giebeler v M & B Associates, 1214

Gilbert v Cobb Exchange Bank, 732

Giles v Wyeth, Inc., 559

Gillespie v Pulsifer, 389

Gilmer v Interstate/Johnson Lane Corp., 351, 938

Gingerich v Protein Blenders, Inc., 451

Girl Scouts of Manitou v GSUSA, 969, 976

Gladhart v Oregon Vineyard Supply Co., 504

Glass Service Co. v State Farm Mutual Automobile Ins. Co., 285

Glen R. Sewell Street Metal v Loverde, 430

Gobe Media Group, LLC v Cocneros, 1018

Golden State Porcelain Inc. v Swid Powell Design Inc., 519

Golden v Golden, 377–378

Golden v Oahe Enterprises, Inc., 1052

Golden Years Nursing Home, Inc. v Gabbard, 645

Goldfinger v Brown, 1059

Goldman v O. J. Simpson, 810

Gonzalez v Don King Productions, Inc., 289

Gonzalez v Kay, 753

Gonzalez v Morflo Industries, Inc., 573–574

Gonzalez v Old Kent Mortgage Co., 669

Gordon v Gordon, 476, 607

Gorgone v District of Columbia Bd. of Zoning Adjustment, 1205

Gorham v White, 226

Gorman v Farm Bureau Town & Country Insurance Co., 822

Gornicki v M & T Bank, 697

Gotham Partners, L.P. v Hallowood Realty Partners, L.P., 1015

Gottschalk v Benson, 226

Grabert v Department of Public Safety & Corrections, 186

Grabert v State through Dept. of Public Safety & Corrections, 186

Grace v Corbis Sygma, 469

Grace v USCAR, 916

Graff v Bakker Brothers of Idaho, Inc., 553

Gramacy Equities Corp. v DuMont, 997

Grand Rapids Auto Sales, Inc. v MBNA America Bank, 683–684

Granholm v Heald, 74–75

Gratz v Bollinger, 20

Graves v Norred, 824

Gray v Edgewater Landing, Inc., 1052

Gray v First Century Bank, 745

Graziano v Grant, 286

Great Atlantic & Pacific Tea Co., Inc. v FTC, 101

Great Southern Wood Preserving, Inc. v American Home Assur. Co., 544

Great West Casualty Co. v Flandrich, 490–491, 497

Greater Louisville Auto Auction, Inc. v Ogle Buick, Inc., 552

Greater New Orleans Broadcasting Association, Inc., v U.S., 79

Green v Hocking, 762

Green Tree Financial Corp. v Randolph, 36

Greenman v Yuba Power Products, 568

Greenpeace, American Oceans Campaign v National Marine Fisheries Service, 125

Greenstein, Logan & Co. v Burgess Marketing, Inc., 1114

Greentree Properties, Inc. v Kissee, 442

Greenwald v Kersh, 381

Griffith v Clear Lakes Trout Co., Inc., 507

Griggs v Duke Power Co., 941, 950, 936

Groseth International Harvester, Inc. v International Harvester, 979–980

Gross v FBL Financial Services, Inc., 950

Grove v Charbonneau Buick-Pontiac, Inc., 390–391

GS Petroleum, Inc. v R and S Fuel, Inc., 1039

Guardian Life Ins. Co. of America v Weisman, 653

Guerra v Hertz Corp., 748

Gustafson v Bell Atlantic Corp., 913

H

H. J., Inc. v Northwestern Bell Corp., 183

H. Rich Corp. v Feinberg, 1041

Haag v Bongers, 892–893

Hackbart v Cincinnati Bengals, Inc., 202

Hadfield v Gilchrist, 472–473

Hagan v Adams Property Associates, Inc., 1030

Hakimi V Cantwell, 354

Haley v Talcott, 1021

Hallday v Sturm, Ruger, & Co., Inc., 564

Halloum v Intel Corp., 901

Hamer v Sidway, 344

Hammann v City of Omaha, 117

Hammer Construction Corp. v Phillips, 416

Hampton Roads Seventh-Day Adventist Church v Stevens, 1236

Hanan v Corning Glass Works, 389

Hanewald v Bryan's Inc., 1074

Hanks v Powder Ridge, 201

Hansen v Smikahl, 1188

Hanson-Suminski v Rohrman Midwest Motors Inc., 317

Harbour v Arelco, Inc., 349

Hardesty v American Seating Co., 200

Harlan v Roadtrek Motorhomes, Inc., 559

Harley-Davidson v Grottanelli, 214, 236

Harmon Cable Communications v Scope Cable Television, Inc., 411

Harms v Northland Ford Dealers, 436–437

Harper v Inkster Public Schools, 1122

Harris v Ivax Corp., 1096

Harshman v Pantaleoni, 1000

Hauter v Zogarts, 577

Hayes v Carlin America, Inc., 399

Hayes v Collins, 1032, 1050

Hayes v Larsen Mfg. Co., Inc., 562

Hayes v Shelby Memorial Hospital, 958

Head v Phillips Camper Sales & Rental, Inc., 588

Heath v Heath, 461

Heckler v Chaney, 119

Hegyes v Unjian Enterprises, Inc., 209–210

Helms v Certified Packaging Corp., 765, 774

Helvey v Wabash County REMC, 528

Henderson v Quest Expeditions, Inc., 448

Henley v Dillard Department Stores, 192

Henry v Taco Tia, Inc., 978

Hentges v Thomford, 884

Herbert Rosenthal Jewelry Corp. v Kalpakian, 240

Herman v Hogar Praderas De Amor, Inc., 904

Herman & MacLean v Huddleston, 1109

Herman v Monadnock PR-24 Training Council, Inc., 886

Hertz v Klein Mfg., Inc., 473

Hess v Reg-Ellen Machine Tool Corp., 1066

Hewitt Associates, LLC v Rollins, Inc., 286, 302

Hialeah Automotive, LLC v Basulto, 30

Hieber v Uptown Nat'l Bank of Chicago, 694

Hill v Lindner, 1202

Hill v London, Stetelman, and Kirkwood, Inc., 1229

Hill v Perrones, 418

Hill v Southeastern Floor Covering Co., 1149, 1157

Hinc v Lime-O-Sol Company, 290

Hinger v Parker & Parsley Petroleum Co., 888

Hinton v Sealander Brokerage Co., 1217

Hiram College v Courtad, 275

Hocking v Dubois, 1108

Hoffman v Altec Int'l Inc., 1063

Hoffman v Red Owl Stores, Inc., 346

Hold Fast Tattoo, LLC v City of North Chicago, 1206, 1208

Holland v High-Tech Collieries, Inc., 327

Holly Hill Acres, Ltd. v Charter Bank of Gainesville, 636

Hollywood Fantasy Corp. v Gabor, 336

Holmes v Holmes, 1004

Holzman v Blum, 870

Holzman v de Escamilla, 1029

Home Basket Co., LLC v Pampered Chef, Ltd., 517–518

Home Oil Company, Inc. v Sam's East, Inc., 91

Home Pride Foods, Inc. v Johnson, 231

Home Shopping Club, Inc. v Ohio International, Ltd., 593

Homes v O'Bryant, 333

Hommel v Micco, 1029–1030

Honeywell International Inc. v Air Products and Chemicals, Inc., 290

Hooks v McCall, 209

Hooper v Yakima County, 269

Hopkins v BP Oil, Inc., 381

Hopper Furs, Inc. v Emery Air Freight Corp., 500–501

Horbach v Kacz Marek, 513

Hornell Brewing Co., Inc. v Spry, 595

Howard Const. Co. v Jeff-Cole Quarries, Inc., 512

H.P.B.C., Inc. v Nor-Tech Powerboats, Inc., 507

Hsu v Vet-A-Mix, Inc., 287

Huang v Gateway Hotel Holdings, 898

Huang Group v LTI, 1142

Hubbard v Tomlinson, 1078

Huger v Morrison, 436

Hughey v United States, 163

Hugo Boss Fashions, Inc. v Sam's European Tailoring, Inc., 510

Humlen v United States, 859

Hunter's Run Stables, Inc. v Triple H, Inc., 526

Hurd v Wildman, Harrold, Allen, and Dixon, 323

Hurwitz v Padden, 1028

Husky Industries v Craig, 875–876

Hutton v Public Storage Management, Inc., 471

Hyatt Corp. v Palm Beach Nat. Bank, 650, 658

Hyundai Motor America, Inc. v Goodin, 557

I

Ibanez v Farmers Underwriters Ass'n, 1080

Iberlin v TCI Cablevision of Wyoming, 761

IBP, Inc. v Mercantile Bank of Topeka, 694, 709

Idaho Bank & Trust Co. v First Bankcorp of Idaho, 1118

Idaho Migrant Council, Inc. v Warila, 384

IFC Credit Corp. v Nuova Pasta Co., 1147

IFC Credit Corp. v Specialty Optical Systems, Inc., 623

Ihrig v Frontier Equity Exchange, 1066

IIC Holdings, LLC v HR Software Acquisition Group, Inc., 1019

Ileto v Glock, Inc., 78

Illinois v V&M Industries, 1073

Immunomedics, Inc. v Does 1–10, 264

Imports, Ltd., v ABF Freight Systems, Inc., 491–492

In re 212 East 52nd Street Corp., 1043

In re 75,629 Shares of Common Stock of Trapp Family Lodge, Inc., 1044–1045

In re Abbott Laboratories Derivative Shareholder Litigation, 1146

In re Adoption of Smith, 308

In re AmeriDebt Inc., 797

In re Armstrong, 624

In re Baby M, 358

In re Bear Stearns Litigation, 1155

In re Bedrock Marketing, LLC, 625

In re Bilski, 228

In re Blasco, 628

In re Borden, 775

In re Boss Trust, 321

In re Breast Implant Product Liability Litigation, 527

In re Cady, Roberts & Co., 1108

In re Cassell, 1221

In re Channel Home Centers, Inc., 688
In re City of New York, 1168
In re Commercial Money Center, Inc., 769
In re Comverse Technology, Inc., 1071
In re Cottage Grove Hospital, 765
In re Countrywide Litigation, 1113
In re Dell Securities Litigation, 1123
In re Delphi Corp., 290–291, 302
In re Devel, 226
In re Estate of Bolinger, 985
In re Estate of Gordon, 1255
In re Estate of H. H. Herring, 467
In re Estate of Morris P. Van Der Veen, 1247, 1252
In re Estate of Norris, 713
In re Estate of Novak, 282
In re Estate of Sharek, 1244
In re Estate of Speers, 1238, 1252
In re Estate of Tolin, 1255
In re Estate of Walter Brownlee, Sr., 460
In re Ferguson, 228–229
In re Ford Motor Co. E-350 Van Products Liability Litigation, 559
In re Franchise Pictures LLC, 765
In re Frederickson, 797
In re Harms, 499
In re Hornsby, 817–818
In re Hubert Plankenhorn, 286–287, 302
In re IMAX Securities Litigation, 1123
In re Intuit Privacy Litigation, 249
In re Jackson's Estate, 389
In re Jairath, 818
In re Jasper Seating, Inc., 539
In re Jass, 798, 814
In re Jim Ross Tires, Inc., 774
In re Kang Jin Hwang, 642
In re Klingman, 1238
In re Landmark Land Co. of California, 1146
In re Lee, 815
In re Lingenfelter's Estate, 1254
In re Lockovich, 790
In re Looper, 811, 815

In re Lucent Technologies Inc., Securities Litigation, 1096
In re Lull, 768, 779, 786
In re Marriage of Sharp, 1249
In re Mayco Plastics, Inc., 582
In re Mercer, 809
In re Michelle's Hallmark Cards & Gifts, Inc., 789
In re Mines Tire Co., Inc., 789
In re Moltech Power Systems, Inc., 602
In re MoneyGram Intern., Inc. Securities Litigation, 1113
In re Musselman, 797
In re Mutual Funds Investment Litigation v Janus Capital Group, 1094
In re Nantucket Island Associates Limited Partnership Unit Holders Litigation, 1015
In re Northrup, 779
In re Okamoto, 816
In re Omega Door Co., Inc., 765
In re Orso, 815–816
In re Owens Corning et al., Debtors in Possession, 444
In re Pacific/West Communications Group, Inc., 774
In re Price, 766
In re Quality Processing, Inc., 534
In re Rabin, 807
In re Rafter Seven Ranches LP, 567, 586
In re Seagate Technology, LLC, 229
In re SGE Mortgage Funding Corp., 668
In re S.M. Acquisition Co., 584
In re Smith, 117
In re Smith Min. and Material, LLC, 804
In re SpecialCare, Inc., 789
In re T & R Flagg Logging, Inc., 769
In re The Holladay House, Inc., 765
In re Thomas, 551–552
In re Thriftway Auto Supply, Inc., 789
In re Toys R Us, Inc., Privacy Litig., 249
In re Verizon Internet Services, Inc., 263
In re Walt Disney Co. Derivative Litigation, 1142, 1143, 1155

In re Westinghouse Uranium Litigation, 594
Indianapolis-Marion County Public Library v Charlier Clark & Linard, P.C., 1118
Industrial Machinery & Equipment Co. Inc. v Lapeer County Bank & Trust Co., 789
Industrial Mechanical, Inc. v Siemens Energy & Automation, Inc., 734
Ingram v Earthman, 636–637
Integrated, Inc. v Alec Fergusson Electrical Contractors, 390
Inter-Americas Ins. Corp., Inc. v Imaging Solutions Co., 585
Intersparex Leddin KG v AL-Haddad, 853
Intrastate Piping & Controls, Inc. v Robert-James Sales, Inc., 512
Ioviero v CigaHotel, Inc., aka Landia I.S., Inc., 1053
Irwin v West End Development Co., 1078–1079
Isbell v City of San Diego, 1211
Island City Flying Service v General Electric, 893–894
Island Development Corp. v District of Columbia, 420
Iwen v U.S. West Direct, 362

J

J. M. v Shell Oil Co., 974
J. O. Hooker's Sons v Roberts Cabinet, 506
J. Walter Thompson, U.S.A., Inc. v First BankAmericano, 702
Jackson Hole Traders, Inc. v Joseph, 588, 592
Jackson v DeWitt, 402
Jackson v NestlT-Beich, Inc., 574
Jacob v Harrison, 639
Jacob & Youngs, Inc. v Kent, 417
Jacobs v State, 169
Janich v Sheriff, 959
Jauquet Lumber Co., Inc. v Kolbe & Kolbe Millwork, Inc., 99
Jefferson Parish Hosp. Dist. No. 2 v Hyde, 101

Jefferson Randolf Corporation v PDS, 446
Jenkins Subway, Inc. v Jones, 421
Jennie-O-Foods, Inc. v Safe-Glo Prods. Corp., 507
Jennings v Radio Station KSCS, 346
J.M. Beeson Co. v Sartori, 417
J.M. Smucker Co. v Rudge, 744
John Carlo, Inc. v Secretary of Labor, 920
John Hancock Mutual Life Ins. Co. v Harris Trust, 913
Johnny Dell, Inc. v New York State Police, 552
Johnson v Santa Clara Transportation Agency, 948
Jom Investments, LLC v Callahan Industries, Inc., 397
Jones v Frickey, 295
Jordan v Civil Service Bd., Charlotte, 116
Jordan Keys v St. Paul Fire, 281
Joseph Stephens & Co., Inc. v Cikanek, 765
Joy Management Co. v City of Detroit, 1152
Judson v Davis, 1034
Julson v Federated Mutual Ins. Co., 829

K

Kaghann's Korner, Inc. v Brown & Sons Fuel Co., Inc., 584
Kaitz v Landscape Creations, Inc., 505
Kalas v Cook, 520
Kalendareva v Discovery Cruise Line Partnership, 210
Karrer v Georgia State Bank of Rome, 710
Kaskel v Northern Trust Co., 651
Katris v Carroll, 1019
Katzenbach v McClung, 85
Kaufman & Stewart v Weinbrenner Shoe Co., 384
Kaufman, Inc. v Performance Plastering, Inc., 1043
Kauthar Sdn Bhd v Sternberg, 140
Kawasaki Shop v Kawasaki Motors Corp., 979

Kaycee Land and Livestock v Flahive, 1023

K.C. Roofing Center v On Top Roofing, Inc., 1078

Keeley v CSA, P.C., 356

Keiting v Skauge, 426

Kelley Manufacturing Co. v Martin, 1067

Kelly-Stehney & Assoc., Inc. v McDonald's Indus. Products, Inc., 515

Kelo v City of New London, 1179, 1185

Kelsoe v International Wood Products, Inc., 345

Kemp Motor Sales v Statham, 681–682

Kerman v Martin Friedman, CPA, 1129

Kerr v Fernandez, 1186

Kertesz v The Spa Floral, LLC, 1030

Keryakos Textiles, Inc. v CRA Development, Inc., 296, 302

Kim v Chamberlain, 966

Kimbrell's Furniture Co. v Sig Friedman, d/b/a Bonded Loan, 791

Kimta, A. S. v Royal Insurance Co., Inc., 832

Kindrich v Long Beach Yacht Club, 209

King v Lens Creek, Ltd., Partnership, 888

King v Moorehead, 1229

King v Stoddard, 1004

King v Trustees of Boston University, 333

King Jewelry Inc. v Federal Express Corporation, 545, 550

Kinney v Yerusalim, 1219

Kirby v Macon County, 202

Kirby v NMC Continue Care, 615

Kirkpatrick v ETC, International, 148

Kittell v Vermont Weatherboard, Inc., 933

Klein v Sporting Goods, Inc., 1079–1080

Kline v Security Guards, Inc., 925

Klinicki v Lundgren, 1158–1159

Klokke Corp. v Classic Exposition, Inc., 1072

Kmart Corp. v Trotti, 925

KMS Restaurant Corp. v Wendy's International, 970

Knievel v ESPN, 207

Knight Pub. Co., Inc. v Chase Manhattan Bank, N.A., 643

Knoefler v Wojtalewicz, 675

Knutson v Snyder Industries, Inc., 903

Kohn v Darlington Community School District, 1169

Kolb v Paul Revere Life Insurance Co., 827

Konop v Hawaiian Airlines, Inc., 924

Koontz v Rosener, 861

Koslik v Gulf Insurance Co., 827

Kotsch v Kotsch, 868–869

Krajcir v Egid, 638

Kramer Associates, Inc. v IKAM, Ltd., 439

Kramper Family Farm v Dakota Industrial Development, Inc., 350, 361

Krause v Vollmar, 989

Kridelbaugh v Aldrehn Theaters Co., 1053

Kroboth v Brent, 385

KRS International Co. v Teleflex, Inc., 227

KSI Rockville, LLC v Eichengrun, 1018

Kuketz v Brockton Athletic Club, 956

Kunz v SEC, 1090

Kuslansky v Kuslansky, Robbins, Stechel and Cunningham, LLP, 1024

Kvaerner U.S., Inc. v Hakim Plast Co., 614–615

L

L & B Hospital Ventures, Inc. v Health-care International, Inc., 1109

L. B. Foster v Tie and Track Systems, Inc., 305

La Trace v Webster, 561, 573

LaBarge Pipe & Steel Co. v First Bank, 727

Lackawanna Chapter v St. Louis County, 470

Ladd v NBD Bank, 535

Laface Records, LLC v Atlantic Recording Corp., 248

Lam Research Corp. v Dallas Semiconductor Corp., 614

Lamb v Scott, 853

Lamle v Mattel, Inc., 376

Langness v "O" Street Carpet, Inc., 1010

Larson v Johnson, 281–282

Larson v Tandy Corp., 1009

Larson v Wasemiller, 886

Lasday v Weiner, 1071

Lasseigne v American Legion Post 38, 893

Laverman v Destocki, 460

Lawson v Hale, 564

Leal v Holtvogh, 504

Learning Links, Inc. v United Parcel Services of America, Inc., 544

Leary v Foley, 1066

Leavings v Mills, 642

Lechmere, Inc. v NLRB, 905, 908

Lee v Bell South Telecommunications Inc., 913

Lee v First Union Nat. Bank, 737

Leegin Creative Leather Products, Inc. v PSKS, Inc., 90, 99

Leibling, P.C. v Mellon, PSFS (NJ) N.A., 713

Leingang v City of Mandan Weed Board, 439

Lentimo v Cullen Center Bank and Trust Co., 359

Leopold v Halleck, 681

Lever Brothers Co. v United States, 137

Levy v Gold & Co., Inc., 880

Levy v Southbrook International Investments, Ltd., 1101

Lewis v Ariens, 569

Lewis v Carson Oil Co., 195

Lewis v Edwards, 996

Lewis v Handel's Homemade Ice Cream and Yogurt, 566

Libby v Perry, 979

Liberty Mutual Ins. Co. v Enjay Chemical Co., 881

Licitra v Gateway, Inc., 587

Limited Stores, Inc. v Wilson-Robinson, 191

Lincoln National Life Insurance Co. v Calhoun, 823

Lindner Fund v Abney, 1119

Lindquist Ford, Inc. v Middleton Motors, Inc., 270

Lines v Bank of California, 791

Lipcon v Underwriters at Lloyd's, London, 127

Lite-On Peripherals, Inc. v Burlington Air Express, Inc., 542, 550

Lloyd's v Labarca, 832

Lobel v Samson Moving & Storage, Inc., 485

Logsdon v Logsdon, 1254

Lombardo v City of Dallas, 1209

Long v Jeb Breithaupt Design Build Inc., 1178

Long v Time Insurance Co., 824–825, 840

Lopez v Silver Cross, 10

Lorenc v CSX Corp., 1058

Lorillard Tobacco Co. v Roth, 118

Los Angeles News Service v Reuters, 220

Lotona v Aetna U.S. Healthcare Inc, 358

Lotus Development Corp. v Borland International, Inc., 232, 239

Lovering v Seabrook Island Property Owners Ass'n, 1038, 1053

Lowry's Reports, Inc. v Legg Mason, Inc., 253

L-Tec Electronics Corp. v Cougar Electronic Org. Inc., 1043

LTV Aerospace Corp. v Bateman, 527

Lucier v Impact Recreation, LTD., 1224

Lucini Italia Co. v Grappolini, 860–861

Lucy v Zehmer, 304

Lumberman's Mutual Ins. Co. v Franey Muha Alliant Ins., 861

Lundberg v Church Farms, Inc., 869–870

Lynch v Bank of America, N.A., 697

M

M. Fortunoff of Westbury Corp. v Peerless Ins., 486, 497

Maack v Resource Design & Construction, Inc., 317

Mac'Kie v Wal-Mart Stores, Inc., 776

MacArthur v Stein, 986

MADCAP I, LLC v McNamee, 278

Madison v Superior Court, 452

Maersk Sealand v Ocean Express Miami (Quality Print), 493

Magee v Walbro, Inc., 470

Magic Valley Foods, Inc. v Sun Valley Potatoes, Inc., 583, 592

Magnavox Employees Credit Union v Benson, 790

Magnum Real Estate Services, Inc. v Associates, LLC, 371

Maimonides School v Coles, 1235, 1252

Maine Family Federal Credit Union v Sun Life Assur. Co. of Canada, 668, 682–683

Mainstream Marketing Services, Inc. v F.T.C., 118, 121

Major Products Co., Inc. v Northwest Harvest Products, Inc., 628

Mallen v Mallen, 389

Mallin v Paesani, 202

Mallock v Southern Memorial Park, Inc., 1188

Malone v American Business Information, Inc., 931

Mammoth Mountain Ski Area v Graham, 207–208

Manchester Equipment Co. Inc. v Panasonic Industrial Co., 389–390

Mandeville Island Farms v American Crystal Sugar Co., 99

Mannish v Lacayo, 879

Marc Rich v United States, 153

Marcus Dairy, Inc. v Rollin Dairy Corp., 505

Marino v Perna, 617

Marks v Minnesota Mining and Manufacturing Co., 1048

Marsh v Rheinecker, 272

Marsh Advantage America v Orleans Parish School Board, 1046

Marshall Produce Co. v St. Paul Fire & Marine Ins. Co., 844

Martellini v Little Angels Day Care, Inc., 1204

Marten v Staab, 300

Martin v Cook, 791

Martin v Martin Brothers Container Corp., 1044

Martin v OSHRC, 919

Martin Printing, Inc. v Sone, 371

Marx v Akers, 1070

Marx v Whitney National Bank, 713

Maryland Heights Leasing, Inc. v Mallinckrodt, Inc., 208

Maryott v Oconto Cattle Co., 777

Maschmeier v Southside Press, Inc., 1079

Mason v Fakhimi, 445

Mass. v Cheromcka, 169

Massachusetts v EPA, 1192, 1207

Massey v Jackson, 437

Master Homecraft Co. v Zimmerman, 639

MasterCard v Town of Newport, 762

Mastrobuono v Shearson Lehman Hutton, 1104

Mawer-Gulden-Annis, Inc. v Brazilian & Colombian Coffee Co., 894

Max Duncan Family Investments, Ltd. v NTFN Inc., 631, 669

Mayberry v Volkswagen of America, Inc., 562

MCA Television Ltd. v Public Interest Corp., 95

McCarthy v Tobin, 287

McClain v Real Estate Board of New Orleans, Inc., 90

McClellan v Cantrell, 816

McCune & McCune v Mountain Bell Tel. Co., 999

McDaniel v 162 Columbia Heights Housing Corporations, 776

McDaniel v Hensons, Inc., 881

McHugh v Santa Monica Rent Control Board, 122–123

McInnis v Western Tractor & Equipment Co., 616

McLane v Atlanta Market Center Management Co., 863

McLaren v Microsoft Corp., 261

McLaughlin v Heikkila, 293, 305

McLaughlin v Richland Shoe Co., 903–904

McLaughlin's Estate v Chicken Delight, Inc., 979

McLaurin v Noble Drilling Inc., 888

McLeod v Sears, Roebuck & Co., 788

McLinden v Coco, 374

McMahon v A, H, & B, 349

McMahon v Bunn-O-Matic Corp., 557

McMillan v First Nat. Bank of Berwick, 169

McNeil-PPC, Inc. v Pfizer Inc., 743

MD Drilling and Blasting, Inc. v MLS Construction, LLC, 292

Means v Clardy, 630

Mears v Nationwide Mut. Ins. Co., 288

Medina v Graham's Cowboys, Inc., 885, 894

Medistar Corp. v Schmidt, 341, 344, 447

Mehl v Mehl, 1009

Melcher v Apollo Medical Fund Management, 1019

Melodee Lane Lingerie Co. v American District Telegraph Co., 452

Memorial Hospital v Baumann, 892

Memphis Light, Gas and Water Division v Craft, 84

Mercantile Bank of Arkansas v Vowell, 712–713

Mercedes-Benz of North America, Inc. v Garten, 576–577

Merrill v Jansma, 1229

Meteor Motors v Thompson Halbach & Associates, 355

Metro-Goldwyn-Mayer Studios, Inc. v Grokster, Ltd., 225

Metropolitan Life Ins. Co. v Ward, 78

Metropolitan Park District of Tacoma v Griffith, 431

Metty v Shurfine Central Corporation, 565

Meyer v Mitnick, 462–463

Meyers v Henderson Construction Co., 527

MIC v Battle Mountain Corp., 1038

Michael v Mosquera-Lacy, 743

Mid Continent Casualty Co. v JHP Development Inc., 832

MidAmerica Construction Management, Inc. v MasTec North America, Inc., 411

Middlesex Mut. Assur. Co. v Vaszil, 720

Midfirst Bank v C. W. Haynes & Co., 675

Miles v Raymond Corp., 558

Miller v Calhoun/Johnson Co., 323, 674, 681

Miller v LeSea Broadcasting, Inc., 443

Miller v Thane International, Inc., 1094

Miller's Executor v Shannon, 1254

Milliken & Co. v Duro Textiles, LLC, 1048

Mills v Kimbley, 1201

Mills v U.S. Bank, 652

Mineral Deposits, Ltd. v Zigan, 240

Miniat v EMI, 1139

Minjak Co. v Rudolph, 1230–1231

Miranda v Arizona, 180

Mirano Contracting, Inc. v Perel, 277

Mirza v Maccabees Life and Annuity Co., 837

Mission West v Republic, 983

Missouri v III Investments, Inc., 1066

Mitchell v Badcock Corp., 429

Mitchell v T.G.I. Friday's, 565, 573

MKL Pre-Press Electronics v La Crosse Litho Supply, LLC, 420

ML-Lee Acquisition Fund, L.P. v. Deloitte & Touche, 1118

Money Mart Check Cashing Center, Inc. v Epicycle Corp., 681

Montano v Allstate Indemnity, 835

Moore v Beye, 190

Moore v Lawrence, 388

Moore v Lera Development Inc., 863–864

Moore v Meads Fine Bread Co., 100–101

Moreno v Hanford Sentinel, Inc., 208

Moretz v Miller, 1249

Morgan v American Security Ins. Co., 823

Moritz v Pines Hotel, Inc., 893

Morris v International Yogurt Co., 761

Morrison v Chilton Professional Automotive, Inc., 968

Morrison v Thoelke, 298–299

Morton's of Chicago v Crab House Inc., 300

Moseley v Zieg, 1187

Motor Vehicles Manufacturers Ass'n v State Farm Mutual Ins. Co., 110, 121

Mount Vernon Fire Insurance Co. v Belize NY, Inc., 841

Mountain Farm Credit Service, ACA v Purina Mills, Inc., 789

MPI v Jorge Lopez Ventura, 372

Muehlbauer v General Motors Corp., 605

Muick v Glenayre Electronics, 263

Multi-Tech Systems, Inc. v Floreat, Inc., 506

Murphy v Crosland, 1043

Murray v Accounting Center of Lucas County, Inc., 357

Murray v Conseco, Inc., 1146

Myers v Wild Wilderness Raceway, L.L.C., 1201

N

Naquin v Air Engineered Systems & Services, Inc., 1081

National Bank v Univentures, 637

National Football League v PrimeTime 24 Joint Venture, 220

National Hispanic Circus, Inc. v Rex Trucking, 490

Nation-Wide Check Corp. v Banks, 637

NE Ohio College of Massotherapy v Burek, 851

Neiman v Provident Life & Accident Insurance Co., 348

Nelson v Baker, 303

Nemard Construction Corp. v Deafeamkpor, 363

Nesbitt v Dunn, 321

Net Jets Aviation, Inc. v LHC Communications, LLC, 1021

Neuhoff v Marvin Lumber and Cedar Co., 341

New Hanover Rent-A-Car, Inc. v Martinez, 356

New Mexico v Herrera, 633, 635

New Mexico v Howell, 186

New York v Jennings, 185

New York v Trans World Airlines, 70

New York Life Ins. Co. v Estate of Haelen, 863

New York Trans Harbor, LLC v Derecktor Shipyards, 401

Newdow v U.S. Congress (Newdow I), 19

Newdow v U.S. Congress (Newdow II), 19

Newdow v U.S. Congress (Newdow III), 19

Newman v Physical Therapy Associates of Rome, Inc., 478

Next Century Communications v Ellis, 319

Nichols v Lowe's Home Center, Inc., 197

Nike, Inc. v McCarthy, 363

Nintendo of America v NTDEC, 136

Nissho Iwai Europe PLC v Korea First Bank, 728

NLRB v Fruit and Vegetable Packers, Local 760 (Tree Fruits, Inc.), 912

NLRB v Jones & Laughlin Steel, 73

NLRB v Retail Clerks, Local 1001 (Safeco Title Ins. Co.), 912

NLRB v Town & Country Electric, Inc., 908

NLRB v Transportation Management Corp., 905, 909

Noram Investment Services, Inc. v Stirtz Bernards Boyden, 1134–1135

Norfolk Southern Ry. Co. v Kirby, 493

North Carolina ex rel. Cooper v Tennessee Valley Authority, 1201

North Coast Women's Care Medical Group, Inc. v San Diego County Superior Court, 79

Northeast Harbor Golf Club v Harris, 1149

Northeast Realty, LLC v Misty Bayou, LLC, 1020

Northern Insurance Company of New York v 1996 Sea Ray Model 370DA Yacht, 537, 550

Northville Industries v National Union Fire and Ins. Co., 831

Nostrand Gardens Co-op v Howard, 1230

Nursing Home Pension Fund, Local 144 v Oracle Corp., 36

Nycal Corp. v KPMG Peat Marwick LLP, 1120

O

Oakes Logging, Inc. v Green Crow, Inc., 414

Oakley Fertilizer, Inc. v Continental Ins. Co., 510

O'Banner v McDonald's Corp. (653 NE2d 1267), 974

O'Banner v McDonald's Corp. (670 NE2d 632), 974

O'Bryan v Ashland, 1114

Ocean Atlantic Development Corp. v Aurora Christian Schools, Inc., 287

Ochoa v Ford, 295

O'Connor v Ortega, 925

Ocwen Loan Servicing, LLC v Branaman, 628

Oheka Management, Inc. v Home Theater Interiors, LLC, 563, 573

Okefenokee Aircraft, Inc. v Primesouth Bank, 770

Olander Contracting v Wachter, 383

Oliveira v Lombardi, 522

Omnicom v Giannetti Investment Co., 991–992

Oncale v Sundowner Offshore Services, Inc., 942

Oneal v Colton Consolidated School District, 430

O'Neal v Home Town Bank of Villa Rica, 339

O'Neill v Dunham, 1224

Orange Bowl Corp. v Warren, 403

Orr v Orr, 79

Ortega v O'Connor, 925

Ortiz v Chicago, 209

Osakeyhtio v EEC Commission, 139

Ossining Union Free School District v Anderson, 1118

Ost v West Suburban Travelers Limousine, Inc., 897

Overman v Brown, 303

Overton v Reilly, 958

P

Paden v Murray, 319, 327

Paduano v City of New York, 123

Page v American National Bank & Trust Co., 208

Palmer v BRG of Georgia, Inc., 101–102

Palsgraf v Long Island Rail Road Co., 198–199, *199*

Pan American World Airways, Inc., v Aetna Casualty & Surety Co., 830

Pankas v Bell, 327

Pankratz Implement Company v Citizens National Bank, 774

Pantano v McGowan, 294

Pantoja-Cahue v Ford Motor Credit Co., 782

Pappas v Hauser, 304

Paraskevaides v Four Seasons Washington, 495, 498

Parrino v Sperling, 574

Partipilo v Hallman, 276

Patel v Patel, 994

Paten v Thoroughbred Power Boats, Inc., 1047

Patterson Custom Homes v Bach, 859

Paul Frank Industries Inc. v Paul Sunich, 215

Payday Today, Inc. v Hamilton, 753

Payne v Western & Atlantic Railroad Co., 898

Payout v Coral Mortgage Bankers, 376

PAZ Securities, Inc. v SEC, 1103

Peace v Doming Holdings Inc., 286

Peavy v Bank South, 659–660

Peddy v Montgomery, 308

Pee Dee Nursing Home v Florence General Hospital, 871

Pelican Plumbing Supply, Inc. v J. O. H. Construction Co., Inc., 636

Pena v Salinas, 844

Pennsylvania v Baldassari, 407

Pennsylvania v Bunting, 166

Pennsylvania v Suders, 943

Pennsylvania Dept. of Banking v NCAS of Delaware, LLC, 677, 741

People v Neff, 163

PepsiCo, Inc. v Pacific Produce, Ltd., 150–151

Pepsi-Cola Bottling Co. of Pittsburgh, Inc., v PepsiCo, Inc., 271

Pepsi-Cola Co. v Steak 'N Shake, Inc., 517

Perfect 10 v Amazon.com, Inc., 223

Perini Corp. v First Nat'l Bank, Redland Co., Inc. v Bank of America Corp, 695

Perkins v Standard Oil Co., 386

Peronto v Case Corp., 922

Pero's Steak and Spaghetti House v Lee, 670

Perry v Saint Francis Hospital, 463

Pettes v Yukon, 988

PGI, Inc. v Rathe Productions, Inc., 966, 976

Philbrick v eNom Inc., 218

Philip Morris, Inc. v Star Tobacco Corp., 217

Philip Werlein, Ltd. v Daniels, 872

Philipp Lithographing Co. v Babich, 1003

Phillips v Grendahl, 756, 759

Phillips v Montana Education Ass'n, 1156

Phillips v Rogers, 390

Phipps v Clark Oil & Refining Corp., 932–933

Physical Distribution Services, Inc. v R. R. Donnelley, 404

Physicians Mutual Ins. Co. v Savage, 390

PIC Realty Corp. v Southfield Farms, Inc., 275

Pico v Cutter Dodge, Inc., 285

Pierce v First Nat'l Bank, 535

Pinchuck v Canzoneri, 359–360

Pinnock v International House of Pancakes, 1222

Plaisance v Scottsdale Insurance Co., 822

Plano Lincoln Mercury, Inc. v Roberts, 600

Platone v Flyi, Inc., 901

Playboy Enterprises, Inc. v Welles, 219

Plessy v Ferguson, 8

Poly America, Inc. v NLRB, 911

Pope v McWilliams, 1242

Porteous v St. Ann's Café & Deli, 565

Porter County Development Corp. v Citibank (South Dakota), N.A., 669, 680

Potomac Leasing Co. v Vitality Centers, Inc., 365

Potter v Hughes, 1070

Potter v Tyndall, 577

Power & Pollution Services, Inc. v Suburban Power Piping Corp., 431

Prate Installations, Inc. v Thomas, 426

Pratt & Whitney, 261–262

Pravin Banker Associates v Banco Popular del Peru, 399

Praxair, Inc. v General Insulation Co., 557

Precision Instrument Co., Inc., 581

Precision Mirror & Glass v Nelms, 584

Premier Title Co. v Donahue, 384

Prenger v Baumhoer, 334

Presley v City of Memphis, 466

Presley Memorial Foundation v Crowell, 458

Presto Mfg. Co. v Formetal Engineering Co., 614

Presto-X-Co. v Ewing, 363

Prince v O'Brien, 985

Princeton University Press v Michigan Document Services, Inc., 223

Procan Construction Co. v Oceanside Development Corp, 315

Procter & Gamble v Investbanka, 434

Production Credit Ass'n of Manaan v Rub, 339

ProGrowth Bank, Inc. v Wells Fargo Bank, N.A., 773, 786

Pruitt v Main & Tower, Inc., 887

Public Employees Retirement System of Ohio v Betts, 949

Puget Sound National Bank v Washington Department of Revenue, 401

Puget Sound Service Corp. v Dalarna Management Corp., 320–321

Pugliese v Mandello, 966

Purina Mills, LLC v Less, 269, 602

Purkett v Key Bank USA, Inc., 790

Pyeatte v Pyeatte, 282–283

Q

Qatar v First American Bank of Virginia, 662

Quadrtech Corp., 907

Qualcomm, Inc. v Broadcom, Inc., 27

Qualitex Co. v Jacobson Products Co., Inc., 215

Quality Components Corp. v Kel-Keef Enterprises, Inc., 562

Quality King v L'Anza Research, 137

Quicksilver Resources, Inc. v Eagle Drilling, LLC, 402

Quill v North Dakota, 75

Quilling v National City Bank of Michigan/Illinois, 701

Quon v Arch Wireless Operating Co., Inc., 247, 260

R

Rad Concepts, Inc. v Wilks Precision Instrument Co., Inc., 581

Radley v Smith and Roberts, 404

Ragan v Columbia Mutual Ins. Co., 827

Ragsdale v Volverine World Wide, Inc., 916

Ralls v Mittlesteadt, 879

Ramos v Granajo, 1230

Ramsey v Ellis, 277

Ramsey v Taylor, 1242, 1252

Randi W. v Muroc Joint Unified School District, 195

Rangen, Inc. v Valley Trout Farms, Inc., 527

Raritan River Steel Co. v Cherry, Bekaert & Holland, 1119

Raytheon v Fair Employment and Housing Commission, 958–959

Receivables Purchasing Co., Inc. v R & R Directional Drilling, LLC, 773

Record v Wagner, 869

Red Devil Fireworks Co. v Siddle, 363–364

Red Hill Hosiery Mill, Inc. v Magnetek, Inc., 566

Reebok Int'l, Ltd. v Marnatech Enterprises, Inc., 152

Reeves v Sanderson Plumbing Products Co., Inc., 949

Regent Corp., U.S.A. v Azmat Bangladesh, Ltd., 629

Reich v Republic of Ghana, 596

Reid v Boyle, 371

Reiman v Moore, 1231

ReMapp Intern. Corp. v Comfort Keyboard Co., Inc., 517

Remora Investments, LLC v Orr, 1019

Rent-A-Center, Inc. v Hall, 529

Reserve Mining Co. v Minnesota Pollution Control Agency, 122

Resource Lenders, Inc. v Source Solutions, Inc., 215

Retail Property Investors, Inc. v Skeens, 1068

Revlon, Inc. v United Overseas, Ltd., 151–152

Reynolds v Hartford Financial Services Group, Inc., 755

R.H. Freitag Mfg. Co. v Boeing Airplane Co., 389

Rhodes v Guiberson Oil Tools, 949, 955

Rhodes v Pioneer Parking Lot, Inc., 477

Ricci v DeStefano, 937

Rice v Flood, 864

Rich v Brookville Carriers, Inc., 852

Rich Products Corp. v Kemutec, Inc., 508

Richards v Powercraft Homes, Inc., 1178

Riegel v Medtronic, 69

Rite Aid Corp. v Levy-Gray, 504

Ritz v Selma United Methodist Church, 464

Rivera v Brickman Group, Ltd., 905

Rizzo v The MacManus Group, Inc., 1094

RKR Motors Inc. v Associated Uniform Rentals, 445

RNR Investments, Ltd. v People's First Community Bank, 993

Roach v Bynum, 1036

Robinson v State Farm Mutual Automobile Ins. Co., 828

Rockland Industries, Inc. v E+E (US) Inc., 595–596

Rockwell v Sun Harbor Budget Suites, 885

Rodriguez v Learjet, Inc., 609, 613

Rogath v Siebenmann, 559

Rogers v Desa International, Inc., 227

Rogers v Salisbury Brick Corp., 451

Ronson v David S. Talesnick, CPA, 1114, 1132

Roof Techs Int. Inc. v State, 269

Rosenbach v Diversified Group, Inc., 1114

Rosenfeld v Basquiat, 516–517

Rossetti v Busch Entm't Corp., 504

Rosso v Rosso, 1063

Rothschild Sunsystems, Inc. v Pawlus, 891

Rovell v American Nat'l Bank, 697–698, 709

Rowe v New Hampshire Motor Transport Association, 74

Roy Supply, Inc. v Wells Fargo Bank, 689

Royal Indemnity Co. v Security Guards, Inc., 447

RPR & Associates v O'Brien/ Atkins Associates, P.A., 269

Rubin v United States, 1108

Rubin v Yellow Cab Co., 894

Rudolf Nureyev Dance Foundation v Noureeva-Francois, 459

Russ v Woodside Homes, Inc., 446

Ruth v Triumph Partnerships, 754

Rutledge v High Point Regional Health System, 740

Ruvolo v Homovich, 566

S

Sabia v Mattituck Inlet Marina, Inc., 348

Sabine Pilot Service, Inc. v Hauck, 930

Sabritas v United States, 142–143

Sadeghi v Gang, 295, 302

Salazar v Church's Fried Chicken, Inc., 958

Salisbury v Chapman and Realty World, Inc., 980

Salsbury v Northwestern Bell Telephone Co., 333

Salsman v National Community Bank, 711

Salute v Stratford Green Apartments, 1214

Samsung Electronics America, Inc. v Blu-Ray Class Action Litigation, 558

San Diego Air Sports Center, Inc. v FAA, 111, 121

San Francisco Police Officers Ass'n v San Francisco, 948

Sanitary Linen Service Co. v Alexander Proudfoot Co., 345

Sannerud v Brantz, 196

Santa's Workshop v Hirschfeld, Inc., 1051–1052

Saputa v Cantanese, 1231

Sargent v Ross, 1231

Sassy Doll Creations Inc. v Watkins Motor Lines Inc., 490

Savidge v Metropolitan Life Ins. Co., 661

Saxton v AT&T Co., 960

Saxton v Pets Warehouse, Inc., 504

Saylor v Villcar Realty, L.L.C., 1225

SCADIF, S.A. v First Union Nat. Bank, 630

Scarborough v Winn Residential LLP/Atlantic Terrace Apartments, 1220

Schiffer v United Grocers, Inc., 625

Schmidt v Farm Credit Services, 1147

Schmidt v Prince George's Hospital, 311, 325

Schock v Ronderos, 550–551

Schoen v Freightliner LLC, 192

Schottenstein Trustees v Carano, 401

Schulingkamp v Carter, 648, 658

Schultz v Bank of the West, C. B.C., 790

Schultz v Barberton Glass Co., 208

Schwartz v Family Dental Group, PC, 985

Scott v Beth Israel Med. Ctr., 246

Scottish Heritable Trust v Peat Marwick Main & Co., 1122

Scotwood Industries, Inc. v Frank Miller & Sons, Inc., 589

SEC v Banca Della Suizzera Italiana, 141

SEC v Bilzerian, 1102

SEC v Chester Holdings, Ltd., 1113

SEC v Edwards, 1087, 1105

SEC v ILN, Inc., 1109–1110

SEC v Infinity Group Co., 1086

SEC v Materia, 1099

SEC v Pentagon Capital Management, PLC, 1094

SEC v Shiner, 1086

SEC v Wallenbrock, 1087

Security Bank and Trust Co. v Federal Nat'l Bank, 692

Security First v U.S. Die Casting, Inc., 1066–1067

Security Safety Corp. v Kuznicki, 451

Security State Bank v Burk, 723, 730

Security Title Agency, Inc. v Pope, 1149–1150, 1155

Seeman v Sterling Ins. Co., 829

Sega Enterprises, Ltd. v Maphia, 264

Selden v Burnett, 1119

Selectouch Corp. v Perfect Starch, Inc., 604

Sellon v City of Manitou Springs, 1210

Semitekol v Monaco Coach Corp., 567

Semple v Federal Express Corp., 900, 928

Service Corp. Intern. v Aragon, 741

Sharbino v Cooke Family Enterprises, Inc., 610

Sharon v City of Newton, 448

Shatterproof Glass Corp. v James, 1132–1133

Shaw v Delta Airlines, Inc., 1009

Shawnee Hospital Authority v Dow Construction, Inc., 419

Sheffield v Darby, 577

Sheppard v Griffin, 999

Sherwood v Walker, 316

Sherwood Estates Homes Ass'n, Inc. v McConnell, 1209

Shipes v Hanover Ins. Co., 828

Shipler v General Motors Corp., 199–200

Shmueli v Corcoran Group, 465

Shoaf v Warlick, 1064

Shoars v Epson America, Inc., 924

Shoreline Communications, Inc. v Norwich Taxi, LCC, 403

Shurgard Storage Centers v Lipton-U City, LLC, 315, 325

Siesta Sol, LLC v Brooks Pharmacy, Inc., 516

Silveira v Las Gallina Valley Sanitary District, 1196

Silvernail v Silvernail, 983

Simcala v American Coal Trade, Inc., 290

Simmons v Washing Equipment Technologies, 563

Simonetti v Delta Air Lines Inc., 251

Simpson v Goodman, 459

Sippy v Christich, 328

Sirius LC v Erickson, 632, 635

SKF USA, Inc. v U.S. Customs and Border Protection, 88, 144

Slodov v Animal Protective League, 505

Smith v Augustine, 1079

Smith v Brown & Jones, 996

Smith v City of Jackson, Mississippi, 950

Smith v Gordon, 674

Smith v Locklear, 338

Smith v Penbridge Associates, Inc., 592

Smith v Redd, 1011

Smith v Van Gorkom, 1142, 1144, 1155

Smith v Vaughn, 631, 632, 635

Smith v Watson, 500

Smith & Edwards v Golden Spike Little League, 967

Smith Land & Improvement Corp. v Celotex, 1208–1209

Smith-Hoy v AMC Property Evaluations, Inc., 972

SMS Financial, L.L.C. v ABCO Homes, Inc., 659

Smyth v Pillsbury Co., 261, 930

Snug Harbor Realty Co. v First National Bank, 660

Softa Group, Inc. v Scarsdale Development, 587

Solow v Heard McElroy & Vestal, LLP, 1117

Sony Music Entertainment Inc. v Does 1–40, 249, 260–261

South Carolina Ins. Co. v Collins, 844

South Central Bank of Daviess County v Lynnville Nat. Bank, 700, 709

Southeast Alaska Construction Co. v Alaska, 445

Southern Energy Homes, Inc. v AmSouth Bank of Alabama, 732–733

Southern Farm Bureau Casualty Co. v Allard, 842–843

Southern Nuclear Operating Co. v NLRB, 910

SouthTrust Bank of Alabama, N.A. v Webb-Stiles Co., Inc., 727, 730

Specialty Tires, Inc. v CIT, 422–423, 428

Speed v Muhana, 378

Spiegler v School District of the City of New Rochelle, 408

Spray-Tek, Inc. v Robbins Motor Transp., Inc., 544

Spur Industries, Inc. v Del E. Webb Development Co., 1202, 1208

St. Bernard Savings & Loan Ass'n v Cella, 669

St. Louis v Institute of Med. Ed. & Res., 1038

St. Paul Mercury Insurance Company v Merchants & Marine Bank, 778

St. Paul Reinsurance Co., Ltd. v Club Services Corp., 861

St. Paul-Mercury Indemnity Co. v Donaldson, 733

Stafford v JHL, Inc., 447

Stahl v St. Elizabeth Medical Center, 675

Standard Insurance Co. v Carls, 841–842

Stanford v Neiderer, 861

Stark v Zeta Phi Beta Sorority Inc., 193

State v Arkell, 184–185

State v Cardwell, 504

State v Christensen, 7

State v Christy Pontiac-GMC, Inc., 1156–1157

State v Martinez, 168

State v McWilliams, 630

State v Moore, 169

State v Morris, 5

State v Steenberg Homes, Inc., 1152

State v Weaver, 170

State v Westwood Squibb Pharmaceutical Co., 1047

State Casualty v Johnson, 1008

State Department of Ecology v Lundgren, 1152

State ex rel. Cordray v Midway Motor Sales, Inc., 747

State Farm Insurance v Campbell, 204

State Farm Mutual Automobile Co. v Campbell, 828

State Oil v Khan, 94, 99

State Sec. Check Cashing, Inc. v American General

Financial Services (DE), 653

State Street Bank v Signature Financial Group, 227

Steel Industries, Inc. v Interlink Metals & Chemicals, Inc., 594

Steele v Ellis, 552

Stenzel v Dell, Inc., 585

Stephans Industries, Inc. v Haskins & Sells, 1116

Stephan's Machine & Tool, Inc. v D&H Machinery Consultants, Inc., 617

Sterling Power Partners, L.P. v Niagra Mohawk Power Corp., 504

Sterling v Sterling, 369

Stevens v Hyde Athletic Industries, Inc., 762

Stinchfield v Weinreb, 876

Stone v CDI Corp, 470

Stoneridge Investment Partners, LLC v Scientific Atlanta, Inc., 1097

Street v Board of Licensing of Auctioneers, 300

Streetscenes, LLC v ITC Entertainment Group, Inc., 855

Stricker v Taylor, 297

Stronghaven Inc. v Ingram, 436

Stuart v Chawney, 1204

Studebaker v Nettie's Flower Garden Inc., 884

Succession of Gourgis, 1240

Summers v Dooley, 991

Summers v Max & Erma's Restaurant, Inc., 565

Sun Kyung Ahn v Merrifield Town Center Ltd. Partnership, 757

Sun Life Assurance Co. v Paulson, 823

Sundamerican Bank & Trust Co. v Harrison, 1121

Sunrich v Pacific Foods of Oregon, 601

Sun-Sentinel Company v U.S. Dept. of Homeland Security, 107

Suntrust Bank v Houghton Mifflin Co., 224

Susman v Cypress Venture, 1000

Suzuki Motor Corp. v Consumers Union, 196

Swanson v Beco Const. Co., Inc., 581

SWAT 24 v Bond, 358

Sykes Corp. v Eastern Metal Supply, Inc., 661–662

Syrovy v Alpine Resources, Inc., 527–528

T

Taback v Town of Woodstock Zoning Board of Appeals, 1209

Tackney v United States Naval Academy Alumni Association Inc., 966

Tacoma News, Inc. v Tacoma-Pierce County Health Dept., 122

Tague v Autobarn Motors, Ltd., 758

Tambe Electric v Home Depot, 391

Tampa Bay Economic Development Corp. v Edman, 629

Tate v Action-Mayflower Moving & Storage, Inc., 501–502

Tate v Illinois Pollution Control Board, 124

Taylor v Baseball Club of Seattle, 201

Taylor v NationsBank Corp., 1253

Taylor v Ramsay-Gerding Construction Co., 854, 868

Temple Steel Corp. v Landstar Inway, Inc., 489

Tempur-Pedic Intern., Inc. v Waste to Charity, Inc., 538, 550

Tennessee v Baker, 183

Tennessee UDC v Vanderbilt University, 462

Terry & Wright v Crick, 1187

Texas Farm Bureau Mutual Insurance Co. v Sears, 899

Textor Construction, Inc. v Forsyth R-III School District, 450

Thayer v Dial Industrial Sales, Inc., 273

Thayer v Hicks, 1133–1134

The Clark Const. Group, Inc. v Wentworth Plastering of Boca Raton, Inc., 723

The Paper Magic Group, Inc. v J.B. Hunt Transport, Inc., 490

The Steelworkers v Weber, 948

Thomaier v Hoffman Chevrolet, Inc., 528

Thomas v Bryant, 339

Thompson v First Citizens Bank & Trust Co., 380

Thompson v San Antonio Retail Merchants Ass'n, 760

Thompson & Green Machinery Co. v Music City Lumber Co., Inc., Music City Sawmill Co., Inc., 1051

Thor Food Service Corp. v Makofske, 328

Thornton v Windsor House, Inc., 409

Thorton v D.F.W. Christian Television, Inc., 381

Tibbetts v Crossroads, Inc., 363

Tidelands Life Ins. Co. v France, 822

Time Warner Cable, Inc. v Directv, Inc., 744

Tingler v State Board of Cosmetology, 117

Tips v Hartland Developers, Inc., 434–435, 440, 449

TK Power, Inc. v Textron, Inc., 506

To-Am Equipment Co. v Mitsubishi-Caterpillar Forklift of America, 978

Tobin v Liberty Mutual Insurance Co., 953

Tonelli v United States, 884

Top of Iowa Co-Op v Sime Farms, Inc., 534

Torres v Banc One Leasing Corp, 523

Town of Freeport v Ring, 644

Trabing v Kinko's, Inc., 899

TradeWinds Environmental Restoration, Inc. v Brown Brothers Construction, LLC, 1033

Traffic Control Sources, Inc. v United Rentals Northwest, Inc., 400

Transamerican Ins. Co. v Tab Transportation, 826

Transamerican Leasing, Inc. v Institute of London Underwriters, 833

Transport Equipment Co. v Guaranty State Bank, 790

Travelers Cas. and Sur. Co. of America v Ernst & Young LLP, 1118

Travelers Cas. and Sur. Co. of America v Wells Fargo Bank N.A., 668

Travis v Paepke, 339

Tresch v Norwest Bank of Lewistown, 390

Trevino v MERSCORP, Inc., 1072

Triple Crown America, Inc. v Biosynth AG, 508

Troccoli v Lab Contract Industries, Inc., 1068

Truck South Inc. v Patel, 314

Trujillo v Apple Comuter, Inc., 564

Trustees of the National Elevator Industry Pension Fund v Lutyk, 1072

Tschiras v Willingham, 318

Turgeon v Howard University, 938

Turtle Island Restoration Network v Evans, 143

Two Pesos, Inc. v Taco Cabana, Inc., 217

Tyson Foods Inc. v Guzman, 197–199

U

UAW v Johnson Controls, Inc., 946

Uberti v Lincoln National Life Ins. Co., 827

Udolf v Reiner, 855

Ulanet v D'Artagnan, Inc., 1047

Ulmas v Acey Oldsmobile, Inc., 596

Ultramares Corp. v Touche, 1117

Underhill v Hernandez, 138

Unichem Corp. v Gurtler, 1159

Union Light & Power Co. v DC Department of Employment Services, 923

Union Miniere, S.A. v Parday Corp., 850

Union Nat'l Bank v Fern Schimke, 731

Union Pacific Railroad v Novus International, Inc., 396

Unisource Worldwide, Inc. v Valenti, 357

United Catholic Parish Schools of Beaver Dam Educational Ass'n v Card Services Center, 668

United Consumers Club v Griffin, 746

United Resource Recovery Corp.v Ranko Venture Management Inc., 339

United States v Acheson, 257

United States v Alcoa, 138

United States v American Library Association, 86

United States v Autorino, 169

United States v Ballistrea, 184

United States v Best Foods, Inc., 1194

United States v Bloom, 430

United States v Campbell, 183–184

United States v Chestman, 1098

United States v Falcone, 1106

United States v Faulkner, 169

United States v Harrell, 164

United States v Heckenkamp, 7

United States v Hilton, 257

United States v Hunter, 255

United States v Kravitz, 186

United States v Lopez, 84

United States v Microsoft, 94

United States v Midwest Video Corp., 108

United States v Morrison, 73

United States v Morton Salt Co., 114

United States v Nippon Paper Industries Co. Ltd., 137

United States v O'Hagan, 40, 1100, 1106

United States v Park, 158

United States v Pepper's Steel, Inc., 831

United States v Perez, 135

United States v Peterson, 255

United States v Wegematic Corp., 594

United States v Wilson, 73

United States Steel Corp. v Commissioner, 153–154

Universal Premium Acceptance Corp. v York Bank's Trust Co., 630

University of Colorado v American Cyanamid Co., 200

University of Georgia Athletic Ass'n v Laite, 238

Unlimited Adjusting Group, Inc. v Wells Fargo Bank, N.A., 644

Unr-Rohn, Inc. v Summit Bank, 670

U.S. Airways v Barnett, 952

U.S. Leather v H&W Partnership, 992

U.S. Material Supply, Inc. v Korea Exchange Bank, 724

U.S. Surgical Corp. v Orris, Inc., 529

U.S. v Able Time, Inc., 150

U.S. v Angevine, 263

U.S. v Bell, 172

U.S. v Booker, 160

U.S. v Erickson, 157, 182

U.S. v Inn Foods, Inc., 142

U.S. v King, 256–257, 261

U.S. v Park, 182

U.S. v Park Place Associates, 30

U.S. v Philip Morris USA Inc., 79

U.S. v Prince, 164

U.S. v Quattrone, 185–186

U.S. v Skilling, 160

U.S. v Tudeme, 169

U.S. v Welch, 167

USDA v Moreno, 85–86

USX Corp. v M. DeMatteo Construction Co., 417

Utah Pie Co. v Continental Baking Co., 91, 99

V

Vader v Fleetwood Enterprises, Inc., 758

Vallot v All American Ins. Co., 845

Varity Corp. v Howe, 913–914

Vassi/Kouska v Woodfield Nissan Inc., 351

Venmar Ventilation, Inc. v Von Weise USA, Inc., 505

Venture Tape Corp. v McGills Glass Warehouse, 215–216, 236

Verlinden B.V. v Central Bank of Nigeria, 139

Vial v Provo City, 1205

Victoria's Secret Stores v Artco, 219

Villas West II of Willowridge Homeowners Ass'n, Inc. v McGlothin, 1204

Villette v Sheldorado Aluminum Products, Inc., 577–578

Virginia v Browner, 108

Vukovich v Coleman, 356

VW Credit, Inc. v Coast Automobile Group, Ltd., 971

W

W. I. Carpenter Lumber Co. v Hugill, 733

Wagner v Bank of America, 652

Wagner v McNeely, 614

Waldron v Delffs, 643

Wales v Roll, 993

Wales Trucking Co. v Stallcup, 1210

Wall v Hodges, 1255

Wall Street Network, Ltd. v New York Times Company, 506, 525

Wallace v Iowa State Bd. of Educ., 117

Wal-Mart Stores, Inc. v AIG Life Insurance Co., 423

Wal-Mart Stores, Inc. v Binns, 191

Wal-Mart Stores, Inc. v Samara Bros, Inc., 217

Walsh v Telesector Resources Group, Inc., 269

Walter v George Koch Sons, Inc., 563

Walton v Mariner Health, 878

Walz v Todd & Honeywell, Inc, 875

Warfield v Beth Israel Deaconess Medical Center, Inc., 29

Warner-Jenkinson v Hilton Davis Chemical Co., 230

Washington v Riley, 174

Washington National Ins. Co. v Sherwood Associates, 413

Washington Sports and Entertainment, Inc. v United Coastal Ins., 832

Washington State Grange v Washington Republican Party, 9

Wasniewski v Quick and Reilly, Inc., 461

Wassenaar v Panos, 452

Waterbury Hospital v NLRB, 932

Waters v Key Colony East, Inc., 451

Waton v Waton, 373

Webb v Interstate Land Corp., 788

Webster v Blue Ship Tea Room, 575

Weil v Murray, 586, 592

Welch v Choa, 901

Weldon v Trust Co. Bank of Columbus, 690, 711

Welsh v U.S., 940

Wermer v ABI, 424

Werner Enterprises, Inc. v Ace Seguros, 499

West Pinal Family Health Center, Inc. v McBride, 441

Westby v Gorsuch, 329–330

Western Casualty & Surety Co. v Citizens Bank of Las Cruces, 663

Weston v Weston Paper and Manufacturing Co., 1078

Weyerhaeuser v Ross-Simons, 91

Whelen Associates v Jaslow Dental Laboratory, 232

Whirlpool v Marshall, 920, 932

Whithorn v Whithorn Farms, Inc., 1071

Wilcox Manufacturing, Inc. v Marketing Services of Indiana, Inc., 313

Wilkie v Eutice, 383

William C. Cornitius, Inc. v Wheeler, 304

William Iselin & Co. v Landau, 1133

Williams v Countrywide Home Loans, Inc., 1182

Williams v First Tennessee National Corp., 899

Williams v Great Falls, 1201

Williams v Smith Avenue Moving Co., 465

Williams Controls v Parente, Randolph, Orlando, & Associates, 1131–1132

Williamson v Strictland & Smith Inc., 480

Willis Mining v Noggle, 504

Wilson v Brick Tp. Zoning Bd. of Adjustment, 1206

Wilson v Layne, 5, 11

Winchell v Guy, 1172, 1185

Wisconsin Electric Power Co. v Union Pacific Railroad Co., 424–425

Wisconsin v Tolliver, 168

Wombles Charters, Inc. v Orix Credit Alliance, Inc., 782

Woodhull Corp. v Saibaba Corp., 415

Woodman v Kera, LLC, 448

Woodsland Furniture, LLC v Larsen, 217

Woodson v Scott Paper Co., 935

World Diamond Inc. v Hyatt Corp., 495

World Radio Laboratories, Inc. v Coopers & Lybrand, 1122

Wright v Mallet, 459

Wright v Universal Maritime Service Corp., 37

Wujin Nanxiashu v Ti-Well International, 1150

Wyeth v Levine, 69, 560

Wyman-Gordon Co. v NLRB, 930–931

X

XL Disposal Corp. v John Sexton Contractors Co., 395

Xpert Automation Systems Corp. v Vibromatic Co., 231

Y

Yarde Metals, Inc. v New England Patriots Ltc., 365

Yates v State, 17–18

Yelverton v Lamm, 852

Young v Pileggi, 328

Young v Taylor-White LLC, 884

Young v Virginia Birth-Related Neurological Injury Compensation Program, 272

Youse v Employers Fire Ins. Co., 834

Yu Fang Tan v Arnel Management Co., 1225, 1228

YYY Corp. v Gazda, 630

Z

Z&Z Leasing, Inc. v Graying Reel, Inc., 1211

Zadrozny v City Colleges of Chicago, 283

Zeigler v Cardona, 837

Ziegler Furniture and Funeral Home, Inc. v Cicmanec, 674, 675

Zuckerman v Antenucci, 997–998

Zuni Public School Dist. No. 89 v Department of Educ., 108

subject index

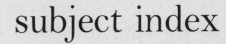

A

abate, 1244
abatement, 1222
absolute guaranty, 719
absolute privilege, 194
abstract of title, 1176
acceptance
  defined, 294, 508, 585,
    1059, 1176
  effect of, 295
  by telephone/electronic
    communication, 299
  time and manner of,
    296–298
acceptance of offer 294–300
  auction sales, 300
  communication of,
    298–300
  counteroffer, 293
  death or disability and, 294
  effect of, 295
  firm offer, 292–293
  lapse of time, 293–294
  manner and time of,
    296–298
  privilege of offeree, 294
  revocation of, 292–293
  silence as, 296–298
  subsequent illegality, 294
  by telephone and electronic
    communication, 299
  unordered goods and
    tickets, 297–298
  what constitutes acceptance,
    294
  who may accept, 295
acceptor, 625
accommodation party, 625
accord and satisfaction, 419
accountant liability and
  malpractice
  choice of remedy, 1115
  comparative negligence,
    1123
  defenses to, 1122–1123
  destruction of records, 1129
  environment of, 1115–1116
  fraud practice liability to
    third parties, 1123–1124
  general principles of,
    1113–1117

  liability to third parties:
    beyond privity,
    1117–1121
  limitation of, 1116–1117
  maintaining auditor
    independence,
    1127–1128
  nonliability parties,
    1121–1122
  parties affected by decision
    of accountant's client,
    1122
  Sarbanes-Oxley provisions,
    1124–1129
  scope of limitation, 1116
  theories of, 1125
  tort liability, 1115
  what constitutes
    malpractice, 1113
acknowledgment, 1236
acquired distinctiveness, 213
act-of-state doctrine, 138
Adams, Mike, 253
adeemed, 1244
Adelphia Corporation, 159
adjustable rate mortgage
  (ARM), 1181
administrative agency 105–121
  administrative decision
    form, 115–116
  adminstrative hearing, 115
  adoption of regulations,
    108–109, 110–112
  agency research of issues,
    109
  appeal from administrative
    action, 116–119
  authority of, 108
  cease-and-desist order, 116
  consent decrees, 115
  constitutional limitations on
    administrative
    investigations, 112–114
  defined, 105
  enforcement, preliminary
    steps, 114
  enforcement or execution of
    the law, 112
  executive power of,
    112–114
  exhaustion of administrative
    remedies, 116

  finality of administrative
    determination, 116–119
  inspections, 113
  judicial power of, 114–121
  legislative power of,
    107–112
  liability of, 120
  nature of, 105–107, 120
  open operation, 106, 121
  options after public
    comment period,
    111–112
  procedural issues, 117
  production of papers and
    records, 113–114
  proposed regulations,
    110–111
  public comment period on
    proposed rules, 111
  punishment and
    enforcement powers,
    116
  purpose of, 105
  regulations as laws,
    107–108
  rule adoption, 112
  as specialized court,
    114–116
  steps in agency rulemaking,
    113
  uniqueness of, 105–106
Administrative Dispute
  Resolution Act of 1990, 115
administrative law, 105
administrative law judge (ALJ),
  115
Administrative Procedure Act,
  106
administrative regulation, 8
administrator, administratrix,
  372, 1240
adminstrative chain of
  command, 106
admissibility, 26
ADR. See alternative dispute
  resolution (ADR)
adverse possession, 1179
advertising
  corrective/retractive, 743
  deception, 742, 744, 759
  false or misleading, 88–89,
    742, 759

  fraudulent, 742
advising bank, 727
affidavit, 1236
affirm, 17
affirmative action programs,
  947–948
after-acquired goods, 767
A.G. (Aktiengesellschaft), 133
age, discrimination based on,
  949–950
Age Discrimination in
  Employment Act (ADEA),
  937, 944, 949, 955
agency 850–868
  accounting, 861, 867
  agent, 850
  agent employment
    according to contract,
    862
  agent loyalty, 859–861, 867
  agent's acts adverse to
    principal, 858
  agent's authority, 856–859,
    867
  agent's compensation, 862
  agent's duties and liabilities
    after, 862
  apparent authority,
    853–854, 856, 866
  attorney, 858
  attorney in fact, 853
  authorization by
    appointment, 853
  authorization by conduct,
    853–854
  binding contract, 857, 867
  classification of agents,
    852–853
  conditions for ratification,
    855–856
  coupled with an interest,
    853
  creating, 853–856
  customary authority, 856,
    867
  defined, 696, 850
  definitions and distinctions,
    850–852, 867
  disability of principal under
    UDPAA, 864, 867
  durable power of attorney,
    864, 867

duties and liabilities of agent during, 859–861, 867
duty to ascertain extent of agent's authority, 857–858, 867
effect of proper exercise of authority, 857
effect of termination of authority, 865–866
employees, 850
express authorization, 853, 866, 867
general agent, 852, 867
incidental authority, 856, 867
independent contractor, 850–852, 867
information, 861
intent to ratify, 854–855
limitations on agent's authority, 858–859, 867
nature of agency relationship, 850–853, 867
obedience and performance, 861
obvious limitations on authority, 858
power of attorney, 853
principal, 850
principal's duties and liabilities to agent, 862–863
protection of agent's authority, 865
proving agency relationship, 856
by ratification, 854–856
reasonable care, 861, 867
relationships, 851
scope of agent's authority, 856–857, 867
secret limitations on authority, 859
special agent, 852, 867
termination by act of parties, 863, 867
termination by operation of law, 863, 867
termination of, 863–866, 867
termination of coupled with an interest, 865
Uniform Durable Power of Attorney Act (UDPAA), 864, 867
universal agent, 853, 867
agent 132, 695, 850
contracting, 889
soliciting, 889

airbill, 487
Alien Registration Card, 926
alteration, 675
alter ego theory, 1073
alternative dispute resolution (ADR), 28–33
alternative payees, 649
Amazon.com, 247
ambiguous, 379, 634
American Law Institute (ALI), 504
American rule, 447
American Society of Composers, Authors, and Publishers (ASCAP), 222
Americans with Disabilities Act (ADA), 937, 944, 950, 955, 1214, 1219
Americans with Disabilities Amendments Act of 2008 (ADAAA), 950
anatomical gifts, 463
annual percentage rate (APR), 748
answer, 24
antenuptial agreement, 373
anticipatory breach, 434
anticipatory repudiation, 434
anticompetitive behavior remedies, 97, 98
antidiscrimination, and leases, 1214
antidumping laws, 127, 149
antilapse statutes, 1245
antiracketeering acts, federal and state, 147
Antitrust (film), 98
antitrust law exemption, 967
antitrust laws, 127, 137–140
Antitrust Modernization Committee, 91
AOL, 95
apparent authority, 856
appeal, 17
appelate jurisdiction, 17
appropriation, 250
arbitration 29–30
code of, 1103–1104, 1105
as contract provision, 33
defined, 26
ARM. *See* adjustable rate mortgage
Arms Control Export Act, 136
arson, 172
Arthur Andersen, 170, 1128
Article 2, 504
articles of incorporation, 1032
ASCAP. *See* American Society of Composers, Authors, and Publishers

Asian-Pacific race, 938
assault, 189–190
assessments and taxes, duty of lease, 1222
assignee
defined, 396, 666
rights of, 667
assignment 396–404, 405
burden of performance, 399–400, 405
consumer protection liability of assignee, 402
continuing liability of assignor, 401–402
credit transaction, 400–401
defenses and setoffs, 403
defined, 396–397, 1226
delegation of duties, 403–404, 406
form of, 397
future rights, 399
intention to delegate duties, 404
liability of assignee, 402–403, 406
nonassignable rights, 399–401
notice of, 397–398, 406
personal services contracts, 400
prohibition of assignment of rights, 399
purpose of, 399
rights of assignee 401, 405
right to money, 399
warranties of assignor, 403, 406
assignor, 396
association tribunal, 31
assumption, 1183
attestation clause, 1236
attorney, recovery of fees by, 28
attorney-client privilege, 23
attorney in fact, 853
attractive nuisance doctrine, 1171
authorities, 1033
automated teller machine (ATM) 169, 703
unauthorized use of 169
automatic perfection, 769
automatic stay, 801
Automobile Dealers' Day in Court Act (ADDCA), 970, 976

automobile insurance, 835–836, 840
avoidance of contract, 316

B

Baby Boom (film), 342
bad check laws, 688
bailee, 469, 505
bailee's lien, 472
bailments 505
bailee's interest, 470, 474
bailor's interest, 470, 474
breach of duty of care: burden of proof, 472, 474
classification of ordinary, 470–471
contract modification of liability, 473
definition, 469
delivery and acceptance, 470, 474
duties and rights of bailee, 471–472, 474
elements of, 469–470
liability for defects in bailed property, 473, 474
for mutual benefit, 471
nature of parties' interest, 470, 474
passage of title, 536, 537
of personal property, 469
renting of space distinguished, 471
bailor, 469
balance sheet test, 804
bank liability, 696–702
bankruptcy, 50, 426. *See also* specific type of bankruptcy
automatic stay, 801, 813
creditors, list of, 802
debt counseling, 796–797
debtor, insolvent, 804
debtor's duties and exemptions, 807–808
declaration of, 796–801
discharge in, 808–810, 814
discrimination, debtor's protection against, 808
federal bankruptcy law, 794–795
fraudulent transfer, 804
grounds for relief, 801
lawyers as debt relief agencies, 796
nondischargeable debts in, 810
order of relief, 802
partnership, 1000

petitioning creditors, 798–801

preferential transfers, 804–805, 813

priority of claims, 805–807, 814

proof of claim, 805

reforms, 757

self-settled trust, 805

trustee in bankruptcy, 802

types of proceedings, 794–795

voidable preferences, 804–805

Bankruptcy Abuse Prevention and Consumer Protection Act of 2005 (BAPCPA), 794

bankruptcy case, anatomy of, 803

bankruptcy courts, 794

bankruptcy estate, administration of, 803–804

Bankruptcy Reform Commission, 794

banks and USA Patriot Act, 164–165

Bank Secrecy Act, 164

Barbarians at the Gate (film), 1048

Barefoot in the Park (film), 1227

battery, 190

battle of the forms, 510

bearer, 631

bearer paper, 633

Bear Stearns, 46–47, 88

bedrock view, 70

Beech Nut Baby Food Company, 89

Beethoven (film), 523

beneficiary 705, 837, 1235

of trust, 1248–1249

of will, 1235–1236

beneficiary contracts

creditor beneficiary, 393

definitions, 393–394

description, 394

donee beneficiary, 393

incidental beneficiaries, 395–396, 405

limitations on intended third party, 395

modification or termination of third party contract, 394–395

necessity of intent, 394

third party beneficiary contracts, 393–396, 405

beneficiary's bank, 705

benefit of the bargain, 440

bequest, 1234

Berne Convention, 136, 220, 221

Berne Convention Implementation Act of 1988, 221

best technology available, 1193

bicameral, 67

bilateral contract, 272

bill of exchange, 623

bill of lading, 487, 535

Bill of Rights, 79

bill of sale, 520

Bilzerian, Paul, 808

Black Americans, 938

BlackBerry service provider, 16

blackmail, 166, 181

Blanchard, Kenneth, 55

blank indorsement, 645

blocking laws, 140

blogging, 244, 251

blue-pencil rule, 357

blue sky laws, 1084

Boeing Co., 136

boilerplate language, 510

bona-fide, 799

bond, 1058

bond indenture, 1058

book value, 1056

breach, 434, 599

breach of contract, 434–450, 1115. *See also* breach of sales contract

action for an injunction, 443

action for specific performance, 442–443, 449

American rule, 447

anticipatory breach, 434–436

anticipatory repudiation, 434–436

antimodification clause, 438

attorney's fees, 446–447

contract provisions affecting remedies and damages, 444–448

cure of breach by waiver, 436

defined, 434

direct and consequential damages, 440, 448–449

effect of liquidates damages, 445

existence and scope of waiver, 436–438

insurance, 828

liability release forms, 448

limitation of remedies, 444

liquidated damages, 444–446, 449

mitigation of damages, 441–442

monetary damages, 440–442

quasi-contractual or restitution remedy, 438–440

recission, 442

reformation of contract by a court, 443

remedies for, 438–444

reservation of rights, 438, 449

waiver of, 436–438

breach of sales contract

action for breach of warranty, 604–605

action for specific performance, 607

buyer's action for damages for nondelivery, 604

buyer's remedies under UCC article 2, 607

buyer's resale of goods, 606–607

cancellation by buyer, 605–606

cancellation by seller, 600

contract provisions on remedies, 608–611

damages, exclusion of, 609

damages, limitation of, 608–609

damages, other types, 602, 604, 606

defenses, preservation of, 611

defenses, waiver of, 610, 612

down payment and deposits, 609, 610

lease by Collins Entertainment Corporation, 602

measure of damages, 605

notice of, 605

notice of third-party action against buyer, 605

preservation notice, 611

prohibition of waiver, 611

rejection of improper tender, 603

remedies, 599–613

resale by seller, 600, 612

revocation of acceptance, 603, 612

secured transaction, 602

seller's action for damages under market price formula, 601

seller's action for lost profits, 601

seller's action for the purchase price, 602

seller's lien, 600

seller's nonsale remedies, 602–603

seller's remedies under UCC Article 2, 603

seller's remedy of stopping shipment, 600

statute of limitations, 599

time limits for, 599

breach of the peace, 782

Breaking Away (film), 58

bribery 166, 181

commercial, 166

of public officials, 149

Broadcast Music, Inc. (BMI), 222

bubble concept, 1191

Buckley Amendment, 6

Buffett, Warren, 56

Built to Last (Collins, J. and Porras, J.), 45

bulk transfer law, 515

bulk transfers, 515

bundle of rights, 4

Bureau of Citizenship and Immigration Services, U.S. (USCIS), 926–927

Bureau of Industry and Security (BIS), 134–135

Burger King Corporation, 969

burglary, 172

business

criminal procedure rights for, 177–180

due process rights, 180

Fifth Amendment Rights, 179–180, 181

Fourth Amendment Rights, 177–180

regulate of, 88–89

regulation of, 354–360

sale of, 356

business ethics

defined, 40

and financial performance, 45–46

importance of, 44–51

and regulation, 46–51

universal standards for, 41

business judgment rule, 1142

business organizations

cooperatives, 967–968, 976

corporations, 965, 975

franchises, 968–975

joint ventures, 965–966, 976

partnerships, LLPs, and
   LLCs, 964–965, 975,
   986, 1005
principal forms, 964–965
types of, 964–977
unincorporated associations,
   966–967
business records, 178
business transactions,
   international, 41–42
bylaws, 1036

C

cancellation provision, 335
The Candidate (film), 81
capital, distribution of, 1069
capital stock, 1056
Capper-Volstead Act of 1922,
   968
cargo insurance, 832
Carmack Amendment to
   Interstate Commerce Act,
   490
carrier, 485
case law, 8
cashier's check, 624, 689
cash on delivery (COD), 540
cash surrender value, 836
cash tender offer, 1101
causation, 198
cause of action, 399
cease-and-desist order, 116
certificate of deposit, 623
certificate of incorporation,
   1032
certificate of stock, 1057
certified check, 695
certified public accountant,
   1113–1114
cestui que trust, 1248
CF (cost and freight), 540
challenged for cause, 25
Chapter 7 bankruptcy,
   794–795, 813
Chapter 11 bankruptcy 795,
   810–812, 813
   plan confirmation, 812
   reorganization plan,
      811–812, 814
Chapter 13 bankruptcy 795,
   1032
   discharge of debtor,
      812–813
   payment/debt adjustment
      plans, 795, 812–813
   plan confirmation, 812
   plan contents, 812
charitable subscriptions, 333,
   340–341

Chavez, Julio Cesar, 288
check, 624, 678–696, 708
   agency status of collecting
      bank, 695–696
   alteration of, 698–699, 708
   bank liability, 696–702
   bank reporting
      requirements, 693, 708
   banks and privacy, 693, 708
   bank's duty of care, 696
   certified, and stop payment
      order, 695, 708
   certified checks, 690, 708
   certified checks and stop
      payment, 691, 708
   check and draft, differences,
      688, 708
   check clearing, 645
   customer-bank relationship,
      693, 708
Check Truncation Act (CTA),
   701
child labor, 905
Children's Online Privacy
   Protection Act (COPPA),
   250
Chinese Foreign Equity Joint
   Venture Law, 134
choice-of-law clause, 127
chose in action, 458
CIF (cost, insurance and
   freight), 540
CISG. *See* Contracts for the
   International Sale of Goods
   (CISG)
civil disobedience, 41
Civil Rights Act of 1964
   Title VII, 935–938, 939,
      954
Civil Rights Act of 1991, 935,
   953
claims, 399, 805, 1243
Class Action (film), 205
Clayton Act, 90, 95, 98
Clean Air Act of 1963, 1191
Clean Water Act, 1192
Clear and Present Danger (film),
   120
close-connection doctrine, 669
close corporation, 1033
Coca-Cola Bottling Company,
   968
COD. *See* cash on delivery
codes of ethics, 51
codified law, 40
coinsurance clause, 834
collateral
   after-acquired, 767
   compulsory deposition of,
      783

consumer goods, 767
creditor's possession and
   disposition of, 782
debtor's right of
   redemption, 784, 786
defined, 633, 764
disposition of, 784
electronic chattel paper, 768
liability for deficit, 785
nature and classification of,
   766–768, 785
notice of intention, 783,
   786
postdisposition accounting,
   784–785
proceeds, 767
purchase money security
   interest in inventory,
   778
status of repair or storage
   lien, 779
tangible, 785
collateral heirs, 1245
collective bargaining 905
   employer duty of, 910
Collins, James C., 45
Columbia Health Care, 45
Columbo (television series), 181
comity, 138
commerce clause, 72, 73
Commerce Control List (CCL),
   135
Commerce Country Chart, 135
Commercial General Liability
   (CGL) policies, 831–832
commercial impracticability,
   590
commercial lease, 522
commercial paper, 622
commercial unit, 584
commissiion merchant, 493
commission, 493
common carrier, 485
common law, 8
common law rule, 1171
common stock, 1057
communication, privacy of,
   6–7
Communications Act of 1934,
   164
community property, 468
comparative negligence, 199,
   201, 1123
compensatory damages, 440,
   741
complaint
   defined, 23
   disposition of, 33
composition of creditors,
   338

Comprehensive Environmental
   Response, Compensation,
   and Liability Act
   (CERCLA), 1193
computer crime
   computer as victim, 173
   computer raiding, 174
   diverted delivery, 174
   economic espionage, 175
   unauthorized use of
      computer, 173, 174
Computer Fraud and Abuse
   Act (CFAA), 250, 255
computer software, warranty
   liability and damage
   provisions, 506
computer viruses, 254
concealment, 722
condition
   concurrent, 413
   defined, 411
condition precedent, 411
condition subsequent, 412
condominium, 1172
confidential relationship, 321
conflict of interest 1088
   defined, 53
conflicts of law, 23
conglomerate, 1045
Congress 47
   silence of, 70
Congressional Enabling Act,
   108–109
consequential damages, 440,
   448–449, 604
consideration
   adequacy of, 333–334
   benefit-detriment approach,
      332
   cancellation provision, 335
   completion of contract and,
      337
   compromise and release of
      claims, 337–338
   conditional promises, 336
   defined, 332
   exceptions to, 340–342
   forbearance as, 334–335,
      342
   general principles of,
      332–336
   gifts as, 332–333
   illusory promises and,
      335–336
   Internal Revenue Service
      and, 334
   moral obligation, 339
   past, 338–339
   preexisting legal obligation,
      336–338

special situations, 336–340
and value compared, 668
consignee, 547
consignment, 547
consignor, 547
consolidation (of corporations),
1044
conspiracy, 163
Constitution. *See* U.S.
Constitution
constitution, 7–8, 67
constitutional law, 7–8, 11
constructive bailment, 471
constructive delivery, 460
constructive eviction, 1217
consumer, 737
consumer credit, 755
Consumer Credit Protection
Act (CCPA), 419
consumer goods, 767
consumer lease, 521
Consumer Leasing Act of 1976,
747
Consumer Product Safety Act,
752
Consumer Product Safety
Commission, 752
Consumer Product Safety
Improvement Act, 560
consumer protection
action by attorney general,
740–741
action by consumer, 741
advertising, 742–743
areas of, 742–758
automobile lemon laws, 758
civil and criminal penalties
under statutes, 741–742
consumer, 738
consumer contract,
746–748
consumer protection
movement, 737
credit, collection, and billing
methods, 752–754
credit, limitations on,
747–748
credit cards, 749–751
credit counseling, 748
credit disclosures, 748
credit repair organizations,
757
credit reporting agencies/
credit bureaus, 755
credit standing and
reputation, 755–757
damages, 741–742
Equal Credit Opportunity
Act (ECOA), 752
erroneous credit report, 757

expansion of, 737–738
from false information,
755–757
franchises, 758
general principles, 737–742
government agency action,
740
home-solicited sales, 745
improper collection
methods, 752–754
Interstate Land Sales Full
Disclosure Act
(ILSFDA), 757
invalidation of contract, 741
invasion of privacy, 752
labeling and marking
products, 744–745
legal environment of
consumer, 742
legislation, 354
liability under consumer
protection statutes, 738
medical information, 756
privacy, 755
product safety, 752
real estate development
sales, 757
remedies, 740
replacement or refund, 741
selling methods, 745–746
service contracts, 757
telemarketing, 746
unconscionability, 748
unfair or deceptive acts or
practices (UDAP)
statutes, 737
when there is liability under
statutes, 738–740
contact rule, 1118
contemplated action, guidelines
for analyzing, 43
contract. *See also* breach of
contract; contract discharge
avoidance of, 316
avoidance of hardship, 385
completion of, 337
conduct and custom, 385
construction, rules of,
381–385
in cyberspace, 252–253
defined, 252, 268
duress, 380
effects of invalidity,
357–358
electronic forms, 368–388
evidenced by a writing, 369
fraud, 380
good faith adjustment, 337,
342
hurdles in the path of, 370

illegal, 348–349
insurance, 822–829
international, 127
interpretation, 381–385,
386
lawsuit by third person, 403
mistakes, 314–317, 325,
380
modification of, 380
nature of writing, 383–384,
386
nondisclosure, 320–321
oral, 368, 378
oral extension of, 370–371
parties in agreement,
381–382, 386
reformation, 316–317
sale of business, 356
sale of goods, 373
under seal, 270
statutory regulation, 354
strict construction against
drafting party, 384, 386
terms of, 382–385
third-party beneficiaries,
393–396
third persons and, 393–407
unilateral mistakes,
314–315, 325
U.S. law of, 127
whole contract, 382
words and reference,
381–382, 386
writing, 368–388
written note or
memorandum, 374–375
contract carrier, 486
contract completed within one
year, 369
contract discharge 411–429
accord and satisfaction, 419
by action of parties,
418–420
act of other party, 421–422
adequacy of performance,
415–418
by agreement, 419
bankruptcy, 426
causes, 416
change of law, 421
classifications of conditions,
411–413
commercial impracticability,
422
comparison to common law
rule, 424
consumer protection
recission, 419
contractual limitations, 426
damages, 415

death or disability, 421
destruction of subject
matter, 421
developing doctrines,
422–424
discharge by performance,
413–418
external causes, 420–427
fault of complaining party,
418
force majeure, 424
frustration of purpose
doctrine, 423
impossibility, 420–422
nature of performance,
413–414
normal discharge, 413
operation of law, 426
payments, 414
performance, 411
performance to satisfaction
of contracting party, 418
statute of limitations, 426
substitution, 419
temporary impossibility,
425–426
time limitation for
litigation, 426
time of performance,
414–415
by unilateral action,
418–419
weather, 425
contracting agent, 889
contract interference, 196
contract of adhesion, 351
Contracts for the International
Sale of Goods (CISG), 520,
521, 525
contractual capacity 308–326
contracts for necessaries,
310
contracts minors cannot
avoid, 312
deception, 317–321
defined, 308–309
discrimination, 309
duress, 323
factual incapacity, 309
influence, 322
intoxicated persons,
313–314
minors' avoidance of, 309
pressure, 322–323
ratification of former
minor's contract, 311
recovery of property by
minor, 310
restitution by minors of
status quo ante, 310

status incapacity, 308–309
third person liability/parent
or cosigner, 312
contractual liability, 312–313
contribution, 721, 722, 729
contributory negligence
of accountant's client or
third party, and liability,
1122
defined, 200
control, 770
conversion, 494
convicts, renting to, 1219
cookies (computer) and
privacy, 249
cooperative, 1173
Copyright Act, 220
copyright notices, 221
copyright protection devices
and crime, 176
Copyright Royalty Tribunal,
222
copyrights
defined, 220
duration, 221
ownership and the Internet,
222
piracy, 222
works applicable, 221–222
corporate directors
conflict of interest,
1140–1142
meetings of, 1142
power of, 1139, 1141
protection of, 1144–1146
qualifications, 1139
removal of a director, 1146
corporation
act of shareholder in
creating liability, 1075
application for
incorporation, 1040
asset sales, 1047–1048
benefits, paying employee,
1037
bond issues, 1037
borrowing money, 1036
bylaws, 1036
capital distribution, 1069
certificate of incorporation,
1040
charitable contributions,
1037–1038
classifications of,
1033–1034
close corporation,
1033–1034
conglomerate, 1045–1046
consolidation, 1044,
1046

consolidations, mergers, and
conglomerates,
1043–1048
contracts, making, 1036
creation and termination of,
1038–1043
de facto corporation, 1041
defined, 1032
dissolution, judicial, 1043
dividends, 1068–1069
doing business in another
state, 1037
domestic and foreign, 1033
by estoppel, 1041–1042
executing negotiable
instruments, 1037
forfeiture of charter,
1042–1043
formation, 1032–1050
governments and,
1034–1035
incorporation, proper and
defective, 1040–1042
incorporation of,
1039–1040
insolvency, bankruptcy, and
reorganization, 1042
legality, 1046
liability of successor
corporation, 1046–1048
malpractice liability of an
associate, 1075
merger, 1044, 1045, 1046
name, 1036
nature and classes,
1032–1035
nonprofit, 1034
participating in an
enterprise, 1037
particular powers,
1036–1038
perpetual life, 1036
as a person, 1032
powers of, 1035–1038
power to regulate, 1035
professional, 1034
professional corporation,
1075
promoters, 1038–1039
property, acquiring, 1037
property, transferring, 1037
public, private, and quasi-
public, 1033
public authorities, 1033
seal, 1036
special service, 1033
stock, 1036
stock, buying back, 1037
subchapter S corporation,
1034

ultra vires acts, 1038
corporation by estoppel, 1041
corporation de jure, 1040
corporation management
liability
active participation, 1152
business judgment rule,
1142
civil liability of corporation,
1153–1154
for corporate debts, 1153
criminal liability,
1152–1153
indemnification of officers
and agents, 1153
of management to third
persons, 1150–1151
protection of shareholders,
1153
corporation officers
agents and employees,
1146–1150
liability and fiduciary duties,
1148–1149
powers of, 1147
president, 1147
correspondent bank, 727
corrupt influence, 166–168,
181
cosignee, 485
cosignor, 485
cost, insurance and freight
(CIF), 540
cost and freight (CF), 540
cost of completion damages,
416
cost plus, 513
co-sureties, 721, 722
cotenancy, 466
Council on Environmental
Quality (CEQ), 1199
counterclaim, 24
counterfeiting, 166–167
counteroffer, 293
course of dealing, 514
court
city, 22
defined, 16
federal district, 18
general trial, 21
justice, 22
municipal, 22
small claim, 22
specialty, 21
state appellate, 22
state supreme, 22
types of, 16–18
Court of Appeals, U.S., 18–19,
144
Court of First Instance, 130

Court of International Trade,
144
court procedure, 22–28
court system 16–22
federal, 18–21
participants in, 22–23
covenant against encumbrances,
1177
covenant of further assurances,
1178
covenant of quiet enjoyment,
1177, 1217
covenant of right to convey,
1177
covenant of seisin, 1177
covenants of title, 1177
Credit Card Accountability,
Responsibility and
Disclosure Act (CARD) of
2009, 748
Credit Card Fraud Act of 1984,
170
credit cards 749–751, 759
balance transfers, 750–751
crime and, 169–170
gift cards, 751
late payment fee, 750
preservation of consumer
defenses, 751–752
privacy rights, 248
surcharge prohibited, 750
unauthorized use, 750, 759
unsolicited, 749
creditor, 704, 719, 764
Credit Repair Organization Act
of 1996, 757
credit transfer, 705
crimes, 156–183. See also
individual crimes
agency, 879, 882–889
agent's, 887
business and white-collar
crime penalties,
159–160
civil wrongs, 349–350
common law, 172–173
compliance program/ethics
program, 160
corporate liability, 156,
158
corporate officers/directors
and, 158
criminal liability, 156
damages, action for, 163
deterrence for corporations,
159
forfeiture, 159
general principles, 156–163
indemnification for unjustly
convicted, 163

indemnification of victims, 162–163
interstate commerce, 164
nature and classification, 156
production, competition and marketing, 164–165
responsibility and, 156, 158–162, 181
Sarbanes-Oxley reforms, 161
security crime, 164
Crime Victims Fund, 163
criminal procedure rights for business, 177–180
cross-examination, 26
cumulative voting, 1065
customary authority, 856
customer information, 693, 708
Customs and Border Protection Service, U.S., 142
customs duties, 142
cybercrime, 254–255
cyberlaw 243–261
   appropriation in, 250
   criminal law issues, 254–257
   cybersquatters, 218
   defamation in, 250–252
   defined, 243
   employer monitoring issues, 245–246
   evil twins phenomenon, 255
   First Amendment rights, 257
   fraud in, 252–253
   freedom of speech, screen names, and privacy, 248
   free-riders, 256
   intellectual property issues, 253–254
   introduction to, 243
   issues in, 243
   misrepresentation in, 252–253
   pharming and phishing, 255
   piggybacking, 256
   privacy issues, 244–247
   securities issues in, 258–259
   statutory protections for privacy, 249–255
   tort issues, 244
   Web user information and privacy, 247–248

D

damages
   breach of sales contract, 602, 604, 606

compensatory, 440, 741
consequential, 440, 448–449, 604
cost of completion damages, 416
direct, 440
effect of liquidities, 445
exclusion of, 609
exemplary, 200
limitation of, 608–609
liquidated, 444, 446–449, 608
measure of, 605
mitigation of, 441–442
monetary, 440–442
nominal, 440
other types of, 602, 604, 606
for personal injury, 198–200
punitive, 200, 440, 742
treble, 97
debenture, 1058
debit transfer, 705
debt
   liquidated, 337
   unliquidated, 338
debtor, 396, 704, 719, 764
debtor-creditor relationship
   creation of, 718
   definitions, 718–719
   indemnity contract distinguished, 719
   nature of, 718–730
   rights of sureties, 719–721
   suretyship and guaranty, 718–723, 729
debt or default, 371, 386
decedent
   death of distributee and, 1247
   defined, 372, 1234
   murder of, 1246
decedents' estates. See Estates
deceptive advertising, 738–739
deed, 1058, 1174
deed of trust, 1248
de facto, 1041
defamation, 193–195, 250
default
   rights of parties after, 781–785
   rights of parties before, 775–776
defendant, 22
definiteness
   "best effort" clauses, 290
   definite by incorporation, 289
   divisible contracts, 290

exceptions to, 290, 291
   implied terms, 289
definite time, 630
delegated powers, 68
delegation, 403
delegation of duties
   defined, 403
   under the UCC, 404
delivery
   constructive, 460
   of deeds, 1174
   defined, 643
   and quantity, 584
   and shipment terms, 539
   symbolic, 460
   transfer by, 656
delivery and assignment compared, 689
Delta Airlines, 251
demand draft, 688
demand paper, 688
demurrer, 24
Department of Homeland Security, 926
Department of Labor, 109
Department of Transportation red light study, 109
deposition, 24
depositor, 481
deregulation, 70, 88
derivative action, 1069
developing countries, and regional trade groups, 132
development statement, 757
devise, 1234
devisee, 1234
Digital Millenium Copyright Act (DMCA), 176, 181, 254
direct damages, 440
direct deposit and withdrawal, 703
directed verdict, 26
direct examination, 26
disability
   defined, 837
   discrimination based on, 950
Disadvantaged Business Enterprise (DBE) program, 947
discharge by
   action of parties, 418
   agreement, 419
   external causes, 420–427
   impossibility, 420–422
   operation of law, 426
   unilateral action, 418–419
discharge in bankruptcy, 808

discharge of contracts, normal, 413
disclaimer
   particular language for, 567
   postsale, 568
   validity of, 567
disclaimer of warranties, 567
disclosed principal
   action of authorized agent of, 875
   defined, 876
   unauthorized action of agent of, 875
discovery, 24
discrimination
   age, 949–950
   height, weight and physical ability, 941
   and leases, 1214
   national origin, 945
   against persons with disabilities, 950
   pregnancy, 941
   race and color, 938
   religion, 938–940
   reverse, 947–948
   sex, 940–941
   theories of, 935–937
   unlawful, 939
dishonor
   defined, 678
   notice of, 678
   time for notice of, 692
dishonor of a check, 692–693
disinherited, 1239
Disney Company, 196
disparate impact theory, 935, 939
disparate treatment theory, 939
dispute resolution, 28–33
Dispute Settlement Body, 129
distinctiveness, 213
distribution per stirpes, 1246
distributor, 132
district court, federal, 18
divestiture order, 95
dividends
   at directors' discretion, 1068–1069
   effect of transfer of shares, 1069
   form of, 1069
   funds available for declaration of, 1068
divisible contract, 290
document of title, 481, 535
Doha Round, 129
domestic corporation, 1033
dominant tenement, 1164

donee, 459
donor, 459, 1248
Do Not Call Registry, 746
double indemnity, 837
Double Indemnity (film), 839
Double Jeopardy (film), 181
double taxation, 133, 965
draft
    defined, 623
    demand, 688
    negotiable instrument, 623,
        624, 634
    time, 688
drawee
    defined, 625, 677
    negligence of, 653
drawer, 625, 678
dual motive cases, employee
    dismissal, 909
due diligence, 1203
due process, 4, 77, 180
due process clause, 77
dumping, 143
duress, 323, 325, 380, 386,
    674, 680
duty
    breach of, 198, 205
    countervailing, 145
    defined, 4, 396
duty of care
    bank's, 696
    breach of, 472
duty or legal obligation,
    preexistig, 336–338
duty to deliver, seller's, 583
duty to exercise reasonable care,
    197

E

easement
    defined, 1164
    by implication, 1164
    termination of, 1165
Ebbers, Bernie, 179
e-commerce and cyberlaw, 7
    buzz or guerilla marketing,
        745
    check clearing/Check 21,
        645
    complying with regulations
        online, 112
    computer bullies, 175
    contract formation, 297
    electronic checking, 626
    electronic contract, 523
    electronic presentment,
        679
    electronic record keeping,
        1086

electronic signatures,
    375–376, 826
e-mail's revelations, 96
Google mistrial, 32
identity theft, 749
infringement, 564
Internet and interstate, 76
nuisance and electrical
    current, 1203
payroll card, 689
privacy in the workplace,
    248
real estate listings, 1173
rejection of goods in
    cyberspace, 587
search engines, 774
stock selling scams, 1103
supply chain and risk
    management, 543
trademarks, 219
video wills, 1237
e-commerce and the law
consequential damages and
    software, 611
destruction of documents,
    1129
Economic Crime Package,
    2001, 159
economic crisis of 2008, 747
economic duress, 323, 325
Economic Espionage Act
    (EEA), 175, 181, 255
economic strikers, 911
Edmundo, 335
EEC. *See* European Economic
    Community
EEOC. *See* Equal Employment
    Opportunity Commission
effects doctrine, 138
effluent guidelines, 1192
EFT. *See* electronic funds
    transfer
Ehrlich, David, 369
electoral college, 67
Electronic Communications
    Privacy Act of 1986
    (ECPA), 245, 924, 928
electronic digital interchange
    (EDI), 252
electronic forms (contracts),
    368–388
Electronic Funds Transfer Act
    (EFTA), 703, 708
electronic funds transfer (EFT)
    703, 708
    crime, 175, 181
Electronic Fund Transfers Act
    (EFTA), 175–176
electronic presentment, 696
electronic promissory notes, 622

electronic signatures, 826
Electronic Signatures in Global
    and National Commerce
    Act (E-sign), 253, 375–376,
    523, 622
electronic tracking, 535
eleemosynary corporation, 1034
e-mail
    mailbox rule, 300
    privacy and, 244, 246
embezzlement, 170
eminent domain, 1178
emissions offset policy, 1191
employee privacy 923–926
    drug and alcohol testing,
        925–926
    Electronic Communications
        Privacy Act of 1986
        (ECPA), 924
    e-mail monitoring, 924
    Federal Wiretapping Act, 923
    monitoring telephone
        conversations, 923–924
    property searches, 924–925
    source of privacy rights, 923
Employee Retirement Income
    Security Act (ERISA),
    912–914, 928
employees' health and safety
    918–921
    common law status of
        employer, 921
    compensation for
        employees' injuries,
        921–923
    employer duties, 919
    enforcement, 919–920
    Federal Employees'
        Compensation Act, 922
    Occupational Safety and
        Health Act of 1970
        (OSHA), 918–921
    Occupatoinal Safety and
        Health Review
        Commission (OSHRC),
        919
    standards, 919
    state "right-to-know"
        legislation, 921
    statutory changes,
        921–922
    workers' compensation
        statutes, 921, 922
employer/employee relations,
    privacy and, 245, 246
employer-related immigration
    laws. *See* immigration laws,
    employer-related
employment, regulation of
    897–929

characteristics of
    employment
    relationship, 897, 927
child labor provisions, 905
collective bargaining, 905
collective bargaining
    contracts, 897
compensation, 903
creation of employment
    relationship, 897, 927
duties of employee,
    902–903
election conduct, 907
employee reactions,
    899–900
employer and union unfair
    labor practices charge,
    906
employer duty to bargain
    collectively, 910
employment-at-will
    doctrine and exceptions,
    898–899
employment contracts, 356,
    897–898
ERISA (Employee
    Retirement Income
    Security Act), 912–914
federal wage and hour law,
    903–904
inventions by employee,
    902–903
justifiable discharge,
    900–901
Labor-Management
    Reporting and
    Disclosure Act
    (LMRDA), 912
labor relations laws,
    905–912
National Labor Realtions
    Act (NLRA), 905, 907
overtime pay, 905
pension plans and federal
    regulation, 912–914
reductions in force, 901
rights of employee,
    903–905
right to work, 910–911
Sarbanes-Oxley Act,
    901–902
services of employee, 902
strike and picketing activity,
    911–912
subminimum wage
    provisions, 904
trade secrets, 902
24-hour rule, 907
union activity, 907–909
union affairs, 905

wage issues, 904–905
whistleblower protection, 901–902
employment-at-will doctrine, 898
employment contract, 356, 897–898
employment practices, 109
en banc, 19
encoding warranty, 696
Endangered Species Act (ESA), 1197
endowment insurance, 836
English civil law, 9
Enron Corporation, 45, 159, 161, 170, 1124, 1128
entertainment. *See* sports and entertainment law
environmental impact statement (EIS), 1196
environmental law. *See also* land use controls
   air pollution regulation, 1191–1192
   civil remedies, 1200–1201
   Clean Water Act, 1192
   criminal penalties, 1200
   enforcement of, 1198–1203
   Environmental Protection Agency (EPA), 1191, 1192–1193, 1196, 1197, 1198, 1200
   environmental quality regulation, 1196
   modern legislation and requirements, 1191
   nuisance and technological environment, 1202
   other regulations, 116, 1197–1198
   parties responsible for enforcement, 1199
   private and public nuisances, 1201–1202
   private remedies, 1201–1203
   remedy for nuisance, 1202
   solid waste disposal regulation, 1193–1196
   state environmental regulation, 1198
   statutory environmental law, 1191–1198
   U.S. Supreme Court and, 1192
   water, competition for, 1198
   water pollution regulation, 1192–1193

Environmental Protection Agency (EPA), 1191, 1192–1193, 1196, 1197, 1198, 1200
Equal Employment Opportunity Commission (EEOC), 9, 109, 937–938, 954
Equal Employment Opportunity Law 935–956
   affirmative action and reverse discrimination, 947–948
   age discrimination, 949–950
   arbitration option, 937–938
   bona fide occupational qualification exception, 945
   Civil Rights Act of 1964, Title VII, 935–938, 954
   Civil Rights Act of 1991, 935, 954
   damages, 937
   discrimination, theories of, 935–937
   discrimination against persons with disabilities, 950–953, 955
   employment discrimination, 935
   equal pay, 948
   exclusions from ADA coverage, 953
   extraterritorial employment, 953
   failure to take action, 953
   height, weight, and physical ability requirements, 941
   national origin, 945, 954
   pregnancy-related benefits, 941
   Presidential Executive Order 11246, 948
   procedure, 937
   protected classes and exceptions, 938–948
   protection against retaliation, 944
   proving a disability discrimination case, 951–952
   race and color, 938, 954
   reasonable accomodation under the ADA, 952
   religion, 938–940, 954
   right to sue letter, 937, 954
   seniority system, 947
   sex, 940–941, 954
   sexual harassment, 941–943

testing and educational requirements, 946
   Title VII exceptions, 945–947
   unlawful discrimination, 939
Equal Pay Act (EPA), 937, 944, 948, 955
equal protection of the law, 78–79
equitable title, 1249
equity, 9
equity, principles of, as law classification, 9–10
Erin Brockovich (film), 1206
ERISA. *See* Employee Retirement Income Security Act
escalation clause, 1219
escheat
   defined, 465–466
   right of, 1246
escrow payment of rent, 1222
esculpatory clause, 447
E-sign, 252, 253, 375–376
espionage, economic, 175
estate. *See also* trusts
   appointment of personal representative, 1243
   intestate distribution of, 1245–1247
   promise to pay, 372–373, 386
   proof of claims against, 1243
   when administration not necessary, 1242–1242
estate in fee, 1169
estates
   administration of, 1240–1247
   probate of will, 1240–1242
   testate distribution of, 1244–1245
   wills, 1234–1240
estoppel, 536
ethical behavior, categories of 51–55
   conflict of interest, 53–54
   doing no harm, 54
   fairness, 54
   loyalty, 53–54
   maintaining confidentiality, 54
   promise keeping, 52–53
   truth, 51–52
ethical dilemmas 51–59
   Blanchard and Peale Three-Part Test, 55–56
   Front-Page-of-the-Newspaper Test, 56

Laura Nash Model, 56
Wall Street Journal Model, 57–58
ethical values, 59
ethics, business 40–51, 59
   action guidelines, 43
   financial performance and, 45–46
   importance of, 44–51
   regulation and, 46–51
   social forces and the law, 40–60
   universal standards and, 41
ethics, situational, 41–42
Ethics and the law
   blogging and defamation, 251
   bribery, 176
ethics and the law
   auditing firms and, 1126
   background checks, 52
   bankruptcy and employee pensions, 809
   bankruptcy records, 795
   bill collection, 754–755
   bribery, 147
   Burger King case, 57
   cashier's check and bankruptcy, 700
   compensation of corporate officers, 1151
   consideration, 339
   contractual capacity, 314
   credit counseling business, 797
   creditors authority over debtors, 726
   donation and title, 538
   eminent domain, 1181
   estate of Brooke Astor, 1243
   holder in due course status, 672
   indorsement, 651
   insurance industry and September 11 attacks, 830
   land development sale, 880
   logging and overharvesting, 1199
   management bonuses, 44
   Marsh & McLennan, 93
   negotiable instruments, 631–632
   product liability, Mattel Toy Co., 571
   recission of agreement, 610
   reorganization as LLP, 1025
   repossession, 784
   return of goods, 589
   sales contract, 508

surrogacy contract, 358
water conservation
    requirement, 109
withholding of documents,
    27
EU (European Union), 129,
    130, 149
European Commission, 130
European Council, 130
European Court of Justice
    (ECJ), 130
European Economic
    Community 130
    Single European Act, 131
European Economic
    Community (EEC), 130
European Parliament, 130
European Union (EU), 129,
    130, 149
eviction proceedings, 1220,
    1223
evil twins phenomenon,
    255
exculpatory clause, 1117
executed contract, 272
execution, 26
Executive branch, 67
executor, executrix, 372, 1240
executory contract, 272
exemplary damages, 200
exhaustion of administrative
    remedies, 116
existing goods, 505, 533, 539
exoneration, 720
expert witness, 25
exploitation, protection from,
    50
export, 132
Export Administration Act,
    134, 149
Export Administration
    Regulations, 135
Export Control Classification
    Numbers (ECCNs), 135
export controls as foreign
    policy, 143
Exporter Assistance Staff,
    Department of Commerce,
    136
export licence, 135
export sale, 132
ex post facto law, 69
express authorization, 853
express contract, 270
express warranties, 558
express warranty, 558–561
extortion and blackmail, 166,
    181
Exxon Mobil Oil Company,
    968

F

Facebook, 245
facilitation payments, 167
factor, 493, 547
factorage, 493
Fair Credit and Change Card
    Disclosure Act, 748
Fair Credit Reporting Act
    (FCRA), 755
Fair Debt Collections Practices
    Act, 50
Fair Housing Act, 1214
Fair Labor Standards Act
    (FLSA), 903, 927
fair use, 254
false claims and pretenses,
    168–169, 181
false imprisonment, 190, 205
family and medical leave,
    916–917, 928
    defenses, 917–918
    discrimination and
        retaliation protection,
        918
    military service leave under
        USERRA, 917
    protections, 917
Family and Medical Leave Act
    of 1993 (FMLA), 916
Family Educational Rights
    and Privacy Act, 1974
    (FERPA), 6
The Family Man (film), 58
Fanning, Shawn, 253
farmers' cooperatives, antitrust
    exemption, 967–968
FAS (free alongside ship), 540
Federal Anticybersquatting
    Consumer Protection Act,
    218
Federal Arbitration Act, 30,
    351, 937
Federal Circuit, 18
federal court system, 19
federal deregulation, effect of, 70
federal district court, 18
Federal Employees'
    Compensation Act, 922
Federal Judicial Circuits, 20
Federal Motor Carrier Safety
    Administration, 486
Federal Omnibus
    Transportation Employee
    Testing Act, 925
federal powers
    banking power, 77
    constitutional limitations on
        government, 77
    financial powers, 76–77

as general welfare power,
    72–73
    power to regulate
        commerce, 72–74
    spending power, 76
    taxation power, 76
Federal Register, 107, 110
Federal Register Act, 110
federal regulations, 69, 82
Federal Reserve, 47, 89
Federal Rules of Civil
    Procedure, 24
federal securities regulation.
    See securities regulation
Federal Sentencing Guidelines,
    159
federal supremacy law, 69–70, 81
federal system, 67
Federal Tort Claims Act
    (FTCA), 202–203, 884
Federal Trade Commission Act,
    89
Federal Trade Commission
    (FTC)
    consumer protection, 737
    creation of, 89
    privacy, 248
    structure of, 105
    telemarketers and, 88
    unfair competition and, 114
Federal Trademark Dilution
    Act, 218, 254
Federal Wiretapping Act, 923
FedEx, 89, 298
fee simple defeasibles, 1170
fee simple estate, 1169
felony, 156, 181
field warehousing, 484, 769
Fifth Amendment Rights for
    business, 179–180, 181
finance lease, 522
financial performance, and
    ethics, 45–46
financing statement
    content of, 771, 773–774
    defective filing, 774
    defined, 771
    sample UCC-1, 772
Finke, Nikke, 196
fire insurance, 833–834, 839,
    840
fire insurance policy, 833
firm offer, 293, 507
First Amendment, 79
first-in-time provision, 777
first-to-perfect basis, 778
fixture
    defined, 1167
    moveable machinery and
        equipment, 1168

tests of, 1168
    trade, 1168
flexible rule, 1121
floating lien, 767
FMLA. See Family and Medical
    Leave Act of 1993
FOB place of shipment, 539
food labeling regulations, 49
forbearance, 334, 342
forcible entry and detainer, 1223
for deposit only, 647–648
foreclosure, 1183
foreign corporation, 1033
Foreign Corrupt Practices Act
    (FCPA), 146–147, 149,
    167, 1152
foreign unfair trade restrictions,
    relief from, 143–146
foreseeable user rule, 1119–1120
forged indorsement, 652
forgery
    alteration reporting time
        and, 700–702
    check, 649, 697–698,
        700–702, 708
    in credit card transactions,
        170
    defined, 168
    implied warranties and,
        655–666
    of indorsement, 181, 652,
        653, 674, 680, 697, 708
    preclusion rule, 697
    protection by article 4 of
        UCC, 698
    of will, 1242
formal contracts, 270
Fourth Amendment, 4–5, 79,
    177–180, 181, 924
franchise
    defined, 758
    franchise agreement,
        969–970
    franchise disclosure rule,
        972, 973–974
    liability, 974, 976
    special protection under
        federal law, 970–971
    types of, 968
    vicarious liability claims
        against, 972, 974–975
franchisee, 758
franchising, 133
franchisor, 758
fraud
    agency, 883
    contract, 317–319, 325
    corporate, 171, 181
    cybercrime, 252–253, 255
    imposter, 838

in lease agreement, 1216
product liability, 568
protection from, 50
statements, 319, 325
statute of, 368–378, 386
suretyship/guarantee and, 722
telemarketing, 746
fraud in the inducement, 673
fraud-on-the-market, 1097
Freedom of Access to Clinic Entrances Act, 73
Freedom of Information Act, 106, 107
Freedom of speech
commercial speech, 79
right to, 4
free enterprise system, 88
freight fowarder, 136
freight insurance, 833
French Kiss (film), 707
Friedman, Milton, 43, 88
FTC. *See* Federal Trade Commission (FTC)
full warranty, 560
funds transfer, 702–707
automated teller machine (ATM), 703
characteristics of, 704
choice of law, 706
clearing house, 706
credit and debit transfer, 705
definitions, 705
direct deposit and withdrawal, 703
effect of error, 707
EFTA and consumer transfers, 705, 708
electronic funds transfer, 703, 708
errors in, 706–707
failure to act, 707
Internet banking, 703
laws governing, 704
liability for loss, 707
pattern of, 704–705
pay-by-phone system, 703
payment order, manner of transmitting, 706
point-of-sale terminal, 703
regulation and rules, 706, 708
reimbursement of the bank, 706
scope of UCC Article 4A, 705, 708
types of electronic systems, 703
unauthorized order, 707
fungible goods, 534

Funny Farm (film), 301
Fun with Dick and Jane (film), 785
Furst, Jeffrey, 985
future goods, 505, 533

G

Gabor, Zsa Zsa, 335–336
gambling, wagers, lotteries, 353–354
game laws, 464
Garcia, Freddie, 201
garnishment, 26
Gates, Bill, 44
general agent, 852
General Agreement on Tariffs and Trade (GATT), 129
general corporation code, 1034
general jurisdiction, 16
general legacies, 1244
generally accepted accounting practices (GAAP), 1113, 1130
generally accepted auditing standards (GAAS), 1113, 1130
General Motors, 199, 970
general partner, 1014
general partnership, 1022
Gesellschaft mit beschränkter Haftung (GmbH), 133
gift
defined, 505
inter vivos, 459–460
as personal property, 458–459
gift causa mortis, 461
Gonzalez, Miguel Angel, 288
Good Burger (film), 975
Goodbye Girl, The (film), 448
good faith, 350, 384, 581, 668
goods
acceptance of, 508, 509
damage to, 532, 543–544
defined, 504
existing, 505, 539
fungible, 534
future, 505, 533
identification of, 533
lease of, 521–523
nature of, 505
returnable, 545
sale of, 504504
seizure of, 532
seller's obligation to deliver, 539
title to, 535–536, 540
Google, 6

Goonies, The (film), 474
government, branches of, 67
government of the United States, 68
Gramm, Phil, 808
Gramm, Wendy, 808
grantee, 1174
grantor, 1174
gratuitous bailment, 471
gray market goods, 137
grease payments, 167
green card (Alien Registration Card), 926
gross return of partnership, 987–988
guarantor, 718
guaranty, 718
guaranty of collection, 719
guaranty of payment, 719
guest, 494
Guzman, Gustavo, 197, 198

H

Hanks, Gregory, 201
hearsay evidence, 755
height discrimination, 941
Henley, Don, 192
holder, 642, 666, 667, 680
holder in due course, 642, 666, 687
holder through a holder in due course, 671
holographic will, 1240
Home Equity Loan Consumer Protection Act, 748
homeowners insurance, 833–835, 840
Hoosiers (film), 58
hotelkeeper, 494
House of Representatives, 67
Housing and Urban Develpment, Department of, 757
housing laws, 1219
hull insurance, 832

I

identification, 533
identified, 533
identity theft, 255, 749
Iger, Robert, 196
illusory promise, 335
Immigration Act of 1990, 926
Immigration and Naturalization Act (INA), 926
Immigration and Naturalization Service, 926

immigration laws, employer-related 926–927, 928
employer liability, 926
employer verification and special hiring programs, 926
green card, 926
Immigration and Naturalization Act (INA), 926
Immigration Reform and Control Act of 1986 (IRCA), 926
"specialized knowledge" personnel, 927
U.S. Bureau of Citizenship and Immigration Services (USCIS), 927
visa classification, 926–927
Immigration Reform and Control Act of 1986, 926
impeach, 24
implied contract, 270
implied warranty, 403, 562
implied warranty of merchantability, 564
impostor rule, 652
imprisonment, false, 190–191
incidental authority, 856
incidental damage, 602
income, 1248
incontestability clause, 837
incorporation by reference, 382
incorporator, 1039
Incredible Shrinking Woman, The (film), 571
indemnity, 719–721, 721, 729
indemnity contract, 719
indenture trustee, 1058
independent contractor, 850
individual intent, enforcement of, 49
indorsee, 646
indorsement, 644
indorser, 678
influence, improper, 166–167
informal contract, 270
informal settlements, 115
infringement, 254
injunction, 443, 1200
injury, work related, 198–199
inland marine, 832
The In-Laws (film), 148
in pari delicto, 349
insider, 804, 1098
insider information, 1098
insolvency, 804
instruction, 26
instrument
bearer, 643–644, 655

demand, 631
fraud as to nature of, 674
lost, 654–655
negotiable, 622–624,
631–632, 1037
nonnegotiable, 625
order, 644–652
overdue or dishonored,
669–670
insurable interest, 533
insurance 822–841
antilapse and cancellation
statutes and provisions,
825–826
automobile, 835–836
beneficiary, 837, 840
breach of contract, 828
business liabillity, 831–832
cash surrender value, 836
claims, burden of proof, 827
coinsurance, 834, 839
commercial, 146
contract, 822–829
disability, 837
double indemnity, 837
endowment, 836
exclusion, 837
fire and home insurance,
833, 839, 840
imposter fraud, 838
incontestability clause, 837,
840
insurable interest, 822–824,
839
insurer bad faith,
827–828
kinds of, 830–838
lienholder, 822
life, partnership, 823
life insurance, 822–824,
836–838, 840
marine, 832–833
no-fault, 836
parties, 822
Personal Auto Policy (PAP),
835
policy, 822, 839
property, insurable interest
in, 822
risk managers, 830
statutory provisions of
contract, 825
subrogation, 829
term, 836
time limitations on insured
claims, 828–829
whole life insurance, 836
insurance agent, 822
insurance broker, 822
insured, 822

insurer, 822
integrity, 52
intellectual property rights,
244, 253
cyberspace, 253–254
international trade and,
136–137
Internet and, 212–237
intended beneficiary, 393
intended user rule, 1121
intentional infliction of
emotional distress, 192
intentional tort, 189
interest in the authority, 853
interest in the subject matter,
853
interference (to right of
possession), 1217
interlineation, 1237
interlopers, 1121–1122
intermediary bank, 705
Internal Revenue Service (IRS),
133
International Bank for
Reconstruction and
Development. *See* World
Bank
international business
transactions, 41–42
International Monetary Fund
(IMF), 132
international trade
agency requirements, 132
antidumping laws and
export subsidies, 144
antitrust laws, 137–140
arbitration alternative, 128
barriers, nontariff, 143
barriers to trade, 142–143
commercial insurance, 146
conflicting ideology, 128
counterfeit goods, 136
economic injury relief,
143–146
export assistance, 136
export controls as foreign
policy, 143
export regulations, 134–136
export sales, 132
expropriation, 146
financing/currency, 128
Foreign Corrupt Practices
Act, 1977, 146–147
foreign distributorships,
132–133
foreign import restrictions,
143
forms of business
organizations, 132–134
general principles, 127–134

government regulation,
134–148
intellectual property rights,
136–137
joint ventures, 134
laws applicable, 127–128
legal background, 127–129
legal environment of,
127–150
licensing, 133, 135
offshore tax evasion, 141
organizations, comferences,
treaties, 129–132
sanctions, 135
section 301 authority, trade
retaliation, 145
securities and tax fraud
regulation, 140–141
trade restrictions, relief, 145
wholly owned subsidiaries,
133
International Trade
Administration (ITA), 144
International Trade
Commission (ITC), 144
Internet
banking, 703
cyberspace crime, 254–257
domain names and, 218–220
negotiable instruments, 622
personal postings, 246
surfing, 244
web user information,
247–250
Internet Corporation for
Assigned Names and
Numbers (ICANN), 220,
254
Internet Service Providers
(ISP), user information and,
248
interrogatories, 25
interstate commerce, 73–74, 905
Interstate Commerce Act
Carmack Amendment, 490
Interstate Commerce
Commission. *See* Federal
Motor Carrier Safety
Administration
Interstate Commerce
Commission Termination
Act (ICCTA), 486–487
Interstate Land Sales Full
Disclosure Act (ILSFDA),
757
inter vivos gift, 459
intestate, 1234
intestate succession, 1245
invasion of privacy, 192, 246
invitee, 1171

involuntary bankruptcy, 798
IRS (Internal Revenue
Serrvice), 133
issuer, 481, 724
It Could Happen to You (film),
405
Ito, Lance, 5

J

Jacob, Mark S., 250
Jaws (film), 58
Jerry Maguire (film), 324
Johnson Controls Battery
Group, 145
joint and several liability, 200
joint tenancy, 467
joint ventures 134
contract joint ventures, 134
defined, 134
equity joint ventures, 134
Jones, Brian, 197, 198
judge, 22
judgment, execution of, 28
judgment lien, 1167
judgment n.o.v., 28
judicial branch, 67
judicial triage, 31
jurisdiction, 16
jurisdictional rule of reason, 138
jury, 23
challenged for cause, 25
selection, 25

K

King, Don, 288
known user rule, 1119

L

labeling, false or misleading,
88–89
Labor-Management Reporting
and Disclosure Act
(LMRDA), 905, 912
labor relations laws, 905–912
labor unions
affairs, 905
elections, 912
firing emloyees for union
activity, 908–909
regulation of internal affairs,
912
land, 1164
landlords, 1214
liability to tenant,
1224–1226
liability to third persons,
1226

remedies of, 1223
land sale agreement, 371, 386
land use controls, 1203–1206
  nonconforming use, 1205
  restrictive covenants in
    private contracts,
    1203–1204
  variance, 1205
  zoning, public, 1204–1206
Lanham Act, 136, 137, 212,
  217
larceny, 172
law, 4. *See also* specific right
  business ethics and social
    forces, 40–60
  classifications of, 9–10
  codified, 40
  conflict of, 23
  constitutional, 7–8, 11
  English common, 9
  equal protection of, 77–78
  ethics and, 6, 27, 40
  legal rights, 4
  nature and sources of, 4–12
  Roman, 9
  social order and, 4, 11
  sources of, 7–8
  statutory, 8
  types of, 8
  uniform state, 9
lawsuit, 16
  application, 23
  commencement, 23–24
  defendant's response and
    pleadings, 24
  designation of expert
    witness, 25
  discovery, 24, 25
  initial steps, 23–25
  motion for summary
    judgment, 25
  service of process, 24
lawyers, 23
Lay, Kenneth, 45, 179, 1244
leasehold estate, 1169
leases, 1214–1229
  classification of tenancies,
    1215
  creation of, 1214
  definition and nature of,
    521, 1214
  illegal activity on property,
    1219–1220
  improvements, 1222
  landlord's liability in,
    1224–1226
  notice of termination, 1216
  possession, 1217–1218
  protection and retaliation,
    1222

remedies of landlord, 1223
renewal of, 1216–1217
rent, 1218–1219
repairs and condition of
  premises, 1219,
  1221–1222
rights and duties of parties,
  1217–1223
taxes and assessments, 1222
tenants' deposit, 1222
tenant's liability in, 1226
termination of, 1215–1216
transfer of rights,
  1226–1227
use of premises, 1218
leases of goods, 521–523
  commercial lease, 522
  consumer lease, 521–522
  default, 522–523
  finance lease, 522
  form of lease contract, 522
  warranties, 522
Ledger, Heath, 1239
legacies, abatement of, 1244
legacy, 1234
legality and public policy
  agreement not to compete,
    355–358
  agreements contrary to, 353
  business, regulation of,
    354–360
  contracts, statutory
    regulation, 354
  contracts in restraint of
    trade, 355
  crimes and civil wrongs,
    349–350
  gambling, wagers, and
    lotteries, 353–354
  general principles, 348–352
  good faith and fairness, 350
  illegality, effect of, 348–349
  legal violation, effects, 354
  licensing, 354–355
  partial illegality, 349
  protection of one party, 349
  public welfare agreements,
    352–354
  unconscionable clauses,
    350–351, 360
  unequal guilt, 349
  usurious contracts, 358–359
legal title, 1249
legatee, 1234
legislative branch, 67
Lehman Brothers, 46–47, 88
lemon laws (automobile), 758,
  759
lessee, 1214
lessor, 1214

letter of credit
  contracts involved in, 725
  defined, 128, 724–726
  duration, 728, 729
  duty of issuer, 728
  form, 728
  independence rule, 726
  parties to, 727–728, 729
  reimbursement of issuer, 728
  strict compliance rule, 726
letters of administration, 1243
letters testamentary, 1243
Lewis, Neda, 194
liability, 189. *See also*
  nonliability; product liability
  cumulative theories of, 570
  employee e-mail, 244–245
  employer, 162
  immigration laws,
    employer-related,
    926–927
  industrial accidents, 921
  nature of harm, 556–557
  strict, 203–204
  strict tort liability, 568–570,
    572
  theories of, 556
  for torts of agent or
    employee, 887, 890
  UCC warrants and, 557
  who is liable in product
    liability, 557
liability insurance, 833
liability of holder and stop
  payment order, 695
libel, 193, 205
license, 1166
licensee, 1171
licensing, 88, 133, 354–355
liens, 1167, 1223
life estate, 1169
limitation-of-liability clause,
  447, 1117
limited covenant, 1178
limited defenses, 678
limited liability companies
  (LLCS), 964, 975
  assignment, 1021
  capital contributions, 1018
  characteristics of,
    1017–1023
  comparison of general,
    limited and limited
    liability partnership,
    1022
  disregarding the LLC entity,
    1021
  dissolution of, 1021
  distinguished from limited
    partnership, 1023

distinguished from
  subchapter S
  corporation, 1023
distributions, 1019–1020,
  1026
formation, 1018, 1026
LLC property, 1020
management, 1018–1019
operating agreement/
  partnership agreement,
  1018, 1026
and other entities,
  1023–1024
tax classification, 1021
usage, 1024
limited liability partnerships
  (LLPs)
  business organization, 964,
    975
  compared to LPs and LLCs,
    1022
  extent of limited liability,
    1024–1025
  registration and usage, 1025
limited partner, 1014
limited partnership (LP),
  1014–1017
  capital contributions, 1015
  certificate of, 1015
  characteristics of,
    1015–1017
  comparison with general
    partnership, LLC and
    LLP, 1022
  dissolution, 1017
  firm name, 1015
  formation of, 1014–1015
  general members, 1014,
    1017, 1026
  limited members, 1014,
    1017, 1026
  limited partnership
    agreement, 1015
  management and control,
    1015, 1026
  right to sue, 1016–1017
  safe harbor activities, 1016,
    1026
limited partnership liability,
  1014
limited (special) jurisdiction, 17
limited warranty, 560
lineals, 1245
Lipcon, Irmgard, 127
Lipcon, Mitchell, 127
liquidated damages, 444, 608
liquidated damages clause, 445
liquidation, 794
litigation
  alternatives to, 28–33, 34

process, 16
"Little FTC Acts," 737
living-document view, 70
living trust, 1248
living will, 1240, 1241
LLC. *See* limited liability companies
Llewellyn, Karl, 668–669
Lloyd's of London, 127, 146
loans
    subprime lending market, 747
    title loans, 747
location and application of law, 23
Long, Kenneth, 199
loss, risk of. *See* title and risk of loss
lottery, 353
Lundstrom, Carl, 254

M

Mackey, John, 251
Madrid System of International Registration of Marks (the Madrid Protocol), 136, 213
Mailbox rule, 298, 302, 509
mailbox rule, 300
maker, 624, 677
malpractice, 198, 1113–1114
marine insurance, 832
mark
    abandonment of exclusive right, 216
    dilution of, 218
    improper use of, 215
    registrable, 213–215
marketing, target, 248
market power, 92
Market Reform Act of 1990, 1085
market value, 1057
marriage promises, 373, 386
Marsh & McLennan, 45, 245
Martorano, James, 985
mask work, 233
mass picketing, 912
maturity date, 1058
McGuire, Mark, 179
McNealy, Scott, 246
McNeil, 57
means test, 796, 800, 802, 813
mechanic's lien, 1167
MedArb dispute resolution, 30
mediation, 30
Medicare, 918
Medistar, Corporation, 446–447
Meet Joe Black (film), 1075

Melvin and Howard (film), 1251
mentally incompetent persons
    appointment of guardian, 313, 324
    effect of incompetency, 312, 324, 325
merchant, 507
mergers, 95–96, 1044
Merrill Lynch, 47, 88
Mesa, José, 201
Mexico trade agreements, 131
Microsoft, 93–95
Midnight Run (film), 360, 1129
minimum wage, 903–904
minitrial, 32
minors
    age misrepresentation, 309–310
    contractual capacity of, 308–312, 324
    contractual liability of parents, 310–311, 324
minor's contract, 309–312, 324
Miranda rights/warnings, 180
mirror image rule, 509
misdemeanor, 156, 181
misrepresentation 252, 1116
    cyberspace, 252–253
    intentional, 317
    negligent, 320, 325
mistrial, 26
Model Business Corporation Act (MBCA), 1035
monetary policy, 71
money, 629
money laundering, 164–165
Money Laundering Control Act, 164
money order, 624, 689
monopolies, 92–96, 355
monopolization, 92–94
moral obligation, 339
moral relativism, 41–42
moral standard, 40
mortgage market, 47
mortgages, 1180–1183
    adjustable-rate, 1181
    characteristics of, 1181
    creative financing, 1181–1182
    form of, 1181
    property subject to, 1181
    recording of, 1182
    responsibilities of parties in, 1182
    reverse, 1181
most-favored-nation clause, 129
motion for summary judgment, 25

motion to dismiss, 24
Motor Vehicle Information and Cost Savings Act, 746
murder, and inheritance, 1246
mutuality of obligation, 335
MySpace.com, 245

N

NAFTA. *See* North American Free Trade Agreement
Napster, 253
Nash, Laura, 56
National Automobile Underwriters Association, 835
National Bureau of Casualty Underwriters, 835
National Conference of Commissioners on Uniform State Laws, 9, 504, 1014
National Do Not Call Registry, 746
National Environmental Policy Act (NEPA), 1196
nationalization, 146
National Labor Relations Act (NLRA), 905, 907, 928
National Labor Relations Board (NLRB), 114, 905, 907, 927
national origin, discrimination based on, 945, 954
National Securities Market Improvement Act (NSMIA), 1084
Native American, 938
natural law, 41
necessaries, 310
negligence
    breach of duty, 198
    causation, 198–200
    defenses to, 200–203
    defined, 189
    duty to exercise reasonable care, 197–198
    product liability, 568, 572
negotiability, 625
negotiable bill of lading, 487
negotiable instruments, 622–635
    absence of representative capacity or identification of principal, 627
    acceptor, 625
    ambiguous language, 634
    authentication of, 626, 627
    bearer paper, 633, 642
    certificate of deposit, 623
    check, 624, 634

definite time of payment, 630
definition, 622–623
demand instrument, effective date on, 631
draft or bill of exchange, 623
drawee, 624, 625, 634
drawer, 624, 625
electronic promissory notes, 622
Electronic Signatures in Global and National Commerce Act (E-sign), 622
kinds, 623–624
maker, 624, 634
missing date, 631
order paper, 632, 644
parties to, 624–625, 634
payee, 624, 625, 634
payment in money, 629, 634
payment on demand, 630
promise or order to pay, 627, 634
promissory notes, 623
secondary obligor, 625
signatures, 629
statute of limitations, 634
sum certain, 623, 629–630, 634
time of payment, 630
types of, 622–625, 634
unconditional promise or order, 627
Uniform Electronic Transactions Act (UETA), 622
written record, 626
negotiable instruments,
    liabilities of parties under
    dishonor and notice of dishonor, 678, 680
    holder-in-due-course-protections, 667–671
    ordinary holders and assignees, 666–667, 680
    payment rights and defenses, 677
    presentment, attaching liability, 678
    rights and liabilities, 666–672
    roles of parties and liability, 677–678
    types, 666
negotiable instrument transfers 642–658, 650–651
    alteration, 675
    bank indorsement, 649

bearer instruments, 643–644, 655, 657
blank indorsement, 645, 657
contract defenses, 672
correction of name by indorsement, 648–649
defenses, classification of, 672
defenses to payment of, 672–677, 676
definition of, 642, 657
denial of holder-in-due-course protection, 675–677, 680
dummy payee, 653
duress depriving control, 674
effect of, 642
effect of incapacity or misconduct, 654
embezzlement, 643
Federal Trade Commission Rule, 676, 680
forged and unauthorized indorsements, 652–655, 657, 674, 680
fraud as to the nature of terms of the instrument, 674
fraud in the inducement, 673, 680
good faith, 668–669
holder in due course limited defenses, 672–673, 680
holder through a holder in due course, 671
how negotiation occurs, 642–652
ignorance of defenses and adverse claims, 670
illegality, 675
impersonating payee, 652–653
imposter rule, effect of and limitations of, 653
incapacity and, 673, 674
indorsement, 644, 652
instrument overdue or dishonored, 669–670
lost instruments, 654–655
miscellaneous defenses, 673
multiple payees and indorsements, 649–650
negligence of drawee not required, 653
order instruments, 644–652, 655
order or bearer character of an instrument, 642–643, 657

problems in negotiation of, 652
qualified indorsement, 646–647, 657
quasi-forgery: imposter rule, 652
restrictive indorsement, 647–648, 657
special indorsement, 646, 657
universal defenses against all holders, 673–675, 680
value, 668
warranties, 655–656
negotiable warehouse receipt, 482
negotiation 642
    rules of, 288
    warranties in, 655
Neij, Fredrik, 254
Network Solutions Inc., 254
New Century Financial, 88
New Kids on the Block, 985
Newspaper Preservation Act of 1970, 97
New York Unjust Conviction and Imprisonment Act, 163
Nichols, Rhonda, 197
Nike labor practices (Sweating It Out on Free Speech), 80–81
Nine to Five (film), 496
NLRB. *See* National Labor Relations Board
no-fault insurance, 836
Noise Control Act, 1197
nominal damages, 440
nonattainment areas, 1191
noncompete clauses, 357
noncompetition covenant, 356
nonconforming use, 1205
nonconsumer lease, 522
nondisclosure, 320–321
nonliability
    concealment, active, 321
    confidential relationship, 321
    defect or condition unknown, 321
    exceptions, 321
    general rule of, 320
nonnegotiable bill of lading, 487
nonnegotiable instrument, 625
nonnegotiable warehouse receipt, 482
North American Free Trade Agreement (NAFTA), 129, 131, 149

notice of dishonor, 678
notice of termination, 1216
notice-race statute, 1176
notice statute, 1176
Notting Hill (film), 205
novation, 401
nuisance, 1201

O

obligation, mutuality of, 335
obligations and performance
    adequate assurance of performance, 582, 591
    buyer's duties, 584–588
    buyer's responsibilities upon revocation of acceptance, 588
    cure of defective tender or delivery, 584
    duties of the parties, 583–590
    failure to give assurance, 582
    form of assurance, 582
    form of payment, 588
    general principles, 581–582
    notification of revocation of acceptance, 587
    obligation of good faith, 581
    place, time, and manner of delivery, 583
    quantity delivered, 584
    repudiation of contract, 582
    revocation of acceptance, 586
    right to examine goods, 584
    right to refuse or return the goods, 584, 589
    sales contract, 581
    seller's duty to deliver, 583
    time of payment, 588
    time requirements of obligations, 581
    what constitutes acceptance of goods, 585
    when duties are excused, 590
obligee, 268, 396, 719
obligor, 268, 396, 718
obstruction of justice/Sarbanes-Oxley, 170
Occupational Safety and Health Act of 1970, 116
Occupational Safety and Health Administration (OSHA), 902
ocean marine, 832
O'Connor, Sandra Day, 41

offer, 289, 507
    communication of offer to offeree, 291
    contractual intention, 285–286
    counteroffer, 293
    death/disability of either party, 294
    definiteness, 286–289
    lapse of time, 293–294
    offer defined, 285
    rejection of offer by offeree, 293
    requirements of, 285–291
    subsequent illegality, 294
    termination of offer, 291–293
offeree, 269
offeror, 269
Office of Federal Contract Compliance Programs (OFCCP), 948
Oil Pollution Act, 1197
Older Workers Benefit Protection Act (OWBPA) of 1990, 949
ombudsman, 33
Omnibus Trade and Competetiveness Act of 1988, 145
One Minute Manager (Blanchard, K.), 55
onsent decrees, 115
OPEC. *See* Organization of Petroleum Exporting Countries
opening statements, 26
open meeting law, 107, 121
operation of law, 426
opinion or value, statement of, 317–318
oppression, protection from, 50
option contracts, 272, 292
oral contract, 378
order of relief, 802
order paper, 632
Organization of Petroleum Exporting Countries (OPEC), 132
Organized Crime Control Act, 165
original jurisdiction, 16
originator, 705
OSHA standards and regulations, 920, 928
output contract, 290, 513
outstanding, 1056
overdraft, 693
Overseas Private Investment Corporation (OPIC), 146

P

Parenthood (film), 954
Parker, Sean, 253
parol evidence rule 378–381,
    514, 524
  exclusion of, 378–379
  when not applied,
    379–380
partially disclosed principal,
    876
partnerships, 983–1007
  alienation of interest, 1000
  arbitration, 994
  assignment and creditors,
    996
  assignment of partner's
    interest, 990
  authority of partners,
    990–994
  bankruptcy, 1000
  cessation of business, 993
  characteristics of, 984
  compensation, 996
  confession of judgment, 994
  continuation of partnership
    business, 1005
  contribution and indemnity,
    996
  contribution of skill or
    labor, 988
  control, 986
  creditors of, 1004
  customary authority of
    individual partners,
    991–992, 1006
  death of partner, 1000,
    1005
  definition, 983–984
  determining existence of,
    985–988
  dissociation under RUPA,
    1002
  dissolution of, 999–1005
  distribution of assets,
    1004–1005, 1006
  distribution of capital, 997
  duties of partners, 994–995,
    1006
  effect of dissolution on
    partner's liability, 998,
    1006
  enforcement and satisfaction
    of creditor's claims,
    998–999, 1006
  express authority of
    individual partners, 991,
    1006
  expulsion, 1000
  fixed payment, 988

  formation of business
    organization, 986
  general partnerships, 983
  gross returns, 987–988, 1006
  illegality, 1000
  impracticability, 1001
  incapacity of partner, 1001
  inspection of books, 996,
    1006
  lack of success, 1002, 1006
  liability, 988–989
  liability of partners and
    partnership, 997–998
  limitation on authority of
    individual partner to
    bind partnership, 993
  limited liability partnerships
    (LLPs), 983
  limited partnerships (LPs),
    983
  liquidation, 1005
  loyalty and good faith,
    994–995
  management, 996, 1006
  misconduct of partner,
    1001, 1006
  nature and creation, 983–990
  nature and extent of partner's
    liability, 997–998
  nominal partner, ostensible
    partner, or partner by
    estoppel, 988
  obedience, 995
  partnership agreement,
    984–985, 987, 1000,
    1005
  payment of interest, 996
  personal obligations, 994
  profit and loss sharing, 987,
    1006
  prohibited transactions,
    993–994
  property, 989
  purported partnership, 989
  repayment of loan, 996
  Revised Uniform
    Partnership Act (RUPA),
    983
  rights of partners, 984,
    995–997
  share of profits, 996, 1006
  suretyship, 994
  tenancy in, 989–990
  as to third persons,
    988–989
  Uniform Partnership Act
    (UPA), 983
  winding up partnership
    affairs, 1004, 1005,
    1006

  withdrawal, 1000
part-payment checks, 338
part performance doctrine, 369
party, 624
par value, 1056
past consideration, 338
Patent and Trademark Office,
    U.S., 212
Patent Cooperation Treaty, 136
Patriot Act, 48, 164, 693
payable in order, 631
pay-by-phone system, 703
payee, 625
payment after depositor's death,
    694
payment on forged or missing
    indorsement, 698, 708
payment order, 705
payment over s stop payment
    order, 697
Peale, Norman Vincent, 55
Peanut Corporation of
    America, 46
Pension Benefit Guaranty
    Corporation (PBGC), 914
pension plans
  administration, 912–913
  enforcement, 914
  ERISA, 912–914
  and federal regulation,
    912–914
  fiduciary standards and
    reporting, 913–914
  funding, 914
  termination insurance, 914
  vesting, 914
per capita, 1246
peremptory challenge, 26
perfected security interest, 769
perfection
  consumer goods, 775, 785
  lapse of time, 775
  loss of, 775
  motor vehicles, 775
  possession of collateral, 775
  removal from state, 775
  secured transactions,
    769–775, 786
performance, 434, 448
periodic tenancy, 1215, 1216
perjury, 167, 181
Personal Auto Policy (PAP),
    835
personal injury, 557
  landlord's liability to tenant,
    1224–1226
  liability for injury on
    premises, 1223–1226
personal property, 458–469
  abandoned, 464

  anatomical gifts, 463
  community property,
    468–469, 474
  conditional gifts, 462
  conversion, 465
  delivery of inter vivos gift,
    459–460
  donor's death, 460
  escheat, 465–466
  finding lost property,
    463–464, 474
  gifts, 458–463, 474
  gifts causa mortis, 461
  intent to make a gift, 459
  inter vivos gift, 459
  joint tenancy, 467, 474
  multiple ownership of,
    466–468
  occupation of, 464–465, 474
  survivorship, 467–468, 474
  tenancy by entirety/
    entireties, 468
  tenancy in common,
    466–467, 474
  title to, 458
  unclaimed property,
    465–466
  wild animals, 464
personal representative, 372,
    1240, 1243
per stirpes, 1246
pet restrictions, in leases, 1218
Petroleum Marketing Practices
    Act (PMPA), 971, 976
pharming, 255
phishing, 255
physical ability, discrimination
    based on, 941
physical duress, 323, 325
picketing, 911–912
piracy, 222
Pirate Bay Web site, 254
plaintiff, 22
pleadings, 24
pledge, 722
point-of-sale terminal, 703
police power, 68, 88, 98, 1034
policy, 822
Porras, Jerry J., 45
positive law, 40
possession, 1217
possibility of reverter, 1170
Postal Reorganization Act, 298
Postal Service, U.S., 89, 298
postdate, 633, 688
power of attorney, 853
precedent, 8
preclusion rule, 697
predatory lending, 747
Predicate Act, 165

preemptive right, 1066
preemtion, 69
preferences, 803
preferential transfers, 804
preferred stock, 1057
Pregnancy Discrimination Act
    (PDA), 941
premature payment of
    postdated check, 696
prenuptial agreement, 373
prescription, 1165
presentment, 678, 690–692
price discrimination, 90, 92, 98
price fixing, 89–90, 94
prima facie, 469
primary party, 677
primary picketing, 912
primum non nocere, 54
principal, 132, 718, 850, 1248
principal debtor, 718
principal register, 212
print art, 227
privacy
    cyberspace, 244
    Internet user information,
        248
    invasion of, 192
    job applicant screening, 245
    monitoring employees, 245,
        246
    protection in cyberspace,
        249
    right to, 4–6, 11, 107
    technology and, 6–7
    web user information,
        247–250
Privacy Act of 1974, 249
private carrier, 486
private corporation, 1033
private law, 8
private nuisance, 1201
Private Securities Litigation
    Reform Act (PSLRA), 165,
    1085, 1095
privileges and immunities
    clauses, 78
privity, 268, 557
probate, 1240
procedural law, 9
process, 24
Proctor & Gamble (P&G),
    434
product disparagement, 196
product liability, 556–573. *See
    also* liability; warranties
    cumulative theories of
        liability, 570
    disclaimer of warranties,
        567–568
    express warranties, 558–561

fraud, 568
general principles, 556
implied warranties,
    561–566
negligence, 568
other theories of, 568–570
strict tort liability,
    568–570
product safety, 752, 759
profit, 1166
promisee, 268
promisor, 268
promissory estoppel, 340, 341,
    342
promissory note, 623
promoters, 1038
proof of claim, 805
proof of harm, 319
property
    ademption of, 1244–1245
    continued use of, 1218
    destruction of, 1216
    possession and preservation
        of trust property, 1249
    protection of, 49
property report, 757
pro-rata, 776
prosecutor, 22
prospectus, 1089
protection of person, 48
proxy, 1065
Public Company Accounting
    Oversight Board (PCAOB),
    1125
public corporation, 1033
public health, safety and
    morals, protection of, 49
public housing, tenant
    screening for, 1219
public nuisance, 1201
public policy, 353. *See also*
    legality and public policy
public warehouses, 480
pump-and-dump, 259
punitive damages, 200, 440,
    742
purchase money security
    interest (PMSI), 766
purity standards, 88

Q
qualified indorsement, 646
qualified privilege, 194
quantum meruit, 275
quasi contract, 273
quasi-judicial proceedings, 77
quasi-public corporation, 1033
quitclaim deed, 1174
quorum, 1138

R
race and color, discrimination
    and, 938
race-notice statute, 1176
race statute, 1176
Racketeer Influenced and
    Corrupt Organization
    (RICO) Act, 165
racketeering, 165
Railway Labor Act, 907
real property, 458, 1164–1186.
    See also mortgages
    adverse possession,
        1179–1180, 1184
    buyers, additional
        protection, 1176
    common law rule, 1171
    condition of, liability ro
        third persons,
        1170–1171, 1184
    condominiums,
        1172–1173, 1184
    co-ownership of,
        1172–1173, 1184
    deeds, 1174–1176
    default on, 1183, 1184
    easements, 1164–1166
    eminent domain,
        1178–1179, 1180, 1184
    expense collection, 1173
    fee simple estate,
        1169–1170
    fitness for use, 1178,
        1184
    fixtures, 1167–1168
    foreclosure, 1183, 1184
    freehold estate, 1169, 1184
    future interests, 1170
    grantee's covenants, 1178
    grantor's warranties,
        1177–1178, 1184
    land, 1164, 1184
    leasehold estate, 1169, 1184
    licenses, 1166
    liens, 1166–1167
    life estate, 1170
    movable machinery and
        equipment, 1168
    multiple ownership, 1172,
        1184
    nature of, 1164–1169
    ownership, nature and form
        of, 1169–1170, 1184
    profits, 1166
    redemption, 1183
    takings clause, 1178
    tort liability, condominium,
        1173
    trade fixtures, 1168

transfer by deed,
    1174–1178
transfer of interest,
    1182–1183
transferring, other methods,
    1178–1180
warranties of title,
    1177–1178, 1184
warranty deed, form of,
    1175
recission, 419
recognizance, 270
record, 688
recorder, 1176
Recording Industry Association
    of America (RIAA), 254
records and documents,
    privileged, 178
re-cross-examination, 26
redemption, 1183
re-direct examination, 26
reductions in force, 901
reference to a third person, 31
reformation, 316
registered bonds, 1058
registration of marks,
    international, 213
registration requirements, 1089
registration statement, 1088
regulation, government
    competition and prices,
        88–99
    markets and competition,
        89–96
    power to protect business, 97
    prices, 89–92
    production, distribution
        and financing, 88–89
    unfair competition, 89, 98
regulation of business, 47, 72
Regulatory Flexibility Act, 110
Rehabilitation Act, 937, 950
Rehnquist, William, 41
rejection of offer, 293
religion, discrimination and,
    938–940
remainder interest, 1170
remand, 17
remedy, 438
rent. *See also* Leases
    escalation of, 1219
    escrow payment of, 1222
    nonpayment of, and
        remedies of landlord,
        1223
rent-a-judge plan, 31–32
repossession, 783, 784, 786
representative capacity, 627
repudiation, 582
reputation, importance of, 46

requests for production of documents, 25
requirements contract, 290, 513
Research in Motion, Ltd. (RIM), 16
reservation of rights, 438
Resource Conservation and Recovery Act (RCRA), 1193
Resource Recovery Act, 1193
respondeat superior, 883
responsible corporate officer doctrine, 1152
restraint of trade, 137, 355
restrictive covenants, 1203
restrictive indorsement, 647
retaliation, tenant protection from, 1222
Retirement Equity Act of 1984, 914
reverse, 17
reverse discrimination, 947–948
reverse mortgage, 1181
reversible error, 17
reversionary interest, 1226
Revised Model Business Corporatoin Act (RMBCA), 1139
Revised Uniform Limited Partnership Act (RULPA), 1014
Revised Uniform Partnership Act (RUPA), 983
revocation of a will 1237–1239
   by act of testator, 1238
   by operation of law, 1238–1239
revoke, 1237
Reynolds, Burt, 808
right of
   escheat, 1246
   first refusal, 273
   possession, 1217
   privacy, 5
   survivorship, 467–468
rights 4, 396
   individual, 4
   legal, 4
   personal, protection of, 49
rights of assignee, holder, and holder-in-due-course, 667
right to
   cure, 585
   due process, 4
   freedom of speech, 4
   privacy, 4–6, 11
   vote, 4

right to know (Sunshine laws), 107, 121
right to sue letter, 937, 954
right-to-work laws, 910
riots and civil disorders, 172
risk 830
   assumption of, 201–202, 205
risk of loss, 541
Riviera, Jesse, 222
robbery, 172
Robinson-Patman Act, 90
Roman law, 9
Roto-Rooter, 968
run with the land, 1178
RV (film), 548

S

Safe Drinking Water Act, 1197
safe harbor provisions, 219
safe harbor rules, 1095–1096
sale(s)
   on approval, 545
   asset sales, 1047–1048
   auction, 300, 548
   on buyer's specification, warranty on, 564
   contract for, 505
   distinguished from other transactions, 505–507
   of food or drink, warranty, 565
   formation of sales contracts, 507–512
   of goods, 524, 373504
   home-solicited, 745
   illegal, effect of, 512
   lease of goods, 505
   nature of, 504–515
   not in the ordinary course of business, 780–781
   in the ordinary course of business, 779
   or return, 547
   particular (and warranties), 564
   real estate development, 757
   on secondhand/used goods, warranty on, 564–565
   subject matter of, 504–505
sales contract
   acceptance, 508–512
   admission, 519
   amount of sale, 515
   authentication/signature, 515–516
   boilerplate language, 510
   change in terms:
      modification of contract, 513–514

contradicting terms, parol evidence rule, 514, 524
death of client, 520
duties of parties, 583
exception to signature requirements, 516
formation, 507–512, 524
form of, 515–520
illegality, 512
indefinite duration term, 513
international sales, uniform law, 520–521
interpreting contract terms, 514–515, 524
merchant's confirmation memorandum, 516, 524
merchant *versus* nonmerchant parties, 507
nature of writing required, 515–518
necessary information, 507
noncode requirements, 519–520
noncompliance, effect of, 518
offer, 507–508
output and requirements contract, 513
payment, 519
price, 513
receipt and acceptance, 519
records, 517
requirement of a writing, exceptions to, 518
seller's duty to deliver, 583
specially manufactured goods, 518–519
terms in the formed contract, 512–515, 524
terms under UCC, 511
unconscionability, 512
written terms, 515
Samara Brothers, 217
sample, warranty of conformity to, 559
Santa Clause, The (film), 386
Sarbanes-Oxley Act of 2002 (SOX), 109, 159, 170, 171, 181, 1086
   auditor/accounting-related provisions, 1124–1129
   certification of company reports, 1092–1093
   destruction of records, 1129
   employment, 901–902
   reforms, 161
   standards of professional conduct, 1102

transaction reports, 1101
Schmidt, David, 446
Schoen, Erica, 192
screen name privacy, 248
SDRs (special drawing rights), 132
search, unlawful, 5, 11
search and seizure warrants, 177
search engine
   defined, 253
   identification, 774
Search Engine Promotion Code of Ethics, 253
search warrant, 177
Sears, 58
seasonable, 585
secondary goods, warranty on, 564–565
secondary meaning, 213
secondary obligors (secondary parties), 678, 690
secondary picketing, 912
secrecy laws, 140
section 301 authority
   trade retaliation, 145
secured interest, 780
secured party, 764
secured transaction 602, 764–787
   authentication, 765
   automatic perfection, 770
   automobile lemon laws, 758, 759
   collateral, 766–768
   correction statements, 776
   creation of, 764–768
   creditor's possession and disposition of collateral, 782
   creditor's retention of collateral, 782–783
   definitions, 764–765
   identification of debtor, 771
   loss of perfection, 775
   nature of creditor's interest, 764
   nature of debtor's interest, 765
   perfected security interest, 769
   perfection of, 769–775
   priorities, 776–781, 785
   purchase money security interest (PMSI), 766
   repossession of collateral, 769
   rights in the collateral, 766
   rights of parties after default, 781–785

rights of parties before default, 775–776
sales in ordinary course of business, 779, 785
sales not in course of ordinary business, 780–781, 785
secured party *versus* buyer of collateral from debtor, 779–781
secured party *versus* secured party, 777
secured party *versus* unsecured party, 776–777
security interest, 764, 785
statement of account, 775
temporary perfection, 770
termination statement, 776
unsecured party *versus* unsecured party, 776
value, 766
securities, 1086
Securities Act of 1933, 1085, 1087–1091, 1105
Securities Acts Amendments of 1990, 1085
Securities and Exchange Commission (SEC) 47
  actions, 1093
  Regulation FD (Fair Disclosure), 1100
  Rule 504, 1091
  Rule 506, 1090
Securities Enforcement Remedies and Penny Stock Reform Act of 1990, 1085
Securities Exchange Act of, 1934, 140, 1085, 1091–1098, 1105
securities regulation, 1084–1106
  aiders and abettors, 1096–1097
  antifraud provision of 1934 act, 1093, 1105
  applicability of 1933 act, 1089
  arbitration of securities disputes, 1103–1104, 1105
  auditor disclosure, 1098
  certifications and disclosure control, 1092–1093
  civil liability of sellers of securities, 1091
  class-action reforms, 1096
  criminal liability, 1091
  definition of security, 1086–1087

disclosure of ownership and short-swing profits, 1101
federal laws, 1085–1086
federal regulation, 1085–1103
fraud-on-the-market doctrine, 1097
industry self-regulation, 1103–1104
lawyer reporting of wrongdoing, 1098
liability for false/misleading statements, 1091, 1105
liability for "material misstatements or omissions of fact," 1094
liabillity, 1091
litigation reform, 1095, 1096
misappropriators, 1099
National Securities Market Improvement Act (NSMIA), 1084
principal reports, 1092
private actions, 1093–1094
prospectus, 1089
registration, 1088–1092
regulation A offerings, 1089
regulation FD, 1100–1101
regulation of accountants and attorneys by the SEC, 1102
remedy for investors, 1101
restricted securities, 1091
rule 504-506 exemptions, 1091
safe harbor rules, 1095–1096
Securities Act of 1933, 1087–1091
Securities Exchange Act of 1934, 1091–1098
state blue sky laws, 1084, 1105
state regulation, 1084
tender offers, 1101–1102
trading by insiders and tippees, 1098
trading on insider information, 1098–1101, 1105
security agreement, 765
security interest
  creation of, 765
  defined, 764
  in inventory, purchase money, 766
  perfected, 769
  purchase money, 778
  security registration periods, 1090

security procedure, and EFTs, 703
self-help repossession, 782
self-incrimination, 114
self-incrimination rights for business, 179–180, 181
self-proved wills, 1236
seller's action
  for damages under market price formula, 601
  for lost profits, 601
  for the purchase price, 602
seller's breach in risk of loss, 544–545
seller's nonsale remedies, 602–603
seller's remedy of stopping shipment, 600
selling on consignment, 493
semiconductor chip product, 233
Senate, 67
Sentencing Commission, U.S., 159
September 11th terrorist attacks, 830
service contract, 505
service mark, 212–220
servient tenement, 1164
settlor, 1248
severalty, 466
sex, discrimination based on, 940–941
sex offenders (registered), renting to, 1219
sexual harassment 244, 941–943
  employer procedure, 943
  hostile work environment, 941–942
  by nonsupervisors, 943
  rationale, 942–943
  tangible employment action, 941
shared powers, 68
shareholders
  action without meeting, 1139
  alter ego theory, 1073
  exceptions to limited liability, 1073–1075
  extent of management control by, 1138–1139
  ignoring the corporate entity, 1071–1073
  liability of, 1071–1075
  meetings, 1138
  meetings of, 1138, 1154
  obtaining advantages of corporate existence, 1073

piercing the corporate veil, 1071–1072, 1076
quorum, 1138
unauthorized dividends, 1074–1075
unpaid subscriptions, 1074
wage claims, 1073
shareholder rights, 1056–1058, 1063–1071. *See also* stocks and bonds
  financial statements, 1068
  form of books, 1068
  inspection of books, 1066–1068, 1076
  ownership rights, 1064, 1076
  preemptive offer of shares, 1066, 1076
  right to vote, 1064–1065, 1076
  shareholder's actions, 1069–1071, 1076
  shares, transfer of, 1064
  stock, certificates of, 1064
  votes, number of, 1065, 1076
  who may vote, 1064
shares
  acquisition of, 1058
  duration of, 1058
  fractional, 1058
  lost, destroyed, or stolen, 1063
  restriction on transfer, 1060
  transfer of, 1064, 1069
Shatner, William, 744
Shell Oil Company, 971
Sherman Antitrust Act, 89–90, 92, 97, 98, 968
Shipler, Penny, 199
shipment
  rejection of, 492
  stopping, 600
shipment contracts
  passage of title, 540
  risk of loss, 541
shipment terms, 539
shopkeeper's privilege, 191
shopkeeper's tort, 190
shop right, 903
short-swing profit, 1101
signatures, digital, 253
Silvernail, Paul, 983
Silvernail, Sr., David, 983
Simplification Regulations 1996, 135
Simpson, Jessica, 744
Simpson, O.J., 5
Single European Act, 131
sinking fund, 1058

situational ethics, 41–42
Sixth Amendment, 180, 181
Skilling, Jeffery, 45
Skylarov, Dmitri, 176
slander, 193, 205
slander of title, 196
Small Business Job Protection
    Act of 1996, 1034
small claims court, 22
social forces, business ethics and
    the law, 40–60
social forces movement, 47
social problems and business,
    43–44
Social Security, 918
Soft Drink Interbrand
    Competition Act, 97
software warranty liability and
    damage provisions, 506
soliciting agent, 889
solid waste disposal regulation,
    1193–1196
Sonny Bono Copyright Term
    Extension Act of 1998, 221
Sotheby's Auction House, 90
sovereign compliance doctrine,
    138
sovereign immunity doctrine,
    139
SOX Act. See Sarbanes-Oxley
    Act of 2002 (SOX)
spamming, 177
special agent, 852
special drawing rights (SDRs),
    132
special hiring programs, 926
special indorsement, 646
special jurisdiction, 17
special service corporation,
    1033
specialty court, 21
specific legacies, 1244
specific lien, 481
specific performance
    court order, 10
    defined, 439
speech, freedom of, 248
spendthrift trust, 1249
Spielberg, Steven, 368, 374
Spitzer, Eliot, 45
sports and entertainment law
    bankruptcy, 799
    celebrity issues and
        antitrust, 95
    deceptive advertising, 744
    easement, 1167
    endorsement contracts,
        412–413
    Friends television show
        contracts, 435

gambling, 171
Heath Ledger's probate,
    1239
landlord liability, 1224
morals clause, 53
sports exception doctrine
    and liability, 202
steroid use, 10
zoning, nonconforming,
    1205
spot zoning, 1206
stability and flexibility, in
    business transactions, 50
stakeholder
    analysis, 42
    behavior and ethics of,
        42–44
stale check, 693
Standard & Poor's, 244
standby letter, 724
stare decisis, 8, 11
Starr, Maurice, 985
state, protection of, 48
state court systems, 21–22
state laws, uniform, 9
state powers, 67
status quo ante, 310
statute, 1176, 1245
statute of frauds
    contracts evidenced by a
        writing, 369–374
    effect of noncompliance,
        377–378
    note or memorandum,
        374–375, 377
    validity of oral contracts,
        368, 515
statute of limitations, 426, 599
    action to force liability, 702
    negotiable instruments, 634
    tort, 599
    UCC, 599
statutory law, 8
stay of foreclosure, 1183
Stewart, Martha, 25
stirpes, 1246
stirpital distribution, 1246
stocks and bonds
    acquisition of shares,
        1058–1063
    capital and capital stock,
        1056
    characteristics of bonds,
        1058, 1076
    classification by preference,
        1057, 1076
    cumulative preferred, 1057
    duration of shares, 1058
    fractional shares, 1058
    interest transfer, 1061

kinds of stock, 1057–1058,
    1076
lost, destroyed, or stolen
    share certificates, 1063
nature of acquisition, 1059
nature of stock, 1056–1057,
    1076
participating preferred
    stock, 1057
restrictions on transfer,
    1010–1061
secured transaction, 1061
statute of frauds, 1059
stock certificate and
    uncertificated shares,
    1057
subscription, 1059–1060
subscription after
    incorporation,
    1059–1060
subscription before
    incorporation, 1059
terms and control, bonds,
    1058
transfer of shares,
    1060–1061
valuation of, 1056–1057
stock subscription, 1059
stop payment, 694–695, 708
Stored Communications Act,
    245
straight bill of lading, 487
strict liability, 189, 205
strict tort liability, 556
strikes, and rights of strikers,
    911
subchapter S corporation, 1034
subject matter jurisdiction, 16
sublease, 1226–1227
sublessee, 1219
Subprime lending market,
    747
subprime mortgage market,
    47, 88, 1121
subrogation, 720, 829
substantial impairment, 587
substantial performance, 415
substantive law, 9
substitute check, 689, 701
substitution, 419
sufficient funds, 687
Sullivan, Scott, 808
sum certain, 629
summary jury trial, 31
summation, 26
Sunde, Peter, 254
Sunshine Act of 1976, 107
Superfund Amendment and
    Reauthorization Act, 1193
superfund sites, 1193

Supplemental Security Income
    (SSI) program, 918
supply chain management 532,
    548
    bill of lading, 486–487
    boarders or lodgers, 496
    carrier's liability for delay,
        490
    carrier's limitation of
        liability, 490
    COD shipment, 491
    common carriers, 485–493
    complexities in
        intercontinental and
        domestic shipping, 492
    definitions, 480
    duration of hotel guest
        relationship, 494–495
    duties of common carrier,
        488
    effect of factor transaction,
        493–494
    factors and consignments,
        493–494
    field warehousing, 483–485
    hotelkeepers, 494–496
    legal aspects of, 480–498
    lien of warehouse, 481
    limitation of liability of
        warehouses, 485
    negotiable warehouse
        receipts, 482, 484
    notice of claim, 491
    nonnegotiable warehouse
        receipts, 482
    rejected shipment, 492
    rights of common carrier,
        488
    statutory regulations, 480
    warehouses, 480–485
    warranties, 483
    warranties of bill of lading,
        488
Supreme Court, U.S., 19–21,
    144
sureties
    defenses of, 721–723
    ordinary contract defenses,
        721
    surety defined, 718
    no release of, 723
    release of, 724
surety, guaranty, and indemnity
    relationships, 719
suretyship, 371, 718
suretyship defenses, 722
surfboard transaction diagram,
    397
survivorship, right of,
    467–468

Swiss Financial Markets Supervising Authority, 141
Switzerland secrecy treaty with U.S., 141
sworn testimony, 27
symbolic delivery, 460

T

takeover laws, 96
target marketing, 248
tariff, 142
Tariff Act of 1930, 137, 144
taxes and taxation
  double taxation, 133, 965
  evasion of taxes, 13
  landlord payment of taxes, 1222
  offshore, 141
  Social Security taxes, 918
tax lien, 1167
Taylor, Delinda, 201
technology
  legal issues and, 243
  privacy and, 6–7
Teerlink, Richard, 46
telemarketing, 746
Telephone Consumer Protection Act (TCPA), 746
teller's check, 623, 689
temporary insider, 1098
temporary perfection, 770
tenancy at sufferance, 1215
tenancy at will, 1215
tenancy by entirety/the entireties, 468
tenancy for years, 1215, 1216
tenancy in common, 466
tenants
  assignment of lease and sublease, 1226–1227
  defined, 1214
  deposit, 1222
  landlord's liability to, 1224–1226
  liability to third persons, 1226
tender, 413, 540
tender of performance, 427
termination and authority, agent's protection from, 865
termination by notice, 215
termination insurance, ERISA and, 914
termination of agency, 880, 882
termination of easement, 1165
termination of employment contract, 898
termination of lease, 1216

termination statement, 776
term insurance, 836
terrorist attacks, September 11, 2001, 830
testamentary capacity, 1234
testamentary intent, 1236
testamentary trust, 1248
testate, 1234
testator, testatrix, 1234
testimony under oath, 27
thievery, 677
third-party beneficiary, 393
third person arbitration, 31
third persons in agency 875–891
  action of authorized agent of disclosed principal, 875, 890
  agent's contracts, 880–881
  agent's knowledge, 882
  agents statements, 882
  contract, execution of, 878–879, 890
  employees with criminal records, 885
  enforcement of claim by third person, 889
  exceptions to owner's immunity, 888–889
  fraud, 883
  government regulation of employee crimes, 884
  hiring, need for due care in, 885
  independent contractor, undisclosed, 889
  intentinal act, 883
  liability, assumption of, 877–878
  liability for torts of agent or employee, 887, 890
  liability of agent to third person, 875–879
  liability of principal the third person, 879–882
  negligent act, 883
  negligent hiring and retention of employees, 885–886
  negligent retention, 885
  negligent supervision and training, 886
  owner's liability for crimes of independent contractor, 887–889, 890
  payment to agent, 881–882
  principal: disclosed, partially disclosed, and undisclosed, 876–877, 890

principal, disclosure of, 876–877, 890
principal's liability for agent's torts and crimes, 882–889
respondeat superior, doctrine of, 883
simple contracts with principal disclosure, 880–881
torts and crimes, 879
transactions with sales personnel, 889, 890
unauthorized action, 875–876
vicarious libility for torts and crimes, 882–884
time draft, 688
time for notice of dishonor, 692
time for presentment for payment, 691–692
time limitations, 700–702, 708
Time Warner, 95, 744
tippee, 1098
title. *See also* title and risk of loss
  abstract of, 1176
  covenants of, 1177
  document of, 481, 535
  passage of, 536, 537
  slander of, 196
  warranty of, 1177, 1184
title and risk of loss, 532–550
  auction sales, 548
  authorization, 536
  bailments or sale by and entrustee, 537–539
  CF, CIF, and COD, 540, 548
  consignments and factors, 547
  contract for delivery at destination, 543
  contract for shipment to buyer, 543, 548
  creditors' claims, 532–533, 548
  damage or destruction of goods, 543–544
  delivery and shipment terms, 539–540
  determining rights, 533–548
  effect of seller's breach in risk of loss, 544–545
  electronic tracking, 535
  estoppel, 536
  existing goods, 533, 548
  FAS, 540, 548

FOB place of destination, 539, 548
FOB place of shipment, 539, 548
fungible goods, 534
future goods, 533–534, 548
identification, effect of, 534, 548
insurable interest, 534
insurance, 533, 548
  in nonshipment contracts, 542, 548
passage of title, 536–541
potential problems and transactions, types of, 532–533
returnable goods transactions, 545–547
sale on approval, 545–547
sale or return of goods, 547, 548
self-service stores, 547
  in shipment contracts, 542–543, 548
stolen property, 536
voidable title, 536
title to property, protection of, 49
Title VII of the Civil Rights Act of 1964. *See under* Civil Rights Act of 1964
tort liability, 202–203, 1115
torts, 188–207, 205, 243, 317
  agency, 879, 882–889
  assault, 189
  battery, 190
  defined, 188
  general principles, 188–189
  intentional, 189–197
  liability of agent or employee, 887, 890
  public policy and, 203–204
  strict liability, 189
  types of, 189, 205
Toxic Substances Control Act (TOSCA), 1193
trade. *See also* international trade
  furtherance of, 50
  restraint of, 137, 355
Trade Act of 1974, 145
trade associations and dispute settlement, 31
trade dress, 216
trade dress protection, 216–217
trade libel, 196
trademark, 212–220
trade secret, 230
transfer
  credit, 705

debit, 705
by delivery, 1061
funds, 705
transferee, 1174
transfer of real property by deed
additional protection of
buyer, 1176
classification of, 1174
defined, 1174
delivery and acceptance, 1174
execution of deed, 1174
grantee's covenants, 1178
grantor's warranties, 1177
recording of deed, 1176
transfer of the tenant, 1216
traveler's check, 624
treasury stock, 1037
Treaty of Maastricht, 130, 131
Treaty of Mutual Assistance in
Criminal Matters, 141
Treaty of Rome, 130, 131
treble damages, 97
trespass, 196–197, 1171
trial 25–26, 28, 34
judicial triage, 32
jury instructions and
verdict, 28
jury selection, 25
minitrial, 32
motion for directed verdict,
26
motion for mistrial, 26
motion for new trial;
motion for judgment
n.o.v., 28
opening statement, 26
posttrial procedures, 28
presentation of evidence, 26
summary jury trial, 31
summation, 26
trial *de novo*, 30
tripartite, 67
tripartite structure, 106, 121
trust, and ethics, 44–45
trust agreement, 1248
trust corpus, 1248
trustee
defined, 1248
duties, 1249
trustee in bankruptcy, 802
trustor, 1248
trusts, 1247–1250
creation of, 1248
definitions, 1248
duties and powers of trustee,
1249–1250
remedies for breach of trust,
1250
termination of, 1250
trust principal/income
allocation, 1249–1250

truth, 51–52
Truth in Lending Act (TILA),
748
Turtle Law, U.S., 143
Twain, Mark, 51
tweeting, 244
24-hour rule, 907
tying, 94
Tylenol, 57
Tyson Foods, 197, 198

U

ultra vires, 1038
unauthorized collection,
699–700
unauthorized indorsement, 652
unauthorized signature or
alteration, 701–702, 708
Uncle Buck (film), 427
unconscionability
in contracts, 350–351, 360
defined, 512, 1214
underwriter, 822
undisclosed principal, 877
undue influence, 322
unemployment benefits,
915–918
eligibility, 915–916
funding, 916
unfair competition, 89
unfair labor practices, 906f
Unfair or Deceptive Acts or
Practices (UDAP) statutes,
737
Uniform Anatomical Gift Act,
463
Uniform Arbitration Act, 28
Uniform Commercial Code
(UCC), 9, 127, 302, 424,
493, 581, 591
acceptance, 508, 509
Article 2, 493, 504,
506–512, 515, 520,
532, 540, 558, 599, 608
Article 3, 505, 622, 624,
625, 634, 642, 644,
668, 689, 693, 1062
Article 4, 505, 693
Article 6, 515
Article 7, 480, 481, 483,
535, 603
Article 8, 504, 1036, 1061
Article 9, 515, 602, 764,
771–774, 776, 783, 784
collateral, 767
deficit liability, 785
delegation of duties, 404
doctrine of firm offer, 293
international trade and, 127
letter of credit, 724

loss of goods, 543
sales contracts, 507, 511,
513, 519
Section 2-318, 557
Section 2-710, 602
secured transaction, 764
statute of frauds, 516, 524
time limits for suits, 599
warranties, 473, 556, 557,
569, l, 563
Uniform Computer
Information Transactions
Act (UCITA), 9, 252
Uniform Consumer Credit
Code (UCCC), 398
Uniform Disposition of
Unclaimed Property Act, 466
Uniform Domain Name
Dispute Resolution Policy,
254
Uniformed Services
Employment and Re-
Employment Rights Act
(USERRA), 917–918
Uniform Electronic
Transactions Act (UETA),
9, 252, 375, 523
Uniform Gifts to Minors Act
(UGMA), 461
Uniform Limited Partnership
Act (ULPA), 1014
Uniform Partnership Act
(UPA), 983, 1014
Uniform Probate Code (UPC),
1234
Uniform Securities Act, 1084
Uniform Simultaneous Death
Act, 1247
Uniform Unclaimed Property
Act (UUPA), 466
unilateral contract, 272
United Nations Conference on
Trade and Development
(UNCTAD), 130
United Nations Convention on
Contracts for the
International Sale of Goods
(CISG), 128, 130, 148,
611–612
United Parcel Service (UPS),
89, 298
United States–Canada Free Trade
Agreement of 1989, 131
United States government, 68.
See also U.S. Constitution
universal agent, 853
universal defenses, 673
unknown user, 1121
unlawful search, 5, 11
UPC. *See* Uniform Probate
Code (UPC)

Uruguay Round Agreement,
129, 144
U.S. Code, 18
U.S. Constitution, 4, 67–70
charateristics of, 71–72
delegates and shared powers,
68
and Federal System, 67
Fifth Amendment,
179–180
as foundation of legal
environment, 67–83
Fourth Amendment,
177–180
interpreting and amending,
70, 71, 81
limitations on government,
77–79
other powers, 68–69
powers of, 81
prohibited powers, 69
and the states, 68–70
U.S. Patriot Act, 48, 164, 693
U.S. Supreme Court, 19–21
usage of trade, 385, 514
usury, 358, 359, 361
uttering, 168

V

valid contract, 271
value, 668, 766
values, ethical, 59
variance, 1205
vicarious liability, 882
victim compensation,
162–163
Victims of Crime Act of 1984,
163
Victoria's Secret stores, 220
video wills, 1237
viruses, computer, 254
voidable contract, 271
voidable title, 536
void agreement, 271
voir dire, 25, 34
voluntary bankruptcy, 796
vote, right to, 4
voting
cumulative, 1065
by proxy, 1065
straight, 1065
voting agreements and trusts,
1065
voting trust, 1065

W

Wage and Hour Act, 903
Wahlberg, Mark, 368, 374
waiver

defenses, 610
defined, 419, 436
existence and scope of, 436–438
prohibition of, 611
Wall Street (film), 1104
Wal-Mart stores, 217
warehouse 480
defined, 480
liability of, 485
lien of, 481
public, 480
rights and duties, 480
warehouse receipt, 481, 484, 535
Warg, Gottfrid Svartholm, 254
warrant, 255
warranties. *See also* product liability; warranties, implied
beneficiary of implied warranties, 656
bill of lading and, 487
conspicuousness, 567
description of goods as warranties, 558
disclaimer of warranties, 567–568
express, 558–561
notice of breach of, 656
other parties', 656
qualified indorser, 656
scope of, 655
transfer by delivery, 656
UCC, 557, 569

unqualified indorser, 655–656
warranty defined, 480, 556
what is not warranted, 655
warranties, implied, 561–566, 572, 655–656
additional implied warranties of merchant sellers, 563–564
breach of warranty, 566
Convention on Contracts for the International Sale of Goods (CISG), 566
definition, 562
against encumbrances, 562
of fitness for a particular purpose, 562
against infringement, 563–564
international sale of goods, 566
merchantability or fitness for normal use, 564, 572
necessity of defect, 566
in particular sales, 564
sale of food or drink, 565
sale of secondhand or used goods, 564–565
sale on buyer's specifications, 564
of sellers, 562
warranty of title, 562
warrants, search and seizure, 177

warranty against encumbrances, 562
warranty deed, 1174
Warranty Disclosure Act, 747
warranty of habitability, 1221
warranty of title, 562, 1177
wasting assets corporation, 1068
way of necessity, 1164
weight, discrimination based on, 941
welfare, public, agreements affecting, 352–354
whistleblower protection, 901–902
White Americans, 938
White-Collar Crime Penalty Enhancement Act of 2002, 161
white-collar crimes, 163–173
White-Collar Criminal Charges, 160–161
whole life insurance, 836
Williams Act, 1101, 1105
wills, 1234–1240
beneficiaries, 1235–1236
construction of, 1244
definitions, 1234
disinheritance, 1239
election to take against, 1239
form, 1236–1237
holographic, 1240

living wills, 1240, 1241
modification of, 1237
parties to will, 1234–1236
probate of, 1240–1242
revocation of, 1237–1239
special types of, 1239–1240
testamentary intent, 1236
will contest, 1242
witness, expert, 25
women and contractual capacity, 308–309
Woods, Tiger, 250
workplace and the Internet, privacy issues, 244–247
World Bank, 132
WorldCom, 96, 159, 161, 1124
World Intellectual Property Organization (WIPO), 220
World Trade Center terrorist attack, 425
World Trade Organization (WTO), 129, 145, 148
World Wide Web, 243
writ of *certiorari*, 20
wrongfully dishonored, 695

Z

zoning, 49, 1204